CREATING SOCIAL CHANGE

HOLT, RINEHART AND WINSTON MARKETING SERIES

Paul E. Green, Adviser
Wharton School, University of Pennsylvania

Philip Kotler, Adviser
Northwestern University

James F. Engel, The Ohio State University
Henry F. Fiorillo, Canadian Breweries, Ltd. and University of Toronto
Murray A. Cayley, Imperial Oil Company
  Market Segmentation: Concepts and Applications

James F. Engel, David T. Kollat, Roger D. Blackwell
All of The Ohio State University
  Consumer Behavior
  Cases in Consumer Behavior
  Research in Consumer Behavior

Ronald R. Gist, University of Denver
  Cases in Marketing Management
  Marketing and Society: A Conceptual Introduction
  Readings: Marketing and Society

Charles S. Goodman, University of Pennsylvania
  Management of the Personal Selling Function

Paul E. Green, University of Pennsylvania
Vithala R. Rao, Cornell University
  Applied Multidimensional Scaling: A Comparison of Approaches and Algorithms

David T. Kollat, Roger D. Blackwell, James F. Robeson
All of the Ohio State University
  Strategic Marketing

Philip Kotler, Northwestern University
  Marketing Decision Making: A Model Building Approach

John C. Narver, University of Washington
Ronald Savitt, Boston University
  The Marketing Economy: An Analytical Approach
  Conceptual Readings in the Marketing Economy

Vern Terpstra, The University of Michigan
  International Marketing

Thomas R. Wotruba, San Diego State College
  Sales Management: Planning, Accomplishment, and Evaluation

Thomas R. Wotruba, San Diego State College
Robert M. Olsen, California State College, Fullerton
  Readings in Sales Management: Concepts and Viewpoints

Gerald Zaltman, Northwestern University
Philip Kotler, Northwestern University
Ira Kaufman, University of Manchester
  Creating Social Change

CREATING

SOCIAL CHANGE

GERALD ZALTMAN *Northwestern University*

PHILIP KOTLER *Northwestern University*

IRA KAUFMAN *University of Manchester*

HOLT, RINEHART AND WINSTON, INC.
New York Chicago San Francisco Atlanta
Dallas Toronto Montreal London Sydney

Gerald Zaltman   Philip Kotler   Ira Kaufman

CREATING SOCIAL CHANGE

Library of Congress Catalog Card Number: 73–167810

ISBN: 0–03–080262–8

Printed in the United States of America

2 3 4 5   006   9 8 7 6 5 4 3 2 1

TO OUR WIVES

JEAN

NANCY

DENISE

PREFACE

The present decade is as critical as it is unique. It is critical because of the extreme pervasiveness of the social change processes affecting the structure and functioning of our society. The course that these changes follow and the end results during the 1970s will mold the character of life in this country and abroad for decades to come. We are also living in a unique time period. At no other time in history have such important change processes been present together with a relatively sophisticated social technology. When we speak of social technology, we mean the capability of dealing with—of controlling or helping to guide—human behavior.

At any given time social technology consists of the accumulated inventory of behavioral knowledge giving us a better understanding of individual and social behavior. In many instances our understanding of behavioral phenomena enables us to intervene in individual and social life and to organize, plan, implement, and control behavioral processes to the betterment of society in general. Of course, our ability to influence behavior is far from total and perhaps fortunately so because not all change is necessarily good. Nevertheless, scattered throughout the behavioral sciences are many sound guidelines for managing social change. We feel that the current state of the art for organizing, planning, implementing, and controlling social change processes is at a sufficiently high level to warrant our bringing together the best of these guidelines and placing them in a single volume under the title, *Creating Social Change*.

The need for a book which integrates social science knowledge with managerial processes is great. A statement by Bernard Berelson concerning family planning applies with equal force to other social sectors: "If there is one deficiency in this field that is more serious than any other . . . *it is a general lack of adequate implemental machinery.* We don't have a cadre of people who can organize a governmental program, for example, and apply it to a large population and run it successfully." It was this challenge laid down by Berelson which more than any other single stimulus motivated us to prepare *Creating Social Change.*

Although it is a collection of readings, we feel that this book makes a number of needed contributions to the field. First, some of the papers were either prepared especially for this volume, significantly revised for this volume, or not previously published for wide circulation. The format of the book presents an innovative frame of reference for viewing social change processes. Part One emphasizes five basic components of all social change efforts: the cause, change target, change agency, channel, and change strategies (the five C's). Part Two presents a total view of strategies and tactics available to social action programs and suggests a typology of strategies. Part Three is more explicitly management-oriented with a chapter each on organizational strategy, planning, implementing programs, and controlling programs. The Five C's of Part One are the elements on which these management considerations must focus, and the strategies and tactics of Part Two are the mechanisms and manifestations of the management process. Treating the Five C's and strategies sections first enhances considerably the understanding of and insight into the social change management process. This process is essential in social change for it links social problems and needs with potentially successful solutions.

Overall, the book emphasizes a model-building or systems approach to social change. This is another unique feature. It stresses the need for the change agent to develop a model of his particular area of concern, examine the interactions among the parts of the model, and find points where he can gain leverage for implementing his objectives.

The single most important criterion used in selecting papers was the contribution each paper made toward our understanding of and our ability to improve action-oriented social change programs. Some of the papers are primarily theoretical in nature, but most are empirically based. In all instances, particularly with the help of the editorial introductions, the implications of the papers for change agents are clear.

An additional criterion used in selecting papers involved the degree to which they could be generalized to other contexts. Thus, while the majority of papers are rooted in a particular social context, they have nearly equal relevance beyond those boundaries.

The papers cover a myriad of areas: health and social services, education, political affairs, social deviance, modernization and national development, and race relations to name a few. They also cover a broad range of several crucial issues of this decade: family planning, pollution control, drug abuse, juvenile delinquency, innovation in education, political reform, ghetto problems, racial integration, and so on. We feel that this volume will prove very useful in departments of anthropology, economics, environmental sciences, psychology, and sociology and in the professional schools of business, education, law, nursing, public health, and social work. Moreover, it should be of no less value to practitioners of social change (as distinguished from the university-oriented academicians) and provide invaluable insight from that vantage point.

Creating Social Change has been used successfully in university courses on social change and related courses involving students from most of the departments and schools just mentioned. We have also had the benefit of extensive advice from many colleagues and practitioners interested in social change and from fellow faculty members. We are deeply grateful for their assistance in the preparation of this volume.

Special thanks are also due to Mrs. Edith Bass and Mrs. Marion Davis for their invaluable and unexcelled clerical and secretarial assistance. Finally, and most importantly, we must acknowledge our deepest gratitude to the many authors whose efforts are represented here who were kind enough to let us reproduce their papers.

December 1971   G. Z.
Evanston, Illinois   P. K.
Manchester, England   I. K.

CONTENTS

OUTLINE OF INTEREST AREAS

EDUCATION
Chin and Benne   18.
Eicholtz and Rogers   57.
Lippitt   47.
Watson   56.

FAMILY PLANNING
Demerath   60.
Simon   49.
Smith   9.
Wilder and Tyagi   32.

GOVERNMENT SERVICES
Alexander and Podair   54.
Evans   58.
Hapgood and Bennett   52.

HEALTH AND PUBLIC SAFETY
Campbell   59.
ENACT   50.
Levanthal   31.
National Tuberculosis and Respiratory Disease
Association   55.
Zeigler   30.

MANAGEMENT
Argyris   34.
Demerath   60.
Granger   45.
Kahneman and Schild   16.
Kaufman   20.
Kotler and Zaltman   48.
Stein   44.
Zaleznik and Moment   3.

MODERNIZATION
Doob   5.
Hapgood and Bennett   52.
Jones   19.
Rogers   15.

POLITICAL AFFAIRS
Bondurant   22.
Fagen   17.
Huntington   20.
Lipsky   21.
Milbrath   33.
Nieburg   12.
Singer   43.
Tedeschi, Bonoma, Schlenker, and Lindskold   11.
Wiebe   14.

RACE RELATIONS
Carmack   37.
Dubey   41.
Evans   58.
Hundley   25.
Oppenheimer and Lakey   23.
Walton   27.

SOCIAL DEVIANCE
Blumberg, Shipley, and Shandler   36.
Etzioni   46.
Lenrow   35.

SOCIAL WORK
Dubey   41.
Pruger and Specht   40.
Rothman   39.
Specht   24.
Strong   7.
Taylor   53.

MULTI-CONTEXT
Bandura   4.
Brown   28.
Cartright   6.
Deutsch   10.
Katz, Levin, and Hamilton   8.
Kelman   51.
Kotler   13.
Martindale   1.
Oppenheimer and Lakey   42.
Rokeach   29.
Schein   38.
Schelling   26.

CREATING SOCIAL CHANGE

PART ONE

OVERVIEW OF SOCIAL CHANGE

Editors' Introduction
to Part One

The roots of life in the United States are changing. Significant changes are occurring in personal styles and values, technological innovations, and social institutions. American society in the latter half of the twentieth century has been aptly described as "The Temporary Society": adaptive, rapidly changing, imaginative, creative, essentially an innovation unto itself.[1] Technological and intellectual changes have in turn fostered a new sensitivity and awareness of social problems and a desire to cope with them. The growing desire to attack social problems is manifested by substantial numbers and types of persons engaged, many for the first time, in social action—housewives, students, businessmen, educators, minorities, religious leaders, and so on.

With this growing interest in the problems of American society, *social change* has become a popular term. It has been used to describe changes in birth control practices, social and economic life styles of our urban ghettos, and the philosophies of organized groups. An adequate working definition of social change has been provided by Everett Rogers. "*Social change* is the process by which alteration occurs in the structure and function of a social system."[2] The diverse implications of even such a brief definition can be grouped into three categories. First, there is the source of the impetus to change. Second, it is necessary to consider the various ways in which change manifests itself.

[1] W. G. Bennis, "The Temporary Society," *Innovation*, No. I, May 1969.
[2] E. Rogers, *Modernization Among Peasants* (New York: Holt, Rinehart and Winston, 1969).

1

Finally, the consequences of change must be anticipated and studied. Consider the impetus first.

The impetus of social change may have its origins inside the social system or from outside the social system. Moreover, and somewhat more important in this case, regardless of the source, the impetus may be a planned series of change efforts or may be an unplanned sequence of events. Planned social change refers to deliberate efforts by change agents to affect a change in a target system of individuals. In different contexts the concept of planned social change has been referred to as social planning,[3] planned change,[4] social communication engineering,[5] social marketing,[6] and change management.[7] It has pervaded many of the American institutions attempting to guide and engineer programs of change in society. Planned social change "originates with a declared intention of objectives; it starts with a purpose of altering the free play of those social consequences that have ensued from demographic, physiographic and technological change."[8] After the innovator determines his objectives, he proceeds to develop an action plan. His basic strategy relies on concepts of power, persuasion, and reeducation, the mix varying from situation to situation. These strategies for planned social change will be discussed in Part Two.

Unplanned social change is a result of natural forces causing changes in society. Saul Alinsky, noted for his community organizing, suggests that many tactics for social change

are unplanned: "So many tactics on the scene of action aren't planned or engineered. Often they're irrational. They just happen."[9] Halpin describes unplanned social change as "free change"—an unintended consequence of the interaction of the forces of society. The distinction between planned and unplanned change can be clarified by using cultural change as a context. C. Arensberg and A. Niehoff[10] describe cultural borrowing as the passing of ideas and techniques between cultures. Such borrowing causes unplanned social change, since it just occurs and is not directed. On the other hand, planned social change ensues as change agents are deliberately brought from one culture or social system to another to introduce new techniques.

The study of unplanned change is an important first step in the effective planning of change. It provides the change agent with valuable insight into the basic mechanisms affecting changes in the structure and function of the society that he is attempting to change. The agent will be able to determine which factors have to be accepted as given and which are more amenable to change. For this reason some instances reflecting unplanned change are included in this volume. The manifestation of social change reveals the occurrence of changes in aspects of society. By distinguishing between short- and long-term change and micro, intermediate, and macro levels of societal change, one can cross classify these two important dimensions. As a result, six types of social change can be identified.

[3] M. Andrews, *Social Planning by Frontier Thinkers* (New York: Richard Smith, 1944).

[4] R. Lippitt, J. Watson, and B. Westley, *Dynamics of Planned Change* (New York: John Wiley & Sons, 1958).

[5] M. Rees and W. Paisley, "Social and Psychological Predictors of Adult Information Seeking and Media Use," *Adult Education Journal*, Vol. XIX, No. 1 (1968), p. 27.

[6] P. Kotler and G. Zaltman, "Social Marketing: An Approach to Planned Change," in this book, Reading 48.

[7] I. Kaufman, "Change Management: The System and the Process," in this book, Reading 2.

[8] A. Halpin, "Change the Mythology," *Theory into Practice* (Columbus: Ohio State University, College of Education), Vol. VIII, No. 1 (February 1969).

[9] S. Alinsky, "The Professional Radical Moves in on Rochester," *Harper's Magazine* (July 1965).

[10] C. Arensberg and A. Niehoff, *Introducing Social Change* (Chicago: Aldine Publishing, 1964), p. 59.

The time dimension is a highly relative phenomena. It may be measured in terms of days, weeks, months or years, depending upon the context of the change.

Type 1 refers to changes in one's attitudes and behavior. This can be exemplified by the persuasion of an individual to adopt a birth control practice. The effects of this change over the long term (Type 2) might be reflected in inter-generational upward mobility. For example, the parents with less children have more money to spend for their own pleasure or educating their children; this might result in improved mobility for their offspring.

The third type of social change is illustrated by changes in group norms, values, and membership. The long-term results of such changes might be organizational change (Type 4). The organization or group can change in structure as well as function. For example, the party platform on civil rights of the Democratic Party has evolved over the years as a result of different leadership and values.

Type 5 is characterized by grand and relatively rapid changes as a result of an invention or revolution. For example, the medical discovery of the birth control pill and the widespread use of the pill caused many changes in the life style and practices of adopters. This case differs from the first type in two ways. To begin, the invention affects society's population control problems (urban growth, and so forth). Secondly, the existence of such a product in many cases will not require a change in values or attitudes for adoption. The long-term ramifications (Type 6) of such an invention are broad. They could be as minor as changing female occupational behavior or as major as facilitating the modernization process of an underdeveloped country.

The final dimension of social change is its consequences. Changes in the social systems can be viewed as either structural or functional or both together. The urban riots of 1966 and 1968 caused the creation of many new agencies to handle minority problems. To this extent, the riots helped change the structure of federal, state, and, in some cases, local governments. Student protests, on the other hand, do not always succeed in changing the administration of the school; but often they do succeed in sensitizing the administration to their desires. This is a change in function. Frequently these changes are dynamic effects of each other and cannot be isolated. The importance of these dimensions is reflected in the goals of the initiating organization, which will be discussed in Part Three.

The aim of Part One is to present an overview of the different meanings and contexts of social change. Section I contrasts different leading perspectives, while Section II distinguishes four essential elements in all social change efforts.

Section I, beginning with Don Martindale's "The Crisis in the Contemporary Theory of Social and Cultural Change," examines some grand theories of social change. Martindale compares five schools of sociological thought: positive organicism, conflict theory, sociological formalism, social behaviorism, and sociological functionalism. His discussion emphasizes the need for a complete reexamination of

Time Dimension	Level of Society		
	Micro (Individual)	*Intermediate (Group)*	*Macro (Society)*
Short term	*Type 1* 1) Attitude change 2) Behavior change	*Type 3* 1) Normative change 2) Administrative change	*Type 5* 1) Invention-Innovation 2) Revolution
Long term	*Type 2* Life-cycle change	*Type 4* Organizational change	*Type 6* Socio-cultural evolution

the theories of sociocultural change. No one theory, of course, is adequate to explain all essential aspects of social change.[11]

Moving from grand theories of social change to a more middle-range approach, Kaufman in "Change Management: The Process and the System" develops a macrobehavioral model of social change using the management process as a frame of reference. This model uses a systems approach in trying to better understand social change. The author views the change management system as having three major subsystems—organizational, communication, and change target. His description of each subsystem includes a discussion of the activities involved in the process of managing change.

Still another perspective on social change is exemplified in Abraham Zaleznick and David Moment's "Change." The authors treat the interpersonal change process from four points of view: culture, organization, group, and individual. They trace the interaction between forces of conservation and change at each of the four levels. Their paper stresses interpersonal relations, one of the most important influences in adopting or rejecting change.

Following the overview of social change, Section I considers three disciplinary frameworks for explaining the occurrence of social change. The social-psychological perspective emphasizes the psychological mechanism involved in social interaction and change. For example, attitude change can be viewed as a process of unfreezing, changing, and refreezing, which was conceived by Kurt Lewin and later elaborated upon by E. Schein.[12] This three-stage process is precipitated by an alteration in one's state of cognitive balance (equilibrium). At this point the individual is motivated to change (unfreezing), then develops new responses (changing) and finally

integrates and stabilizes change (refreezing).

In "Strategies of Attitude Change" Albert Bandura distinguishes three approaches to producing attitudinal-behavioral change.[13] The first approach attempts to change beliefs by exposure to persuasive communication. The second approach attempts to alter affective (emotional) evaluations of and behaviors toward an object. The third approach attempts to change the behavior, in the hope that attitude change will then occur. Bandura's analysis is particularly significant because he integrates applications of social modeling with the strategy of attitude change. The outgrowth of the work done on attitude change is the persuasive strategies of Part Two.

Leonard Doob in "Psychological Aspects of Planned Developmental Change" considers change from the point of view of economic development planners. He presents a series of psychologically relevant principles and analyzes the five psychological processes of predispositions, perceptions, other people, personality traits and learning in terms of three kinds of change. Doob views change as antecedent (before the fact), consequent (the result) and concomitant (spiraling process). Thus, fifteen principles emerge in his discussion.

The final aspect of social psychological change concentrates on interpersonal relations. Dorwin Cartwright in "Achieving Change in People: Some Applications of Group Dynamics Theory," discusses a series of propositions based on Lewin's original work. His basic approach involves using group pressure to change people. The pressure to change is exerted by confrontations and discussions with a peer group.

Turning to the individual, Stanley Strong in "Counseling: An Interpersonal Influence Proc-

---

[11] See J. McLeish, *The Theory of Social Change,* London (Routledge & Kegan Paul, 1969) for an additional elaboration on the theories of social change.

[12] E. Schein, "The Mechanisms of Change," in W. Bennis, E. Schein, F. Steele and D. Berlew (eds.), *Interpersonal Dynamics* (Homewood, Illinois: Dorsey Press, 1964), pp. 362–378.

[13] See M. Rokeach, *Beliefs, Attitudes and Values* (San Francisco: Jossey-Bass, 1969) for a highly relevant discussion of the linkage between changes in attitudes, values, and behavior.

ess" surveys the opinion change research in the areas of expertness, trustworthiness, attractiveness and involvement. His thesis is that behavior change is a two-phase interpersonal influence process. Initially, the counselor must enhance his client's perceptions of the above four variables. Secondly, the counselor can use the "influence power" that he has acquired to pursue changes in the direction of the client's goals. Both the Cartwright and Strong papers reflect the principles used in the reeducative strategy examined in Part Two.

The second disciplinary perspective is diffusion-communication theory. The diffusion viewpoint emphasizes the "process of spreading a new idea or innovation from its source of invention or creation to its ultimate users or adopters."[14] In the same light, communication research attempts to delineate the best ways to deliver messages of change to groups of people. Thus, diffusion-communication theory provides a means to explain how new social ideas are transferred from individual to individual and from group to group.

Elihu Katz, Martin Levin, and Herbert Hamilton, in "Traditions of Research on the Diffusion of Innovation," discuss several studies of diffusion in terms of seven characteristics of the process of diffusion—acceptance, trial, item, adopter unit, channels, social structure, and culture. This classification is very useful in comparative analysis as it makes it possible to generalize across disciplines and innovations.

In "Motivation, Communications Research, and Family Planning," M. Brewster Smith applies communications research findings to the problem of family planning. He presents a four-stage adoption paradigm for family planning. One's movement through the process is dependent upon the creation of a relevant cognitive structure, a positive motivational structure, and a feasible behavioral structure. Smith's major contribution is the linkage of theoretical communication principles with operational strategies for change.

The final disciplinary perspective on change

is conflict theory which is an outgrowth of Machiavellian politics and Marxian dialectics. This perspective is cogently stated by Saul Alinsky: "change means movement, movement means friction, friction means heat, and heat means controversy. The only place where there is no friction is in outer space or a seminar on political action."[15] The friction and controversy is the essense of conflict. Conflict can be manifested in many different ways. It can be nonviolent (voting majority, strike), quasi-nonviolent (threats), and violent (riots, revolution).[16] Conflict can be used in any of these three ways to achieve social change. The success of such a social change effort is based on the management of this conflict. This concept is the basis of the next three readings.

Morton Deutsch in "Conflicts: Productive and Destructive" views the specific conditions and processes related to the productive and destructive consequences of conflict. In terms of productive conflict, he describes creative thinking, motivation, cooperative problem-solving, and controlled competitive conflict as resultants. On the other hand, destructive or "escalated" conflict is related to three processes: competition to win, misperception and biased perception, and commitment. Deutsch, then, considers modes of conflict resolution and their anticipated results. He concludes by stressing the importance of coping and managing conflict in "seeking peaceful social change."

James Tedeschi, Thomas Bonoma, Barry Schlenker, and Svenn Lindskold in "Power, Influence, and Behavioral Compliance" discuss how behavior can be changed under conditions of social conflict and limited communications. The authors present the paper in two parts: a general overview of theories of power and influence and a dyadic theory of influence. The dyadic theory of influence is an integration of T. Parson's work on influence, J. R. P. French and B. Raven's work on power and H. D. Lasswell and A. Kaplan's work on economic power. The authors present a model with three essential components: a source, a

---

[14] E. Rogers, *Diffusion of Innovation* (New York: Free Press, 1962), p. 13.

[15] G. Astor, "The Apostle," *Look Magazine* (June 25, 1968), p. 63.

[16] W. B. Cameron, *Modern Social Movements* (New York: Random House, 1964).

signal system and a target. The remainder of the paper describes research findings on the different types of power that support their theory of influence.

H. L. Nieburg's "The Threat of Violence and Social Change" examines the use of occasional violence as an essential element of peaceful social change. The author suggests that the threat of violence lends credibility to a social cause. In distinguishing between force and violence, Nieburg discusses "their roles" in pressuring for political and social change. He concludes by discussing some concrete examples in both the international and domestic areas. The principles discussed in the Deutsch, Tedeschi, *et al.*, and Nieburg papers are the basis for the power strategies of Part Two.

In Section II, five essential components of any effort of planned social change are isolated: cause, change agency, change target, channel, and change strategy. The "five C's" provide the initiator of social change with a clear perspective of the salient features of a social change program.

In "Elements of Social Action," Philip Kotler considers the conceptual content of each of the five C's. He classifies causes into those directed at helping, protest, and revolution. Looking at the change agency he views those who serve the agency as two types—leaders and supporters—and delineates several types under each. The change targets are the third element. They are the objects of the change effort. The fourth element, channels, has two dimensions: channels for influence and channels for response. The change strategy is the last elements of the Five Cs and represents the basic approach used to influence the change targets. Kotler illustrates the typology by discussing various causes.

G. D. Wiebe's "Merchandising Commodities and Citizenship on Television" describes four different causes and four dissimilar public information campaigns. The causes are war bonds, civil defense, juvenile delinquency, and citizenship behavior. Wiebe's objective was to present the four causes as case studies, in order to get a perspective of some of the principles of mass communication theory. Each case is analyzed in terms of five factors essential for a successful mass persuasion effort. This paper will enable the reader to understand the adjustments necessary in attempting to plan changes for different causes.

In Everett Roger's "Change Agents, Clients, and Change," the focus is on the change agent and his relationship with the client. Rogers describes the seven functions of a change agent in attempting to modify the client's behavior. The success of the "client modification" is dependent upon four liaison variables of a change-agent–client relationship. They are reciprocity, homophily (attribute similarity), empathy, and credibility. The importance of the reading lies in its attempt to isolate important variables entering into a change-agent–client relationship. This knowledge should aid the change agent in planning future encounters.

D. Kahneman and E. O. Schild in "Training Agents of Social Change in Israel" describe a training approach for a change agent. They contend that the essential activities of the change agent are the preliminary analysis of the problem and the strategic planning toward the desired change. With this end, they conceived of an accounting scheme to analyze the causes of deficient planning. The concluding portion of their paper describes the main phases of a training program to accomplish the objectives set forth above.

Turning to the role of channels in social action, Richard Fagen in "Components of Communication Networks" views four different types of channels. A channel is considered any structure or institution used to carry communication. Fagen's classification of organizations, groups, mass media, and special channels is cast in a political context, but it is generalizable to any fact of social change. Each channel category is characterized by specific attributes.

The discussion of change strategy begins with Robert Chin and Kenneth Benne's paper, "General Strategies for Effecting Change in Human Systems." Chin and Benne make an impressive attempt to classify the many change strategies that can be identified. They discuss three types of strategies for bringing about change. The empirical-rational strategies assume that man is essentially a rational being who will act according to his perceived self-interest. In fact, social change effort is directed to linking the change object with the client's self-interest. The second set of strategies, termed normative-reeducative, view man as living in a complex sociocultural world where reality is viewed through a colored looking glass of attitudes, values, and beliefs. To bring about change, it is necessary to alter the attitudes, values, and beliefs supporting existing norms. The third group of strategies are power-coercive strategies. Here the view is that man or society is essentially fixed in the status quo and will usually require the application of force before change will come about.

"Strategies and Tactics of Planned Organizational Changes" by Garth Jones presents a second typology of strategies which sheds further light on the nature of strategies and the way that strategies can be grouped together. One type of strategy is coercive in nature. It involves the use of threat or force. This will occur when an imbalance of power exists, which is often due to the unequal distribution of and control over resources. Normative strategies, the second type, rely on the internalization of social norms and full socialization into society's institutions. Behavior is generally controlled or altered by manipulating symbols and administering rituals. The third type, utilitarian strategies, are characterized by control over material resources and rewards which the client system receives if it complies with demands made by the change agent. The reading concludes with a discussion of tactics that can implement strategies.

PERSPECTIVES ON THE PROCESS
OF SOCIAL CHANGE

A. GENERAL DISCUSSION

1. The Crisis in the Contemporary Theory of Social and Cultural Change

Don Martindale*

Even the most elementary review of the current forms of sociological theory of social change, on the one hand, and of the traditional theories of social change, on the other, indicates four things: (1) Theories of social change can be reduced to a few basic models; (2) traditionally theories of social change have been developed in great profusion around these basic models; (3) recent sociological theories have only weakly and uncertainly exploited the traditional models; (4) nevertheless, one of the primary justifications for the development of sociology in the first place was its interest in social and cultural change. The relation between the theory of social change and general sociological theory may help clarify this situation.

Sociological theory attempts to account for the nature and forms of social life; the theory of social change attempts to account for the origin and transformation of these forms. No general sociological theory is complete unless it develops its explanations of social and cultural change. On the other hand, it is also evident that all eclectic theories of social change must prove unsatisfactory in the long run. Only when a decision has been reached as to the nature and forms of social life can the

Reprinted in part from Don Martindale, *Social Life and Cultural Change* (Princeton: D. Van Nostrand 1961), pp. 12–30. Copyright © 1962 by Litton Educational Publishing, Inc. By permission of D. Van Nostrand Company.
* Professor of Sociology, University of Minnesota.

problem of their origin and transformation be systematically developed. The basic types of general sociological theories have very different implications for special theories of social and cultural change.

The types of sociological theory which have been advanced since the origin of science about a hundred years ago have been reviewed elsewhere,[1] making it unnecessary to examine them in detail here. The five types of sociological theory are: positivistic organicism, conflict theory, sociological formalism, social behaviorism, and functionalism. Some of these schools have developed major subbranches: positivistic organicism partly subdivided into traditional organicism, biological organicism; and voluntaristic positivism, before it disintegrated in recent times into pure organicism and pure positivism. Sociological formalism subdivided into a neo-Kantian and a phenomenological branch. Social behaviorism was subdivided from the beginning into pluralistic behaviorism, symbolic interactionism, and social action theory. Functionalism is divided into macrofunctionalism and microfunctionalism. The manner in which these general theories have accounted for human social life have provided them with very different affinities for theories of social and cultural change.

Positivistic Organicism's Linkage with Progress and Evolution

Positivistic organicism, the first general school of sociological theory, created by Auguste Comte, Herbert Spencer, and Lester Ward took mankind as a whole to be the object of study of sociology. Mankind (humanity), or in its major manifestation, society, was thought to be an organic unit. The proper means of study of this organic unit was the examination of the methods and techniques which had proved their worth in the physical sciences.

All of the positivistic organicists were convinced that the happenings of humanity or society were in part determined by the natural and biological environment. However, the primary causes of social events were other social events. Hence, when humanity or the many societies in which human beings were distributed changed, the source of these changes was to be sought in social events themselves. The primary object of the new science, according to its founders, was to explain these same social and cultural changes.

The theories of progress developed broadly and loosely in the eighteenth century, particularly by Condorcet, and advanced in the early nineteenth century, particularly by Saint-Simon, formed the starting point for Comte's thinking which centered in the explicit search for a law of progress which he formulated in his *Cours de philosophie* completed in six volumes between 1830 and 1842. Human progress, he argued, is ruled by the law of the three stages in which men account for the phenomena of the world.

In the earliest attempt by men to explain phenomena, their thinking is theological in nature (events are explained as caused by deities and demons). Later, as men grow more sophisticated, they reject such anthropomorphizing, explaining events in terms of presumed abstract principles or essences. However, in time they recognize that such metaphysical explanations are also inadequate and thinking advances to a positive stage in which explanations are made on the basis of scientific methods. This law of the three stages operates, according to Comte, in every area of human mental life and development.

> The movement of history is due to the deeply rooted though complex instinct which pushes man in all ways to ameliorate his condition incessantly, to develop in all ways the sum of his physical, moral, and intellectual life. And all the phenomena of his social life are closely cohesive, as Saint-Simon had pointed out. By virtue of this cohesion, political, moral, and intellectual progress are inseparable from material progress, and so we find that the phases of his material development correspond to intellectual changes.[2]

[1] Don Martindale, *The Nature and Types of Sociological Theory* (Boston: Houghton Mifflin, 1960).

[2] J. B. Bury, *The Idea of Progress* (New York: Dover Publications, 1932), p. 293.

Humanity develops in terms of these imminent forces. In the nineteenth century the rise of the biological sciences became a dominant factor in social thought. Darwin himself had been strongly inclined toward the fusion of the concepts of progress and evolution.

> As all the living forms of life are the lineal descendents of those which lived long before the Cambrian epoch, we may feel certain that the ordinary succession by generation has never once been broken, and that no cataclysm has desolated the whole world. Hence we may look with some confidence to a secure future of great length. And as natural selection works solely by and for the good of each being, all corporeal and mental endowments will tend to progress toward perfection.[3]

The major synthesis of the doctrines of progress and evolution, however, was made by Spencer, who was an evolutionist even before Darwin. Evolution was extended by him to sociology and ethics. Human nature was not conceived to be fixed, but undergoing indefinite variation. This very property made humanity perfectible. Evil is not a fixed element in either the human being or the social constitution, but results from the maladaptation of the organism to the conditions of life. Modification of forms continues until adaptation is complete in the mental and moral, as well as the biological life spheres. Civilization is the end product of the adaptations already accomplished.

> Always towards perfection is the mighty movement—towards a complete development and a more unmixed good; subordinating in its universality all petty irregularities and fallings back, as the curvature of the earth subordinates mountains and valleys. Even in evils the student learns to recognize only a struggling beneficence. But above all he is struck with the inherent sufficingness of things.[4]

One effect of this fusion of the concepts of progress and evolution and of the conception of the evolution of human society toward more progressive forms was to set in motion the employment of societal typologies intended to epitomize early and late stages in the historical process. Examples of famous societal types are shown in Table 1.1.

It is unnecessary to trace the rich profusion of progress-evolutionary theories of social change. Nor is it necessary to document in detail the reason for their collapse. It is sufficient to note, simply, that the breakdown of the theory of social and cultural change which at one time was almost coextensive with sociology itself shook the new social science to its very foundations.[5]

The critical difficulties which brought the progress-evolution theory of social change into difficulty and eventually brought about its downfall were: it rested on value premises, its basic propositions were taken as fixed rather than formulated as hypotheses for test, and it lacked an adequate method. Social evolutionism had assumed that human development was unilinear. Contemporary preliterates, who would seem to violate the assumption of the unilinear development of human society, were conceived to have been delayed by local cir-

TABLE 1.1   Types of Society

Thinker	Early	Late
Auguste Comte	Theological society	Positivistic society
Herbert Spencer	Militaristic society	Industrial society
Henry Sumner Maine	Status-dominated society	Contract-dominated society
Ferdinand Tönnies	Gemeinschaft	Gesellschaft
Robert Redfield	Folk society	Secular society

[3] Charles Darwin, *The Origin of Species* (New York: P. F. Collier, 1909), p. 528.
[4] Herbert Spencer, quoted by Bury, *op. cit.*, p. 340.
[5] For some of the details, see Don Martindale, "Sociological Theory and the Ideal Type," in Llewellyn Gross (editor), *Symposium on Sociological Theory* (Evanston, Illinois: Row, Peterson & Company, 1959), pp. 57–91.

cumstances at an early evolutionary stage in the development of mankind. A potential source of negative evidence against the progress-evolution theory was thus turned into an asset, since one now felt free to use evidence gathered from contemporary preliterates to reconstruct the evolution of society.

Considerable difference of opinion existed between different evolutionists as to where humankind began its ascent and where its odyssey would terminate. These points on the evolutionary series were usually assumed arbitrarily in terms of the value premises of the given thinker. Often some recently reported preliterate group (such as the Australian preliterates which Durkheim considered the lowest stage of surviving primitivism) was taken as the starting point of the evolutionary series. The highest stage of evolution was usually taken to be the sociologist's own society—Paris, London, Boston. A hypothetical line was arbitrarily drawn between these points and various kinds of historical and ethnographic evidence, usually torn out of the social context of particular societies, was arbitrarily strung on this hypothetical line. No mechanism for the social evolutionary process, equivalent to the germ plasm of living species, could be specified which might operate as the foundation of social evolution. Such procedure permitted so many contradictory organizations of the same facts that in the long run the entire progress-evolution theory of social change fell into disrepute.

The Cyclical Theories of the Heirs of Positivistic Organicism

The downfall of the progress-evolution theory of social change was itself one of the major components in the modification and eventual disintegration of positivistic organicism. From the beginning tension had existed between the positivistic and organismic elements of this school of theory.[6] One result of this tension was the development of volun-

taristic organicism which retained the organismic theory of society but placed far greater emphasis on the *drive* or *feeling* life of man than had the founders[7] of sociology. With this development came the inclination toward a different theory of social change.

Among the philosophic forerunners of voluntaristic positivism, Nietzsche had inclined, in his doctrine of eternal recurrence, toward a cyclical theory of social and cultural change. Among the sociological exponents of voluntaristic positivism, Pareto inclined toward a cyclical theory of social change. The most basic events of social life were found by Pareto in *residues* (the underlying drives of society) and in derivations (variable conscious elements). Two of these residues or powerful voluntaristic proclivities, the residue of combinations (a tendency to innovate) and the residue of persistence of aggregates (the tendency toward conservation), were particularly important.[8] Two principal social types and two major social classes embody these residues: the speculators (the residue of combinations) and the *rentiers* (the residue of persistence of aggregates). *Rentiers* are the lions of society. They are conservative, cautious, suspicious of change, and quite ready to use force to maintain order. However, they also have a fatal tendency to be lazy. They are easily persuaded to allow the foxes (combiners, *entrepreneurs*, schemers, inventors) to penetrate their ranks by craft and trickery. In the end the *rentiers* find themselves dethroned. History is "the graveyard of aristocracies." However, in time the deceit and trickery of the speculators become unbearable, and the lions regain the will to power to put them down by force. History is a "circulation of the Elite."

Not all the heirs of positivistic organicism retained the positivistic elements of the original theory. Certain persons retained and purified the organicism of the original theory, but dropped its positivistic forms. All of the main

---

[6] See Don Martindale, *The Nature and Types of Sociological Theory, op. cit.*, pp. 52 ff.

[7] *Ibid.*, pp. 99–100.

[8] See Don Martindale, *The Nature and Types of Sociological Theory, op. cit.*, pp. 110 ff.

representatives of a purified contemporary organicism have promoted cyclical theories of social and cultural change. This is illustrated by the works of Oswald Spengler, Arnold Toynbee, and Pitirim Sorokin.[9]

Sorokin is the best example, sociologically speaking, of this trend among the pure organicists toward cyclical theories of social and cultural change. He has developed his doctrines not only in *Social and Cultural Dynamics* but in *Society, Culture, and Personality.*[10] As Speier has noted, Sorokin was as interested in demolishing the theory of progress as in developing an alternative for it:

> *Social and Cultural Dynamics* is a very ambitious study. It covers the history of civilization for the last twenty-five hundred years and contains numerous excursions into the history of many civilizations in order to ascertain the forms and kinds of socio-cultural change.
>
> Fundamentally, the work is a gigantic re-examination of the theory of progress which, in popular form, has dominated the philosophic views of many social scientists in the nineteenth century and has exerted a deep influence upon the mores of modern Western society. The theory contained not only the prospect of an ever-increasing efficiency of man's control over nature—making for greater safety and comfort—but also of an ever-increasing liberation of man from prejudices, ignorance, and destructive passions.[11]

Sorokin treats personality, society, and culture as three successively more comprehensive systems of human phenomena. His distinction primarily concerns the third. "The cultural aspect of the superorganic universe consists of meanings, values, norms, their interaction and relationships, their integrated and unintegrated groups ('systems' and 'congeries') as

they are objectified through overt actions."[12] When one studies the socio-cultural universe, "the individuals and groups function not for their own sake but mainly as the agents and instrumentalities of meanings, values, and norms.[13] It is Sorokin's contention that this cultural universe of meanings, values, and norms which "contains billions of small systems" forms progressively larger systems:

> Among the comparatively vastest of these systems are the integrated systems of science, philosophy, religion, ethics, law, the fine arts, and the systems of oral and written language as the main vehicles for the objectification of any system or congeries of meanings.[14]

Such vast cultural systems in turn are said to be integrated into the "vastest known ideological super-systems." There are three such great integrations of culture. Their natures consist of their conception of the ultimate nature of truth, reality, and life.

> Some ideological cultures answer that *true reality and true value is sensory*, that beyond the reality and value perceived by our sense organs there is no other reality and no value. Having answered it in this way, such ideological cultures build upon this answer their vastest supersystem in which most of their scientific, philosophical, ethical, and other systems articulate exactly this major premise. Such ideological supersystems can be called *sensate.* Other highly integrated ideological cultures answer the problem by stating that *the true reality and true value is the supersensory, super-rational God* ("Tao," "World Soul," "Brahman," etc.), *the sensory reality and value being either a mere illusion, or the least important, least real, sometimes even negative, reality and value.* The vastest ideo-

---

[9] See Oswald Spengler, *The Decline of the West,* trans. by Charles Francis Atkinson (New York: Alfred A. Knopf, 1926); Arnold Toynbee, *A Study of History* (New York: Oxford University Press, 1934–1954), 10 vols.

[10] Pitirim Sorokin, *Society, Culture, and Personality* (New York: Harper & Bros., 1947).

[11] Hans Speier, *Social Order and the Risks of War* (New York: George W. Stewart, 1952), p. 208.

[12] Sorokin, *Society, Culture, and Personality, op. cit.,* p. 313.

[13] *Ibid.,* p. 313. The reification of culture should be noted. It uses individuals as its instruments!

[14] *Ibid.,* p. 317.

logical supersystem built upon this premise can be called *ideational*.

Still other highly integrated cultures assume that *the true reality and value is partly sensory, partly rational, partly supersensory and superrational infinite manifold*. The ideological supersystem erected upon this major premise can be called *idealistic*.[15]

Examples of sensate culture are found in Greece and Rome after the fourth century B.C., in the West since the fifteenth century A.D., in some periods of Chinese history, and in some primitive tribes of our day, for example, the Dobu. Examples of ideational culture are found in Taoist China, Greece (prior to the fifth century B.C.), Brahmanistic and Buddhistic India, Christian medieval Europe, and certain modern primitive tribes, for example, the Hopi and Zuni in North America. Examples of idealistic culture are found in Confucianist China, ancient India, ancient Greece of the fifth century B.C., and Europe in the thirteenth and fourteenth centuries.

Perhaps the most significant of all the criticisms that have been directed at Sorokin's constructions is that historical phenomena are not being studied to understand them, but to evaluate them. Moreover, this evaluation is being conducted in terms of a comparatively limited scheme of values. The methodological weakness of Sorokin's procedure has been summarized by Speier:

> In many respects Sorokin's sociological approach to history reminds one of the methodology of the old unilateral evolutionists in ethnological theory, who started out with an assumed and prearranged scheme of universal evolution and then searched for the material to round out the skeleton outline and vindicate the evolutionary scheme, having little regard for the cultural context from which they wrenched their data.[16]

In Speier's view, Sorokin's philosophy is a kind of vulgarization of early Christian thinking.

The distinction between sense, reason, and faith is retained as a universal principle of division of the types of man, cultures, and "systems" within each culture. The hierarchization of these values, however, is blurred. The idea of a supreme good is given up in favor of a relativistic point of view tempered by eclectic professions of absolute standards. Throughout his work some kind of hierarchy of the three values is implied, as is particularly evident from the expressions of contempt, disgust, and revulsion in which Sorokin indulges whenever he describes the "sensate sewers" of our time.[17]

The substitution in Sorokin's studies of evaluation for scientific analysis is carried further in his relativization of truth and the development of a concept of integral truth, said to be as different from the truths of faith, of reason, and of the senses as each is different from the other. Integral truth is said to fuse the empirical truth of the senses, the rational truth of reason, and the superrational truth of faith into a higher unity.[18] This proposal moves Sorokin's theories not only outside of the circle of positivism but outside of science as well.

The Theories of Social Change of Conflict Theory

Long before positivistic organicism had run its course and had begun to modify and eventually abandon the theoretical formula on which the theory first rested, a deeper ground movement in general sociological theory was manifested in the rise of conflict theory. Conflict theory arose as a realistic protest against many superficialities in early organismic theories. By and large, the conflict theorists retained and even intensified the positivism of early sociology. However, in place of the conception of society as an organism, social reality was thought to be a process of conflict of individuals and of groups over scarce values.[19]

It is useful to distinguish various conflict

[15] *Ibid.*, p. 320.

[16] Speier, *op. cit.*, p. 210.

[17] *Ibid.*, pp. 211–212.

[18] Pitirim A. Sorokin, *Social and Cultural Dynamics* (New York: American Book Co., 1937–1941), Vol. IV, p. 762.

[19] See Don Martindale, *The Nature and Types of Sociological Theory, op. cit.*, pp. 127 ff.

ideologies developed in the nineteenth and twentieth centuries from sociological conflict theory proper. An ideology is a social and political program rather than a scientific explanation. The two main conflict ideologies, Marxian socialism and social Darwinism, were not primarily developed by professional sociologists, but by persons interested in practical economic and political reform. Both major conflict ideologies, however, elaborated interesting theories of social change.

Theories of Social and Cultural Change of the Conflict Ideologies

Marxism, which had in part developed in reaction to Hegelian idealism, took over its theory of imminent development in a conception of dialectical materialism. This was a form of progress theory in which the mechanism of social development was located in economically based class conflicts. As its position was formulated in the *Communist Manifesto*, "the history of all human society past and present has been a history of class struggles."[20] These class struggles in the past occurred under slavery and under feudalism. At the present time they are forming under capitalism. In each stage the nature of social life is determined by the system of social relations which, in turn, rests on the kind of mastery of nature its technology makes possible. Under each system of technology and production in the past, a division arose in time between the owners of the means of production and the workers. The former were able to skim off the surplus productivity of labor. However, in the end, class struggles broke out and the workers took production into their own hands, advancing social development to a new level of efficiency. The cycle of revolutions was accompanied by a rising level of achievement. The positive achievements of capitalism are themselves more extraordinary than the Egyptian pyramids, Roman aqueducts, or Gothic cathedrals. As Marxian theorists saw it, contemporary society is now on the threshold of the next highest step which, through the dictatorship of the proletariat, may open the way to the classless society of the future.

Among the many objections that have been raised against the Marxian theory of social change are the following: It provided a one-factor analysis of social change; its conception of the social classes was oversimplified; it made predictions about social and economic developments (for example, the disappearance of the middle class into the two great classes of capitalists and proletariat) which have not in fact come to pass. However, though Marxism completely failed to establish a general theory of social change, it left no doubts that many social changes are best traced to economic conflicts.

The social Darwinists also developed a conflict ideology in which a concept of social change was involved. The kind of conflict it presupposed was not a struggle of classes but a biological struggle to survive. Moreover, many social Darwinists were inclined to conceive social change in pessimistic terms, presenting one of the few contemporary ideas of change as degeneration. Malthus argued that for all species of living things, including the human species, there is a tendency for population to outstrip the food supply. In the end the effect on population is to drag the level of life down to the point where people are just able to survive. Voluntary methods of population check, he thought, entail an extensive corruption of morals which can be worse than the effects of an excess of population. Moreover, the natural checks on population by vice, unwholesome occupations, poverty, sickness, and war are never sufficient to prevent the encounter of man with his destiny.

> It seems evident that no improved form of government, no plans of emigration, no benevolent institutions, and no degree or direction of national industry, can prevent the continued action of a great check to increase in some form or other; it follows that we must submit to it as an inevitable law of nature.[21]

[20] Karl Marx and Friedrich Engels, *The Communist Manifesto* (New York: International Publishers, 1930), p. 25.
[21] Thomas Malthus, *Essay on Population* (New York: The Macmillan Co., 1894), p. 97.

From Malthus' day to the present, gloomy predictions on the future of human society under the pressures from population have been advanced.

As has been pointed out many times, here again, as in the case of the Marxian theory of social change, only a single factor has been specified. Furthermore, there is a playback from social life on population which has not been adequately accounted for in the idea that the voluntary control of population results in moral corruption. Many societies seem to have stabilized their populations for long periods without either having first reduced the level of life to a starvation level or having permanently corrupted their ethical life. However, here again the proposition was established beyond doubt that though demographic factors can never account for the whole of social change, they play a role in it.

Early Conflict Theorists Subscribe to a Modified Progress Theory

By and large, the early conflict theories accepted the dominant interpretation of their period, conceiving social and cultural change as progressive. They differed primarily from the positivistic organicists in attributing social progress to the establishment of equilibria of interests in the course of a struggle for social, economic, and political power. They assumed a more or less constant tendency to shift the scene of the contest to the more comprehensive arenas of power. In one form or another, this is assumed or stated by all the major conflict theorists, among whom are Walter Bagehot, William Graham Sumner, Ludwig Gumplowicz, Gustav Ratzenhofer, George Vold, and Ralf Dahrendorf.

Ratzenhofer, who conceived the social process as a product of conflicting interests, illustrates the tendency in his *Sociological Knowledge*.[22] He argued that conflicting interests lead man successively to form more comprehensive social structures. Or, perhaps, it would be better to say that the contests of men terminate with the formation of structures of in-

creasing size. Any given structure, once formed, becomes the agency in further struggle, hence were formed: the horde, the settled race, the state, the hegemony with world control, and, finally, the international coalition. This societal evolution is accompanied by an ethical and cultural evolution in which the stages are: fellows, community of interests, political self-control in the interest of peace, universal freedom and equality of legal rights, diplomacy, and international peace.

When the theories of progress developed by the positivistic organicists began to tumble into ruins, they tended to cast doubt upon those of the conflict theorists as well. However, the nature of their analytical mechanism did not commit the conflict theorists to value premises in quite the same manner or to unilinear schemes of social development. Most conflict theorists could have accepted the idea that the formation of more comprehensive structures of power may take many different directions at different times and places. The fact that these points have not been made is due more to the fact that conflict theory itself had lacked adherents than to properties of its theories. The comparative lack of adherents to conflict theory is possibly a product of the frequent failure to distinguish between conflict ideology and sociological conflict theory. The conflict ideologists tended to pass over into politics and out of the field of sociology, and sociologically inclined students in distinguishing themselves from the conflict ideologists have usually embraced other types of theory.

The Lack of a Theory of Social Change by the Sociological Formalists

As a movement in general theory, sociological formalism was produced in part by the crisis of positivistic organicism, particularly by the disaster suffered by its theories of social change. Formalism was an attempt to reconstitute sociology by means of the kind of analysis that Immanual Kant employed in his

[22] Gustav Ratzenhofer, *Die Sociologische Erkenntniss* (Leipzig: F. A. Brockhaus, 1907).

epistemology.[23] The formalists proposed to analyze social life in terms of social relations or forms, as they described them, following Kant's epistemological distinctions. For this purpose they relegated the study of the content of social life to other social sciences. Because of various technical problems in neo-Kantian sociology, formalism tended to shift to the analysis of the presumed depth levels of phenomenal experience along lines outlined by the phenomenologists.

The formalists cut their ties with history, and simultaneously thrust most of the problems of social change aside. The various changes of social life assumed relevance for them only to the degree that social forms or relations were manifested in them. Under these circumstances, though occasional observations about one or another type of social change were made by various formalists, the development of a general theory of social change was not attempted.

The Social Behavioristic Receptivity to Social Change

Social behaviorism arose in the same atmosphere as formalism and in response to the same problems. However, the school defined the basic materials of sociology as social behavior rather than social structure in the manner of organismic positivism and conflict theory or as social relations in the manner of the formalists.[24] Moreover, while social behaviorism agreed that modification of the positivistic assumptions of the early schools was necessary, it did not accept the antipositivistic inclinations of certain of the formalists. It undertook the development of new empirical methods. Three branches of social behaviorism emerged, differentiated by their peculiar definition of social behavior and their methodological preferences: pluralistic behaviorism, symbolic interactionism, and social action theory. Two of the branches of social behaviorism—pluralistic behaviorism and social ac-

tion theory—had strong interests in theories of social change.

Pluralistic Behaviorism

Pluralistic behaviorism was developed by Gabriel Tarde in France, modified by E. A. Ross and F. H. Giddings in America, and transmitted in recent times to William F. Ogburn, F. Stuart Chapin, and others. As Tarde saw the matter, social life at bottom always consists of the acts of individuals. These acts, in turn, rest on beliefs and desires. Social structures are merely complex arrangements of these unit acts. Nevertheless, one can get his most immediately accurate description of social life by noting the differences between unit acts and counting their frequencies. Such acts will either be repetitions (imitations) of the acts of others or nonrepetitions (innovations). From this perspective, every individual is a potential source of change.

Tarde was convinced that one could establish laws of imitation. For example, he thought that imitations are refracted by their medium. The laws of imitation include the fact that they tend to move from upper to lower classes and from city to country. Finally, considered as a whole, ages of custom- and of fashion-imitation alternate with one another. Such ideas, modified in minor ways by Giddings and Ross, supplied the foundation for the theories of collective behavior in the early twentieth century. The new method of social statistics evolved rapidly in connection with this type of social behaviorism.

Although the pluralistic behaviorists were not committed to the view that only society as a whole changes, since its position emphatically implied that every person was a potential innovator, it became one of the few points in sociological theory where a theory of progress was retained despite the collapse of the progress-evolution formulas elsewhere. The device by which certain recent pluralistic behaviorists managed to save the progress for-

---

[23] See Don Martindale, *The Nature and Types of Sociological Theory, op. cit.*, pp. 211 ff.

[24] See Don Martindale, *The Nature and Types of Sociological Theory, op. cit.*, pp. 285 ff.

mula was the distinction between material and nonmaterial culture. Culture was defined statistically, rather than structurally, as the accumulated products of human society. With Tarde inventions and discoveries were treated as the specific source of social change.

If the primary source of cultural change is located in the material culture and if non-material culture is assumed primarily to consist of adaptation to this, the illusion of continuous growth can be maintained. If one compares the products of Greek drama with modern movies and asks which is higher, it is no foregone conclusion that the movies will come out on top. However, if one compares the material culture of ancient Greece with that of modern America, the story is quite different. There is little question that classical Greek plumbing was quite inferior to that of modern America. Many times the question has been asked: Why has the cultural-lag theory persisted in the face of all the criticism which over the years has been raised against it? This can only be attributed to the powerful wish by contemporary men to retain the doctrine of progress in the teeth of apparently fatal objections to it.

As Ogburn conceived it, the real source of cultural progress was located in such material inventions as tools, weapons, and technical processes. Adaptive culture consists of all other things which must be adjusted to this material base. Many things may interfere with the easy adaption of nonmaterial to material culture: vested interests in tradition, fear of change, reluctance to change one's habits, lack of education or wrong education, social pressure, and avoidance of the unpleasant. As a result, "material-culture changes force changes in other parts of culture such as social organization and customs, but these latter parts of culture do not change as quickly. They lag behind the material-culture changes, hence we

are living in a period of maladjustment."[25] However, Ogburn left no doubt where things had to go.

Unfortunately for the clarity of his argument, Ogburn went on to offer another kind of lag theory, best described as a biological lag. Here the contrast was traced, not between two parts of culture, but between biology and culture. It was argued that "man is the same biologically as he was in the late ice age, while his culture has suddenly become vastly different."[26] As a Stone Age man living in a contemporary city, man is exposed to severe psychological tensions, accounting for such problems as war, crime, sexual aberrations, and disease. Between these two types of theories, cultural and biological lag, contradictory interpretations of the same facts are possible.[27]

The fundamental elasticity of the pluralistic behavioral approach to social change was appreciated much more fully by Chapin than by Ogburn. In his study Chapin retained the culture-lag hypothesis to account for the accumulation of material culture. However, his compromise formula which viewed cultural change as selectively accumulative in time, but "cyclical or oscillatory in character," took account of the possibility that particularly in nonmaterial culture, cycles of varying scope may appear. Cycles of social change, he argued, are of several orders. Cycles of the first order occur in the material culture. They may be minor, illustrated by the displacement of one machine industry by another in a business cycle, or major, illustrated by the rise and fall of a system of technology, for example, the slave system. Cycles of the second order in the nonmaterial culture are illustrated by the rise and fall of religious sects or the rise and fall of social structures. Cycles of the third order relate to large cultural composites, for example, national cultures. These cycles vary in scope from the rise and fall of classes or

[25] William F. Ogburn, *Social Change with Respect to Culture and Original Nature* (New York: B. W. Huebsch, 1922), p. 193.

[26] *Ibid.*, p. 286.

[27] For a critique, see Don Martindale, "Social Disorganization: The Conflict of Normative and Empirical Approaches," in *Modern Sociological Theory*, ed. by Howard Becker and Alvin Boskoff (New York: Dryden Press, 1957), pp. 340–367.

dynasties to the rise and fall of whole civilizations.[28]

Social Action Theory

Like pluralistic behaviorism, social action theory treated social reality as consisting of particular interhuman acts. Comparable to the pluralistic behavioral insistence that interhuman behaviors have beliefs and desires at their core was the concern of social action theory with the meaningful dimensions of interhuman behavior. For social action theory, too, only individuals innovate, though they often do so in the name of the groups in which they operate. Over and again, for example, new social arrangements were conceived by Max Weber to emerge in the activities of a charismatic leader, that is, a person perceived by his followers as extraordinary and to be followed for this reason. This instance was merely one of many where the role of the individual as innovator was emphasized.

While the social action theorists (Max Weber, Robert MacIver, Thorstein Veblen, John R. Commons, and others) never assembled their many suggestions about social change and their many studies of specific short-time and long-time developments into an integrated theory of social change, various special problems of social change were ever foremost in their thoughts. Veblen, for example, was occupied throughout his life with the rise of capitalism and its consequence for other aspects of contemporary culture. Commons, too, studied the rise of many of the institutions of capitalism—the formation of unions, the development of labor legislation, the influence of immigration on labor conditions. Commons' study of the *Legal Foundations of Capitalism*[29] is a classic in the study of the interrelation and mutual interplay of legal and economic institutions. MacIver was profoundly concerned with the rise and transformation of political institutions.

Finally, Max Weber carried out many profoundly influential studies of specific historical developments. Such was his study of the evolution of the agrarian institutions of antiquity, the role of the religious psychology cultivated among certain Protestant sects in the development of capitalism, the rise of rational musical patterns in Western polyphonic music, the rise and influences of bureaucratic administration in all large-scale modern structures. In the course of these and many other studies, numerous generalizations about social change were established: the emergence of charismatic leaders in times of crisis; the necessity for routinization of charisma, if charismatic change is to be conserved; the influence of the style of life of the stratum which primarily bears it on a social movement as a whole; the interadjustment of major areas of institutional life (such as economics to politics and religion, and vice versa).

While none of the social-action theorists was willing to subscribe either to an unqualified progress theory or to an unqualified conception of social and cultural cycles, all of them were convinced that long-time trends are discernible in certain areas (for example, technology and science), and some social and cultural changes are cyclical in character. The social action theorists have produced a large number of generalizations usually employed by sociology at present to account for various special changes without anchoring these ideas in a single identifiable theory of social change.

The Functionalistic Approach to Social and Cultural Change

Since the role of functionalism in the theory of social and cultural change has been commented on, it is unnecessary to discuss it in detail. Contemporary functionalism is a return to a modified form of the organicism of the founders conjoined to an up-dated positivism.[30] The observation was made earlier that,

---

[28] F. Stuart Chapin, *Cultural Change* (New York: The Century Company, 1928), pp. 208–209.

[29] John R. Commons, *The Legal Foundations of Capitalism* (Madison: University of Wisconsin Press, 1957).

[30] See Don Martindale, *The Nature and Types of Sociological Theory, op. cit.,* pp. 441 ff.

in view of the functionalistic assumption of the causal priority of the system over its parts and their reification of the equilibrium states of social systems, the functionalists were put in the position of holding that social change was in principle impossible except for the intrusion of outside factors.

In terms of the review of the relation between theories of social and cultural change and general sociological theory, this statement appears not altogether true. Functionalism is not in principle prevented from accounting for change arising internal to the system (except for dysfunctions which call for adjustment), but it was put into position where only the imminent evolution of the system adequately accounts for change. In short, the character of functionalistic theory seems to force it into the position where it must account for social and cultural change in the same manner as was originally attempted by the positivistic organicists. However, the memory of the disaster suffered by the early forms of imminent evolutionism is too fresh to make the prospect of a theory of social change which rehabilitates the doctrine of imminent evolutionism very appealing. Functionalism has been left in the unenviable position where the one major alternative open to it is unacceptable.

Postscript to the Functionalistic Theory of Change

Since the above section was written the *magnum opus* of macrofunctionalism, the two huge volumes of *Theories of Society* edited by Talcott Parsons, Edward Shils, Kaspar D. Naegele and Jesse R. Pitts, has appeared. In this "Aristotelian synthesis" of macrofunctionalism a vast number of fragments from pre-1935 sociological writings have been organized exclusively within a functionalistic framework. This enterprise somewhat resembles that of Italian masons of the Renaissance period who chiseled the marbles of the Roman ruins to fragments which they polished and cemented into the entryways and baths of prosperous bourgeois merchants of the cities.

Long introductions have been added by the editors to their mosaic tile designs, in which functionalistic theory has been brought to full integration and completeness.

Talcott Parsons, who has grown restive under the frequent observation by contemporary critics that functionalism has troubles with its theory of social change,[31] undertook in his sections of *Theories of Society* to develop the functionalistic theory of social change. His arguments have special interest here; they supply basic confirmation for the contention in the preceding section that the nature of functionalistic theory forces it toward an evolutionary position. At the same time, the judgment expressed earlier—that the memory of the early disaster suffered by social evolutionism was too fresh to make rehabilitation of this theory very appealing—was in error. By way of a series of euphemisms Parsons has taken this very step; he has refurbished social evolutionism.

In "An Outline of the Social System" which compactly summarizes macrofunctionalism, Parsons conceives society as a system surrounded by three others (personality, the organism, and culture). A society is said to be in equilibrium when its boundaries with the other three systems are maintained intact. Social equilibrium consists in "boundary maintenance"; social change consists in boundary-breaking. "If a subboundary is broken, resources within the larger system counteract the implicit tendency to structural change."[32]

Social change conceived as boundary destruction and equilibrium restoration, is said to have two sources, exogenous and endogenous. An exogenous factor is one arising outside the social system; an endogenous factor is one arising internal to the social system. The external (exogenous) sources of social change are internal to the other systems (personality, the organism, culture) which are said to border society. In Parsons' inimitable language:

The exogenous sources of social change consist in endogenous tendencies to change in the

---

[31] See Parsons' answer to Llewellyn Gross in the *American Journal of Sociology* for September 1961.

[32] Talcott Parsons, *Theories of Society* (Glencoe: The Free Press, 1961), Vol. 1, p. 71.

organisms, personalities, and cultural systems articulated with the social systems in question.

Examples of such external causes of social change are properties of the geographical environment, biological heredity, the occurrence of great men, and population pressure. Endogenous sources of social change are strains between the parts of society.

> The most general, commonly used term for an endogenous tendency to change is a "strain." *Strain* here refers to a condition in the *relation* between two or more structured units (i.e., subsystems of the system) that constitutes a tendency or pressure toward changing that relation to one incompatible with the equilibrium of the relevant part of the system.[33]

In other words, a strain is a strain.

There are, Parsons argues, two main types of change depending on the source (exogenous or endogenous) of the model for re-equilibrium once the forces to repair boundary destruction are set in motion.

> The first . . . is the one where the principal model component comes from outside the society. This has been true of the contemporary undeveloped societies. . . .
> The second . . . is that occurring when the cultural model cannot be supplied from a socially exogenous source, but must . . . be evolved from within the society. This is the situation to which Max Weber's famous category of charismatic innovation applies.[34]

However whatever the source of its re-equilibrium model, social change normally inclines toward a "functional differentiation" of originally "functionally diffuse" structures. "The process of functional differentiation is one of the fundamental types of social change and has evolutionary aspects."[35]

Elsewhere in the same volume Parsons makes this revived social evolutionism even more explicit. Originally, he argues, all soci-

eties were primitive, undifferentiated, and characterized by "ascriptive solidarities."

> In the structure of primitive or relatively undifferentiated societies, ascriptive components are overwhelmingly predominant. The first focus of the ascriptive structure is generally kinship.[36]

"Ascriptive solidarity" is another name for functional diffuseness. The original ascriptive solidarities are said to undergo functional differentiation in time.

> The above outline of comparative social structure has been sketched from a frankly evolutionary frame of reference. We have taken the concept of ascriptive solidarities as not merely designating one structural type, but as a broad evolutionary base line. In the process, old ascriptive solidarities are "whittled away," and in a wide variety of ways new ones are created. . . . However, the *relative* importance of ascriptive solidarity tends to decline, though the process is uneven and reversions are common. . . .[37]

Thus, by way of a series of euphemisms Parsons has rehabilitated the social evolution hypothesis. His very terminology is a thinly disguised version of older formulas. "Ascriptive solidarity" means that individuals are bound to each other by some generalized bond such as by the fact that they are family members, neighbors, or brothers of a fraternal organization. This is exactly what Henry Sumner Maine meant when he described ancient man's relation to his fellows as a "status." By "functional differentiation" Parsons means that individuals are related to one another as interlocked specialists in a division of labor. This is exactly what Henry Sumner Maine meant by the observation that in contemporary societies a man's relation to his colleagues tends to become very precisely defined as in the case of a "contract." In new language Parsons has revived Maine's old formula that human society

---

[33] *Ibid.,* p. 71.
[34] *Ibid.,* p. 78.
[35] *Ibid.,* p. 76.
[36] *Ibid.,* p. 242.
[37] *Ibid.,* p. 263.

everywhere evolves, despite occasional set-backs, *from status to contract.*

Since the days when Spencer argued that society evolves from "incoherent homogeneity" to "coherent heterogeneity" to Parsons' argument, nearly one hundred years later, that society evolves from "ascriptive solidarity" to "functional differentiation," the sociological theory of change seems to have made one full circle. Inasmuch as the many objections raised against the evolutionary hypothesis when applied to human society are still largely unanswered, one can expect that they will now be redirected at the functionalists. And sociology is ready for another round.

Summary

Though three major positions on social and cultural change have been sporadically promoted in contemporary sociology, the culture-lag theory, the cultural-cycle theory, and the intrusive-disturbance theory, this branch of contemporary sociological theory is experienced by many sociologists as in crisis.

The great profusion of historical forms of the theory of social change can be reduced to four basic types: (1) the theory that social and cultural changes are nonexistent or of little importance, (2) the theory that social and cultural changes are degenerative, (3) the theory that social and cultural changes are progressive, and (4) the theory that they are cyclical. The three positions in contemporary sociology fall into the first, third, and fourth types.

In contrast to its weak development in current sociology, the theory of social change was one of the most strongly developed branches of theory in early sociology. Five schools of sociological theory have developed: positivistic organicism, conflict theory, sociological formalism, social behaviorism, and sociological functionalism. In positivistic organicism social change was conceived as progressive and evolutionary. However, the theory collapsed when it was demonstrated to rest on value premises and inadequate methods. Later members of this school of theory had recourse to various cyclical theories of social and cultural change. In its early days conflict theory developed specialized forms of the theory of social progress, resting on mechanisms of individual and group conflict rather than on imminent evolution of organismlike structures. Conflict theory has declined for lack of proponents rather than for any structural defect. Formalism was the first school explicitly to renounce its ties with history and to shift the whole theory of social change to an insignificant place in its considerations. Of all contemporary schools, social behaviorism has been most receptive to various theories of social change. The culture-lag theory of the pluralistic behaviorists has attempted to preserve some of the old progress formulas by means of its distinction between material and nonmaterial culture. The social-action theories have been receptive to a variety of explanations of special social changes without, however, integrating its many ideas on social change into a single consistent form.

Contemporary functionalism, which has dominated American sociological theory since World War II, rests on a theoretical formula similar to that of positivistic organicism. However, though its general theory forces it toward an imminent evolutionary theory of change, there has been great hesitation until recently to reconstruct a formula which suffered so severe a disaster in the past.

For all these reasons many contemporary sociologists feel that the theory of social and cultural change is in greater need of re-examination than any other branch of the discipline.

Selected Bibliography

Bury, J. B., *The Idea of Progress* (New York: Dover Publications, 1932).

Chapin, F. Stuart, *Cultural Change* (New York: Appleton-Century-Crofts, 1928).

Commons, John R., *The Legal Foundations of Capitalism* (Madison: University of Wisconsin Press, 1957).

Martindale, Don, *The Nature and Types of Sociological Theory* (Boston: Houghton Mifflin, 1960).

Marx, Karl, and Friedrich Engels, *The Communist Manifesto* (New York: International Publishers, 1930).

Moore, Wilbert E., "A Reconsideration of Theories of Social Change," *American Sociological Review*, Vol. 25, No. 6, December, 1960, pp. 810 ff.

Ogburn, William F., *Social Change with Respect to Culture and Original Nature* (New York: B. W. Huebsch, 1922).

Sorokin, Pitirim A., *Social and Cultural Dynamics* (New York: American Book Co., 1937–1941), 4 vols.

Speier, Hans, *Social Order and the Risks of War* (New York: George W. Stewart, 1947).

Weber, Max, *The Protestant Ethic and the Spirit of Capitalism* (New York: Charles Scribner's Sons, 1958).

2.   Change Management: The Process and the System

Ira Kaufman*

Date Line: Urban America, 1970

"There are many things which must be changed in the United States for the betterment of the citizens and their way of life," said John Doe, middle-class American.

This statement exemplifies the growing desire to institute changes in many aspects of American society. Americans, like John Doe, are not unanimous in their concern for every social cause or the method to bring about these changes. Some concerned Americans will passively agree, with John Doe's statement, while others will actively strive to institute these changes. Notwithstanding their techniques, the second group or change agents have at least one thing in common. It is their desire to direct social changes. The organizations working toward peace, family planning, racial equality, or consumer protection, each evolve different campaigns to gain the support of the American public for their cause. Each organization attempts to change the public's attitudes and consequent actions in the direction of the goals of the organization.

Although many organizations attempt to direct change, few agencies have impressive records. The reasons for failure range from an unworthy cause to an ineffective organization. Most agencies working for social change do not approach the problem in an organized, analytical fashion. Often their tactics are neither pretested, coordinated or evaluated; therefore their efforts are diffuse and marginally effective.[1] A solution has been posed in terms of "conflict management."[2] It is suggested that conflict management must diagnose problems and mobilize men, media, and resources to solve social problems.

The objective of this paper is to develop a model of change management which will provide change agents with a managerial approach in directing social change. One can define directed social change as a *planned attempt to modify the attitudes and behavior of target individuals or groups by agencies of change seeking to introduce ideas or innovations into a social system in order to achieve the goals of the agency or constituency.*

A model of change management focuses on the four activities of management: organizing-analyzing, planning, implementing, and evaluation-controlling. The change management system is a model of the process of social

Some of the ideas presented in this selection were originally conceived in Ira Kaufman and Ronald Stiff, "A Social Marketing Approach to Defensive Driving," Northwestern University, April 1970.

* Lecturer, Manchester Business School, University of Manchester.

[1] See Bernard Berelson, "On Family Planning Communication," in Donald Bogue (ed.), *Mass Communication and Motivation for Birth Control* (Chicago: University of Chicago Community and Family Study Center, 1967), p. 49.

[2] Ed Butler, "There Ought to Be a Law," *RAP Magazine* (Winter 1970).

change cast in this die. It is comprised of three interrelated interdependent subsystems which provide feedback to the other subsystems. Each of the subsystems corresponds to four major managerial activities and each will be treated separately.

The Change Management System

Previous discussions of directed social change have focused on either a microbehavioral or macrobehavioral approach to social change. The microbehavioral[3] view of social change attempts to relate the new attitudes and behavior of an individual with one's characteristics and dispositions. This approach is useful to the change agent in the understanding of his change targets. The theory is developed in terms of a black box model, while the analysis attempts to uncover the causal linkages between the boxes. This approach is exemplified by models of attitude change,[4] adoption,[5] and consumer behavior.[6]

The second approach to directed social change takes a macrobehavioral view of the situation. It attempts to provide change agents with certain guidelines and strategies which will increase a change target's probability of changing. The theoretical underpinnings of this approach lie in the results of descriptive surveys and practical experience. Much of the work done in cultural change and modernization is based on this approach.[7]

The model proposed in this paper will integrate these two approaches. It will use a systems approach to achieve this end. This model will be called the *change management system*. *Change management can be defined as the organization, planning, implementation, and evaluation of social programs whose ultimate goal is social change.*

The change management system has been conceived as an open system. An open system is any system that adapts to its environment by changing the structure and processes of its internal components.[8] Four basic concepts characterize any systems model: boundary, tension, equilibrium, and feedback.[9] In the case of the change management system, the system boundary refers to any variables in the environment that affect the ultimate response to the decision object of the change effort. The tension within the system describes the stress and conflict caused by different components within the system. Tension will be characterized by the internal dynamics of a change agency: such as the creativity and innovation of the members or structural changes of the organization.[10] The third characteristic of systems—equilibrium—relates a system's tendency to balance the various forces acting upon it. The change management system will dynamically adapt itself to a new equilibrium state in response to internal (organizational) and external (environmental) disruptions.

[3] See Philip Kotler, *Marketing Decision Making: A Model Building Approach* (New York: Holt, Rinehart and Winston, 1971) for a discussion of microbehavioral models in a marketing context.

[4] See Irving Janis and Carl Hovland, "An Overview of Persuasibility Research," Irving Janis, *et al.* (eds.), *Personality and Persuasibility* (New Haven: Yale University Press, 1959).

[5] See Everett Rogers, *Diffusion of Innovations* (New York: The Free Press, 1962).

[6] See John Howard and Jagdish Sheth, *The Theory of Buyer Behavior* (New York: John Wiley & Sons, 1969).

[7] See Daniel Lerner, *The Passing of Traditional Society* (New York: The Free Press, 1958). Also, Herbert Hyman, Gene Levine, and Charles Wright, *Inducing Social Change in Developing Countries* (New York: U.N. Research Institute for Social Development, April 1967).

[8] Walter Buckley, "Society as a Complex Adaptive System," in W. Buckley (ed.), *Modern Systems Research for the Behavioral Scientist* (Chicago: Aldine Publishing, 1968), pp. 490–491.

[9] Robert Chin, "The Utility of System Models and Developmental Models for Practitioners," in W. Bennis, K. Benne, and R. Chin (eds.), *Planning of Change* (New York: Holt, Rinehart and Winston, 1969), p. 299.

[10] *Ibid.*, p. 301.

Finally, feedback emphasizes the self-control and adaptive nature of the system. It focuses on changing those operating processes or structures which are not permitting goal optimization.[11] The change management system has sensing mechanisms which provide feedback. This enables a change agency to adjust its strategies and tactics to be more in line with its objectives.

The change management system has three subsystems: organizational, communication, and change target (Figure 2.1). The three subsystems of the change management system parallel the four central activities of management. The organizational subsystem is a major input of the system. It creates a structure that will *analyze*, *plan*, and *administer* the change program to be used to perpetuate the issue. The communications subsystem serves to transform the organizational input. It is the actual structure by which the organization's change program is *implemented*. Finally, the change target subsystem is the output of the system. This subsystem will process all the stimuli of the communication subsystem concerning the issue and respond accordingly. The organization can use responses as a means for *evaluation* of the change program. This evaluation will enable the organization to control its progress toward previously set goals.

Within each subsystem of the change management system, there is a process. This process is the "actions and interactions of the components of the ongoing system in which varying degrees of structure arise, persist, dissolve or change."[12] In effect, the collapsing of the three structural subsystems into one grand entity would change the model to that of a change management process. The change management process was created to present to those interested in social change a logical flow of events and decision states. Each decision state will reflect the previous choices made while molding the pattern of future decisions. The model proposes a process view of social change using a management perspective. For explication and conceptual clarification, one can think of the change management system as three interrelated subsystems with a process integrating the entire system. Each subsystem will be discussed in terms of an input and an output.

Before discussing each subsystem, one must consider the environmental input. The environment acts as an exogenous input to the change management system. This affects the endogenous input of the organizational subsystem as well as the other two subsystems. The environment is composed of four major influences: political, social, economic, and technological. Any of those environmental influences can affect the equilibrium state of the change management system, thus forcing an adjustment in many aspects of the system. Any agency seeking to direct change must consider the dynamics of the environment in order to achieve success. Examples of environmental influences are discussed relative to each subsystem.

Organizational Subsystem

Inputs

Within the organizational subsystem, the input to the process can begin in either of two ways. First, a *social cause* or *issue* can exist which motivates a *group* or *individual* to organize a *change agency*. The second alternative is the recognition of an existing social cause or issue by an established group. Regardless of which way it was formed, the change initiator must create a formal structure to direct social change. This organization may be a recasting of an old structure or a newly created group. Thus, the organization must mobilize its efforts, in order to adapt to the role of a change agency.

In either case, the membership of the change agency must choose a *change philosophy*. The philosophy is the general approach used by the organization to accomplish social change. This approach can be one of: directed change (persuasive, power or reeducative strategies, discussed on page 28), equilibrium maintenance (status quo), or exogenous

[11] Buckley, *op cit.*, p. 494.
[12] *Ibid.*, p. 497.

Figure 2.1. Change Management System.

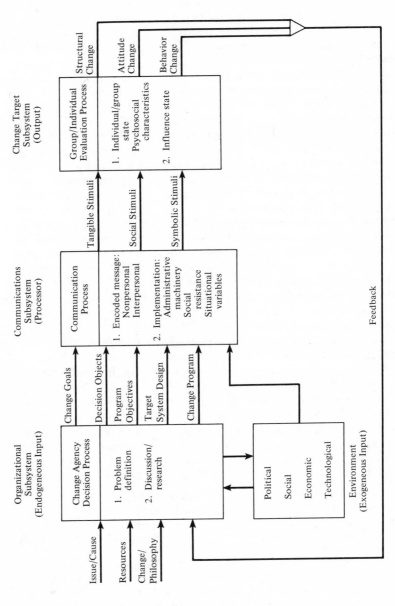

change (technological advances, laws, sociali-zation).[13] Each of these approaches is then modified by a change agency's desire for ei-ther radical revolutionary change or incre-mental, evolutionary change. Using directed, incremental change as their change philoso-phy, Planned Parenthood attempts to alter the birth control practices of society. The equilib-rium maintenance approach is employed not to change individuals' attitudes and behaviors, but rather to retain their past allegiance. This is exemplified by an organization such as the Klu Klux Klan. The Klan is attempting to keep the South segregated in the face of a declining interest in the cause and the organization. The third approach, exogenous change, allows somewhat "natural processes" to dictate the changes in society. For example, the American legislative and judicial systems pass and en-force laws which will have profound changes in American life. The Civil Rights Law will create social changes by socializing and edu-cating the southern youth. This approach is contrasted by the use of directed change by many of the active civil rights groups (i.e., Southern Christian Leadership Council). The change management system will be explained in terms of the directed incremental change approach, but each of the other two ap-proaches are amenable to the same analysis.

Besides their guiding philosophy, each or-ganization will be characterized by five essen-tial resources: political pressure, economic wealth, social prestige, expertise, and creative talent. The presence or lack of these resources will greatly affect the success of a change agency. The first three resources can be dis-cussed in terms of one dimension—*power*. The wielding of power in society by a change agency is dependent upon that organization's ability to mobilize its political, economic and social resources. The second dimension—*peo-ple*—affects the successful use of power. The presence of experienced, creative organiza-tional members will enable a change agency to effectively implement the power it attains.

Processor

The first event in transforming the inputs is the *definition* of the social cause. The organi-zation defines the problem and considers al-ternative actions. This is usually accomplished by a discussion, research, or combination ap-proach. This first approach to problem defini-tion is membership discussion sessions, which are based upon the member's experience and are exemplified by a brainstorming session. Al-though often shortsighted, the discussion tech-nique is generally adopted. It features a use-ful, pragmatic, short-run approach to social change. In an attempt to improve upon the problem definition stage, social scientists have attempted to employ research. This second approach has been referred to as "reforms as experiments."[14] It involves three stages: de-sign, analysis, and utilization. In the design stage[15] the problem is first formulated in terms of a model. A field or laboratory experi-ment is then designed to test the most viable decision objects and complimentary social change tactics of the model. The second stage,[16] suggests the analyzing of the experi-

---

[13] See Louis Barnes, "Organizational Change and Field Experiment Methods," in Victor Vroom (ed.), *Methods of Organizational Research* (Pittsburgh: University of Pittsburgh, 1967), for a typology of organizational change.

[14] Donald T. Campbell, "Reforms as Experiments," *American Psychologist*, Vol. XXIV (April 1969), pp. 409–429.

[15] See Leslie T. Wilkins, "Problem into Model," *Social Deviance* (Englewood Cliffs, N. J.: Prentice-Hall, 1965), pp. 178–189, for a discussion of modeling social problems. Also Donald T. Campbell and Julian Stanley, *Experimental and Quasi-Experimental Designs for Research* (Chicago: Rand McNally, 1963), for an excellent discussion of types of research designs.

[16] See Fred Kerlinger, *Foundations of Behavioral Research* (New York: Holt, Rinehart and Winston, 1964), for a comprehensive survey of techniques used to analyze behavioral data. Also, Raymond Bauer and Robert Buzzell, "Mating Behavioral Science and Simulation," *Harvard Business Review*, (1964), pp. 116–124, for an application of a research strategy and an analytical technique to aid decision-making.

mental data. Finally, in the utilization stage,[17] the results of the analysis are used to improve the understanding of the problem and the possible solutions.

Output

The utilization of research and discussion session resolutions are the initial outputs. They are manifested in many ways. The organization will have clarified its *change goals* and decided upon their decision objects. The change goals refer to the long-term desires of the organization. These could involve any of the following changes: attitude change, individual behavior change, and structural change. The decision object is referred to as *a material or nonmaterial entity toward which an individual is predisposed and considers acting upon.*[18] It is what an individual must decide to adopt or reject; thus the decision object is the entity that the change agency has created as the focus of its change efforts. The decision object can be a person or a group of people (political candidate), economic product (automobile), issue (family planning), or a program (political platform). The decision object can be conceived as the end of the organization or as a means toward that end. The *ultimate decision object* is the desired end toward which the organization works. Most organizations working for social change realize the impossibility of achieving their end within a short period of time. For this reason, they choose *subsidiary decision objects*, which act as means toward an end.

To clarify some of the concepts discussed one can use Planned Parenthood as an example. The organization's change goal is for social change to provide a healthy, livable world. Its ultimate decision object is family planning; the organization feels it cannot attain its change goals if parents do not plan and control the size of their families to a reasonable number. The leaders realize they cannot achieve their end of world-wide family planning immediately; therefore, the organization chose to support subsidiary decision objects. The setting up of clinics, the disseminating of information, and the lobbying for the legalization of abortions fall in the second category of social objects.

A second series of outputs reflects the actual planning of the change program. The change programs are planned and developed to communicate and motivate an individual to adopt the decision object. This begins by outlining *program objectives* for the subsidiary social objects being "marketed." These objectives are for the short run and are specific to each decision object. They are the short-term behaviors that are instrumental in achieving the ultimate goal. Program objectives will differ with respect to the type of decision object being "marketed." In the case of an issue, attending your first antipollution meeting might be the objective; while, in the case of a person, a voter's awareness of Richard Nixon's new image may be the objective.

The next major decision in the process is to select "which people" you will attempt to change. These segments of society are referred to as a *change target system*. Each change target system would ideally be a homogeneous group of individuals who would be more likely to respond to one type of appeal than another. These targets can either be protagonists or antagonists to the cause. For example, Planned Parenthood might select cardinals of the Catholic Church as targets, most of these cardinals are against birth control. It has been suggested that each change target system should have three requirements: that they are

---

[17] See Mark Chesler and Mary Flanders, "Resistance to Research and Research Utilization: The Death and Life of a Feedback Attempt," *Journal of Applied Behavioral Science*, Vol. IV (October–December 1967), pp. 469–487. Also, Ronald Lippitt, "The Use of Social Research to Improve Social Practice," *American Journal of Orthopsychiatry*, Vol. XXXV (July 1965), pp. 663–669, for a discussion of the utilization of research information.

[18] The concept of decision object is similar to that of social or psychological (attitude) object discussed by L. L. Thurstone, "The Measurement of Social Attitudes," *Journal of Abnormal and Social Psychology*, No. 6, (1931), pp. 249–269, except that it involves a decision to act.

measurable, accessible, and substantial enough to incur the expense of reaching.[19] The segmenting of change target systems will allow the change agency to employ the most effective appeals. This is called *target segmentation* and can be defined as *the development and pursuit of different change programs by the same organization for essentially the same decision object but for different components of the total audience.*[20]

The creation of the *change program* is the final output. The change program includes the specific change tactics used by the change agency to effect changes in specific change target systems. In other words, the varieties of communicated stimuli that are disseminated to change targets about a specific product, idea, or person represent the change program for that decision object. In any campaign for social change one can view the mix of tactics used in the change program as the key determinant of success.

Each change program is molded about some combination of the three basic strategies to changing people—power, persuasion, and reeducation. These strategies are paralleled by three theoretical processes for influencing people—compliance, identification, and internalization.[21] The power approach is characterized by the use of political, economic, and social reward sanctions. One is "forced" for his own good to change his behavior. One will comply to this influence if his actions are under surveillance of the power figure. The second approach focuses on using persuasive appeals to one's rational psyche. In this case the behavior change is dependent on the expected external rewards of the new alternative behavior. One will adopt a new behavior if it can be identified with a person or group the individual

wants to relate to. The last strategy is concerned with reeducative practices toward the norms of the organization or society. This strategy creates behavior change by confronting individuals and sensitizing them to more rewarding behaviors. The individual, in this case, sees the behavior as relevant and "intrinsically rewarding"; thus, he internalizes it.

Each change program is composed of three basic change variables—influence structures, cost, and channels. The influence structures reflect the way that a decision object is presented. The cost involves the expected value (rewards–costs) of accepting the decision object. The channels include two dimensions: the media outlets for the message and the physical outlets to "dispense" the decision object.

The influence structure functions as a "generalized mediating mechanism to facilitate social transactions, to persuade people toward some action or inaction, and to serve as a transferable form of social wealth."[22] More simply, an influence structure is the means used to influence a change target. One can conceive of three types of influence structures: mass, intergroup, and interpersonal. Each structure is characterized by levels of interaction, type of exposure, manifestation of the influence, mechanisms mediating the influences, and results of the influence (Figure 2.2).

For example, usually the change agency begins by attempting to influence the masses or major segments of society. To do so the agency usually mobilizes the mass media to inform the client of the decision object. While mass influence is being employed, the group will try to influence a small segment of society at a more personal level. Intergroup influence

[19] Philip Kotler, *Marketing Management: Analysis, Planning, and Control.* (Englewood Cliffs, N. J.: Prentice-Hall, 1967), p. 45.

[20] Adapted from Ronald Frank, "Market Segmentation Research: Findings and Implication," F. Bass, C. King and E. Pessemier (eds.), *Applications of the Sciences in Marketing Management,* (New York: John Wiley & Sons, 1968).

[21] Herbert Kelman, "Processes of Opinion Change," *Public Opinion Quarterly,* Vol. 25 (1961), pp. 51–78.

[22] Based on Otto Lerbinger, "Influence: The Generalized Medium of Public Communication," in Otto Lerbinger and Albert J. Sullivan (eds.), *Information Influence & Communication,* (New York: Basic Books, 1965), p. 253.

Figure 2.2. Influence Structures.

Characteristics	Type of Influence Structure		
	Mass ——————⟶	Intergroup ——————⟶	Interpersonal
Change agency—target interaction	Agency to society or major segment	Agency to minor segment of society	Individual to individual
Type of exposure	Mass media	Audience participation, selected media	Face to face
Manifestation	Advertising	Speeches, group discussion, or confrontation	Personal incentives, personal selling, bargaining
Mediating mechanisms	Reinforcement repetition	Rational persuasion, group dynamics	Personal influence, coercion
Result of influence	Informs and reminds of decision object	Gives target additional understanding of decision object	Adoption or rejection of decision object

generally involves a few group members trying to influence a larger audience. The final type of influence, interpersonal, is the most direct and the most effective. Interpersonal influence is a consequence of one or both of the individuals having been affected by either the mass or intergroup influence. The outcome of this exchange of views at the interpersonal level will have the greatest affect on adoption.

The selection of an influence structure or mix of influence structures is guided by the basic strategy of the change programs. The basic strategy will affect not only the selection of the influence structure but also the manifestation of the influence structure. An influence structure can be manifested as either a tactic or an activity (Figure 2.3). A tactic is a *pure instrument or mode of influencing a change target*. A tactic can be used alone or in combination. When a mix of tactics is used, it is called a *change activity*. For example, the change activity, lobbying, employs seven different tactics:[23] advertising (paid or donated nonpersonal promotion), publicity (not paid for nonpersonal exposure in mass media, i.e., news story), direct mail (sending of literature by mail), speeches, personal selling (interpersonal oral presentation), leafletting (giving of pamphlets or papers), and word-of-mouth ad-

vertising (unsolicited discussions among people). In the case of both tactics and change activities their basic appeal is reflected in the change strategy or mix of strategies used by the change agency.

Thus, each influence structure involves the mediating of influence to different people, through different outlets, using different tactics and activities, and with different results. Using birth control as the decision object, one can view the three types of influence. Initially, advertisements might be run on television (mass influence) to remind and inform the public of the need to practice birth control. Secondly, Planned Parenthood might organize a population teach-in or a local community discussion group (intergroup influence) to give a segment of society a greater appreciation of the problem. Finally, the word-of-mouth discussion among friends and neighbors (interpersonal influence) will greatly influence the final decision of an individual to adopt or reject the practice of family planning.

The second element of the change program is the cost variable. It refers to the amount of resources an individual must expend to alter his behavior. There are three dimensions of cost which an individual must consider before

[23] See Kotler, *op. cit.*, p. 451, for a description of some of these tactics.

Figure 2.3. Manifestations of Influence Structures.

Change Activities

Structure	Influence / Tactics	Teach-in	Lobbying	Fund Raising	Nonviolent Demonstrations (Rally)	Violent Demonstrations (Riots)	Sensitivity Groups	Negotiating, Bargaining	Strikes, Boycotts	Disruption
Mass	Advertising	✓	✓	✓	✓				✓	✓
	Publicity	✓	✓	✓	✓				✓	✓
	Direct mail	✓								
Intergroup	Speeches	✓		✓	✓				✓	✓
	Group discussion	✓					✓			
	Group confrontation				✓	✓	✓		✓	✓
Interpersonal	Personal selling	✓	✓	✓	✓	✓		✓	✓	✓
	Personal incentive		✓		✓	✓		✓	✓	✓
	Counseling (individual confrontation)						✓			
	Word-of-mouth advertising	✓		✓	✓	✓				
	Bargaining		✓		✓			✓	✓	✓
	Leafletting	✓	✓	✓	✓				✓	✓

adopting a decision object. The material aspect of cost involves the amount of money the adopter will have to expend. The psychic cost involves the prestige, status, mental ease, and so forth, which an individual gains or loses as a result of adoption. The third cost is that of effort. Effort involves the mental and physical effort expended as well as the time and convenience factors affecting adoption of the decision object. Each of these costs are weighted by the individual and compared relative to the costs and rewards of the alternatives. Thus, if Planned Parenthood was concentrating on using cost as a variable, it would lobby for tax credit for no children, increase the prestige of limited family size, and reduce the price of contraceptive devices. This approach would be to increase the rewards and decrease the costs to such an extent as to make people want to control the size of their families.

The channels are outlets where information is disseminated or the decision object is available for adoption. They refer to the "where and how" an individual may positively respond to a message, thus motivating one toward behavioral change. The channels are characterized by location, availability, and adequacy. For example, the telephone is a channel for information seeking, while the number and location of birth control clinics are channels affecting the adoption of the practice. Therefore, although one might perceive great rewards in and be persuaded to practice birth control, he might not adopt the practice because the channels are not adequate. In the context of antismoking campaigns, Gerhart Wiebe made the distinction between media outlets and physical outlets:

No general advertising campaign is successful unless there is a "retail store" in which the advertised product can be sold to individuals.

He asked those concerned with selling the findings reported in the Surgeon General's Report to find a "retail store," a vehicle for individual contact to potentiate the effects of mass communications.[24]

On viewing the change program in general, one can sense that the change target system and the type of social object being communicated will set the parameters of the change program. In the case of most economic goods the marketing-advertising campaigns, a type of change program, focus on changing low involvement,[25] inconsequential beliefs (i.e., Crest toothpaste has a good taste). As Milton Rokeach states, "the more competitive the advertising the more it addresses itself to psychologically inconsequential beliefs about the relative merits of different brands."[26] On the other hand, the change programs for nonmaterial decision objects must be aimed at beliefs in which one is more involved.[27] These more involved beliefs relate to one's authority figures (i.e., church) or to those beliefs which are derived from one's authority figures.[28] Both of these beliefs are harder to change and more central to the individual. Thus, change programs for family planning must use appeals that will change these more central beliefs. Planned Parenthood must change (or challenge) a Catholic's beliefs concerning the Church's position on birth control.

The distinction between the three types of variables has been formulated to understand their function in a change program. The three variables must be integrated into a well-balanced program. Each decision object might use a different mix of these variables, but each variable must be considered for the program to be successful. The change program is analogous to an automobile engine. It must have the proper mix of air, gasoline, and electric

[24] Bernard Mausner, "The Beaver College Conference on Behavioral Studies in Smoking," in Edgar Borgatta and Robert Evans (eds.), *Smoking, Health, and Behavior,* (Chicago: Aldine Publishing Co., 1968).

[25] Herbert Krugman, "The Impact of Television Advertising: Learning without Involvement," *Public Opinion Quarterly* (Fall 1965), pp. 349–356.

[26] Milton Rokeach, *Beliefs, Attitudes, and Values,* (San Francisco: Jossey-Bass, 1968), Chap. 8.

[27] Krugman, *op. cit.*

[28] Rokeach, *op. cit.,* Chap. 1.

sparks for it to run smoothly. Otherwise, it will stall out or waste a great deal of gas.

Communications Subsystem

The second subsystem of the change management system is the communications subsystem. It acts as a boundary between the change agency and the change target. Thus, the communications subsystem serves to both encode and carry the change agency's and the environment's messages to the change target. In other words, this subsystem transforms inputs into stimuli.

Inputs

The inputs to the communications subsystem are twofold. Initially, the outputs of the organizational subsystem—the change goals, decision object, and change program—are endogenous inputs to the change management system. An exogenous input which affects both the organizational and communications subsystem is the environment. This includes the social, political, economic, and technological influences.

Processor

After planning the most effective strategies, the change agency must implement the program, which necessitates the implanting of encoded stimuli in the target communication networks. These networks can be of the nonpersonal, mass media type or the interpersonal type. The choice of these networks has been decided as a channel strategy of the change program. For the change program to achieve any degree of success, the change agency must manage the communication process. The communication process, in turn, is primarily affected by the interaction of the organizational subsystem and the environment. This interaction involves three essential elements—administrative machinery, social resistance, and environmental variables.

The administrative machinery represents the individuals in the organization who are responsible for implementing the change program. This group must have a strong leader who will coordinate, motivate, and control the group's efforts. The administrative machinery

of any change agency has many levels. For example, the Democratic National Committee has a central leadership committee with fifty state organizations and thousands of city and local precinct organizations. Many change programs are successful in creating awareness of a social object by a national mass media campaign but fail to create behavioral changes because of the lack of local administrative machinery.

The second element affecting the communication process and implementation is social resistance, which brings to the forefront the social and institutional mores of a social system. The change agency must recognize the consequence of its change goals on the local communication networks and devise its tactics accordingly. For example, Planned Parenthood had planned to use free public service advertising in mass media. A predominantly Catholic community, a target of the program, does not favor the objectives of Planned Parenthood and lobbies against any free use of the local communication networks. In this case, Planned Parenthood must be able to overcome the resistance in order to implement their change program.

The final element affecting implementation is situational variables. These variables include time and situational and physical realities of the environment. The importance of time cannot be underestimated. Any change program requesting attendance of community members must consider conflicts with other activities, season of the year, and time of the day. In addition, the change agency must be responsive to abrupt shifts in the mood of its change targets. Again in the family planning context, the Pope's reaffirmation of the Church's position against birth control a few days before the opening of a clinic might prove disastrous to its initial success.

Considering these three elements, a change agency might understand a basic reason for the failure of change programs. Much work is often done organizing and planning for social change, but little is done to implement these ideas. The change agency often thinks the implementation will just get done by the organization. Such reasoning, of course, is a fallacy and must be corrected for change programs to be successful. Change management will only be effective if each activity of the process is properly managed.

Outputs

The output can be considered the sum of all social influences and change efforts to which an individual is exposed.[29] The outputs of the communications subsystem can be characterized as three types of stimuli: tangible, symbolic, and social. The tangible stimuli concerning any decision object refer to the actual attributes of that object. For example, a message discussing the offering of an adult education course would have the course name, the fee, the location, and offering times as tangible stimuli. The symbolic stimuli are the images an individual perceives about the decision object. In the same example, the perceived rewards, the image of the course content, and possible course attendees would be examples of symbolic stimuli. The third type of stimuli, social, are described by those significant others who influence one's decision-making process. The significant others include family, reference groups, and organizations which prove to be powerful, attractive, or credible in influencing an individual's decision.[30] Thus, social stimuli are inputs from significant others concerning a decision object. In the adult education example a company's "urging" of an employee's attendance, favorable discussion among friends, or active community interest in the course are types of social stimuli.

Change Target Subsystem

The last subsystem in the change management system is the change target subsystem. Here the change target (individual or group) receives stimuli from the communications subsystem and then passes through a series of evaluation states in response to the stimuli. Depending upon the change target, the evaluation process can be on the group or individual level. For this reason, one can consider an individual change system and a group change system to model their respective decision-making process. In the case of the former the output is attitude and/or behavior change, while in the latter it is individual attitude-behavior change or structural change.[31] The individual change system will be discussed extensively since many of the concepts can be transferred to the group level.

The individual change system is a microbehavioral model of individual change. It is an interdisciplinary approach attempting to synthesize the inquiry and action approaches of four fields of individual change—communication, attitude theory, diffusion, and consumer behavior. More specifically, this paradigm is built upon the salient attributes of William McGuire's attitude change model,[32] Everett Roger's adoption model,[33] and John Howard and Jagdish Sheth's buyer behavior model.[34]

The individual change system is basically an input-output model (Figure 2.4). It is comprised of three essential elements—input, processor, and output. The inputs to the individual change system are the outputs of the communications subsystem. The processor is the element of the system which considers alternative modes of response. In essence, the processor is an individual's evaluation process. Any decision is a result of the inputs to the processor and the interaction of individual and influence states. These two states corre-

[29] Howard and Sheth, *op. cit.*, p. 63.

[30] Herbert Kelman, "Compliance, Identification, and Internalization: Three Processes of Opinion Change," *Journal of Conflict Resolution*, Vol. 2 (1968), pp. 51–60.

[31] See Harold Leavitt, "Applied Organizational Change in Industry: Structural, Technological, and Humanistic Approaches," in James March (ed.), *Handbook of Organizations* (Chicago: Rand McNally, 1965), for a thorough discussion of organizational change.

[32] William McGuire, "Personality and the Susceptibility to Social Influence," in E. Borgatta and W. Lambert (eds.), *Handbook of Personality Theory and Research*, (Chicago: Rand McNally, 1968).

[33] Rogers, *op. cit.*

[34] Howard and Sheth, *op. cit.*

Figure 2.4. Individual Change System.

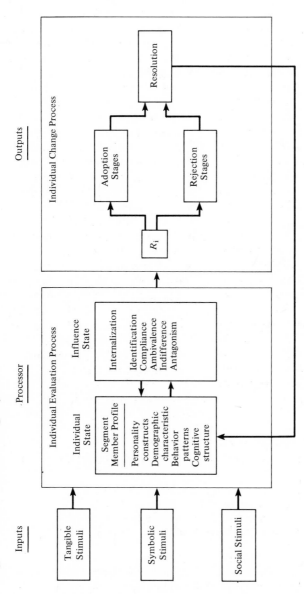

spond to the internal (dispositional) and the external (situational) components of personality.[35] The individual state is what Kurt Lewin described as the "life space" of an individual. It is all the facts that have existence or demonstratable effects for the individual under study. Each individual is a member of a segment of society and has a profile of characteristics unto himself. The influence states are mediating processes that aid the individual in interpreting inputs and making responses. *This evaluation process is dynamic in nature and occurs before each response.*

The final element is output. The output is the measurable mental-behavioral responses of the individual. The aggregate of these response states comprise the individual change process. Within the individual change process an individual can pass within and between two series of response states. The adoption stages elucidate the process of becoming aware of a message, becoming interested in that message, and acting upon the message. On the other hand, the rejection stages consider the nonexistence of a message, the non-involvement in or resistance to a message, and the rejection of the message. In either the case of adoption or rejection the individual must pass through a final stage. This involves resolving the discrepancies between one's actions and feelings. The expansion of these three elements reveals the dynamic nature of the system while describing the interactions of the process components. The following is a treatment of each element.

Inputs

The inputs to the individual change system are the outputs of the communications subsystem. These include tangible, intangible, and social stimuli.

Processor

The processor shows how an individual processes and evaluates the stimuli he receives concerning a decision object. The individual evaluation process occurs dynamically

throughout one's entire decision of whether or not to adopt a decision object. Each evaluation of the incoming stimuli is a function of the interaction of two states—the individual and the influence.

Individual State

The individual state describes a member of a segment of society with a profile (segment member profile) of personality constructs, demographic characteristics, past behavioral patterns, and a cognitive state. Each of the four conditions are not independent with respect to each other and also change with time.

One's *personality constructs* are the first elements of the individual's profile. The theory of personal constructs is based on a fundamental postulate, "A person's processes are psychologically channelized by the ways in which he anticipates events and that these ways exist in the form of constructs." The personality construct is an abstraction of the way an individual construes things as being alike or different from one another. An individual's system of constructs is hierarchical in nature and form his personality. An individual's *demographic characteristics*, the second element, change as one develops. One's demographics are any characteristics that "paint a picture of an individual's position in society." They include race, religion, education, housing, income, etc. The third element of the profile, *behavioral patterns*, is closely akin to demographic characteristics. The major distinction lies in that *not all* behaviors and experiences "paint a picture of one's social positions." Behavioral patterns are tangible activities in which an individual participates or has participated. Those activities include the entire gamut of behavior—organizational membership, community activities, past experiences, information seeking, general deportment, and so on. The last element, *cognitive structure*, refers to an individual's mapping of the relationship between needs, values, beliefs, and attitudes with regard to a decision object. This state of mind is a function of one's personality

[35] Kurt Lewin, *A Dynamic Theory of Personality* (New York: McGraw-Hill Book Company, 1967).

constructs. It constantly adapts to changes in demographics and to the experiences of past behavioral actions. One's cognitive structure acts as a filter for communicated stimuli. If an individual will "allow" a stimulus to disrupt the balanced cognitive state, one will enter the individual change process.

The interaction of the four elements results in an individual belonging to many segments in society. A segment is a group of individuals who have at least one behavioral characteristic in common. For example, an individual might be a risk-taker who subscribes to many adventure-oriented magazines and who has had two traffic accidents and thinks traffic safety is unimportant. The interaction of these four elements might mean that this individual and those like him should be persuaded to drive more defensively. A reform agency, such as the National Safety Council, is interested in reaching this segment of society. By analyzing their demographic characteristics and behavioral patterns, the agency might find it is effective to use adventure-oriented magazine advertisements. Thus, agencies interested in changing segments of society should analyze their segment member profiles to choose the most effective media to communicate their messages.

INFLUENCE STATES

The influence states are five different states of mind. These states of mind describe at what level an individual can be affected by the stimuli he receives. The segment member profile mediated by these states of mind interpret stimuli. The interpretation and evaluation of the stimuli will result in a positive, undecided, or negative response in regard to a decision object. The interaction of the segment member profile and influence state will take place before each response.

An individual can respond positively to stimuli at one of three levels—*compliance*, *identification*, and *internalization*. These levels of influence had been discussed previously in the context of the change strategy. The change agency must consider a level of influence and create tactics which are complementary.

The second major class of influence states considers when an individual is undecided as to his action concerning a decision object. Such a state of mind can be called *ambivalence*. It is defined as the coexistence within an individual of positive and negative feelings toward a decision object drawing him in opposite directions. This frequently occurs when an individual considers the importance of the punishments in a compliance situation and his true feelings toward the decision object.

The last class of influence states are those causing a negative response to a decision object. These include *indifference* and *antagonism*. Indifference is considered a state of mind at which there is an absence of feeling or interest in the decision object. On the other hand, antagonism is defined as a conflict with or hostility for a decision object. Both indifference and antagonism will certainly lead to rejection unless an individual is thrust in a compliant situation.

Outputs

The final element of the individual change system is the output. The output of each stimuli passing through the evaluation process is a response state. The summation of response states leading to an ultimate decision is called the *individual change process*. The individual change process has two parallel series of response states—the adoption stages and the rejections stages (Figure 2.5). In either the case of adoption or rejection, the individual must resolve his actions and feelings in the last stage.

The individual change process will be discussed in terms of both an operational and conceptual development of each stage. Since the individual change process is dynamic by definition, its presentation will also be dynamic. Thus, the discussion of each stage will include the evaluation process preceding the response, the response alternatives, the manifestation of the response, and the selective processes.

Before entering any mental-behavioral stage, the processor will have made a conscious or unconscious evaluation of the alternatives. The evaluation process is mediated

Figure 2.5. Individual Change Process.

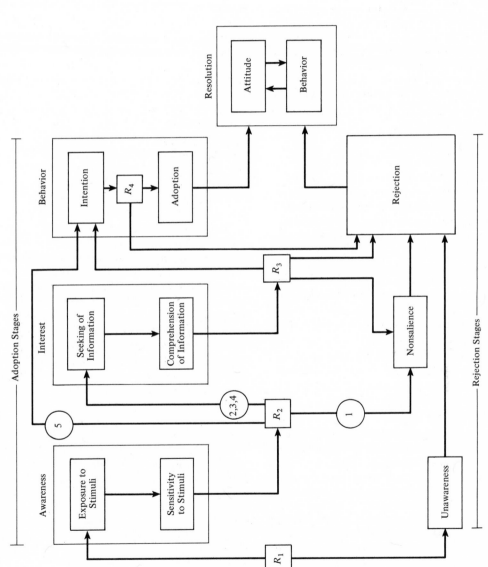

within each stage of the individual change process by "selective processes."[36] These processes are a function of the individual state. They aid an individual in seeking out information and environments that are compatible to him. The relevancy of each process will be discussed in terms of its applicability to each stage. The output (response) of the processor will lead the individual to one of two decision paths, adoption or rejection. In either case the decision and the outcomes are feedback to the processor for use in future evaluations. Since rejection and adoption are complimentary processes, the discussion will focus on each response state ($R_1 . . . R_4$) and its alternative decision paths. The following is a treatment of each stage.

AWARENESS-UNAWARENESS STAGE

When a stimulus is presented to a population, some individuals become aware of it and others do not. Thus, in the first response state (R_1 in Figure 2.5) an individual enters the stage of awareness or unawareness. Unawareness will be defined as the inability to recall a stimulus.[37]

In the case of awareness the individual becomes physically exposed to a stimulus and can identify it. After being exposed, he evaluates the importance and relevance of the stimuli; this is his sensitivity to the stimuli. The mediating processing between exposure and sensitivity is commonly labeled selective attention.

INTEREST-NONSALIENCE STAGE

At R_2 one enters either the interest or nonsalience stage. The decision is based on the consideration of both one's attitude[38] (A) and behavioral intention (B) toward the deci-

sion object. The individual has five alternatives: (1) reject A and B; (2) consider A and resist B; (3) resist A, consider or accept B; (4) consider A and B; (5) accept A and B. In the first alternative he would "pass into" the nonsalience stage of the rejection decision path. After being exposed to the stimuli, the individual felt it was unimportant or meaningless to him. This stage leads to ultimate rejection. In the second, third, and fourth alternatives he would most likely elect to seek information before finalizing a decision. The fifth and last alternative suggests that the individual will proceed immediately to the behavioral stage. This occurs when an individual has previously sought information on a decision object and new information is not needed to make a decision. It is exemplified by consumer impulse buying, stimulation of an ever present salient interest, or a compliance influence state.

An individual passing from awareness to interest can be described by his information-seeking behavior. The second stage, interest, involves two activities mediated by a selection process. The first is the active seeking of information by mail, telephone, interpersonal relations, and so forth. The information will be perceived and retained differently by each individual. These are called selective perception and retention; they are a function of the segment member's profile. Comprehension is the second activity of the interest stage. The comprehension of the message will determine one's evaluation and will effect one's response at R_3.

BEHAVIOR STAGE

At R_3 an individual has been exposed to a stimulus and has responded for information: now he must choose whether to adopt or re-

[36] A. H. Hastorf and H. Cantril, "They Saw a Game: A Case Study," *Journal of Abnormal and Social Psychology,* Vol. 49 (1954), pp. 129–134.

[37] See Ernest Hilgand, "What Becomes of the Input from the Stimulus," in Charles Eriksen (ed.), *Behavior and Awareness,* (Durham, N. C.: Duke University Press, 1962), pp. 48–49, for a description of five circumstances of unawareness.

[38] Attitude is defined as a combination of the value and instrumentality of the decision object. See Martin Fishbein, "A Behavior Theory Approach to Relations Between Beliefs About an Object and Attitude Toward an Object," in M. Fishbein (ed.), *Attitude Theory and Measurement* (New York: John Wiley & Sons, 1967).

ject the behavior. At this point he has only four alternatives: (1) reject A and B; (2) consider or accept A, reject B; (3) resist A, accept B; (4) accept A and B. In case one he would again pass into the nonsalience stage. The second and third cases would involve a resolution between attitude and behavior, but in the second case one would "pass into" the rejection stage, while the individual choosing case three would continue toward adoption. The last alternative would also continue toward adoption.

The third mental-behavioral stage is the behavior itself. This stage is composed of people intending to adopt a decision object and those who actually adopt it. Between intention and adoption the individual has a final series of evaluations. These evaluations will result in R_4 and a decision to adopt or reject. The decision to reject at R_4 is affected by many conditions. In the case of a family-planning lecture or adult education class the conditions range from situational factors, such as weather and location, to attitudinal conditions, such as the relative rewards of an educational activity versus an unexpected, important social event.

RESOLUTION STAGE

Resolution is the last stage of the individual change process. After an individual has either adopted or rejected a decision object, he enters the resolution stage. It is at this point that individuals resolve the inconsistencies between their attitude toward the decision object and their actual behavior. Resolution is based on the premise that all people have a certain need for a tolerable level of internal consistency between feelings and action; the strength of the need will determine the activity of this stage.

The final element of the individual change process is the feedback loop. It allows the individual to learn from his past activities and change his profile with respect to these experiences. For example, the smoker who believes cigarettes cause lung cancer can resolve the inconsistency by rationalizing (rejecting anti-

smoking stimuli) or stopping (adopting stimuli) smoking. If he stops or rationalizes, he will feedback these results to "update his segment member profile." If the rationalizer is eventually stimulated by an effective message (possibly death of a fellow smoker), he will pass directly from awareness to behavior. Thus, the feedback loop is a conceptual method for describing learning in the individual change system.

Feedback

The final element of the change management process involves the evaluation feedback mechanism. This mechanism is similar to the feedback loop in the individual change system. Here the feedback is not to the individual but to the change agency. The responses of the change targets allows the organization to gauge the success of its efforts. It will enable the organization to modify ineffective strategies and refine those that are effective. The function of evaluation can be formally designated to a research department or handled informally by judging the gross effects of a change program. In most organizations initiating social change evaluation is an informal activity. In cases of success their only feedback for all their efforts is the passage of a bill, the decline of the birth rate, and so forth. In the cases of failure most change agencies cannot understand "what went wrong"; therefore, they cannot evaluate their change program and the necessary adjustments. Thus, "an efficient steering of social action presupposes that fact-finding methods have to be developed which permit a sufficiently realistic determination of the nature and position of the social goal and the direction and the amount of the locomotion resulting from a given action."[39]

Conclusion

In summary, the change management system is composed of an organizational, communications, and change target subsystems. In the organizational subsystem the change agency goes through a decision process involv-

[39] Kurt Lewin, "Frontiers in Group Dynamics," *Human Relations*, Part IIB (1947), pp. 147–153.

ing the *analysis* and *planning* of change efforts. The communications subsystem describes the *implementation* of the communications process. It is at this point that a message is encoded in the communications networks. Finally, the change target subsystem is the ultimate recipient of the stimuli. In this subsystem an individual or group evaluates the stimuli and elicits a behavior. The resultant behavior becomes feedback that can be audited and *evaluated* by the change agency.

The development of the change management system is based on the work of many applied behavioral scientists.[40] Its paradigm was developed to give the change agency a managerial perspective. It will enable the change agency to view the sequential events ideally necessary to plan and implement social change. Most organizations promoting social change do not see the linkage between theoretical inquiry results and practical application. They infrequently plan and research alternatives before trying to implement changes. On the whole, they may achieve minimal success for their massive efforts.

The change management system is conceived as a framework for alerting the change agency to the level at which it is operating and the general opportunities and problems it faces in planning social change.

[40] W. Bennis, K. Benne, and R. Chin, *The Planning of Change* (New York: Holt, Rinehart and Winston, 1969). Also, Ronald Lippitt, J. Watson, and B. Westley, *Dynamics of Planned Change* (New York: Harcourt Brace Jovanovich, 1958).

3.   Change

Abraham Zaleznik* • David Moment**

We have organized our study of interpersonal relations in organizations according to: (1) group processes, (2) the individual and interpersonal dynamics, (3) organizational aspects, and (4) leadership and change. The first three sections each analyzed particular processes and their interrelationships. The final section, beginning with the preceding chapter on leadership, has thus far discussed the personality of the individual as leader in relation to the social processes of the group and within the constraints of the organizational and environmental systems. Our analysis of change will start with the nature of organic processes in general, drawing upon some of the concepts and problems represented in general systems theory. We shall then discuss problems of planned changes in individual, group, and organizational behavior and attitudes, citing some research findings on these processes. A laboratory learning model for change will precede the conclusion of our study.

We are concerned with changes in human behavior and attitudes. Other classes of change, such as technological change and economic development, ultimately involve problems of behavior and attitude change in individuals, groups, and organizations. Although the substance of particular technical and economic plans are of upmost importance, we shall not deal with them directly. Some of the social implications of technology and economic reward systems were discussed earlier, but our major focus is on the dynamics of change in individuals, groups, and organizations.

The General Theory of Change

Organic processes take place in the relationships among living units. The units are arranged into systems of increasing complexity,

Reprinted in part from Abraham Zaleznik and David Moment, "Change," *The Dynamics of Interpersonal Behavior* (New York: John Wiley & Sons, 1964), pp. 445–460. Used by permission.
° Cahneys-Pabb Professor of Social Psychology of Management, Graduate School of Business, Harvard University.
°° Professor, Graduate School of Business, Harvard University.

starting with the individual cell. Combinations of particular kinds of cells make up organs such as the liver, the heart, or the lungs. Such organs exist in functional relationships to other organs and to the next larger unit. They are connected by such systems as the nervous system, the circulatory system, and the respiratory system, to make up the total individual organism, the living plant or animal. However, even the total individual cannot exist without other individuals; each unit is engaged in exchange processes with other individuals and with groups. The individual human is dependent on animal and vegetable systems, weather systems, and in modern life social groups and larger social organizations.

The major attribute of organic processes— as opposed to mechanical processes such as an internal combustion engine—which must lie at the base of any theory of individual and social change, is the inherent regenerative potential of the life processes and the eventual death of the individual unit. Organic systems reproduce and maintain themselves, even though each individual member is destined to eventually perish. Such processes maintain temporal continuity in the identity of the individual, the group, the complex organization, the total society, and the civilization in spite of the transient existence of the individuals comprising the larger entity at any one time.

Basic Forces toward Conservation and Change

The processes by which continuity is maintained provide the media in which both resistance to change and the consummation of change takes place. The development of the individual over his life provides a model for the workings of processes of continuity and discontinuity within the individual, the group, and the organization over time.

At age 40, John Jones is the same individual as he was at birth in certain important respects. But he is strikingly different in other respects. The maintenance of the continuity of his identity is crucial for both his personality and the groups of which he is a part. If today and tomorrow he does not feel and behave as the same John Jones he was yesterday, he is suffering severe emotional or mental illness and cannot function coherently. On the other hand, if the groups with which he interacts do not accept him today as the same person he was yesterday and will be tomorrow, severe social pathology exists, and he and the groups cannot function co-operatively.

This required continuity of individual and social identity is the basis of forces toward conservation and the maintenance of the *status quo*. It implies that, in some respects, conditions must *not* change in order for the individual and the group to continue to function effectively. John Jones and his social world would collapse if he felt and acted like a responsible, adult person at work one day, a "beatnik" the next, and an infant the following day. Hence, the time-binding sameness of identity along with social trust in its predictability become tremendously strong forces toward conservation and resistance to change in individuals, groups, and organizations.

With all his sameness of identity, John Jones, age 40, is clearly not the infant John Jones in many important respects. Most obviously, his physical appearance and capabilities are different. The social world behaves differently toward him as an adult than it did when he was an infant. And it expects and counts on different behaviors from him. The inherent biological growth of the individual and the social expectation that he will grow up constitute forces toward change in the individual and his social relationships. Hence, along with inherent forces toward conservation, the life processes contain inherent forces toward change. Paradoxically, the socially expected sequence of changes may become a form of extreme conservation; for example, the expectation that the son would follow in his father's footsteps. Thus, natural processes of change may become institutionalized into sets of conservative forces.

One characteristic inherent in organic processes is the polarity between forces toward conservation and maintenance of identity, on the one hand, and forces toward change, adaptation, growth, and development on the other. Both sets of forces fight a losing battle for the individual; he will not live forever no matter how effectively he maintains himself.

The processes of growth and development can only be culminated in an eventual return to nonexistence. Thus, the amazing thing about life processes is how they strive against the inevitable; life *is* hope in this respect. The institutionalization of this hope, this tremendous output of energy directed toward fighting a losing battle, becomes the basis for the continuity of identity of the larger unit, which persists in spite of the loss of identity of its individual members, Superordinate goals, systems of philosophical and religious belief and transcendental causes, become the outside sources of identity continuity to the individual. The institutionalization of hope into external causes defends the individual and the group against the most immobilizing form of anxiety, the awareness of the condition of nonexistence or the fear of death.

Our discussion has pointed to the tremendously strong bases on which forces resisting and facilitating change rest; these bases distinguish life processes, especially those involving humans, from mechanical processes. The piston in an internal combustion engine is not aware of the fact that it is being used up; it doesn't fight against the process. Humans and their groups do care. They devote considerable energy to expressing their concern.

The workings of the processes of conservation and change have been described from the point of view of the individual, the group, the complex organization, and an entire culture. Since the problems of behavioral and attitudinal change cut across all of these levels of analysis, we shall briefly discuss some of the theories relevant to each.

Culture Change

One of the causes which has captured the imagination of, and has become an object of identification for, many Americans since the Second World War has been helping the economically underdeveloped nations of the world. The exotic flavor of this cause is important because the same, well-meaning Americans who enthusiastically contribute time and effort to helping Africans and Asians do not seem to devote as much attention to the less exotic, but physically closer, needs for development within their own families, work relationships, neighborhoods, communities, geographic regions, and nation. Somehow, remoteness in space, time, and experience is a stronger motivation toward understanding and help than the familiarity of problems such as slums, delinquency, unequal opportunities, and intergroup conflict.

The distinctness of cross-cultural differences not only captures the imagination and interest, it also makes the job of understanding, in both its intellectual and emotional senses, appear to be easier. People can more easily accept that the Greeks have different work, eating, and child-raising practices than they can accept a similar observation about their neighbors. However, the earliest attempts at offering cross-cultural help were often accompanied by serious misunderstanding on the part of the well-meaning helpers; the ingratitude of those being "helped" was attributed to ignorance and stubbornness rather than to the existence of strong cultural patterns which change tended to disrupt.[1] Offering help was not a simple matter of two members of the same group in interaction; the intent was to change the recipient culture.

Cross-cultural helpers may become exasperated when a particular technical improvement or health measure is accepted readily in one culture but rejected by another, or when one culture accepts one kind of change and rejects another. At first glance, the patterns of acceptance and rejection seem to be arbitrary. Uniformities of rejection lie at deeper levels; the social-emotional meaning of a particular technical object or activity pattern may vary from culture to culture, and the significance attached to objects and activities may vary within a culture in ways which bear little relationship to the meaning of the object or activity to the outsider. Moreover, the social-emotional interpretation of helping and receiving help vary from culture to culture.

Edward T. Hall[2] discusses three distinct levels of culture discovered and described by anthropologists: fomal, informal, and techni-

[1] See, for example, Mead, *Cultural Patterns and Technical Change.*
[2] Hall, *The Silent Language.*

cal. Each of these levels transfers the learning of sentiments and practices in a different manner, and each of them features a different strength of emotional resistance to change. Formal traditions are unquestioned imperatives, things that are *done* or *not done* in a particular culture. To our culture, wearing clothing in public is a formal tradition. The child is taught that this is done; no other explanation is offered or even thought of. Formal traditions are learned by precept or admonition.

Informal traditions, on the other hand, are learned by imitating models. These involve doing as certain other people do. Again, the tradition is not explained or deliberately throught out. But, unlike formal traditions, informal traditions may change as models change. General styles of clothing would fit this level; men wear trousers and women wear skirts; the child is taught to dress and act like a little man or a little lady.

The technical level of culture is fully explained by teacher to student; it includes practices which are consciously describable. The child is taught how to tie shoelaces, how to tie a cravat, and when to wear particular kinds of clothing. The questions of whether or not to wear shoes, a formal matter, and whether to wear boys' shoes or girls' shoes, an informal matter, are not involved. Hall points out that all cultural behavior patterns contain all three levels.[3]

According to Hall's analysis, in matters of externally introduced changes, the level of the culture involved and the nature of the emotional aspects of the change are important matters. The degree and kind of affect involved in the three levels of culture differs markedly. Violations of the formal level are perceived with shock and considered "unnatural" events; an adult walking down a city street naked would meet with such a reaction. The violation of an informal tradition, on the other hand, would cause discomfort and invoke conventional social controls, such as giggling, kidding, or embarrassed nervousness.

But social processes are not traumatically interrupted by informal violations, as they tend to be with violations of formal traditions.

In contrast, technical levels of cultural practices are relatively free of affect; the "right way" can be logically explained. However, the fastidious technician will get emotionally disturbed if the technical rules of the game are violated. In Hall's words, ". . . the formal is supported by technical props. It is the technical that people often resort to when all else fails."[4] Thus, technical devices, such as explicit laws, rules, and regulations, may be invoked when a formal tradition is violated, or the devices may become formalized.

The problem in efforts toward cross-cultural change is that the levels and emotional significances attached to the same practice may differ drastically between two cultures. Hall and Mead[5] give many examples of misunderstandings that arise as a result of these differences. Some of them involve agriculture, dietary practices, and community sanitation, which to the American advisor, are primarily technical problems. In many cultures, however, these activities involve formal, religious traditions, as well as informal traditions, and attempted changes meet with strong resistance. Even in the United States, where health and medical practices are, by and large, treated technically, attempts to fluoridate town water supplies have met strong opposition. Groups felt that their formal traditions were being threatened by having nature, as they defined it, violated and by having something done to them against their will.

The idea of several levels of culture carries with it two important elements which tend to apply to other processes. One is that of differential awareness or consciousness on the part of individual members as to the existence of underlying rules of behavior. Few people give any thought to the formal tradition of wearing clothing in public and would be ill at ease to think of the practice as anything but natural; alternatives are normally not conceivable.

In addition to differing levels of awareness,

---

[3] *Ibid.*, pp. 63 ff.
[4] *Ibid.*, p. 77.
[5] Hall, *op. cit.*, Mead, *op. cit.*

the idea of levels of culture also describes a hierarchy of emotional involvement and a directly proportional set of forces which tend to resist changes and to maintain the predictable status quo. The purely technical can be changed easily; the purely formal is the most persistently unchangeable. But the several levels are all contained in any one practice, so that some continuity of tradition will be maintained at one or more levels, even when another level is apparently changed. The form may change while the function persists, as in the case of the substitution of animals for human sacrifices in some cultures. On the other hand, the form may persist while the function changes, as with buttons on men's coat sleeves which are reputed to have been used originally to discourage men from wiping their noses on their coat sleeves.

The process of culture change includes another element which will arise later in our discussion of planned change. This is the fact that change processes involve the raising to awareness and explicit examination of processes that have been taken for granted. Conscious examination of the otherwise unconscious emotional attachment to traditions is a major focal point in the process of change in cultural settings.

Organizational Change

Roethlisberger and Dickson's description of the industrial organization closely parallels the three levels of culture described by Hall.[6] The same three terms are used, that is, formal, informal, and technical, but in different ways. We have abbreviated Roethlisberger and Dickson's scheme as follows:

> Technical Organization
> Human Organization
>   Individual
>   Social Organization
>   Formal Organization
>   Informal Organization[7]

Technical organization refers to the requirements of the productive processes, such as tools, materials, conversion processes, and products. Above the level of the individual, the human organization features two important levels: the formal and informal organizations. This is where Roethlisberger and Dickson's definitions differ from Hall's. The formal organization corresponds to Hall's technical level of culture; in industry it consists of the explicit sets of rule and regulations which prescribe the authority hierarchy and the relationships between the technical organization, that is, the logics of work, and the social organization. In other words, who is supposed to do what with whom and for whom.

The informal organization, as described by Roethlisberger and Dickson, consists of actual behavior patterns and sentiments, regardless of the formal prescriptions. Since the actual behaviors and sentiments of work groups are based on largely unrecognized social norms, values, and traditions, they correspond to Hall's formal and informal levels of culture.

The concept of equilibrium is central to Roethlisberger and Dickson's description of the total organization. It is implicit in Hall's description of levels of culture. Briefly stated here, the concept refers to a state of balance that exists among parts of a system. Thus, any change in one part is accompanied by changes in the other parts. Any change in external pressures on the total system will result in tendencies within the system to maintain, or return to, its original condition. Any particular activity pattern within the total organization contains elements of the technical, formal, and informal systems. An attempted change in a technical procedure, for example, will affect other technical procedures, formal activities, and especially the informal organization of interactions, activities, and sentiments.

Countless field studies of change in organizational systems attest the resistances of the informal organization to changes at the technical or formal levels.[8] These resistances rep-

---

[6] Roethlisberger and Dickson, *Management and the Worker,* pp. 565 ff.

[7] *Ibid.*

[8] See, for example, Zaleznik, *Foreman Training in a Growing Enterprise,* and the Lightner series of cases which are included in Zaleznik and Moment, *Cases on Interpersonal Behavior in Organizations.*

resent the conservative forces operating within the organization of face-to-face relationships among individuals. Such relationships tend to have the most real and immediate impact on individual members.

Attempted changes in organizational behavior patterns are usually introduced in terms of specific and explicit modifications of technical or formal requirements. They do not, however, normally address the informal patterns of behavior and sentiments. One reason is that the leaders who attempt to initiate change, as well as the members of the groups themselves, are not too aware of the existence of such patterns. A second reason is that even if the change agent is aware of the informal, implicit organization, he has no socially legitimate way of addressing it without overstepping the boundaries of his formal and technical role. As a result, organizational changes which are consummated successfully inevitably involve *informal* behavior patterns. The formal boss, for example, will step out of his boss role and address members of the work group as individuals, even though his formal job definition may exclude, or even prohibit, this kind of behavior.

Analysis of culture change has highlighted the existence of several levels of culture, the different kinds and degrees of emotional attachment at each level, and the need for making the implicit explicit in order to consummate culture change. Organizational analysis adds the importance of the concept of equilibrium. Change takes place through existing internal behavior patterns, even when imposed from without by purely external agents. The study of changes in group behavior confirms these generalizations and principles.

Group Change

Since the small group has a characteristic culture and social organization, the observations regarding processes of change in larger cultures and in formal organizations are applicable. The major difference is the relative ease with which an entire small group can be observed, its attributes measured, and experiments performed. Consequently, the dynamics of the change process may be described in more specific detail in the case of the small group.

The identity and continuity of the group are closely related to its social structure and norms. One function of its norms is to maintain the stability and predictability of its social relationships. Externally imposed changes in its task requirements and formal relationships to outsiders will invariably change the group's social structure and violate or invalidate some of its norms. Thus, the equilibrium of the group can be maintained only through the existence of resisting or compensating forces.

A major aspect of the change problem in groups is the group attitude toward external authority. Obviously, when alienation and hostility exist toward the authorities which impose change, strong group reaction may be predicted. A common pattern under this condition is one of surface compliance and informal sabotage. Such sabotage can take the form of the group's insistence on following all formal rules and procedures, to the detriment of task performance and to the embarrassment of the authorities.

Research on leadership behavior has highlighted the importance of the leader's behavior to the group's performance, satisfaction, and ability to change. Leadership behaviors which allow and actively encourage the group to address its problems explicitly tend to be more effective. In studies of leadership, the part *group* processes play in the outcomes is of utmost importance. Research findings related to group processes, leadership behavior, and group change will be discussed later in this chapter.

The small group is the major source of emotional support for the individual, as well as the major source of pressures to conform socially. Asch demonstrated that group pressure can change the unsupported individual's perceptions of physical stimuli and that the individual's ability to resist social pressure is tremendously increased if he is supported by even one other person.[9]

[9] Asch, "Effects of Group Pressure upon the Modification and Distortion of Judgments." See also Schein, *Coercive Persuasion,* p. 242.

Our general comments on group change have added one more important observation to our discussion of change in larger social systems. Prospective changes affect cultural and organizational systems at several levels of awareness and emotional strength. But they are invariably brought to bear in systems of small, face-to-face, group interactions. The small group is a strategic focus for practical, applied change programs as well as for research because it transforms social abstractions, such as culture, values, and tradition, into concrete, observable, and to some degree controllable interpersonal events.[10] The small group setting is where reality testing, on the one hand, and emotional contagion, on the other, actually take place. At the same time, the small group is the primary unit with which authority figures, including agents of change, must deal in practical affairs. The group's attitude toward authority, its conservative forces which resist change, and its potential for adaptation and development all affect the strategic interaction between the authority figure and the group.

The object of change, in planned change programs and in the study of change processes, is the behavior and attitudes of *the individual*. The analysis and understanding of cultural, organizational, and group processes are indispensable for understanding problems of change in the individual. But the basic dynamic forces of all these other systems, in conservation and in adaptation and development, lie rooted in the dynamics of the individual's personality. The emotions attached to the various levels of cultural traditions are the emotions of individuals. The logics of technical organization, sets of formal organizational rules and procedures, and the norms of the informal group all exist as ideas and sentiments within individuals. The workings of social processes of behavior control, resistance to change, and reality testing for change take place as intrapersonal and interpersonal processes, in their most fundamental forms. We shall conclude our discussion of the general theory of change with a brief examination of its meaning to the individual's personality.

Individual Change

The concept of individual identity, as developed by Erikson,[11] is a convenient point at which to begin our examination of change in individual behavior and attitudes. When we demand that a person change his behavior and attitudes, we are, in effect, asking him to become someone else. Since he may not have a very well-developed sense of identity to begin with, the demand for change may cause an identity crisis. This has been one consequence of the leadership training programs described in our discussion of the leader.

The individual's identity problem and its relationship to the consistency of his behavior and attitudes involves several levels of his personality. Unconscious and conscious processes, the self he presents to his various publics, and his private self are all related to such dimensions as level of awareness, overt behavior and internal processes, and personal role differentiation. The equilibrium problem is clearly evident in this complex set of subsystems contained within the individual's personality. A change in any one of these levels or processes is accompanied by balancing changes in other levels or processes. In addition to the interrelationships among these systems, the total personality and its parts all respond homeostatically to external disturbances; they exhibit a tendency to return to their initial state of equilibrium.

Freud and others have discussed the tendency of the person to long to "return to the womb," the most comfortable, initial human condition.[12] This is accompanied by an opposing tendency to be active: to experience a variety of human events, to attain competence in interacting with the environment, and to continue to develop into something more than the animal that the individual is biologically.[13]

---

[10] See Schein, *op. cit.*

[11] Erikson, "Identity and the Life Cycle."

[12] For example, see Schachtel, *Metamorphosis*, pp. 8–9.

[13] See, for example, White, "Motivation Reconsidered: The Concept of Competence."

Ego processes and the mechanisms of defense are the work centers and work procedures by which the individual's relationships to the environment and to his internal responses are governed. Some ego processes are relatively conflict free, such as mathematical ability and physical skill in playing games or working. Other ego processes are potentially laden with conflict; one of these, interpersonal relations, is especially relevant to the problems of the leader and group member. Rapaport has described the ego as vacillating between *autonomy*, where conflict-free competences may be exercised freely in relation to external realities, and *dependence* upon unconscious, emotional-laden, overdetermined internal sources of energy and direction.[14]

The problems of individual change with which we are concerned invariably involve the individual's relationship to external authority. To change behavior and attitudes in response to *impersonal* external demands is a relatively simple problem for the individual. His application of relatively conflict-free competence to solving external problems may sometimes be thwarted by feelings of frustration and anger, but by and large he can go on trying, limited only by fatigue and lack of ability. On the other hand, to change in response to the demands of other *persons* is an entirely different matter; it involves an emotional response to who the other person is and what he is doing to the individual interpersonally. To be told or advised what to do or think by another person is quite different from discovering or learning what to do or think by one's self. Feelings of counterdependence, rebelliousness, hostility, and anger are not the only interpersonal emotions involved in external demands for individual change; the opposite feelings of comfortable dependency, affection, wanting to be close and friendly, wanting to please, and wanting to comply can also emotionally color such responses. Although many leaders and agents of change would favor the latter emo-

tional response, it represents no more autonomy, development, or learning to deal with reality than does the more agressive and hostile one, even though it may appear to facilitate change. There is an important difference between *conformity*, which represents no change on the part of the individual, and individual change at deeper levels in the direction of autonomy and enhanced reality orientation.

Growth, learning, self-actualization, the development of competence, ego-autonomy, improved potential for adaptation, and similar concepts point to the ideal of individual development aimed for by responsible agents of change. In the case of the individual, these ideals are usually pursued through therapy in which the counselor, psychiatrist, or psychoanalyst are the agents of change. Current trends in leadership training attempt to prescribe these same goals for the administrator, group leader, and community leader; the change agent is considered the helper and facilitator of individual, group, and organizational change toward the ideal.

In some early forms of individual therapy, the agent was often defined out of the situation. The individual was the object of change and the therapist was the external expert who intervened; but he was not part of the change process, which was considered to be entirely internal to the individual subject. Hypnosis and shock treatment are examples of this situation. In another view, the therapy situation was primarily a special kind of human relationship; the change agent and the subject were involved together in a process of changing their relationship to each other, as well as changing their internal conditions through "therapeutic interaction."[15]

The problem of individual change necessarily involves changes in object relationships for the individual. It also involves changes in the way the individual thinks about himself, about other people, and about his relationship to his work. In addition, his emotional re-

---

[14] Rapaport, "The Autonomy of the Ego," and "The Theory of Ego Autonomy: A Generalization."

[15] Harry Stack Sullivan emphasized the *interpersonal* nature of the disturbance and of the treatment. See Reference.

sponses and intellectual processes will be modified, and his motivations will be open to personal questioning. Such changes normally take place within individuals as they develop from infants to mature adults over the lifetime. However, the same processes which result in stable self-identification and the ability to function effectively with others at work tend to solidify the mechanisms of defense and prevent further learning and development along some lines. The process of individual change must be examined, therefore, as a form of therapy, even though the subjects are in all significant respects "normal." Since the modern environment for the individual is *not* stable and normal, special attention must be given to the problem of helping stable individuals continue to learn in the midst of rapid, continuing change in their social and technical environments.

Individual change is an *interpersonal* process, as well as a process in which *intrapersonal* aspects of the individual are altered. This points up the problem of distinguishing between conformity and significant change. Many change programs, such as executive development programs, supervisor training, and human relations training groups, contain pure socialization elements as well as self-education elements. For example, the newly-promoted executive learns how to behave as a member of his new status group; much of his training for the new role is purely social in nature. Similarly, members of human relations training groups often learn to conform to a new and different set of norms: medical students learn to act like doctors and officer candidates learn to act like officers. This kind of learning has to do with entry into a new group, rather than improved personal competence of a more significant nature.

Pure social conformity is manifested in the apparent changes in behavior and attitudes which accompany the individual's transition from membership in one group to membership in another. Since the individual usually learns and changes over his lifetime as a result of his experiences, social and otherwise, it is

difficult to separate pure socialization processes from more basic changes in personality structure. This means that the agent of change, if he is concerned with significant learning rather than conformity, has to make a special effort to distinguish between the socialization processes to which he and the client are subjected, and more basic and permanent personality change.

From the point of view of external agents of change, an important set of characteristics are the individual's motivation to self-examination and change, his intellectual and emotion readiness to change, and the resistances to change which are inherent in his particular personality structure at the time. The fine and delicate edge between forces toward change and conservation is where the change agent must focus his attention. In the development of the personality system of the individual, the timing of environmental demands in relation to his biological and psychological readiness is a crucial factor. Such demands occur according to implicit social plan or accident in some instances and according to explicit plan in others. The age at which the child enters school is determined by social plan and is characterized by close limits and tight control. On the other hand, the age of marriage, though generally prescribed by a broader social plan, often occurs by accident. In either case, the experience is not consummated satisfactorily unless the timing is right in relation to the physical and psychological readiness of the individual.

Even though subjects have the physical appearance of mature adults, their readiness for change cannot be taken for granted by agents of planned change. Concepts and findings of developmental theory suggest that it is important to examine the positions in the cycle of development where learning is rapid and where useful analogs may be sought for the implementation of change. Two learning phases in the life cycle contain some interesting parallels. One occurs during the so-called latency period of development and the second during adolescence.[16]

The latency period is the phase of develop-

[16] These ideas are also presented in Moment and Zaleznik, *Role Development and Interpersonal Competence,* pp. 164 ff.

ment marked by rapid learning of basic cognitive skills and content. The capacity to learn during this phase depends on the recession of certain instinctive processes that were dominant in earlier development phases. Where the instinctive processes of fantasy and activity stay in the forefront, however disguised, there tends to be a failure in learning. In essence, the learning process of the latency period is predicated upon the existence of a *moratorium* in instinctual development.[17] When the moratorium is well established internally, the learning process for the individual tends to be rapid and productive.

The second period which serves as a useful analog to the problem under consideration is that of adolescence. This period is marked by rapid change of another kind. The greatest changes are biological and social. The individual matures sexually and experiences an increase in the magnitude of instinctual drives. Accompanying this change is a period of social experimentation characterized mainly by: emphasis on peer relations and withdrawal from parental control; role experimentation in highly ritualized forms; and highly unstable patterns of behavior, with rapid fluctuation in mood and action.

The behavior of the adolescent is understood best in the light of the social tasks facing him in anticipation of later life tasks. At the conclusion of the period of adolescence, the individual must make a series of significant decisions. He must choose a career and select the mate with whom he will share his work, family, and community life. The learning problem of the adolescent period is the establishment of a sense of identity in which occupational and sex roles assume paramount importance.[18] The experimental behavior of the adolescent in formulating his identity is sanctioned by society and made possible by the establishment of a second moratorium in development. The role responsibilities of the growing person are suspended in anticipation of his later full acceptance of the diverse and complex roles of adulthood.

It is significant to note the correlation between the existence of these two moratoria and the rapidity of experimentation and learning. It is also significant to note that the moratorium of the adolescent period is the last fully sanctioned period of experimentation in the individual's life. Beyond adolescence any dramatic developmental experience will depend upon an individual's self-declared moratorium.

During adult phases of development, the main type of socially recognized moratorium occurs when the individual presents himself for psychotherapeutic help. Within this highly specialized relationship, rapid learning and experimentation can take place. But this type of learning is available mainly to persons who have experienced severe alienation from their social environment or for whom the maintenance of relationships causes severe pain and anxiety.

It is difficult to establish moratoria for adults who are fully engaged in working and family life. Such individuals do not define themselves as sick or in need of significant personal change. But for some, the changing demands of their work and social environments seem to call for a significant learning experience supported by their society.

In our brief overview of changes in cultures, organizations, groups, and individuals, several uniformities stand out which must be taken into account by any general theory of change in groups and individuals:

1. Change processes involve at least two, and possibly three or more, levels of meaning. These levels are described by such terms as overt and covert, manifest and latent, conscious and unconscious, formal and informal, form and function. For the unit undergoing change, continuity will always be maintained at some level while changes take place at other levels; forced discontinuities must be supported by reinforced continuity of identity or complete disintegration will result.

2. During processes of change, the implicit or latent meanings of behavior and attitude patterns

---

[17] Erikson, *op. cit.*, p. 111.
[18] *Ibid.*, p. 110.

are raised to awareness for conscious examination; new patterns are substituted for old in such a way as to maintain the continuity and identity of the system. Some old patterns may be retained, but conscious examination may change their meanings.

3. Face-to-face interaction settings are strategic in the change process; the counseling relationship and the small group process provide testing-out and acting-out opportunities for the individual. Interaction by itself is not sufficient to ensure change; individual and group behavior and attitudes are reinforced, as well as tested, in social processes. Although individual change takes place through social interaction, socialization, as reflected in conformity, also takes place.

4. For the individual, significant changes normally take place during the specific periods of his life when social demands are relaxed and when he is physically and psychologically ready for change.

We have introduced the term "change agent" to refer to the person who consciously attempts to initiate change in a system; the term focuses attention on problems of planned change. However, it may be misleading when applied descriptively to natural process of change.

Throughout history there have been many people who were change agents and leaders by intent. But the complexity of human processes has made it difficult to assess the degree to which the consequences of their behaviors matched their intentions and the degree to which their roles in the changes were merely incidental to other influences. The teacher teaches, but the degree to which his behavior causes the student to learn is another question. Thus, our attempts to understand processes of change and the change agent's role must be tempered with the critical awareness that "contributing to" or "influencing" change processes is quite different from "causing" change, or "making change happen." Some of the most significant agents of change could not have been aware of the extent of their influence, for example, Darwin, Einstein, and Freud. Conversely, overly self-conscious efforts at change, such as various moral reform movements, often have less influence on human events than they intend.

References

Asch, S. E. "Effect of Group Pressure Upon the Modification and Distortion of Judgments," *Groups, Leadership, and Men,* Harold Guetzkow, Ed. Pittsburgh: Carnegie Press, 1951.

Erikson, Erik H. "Identity and the Life Cycle," *Psychological Issues,* Vol. I, No. 1, 1959.

Hall, Edward T. *The Silent Language.* New York: Doubleday, 1959.

Mead, Margaret, Ed. (UNESCO) *Cultural Patterns and Technical Change.* New York: New American Library of World Literature, 1955.

Moment, David, and Zaleznik, Abraham. *Role Development and Interpersonal Competence.* Boston: Division of Research, Harvard Business School, 1963.

Rapaport, David. "The Autonomy of the Ego," *Bulletin of the Menninger Clinic,* Vol. 15, No. 4, July 1951.

Roethlisberger, Fritz J., and Dickson, William J. *Management and the Worker.* Cambridge: Harvard University Press, 1943.

Schachtel, Ernest G. *Metamorphosis.* New York: Basic Books, 1959.

Schein, Edgar H. "The Chinese Indoctrination Program for Prisoners of War: A Study of Attempted Brainwashing," *Reading in Social Psychology,* Maccoby, Newcomb, and Hartley, Eds. New York: Holt, 1958.

Sullivan, Harry Stack. *The Interpersonal Theory of Psychiatry.* New York: Norton, 1953.

White, Robert W. "Motivation Reconsidered: The Concept of Competence," *Psychological Review* Vol. 66, No. 5, September 1959.

Zaleznik, Abraham. *Foreman Training in a Growing Enterprise.* Boston: Division of Research, Harvard Business School, 1951.

B. SOCIAL PSYCHOLOGICAL PERSPECTIVES

4. Strategies of Attitude Change

Albert Bandura*

Belief-Oriented Approach

Three general approaches can be employed either singly or in various combinations to induce attitudinal changes. The informational or belief-oriented approach attempts to effect modifications in people's attitudes by altering their beliefs about the attitude object through exposure to various forms of persuasive communications. It is assumed that people can be induced to change their evaluations of an attitude object by presenting them with new information about its characteristics.

Most of the research generated by this informational approach (Cohen, 1964; Hovland & Janis, 1959; Hovland, Janis, & Kelley, 1953; Rosenberg et al., 1960) has been expressly designed to isolate the conditions under which a given communication will have its maximal effect upon recipients' attitudes. Three general sets of variables, namely the nature of the communicator, the communication, and the recipients, have been most extensively investigated. Studies of the persons being influenced have generally been concerned with their personality characteristics, the level of their intelligence or sophistication, the nature of their pre-existing attitudes, and the strength of their commitment to a given position. The effects of communicator variables in enhancing attitudinal modification are typically analyzed in terms of attributes such as expertness, trustworthiness, prestige, impartiality, social power, and concealment of the persuader's manipulative or propagandistic intent. The form and organization of persuasive arguments, which can also significantly influence attitude formation and change, involves such matters as the optimal order of presenting weak and major arguments, the sequence of supporting and opposing arguments, the degree of explicitness with which conclusions are stated, the amount of repetition, the degree of discrepancy between the subject's views and the ones advocated, the affective properties of the contents, and whether the influence program relies upon a one-sided presentation or also includes some consideration and refutation of counterarguments. Research findings show that the effects of these different variables rarely produce simple effects; rather their direction and magnitude are dependent in part upon the simultaneous influence of other factors. For example, the amount of attitude change may increase as a direct function of degree of discrepancy of opinions advocated by a highly respected source, whereas a less credible persuader may exert a decreasing influence the more divergent his opinions (Aronson, Turner, & Carlsmith, 1963; Bergin, 1962). To complicate matters further, a given variable may have differential immediate and long-term effects upon attitudes. With the

Reprinted in part from Albert Bandura, "Strategies of Attitude Change," *Principles of Behavior Modification* (New York: Holt, Rinehart and Winston, 1969), pp. 599–615. Copyright © 1969 by Holt, Rinehart and Winston, Inc. Reprinted by permission of Holt, Rinehart and Winston, Inc.
* Professor of Psychology, Stanford University.

passage of time, relevant content may be retained but the source forgotten, thus reducing initial credibility influences (Hovland & Weiss, 1951; Hovland, Lumsdaine, & Sheffield, 1949; Kelman & Hovland, 1953).

Most of the preceding investigations of persuasive communications have been primarily guided by a set of empirical principles rather than a systematic theory. However, these principles are organized around the basic assumption that attitude change is governed to a large extent by anticipations conveyed through communications of rewarding and punishing consequences for certain courses of action. A competent or prestigious communicator is generally more influential than a less competent one because the former's behavioral recommendations, if executed, are more likely to result in favorable outcomes. As noted below, the content of communications often includes incentive references or is expressly designed to alter the valence of the attitude object.

Although belief changes can be induced by exposure to communication stimuli, there is little evidence that mere presentation of information about the attitude object alters people's behavior toward it to any great extent. Higher-order conditioning processes are therefore frequently employed to augment the potency of persuasive communications. One method, which relies upon the phenomenon of vicarious reinforcement, increases the likelihood that an observer will respond in the recommended manner by depicting reinforcing consequences accruing to a performing model. In positive appeals, performance of the behavior suggested by the communicator results in a host of rewarding effects. Thus, smoking a certain brand of cigarettes or using a particular hair lotion wins the loving admiration of voluptuous belles, enhances job performance, masculinizes one's self-concept, actualizes individualism and authenticity, tranquilizes irritable nerves, invites social recognition and amicable responsiveness from total strangers, and arouses affectionate reactions in spouses. Laboratory studies (Bandura, 1968) disclose that, according to their nature, depicted consequences to a performer not only

facilitate or inhibit response tendencies, but their effects may outweigh the previously acquired value system of the viewers (Bandura, Ross, & Ross, 1963).

Negative appeals, on the other hand, portray the adverse consequences which result from failure to comply with a communicator's behavioral recommendations. Although vicarious punishment may inhibit existing response dispositions to some extent, it is a less reliable procedure for producing desired attitudes and corresponding patterns of behavior. Display of noxious or revolting outcomes tends to arouse strong emotional responses which may give rise to avoidance of disturbing material and associated recommendations (Janis, 1967) or endow the attitude object itself with negative valence.

Belief changes achieved by persuasive arguments may temporarily increase the likelihood of advocated courses of action, but it is doubtful that this type of approach can by itself produce enduring effects unless favorable incentive conditions, which govern persistence of induced changes, are arranged as well. That is, if a person were to act on his beliefs, the effects of adverse outcomes would eventually negate the influence of persuasive communications. An uncomely brunette, for example, who has been persuaded that "blondes have more fun" may dye her hair a flaxen tint, but if her dismal dating plight should remain unchanged she is likely to discard the belief and revert to her natural hue.

Some research indicates that susceptibility to counterinfluence and rate of extinction of newly established beliefs can be temporarily attenuated by preparatory communications (Janis & Herz, 1949, cited in Hovland, Janis, & Kelley, 1953; McGuire, 1964). These serve to stimulate rehearsal of refutations of opposing arguments or to instill expectations in recipients that although they will at first encounter failure experiences and other adverse outcomes, if they adhere to their convictions they will eventually achieve success. A person who has been led to anticipate unfavorable initial outcomes may discount subsequent failures for a time. However, where discrepancies exist between assumed and actual schedules of reinforcement, both his behavior and his beliefs probably will gradually adjust to existing reinforcement conditions.

Because of ease of application, persuasion techniques presented through verbal or pictorial devices are widely employed on a mass basis in efforts to control consumer behavior, to influence voting choices, and to indicate either positive or negative evaluative responses toward particular attitude objects and social issues. The efficacy of mass persuasion methods is often diminished, however, by the limited control that influence agents can exercise over people's attention to communication stimuli, and by lack of direct means of immediately reinforcing the audience members for performing the recommended behavior. On the other hand, under conditions where selected communication stimuli are capable of attracting and holding viewers' attention and the advocated actions do, in fact, result in favorable consequences, mass appeals may initiate lasting changes in people's beliefs and behavior.

Affect-Oriented Approach

A second general strategy for inducing attitudinal changes involves an affect-oriented approach. In this paradigm, both evaluations of, and behavior toward, particular attitude objects are modified by altering their affective properties. These emotional changes are typically achieved through procedures based upon the principle of classical conditioning. As shown in preceding chapters, attitudinal and behavioral reversals can be produced by contiguous association of objects that are highly positive in valence with noxious experiences in aversive forms of counterconditioning, or by pairing subjectively distressing stimuli with positively reinforcing events in desensitization operations. The most convincing demonstrations of transfer effects of emotional reconditioning are furnished by studies in which the affective properties of attitude objects are independently measured, usually in terms of appropriate physiological indices, with adequate controls for nonspecific social influences (Marks & Gelder, 1967).

Although the use of association principles to facilitate attitudinal changes has been widespread, there has been surprisingly little research into the effectiveness of this approach. There is some evidence that evaluative responses can be altered by presenting persuasive messages or objects contiguously with appetizing foods (Janis, Kaye, & Kirschner, 1965; Razran, 1938), unpleasant odors (Razran, 1940), or sexually arousing stimuli (Smith, 1968). In an effort to determine whether extraneous gratification facilitates attitudinal change by a conditioning mechanism or by creating a positive attitude toward the donor, Dabbs & Janis (1965) compared the attitudinal effects of food consumption occurring contiguously or noncontiguously with exposure to persuasive messages under two different endorsement conditions. For half the subjects the experimenter positively endorsed the messages while for the remaining subjects he personally disagreed with the conclusions advocated by the communication. Neither the contiguity nor the endorsement variable alone produced a significant effect, but contiguous food combined with positive endorsement increased acceptance of unpopular opinions. These findings, however, must be accepted with reservation because attitude measures are of questionable validity when obtained by the same person who positively or negatively endorses the opinions being rated.

In naturalistic influence situations the method that is most frequently employed to induce changes in the affective value of an object involves higher-order associations of symbolic stimuli. In this procedure, the names and attributes of attitude objects are paired with verbal stimuli or pictorial presentations likely to evoke in listeners strong emotional responses on the basis of prior first-order conditioning. In several laboratory investigations of this learning process (Insko & Oakes, 1966; Staats & Staats, 1957), formerly neutral nonsense syllables have been contiguously associated with emotionally toned adjectives. The syllables take on negative valence through repetitive pairings with adjectives having negative connotations (e.g., ugly, dirty), whereas these same items are evaluated as pleasant after they have been associated with positively conditioned words such as beautiful, tasty, and happy. Pre-existing attitudinal responses toward familiar names of persons and nations have also been significantly altered through conditioning methods utilizing emotional words as the evocative stimuli (Staats & Staats, 1958).

A study by Das & Nanda (1963) further reveals that developed conditioned evaluative responses tend to generalize along previously established associative networks, thus resulting in widespread effects. After nonsense syllables had been contiguously associated with the names of two aboriginal tribes, favorable and unfavorable attitudes were developed toward the syllables. In a subsequent test subjects ascribed positive and negative attributes to the tribes in accordance with the evaluative responses conditional to their corresponding nonsense syllables.

It should be noted in this context that, unlike laboratory analogues of attitudinal learning in which single emotional words are presented in discrete trials, in real-life situations considerably more intense emotional reactions are typically elicited in audiences by the cumulative impact of long series of emotionally toned descriptions or pictorial presentations.

The above studies, though relevant to the issue of attitudinal modification through affective manipulations, would have greater implications had they included more extensive assessment of emotional changes. Of much greater import would be evidence that exposure to communication stimuli does, in fact, endow attitude objects with emotion-arousing properties, and that alterations in the effective domain are associated with corresponding changes in individuals' overt behavior toward the objects in question.

Another method of inducing affective changes that have considerable behavioral consequences relies upon modeling processes (Bandura, 1968). This outcome is achieved by associating attitude objects or their descriptions with affective modeling cues capable of arousing in viewers analogous emotional responses. Attitudinal modification through modeling is illustrated in an ingenious experi-

ment by Duncker (1938). In an initial test of food preferences children chose powdered chocolate with a pleasant lemon flavor over a very sweet sugar with a disagreeable medicinal taste. Later, a story was read to the children in which a stalwart astute hero abhorred a sour-tasting foodstuff similar to the children's preferred food and enthusiastically relished a sweet-tasting substance. The reactions of the admired hero reversed the children's initial food preference, as measured immediately after the story session and in six successive tests in which the children chose between powdered chocolate and medicated sugar. Moreover, brief recall of the story reinstated the experimentally induced preferences that had declined gradually over time. More recently, Carlin (1965) found that young children showed a greater preference for deferred gratification after they saw an adult model display positive affective reactions while waiting for delayed rewards than they did after they observed the model express negative emotional reactions and devalue the goal object during the imposed delay period.

In the foregoing studies both evaluative judgments and emotional responses were modeled. The observed changes therefore cannot be attributed solely to the influence of affective modeling cues. There is some reason to believe from evidence provided by Culbertson (1957) that the modeling of preferences and beliefs without strong affective displays can alter attitudes. Observers who witnessed others express favorable attitudes toward integration subsequently exhibited a decrease in prejudicial attitudes.

The potency of modeling for inducing attitudinal changes is further demonstrated in the experiment by Bandura, Blanchard, & Ritter (1969) that was previously described. Snakephobic subjects were administered eight evaluative dimensions of the semantic differential technique and six attitude scales on which they rated how much they would like or loathe different types of encounters with reptiles. Subjects were then given factual information about the characteristics and habits of snakes in order to control and to assess the possible influence of incidental information before any treatment procedures were applied. After the test for snake avoidance behavior, the attitude measures were again administered. In the next phase of the experiment subjects received either systematic desensitization, symbolic modeling, live modeling combined with guided participation, or no treatment. Following completion of the treatment series the attitude measures were again administered prior to, and immediately after, the snake avoidance test.

The results are summarized graphically in Figure 4.1. Subjects loathing of reptiles was not altered in the slightest by factual information and exposure to the test snake. The refractory quality of these negative attitudes is further shown by the control subjects, whose evaluative reactions remained unchanged across repeated assessments. Both symbolic modeling and desensitization, which successfully extinguished negative emotional responses to snake stimuli, produced extensive attitudinal changes. The treatment condition that neutralized the anxiety-arousing properties of snakes and enabled subjects to interact with the repugnant attitude object without any adverse consequences achieved the greatest modification in attitudinal behavior. In a study designed to assess the relative influence of information, modeling, and guided contact in the latter method, Blanchard (1969) found that modeling accounted for approximately 80 percent of the attitude change. Information, on the other hand, increased subjects' emotional arousal to modeling displays and had, if anything, a slightly adverse effect.

The attitudinal consequences of affective change are also disclosed in desensitization studies involving more general attitudes dealing with sex, aggression, and other interpersonal contents. These findings indicate that the cognitive evaluative component of attitudes can be substantially modified through direct manipulation of the affective properties of the attitude object without involving informational references of a favorable or unfavorable sort. Essentially similar results are reported by Rosenberg (1960), who has shown that a negative affect induced through posthypnotic suggestions produces a correspond-

Figure 4.1. Attitudinal Changes for Subjects Who Received Either One of the Three Treatment Procedures or Served as Untreated Controls. The numeral 1 indicates subjects' attitudes prior to the behavioral test, and the numeral 2 shows their attitudes immediately after the test of avoidance behavior. (Bandura, Blanchard, and Ritter 1969.)

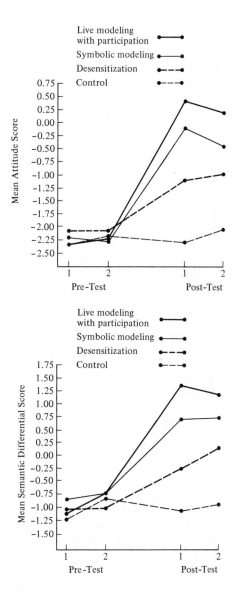

ing change in beliefs about the attitude object.

Behavior-Oriented Approach

The third approach to the modification of attitudes, which is frequently employed in experimental social psychology (Brehm & Cohen, 1962; Festinger, 1957), relies upon a behavior-oriented strategy. Change programs conducted within a social-learning framework likewise favor this type of approach, although they receive little mention in discussion, of attitude theory because until recently the cognitive consequences that undoubtedly accompany behavioral modifications have rarely been systematically assessed. Before specific experimental findings bearing on behavioral approaches are discussed, the conceptual scheme underlying most of this research will be presented briefly.

Investigations of the process of attitude change have, in large part been guided by various models of cognitive consistency. Among the more prominent theoretical positions are those of *congruity* (Osgood & Tannenbaum, 1955), *balance* (Adelson & Rosenberg, 1958; Heider, 1958), and *cognitive dissonance* (Festinger, 1957). Although these formulations differ somewhat in the types of events that are interrelated and the methods used to disrupt internal equilibrium, they have in common the view that a person's cognitions about himself and his environment are organized into an internally consistent system. It is further assumed, albeit implicitly, that there exists a strong drive for self-consistency. Consequently, the introduction of new information that contradicts existing attitudes or beliefs creates an aversive motivational state that instigates the individual to eliminate or reduce it by making cognitive adjustment designed to achieve a new mental equilibrium. These consistency doctrines thus assume that disruption of internal congruity between cognitive elements constitutes a basic determinant of attitude change.

In laboratory investigations the requisite cognitive disequilibrium is usually created through exposure to persuasive communications which counter subjects' initial attitudes.

Research stimulated by the cognitive dissonance model is especially relevant to the issue under discussion because, unlike the other consistency enterprises, the method most often employed to induce attitudinal changes involves getting a person to engage in attitude-discrepant behavior under conditions of minimal external inducement.

There are several reasons for selecting change in behavior as a primary mode of attitude change. First, it is much easier to arrange reinforcement contingencies for altering specific overt actions than for changing personal convictions, which have a more private character and are often more difficult to define. By skillful management of incentives a person can be induced to take progressively more favorable actions toward attitude objects. Second, diverse opinions usually exist about possible effects of engaging in certain forms of behavior. Consequently, such beliefs are more readily modifiable than cognitive representations of the behavior itself, which, because of its objective status, is more firmly fixed. Thus, for example, it is easier to alter one's opinions about the effects of smoking than to deny that one is, in fact, smoking, or to discontinue smoking altogether. Third, in many cases behavior is so powerfully maintained by its immediate consequences that any induced cognitive modification is likely to exert, at most, weak and transitory influence upon corresponding actions. A psychotherapist, for example, who contracted to cure chronic alcoholism or debilitating compulsive rituals by exposing his clients to discrepant information about the physiological hazards of excessive drinking or the irrationality of needless, arduous compulsions would, in a short time, suffer insolvency. Obviously, in instances where behavior is highly resistant to change, modification of response consequences is essential for effecting enduring alterations in performance to which attitudes would eventually be expected to adapt.

In the prototypic dissonance experiment, subjects' attitudes toward a particular issue or object are assessed through self-ratings, after which they are prompted, in one way or another, to engage in behavior which contradicts their private views. The same rating scales are later readministered, and the change scores are taken to represent the degree of attitude alteration. These studies (Brehm & Cohen, 1962; Cohen, 1964; Festinger, 1957) demonstrate that induced behavioral changes typically produce a corresponding modification in subjects' attitudes. After it was demonstrated that behavioral change has attitudinal consequences, subsequent research was primarily concerned with identifying the variables governing the amount of attitudinal change effected by performance of discrepant behavior. The conditions selected for investigation are based upon the general assumption that the less compelling the reasons for engaging in the contradictory behavior, the greater the dissonance and hence, the more attitude change is required to reduce it. Thus, persons who engage in attitude-discrepant behavior because of large rewards or strong coercive pressures have ample external justification for their actions and presumably, therefore, experience little dissonance and change of attitude. On the other hand, it is assumed that those who behave contrary to their private opinions under conditions of minimal external inducement are obliged to discover new attractions in the disagreeable activity to justify to themselves their voluntary performance of inconsistent actions.

According to dissonance theory, inconsistent action will produce the greatest amount of attitude change under conditions where small incentives, just sufficient to get the person to comply, are employed; there are minimal threats or coercive inducements; few reasons are given for taking the discrepant stand; the person receives a high degree of choice in committing himself to the counterattitudinal performance; there is high expenditure of effort in the attainment of the goal object or in the enactment of the discrepant behavior; the inducing agent is viewed unfavorably; and the person being influenced displays high self-esteem. It should be noted here that in naturalistic situations it is ordinarily no easy task to get people to perform personally repugnant actions for any length of time under such unfavorable incentive conditions.

Evaluation of the major theoretical issues and voluminous empirical findings bearing on dissonance-arousing variables goes beyond the scope of this book. For the interested reader, detailed reviews are available elsewhere (Abelson, Aronson, McGuire, Newcomb, Rosenberg & Tannenbaum, 1968; Chapanis & Chapanis, 1964; Elms, 1967; Feldman, 1966). The empirical studies have generally yielded conflicting results; consequently, the precise conditions under which induced discrepant performance will have greatest effect on attitudes still remain somewhat obscure. A major difficulty in verifying derivations from dissonance theory and in drawing conclusions from experimental data arises because there exists no independent measure of the degree to which the postulate state of dissonance has been aroused by a given procedure. Since the induction operations typically involve a complex set of events, experimental outcomes are open to numerous alternative explanations, which complicate interpretation. For a graphic illustration of the ambiguity concerning the independent variables in forced compliance studies, the reader is referred to the spirited debate between Aronson (1966) and Rosenberg (1966) who interpret the same experimental manipulation as having created opposite amounts of cognitive dissonance!

One theoretical issue, because of its obvious relevance to the role of incentives in change processes, warrants discussion in this context. It is widely believed that experimental findings concerning the effects of incentives upon attitude change brought about by divergent behavior contradict derivations from "conventional reinforcement theory." In fact, because of inadequate application of incentives, results of those studies are of limited relevance to reinforcement principles. Moreover, as will be discussed later, contrary to common belief both dissonance and reinforcement theory offer the same nonobvious implications.

In these experiments subjects are induced to write essays, enact prescribed roles, or otherwise publicly espouse a set of opinions that contradict their private feelings and beliefs. Some subjects are offered small monetary incentives (15¢, 50¢) for assuming the discrepant position, while others are promised more generous rewards ($5, $20). Several experiments (Brehm & Cohen, 1962; Festinger & Carlsmith, 1959) report an inverse relationship between size of monetary incentive and attitude change; other investigations have yielded both positive and inverse relationships (Carlsmith, Collins, & Helmreich, 1966; Linder, Cooper, & Jones, 1967), no incentive effects of statistically significant magnitude (Elms & Janis, 1965; Janis & Gilmore, 1965; Nuttin, 1966), or evidence that higher monetary incentives produce greater degrees of attitude change (Collins, 1969; Rosenberg, 1965).

The conditions governing the relationship between incentives and attitude change cannot be reliably identified unless data are presented for two other critical relationships, namely, the amount of counterattitudinal behavior engaged in as a function of different magnitudes of reward, and the degree to which variations in amount of discrepant behavior are associated with extent of attitude change. In experiments where the amount and quality of counterattitudinal performance are measured, outcomes are often uninterpretable because the material rewards, which supposedly serve as external inducements for discrepant behavior, are applied in such a loose contingency that their incentive function is virtually obliterated. Rewards are offered for any performance subjects choose to display, but otherwise the incentives are not explicitly made contingent upon the number, persuasiveness, and elaborated quality of arguments.

Even experiments conducted by proponents of incentive principles have limited bearing on incentive theory because rewards are offered without specific performance requirements. If incentives facilitate attitude change because they motivate individuals to generate positive arguments counter to their own beliefs (Janis, 1968), then subjects should be rewarded on the basis of the number of favorable arguments that they produce. An adequate test of the predictive efficacy of incentive theory would also require independent evidence that variations in reward actually produce a differential number and variety of arguments.

When rewards are provided without regard to response output, there is no reason to expect them to have any consistent behavioral or attitudinal effects. This is borne out by the actual findings. A number of limiting conditions under which the consistency theories hold have been proposed, including freedom of choice, commitment, public or private performance, anticipated consequences of influencing others in the counterattitudinal direction, and self-devaluative consequences. However, none of these explanations adequately reconciles all the divergent results.

The positive influence of incentives is also frequently nullified in dissonance experiments by introducing monetary rewards in the context of inordinate social pressures upon subjects to perform the disagreeable task. In the procedure most often employed, a flustered experimenter explains to an unwitting subject that an unexpected emergency has arisen because the regular assistant has just phoned saying that he will be unable to conduct the study with the next subject, who has already arrived and is waiting for his scheduled session. Would the subject be willing for a small or a large fee, to substitute for the absent assistant by informing the waiting subject that a boring task is interesting and enjoyable? It is hardly surprising that, given such compelling reasons, the same amount of discrepant behavior is enacted regardless of incentive size (Carlsmith, Collins, & Helmreich, 1966; Festinger & Carlsmith, 1959), and subjects are willing to perform the disagreeable task even without any monetary rewards at all (Nuttin, 1966). Indeed, given this "sudden, unexpected, and pressing" crisis, and urgent appeals to the subject to help the experimenter "out of a jam," none of the experimental conditions, regardless of the appended fee, can be considered as providing insufficient justification for compliance. By contrast, when the inordinate social pressures are absent and the monetary rewards serve as the main justification for developing counterattitudinal arguments, as in essay-writing situations, increased incentives often produce increasing amounts of attitude change (Carlsmith, Collins, & Helmreich, 1966). Other investigators (Elms,

1967; Janis & Gilmore, 1965; Rosenberg, 1966) have therefore attributed the effects of differential payments to arousal of resentment, suspicion, and other interfering emotional responses rather than to their intended positive incentive value.

Although there is abundant evidence that performance of counterattitudinal behavior can be a highly efficacious means of altering existing attitudes, divergent findings regarding contributory conditions suggest that more than one mediating process is probably involved. Some of these alternative mechanisms are discussed below.

Individuals undergo considerable social training to be logical and consistent in their beliefs. To the extent that contradictory beliefs engender critical reactions from others and other negative consequences, inconsistency may become an aversive condition that instigates emotional arousal and cognitive modifications designed to remove the source of discomfort. Hence, dissonance processes may be involved to some extent under conditions where people have voluntarily committed themselves to perform disagreeable behavior with weak external inducement and are therefore compelled to modify their beliefs to justify their contradictory actions. Because of the many limiting conditions under which dissonance effects are believed to occur, the phenomenon could not be highly prevalent. Dissonance reduction must, therefore, be only one of several processes activated by counterattitudinal performance.

Whenever a given action has been rewarded, reinforcement effects tend to generalize across similar classes of behavior, with the result that the incidence of corresponding verbal responses is likewise increased to some degree (Lovaas, 1961). Cognitive equivalents of the reinforced overt behavior are also affected in a similar manner (Miller, 1951) even though they have never been directly involved in the reinforcement contingency. Thus, in situations where counterattitudinal behavior is contingently rewarded, analogous changes in the cognitive domain may partly reflect a *response generalization* process.

A third interpretation of role-enactment effects, advanced by Janis & King (1954), Janis & Gilmore (1965), and Rosenberg (1965), emphasizes the *self-persuasive* consequences of recalling and developing numerous positive arguments. According to this point of view, favorable incentive conditions are likely to produce a greater amount of improvisation and more persuasively elaborated arguments upholding the opposed point of view. In the course of role-playing the person becomes influenced by the merits of his own convincing arguments.

Although there is some evidence that degree of attitude change is positively related to amount and quality of counterattitudinal behavior, incentive size alone has no consistent effects upon either improvisation or attitude change (Janis & King, 1954; Janis & Gilmore, 1965; Kelman, 1953; Rosenberg, 1965). However, Janis has shown that large incentives furnished by a favorable source produce better quality of performance and greater modification in attitudes than do small monetary rewards offered by an unfavorable sponsor for taking a contradictory stand. Rosenberg (1966) also offers the interesting proposition that self-persuasive consequences of behavioral rehearsal may depend upon the performer's psychological set. As in the case of influences from external sources, a person who labels his counterattitudinal advocacy as manipulative and deceptive may be considerably more resistant to his own persuasive arguments than if he undertakes the task with a positive self-searching orientation. This factor, if operative, might account for some of the conflicting results. Bem (1967) similarly argues that the self-persuasive effects of observing one's own behavior may be partly determined by the stimulus conditions under which it occurs.

To the extent that attitudinal changes are partly governed by the amount of discrepant behavior engaged in, the selection of incentive magnitude as the critical variable for testing predictions from dissonance and reinforcement theory was an unfortunate choice, because variations in amount of reward have no consistent effects upon performance by human subjects (Bruning, 1964; Elliott, 1966; Lewis &

Duncan, 1961). This is analogous to manipulating a variable that has no uniform effect upon the amount of dissonance arousal. In order to furnish a critical test of reinforcement theory, it is necessary to vary an incentive property that has reliable behavioral consequences, since the only reason for employing rewards is to alter the incidence of the crucial behavior. In view of evidence that variable, intermittent reinforcement results in higher performance than the same rewards administered on a fixed schedule, a more appropriate incentive variable, from the standpoint of reinforcement theory, would be the pattern in which counterattitudinal behavior is rewarded. For most incentive characteristics, the supposedly rival theories predict the same outcome, though for different reasons. Consider, for example, situations in which counterattitudinal behavior is generously reinforced on a fixed-interval schedule in one case, and much less frequently on a variable-ratio schedule in a contrasting treatment. The less favorable incentive condition would be expected to produce more attitudinal change because, according to dissonance theory, it provides less justification and hence greater dissonance, and according to reinforcement theory, because it generates more self-persuasive behavior.

It should also be noted in passing that, as far as behavior change programs are concerned, there are no reinforcement theories that prescribe the use of excessive rewards. On the contrary, it is most advantageous for several reasons to employ incentive conditions just sufficient to elicit the desired behavior. First, the aim is to produce enduring alterations in behavior, and partially reinforced behavior is most resistant to extinction. Second, in a well-designed program artificial, external inducements, initially required to elicit the desired responsiveness, are gradually reduced as the behavior produces natural and self-evaluative reinforcing consequences. Since reductions in incentives generate disruptive emotional effects, a change agent would be inviting unnecessary trouble by the use of needlessly large rewards.

The discussion thus far has focused on internal readjustments prompted by inconsistent action and alternative mediating processes that might account for the phenomenon. A fourth mechanism mediating role-enactment effects—an *experiential consequences* process—highlights the fact that a change in behavior provides a person with a variety of new experiences with the attitude object. Information gained from these new social interactions and observations can, in itself, produce substantial reorganization of attitudes (Kelman, 1961). Thus, for example, a prejudiced person who has been induced to behave positively toward members of a minority group may adopt a more favorable attitude not so much because of stress created by intrapsychic inconsistency, but because close positive associations with minority groups furnish additional evaluative knowledge and rewarding outcomes for the participants. Direct experiential consequences of behavioral change, depending upon their nature, may far outweigh the influence of intrapsychic tensions in initiating and maintaining attitudinal changes.

Another important aspect of this process concerns the effects of induced behavioral modifications upon the social environment of a monitoring membership group. If a person behaves in a discrepant manner, he may be virtually forced into association with the outgroup through ostracism. Under these circumstances "consistency" may be enforced and maintained through external, social mediation rather than intrapsychic compromises. Experiential consequences of behavioral change are likely to play a major role in determining how long induce attitudinal changes will endure.

Modification of Self-Attitudes

Of particular relevance to social approaches for developing and modifying attitudes is the evidence provided by Breer & Locke (1965) that task experiences can exert strong influence upon performers' attitudes. In these studies individuals are either differentially rewarded or experience differential success for performing tasks in two different ways. After the performance experiences, subjects' preferences for similar activities and more abstract values only indirectly related to the tasks themselves are measured. The overall results, based upon numerous investigations of attitudes toward individualism, equalitarianism, theism, and achievement, show that significant attitudinal changes can be induced by providing individuals with successful task experiences. For example, college students who worked better in groups than alone became more collectivistic in their attitudes, whereas subjects who experienced greater success when performing tasks independently adopted a more individualistic orientation. These studies also provide some evidence that attitudes induced by success tend to generalize to related types of activities and to abstract preferences.

Change agents are often concerned not only with altering individual's evaluations of different forms of behavior but in modifying their self-attitudes as well. Indeed, in some schools of psychotherapy, such as the client-centered approach (Rogers, 1959), self-concept changes are routinely selected as one of the primary treatment objectives. According to this point of view, self-attitudes can be modified most effectively through intrapsychic exploration under conditions where the change agent displays empathy, noncontingent positive regard, and genuineness. The individual's difficulties presumably stem from the fact that experiences that are incompatible with his faulty self-conception are consistently denied or inadequately symbolized. Self-examination in a positive, nonevaluative relationship will lead him to attend to warded-off experiences and accept them as part of himself; this, in turn, produces increased feelings of self-worth, self-acceptance, and greater freedom of action. This approach is predicated on the basic assumption that the person already has developed highly competent repertoires of behavior, most of which are inherently satisfy-ing, but which are neither accepted nor actualized because of the faulty self-evaluative contingencies that he has adopted from misguided socialization agents.

Undoubtedly many competent people do experience a great deal of self-generated distress and many self-imposed constraints as a result of adherence to ill-advised or excessively high standards of self-reinforcement. To the extent that a change agent differentially reinforces realistic standard-setting behavior and elicits emulation of more lenient self-evaluative standards as conveyed through his comments and actions, the client's habitual self-attitudes are likely to undergo change. However, results of outcome studies presented earlier indicate that this objective may not be too readily achieved on the basis of the types of conditions prescribed by the client-centered approach.

In many cases, of course, unfavorable self-attitudes stem from behavioral deficits and are repeatedly reinforced through failure experiences occasioned by the person's inability to meet realistic cultural expectations. It is obvious that for such persons no amount of self-exploration will yield esteem-producing vocational skills, academic capabilities, interpersonal competencies, and rewarding avocational proficiencies which would support realistic positive self-evaluations. Here the primary concern must be with self-development rather than self-exploration. Evidence that attitudes are significantly influenced by rewarding performance feedback indicates that enduring positive self-evaluations can be most effectively achieved by arranging optimal conditions for the individual to acquire the requisite competencies. On the other hand, the likelihood is exceedingly small that favorable self-attitudes, however induced, could survive in the face of disconfirming performance experiences.

References

Abelson, R. P., Aronson, E., McGuire, W. J., Newcomb, T. M., Rosenberg, M. J., & Tannenbaum, P. H. *Theories of cognitive consistency: A sourcebook.* Chicago: Rand McNally, 1968.

Abelson, R. P., & Rosenberg, M. J. Symbolic psycho-logic: A model of attitudinal cognition. *Behavioral Science,* 1958, 3, 1–13.

Adams, J. K. Laboratory studies of behavior without awareness. *Psychological Bulletin*, 1957, 54, 393–405.

Aronson, E. The psychology of insufficient justification: An analysis of some conflicting data. In S. Feldman (Ed.), *Cognitive consistency*. New York: Academic Press, 1966. Pp. 109–133.

Aronson, E., Turner, J. A., & Carlsmith, J. M. Communicator credibility and communication discrepancy as determinants of opinion change. *Journal of Abnormal and Social Psychology*, 1963, 67, 31–36.

Ayllon, T., & Azrin, N. H. Reinforcement and instructions with mental patients. *Journal of the Experimental Analysis of Behavior*, 1964, 7, 327–331.

Bandura, A. Social-learning theory of identificatory processes. In D. A. Goslin (Ed.), *Handbook of socialization theory and research*. Chicago: Rand McNally, 1968.

Bandura, A., Blanchard, E. B., & Ritter, B. The relative efficacy of desensitization and modeling approaches for inducing behavioral, affective, and attitudinal changes. Unpublished manuscript, Stanford University, 1968.

Bandura, A., & Perloff, B. Relative efficacy of self-monitored and externally imposed reinforcement systems. *Journal of Personality and Social Psychology*, 1967, 7, 111–116.

Bandura, A., Ross, D., & Ross, S. A. Vicarious reinforcement and imitative learning. *Journal of Abnormal and Social Psychology*, 1963, 67, 601–607.

Bem, D. J. Self-perception: An alternative interpretation of cognitive dissonance phenomena. *Psychological Review*, 1967, 74, 183–200.

Bergin, A. E. The effect of dissonant persuasive communications upon changes in a self-referring attitude. *Journal of Personality*, 1962, 30, 423–438.

Blanchard, E. B. The relative contributions of modeling, informational influences, and physical contact in the extinction of phobic behavior. Unpublished doctoral dissertation, Stanford University, 1969.

Bourne, L., E., Jr. *Human conceptual behavior*. Boston: Allyn & Bacon, 1966.

Breer, P. E., & Locke, E. A. *Task experience as a source of attitudes*. Homewood, Ill.: Dorsey, 1965.

Brehm, J. W., & Cohen, A. R. *Exploration in cognitive dissonance*. New York: Wiley, 1962.

Bridger, W. H., & Mandel, I. J. A. comparison of GSR fear responses produced by threat and electric shock. *Journal of Psychiatric Research*, 1964, 2, 31–40.

Bridger, W. H., & Mandel, I. J. Abolition of the PRE by instructions in GSR conditioning. *Journal of Experimental Psychology*, 1965, 69, 476–482.

Brown, R. W. *Social psychology*. New York: Free Press, 1965.

Bruning, J. L. Effects of magnitude of reward and percentage of reinforcement on a lever movement response. *Child Development*, 1964, 35, 281–285.

Carlin, M. T. The effects of modeled behavior during imposed delay on the observer's subsequent willingness to delay rewards. Unpublished doctoral dissertation. Stanford University, 1965.

Carlsmith, J. M., Collins, B. E., & Helmreich, R. L. Studies in forced compliance: I. The effect of pressure for compliance on attitude change produced by face-to-face role playing and anonymous essay writing. *Journal of Personality and Social Psychology*, 1966, 4, 1–13.

Chapanis, N. P., & Chapanis, A. Cognitive dissonance: Five years later. *Psychological Bulletin*, 1964, 61, 1–22.

Chatterjee, B. B., & Eriksen, C. W. Cognitive factors in heart rate conditioning. *Journal of Experimental Psychology*, 1962, 64, 272–279.

Clark, D. F. The treatment of monosymptomatic phobia by systematic desensitization. *Behavior Research and Therapy*, 1963, 1, 63–68.

Cohen, A. R. *Attitude change and social influence.* New York: Basic Books, 1964.

Collins, B. E. The effect of monetary inducements on amount of attitude change produced by forced compliance. In A. C. Elms (Ed.), *Role playing, reward, and attitude change.* Princeton, N. J.: Van Nostrand, 1969.

Culbertson, F. M. Modification of an emotionally held attitude through role playing. *Journal of Abnormal and Social Psychology*, 1957, 54, 230–233.

Dabbs, J. M., Jr., & Janis, I. L. Why does eating while reading facilitate opinion change? An experimental inquiry. *Journal of Experimental Social Psychology*, 1965, 1, 133–144.

Das, J. P., & Nanda, P. C. Mediated transfer of attitudes. *Journal of Abnormal and Social Psychology*, 1963, 66, 12–16.

Duncker, K. Experimental modification of children's food preferences through social suggestion. *Journal of Abnormal and Social Psychology*, 1938, 33, 489–507.

Ekman, P., Krasner, L., & Ullmann, L. P. Interaction of set and awareness as determinants of response to verbal conditioning. *Journal of Abnormal and Social Psychology*, 1963, 66, 387–389.

Elliott, R. Reaction time and heart rate as functions of magnitude of incentive and probability of success: A replication and extension. *Journal of Experimental Research in Personality*, 1966, 1, 174–178.

Ellis, R. A., & Lane, W. C. Structural supports for upward mobility. *American Sociological Review*, 1963, 28, 743–756.

Elms, A. C. Role playing, incentive, and dissonance. *Psychological Bulletin*, 1967, 68, 132–148.

Elms, A. C., & Janis, I. L. Counternorm attitudes induced by consonant versus dissonant conditions of role-playing. *Journal of Experimental Research in Personality*, 1965, 1, 50–60.

Feldman, S. *Cognitive consistency.* New York: Academic Press, 1966.

Festinger, L. *A theory of cognitive dissonance.* Evanston, Ill.: Row, Peterson, 1957.

Festinger, L. Behavioral support for opinion change. *Public Opinion Quarterly*, 1964, 28, 404–417.

Festinger, L., & Carlsmith, J. M. Cognitive consequences of forced compliance. *Journal of Abnormal and Social Psychology*, 1959, 58, 203–210.

Heider, F. *The psychology of interpersonal relations.* New York: Wiley, 1958.

Hernández-Péron, R., Scherrer, H., & Jouvet, M. Modification of electric activity in cochlear nucleus during "attention" in unanesthetized cats. *Science*, 1956, 123, 331–332.

Hirsch, J. Learning without awareness and extinction following awareness as a function of reinforcement. *Journal of Experimental Psychology*, 1957, 54, 218–224.

Hislop, M. W., & Brooks, L. R. Suppression of concept learning by verbal rules. *Journal of Experimental Psychology*, in press.

Holmes, D. S. Verbal conditioning, or problem-solving and cooperation? *Journal of Experimental Research in Personality*, 1967, 2, 289–294.

Homme, L. E. Perspectives in psychology: XXIV. Control of coverants, the operants of the mind. *Psychological Record*, 1965, 15, 501–511.

Horn, G. Electrical activity of the cerebral cortex of the unanesthetized cat during attentive behavior. *Brain*, 1960, 83, 57–76.

Hovland, C. I., & Janis, I. L. (Eds.), *Personality and persuasibility.* New Haven: Yale University Press, 1959.

Hovland, C. I., Janis, I. L., & Kelley, H. H. *Communication and persuasion: Psychological studies of opinion change.* New Haven: Yale University Press, 1953.

Hovland, C. I., Lumsdaine, A. A., & Sheffield, F. D. *Experiments on mass communication.* Princeton, N.J.: Princeton University Press, 1949.

Hovland, C. I., & Weiss, W. W. The influence of source credibility on communication effectiveness. *Public Opinion Quarterly,* 1951, 15, 635–650.

Insko, C. A., & Oakes, W. F. Awareness and the "conditioning" of attitudes. *Journal of Personality and Social Psychology,* 1966, 4, 487–496.

Janis, I. L. Attitude change via role-playing. In R. P. Abelson, E. Aronson, W. J. McGuire, T. M. Newcomb, & P. H. Tannenbaum (Eds.), *Theories of cognitive consistency: A sourcebook.* Chicago: Rand McNally, 1968.

Janis, I. L. Effects of fear arousal on attitude change: Recent developments in theory and experimental research. In L. Berkowitz (Ed.), *Advances in experimental social psychology.* Vol. III. New York: Academic Press, 1967. Pp. 167–224.

Janis, I. L., & Gilmore, J. B. The influence of incentive conditions on the success of role playing in modifying attitudes. *Journal of Personality and Social Psychology,* 1965, 1, 17–27.

Janis, I. L., Kaye, D., & Kirschner, P. Facilitating effects of "eating-while-reading" on responsiveness to persuasive communications. *Journal of Personality and Social Psychology,* 1965, 1, 181–186.

Janis, I. L., & King, B. T. The influence of role playing on opinion change. *Journal of Abnormal and Social Psychology,* 1954, 49, 211–218.

Johnson, II., & Eriksen, C. W. Preconscious perception: A re-examination of the Poetzl phenomenon. *Journal of Abnormal and Social Psychology,* 1961, 62, 497–503.

Kanfer, F. H. Verbal conditioning: A review of its current status. In T. R. Dixon & D. L. Horton (Eds.), *Verbal behavior and general behavior theory.* Englewood Cliffs, N. J.: Prentice-Hall, 1968. Pp. 254–290.

Kaufman, A., Baron, A., & Kopp, R. E. Some effects of instructions on human operant behavior. *Psychonomic Monograph Supplements,* 1966, 1, 243–250.

Keller, L., Cole, M., Burke, C. J., & Estes, W. K. Reward and informational values of trial outcomes in paired-associate learning. *Psychological Monographs,* 1965, 79 (12, Whole No. 605).

Kelman, H. C. Attitude change as a function of response restriction. *Human Relations,* 1953, 6, 185–214.

Kelman, H. C. The induction of action and attitude change. *Proceedings of the XIV International Congress of Applied Psychology.* Copenhagen: Munksgaard, 1961.

Kelman, H. C., & Hovland, C. I. Reinstatement of the communicator in delayed measurement of opinion change. *Journal of Abnormal and Social Psychology,* 1953, 48, 327–335.

Klein, G. S., Spence, D. P., Holt, R. R., & Gourevitch, S. Cognition without awareness: Subliminal influences upon conscious thought. *Journal of Abnormal and Social Psychology,* 1958, 57, 255–266.

Krasner, L. Studies of the conditioning of verbal behavior. *Psychological Bulletin,* 1958, 55, 148–170.

Krasner, L., & Ullmann, L. P. Variables affecting report of awareness in verbal conditioning. *Journal of Psychology,* 1963, 56, 193–202.

Krasner, L., Ullmann, L. P., Weiss, R. L., & Collins, B. J. Responsivity to verbal conditioning as a function of three different examiners. *Journal of Clinical Psychology*, 1961, 17, 411–415.

Krauss, I. Sources of educational aspirations among working-class youth. *American Sociological Review*, 1964, 29, 867–879.

Lazarus, R. S., & McCleary, R. A. Autonomic discrimination without awareness: A study of subception. *Psychological Review*, 1951, 58, 113–122.

Levin, S. M. The effects of awareness on verbal conditioning. *Journal of Experimental Psychology*, 1961, 61, 67–75.

Levitt, T. *Industrial purchasing behavior: A study of communications effects.* Boston: Harvard University Press, 1965.

Levy, L. H. Awareness, learning, and the beneficient subject as expert witness. *Journal of Personality and Social Psychologyy*, 1967, 6, 365–370.

Lewis, D. J., & Duncan, C. P. Effects of variable magnitude of reward on a lever-pulling response. *Journal of Experimental Psychology*, 1961, 62, 203–205.

Linder, D. E., Cooper, J., & Jones, E. E. Decision freedom as a determinant of the role of incentive magnitude in attitude change. *Journal of Personality and Social Psychology*, 1967, 6, 245–254.

Lovaas, O. I. Interaction between verbal and nonverbal behavior. *Child Development*, 1961, 32, 329–336.

Maccoby, N., Romney, A. K., Adams, J. S., & Maccoby, E. E. *"Critical periods" in seeking and accepting information.* Stanford: Stanford University Institute for Communication Research, 1962.

Mackay, H. A., & Laverty, S. G. GSR changes during therapy of phobic behavior. Unpublished manuscript. Queen's University, Ontario, 1963.

Mandel, I. J. & Bridger, W. H. Interaction between instructions and ISI in conditioning and extinction of the GSR. *Journal of Experimental Psychology*, 1967, 74, 36–43.

Marks, I. M., & Gelder, M. G. Transvestism and fetishism: Clinical and psychological changes during faradic aversion. *British Journal of Psychiatry*, 1967, 113, 711–729.

McGuire, W. J. Inducing resistance to persuasion. In L. Berkowitz (Ed.), *Advances in experimental social psychology.* Vol. I. New York: Academic Press, 1964. Pp. 191–229.

Miller, M. M. Treatment of chronic alcoholism by hypnotic aversion. *American Medical Association Journal*, 1959, 171, 1492–1495.

Miller, M. M. Hypnotic-aversion treatment of homosexuality. *Journal of the National Medical Association*, 1963, 55, 411–415.

Miller, N. E. Learnable drives and rewards. In S. S. Stevens (Ed.), *Handbook of experimental psychology*, New York: Wiley, 1951. Pp. 435–472.

Mischel, W. *Personality and assessment.* New York: Wiley, 1968.

Newcomb, T. M., Turner, R. H., & Converse, P. E. *Social psychology: The study of human interaction.* New York: Holt, Rinehart & Winston, 1965.

Nuttin, J. M., Jr. Attitude change after rewarded dissonant and consonant "forced compliance." *International Journal of Psychology*, 1966, 1, 39–57.

O'Connell, D. C., & Wagner, M. V. Extinction after partial reinforcement and minimal learning as a test of both verbal control and PRE in concept learning. *Journal of Experimental Psychology*, 1967, 73, 151–153.

Osgood, C. E., & Tannenbaum, P. H. The principle of congruity in the prediction of attitude change. *Psychological Review*, 1955, 62, 42–55.

Philbrick, D. B., & Postman, L. A further analysis of "learning without awareness." *American Journal of Psychology*, 1955, 68, 417–424.

Postman, L., & Sassenrath, J. The automatic action of verbal rewards and punishments. *Journal of General Psychology*, 1961, 65, 109–136.

Premack, D. Reinforcement theory. In D. Levine (Ed.), *Nebraska symposium on motivation: 1965*. Lincoln: University of Nebraska Press, 1965. Pp. 123–180.

Razran, G. H. S. Conditioning away social bias by the luncheon technique. *Psychological Bulletin,* 1938, 35, 693.

Razran, G. H. S. Conditioned response changes in rating sociopolitical slogans. *Psychological Bulletin,* 1940, 37, 481.

Razran, G. Conditioning and perception. *Psychological Review,* 1955, 62, 83–95.

Razran, G. The observable unconscious and the inferable conscious in current soviet psychophysiology. *Psychological Review,* 1961, 68, 81–147.

Rogers, C. R. A theory of therapy, personality, and interpersonal relationships, as developed in the client-center framework. In S. Koch (Ed.), *Psychology: A study of a science. Vol. III. Formulations of the person and the social context*. New York: McGraw-Hill, 1959. Pp. 184–256.

Rokeach, M. Attitude change and behavioral change. *Public Opinion Quarterly,* 1966, 30, 529–550.

Rosenberg, M. J. An analysis of affective-cognitive consistency. In M. J. Rosenberg, C. I. Hovland, W. J. McGuire, R. P. Abelson, & J. W. Brehm (Eds.), *Attitude organization and change: An analysis of consistency among attitude components*. New Haven: Yale University Press, 1960. Pp. 15–64.

Rosenberg, M. J. When dissonance fails: On eliminating evaluation apprehension from attitude measurement. *Journal of Personality and Social Psychology,* 1965, 1, 28–42.

Rosenberg, M. J. Some limits of dissonance: Toward a differentiated view of counter-attitudinal performance. In S. Feldman (Ed.), *Cognitive consistency*. New York: Academic Press, 1966. Pp. 135–170.

Rosenberg, M. J., Hovland, C. I., McGuire, W. J., Abelson, R. P., & Brehm, J. W. *Attitude organization and change: An analysis of consistency among attitude components*. New Haven: Yale University Press, 1960.

Rosenthal, R., Persinger, G. W., Vikan-Kline, L. I., & Fode, K. L. The effect of experimenter outcome-bias and subject set on awareness in verbal conditioning experiments. *Journal of Verbal Learning and Verbal Behavior,* 1963, 2, 275–283.

Sasmor, R. M. Operant conditioning of a small-scale muscle response. *Journal of the Experimental Analysis of Behavior,* 1966, 9, 69–85.

Sassenrath, J. M. Transfer of learning without awareness. *Psychological Reports,* 1962, 10, 411–420.

Schanck, R. L. A. study of a community and its groups and institutions conceived of as behavior of individuals. *Psychological Monographs,* 1932. 43 (2, Whole No. 195).

Scobie, S. R., & Kaufman, A. Intermittent punishment of variable interval and variable ratio responding. *Journal of the Experimental Analysis of Behavior,* 1969, 12, 137–147.

Shepard, R. N., Hovland, C. I., & Jenkins, H. M. Learning and memorization of classifications. *Psychological Monographs,* 1961, 75 (13, Whole No. 517).

Sidman, M. Avoidance behavior. In W. K. Honig (Ed.), *Operant behavior*. New York: Appleton-Century-Crofts, 1966. Pp. 448–498.

Skinner, B. F. *Science and human behavior,* New York: Macmillan, 1953.

Smith, G. H. The influence of a female model on perceived characteristics of an automobile. Paper read at the meeting of the American Psychological Association, San Francisco, August, 1968.

Spence, D. P. Conscious and preconscious influences on recall: Another example of the restricting effects of awareness. *Journal of Abnormal and Social Psychology,* 1964, 68, 92–99.

Spence, D. P., & Holland, B. The restricting effects of awareness: A paradox and an explanation. *Journal of Abnormal and Social Psychology,* 1962, 64, 163–174.

Spence, K. W. Cognitive and drive factors in the extinction of the conditioned eye blink in human subjects. *Psychological Review,* 1966, 73, 445–458.

Spilberger, C. D., Berger, A., & Howard, K. Conditioning of verbal behavior as a function of awareness, need for social approval, and motivation to receive reinforcement. *Journal of Abnormal and Social Psychology,* 1963, 67, 241–246.

Spielberger, C. D., Bernstein, I. H., & Ratliff, R. G. Information and incentive value of the reinforcing stimulus in verbal conditioning. *Journal of Experimental Psychology,* 1966, 71, 26–31.

Spielberger, C. D., & De Nike, L. D. Descriptive behaviorism versus cognitive theory in verbal operant conditioning. *Psychological Review,* 1966, 73, 306–326.

Spielberger, C. D., Levin, S. M., & Shepard, M. C. The effects of awareness and attitude toward the reinforcement of the operant conditioning of verbal behavior. *Journal of Personality,* 1962, 30, 106–121.

Staats, A. W., & Staats, C. K. Attitudes established by classical conditioning. *Journal of Abnormal and Social Psychology,* 1958, 57, 37–40.

Staats, C. K., & Staats, A. W. Meaning established by classical conditioning. *Journal of Experimental Psychology,* 1957, 54, 74–80.

Thorndike, E. L. A theory of the action of the after-effects of a connection upon it. *Psychological Review,* 1933, 40, 434–439.

Verplanck, W. S. Unaware of where's awareness: Some verbal operants—notates, monents, and notants. In C. W. Eriksen (Ed.), *Behavior and awareness.* Durham, N.C.: Duke University Press, 1962. Pp. 130–158.

5. Psychological Aspects of Planned Developmental Change

Leonard W. Doob*

To distill guiding principles of a psychological nature from the voluminous literature on social change requires almost foolhardy courage. There are concrete studies, including those which simply recount or reconstruct the history of a changing society (for example, Kluckhohn and Leighton, 1946) and a very few which report the results of two field trips separated by a period of time (for example, Lewis, 1951; Mead, 1956). There are generalizations based upon concrete studies that are carefully cited (especially Keesing, 1953; Havighurst and Neugarten, 1955), and there also are those derived from the writer's own brilliance, insight, or preoccupations (for example, Redfield, 1953). The generalizations themselves, moreover, are phrased variously; some refer to human potentialities, others to institutions, and yet others to specific culture traits.

Under these circumstances, I can seek only to condense and improve twenty-seven hypotheses formulated elsewhere (Doob, 1960: 324–26) by designing a psychological schema that springs from three sources. The first has already been revealed, the distinction concern-

Reprinted in part from Leonard W. Doob,"Psychological Aspects of Planned Developmental Change," in Art Gallaher, Jr. (ed.), *Perspectives in Developmental Change.* (Lexington: University of Kentucky Press, 1968), pp. 45–56.

* Professor of Psychology, Yale University.

ing three kinds of change (antecedent, consequent, and concomitant).[1] Then, secondly, a potentially useful set of psychological processes, important variables through which the changes occur, is suggested below. Though the selection is arbitrary, an eclectic series of variables is offered which are related not only to the points already made about the three kinds of change (especially to the need to be acquainted with people's predispositions) but also to the general learning process:

A. *Predisposition*: the preexisting beliefs and values people bring to a learning situation.

B. *Perception*: the ways in which they appraise the situation at hand.

C. *Other people*: the attitudes they have toward others who are involved in the situation.

D. *Personality traits*: their characteristic mode of reacting in general or in specific situations.

E. *Learning*: the actual learning that does or does not take place, including the learners' general abilities.

Thus, fifteen principles emerge as the product of three kinds of change multiplied by five psychological processes.

The third source for principles derives from the fact that developmental change involves many people who interact with one another, not only at a given moment but also over generations; consequently, the learning is so complex that it must be considered separately on this mass level. In addition, the five principles under each of the three kinds of change are accompanied by supplementary statements of a different sort, as the italicized words in each instance would suggest:

Antecedent change: one or more of the ways in which the italicized concept might conceivably be *weighted* is shown. Such weighting extends the scope of a principle by supplying additional empirical generalizations or subprinciples.

Consequent change: so many changes can occur in people that a complete inventory of behavior would be necessary to include all the variations. Short of that inventory, abstract terms must seek to categorize the critical process which is italicized in the statement of the principle and then followed by a trio or so of *possibilities* representing specific findings that are salvageable from the literature on social change. In order to suggest such possibilities, moreover, a basic assumption must be made: the people in question have undergone either many or important changes.

Concomitant change: here another type of presentation is offered, that of an *illustrative* subprinciple which might be deduced from the principle itself and especially from the section containing the variable in italics.

The principles are arranged below in the manner that has been forecast. Under each of the five psychological processes, the order is antecedent, consequent, and concomitant change.

Psychological Processes

A. Predispositions

1. People are likely to accept a proposed change when it is not in *conflict* with traditional beliefs and values which are proving satisfactory.

Suggestive weightings: (a) "conflict": "incompatibility" or "incongruence" between the change and the traditional trait from an anthropological standpoint is likely to produce psychological conflict within people (Kushner and others, 1962: 10–11) as well as social conflict between them; a change that is "new and in a new context" (Mead, 1955:285) is likely to produce less conflict than one in an old context. (b) "satisfactory": beliefs and values are satisfactory when they have existed within people or their society for a relatively long

---

[1] Editors' note: The three kinds of change are defined in the following way: Antecedent—"precipitating circumstances inducing or compelling people to produce or accept change." Consequent—"what happens to people as a consequence of adopting changes." Concomitant—"one group of people changes and produces change as a result of which another group must change."

time and when they are associated with the achievement of basic goals; beliefs and values associated with an existing religion are likely to be considered satisfactory and hence to be influential.

2. Having changed in many or important respects, people are likely to exhibit changes in their *modes of expressing* beliefs and values.

Possibilities: a decrease in dogmatism, a more favorable attitude toward change as such, and greater skill in encoding or verbalizing internal feelings.

3. While changing, people are likely to experience *discrepancies* among their beliefs and values, which may result in additional change.

Illustration: beliefs and values change at different rates, so that at any moment there may be a gap between what people value from the past and their new beliefs in the present.

B. Perception

4. People are likely to accept a proposed change when it appears to have *advantages* which can be intelligibly *demonstrated* in the present or which are anticipated in the future.

Suggestive weightings: (a) "advantages": the advantage obtained from accepting a change may include not only the goals thereby obtained but also the prestige from adopting it (Linton, 1940:488). (b) "demonstrated": since changes can be learned only after all or some of their components have been perceived, demonstrability depends in part upon the initiative of innovators and upon the channels of communication and transportation available to them (and those channels in turn depend upon—and here a host of other factors would have to be listed ranging from natural resources or the size of a society to its social classes or castes); the demonstrability of an advantage depends upon people's previous experience and upon their present attitudes and knowledge; the demonstrability of the advantages to be obtained from modifying a material trait is often but not always easier to perceive and to appreciate than those from a nonmaterial one; the feasibility of a change as a

whole is likely to be better appreciated when people can experience it or attempt it "on a limited basis" (Rogers, 1962:131–32).

5. Having changed in many or important respects, people are likely to perceive events somewhat *differently*.

Possibilities: differences in set resulting from the structure and vocabulary of a newly learned language, dialect, or set of terms and labeling correctly or incorrectly—from the viewpoint of the planner—the old or the new referent of change, or both.

6. While changing, people are likely to become *sensitive* to relevant aspects of their environment.

Illustration: people undergoing significant change are likely to acquire pseudosociological and pseudopsychological knowledge concerning their society and their contemporaries.

C. Other People

7. People are likely to accept a proposed change when it is introduced by people whom they consider *important and competent* and who have *adequately consulted* them or their respected leaders.

Suggestive weightings: (a) "important and competent": the higher the social status of the innovator within the society, the more influential he is likely to be. (b) "adequately consulted": a consultation is considered adequate when the explanation appears intelligible in the light of available knowledge and when people are convinced that their own interests are being taken into account.

8. Having changed in many or important respects, people are likely to alter their attitudes toward some but not all the *people in their milieu*.

Possibilities: continued approval of family forms but, as anthropologists suggest (for example, Hunt, 1957:318), the attitudes vary, too, with the type of prevailing family structure; disapproval of traditional political leaders.

9. While changing, people are likely to try to join, seek support from, or remain in *groups* providing support for exhibiting the innovation.

Illustration: important changes are accompanied by the founding of, and increase in, associations related to the change.

D. Personality Traits

10. People are likely to accept a proposed change when it is in accord with the *modal personality traits* of their society or with a *goal* they are seeking.

Suggestive weightings: (a) "modal personality traits": some very general personality traits which exist modally in a society—such as "adaptability" or "rigidity"—facilitate all types of change. (b) "goal": people seek goals which stem from tradition and from special problems existing during a particular historical period.

11. Having changed in many or in important respects, people are likely to acquire new traits which represent *basically different orientations*.

Possibilities: the ability to tolerate the delay in receiving rewards and punishments, to display initiative, to be self-confident, and to act independently.

12. While changing, people are likely to be *discontented*.

Illustration: People usually tend to be insecure, aggressive, or display other signs of discontent while changing.

E. Learning

13. People are likely to accept a proposed change when it makes demands whose components they have *already learned* or *feel confident* they can learn.

Suggestive weightings: (a) "already learned": the components of a change already known or mastered by people depend in part upon their cultural heritage, the political system under which they live, and other variables. (b) "feel confident": as they learn some of the components involved in a change, people's confidence in general regarding that change increases.

14. Having changed in many or important respects, people are likely to develop *new kinds of abilities*.

Possibilities: to store information differently or to think more abstractly.

15. While changing, people usually learn to *adapt* to novel situations.

Illustration: changing people learn to learn more readily.

Interaction

16. Over time, generally long periods of time which may include generations, almost infinitely varied changes are possible in any group or society; but at a given instant, usually but not always, significant changes occur slowly.

17. Planned or unplanned changes are likely to have, beyond their immediate effects, additional consequences, some or many of which may be quite unforeseeable.

The principles provoke some more general issues. First, in reference to "satisfactory," a suggestive weighting for the first principle, one might ask: at what point in the life cycle are habits learned which prove satisfactory and hence resist change? According to what has become the conventional view, those acquired in early childhood are likely to be stable (Brumer, 1956:194); according to another, early socialization in "primitive societies," being "loose, vague, [and] unsystematic," tends to produce habits considered secular rather than sacred and therefore changeable (Hart, 1955:139, 143). The critical point from a psychological standpoint is not the age at which a habit is learned but the degree of reinforcement it receives—if it is learned early and thereafter reinforced or if it is learned late and thereafter also reinforced, it will persist. The former situation seems to prevail more frequently than the latter, for the important values of a society tend to be transmitted to the very young. Here is perhaps a clear-cut illustration of how a psychological approach reconciles an apparent contradiction by reducing the alternatives to a common denominator.

Principle 7 refers as a suggestive weighting to an "adequate" consulting of the people who are to be changed. But what if they are not consulted at all? A tyrant might say that the change can nevertheless be brought to pass. The answer is: yes, it can be; but, if they step forth in opposition, then people have to be guarded or crushed, and guarding or crushing requires an expenditure of energy, and to that degree, if negatively, their desires are taken into account. Under most but not all conditions change is painful, or at least it is likely to be anticipated; for this reason, those confronted with change must become convinced that they are not going to lose whatever gains they think they possess and must believe that they will not have their present misery increased. If they can play some part in the decision, they probably will be convinced that they have at least defended their interests; perhaps their very participation makes them feel committed to cooperate. These views reflect more than a crude, ethnocentric bias in favor of the democratic conviction that people like to feel they are masters of their destiny, for the alternative of consultation with leaders is included. Men may not wish, moreover, to play a direct role in the decisions affecting themselves—making decisions is difficult and may carry with it a feeling of responsibility—and so the privilege or the responsibility gladly is allocated to others whom they respect and trust, the formal or the informal leaders.

The weight given each principle fluctuates with the situation at hand and with the point in time at which the situation is examined. After being changed in some respects and after deriving satisfaction from that change, people then may become generally receptive to the notion of change. When the Manus in the Admiralty Islands of New Guinea had observed American soldiers and had "grasped the idea that there was a total civilized way of life, not an unrelated assemblage of detailed superior weapons, gadgets, and religious beliefs," they were ready to accept many additional innovations from the outside (Mead, 1956:172). Although insufficient psychological evidence has been recorded in connection with this change, it may be guessed that the islanders, having adopted many small changes and admiring the material culture of the American soldiers, if not the Americans themselves, developed a "basically different orientation" (Principle 11), as a result of which

they found additional changes compatible with their "beliefs and values" (Principle 1) and their own personality traits (Principle 10).

All the variables requiring weights are psychological in the last analysis, which means that they must be referred to specific people. Thus, according to Principle 1, people must believe on a purely consciously level not only that the status quo is not "satisfactory"—the "felt need" mentioned by the proponents of community development—but also that the innovation will produce improvement. From the viewpoint of an outsider the need for change may be apparent—malnutrition, they say, can be eliminated by producing and consuming another type of crop—yet the people themselves may be content with their present diet and reject the substitute food (Erasmus, 1961:18–25). Weightings based upon objective facts, consequently, must be tentative until their actual psychological effects are ascertained.

A real problem inherent in the psychological approach arises from the fact that the people to whose predispositions, perception, etc., all the principles refer are not specified and cannot be specified except through information that transcends psychology. Anthropologists (for example, Adair and Vogt, 1949; Dozier, 1951) indicate that changes are accepted or rejected as a function of their relation to the preexisting culture: are the changes "congenial," "congruent," "compatible," or not? In psychological terms this means that they are or are not "in conflict," as Principle 1 above states, with the "traditional beliefs and values" of some, but not all, people in the society. It is conceivable, therefore, that a change will be accepted when it is congruent with the opinions and feelings not of the marginal but of the minority who control the society. In this sense the principle is a useful guide only to the latter and not to the former, and hence it cannot forecast the outcome for the society as a whole. Once a change is introduced by the minority, moreover, it may be perceived differently by the majority and by then no longer be in conflict with their beliefs and attitudes, a process which again is not subsumed under the principle itself. The planner can be sure only of the appearance of individual differences: people always react to any situation as a function of more or less unique individual (for instance, age or sex) or group (for example, social or economic class) differences. The importance of particular people must be independently ascertained.

Precisely the same problem arises concerning the role of an adopted change. For the individual a changed habit interacts with previous habits. For the society a changed person or a changed group interacts with unchanged persons or groups. There is no reason to imagine that the same principles are useful to understand or predict both intraindividual and interindividual conflict or interaction.

Turning now to Principle 16, the first of the two on interaction, we believe passing reference to the doctrine of cultural relativity is sufficient to establish the tentative validity of the "almost infinitely varied changes" which people can be made to reveal. Immediately, however, an objection must be whispered: there are biologically determined limits. But what of psychological limitations? Centuries of speculation and research certainly have not provided an adequate reply either for the individual or for society. Muzziness still pervades the concept of "adjustment" in psychiatry, for example, and the solution for each patient remains the healthy, pragmatic one of what is best for this patient under the particular circumstances that are likely to confront him in his lifetime.

The pessimistic note in Principle 16 concerning the slowness of change stems from evidence indicating that habits established during early childhood survive and can be modified only with great difficulty. In this basic sense, people tend to be conservative. It has been shown that men and women—at least Americans who have been investigated—resort to various devices to retain their viewpoints and feelings, such as deliberately avoiding exposure to a contrary viewpoint (Klapper, 1960:19–23) or discounting the sources of the communication to which they have been exposed (Hovland and others, 1953:73–74). Language itself is a moderating influence.

Aside from reminding people of their national or ethnic identity, to some extent it structures the way in which they perceive and store information about the external world.

The basically conservative nature of people does not, of course, preclude planning. Communications can reach them if certain conditions are satisfied. There must be one or more communicators wishing to communicate; they must have at their disposal appropriate media of communication; they must conform to certain formal and informal restrictions existing in any society; their potential audience must be assembled at a site where such communications can be received; and the audience must be in a mood to perceive and to learn. As previously indicated, stability of habits will depend not on the age at which habits are acquired, but on the kinds of reinforcements that appear throughout life. Under certain conditions, for example, people can undergo violent change apparently without suffering great psychic damage. It already has been indicated that the process of change also may be suddenly accelerated when a favorable attitude toward the notion of change is acquired. Principle 17, in fact, suggests that basic changes are likely to lead to changes in innumerable related habits. The question for the planner really is to try to anticipate the nature of the changes. Some have been singled out—such as conversion to a religious group with a broad *Weltanschauung*, the material aspects of modern civilization, a political movement (conservatism, communism), and various forms of nationalism and patriotism—but their precise effects upon separate habits are not clear (Doob, 1964b:127–31). Future research, moreover, may reveal new devices to produce change. For example, if people can be immunized against change by being exposed to doses of a contrary viewpoint (McGuire and Papageorgis, 1961), conceivably they might also learn that their situation is improved by certain alterations in their life's regimen.

The last principle might well be called the perplexity of unforeseeability. The "probably unforeseeable" consequences reflect the multivariate situation confronting the planner or the analyst. So many factors interact in real life or in a real person that it is difficult or impossible to anticipate the outcome (see, for example, Gouldner, 1957:99–102). When people learn any new form of behavior, wittingly or not, they modify it somewhat to conform to their abilities or background; this apparently is also true of social innovations (Barnett, 1953:329–34). Even then, foreseeable consequences may be disrupted by unforeseen events.

All that the planner can hope to do is to reduce this sphere of unpredictability as much as possible. Thus, no one can foresee exactly what will happen when people in a developing area are taught to read and write, but certainly it may be anticipated that they then will want "some of the comforts and benefits of civilization" (Chadwick, 1949:34)—and only the context and future development can disclose the particular ones they crave.

References Cited

Adair, John, and Evon Vogt. 1949: "Navaho and Zuni Veterans: A Study of Contrasting Modes of Culture Change," *American Anthropologist,* LI, 547–61.

Barnett, H. G. 1953: *Innovation: the Basis of Cultural Change,* McGraw-Hill, New York.

Bruner, Edward M. 1956: "Cultural Transmission and Cultural Change," *Southwestern Journal of Anthropology,* XII (1), 191–99.

Chadwick, E. R. 1949: "The Anatomy of Mass Education," *Mass Education Bulletin,* I, 30–36.

Doob, Leonard W. 1960: *Becoming More Civilized: a Psychological Exploration,* Yale University Press, New Haven. 1964b *Patriotism and Nationalism: Their Psychological Foundations,* Yale University Press, New Haven.

Dozier, Edward P. 1951: "Resistance to Acculturation and Assimilation in an Indian Pueblo," *American Anthropologist,* LIII, 56–66.

Erasmus, Charles J. 1961: *Man Takes Control: Cultural Development and American Aid,* University of Minnesota Press, Minneapolis.

Gouldner, Alvin W. 1957: "Theoretical Requirements of the Applied Social Sciences," *American Sociological Review,* XXII (2), 92–102.

Hart, C. W. M. 1955: "Contrasts Between Prepubertal and Postpubertal Education," in *Education and Anthropology,* ed. G. D. Spindler, Stanford University Press, Stanford.

Havinghurst, Robert J., and Beatrice Neugarten. 1955: *American Indian and White Children,* University of Chicago Press, Chicago.

Hovland, Carl I., Irving L. Janis, and Harold H. Kelly. 1953: *Communication and Persuasion,* Yale University Press, New Haven.

Hunt, Chester L. 1957: "Cultural Barriers to Point Four," in *Underdeveloped Areas,* ed. L. Shannon, Harper and Row, New York, 316–21.

Keesing, Felix M. 1953: *Culture Change,* Stanford University Press, Stanford.

Klapper, Joseph T. 1960: *The Effects of Mass Communication,* The Free Press, Glencoe, Ill.

Kluckhohn, Clyde, and Dorothea Leighton. 1946: *The Navajo,* Harvard University Press, Cambridge, Mass.

Kluckhohn, Florence Rockwood, and Fred L. Strodtbeck. 1961: *Variations in Value Orientations,* Row Peterson, Evanston, Ill.

Kushner, Gilbert, and others. 1962: *What Accounts for Sociocultural Change?* Institute for Research in Social Science, University of North Carolina, Chapel Hill.

Lewis, Oscar. 1951: *Life in a Mexican Village,* University of Illinois Press, Urbana.

Linton, Ralph (ed.). 1940: *Acculturation in Seven American Indian Tribes,* Appleton-Century, New York.

McGuire, William J., and Demetrios Papageorgis. 1961: "The Relative Efficacy of Various Types of Prior Belief-Defense in Producing Immunity Against Persuasion," *Journal of Abnormal and Social Psychology,* LXII (2), 327–37.

Mead, Margaret (ed.). 1955: *Cultural Patterns and Technical Change,* Mentor Books, New York. 1956: *New Lives for Old: Cultural Transformation, 1928–1953,* William Morrow and Co., New York.

Redfield, Robert. 1953: *The Primitive World and its Transformations,* Cornell University Press, Ithaca.

Rogers, Everett M. 1962: *Diffusion of Innovations,* The Free Press of Glencoe, New York.

6. Achieving Change in People: Some Applications of Group Dynamics Theory

Dorwin Cartwright*

I

We hear all around us today the assertion that the problems of the twentieth century are problems of human relations. The survival of civilization, it is said, will depend upon man's ability to create social inventions capable of harnessing, for society's constructive use, the vast physical energies now at man's disposal. Or, to put the matter more simply, we must learn how to change the way in which people behave toward one another. In broad outline, the specifications for a good society are clear, but a serious technical problem remains: How can we change people so that they neither restrict the freedom nor limit the potentialities for growth of others; so that they accept and respect people of different religion, nationality, color, or political opinion; so that nations can exist in a world without war, and so that the fruits of our technological advances can bring economic well-being and freedom from disease to all the people of the world? Although few people would disagree with these objectives when stated abstractly, when we become more specific, differences of opinion quickly arise. How is change to be produced? Who is to do it? Who is to be changed? These questions permit no ready answers.

Before we consider in detail these questions of social technology, let us clear away some semantic obstacles. The word "change" produces emotional reactions. It is not a neutral word. To many people it is threatening. It conjures up visions of a revolutionary, a dissatisfied idealist, a trouble-maker, a malcontent. Nicer words referring to the process of changing people are education, training, orientation, guidance, indoctrination, therapy. We are more ready to have others "educate" us than to have them "change" us. We, ourselves, feel less guilty in "training" others than in "changing" them. Why this emotional response? What makes the two kinds of words have such different meanings? I believe that a large part of the differences lies in the fact that the safer words (like education or therapy) carry the implicit assurance that the only changes produced will be good ones, acceptable within a currently held value system. The cold, unmodified word "change," on the contrary, promises no respect for values; it might even tamper with values themselves. Perhaps for this very reason it will foster straight thinking if we use the word "change" and thus force ourselves to struggle directly and self-consciously with the problems of value that are involved. Words like eduation, training, or therapy, by the very fact that they are not so

Reprinted from Dorwin Cartwright, "Achieving Change in People: Some Applications of Group Dynamics Theory," *Human Relations,* Vol. IV (1951), pp. 381–393.

° Professor, Research Center for Group Dynamics, University of Michigan.

disturbing, may close our eyes to the fact that they too inevitably involve values.

Another advantage of using the word "change" rather than other related words is that it does not restrict our thinking to a limited set of aspects of people that are legitimate targets of change. Anyone familiar with the history of education knows that there has been endless controversy over what it is about people that "education" properly attempts to modify. Some educators have viewed education simply as imparting knowledge, others mainly as providing skills for doing things, still others as producing healthy "attitudes," and some have aspired to instill a way of life. Or if we choose to use a word like "therapy," we can hardly claim that we refer to a more clearly defined realm of change. Furthermore, one can become inextricably entangled in distinctions and vested interests by attempting to distinguish sharply between, let us say, the domain of education and that of therapy. If we are to try to take a broader view and to develop some basic principles that promise to apply to all types of modifications in people, we had better use a word like "change" to keep our thinking general enough.

The proposal that social technology may be employed to solve the problems of society suggests that social science may be applied in ways not different from those used in the physical sciences. Does social science, in fact, have any practically useful knowledge which may be brought to bear significantly on society's most urgent problems? What scientifically based principles are there for guiding programs of social change: In this paper we shall restrict our considerations to certain parts of a relatively new branch of social science known as "group dynamics." We shall examine some of the implications for social action which stem from research in this field of scientific investigation.

What is "group dynamics"? Perhaps it will be most useful to start by looking at the derivation of the word "dynamics." It comes from a Greek word meaning force. In careful usage of the phrase, "group dynamics," refers to the forces operating in groups. The investigation of group dynamics, then, consists of a study of

these forces: what gives rise to them, what conditions modify them, what consequences they have, etc. The practical application of group dynamics (or the technology of group dynamics) consists of the utilization of knowledge about these forces for the achievement of some purpose. In keeping with this definition, then, it is clear that group dynamics, as a realm of investigation, is not particularly novel, nor is it the exclusive property of any person or institution. It goes back at least to the outstanding work of men like Simmel, Freud, and Cooley.

Although interest in groups has a long and respectable history, the past fifteen years have witnessed a new flowering of activity in this field. Today, research centers in several countries are carrying out substantial programs of research designed to reveal the nature of groups and of their functioning. The phrase "group dynamics" has come into common usage during this time and intense efforts have been devoted to the development of the field, both as a branch of social science and as a form of social technology.

In this development the name of Kurt Lewin has been outstanding. As a consequence of his work in the field of individual psychology and from his analysis of the nature of the pressing problems of the contemporary world, Lewin became convinced of society's urgent need for a *scientific approach* to the understanding of the dynamics of groups. In 1945 he established the Research Center for Group Dynamics to meet this need. Since that date the Center has been devoting its efforts to improving our scientific understanding of groups through laboratory experimentation, field studies, and the use of techniques of action research. It has also attempted in various ways to help get the findings of social science more widely used by social management. Much of what I have to say in this paper is drawn from the experiences of this Center in its brief existence of a little more than five years (Cartwright, 1950).

II

For various reasons we have found that much of our work has been devoted to an attempt to gain a better understanding of the ways in which people change their behavior or resist efforts by others to have them do so. Whether we set for ourselves the practical goal of improving behavior or whether we take on the intellectual task of understanding why people do what they do, we have to investigate processes of communication, influence, social pressure—in short, problems of change.

In this work we have encountered great frustration. The problems have been most difficult to solve. Looking back over our experience, I have become convinced that no small part of the trouble has resulted from an irresistible tendency to conceive of our problems in terms of the individual. We live in an individualistic culture. We value the individual highly, and rightly so. But I am inclined to believe that our political and social concern for the individual has narrowed our thinking as social scientists so much that we have not been able to state our research problems properly. Perhaps we have taken the individual as the unit of observation and study when some larger unit would have been more appropriate. Let us look at a few examples.

Consider first some matters having to do with the mental health of an individual. We can all agree, I believe, that an important mark of a healthy personality is that the individual's self-esteem has not been undermined. But on what does self-esteem depend? From research on this problem we have discovered that, among other things, repeated experiences of failure or traumatic failures on matters of central importance serve to undermine one's self-esteem. We also know that whether a person experiences success or failure as a result of some undertaking depends upon the level of aspiration which he has set for himself. Now, if we try to discover how the level of aspiration gets set, we are immediately involved in the person's relationships to groups. The groups to which he belongs set standards for his behavior which he must accept if he is to remain in the group. If his capacities do not allow him to reach these standards, he experiences failure, he withdraws or is rejected by the group and his self-esteem suffers a shock.

Suppose, then, that we accept a task of therapy, of rebuilding his self-esteem. It would appear plausible from our analysis of the problem that we should attempt to work with variables of the same sort that produced the difficulty, that is to work with him either in the groups to which he now belongs or to introduce him into new groups which are selected for the purpose and to work upon his relationships to groups as such. From the point of view of preventive mental health, we might even attempt to train the groups in our communities—classes in schools, work groups in business, families, unions, religious and cultural groups—to make use of practices better designed to protect the self-esteem of their members.

Consider a second example. A teacher finds that in her class she has a number of trouble-makers, full of aggression. She wants to know why these children are so aggressive and what can be done about it. A foreman in a factory has the same kind of problem with some of his workers. He wants the same kind of help. The solution most tempting to both the teacher and the foreman often is to transfer the worst trouble-makers to someone else, or if facilities are available, to refer them for counselling. But is the problem really of such a nature that it can be solved by removing the trouble-maker from the situation or by working on his individual motivations and emotional life? What leads does research give us? The evidence indicates, of course, that there are many causes of aggressiveness in people, but one aspect of the problem has become increasingly clear in recent years. If we observe carefully the amount of aggressive behavior and the number of trouble-makers to be found in a large collection of groups, we find that these characteristics can vary tremendously from group to group even when the different groups are composed essentially of the same kinds of people. In the now classic experiments of Lewin, Lippitt, and White (1939) on the effects of different styles of leadership, it was found that the same group of children displayed markedly different levels of aggressive behavior when under different styles of leadership. Moreover, when individual children were transferred from one group to another, their levels of aggressiveness shifted to conform to the atmosphere of the new group. Efforts to account for one child's aggressiveness under one style of leadership merely in terms of his personality traits could hardly succeed under these conditions. This is not to say that a person's behavior is entirely to be accounted for by the atmosphere and structure of the immediate group, but it is remarkable to what an extent a strong, cohesive group can control aspects of a member's behavior traditionally thought to be expressive of enduring personality traits. Recognition of this fact rephrases the problem of how to change such behavior. It directs us to a study of the sources of the influence of the group on its members.

Let us take an example from a different field. What can we learn from efforts to change people by mass media and mass persuasion? In those rare instances when educators, propagandists, advertisers, and others who want to influence large numbers of people, have bothered to make an objective evaluation of the enduring changes produced by their efforts, they have been able to demonstrate only the most negligible effects (Cartwright, 1949). The inefficiency of attempts to influence the public by mass media would be scandalous if there were agreement that it was important or even desirable to have such influences strongly exerted. In fact, it is no exaggeration to say that all of the research and experience of generations has not improved the efficiency of lectures or other means of mass influence to any noticeable degree. Something must be wrong with our theories of learning, motivation, and social psychology.

Within very recent years some research data have been accumulating which may give us a clue to the solution of our problem. In one series of experiments directed by Lewin, it was found that a method of group decision, in which the group as a whole made a decision to have its members change their behavior, was from two to ten times as effective in producing actual change as was a lecture presenting exhortation to change (Lewin, 1951). We

have yet to learn precisely what produces these differences of effectiveness, but it is clear that by introducing group forces into the situation a whole new level of influence has been achieved.

The experience has been essentially the same when people have attempted to increase the productivity of individuals in work settings. Traditional conceptions of how to increase the output of workers have stressed the individual: select the right man for the job; simplify the job for him; train him in the skills required; motivate him by economic incentives; make it clear to whom he reports; keep the lines of authority and responsibility simple and straight. But even when all these conditions are fully met we are finding that productivity is far below full potential. There is even good reason to conclude that this individualistic conception of the determinants of productivity actually fosters negative consequences. The individual, now isolated and subjected to the demands of the organization through the commands of his boss, finds that he must create with his fellow employees informal groups, not shown on any table of organization, in order to protect himself from arbitrary control of his life, from the boredom produced by the endless repetition of mechanically sanitary and routine operations, and from the impoverishment of his emotional and social life brought about by the frustration of his basic needs for social interaction, participation, and acceptance in a stable group. Recent experiments have demonstrated clearly that the productivity of work groups can be greatly increased by methods of work organization and supervision which give more responsibility to work groups, which allow for fuller participation in important decisions, and which make stable groups the firm basis for support of the individual's social needs (Coch & French, 1948). I am convinced that future research will also demonstrate that people working under such conditions become more mature and creative individuals in their homes, in community life, and as citizens.

As a final example, let us examine the experience of efforts to train people in workshops, institutes, and special training courses. Such efforts are common in various areas of social welfare, intergroup relations, political affairs, industry, and adult education generally. It is an unfortunate fact that objective evaluation of the effects of such training efforts has only rarely been undertaken, but there is evidence for those who will look that the actual change in behavior produced is most disappointing. A workshop not infrequently develops keen interest among the participants, high morale and enthusiasm, and a firm resolve on the part of many to apply all the wonderful insights back home. But what happens back home? The trainee discovers that his colleagues don't share his enthusiasm. He learns that the task of changing others' expectations and ways of doing things is discouragingly difficult. He senses, perhaps not very clearly, that it would make all the difference in the world if only there were a few other people sharing his enthusiasm and insights with whom he could plan activities, evaluate consequences of efforts, and from whom he could gain emotional and motivational support. The approach to training which conceives of its task as being merely that of changing the individual probably produces frustration, demoralization, and disillusionment in as large a measure as it accomplishes more positive results.

A few years ago the Research Center for Group Dynamics undertook to shed light on this problem by investigating the operation of a workshop for training leaders in intercultural relations (Lippitt, 1949). In a project, directed by Lippitt, we set out to compare systematically the different effects of the workshop upon trainees who came as isolated individuals in contrast to those who came as teams. Since one of the problems in the field of intercultural relations is that of getting people of good will to be more active in community efforts to improve intergroup relations, one goal of the training workshop was to increase the activity of the trainees in such community affairs. We found that before the workshop there was no difference in the activity level of the people who were to be trained as isolates and of those who were to be trained as teams. Six months after the workshop, however, those who had been trained as isolates

were only slightly more active than before the workshop whereas those who had been members of strong training teams were now much more active. We do not have clear evidence on the point, but we would be quite certain that the maintenance of heightened activity over a long period of time would also be much better for members of teams. For the isolates the effect of the workshop had the characteristic of a "shot in the arm" while for the team member it produced a more enduring change because the team provided continuous support and reinforcement for its members.

III

What conclusions may we draw from these examples? What principles of achieving change in people can we see emerging? To begin with the most general proposition, we may state that the behavior, attitudes, beliefs, and values of the individual are all firmly grounded in the groups to which he belongs. How aggressive or cooperative a person is, how much self-respect and self-confidence he has, how energetic and productive his work is, what he aspires to, what he believes to be true and good, whom he loves or hates, and what beliefs and prejudices he holds—all these characteristics are highly determined by the individual's group memberships. In a real sense, they are properties of groups and of the relationships between people. Whether they change or resist change will, therefore, be greatly influenced by the nature of these groups. Attempts to change them must be concerned with the dynamics of groups.

In examining more specifically how groups enter into the process of change, we find it useful to view groups in at least three different ways. In the first view, the group is seen as a source of influence over its members. Efforts to change behavior can be supported or blocked by pressures on members stemming from the group. To make constructive use of these pressures the group must be used *as a medium of change*. In the second view, the group itself becomes the *target of change*. To change the behavior of individuals it may be necessary to change the standards of the group, its style of leadership, its emotional atmosphere, or its stratification into cliques and hierarchies. Even though the goal may be to change the behavior of *individuals*, the target of change becomes the group. In the third view, it is recognized that many changes of behavior can be brought about only by the organized efforts of groups *as agents of change*. A committee to combat intolerance, a labor union, an employers association, a citizens group to increase the pay of teachers— any action group will be more or less effective depending upon the way it is organized, the satisfactions it provides to its members, the degree to which its goals are clear, and a host of other properties of the group.

An adequate social technology of change, then, requires at the very least a scientific understanding of groups viewed in each of these ways. We shall consider here only the first two aspects of the problem: the group as a medium of change and as a target of change.

The Group as a Medium of Change

Principle No. 1

If the group is to be used effectively as a medium of change, those people who are to be changed and those who are to exert influence for change must have a strong sense of belonging to the same group.

Kurt Lewin described this principle well: "The normal gap between teacher and student, doctor and patient, social worker and public, can . . . be a real obstacle to acceptance of the advocated conduct." In other words, in spite of whatever status differences there might be between them, the teacher and the student have to feel as members of one group in matters involving their sense of values. The chances for re-education seem to be increased whenever a strong we-feeling is created (Lewin, 1948). Recent experiments by Preston and Heintz have demonstrated greater changes of opinions among members of discussion groups operating with participatory leadership than among those with supervisory leadership (1949). The implications of this principle for classroom teaching are far-reaching. The same may be said of supervision in the factory, army, or hospital.

Principle No. 2

The more attractive the group is to its members the greater is the influence that the group can exert on its members.

This principle has been extensively documented by Festinger and his co-workers (1950). They have been able to show in a variety of settings that in more cohesive groups there is a greater readiness of members to attempt to influence others, a greater readiness to be influenced by others, and stronger pressures toward conformity when conformity is a relevant matter for the group. Important for the practitioner wanting to make use of this principle is, of course, the question of how to increase the attractiveness of groups. This is a question with many answers. Suffice it to say that a group is more attractive the more it satisfies the needs of its members. We have been able to demonstrate experimentally an increase in group cohesiveness by increasing the liking of members for each other as persons, by increasing the perceived importance of the group goal, and by increasing the prestige of the group among other groups. Experienced group workers could add many other ways to this list.

Principle No. 3

In attempts to change attitudes, values, or behavior, the more relevant they are to the basis of attraction to the group, the greater will be the influence that the group can exert upon them.

I believe this principle gives a clue to some otherwise puzzling phenomena. How does it happen that a group, like a labor union, seems to be able to exert such strong discipline over its members in some matters (let us say in dealings with management), while it seems unable to exert nearly the same influence in other matters (let us say in political action)? If we examine why it is that members are attracted to the group, I believe we will find that a particular reason for belonging seems more related to some of the group's activities than to others. If a man joins a union mainly to keep his job and to improve his working conditions, he may be largely uninfluenced by the union's attempt to modify his attitudes toward national and international affairs. Groups differ tremendously in the range of matters that are relevant to them and hence over which they have influence. Much of the inefficiency of adult education could be reduced if more attention were paid to the need that influence attempts be appropriate to the groups in which they are made.

PRINCIPLE No. 4

The greater the prestige of a group member in the eyes of the other members, the greater the influence he can exert.

Polansky, Lippitt, and Redl (1950) have demonstrated this principle with great care and methodological ingenuity in a series of studies in children's summer camps. From a practical point of view it must be emphasized that the things giving prestige to a member may not be those characteristics most prized by the official management of the group. The most prestige-carrying member of a Sunday School class may not possess the characteristics most similar to the minister of the church. The teacher's pet may be a poor source of influence within a class. This principle is the basis for the common observation that the official leader and the actual leader of a group are often not the same individual.

PRINCIPLE No. 5

Efforts to change individuals or subparts of a group which, if successful, would have the result of making them deviate from the norms of the group will encounter strong resistance.

During the past few years a great deal of evidence has been accumulated showing the tremendous pressures which groups can exert upon members to conform to the group's norms. The price of deviation in most groups is rejection or even expulsion. If the member really wants to belong and be accepted, he cannot withstand this type of pressure. It is for this reason that efforts to change people by taking them from the group and giving them special training so often have disappointing results. This principle also accounts for the finding that people thus trained sometimes display increased tension, aggressiveness to-

ward the group, or a tendency to form cults or cliques with others who have shared their training.

These five principles concerning the group as a medium of change would appear to have readiest application to groups created for the purpose of producing changes in people. They provide certain specifications for building effective training or therapy groups. They also point, however, to a difficulty in producing change in people in that they show how resistant an individual is to changing in any way contrary to group pressures and expectations. In order to achieve many kinds of changes in people, therefore, it is necessary to deal with the group as a target of change.

The Group as a Target of Change

PRINCIPLE No. 6

Strong pressure for changes in the group can be established by creating a shared perception by members of the need for change, thus making the source of pressure for change lie within the group.

Marrow and French (1945) report a dramatic case-study which illustrates this principle quite well. A manufacturing concern had a policy against hiring women over thirty because it was believed that they were slower, more difficult to train, and more likely to be absent. The staff psychologist was able to present to management evidence that this belief was clearly unwarranted at least within their own company. The psychologist's facts, however, were rejected and ignored as a basis for action because they violated accepted beliefs. It was claimed that they went against the direct experience of the foremen. Then the psychologist hit upon a plan for achieving change which differed drastically from the usual one of argument, persuasion, and pressure. He proposed that management conduct its own analysis of the situation. With his help management collected all the facts which they believed were relevant to the problem. When the results were in, they were now their own facts rather than those of some "outside" expert. Policy was immediately changed without further resistance. The important point here is that facts are not enough. The facts must be the accepted property of the group if they are to become an effective basis for change. There seems to be all the difference in the world in changes actually carried out between those cases in which a consulting firm is hired to do a study and present a report and those in which technical experts are asked to collaborate with the group in doing its own study.

PRINCIPLE No. 7

Information relating to the need for change, plans for change, and consequences of change must be shared by all relevant people in the group.

Another way of stating this principle is to say that change of a group ordinarily requires the opening of communication channels. Newcomb (1947) has shown how one of the first consequences of mistrust and hostility is the avoidance of communicating openly and freely about the things producing the tension. If you look closely at a pathological group (that is, one that has trouble making decisions or effecting coordinated efforts of its members), you will certainly find strong restraints in that group against communicating vital information among its members. Until these restraints are removed there can be little hope for any real and lasting changes in the group's functioning. In passing it should be pointed out that the removal of barriers to communication will ordinarily be accompanied by a sudden increase in the communication of hostility. The group may appear to be falling apart, and it will certainly be a painful experience to many of the members. This pain and the fear that things are getting out of hand often stop the process of change once begun.

PRINCIPLE No. 8

Changes in one part of a group produce strain in other related parts which can be reduced only by eliminating the change or by bringing about readjustments in the related parts.

It is a common practice to undertake improvements in group functioning by providing training programs for certain classes of people in the organization. A training program for foremen, for nurses, for teachers, or for group workers is established. If the content of the training is relevant for organizational change, it must of necessity deal with the relationships these people have with other subgroups. If nurses in a hospital change their behavior significantly, it will affect their relations both with the patients and with the doctors. It is unrealistic to assume that both these groups will remain indifferent to any significant changes in this respect. In hierarchical structures this process is most clear. Lippitt has proposed on the basis of research and experience that in such organizations attempts at change should always involve three levels, one being the major target of change and the other two being the one above and the one below.

IV

These eight principles represent a few of the basic propositions emerging from research in group dynamics. Since research is constantly going on and since it is the very nature of research to revise and reformulate our conceptions, we may be sure that these principles will have to be modified and improved as time goes by. In the meantime they may serve as guides in our endeavors to develop a scientifically based technology of social management.

In social technology, just as in physical technology, invention plays a crucial role. In both fields progress consists of the creation of new mechanisms for the accomplishment of certain goals. In both fields inventions arise in response to practical needs and are to be evaluated by how effectively they satisfy these needs. The relation of invention to scientific development is indirect but important. Inventions cannot proceed too far ahead of basic scientific development, nor should they be allowed to fall too far behind. They will be more effective the more they make good use of known principles of science, and they often make new developments in science possible. On the other hand, they are in no sense logical derivations from scientific principles.

I have taken this brief excursion into the theory of invention in order to make a final point. To many people "group dynamics" is known only for the social inventions which have developed in recent years in work with groups. Group dynamics is often thought of as certain techniques to be used with groups. Role playing, buzz groups, process observers, post-meeting reaction sheets, and feedback of group observations are devices popularly associated with the phrase "group dynamics." I trust that I have been able to show that group dynamics is more than a collection of gadgets. It certainly aspires to be a science as well as a technology.

This is not to underplay the importance of these inventions nor of the function of inventing. As inventions they are all mechanisms designed to help accomplish important goals. How effective they are will depend upon how skillfully they are used and how appropriate they are to the purposes to which they are put. Careful evaluative research must be the ultimate judge of their usefulness in comparison with alternative inventions. I believe that the principles enumerated in this paper indicate some of the specifications that social inventions in this field must meet.

References

Cartwright, D. Some principles of mass persuasion: Selected findings of research on the sale of United States War Bonds. *Hum. Relat.*, 1949, 2, 253–267.

Cartwright, D. *The Research Center for Group Dynamics: A report of five years' activities and a view of future needs.* Ann Arbor: Institute for Social Research, 1950.

Coch, L., & French, J. R. P., Jr. Overcoming resistance to change. *Hum. Relat.*, 1948, 1, 512–532.

Festinger, L., Schachter, S., & Back, K. *Social pressures in informal groups: A study of a housing project.* New York: Harper, 1950.

Lewin, K. *Resolving social conflicts.* New York: Harper, 1948.

Lewin, K. *Field theory in social science.* New York: Harper, 1951.

Lewin, K., Lippitt, R., & White, R. K. Patterns of aggressive behavior in experimentally created "social climates." *J. soc. Psychol.*, 1939, 10, 271–299.

Lippitt, R. *Training in Community relations.* New York: Harper, 1949.

Marrow, A. J., & French, J. R. P., Jr. Changing a stereotype in industry. *J. soc. Issues*, 1945, 1, 33–37.

Newcomb, T. M. Autistic hostility and social reality. *Hum. Relat.*, 1947, 1, 69–86.

Polansky, N., Lippitt, R., & Redl, F. An investigation of behavioral contagion in groups. *Hum. Relat.*, 1950, 3, 319–348.

7. Counseling: An Interpersonal Influence Process

Stanley R. Strong*

Goldstein and his associates have argued that extrapolation of certain principles and research findings in social psychology to counseling psychology can increase our understanding of counseling and our effectiveness as counselor (Goldstein, 1966; Goldstein & Dean, 1966; Goldstein, Heller, & Sechrest, 1966). Re-

search on opinion change seems particularly promising for this purpose because of the focus on communication. In opinion-change research, a communicator attempts to influence his audience in a predetermined direction; in counseling, the counselor attempts to influence his client to attain the goals of coun-

Reprinted from Stanley R. Strong, "Counseling: An Interpersonal Influence Process," *Journal of Counseling Psychology*, Vol. XV (1968), pp. 215–224.

* Research Psychologist, Student Life Studies, Department of Psychology, University of Minnesota.

seling. Verbal communication is the main technique used by an opinion changer in influencing his audience; verbal communication is also the counselor's main means of influencing his client. For both, these communications present opinions or conceptions different than or discrepant from the opinions or conceptions of the audience or client. Finally, characteristics of the communicator as perceived by the audience, characteristics of the audience, and characteristics of the communication affect the success of influence attempts. These characteristics have been given much attention in both fields.

The purposes of this paper are to (a) review the opinion-change research on communicator and audience variables which affect the success of influence attempts, (b) suggest aspects of counseling which have similar effects, and (c) present a two-phase model of counseling based on these considerations.

Opinion-Change Variables: Theories and Research

Festinger's (1957) cognitive dissonance theory has been the basis of much of the opinion-change research and is used to organize this review. Zimbardo (1960) has summarized the theory as follows:

> Dissonance theory assumes a basic tendency toward consistency of cognitions about oneself and about the environment. When two or more cognitive elements are psychologically inconsistent, dissonance is created. Dissonance is defined as a psychological tension having drive characteristics. Thus, the existence of dissonance is accompanied by psychological discomfort and when dissonance arises, attempts are made to reduce it [p. 86].

Applied to opinion-change research, the theory suggests that an individual will experience dissonance when he knows another person—a communicator—holds an opinion contrary to his own (Festinger, 1957, p. 178). The magnitude of dissonance created by the contrary opinion is a function of the degree of perceived discrepancy between the two opinions —the greater the perceived discrepancy, the greater the dissonance.

Five means of reducing dissonance can be drawn from the theory: (a) The individual can change his opinion to that of the communicator; (b) he can discredit the communicator and thus reduce the importance or cognitive weight of the communicator's assertions; (c) he can devaluate the importance of the issue which reduces the cognitive weights of both positions, and thus the absolute amount of dissonance created by their incompatibility; (d) he can attempt to change the communicator's opinion and, if successful, eliminate the discrepancy; and (e) he can seek to add cognitions consonant with his opinion and thus reduce the relative cognitive weight of the communication.

The avenue of dissonance reduction used by the recipient of a discrepant communication depends on the circumstances of the influence attempt. If the communicator cannot be discredited, if issue importance cannot be devaluated, if counter-persuasion cannot be exerted, and if social support cannot be found, the recipient's cognitive change is a direct function of the cognitive change advocated by the communicator. However, cognitive change is unlikely when alternative means of dissonance reduction are available. An individual's cognitions are interrelated so that a change of one cognition necessitates changes of other cognitions. The resulting psychological effort increases resistance to changing any singular cognitive element (Festinger, 1957, p. 27).

The avenues of dissonance reduction are reciprocal; an easily discredited communicator will achieve little opinion change and much derogation, while a highly credible communicator may achieve much opinion change with little derogation. Clients uninvolved in the topic of an interpretation will disclaim the importance of the issue with little cognitive change, while those highly involved may show much change with little devaluation of the topic.

The thrust of the theory is that arousal of client cognitive dissonance is a function of the psychological discrepancy between his cognitive constructs and the content of counselor communications. The client will change his cognitive constructs in the direction advocated by the counselor only if other means of dissonance reduction are controlled. The studies reviewed below deal with communicator and audience variables that control or moderate the use of one or another avenue of dissonance reduction.

Communicator characteristics which control communicator derogation are the communicator's perceived credibility and his perceived attractiveness. According to Hovland, Janis, and Kelley (1953, p. 21), communicator credibility has two components: ". . . (1) The extent to which a communicator is perceived to be a source of valid assertions (his 'expertness') and (2) the degree of confidence in the communicator's interest to communicate the assertions he considers most valid (his 'trustworthiness')." A communicator's attractiveness is based on his perceived similarity to, compatibility with, and liking for the influence recipient.

The communication recipient's involvement in the influence situation is a result of the intrinsic value of the issue, the effort required of him, or the personal importance of his response. Involvement controls recipient devaluation of issue importance. None of the opinion-change studies deal with dissonance reduction by securing social support or by counterpersuasion. These avenues are usually blocked by not allowing communication recipients to talk to the communicator or to each other.

Expertness

Perception of a communicator as a source of valid assertions is influenced by (a) objective evidence of specialized training such as diplomas, certificates, and titles, (b) behavioral evidence of expertness such as rational and knowledgeable arguments and confidence in presentation, and (c) reputation as an expert.

Aronson, Turner, and Carlsmith (1963) studied the effects of reputation as an expert on opinion change. They asked coeds to rank nine stanzas from modern poems by the way the poet used form to aid in expressing his meaning. The coeds then read a passage describing uses and abuses of form in which the nine stanzas were examples. For each coed, stanza evaluation in the passage was set at small, moderate, or large discrepancy from her rankings. For half of the coeds, the passage was attributed to T. S. Eliot; for the other half, the passage was attributed to a student from a small teachers college. After reading the passage, the coeds reevaluated (reranked) the stanzas and, to measure derogation, indicated their strength of agreement with statements about the author. Results indicated the operation of communicator credibility in controlling the means of dissonance reduction in that opinion change was a linear function of discrepancy for the expert source—the greater the discrepancy, the greater the change—while it was a curvilinear function of discrepancy for the mildly credible source—opinion change increased from small to moderate discrepancy and decreased from moderate to large discrepancy. Derogation of the mildly credible source was high, while derogation of the highly credible source was low. However, derogation did not increase with discrepancy, but was constant across the discrepancy continuum.

Bockner and Insko (1966), Bergin (1962), and Browning (1966) reported similar results using objective evidence of expertness. Bockner and Insko asked undergraduates to read an article on the number of hours of sleep required by students. For half of the students, the article was attributed to "Sir John Eccles, Nobel prize winning physiologist." For the other half, it was attributed to "Mr. Harry J. Olsen, director of the Fort Worth Y.M.C.A." Amount of sleep advocated in the communications was varied from 8 to 0 hours. As before, opinion change was a linear function of discrepancy for the highly credible source, while it was a curvilinear function of discrepancy for the mildly credible source. In addition, disparagement of the mildly credible source was a linear function of discrepancy, but was not for the highly credible source.

Bergin (1962) studied source-expertness effects on an issue more relevant to counseling—self-rating of masculinity-femininity. Sixty introductory psychology students rated themselves on a masculinity-femininity scale before and after treatment. They were randomly assigned to high- or low-credibility conditions and to low-, moderate-, or high-communication-discrepancy conditions. In the high-credibility condition, each student reported to a receptionist who directed him to an office decorated with diplomas, certificates, and a picture of Freud. The communicator, dressed in a white coat, tested him with complex instruments allegedly yielding an extremely accurate picture of his personality. After the tests, the communicator showed the student his ratings on masculinity-femininity and other scales. In the low-credibility condition, each undergraduate was rated by a high school student who obviously knew little about personality evaluation. Changes between pre and post self-ratings were a linear function of discrepancy in the high-credibility condition, but not in the low-credibility condition. Intensity of communicator disparagement was a function of discrepancy in the low-credibility condition, but not in the high-credibility condition.

Browning (1966) studied the effects of therapist-perceived expertness (prestige) on client acceptance of interpretations in therapy. Twenty-four college-student volunteers, judged nonpsychiatric, were randomly assigned to either "high- or low-prestige therapists." The same therapist served in both conditions. After an initial interview devoted to orientation to therapy, each client received 24 interpretations spaced over from two to four interviews. A significantly greater number of large discrepancy interpretations were accepted by clients in the high-prestige-therapist condition than in the low-prestige condition.

Few investigators have developed perceived expertness behaviorally, that is, with communicator rational and knowledgeable arguments and confidence. Bergin's "expert" made some use of this source by his confidence and his impressive instruments. Brehm and Lipsher (1959) studied the effects of supporting reasons for discrepant opinions with high school students. One hundred and fourteen students gave their opinions on a number of current social and political issues. Three weeks later they were asked to evaluate and react to the opinions of "students from another class." Half of the communications included supporting reasons for discrepant opinions, half did not.

Degree of opinion discrepancy was varied. Students receiving supporting reasons for discrepant opinions rated the communicators more "trustworthy" than those not receiving supporting reasons. This may mean that, when supporting reasons were given, students perceived the opinions to be more valid, and thus viewed the communicator as more expert. Opinion-change data were inconsistent, but communications with supporting arguments tended to result in greater opinion change than those without such support.

These studies show that a communicator's perceived expertness controls the extent to which his discrepant communications will lead to opinion change rather than to his own disparagement. They also show that the greater the communicator's perceived expertness, the more discrepant his communications can be without generating derogation.

Trustworthiness

A communicator's perceived trustworthiness is a function of (a) his reputation for honesty, (b) his social role, such as physician, (c) his sincerity and openness, and (d) his perceived lack of motivation for personal gain. All of these attributes have been used to manipulate perceived trustworthiness.

Hovland and Weiss (1951) asked undergraduates to read an article on one of four issues: antihistamine drugs, atomic submarines, the steel shortage, or the future of movie theaters. One-half of the communications on each issue were attributed to a highly trustworthy source such as the *New England Journal of Biology and Medicine*, Robert J. Oppenheimer, etc. The other half were attributed to a less trustworthy source, such as a "pulp" pictorial magazine, *Pravda*, etc. Students rated presentations and conclusions more fair and justified and more of them changed their opinions in the advocated direction when articles were attributed to high-trustworthy sources than when they were attributed to low-trustworthy sources. Although opinion-change differences due to source trustworthiness were not significant on retest 4 weeks later, further research showed that when the source was reinstated at retest significant differences were retained (Kelman & Hovland, 1953).

Hovland and Mandell (1952) studied source-trustworthiness effects on opinions of the need to devaluate United States currency. The high-trustworthy communicator was an economist from a leading university; the low-trustworthy communicator was an import executive. College-undergraduate subjects were informed that importers would gain from currency devaluation. The high-trustworthy communicator was judged to do a better job and to be more fair and honest in his presentation than the low-trustworthy communicator, but opinion-change differences were not significant.

Zagona and Harter (1966) studied source-trustworthiness effects on attitudes about smoking. Three communication sources were the *Surgeon General's Report on Smoking and Health*, *Life*, and an advertisement by the American Tobacco Company. They summarized their results as follows: ". . . as credibility of the source increased, the percentage of subjects who agreed with the information and perceived it as trustworthy also increased [p. 155]."

Two studies suggest that trustworthiness is more important than expertness in facilitating opinion change. Kelman and Hovland (1953) played a recording of an "educational radio program" on juvenile delinquency to senior high school students. The students were asked to "judge its educational value." In the course of the program, a guest speaker was introduced who urged extreme leniency in the treatment of juvenile delinquents. In the high-trustworthy condition, the speaker was introduced as an experienced, well-informed, highly trained, sincere, and honest judge in a juvenile court. In the neutral-trustworthy condition, the guest speaker was introduced as a "member of the studio audience chosen at random." In the third condition, the guest speaker was also a "member of the studio audience chosen at random." However, the introductory interview revealed that he had been a delinquent as a youth and was currently out of jail on bail for a charge of dope peddling. Each speaker presented identical content. A significantly greater proportion of the positive communicator's audience judged the presentation to be fair and changed their opinions in the advocated direction than did the negative communicator's audience. Proportions of the audience judging the neutral communicator to be fair and changing their opinions in the direction he advocated were only slightly less than for the positive communicator. This suggests that although the neutral communicator had no "expert" credentials he was perceived as sincere and honest and thus was as influential as the expert.

Walster, Aronson, and Abrahams (1966) presented seventh graders with "news stories" in which a public prosecutor or a convict urged stronger or weaker court power. The students were told that prosecutors would obtain more convictions with stronger court power which would enhance their personal prestige and income. Obviously, criminals would benefit personally from weaker court power. The prosecutor obtained greater opinion change than the convict when they both argued for weaker court powers. However, the opposite was true in the arguments for stronger court powers. Apparently the convict's appeal, clearly against his best interest, resulted in greater trust and perceived sincerity and thus greater opinion change. The prosecutor, arguing for a change from which he would personally benefit, was perceived to be less trustworthy and sincere and obtained less opinion change in spite of his greater prestige.

These studies show that a communicator's perceived trustworthiness affects the extent to which he is able to effect opinion change. Results from Kelman and Hovland, and Walster *et al.* suggest that trustworthiness is more important than perceived expertness. Perceived untrustworthiness can obviate the influence of expertness; perceived trustworthiness can compensate for ambiguous expertness.

Attractiveness

Communicator attractiveness is usually manipulated by assuring subjects that they will like the communicator, that they are compatible with him, or that the communicator is similar to them in background, opinions, etc. Assurances of liking, compatibility, or similarity are usually "based" on personality or opinion questionnaire "results."

A series of studies by Byrne and his associates (Byrne, 1961; Byrne & Blaylock, 1963; Byrne, Griffitt, & Golightly, 1966) has shown that opinion similarity increases perceived liking as well as perceived intelligence, adjustment, morality, and knowledgeableness of the similar party. They have also shown that liking is associated with greater perceived similarity than is actually the case (Byrne & Blaylock, 1963), and that perceived similarity of opinions on important issues produces more liking than perceived similarity on unimportant issues (Byrne, 1961).

An early study of the effects of liking on interpersonal influence was done by Back (1951). He randomly paired introductory psychology students, but informed them that they were matched extraordinarily well (high attraction) or not exactly, but reasonably well (low attraction), according to the results of previous self- and "preferred other" descriptions. Each pair was brought together to discuss stories they had written in private, based on what they thought were the same photographs. Actually, the photographs were slightly different to insure different interpretational details. After their discussion, they returned to their separate rooms to "write what you now think to be the best story." Back found that students in the high-attraction pairs attempted to influence each other more often and revised their stories more than did students in the low-attraction pairs. Sapolsky (1960) reported the same effects in verbal conditioning. Subjects told that they were well matched with the experimenter according to questionnaire results responded more to reinforcement than those led to believe they were less well matched.

Brock (1965) studied the effects of perceived similarity on interpersonal influence in the paint department of a large department store. After a customer selected the paint he wanted, the clerk urged him to purchase a different brand and grade of paint. The clerk began his influence attempt with a description of his recent experience with the paints on a similar size job (similar condition) or on a much larger job (dissimilar "expert" condition). The clerks were significantly more successful in influencing customers' buying decision when they were perceived as similar than as dissimilar but expert. Burnstein, Stotland, and Zander (1961) have demonstrated that perceived similarity in background facilitates interpersonal influence. Berscheid (1966) has shown that perceived similarity based on opinions relevant to the topic of influence facilitates interpersonal influence more than perceived similarity based on opinions irrelevant to the influence topic.

These studies show that the influence recipient's liking for the communicator, his perceived compatibility with the communicator, and his perceived similarity significantly increase the communicator's ability to influence him. Results from Byrne (1961) and Berscheid (1966) suggest that perceived similarity on relevant, important issues facilitates influence more than similarity on irrelevant or less important issues.

Involvement

The influence recipient's involvement in the influence process can be manipulated by using issues of different intrinsic importance to the recipient, by varying the consequences or personal significance of the recipient's opinion, and by varying the amount of physical or psychological effort required by the process. Unfortunately, the effects of involvement on interpersonal influence have been investigated in very few studies. Involvement is usually held at a moderately high level across conditions by the intrinsic importance of current social and political issues. However, some evidence suggests the effects of these three sources of involvement on opinion change.

Zimbardo (1960) mentioned an unpublished study by Brehm and Lipsher in which they

. . . manipulated involvement using issues which varied in the degree to which subjects were concerned with them. They found that the amount of opinion change in the direction of the communicator was greater for issues of high concern than for the issue of low concern [pp. 91–92].

Bergin's (1962) results indicate that the theoretical model of opinion change presented here applies to issues of considerable personal importance, that is, self-conceptions of masculinity-femininity.

Zimbardo (1960) studied the effects of involvement by varying the consequences of subjects' opinions. He asked coeds to read a short case history of a juvenile delinquent and to give their opinion of the locus of blame for the youth's crimes. Then they were exposed to an opinion discrepant from their own, obstensibly that of their friend with whom they had signed up for the experiment. After the exposure, they were asked to make a "fresh" evaluation of the problem. Derogation was controlled by the friendship pairs and by a pre-communication task in which the friend was established as an expert in judging juvenile delinquents from photographs. Communication discrepancy was set at high and low values. High involvement was induced by telling the coeds that their opinions revealed their personalities and social values. In the low-involvement condition coeds were told that "although they should read the case study carefully, they should not expect too much from it [p. 88]." It was too short and unrepresentative, and previous results had shown that their reactions would reveal nothing about their personalities or social values. Results were significantly influenced by both discrepancy and involvement. Opinion change was greater with large discrepancy than with small discrepancy and with high involvement than with low involvement. Interaction between the two main effects was not statistically significant.

Cohen (1959) manipulated involvement by varying the subjects' perceptions of effort necessary to understand a persuasive communication. Thirty-six undergraduates read a statement arguing that placing juvenile delinquents in foster homes would decrease delinquency. Three weeks earlier, and immediately after reading the statement, the students filled out an opinion questionnaire containing the target question. High involvement was induced for one-half of the students by telling them that the communication was difficult and required much effort to understand. The other students were told that the passage was relatively simple and easy to understand. Students were also classified into high and low groups according to the discrepancy of their initial opinion from the advocated opinion. Cohen found a significant interaction between effort and discrepancy: in the high-effort condition, students with high initial discrepancy changed their opinions more than students with low initial discrepancy; in the low-effort condition, students with low initial discrepancy changed their opinions more than those with high initial discrepancy. Overall, high-discrepancy students changed more than low-discrepancy students.

These studies indicate that opinion change is facilitated when influence recipients are highly involved in the influence process. All three modes of involvement are effective in enhancing opinion change. In addition, there is evidence from studies not directly dealing with interpersonal influence that effort, unjustified by reward, greatly enhances cognitive change (Aronson, 1961; Aronson & Mills, 1959).

Conclusion

The research reviewed here shows the importance of perceived expertness, trustworthiness, attractiveness, and involvement in interpersonal persuasion. These variables control the means of reducing dissonance raised by a discrepant communication. At high values they deter dissonance reduction by discrediting the communicator and devaluating the issue and thus enhance opinion and attitude change. These results suggest that interpersonal persuasion can be conceptualized as a two-phase process. First, communicator credibility and attractiveness and audience involvement are enhanced to increase the probability of success of later influence attempts; second, statements intended to bring about the desired opinion and attitude changes are communicated. Let us now identify those processes and techniques in counseling which implement the first phase of the influence process.

Opinion-Change Variables: in Counseling

Expertness

Counseling has expended considerable effort to provide the practitioner with objective indexes of his specialized training, knowledge, and expertise. Diplomas, state certifications, and certificates of membership in professional organizations adorn the walls of the counselor's office. Shelves filled with professional books and periodicals and stacks of confidential letters, announcements, and folders on desks attest to the counselor's expertise. Raven (1965), Schofield (1964, p. 107), and Frank (1963, p. 129) have pointed out the importance of these evidences of "expert power" in interpersonal persuasion.

Less obvious, but perhaps more important, are the evidences of expertise in the counselor's behavior. Most counselors pay considerable attention to structuring the interview. They point out the roles and requirements of the client and the counselor in the interview, the sequences of the process, and events likely to occur as they work toward problem solution. Such structuring, whether explicit or implicit, gives evidence of the counselor's expertise. Since the client must perceive that the counselor knows what he is doing, explicit structuring may be more effective than implicit structuring. There is some evidence that explicit structuring does enhance counseling effectiveness (Traux, 1966). Structuring also enhances the counselor's "informational influence" (Raven, 1965). The client is provided a "rational" framework to view his problem, the means of problem solution, and the importance of his efforts and further information. He is thus more able to guide his own efforts toward problem solution. Frank (1963, p. 146) has suggested that the counselor's confidence in his therapeutic theory and procedure enhances his counseling effectiveness. Such confidence enhances the client's perception of the counselor's expertise.

Trustworthiness

A major contribution to the counselor's perceived trustworthiness is his socially sanctioned role as an extender of help, a source of assistance in problems of living, or what Raven (1965) has termed "legitimate influence." The client, in coming to the counselor, accepts this role. Professional organizations for counselors have established codes of ethics to insure that counselors keep the client's welfare uppermost in their day-to-day transactions (American Personnel & Guidance Association, 1961; American Psychological Association, 1959). Behaviorally, counselors communicate a sincere, deep interest in the client's welfare. Frank (1963) has suggested that, "The attitudes of the therapist that seem to contribute most to the patient's trust in him are a steady, deep interest, an optimistic outlook, and a dedication to the patient's welfare [p. 115]." As further evidence that he is trustworthy, that he has no selfish or devious motives, the counselor assures the client that any information the client may divulge or that the counselor may obtain is completely confidential. Thus, the counselor establishes the client's perception of his personal trustworthiness by paying close attention to the client's statements and other behavior, by communicating his concern for the client's welfare, by avoiding statements indicating exhibitionism or perverted curiosity, and by assuring confidentiality of all transactions.

Attractiveness

The counselor's attractiveness to the client depends heavily on the counselor's behavior in the interview. A counselor may have a reputation as likable and compatible among potential clients which is generated by satisfied clients. This reputation, however, is ultimately a function of interview performance.

In the interview, liking is directly engendered by the counselor's unconditional positive regard or nonpossessive warmth for the client. Traux and Carkhuff (1967, pp. 58–68) have defined unconditional positive regard as valuing and caring for the client as a separate person regardless of the "goodness" or "badness" of his behavior. While this counselor characteristic may be regarded as an attitude, Traux and Carkhuff have shown that it is a measurable attribute of counselor behavior. Such nonpossessive caring, valuing, or liking for the client can be expected to generate reciprocal liking for the therapist as has been shown by Byrne (1961) and Mills (1966). Attractiveness derived from similarity and compatibility is engendered by counselor accurate empathy or therapeutic understanding. Traux and Carkhuff (1967) see accurate empathy as involving ". . . both the therapist's sensitivity to current feelings and his verbal facility to communicate this understanding in a language attuned to the client's current feelings [p. 46]." They pointed out that the counselor's own experiences and feelings are a major source of his sensitivity and understanding. Thus, when the counselor communicates his understanding, he is communicating his similarity to the client. Even when the communication is largely derived from theoretical and pragmatic knowledge of human nature, such understanding would seem to enhance the client's perception of counselor similarity and compatibility. Another means of enhancing perceived similarity is counselor revealment of experiences, feelings, or problems similar to those revealed by the client. This technique is potentially very powerful because of its immediate and unambiguous communication of real similarity. Its use, however, requires considerable clinical skill in judging when such self-revealment will be perceived by the client as real similarity and not as a "slip from role" or exhibitionism.

Involvement

Client involvement in counseling is enhanced in a number of ways. Counseling often begins with relatively high involvement in that the topic of conversation is a problem in living which is personally troubling to the client. Obviously, such a topic is intrinsically important to the client. Often, however, the client's involvement in counseling needs to be carefully enhanced to increase the probability of "appropriate" client change rather than a "flight into health" or premature termination of counseling. Two counseling techniques

which enhance client involvement are reconnaissance (Sullivan, 1954, pp. 59–93), or scanning and focusing (Sundberg & Tyler, 1962, p. 115), and problem elaboration (Kelly, 1955, pp. 937–975). Clients expend considerable effort in these counseling processes. These exploratory procedures also enhance the client's perception of the importance of his problems and the many aspects of his life affected by the problem behavior. In addition to enhancing involvement and interpersonal intimacy, these processes provide the counselor with diagnostic understanding of the problem necessary for directing later influence attempts.

One of the most important techniques for enhancing client involvement is reflection of feeling or accurate empathy. Traux and Carkhuff (1967) have compiled impressive evidence that high levels of therapist accurate empathy (as well as nonpossessive warmth and genuineness) are causally related to client depth of self-exploration. They have conceptualized self-exploration in terms of client statements concerning self-worth, emotionally tinged experience, perceptions of relationships with others, emotional turmoil, or "expressions of more specific feelings of anger, affection, etc. [p. 195]." Such self-revealment obviously requires much effort and enhances problem-area saliency and importance to the client. Reconnaissance, problem elaboration, exploration of feelings (accurate empathy), all enhance the client's involvement by requiring much effort on his part and by increasing the perceived importance of the problem. There is a strong interaction between the processes enhancing client involvement and those enhancing perceived counselor characteristics. The counselor's communication of therapeutic understanding, nonpossessive warmth and genuineness and his smoothness and self-assurance in guiding the various processes enhance his perceived expertness, trustworthiness, and attractiveness, as well as client involvement.

Two-Phase Model of Counseling

The thrust of this paper is that counseling for attitude and behavior change is best conceptualized as a two-phase interpersonal influence process. The counseling processes and techniques discussed increase (a) the counselor's influence power over the client by enhancing his perceived credibility (expertness and trustworthiness) and attractiveness (liking, similarity, and compatibility), and (b) the persuasibility of the client by enhancing his involvement in counseling. As a result of these processes and techniques, the probability of client change in reaction to counselor influence attempts is maximized; the probability of the client's use of other avenues of reducing aroused dissonance is minimized. In the second phase, the counselor makes maximum use of the influence power he has built to implement the desired changes in client cognitive framework and behavior. The exact techniques he uses will depend on his diagnosis of the problem, the facilities available, his own expertise, and his guiding theoretical model. He may use interpretation, suggestion, advice, urging, information, homework assignments, reinforcement, role playing, modeling, behavioral enactment and practice, and other techniques. This agrees with Carkhuff (1966) who has suggested a similar two-phase model of counseling in which, during the second phase, the counselor does ". . . whatever is necessary to enable the client to achieve his goals [p. 408]."

References

American Personnel and Guidance Association Committee on Ethics. Code of ethics. *Personnel and Guidance Journal*, 1961, 40, 206–209.

American Psychological Association, Committee on Ethical Standards of Psychologists. Ethical standards of psychologists. *American Psychologist*, 1959, 14, 279–282.

Aronson, E. The effect of effort on the attractiveness of rewarded and unrewarded stimuli. *Journal of Abnormal and Social Psychology*, 1961, 62, 373–380.

Aronson, E., & Mills, J. The effect of severity of initiation on liking for a group. *Journal of Abnormal and Social Psychology*, 1959, 59, 177–181.

Aronson, E., Turner, J., & Carlsmith, J. M. Communicator credibility and communication discrepancy as determinants of opinion change. *Journal of Abnormal and Social Psychology*, 1963, 67, 31–36.

Back, K. W. Influence through social communication. *Journal of Abnormal and Social Psychology*, 1951, 46, 9–23.

Bergin, A. E. The effect of dissonant persuasive communications upon changes in a self-referring attitude. *Journal of Personality*, 1962, 30, 423–438.

Berscheid, E. Opinion change and communicator-communicatee similarity and dissimilarity. *Journal of Personality and Social Psychology*, 1966, 4, 670–680.

Bockner, S., & Insko, C. A. Communicator discrepancy, source credibility, and opinion change. *Journal of Personality and Social Psychology*, 1966, 4, 614–621.

Brehm, J. W., & Lipsher, D. Communicator-communicatee discrepancy and perceived communicator trustworthiness. *Journal of Personality*, 1959, 27, 350–361.

Brock, T. C. Communicator-recipient similarity and decision change. *Journal of Personality and Social Psychology*, 1965, 1, 650–657.

Browning, G. J. An analysis of the effects of therapist prestige and levels of interpretation on client responses in the initial phase of psychotherapy. *Dissertation Abstracts*, 1966, 26, 4803.

Burnstein, E., Stotland, E., & Zander, A. Similarity to a model and self-evaluation. *Journal of Abnormal and Social Psychology*, 1961, 62, 257–264.

Byrne, D. Interpersonal attraction and attitude similarity. *Journal of Abnormal and Social Psychology*, 1961, 62, 713–715.

Byrne, D., & Blaylock, B. Some similarity of attitudes between husbands and wives. *Journal of Abnormal and Social Psychology*, 1963, 67, 636–640.

Byrne, D., Griffitt, W., & Golightly, C. Prestige as a function in determining the effect of attitude similarity-dissimilarity on attraction. *Journal of Personality*, 1966, 34, 434–444.

Carkhuff, R. R. Counseling research, theory, and practice—1965. *Journal of Counseling Psychology*, 1966, 13, 467–480.

Cohen, A. Communication discrepancy and attitude change: A dissonance theory approach. *Journal of Personality*, 1959, 27, 386–396.

Festinger, L. *A theory of cognitive dissonance.* Evanston, Ill.: Row, Peterson, 1957.

Frank, J. D. *Persuasion and healing.* New York: Schocken Books, 1963.

Goldstein, A. P. Psychotherapy research by extrapolation from social psychology. *Journal of Counseling Psychology*, 1966, 13, 38–45.

Goldstein, A. P., & Dean, S. J. *The investigation of psychotherapy: Commentaries and readings.* New York: Wiley, 1966.

Goldstein, A. P., Heller, K., & Sechrest, L. B. *Psychotherapy and the psychology of behavior change.* New York: Wiley, 1966.

Hovland, C. I., Janis, I. L., & Kelley, H. H. *Communication and persuasion: Psychological studies of opinion change.* New Haven: Yale University Press, 1953.

Hovland, C. I., & Mandell, W. An experimental comparison of conclusion-drawing by the communicator and by the audience. *Journal of Abnormal and Social Psychology*, 1952, 47, 581–588.

Hovland, C. I., & Weiss, W. The influence of source credibility on communication effectiveness. *Public Opinion Quarterly*, 1951, 15, 635–650.

Kelly, G. A. *The psychology of personal constructs.* Vol. 2. *Clinical diagnosis and psychotherapy.* New York: Norton, 1955.

Kelman, H. C., & Hovland, C. I. "Reinstatement" of the communicator in delayed measurement of opinion change. *Journal of Abnormal and Social Psychology*, 1953, 48, 327–335.

Mills, J. Opinion change as a function of the communicator's desire to influence and liking for the audience. *Journal of Experimental Social Psychology*, 1968, 2, 152–159.

Raven, B. H. Special influence and power. In L. D. Steiner & M. Fishbein (Eds.), *Current studies in social psychology.* New York: Holt, Rinehart & Winston, 1965.

Sapolsky, A. Effect of interpersonal relationships upon verbal conditioning. *Journal of Abnormal and Social Psychology*, 1960, 69, 241–246.

Schofield, W. *Psychotherapy, the purchase of friendship.* Englewood Cliffs, N. J.: Prentice-Hall, 1961.

Sullivan, H. S.: *The psychiatric interview.* New York: Norton, 1954.

Sundberg, N. D., & Tyler, L. E. *Clinical psychology, an introduction to research and practice.* New York: Appleton-Century-Crofts, 1962.

Traux, C. B. Therapist empathy, genuineness, and warmth and patient therapeutic outcome. *Journal of Consulting Psychology*, 1966, 30, 395–401.

Traux, C. B., & Carkhuff, R. R. *Toward effective counseling and psychotherapy: Training and practice.* Chicago: Aldine, 1967.

Walster, E., Aronson, E., & Abrahams, D. On increasing the persuasiveness of a low prestige communicator. *Journal of Experimental Social Psychology*, 1965, 2, 325–342.

Zacona, S. V., & Harter, R. Credibility of source and recipient's attitude: Factors in the perception and retention of information on smoking behavior. *Perceptual and Motor Skills,* 1969, 23, 155–168.

Zimbardo, P. G. Involvement and communication discrepancy as determinants of opinion conformity. *Journal of Abnormal and Social Psychology,* 1960, 60, 86–94.

C. DIFFUSION AND COMMUNICATION PERSPECTIVE

8. Traditions of Research on the Diffusion of Innovation[a]

Elihu Katz* • Martin L. Levin** • Herbert Hamilton***

The process of diffusion is defined as the (1) acceptance, (2) over time, (3) of some specific item—an idea or practice, (4) by individuals, groups or other adopting units, linked to (5) specific channels of communication, (6) to a social structure, and (7) to a given system of values, or culture. The elements of this definition are treated as an "accounting scheme" in terms of which diffusion studies in the fields of sociology, anthropology, rural sociology, mass communications, etc., are reviewed and problems of research design are explicated.

It is hardly news that the diffusion of innovation is one of the major mechanisms of social and technical change. Indeed, around the turn of the century anthropologists were greatly impressed with the significance of diffusion, even overly impressed. In sharp contrast to the European diffusionists,[1] however, the Americans avoided grand, all-embracing theories of cultural development. Instead they worked modestly, investigating rather specific items—elements of the maize-complex, the

[a] Preliminary formulations of portions of this paper were presented at the meetings of the American Sociological Association, Chicago, 1959, and the American Anthropological Association, Mexico City, 1959. We wish to thank Robert L. Crain and Manning Nash for reading and commenting on the present version; readers of the earlier version are too numerous to mention. The overall project of which this paper is a part has received the support of the Foundation for Research on Human Behavior and the Social Science Research Committee of the University of Chicago.

Reprinted from Elihu Katz, Martin Levin, Herbert Hamilton, "Traditions of Research on the Diffusion of Innovation," *American Sociological Review,* Vol. XXVIII, No. 2 (April, 1963), pp. 237–252.

* Director, Communications Institute, Hebrew University.
** Associate Professor, Department of Sociology, Emory University.
*** Professor, Department of Sociology, Loyola University of Chicago.

[1] Robert H. Lowie, *History of Ethnological Theory* contains an excellent treatment of the early anthropological movements and schools, including evolutionism and diffusion. In this connection also see Alexander Goldenweiser's "Cultural Anthropology" in Harry Elmer Barnes (ed.), *History and Prospects of the Social Sciences,* New York: Alfred A. Knopf, 1925. A. L. Kroeber's article "Diffusionism" in the *Encyclopedia of the Social Sciences* is a brief, interesting description of the early diffusionist work in the context of the development of anthropology, and Melville Herskovits, *Men and His Works,* Chapters 30 and 31, New York: Alfred A. Knopf, 1938, can also be examined with profit as an informative survey of the various early movements in anthropology. For various sides of the argument concerning the early work on diffusion see G. Elliot Smith, *et al., Culture: The Diffusion Controversy,* New York: Norton, 1927.

horse-complex, the sundance—tracing their distribution in space and, insofar as possible, in time. The work remained primarily historical and descriptive, although some important generalizations about the generic aspects of diffusion were advanced.[2]

Influenced in part by these anthropologists, several empirically minded sociologists of the 20's and 30's also demonstrated an interest in diffusion.[3] Studies were made of the spread of the city-manager plan, of a third-party movement, of amateur radio as a hobby, and the like. The guiding theoretical concerns had to do with the influence of the metropolis on its satellites, the effectiveness of natural and legal boundaries as barriers of diffusion, and flow of innovation from region to region across the country, as well as the hypothesis of a "concentric circle" pattern of diffusion which was shared with the anthropologists. The underlying assumption was always that informal communication among adopters was the key to diffusion.

In both of these fields, diffusion studies came to a halt by about 1940.[4] In anthropology, attention shifted to the closely related

[2] Among the more suggestive of these studies for our purposes are the following: Robert H. Lowie, "Plains Indians Age Societies," *Anthropological Papers,* American Museum of Natural History, 11 (1916), pp. 877–1031; Robert H. Lowie, "Ceremonialism in North America," *American Anthropologist,* 16 (October–December, 1914), pp. 602–631; Paul Radin, "A Sketch of the Peyote Cult of the Winnebago: A Study in Borrowing," *Journal of Religious Psychology,* 7 (January, 1914), pp. 1–22; Leslie Spier, "The Sun Dance of the Plains Indians: Its Development and Diffusion," *Anthropological Papers,* American Museum of Natural History, XVI (1921), pp. 451–527; Clark Wissler, "Material Culture of the North American Indians," *American Anthropologist,* 16 (October–December, 1914), pp. 477–505; Clark Wissler, "Costumes of the Plains Indians," *Anthropological Papers,* American Museum of Natural History, 17 (1915), pp. 39–91; Clark Wissler, "The Ceremonial Bundles of the Blackfoot Indians," *Anthropological Papers,* American Museum of Natural History, VII (1914), pp. 65–289.

[3] See, for example, Raymond V. Bowers, "The Direction of Intra-Social Diffusion," *American Sociological Review,* 2 (December, 1937), pp. 826–836; F. S. Chapin, *Cultural Change,* New York: Century, 1928; Edgar C. McVoy, "Patterns of Diffusion in the United States," *American Sociological Review,* 5 (April, 1940), pp. 219–227; H. Earl Pemberton, "Culture Diffusion Gradients," *American Journal of Sociology,* 42 (September, 1936), pp. 226–233.

[4] In the 1920's and 1930's, a method of diffusion research commonly referred to as "age-area" analysis was developed. This method involved reconstructing the temporal movement and spread of cultural traits and complexes from geographic data on the spatial distribution of the cultural elements under investigation. Especially noteworthy in this regard was the work of Clark Wissler, who developed it to its most refined degree. See his *Man and Culture,* New York: Thomas Y. Crowell Co., 1923, and *The Relation of Nature to Man in Aboriginal America,* New York: Oxford University Press, 1926. While a very important contribution to the field in its day, this approach was subjected to a searching critique by Roland Dixon in *The Building of Culture,* New York: Scribners, 1928. This kind of criticism, no doubt, contributed appreciably to the subsequent decline of distributional diffusion studies generally. Still, there has been a continued production of such studies and, indeed, one occasionally encounters especially interesting investigations at least partly employing this approach, such as the recent work by David F. Aberle and Omer C. Stewart, "Navaho and Ute Peyotism: A Chronological and Distributional Study," *University of Colorado Studies,* Series in Anthropology No. 6, 1957. Furthermore, those interested in archaeology seem to have maintained an even more central concern for diffusion analysis along these distributional lines. See, for example, the spirited discussion of the paper by Munro S. Edmondson, "Neolithic Diffusion Rates," *Current Anthropology,* 2 (1961), pp. 71–102.

problem of acculturation[5] in which emphasis is placed on ongoing (rather than historical) situations of intergroup contact, on patterns of culture traits rather than single items and, typically, on pairs of interacting societies rather than longer chains of connected groups.[6]

It is less clear why diffusion studies failed to hold the interest of sociologists, though they were never as prevalent as in anthropology. It seems a reasonable guess, however, that the revolution in communication which began with the rapid spread of radio in the late 20's and early 30's diverted their attention.

The Revival of Interest in Diffusion Research

But the mass media are incapable of influencing people (though they may inform them) as directly or as simultaneously as had been imagined.[7] Indeed, the study of mass media "effects," with its primarily psychological bias, is now broadening to take account of the *social* processes involved in the spread of influence and innovation.[8] This seems an altogether reasonable next step for former students of mass media "campaigns." For, if the mass media are not as all-powerful as was originally imagined, the problem of understanding the furious rate at which new ideas and behavior travel through society still remains. In short, there is a revival of interest in diffusion processes.[9]

The sociologists of communication who found themselves interested in diffusion discovered, somewhat to their surprise, that relevant studies were being carried on in a number of closely related fields. The most conspicuous case is that of rural sociology which has accumulated, over the last two decades, several hundred studies of the communication and acceptance of new farm practices.[10] Similarly, researchers in the field of education have

[5] Acculturation or culture contact studies were heralded by Robert Redfield, Ralph Linton and Melville J. Herskovits, in their "Memorandum on the Study of Acculturation," *American Anthropologist*, 38 (January–March, 1936), pp. 149–152.

[6] Indeed, a large segment of diffusion studies has tended to concern itself with adjustive responses to contact rather than the transmission of items between groups. This paper will explicitly avoid consideration of the now predominant concern with the social and cultural consequences of change. Our focus is on the processes of *communication* of change. Studies concerned with non-diffusion aspects of change are helpful, however, in drawing attention to the interrelationships among diffusion processes, socialization processes and adjustive processes in culture change. For an interesting empirical study illustrative of the link between socialization processes and (resistance to) acculturation, see Edward M. Bruner, "Primary Group experience and the Processes of Acculturation," *American Anthropologist*, 58 (August, 1956), pp. 605–623.

[7] For a discussion of some of the social and psychological factors involved in the transmission of influence via the mass media, see Joseph T. Klapper, *The Effects of Mass Communication*, New York: Free Press, 1960, Part One.

[8] The design of research in mass communication has recently begun to take account of interpersonal relations as structures which relay and reinforce (or block) the flow of influence and innovation. See Elihu Katz, "The Two-Step Flow of Communication: An Up-to-Date Report on an Hypothesis," *Public Opinion Quarterly*, 21 (Spring, 1957), pp. 61–78.

[9] In the few relevant studies so far, the tendency has been to follow a communication as it passes from one individual to the next, to establish the nature of the relationship between the interacting individuals and thus to infer the relevant social network; in other words, structures of social relations are derived from the flow of interpersonal communication. The alternative method—that of mapping the potentially relevant structures of social relations *prior* to tracing the flow of influence would seem to be somewhat more desirable, if more difficult.

[10] For an overview of work in this field together with selected bibliography, see Herbert F. Lionberger, *Adoption of New Ideas and Practices*, Ames, Iowa: Iowa State University Press, 1960.

tried to understand the rate of acceptance of innovations by school systems and have looked at such things as the spread of the kindergarten or supplementary reading.[11] Public health is interested in the acceptance of new health practices—the Salk vaccine, for example.[12] Marketing researchers, of course, are interested in the spread of acceptance of new products (although they have done far less work on this problem than one might imagine);[13] folklorists have documented the extent to which children's games, for example, have spread from region to region;[14] and so on. Like sociology, anthropology has also experienced something of a return to some of the interests of the more sober schools of diffusion, as a by-product of the current effort to evaluate the progress of the varied programs for planned change in underdeveloped areas of the world.[15]

The State of Diffusion Research

Ironically, it almost seems as if diffusion research in the various research traditions can be said to have been "independently invented"! Indeed, diffusion researchers in the several traditions which we have examined scarcely know of each other's existence. The recent "discovery" of rural sociology by students of mass communications and vice versa is a good case in point.[16] As a result, each tradition has emphasized rather different variables and a characteristically different approach. This paper attempts to integrate these diverse points of view.

To accomplish this, we shall first propose a working conception of diffusion from a sociological point of view. This will be done in terms of a tentative set of component elements, each of which can be formulated as a key variable (sometimes as several variables) intrinsic to, or bearing upon, the diffusion process. Taken together, they constitute a kind of "accounting scheme" for the study of diffusion.

Following the enumeration of the component elements, each will be considered in some detail, paying particular attention to problems of conceptualization and operational definition. Then, we shall attempt to "locate" the characteristic emphases of each of the research traditions in terms of one or more of these elements of the diffusion process.

---

[11] See Paul R. Mort and Frances G. Cornell, *American Schools in Transition,* New York: Teachers College, Columbia University, 1941; and Walter Cocking, "The Regional Introduction of Educational Practices," New York: Bureau of Publications, Teachers College, Columbia University, 1951.

[12] For numerous references, see Steven Polgar, "Health and Human Behavior: Areas of Interest Common to Social and Medical Sciences," *Current Anthropology,* 3 (April, 1962), pp. 159–179, particularly the section on Health Action Programs and, to a certain extent, the section on Dynamics of Health Status. Anthropologists have been particularly active in this area.

[13] The most interesting study, from our point of view, is *The Tastemakers* (Vol. I), a report of the Public Opinion Index for Industry, Princeton, New Jersey: Opinion Research Corporation, April 1959.

[14] See, for example, Iona and Peter Opie, *The Lore and Language of Schoolchildren,* London: Oxford University Press, 1959.

[15] There is a burgeoning literature on this subject. See the studies reported in recent volumes of *Human Organization* and *Economic Development and Cultural Change;* the several collections of case studies, particularly Benjamin Paul, (ed.), *Health, Culture and Community,* New York: Russell Sage Foundation, 1955; and recent volumes such as Charles Erasmus, *Man Takes Control,* Minneapolis: University of Minnesota Press, 1961; and George M. Foster, *Traditional Cultures and the Impact of Technological Change,* New York: Harper, 1962.

[16] For an account of the confrontation between students of mass communication and of rural sociology, see Elihu Katz, "Communication Research and the Image of Society: Convergence of Two Traditions," *American Journal of Sociology,* 65 (March, 1960), pp. 435–440.

Defining Diffusion

Viewed sociologically, the process of diffusion may be characterized as the (1) *acceptance*, (2) over *time*, (3) of some specific *item* —an idea or practice—(4) by individuals, groups or other *adopting units*, linked (5) to specific *channels* of communication, (6) to a *social structure*, and (7) to a given system of values, or *culture*.

Altogether, there are very few studies in any of the traditions of diffusion research which have incorporated *all* of these elements. In fact, the traditions differ from each other precisely in their tendency to "favor" certain of the elements rather than others.

Now we shall consider each of the components in turn.

Acceptance

Acceptance is the dependent variable in most studies of diffusion though, strictly speaking it is time-of-acceptance that is really of interest. Ideally, in other words, diffusion studies seek to classify acceptors in terms of the timing of their acceptance of an item or to compare the relative rate of acceptance in one community with another. More often than not, however, information about time is lacking and, instead, one learns—for a given point in time—which individuals have and have not accepted an innovation or what proportion of community members in different communities have accepted.

Most diffusion studies define acceptance rather arbitrarily. Where information on time is available, date of "first use" is frequently employed as the measure of acceptance, the season of first-use of hybrid corn, for example.[17] But, obviously, first-use may or may not be followed by continued use, and some recent studies, therefore, have insisted on the distinction between "trial" and "adoption." Thus, a measure of "sustained use" might be appropriate for some purposes but, for other purposes, it may be of interest to consider only "ever use."[18]

For anthropologists, however, this is a much more serious matter. First of all, anthropologists tend to be skeptical about the extent to which a given item is perceived and used in the same manner in different societies. If the sewing machine is prominently displayed on the open porch, but never used for sewing, it may be argued that it is no longer the "same" item. For anthropologists, that is, acceptance tends to refer not to the form of an item alone but to form-meaning-function.[19] Consider the acceptance of Christianity, for example, as discussed in the anthropological literature. With respect to its appearance in a given society, anthropologists would tend to ask: (1) Is it the "same" item? (2) Is it internalized in the personalities of the group? (3) Is it central to the social institutions of the group? Indeed, one of the factors underlying the distinction between "acculturation" (a prestigeful concept) and "diffusion" (a less prestigeful one) in anthropology, appears to be related to the "level" of acceptance (internalization and centrality) involved.[20]

[17] See Bryce Ryan and Neal Gross, "The Diffusion of Hybrid Seed Corn in Two Iowa Communities,"*Rural Sociology,* 7 (March, 1943), pp. 15–24.

[18] Gaining acceptance for most contraceptive techniques, for example, is much more a problem of "sustained use" than of "first use." See Reuben Hill, J. Mayone Stycos and Kurt Back, *The Family and Population Control,* Chapel Hill: University of North Carolina Press, 1959. Obviously, the distinction is appropriate wherever first use does not lead directly to continued use. See A. Apodaca, "Corn and Custom," in E. H. Spicer (ed.), *Human Problems in Technological Change,* New York: Russell Sage Foundation, 1952, for a study of the acceptance of an innovation which was later discontinued.

[19] The form-meaning-function distinction is stressed particularly in Ralph Linton, *The Study of Man,* New York: Appleton-Century, 1936, pp. 402–404.

[20] For good examples of the applicability of the notion of levels of incorporation of an innovation into a receiving society, see Edward P. Dozier, "Forced and Permissive Acculturation," *American Indian,* 7 (Spring, 1955), pp. 38–44; and Edward H. Spicer, "Spanish-Indian Acculturation in the Southwest," *American Anthropologist,* 56 (August, 1954), pp. 663–678.

This is a good example, perhaps, of the utility of confronting several traditions with each other within a manageable framework. Obviously, some kind of distinction must be made between mere external acceptance of a form and its internalization; and, obviously, attention must be given to the extent to which function travels together with form. But these ideas should not be treated merely as *cautionary;* they are also suggestive of hypotheses. Indeed, writing in a very similar vein, Gabriel Tarde—the social theorist of diffusion *par excellence*—suggested that "inner" changes precede "outer" changes in the sense that the diffusion of an idea precedes the diffusion of the tangible manifestation of that idea or, in other words, that there is a "material lag" rather than a "cultural lag" in the transfer of items across societal boundaries. Some theorists would agree; others, obviously, would not.[21] In any case, the implication is that diffusion research ought not to be misled by the argument over whether "mere diffusion" or penetration to deeper levels is more important but, rather, whether these correspond to separable episodes in the spread of any given item and, if so, how they are related.

Time

If any one of the elements may be said to be more characteristic of the diffusion process than the others, it is time. It is the element of time that differentiates the study of diffusion both from the study of mass communication "campaigns" with their assumed immediacy of impact and from traditional distributional studies. Diffusion takes time; for example, it took ten years for hybrid corn—an unusually successful innovation—to reach near-complete acceptance in Iowa communities. Nevertheless, there are very few studies, so far, that have taken systematic account of time in the study of diffusion.

In part, this neglect is a result of the difficulty of obtaining data. Studies which have taken account of time have relied on one of the following three methods: *recall* (where a respondent, or an informant, dates the acceptance of an innovation), *records* (where time-of-acceptance is a matter of record, for some reason), and *inferences* (such as in the archaeological dating methods of stratigraphy or Carbon-14).

Some of the early diffusion studies by sociologists had access to data on time because they studied innovations intended for adoption by municipalities—the city manager scheme, for example.[22] A current study of the diffusion of fluoridation has such data for the same reason.[23] The dates of acceptance of such innovations are a matter of public record.

Anthropologists who were studying diffusion in the 20's and 30's gave considerable thought to the development of a methodology for inferring time from spatial distributions. Clark Wissler, for example, was able to demonstrate that a particular distribution of pottery around a hypothesized point of origin did, indeed, correspond to a known succession of types of pottery as established stratigraphically.[24] Wissler further indicated that "students of culture generally assume that widely distributed trait complexes are the older," though he immediately cautions that such an assumption may result in serious error insofar as the rates of diffusion of different sorts of items may vary.

Early sociological students of diffusion faced a similar obstacle though they had more

[21] In his analysis of the diffusion of the sun dance, Spier explicitly cites his data as evidence, at least in this case against Tarde. See Leslie Spier, *op. cit.,* p. 501.

[22] See, for example, McVoy, *op. cit.*

[23] See Robert L. Crain, "Inter-City Influence in the Diffusion of Fluoridation," unpublished Ph.D. dissertation, Department of Sociology, University of Chicago, 1962.

[24] See *Man and Culture, op. cit.* Also see the work of Margaret T. Hodgen, "Geographical Diffusion as a Criterion of Age," *American Anthropologist,* 44 (1942), pp. 345–368. The article by Edmondson, *op. cit.,* is based on Carbon-14 datings.

data on time. It is relatively easy to establish, for example, the date on which 10 per cent of the population of a city or state owned a refrigerator or a radio. Then, treating the city or the state as if they were "adopters" of refrigerators and radios makes it tempting to suggest that certain cities are influencing others to adopt or that there seems to be a certain kind of geographical movement from state to state. A genuinely pioneering (though perhaps unconvincing) effort to strengthen this sort of tenuous ecological analysis with data gathered from individuals was made by Bowers in the 30's.[25] Bowers studied the diffusion of amateur radio as a hobby and demonstrated, for example, that the proportion of amateurs to population was at its highest in 1914–15 in cities of 25,000–100,000; five years later the peak was in cities of 10,000–25,000; during the following five years, the heaviest concentrations were in still smaller cities. From this distribution, he infers that people in the larger cities had influenced those in smaller places. Then, by means of a mail questionnaire, an attempt was made to test this inference by asking licensed amateur radio operators to report on the sources which were influential in their decisions to become "hams."

If students of pre-history sorely felt the lack of data on time, it is a nice anomaly that students of "consumer" innovations in the mid-twentieth century are experiencing the same problem. It may be possible to ask a farmer to try to recall the season during which he first planted hybrid corn, but it is very difficult to be certain that such information is reliable. How much more is this the case for innovations which are less central to their adopters and inherently less datable than is the season

of first use of a new kind of seed? One can perhaps ask about the date of purchase of major appliances, but it is almost impossible to rely on recall for most other things. A promising source for data of this kind is the type of consumer panel in which households are asked to keep a record of all their purchases, entering them in some sort of log on a daily or weekly basis; however, there are many difficulties with this procedure.[26] Occasionally, unusual opportunities present themselves for obtaining data on adoption dates. The study of the diffusion of new drugs among physicians, for example, had access to prescriptions on file in local pharmacies, making it possible to date each doctor's first use of a new drug.[27]

Time is a crucial ingredient in the diffusion process, however, not simply because it enables the researcher to identify the characteristics of early-adopting individuals or to establish the direction of the flow of influence. It is also important because it provides a basis for the charting of diffusion curves, thus making possible the development of mathematical descriptions of variations in the diffusion process. Time, and the number of adopters at a given time, are continuous and easily quantified variables; hence, the study of diffusion is one of the areas of social science which lends itself immediately to the construction of mathematical models. For example, one can construct theoretical models of the diffusion process given certain assumptions and compare the results with those actually observed in the real world. On the basis of such a comparison, one can infer whether a given item is "contagious" or not, that is, whether the item spread as a function of the extent of previous adoptions or the character of contacts with previous adopt-

---

[25] See Bowers, *op. cit.*

[26] There is considerable difficulty in maintaining the representativeness of the consumer-panel sample, and constant programmed turnover is one of the strategies of doing so; for diffusion research, however, turnover represents a complication. Moreover, if one approaches the diffusion problem in a situation where individual adopters are widely dispersed—such as in a national study of some consumer innovation, for example—one must cope with the added complexity of differing beginning dates in different regions, etc.

[27] See James S. Coleman, Elihu Katz and Herbert Menzel, "The Diffusion of an Innovation among Physicians," *Sociometry*, 20 (December, 1957), pp. 253–270.

ers.[28] Hagerstrand, a geographer, was able to demonstrate that the most probable adopter of a new farm practice is the farmer living in the vicintiy of someone who has just adopted it; and on the macro-level an innovation spreads from primary centers until the original source of influence is exhausted, whereupon some new center springs up.[29] Crain found essentially the same phenomenon at work in the case of fluoridation where the unit of adoption is a municipality rather than an individual.[30] Similarly, attempts have been made to specify, *a priori*, the probable influence of different patterns of social relations on the spread of innovation. The work reported by Stuart Dodd is a good example.[31] The same kind of logic suggests that similar innovations may be described by similar curves of diffusion and, if this is so, part of the problem of classifying innovations (to be discussed below) will be open to solution.[32]

A Specific Item

The discussion of acceptance has already made clear part of the problem of specifying the particular item under study. Obviously, one would like to ascertain whether the meaning of a given item for one individual, or for one society, is the same as it is for another. In a related sense, one would also like to know whether or not a given item is part of a larger "complex" of items to which it adheres. On the other hand, this does not preclude—as some people seem to think—the legitimacy of studying the diffusion of an isolated item, concentrating on form alone regardless of possible "adhesions" and regardless of possible variations in function. In any event, these problems are somewhat reduced when the items involved are practices more than ideas, items of lesser rather than greater pervasiveness, and when the study is concentrating on diffusion

---

[28] An impressive amount of work is going on in this area, much of it beyond the competence of the present authors. The major contributions include the following: Stuart C. Dodd, "Diffusion Is Predictable: Testing Probability Models for Laws of Interaction," *American Sociological Review*, 20 (August, 1955), pp. 392–401; and Stuart C. Dodd and Marilyn McCurtain, "The Logistic Law in Communication," in National Institute of Social and Behavioral Science, Symposia Studies Series No. 8, *Series Research in Social Psychology*, Washington, D.C., 1961; Melvin DeFleur and Otto Larsen, *The Flow of Information*, New York: Harper, 1958; Georg Karlsson, *Social Mechanisms*, Glencoe, Ill.: The Free Press, 1958; Torsten Hagerstrand, "Monte Carlo Simulation of Diffusion," University of Lund, Sweden, 1960 (unpublished); and James S. Coleman, "Diffusion in Incomplete Social Structures," Baltimore: Department of Social Relations, Johns Hopkins University, 1961 (unpublished). Two economists who have worked intensively with diffusion curves are Zvi Griliches, "Hybrid Corn: Explorations in the Economics of Technological Change," *Econometrica*, 25 (October, 1957), pp. 501–522; and Edwin Mansfield, "Technical Change and the Rate of Imitation," Pittsburgh: Graduate School of Industrial Administration, Carnegie Institute of Technology (unpublished). See also a noteworthy series of articles by bio-physicist Anatol Rapoport entitled, "Spread of Information through a Population with Socio-Structural Bias," *Bulletin of Mathematical Biophysics*, 15 and 16 (1953–54). Related work in the epidemiology of contagious disease is that of N. T. J. Bailey, *The Mathematical Theory of Epidemics*, London: Charles Griffin, 1957. Steven Polgar has written a paper that is relevant here on "The Convergence of Epidemiology and Anthropology," School of Public Health, University of California at Berkeley (unpublished).

[29] Hagerstrand, *op. cit.*

[30] Crain, *op. cit.*

[31] Dodd and McCurtain, *op. cit.*

[32] This is more difficult than it sounds, perhaps, but it is a lead worth following.

within a particular culture rather than across cultures. This, perhaps, makes somewhat clearer why anthropologists, more than others, have raised questions in this area.

The major problem of specifying the item in diffusion research derives from these considerations. It is the problem of how to classify items so that the results obtained are generalizable to other items. This problem is not unique to diffusion research, of course, but it is perhaps particularly obvious in this context. Suppose one studies the diffusion of hybrid corn, or of fluoridation, or of 2–4–D weed spray. Unless some scheme of classification exists which would make it possible to say that a given new item is rather more like a 2–4–D weed spray than it is like hybrid corn, each study simply becomes a discrete case which cannot be generalized.

Such a classification system is particularly difficult because, like all "content analysis," one must make guesses about the meaning of the item to its potential audience. Of course, to a certain extent this can be studied empirically. Suppose, for example, that the dimension of "radicalness"—that is, the extent to which an innovation is a major departure from some previous mode of acting—were an important one, as many observers seem to think. One might pre-test the actual use of an innovation—a visual telephone, for example—to discover the kinds of behavioral and attitudinal changes which it implies in order to rank it, at least as perceived by its early users, on a radicalness scale.

But the trouble is that nobody is quite sure what dimensions of an item are relevant, and very little research has been done to try to find out. There are some exceptions, however, Wilkening in the United States and Emery and Oeser in Australia have traced the spread

of several different agricultural innovations through the same communities and, on the basis of their differential rates and patterns of acceptance, have speculated about some of the dimensions which affect diffusion.[33] A major study of the diffusion of educational practices also speculates about why different sorts of innovations seem to spread in different patterns.[34] Dimensions that have been suggested by these authors and others center on economic-sounding considerations such as (1) extent of capital outlay required; (2) extent of anticipated profitability; (3) certainty of profitability or efficacy, and extent of possible loss or danger (risk). Of course, these are not strictly financial matters at all.

The most promising works on this problem have been several attempts to explicate the most traditional of the dimensions in terms of which innovations have been classified: material vs. non-material items. Barnett and others have suggested that material items find more ready acceptance because (1) they are more easily communicated; (2) their utility is more readily demonstrable; and (3) typically, they are perceived as having fewer ramifications in other spheres of personal and social life.[35] Following Barnett, Menzel classified several different kinds of medical innovations in terms of his estimates of their (1) communicability, (2) risk, and (3) pervasiveness, hypothesizing that early adopters of each item would have certain characteristics.[36] He suggested, for example, that integration into the local medical community would be characteristic of early adopters of a new drug which "required" communication but neither risk nor pervasiveness, whereas acceptance of a psychotherapeutic technique would be likely to "require" a certain emancipation from the local community and thus lesser integration. The results ob-

[33] Eugene A. Wilkening, *Acceptance of Improved Farm Practices in Three Coastal Plains Communities,* Raleigh: North Carolina Agricultural Experiment Station, Bulletin 98, 1952; and F. E. Emery, Oscar Oeser and Joan Tully, *Information Decision and Action: A Study of the Psychological Determinants of Changes in Farming Techniques,* Carleton: Melborne University Press, 1958.

[34] Mort and Cornell, *op. cit.*

[35] Barnett, *op. cit.*, pp. 374–377.

[36] Herbert Menzel, "Innovation, Integration and Marginality," *American Sociological Review,* 35 (October, 1960), pp. 704–713.

tained were promising and represent the opening up of an important direction for diffusion research.

Units of Adoption

Another way in which items can be usefully classified is in terms of the units of adoption for which they are intended. Most studies in sociology, rural sociology and marketing have considered only consumer-type items, those intended for adoption by an individual. But some innovations are intended for—indeed, they may "require"—groups, in the sense that it "takes two to tango" or to telephone, or to perform the peyote ritual, etc.). And among such group-oriented innovations, a further distinction seems useful. There are items which require collective adoptions but permit any given individual to adopt or not (the telephone, for example); there are other items, however, where the group adopts as a single unit leaving no room for individual options (fluoridation, for example).

Just as the item may "require" one or another adopting unit, a given culture may "prescribe" one rather than another adopting unit as appropriate. The *kibbutz* prescribes a group decision even for consumer-type innovations intended for use by individuals: similarly, the simultaneous conversion of an entire village to Christianity reflects the acceptance of a corporate decision, made by the chief perhaps, as binding upon all. Anthropologists are much more likely than those in other traditions to focus on the group as an adopting unit. Sometimes, this is just another way of talking about individuals as, for example, when it is reported that Village A adopted a certain kind of plow but Village B did not. But, often, the group is indeed the unit of adoption in the sense that the group "decides," or the culture "prescribes," that there be a collective decision.

Thus, the unit of adoption may vary as a function of the "requirements" of the item or the "prescription" of the culture. And, just as in the case of the other elements in the diffusion process, the adopting unit functions as a variable to facilitate or block the flow of acceptance of innovation. For example, items which "require" collective adopting units may be resisted, therefore, by cultures which "prescribe," or favor, the individual as the unit of adoption and vice versa. Resistance to fluoridation, in the United States, in terms of minority rights is one such example; resistance to consumer innovations by Israeli *kibbutzim* is another. By the same token, an appeal for acceptance of an innovation is less likely of success when directed to the "wrong" adopting unit—as when family planning campaigns aim at, say, the wife, but the culture "prescribes," or the technique "requires," joint agreement by both spouses.[37]

Channels

So far, almost nothing has been said about the channels which transmit information and influence concerning an innovation. Indeed, except for occasional studies which noted the role of highways or of caravan routes, channels—like time—are missing in most of the early studies of anthropologists and sociologists. Even when it seemed certain, from distributional evidence or other inferences, that an innovation traveled from Tribe A to Tribe B, it was often unclear *how* this took place. On the other hand, if there is any single thing that is most wrong with contemporary studies of diffusion in the fields of mass communication, rural sociology and marketing research, it is that there is too much emphasis on channels. The typical design for research in these fields has been based, almost exclusively, on the assumption that people can be asked to recall the channels of information and influence that went into the making of their decisions to adopt an innovation or to make some sort of behavioral change. This approach in mass media research is known as "reconstruc-

---

[37] For further discussion of the points raised in this section, see Elihu Katz, "Notes on the Unit of Adoption in Diffusion Research," *Sociological Inquiry*, 32 (1962), pp. 3–9.

tion" or "reason analysis."[38] It is of some methodological interest, too, because it reverses the usual experimental design of "campaign" studies which begin with stimuli and try to track down their effects. Reason analysis, instead, begins with an effect and seeks to reconstruct how it came about. It is this approach which is, in a sense, responsible for the rediscovery of the importance of interpersonal relations in the flow of influence and innovation in modern society. It is only very recently that students of mass communications and marketing have begun to include interpersonal relations among the channels of diffusion. This contrasts sharply with the rural sociologists who have long been aware—though they have not formulated it systematically until rather recently—that there is a "two-step flow" from the county agent to an influential farmer and thence to other farmers.

While a concern with channels is the pre-dominant emphasis in several fields, it is a conspicuous lack in several others. Early anthropological studies, particularly those dealing with historical instances of diffusion, have been criticized for their (necessary, in part) lack of attention to process. Still, there were occasional studies pointing to probable means of transportation and communication such as Wissler's research on the horse in relation to the diffusion of Plains Indian culture traits[39] or the analyses of the role of roads and highways by various authors,[40] and there was even a noteworthy study of the personalities and roles of key agents in the transmission of change.[41] More recent anthropological studies of acculturation of technical assistance campaigns have given close attention to the character of the contacts between donor and recipient societies, a subject to which we shall return in the section on social structure below.

An interesting new development in decision-

---

[38] For discussions of "reason analysis," see Paul F. Lazarsfeld and Morris Rosenberg (eds.), *The Language of Social Research*, Glencoe: The Free Press, 1955; and Hans Zeisel, *Say It with Figures*, New York: Harper, 1957.

[39] Clark Wissler's "The Influence of the Horse in the Development of Plains Culture," *American Anthropologist*, 16 (January–March, 1944), pp. 1–25, is the early classic paper on the role of "physical" means of transportation as a facilitator of diffusion. Also see the later study of Erna Gunther, "The Westward Movement of Some Plains Traits," *American Anthropologist*, 52 (April–June, 1950), pp. 174–180.

[40] See, for good examples, Stuart Rice, *Quantitative Methods in Politics*, New York: Knopf, 1928, pp. 154–155; A. T. and G. M. Culwick, "Culture Contact on the Fringe of Civilization," *Africa*, 8 (April, 1935), pp. 163–170; and, more recently, Charles J. Erasmus, "Agricultural Changes in Haiti: Patterns of Resistance and Acceptance," *Human Organization*, 2 (Winter, 1952), pp. 20–26. Some of these studies, it should be noted, are concerned rather more with channels of *distribution* than with channels of communication.

[41] Paul Radin, *op. cit.*, pp. 1–22. More recent examples include Richard N. Adams, "Personnel in Culture Change," *Social Forces*, 30 (December, 1951), pp. 185–189; Homer G. Barnett, "Personal Conflicts and Social Change," *Social Forces*, 20 (December, 1941), pp. 160–171; Wesley L. Bliss, "In the Wake of the Wheel," in Spicer (ed.), *Human Problems in Technological Change*, pp. 23–32; Henry F. Dobyns, "Experiment in Conservation," in Spicer, *ibid.*, pp. 209–223; Allan R. Holmberg, "The Wells That Failed," in Spicer, *ibid.*, pp. 113–123; Bertram Hutchinson, "Some Social Consequences of Nineteenth Century Missionary Activity Among the South African Bantis," *Africa*, 27 (April, 1957), pp. 160–175; I. Schapera, "Cultural Changes in Tribal Life," in Schapera (ed.), *The Banta-Speaking Tribes of South Africa*, London: Routledge and Sons, Ltd., 1937; Omer Stewart, *Washo-Northern Paiute Peyotism: A Study in Acculturation*, Berkeley: University of California Press, 1944; Fred Voget, "Individual Motivation in the Diffusion of the Wind River Shoshone Sundance to the Crow Indians," *American Anthropologist*, 50 (October–December, 1948), pp. 634–646; Fred Voget, "A Shoshone Innovator," *American Anthropologist*, 52 (January–March, 1950), pp. 52–63.

making research has been the attempt, by several rural sociologists, to explore the psychological stages of the decision-making process and then to discover which media function most effectively within each stage.[42] For example, for the initial "awareness" stage of receiving information, the mass media are obviously more efficient than interpersonal relations, but the reverse is true for the stage of "acceptance." The importance of this work is that it makes even more salient one of the central themes of this decision-making tradition, which is that the channels are better viewed as complementary rather than competitive. In other words, it has become clear to many of those who have studied the role of the media in the making of decisions that different media are appropriate for different tasks and, consequently, that there is little worth to the gross question, which medium is more effective?

Where these studies begin to be more interesting is when they are carried out within a larger framework of structural and cultural factors. Ryan and Gross, for example, used the decision-making approach to confirm the hypothesis which they found implicit in the logistic growth curve obtained for the spread of hybrid corn: that early adopters influenced the acceptance of the new seed by later adopters.[43]

What should be clear by now, however, is that the place of many of these channel studies needs to be reconceptualized. To the extent that they focus on interpersonal channels—that is, on the "relay" functions of interpersonal networks—they are concerned with social structure. And, if the sequence of events is taken into account whereby some persons are influenced by the mass media and others influenced by other persons, we have the beginnings of a diffusion study.

Ideally, a diffusion study should classify individuals according to their place in a social structure—that is, according to their relationships with other people. What we need to know is when this kind of differential placement in the social structure is also related to differential access to, or acceptance of, influence stemming from outside the group regardless of whether the channel of influence is television or a troubadour or a traveling salesman. Then, we want to know whether differential placement in relationship to others has something to do with passing on, or reinforcing, information concerning the innovation. Thus studies of "who influences whom" fall into place both as structural studies and channel studies. Their content ranges from the role of a prestigeful person in introducing the sun dance to the Crow Indians[44] to the influential role of women with large families in the realm of marketing.[45]

In short, what is needed is a wedding of studies of the channels of decision-making and the social-structural approach to the study of diffusion so that influence and innovation can be traced as to how they make their way into a social structure from "outside" and as they diffuse through the networks of communication "inside."

Social Structure

From the point of view of diffusion research, then, the social structure functions in several different ways. First of all, it constitutes a set of boundaries within which items diffuse. Secondly, as has already been demonstrated, the social structure describes the major channels of person-to-person communication through which diffusion flows. Additionally, social structure has to do with the distribution and differentiation of statuses and roles and the characteristic patterns of interaction among the occupants of varying positions. At least as far as diffusion is concerned, each

---

[42] See James H. Copp, Maurice L. Sill and Emory J. Brown, "The Function of Information Sources in the Farm Practice Adoption Process." *Rural Sociology*, 23 (June, 1968), pp. 146–157; and Everett M. Rogers and George M. Beal, "The Importance of Personal Influence in the Adoption of Technical Changes," *Social Forces*, 36 (May, 1957), pp. 329–334.

[43] Ryan and Gross, *op. cit.*

[44] See Fred Voget, "Individual Motivation . . . ," *op. cit.*

[45] See Katz and Lazarsfeld, *op. cit.*, Part III.

of these functions may be seen to follow from the definition of social structure in terms of the frequency and the character of interpersonal contacts.

Consider boundaries, for example. Apart from making it possible to talk about the rate and extent of spread of an item within a system, boundaries are of interest to diffusion research because the frequency and character of social relations across a boundary differ from those within a boundary. Some studies have taken as problematic the determination of the effective boundaries within which diffusion takes place. For example, in his pioneering study of the diffusion of political influence, Stuart Rice discovered that state boundary lines acted as barriers to the diffusion of political influence except, interestingly, when residents of both sides of a state boundary shared a common marketing area.[46] A number of studies have dealt with the boundaries which arise in connection with systems of social and ethnic stratification. Acceptance of an innovation by a lower social stratum, for example, may block acceptance by higher strata and, by the same token, upper-status groups—as Gillin has shown—may actually try to block the diffusion of symbolically meaningful items to groups of lesser status.[47] The approach fits very well with classical sociological ideas about fashion changes in stratified societies.[48] The same kind of thinking is characteristic of studies which have treated intergroup cleavages and rivalries within societies as boundaries to diffusion.[49] Several studies have inquired into the strategies of boundary-maintenance: Freed, for example, has analyzed the ways in which the traditional Amish and Eastern-European Jewish communities managed to constitute social structures limiting incursions of influence from the world outside.[50] Finally, a number of anthropologists have confronted the problem of classifying the character of the social relations that exist across boundaries. Spicer, for example, tries to classify the variable relations between the Spanish conquerors and certain Indian tribes in terms of dimensions such as directed vs. non-directed, forced vs. permissive, hostile vs. friendly, and the like. From an analysis of these social interrelations, and the communications channels which they imply, have come various ideas about the kinds of items and changes which are likely to be associated with them.[51]

Curiously, more work has been done on the implications for diffusion of the structure of social relations across boundaries than within

[46] Stuart Rice, *op. cit.*

[47] See John Gillin, "Parallel Cultures and the Inhibition to Acculturation in a Guatemalan Community," *Social Forces,* 24 (October, 1945), pp. 1–14; on this same theme, see the theoretical discussion by George Devereux and Edwin Loeb, "Antagonistic Acculturation," *American Sociological Review,* 8 (April, 1943), pp. 133–147.

[48] See Georg Simmel, "Fashion," reprinted in *American Journal of Sociology,* 62 (May, 1957), pp. 541–558.

[49] For example, Homer Barnett, "Applied Anthropology in 1860," *Applied Anthropology,* 1 (April–June, 1942), pp. 19–32.

[50] Stanley A. Freed, "Suggested Type Societies in Acculturation Studies," *American Anthropologist,* 59 (February, 1957), pp. 55–68. Also see Joseph W. Eaton, "Controlled Acculturation: A Survival Technique of the Hutterites," *American Sociological Review,* 17 (June, 1952), pp. 333–340; and Eric Wolf, "Aspects of Group Relations in a Complex Society: Mexico," *American Anthropologist,* 58 (December, 1956), pp. 1065–1078.

[51] Thus, the combination of directed, permissive, friendly, intense and intimate contacts in the case of the Cahita led to the "fusion" of native and donor cultural elements while, in the case of the Athabascan, undirected, unforced, but hostile, intermittent and impersonal relations led to what Spicer calls "reorientation" or the adoption of a limited number of traits which, however, were extensively modified by the recipient culture. See Edward H. Spicer, "Spanish-Indian Acculturation in the Southwest," *op. cit.* For a related attempt to classify types of intergroup relations, see Edward P. Dozier, "Forced and Permissive Acculturation," *op. cit.*

boundaries. Certainly very few studies have been done on the basic problem of comparing the ways in which different kinds of structural arrangements within a group condition the diffusion of a given item. There are some notable exceptions, however. Larsen and Hill, for example, studied the differential patterns of spread of a message in a working class and in a college community, and also in summer-camp communities of varying degrees of stability.[52] Lionberger studied variations in the flow of information as between residents in matched neighborhoods and "non-neighborhoods,"[53] and Stuart Dodd found that variations in social relations resulting from differences in city size and population density affect the rate and extent of diffusion of airborne leaflets.[54] Asking a different question about social-structural relations, Albert argues, on the basis of a comparison of the rate of acceptance of European influences in Ruanda and Urundi that, under certain conditions, innovation will diffuse more rapidly in more centrally organized societies.[55] Oscar Lewis has reported several cases of attempted assistance to underdeveloped communities where the social structure of these communities played a key role in the fate of the project.

Based on his restudy of the Mexican village of Tepoztlán, Lewis describes an effort to introduce a modern medical service which encountered resistance from those sectors of the village that would now be called the power structure of the community.[56] In a second study Lewis describes the strategic significance of intro-community factions and cleavages for the eventual fate of innovations entering a village in India.[57] To the extent that a society is more complex, networks of social relations become increasingly specialized. Thus, in the study of the diffusion of new drugs among doctors, networks of professional relations and networks of social relations were both found to carry influence, though at rather different rates and at rather different phases of the diffusion process.[58] A related point is made by Edmondson to the effect that the uniform rate of spread which he finds in his study of rates of culture-trait diffusion in the Neolithic may be a product of the essential similarity in the roles of all potential adopters; he speculates that the rise of specialists might change the picture substantially.[59]

More typical of current diffusion research is the use of social-structural factors to classify *individuals* rather than groups, both in terms

[52] See Otto N. Larsen and Richard J. Hill, "Mass Media and Interpersonal Communication," *American Sociological Review*, 19 (August, 1954), pp. 426–433; and "Social Structure and Interpersonal Communication," *American Journal of Sociology*, 63 (March, 1958), pp. 497–505.

[53] Herbert F. Lionberger and Edward Hassinger, "Neighborhoods as a Factor in the Diffusion of Farm Information in a Northeast Missouri Farming Community," *Rural Sociology*, 19 (December, 1954), pp. 377–384.

[54] See Stuart Dodd, "Formulas for Testing Opinions," *Public Opinion Quarterly*, 22 (Winter, 1958–59), pp. 537–554.

[55] Ethel M. Albert, "Socio-Political Organization and Receptivity to Change: Some Differences between Ruanda and Urundi," *Southwestern Journal of Anthropology*, 16 (Spring, 1960), pp. 46–74.

[56] Oscar Lewis, "Medicine and Politics in a Mexican Village," in Benjamin Paul (ed.), *Health, Culture and Community, op. cit.*, pp. 403–434.

[57] Oscar Lewis, *Group Dynamics in a North-Indian Village, A Study of Factions*, New Delhi, India: Programme Evaluation Organization, Planning Commission, 1954. The importance of social cleavages and factions in relation to the adoption and use of new items is suggested by other studies as well, including A. R. Holmberg, "The Wells That Failed," in Edward Spicer (ed.), *Human Problems in Technological Change*, New York: Russell Sage Foundation, 1952, pp. 113–123; and also J. D. N. Versalius, "Social Factors in Asian Rural Development," *Pacific Affairs*, 30 (June, 1957), pp. 160–172.

[58] Coleman, Katz and Menzel, *op. cit.*

[59] Edmondson, *op. cit.*

of relative status and in terms of differential roles. A large number of rural studies take account of such factors as size-of-farm, age, education, membership in formal organizations and the like.[60] While it is true that, in general, these variables are related to the acceptance of innovation in predictable ways, there are occasional surprises. A number of studies have shown that older people are more likely to accept certain innovations (those that contain a "revivalistic" element, for example)[61] and, similarly, another study found persons of lesser education to be earlier acceptors of the Salk Vaccine under certain circumstances.[62] It is true that these standard variables do account for a considerable part of the variance in many studies, but they leave very many questions unanswered. And there are, of course, other structural variables which have been examined. Thus, Wilkening has studied the effect on innovation in farming of authoritarian vs. non-authoritarian family heads.[63] Larsen and Hill, and Lionberger, are concerned with the ways in which social status within a primary group makes people differentially accessible to others both inside and outside the group.[64] The study of the diffusion of a new drug among physicians focuses on the consequences of differential integration in the medical community for time-of-adoption,[65] while a pioneering study in the field of marketing is concerned with the influence of a composite variable called "mobility" on time-of-adoption of new consumer goods.[66]

By the same token, group members have been studied in terms of the frequency and character of their contacts *outside* the group. Rural-sociological studies have taken accounts of such things as trips to the city, visiting outside the region, and personal contacts with agents of change such as salesmen, county agents and others who come into the community from the "outside world."[67] Certain anthropologically oriented studies of technological change in developing areas have taken similar account of contacts outside the community as a factor making for individual differences in the acceptance of innovation.[68] This kind of thinking, of course, leads directly to questions concerning the applicability of the hypothesis of the "two-step flow of communication" not only to mass communications

[60] For the influence of such variables on the acceptance of new farm practices see Lionberger, *Adoption of New Ideas and Practices, op. cit.*, Chaps. 8 and 9.

[61] See Fred Voget, "Individual Motivation . . . ," *op. cit.*, and the literature on nativistic movements generally.

[62] See John C. Belcher, "Acceptance of the Salk Polio Vaccine," *Rural Sociology*, 23 (June, 1958), pp. 158–170. Other studies of the diffusion of acceptance of the Salk Vaccine in other circumstances find the usual inverse relationship with education, social status, etc. Compare John A. Clausen, Morton A. Seidfeld and Leila C. Deasy, "Parent Attitudes toward Participation of Their Children in Polio Vaccine Trials," *American Journal of Public Health*, 44 (December, 1954), pp. 1526–1536.

[63] Eugene A. Wilkening, "Changes in Farm Technology as Related to Familism, Family Decision Making and Family Integration," *American Sociological Review*, 19 (February, 1954), pp. 29–37.

[64] Larsen and Hill, "Social Structure and Interpersonal Communication," *op. cit.*; Herbert F. Lionberger, "The Relation of Informal Social Groups to the Diffusion of Farm Information in a Northwest Missouri Farm Community," *Rural Sociology*, 19 (September, 1954), pp. 233–243.

[65] Coleman, Katz and Menzel, *op. cit.*

[66] See *The Tastemakers, op. cit.*

[67] For example, Ryan and Gross, *op. cit.*: F. E. Emery and O. A. Oeser, "*Information, Decision and Action,* Melbourne: Melbourne University Press, 1958.

[68] For example, Rose K. Goldsen and Max Ralis, *Factors Related to the Acceptance of Innovations in Bang Chan, Thailand,* Ithaca: Cornell Thailand Project, Interim Reports Series, No. 3, 1957.

but to interpersonal diffusion as well: Does influence tend to flow from individuals with relatively more contact with the "outside world" (not only the mass media) to those who stay "at home?"

Value Systems

Social structures function, too, as anchorages for shared attitudes and values or, in other words, for culture. By the same token, roles are anchorages for certain individual differences in outlook and personality, though roles are not the only factor associated with personality. Attitudes, values and personality represent one of the major sets of variables that have been related to the acceptance of innovation and, if we consider them both at the level of the individual and of the group, it becomes possible to point out some interesting parallels between ostensibly unrelated traditions of research.

The central idea is that of "compatibility" or "fit" between the culture of a group or the personality of the individual and the elements of a proposed innovation. On the group level, there are a number of anthropological studies underlining this principle.[69] Among early studies, Lowie's, Wissler's, Radin's and Spier's studies on various aspects of diffusion among American Indians all emphasize the role of culture in making for selective borrowing.[70] Somewhat later, Elsie Clews Parsons also stressed that traits were taken over by Mexican Indian townspeople from the Spanish and from others when they could "be fitted into an old form of behavior and (were) compatible with existing emotional attitudes."[71] Since these early studies, anthropologically oriented research on diffusion has typically taken account of this principle. Furthermore resistance to proposed innovations as well as acceptance has often been explained in terms of this conception; in such cases, of course, the emphasis is upon the incompatibility between the receiving culture and the innovation.[72]

[69] For a general discussion, and many specific examples, see Homer G. Barnett, *Innovation*, New York: McGraw-Hill, 1953. This general conception has long been a fundamental postulate of anthropological thinking about cultural change. See, for example, in addition to the references cited in footnote 2, Boas' thinking in an early paper (1911) later reprinted in *Race, Language and Culture*, New York: Macmillan, 1940, p. 299. Somewhat later Linton ably stated the important elements of earlier anthropological thinking on this problem in *The Study of Man*, New York: Appleton Century Co., 1936. It should be noted that virtually from the beginning this conception of cultural compatibility has been applied to two distinctly different aspects of change phenomena. On the one hand, the compatibility conception has been applied to the problem of what might be called symbolic" or "meaningful" fit between an innovation and the "mentality" of human targets of change; or perhaps more accurately, the compatibility between the meanings and symbolic significance of the innovation as perceived by the actors in question and their own system of values, attitudes and moods. On the other, the notion of compatibility has been applied to what might be referred to as "functional fit," i.e., the problem of the compatibility between the innovation and the adopting system viewed from the standpoint of the *consequences* of accepting and using the innovation.

[70] Ci. footnote 2, above.

[71] See Elsie Clews Parsons, *Mitle, Town of the Souls*, Chicago: University of Chicago Press, 1936, p. 536.

[72] For example, Charles J. Erasmus, *op. cit.*, describes a situation among Haitian farmers, especially the backward ones, where the strong acceptance of a norm opposing "too much" material success acts to block and/or delay the diffusion of improved agricultural methods. Others who have emphasized this point include Charles P. Loomis and Glen Gresham, "The New Mexican Experiment in Village Rehabilitation," *Applied Anthropology*, 2 (June, 1943), pp. 13–37; F. L. Bailey, "Suggested Techniques for Inducing Navaho Women to Accept Hospitalization

But all too few of these studies are comparative in the sense of setting out to demonstrate that a given item is accpetable to relatively comparable groups which, however, differ in values. One such example may be found in Oliver's study of the greater acceptability of new plant foods in a community many of whose rituals centered on the pig as compared wtih a community where *taro*, a plant, was a center of ritual and an important element in many institutional relations.[73] Hawley reports on a similar comparative situation where Catholicism found greater acceptance among the patrillineally oriented Eastern Pueblo but was incompatible with the matrillineally oriented Western Pueblo.[74] In much the same way, Saxon Graham seeks to explain the differential penetration of television and other leisure-time innovations in the middle and working classes in terms of the hospitality offered by the different sets of values of the two classes.[75]

On the individual level, the notion of compatibility, or fit, is equally applicable. Here can be located the whole tradition of motivation research in marketing. For motivation research is, in essence, the exploration of the symbolic meaning attributed by consumers to given items, seeking, ultimately, to tailor the item or its image to the consumer's personality.[76] Studying the introduction of television in England, Himmelweit established that even when class membership is held constant, different value orientations characterize early and late adopters.[77] The former seemed more present-oriented while the latter were more future-oriented and perhaps inner-directed. In addition, rural sociologists have occasionally dealt with the problem of the functional compatibility of a new practice in relation to the personality characteristics of the individual.[78]

In any case, this classification brings very different research traditions into touch. Nevertheless, although the long-run aim may be the same, the dependent variables tend to be different. Hawley and Gram, for example, are concerned with the comparative extent of penetration of the item being studied in groups with different values. On the individual level, Himmelweit is concerned with the acceptance of TV by a given date. Motivation researchers, however, hardly ever study actual

During Childbirth," *American Journal of Public Health,* 38 (October, 1948), pp. 1418–1423; Morris E. Opler and Rudra Dott Singh, "Economic, Political and Social Change in a Village of North Central India," *Human Organization,* 11 (Summer, 1952), pp. 5–12; Bertram Hutchinson, "Some Social Consequences of Missionary Activity among the South African Bantu," *Africa,* 27 (April 1957), pp. 34–46.

[73] Douglas L. Oliver, "A Case of a Change in Food Habits in Bougainville, British Solomon Islands," *Applied Anthropology,* 1 (January–March, 1942), pp. 34–46.

[74] Florence Hawley, "The Role of Pueblo Social Organization in the Dissemination of Catholicism." *American Anthropologist,* 48 (1946), pp. 407–415.

[75] Saxon Graham, "Class and Conservatism in the Adoption of Innovations," *Human Relations,* 9, 1 (1956), pp. 91–100.

[76] See George H. Smith, *Motivation Research in Advertising and Marketing* (New York: McGraw-Hill, 1953). An excellent example of work in this tradition is the early study of Maison Haire, "Projective Techniques in Marketing Research," *Journal of Marketing,* 14 (April, 1950), pp. 649–656, demonstrating that the initial resistance to instant coffee was based on an image that the product symbolized housewifely laziness.

[77] Hilde Himmelweit, *et al., Television and the Child,* London: Oxford University Press, 1958.

[78] For example, Irving A. Spaulding, "Farm Operator Time-Space Orientations and the Adoption of Recommended Farming Practices," Rhode Island Agricultural Experiment Station Bulletin, No. 330, 1955; Everett M. Rogers, "Personality Correlates of the Adoption of Technical Practices," *Rural Sociology,* 22 (September, 1957), pp. 267–268.

acceptance; their dependent variable is more likely to be "propensity to accept" and even this is often vaguely defined. Indeed, it may be said that this entire line of work requires that a distinction be made between the potential adopter's perception of the compatibility of an item and some objective evaluation of its compatibility, particularly over a longer period. This distinction parallels, to some extent, the earlier allusions to the difference between first use of an item and continued use. The item may be perceived as attractive to begin with, but experience with the item may involve unanticipated consequences which prove the longer-run incompatibility. Thus, the ease with which Puerto Rican women were willing to begin use of contraception does not jibe with the difficulties of inducing them to continue regular use.[79] In turn, this raises a more general question concerning the tendency to overlook the fact that most innovative items consist of complex elements some of which may "fit" while others may not.

Apart from the notion of functional fit, however, there are other subheadings within the cultural dimension which must be accounted for. Thus, there is a set of ideas, both on the group and on the individual level, which would seem to have more to do with a general orientation toward innovation than with the specific compatibility between certain innovations and certain values. Rural sociologists have conducted several studies of variations in ethnic attitudes toward innovation.[80] On the individual level, too, early vs. late adopters, or adopters vs. non-adopters, have been studied in terms of orientations such as sacred-secular, scientific-traditional, cosmopolitan-local and the like.[81]

Conclusions

We have tried (1) to present an overview of the basic elements of the process of diffusion, and (2) to indicate, with respect to this accounting scheme, where each of a variety of research traditions has contributed as well as where it has fallen short, and (3) to specify problems which deserve further study.[82] We have drawn specifically on the early work on diffusion in anthropology, sociology and education, and on more contemporary work stemming from the sociology of mass communication, rural sociology, studies of acculturation and of technical change, public health and marketing. We have hardly begun to explore the work in folklore, geography, archeology, and other fields.

---

[79] See Hill, Stycos and Back, *op. cit.* Also see Apodaca, "Corn and Custom," in Spicer (ed.), *op. cit.*

[80] For example, Harold A. Pederson, "Cultural Differences in the Acceptance of Recommended Farm Practices," *Rural Sociology,* 16 (March, 1951), pp. 37–49; C. R. Hoffer, "Acceptance of Improved Farm Practices among Farmers of Dutch Descent," Michigan State College Agricultural Experiment Station, Special Bulletin No. 316, June 1942.

[81] For example, Emery and Oeser, *op cit.*; Ryan and Gross, *op. cit.*

[82] It deserves to be noted that, in 1952, a subcommittee of the Rural Sociological Society proposed a classification system for diffusion studies which resembles this one in part. It divided studies into those emphasizing (1) differential acceptance of farm practices as a function of status, role, and motivation; (2) differential acceptance as a function of socio-cultural systems; (3) diffusion as the study of cultural change; and (4) diffusion as a problem of the communication of information. The present paper differs, first of all, in that it advocates the integration of these several approaches in each study, though it also views the elements of the diffusion process as headings in terms of which to organize the various traditions of diffusion research. Secondly, as far as the specific classification schema is concerned, our inclination is to view categories one and two as parallel; accordingly we have grouped the individual (category one) and group (category two) factors together, dividing them only according to whether they are cultural or structural in emphasis.

From the point of view of further development of the basic components, we have suggested (1) that the dependent variable, which we have been calling *acceptance*, must be more clearly defined; (2) that considerable ingenuity is needed to date the acceptance of innovations by their adopters, for *time* is the key to diffusion research; (3) that considerable effort must be invested in the development of a "content analytic" scheme for classifying *the item* which is diffusing; (4) that attention must be given to the *unit of adoption* "required" by an item in the light of the unit which is "prescribed" or the unit which is the "target" of a communication campaign; (5) that interpersonal *channels* of communication must be viewed as elements of social structure; (6) that work is urgently needed on the comparative study of the same item diffusing in different *social structures* and, finally, (7) that the notion of "compatibility" between a given *culture* or personality and an item must be formulated much more strictly.

From the point of view of the various traditions, we have tried to suggest how the work of each tradition contributes to a generic design for diffusion research. Thus, anthropology brings into clear focus the group as the unit of adoption, and intergroup, rather than intragroup, contacts; it devotes considerable attention to the structure of social relations between donor and recipient as central to an understanding of the fate of an item moving from one group to the other; it raises the question of "levels" of acceptance. Another contribution of the work in anthropology centers around the concept of compatibility—that is, the extent to which a given culture is receptive to a given new item. But almost no attention is given to channels, and little information is available about the progress of an item over time.

Early sociological work on diffusion also focused on corporate units of adoption (the municipality) as did educational research (the school system). In both these traditions, measures of time-of-adoption were explicitly formulated. Geographical proximity and urban-rural relations are the typical social structures in which channels of communication are thought, in some mysterious way, to inhere.

More recent work in mass communication, rural sociology, public health and marketing has focused explicitly on the individual as the unit of adoption and on his perception of the channels of communication which influence his decision to adopt. Rural sociology has continually taken account of interpersonal relations as a channel but this has not been true of mass communication or marketing research until recently. In each of these fields, there appears to be a growing interest in exploring the social structures in which adopting units are linked, and to introduce time as a variable. If it becomes possible to combine this approach satisfactorily and still take account of the ways in which other channels of communication, including the mass media, impinge on these structures, the problem of designing diffusion research for modern society will be well on its way to solution. But there are no easy answers so far.

9. Motivation, Communications Research, and Family Planning

M. Brewster Smith*

Introduction

The fertility of a population can be viewed as the resultant of many individual acts and decisions, made within a framework of biological and environmental constraints. Questions of human motivation and motivational change thus have an important bearing on the viabil-

Reprinted from M. Brewster Smith, "Motivation, Communications Research, and Family Planning," *Public Health and Population Change*, edited by Mindel C. Sheps and Jeanne Clare Fidley (Pittsburgh: University of Pittsburgh Press, 1965), pp. 70–89. By permission of the University of Pittsburgh Press. © 1965 by the University of Pittsburgh Press.
* Professor of Psychology, University of California, Santa Cruz.

ity of efforts to attain social control over population growth. Such questions enter the picture in two logically separable respects. On the one hand, the number of children desired by fecund couples varies from society to society, and, over time, within the same society. What factors lead parents to aspire to a particular size of family, and how may their desires be influenced in the direction of the small families required for slowly growing populations in an era of low mortality? On the other hand, couples differ in the extent to which they are motivated to employ rational and effective means of limiting their families to the size they desire. What motivational factors are involved in the acceptance and effective use of birth control, and how may the more effective use of birth control procedures be promoted?

These two kinds of motivational questions are thus respectively concerned with the private ends and means that affect fertility and population growth. So long as the sizes of families that actually prevail in a population exceed the size that is typically desired—as when effective birth control techniques are not generally employed—the second type of question, concerned with the promotion of birth control, should have the top priority because of its strategic relevance to population growth. But in populations (typical of the economically well-developed countries) in which birth control has gained widespread acceptance, questions concerning the motivation of desired family size become increasingly important from the standpoint of population policy. The main body of this paper is focused on the first problem: What implications can be drawn from social psychological research and theory that can contribute to the acceptance and promulgation of effective birth control practices? At the end, I will revert to the problem

of desired family size in connection with a discussion of research needs.

Practitioners and scientists in other fields often look to the student of human motivation for near-magical solutions to problems that *they* cannot handle—and are ready with contempt when the magical solution is not forthcoming. If he is mindful of these ambivalent expectations, the social psychologist who ventures into the strange territory of population control and family planning will be wise to assume a posture of extreme modesty. In order to appreciate what research on communications and motivation *can* contribute, we had best begin by examining some of the reasons why such modesty is called for—not by way of apology, but to clear the ground so that relevance can be established.

Types of Communications Research

The years since World War II have seen the burgeoning in the United States of research on persuasive communication, and the emergence of a body of tentative empirical generalizations that Nathan Maccoby[1] has dignified as "the new scientific rhetoric." In spite of substantial progress in this field, however, communications research has been addressed to much easier problems than those confronted in the motivational aspect of family planning, and its empirical propositions have been worked out in much simpler, more promising settings.

One impressively cumulative research tradition has used controlled experimentation to identify factors that determine the effectiveness of communication once the recipient has been exposed to the message.[2] This body of work on "captive audiences," primarily the contribution of psychologists, has yielded a considerable array of generalizations. But

[1] N. Maccoby, "The New 'Scientific' Rhetoric," *The Science of Communication*, ed. W. Schramm (New York: Basic Books, 1963).

[2] A key reference in this tradition is C. I. Hovland, I. L. Janis, and H. H. Kelley, *Communication and Persuasion* (New Haven: Yale University Press, 1953). The more recent literature is reviewed, and a selection of empirical generalizations provided, in I. L. Janis and M. B. Smith, "Effects of Education and Persuasion on National and International Images," *International Behavior: A Social Psychological Interpretation*, ed. H. C. Kleman (New York: Holt, Rinehart, and Winston, 1965).

apart from the simplification involved in starting with the captive audience, research in this tradition has characteristically chosen its ground so as to increase the likelihood of obtaining substantial effects, which facilitate the comparison of various factors in the modification of attitudes and practices. It has dealt more with short-term effects than with long-term ones, more with trivial or superficial issues than with emotionally laden and central ones, and more with changes in beliefs and feelings than with consequential behaviors. It has also been heavily based on conveniently available American student populations. Thus, we cannot be sure that the same variables will remain important or have the same weights when communication with widely differing kinds of audiences on very different topics is at issue, but we can certainly expect that the magnitude of effects achieved will often be substantially smaller than in these experimental studies.

A second tradition, to which sociologists have been the main contributors, has used techniques of interview survey research in field studies of the effects of the mass media.[3] In contrast with the results of experimental studies, the typical finding in these field studies of "free" audiences has been one of rather minimal effects, primarily in the direction of reinforcing or activating existing attitudes, not of conversion. Again, the research has been primarily on American publics, and the range of issues explored has not been great. Voting and purchasing, as identifiable acts, have nevertheless made available a research focus on consequential behavior that goes beyond attitudes and beliefs.

Field research in this tradition becomes most relevant to population planning when it has been directed at the role of communications in the promulgation and diffusion of new techniques and practices. Converging evidence seems to point to a two-step linkage in which the public media have their effect primarily upon a limited subpopulation of "opinion leaders" (it turns out that they are different people depending on the issue), who in turn spread the message in their own spheres of personal influence.[4] But the kinds of decisions involved in buying a new product, adopting a new drug, introducing a new farming practice (all topics of studies in this vein) are a large step from those involved in family planning.

Even the most cursory thought about family planning highlights ways in which its motivational context differs so radically from the setting of most recent communications research as to represent a difference in kind, not in degree. The neutral language in which family planning is discussed scientifically and professionally should not let us forget that we deal here with sex and the marriage bed, around which surely are woven some of the strongest and least rational motives, the most intimate and private relationships, and the firmest institutional norms and taboos known to man. The very idea of introducing planful rationality in this "sacred" area could initially have been conceived only in a society trained to give unprecedented priority to rational-technical considerations by long experience with them in more public, less emotionally charged spheres of urban and industrial life.[5] Yet we are under imperatives to promote birth control in tradi-

---

[3] See J. T. Klapper, *The Effects of Mass Communication* (Glencoe: Free Press, 1960), for a recent review of findings from this research tradition. An attempt at reconciling the general trend of results in experimental and in field studies is made by C. I. Hovland, "Reconciling Conflicting Results Derived From Experimental and Survey Studies of Attitude Change," *American Psychologist*, XIV (Jan., 1959), pp. 8–17.

[4] E. Katz, "The Diffusion of New Ideas and Practices," *The Science of Communication*, ed. W. Schramm (New York: Basic Books, 1963); E. Katz and P. F. Lazarsfeld, *Personal Influence: The Part Played by People in the Flow of Mass Communication* (Glencoe: Free Press, 1955).

[5] Methods of population control have of course been practiced in many traditional societies. But the use of such methods may reflect adaptations gradually developed in the culture, rather than deliberate decisions of rational planning.

tional societies that are just beginning to attain a modicum of rationality in their public, economic, and political spheres! Any attempt to extrapolate to the motivation of family planning from research on other topics runs the risk of sheer fatuity.

On this appraisal, the social psychologist who shares concern with the population problem has several options. On the one hand, he may proclaim the irrelevance of existing social psychological research and call for an enormous expansion of basic research on the motivation of change in birth-producing or birth-limiting decisions and behavior. It always seems both easy and virtuous to ask for more research, and more is obviously needed here, but I will nevertheless reject this option with respect to the promotion of family planning. For all its limitations, existing research has its relevance in ways I hope to suggest below. And I agree with Berelson[6] that given the current urgencies and limitations of resources, the highest priorities for investment ought to be assigned in other directions.

A second option that I will follow in part is to draw cautiously on the results of existing research for hypotheses that seem relevant to social intervention in population control. The research will seldom warrant prescriptive advice to the practitioner. It may help to sensitize him, however, to potentially important factors that he has not considered explicitly. Particularly the negative conclusions of communications research—conclusions about circumstances in which persuasive communication is likely to be *ineffective*—may, *a fortiori*, help him to avoid wasted effort in the more difficult case of family planning. To the extent that action programs incorporate features extrapolated from the results of research on other topics and contexts, these action hypotheses need to be checked in program evaluation—but so do all the hunches and insights around which programs are built, whatever their source.

In addition, the present fund of research experience can be drawn upon for aid in the better *theoretical* definition of the practical problem. Often to redefine a problem is to see the contingencies that bear upon its solution in a different light. My impression is that in the present modest state of research in motivation and communication, the greatest probable contribution of social psychology lies in this direction. With these preliminaries behind us, I therefore begin with an attempt to illustrate this third option.

Some Theory with Practical Implications

A little theory can often cast a useful searchlight upon silly practice. My favorite example comes from a wartime venture in venereal disease control, so far as I know unrecorded. The American troop information officers in Manila —high-ranking recruits from Madison Avenue —had the inspiration of modelling their appeals over Armed Forces Radio on a recently notorious and perhaps successful campaign of cigarette advertising, in which the advertisers of Lucky Strikes had filled the media for weeks with the unexplained slogan, LS/MFT, at long last announcing—after suspense had presumably built up to the point of nationwide breathlessness—LS/MFT: Lucky Strikes Mean Fine Tobacco. The Manila version, also repeated sententiously for weeks, went: VD/MT. . . . VD/MT—with the final elucidation to a supposedly breathless audience: VD/MT . . . Venereal Disease . . . Means Trouble! A moment's theoretical consideration of the radically different behavioral objectives involved in raising the saliency for smokers of one among many closely similar alternative brands, and in motivating soldiers to avoid intercourse or employ prophylactic measures, should have stopped this pretentious effort.

The modification of birth-producing practices is a special and difficult case of the more general problem of the induction of another's behavior by an outside agent. One of the most cogent analyses of the psychological processes involved in such "behavior induction" remains

[6] B. Berelson, "Communication, Communications Research, and Family Planning," *Emerging Techniques in Population Research* (New York: Milbank Memorial Fund, 1963), pp. 159–171.

that of Dorwin Cartwright,[7] which he presented in the context of selected findings from research on the sale of United States war bonds in World War II. To quote Cartwright:

> What happens psychologically when someone attempts to influence the behavior of another person? The answer, in broad outline, may be described as follows: To influence behavior, a chain of processes must be initiated within the person. These processes are complex and interrelated, but in broad terms they may be characterized as (i) creating a particular cognitive structure, (ii) creating a particular motivational structure, and (iii) creating a particular behavioral (action) structure. In other words, behavior is determined by the beliefs, opinions, and "facts" a person possesses; by the needs, goals, and values he has; and by the momentary control held over his behavior by given features of his cognitive and motivational structure. To influence behavior "from the outside" requires the ability to influence these determinants in a particular way.
>
> It seems to be a characteristic of most campaigns that they start strongly with the first process, do considerably less with the second, and only lightly touch upon the third. To the extent that the campaign is intended to influence behavior and not simply to "educate," the third process is essential.[8]

Cartwright's entire analysis is so pertinent that if space permitted, I would like to summarize it at greater length. He points out that to *create the desired cognitive structure*—gain acceptance for the relevant facts and beliefs—the message must first reach the sense organs of the persons to be influenced. Once it is received, whether the message is accepted or rejected will depend on how the person identifies it with more general categories to which it appears to belong. He will tend to fit new messages into his stock of categories in ways that serve to protect him from unwanted changes in his cognitive structure (change is resisted). *Creation of the required motiva-*

tional structure in a person involves getting him to see the given action as a step toward some desired goal—the more goals that are seen as attainable by a single path, the more likely the path is to be taken. Finally—and it is the implications of this last step that I want to develop here—*creating the required behavioral structure* so that the given action will in fact occur depends on establishing conditions such that the appropriate cognitive and motivational systems gain control of the person's behavior at a particular point in time. Cartwright suggests and illustrates three subprinciples in this connection:

> The more specifically defined the path of action to a goal (in an accepted motivational structure), the more likely it is that the structure will gain control of behavior.
>
> The more specifically a path of action is located in time, the more likely it is that the structure will gain control of behavior.
>
> A given motivational structure may be set in control of behavior by placing the person in a situation requiring a decision to take, or not to take, a step of action that is a part of the structure.[9]

In the case of war bond sales, the advantages of specifying the path of action concretely (the first two of the foregoing principles) were illustrated by the substantially greater effectiveness of campaign appeals that said, in effect, "Buy an extra $100 bond during the drive from the solicitor where you work," than of appeals of an earlier, expensive campaign that in substance merely recommended, "Buy War Bonds." The effective technique of personal solicitation, which required the solicited person to make a decision to buy or not to buy a bond then and there, embodied the third principle. It is easy to think of parallels in communications advocating birth control.

But the search for parallels reveals instructive differences between the two cases. Buying a bond is a single well-defined act, to which the principles just noted can be readily ap-

[7] D. Cartwright, "Some Principles of Mass Persuasion: Selected Findings of Research on the Sale of United States War Bonds," *Human Relations*, II, No. 3, (1949), pp. 253–267.

[8] *Ibid.*, p. 255.

[9] *Ibid.*, pp. 264–265.

plied; the barrage of wartime appeals and solicitation was designed to make it easy to buy, difficult to refuse. By the technique of payroll deduction, moreover, one decision can be made to commit the person to a whole series of purchases, which become equivalent to a single act rather than a set of independent actions. Once committed, the war bond subscriber has to make a separate decision to terminate his purchases—and the promotional campaign, of course, does nothing to encourage *such* decisions. In the sphere of birth control, however, all of the methods that depend on modifying the conditions of each specific act of sexual intercourse fall outside the scope of ready influence, according to these principles. It is simply not possible to arrange the equivalent of war bond solicitation to guide the decision processes affecting each separate act of intercourse. Neither is it possible, where these methods are at issue, to secure the kind of externally binding commitment to their practice that is represented by payroll deduction. The behavioral objective for their advocates must therefore be *not* the motivation of specific acts, but rather the establishment of consistent habits or the development in people of strong and consistent internalized controls. Both of these objectives are intrinsically much more complex and difficult to achieve. It is dubious whether even the best planned promotional campaigns can often attain them.

The present analysis therefore highlights the probable relevance of a dimension along which techniques of birth limitation may vary, ranging from fully committing single acts (male and female sterilization), through infrequent acts the motivation of which can be separately induced (the insertion of intrauterine rings, long-term medication, perhaps abortion), to the entire range of chemical-mechanical procedures that must be carried out daily or before each occasion of intercourse. Included in this last, least promising category are not only the rhythm method and withdrawal, but also the daily "pill," since each of these techniques requires multiple decisions to act or refrain from acting.

The initial middle-class leadership of the birth control movement has favored techniques that fall in the latter category, perhaps just because they seem to maximize voluntary decision—planfulness—about parenthood and thus appeal to middle-class values. It should be recognized, however, that any procedure that maximizes and multiplies voluntary decisions is *disadvantageous* from the standpoint of permitting coordinated social intervention to limit births. If, as seems likely, promotional methods cannot instill sufficiently consistent contraceptive habits and self-discipline in enough people to achieve acceptable target reductions in birth rates, consideration might well be given to focusing promotion on more attainable goals. Sterilization and chemical or mechanical procedures that require attention only at infrequent occasions would seem to be more feasible subjects for promotional campaigns.

Note in passing that the dimension I have been emphasizing is closely related to one emphasized by Berelson[10] in his grid of three main factors which he proposes for the orientation of field experiments on the promotion of birth control. Berelson ventures that the practically important variables which in combination define a framework for the planning of program testing are, first, the nature of the *society* (traditional or modern), second, the nature of the *contraceptive method* (hard to use or easy), and, finally, the nature of the *approach* (through whom the informational, educational, or promotional campaign is addressed saying what, to whom).

For his second variable, he contrasts the traditional methods of withdrawal, condom, foam tablet, rhythm, etc., with the steroid pill and intrauterine device, saying that:

> What makes [the former] methods hard to use is the requirement for sustained motivation, the need in most cases to do something preparatory at the time of intercourse, and in some cases the sheer bother and nuisance value. Beyond such problems is the further difficulty that such methods are not always effective—so that the user or potential user

[10] Berelson, *op. cit.*, pp. 163–165.

may feel justified in thinking that the result is not going to be worth the effort.

Berelson calls for field studies aimed at providing an adequate basis for such gross administrative decisions as whether the "hard" methods can be effectively promoted in traditional societies, even with maximum effort.

Clearly Berelson is making much the same distinction as mine. But his unduly pessimistic dismissal of motivational theory leads him to couch the distinction in the more common-sense terms of "hard" vs. "easy," which in turn leads him to neglect ways in which male sterilization (easy) and female sterilization (hard) both carry one feature of his "easy" list to an even higher degree.

The kind of motivational theory that I have borrowed from Cartwright differentiates analytically the cognitive, attitudinal, and decisional components of the problem of motivating a change in behavior. One may also look at the process temporally. In their generally perspicacious distillation of the literature of communication research for the guidance of written communication on birth control, Bogue and Heiskanen[11] offer as their first principle that "The complete adoption of a new idea or a new mode of behavior is not a simple act, but is a PROCESS comprised of several steps or stages." For the adoption of birth control practices, they suggest the following four stages as a useful framework:

Stage I. *Awareness and Interest.* This stage includes *learning that birth control is possible, respectable, and practical; becoming interested in it; and wanting to learn about it.*

Stage II. *Information-Gathering, Evaluation, and Decision to Try.*

Stage III. *Implementation.* This stage includes *taking action, learning how to use, correcting mistakes, and overcoming wrong ideas.*

Stage IV. *Adoption and Continued Use.* This is the stage of full adoption. Couples who arrive at this stage feel that birth control is right and normal. They would be uncomfortable or fearful to have sex relations without it unless they positively wanted a pregnancy to occur.[12]

While such a scheme of stages certainly does not represent an ambitious level of theorizing, it again illustrates the advantage that even low-level theory can provide; it functions as a scanning device in terms of which judgments are called for that might otherwise be neglected. Thus, we are reminded that individuals and populations will be located at different steps along this continuum: the planning of communication strategy obviously requires information about the target population in this respect. Special surveys may be required. Further, the advantages become apparent of developing materials and approaches geared to the readiness and interests characteristic of a particular stage—and of finding or devising channels of distribution that match the materials to the readiness of the recipient. Once such a scheme is proposed, the consequences are obvious.

Some Implications of Research on Communication

Of all the results of communications research, the central finding that ought to be kept before all would-be communicators is the fact of resistance. In general, people's beliefs, attitudes, and behavior tend to be stable. Demands and arguments for change, uncomfortable new facts that do not fit neatly into accustomed categories, are likely to be resisted. Whenever communications attempt to change pre-existing beliefs, attitudes, and habits that engage important goals and values, strong resistances are likely to arise at each stage of the communication process. Thus, some communications are so strongly resisted that they fail to achieve even the first step of eliciting audience *exposure* to the message. The self-selective tendency by which audiences become restricted to the already informed and converted is a recurring and major source of frustration to organizers of persuasive campaigns.[13]

[11] D. J. Bogue and V. S. Heiskanen, *How to Improve Written Communication for Birth Control* (Chicago: University of Chicago Family Study Center, and New York: National Committee on Maternal Health, Inc., 1963).

[12] *Ibid.*, pp. 7–9.

[13] H. H. Hyman and P. B. Sheatsley, "Some Reasons Why Information Campaigns Fail," *Public Opinion Quarterly*, XI, No. 3 (1947), pp. 412–423.

Other communications that are somewhat more successful at the outset may end up by being just as ineffective because resistances are mobilized in members of the audience while they are exposed to the message, which interfere drastically with *attention, comprehension,* or *acceptance.*[14] No change or even "boomerang effects" may occur as a consequence of selective inattention to disturbing ideas, misperception of the message, or subsequent selective forgetting.[15] And as we have seen, even when a persuasive message is accepted, the recipient may fail to act upon it or lack the skill to act effectively.

Much effort is wasted in futile persuasive efforts because this paramount fact of resistance is neglected or underestimated. Before any major campaign in the difficult area of human reproductive practices is embarked upon, the would-be communicator should consider his chances of overcoming resistance sufficiently to justify his investment. Some pilot testing of materials and approach is normally called for before any substantial outlay of funds and effort is warranted.

One touchstone for distinguishing promising from unpromising situations is suggested by Hovland, Janis, and Kelley[16] in their analysis of an essential difference between instruction and persuasion. They point out that in communication consensually defined as instructional, in which acceptance is more readily elicited, the setting is typically one in which the recipients anticipate that the communicator is trying to help them, that his conclusions are incontrovertible, and that they will be socially rewarded rather than punished for adhering to his conclusions. In situations commonly regarded as persuasive, on the other hand, interfering expectations are likely to be aroused which operate as resistances. These interfering expectations seem to be of three major kinds: (1) expectations of being manipulated or exploited by the communicator (distrust); (2) expectations of being "wrong" —out of tune with reality as they understand it; and (3) expectations of social disapproval (from people important to them whose norms do not accord with the communicator's position).

The situations encountered by communicators in the sphere of population control surely cover the full range between these two ideal types. The more that inculcation of the desired knowledge and practices can be conducted via the established educational, medical, and religious institutions of the community, the more the "instructional" conditions should apply. Conversely, the more the campaign is seen as a foreign body at variance with the natural and established order, the more closely the "persuasive" type is approximated under conditions that maximize the likelihood of resistance. To the extent that the latter conditions prevail, it is always an open question whether the effort is warranted.

Janis and Smith[17] summarize the research evidence concerning the major sources of resistance to persuasive communication, classifying them under two rubrics: resistance due to the anchorage of a person's attitudes and practices in his group affiliations, and resistance due to anchorage in personality needs. Factors related to the former source of resistance have been extensively studied, documenting the obvious but important point, among others, that the more strongly attached a person is to his group, the more he is likely to resist "counter-norm communications" at variance with the standards and precepts of the group to which he belongs. Techniques of persuasion that emphasize a community orientation, legitimation by established leaders, discussion and group support and the like are intended to take these sources of resistance into account.[18]

---

[14] Hovland, Janis, and Kelley, *op. cit.,* pp. 287–293.

[15] Klapper, *op. cit.,* pp. 18–26.

[16] Hovland *et al., op. cit.,* pp. 293–298.

[17] Janis and Smith, *op. cit.*

[18] See R. Lippitt, J. Watson, and B. Westley, *The Dynamics of Planned Change* (New York: Harcourt, Brace, 1958), for a well-conceptualized account of a group-oriented approach to the induction of planned change, with consideration of relevant evidence.

Resistance to change anchored in personality needs arises inevitably from the fact that each person has a major investment in his own pattern of beliefs, attitudes, and behaviors that he has worked out in the give-and-take of living or adopted from his parents and mentors. Attitudes and practices are particularly obdurate to rational persuasion insofar as they form part of the person's armament for dealing with his unrecognized inner problems, containing and allaying his anxiety, and helping him to maintain adequate "face" toward self and world. It is in this respect that strong personality-anchored resistances may especially be anticipated in the intimate and emotionally charged area of sexual beliefs and practices. One implication, to the extent that such defensive sources of resistance are otherwise likely to be evoked, is that those techniques of birth control that dissociate the contraceptive decision from the intimacy of sexual life should meet with less resistance than others: the oral "pill" and, to a lesser extent, the implanted intrauterine device (which is associated with the sexual anatomy but not with specific sexual acts). And here, of course, lies the great obstacle to sterilization, where the motivational advantage that it requires only a single act of decision is counterbalanced by the fantasies of impotence, castration, or defeminization that it may invoke.

We have already noted a special source of personal and perhaps cultural resistance that becomes particularly relevant as efforts at population control are directed toward the rural and urban poor of traditionally oriented societies, or even of modern ones. Rationality, planfulness, capacity for delayed gratification, and broad time perspectives, all middle-class virtues that are called for by some approaches to birth control, become psychological luxuries that the extremely deprived, the hope-foresaken of the "culture of poverty"[19] can ill afford. Culturally supported attitudes of resignation, fatalism, and present—rather than future—orientation are presumably clung to because they permit a measure of equanimity in the face of predictable frustrations; gratifications are grasped heedlessly when they are available because there is no warrant for confidence that forbearance will pay off. Programs aimed at reducing birth rates in such populations will obviously encounter the passive resistance of apathy and erratic performance, if they make demands on resources of planfulness and committing decision-making that are unavailable.[20]

The emphasis in the foregoing has advisedly been placed on obstacles and resistances to persuasive communication as an avenue toward population control, since an over-valuation of the power of the "persuader" seems to be a contemporary culture trait shared by professionals and laity alike. Yet research does suggest circumstances under which persuasive efforts are likely to meet with more success.

One such type of situation is that to which Katz and Schanck called attention a number of years ago, with the label *"pluralistic ignorance."* "People will stay in line because their fellows do, yet, if they only knew that their comrades wanted to kick over the traces too, the institutional conformity of the group would quickly vanish. . . ."[21] Where there are taboos or strong barriers against free communication, as is so likely to be the case in regard to sexual matters, states of pluralistic ignorance are especially likely to develop. Surveys of individual attitudes in the area of family planning will often turn up such instances,

---

[19] O. Lewis, *Five Families: Mexican Case Studies in the Culture of Poverty* (New York: Basic Books, 1959); J. Blake, *Family Structure in Jamaica* (Glencoe: Free Press, 1961); L. Rainwater, *And the Poor Get Children* (Chicago: Quadrangle Books, 1960).

[20] As noted in other papers in this Symposium, the increasingly uprooted urban concentration may be more amenable than a traditional peasantry to innovation. Other accompaniments of modernization such as the reduction of high infant mortality and compulsory education may make individuals more accessible to new ideas, and freer from the restraints of group-anchored resistances.

[21] D. Katz and R. L. Schanek, *Social Psychology* (New York: Wiley, 1938), pp. 174–175.

which then suggest points of vulnerability in the traditional norms that persuasion can capitalize upon.

Thus in their Puerto Rican survey, Hill, Stycos, and Back unearthed pluralistic ignorance that was giving vulnerable support to the *machismo* tenet that men are expected to want large families, especially of sons, as a proof of their masculinity. In fact, however, the men turned out to be even more oriented than their wives to small families. Their wives were unaware of this fact.[22] To the extent that such constellations of misinformation prevail, programs that seek to induce freer communication can contribute to the emergence and stabilization of more appropriate norms.

A second class of situations that affords optimal opportunities for influence involves the "captive audience." We noted at the outset, as a limitation on the generalizability of psychologists' experimental studies, that they have tended to focus on captive audiences with which exposure to the intended message is guaranteed. Certainly, results from such studies cannot be generalized to situations in which people are freely exposed to competing messages in the mass media, but there *are* important types of situations in which one can count on people receiving the desired message. In these situations there are many reasons to expect communications to be more effective, especially when the circumstances permit prolonged and repeated exposure under favorable institutional auspices. An ideal case is provided when the schools are available for instruction in family planning or for the promulgation of small-family values. Whatever messages can be channelled through the classroom not only have the advantage of a guaranteed audience; they participate in the context of "instruction" which as we have seen is likely to circumvent the resistances to which "persuasion" is vulnerable.

While no other case comes to mind that presents equivalent opportunities, there are others that share some of its advantages. For example, a program that enlists the participation of the specialists who officiate at childbirth—be they physicians, nurses, or midwives —gains access for communicating with women during a period when they may be expected to be especially receptive to information about family planning.

Political and Logistical Considerations as Strategic Factors

This selective and speculative survey points to tentative conclusions that come to me almost as a surprise. Existing knowledge, for all its uncertainty, calls into serious question the effectiveness of current effort and practice to attain population control by persuasive means. Even were the many "pilot" ventures to be regularized and multiplied, it seems to me unlikely that enough people would be reached, enough persuaded, enough confirmed in consistent birth-limiting practices, to achieve the socially desirable degree of reduction in birth rates. These doubts follow from the minor impact of persuasive campaigns under most circumstances, the major fact of resistance, and the motivational complexity of many of the widely recommended techniques of birth control. The most strategic class of factors that govern the effectiveness of persuasive communication in this application seem to me to be essentially *political*, not scientific or technical.

Thus, access to the schools and other respected and central social institutions—particularly medical—for the free and legitimate communication of facts and recommendations about family planning is clearly a political matter. Where the dissemination of birth control information is illegal, common agreement would see the strategic problem as one of how to get the law changed—not as a need for research on how to achieve more effective clandestine dissemination. So with the school: there is good reason to believe that schools could play a much more effective role than presently available channels; the political problem of access thus becomes more strategic than research on how to achieve more effective persuasion outside the legitimate institutional framework.

[22] R. Hill, J. M. Stycos, and K. W. Back, *The Family and Population Control: A Puerto Rican Experiment in Social Change* (Chapel Hill: University of North Carolina Press, 1959).

Political considerations are also involved in social decision about the acceptability of particular techniques of birth control, regardless of their effectiveness. The acceptability of the rhythm method and the inacceptability of all others to the Catholic Church is of course a matter of engrossingly strategic politics outside and within the Church. But quite parallel issues involve non-Catholics in value conflicts and potentially political disputes about such undoubtedly effective means as abortion and voluntary sterilization.

Gains on the political front would permit persuasive efforts to be directed to a larger extent than is presently the case in most countries toward objectives and via channels that have a fair chance of circumventing human resistances and producing substantial differences in people's reproductive habits and attainments. *Logistical* problems would then emerge as a close second to political ones in strategic relevance. Well-supplied and -staffed clinics must be readily available if favorable motivation is to be converted into the desired action. Health educators in large numbers would be needed to convert existing pilot programs into operational ones. Not least, persuasive efforts toward population control will be immeasurably furthered by the cheap and ready availability of chemical and mechanical means of contraception that are designed to fit the specifications of human motivation as well as of human reproductive physiology. The more effectively the design problem is solved, however, the more strategic will political factors become in determining the logistical availability of the perfected techniques!

The Need for Research

In spite of the uncertain and far from adequate state of psychological knowledge about persuasive communication, therefore, I cannot assign high priority in the grand strategy of population control to basic research in this area. There are too many greater urgencies. But there is great need for the feeding back of dependable knowledge of results to guide the development of more effective persuasive programs, and equal need for dependable knowledge about the relevant beliefs, attitudes, and practices of each population that becomes the target of persuasion. The efforts that are called for fall at various locations on the continuum between informal observation and appraisal, systematic surveys and evaluations, and well-controlled experimentation in the field. A limited number of full-scale field experiments—the Puerto Rico study[23] is in many respects a model—should amply repay the investment required, in providing the grist from which fresh insights can be developed into the processes by which limitation in birth rate can be induced. But the larger share of investment should go toward incorporating modest provisions for fact-finding, pre-testing, and evaluation into all major action programs. Were this investment made (at a level of ambitiousness roughly proportional to the scope of the associated action program), wasted efforts could be avoided and cumulative wisdom developed about sound practice.

Applied research and program evaluation, then, fits the short-term urgencies concerning the promulgation of birth control techniques. The other motivational problem noted at the outset—that of individual goals for family size and how they may be modified—acquires its priority in a broader time perspective. There is time for basic research on this problem, and there is need. If, as has been suggested, American couples are converging on preference for families of two to four children, what are the factors that tip the decision (which in the long run has vast consequences for population growth) toward the higher or the lower number? How may these preferences be modified? Surveys on American samples provide some leads.[24] Other hypotheses have been sug-

[23] *Ibid.*

[24] See R. Freedman, P. K. Whelpton, and A. A. Campbell, *Family Planning, Sterility, and Population Growth* (New York: McGraw-Hill, 1959); C. Westoff, R. G. Potter, P. Sagi, and E. Mishler, *Family Growth in Metropolitan America* (Princeton: Princeton University Press, 1961); C. Westoff, R. G. Potter, and P. Sagi, *The Third Child* (Princeton: Princeton University Press, 1963).

gested in speculative essays by psychologists[25] and by popular writers.[26] Elsewhere Judith Blake advocates an indirect approach via the encouragement of female employment outside the home. Basic research now by psychologists and sociologists could provide knowledge that will be badly needed when effective birth control programs have succeeded in narrowing the gap between desire and achievement in family size.

Concluding Remarks

Apart from the priorities that I see as inherent in the field of population control, I hope that my colleagues in psychology will move the field of population research to a position considerably higher in their own scheme of priorities than the less than marginal position which it presently occupies. Because of the intimacy with which fundamental human passions and relationships are involved, the motivational and decisional processes associated with human fertility should provide a rewarding context in which psychologists may come to grips in research with important aspects of personality and social psychology.

Acknowledgement

I am indebted to Mr. Richard Gardner for bibliographic assistance.

[25] E.g., L. W. Hoffman and F. Wyatt, "Social Change and Motivations for Having Larger Families: Some Theoretical Considerations," *Merrill-Palmer Quarterly*, VI (1960), pp. 235–244.
[26] E.g., B. Frieden, *The Feminine Mystique* (New York: Norton, 1963).

D.   CONFLICT PERSPECTIVES

10.   Conflicts: Productive and Destructive[a]

Morton Deutsch*

It is a great honor and delight for me to receive the Kurt Lewin Memorial Award. As you know, Kurt Lewin has had a profound influence on my life and work. I have been influenced by his value orientations as well as his theoretical orientations. He believed that an intellectually significant social science has to be concerned with the problems of social action and social change and that intelligent social action has to be informed by theory and research. He rejected both a heartless science and a mindless social action. I am proud to have had this remarkable man as a teacher and as a guide.

[a] Kurt Lewin Memorial Address given at the meetings of the American Psychological Association, September 1, 1968, in San Francisco. Preparation of this paper was supported by a contract with the Office of Naval Research, Nonr-4294(00), and a grant from the National Science Foundation, GS–302.

Reprinted from Morton Deutsch, "Conflicts: Productive and Destructive," *Journal of Social Issues*, Vol. XXV, No. 1 (January 1969), pp. 7–41. Abridgement.

* Professor, Teachers College, Columbia University.

I wish to discuss the characteristics of productive and destructive conflict and to consider the conditions which give rise to one or another type. Although actual conflicts are rarely purely benign or malign, it is useful for analytic purposes to consider the simple cases. Doing so highlights not only the differences in the outcomes of conflict but also the differences in types of processes by which the outcomes are derived.

Let me start with the dull but necessary chore of defining some of the key terms that I shall be using. A *conflict* exists whenever *incompatible* activities occur. The incompatible actions may originate in one person, in one group, in one nation; and such conflicts are called *intra*personal, *intra*group, or *intra*national. Or they may reflect incompatible actions of two or more persons, groups or nations; such conflicts are called *inter*personal, *inter*group, or *inter*national. An action which is incompatible with another action prevents, obstructs, interferes with, injures, or in some way makes it less likely or less effective.

A conflict may arise from differences in information or belief (my wife thinks our son's mosquito bites are better treated by calamine lotion, while I think caladryl is better). It may reflect differences in interests, desires or values. (I prefer to invest our savings in the stock market while my wife would prefer to spend it on winter vacations). It may occur as a result of a scarcity of some resource such as money, time, space, position (the more closet space that my wife uses for her clothing, the less space there is for my files). Or it may reflect a rivalry in which one person tries to outdo or undo the other.

"Competition" and "Conflict"

The terms "competition" and "conflict" are often used synonymously or interchangeably. I believe such usage reflects a basic confusion. Although "competition" produces "conflict," not all instances of "conflict" reflect competition. Competition implies an opposition in the goals of the interdependent parties such that the probability of goal attainment for one decreases as the probability for the other increases. In conflict which is derived from competition, the incompatible actions reflect incompatible goals. However, conflict may occur even when there is no perceived or actual incompatibility of goals. Thus, if my wife and I are in conflict about how to treat our son's mosquito bites, it is not because we have mutually exclusive goals; here, our goals are concordant. The distinction between "conflict" and "competition" is not one which I make merely to split hairs. It is an important one and is basic to a theme that underlies this paper: conflict can occur in a cooperative or competitive context and the processes of conflict resolution which are likely to be displayed will be strongly influenced by the context within which conflict occurs.

I am concerned with psychological or perceived conflict—i.e., conflicts which exist psychologically for the parties involved. I do not assume that perceptions are always veridical nor do I assume that actual incompatibilities are always perceived. Hence, it is important in characterizing any conflict to depict the objective state of affairs, the state of affairs as perceived by the conflicting parties, and the interdependence between the objective and perceived realities. Let me illustrate some of the possibilities of misperception. I may perceive an incompatibility where there is none (my wife's clothes and my files may both be able to fit into our closets even though neither of us believes so); I may perceive an incompatibility as noncontingent but, in reality, it is contingent upon changeable features of the situation (her clothes and my files can both fit if I remove some shelves from the closet that are rarely used); I may experience the frustration and annoyance of incompatible actions without perceiving that they are due to conflict (my closet space may have become cramped and overcrowded because my wife has placed various objects into my space without my being aware of this); or I may perceive an incompatibility but make the wrong attribution so that I perceive the nature of the conflict incorrectly (I may blame my son for having put some of his things in my closet when it was done by my wife).

The possibility that the nature of a relationship may be misperceived indicates that the lack of conflict as well as the occurrence of conflict may be determined by misunderstanding or misinformation about the objective state of affairs. Thus, the presence or absence of conflict is never rigidly determined by the objective state of affairs. Apart from the possibility of misperception, psychological factors enter into the determination of conflict in yet another crucial way. Conflict is also determined by what is valued by the conflicting parties. Even the classical example of pure conflict—two starving men on a lifeboat with only enough food for the survival of one—loses its purity if one or both of the men have social or religious values which can become more dominant psychologically than the hunger need or the desire for survival.

The point of these remarks is that neither the occurrence nor the outcomes of conflict are completely and rigidly determined by objective circumstances. This means that the fates of the participants in a situation of conflict are not inevitably determined by the external circumstances in which they find themselves. Whether conflict takes a productive or destructive course is thus open to influence even under the most unfavorable objective conditions. Similarly, even under the most favorable objective circumstances, psychological factors can lead conflict to take a destructive course. I am not denying the importance of "real" conflicts but rather I am asserting that the psychological processes of perceiving and valuing are involved in turning objective conditions into experienced conflict.

"Constructive" and "Destructive"

In the next section, I shall characterize the typical development and course of destructive and constructive conflicts. Here let me clarify what I mean by the value-laden terms "constructive" and "destructive." At the extremes, these terms are easy to define. Thus, a conflict clearly has destructive consequences if the participants in it are dissatisfied with the outcomes and all feel they have lost as a result of the conflict. Similarly, a conflict has productive consequences if the participants all are satisfied with their outcomes and feel that they have gained as a result of the conflict.

Also, in most instances, a conflict whose outcomes are satisfying to all the participants will be more constructive than one which is satisfying to some and dissatisfying to others.

My characterization of destructive and constructive conflicts obviously has its roots in the ethical value "the greatest good for the greatest number." Admittedly, there are still considerable theoretical and empirical difficulties to be overcome before such a value can be operationalized with any generality or precision. It is, of course, easier to identify and measure satisfactions-dissatisfactions and gains-losses in simple laboratory conflict situations than it is in the complex conflicts of groups in everyday life. Yet even in the complex situations, it is not impossible to compare conflicts roughly in terms of their outcomes. In some instances, union-management negotiations may lead to a prolonged strike with considerable loss and ill-will resulting to both parties; in other instances it may lead to a mutually satisfying agreement where both sides obtain something they want. In some cases, a quarrel between a husband and wife will clear up unexpressed misunderstandings and lead to greater intimacy while in others it may produce only bitterness and estrangement.

One more definitional point. It is often useful to distinguish between the "manifest" conflict and the "underlying" conflict. Consider the conflict of an obsessional patient over whether or not she should check to see if she really turned off the stove, or the argument of two brothers over which TV program is to be tuned in, or the controversy between a school board and a teachers' union over the transfer of a teacher, or an international dispute involving alleged infractions of territory by alien aircraft. Each of these manifest conflicts may be symptomatic of underlying conflict: the obsessional patient may want to trust herself but be afraid that she has impulses which would be destructive if unchecked; the two brothers may be fighting to obtain what each considers to be his fair share of the family's rewards; and so on. "Manifest" conflict often cannot be resolved more than temporarily unless the underlying conflict is dealt with or unless it can be disconnected and separated from the underlying conflict so that it can be treated in isolation.

I shall now turn to the basic questions to which this paper is addressed. What are the characteristic symptoms and courses of conflicts which end up one way or the other? What are the factors which make a conflict move in one direction or the other? I do not pretend that I have complete or even satisfying answers. Nevertheless, I hope that you will agree that these are questions which warrant attention.

The Course of Destructive Conflict

Destructive conflict is characterized by a tendency to expand and to escalate. As a result, such conflict often becomes independent of its initiating causes and is likely to continue after these have become irrelevant or have been forgotten. Expansion occurs along the various dimensions of conflict: the size and number of the immediate issues involved; the number of the motives and participants implicated on each side of the issue; the size and number of the principles and precedents that are perceived to be at stake; the costs that the participants are willing to bear in relation to the conflict; the number of norms of moral conduct from which behavior toward the other side is exempted; and the intensity of negative attitudes toward the other side.

The processes involved in the intensification of conflict may be said, as Coleman (1957, 14) has expressed it, "to create a 'Gresham's Law of Conflict': the harmful and dangerous elements drive out those which would keep the conflict within bounds." Paralleling the expansion of the scope of conflict there is an increasing reliance upon a strategy of power and upon the tactics of threat, coercion, and deception. Correspondingly, there is a shift away from a strategy of persuasion and from the tactics of conciliation, minimizing differences, and enhancing mutual understanding and good-will. And within each of the conflicting parties, there is increasing pressure for uniformity of opinion and a tendency for leadership and control to be taken away from those elements that are more conciliatory and invested in those who are militantly organized for waging conflict through combat.

Three Interrelated Processes . . .

The tendency to escalate conflict results from the conjunction of three interrelated processes: (a) competitive processes involved in the attempt to win the conflict; (b) processes of misperception and biased perception; (c) processes of commitment arising out of pressures for cognitive and social consistency. These processes give rise to a mutually reinforcing cycle of relations which generate actions and reactions that intensify conflict.

Other factors, of course, may serve to limit and encapsulate conflict so that a spiraling intensification does not develop. Here, I am referring to such factors as: the number and strength of the existing cooperative bonds, cross-cutting identifications, common allegiances and memberships among the conflicting parties; the existence of values, institutions, procedures, and groups that are organized to help limit and regulate conflict; and the salience and significance of the costs of intensifying conflict. If these conflict-limiting factors are weak, it may be difficult to prevent a competitive conflict from expanding in scope. Even if they are strong, misjudgment and the pressures arising out of tendencies to be rigidly self-consistent may make it difficult to keep a competitive conflict encapsulated.

Competitive Effects

Elsewhere (Deutsch 1962a, 1965a, in preparation) I have characterized the essential distinctions between a cooperative and competitive process and described their social psychological features in some detail. Here, I shall only highlight some of the main features of the competitive process. In a competitive encounter as one gains, the other loses. Unlike the cooperative situation where people have their goals linked so that everybody "sinks or swims" together, in the competitive situation if one swims, the others must sink.

Later in the paper, I shall detail some of the factors which lead the parties in a conflict to define their relationship as a competitive one.

For the moment, let us assume that they have competitively defined their conflict and let us examine the consequences of doing so and also why these consequences tend to expand conflict. Typically, a competitive process tends to produce the following effects:

(a) Communication between the conflicting parties is unreliable and impoverished. The available communication channels and opportunities are not utilized or they are used in an attempt to mislead or intimidate the other. Little confidence is placed in information that is obtained directly from the other; espionage and other circuitous means of obtaining information are relied upon. The poor communication enhances the possibility of error and misinformation of the sort which is likely to reinforce the preexisting orientations and expectations toward the other. Thus, the ability to notice and respond by the other away from a win-lose orientation becomes impaired.

(b) It stimulates the view that the solution of the conflict can only be of the type that is imposed by one side on the other by superior force, deception, or cleverness—an outlook which is consistent with the definition of the conflict as competitive or win-lose in nature. The enhancement of one's own power and the complementary minimization of the other's power become objectives. The attempt to create or maintain a power difference favorable to one's own side by each of the conflicting parties tends to expand the scope of the conflict as it enlarges from a focus on the immediate issue in dispute to a conflict over who shall have the power to impose his preference upon the other.

(c) It leads to a suspicious, hostile attitude which increases the sensitivity to differences and threats, while minimizing the awareness of similarities. This, in turn, makes the usually accepted norms of conduct and morality which govern one's behavior toward others who are similar to oneself less applicable. Hence, it permits behavior toward the other which would be considered outrageous if directed toward someone like oneself. Since neither side is likely to grant moral superiority to the other, the conflict is likely to escalate as one side or the other engages in behavior that is morally outrageous to the other side. Of course, if the conflicting parties both agree, implicitly or explicitly, on the rules for waging competitive conflict and adhere to the agreement, then this agreement serves to limit the escalation of conflict.

Misjudgment and Misperception

In our preceding discussion of the effects of competition, it was evident that impoverished communication, hostile attitudes, and oversensitivity to differences could lead to distorted views of the other which could intensify and perpetuate conflict. In addition to the distortions that are natural to the competitive process, there are other distortions which commonly occur in the course of interaction. Elsewhere (Deutsch 1962b, 1965b) I have described some of the common sources of misperception in interactional situations. Many of these misperceptions function to transform a conflict into a competitive struggle even if the conflict did not emerge from a competitive relationship.

Here let me illustrate with the implications of a simply psychological principle: *the perception of any act is determined both by our perception of the act itself and by our perception of the context in which the act occurs.* The contexts of social acts are often not immediately given in perception and often they are not obvious. When the context is not obvious, we tend to assume a familiar context—a context which is most likely in terms of our own past experience. Since both the present situations and past experience of the actor and perceiver may be rather different, it is not surprising that they will interpret the same act quite differently. Misunderstandings of this sort, of course, are very likely when the actor and the perceiver come from different cultural backgrounds and are not fully informed about these differences. A period of rapid social change also makes such misunderstandings widespread as the gap between the past and the present widens.

Given the fact that the ability to place oneself in the other's shoes is notoriously underdeveloped in most people and also that this ability is further impaired by stress and inadequate information, it is not astonishing that certain typical biases emerge in the perceptions of actions during conflict. Thus, since most people are motivated to maintain a favorable view of themselves but are less strongly motivated to hold such a view of others, it is not surprising that there is a bias toward perceiving one's own behavior toward the other as being more benevolent and more legitimate than the other's behavior toward oneself. Here I am simply restating a well-demonstrated psychological truth: namely, the evaluation of an act is affected by the evaluation of its source: the source is part of the context of behavior. Research, for example, has shown that American students are likely to rate more favorably an action of the United States directed toward the Soviet Union than the same action directed by the Soviet Union toward the United States. We are likely to view American espionage activities in the Soviet Union as more benevolent than similar activities by Soviet agents in the United States.

If each side in a conflict tends to perceive its own motives and behavior as more benevolent and legitimate than those of the other side, it is evident that conflict will spiral upward in intensity. If "Acme" perceives its actions as a benevolent and legitimate way of interfering with actions that "Bolt" has no right to engage in, "Acme" will certainly be amazed by the intensity of "Bolt's" hostile response and will have to escalate his counteraction to negate "Bolt's" response. But how else is "Bolt" likely to act if he perceives his own actions as well-motivated? And how likely he is to respond to "Acme's" escalation with still further counter-escalation if he is capable of so doing!

To the extent that there is a biased perception of benevolence and legitimacy, one could also expect that there will be a parallel bias in what is considered to be an equitable agreement for resolving conflict: should not differential legitimacy be differentially rewarded? The biased perceptions of what is a fair compromise makes agreement more difficult and, thus, extends conflict. Another consequence of the biased perception of benevolence and legitimacy is reflected in the asymmetries between trust and suspicion, and between cooperation and competition. Trust, when violated, is more likely to turn into suspicion than negated suspicion is to turn into trust. Similarly, it is easier to move in the direction from cooperation to competition than from competition to cooperation.

Other Processes Leading to Misperception

There are, of course, other types of processes leading to misperceptions and misjudgments. In addition to the distortions arising from the pressures for self-consistency and social conformity (which are discussed below), the intensification of conflict may induce stress and tension beyond a moderate optimal level and this over-activation, in turn, often leads to an impairment of perceptual and cognitive processes in several ways: it reduces the range of perceived alternatives; it reduces the time-perspective in such a way as to cause a focus on the immediate rather than the over-all consequences of the perceived alternatives; it polarizes thought so that percepts tend to take on a simplistic cast of being "black" or "white," "for" or "against," "good" or "evil"; it leads to stereotyped responses; it increases the susceptibility to fear- or hope-inciting rumors; it increases defensiveness; it increases the pressures to social conformity. In effect, excessive tension reduces the intellectual resources available for discovering new ways of coping with a problem or new ideas for resolving a conflict. Intensification of conflict is the likely result as simplistic thinking and the polarization of thought pushes the participants to view their alternatives as being limited to "victory" or "defeat."

Paradoxically, it should also be noted that the very availability of intellectual and other resources which can be used for waging conflict may make it difficult, at the onset of conflict, to forecast the outcome of an attempt to impose one's preference upon the other. Less inventive species than man can pretty well predict the outcome of a contest by force through aggressive gesturing and other display of combat potential; thus, they rarely have to engage in combat to settle "who shall get what, when." The versatility of man's techniques for achieving domination over other men makes it likely that combat will arise because the combatants have discordant judgments of the potential outcomes. Unlike his hairy ancestors, the "naked ape" cannot agree in advance who will win. Misjudgment of the other side's willingness and capability of fighting has sometimes turned controversy into combat as increased tension has narrowed the perceived outcomes of conflict to victory or defeat.

Processes of Commitment

It has long been recognized that people tend to act in accord with their beliefs; more recently, Festinger has emphasized in his theory of cognitive dissonance that the converse is also often true: people tend to make their beliefs and attitudes accord with their actions. The result of this pressure for self-consistency may lead to an unwitting involvement in and intensification of conflict as one's actions have to be justified to oneself and to others. The tragic course of American involvement in the civil war in Vietnam provides an illustration.

In an unpublished paper presented over two years ago (1966) I wrote:

How did we get involved in this ridiculous and tragic situation: a situation in which American lives and resources are being expended in defense of a people who are being more grievously injured and who are becoming more bitterly antagonistic to us the more deeply we become involved in their internal conflict? How is it that we have become so obsessed with the war in South Vietnam that we are willing to jettison our plans for achieving a Great Society at home, neglect the more important problems in South America and India, and risk destroying our leadership abroad? Not so long ago, we had a different view of the importance of Vietnam. In 1954, despite urgent French pleas, President Eisenhower refused to let the American military intervene even if all of Vietnam should fall. Senator Lyndon B. Johnson, at the time, vehemently opposed the use of American soldiers in this far-off land.

Now that we are massively involved in South Vietnam, we hear many different rationalizations of our involvement: Dean Rusk has cited the SEATO treaty commitment but as Richard N. Goodwin has pointed out in *The New Yorker* (April 16, 1966): "No adviser in the highest councils ever urged action on the basis of the SEATO treaty; none, as far as I know, ever mentioned the existence of such a pledge. And, in fact, there was no such commitment." Efforts to justify our involvement in terms of showing the communists that internal subversion does not pay are also not convincing: would they not have already learned from Greece, Malaya, the Phillipines, the Congo and Burma, if this was the lesson that had to be taught? Similarly, how persuasive is the "domino theory" when such big dominoes as China, itself, and also such small ones as Cuba have fallen without creating any noticeable domino effect? Nor can we claim "defense of freedom" as our justification when we consider how undemocratic the governments of South Vietnam have been—from Diem's to Ky's.

Why then are we involved in the war in South Vietnam?

CONTINUED INVOLVEMENT JUSTIFIES PAST INVOLVEMENT . . .

The most direct statement of the reason for our continued involvement is the fact that we are involved: our continued involvement justifies our past involvement. Once involved it is exceedingly difficult to disengage and to admit, thereby, how purposeless and unwitting our past involvement has been. I am stating, in other words, that we are not involved because of any large strategic or moral purpose and that any such purposes we now impute to our involvement are *ex post facto* rationalizations.

As a nation, we stumbled into the conflict in South Vietnam under the mistaken assumption that "victory might come easily and with little pain." At every step of increasing involvement, we were led to believe that with some small additional help (economic aid, then military advisers, then the use of American helicopters, then the combat use of American soldiers, then massive air intervention by American planes, then bombing of the North, then massive intervention of American troops, and so on) we would not risk a major conflict but yet would help to build an independent, stable country that could stand on its own feet. We have over and over again acted on the tempting assumption that with just a little more investment we would prevent the whole thing from going down the drain.

This type of assumption is one with which

we are familiar in connection with the psychology of gambling. We all know of the losing gambler, getting deeper and deeper into a hole, who keeps on betting with the hope that by so doing he will recover his initial losses. Not all losing gamblers submit to the gambler's temptation of course. But those whose sense of omnipotence is at stake, those who are too proud to recognize that they cannot overcome the odds against them are vulnerable to this type of disastrous temptation. Are we, as a nation, so committed to a view of ourselves as omnipotent that we cannot recognize that we are making the wrong gamble?

GRADUAL AND UNWITTING COMMITMENT

In addition to the gambler's temptation, I shall describe briefly three other processes of gradual and unwitting commitment. One is the much-discussed process of *dissonance-reduction*. As Festinger (1961) has pointed out: "rats and people come to love the things for which they have suffered." Presumably they do so in order to reduce the dissononce induced by the suffering and their method of dissonance-reduction is to enhance the attractiveness of the choice which led to their suffering: only if what one chose was really worthwhile would all of the associated suffering be tolerable. Have we not increased what we perceive to be at stake in the Vietnam conflict as it has become more and more costly for us? We are now at the point where we are told that our national honor, our influence as a world leader, our national security are in the balance in the conflict over this tragic little land.

Silvan Tomkins (Tomkins and Izard, 1965) has described a process of *circular, incremental magnification* which also helps to explain the widening of involvement and the monopolization of thought. He suggests that it occurs if there is a sequence of events of this type: threat, successful defense, breakdown of defense and re-emergence of threat, second successful new defense, second breakdown of defense and re-emergence of threat, and so on until an expectation is generated that no matter how successful a defense against a dreaded contingency may seem, it will prove unavailing and require yet another defense. This process is circular and incremental since each new threat requires a more desperate defense and the successive breakdown of each newly

improved defense generates a magnification of the nature of the threat and the concurrent affect which it evokes. The increasing and obsessive preoccupation with Vietnam may, in part, reflect just such a process: time and time again, we have assumed that a new and more powerful defense or assault against the Vietcong would do the trick only to find that a new and more powerful military commitment was required. By now, according to newspaper reports, Vietnam almost monopolizes the thinking of our national leaders and the attention given to more fundamental concerns is minimized.

SITUATIONAL ENTRAPMENT

Let me, finally, turn to an everyday process of unwitting involvement: *situational entrapment*. The characteristic of this process is that behavior is typically initiated under the assumption that the environment is complaint rather than reactive—that it responds as a tool for one's purposes rather than as a self-maintaining system. Well-intentioned actions sometimes produce effects opposite to those intended because the actions do not take into account the characteristics of the setting in which they take place. By now, we are all aware that an unintended consequence of some public health measures in Latin America was the population explosion. Only now, are we beginning to recognize that some consequences of the types of aid we have given to some underdeveloped countries is to hinder their economic development and to foster a need for ever-increasing aid. Similarly, one may propose that the nature of the American intervention in Vietnam has served to weaken the opposition to the Vietcong, demoralize those in Vietnam who were able and willing to rely on the Vietnamese to solve their problems without foreign control, increase the strength and resolution of the Vietcong, and otherwise produce the responses which would require an increasing involvement and commitment of American resources and men just to prevent an immediate overturn of the situation.

I have used the war in Vietnam to illustrate the process of unwitting involvement in the intensification of conflict. It could also be used to indicate the consequences of a competitive process of resolving our conflicts with Communist China, North Vietnam, and the Vietcong. There has been little in the way of open and honest communication, there has been massive and mutual misperception and misunderstanding, there has been intense mutual suspicion and hostility, there has been derogation of the possibilities of agreement other than those imposed by force, there has been a widening of the scope of the issues in conflict and an escalation of the force employed, and there was an increasing attempt to polarize loyalties and allegiances about this one area of conflict.

A destructive conflict such as the one in which we have been engaged in Vietnam can be brought to a conclusion because the costs of continuing the conflict becomes so large in relation to any values that might be obtained through its continuance that its senselessness becomes compellingly apparent. The senselessness is likely to be most apparent to those who have not been the decision-makers and thus have little need to justify the conflict, and to those who bear the costs most strongly. Destructive conflict can, also, be aborted before running its full course if there is a strong enough community or strong third parties who can compel the conflicting parties to end their violence. We in the United States are in the unfortunate position that relative to our prestige and power there is neither a disinterested third party nor an international community that is powerful enough to motivate us to accept a compromise when we think our own interests may be enhanced by the outcome of a competitive struggle. Peace in Vietnam might have occurred much earlier if the UN, or even our friends, could have influenced us.

Productive Conflict

It has been long recognized that conflict is not inherently pathological or destructive. Its very pervasiveness suggests that it has many positive functions. It prevents stagnation, it stimulates interest and curiosity, it is the medium through which problems can be aired and solutions arrived at; it is the root of personal and social change. Conflict is often part of the process of testing and assessing oneself and, as such, may be highly enjoyable as one experiences the pleasure of the full and active use of one's capacities. Conflict, in addition,

demarcates groups from one another and, thus, helps to establish group and personal identities; external conflict often fosters internal cohesiveness. Moreover, as Coser (1956, 154) has indicated:

> In loosely-structured groups and open societies, conflict, which aims at a resolution of tension between antagonists, is likely to have stabilizing and integrative functions for the relationship. By permitting immediate and direct expression of rival claims, such social systems are able to readjust their structures by eliminating the sources of dissatisfaction. The multiple conflicts which they experience may serve to eliminate the causes for dissociation and to re-establish unity. These systems avail themselves, through the toleration and institutionalization of conflict, of an important stabilizing mechanism.

I stress the positive functions of conflict, and I have by no means provided an exhaustive listing, because many discussions of conflict cast it in the role of the villain as though conflict *per se* were the cause of psychopathology, social disorder, war. The question I wish to raise now is whether there are any distinguishing features in the process of resolving conflict which lead to the constructive outcomes? Do lively, productive controversies have common patterns that are distinctive from those characterizing deadly quarrels?

In the Literature . . .

I must confess that as I started to work on this paper I had expected to find in the social science literature more help in answering these questions than I have found so far. The writings, for example, on personality development, unfortunately, have little to say about productive conflict; the focus is on pathological conflict. Similarly, the voluminous literature on social conflict neglects productive conflict between groups. It is true that the long standing negative view of social conflict has yielded to an outlook which stresses the social functions of conflict. Nevertheless, apart from the writings of people connected with the "non-violence" movement little attempt has been made to distinguish between conflicts that achieve social change through a process that is destructive from one that is mutually rewarding to the parties involved in the conflict. Yet change can take place either as it has at Columbia, through a process of confrontation which is costly to the conflicting groups, or it can take place through a process of problem-solving, as it has at Teachers College, which is mutually rewarding to the conflicting groups.

My own predilections have led me to the hunch that the major features of productive conflict resolution are likely to be similar, at the individual level, to the processes involved in creative thinking and, at the social level, to the processes involved in cooperative group problem-solving. Let me first turn to the process involved in creative thinking. For an incisive, critical survey of the existing literature I am indebted to Stein (1968).

Creative Thinking

The creative process has been described as consisting of several overlapping phases. Although various authors differ slightly in characterizing the phases, they all suggest some sequence such as the following:

(a) An initial period which leads to the experiencing and recognition of a problem which is sufficiently arousing to motivate efforts to solve it.

(b) Second, a period of concentrated effort to solve the problem through routine, readily available, or habitual actions.

(c) Then, with the failure of customary processes to solve the problem, there is an experience of frustration, tension, and discomfort which leads to a temporary withdrawal from the problem.

(d) During this incubation period of withdrawal and distancing from the problem it is perceived from a different perspective and is reformulated in a way which permits new orientations to a solution to emerge.

(e) Next, a tentative solution appears in a moment of insight often accompanied by a sense of exhilaration.

(f) Then, the solution is elaborated and detailed and tested against reality. And

(g) finally, the solution is communicated to relevant audiences.

There are three key psychological elements in this process:

(a) the arousal of an appropriate level of motivation to solve the problem;

(b) the development of the conditions which permit the reformulation of the problem once an impasse has been reached; and

(c) the concurrent availability of diverse ideas which can be flexibly combined into novel and varied patterns.

Each of these key elements are subject to influence from social conditions and the personalities of the problem-solvers.

The Arousal of the Optimal Level of Motivation

Consider the arousal of an optimal level of motivation, a level sufficient to sustain problem-solving efforts despite frustrations and impasses and yet not so intense that it overwhelms or that it prevents distancing from the problem. Neither undue smugness nor satisfaction with things as they are nor a sense of helplessness, terror, or rage are likely to lead to an optimal motivation to recognize and face a problem or conflict. Nor will a passive readiness to acquiesce to the demands of the environment; nor will the willingness to fit oneself into the environment no matter how poorly it fits oneself. Optimal motivation, rather, presupposes an alert readiness to be dissatisfied with things as they are and a freedom to confront one's environment without excessive fear, combined with a confidence in one's capacities to persist in the face of obstacles. The intensity of motivation that is optimal will vary with the effectiveness with which it can be controlled: the more effective the controls, the more intense the motivation can be without its having disruptive consequences.

Thus, one of the creative functions of conflict resides in its ability to arouse motivation to solve a problem which might otherwise go unattended. A scholar who exposes his theories and research to the scrutiny of his peers may be stimulated to a deeper analysis when he is confronted with conflicting data and theoretial analysis by a colleague. Similarly, individuals and groups who have authority and power and who are satisfied with the status quo may be aroused to recognize problems and be motivated to work on them as opposition from the dissatisfied makes the customary relations and arrangements unworkable and unrewarding. They may be motivated also by being helped to perceive the possibilities of more satisfying relations and arrangements. Acceptance of the necessity of a change in the status quo rather than a rigid, defensive adherence to previously existing positions is most likely, however, when the circumstances arousing new motivations suggest courses of action that contain minimal threat to the social or self-esteem of those who must change.

Threats Induce Defensiveness

Thus, although acute dissatisfaction with things as they are, on the one hand, and the motivation to recognize and work at problems on the other, are necessary for creative solutions, they are not sufficient. The circumstances conducive to creativity are varied, but they have in common that "they provide the individual with an environment in which he does not feel threatened and in which he does not feel under pressure. He is relaxed but alert" (Stein, 1968). Threat induces defensiveness and reduces the tolerance of ambiguity as well as openness to the new and unfamiliar; excessive tension leads to a primitivization and stereotyping of thought processes. As Rokeach (1960) has pointed out, threat and excessive tension leads to the "closed" rather than "open" mind. To entertain novel ideas which may at first seem wild and implausible, to question initial assumptions or the framework within which the problem or conflict occurs, the individual needs the freedom or courage to express himself without fear of censure. In addition, he needs to become sufficiently detached from his original viewpoints to be able to see the conflict from new perspectives.

Although an unpressured and unthreatening environment facilitates the restructuring of a problem or conflict, and, by so doing, makes it more amenable to solution, the ability to re-

formulate a problem and to develop solutions is, in turn, dependent upon the availability of cognitive resources. Ideas *are* important for the creative resolution of conflict, and any factor which broadens the range of ideas and alternatives cognitively available to the participants in a conflict will be useful. Intelligence, the exposure to diverse experiences, an interest in ideas, a preference for the novel and complex, a receptivity to metaphors and analogies, the capacity to make remote associations, independence in judgment, the ability to play with ideas are some of the personal factors which characterize creative problem-solvers. The availability of ideas is also dependent upon social conditions such as the opportunity to communicate with and be exposed to other people who may have relevant and unfamiliar ideas (i.e., experts, impartial outsiders, people with similar or analogous situations), a social atmosphere which values innovation and originality and which encourages the exchange of ideas, and a social tradition which fosters the optimistic view that, with effort and time, constructive solutions can be discovered or invented to problems which seem initially intractable.

Let me note that in my view the application of full cognitive resources to the discovery and invention of constructive solutions of conflict is relatively rare. Resources are much more available for the waging of conflict. The research and development expenditures on techniques of conflict-waging or conflict suppression, as well as the actual expenditures on conflict-waging, dwarf the expenditures for peace-building. This is obviously true at the national level where military expenditures dominate our national budget. I would contend that this is also true at the interpersonal and intergroup levels. At the interpersonal level, most of us receive considerable training in waging or suppressing conflict and we have elaborate institutions for dealing with adversary relations and for custodial care of the psychological casualties of interpersonal conflict. In contrast, there is little formal training in techniques of constructive conflict resolution, and the institutional resources for helping people to resolve conflicts are meagre indeed.

Cooperative Problem-solving

In a cooperative context, a conflict can be viewed as a common problem in which the conflicting parties have the joint interest of reaching a mutually satisfactory solution. As I have suggested earlier in the paper, there is nothing inherent in most conflicts which makes it impossible for the resolution of conflict to take place in a cooperative context through a cooperative process. It is, of course, true that the occurrence of cooperative conflict resolution is less likely in certain circumstances and in certain types of conflict than in others. We shall consider some of the predisposing circumstances in a later section.

There are a number of reasons why a cooperative process is likely to lead to productive conflict resolution:

(a) It aids open and honest communication of relevant information between the participants. The freedom to share information enables the parties to go beneath the manifest to the underlying issues involved in the conflict and, thereby, to facilitate the meaningful and accurate definition of the problems they are confronting together. It also enables each party to benefit from the knowledge possessed by the other and, thus, to face the joint problem with greater intellectual resources. In addition, open and honest communication reduces the likelihood of the development of misunderstandings which can lead to confusion and mistrust.

(b) It encourages the recognition of the legitimacy of each other's interests and of the necessity of searching for a solution which is responsive to the needs of each side. It tends to limit rather than expand the scope of conflicting interests and, thus, minimizes the need for defensiveness. It enables the participants to approach the mutually acknowledged problem in a way which utilizes their special talents and enables them to substitute for one another in their joint work so that duplication of effort is reduced. Influence attempts tend to be limited to processes of persuasion. The enhancement of mutual resources and mutual power become objectives.

(c) It leads to a trusting, friendly attitude which increases sensitivity to similarities and common interests, while minimizing the salience of differences. However, one of the common pathologies of cooperation (Deutsch, 1962a) is expressed in premature agreement: a superficial convergence in beliefs and values before the underlying differences have been exposed.

It can be seen that a cooperative process produces many of the characteristics that are conducive to creative problem-solving—openness, lack of defensiveness, full utilization of available resources. However, in itself, cooperation does not insure that problem-solving efforts will be successful. Such other factors as the imaginativeness, experience, and flexibility of the parties involved are also determinative. Nevertheless, if the cooperative relationship is a strong one, it can withstand failure and temporarily deactivate or postpone conflict. Or, if it cannot be delayed, cooperative relations will help to contain destructive conflict so that the contest for supremacy occurs under agreed-upon rules.

Controlled Competitive Conflict

So far my discussion has centered on unregulated conflict. I have considered characteristics of a destructive competitive process in which the outcomes are determined by a power struggle and also those of a cooperative process in which the outcomes are determined by joint problem-solving. However, it is evident that competitive conflict, because of its destructive potential, is rarely unregulated. It is limited and controlled by institutional forms (e.g., collective bargaining, the judicial system), social roles (mediators, conciliators, referees, judges, policemen), social norms ("fairness," "justice," "equality," "nonviolence," "integrity of communication," etc.), rules for conducting negotiations (when to initiate and terminate negotiations, how to set an agenda, how to present demands, etc.), and specific procedures ("hinting" versus "explicit" communication, public versus private sessions, etc.). These societal forms may be aimed at regulating how force may be employed (as in the code of a duel of honor or in certain rules of warfare), or it may be an attempt to ascertain the basic power relations of the disputants without resort to a power struggle (as is often the case in the negotiations of collective bargaining and international relations), or it may be oriented toward removing power as the basis for determining the outcome of conflict (as is often the case in judicial processes).

With regard to regulated conflict, it is pertinent to ask what are the conditions which make it likely that the regulations will be adhered to by the parties in conflict? In a duel of honor, when would a duelist prefer to die rather than cheat? These questions, if pursued along relevant intellectual lines would lead to an examination of different forms of rule violation and social deviance, their genesis and control. Such an investigation is beyond the scope of this paper. However, it seems reasonable to assert that adherence to the rules is more likely when: (a) the rules are known, unambiguous, consistent, and unbiased; (b) the other adheres to the rules; (c) violations are quickly known by significant others; (d) there is significant social approval for adherence and significant social disapproval for violation; (e) adherence to the rules has been rewarding while uncontrolled conflict has been costly in the past; and (f) one would like to be able to employ the rules in future conflicts. Undoubtedly, the most critical influence serving to encapsulate and control competitive conflict is the existence of common membership in a community which is strong enough to evoke habitual compliance to its values and procedures and also confident enough of its strength to tolerate internal struggles.

There are several productive possibilities which inhere in regulated conflict. It provides a basis for resolving a conflict when no other basis for agreement can be reached: "first choice" goes to the winner of the contest. However, the winner is not necessarily the sole survivor as may be the case in an uncontrolled test of power. The values and procedures regulating the conflict may select the winner on some other basis than the relative combat strength of the contestants. A conflict between husband and wife or between the United States and one of its citizens may be settled by a judicial process which permits the contestant with a stronger legal claim to win even though his physical prowess may be weaker. Or, the rules may make the contest

one of intellectual rather than physical power. Thus, by the regulation of conflict a society may encourage the survival of certain values and the extinction of others because the rules for conducting conflict reflect the values of the society.

Also, insofar as a framework for limiting a conflict exists it may encourage the development of the conflict sufficiently to prevent "premature cooperation." The fear of the consequences of unrestrained conflict may lead to a superficial, unsatisfying and unstable agreement before the underlying issues in the conflict have been worked through. The freedom to push deeper into a conflict because some of its potential dangers have been eliminated is, of course, one of the characteristics of creative conflict resolution. However, for the conflict to be contained as it deepens, there must be a community which is strong enough to bind the conflicting parties to the values and procedures regulating conflict. If the direct or mediated cooperative interests of the conflicting parties are weak, the control process is likely to fail or be subverted; the agreements arrived at will be challenged and undermined; conflict will escalate and take a destructive turn. Effective regulation presupposes a firm basis of confidence in the mutual allegiance to the procedures limiting conflict.

Conditions Which Influence the Course of Conflict Resolution

I now turn to a consideration of the factors which tend to elicit one or the other process of conflict resolution. First, I shall consider the question: What gives rise to a destructive or constructive course of conflict? Next, I shall consider the more difficult question: What can be done to change a destructive conflict into a constructive one?

Factors Determining the Course of Conflict

There are innumerable specific factors which may influence the course which a conflict takes. It is useful to have some simplifying outline that highlights central determinants and permits a proliferation of detail as this becomes necessary.

Process

In the preceding sections, I have indicated that the characteristic strategies and tactics elicited by cooperative and competitive processes tend to be self-confirming and self-perpetuating. The strategy of power and the tactics of coercion, threat, and deception result from and result in a competitive orientation. Similarly, the strategy of mutual problem-solving and the tactics of persuasion, openness, and sharing elicit and are elicited by a cooperative orientation. However, cooperation which is reciprocated by competition is more likely to end up as mutual competition than mutual cooperation.

Prior Relationship

The stronger and the more salient the existing cooperative as compared with the competitive bonds linking the conflicting parties, the more likely it is that a conflict will be resolved cooperatively. The total strength of the cooperative bonds is a function of their importance as well as their number. There are obviously many different types of bonds that could be enumerated: superordinate goals, mutually facilitating interests, common allegiances and values, linkages to a common community, and the like. These bonds are important to the extent that they serve significant needs successfully. Thus, experiences of successful prior cooperative relationships together enhance the likelihood of present cooperation; experiences of failure and disillusionment in attempts to cooperate make it unlikely. On the other hand, the past experience of costly competitive conflict does not necessarily enhance the probability of cooperation, although this is a possible result.

The Nature of the Conflict

Here I wish to highlight several major dimensions of conflict: the size (scope, importance, centrality), rigidity, and interconnectedness of the issues in conflict.

Roger Fisher (1964), in a brilliant paper entitled "Fractionating Conflict," has pointed out that "issue control" may be as important as "arms control" in the management of conflict. His thesis is the familiar one that small con-flicts are easier to resolve than large ones. However, he also points out that the participants may have a choice in defining the conflict as a large or small one. Conflict is enlarged by dealing with it as a conflict between large rather than small units (as a conflict between two individuals of different races or as a racial conflict), as a conflict over a large substantive issue rather than a small one (over "being treated fairly" or "being treated unfairly at a particular occasion"), as a conflict over a principle rather than the application of a principle, as a conflict whose solution establishes large rather than small substantive or procedural precedents. Many other determinants of conflict size could be listed. For example, an issue which bears upon self-esteem or change in power or status is likely to be more important than an issue which does not. Illegitimate threat or attempts to coerce are likely to increase the size of the conflict and thus increase the likelihood of a competitive process.

"Issue rigidity" refers to the availability of satisfactory alternatives or substitutes for the outcomes initially at stake in the conflict. Although motivational and intellectual rigidity may lead the parties in conflict to perceive issues more rigidly than reality dictates, it is also evident that certain issues are less conducive to cooperative resolution than others. "Greater power over the other," "victory over the other," "having more status than the other" are rigid definitions of conflict since it is impossible on any given issue for both parties in conflict to have outcomes which are superior to the other's.

Many conflicts do not, of course, center on only one issue. If the issues are separable or sufficiently uncorrelated, it is possible for one side to gain on one issue and the other side to find satisfaction in another issue. This possibility is enhanced if the parties do not have the same evaluations: if issue A is important to one and not the other, while the reverse is true for issue B.

The Characteristics of the Parties in Conflict

Ideology, personality, and position may lead to a more favorable evaluation of one process than the other. The strategy and tactics associated with competitive struggle may seem more manly or intriguing than those associated with cooperation: consider the contrasting popular images of the soldier and of the diplomat. Similarly, the characteristics of the individual parties to a conflict will help determine the size and rigidity of the issues that they perceive to be in conflict and also their skill and available resources for handling conflict one way or another.

In addition, conflict and dissension within each party may affect the course of conflict between them. Internal conflict will often either increase external belligerence as a tactic to increase internal cohesiveness or lead to external weakness and possibly tempt the other side to obtain a competitive advantage. Internal instability also interferes with cooperative conflict resolution by making it difficult to work out a durable, dependable agreement.

Estimations of Success

Many conflicts have an unplanned, expressive character in which the course of action taken is an expression both of the quality of the relationship between the participants and of the characteristics of the individual participants. Other conflicts are guided by an instrumental orientation in which courses of action are consciously evaluated and chosen in terms of how likely they are to lead to satisfying outcomes. Many factors influencing the estimations of success of the different processes of conflict resolution could be listed. Those who perceive themselves to have a clear superiority in power are likely to favor an unregulated competitive process; those who perceive themselves as having a legal superiority in "rights" are likely to favor adversary relations that are regulated by legal institutions; those who are concerned with the long-range relationships, with the ability to work together in the future are more likely to favor a cooperative process. Similarly, those who have been excluded from the cooperative process and expect the regulations to be stacked against them may think of the competitive process as the only one offering any potential of satisfaction.

Third Parties

The attitudes, strength, and resources of interested third parties are often crucial determinants. Thus, a conflict is more likely to be resolved cooperatively if powerful and prestigeful third parties encourage such a resolution and help to provide problem-solving resources (institutions, facilities, personnel, social norms and procedures) to expedite discovery of a mutually satisfactory solution.

Changing the Course of Conflict

From much that I have stated earlier, it is evident that I believe that a *mutually* cooperative orientation is likely to be the most productive orientation for resolving conflict. Yet it must be recognized that the orientations of the conflicting parties may not be mutual. One side may experience the conflict and be motivated to resolve it; the other side may be content with things as they are and not even aware of the other's dissatisfaction. Or both may recognize the conflict but one may be oriented to a win-lose solution while the other may be seeking a cooperative resolution. We have suggested earlier that the usual tendency for such asymmetries in orientation is to produce a change toward mutual competition rather than mutual cooperation. It is, after all, possible to attack, overcome, or destroy another without his consent but to cooperate with another, he must be willing or, at least, compliant.

How can Acme induce Bolt to cooperate in resolving a conflict if Bolt is not so inclined or if Bolt perceives his interests as antagonistic to Acme's? There is, obviously, no single answer to this question. What answer is appropriate depends upon such factors as: the nature of the conflict, the relative power of Acme and Bolt, the nature and motivation of Bolt's noncooperation, the particular resources and vulnerabilities of each party, and their relationships to third parties. However, it is evident that the search for an answer must be guided by the realization that there are dangers in certain types of influence procedures. Namely, they may boomerang and increase open resistance and alienation or they may merely elicit a sham or inauthentic cooperation with underlying resistance. Inauthentic cooperation is more difficult to change than open resistance because it masks and denies the underlying alienation.

Let me offer some hypotheses about the types of influence procedures which are likely to elicit resistance and alienation:

(a) *Illegitimate techniques* which violate the values and norms governing interaction and influence that are held by the other are alienating (the greater the violation, the more important and the more numerous the values being violated, the greater will be the resistance). It is, of course, true that sometimes an adaptation level effect occurs so that frequently violated norms lose their illegitimacy (as in parking violations); at other times, the accumulation of violations tends to produce an increasingly negative reaction.

(b) *Negative sanctions* such as punishments and threats tend to elicit more resistance than positive sanctions such as promises and rewards. What is considered to be rewarding or punishing may also be influenced by one's adaptation level; the reduction of the level of rewards which are customarily received will usually be viewed as negative.

(c) Sanctions which are *inappropriate* in kind are also likely to elicit resistance. Thus, the reward of money rather than appreciation may decrease the willingness to cooperate of someone whose cooperation is engendered by affiliative rather than utilitarian motives. Similarly, a threat or punishment is more likely to be effective if it fits the crime than if its connection with the crime is artificial. A child who breaks another child's toy is punished more appropriately if he has to give the child a toy of his own as a substitute than if he is denied permission to watch TV.

(d) Influence which is *excessive* in magnitude tends to be resisted; excessive promise or reward leads to the sense of being bribed, excessive threat or punishment leads to the feeling of being coerced.

These factors summate. Illegitimate threat which is inappropriate and excessive is most likely to elicit resistance and alienation while an appropriate legitimate reward is least likely to do so. Inauthentic cooperation, with covert resistance, is most likely when resistance is high and when bribery or coercion elicits overt compliance.

What Action Induces Cooperation?

I have, so far, outlined what one should *not* do if one wants to elicit authentic cooperative conflict resolution. Let me turn now to the question of what courses of action can be taken which are likely to induce cooperation. In so doing, I wish to focus on a particularly important kind of conflict: conflict between those groups who have considerable authority to make decisions and relatively high control over the conventional means of social and political influence and those groups who have little decision-making authority and relatively little control over the conventional means of influence.

Although there have always been conflicts between the ruler and the ruled, between parents and children, and between employers and employees, I suggest that this is the characteristic conflict of our time. It arises from the increasing demand for more power and prosperity from those who have been largely excluded from the processes of decision-making usually to their economic, social, psychological, and physical disadvantage. The racial crisis in the United States, the student upheavals throughout the world, the revolutionary struggles in the underdeveloped areas, the controversies within and between nations in Eastern Europe, and the civil war in South Vietnam: all of these conflicts partly express the growing recognition at all levels of social life that social change is possible, that things do not have to remain as they are, that one can participate in the shaping of one's environment and improve one's lot.

Role Satisfaction

It is evident that those who are satisfied with their roles in and the outcomes of the decision-making process may develop both a vested interest in preserving the existing arrangements and appropriate rationales to justify their positions. These rationales generally take the form of attributing superior competence (more ability, knowledge, skill) and, or, superior moral value (greater initiative, drive, sense of responsibility, self-control) to oneself compared to those of lower status. From the point of view of those in power, lack of power and affluence is "little enough punishment" for people so incapable and so deficient in morality and maturity that they have failed to make their way in society. The rationales supporting the status quo are usually accompanied by corresponding sentiments which lead their possessors to react with disapproval and resistance to attempts to change the power relations and with apprehension and defensiveness to the possibility that these attempts will succeed. The apprehension is often a response to the expectation that the change will leave one in a powerless position under the control of those who are incompetent and irresponsible or at the mercy of those seeking revenge for past injustices.

If such rationales, sentiments, and expectations have been developed, those in power are likely to employ one or more defense mechanisms in dealing with the conflict-inducing dissatisfactions of the subordinated group: *denial*, which is expressed in a blindness and insensitivity to the dissatisfactions and often results in an unexpected revolt; *repression*, which pushes the dissatisfactions underground and often eventuates in a guerrilla-type warfare; *aggression*, which may lead to a masochistic sham cooperation or escalated counter-agression; *displacement*, which attempts to divert the responsibility for the dissatisfactions into other groups and, if successful, averts the conflict temporarily; *reaction-formation*, which allows expressions of concern and guilt to serve as substitutes for action to relieve the dissatisfaction of the underprivileged and, in so doing, may temporarily confuse and mislead those who are dissatisfied; *sublimation*, which attempts to find substitute solutions— e.g., instead of increasing the decision-making power of Harlem residents over their schools, provide more facilities for the Harlem schools.

What Can a Less Powerful Group Do?

What can a less powerful group (Acme) do to reduce or overcome the defensiveness of a more powerful group (Bolt) and to increase the latter's readiness to share power? Suppose, in effect, that as social scientists we were consultants to the poor and weak rather than to the rich and strong, what would we suggest? Let me note that this would be an unusual and new position for most of us. If we have given any advice at all, it has been to those in high power. The unwitting consequence of this one-sided consultant role has been that we have too often assumed that the social pathology has been in the ghetto rather than in those who have built the walls to surround it, that the "disadvantaged" are the ones who need to be changed rather than the people and the institutions who have kept the disadvantaged in a submerged position. It is not that we should detach ourselves from "Headstart," "Vista," and various other useful training and remedial programs for the disadvantaged. Rather, we should have an appropriate perspective on such programs. It is more important that the educational institutions, the economic and political systems be changed so that they will permit those groups who are now largely excluded from important positions of decision-making to share power than to try to inculcate new attitudes and skills in those who are excluded. After all, would we not expect that the educational achievements of black children would be higher than they are now if school boards had more black members and schools had more black principals? Would we not also expect that the occupational attainment of blacks would be higher (and their unemployment rate lower) if General Motors, A.T. and T., and General Electric had some black board members and company presidents as well as white ones? Again, would we not expect more civil obedience in the black community if Charles Evers rather than James Eastland were chairman of the Senate Judiciary Committee and if the House had barred corrupt white congressmen as well as Adam Clayton Powell? Let us not lose sight of what and who has to be changed, let us recognize where the social pathology really is!

Attention, Comprehension, Acceptance

But given the resitance and defensiveness of those in high power, what can we recommend to those in low power as a strategy of persuasion? As Hovland, Janis, and Kelley (1953) have pointed out, the process of persuasion involves obtaining the other's *attention, comprehension,* and *acceptance* of the message that one is communicating. The process of persuasion, however, starts with the communicator having a message that he wants to get across to the other. He must have an objective if he is to be able to articulate a clear and compelling message. Further, in formulating and communicating his message, it is important to recognize that it will be heard not only by the other, but also by one's own group and by other interested audiences. The desirable effects of a message on its intended audience may be negated by its unanticipated effects on those for whom it was not intended. I suggest that the following generalized message contains the basic elements of what Acme must communicate to Bolt to change him and, in addition, it is a message which can be overheard by other audiences without harmful consequences. Admittedly, it must be communicated in a way which elicits Bolt's attention, comprehension, and acceptance of its credibility rather than in the abstract, intellectualized form in which it is presented below. And, of course, the generalized objective of equality must be detailed in terms of specific relations in specific contexts.

I am dissatisfied with our relationship and the effects it has. I think it can be improved in ways which will benefit you as well as me. I am sufficiently discontent that I can no longer continue in any relationship with you in which I do not participate as an equal in making the decisions which affect me as well as you, except as a temporary measure while we move toward equality. This may upset and discomfort you but I have no alternative other than to disengage myself from all forms of inauthentic cooperation: my dignity as well as pressure from my group will no longer allow me to engage in this self-deception and self-abasement. Neither coercion nor bribery will be effective; my self-respect and my group will force me to resist them. I remain prepared to cooperate with you as an equal in working on joint problems, including the problems involved in redefining our relationship to one another. I

expect that changing our relationship will not be without its initial difficulties for both of us; we will be uncertain and perhaps suspicious, we will misunderstand and disagree and regress to old habits from time to time. I am willing to face these difficulties. I invite you to join with me to work toward improving our relationship, to overcome your dissatisfactions as well as mine. I believe that we both will feel more self-fulfilled in a relationship that is not burdened by inauthenticity.

It would take too long to detail all of the elements in this message and their rationales. But essentially the message commits Acme irreversibly to his objective, self-esteem and social esteem are at stake; he will be able to live neither with himself nor his group if he accepts an inferior status. This is done not only in words but also by the style of communicating which expresses a self-confident equality and competence. It provides Bolt with the prospect of positive incentives for changing and negative ones for not changing; Acme maintains a cooperative stance throughout and develops in action the possibility of a true mutual exchange by expressing the awareness that dissatisfactions are not onesided. It also inoculates against some of the expected difficulties involved in change. It should be noted that Acme's statements of the threats faced by Bolt if change is not forthcoming (the instrumental threat of noncooperation, the moral threat that the status quo violates important social norms concerning human dignity and authenticity, the threat of resistance to coercion) are neither arbitrary, illegitimate, coercive, nor demanding to Bolt—i.e., they are not strongly alienating.

Rage or Fear Handicaps . . .

Rage or fear in the low power group often makes it impossible for them to communicate a message of the sort that I have described above. Rage leads to an emphasis on destructive, coercive techniques and precludes offers of authentic cooperation. Fear, on the other hand, weakens the commitment to the steps necessary to induce a change and lessens the credibility that compliance will be withdrawn if change does not occur. Although it is immediately destructive, rage is potentially a more useful emotion than fear since it leads to bold actions which are less damaging to the development of a sense of power and, hence, of self-esteem. And these latter are necessary for authentic cooperation. Harnessed rage or outrage can be a powerful energizer for determined action, and if this action is directed toward building one's own power rather than destroying the other's power, the outrage may have a socially constructive outcome.

In any case, it is evident that when intense rage or fear are the dominant emotions, the cooperative message that I have outlined is largely irrelevant. Both rage and fear are rooted in a sense of helplessness and powerlessness: they are emotions associated with a state of dependency. Those in low power can overcome these debilitating emotions by their own successful social action on matters of significance to them. In the current slang, they have got to "do their own thing", it cannot be given to them nor done for them. This is why my emphasis throughout this discussion has been on the sharing of power, and thus increasing one's power to affect one's fate, rather than on the sharing of affluence. While the sharing of affluence is desirable, it is not sufficient. In its most debilitating sense, "poverty" is a lack of power and not merely a lack of money. Money is, of course, a base for power but it is not the only one. If one chooses to be poor, as do some members of religious or pioneering groups, the psychological syndrome usually associated with imposed poverty—a mixture of dependency, apathy, small time perspective, suspicion, fear, and rage—is not present.

Authentic Cooperation

Thus, the ability to offer and engage in authentic cooperation presupposes an awareness that one is neither helpless nor powerless, even though one is at a relative disadvantage. Not only independent action but also cooperative action requires a recognition and confirmation of one's capacity to "go it alone" if necessary. Unless one has the freedom to choose not to cooperate, there can be no free choice to cooperate. "Black power" is, thus, a

necessity for black cooperation: of black cooperation with blacks as well as with whites. Powerlessness and the associated lack of self and group esteem are not conducive either to internal group cohesiveness or to external cooperation. "Black power" does not, however, necessarily lead to white cooperation. This is partly because, in its origin and rhetoric, "black power" may be oriented against "white power" and thus is likely to intensify the defensiveness of those with high power. When "black power" is primarily directed against "whitey" rather than for "blacks," it is, of course, to be expected that "whitey" will retaliate. The resulting course of events may provide some grim satisfaction to those despairing blacks who prefer to wield even short-lived destructive power rather than to be ineffectual and to those whites who prefer to be ruthless oppressors rather than to yield the psychic gains of pseudo-superiority.

However, even if "power" is "for" rather than "against" and provides a basis for authentic cooperation, cooperation may not occur because it is of little import to the high power group. It may be unaffected by the positive or negative incentives that the low power group control; it does not need their compliance. Universities can obtain new students; the affluent nations no longer are so dependent upon the raw materials produced in the underdeveloped nations; the white industrial society does not need many unskilled Negro workers.

What Can the Group Do for Itself?

What can the low power group do in such situations? First of all, theoretically it may be possible to "opt out" more or less completely—to withdraw, to migrate, to separate so that one is no longer in the relationship. However, as the world and the societies composing it become more tightly knit, this option becomes less and less available in its extreme forms. Black communities can organize their own industries, schools, hospitals, shopping centers, consumer cooperatives, and the like but only if they have resources, and these resources would be sharply curtailed if their relationship with the broader society were completely disrupted. Similarly, students can organize their own seminars, their own living communes, their own bookstores, but it would be difficult for them to become proficient in many of the sciences and professions without using the resources available in the broader academic community. Self-imposed "apartheid" is self-defeating. "Build baby build" is a more useful slogan than "out baby out" or "burn baby burn."

Through building its own institutions and developing its own resources a low power group makes itself less vulnerable to exploitation and also augments its power by providing itself with alternatives to inauthentic cooperation. In so doing, it increases the likelihood that those in high power will be responsive to a change: the positive incentives for changing and the negative incentives for not changing take on greater value. Moreover, such self-constructive action may help to reduce the fears and stereotypes which underlie much of the defensiveness of high power groups.

In addition to the strategy of developing one's own resources and building one's own institutions, there are still other strategies that can be followed by a low power group in the attempt to influence a reluctant or disinterested high power group. The various strategies are not incompatible with one another. I list several of the major ones: (a) augment its power by collecting or activating subgroups within the high power group or third parties as allies; (b) search for other kinds of connections with the high power group which, if made more salient, could increase its affective or instrumental dependence upon the low power group and thus change the power balance; (c) attempt to change the attitudes of those in high power through education and moral persuasion; (d) use existing legal procedures to bring pressures for change; and (e) use harassment techniques to increase the other's costs of adhering to the status quo.

The effectiveness of any strategy of influence is undoubtedly much determined by the particular circumstances so that no strategy can be considered to be unconditionally effective or ineffective. Nevertheless, it is reasonable to assume that low power groups can rarely afford to be without allies. By definition, a low power group is unlikely to achieve many of its objectives unless it can find allies among significant elements within the high power group or unless it can obtain support from other ("third party") groups that can exert influence on the high power group. There is considerable reason to expect that allies are most likely to be obtained if: (a) they are sought out rather than ignored or rejected; (b) superordinate goals, common values, and common interests can be identified which could serve as a basis for the formation of cooperative bonds; (c) reasonably full communication is maintained with the potential allies; (d) one's objectives and methods are readily perceived as legitimate and feasible; (e) one's tactics dramatize one's objectives and require the potential allies to choose between acting "for" or "against" these objectives and, thus, to commit themselves to taking a position; and (f) those in high power employ tactics, as a counterresponse, which are widely viewed as "unfitting" and thus produce considerable sympathy for the low power group.

Civil Disobedience

There is no time here to elaborate on procedures and tactics of building allies; this is what politics is all about. However, let me just comment about the nonviolent, civil disobedience, confrontation tactics which have been employed with considerable success by civil rights and student groups. These methods have tended, with continuing usage, to have less effect in arousing public response and sympathy for the low power groups involved. In part, this is because many of those in high power have learned that to employ coercion as a response to a nonviolent tactic of civil disobedience is self-defeating; it only serves to swing much of the hitherto uninvolved public behind the demonstrators. This is, of course, what happened in Selma and Birmingham as well as at Columbia University and Chicago when unfitting force was used. These techniques also have become less effective because repeated usage vulgarizes them; a measure which is acceptable as an unusual or emergency procedure becomes unacceptable as a routine breeder of social disruption. Let me note parenthetically that I have discussed "nonviolent, confrontation" tactics as a method for gaining allies and public support rather than as a procedure for directly changing the attitudes of those in high power who are strongly committed to their views. I have seen no evidence that would suggest it has any significant effects of the latter sort.

Finding allies and supporters is important not only because it directly augments the influence of a low power group but also because having allies enables the low power group to use each of the other change strategies more effectively. I shall not discuss the other strategies in detail but confine myself to a brief comment about each. A low power group can increase the dependence of a high power group on it by concentrating its power rather than by allowing it to be spread thinly. Thus, the political power of the Negro vote could be higher if it were able to decide the elections in a half-dozen states such as New York, California, Pennsylvania, Illinois, Ohio, and Michigan than if the Negro vote was less concentrated. Similarly, [Negroes'] economic power would be greater if they were able to obtain control over certain key industries and key unions rather than if they were randomly dispersed.

Education, moral persuasion, and the use of legal procedures to bring about social change have lately come into disrepute because these strategies do not bring "instant change" nor do they produce as much *esprit de corps* as strategies which give rise to direct action techniques. Nevertheless, it would be a mistake to underestimate the importance of beliefs, values, and the sense of legitimacy in determining individual and social action. Similarly, to engage in anti-intellectualism or to ignore the significance of intellectual work in establishing true knowledge is an error. Truth threatens arbitrary power by unmasking its unreasonableness and pretensions. Anti-intellectualism is a tool of the despot in his struggle to silence or discredit truth. Also, it would be a mistake to ignore the tremendous changes in beliefs and values concerning human relationships which have occurred during the recent past. Much of

the evil which now occurs is not a reflection of deliberate choice to inflict such evil but rather the lack of a deliberate choice to overcome self-perpetuating vicious cycles. Obviously, a considerable educational effort is needed to help broaden the understanding of conflict and to accelerate growth in the ability to include others in the same moral community with oneself even though they be of rather different social, economic, and ethnic background.

Harassment

Harassment may be the only effective strategy available to a low power group if it faces an indifferent or hostile high power group. Although sharp lines cannot be drawn, it is useful to distinguish "harassment," "obstruction," and "destruction" from one another. "Harassment" employs legal or semilegal techniques to inflict a loss, to interfer with, disrupt or embarrass those with high power; "obstruction" employs illegal techniques to interrupt or disrupt the activities and purposes of those in high power; "destruction" employs illegal, violent techniques to destroy or to take control over people or property. Obstructive and destructive techniques invite massive retaliation and repression which, if directed against harassment techniques, would often seem inappropriate and arouse sympathy. However, a clearly visible potential for the employment of obstructive and destructive techniques may serve to make harassment procedures both more acceptable and more effective.

There are many forms of harassment which can be employed by low power groups: consumer boycotts; work slowdowns; rent strikes; demonstrations; sit-ins; tying up phones, mail, government offices, businesses, traffic, etc. by excessive and prolonged usage; ensnarling bureaucratic systems in their own red tape by requiring them to follow their own formally stated rules and procedures; being excessively friendly and cooperative; creating psychological nuisances by producing outlandish behavior, appearances, and odors in stores, offices, and other public places; encouraging contagion of the ills of the slum (rats, uncollected garbage, etc.) to surrounding communities; etc. Harassment, as is true for most procedures, is undoubtedly most effective when it is employed to obtain well-defined, specific objectives and when it is selectively focussed on key persons and key institutions rather than when it is merely a haphazard expression of individual discontent.

In Conclusion . . .

As I review what I have written in this last section, where I have functioned as a self-appointed consultant to those in low power, I am struck by how little of what I have said is well-grounded in systematic research or theory. As social scientists we have rarely directed our attention to the defensiveness and resistance of the strong and powerful in the face of the need for social change. We have not considered what strategies and tactics are available to low power groups and which of these are likely to lead to a productive rather than destructive process of conflict resolution.

We have focused too much on the turmoil and handicaps of those in low power and not enough on the defensiveness and resistance of the powerful; the former will be overcome as the latter is overcome.

Is it not obvious that with the great disparities in power and affluence within nations and between nations that there will be continuing pressures for social change? And is it not also obvious that the processes of social change will be disorderly and destructive unless those in power are able or enabled to lower their defensiveness and resistance to a change in their relative status? Let us refocus our efforts so that we will have something useful to say to those who are seeking radical but peaceful social change. Too often in the past significant social change in the distribution of power has been achieved at the cost of peace; this is a luxury that the world is no longer able to afford.

References

Coleman, J. S. *Community conflict*. Glencoe: Free Press, 1957.

Coser, L. *The functions of social conflict*. Glencoe: Free Press, 1956

Deutsch, M. Cooperation and trust: some theoretical notes. In M. R. Jones (Ed.), *Nebraska symposium on motivation*. Lincoln: University of Nebraska Press, 1962. (a)

Deutsch, M. A psychological basis for peace. In Q. Wright, W. M. Evan, and M. Deutsch (Eds.), *Preventing World War III: some proposals*. New York: Simon and Schuster, 1962. (b)

Deutsch, M. Conflict and its resolution. Presidential address before the Division of Personality and Social Psychology of the American Psychological Association, September 5, 1965. (a)

Deutsch, M. A psychological approach to international conflict. In G. Sperrazzo (Ed.), *Psychology and international relations*. Washington, D.C.: Georgetown University Press, 1965, (b)

Deutsch, M. Vietnam and the start of World War III: some psychological parallels. Presidential address before the New York State Psychological Association, May 6, 1966.

Deutsch, M. *The resolution of conflict*. New Haven: Yale University Press, (in preparation).

Festinger, L. The psychological effects of insufficient reward. *American Psychologist*, 1961, 16, 1–11.

Fisher, R. Fractionating conflict. In R. Fisher (Ed.), *International conflict and behavioral science: the Craigville papers*. New York: Basic Books, 1964.

Hovland, C. I., Janis, I. L. and Kelley, H. H. *Communication and persuasion*. New Haven: Yale University Press, 1953.

Rokeach, M. *The open and closed mind*. New York: Basic Books, 1960.

Stein, M. I. *The creative individual*. In manuscript, 1968.

Tomkins, S. S. and Izard, C. C. (Eds.), *Affect, cognition, and personality*, New York: Springer Publishing Co., 1965.

11. Power, Influence, and Behavioral Compliance

James T. Tedeschi* • Thomas V. Bonoma**
Barry R. Schlenker*** • Svenn Lindskold****

Social psychologists have traditionally been concerned with problems of social conflict, power, influence, and persuasion. Yet, when one looks for systematic theory and evidence regarding the determinants of behavioral compliance to rules, norms, or influence attempts, few prescriptions can be garnered by the practical man of affairs for developing policy in matters of law and order. In a day when shouts of black power, student protests, and antiwar demonstrations reverberate through the legitimate institutions of the country and when violence commissions report the degree of disorder existing in the urban centers of America, lack of social scientific evidence upon which to base policy is a disquieting comment upon the relevance of social scientific research.

For the past forty years, social psychologists have focused much of their interest upon the processes of attitude formation and change. The assumption motivating such research is that once we know how to measure attitudes, how to understand structural factors involved in belief systems, and how to produce attitude change, then the basis for predicting and controlling behavior will have been established. Unfortunately, after thousands of experiments have been performed and scores of theories have been developed, little evidence has been produced to prove that attitudes mediate behavior in any direct fashion. It is noteworthy that relatively few studies even attempt to establish the relationship between attitudes and behavior, but rather, studies are more concerned with the effects of behavior on attitudes (Festinger, 1964; Rokeach, 1968).

A plausible argument can be made that attitudes and behaviors actually follow different psychological laws and serve parallel but separate functions for the individual. For example, behavior may occur as a simple function of the cost-reward structure of the perceived environment, whereas the verbal expression of attitudes may serve the function of rationalizing the actions as "good" or at least necessary. Durkheim (1951) suggested that persons need to view their own actions as "good." A person who cannot find sufficient justification for his actions in his personal value system is likely to change his attitudes in a manner consonant with his behavior so that he can rationalize his conduct (Festinger, 1957). In addition to the function of rationalization for behavior, expressed attitudes can be used to legitimate a power position (authority) or as influence techniques to gain power over the behavior of other pepole. Also, it is clear that verbal behavior is seldom rewarded or punished to the same degree or in the same circumstances as are other behaviors. A person is brought to trial for a behavior he has allegedly shown, but a man who expresses remorse for his crime is likely to gain a more lenient sentence or to be paroled.

The above arguments provide reason to reject the basic assumption underlying most social-psychological research pertaining to the social influence processes—that a person's attitudes directly mediate his behaviors. Once this assumption is rejected, a number of different research strategies are suggested: (1) study how people use their attitudes for purposes of influence and power, (2) study how individuals use their attitudes to rationalize their behaviors, or (3) focus upon how influence attempts gain behavioral compliance and avoid the pitfalls associated with the labyrinth

Reprinted from J. Tedeschi, T. Bonoma, B. Schlenker, S. Lindskold, "Power, Influence, and Behavioral Compliance," *Law and Society Review*, May 1970, pp. 521–544.
* Professor of Psychology, State University of New York at Albany.
** Instructor of Psychology, State University of New York at Albany.
*** Department of Psychology, State University of New York at Albany.
**** Department of Psychology, Ohio University.

of attitude structures. The last strategy has been adopted by the present authors.

The deliberate attempt by one person to elicit behavioral compliance from another person has been viewed by political scientists, sociologists, and social psychologists as an attempt to use social power or exercise social influence. The concepts of power and influence are sometimes used interchangeably, but some theorists are wont to make fine distinctions between the two terms. The remainder of this paper will review some of the concepts of power and attempt to integrate them into a more comprehensive theory of influence within dyads. Evidence for the theory will be presented and some conclusios of interest to policy makers will be proffered.

Theories of Power and Influence

In our everyday behavior to achieve certain goals and avoid certain unpleasantries, we are inevitably confronted with an obstacle. Whether the obstacle is in the form of the conflicting goals of another with whom we are interacting, or the norms and rules of the group to which we belong, we must decide to reach some mutual accommodation of interests, to exert pressure to achieve an all-or-nothing solution, or to just give up on that particular goal. As long as people desire similar or mutually exclusive goals, and as long as most societies inculcate similar values into their members, social conflict must be engendered. Social conflict may be simply defined as a struggle over values and claims to scarce status, power, and resources in which the aims of the opponents are to neutralize, injure, or eliminate their rivals (Coser, 1956).

In classical sociological thought, conflict was considered dysfunctional and detrimental to the social system. Parsons (1949) thought social conflict was a disease which should be treated by propaganda specialists as a doctor treats his patients. Lewin (1946) desired the social management of conflict to achieve harmony. However, Simmel (1950) has pointed out some of the functional and beneficial effects of change which conflicts permit. Thus, the current view seems to place conflict in the role of a societal stimulant, which, if held within bounds, is essential to the development of progress.

However, whether one views conflict as functional or dysfunctional, beneficial or harmful, it nonetheless pervades all forms of social interaction, and its mitigation can only be temporarily achieved by the exercise of social influence which allows bargaining and the accommodation of interests, or alternatively, a settlement of the conflict in favor of the stronger adversary.

The resolution of conflicting interests has been a central problem in political science and in economics. Social scientists in these disciplines have developed a number of theories of power to help account for both the development and solution of conflicts. However, there has been little agreement as to a definition of power. Schur (1969: 85) defines power as the "ability to determine the behavior of others in accord with one's own wishes." MacIver (1964: 77) similarly considers power to be the "capacity to control, regulate, or direct the behavior of persons or things." Hans Morgenthau (1964) has offered the most general definition of power, which he defines as coextensive with any behavioral changes in one person which can at least partially be attributed to the actions of another person; the latter, as the controlling person or the causative agent, is considered the powerful individual. The breadth of these definitions is almost as broad as the area of social science and yields little precision in theory and no testable predictions either about the use of power or the compliance gained. Yet it can be seen from the above definitions that power and influence are in all social interactions. For example, Deutsch (1966) considers political science to be the study of how compliance is obtained. Similarly, Nieburg (1969) notes that politics is nothing more than the struggle for influence and authority within presently established formal authority structures. In this regard, Lord Acton considered the continental governments, formed atfer the French Revolution, to be based on the people's participation in power, not their security or freedom. Similarly, cries for black power are based not on a vague desire for the value of freedom, but on a share in the socioeconomic power base from which freedom will follow.

The range of a theory of power clearly exceeds the bounds of political science. For example, law was considered by Weber (1954) as orders which are extremely guaranteed by a high probability of coercion, designed to bring about conformity and avenge violations and administered by a group possessing the legitimate right to do so. Thus, whether a subtle and frequently unadmitted power struggle occurs (the word "power" sometimes carries negative connotations in relations between friends) to decide whether the husband plays golf or the wife takes him to the opera, or the more overt struggle for power among nations is the focus of interest, much of social behavior seems ultimately to boil down to the question of how social influence is wielded.

As often happens in the field of science, concepts are continually redefined in an attempt to develop a coherent theory. In this tradition, Harsanyi (1962) suggests that compliance of one party to the wishes of the other constitutes the criterion for the successful exercise of power. In a condition of bilateral power, where each person has some influence over the behavior of the other, the amount of P's power over P and W's joint policy with respect to some controversial issue, "X," is defined as the probability (p) of P's being able to get the joint policy X_p adopted when P favors this policy X_p and W favors a different policy X_w. For Harsanyi, a condition of a power relationship is that two or more individuals have conflicting preferences and a decision must be made as to whose preferences will prevail. Power is a relevant factor in social interactions only where social conflict exists. Harsanyi's analysis has the virtue of attempting to identify the conditions under which power is exercised. However, the possibility of compromise or the failure of a power attempt are not considered nor does the theory indicate the processes by which the conflicting parties resolve their differences.

Parsons (1963) analytically separates the concepts of power and influence. For him, power is a form of abstract currency and legitimacy and relies upon the psychological factor

of trust. The influence processes are conceived as ways of getting results in interaction. In a manner of speaking, it may be said that Parsons' four systems of influence specify the processes by which conflicting parties resolve their differences and, consequently, serve to fill a gap in Harsanyi's theory of power. One form of influence, deterrence, relies on threats, coercion, and punishment for effectiveness. Promises of rewards or inducements constitute a second form of influence. Attempts to restructure the goals or attitudes of target individuals through the use of arguments or propaganda is a process labeled persuasion. Finally, Parsons suggests that the technique of activating commitments by appeals to norms may be effective in gaining compliance because the target individual reassesses what constitutes appropriate behavior for the situation.

Lasswell and Kaplan (1950) have developed a number of base values that they believe serve as basic resources for those who wield power and influence. These base values are respect, moral standing, affection, well-being, skill, wealth, enlightenment, and power (which can be used as a basis for accruing even more power). French and Raven (1959) have also delineated factors which serve as the bases of power. Reward power and coercive power derive from a source's ability to administer reinforcements and punishments and correspond with Parsons' distinction between inducements and deterrence and Lasswell and Kaplan's categories of wealth and power. French and Raven also suggest that a target individual often complies with a source's wishes because the former identifies with or is attracted to the latter—a form of attraction or referent power. Referent power can be viewed as equivalent to the categories of respect and affection in the Lasswell and Kaplan system and both inducements and activation of commitments in Parsons' system. Referent power is clearly related to Schopler and Bateson's (1965) proposal that the dependency needs of the target may be a basis of power for the source. Expert power is defined by French and Raven as a source's ability to persuade a target because of the former's persuasion process and the categories of skill and enlightenment in the typology of Lasswell and Kaplan. Persuasion systems appear also to be equivalent to Jones and Gerard's (1967) notion of information control. The fifth and last basis of power offered by French and Raven depends upon a target's belief that the source of influence deserves compliance because of the latter's role position (legitimate authority). Legitimate power is the only kind of power recognized by some theorists (Parsons, 1963; Gamson, 1968) and is consistent with the categories of moral standing and well-being among the bases of power suggested by Lasswell and Kaplan.

A number of social scientists define power as related to outcome control. March (1955) argues that the greater the power of *P*, the greater the ability of *P* to restrict *W*'s outcomes. Thus, if *P* cannot by his own actions lessen the range or value of outcomes for *W* in a situation, then *P* has no control over the future. Karlsson (1962), a sociologist, argues that the greater the range over which *P* can determine *W*'s rewards, the greater *P*'s power over *W*. At a more operational level of analysis, Thibaut and Kelley (1959) have offered an analysis of outcome control in dyadic interactions where the values in simple two-choice situations yield a matrix of payoffs to the two parties involved. When one player has absolute control over the other's outcomes, regardless of what the latter does, the former is said to possess fate control. Behavior control refers to a situation in which one or both parties in a dyadic interaction partially control the other's outcomes but do not possess fate control.

Many other issues have been raised concerning definitions of power and influence. For example, some reserve power for coercive influence attempts (Bachrach and Baratz, 1963), and others attempt to distinguish between power and force (Lasswell and Kaplan, 1950). However, the above review of concepts of power and influence and some of the factors contributing to compliance indicate that a wide range of phenomena are considered and that the language generally used by theorists (though often heuristic) does not meet the formal criteria expected for scientific theories.

What is clearly needed at this point in the development of social science is a theory of power or influence which takes into consideration some of the analyses and definitions that have so far been offered, and which is clearly and precisely formulated so that testable theorems or predictions can be derived. Science is not just a process of intuitive analysis. It requires that concepts be imbedded in a system of functional relationships which can be empirically evaluated.

Theorists have delineated factors associated with the source of social influence, the types of influence attempts that might be made, the conditions under which influence takes place, and the target's characteristics rendering him influenceable, all of which are important for any theory of social influence. Thus, source characteristics, such as respect, moral standing, affection, wealth, skill, well-being, enlightenment, and power yield credits for future influence attempts. Different means of exercising influence correspond with inducements, deterrence, activation of commitments, and persuasion. The belief by the target-of-influence in the legitimacy of source's authority should be related to the degree of compliance or deference given to the source's influence attempts.

Tedeschi (1968) has developed a theory of social influence within dyads that attempt to capture most of the components of an influence system suggested by the above review of the concepts of power and influence. the theory predicts behavioral compliance by target individuals but also suggests factors relevant to source behaviors. The remainder of this paper will present Tedeschi's theory and will review evidence gathered to evaluate the theory.

A Dyadic Theory of Influence

The theory proposed by Tedeschi is deliberately simplified, first of all, to dyadic interaction and, second, to explicit contingent threats and promises sent from a specified source to a known target. The modes of influence thus correspond to Parsons' categories of deterrence and inducements, French and Raven's types of coercive and reward power, and

Lasswell and Kaplan's bases of wealth and power. The theory is static in that it does not fully discuss opportunities for counterinfluence. The focus is upon behavioral compliance and largely ignores cognitive change (and thus the entire area of social persuasion). The source of influence is presumed to be motivated to maximize gains and has already chosen a target. Although specific characteristics of both source and target are defined operationally and linked to the ongoing influence process, the more complex cognitive factors that presumably help mediate the behaviors of both individuals are deliberately simplified. The result is a testable theory, the value of which will depend upon how well it predicts behavior. The theory is developed in a manner calculated to serve as a basis from which to develop a more complex theory once the simpler components are understood.

The basic components of a theory of influence are a source, a signal system, and a target. The present theory restricts the signal system to explicit contingent threats and promises. A threat takes the form "if-then" and asks for the performance of a behavior or the inhibition of a behavior and specifies the punishment for noncompliance. The punishment is an action, the withholding of an action, the production of a noxious stimulus, or the removal of a positive reinforcement, any of which may be perceived by the target as detrimental, costly, and punishing. Law, the nuclear deterrence system existing between the United States and the Soviet Union, and escalation are all examples of contingent threats. The classical theory of law reasons that if the punishment for noncompliance is large enough, man will stay within the bounds of cultural rules. The deterrence system tries to force decision makers into rational forms of behavior (i.e., aggression below certain specified limits) by the threat of annihilation. Escalation can be viewed as a contingent threat whose punishment is greater than the act which precipitated it (e.g., kill one of my soldiers and I will kill ten of yours). Contingent promises similarly take the form: "if you do X (or not X), then I will do Y," where Y is an action considered beneficial by the target.

Bazelon (1965) has conceptualized the economic system largely in terms of contingent promises. For example, he reviews contracts as mutual contingent promises enforced by a court of law (threat system). Modern paper money can be considered a contract with unknown parties for the future delivery of pleasures which one can decide upon at a later date. A check is a promise from a bank that a bookkeeper will place a mark on his books in the appropriate place. The use of promises in political behavior to gain election support is known by every schoolboy. Advertising is also a promise made by a manufacturer that if their product is used, the purchaser will smell better, have more dates, and be happier than if he went without the product (the credibility of advertisements is another question). Contingent threats and promises thus seem to pervade our lives and are indeed essential for an individual who wants to maximize his outcome attainment when interacting with others who might have dissimilar goals.

The paradigm used for the study of compliance to contingent threats and promises is the message-modified version of the Prisoner's Dilemma game (PDG) developed by Horai and Tedeschi (1969). The important features of the unmodified form of this game are illustrated by Luce and Raiffa (1957:95):

> Two suspects are taken into custody and separated. The District Attorney is certain that they are guilty of a specific crime, but he does not have adequate evidence to convict them at a trial. He points out to each prisoner that he has two alternatives: to confess to the crime the police are sure they have done, or not to confess. If they both do not confess, then the D.A. states he will book them on some very minor trumped-up charge such as petty larceny and illegal possession of a weapon, and they would both receive minor punishments; if they both confess, they will be prosecuted, but he will recommend less than the most severe sentence, but if one confesses and the other does not, then the confessor will receive lenient treatment for turning state's evidence, whereas the latter will get "the book" slapped at him.

Thus, the PDG is a mixed-motive, non-zero-sum game in which both parties can win, both can lose, or one can win while the other loses. In the experimental situation, if both parties cooperate, both can win a certain number of points. If both parties compete, both lose a certain number of points. Finally, if one party competes while the other cooperates, the former will win points while the latter will lose points. A certain degree of conflict is thus built into the situation in that there is a temptation to exploit the other rather than cooperate and face the possibility of being exploited yourself. However, if both parties reason this way, both will continually lose. In the modified PDG, messages (e.g., threats and promises) can be intermittently exchanged by the parties. By using a simulated player as one of the parties, source characteristics, frequency of message use, and strategy selections can be systematically manipulated, and the effects of these independent variables on conflict and compliance can be delineated. All of the studies to be presented used the message-modified PDG as the research tool.

Figure 11.1 presents an overview of the

Figure 11.1.

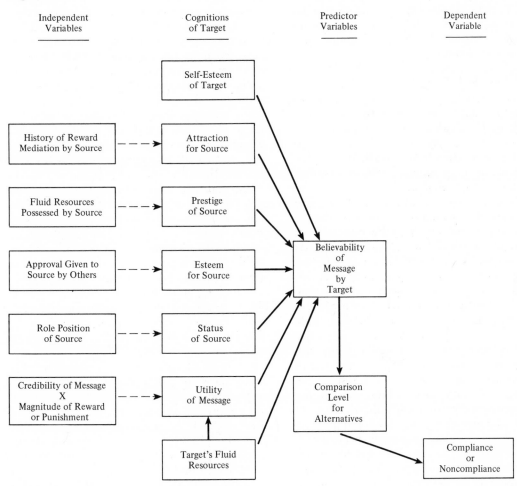

concepts of the theory and indicates the relationships between them. Source characteristics are assumed to be measurable and constitute the independent variables of the theory. Source characteristics must be perceived or interpreted by the target and these second order variables are considered to be cognitive attributes of the taregt which correspond to the objective determination of the characteristics. Each of the second order variables are assumed to have specific functional relationships with the predictor variable, believability of the communication, which if the target cannot or chooses not to "leave the field" for some alternative social relationship, is directly related to behavioral compliance. The specific effects of each of the independent variables on compliance will now be discussed under their appropriate headings.

Reward and Punishment Power

A source of influence who uses promises and threats to obtain compliance to his wishes from a target individual can be expected to be successful in proportion to the degree to which his deeds match his words. If a source offers rewards for compliance but does not follow through by giving the reward when the occasion arises, then the target should begin to doubt his word. Similarly, the believability of threats will be decreased if the target's defiance is not punished. As Nieburg (1969) has observed, the rational goal for the use of violence in carrying out a threat is the demonstration of the will and capability of action, thereby establishing high credibility for future threats. In addition, the degree of magnitude of rewards and punishments should be an important determinant of believability and subsequent compliance. MacIver (1964) notes that obedience to the law is a result of the costs for noncompliance, whether from the actual punishments or from guilt and loss of respect, and the like, being higher than costs of compliance. As has previously been noted, both the classical theory of law and the deterrence system rest on the premise that if the punishment is made severe enough compliance will result.

Source credibility can be operationally de-fined and measured as the proportion of times the source does what he says he will do. Thus, the proportion of times the source rewards compliance to promises is a measure of promise credibility, and the proportion of times the source punishes noncompliance to threats is a measure of threat credibility. It should be noted that these definitions explicitly assume that unsuccessful promises and successful threats have no objective credibility, although there is no presumption that such events either do or do not affect believability. It is quite possible that compliance to threats or noncompliance to promises will have cognitive effects on the targt so that he rationalizes his responses by feeling that he definitely would have been punished had he not complied to the threat, or would definitely not have been rewarded if he had complied to the promise. Such rationalizations could produce increments in believability apart from objective credibility effects.

Since message credibility refers to the probability of an event, and magnitude of reward or punishment refer to the value of the event to the target, the concept of utility, as used by decision theorists and economists, seemed to be applicable to target's perceptions. The concept of utility has been used to express the subjective expected value of a future event perceived by a particular individual and is presumed to mediate the individual's choices (holding all else constant). The relationship between probability and value is usually believed to be multiplicative (Edwards et al., 1965). In a controlled laboratory experiment, both message credibility and value can be specified and measured. If the multiplicative relationship of credibility and value is assumed to be directly related to target's perception of message utility, and utility is assumed to be functionally related to believability, it can be predicted that compliance will be a direct function of message utility. Horai and Tedeschi (1969) were the first to test the relationship of message utility and compliance, and found that compliance to threats was a direct linear function of both credibility and punishment magnitude. The finding that as the negative utility of threats increases, compliance by target individuals also increases has been replicated a number of times (Lindskold et al., 1969; Faley and Tedeschi, 1969).

Tedeschi et al. (1968) found that when the punishment magnitude threatened for noncompliance was no greater than the costs to target for complying, the target resisted the threats, irrespective of message credibility. This result implies that the target is not indifferent when the punishment for noncompliance equals the costs of compliance but in fact derives some satisfaction from depriving the source of the gains to be gotten from the target's compliant behavior. Also, it could be inferred that when significant target values are at stake, threats are unlikely to be effective in gaining compliance.

It is quite clear that promises are not merely symmetrical to threats in that the former offers rewards and the latter offers punishments. Several studies (Lindskold and Tedeschi, 1969a; Lindskold et al., 1970; Schlenker, Bonoma, Tedeschi, et al., 1969) reveal that promise credibility, magnitude of reward, and positive message utility have no effects upon a target's compliance. Apparently, a promisor is perceived as generally benevolent, even when his promises are not fulfilled. In such a situation, the target is predisposed to be cooperative. Demos (1957) has suggested that promises create a moral obligation for the promisor, while threats carry no moral claim against the threatener. Our results suggest that promises connote normative obligations for the target as well as for the source. Apparently, a promisor is perceived as helpful and the normative rule is "help those who help you." Complementary to the effects of threats (when punishment for noncompliance is less than or equal to the costs of compliance), a target of promises ignores the small advantages to be gained by competitive noncompliant actions if he can gain almost as much by compliance. The important factor is that the promise itself, apart from source credibility or the magnitude of reward offered for compliance, carries strong normative connotations which are effective in mediating the target's compliance.

In the experiments so far reviewed, either threats or promises were sent by the source intermittently during the course of continuous dyadic interactions. Contrary to common sense, the use of threats does not exacerbate the ongoing conflict between individuals. However, the use of promises does ameliorate conflict. The strategist formulating policy must determine whether he prefers to use threats to gain compliance and accept a low level of cooperation by the target during other interactions in which threats are not used, or whether he prefers to use promises to gain a slightly lower level of compliance but more cooperative behavior by the target individual during interactions in which direct influence is not wielded.

Attraction Power

The degree of liking of the target for the source of influence may be considered a basis of power for the source. Festinger et al. (1950) demonstrated that the number of friendship choices in a group was positively correlated with conformity to group standards, a result that has been often replicated (Festinger et al., 1952; Gerard, 1953; Schachter, 1951; Lott and Lott, 1960; Thibaut and Strickland, 1956; Walker and Heyns, 1962). If attraction is a mediator of conformity to group norms, it may also be considered an important factor in mediating compliance to threats and promises.

Interpersonal attraction can be measured by various sociometric instruments. Experimental samples of existing friendships, strangers, or enemies can be obtained or attraction can be induced by manipulating attitude similarity in the laboratory (Byrne, 1969). In any case, the degree of the target's liking (or disliking) for source can be induced and measured.

The theory specifies that if a target likes the source, the target is more likely to believe promises of reward and to disbelieve threats of punishment. These predictions assume that the target will find it easy to believe that a friendly source will pay off for compliance to promises but will find it difficult to believe that a friendly source will use coercion. Alternatively, if the target dislikes the source, the target should be all too willing to expect punishment for noncompliance to threats and to disbelieve promises of reward. Thus, positive attraction for the source should lead to compliance to promises, while negative attraction should lead to compliance to threats.

Schlenker, Bonoma, Tedeschi, et al. (1969) have carried out two separate experiments to test the above hypothesis. The first study induced high or low attraction for source and exposed subjects to threats of either low or high credibility. Targets who disliked the source did comply as often to the low as to the high credibility threats, confirming that dislike does cause the target to overestimate message utility, increasing believability, estimated costs for noncompliance, and subsequent compliance. However, targets who liked the source were not prone to underestimate the credibility of the threats; such subjects were realistic in their appraisal of the situation and complied more often to the high than to the low credibility threats. Demos' comment that threats carry no moral obligation for either the source or target seems to be confirmed by the latter result. Dislike is a form of power when threats are used as the mode of influence, but positive attraction is not a basis of power in a coercive relationship. It may be concluded that when a source of threats does not have the resources or the intention of spending resources for punishing noncompliance, he can still be effective in exercising influence if he can gain the target's dislike. The exchange of attraction for power can occur in a coercive relationship. But if positive attraction is maintained, compliance can be gotten only with the resolute enforcement of threats.

In the second study, it was found that neither attraction nor message credibility significantly affected compliance to promise. Again, the operation of reciprocity norms (Gouldner, 1960) which apply to promises and which state that one should help those who help him caused compliance to occur about fifty percent of the time irrespective of credibility or attraction. It would appear that the mere statement of the promisor is enough to gain intermediate levels of compliance to promises even if the source is disliked. However, it was found that those subjects who were highly attracted to the "other" player cooperated more (over the course of the entire interaction) and were more trusting of the other than were subjects in the low attraction condition. Individuals who are highly attracted to one another generally seem to share the same attitudes (Byrne, 1969; Smith, 1957; Newcomb, 1961) and, thus, feel that they have similar goals which will not meet interference by cooperation. Thus, trust, which can be defined as the expectation that another will be helpful (Pruitt, 1965), can develop between highly attracted individuals and overall cooperation will increase without affecting compliance to specific promises. High attraction can be considered a base of power in an inducement relationship only when the interaction is taken as a whole and not when a specific promise of reward is dangled before the individual.

Legitimate Power

Authority derives from a role position rather than from the individual who holds the particular office or decision-making role (Freidrich, 1958). The authority is considered to be legitimized by a process of "reasoned elaboration"—the use of shared norms to demonstrate that the authority is worthy of deferential behavior. In a society of formal groups and organizations, hierarchies in role position as regards authority are often clearly established. The perception by a target individual that another person's role position deserves deference (compliance) is represented in the dyadic theory of influence as the perception of status. Within a group or institution it is assumed that status will be a direct function of role position. Furthermore, status is presumed to have a direct relationship to believability of and compliance to threats and promises.

Faley and Tedeschi (1969) have recently completed an experiment testing the relationship between status of source and compliance to threats by target individuals. They used ROTC cadets as the subject population. Cadets, who were themselves either low or high in authority or role position, were targets of threats from a simulated source, who was believed to be of either high or low status.

The results confirmed the theoretical prediction; low status targets were more compliant (deferential) when the source was of high (rather than of low) status and high status targets were defiant of threats sent by a low status source. A somewhat surprising finding was that high status targets were as compliant to a high status source as were low status targets to the same source. The purely hierarchical notion of the effects of status is challenged by the latter result. Apparently, high status equals are likely to yield to each other's demands—presumably out of respect for rank or because similar deference is expected when the influence relationship is reversed, or because neither wants to be placed in the position of punishing the other. It is possible that, as long as they are equal in rank, the higher the authority positions of the two individuals, the more compliance they give to each other's verbal demands.

Intuitively, it seems reasonable that role position confers control over the allocation of decisions and resources. For this reason, there is a question whether status and message utility are really separate or orthogonal to one another in their effects on a target's level of believability and compliance. The Faley-Tedeschi study clearly shows that the effects of message utility and status are orthogonal to each other, but both contribute to the degree of compliance obtained by a source of threats.

At the moment, no evidence has been gathered concerning the relationship of status and compliance to promises.

Dependency Power

A target may have certain needs that render him susceptible to influence. If an individual feels competent and feels that he deserves approval from others, presumably because of his own history of success in accomplishing objectives and solving problems, then he can be said to have high self-esteem. Such a confident individual could be expected to trust a source who promises rewards for compliance, while a low self-esteem person, who feels incompetent and disapproved of by others, could be expected to distrust the promisor. Thus, the theory predicts that a high self-esteem target is

more likely to believe a promisor and more likely to comply to promises than is a low self-esteem target. On the other hand, a target who has low self-esteem is likely to believe that a threatener will punish him, and will comply more often with threats, particularly when the credibility of the threat is low and compliance is unwarranted.

Lindskold and Tedeschi (1969b) have only partially tested these predictions. Subjects were pretested on a measure of chronic self-esteem and divided into high and low groups. They were then sent either threats or promises by a simulated source who established one hundred percent credibility for each type of message. High self-esteem individuals were more compliant to promises than were low self-esteem targets, confirming the theory's prediction. However, high self-esteem targets were also more compliant to threats. It could be said that since the threats were one hundred percent credible, it was more realistic to comply with them and self-destructive to defy them, an interpretation not inconsistent with the theory. A second study is underway to find out whether targets of low self-esteem will comply more frequently than those of high self-esteem when threats have a low credibility. In any case, it is clear that the needs of the target are implicated in the degree of compliance he gives to influence attempts. The kind of influence attempt that will be successful in gaining compliance from a particular individual and the kind of source behavior which is likely to be most effective will depend upon the personality characteristics of the target. Lasswell and Kaplan's basis of power referred to as "well-being" may reside in the target, or the target and the wielder of power.

Expert Power, Respect, and Esteem

Although the discussion of legitimate power and the study by Faley and Tedeschi indicated that respect for another's authority (legitimacy) is an important factor in the social influence process, Lasswell and Kaplan apparently reserved the term, respect, for the person and not the office he holds. Homans (1961) has not been entirely consistent in his definition but has used the concept of esteem to refer to the perceived approval that another person has gained from those around him. An individual's esteem or respect would thus be orthogonal to his legitimacy and status. Esteem, a target cognition, should be a direct function of how much approval the other person (in this case, the source) is actually receiving from third parties. Homans suggests that a person will receive approval in direct proportion to the value and quantity of help he gives other people. Help is thus exchanged for the socially valuable reinforcer of approval. French and Raven's type of power referred to as "expert power" implies the value of, availability of, and ability to provide help or information. If help is directly related to approval, and approval produces the perception of esteem, then the concept of esteem considerably overlaps, and may even be coextensive with, the notion of expert power.

The present theory specifies that esteem for a promisor is directly related to believability and subsequent compliance by the target individual. A target who perceives another person as generally helpful will err on the side of believing the source's promises when such belief is unwarranted. On the other hand, low esteem for the source should lead the target to make the inference that the source is not generally helpful to others; the target should thus believe threats issued by a source perceived as low in esteem.

A pilot study conducted by Smith et al. (1969) attempted to establish high esteem by allowing the target subject to overhear another person give praise to a confederate for help rendered. Low esteem was established by allowing the subject to overhear another person admonish a confederate for having his father call the chairman of the psychology department in an attempt to affect a grade for a course. Unfortunately, this manipulation was unsuccessful in inducing the appropriate levels of esteem. Probably, the perception that the other was an active manipulator in either induction procedure led to the failure to produce the intended effects. Another attempt will be made to induce different levels of esteem by the manipulation of the perception of a passive or active source who either does or

does not have anything to gain by giving help, or removing himself as an obstacle to the attainment of the other person's goals. At this time, no study of the esteem of another as it affects a subject's behavior or attitudes has ever been done in any context and certainly not in an influence situation.

Prestige Power

A threat from a court jester to his monarch is hardly taken seriously and may just cause robust laughter. The reason for this audience response is that the jester is not perceived as having the capacity to carry out the coercion which a king has. A threat is empty of coercive meaning for the target if the source is completely lacking in the resources required to levy the threatened punishment. Furthermore, even if the source is perceived as possessing the resources to punish noncompliance to his threats, he may still be perceived as unwilling to spend his resources for purposes of punishment, hence lacking the intentions to punish, and be defied by the target.

Analysis of the influence process reveals that when a threat is unsuccessful, the source is placed in the position of either punishing or not punishing the target but has not achieved the gains sought through the target's compliance. As Harsanyi (1962) has pointed out, opportunity costs are incurred by the source whenever he exercises his power. The source may be unwilling to spend the resources needed to punish the target unless there is concern about establishing a precedent (and credibility) for a future influence attempt. Similarly, when a target complies to promises, the source has already gained what he was after and will be tempted not to reward the target, unless concern for future interactions is present.

The target will be sensitive to the capabilities and intentions of the source (Pruitt, 1965; Singer, 1963). The source's available fluid resources will be perceived as his influence capability. The perception of intentions will depend upon how the source behaves in the interaction. Thus, even though a source sends threats, he may use them for the purpose of signaling in order to coordinate cooperative opportunities (Nardin, 1968). Additionally, the purely rational goal in the sending of a threat of violence is not provocation of actual violence but the coordination and accommodation of interests (Nieburg, 1969). Schlenker, Bonoma, Pivnick, et al. (1969) tested the hypothesis that a threat could be perceived as a signal to cooperate. Following the sending of a threat, they had the simulated source behave either totally accommodatively or totally exploitatively. Additionally, they had the simulated source send threats which were phrased in either a compellent or a deterrent form. Schelling (1966) has distinguished between compellent and deterrent threats by stating that the former is phrased in a form, "If you do *not* behave in a certain way, I will punish you," while the latter is phrased, "If you *do* behave in a certain way, I will punish you." The compellent threat thus specifies an action which the source must perform to escape punishment and thus can be perceived as more coercing, hostile, and manipulative than the deterrent threat, which only demands that the target not do a specified action to escape punishment. The results indicated that a subject faced with an accommodative source reciprocated that accommodation by being more compliant himself, while a subject faced with an exploitative source reciprocated exploitation with defiance. Also, subjects who received the more hostile compellent threats were more compliant than were those subjects who received the more static deterrent form of threat.

Singer (1963) has proposed that capability and intentions are multiplicatively related and, like utility, refer to the probability of the occurrence of an event based on the perception of source's intentions and the amount of costs or gains involved, based on the perceived capability of the source. Prestige, the target's perception, is considered to be a direct function of capability times intentions by the present theory. The higher the source's prestige, the more believable his influence attempts should be and the more compliance he should receive from target individuals.

Horai and Tedeschi (1970) manipulated the source's intentions while holding capabil-ity constant. They had a simulated source send threats to target subjects and behave either in a resolutely accommodative (i.e., the source was accommodative after sending a threat and always punished noncompliance), irresolutely accommodative (i.e., the source was accommodative after sending the threat but never punished noncompliance), or resolutey exploitative manner (i.e., the source was exploitative after sending the threat and always punished noncompliance). The results indicated that subjects who faced a resolutely accommodative source reciprocated the accommodative intentions by being both more compliant and more cooperative throughout the interaction, while subjects who faced a resolutely exploitative source reciprocated those exploitative intentions by being least compliant and least cooperative throughout the interaction. Sources who were perceived as irresolute in their accommodative intentions were intermediate on both compliance and cooperation. The results of Schlenker, Bonoma, Pivnick, et al. (1969) and Horai and Tedeschi (1970) indicate that when a source is clearly perceived as being accommodative in his intentions, and yet does not forfeit the capacity to punish noncompliance while striving for positive outcomes for both parties, more compliance ensues than when the source is perceived as being resolute in his intentions to exploit the subject. The Horai and Tedeschi (1970) study is consistent with Osgood's (1962) proposal for a series of unilateral conciliatory gestures which are clearly helpful to the opponent and which are aimed at the reduction of conflict in international affairs. The United States, a powerful nation with the acknowledged capacity to use its power in an enforcing manner, would thus appear to be able to initiate cooperative gestures and have them reciprocated by its targets. The results are also in direct opposition to theorists who desire to see a more aggressive policy on the part of the United States because they feel that a conciliatory response during conflicts will merely encourage aggression and exacerbate the conflicts.

The amount of resources possessed by a source can easily be manipulated while holding intentions constant. However, the study has yet to be done.

Counterinfluence

So far, we have concentrated on the factors which cause the source of threats or promises to be more or less successful in gaining compliance from target individuals. The theory and evidence concerning these matters are potentially useful to those in a position to wield influence and power. However, what about the source himself? How can the relatively powerless affect the behavior of the powerful? Very few studies have been done in the entire field of social psychology concerning the behavior of persons in the position of power, the focus almost always centering on the targets of power.

Without the benefit of systematic theory but under the assumption that some of the same factors that affect the target also affect the behavior of the source, the authors have undertaken several exploratory studies of source behavior. Tedeschi, Horai, et al. (1970) investigated the plausible hypothesis that as opportunity costs to the source for using his punishment power increased, the less likely the source would be to punish noncompliance to threats. Surprisingly, they found that the frequency of sending threats decreased as opportunity costs increased, but no effect of opportunity costs on the use of punishment power was observed. The source of threats evidently considered his own costs before sending threats but once he committed himself by sending the threat, he was likely to punish noncompliance, whatever the costs for doing so.

Schlenker and Tedeschi (1970) induced high or low attraction in sources of threats, promises, or threats and promises for the targets of the influence attempts. Although no effects of attraction were found, the kind of power possessed by the source was important in determining his behavior. The source sent more threats and punished noncompliance more resolutely when he did not also have reward power and sent fewer promises and rewarded compliance less often when he did

not also have coercive power. Thus, a powerful source is likely to be more benevolent and accommodating when he has both reward and punishment power than when he has either alone.

Tedeschi, Novinson, et al. (1970) compared the behavior of a source who was faced with a target who invariably retaliated when the source used his punishment power, with a source who incurred an opportunity cost (equivalent to the retaliation in terms of costs to the source) for using his power. Although the costs were the same in either condition, the source used his punishment power more often when the target was armed with retaliatory capability. These findings confirm those of Deutsch and Krauss (1962) and support the conclusion that conflict is more intense when both parties are armed than when only one is armed. Until recently the London police took this principle seriously.

It is a common belief that passive compliance to threats only encourages the source to send more threats since he is, in effect, being rewarded for his behavior. Halle (1967), in his history of the Cold War, noted that there is a deep-seated tendency in both men and nations to turn on one who appears striken and helpless. Gamson's (1964) "cold warriors" feel that we must avoid conciliatory gestures following conflict intensification by the USSR so as not to encourage further exploitation. Tedeschi, Bonoma, et al. (1970) faced a source with a simulated target who was either completely compliant or always defiant. Within each condition, the simulated target was either honest and open in announcing his intentions to comply or defy the source's threats or dishonest in concealing his intentions. Open defiance was successful in deterring the source from sending threats. Open compliance converted the source into a mutual cooperator; and although the source sent the most threats in this condition of the experiment, the threat was used by the source as a signal to coordinate mutual cooperation rather than for exploitative purposes. These results seem to deny the predictions of Halle and Gamson and further support Osgood's (1962) GRIT proposal, which calls for a clear statement of intentions before a conciliatory gesture to reduce conflict.

Obviously, there is a need to develop a theory of how a source of influence will use his power. Further experiments like those reported above may be necessary to develop a body of data suggestive of the relevant variables and functional relationships that will lead to such a theoretical development.

Conclusions and Implications

A scientific theory of social influence within which is incorporated some of the more important and generally accepted definitions of power is only in its earlier stages of development. A systematic program of research is under way to evaluate, change, and expand the theory. The focus of the theory is on how behavioral compliance is gained from another person under conditions of social conflict and limited communications. This emphasis is a clear break wtih the tradition in social psychology which has been mainly concerned with attitude development and change.

It would probably be premature and also wrong to generalize from the theory and the laboratory results presented above to the serious problems of law and order in American society or to international conflict situations. However, a few such generalizations will be offered as a heuristic exercise and to point out the implications that could derive from the development of a mature and coherent theory of social influence.

Kaiser Wilhelm of Germany and Emperor Hirohito of Japan have both been quoted as pessimistic about the outcomes of the wars that each chose to enter. The Kaiser has been quoted as saying that at least Germany would make India bleed, while Hirohito succinctly expressed his position by noting that sometimes there is no alternative to leaping off a tower (Frank, 1967). If each of these leaders entered war with low expectancy of victory, why did they do so? Historians and strategic analysts, such as Tuchman (1962) and Kahn (1960), suggest each believed that he had no choice and that the alternative to war was perceived as worse than war itself. These his-

torical events bear a striking resemblance to the results obtained in the laboratory when the punishment for noncompliance to threats is perceived by the target as being no worse than the costs of compliance. Given such a least-of-evils choice, when both alternatives are unsavory and relatively equivalent in terms of costs, the individual chooses to defy the source of threats rather than bear the ignominy of compliance and the detrimental costs associated with such surrender.

Analogous is the willingness of a few college students to defy the military draft system and accept incarceration implying that at least for these few, the legal punishment for their defiant actions is no worse in their hierarchy of values than serving in the armed forces. In corporate America, this principle is even more clearly illustrated. The penalties for price fixing and collusion are not severe. The profits to be gained by such activities are so vast that some large corporations have been tempted to violate the law many times (Nossiter, 1964). Only by increasing the penalty for price fixing to the point where it is "cheaper" to comply than to defy the law, while concomitantly establishing high probability of punishment or enforcement, can corporate recidivists be deterred.

An interesting finding in our research is that dislike is a form of power. Observation establishes that the young black militant is openly hostile to whites and challenges middle-class blacks, charging them with Uncle Tomming "the Man." The backlash in America is a reaction to this new form of black militancy. But, the finding that dislike is a form of power may indicate that the black militant is gaining some power and can be expected to be somewhat successful in threatening whites even though he does not have sufficient punishment power to enforce his threats. Thus, many jobs are opening to blacks from the fear that violence may occur if such action is not taken. However, the study by Tedeschi, Bonoma, et al. (1970) indicates that open and honest compliance to some black demands could be successful in converting even the most militant into cooperative partners in social change. The experience at many universities is that compliance to the demands of black students has not led just to more demands but rather has led black students to work closely with college administrators in developing new programs.

A process similar to that advocated by Charles Osgood (1962) for the mitigation of international tension could be employed as a matter of policy in domestic conflicts. Graduated reciprocation in tension reduction (GRIT) involves a series of announcements on the part of the instigating nation to the effect that some low-risk actions will be taken which are designed to benefit the other party. Such unilateral announcements are then followed by the performance of the stated behavior and require no specific reciprocation from the other party. GRIT is a strategy to build trust between nations, calculated to reduce tensions and elicit spontaneous reciprocation from the target nation. Our studies indicate that the proposal has a sound foundation, since both open announcement of accommodative intentions and the behavioral demonstration of good faith do result in mutual cooperation. Perhaps GRIT could be applied to ameliorate the distrust and conflict prevalent between blacks and whites in America.

The experimental findings that high self-esteem individuals are more compliant to both high credibility threats and promises than are low self-esteem individuals is a pessimistic one when applied to black-white problems, juvenile delinquents, criminals, or the deprived poor of America. For centuries the white man has taught the black man to believe that black is ugly and second-best, to accept a subservient blue-collar role in America, and to doubt that black men have the native ability to acquire the skills of a technological society. The consequences of such consistent inculcation is that most lower-class blacks have powerful identity problems and generally low self-

esteem. Speedy social change toward integration may have been obviated by white Americans long ago by rendering blacks relatively uninfluenceable to the threats and promises of a white society. It would appear that a prerequisite for a true integration of American society presupposes that the average Negro believes that black is beautiful and that he is as competent and deserving of approval as the average white person. When black Americans have gained self-respect, they should be as compliant to the laws and norms of society as the average middle-class white American.

Young critics of "the system" are quite aware of the consequences of success in our society. Once an individual begins to work his way up the hierarchy of a structured organization, he receives rewards for the acceptance of responsibility, but he also necessarily becomes more conforming to the norms and goals of the organization. The fact is revealed indirectly by the experimental finding that high-status equals are very compliant to each other's social influence attempts. Giving an individual a stake in the institutions of the society is a way of gaining compliance and conformity to the norms of that society. This lesson has not been entirely lost on the social reformers of America. The disaffected, the poor, and the blacks must be given the skills by which they too can escape the confines of low status, as well as low self-esteem. This type of social therapy may be viewed as a hedge against disorder and possible large-scale violence.

Many other speculative generalizations could be made, but the purpose of demonstrating the potential importance of a general theory of social influence has been accomplished. The task now is to provide a firm scientific foundation that can be used with confidence by policy makers faced with the great issues of our time.

References

Bachrach, P. and M. S. Baratz (1963) "Decisions and nondecisions: an analytical framework." Amer. Pol. Sci. Rev. 57 (September): 632–642.
Bazelon, D. T. (1965) The Paper Economy. New York: Vintage.
Byrne, D. (1969) "Attitudes and attraction," pp. 35–89 in L. Berkowitz (ed.) Advances in Experimental Social Psychology, Vol. 4. New York: Academic Press.

Coser, L. (1956) The Functions of Social Conflict. New York: Free Press.

Demos, R. (1957) "Some reflections on threats and punishments." Rev. of Metaphysics 11 (December): 224–236.

Deutsch, K. W. (1966) The Nerves of Government. New York: Free Press.

Deutsch, M. and R. M. Krauss (1962) "Studies of interpersonal bargaining." J. of Conflict Resolution 6 (March): 52–76.

Durkheim, E. (1951) Suicide. Glencoe, Ill.: Free Press. [Original in French]

Edwards, W., H. Lindman, and L. D. Phillips (1965) "Emerging technologies for making decisions," in New Directions in Psychology, Vol. II New York: Holt.

Faley, T. and J. T. Tedeschi (1969) "Status and the reaction to threats." University of Miami (mimeo).

Festinger, L. (1964) Conflict, Decision and Dissonance. Stanford: Stanford Univ. Press.

———(1957) A Theory of Cognitive Dissonance. Evanston, Ill.: Row, Peterson.

———, A. Pepitone, and T. Newcomb (1952) "Some consequences of deindividuation in a group." J. of Abnormal and Social Psychology 47 (April): 382–389.

Festinger, L., S. Schachter, and K. Back (1950) Social Pressures in Informal Groups: a Study of Human Factors in Housing. New York: Harper & Row.

Frank, J. D. (1967) Sanity and Survival. New York: Vintage.

French, J. R. P., Jr. and B. Raven (1959) "The bases of social power," pp. 118–149 in D. Cartwright (ed.) Studies in Social Power. Ann Arbor, Mich.: Institute for Social Research.

Friedrich, C. J. [ed.] (1958) Authority. Cambridge, Mass.: Harvard Univ. Press.

Gamson, W. A. (1968) Power and Discontent. Homewood, Ill.: Dorsey.

———(1964) "Evaluating beliefs about international conflict," in R. Fisher (ed.) International Conflict and Behavioral Science. New York: Basic Books.

Gerard, H. B. (1953) "The anchorage of opinion in face-to-face groups." Human Relations 6 (May): 249–271.

Gouldner, A. W. (1960) "The norm of reciprocity: a preliminary statement." Amer. Soc. Rev. 25 (April): 161–179.

Halle, L. J. (1967) The Cold War as History. New York: Harper & Row.

Harsanyi, J. C. (1962) "Measurement of social power, opportunity costs, and the theory of two-person bargaining games." Behavioral Sci. 7 (January): 67–80.

Homans, G. C. (1961) Social Behavior: Its Elementary Forms. New York: Harcourt, Brace & World.

Horai, J. and J. T. Tedeschi (1970) "Attribution of intention and the norm of reciprocity." University of Miami (mimeo).

———(1969) "The effects of credibility and magnitude of punishment on compliance to threats." J. of Personality and Social Psychology 12 (June): 164–169.

Jones, E. E. and H. B. Gerard (1967) Foundations of Social Psychology. New York: John Wiley.

Kahn, H. (1960) On Thermonuclear War. Princeton, N.J.: Princeton Univ. Press.

Karlsson, G. (1962) "Some aspects of power in small groups," pp. 193–202 in J. H. Criswell, H. Solomon, and P. Suppes (eds.) Mathematical Methods in Small Group Processes. Stanford: Stanford Univ. Press.

Lasswell, H. D. and A. Kaplan (1950) Power and Society. New Haven: Yale Univ. Press.

Lewin, K. (1946) "Action research and minority problems." J. of Social Issues 2 (November): 34–36.

Lindskold, S. and J. T. Tedeschi (1969a) "The effects of contingent promises on interpersonal conflict." University of Miami (mimeo).

———(1969b) "Self-esteem and sex as factors affecting influencability." University of Miami (mimeo).

Lindskold, S., T. Bonoma, and J. T. Tedeschi (1969) "Impressions of and reactions to a threatening simulated opponent." University of Miami (mimeo).

Lindskold, S., T. Bonoma, B. R. Schlenker, and J. T. Tedeschi (1970) "Source accommodativeness, message utility, and compliance to contingent promises." University of Miami (mimeo).

Lott, B. E. and A. J. Lott (1960) "The formation of positive attitudes toward group members." J. of Abnormal and Social Psychology 61 (September): 297–300.

Luce, R. D. and H. Raiffa (1957) Games and Decisions: Introduction and Critical Survey. New York: John Wiley.

MacIver, R. M. (1964) Power Transformed. New York: Macmillan.

March, J. G. (1955) "An introduction to the theory and measurement of influence." Amer. Pol. Sci. Rev. 49 (June): 431–451.

Morgenthau, H. (1964) Politics Among Nations. New York: Alfred A. Knopf.

Nardin, T. (1968) "Communication and the effect of threats in strategic interaction." Peace Research Society, Papers 9: 69–86.

NewComb, T. (1961) The Acquaintance Process. New York: Holt.

Nieburg, H. L. (1969) Political Violence. New York: St. Martin's.

Nossiter, B. D. (1964) The Mythmakers. Cambridge: Houghton-Mifflin.

Osgood, C. E. (1962) An Alternative to War or Surrender. Urbana: Univ. of Illinois Press.

Parsons, T. (1963) "On the concept of influence." Public Opinion Q. 27 (Spring): 37–62.

———(1949) Essays in Sociological Theory Pure and Applied. New York: Free Press.

Pruitt, D. G. (1965) "Definition of the situation as a determinant of international action," pp. 393–432 in H. C. Kelman (ed.) International Behavior: A Social-psychological Analysis. New York: Holt, Rinehart & Winston.

Rokeach, M. (1968) Beliefs, Attitudes, and Values, a Theory of Organization and Change. San Francisco: Jossey-Bass.

Schachter, S. (1951) "Deviation, rejection & communication." J. of Abnormal and Social Psychology 46 (April): 190–207.

Schelling, T. (1966) Arms and Influence. New Haven: Yale Univ. Press.

Schlenker, B. R. and J. T. Tedeschi (1970) "Interpersonal attraction and the use of threats and promises." U.S. International University (mimeo).

Schlenker, B. R., T. Bonoma, W. P. Pivnick, and J. T. Tedeschi (1969) "Compliance to threats as a function of the wording of the threat and the exploitativeness of the threatener." U.S. International University (mimeo).

Schlenker, B. R., T. Bonoma, J. T. Tedeschi, S. Lindskold, and J. Horai (1969) "Interpersonal attraction and compliance to threats and promises." U.S. International University (mimeo).

Schopler, J. and N. Bateson (1965) "The power of dependence." J. of Personality and Social Psychology 2 (August): 247–254.

Schur, E. M. (1969) Law and Society. New York: Random House.

Simmel, G. (1950) The Sociology of G. Simmel. Glencoe, Ill.: Free Press.

Singer, J. D. (1963) "Inter-nation influence: a formal model." Amer. Pol. Sci. Rev. 57 (June): 420–430.

Smith, A. J. (1957) "Similarity of values and its relation to acceptance and the projection of similarity." J. of Psychology 43 (April): 251–260.

Smith, R. B., I. Haber, B. R. Schlenker, and J. T. Tedeschi (1969) "Source esteem and targets compliance to threats." U.S. International University (mimeo).

Tedeschi, J. T. (1968) "A theory of social influence within dyads." Presented at the Sixteenth International Congress of Applied Psychology. Amsterdam.

———, T. Bonoma, and S. Lindskold (1970) "Threatener's reaction to prior announcement of behavioral compliance or defiance." Behavioral Sci. (forthcoming).

Tedeschi, J. T., N. Novinson, and T. Bonoma (1970) "Fixed costs vs. retaliation as factors influencing the threatener." J. of Conflict Resolution (forthcoming).

Tedeschi, J. T., J. Horai, S. Lindskold, and T. Faley (1970) "The effects of opportunity costs and target compliance on the behavior of a threatening source." J. of Experimental Social Psychology (forthcoming).

Tedeschi, J. T., J. Horai, S. Lindskold, and J. P. Gahagan (1968) "The effects of threat upon prevarification and conflict in the P.D.G." Proceedings of the Annual Meeting of the American Psychology Association.

Thibaut, J. W. and H. H. Kelley (1959) The Social Psychology of Groups. New York: John Wiley.

Thibaut, J. W. and L. H. Strickland (1956) "Psychological set and social conformity." J. of Personality 25 (December): 115–129.

Tuchman, B. (1962) The Guns of August. New York: Dell.

Walker, E. L. and R. W. Heyns (1962) An Anatomy for Conformity. Englewood Cliffs, N.J.: Prentice-Hall.

Weber, M. (1954) Max Weber on Law in Economy and Society. Cambridge: Harvard Univ. Press.

12. The Threat of Violence and Social Change

H. L. Nieburg[*]

The threat of violence and the occasional outbreak of real violence—which gives the threat credibility—are essential elements in peaceful social change not only in international, but also in national communities.[1] Individuals and groups, no less than nations, exploit the threat as an everyday matter. This induces flexibility and stability in democratic institutions.

I refer not only to the police power of the state and the recognized right of self-defense, but also to private individual or group violence, whether purposive or futile, deliberate or desperate. Violence and the threat of violence, far from being meaningful only in international politics, are underlying, tacit, recognized, and omnipresent facts of domestic life, in the shadow of which democratic politics are carried on. They instil dynamism into the structure and growth of the law, the settlement of disputes, the processes of accomodating interests, and they induce general respect for the verdict of the polls.

An effort by the state to obtain an absolute

Reprinted from H. L. Nieburg, "The Threat of Violence and Social Change," *American Political Science Review*, Vol. 56, No. 4 (December 1962), pp. 865–873.

[*] Professor of Political Science, State University of New York at Binghamton.

[1] "Violence" is defined as direct or indirect action applied to restrain, injure, or destroy persons or property.

monopoly over violence, threatened or used in behalf of private interests, leads inexorably— as in a prison—to complete totalitarian repression of all activities and associations which may, however remotely, create a basis of anti-state action. A democratic system preserves the right of organized action by private groups, risking their implicit capability of violence. By intervening at the earliest possible point in private activities, the totalitarian state increases the likelihood that potential violence will have to be demonstrated before it is socially effective. On the other hand, by permitting a pluralistic basis for action, the democratic state permits potential violence to have a social effect with only a token demonstration, thus assuring greater opportunities for peaceful political and social change. A democratic system has greater viability and stability; it is not forced, like the totalitarian, to create an infinite deterrent to all non-state (and thus potentially anti-state) activities. The early Jeffersonians recognized this essential element of social change when they guaranteed the private right to keep and bear arms, in the Second Amendment. The possibility of a violent revolution once each generation is a powerful solvent of political rigidity, making such revolutions unnecessary.

The argument of this essay is that the risk of violence is necessary and useful in preserving national societies.[2] This specifically includes sporadic, uncontrolled, "irrational" violence in all its forms. It is true that domestic violence, no less than international violence, may become a self-generating vortex which destroys all values, inducing anarchy and chaos. Efforts to prevent this by extreme measures, however, only succeed in making totalitarian societies that are more liable to such collapses. Democracies assume the risk of such catastrophes, and thereby make them less likely.

Violence has two inextricable aspects: its actual use (political demonstrations, self-immolation, suicide, crimes of passion, property, or politics, etc.), and its potential (threatened) use. The actual outbreak or demonstration of violence must occur from time to time in order to give plausibility to its threatened outbreak, and thereby to gain efficacy for the threat as an instrument of social and political change. The two aspects, demonstration and threat, therefore cannot be separated. If the capability of actual demonstration is not present, the threat will have little effect in inducing a willingness to bargain politically. In fact, such a threat may instead provoke "pre-emptive" counter-violence.

The "rational" goal of the threat of violence is an accommodation of interests, not the provocation of actual violence. Similarly, the "rational" goal of actual violence is demonstration of the will and capability of action, establishing a measure of the credibility of future threats, not the exhaustion of that capability in unlimited conflict.[3] An investigation of the function of violence begins with an outline of concepts.

I. Political Systems and Consensus

We assume that all human relationships, both individual and institutional, are involved in a dynamic process of consensus and competition. These are opposites only as conceptual poles of a continuum. In real relationships, it is often difficult to distinguish objectively between the two. The distinction is sharp only subjectively, for the participant, and his per-

---

[2] The role of violence in political organizations is vividly demonstrated by a recent event among a group of elks at the Bronx Zoo. A 4-year old bull elk, Teddy, had his magnificent antlers sawed off to one-inch stumps. He had reigned as undisputed boss of a herd of six cow elks and one younger bull. But the breeding season was on, and he was becoming "a bit of a martinet." With his antlers off, he gets a new perspective on his authority and becomes a tolerable leader. A younger bull may try to take over as paramount leader of the herd, but if he does, the veterinarian will saw off his antlers, too. *New York Times,* September 26, 1962, p. 35.

[3] By "rational" here is meant: having a conceptual link to a given end, a logical or symbolic means-ends relationship which can be demonstrated to others or, if not demonstrable, is accepted by others (but not necessarily all as proven).

ception of consensus or competition may change from moment to moment, depending on his political role and the objective circumstances.[4] A political role is defined in terms of the many political systems in which the individual objectively or subjectively (by identification of interests) plays a part. A political system contains a hierarchy of authority and values. Each system has a complex structure of leadership and influence but, because of the nature of its task (maximizing and allocating certain values), policy and decision-making power is usually vested in one or a few roles at the top of the pyramid of authority (the elite). Formal and informal political systems exist at all levels of group life (children's play groups, families, lodges, gangs, work groups, nation-states, international alignments, etc.), interpenetrating each other among and between levels. Each isolated system has an interdependent structure of roles, involving loyalty to certain values, symbols, leaders, and patterns of behavior according to system norms. The discrete individual, part of many different systems, must structure his own hierarchy of commitment to meet the simultaneous demands made upon him by many different roles.

Within the individual, the conflicting demands of these roles create tension. Similarly, within each system conflicting values between members are constantly adjusted as roles change, maintaining a state of tension. And political systems as wholes have an objective, dynamic interrelationship, structured into the hierarchy of macro-systems. Within the latter, each sub-system has a role much like that of the individual in smaller constellations. Each sub-system may be part of several macro-systems, imposing conflicting demands upon it. Consequently, within macro-systems there is maintained a state of constant tension between sub-systems.

This objective tension, existing on all levels, is perceived subjectively in terms both of competition and consensus, depending on the comparative degrees of collaboration and conflict which exist in the situation at any given moment.

So any two or more systems may appear as hostile at any given time. From the viewpoint of the participants, the conceptual framework of competition overrides underlying consensus. Decisions and policies of the rival elites then are rationalized in terms of hostility to the values and leaders of the other system. However, if events transpire to place a higher value on a hostile tactical situation involving the macro-system of which both smaller systems are a part, their relationship will be transformed quickly to a conceptual framework of consensus which will override and mute the unresolved competitive elements. Such an event may also bring about internal leadership changes in both sub-systems, if their elites were too firmly wedded to the requirements of the now-irrelevant competitive situation.

Objectively, tension is always present among all roles and systems; that is, elements of both competition and consensus go together. The subjective emphasis which each pole of the continuum receives depends on the value which the tactical situation places on acts and attitudes of hostility or collaboration among the various systems at various times. Degrees of hostility and collaboration are structured by a hierarchy of values within and among all roles and systems all the time. All are involved in a dynamic process.

Conflict, in functional terms, is the means of discovering or reaching consensus, of creating agreed terms of collaboration. Because of our personal roles in the macro-system of nation-states, we tend to view the Cold War in terms of competition. Similarly, because of our roles in the sub-system of the family group, we tend to view family problems in terms of consensus (until the system breaks down completely).

One can revese these conceptual fields. The Cold War can be viewed in terms of the large areas of consensus that exist between the two

---

[4] Essentially, the perception by an individual of his relationship to others within a framework of hostility or cooperation is the subjective basis of "ideology," using the term as Karl Mannheim does in "Sociology of Knowledge," *Ideology and Utopia* (New York, 1957), pp. 265–66.

power-blocs. For example, the wish to prevent the spread of nuclear weapons to each other's allies: the wish to avoid giving each other's allies the power of precipitating general war between the main antagonists; the common interest in reducing accidental provocations; the common interest in establishing some norms of predictability in each other's behavior; etc. Conflict can therefore be considered merely as the means of perfecting these areas of consensus. In the same way, one can view the family situation negatively in terms of competition and hostility. As in an O'Neill drama, one would dwell on all the things that divide the family members and interpret all actions in terms of maneuvers to subdue each other's will. Consensus then becomes a residual category *hors de combat*, and therefore of no importance. One might dwell upon the collaborative aspects of international affairs or the disruptive aspects of family affairs. A policy-maker should do both in the former area, just as a psychiatrist does both in the latter. The collaborative view of the Cold War should not, however, induce euphoria about the nature of the relationship (as it unfortunately does for some), since so many crimes of violence occur in families, and so many murders involve lovers or ex-lovers.[5]

In performing the exercise, the relativistic nature of the concepts of consensus and competition becomes evident. It is impossible to reach any consensus without competition and every consensus, no matter how stable, is still only provisional, since it represents for all its members a submerging of other values. All collaborating individuals, groups, or nations constantly try to exploit favorable opportunities to improve their roles or to impose a larger part of their own value structures upon a larger political system. In an important sense, all individuals, groups, or nations desire to "rule the world," but are constrained to collaborate with others on less desirable terms because of the objective limits of their own power or the cost of the exertion required.

The commitment required to produce a credible threat of violence, sufficient to induce peaceable accommodation, is one of a very high order. Not all individuals nor all political systems are capable of credibly using the threat of violence in order to induce greater deference by others to their values. People generally recognize the kinds of values which can and cannot elicit the high degree of commitment required to make the threat credible.

By and large, all violence has a rational aspect, for somebody, if not for the perpetrator. Acts of violence can consequently be rationalized (i.e., put to rational use), whether they are directed against others or against oneself. This is true because people who may be anxious to apply the threat of violence to achieve a social or political bargaining position are nevertheless usually reluctant also to pay the costs or take the risks of an actual demonstration of that threat. Incoherent acts of violence can be exploited by elites as a means of improving their roles or imposing a larger part of their values upon a greater political system. The more obvious the logical connection between such an act and the ends sought by the elite, the easier it is to assimilate the act and claim it as a demonstration of the potential violence available to the elite if its demands are ignored. The rapidity with which insurgent movements create martyrs from the demise of hapless bystanders, and the reluctance of governments to give martyrs to the opposition, are evidence of this.

II. Nations, Laws, and Ballots

The nation is a highly organized, formal political system, whose structure is well defined by law and custom, reinforced by sanctions legally imposed by the near-monopoly violence (police power) of the state. The central problem of lawful societies is to develop principles, procedures, institutions and expectations that create conditions of continuity and predictability in the lives of its members. The legal system is an abstract model of the society,

[5] See E. Frankel, "One Thousand Murderers," *Journal of Criminal Law and Criminology*, Vol. 29 (1938–39), pp. 687–88, cited in Marshall B. Guard, *Sociology of Deviant Behavior* (New York, 1957), p. 216.

designed to crystallize relationships of the *status quo*, maintain their continuity in the midst of political and social change, and provide lawful methods of resisting or accommodating change. Law itself tends to maintain the *status quo* and, with the instruments of state power, to resist change. But relationships in organized societies change anyway. The process for codifying changed conditions and relationships is called "politics." Political systems legitimize certain kinds of potential violence within controlled limits; it then becomes force.[6] However, law almost never serves the interests of all equally. Rather, it protects some against others or gives advantages to some over others. By placing the force of the state behind the interests of some, law serves to neutralize the potential violence behind the demands of others. In a sense, it thus raises the threshold of violence required to make social protests against the law efficacious. This guarantees that the law cannot be changed easily or quickly by any group, thus giving it greater permanence and stability.

Pressures for political and social change must therefore be substantial before the threat of violence and the fear of the breakdown of law and order rise above the threshold set by the force held by the state. While the threat and fear remain below the threshold, the *status quo* often responds to challenges against the law by more severe enforcement, augmented police and enlarged prisons. But when the threat and fear come near or cross the threshold, a general tendency toward nonenforcement of the law sets in. The *status quo* interests begin to share with the disaffected groups a desire to evade and to change the law.

Private demonstrations of force are illegal in all domestic societies. Toleration is accorded to threats of potential violence, however, to the extent that the laws and institutions are democratic. In all systems, the state, to deserve its name, must apply adequate force to control outbreaks of actual violence by private sources—or tolerate some more or less recognized "off-limits" areas for outlawry.[7] If the instrumentalities of state power are not equal to broad private threats, indeed, the government in power ceases to rule. Vigilantism or the private threat of violence has then in fact become the last resort of authority in the system. Why do governments sometimes fall when there is a general strike or a street demonstration? Why don't they ignore outbreaks with which they cannot cope? And say: "All right, go ahead and strike, fight each other for control of the streets, snake-dance down the avenue. We will sit here in our offices anyway making decisions!" Governments fall when their capabilities for dealing with threatened violence fail. The emerging political system which proves itself capable of raising a higher threshold of violence (than the established government can or will surmount with its force) becomes *de facto* the highest authority, and *de jure* the new government.

Laws are not merely the rules of a game of economic and political competition. They are also a means of winning the game, if some of the players can, as in fact they do, write the laws. The ideal system may be one in which the rules are written with perfect dispassion,

---

[6] The distinction between "violence" and "force" (one uncontrolled, the other controlled), was common in pre-Lasswellian literature. They are often difficult to distinguish objectively. Assessments of controllability may be almost entirely ideological. I prefer to use "force" to designate the objective capabilities, i.e., the concrete means or instruments for violence.

[7] There are many areas outside the effective—if not the nominal jurisdiction of formal governmental authority, as, for example, "off-limit" slum areas where police seldom penetrate, or the Mafia areas of Sicily. Such areas represent political sub-systems which possess a high degree of sovereignty, tolerated, for one reason or another, by the general government. Within such areas, the *de facto* authority is often the elite able to maintain the highest threshold of potential violence, not the formal government. In such areas, an unwritten law usually makes it a severely punished offense to call upon the authority of the general government.

so that they accord no special advantages to anyone. This ideal is never realized. The process of politics which underlies the making and unmaking of laws is not dispassionate. Indeed, it is one of the most passionate of human affairs. No matter how scrupulously fair may be the original constitution and the representation of governing institutions, the tensions of political systems soon intrude historical hierarchies of advantage. Whoever enjoys early advantages in the game soon enjoys that and more by law, with the heightened threshold of the force available at the beckoning of the state to vouchsafe them. In this manner the law tends always to become to some extent the instrument of the *status quo*, resisting change.

In democratic societies, however, the law also guarantees the right of voluntary association, among other political liberties, and restrains (by a constitutional distribution of authority) arbitrary use of the police power. These permit opponents of the *status quo* to establish and maintain a base of political action that may become formidable. It may then be difficult for the regime to find legal pretexts for controlling this base while its potential for antistate violence is still within the state's control capability. Once its potential equals or grows greater than that of the state, repression is no longer a realistic policy. Changing the law, or treating it as a dead letter, gains precedence over enforcing it, even for *status quo* leaders who wish to preserve what control remains over informal political systems in which they are the elite. Once this process of peaceful political change has been successfully set in motion, both the emerging and the declining political elites have a high interest in maintaining a general freedom to threaten violence without initiating or provoking it, either on the part of the state or by other groups. For the *status quo* elites, there is more to be gained in preserving the continuity of the laws than in initiating and provoking the demonstration of violence at an unpredictable level. For the insurgent elites, there is usually more to be gained in preserving the continuity of the laws than in appealing to the uncertain results of violence.

In democratic systems, the ballot becomes the non-provocative symbol by which the elites may measure their capabilities for threatening direct action. In a real sense, voting is an approximation of picking sides before a street fight. Once the sides are picked, the leaders are able to gauge their bargaining strengths and make the best possible deal for themselves and their cohorts. The appeal to actual battle not only is unnecessary, but also, for the weaker side (the only side with an interest in challenging the results of the count), it does not promise to change the results, and may in fact undermine the authority of the polls as a method for reversing one's future position.

The threat of violence implicit in counting heads is an ambiguous measure of the power available to the political systems into which people group themselves at election time. The extent of voter commitment in these systems is uncertain and probably, in most cases, unequal to demands for supporting action. There are very few national elections in the United States—although many elsewhere—in which the results prefigure a plausible threat of civil war as the means by which the defeated candidates can gain concessions and appointments from the winning side. In general, democratic political leaders share a common interest in resolving disputes without invoking real violence. Neither side can be confident that the loyalty of its voters will stand the test of a demonstration of strength. Voting is a very imperfect register of loyalty, but rather conveys a miscellany of emotions, difficult to penetrate or to order rationally. Strenuous efforts are made by defeated candidates to restrain a show of violence by their own followers. Public concessions of defeat, homiletic congratulations, and avowals of support for the winner, are designed to communicate to their backers the finality of the verdict at the polls, which is subject to revision, not by a demonstration of violence, but by renewed peaceful efforts in the next election.

In 1960, after the close result of the Kennedy-Nixon election, what dangers could have been unleashed if Nixon had publicly repudiated the poll and openly supported minority efforts to hold recounts in California and Illinois? In a situation of this kind, it is clear how close to the surface lies the threat of violence implicit in the voting process.

III. The International Process

Many people blithely argue for law as a substitute for violence, as though there was a choice between the two. They call for international law and world government to eliminate war. This point of view reveals a blissful ignorance of the functions of violence in domestic legal systems. A viable system based on law protects the conditions of group action which make threats of violence tolerable. Law always rests on force, a legitimate monopoly in the hands of the state, and it can be changed by the threat of private violence. The threat of violence and the fear of the breakdown of law and order cast their shadows ahead; they operate to moderate demands and positions, thereby setting into peaceful motion the informal political processes of negotiation, concession, compromise, and agreement. Although there is no centralized monopoly of force in the international forum, the processes of mediation and negotiation function in much the same way. The credible threat of violence in the hands of nations has a similarly stabilizing effect, providing statesmen are attentive to the maintenance of their national capability for demonstrating violence, and providing their ambitions are commensurate to the bargaining position which their armaments achieve. More comprehensive legal codes and a world government may not improve the stability of the world community in any case, since the possibility of civil conflict exists in all political systems. Civil wars are frequently bloodier and more unforgiving than wars between sovereign nations.

In international politics also, the threat of violence tends to create stability and maintain peace. Here the threat is more directly responsive to policy controls. The nation-state has greater continuity than the informal political systems that coalesce and dissolve in the course of domestic social change. The threat of force can be asserted much more deliberately and can be demonstrated under full control, as in "good will" Navy visits, army maneuvers near a sensitive border, partial mobilization, etc. Because of the greater continuity of these macro-systems, the national leaders must strive to maintain the prestige of a nation's might and will. If the reputation of a nation's military power is allowed to tarnish, future bargaining power will be weakened. The country may feel obliged to re-establish that prestige by invoking a test of arms, as a means of inducing greater respect for its position from other nations. Strong nations prefer to demonstrate their military power peaceably in order that their prestige will afford them the bargaining power they deserve without a test of arms.

Because the threat of international violence is a conscious instrument of national policy, it generally lacks the random character of domestic violence. This means that if the armaments of nations fall out of balance, if the prestige of nations is no longer commensurate with their ambitions, if the will to take the risks of limited military conflicts is lacking, if domestic political considerations distort the national response to external threat, then the time becomes ripe for the outbreak of violence that may escalate out of control.

In general, the dangers of escalating international conflict induce greater, not lesser, restraint on the part of national leaders in their relations with each other. Attempts to achieve infinite security—and consequent irresponsibility—for the nation are as self-defeating as similar attempts for a domestic regime.

The functioning of consensus and competition between nations is not fundamentally different from that of domestic politics. The most striking difference is that in domestic politics the level of centralized force available to the state creates a high threshold of stability against the threats brought to bear within the system by private groups. In the international forum, the closest approximation to such a threshold is the array of decentralized forces available to the great powers. An aggressive power interested in modifying the *status quo* must cross the threshold of its own threat of force in order to induce other powers to choose between concessions to its demands or the costs and risk of an arms race. To the extent that the *status quo* powers are able and willing to pay the costs and take the risks, their own threshold can be raised, depriving the challenger of any political advantages from his investment. When all of the great powers are attentive to the equations of potential violence, no nation can hope to gain conclusive political advantages from an arms race. This situation makes possible international agreements or a tacit consensus for stabilizing arms and bringing about political settlements. Diplomatic ceremonials, like the ceremonials of personal relations which we call "manners," serve to minimize the dangers of provocation and threat in the day-to-day relations between nations.

IV. The Domestic Process

Underneath the norms of legal and institutional behavior in national societies lies the great beast, the people's capability for outraged, uncontrolled, bitter and bloody violence. This is common to totalitarian as well as democratic societies, and is a major restraint against completely arbitrary government. Even totalitarian regimes can hope for stability only if they reflect in some degree the changing currents of political interest of the people and if they are willing to recruit members of their elites from the potentially disaffected groups which they rule. Even a totalitarian state must purvey some concept of fairness and flexibility, an ability to change in response to the changing internal and external demands put upon it. Indeed, to the extent that a totalitarian regime permits the threat of violence to be raised against it in the form of political pressure, it loses some of its totalitarian quality. The dynamics of totalitarianism, however, generally make this kind of evolution difficult, if not impossible. Dictatorships of one or a few raise the level of official terror to offset or deter the threat of violence from below. Terror and counter-terror may escalate until the whole system collapses in an orgy of violence. The prospects for raising anything but another such dictatorship out of such wreckage would seem remote, except that people tire of violence and presently respond

to it with passivity. Dictators are sometimes suspected of seeking an escape from this iron logic by provoking international wars which unite the country behind the leader, postponing issues of internal dissension.

The threat to carry political dissent outside peaceable channels can distract the government form the pursuit of other values, can impose upon it as its first and major responsibility the re-establishment of domestic peace and order, and can lure it into shortsighted measures to suppress violence, measures that may instead widen the base of opposition and increase the occasions for anti-government protests.

The mere threat of private violence directed against the government has a very great influence upon government actions. By causing reallocations of the resources of the society into the essentially negative goals of internal security, the opposition may succeed in defeating or crippling the positive goals whose accomplishment might legitimize and strengthen government authority. To avoid this predicament, even totalitarian governments occasionally go out of their way to appease their critics. The alternative to reform is ruthless suppression not only of the sources of the threat, but also of every symptom of united social action. Bowling clubs, assemblies of three or more people on street corners—there is no rational way to identify the first links of the chain which leads to social action. All must be broken up. The hopeless search for infinite security begins in this way; its logical end is the downfall of the regime. With this choice before it, it is easy to see why even a dictatorial regime may prefer social and political reform to the treat of violence. This is why so many kings and tsars rather than destroying their rivals and opponents, often sent them instead on enforced vacations and educational tours abroad.

In democratic societies this sharp dilemma is avoided far short of infinite deterrence. The institutional distribution of authority—constitutionalism—precludes unilateral attempts to centralize all the police powers in the hands of one agent. Also the law proscribes the overt threat of private violence and the existence of para-military forces, although it tolerates and protects the implied threat of violent outbreaks if political accomodation fails. Violence is demonstrated, not in organized forms, but rather in sporadic outbursts. Disgruntled elites who possess a clear capability for causing a planned demontration—who have, that is, organized groups with a deep sense of moral outrage and injustice—avoid incriminating themselves and provoking counter-action against themselves. Instead they carry out "peaceable demonstrations" designed to reveal their numbers and the intensity of their commitment. These may have the bonus effects of provoking violent action against them, causing government intervention, or causing their more inflammable followers to ignite into unplanned outbursts of violence. Such potentials are implicit in the situation.

The leaders of the agitators then are placed in a position of minimum risk and maximum effectiveness, that of playing the role of "responsible leader." They can bargain with formal authorities and with all the other members of the society in this way: "You must accept our just complaints and you must deal with us; otherwise, we will not be able to control our people. Unspeakable things may happen. We do not desire this to happen, but it is up to you to help us prevent it." While playing this role, the reformist leaders may not be unhappy to have their prophesies partially fulfilled by sporadic outbreaks. Events which demonstrate violence (and thus induce other elites to make concessions) do not have to be planned. Once the emotions of a real social movement are churned up, the problem is to keep the events from happening.

The irresponsible elements may be disowned, but the bargaining power of the responsible leaders is enhanced. In the bargaining process, the moderate leaders often accept concessions which fall short of those demanded by some of their more extremist followers. Opportunists or "realists" often inherit the benefits wrought by the blood of martyrs. This is a healthy mode of exploiting the demonstration of violence without condoning it, enabling compromises to be reached which isolate the extremists and render them less

dangerous to the body politic. Most followers in social movements will follow responsible leadership through the gives-and-takes of compromise, because they share the general fear of unlimited violence and counter-violence, with its unpredictable results and the defeat of all rational goals. Accomodations can be reached, even if only provisionally, which preserve the general consensus in maintaining the form and continuity of society and law.

V. Some Concrete Examples

Let us turn to some concrete examples of how violence works its effects in practice.

A classical case of its actual demonstration against the legality of existing authority is the founding of the state of Israel in 1949. The Irgun, an underground terror organization, created conditions in Palestine which made further British occupation impractical. There is some doubt whether the British government would have honored their commitment to the Jewish Agency or honored it when they did, had it not been for the Irgun's role. Yet the Jewish Agency, the responsible and moderate leadership, negotiated the partition of Palestine and played the major role in the founding of the new state, all the while disavowing the terrorist acts and methods of the Irgun. Before the launching of Irgunist terror, the British government stalled the Jewish Agency and accorded it little respect.

More instructive are cases of domestic violence where the actual demonstration is minimal and where the implicit threat is all, as in the current compaign for Negro rights. Until the last decade, little sustained pressure was exerted to improve the Southern Negro's position by governmental action. Even with the growth of Negro voting power in the big cities of the North, Washington authorities have generally shown great respect for the implicit capabilities of violence of well-organized white supremacists. Partly because of the power of the White South in the Congress, in Democratic National Conventions, and in the Electoral College, presidents have acted with restraint in protecting the rights of Southern Negroes. So long as the possibility of violence was asymmetrical, the Whites well-organized and armed, the Negroes apathetic, intimidated, and disorganized, Negro attempts to register to vote, to protest lynchings and other injustices, could easily be tranquillized by the County Sheriffs, the local police, and the KKK. In the last decade, Negroes have been in the throes of a new self-consciousness, confidence, organization, and leadership. The Black Muslims, the Committee on Racial Equality, the NAACP, etc., have now demonstrated that the Southern Negro is capable of social action and of organized demonstrations of strength. As the capability grows for effective counter-violence against White Citizen Council activities—or, what is more significant, non-violent demonstrations which invoke violence by the extremist Whites—the Negro will gain increasing consideration for his demands, increasing support from "moderate" white leaders, and increasing attention and support from the federal authorities. Just as the existence of the White Citizens Councils strengthened the hand of southern moderates in trying to restrain civil rights action from Washington, so the existence of the Black Muslims and CORE now strengthens the position of the NAACP in seeking concessions from Southern Whites and action by the Justice Department. The threat of uncontrolled violent outbursts, hovering just beneath the surface, acts as a moderating influence, maintaining the institutions of peaceful process, inducing *status quo* groups to a greater readiness to yield some privileges, and restraining the responsible leaders of the insurgent Negroes from extremist demands.[8]

The strategy of non-violent social action (passive resistance or pacifism) does not abandon the threat of force as an instrument of social change. Rather, the threat operates within a civilized society by its provocative effects. By provoking the use of force by others, it forces the government to intervene on the behalf of the non-violent demonstrators, while evoking the sympathies of those less intensely involved. But as an international ideology, pacifism or unilateral non-violence may fail to achieve its objectives. Unless those who pursue it succeed in invoking some force in their behalf, they will be destroyed with impunity by their enemies.

The Dukhobor Sons of Freedom (of Vancouver, British Columbia) have adopted a novel tactic of demonstrating violence as they conduct their immemorial campaign against compulsory public education. They set fire to their own homes and barns, standing by and watching the blaze. They also parade naked down the center of city streets. The significance of these demonstrations is plain. Their religion forbids them to threaten or use violence against others. Instead, they symbolically demonstrate their discipline and passionate commitment to their own way of life by inflicting violence upon their own property. The naked marches provoke arrests and imprisonment and the house-burnings force the welfare agencies to provide temporary shelter. Both actions impose on the government responsibilities it is ill disposed to carry out, especially if such demonstrations are to continue indefinitely and involve the entire Dukhobor settlement. In addition, the demonstrations invoke public attention and sympathy for the believers. All of this may well give the local authorities an incentive to ignore Dukhobor defiance of school attendance laws. In fact, this is what has happened during the last 50 years. Efforts to enforce the law have been spasmodic and half-hearted, while the law has been generally evaded.

The relations of suicide and crime to social

[8] The recent violence at Oxford, Mississippi, involving the registration of Negro James Meredith at the State University, is likely to expedite Negro integration throughout the South. By precipitating violence (which resulted in two deaths), the White Extremists may have strengthened the ranks of the Moderates. Fearing a recurrence, white leadership in future situations may be more concerned with controlling the firebrands than in using them to force concessions from the Justice Department. Gunnar Myrdal put his finger on this when he referred to the "positive" aspect of the riots. "The riots make people think," he declared. *New York Times*, October 4, 1962, p. 10.

change form too large a topic for treatment here.[9] Durkheim studied these phenomena as an indicator or measure of social disorganization. They might also be studied in terms of demonstrating violence as an instrument of political and social change. When teenagers commit crimes, their legitimate grievances get more attention. When someone commits suicide, those who sense the circumstances that drove him to it are led to re-examine their own lives, and may be strengthened in convictions concerning the society in which they live. A suicide by an over-extended installment buyer in Chicago led to efforts to reform state and national laws governing loan-shark interest rates and collection of unpaid installment debts. A suicide, apart from its real motives, may be quickly exploited by those with a social cause. In effect, a suicide resembles a resignation from a government: it challenges values and institutions, evoking from all survivers a sense of the unresolved tensions which surround them, threatening the prospects for their own survival.[10] Suicides and crimes, however obscure and ambiguous, threaten the world and thus change it.

VI. Some Concluding Remarks

Several points may be made in conclusion. Demonstrations of domestic violence serve to establish the intensity of commitment of members of the political system. The more intense the commitment, the greater the risks the system will take in challenging the *status quo*. Accordingly, the greater will be the bargaining efficacy of future threats. Social change often occurs legalistically. Rationalization in terms of the continuity of abstract legal models is a useful means of stressing consensus over competition, adding to the stability of the whole society. However, it is obvious that a legal or ideological syllogism is meaningless except in terms of the emotional force which members of the society attach to the first principle. The infinite regress of syllogistic reasoning ends somewhere with a commitment of self. Such commitments cannot be explained or understood by reasoning alone. Efforts to adduce rational principles for explaining social and political change are futile unless one grapples with the often irrational and illogical intensity of self-commitment which marks social movements.

No system can hope to survive unless it can live with and adjust itself to the multitudinous threats of violence which are the basis of social change. Democracies have shown a greater ability to do this. Yet democratic forms can be subverted to become totalitarian in substance, if the search for infinite security in the international forum is reflected internally in a search for infinite deterrence of threats against the social and political *status quo*. Major social changes have major social causes; they are not the result of isolated conspiracies and plots. They cannot be arrested by an effort to stamp out all conspiracies and plots. In healthy democracies, all political leaders and would-be leaders are, in effect, conspirators and plotters. They must be. This kind of activity is the heart of political democracy.

---

[9] See summary of some pertinent research: Andrew F. Henry and James F. Short, Jr., *Suicide and Homicide* (Glencoe, Illinois, 1954), pp. 69–81.

[10] According to numerous press reports, the suicide of Marilyn Monroe led within a few days to a flurry of suicides by women. In the same manner, it may also have led to many decisions to live, which were not recorded.

SECTION **II**

THE FIVE C's: CAUSE, CHANGE AGENCY, CHANGE TARGET, CHANNEL, AND CHANGE STRATEGY

A. GENERAL DISCUSSION

13. The Elements of Social Action

Philip Kotler*

Abstract

   Social action is defined as the undertaking of collective action to mitigate or resolve a social problem. Large scale social action is a relatively recent phenomenon in man's history made possible by the scientific and industrial revolution and abetted by urbanization, mass communication, and technological progress. A paradigm of five elements—called the five C's—is advanced that encompasses a broad range of social action phenomena. A *cause* is a social objective or undertaking that change agents believe will provide some answer to a social problem. Three causes are distinguished: (1) helping causes, which attempt to help the victims; (2) protest causes, which attempt to discipline the offending institutions; and (3) revolutionary causes, which attempt to destroy the offending institutions. A *change agency* is an organization whose primary mission is to advance a social cause. *Change targets* are individuals, groups, or institutions designated as the targets of change efforts. *Channels* are ways in which influence and response can be transmitted between change agents and change targets. A *change strategy* is a basic mode of influence adopted by the change agent to affect the change target. Each concept is subject to important distinctions which are expected to be useful in analyzing, predicting, and planning social action.

° A Montgomery Ward Professor of Marketing, Northwestern University.

Introduction

Social distress has always been a feature of man's existence. War, pestilence, poverty, and oppression have been so characteristic of human history that one is tempted to a functionalist explanation that they somehow serve the needs of the human or natural order. Yet this possibility can never quite be accepted, and one always finds some fraction of mankind engaged in organized collective efforts to banish—or at least mitigate—the amount of social distress.

The ideology of social action—that man can improve his society through organized collective effort—received its major impetus only in the last few hundred years. Before the scientific and industrial revolutions, there was a great amount of social distress but very little social action. Man's afflictions were treated as an inevitable part of the natural order and persuasively rationalized in religious or economic terms. The scientific revolution gave man new understandings of his world, mind, and body and spawned the idea of progress. The industrial revolution opened the possibility of increasing production so substantially that food, clothing, housing, and medicine would be available to all. Other developments—the growing middle class, increasing literacy, popular regimes—gave birth to a humanitarian consciousness which began to consider how social forces could be harnessed to help the needy, the sick, and the oppressed.

In particular, large-scale social action, as a species of social behavior, is a relatively recent phenomena. Today, large numbers of people join or support causes aimed at improving some aspect of society. They raise money for medical causes, give time to the needy, protest social injustice, and even challenge the established social order. Socially concerned people are organized, aided and abetted by a growing number of professional social actionists— lawyers, ministers, social workers, community organizers, social planners, teachers, radicals.

In spite of the increased outpouring and ministrations of concerned individuals and or-

ganizations, over the years, there is little evidence that man has reversed, or even held back, the amount of social misery. Social problems are very difficult to solve, resolve, or mitigate. Etzioni (1969:749) suggested:

> If we observe a society faced with a problem— poverty, riots, unsafe cars—and formulating a program to deal with it, we can be sure that nine times out of ten the problem will not be solved. If we look again, ten or twenty years later, we shall find that the problem may have been trimmed, redefined, or redistributed, but only infrequently will it have been treated to anyone's satisfaction. Thus, we flatly predict that 15 years from now there will still be massive poverty in the United States (despite the "total war" devoted to its eradication), there will still be outbreaks of violence in the streets during hot summers, and there probably will still be tens of thousands of casualties on the highways each year.

Even when social action proves effective, it often succeeds in replacing one social problem with another. The Eighteenth Amendment destroyed the saloons and the whisky trust but created organized crime. Better street lighting in one neighborhood often drives crime into the next. Many men who stop drinking alcohol start increasing their intake of cigarettes. Reducing the birth rate could lead to more affluence and in turn to more pollution. Thus nature continuously confronts man with the fact that every change creates new social imbalances.

Yet man has no choice but to wage war against his problems. It is of interest that in spite of the magnitude of social action no unified theory has been advanced concerning its nature, elements, antecedents, and consequences. The progress of theory is handicapped by the different vocabularies and perspectives of clergymen, politicians, educators, social workers, radicals, and others involved in social action. Each group has formulated situation-specific models of the social action process in which they are engaged. The structural and process similarities between the actions of angry students, Washington lobbyists, and ghetto organizers are rarely given theoretical recognition. Yet persons involved in social action—protesting the war, converting non-believers, motivating dropouts, and disabusing drug addicts—always find their problems are similar.

This article takes a look at the elements that seem to be common to all social action. The first section defines how the following terms will be used: social problem, social change, and social action. The following sections elaborate the five C's of social action: cause, change agency, change targets, channels, and change strategy. These five elements are the building blocks for understanding the phenomenon of social action.

Social Problems, Social Change, and Social Action

This section defines three important concepts that will be used in the following discussion. The first is social problem, in the absence of which social action would have no meaning.

Social problem: a condition or group of conditions in society which is viewed apprehensively or distastefully by some of its members and which is thought to be susceptible to mitigation or elimination through collective action.

Thus social problems depend on the development of a group definition of a situation. Teenager drug usage is essentially a private habit, but it becomes a social problem when some individuals begin to view it apprehensively or distastefully and feel some action should be taken against it. Poverty passes from being a personal affliction to a social problem when a group begins to view it apprehensively or distastefully and they call for social action. Alcoholism is a social problem because people think something should and can be done about it. Death from old age, however, is not a social problem because people see no solution.

The next term is social change:

Social change: alterations in the attributes or functioning of individuals, groups, institutions, or society.

Social change takes place continuously as individuals, groups, institutions, and societies receive and respond to new stimuli. It is important to distinguish between unplanned and planned social change. Social change will take place even in the absence of conscious change agents pursuing social goals. Inventions, crop failures, diseases, historical personages, all have a tremendous potential for altering the relations among men and between men and the natural habitat, perhaps more than the collective effects of planned social change.

Finally, social action has to be defined:

Social action: the undertaking of collective action to mitigate or resolve a social problem.

The aim of social action is social change in a direction deemed desirable by the agents of change. Success is seen in terms of overcoming or mitigating a social problem.

The Five Elements of Social Action

In every instance of social action, it is possible to distinguish five elements, which may be called the five C's of social action. They are defined below:

Cause: a social objective or undertaking that change agents believe will provide some answer to a social problem

Change agency: an organization whose primary mission is to advance a social cause

Change targets: individuals, groups, or institutions designated as the targets of change efforts

Channels: ways in which influence and response can be transmitted between change agents and change targets

Change strategy: a basic mode of influence adopted by the change agent to affect the change target

These elements are examined in the remaining sections of this article.

Causes

There are far more causes in society than there are social problems. Each social problem spawns a number of divergent solutions by different individuals and collectives. When a sufficient number of persons favor that solution, it becomes their "cause." If this cause is pursued with enough vigor, it may be turned into a *function*, that is, acquire functionaries who professionally handle it. The function may take different forms, such as a social agency, a national organization, a social movement, or a political party. By the time the cause becomes institutionalized, it may no longer be clearly tied to the original social problem but rather represent a general solution applicable to many social problems.

A Classification of Causes

A meaningful classification of causes would be helpful in a number of ways. It would show the underlying dimensions that unite or separate different causes. Each class of cause is likely to involve different relationships among the five elements of social action. Furthermore each class of cause may suggest particular mixes of change strategies—power strategies, persuasive strategies, and reeducative strategies. "Lighter" social causes may call for primary reliance on persuasive strategies while "heavier" social causes may require substantial doses of power or reeducation.

Insofar as causes arise to mitigate or eliminate a social problem, it is possible to develop a three way classification of causes based on the nature of the attack on the social problem. The three types of causes are: (1) helping causes, (2) protest causes, and (3) revolutionary causes.[1]

Helping causes represent the mildest form of social action on behalf of the victims of a social problem. There is no effort to attack the social problem at its roots. This is deemed to be impossible, infeasible, or undesirable for that *agency* to do. The agency instead concerns itself with providing aid, comfort, or education to the actual or potential sufferers. Helping causes direct their time and resources to the poor, the drug addicts, the dropouts, the aged and so on. The prime example of a helping agency are the social work agencies for whom social action meant, until recently, working with the victims of social maladies.

Social action meant individual or group case work, with community action representing only a recent development.

Protest causes (also called reform causes) are primarily concerned with identifying the institutions that contribute most to the social problem and altering their behavior in a way which will improve the condition of the victims. The protesters may ask the offending institutions to distribute greater resources to the victims, share some of its powers, or desist from certain practices. Consider the labor movement in this connection. It evolved from a helping movement to a protest movement. Early trade union activity consisted of the effort of laboring men to provide self-help to those among them in need. This was superseded by a protest movement that identified the company as a contributor to the plight of workingmen and sought to effect a redistribution of power and resources in favor of the workingmen. At the same time, most labor movements have not evolved beyond protest movements, being satisfied to discipline the "offenders" rather than eliminate them.

Revolutionary causes take as their social objective the elimination of those parties or institutions that contribute most to the social problem. They take the position that as long as the offending institution exists, no matter how cooperative or benign it may be, the social problem and its victims cannot be helped very much. The social problem is seen to be fathered by the existence of that institution, whether it be private property, the church, the modern university, etc. Revolutionary causes need not take on violent means to pursue their ends. Socialism and communism are both revolutionary movements; however, the former wants to vote private property out through th ballot box, and the latter sees violence as necessary.

[1] Two other types of causes will not be discussed here. *Escapist causes* are those where the victims decide to withdraw psychologically or physically from the offending situation. Withdrawal cannot be considered a form of social action except in a very special sense. *Conservative causes* involve an agency that denies the existence of the social problem or the desirability of increasing social reforms or resources beyond the present level. Conservative causes typically rationalize the order of things and can be considered a form of social action to counter social action.

Stages in the Life Cycle of Causes

In addition to distinguishing classes of causes, it is useful to distinguish cause stages. According to Cameron (1966:27–28):

> There is no characteristic life cycle of social movements. . . . If we quantify the development of a movement by counting members, amounts of income and expenditures, number of outside persons needed, number of pieces of literature, and so on, we find great variations. . . . Some movements grow very slowly . . . others seem blessed with the vitality and reproductiveness of a mushroom and accumulate personnel and property with great rapidity . . . some skyrocket into prominence and then almost as quickly decline.

Although there is great variation in the rates of growth and decline of social movements, many of them pass through certain well-defined *organizational* phases, or stages. Each stage is characterized by a particular set of problems, strategic options, and leadership styles. One of the more typical patterns is illustrated in Figure 13.1, and consists of four organizational stages—the crusading stage, popular cause stage, managerial stage, and bureaucratic stage.

A great number of causes start out as a crusade led by a few zealous individuals who have a knack of dramatizing a social ill. To the extent their message is effective, new supporters are attracted and the cause may reach the stage of a popular movement. As a popular movement, it is still led by the original leaders whose primary quality is total absorption in the cause and concomitant charisma. But as the ranks of this movement swell, new problems must be coped with, such as developing clearer definitions of roles and responsibilities and attracting adequate resources to keep the organization going. New types of leaders start being favored, those who have organizational skills, and the cause passes into the managerial stage. The reins are tightened and more specific goal setting, planning, and coordination take place. Nevertheless, with luck, the new leaders retain some of the original zeal. Finally, the movement passes into a bureaucratic phase in which the original zeal is lost and the cause is in the hands of functionaries whose main concern is organizational survival. The cause is run like any other business with a product to sell, a rigid hierarchy, established policies, much functional specialization, and so on. Even the job of maintaining a following and support is handled as a specialist function.

These four stages are not inevitable or irreversible. The National Polio Foundation, after the successful development of the Salk vaccine, faced either a phasing out or an adoption of a new cause, and chose the latter course with a new zeal. In other cases, a new leader may appear who gives a flabby movement a new vitality. The consumer protection movement was in a slump for years. Then Ralph Nader appeared and transformed it into a popular movement again. On the other hand,

Figure 13.1.   Stages in the Life Cycle of a Cause.

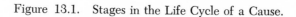
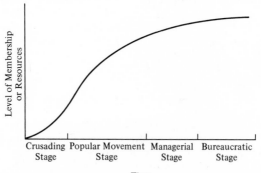

Time

other cause organizations that once commanded power and public attention limp along, such as the Women's Christian Temperance Union, hoping but not being able to regain their former glory.

Change Agency

A change agency is an organization seeking to bring about social change. The change agency might be an *informal group* (e.g., concerned citizens group), a *formal organization* (for example, social agency, political party), or a *political unit* (for example, community, nation, international body).[2]

Those who serve in some relationship to the change agency can be called change agents. This is a broader definition than the one advanced by the staff of the National Training Laboratory (cf. Lippitt, 1958:10–14, 187–208, 226–238) or in the diffusion of innovation literature (Rogers, 1969) which define the change agent as a specialist in change, such as group workers, county agricultural agents, good government groups, community organizers, and so on. The broader definition is taken to permit a broader analysis of the roles played in advancing a cause.

Classification of Change Agent Roles

It is possible to distinguish two major roles, with several breakdowns, that change agents might have to the change agency.

The change agents fall into two groups, *leaders* and *supporters*. The leaders include six types of persons. The *directors* are those who started or head the organization and wield the power. Such names come to mind as Ralph Nader (consumer protection), Francis W.

Willard (WCTU), Eldridge Cleaver (Black Panthers), and so on. The *advocates* are those who wield the pen rather than the power but are close to those in power. For example, the peace movement has many leaders who write and speak to spread the cause of ending the war in Vietnam: John Kenneth Galbraith, David Riesman, Noam Chomsky, Paul Newman, Mary McCarthy, and so on. The *backers* are those who provide the purse. They supply the financial resources to keep the organization operating and are close to those who wield the power. Backers are typically wealthy individuals who become angels for the cause or who are excellent at raising money from others to support the cause. The *technicians* are those who provide professional advice or service, i.e., expertise, to the directors. They may be hired, they may volunteer their services, or they may serve on the staff of the organization. Major technician types are public relation specialists, professional fund raisers, advertising practitioners, community organizers, lawyers, and management consultants. Their attitude toward the cause may range from high enthusiasm to simply the professional sale of their services. The *administrators* are those who run the day-to-day affairs of the organization. They make sure that letters are answered, bills are paid, publicity is developed. Their commitment to the cause may range from intense enthusiasm all the way to "it's another job." Finally, the *organizers* are those who have effective skills in enlisting supporters and running programs and campaigns. These six groups—the directors, advocates, backers, consultants, aliministrators, and organizers—make up the agency's

---

[2] In the limit, the change agency may consist of one person. This person sets out on his own to correct some social problem, using legal, persuasive, or harassment procedures. Thus the anticigarette campaign received a tremendous boost in 1967 when John F. Banzhaf III, a young New York lawyer, filed a petition to the Federal Communications Commission asking them to require the television networks to provide equal time for anticigarette messages. He received a favorable ruling and this began the very effective barrage of antismoking commercials on TV (cf. Whiteside, 1970).

As another example, a mysterious individual called the "Fox" operates in Chicago's South Side to harass the steel companies for their pollution by dumping polluted water on executive carpets, jamming plant sewage systems, and placing antisteel signs throughout the area (cf. Royko, 1970).

leadership. Certain persons may combine a number of leadership roles, especially in earlier stages of the agency, but these roles become more specialized as the agency grows.

Every cause that takes root gains a larger group of supporters or followers. Here three roles can be distinguished. The *workers* (that is, "heelers") are those who are committed enough to the cause to give their time to it. They are the ones who ring doorbells in political campaigns, participate in demonstrations and marches, and help in mailings. *Donors* make contributions of money rather than time to the cause. Finally, there may be a much larger group of *sympathizers* (that is, fellow travelers) who neither work for nor give much money to the cause but give it lip-service support. They are willing to sign petitions, occasionally appear at rallies, and talk in social settings to friends about their feelings. One of the principal jobs of the cause's leaders is to convert sympathizers into donors or active workers.

Thus making up any change agency is a whole range of persons who participate in sundry and complex ways to further the agency's cause. Furthermore, many different change agencies may be involved in any particular area of social concern. For example, Mackenzie (1962) has identified the following groups as active in matters of educational reform: students, teachers, principals, supervisors, superintendents, boards of education, local community, state legislature, state boards or departments of education, state and federal courts, foundations, industrialists, national government, noneducationalists, academicians, teacher training institutions, and professional teacher organizations.

Individual Motives for Participating in a Cause

People participate in social action for a variety of reasons. Aside from the good they might do, they presumably derive satisfaction of one or more psychological needs in the individual's make-up. They may be satisfying consciously or unconsciously an affiliation need, a status need, a power need, or a faith need. *Affiliation seekers* have a strong need to be and work with others. Social causes represent one vehicle for satisfying this need. *Status seekers* have a strong need for respect from others. Thus they join causes that might advance their social status. *Power seekers* have a strong need for power over others. The cause presents them with an opportunity for attention and power. In the extreme, they become demagogues who use the cause to advance their personal ambitions. Finally, *faith seekers* have a strong need for something to believe in that will give meaning to their lives. The cause promises to fill an ideological void or vacuum. When the individuals are particularly frustrated and possibly self-hating, they become what Eric Hoffer (1951) calls the True Believers.

Phases of an Individual's Engagement in a Cause

Those who participate actively in a cause look forward to a certain degree of progress in accomplishing its aims. Disappointments and setbacks, which to some extent are inevitable, will test the real motives, fortitude, and maturity of the various participants. Each individual will pass through several stages marked by growing or abating devotion. The psychological phase pattern in the typical case goes from *enthusiasm* to *frustration* to *reduced expectations* to *adjusted participation*, with occasional returns to earlier emotions with the ups and downs of the cause's successes. Some of the participants will drop out, usually those who joined the cause with unrealistic expectations or more personal motives.

The phase pattern in any particular case is complex and must be modeled carefully. The experiences of Peace Corps volunteers in the Philippines provides a useful example. In two short years, four volunteers resigned and twenty-six others were sent home because they were not able or willing to cope. Even among those remaining, some volunteers became cynical, or hostile, or relented in their efforts and would have liked to find an honorable way to return home if they could face an overwhelming sense of personal failure. Volunteers typically passed through seven stages of coping with their environment (cf. Fuchs, 1967:245-246):

1. The volunteer was curious and waited for signals as to what he should do.

2. He became impatient with the failure of Filipinos to give clear clues and developed a strong desire to accomplish something.

3. He started projects in school and community, sometimes with apparent success, often with failure, and began to realize how deep are the problems inherent in fundamental change.

4. He discovered that Filipinos might simulate change to please him but that nothing had really changed.

5. He reacted by working harder and by trying to push Filipinos to accomplish things his way.

6. He felt depleted and defeated in the realization that pushing did not result in real change.

7. He began to accept and enjoy individual Filipinos for what they were in an almost unconscious recognition that any change in skills and abilities depended on changes in values, and that such shifts could not be effected by action or words except through mutually accepting relationships.

These stages, which had several variations for different Peace Corps volunteers, underscore one of the key needs facing the top leadership of any movement—that of paying special attention to the recruiting, selection, training, and motivation of the cause's supporters.

Change Targets

The change targets are individuals, groups, or institutions designated as the targets of change efforts. The change agency seeks to influence a change in the behavior of the change target. This change is seen as an important step in the solution of the social problem.

Helping causes, by definition, designates the actual or potential victims of the social problem as the change targets. Consider the following examples:

Change Agent	Change Target
Social work agency	The poor
American Heart Association	Smokers, overweight people
Family Planning Association	Mothers, the public
Antidrug groups	Actual or potential users

These helping agencies often talk of the change targets as their clients. Their main target is a *client system*.

Protest causes single out offending institutions as the change targets. Labor movements seek to discipline companies; student movements, universities; and poor movements, government. Their objective is not to destroy the institution but rather wrest concessions from it. They employ direct tactics (confrontation, harassment, negotiation) as well as indirect tactics (public rhetoric and coalitions designed to leverage their pressures against the institution). They describe their target as a *power system*.

Revolutionary causes also single out offending institutions as their change target, but their aim is to destroy or emasculate them. The change target is an *enemy system* that cannot be benign even if its leaders wished it to be. It is a root cause of social distress that has to be extirpated, either through the ballot box or violently.

Although the *ultimate targets* of a cause are victims or offending institutions, the change agency also seeks to influence *intermediate targets* because of their capability of influencing in turn the ultimate targets. There are four key intermediate targets for social action. The first is the *public*. Most social actionists attempt to arouse the sympathies of the public for their cause in the hope that this will influence other institutions or the ultimate targets. The second is the *government establishment*. Social actionists for helping and protest causes typically view the government as a major resource for mitigating the social problem, hoping for reform legislation, judicial decisions, or administrative enforcement to discipline the offending institutions or help the victims. The third intermediate target is the *business establishment*, or technostructure. When business is not involved as the offending institution, it is sought as an ally against the offending institutions. Or the support of noninvolved business firms is sought against other business firms that are the ultimate target. Still another frequent intermediate target is the *professional establishment* (educators, engineers, scientists, lawyers, doctors). Drug control programs enlist the participation of educators, lawyers, and doctors; pollution control programs enlist the support of engineers, scientists, lawyers, and so on. In general, the development of a change program by a change agency requires identifying the key intermediate targets or reference publics, and mapping their influence relations on the ultimate target.

Target Segmentation

Whether the change target is conceived as a client system, power system, or enemy system, change agencies attempt to apply *target segmentation* to aid their efforts. Target segmentation is a major step in effective social action. Too often the target system is stereotyped, and its members and institutions are approached in the same way. Yet the fact is that any target group contains persons at different stages of accessibility and susceptibility to the cause. The change agency must pay attention to these differences and search for the most meaningful dimensions of effective segmentation. The change agent can draw on demographic, geographic, psychographic, behavioral, and social structural variables for segmenting target individuals and institutions.

A notable example of target segmentation, where the public was the target, was performed by Pool and Abelson (1961) in connection with the 1960 political campaign of John F. Kennedy. The American voting population was segmented into 480 types by cross-relating identification data on region, city size, sex, race, socioeconomic status, party, and religion. For example, one voter type was "Eastern, metropolitan, lower-income, white, Catholic, female Democrats" while another voter type was "Border state, rural, upper-income, white, Protestant, male Independents." The political analysts then took the further step of identifying fifty-two issue clusters (for example, foreign aid, attitudes toward the United Nations) and cross-related each voter type's distribution of pros, cons, and indifferents on each issue. The end result was the creation of an analytical and predictive mechanism for estimating the effects of different possible candidate stands on the likely number of votes.

The kind of segmentation variables that count vary with the cause class. In a helping cause, such as working with drug addicts, the change targets can be segmented by (1) the degree of their present addiction, (2) the number of years they have been habituated, and (3) the underlying motives(s). The first dimension leads to distinguishing four classes of persons in relation to drug use: (1) nonusers, (2) ex-users, (3) light-users, (4) heavy-users. The first group, the nonusers, can be subdivided into the susceptibles and the nonsusceptibles. Only the former are a meaningful target group and here the change agency's main effort takes on a persuasive character, particularly the use of fear appeals. The ex-users, on the other hand, need the type of support offered by individual and group therapy, that is, reeducative techniques. Finally, the light- and heavy-users may be reached with the previous approaches plus power tactics, e.g., the threat of imprisonment. In addition, the heavy-users (the addicted) require a higher counseling and medical input than the light-users. This preliminary analysis can be improved considerably by introducing additional variables: the number of years of drug usage and the underlying motivational structure of the user. By cross-relating the significant segmentation variables, distinct drug-user types can be identified and social action and treatment can be tailored to individual segment dynamics.

A different set of variables faces a peace movement group trying to identify its change targets. The relevant power systems include agency's limited resources have to be allocated the university system, and so on. The change among these target systems to gain the great- the military subsystem, the business system, est impact. Even the public is a target system, and a peace movement would want to distinguish at least among the following citizen types:

1. *Militant right*: My country is always right, and I would like to beat the brains out of those who smear it.
2. *Patriots*: We should honor our country.
3. *Four-year voter*: I want to give the Presi-

dent a chance. His problem is a difficult one. Besides, we can vote him out at election time if he doesn't satisfy us.

4. *Spare time opponents*: I don't like our policies in Southeast Asia. I will express my opposition in my spare time but won't participate in anything disruptive.

5. *Peaceful dissenter*: I think my opposition to the war must be expressed in more substantial ways such as demonstrations, rallies, and other forms of peaceful dissent.

6. *Militant dissenter*: I don't feel we should tolerate a group of fascists who run this government and murder innocent people abroad. We must use all means to stop them, including sit-ins, marches on the Pentagon, and even terror and bombs if necessary.

7. *Revolutionary*: I think the whole country is corrupt, and its institutions must be destroyed before we can enter a new age.

The peace organization seeking public support realizes there is little to gain from efforts directed at the first two groups because the chance of conversion is so low and too much effort per target is required. There is more chance of creating popular response by directing effort at group 3 and particularly at group 4. The rhetorics for each group must be appropriately chosen.

The segments chosen for major attention should meet three conditions. The first is *accessibility*, the degree to which meaningful channels exist for reaching the particular change target. Power centers such as the White House, the Pentagon, and the corporate oligarchy are very inaccessible on a direct basis. The second is *substantiality*, the degree to which the segment is large, powerful, or meaningful enough to be worth separate effort. The third is *susceptibility*, the degree to which the target segment is likely to be responsive to change effort. When the peace movement chose universities as their primary target system for change effort, they were influenced mostly by the accessibility and susceptibility of this institution, rather than its substantiality in the total power system.

Channels

Change agents face the problem of selecting effective and efficient channels for reaching their change targets and being reached by them. The task is to determine efficient social contact mechanisms. The channels are often subtle and complicated and various professionals—advertising men, publicists, press agents, local leaders—are often required to help the change agents make a careful determination and selection of channels.

A typology of channels is presented in Table 13.1. The basic division is between influence channels and response channels, with further breakdowns of each. Influence channels describe ways by which change agents can reach change targets; response channels describe ways by which change targets can express their response to change agents.

Influence channels are subdivided in turn into media and personal influence channels. Media influence channels are those which deliver messages to the target audience detached from an interpersonal context. The first of these, the mass media, are print and electronic

TABLE 13.1   Typology of Channels

Typology of Channels

I. Influence Channels
    A. Media Influence Channels
        1. Mass media (Examples: television, radio, magazines, newspapers, billboards)
        2. Specialized media (Examples: the little magazines, newsletters, annual reports, announcements)
    B. Personal Influence Channels
        1. Mass meeting (Examples: rallies, demonstrations, assemblies, programs)
        2. Small groups (Examples: negotiation teams, threat squads)
        3. Individual visitations (Examples: lobbying, personal phone calls)
II. Response Channels
    A. Media Response Channels (Examples: telephone, telegraph, mail, paid advertisements)
    B. Personal Response Channels (Examples: visits to leaders, supporters, branch offices)

channels that reach great numbers of persons at home, work, or play, including many who may not have the slightest interest in the cause. Nevertheless, the mass media may be the most efficient way to spread the message in terms of cost per target audience exposure. The effect of any single exposure, or even set of repeatel exposures, may not be sufficient to trigger the desired response in the target. Instead it may play an important role in conditioning his receptivity to other stimuli, particularly from a personal channel. The mass media are so encompassing and instantaneous in their sweep that they are the only media that make possible a mass distribution of influence.

Specialized media include those print and electronic communication vehicles that are addressed to particular audiences and are not likely to be received by others except by chance. Included are the specialized publications of the professions and the lobbyists and all the announcements, newsletters, and annual reports that are sent out by all organizations. The key characteristic of specialized media is that they are mainly a communication device within the change agency system, that is between leaders and supporters, rather than a channel to outside target groups.

Personal influence channels also offer varied possibilities for reaching change targets. Mass meetings are designed to develop or intensify enthusiasm for a cause. However, like specialized nonpersonal media, they are directed primarily at the cause's present supporters to maintain or increase their spirit or knowledge rather than at other consumer targets. This is because mass meetings generally draw the current supporters and not those whose conversion is ultimately sought. Even mass media tend to reach current supporters more consistently than nonsupporters because mass audiences typically give selective, if not distortive, attention to the contents.

Small groups can be used effectively to reach a limited number of target individuals or groups. While the large demonstration or meeting may prepare the congressman to listen to an angry social action group, the small visiting committee who are admitted to his chambers may close the actual sale. Small

committees or cadres are channels used by larger organizations for a multitude of purposes, including friendly persuasion, social modeling, negotiation, and threat.

Individual visitation can be a highly effective method to reach and convert a target consumer. It signifies personal attention and interest in the consumer and allows a maximum tailoring of the message to the target. The more admired or the more matched the agent is to the target, the more effective the agent is likely to be. Even if the agent is a stranger, certain factors can make a difference in the effectiveness of this channel. The higher the agent's status relative to the target, the more favorable the target's likely response. Fund raisers use this principle in approaching a person who is financially able to give more money than he has been giving. The individual who has given $10,000 last year is approached by an individual who gave $50,000 last year. A second principle is that if the agent is to be on the same status level as the customer, he will be more effective the closer his characteristics match those of the target customer. Thus an insurance agent manages to sell more insurance to persons like himself than to those who differ (cf. Evans, 1963).

The change target who decides to respond to the change agent's appeal can respond through various channels, not necessarily the same ones which carried the influence messages. There are two types of response channels—media response channels (telephone, telegraph, mail, and so on) and personal response channels (visits to the change agent). The probability of a positive response is enhanced by increasing the number and accessibility of response channels. This is illustrated in the celebrated United States bond promotion effort during World War II. The government made purchase as easy as possible by locating bond sales facilities in all post offices and most banks. On a special evening during the war Kate Smith appeared on a radio broadcast urging the American people to increase their bond purchases. A special response channel was set up: a citizen listening to the show could dial a special number and pledge to buy a bond. This additional channel served as a trigger-off mechanism and led to a tremendous sale of bonds in a single evening (cf. Wiebe, 1951–1952:679). Likewise, persons engaged in several other causes, such as in family planning and drug abuse, are beginning to appreciate the critical role played by response channels. In marketing terms, they are opening up new distribution channels for getting their product to the target system, including neighborhood store fronts, door-to-door service, the mails, and the telephone.

The feasibility and effectiveness of the possible channels of influence and response will vary with different types of targets. The *influence channel mix* for reaching the urban poor (e.g., to sell them on better nutrition or inoculation) is different than the mix for reaching and influencing congressmen. The most effective media for reaching the urban poor are broadcast media and individual visitations (D'Onofrio). Television and radio are more effective than newspapers and magazines because of higher illiteracy among the poor and the cost of print media, especially magazines. Individual visitations, especially by clergymen, social workers, physicians, and neighbors have a higher chance of being effective than visits by strangers. Mass meetings have not been particularly effective in drawing large numbers of urban poor although this may change. On the other hand, congressmen are most moved by incoming mail, group visitations, surveys, and other channels that directly bear upon the probability of their continuing in office.

Change Strategies

The change agency faces the problem of determining a realistic set of change goals for the target system and an effective plan for achieving the desired changes. The goals and plan constitute the *change strategy*. The change strategy represents the agent's conception of the most effective influence inputs he can introduce into the system to promote the change. The strategy will be characterized by certain assumptions about power, influence, and communication as they bear on the functioning of the target system. It will provide the basis for designing the change program,

including actions, timing, coalitions, instruments, and organization.

There are three basic ways in which a change agent can attempt to influence a change target—by *coercion, persuasion,* or *education*. Each change strategy works on a different premise concerning the best way to overcome the change target's resistance to the social object. Although an actual change program may combine two or all three strategies, here we will treat them as ideal types.

A power strategy is one that attempts to produce behavioral compliance or cooperation in the change target through the use of agent-controlled sanctions. Agents who resort to a power strategy are primarily concerned with changing the behavior rather than the beliefs or values of the change target. They seek to secure the desired behavior through agent-controlled sanctions such as authority, force, or payment. For change agents in a position of authority over change targets—parents (children), teachers (students), managers (workers), army officers (draftees), judges (defendants)—they can attempt to produce change in the change targets by threatening to withhold rewards or to issue punishment. For change agents who have no authority over the change target, two recourses exist. If the change agent views the change target as an enemy, the power strategy takes the form of force or threat of force—noncooperation, demonstration, harassment, or violence. If the change agent is neither an authority figure, or an enemy of the change target, the power strategy often takes the form of payment—(gifts or bribes) to induce the desired behavior. In general, the resistance, inertia, or indifference of a change target often invites the use of a power strategy involving the use of authority, force, or payment.

A persuasion strategy is one that attempts to induce the desired behavior in the change target through identifying the social object with the change agent's existing beliefs or values. The change agent does not use any external sanctions but rather attempts to find arguments showing that the desired behavior serves the natural interests of the change target. Three types of persuasive arguments are possible, according to Aristotle: *logos*, or appeals to logic; *pathos* or appeals to emotions; and *ethos*, or appeals to values. In the recent television campaign to discourage smoking all three appeals were used. *Logic-laden* commercials attempted to prove that cigarette smoking was harmful to health, *affect-laden* commercials sought to activate smoker's fears of death, and *value-laden* commercials implied that the smoker was immoral or irresponsible to his family because his death would hurt *them*. Persuasion strategies do not try to create or change beliefs or values but rather to activate existing ones through identification with the social object.

A reeducative strategy is one that attempts to induce the desired behavior in the change target through the internalization of new beliefs or values. Here the change agent seeks a deep and lasting change in the behavior of the change target. He does not think that this can be produced through power or persuasive tactics. The key seems to be in attempting to change the beliefs and/or values of the change agent. The reeducative strategists in an anti-smoking campaign will try to formulate messages directed at modifying either the beliefs or the values of the change target. Many people have a primitive belief in their own immortality; they psychologically do not think death will ever touch them, although intellectually they acknowledge it. A *belief-modification* strategy would attempt to alter their psychological beliefs about death so that in coming to a felt awareness of their mortality, they will feel dissonance over continuing to smoke. The strain toward congruity of belief and behavior is expected to lead them to drop the cigarette habit. Alternatively, the reeducative strategist can attempt to change a key value or its centrality in a person's value system. A *value-modification* strategy in the case of smoking is to make the whole issue of health more salient and cogent compared to other values held by the individual. It should be clear that reeducative strategies are the least

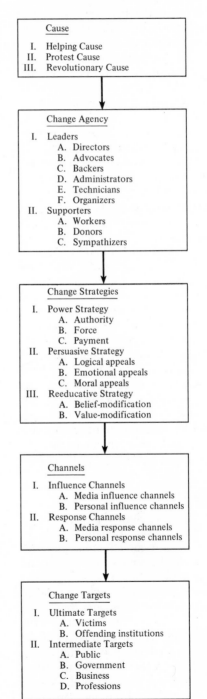

Figure 13.2.   The Elements of Social Action.

direct, most ambitious approaches to behavioral modification. They are mainly handled by skilled practitioners such as psychotherapists in individual situations or milieu therapists in group situations. It is doubtful that reeducative strategies are available or effective as an approach to the public as a whole or offending institutions. Even in a totalitarian society with absolute control over media and official opinion, there are important limitations to how much thought control can be affected. The ability of these regimes to mold public opinion and especially to motivate citizens is not as great as was once thought (cf. Pool, 1967).

Summary

Social action is the undertaking of collective action to mitigate or resolve a social problem. This article proposed a framework that would encompass a large range of social action phenomena—as found in social work, politics, reform movements, and revolutionary causes. Involving five elements—cause, change agent, change target, channel, and change strategy—it provides a useful foundation for social action analysis. Figure 13.2 summarizes this framework.

The direction of flow suggests a cause strategy that is carried through channels to various change targets. The direction is somewhat arbitrary. From a planning point of view, the social action problem may better begin with the designation of change targets, the determination of change strategies, the choice of channels, and then the structuring of the change agency. The framework examined here does not purport to get into the dynamics of the social planning process or the social change process. Rather it is designed as an initial framework for distinguishing the elements—the building blocks—as a prelude to effective social planning.

References

Cameron, Wm. Bruce 1966: *Modern Social Movements*. New York: Random House, 27–28.
D'Onofrio, Carol N. Undated: *Reaching Our "Hard to Reach"—the Unvaccinated*. Monterey: State of California, Department of Public Health.
Etzioni, Amitai 1969: "Toward a Theory of Guided Societal Change." *Social Science Quarterly*, 50 (December), 749–754.
Evans, Franklin B. 1963: "Selling as a Dyadic Relationship—A New Approach." *The American Behavioral Scientist*, 6 (May), 76–79.
Forrester, Jay W. 1971: "Counterintuitive Behavior of Social Systems." *Technology Review*, 43 (January), 53–68.
Fuchs, Lawrence H. 1967: "The Role and Communications Task of the Change Agent—Experiences of the Peace Corps Volunteers in the Philippines," in Daniel Lerner and Wilbur Schramm (eds.), *Communication and Change in the Developing Countries*. Honolulu: East-West Center Press, 245–246.
Hoffer, Eric 1951: *The True Believer: Thoughts on the Nature of Mass Movements*. New York: Harper & Row.
Lippitt, Ronald, *et al.* 1958: *The Dynamics of Planned Change*. New York: Harcourt Brace Jovanovich.
Mackenzie, Gordon N. 1962: "The Social Context of Curricular Change." *Theory into Practice*, 1 (October), 185–190.
Pool, Ithiel de Sola 1967: "The Public and the Polity," in Ithiel de Sola Pool (ed.), *Contemporary Political Science*. New York: McGraw-Hill.
——— and Robert Abelson 1961: "The Simulamatics Project." *Public Opinion Quarterly*, 25 (Summer), 167–183.
Rogers, Everett 1969: *Modernization Among Peasants: The Impact of Communication*. New York: Holt, Rinehart and Winston.
Royko, Mike 1970: "The Fox Fouls Corporate Nest." Chicago *Sun-Times* (December), 3.

Whiteside, Thomas 1970: "Annals of Advertising: Cutting Down." *New Yorker* (December 19), 42ff.

Wiebe, G. D. 1951–1952: "Merchandising Commodities and Citizenship on Television." *Public Opinion Quarterly,* 15 (Winter), 679–691.

B.   CAUSE

14.   Merchandising Commodities and Citizenship on Television

G. D. Wiebe*

While recognizing that citizenship is not soap, this article argues that efforts to "sell" broad social objectives via radio or television are not likely to succeed unless the essential conditions for effective merchandising exist, or can be made to exist. These conditions are primarily that the audience must be forcefully motivated and clearly directed to an adequate, appropriate, and accessible social mechanism. The author demonstrates the importance of these facets by case studies of four programs built around constructive social goals. An earlier version of this paper was delivered before the American Psychological Association in September, 1951.

Dr. Wiebe is Research Psychologist for the CBS Radio Network and Lecturer in psychology at The City College of New York.

The effectiveness of radio, and more recently of television, as advertising media requires no documentation beyond noting that American businessmen have invested hundreds of millions of dollars in radio and television advertising. Social scientists, seeing this enormous and successful motivational phenomenon, ask why these media cannot work with comparable effectiveness in molding behavior and habit patterns in such areas as citizenship responsibility and community participation. To some extent, radio and television have been, and continue to be, effective in these areas. But in these frightening times, the question persists: Why can't you sell brotherhood and rational thinking like you sell soap? If the query is usually stated with less bluntness, it nevertheless poses the same essential question.

We can agree, to begin with, that the answer certainly will not be simply that radio and television can or cannot function in social areas as well as they can in motivating people to buy commodities. The answer will be complex. First of all, we may delimit our problem substantially by noting that the seller of commodities is basically interested in getting as many people as possible to engage in a specified unit of overt behavior. This overt behavior is, with few exceptions, the purchase of his product. The social scientist often disavows the achievement of specified behavior as an objective. In such instances, there is no longer a basis for comparison.

This paper is addressed to such persons as the one who said: "Look here, you claim, and I believe your claim, that radio and television

Reprinted from G. D. Wiebe, "Merchandising Commodities and Citizenship on Television," *Public Opinion Quarterly* (Winter, 1951–1952), Vol. 15, pp. 679–691.
* Dean, School of Public Communication, Boston University.

have caused hundreds of thousands of people to alter certain personal habits and to spend hundreds of thousands of dollars a year to buy the particular commodity involved in this change of habit. Now think what radio and television could do about juvenile delinquency, and many comparable problems, if they could release a similar flow of energy and money in these important areas." Why, he asks, can't radio and television "sell" the reduction of juvenile delinquency like they have sold the use of the home permanent wave? Our answer is that perhaps radio and television can help to achieve social and cultural objectives, given certain conditions. These conditions can most appropriately be studied where they are known to exist; that is, in the merchandising of commodities.

Minimum Conditions for Selling Commodities

The seller of a commodity, whether it be a home permanent or an automobile, assures himself that certain agencies, mechanisms, and conditions exist and are in good working order before he advertises his product. Consider a few of these: He assures himself that the commodity is being produced or manufactured. He assures himself that a smooth distribution system is available. He assures himself that retail outlets exist, and will handle his product. He assures himself that the immediate setting in which the buyer obtains the product is attractive, available, and convenient.

Now, cultural objectives cannot be purchased "at your nearest drug or department store." But nevertheless, there is a fruitful observation to be made here. Note especially the retail outlet as a social mechanism. The advertiser sets up, or affiliates with, a social mechanism in which the behavior motivated by his advertising may be consummated with a minimum expenditure of energy. Then he advertises. The function of radio and television advertising in selling commodities may now be seen in proper perspective. Radio and television advertising perform one basic function. They motivate the potential customer to traverse those last few steps that separate him

from the social mechanism in which he can complete his behavioral intention.

Advertising does not move people to unilateral action. It moves them into interaction with social mechanisms. The emphasis on that phrase "social mechanism," rather than on the people who operate these mechanisms, perhaps carries some connotation of a clanking robot. But the phrase is used advisedly because the people who operate them engage in highly specialized role behavior which is characteristic of the mechanism. I speak primarily of retail sales people. Their behavior is highly structured to conform with the purpose of the social mechanism in which they work. The function of that mechanism is to facilitate the actual purchase of commodities.

It is the crucial importance of the retail store, viewed as a social mechanism which facilitates the desired behavior, that social scientists often seem to overlook when they yearn for behavioral changes comparable to those achieved by advertisers.

Having considered some of the conditions that characterize the advertising and sale of commodities, we may now attempt to generalize our finding in the form of a principle which may be of use to social scientists. Until it has been much more extensively examined and tested, it must, of course, be submitted as an hypothesis.

The success of mass persuasion, in terms of motivating behavior, is a function of the audience member's experience with regard to five factors:

1. the force
2. the direction
3. the mechanism
4. the adequacy and compatibility
5. the distance

A word of explanation regarding each of these five factors seems appropriate. The *force* of the motivation refers to the experience of the audience member which is only partially determined by the content of the radio or television communication. The force of the motivation is a combination of one's predisposition toward the goal prior to the radio or television program *and* the motivation provided by the communication.

The *direction* of motivated persons to the mechanism consists of telling audience members specifically where or how they may easily consummate their motivation in interaction with a social mechanism. The third factor refers simply to the existence of an *implementing social mechanism*. The *adequacy* and *compatibility* of the mechanism refers to whether the mechanism can, and whether it is inclined, to facilitate the goal behavior. The *distance* of the audience member from the mechanism might be rephrased as the audience member's subjective estimate of the intervening energy expenditure required, in comparison with the reward. Distance is used in its common meaning, but it also includes the counteracting, impeding and inhabitory factors that tend to keep the motivated person from achieving the goal of his motivation.

I wish now to discuss four programs, each of which was built around a constructive social objective, each of which had as its stated or clearly implied purpose the motivation of specific overt behavior. The relative success of these programs will be considered in terms of the five factors stated above. No attempt will be made to quantify the degree to which various factors are present. We will proceed in terms of estimates as to whether various factors appear to be relatively strong or weak.

THE CBS-Kate Smith Bond Selling Campaign

Most of you are familiar with the Bond Selling Campaign conducted by Kate Smith over the CBS Network on September 21, 1943. This spectacular event has been studied and reported in book form by Robert K. Merton.[1] Perhaps we can add a bit to the wealth of information contained in that book by considering Kate Smith's bond selling campaign from the point of view of our present discussion. All the elements of good merchandising appear to have been present and in good order.

The force of the motivation appears to have been strong. In 1943, audience members were

[1] *Mass Persuasion*, New York: Harper & Bros., 1946.

strongly predisposed to take tangible, specific part in helping their men in the armed forces. But the task of demonstrating the one-to-one relationship between civilian activities and winning the war was a chronic and perplexing problem to public information officials. Our economy is so complex and ultimate consequences are so far removed from initial causes that those who stayed at home had difficulty in finding a feeling of adequate partnership with their men in the armed forces. This difficulty was not overcome by presentation of the idea that buying bonds aided the prosecution of the war by reducing inflation. Inflation seemed remote and abstract compared to planes and bullets. The hazard of inflation was passed over in favor of another truth; namely, that individuals felt a strong need to experience their bond buying as direct aid to their fighting men. Kate Smith appealed directly and forcefully to this existing need.

As to the direction to the mechanism, the second factor, little was left to the imagination. Miss Smith spoke, repeatedly, as follows:

> "We've worked it out to make it the easiest thing in the world for every one of you to buy a war bond today. Every one of Columbia's stations, including the one that you're listening to now, has a special war bond telephone number. That's all there is to it. Listen for the phone number, jot it down, call that number and order that bond."

People knew exactly how to get in touch with the social mechanism.

The existence of the mechanism, the third factor, is apparent in the quotation above. At 134 CBS stations, extra telephone lines were manned by trained operators. Clerks were mobilized and trained to process the orders.

The mechanism was compatible with the motivation, the fourth requirement, for the mechanism was organized and operated exclusively to service bond buying calls. The adequacy of the mechanism was attested by the phenomenal number of calls that were handled.

The distance of the audience member from the mechanism, the fifth factor, is of special interest. Physical distance was literally reduced to the distance between the listener and his telephone. Psychological distance was also minimized. The listener remained in his own home. There were no new people to meet, no unfamiliar procedures, no forms to fill out, no explanations, no waiting (except that many people got busy signals on their telephones, and this probably had some bandwagon effect to counteract the annoyance). Inhibiting, impeding and counteracting forces were at a minimum. Perhaps the only one that was generally present was the usual reluctance to spend money. Even this was not simply an inhibitor because the appeal was for a personal sharing of deprivation. "Buy more than you can afford," said Kate Smith. "Buy a sacrifice bond." Thus financial sacrifice became compatible with the nature of the motivation.

We have reason, then, to expect this effort at mass motivation to be successful. It was indeed. Audience members called in their orders for bonds at the rate of more than two million dollars an hour, for a total of 39 million dollars in 18 consecutive hours. A year later, profiting by experience but using the same basic sales techniques, Miss Smith sold the phenomenal sum of $112,000,000 worth of War Bonds in 18½ consecutive hours.[2] In these instances, CBS played a multiple role. It provided the motivation and directed it to its own stations, which served as the social mechanism.

Civilian Defense Manpower

The Kate Smith bond selling campaigns were spectacular successes, but most social and cultural objectives cannot be achieved simply by means of telephone calls. Nor can radio or television stations usually undertake the functions of the mechanism. I should like to review, very briefly, a television campaign in which the inadequacy of the social mechanism is demonstrated.[3]

Station WJZ-TV was approached for assistance in mobilizing civilian defense workers.

The Civilian Defense people, to whom we may refer as "CD," were in the position of client. They came to the television station to advertise their product. The management of the station arranged to broadcast a weekly series of television shows. The objective was to persuade citizens of New York City to sign up at designated CD offices for training and continuing responsibility in the local CD organization. These CD offices and their personnel and procedures are, in this instance, the mechanism.

Note that audience members were, in this case, asked to leave their homes, find an unfamiliar address, and voluntarily pledge a substantial amount of their leisure time to be spent at unspecified tasks under the tutelage of unknown persons. Granted that some persons were strongly predisposed in favor of participation in CD, this goal still called for very substantial impact from the television programs.

The series was soon discontinued. Registration facilities were so overburdened by the response that even mimeographed acknowledgments of registration, together with pleas for patience, were running many weeks behind. Teachers, facilities, training manuals, equipment—these and the general administrative provisions were all inadequate.

Without considering each of the five factors in detail, it is apparent that the motivation had force, the direction to the mechanism was specific, the mechanism (namely, the CD organization) existed and was undoubtedly compatible with the motivation. The response is evidence that the distance of the audience member from the mechanism was overcome. But the mechanism was not adequate. While the campaign, insofar as television was concerned, was a notable success, the total campaign must be considered less than successful since hundreds of responsive citizens were, in effect, rebuffed after having responded to what they were led to believe was a dire need in an emergency.

---

[2] Columbia Broadcasting System. Incorporated. *Annual Report For The Fiscal Year Ended December 30, 1944.*

[3] I am indebted to Mr. Robert Saudek of the American Broadcasting Company for the information on which this analysis is based.

An Outstanding Documentary

If the civilian defense incident illustrates a compatible, but inadequate mechanism, a third program will illustrate the complete absence of a mechanism.

In March of 1947, CBS broadcast an hour-long documentary radio program entitled, "The Eagle's Brood." The program dealt with juvenile delinquency. The objective of the program was, directly or indirectly, to reduce the incidence of juvenile delinquency. Unless you had the memorable experience of hearing this program, I must ask you to accept, on faith, my statement that its impact was vivid and compelling. Thus we will assume that the program rated well in terms of the force of the motivation. With regard to the second factor, listeners were not directed to a mechanism.

What of the third factor? Where is the implementing mechanism? In terms of our analogy with the sale of commodities, where was the retail store? The mechanism was absent and the listener was admonished to create it. He was urged to "form a neighborhood council." "You find out," said the script, "who the leaders are in your neighborhood. Not the stuffed shirts . . . but the *real* leaders. You invite representatives of the clubs . . . the churches, the unions, the business groups. . . . You fan each other's interest. You get going." Nor was this an empty admonition. The script cited dramatic and vivid documentation of the effectiveness of neighborhood councils in reducing juvenile delinquency.

Compared with Kate Smith's "pick up the phone and buy your bond" or with the civilian defense program's "stop in and register," the admonition "form a neighborhood council" is certainly formidable.

Could a single radio program motivate people intensely enough so that they would, in fact, set up their own social mechanism? The psychological distance, in this instance, is almost certainly prohibitive. The inhibiting, the impeding, and the counteracting forces are numerous and apparent. It is, I believe, a singular tribute to the people who produced this documentary program, that several listeners wrote in, requesting more information, and stating that they intended to try.

Many social scientists would feel that aside from the actual establishment of neighborhood councils, the success of this program should be measured in terms of attitude changes and in terms of interest engendered among listeners. By these criteria, the program was without doubt successful.[4] These criteria, furthermore, are especially appropriate to the purposes of the broadcast. Let us agree, for the moment, that numerous neighborhood councils with the objective of reducing delinquency could hardly be expected to spring from the single documentary broadcast, moving as it was. Why, then, was it broadcast? We may presume that it was broadcast to provide information and to establish or intensify attitudes and interests which would predispose listeners toward constructive participation if the occasion for such participation should arise; that is, if and when an adequate and compatible social mechanism should come into being.

In terms of our analogy with the sale of commodities, it is as if a manufacturer were to advertise in order to predispose potential customers in favor of buying his product if, in the future, things worked out so that retail stores stocked his product. This situation was not uncommon during the Second World War when many advertised products could not be purchased. The seller was morally certain that he would get back into production of consumer goods in the future, and that his retail outlets would be intact. Meanwhile, his objective was not to motivate buying behavior, but to maintain or to intensify attitudes.

The immediate effects of the documentary broadcast on juvenile delinquency probably compared very favorably with immediate effects derived by those wartime advertisers. In both cases, the social mechanism was not

[4] Elmo Wilson has reported some of these outcomes in "The Effectiveness of Documentary Broadcasts," *Public Opinion Quarterly*, Vol. 12, No. 1 (Spring, 1948), pp. 19–29.

functioning. In both cases, the behavior awaited the activation of facilitating mechanisms.

The Televised Hearings of the Kefauver Committee in New York City

In discussing the Civilian Defense program, we found an inadequate mechanism. In discussing the documentary broadcast on juvenile delinquency, we found the mechanism to be non-existent. The recent Kefauver Committee hearings in New York City, when examined in terms of our five factors, illustrate several other defects not yet discussed.

The students in my Social Psychology class at The City College of New York raised the following question regarding the televised Kefauver hearings: To what extent will aroused citizens implement their attitudes in constructive citizenship behavior? To investigate this question, we formulated a questionnaire, and the students conducted 260 interviews among people of voting age who had seen varying amounts of the hearings on television.

I will not describe the sample beyond the general observation that it is not presented as statistically representative of New York City. It is moderately skewed toward professional and white collar people, toward the male sex and toward the 21- to 35-year-old age group. Thus the respondents might be expected to be somewhat better informed and somewhat more active generally than would a statistically representative sample. The respondents were from 12 different election districts of the city. Our interviews were conducted between 6 and 9 weeks after the close of the New York hearings.

The respondents answered this item: "The Kefauver hearings were about six weeks ago. As you think back to that time, how did you feel about the conditions that were brought to light?" Fifty-one per cent of the respondents indicated strong feelings in their responses. For example: "A shame, a disgrace." "It's deplorable and the voters are at fault." "I was shocked to think of politicians mixing up with racketeers." When people, after an interval of approximately two months, remember and

articulate feelings of shock, protest or anger, we may safely assume that the telecasts were experienced by them as forceful motivation. Hereafter, when we refer to "the sample," we will be referring only to these 134 "most affected" respondents.

The closed hearings of the Kefauver Committee were conducted primarily to gather information as a basis for corrective legislation by Congress. However, from statements made by Mr. Rudolf Halley, Chief Counsel, before the American Television Society, there is no doubt that the televising of the hearings was intended, if not primarily then at least secondarily, to arouse citizens, and to stimulate them to set their house in order. Editors and columnists joined in the stated or implied belief that the televised hearings would go far in reducing apathy among citizens. In the hearings themselves, however, audience members were not told specifically what to do. They were not directed to a mechanism. So, regarding our first two factors, we may say that motivation appears to have been forceful, but the direction of motivated persons to a mechanism was absent.

What of the third factor, an implementing social mechanism? Does one exist? Certainly it does. The political party organizations are such mechanisms. Their representative structure reaches from the individual party member, via representative levels, to the leaders of municipal government. The party in power is directly answerable to the citizen for the calibre of municipal government, and the party out of power traditionally exercises its right to criticize the shortcomings of the incumbents. Both major political party structures, then, are appropriate existing mechanisms for the processing and implementing of individual protests. Fifty-two per cent of our sample enjoyed formal membership in these mechanisms; that is, 52 per cent were enrolled party members.

What of the adequacy of the mechanism? There is probably no mechanism in New York City that is as adequate for representing and implementing rank and file motivation as is the mechanism of political party structure. At its base is a veritable army of committee men, approximately one for each 150 persons of voting age. From this broad base, the representative hierarchy rises through Election District Captains and Assembly District Leaders to the top echelons of officials. The mechanism is, at least theoretically, adequate.

Is the mechanism compatible with the motivation? Is it responsive? Certainly it cannot be compatible unless it is available. Are the committee men available to individuals? The respondents were asked the following question:

"Now I'm not asking you for anybody's name, but I would like to know whether you know your committeeman—just whether you know him or not."

Those familiar with the problems of phrasing questionnaire items will probably agree that this item may tend to invite "yes" answers. At any rate, 25 per cent answered "Yes," while 51 per cent said "No"; and 24 per cent responded, "What's a committeeman?"

These percentages represent all the respondents whether they were enrolled party members or not. When enrolled party members are taken as the base, the percentages on the same item are "Yes," 39 percent; "No," 46 per cent; and "What's a committeeman?", 15 per cent. From these figures we can only conclude that though the mechanism exists, and though it is theoretically adequate, it leaves much to be desired insofar as availability and compatibility are concerned.

But in spite of its limitations, 52 per cent of our respondents *belong* to the mechanism, and 25 per cent know their entrée to it through their committeemen. What, then, did our respondents do? To what did their motivation lead them? In gathering this information, students probed for the role or position of persons with whom the respondent interacted. Thus our information can be subdivided by the deference direction involved, with the following results:

6 percent in spite of probing, maintained that they had done absolutely nothing. They hadn't even talked to anyone about the hearings.

7 per cent had written to their congressmen in Washington.

3 per cent had discussed the hearings with persons below them in deference level—for example, their children.

78 per cent had discussed the hearings with individuals on a lateral deference level—for example, with friends, spouse, or with colleagues on the job.

6 per cent had discussed the hearings with persons above them in deference level.

It is among this last 6 per cent that we must look for those who registered their feelings with a social mechanism. Here is what these people, eight in number, had done:

2 discussed the hearings with their employers.

1 protested to the City Health Department over lax enforcement.

1 talked to "a judge, a colonel and a playground supervisor."

1 prayed for the souls of the racketeers.

2 discussed the hearings with people active in politics.

1 discussed the hearings with "committeemen and women of any party."

Only this last single individual reported that he went consciously and deliberately to the social mechanism which is, on the one hand, directly responsible to the citizen, and on the other hand, directly responsible for municipal government. This, I submit, is a remarkable finding when one considers two factors: first, that the scandal, bribery and corruption in municipal government exposed by the televised hearings had such impact on the people of New York as to seriously disrupt the normal flow of life in that city; and second, that the recently elected incumbent mayor and his high officials declared their independence of these sinister forces and so, presumably, would be sympathetic to an orderly demand for reform via the party hierarchy.

To what extent do these findings indicate an incompatible mechanism? To what extent do these findings have their roots in psychological distance as experienced by audience members? We cannot answer these questions from present data. Almost certainly both conditions are involved. If a mechanism were incompatible, this fact would probably be experienced by the audience member as increased psychological distance. But given a compatible mechanism, psychological or physical distance might still be great through no fault of the mechanism *per se*.

Let us consider only one bit of evidence relating to the fifth factor, the distance of the audience member from the mechanism. Respondents were asked:

"Do you think the Kefauver hearings will improve conditions in the long run, or do you think that things will settle down and be about the same as they were before?"

If audience members were skeptical about the worth of the campaign, this feeling would operate in direct counteraction to the force of the motivation. It would increase the psychological distance of the audience member from the mechanism—as if a person would say, "It was wonderful, it shocked me out of my lethargy, but it won't do any good. You can't change these things."

Will the hearings improve conditions? The responses fall into five categories:

Improve	27	per cent
Maybe improve	25	
About the same	37	
Get worse	1	
Don't know	10	

Varying amounts of skepticism are shown in 73 per cent of the responses. Even in terms of this single observation, we may conclude that the psychological distance, in the case of the Kefauver hearings, was substantial.

By way of summary, we may conclude that the televised Kefauver hearings exhibited several defects when examined as telecasts intended to motivate behavior. First, motivated audience members were not directed to a social mechanism. Secondly, the mechanism does not appear to have been compatible with the motivation. Thirdly, the distance, in terms of inhibiting, impeding and counteracting forces, between the audience member and the mechanism appears to have been formidable.

Conclusions

We may now return to our original question. Can radio and television sell social objectives as they sell soap? On the basis of our discussion we can hazard the following answer: Given a reasonable amount of receptivity among audience members, radio or television programs can produce forceful motivation. The sponsor of the social objective must tell us to what social mechanism the motivation is to be directed. He must see to the existence, adequacy and compatibility of the mechanism and he must consider the distance of audience members from this mechanism in formulating his expectations of results. To the extent that he finds these factors in good order, he is in a situation comparable to that of a commercial sponsor, and he can reasonably expect results comparable with those of a commercial sponsor.

C. THE CHANGE AGENCY AND
CHANGE TARGET

15. Change Agents, Clients, and Change[a]

Everett M. Rogers[*]

A monkey and a fish were caught in a sudden flood. The monkey scrambled up a tree to safety. Noticing the fish struggling against the current, the monkey was filled with humanitarian desire and rescued the fish from the water. To the monkey's surprise, the fish was ungrateful for this technical aid.

Perhaps this Oriental fable illustrates the relationship of the change agent and his peasant clients (Adams 1960). Motivated by a desire to help, but with a contrasting perspective on change and a different style of life than his clients, the efforts of the change agent are often misunderstood and unappreciated. This chapter discusses the role of the change agent, his relationships with clients, and the various strategies of change he employs to bring about desired effects in his clients' behavior. Perhaps the Thoreau and Milne quotations illustrate

the chapter's main themes: (1) the *reciprocity* that characterizes change agent-client relationships, and (2) the greater effectiveness that would be possible if change agents utilized a *strategy* of change.

What Is a Change Agent?

A *change agent* is a professional who *influences innovation decisions* in a *direction deemed desirable* by a *change agency*.[1] A clearer picture of the role of the change agent can be gained through a detailed consideration of the key terms in this definition.

1. *Influence*: The concept of influence refers to interaction between persons that causes changes in the future behavior or attitudes of the participants (Merton 1957:415). Change agents seek to influence the behavior of their clients. The success of their efforts is measured

[a] This chapter was written with the assistance of Robert F. Keith, Assistant Instructor, and Eduardo Ramos, Research Assistant, Department of Communication, Michigan State University.

[1] This definition of change agent is generally consistent with others' conceptions. "Change agent refers to the helper, the person or group who is attempting to effect change (Bennis and others 1962:5). Although these authors do not feel that the change agent must be exogenous to the system, Lippit and others (1958) do. We maintain that he is set off from his clients by the nature of his *professional status* (that is, employment by a change agency), rather than whether he lives in or out (or considers himself a member) of a particular system.

From Everett M. Rogers, "Change Agents, Clients, and Change," *Modernization Among Peasants: The Impact of Communication.* (New York: Holt, Rinehart and Winston, 1969), pp. 169–194. Copyright © Holt, Rinehart and Winston, Inc. Reprinted by permission of Holt, Rinehart and Winston, Inc.

[*] Professor of Communications, Michigan State University.

in terms of (a) client *awareness* of innovations, (b) *persuasion* of the innovation's usefulness, (c) *adoption*, and (d) *reinforcement of continued use*, rather than discontinuance, of the innovations.[2] A change agent must select his strategies of change on the basis of the content of his message, the nature of his audience, the resources at his disposal, and the type of effects he hopes to secure.

2. *Innovation decisions:* Change agents seek to facilitate client decisions to adopt or reject innovations. Individuals adopt new ideas by passing through a cumulative series of stages in the innovation-decision process from (a) awareness (or knowledge) of the innovation, (b) to formation of a favorable attitude toward it, (c) to actual use of the new idea. Efforts in creating awareness and in persuading are aimed at influencing the actual decision. Usually, change agents seek to promote recommended innovations, but they may also oppose new ideas if they feel the innovations would have unfavorable effects on their clients.

3. *Direction deemed desirable:* Change agents operate as tools in the implementation *of planned change* programs. The objectives of these programs presumably represent the change agencies' notion of the directions in which their clients should be changed. Planned change is the alteration of the structure or function of a social system. This results from the efforts by change agents who seek to introduce new ideas in order to reach definite goals. These alterations may occur as the result of mutual undertakings by change agents and their clients, or as the result of coerced change (change without the consent of the client). Most change agents are concerned not only with the promotion of innovations, but also with the development and maintenance of client rapport. However, there are situations when rapport is sometimes ignored in

the interest of expediency; for example, in the case of an epidemic, coerced change may become necessary. The change agent's objectives should reflect the clients' needs if the change agent-client relationship is to be kept intact. Planned change programs that take into account the needs of the clientele to determine change objectives stand the greatest chance of success. Thus, clients have at least some effect on the goals of change agencies. This point suggests that there is a good deal of reciprocity in the agent-client interface; each have influence on the behavior of the other, i.e., reaching mutually satisfying goals through the exchange of knowledge and resources.

4. *Change agency:* Change agents are employees of formal organizations, such as government ministries or commercial companies.

Importance of the Change Agent

When it is asked "Why are change agents important?", we are actually posing the question, "Why is planned change important?" In Chapter I it was shown that spontaneous change is simply not rapid enough to keep pace with the rapidly rising expectations in less developed countries. It is possible to accelerate the rate of adoption of innovations through the promotional efforts of change agents. Ideally, the change agent also serves as a feedback link from peasants to development planners. He is an organized and routinized communication channel by which plans are put into action, and clients' needs are reflected to the planners. Although a change agent is a potential channel for the upward communication of clients' needs, it seems that he seldom fills this role.

Through the change agent, planned change programs can be modified to suit the particular needs of individuals and villages. Change agents serve to localize innovations and situationally legitimize them. The importance of

---

[2] These change agent effects are generally similar to the objective of any purposive communication (Miller 1966:17–18): (1) to increase the acquisition of non-evaluative responses by the receiver (create awareness of new ideas); (2) to affect the acquisition of new evaluative responses by receivers (form attitudes); (3) to alter existing beliefs by affecting the acquisition of different evaluative responses (change attitudes); and (4) to strengthen existing evaluative responses through reinforcement.

change agents in less developed nations is emphasized by the huge government expenditures allotted to their training and maintenance. Alternative communication approaches, such as combining mass media and interpersonal channels in media forums, were discussed in Chapter 6. Nonetheless, change agents are still required to organize and to "service" the media forums.[3]

Role of the Change Agent

There are seven change agent functions in the process of planned change; each function represents a somewhat different objective in the agent-client relationship (Lippit and others 1958).

1. *Develop a need for change:* The change agent is usually involved in the identification of clients' needs. In some instances, peasants recognize needs and approach the change agent for verification or legitimation of the need. In most cases, however, the change agent is faced with the task of making peasants aware of needs. The short planning horizons, low achievement motivation, high fatalism, and low aspirations characteristic of most peasants mean that the change agent must serve a catalytic function for client needs. He must point out new alternatives to existing problems, dramatize these solutions, and then convince his clients they can solve the problems that confront them.

The needs of the peasant clientele must be recognized if change programs are to be successful. Often we "scratch where they do not itch." As a result, change agents are often faced with a high incidence of the discontinuance of innovations following their initial adoption. In one family planning program in India, 40 percent of those who discontinued cited forced (initial) adoption as their main reason for discontinuing the use of contraceptives (Planning Research and Action Institute 1966:62).

Another example from India illustrates the failure of a planned change program when the clients' needs were overlooked. Government officials provided a village with funds to construct irrigation wells which could approximately double crop yields. But the villagers wanted wells for drinking, as they had to carry their water about 2 miles from a river. So the peasants built the wells in the village center rather than in their fields, and drank the water rather than irrigate their crops. If the change agent had based his program upon the felt needs of the villagers, he would have tried to develop a felt need for irrigation by indicating the financial advantages of this innovation.

2. *Establish a change relationship:* Having created or confirmed a need for change, a change agent must foster a belief among his clients that he is competent, trustworthy, and empathetic with his clients' position. This function of the change agent is not easy. Peasants tend to be distrustful in interpersonal relationships, especially with government officials. Nevertheless, establishing rapport and an acceptable level of interpersonal trust between change agent and client is a prerequisite to successful efforts at change.

3. *Diagnose the problem:* The change agent is responsible for analysis of the clients' problem situation in order to determine why existing behaviors do not meet the clients' needs or objectives. To arrive at his own diagnostic conclusions, the change agent must view the situation from his clients' perspective. He must put himself in his clients' shoes.

4. *Examine goals and alternative courses of action, then create the intent to change in the client:* Peasants are often unable to see alternate courses of action that can be taken to meet goals or solve problems. The change agent must try to explore the various avenues that his clients can take to achieve their goals.

When the first innovations are introduced in a traditional village, whose peasants are characterized by authoritarian-submissive attitudes, a change agent may feel that attempts to explore alternative courses of action with his clients are too time-consuming. The clients may expect the change agent to order them to adopt innovations rather than to explore alternatives with them. Perhaps with subsequent

---

[3] Although change agents would be needed in smaller numbers than when they carry the main load in diffusing innovations to villagers.

innovations, the change agent can begin to improve the decision-making faculties of his peasant clients.

5. *Translate intent into action so that the client innovates:* The change agent seeks to influence his villagers' behavior in accordance with his recommendations. In essence the agent works to promote compliance with the program he advocates. One way in which the change agent can promote innovation initiative on the part of peasants is to provide assistance at the trial stage in the innovation-decision process. By helping the client try the innovation, the change agent involves the peasant in actual use of the innovation.[4]

6. *Stabilize change and attempt to prevent discontinuances:* Individuals tend to seek confirming information for decisions they make.[5] Change agents may effectively stabilize new behavior by directing reinforcing messages to those clients who have adopted innovations. By providing support for the new behavior patterns, change agents increase the likelihood that the peasant will continue to use the innovation.

7. *Achieve a terminal relationship:* The goal for any change agent is to develop self-renewing behavior on the part of his clients.[6] The change agent should seek to put himself "out of business" by enabling his clients to be their *own* change agents. The change agent must seek to shift the client from a position of reliance on the change agent to reliance on himself. It is difficult for the change agent to "wean" his clients; often they become more dependent, rather than independent.

Environment or Client Modification

The change agent is capable of altering two aspects of any planned change situation: the environment and the client. *Client modification* involves the change agent in a *direct* relationship with the client in which his effect is determined by behavioral changes on the part of the client. When the change agent restructures the physical or sociocultural environment, he is attempting to influence his clients *indirectly.*

MODIFYING THE ENVIRONMENT

1. *Physical environment:* There are numerous instances of change agents seeking to change the clients' physical milieu. Peace Corps volunteers and community development workers often initiate change at the village level by assisting with the construction of schools, roads, wells, and latrines.[7] Client utilization of the new facilities is not automatic, but such physical changes make the clients' modernization more likely; for example, the improvement of roads may increase villagers' cosmopoliteness.

2. *Social environment:* The social environment must be able to support change. In less developed countries, one often finds a complete absence of the social organization necessary for implementation of change programs, or else existing social institutions are unable to cope with the problems of change. In this case the change agent must help provide the needed social structures. For example, a change agent might organize a marketing co-

[4] However, Deutschmann and Fals Borda (1962a) found that Colombian peasants rarely tried agricultural innovations on a small-scale basis; instead, they jumped immediately to full-scale adoption.

[5] Evidence for this point is provided by Erlich and others (1957) and Mason (1964).

[6] For a more detailed discussion of self-renewal, see Gardner (1964), who expounds the position that both individuals and institutions must be continually changing if they are to be in adjustment with their environment.

[7] It was shown that many innovations fail when introduced to peasants by change agents; however, one of the highest rates of failure must certainly be for latrines. Although latrine construction *can* play an important role in environmental sanitation, most outhouses in peasant villages are idle monuments to change agent ambitiousness. In Colombia, I once observed several thousand newly-built latrines; not one had been used. Villagers were accustomed to defecating in a squatting position, and their culturally-conditioned sphincters were not compatible with the sit-down design of the latrines (Rogers 1969: Chapter 1).

Figure 15.1.   Change Agents Are a Communication Linkage between Clients and the Primary Source of Innovations.

operative in order to introduce greater stability and efficiency into a market system that had previously been erratic and uncoordinated. Village development councils may be formed by change agents to support collective innovations like village wells, roads, schools, and so on.

Modifying the Client

Most commonly, change agents seek to modify their clients' behavior directly. In this case the change agent disseminates information to increase knowledge levels about innovations, and exerts influence to alter or strengthen client attitudes and beliefs to the point where they adopt recommended innovations.

Liaison Role of the Change Agent

Change agents serve as a *linkage* or liaison between two or more social systems.[8] (1) the client social system and (2) the primary innovation source (Figure 15.1). The client social system may be a single village, a number of villages, or selected individuals (for instance, coffee growers) in several villages. In less developed nations the change agency is usually a government ministry or a company seeking to promote adoption of its products. The primary innovation source is usually an experiment station, university, or some other research organization.

Although it is possible for the primary innovation source to be in direct contact with the client system (Figure 15.1), this is a rather unusual situation in less developed nations. Usually, the change agent must communicate the clients' research needs to the scientists, and in turn disseminate innovations from the research organization to the clients.

Change agents often experience *role conflict* due to their liaison position between social systems with conflicting norms and objectives. Although the change agent is a member of a change agency and with the modernized attitudes and beliefs that accompany development activities, he must also relate to his clientele, who are more traditional. When the norms and objectives of the two systems are more discrepant, the change agent is more likely to experience greater role conflict. Over-identification with either system jeopardizes his relationship with the other group. As a result of his position in cross-pressure, between two reference groups with conflicting norms the change agent becomes a member of a "third culture."[9]

Priess (1954) found that more successful extension agents in the United States tended to disregard the expectations of the change bureaucracy in favor of those held by their

[8] Westley and MacLean (1957) posit a general communication model, based upon Newcomb's ABX paradigm, in which C is a role intervening between source and receiver (A and B). C may be a change agent who links B with the source of innovations (the A's). The main function of the C role is the extension of the communication environment of individual B; that is, to link him to more cosmopolite sources of new ideas.

[9] Useem and others (1963) use this concept to describe the position of Indian scholars and technicians who have been exposed to Western culture. However, it seems applicable to the role conflict situation faced by most change agents.

Figure 15.2. Paradigm of Change Agent-Client Communication and Modernization.

Environmental Variables	*Change Agent Variables*	*(Change Strategies) Liaison Variables*	*Client Variables* →	*Modernization of Clients*
1. Physical	1. Education	1. Reciprocity	1. Literacy	1. Innovativeness
2. Sociocultural	2. Technical competence	2. Homophily	2. Social status	2. Political knowledgeability
	3. Age	3. Empathy	3. Mass media exposure	3. Achievement motivation
		4. Credibility	4. Cosmopoliteness	4. Aspirations
			5. Opinion leadership	

clients.[10] It is doubtful that this finding can be generalized to peasant settings because change agents in less developed nations seem more closely aligned with the change agency than with peasant farmers. The latter often lack the education and sophistication to make them a meaningful reference group for the change agent, and they seldom possess the political power of U.S. farmers over the change agency.

Another source of conflict for change agents is interagency and interagent competition. Change agents promoting similar kinds of programs in the same village are often rivals for clients' attention. Local representatives of ministries of public health, community development, and agriculture all compete for villagers' scarce resources.

Change Agents and Client Modernization

The previous discussion suggests a complex, multivariate process of modernization at the client level. The *client* and the *change agent* each bring to the situation individual attributes that effect their interaction. Change agent-client interpersonal relationships are expressed in a series of *liaison variables*, which occur in a physical and sociocultural *environment*. The change agent-client relationship is designed to effect changes in the *level of modernization* of the client, which are achieved by utilizing various *change strategies*. These six primary components are diagrammed in Figure 15.2. The change agent is the source of modernizing messages, which are communicated to his receivers (clients) in order to obtain desired modernization effects.

[10] An example of similar behavior occurred in Pueblo Viejo at the time of our study. The local school teacher, called "El Professor" by the peasants, had come to Pueblo Viejo a few years before from an urban school. His purpose was to gain an understanding of peasant life through close observation. He was a particularly innovative teacher, introducing such practices as class discussion, localized mimeo books, and coeducational schooling. The latter is forbidden by church and state in Colombia, and El Professor was dismissed from his teaching post in Pueblo Viejo by the Ministry of Education. This is one result of change agent conflict between loyalty to clients and to the change agency. The replacement teacher in Pueblo Viejo immediately reinstated such traditional teaching methods as the lecture method, irrelevant, urban-oriented textbooks, and "segregated" classes. What happened to El Professor? He is now a professor at a teacher training institute in Bogotá, where he influences hundreds of future rural school teachers each year, imbuing them with his desire for educational innovativeness.

TABLE 15.1   Variables Related to Change Agent Contact[a]

Variables Related to Change Agent Contact	Number of Research Studies Reporting			Number of Countries in Which Studies Were Done
	Positive Relationship with Change Agent Contact	No Relationship with Change Agent Contact	Negative Relationship with Change Agent Contact	
I. Client attributes				
1. Social status	45	6	5	7
2. Formal participation	24	0	3	4
3. Education	25	3	1	5
4. Opinion leadership	16	1	0	4
II. Modernization variables				
5. Innovativeness	125	8	0	14

[a] The "data" shown in this table come from the Diffusion Documents Center at Michigan State University, where the findings contained in 1290 publications dealing with the diffusion of new ideas have been content-analyzed. The unit of analysis in this table is a research publication.

Change Agent Contact With Clients

Although a great many variables undoubtedly determine change agent effectiveness,[11] attention in this section will focus on the degree of *contact* or communication between change agents and their clients. In order for change agents to have new ideas adopted by their clients, they must have contact with them. The change agents' time and energy are scarce resources, so he must concentrate his interpersonal communication on those clients (1) who will be the most responsive, that is, peasants who are already more modernized, of higher social status, and so on, or (2) who need his assistance the most, that is, villagers who are more traditional.[12] *Most change agents have higher contact with clients who are characterized by greater innovativeness, higher social status, and more education, than their counterparts* (Table 15.1). This "elite-

ness bias," the tendency for change agents to contact their higher status and more modernized clients,[13] is also found in the Colombia villages (Table 15.2), but the correlations are not very strong, and a number are not significant.

When the correlates of change agent contact in Colombia are compared with similar results in India and Kenya (Table 15.2), it can be seen that formal participation, mass media exposure, social status, and cosmopoliteness are most consistently and strongly related to change agent contact. Tables 15.1 and 15.2 also show that those clients who have more change agent contact are typified by a higher degree of modernization, especially innovativeness. Nevertheless, the relationships shown in Table 15.2 are not very strong, and whereas almost all are in the expected direction, many are not significant.

Relatively little variation in change agent

[11] A paradigm that includes a number of such variables that might be studied in future inquiries is shown later in this chapter.

[12] This statement implies that the *change agent* determines which clients he will contact. In reality, the clients also determine whether or not they will seek the change agent for information and advice.

[13] Planners of the U.S. War on Poverty programs insisted that the poverty class be represented by its own leaders on citizen committees to guide the programs. However, in practice few of the poor are eager to seek leadership roles, and even if elected, they lack the needed skills of group problem-solving, parlimentary procedure, and regular meeting attendance. As a result, the relatively more elite *among the poor* eventually gravitate into leadership roles, raising some doubts as to whether the viewpoints of the real poverty class are represented.

TABLE 15.2 Cross-Cultural Comparison of Correlates of Change Agent Contact

Variables Correlated with Change Agent Contact	Zero-Order Correlation with Change Agent Contact				
	Colombian Modern Villages (N = 160)	A Colombian Traditional Village (N = 54)^c	India UNESCO (N = 702)	India Punjab (N = 84)	Kenya (N = 624)
I. Client attributes					
1. Social status	.201^a	[.234]	.177^b	—^{d}	—^{d}
2. Functional literacy	[.086]	[.047]	.158^b	[—.088]	.156^b
3. Level of living	[.029]	[.083]	.134^b	[.109]	250^b
4. Formal participation	.332^b	.337^a	.141^b	.293^b	.172^b
5. Cosmopoliteness	[.146]	.513^b	[—.007]	.438^b	[.077]
6. Education	[—.023]	.297^a	.146^b	[.111]	.123^b
7. Mass media exposure	[.073]	.368^b	.080^a	.366^b	.255^b
8. Opinion leadership	—^{d}	—^{d}	.082^a	.320^b	—^{d}
II. Modernization variables					
9. Agricultural innovativeness	.171^a	.378^b	.165^b	404^b	.313^b
10. Home innovativeness	[.140]	[.184]	.167^b	[.208]	.295^b
11. Achievement motivation	.235^b	[.143]	.166^a	[.196]	[.031]
12. Educational aspirations	[.031]	.585^b		[—.103]	[—.038]
13. Occupational aspirations	[.058]	[.207]	.126$^{b, e}$	.314^b	—^{d}
14. Empathy	.228^b	[.069]	.162^b	[.211]	—^{d}

^{a} Significant at the 5 percent level.
^{b} Significant at the 1 percent level.
^{c} There was no change agent contact in Nazate, so only the 54 peasant respondents in La Cañada could be included here.
^{d} These variables were not measured, and so no correlation with change agent contact could be computed.
^{e} This correlation represents a composite of both occupational and educational aspirations.

contact is explained in a multiple correlation analysis. In Colombia, three variables (formal participation, political knowledgeability, and achievement motivation) account for only 16 percent of the variance; in India, five variables (knowledge about change agents, functional literacy, family literacy, indebtedness, and attitude toward change agents) account for only 11 percent of the variance.[14] There is much room for improvement in attempts to explain variance in change agent contact.

Change Agent-Client Relationships

The nature of relationships between the change agent and his clients involves several variables, that can be viewed as separate concepts, but which must be considered, in reality, as a series of interacting dimensions. They are reciprocity, homophily, empathy, and credibility.

Reciprocity

Gans (1962) describes the change agent-client relationship as one of reciprocity; that is, the behaviors of each affect the other. The change agents (social workers) in Gans' study of Boston's urban poor thought that they were helping their clients to learn middle class values, such as punctuality, respect for property, and so on, which would aid them in the

[14] In the Colombia analysis, empathy, occupational aspirations, family size, farm size, mass media exposure, opinion leadership, level of living, functional literacy, cosmopoliteness, education, and land tenure did not significantly contribute to the multiple correlation. With all the variables included, only 19.5 percent of the variance was explained; thus the deleted variables accounted for only 2.5 percent of the variance. The deleted variables in the India analysis include farm size, level of living, value of agricultural products, mechanization, empathy, mass media exposure, formal participation, knowledgeability, cosmopoliteness, education, and achievement motivation. These variables together account for only 1 percent of the variance in change agent contact.

world of work. The clients, in contrast, felt that they had control by not causing disturbances at settlement house youth parties and by providing the change agents with large (official) work loads, which the social workers needed to justify the donations and appropriations on which they depended for support. In return, the clients expected the change agents not to seek to tamper overly with their lower class values and attitudes. So both the change agents and their clients viewed their relationship as manipulative and reciprocal. Each party had certain resources and activities that the other needed; each thought they were helping the other.

We maintain that there is a certain degree of reciprocity in most change agent-client relationships, whether the change agent is a VLW in an Indian village, a school teacher in rural Colombia, or an extension worker in the United States. Unfortunately, there is little scientific inquiry to date on the exact nature of the reciprocal give-and-take between clients and change agents in less developed countries. Perhaps one reason why lower class and less innovative clients have less contact with change agents is because they do not perceive such a communication exchange as rewarding. They may, in fact, misperceive the change agent as an authoritarian disciplinarian (as, in fact, some change agents may be[15]). Likewise, there are organizational pressures on the change agent to produce results, usually in the form of client adoption of new ideas that he is promoting. This forces him to interact most frequently with those clients who he feels are most responsive to his persuasive efforts. These are usually clients who are more inno-

vative and of higher status, and who are most like (that is, homophilous with) the change agent in his characteristics and attitudes.

Homophily

Homophily is the degree to which pairs of individuals who interact are similar in certain attributes. It has already been pointed out that change agents tend to interact most with their more elite clients.[16] *Communication is more effective when a higher degree of homophily is present;* that is, when source and receiver are more similar in certain attributes. An homophilous pair share common meanings and interests; they are better able to empathize with each other because their roles are similar. Further, greater reciprocity is involved when the change agent and client are more similar to each other.

One implication for change agencies of the homophily-effective communication proposition is that they should select change agents who are as alike their clients as possible. If most of the clients in a target system only possess two or three years of formal schooling, a university-trained change agent will face greater communication difficulties than if he had less education.[17] Evidence for this statement comes from a study by the Allahabad Agricultural Institute (1957) in India. Village-level change agents with only an elementary education were more effective in reaching Indian Villagers than were change agents with high school or university education.

Unfortunately, most change agents must try to communicate with clients who are much different than themselves in formal education, attitudes toward change, technical compe-

---

[15] There is reason to expect that change agents may be more authoritarian in their dealings with their more laggardly and lower status clients than with their more elite clients.

[16] We show the homophilous nature of interpersonal communication between peasants in our Colombian villages in Rogers (1969) Chapter 10. There is a general tendency, albeit a rather weak one, for peasants to interact with those who are similar in innovativeness, mass media exposure, social status, age, literacy, cosmopoliteness, and formal participation. A higher degree of homophily characterizes friendship pairs than information- and opinion-seeking relationships among our Colombian villagers (Chou 1966).

[17] And he will have the most severe problems in communicating effectively with any but the most highly educated of his clients.

tence, and other attributes. In fact, if the clients did not differ from the change agent on these dimensions, the change agent would not have much of a role to play in the modernization process; the clients would already be as modern as the change agent.[18]

The wide subcultural variability within most less developed nations further aggravates the degree of heterophily between change agent and client. For example, because he spoke a different Ibo dialect than his clients, an Ibo extension worker in Eastern Nigeria, employed only about 70 miles from his home village, was forced to communicate with his clients in pidgin English, which only a few of his clients fully understood. Government change agencies in India select village level workers who are usually from a neighboring village,[19] which helps to ensure linguistic and ethnic homophily with peasant clients. In the Colombian villages of study, the extension change agents were university-level graduates in technical agriculture, who had been raised in urban environments.[20] One of the strategies of change they utilized in the modern villages to bridge the "heterophily gap" with their peasant clients was to work through village opinion leaders. Perhaps a reason why most change agents concentrate their efforts on opinion leaders is to halve the social distance[21] between themselves and the majority of their clients, as well as to gain credibility

for their innovations through gaining the tacit endorsement of the leaders. If the opinion leaders are *too* much more innovative than their fellow villagers, the heterophily gap to effective communication that formerly existed between the change agents and their clients, now exists between the opinion leaders and their peers. Many change agents make the strategic mistake of selecting opinion leaders who are too much like change agents, and not enough like their average client. Such too-innovative opinion leaders are often eager to demonstrate new ideas that the change agent is promoting. The problem is that these ambitious opinion leaders are *too* elite; they serve as an unrealistic model for the average client, and he knows it.

So the language of the change agent is often different from the language of the client, and a village opinion leader can only help to bridge this heterophily gap if he is enough like the larger village audience that the change agent is attempting to reach.

Empathy

Ramos (1966) found that Colombian peasants' ability to empathize with the change agent role was closely related to the amount of interpersonal contact the peasant had with the change agent. This finding may reflect the tendency for change agents to have more con-

[18] In fact, a situation approaching this extreme now occurs in some counties in the United States where farmers are becoming almost as well educated and technically competent as county extension agents, at least in certain specialized types of agriculture, such as fruit and vegetable production, poultry-raising, and mink-growing. Once, the county agent was the only college-educated individual in his county. Now the county extension workers are forced to seek graduate-level education in order to "stay ahead" of their clients; nevertheless, increasing numbers of farmers take their problems directly to agricultural scientists at state universities or commercial companies, thus circumventing local extension agents, who the farmers no longer view as credible.

[19] But not from the same village in which the change agent will be assigned to work, as such a high degree of familiarity seems to lead to lower change agent credibility in the clients' eyes.

[20] This is a common background for agricultural extension workers in most Latin American countries.

[21] Ramos (1966) found that the more social distance our Colombian peasants perceived between themselves and the extension workers, the less favorable attitudes they held toward the change agents, the less credibility they placed in them, and the less interpersonal communication they had with the change agents.

tact with those peasants who are more empathic, or, on the other hand, it could indicate that the more contact clients have with change agents, the more familiar they become with the role, and are thus able to empathize more fully with it. Although the empathic ability of the client has been studied in relationship to his innovativeness and change agent contact, no studies have focused on the empathic ability of the change agent.

The change agent's ability to empathize with his clients is undoubtedly an important factor in his success. In fact, a previously discussed proposition about homophily and effective communication should now be modified to account for the degree of empathy, so as to read: *Communication is less effective when a low degree of homophily is present, unless the source has a high degree of empathy with the receiver.* Even though his clients may be much different from himself, an empathic change agent can communicate effectively with them.

If empathy is so important in change agent effectiveness, how can it be increased? One way is in the selection of change agents; those who have actually been in the clients' role are probably better to empathize with it. Thus, agricultural change agencies often seek to employ change agents who come from farm backgrounds. Sometimes novice change agents are given empathy training by living with a peasant family for some weeks or months, so that they are able to see the world through the eyes of their clients.[22] Likewise role-playing (in which the change agent is asked to act hypothetically the role of the client) is sometimes utilized as a technique in the training of change agents to teach them to empathize

with their clients. This kind of initial empathy continuing empathy with clients is most effectively gained by being feedback-minded and receiver-oriented. The change agent's capacity with clients must be maintained over time; to obtain accurate feedback from his clients depends, in part, upon the closeness of his rapport with them.

Perhaps there is an ideal level of change agent empathy with clients. Most change agents do not have enough empathy, but it is possible that a change agent could become so empathetic with his clients that he would no longer wish to change them. In this extreme case, he would perceive his program only through his clients' eyes, that is, unfavorably. Although such an instance is probably rare, one is reminded of the anthropological observer among the Pueblo Indians who joined the tribe (Katz 1963:25).

The most appropriate degree of change agent empathy with clients may depend, in part, on the clients' level of empathy with the change agent. Gans (1962) found that most of the social workers in a Boston slum had a relatively low degree of empathy with their clients, whereas the slum residents were able to take the role of the change agents with greater ease. The clients therefore had a certain advantage in their manipulative engagements with the social workers; the clients understood the nature of the change agents' objectives and could act accordingly, but the lack of empathy in the reverse direction worked to the disadvantage of the social workers. There is no parallel research of this nature among peasants in less developed nations, and it is needed.[23]

[22] While in Colombia I helped organize such a training experience for a group of Latin American agrarian reform officials. Each such change agent was required to live with a peasant family in an isolated village for about two weeks. During the first days of this empathy training, these urban-oriented officials complained bitterly about the bad food, poor living conditions (such as rats which prevented them from sleeping soundly), "stupidity" of their hosts, etc. By the end of their visit, however, most of the trainees seemed to be able to see government change programs through the villager's eyes.

[23] Such inquiry might focus on change agent-client dyads as the unit of analysis. Other variables than change agent and client empathy should be included in this type of investigation, such as perceived reciprocity, authoritarianism, homophily, and credibility.

Figure 15.3. Relative Credibility of Six Sources-
Channels for Agricultural Innovations in the Three
Modern Colombian Villages.

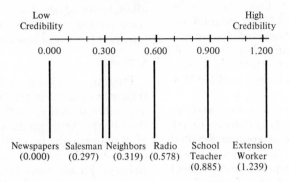

Credibility

Credibility is the degree to which a communication source or channel is perceived as trustworthy and competent by the receiver. A basic proposition from laboratory-experimental studies in communication is that the degree to which an individual's attitudes change is positively related to the credibility with which he perceives the source (or channel[24]) of persuasive messages. If a client perceives that a change agent possesses relatively higher credibility than various other sources and channels, the client can be expected to be more receptive to messages from that change agent.

Among the Colombian respondents, we sought to determine the relative credibility they placed in extension change agents in comparison with five other sources of information about agricultural innovations. The peasants were sequentially presented with these six sources in the form of all possible pairs[25] and asked which source in each combination they

felt was more credible. Figure 15.3 shows the high relative credibility attributed to the extension worker, followed by the school teacher, radio, neighbors, commercial farm salesman, and newspapers. This ranking on credibility is only on the basis of agricultural innovations, and might be quite different from other types of messages such as political or international news. One should also remember (1) that the extension change agent was undoubtedly highly competent in technical agriculture, since he was a university graduate and had been working intensively for five or six years in the villages of study and (2) that the village norms were favorable to innovation and change. Where these conditions are not present, extension change agents may be perceived as less credible. Unfortunately, there is no comparable data from the two traditional villages in Colombia to test this suppostion.[26]

Commercial change agents have much lower credibility in the eyes of the Colombian peasants than the extension worker or the school teacher. The sellers of agricultural

---

[24] It is very difficult to distinguish between source and channel credibility in most non-laboratory communication situations, although the usual convention is to speak of "source credibility."

[25] This method of determining source credibility is called the paired comparison technique. Its advantage is that it simplifies the stimuli alternatives presented to the respondent in each question; its disadvantage is that it can require considerable interview time if the number of alternatives is large.

[26] However, Herzog (1967b) reports almost identical credibility rankings for 1307 Brazilian peasants in 20 modern and traditional villages; newspapers scored 0.300; radio, 0.250; and extension change agents, 1.240.

products like fertilizers, weed sprays, and seeds are not as technically competent (especially in their level of formal education) as the extension worker. Further, they may not be perceived as trustworthy by our peasant respondents who suspect them of a primary interest in profit, rather than in helping the villagers.[27] A similar low credibility for commercial change agents has been found for U.S. farmers (Rogers 1962).

Why do newspapers have such low credibility among the respondents (Figure 15.3)? It may be due to the lack of content devoted to agricultural innovations in Colombia, where none of our interviewees reported this channel in their adoption of a new weed spray.

Figure 15.3 masks *individual* differences in the perceived credibility of the extension change agent. Obviously, some peasants view this change agent as more credible than do others. Generally, the respondents with highest extension worker credibility are those with whom he works most closely; they have a higher degree of change agent contact, more social status, and larger farms. This finding suggests that when communication with change agents is rewarding (as it evidently was in the present case), those clients with greater contact perceive them as more credible. Or perhaps higher credibility leads to greater contact. In any event, future investigation should indicate those factors which lead to higher change agent credibility, as well as the modernization consequences of such credibility.[28]

Strategies for Planned Change

Although the complexity and uniqueness of any specific change situation mitigates against all-inclusive strategies for planned change,[29] some strategy guidelines of a general sort are apparent from past research.

Cultural Fit

Programs of change will be more successful if they are relatively compatible with the existing cultural beliefs, attitudes, and values of the clients. Attempts to eradicate the habitat of the tsetse fly in northern Nigeria, in the hope of reducing the incidence of sleeping sickness disease, were largely unsuccessful because the peasants did not believe there was a relationship between the insect and the illness. Many other change programs fail because they seek to swim against the tide of clients' cultural values. As the discrepancy between existing and advocated positions increases, resistance to change is likely to increase. Change agents must have knowledge of their clients' attitudes and beliefs and their social norms and leadership structure, if their programs of change are to be tailored to fit the clients.

Client Participation

Involving the targets (clients) in the planning of change increases the likelihood of success. Such involvement (1) helps insure that the clients' unique *needs* are considered in planning the change program; (2) increases client commitment to decisions which are made, as a result of their participation in the

[27] The relatively low credibility of commercial change agents is also suggested by the data on communication channels for 2, 4-D weed spray, where farm store personnel are reported most often in creating awareness of the innovation and in informing peasants about how to use the spray at the trial stage, but not in convincing them to adopt at the persuasion stage (where credibility is probably most important). A somewhat similar, but less marked, tendency can also be noted for extension workers, which suggests their proportionately greater credibility (Rogers 1969: Chapter 6).

[28] The research of Herzog (1967b) and McLeod and others (1967) suggests there may not be very high relationships between mass media credibility and such modernization variables as political knowledge.

[29] In fact, one of the most unanimous recommendations of 445 technical assistance workers in 13 less developed countries, who were surveyed by Hyman and others (1967: 179), is the importance of utilizing flexibility in selecting strategies of change. Appropriate strategies should be chosen to suit local conditions.

decision-making processes, and (3) helps legitimize collective innovation decisions (such as the construction of a well or road or formation of a cooperative), if the village power-holders participate in the planning process.

Clients' Evaluation Ability

The underlying strategy of every change agent should be the improvement of his clients' ability to seek information, to define alternatives, to evaluate these alternatives, and to take action to adopt or reject new ideas. In the process of escalating the rate of innovation adoption, change agents sometimes neglect the development of their clients' evaluative capacities.[30] Self-reliance and self-renewing behaviors should be the goals of any strategy for planned change, leading eventually to termination of the clients' dependence upon the change agents.

Opinion Leaders

The time and energy of the change agent are scarce resources. By focusing his communication activities upon opinion leaders in a social system, he may increase the rate of diffusion. Economy of effort is achieved because the time and resources involved in contacting opinion leaders is far less than if each member of the client system were to be reached. Essentially, the leader approach magnifies the change agent's efforts. He can communicate the innovation to a few opinion leaders, and then let word-of-mouth communication channels spread the new idea from there. Even such charismatic and dedicated change agents as Christ and Lenin used disciples to increase and rally their followers to new ideologies (Dahl 1961:96).

Furthermore, by enlisting the aid of leaders, the change agent provides the aegis of local sponsorship and sanction for his ideas. Directed change takes on the guise of spontaneous change. Working through leaders improves the credibility of the innovation, thereby increasing its probability of adoption. In fact, after the opinion leaders in a social system have adopted an innovation, it may be impossible to stop its further spread.

Change agents sometimes mistake innovators for opinion leaders. They may be the same individuals, especially in villages with very modern norms, but often are not. The opinion leaders possess a following, whereas the innovators are the first to adopt new ideas and may not have a following. When the change agent concentrates his communication efforts on innovators, rather than opinion leaders, the results may help to increase awareness knowledge of the innovations, but they are unlikely to persuade many clients to adopt because the innovators' behavior is not likely to persuade the average client to follow suit. A related difficulty occurs when a change agent correctly identifies the opinion leaders in a system, but then procedes to concentrate so much of his attention on these few leaders that they may become *too* innovative in the eyes of their followers, or may be perceived as too friendly and overly identified with the change agent.[31]

Needed Research on Change Agents, Clients, and Change

Several types of needed research, such as on change agent contact, empathy, and change agent credibility, have already been suggested in this chapter. In this section two further types of future inquiry will be described, one dealing with an explanation of change agent success, and the other with a systems analysis of vertical communication in change agencies.

---

[30] When this happens, the change agent has sacrificed long-term progress for the sake of short-run gain. An illustration comes from an agricultural change agent in India, who persuaded his clients to adopt nitrogen fertilizer as the result of an energetic communication campaign, but he did not teach them anything about the principles of how fertilizers stimulate plant growth in the process. The next year, when superphosphate fertilizer became available, the change agent had to repeat his campaign approach, since his clients still had not gained the ability to evaluate innovations by themselves.

[31] Further detail on this point is provided in Rogers (1969) Chapter 10.

Explaining Success and Failure of Village Programs of Planned Change

We already know a good deal, and have ambitious plans to learn more, about the modernization of *individuals* in less developed countries. Unfortunately a parallel type of research on development in which one seeks to explain the relative success of programs of planned change with the *village* as the unit of analysis has been almost ignored. There are vast numbers of single village studies by anthropologists and sociologists; these community ethnologies serve only in a "for-instance" sense to the administrators of national change agencies in less developed countries. Planners of change need to know "less" about "more"; specifically, they require guidelines concerning the kinds of villages in which new change programs should be first launched in order to achieve a high likelihood of success. Further, administrators and planners need an understanding of why the same program of planned change succeeds in certain villages and fails in others. Is success or failure explained by the nature of the village social structure, by the level of modernization of the village (especially its leaders), by the strategies of change utilized by the local change agent, or by a combination of these factors?

These queries can be answered only with data from a *number* of villages that are representative of a less developed nation, or a region or province within it. Two such inquiries are now underway on a multinational basis. One research project,[32] headquartered at Michigan State University,[33] is investigating the relative success of planned change programs in 69 Brazilian communities, 71 Ni-gerian villages, and 108 Indian villages. Pairs of villages are contrasted in this approach; in one member of each pair, the change program has been successful in securing the adoption of new ideas (mostly agricultural), whereas the same program has been relatively unsuccessful in the other village.

Among the antecedent variable utilized in this study are the following:

1. *Village social structure* indicators, such as the degree of clique differentiation, opinion leadership concentration, and the concensus of village leaders.

2. *Village modernization levels* as measured by the degree of institutional development,[34] external communication contact, and the modernization of village leaders.

3. *Change agency variables*, such as the degree of feedback to the local change agent about his program's success, rapport with his clients, and how favorably he is perceived by them.

A paradigm of these, and other, antecedent variables conceptualized as important in explaining the relative success of village change programs is depicted in Figure 15.4. To date, early analysis of the Brazilian data suggests that a rather high percentage of the variance in the dependent variable is explained by the effect of the antecedent variables (Whiting and others, 1967; Fliegel and others, 1967). Further, the change agency variables in the paradigm seem to be especially important in explaining the success of change programs.

A Systems Analysis of Vertical Communications in Change Agencies

Observers of change agencies in countries like India point out that (1) communication

---

[32] The other investigation has recently been initiated by Professors George Dalton and Erma Edelman at Northwestern University. The objective is a secondary analysis of existing social science data about villages in Mexico, Nigeria, and India to explain success-failure of village programs of planned change.

[33] Conducted by faculty members in the Department of Communication; see Whiting (1967) and Fliegel and others (1967).

[34] A concept measured by the presence in the village of cooperatives, schools, various types of businesses, and so on. Such an index was constructed for 24 Mexican villages and for 54 peasant communities in the world by Young and Young (1962). It is hypothesized that the adoption of new ideas is facilitated when village institutions are well-developed, as such an institutional base is needed for the adoption of many innovations.

Figure 15.4. Paradigm of Variables Explaining Success-Failure of Village Programs of Planned Change.

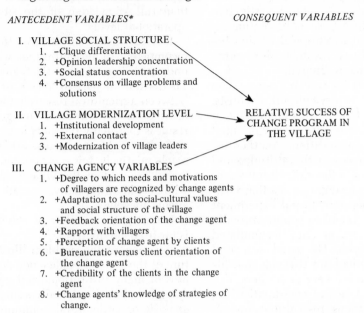

ANTECEDENT VARIABLES*

I. VILLAGE SOCIAL STRUCTURE
    1. –Clique differentiation
    2. +Opinion leadership concentration
    3. +Social status concentration
    4. +Consensus on village problems and solutions

II. VILLAGE MODERNIZATION LEVEL
    1. +Institutional development
    2. +External contact
    3. +Modernization of village leaders

III. CHANGE AGENCY VARIABLES
    1. +Degree to which needs and motivations of villagers are recognized by change agents
    2. +Adaptation to the social-cultural values and social structure of the village
    3. +Feedback orientation of the change agent
    4. +Rapport with villagers
    5. +Perception of change agent by clients
    6. –Bureaucratic versus client orientation of the change agent
    7. +Credibility of the clients in the change agent
    8. +Change agents' knowledge of strategies of change.

CONSEQUENT VARIABLES

RELATIVE SUCCESS OF CHANGE PROGRAM IN THE VILLAGE

* The positive or negative sign preceding each antecedent variable indicates the expected direction of its relationship with the consequent variable.

within a change agency is often a greater problem than (2) communication *from* local change agents to their clients. In other words, it is more difficult to change the change agents' behavior than the farmers'.

When one looks at the nature of the entire communication system in most less developed countries, he is struck by the many dysfunctions that ultimately act to impede the dissemination of innovations and their adoption by peasants. A considerable time has been spent discussing the communication breakdowns that occur at the level of the peasant village, assuming that adaptable, potentially profitable innovations exist as a result of competent research, that effective change agencies are available to transmit this technology from scientist to client, that the peasant has access to adequate credit and markets, and so on.

The research evidence to date leads us to question seriously such implicit assumptions. For example, in the case of agriculture:

1. Most less developed countries lack a ready stock of culturally and climatically adapted agricultural innovations at the present time.[35] Many nonadapted innovations diffused by agricultural change agencies, like extension services, have failed when adopted by peasants. This leads to further reinforcement of negative attitudes toward new ideas in farming and to lower change agent credibility in the farmers' eyes.

[35] There are few innovations with a potential profitability of 20 to 30 percent (over existing practice), which some observers feel is necessary in order to convince villagers to adopt. Some even estimate minimum profitability at a higher level: "To induce farmers to change, the potential pay-off must be high—not 5 to 10 percent but 50 to 100 percent" (President's Science Advisory Committee 1967:16).

Why do we lack adapted innovations? Most agricultural research is done in temperate climates. The results of such investigation must be subjected to extensive adaptation research in tropical and semitropical settings before useful innovations result.[36] More often than not this latter step is ignored.

The farmers' *needs* for research are seldom communicated "up" to agricultural scientists. This may be due to the fact that change agencies like extension services are largely oriented to "downward" communication. Another aspect of the problem lies in the attitudes and communication styles of the agricultural scientists themselves. For example, a leading fertilizer researcher at an agricultural experiment station in one Latin American country proudly showed me a file case of data accumulated from years of research. He acted surprised when asked why he had not disseminated his findings to extension workers or farmers.

2. There is often a lack of coordination between the organizations responsible for research, extension (diffusion), and change agent training in agriculture. Rather than striving through mutual teamwork to improve farm production, these organizations often compete with one another. Similarly, cooperative relationships are seldom found between agricultural agencies and their counter parts in community development, health, and public education, even though all of these organizations are trying to assist the same peasant clients to higher levels of living.

3. Most change agencies are characterized by ineffective vertical communication across hierarchical lines. As a result, national policies seldom reach the local change agent, and feedback from the operational level rarely reaches the top administrator.[37] Those at the top are thus forced to make decisions with less than full knowledge of the situation at the operational level.

4. Local change agents are often technically incompetent in agriculture, as well as in their understanding of the strategies of change. This is due in part to a lack of coordination between agricultural research and the training institutions that produce change agents. The result is that many peasants have little faith in agricultural change agents, extension workers reach relatively few farmers, and those contacted are seldom the village opinion leaders who could informally spread the change agents' messages.

5. Lastly, the number of extension workers is far from adequate.

Our view of the problem illustrates the nature of the general inefficiency and ineffectiveness of many institutionalized communication systems in less developed countries. A *systems analysis* of agricultural communication, from the origin of the innovations to their adoption by farmers, is needed. Such a systems approach to investigating a *total system* of innovation diffusion is a natural outgrowth of various research efforts already underway.

A great deal of useful knowledge about within-village ("horizontal") diffusion of innovations is being learned. Such data give us understanding of the communication system from the viewpoint of the peasant and the local change agent. This is a rich data base upon which to build, but it is just a starting point.

Problems of agricultural communication bear a similarity to those in parallel ministry structures like education. Since 1965, a re-

[36] This adaptation type of research is necessary not only in agriculture, but also for every kind of innovation introduced in less developed nations. When new ideas are not properly adapted, development efforts are like an attempt to transplant cut flowers that do not have roots in the indigenous culture (Dart 1963). The flowers wilt and die because of the eager haste. The whole process suggests an attempt to present the Hoover Dam power system to St. Thomas Aquinas.

[37] This ineffective vertical communication traces, at least in part, to the great heterophily between hierarchical levels in these change agencies; the top administrators differ widely from local change agents in amount of education, attitudes, technical knowledge, and so on. Upward negative feedback is particularly rare, as lower-level bureaucrats do not wish their superiors to know about failures.

search project has been underway on the diffusion of educational practices in Thailand.[38] Data have been gathered from a national sample of Thai secondary schools through interviews with teachers, principals, and their ministry supervisors about ten educational innovations (examples are objective tests, classroom discussion, school libraries, slide projectors, and so on) recommended and promoted by top ministry officials. Many of these innovations, which teachers have been persuaded to adopt, have not been correctly utilized.[39]

The essential feature of systems analysis involves gathering data from all levels in a total system; that is, from all the subsystems, as to how they presently function and the interrelationships or interactions among these subsystems.[40] Such a systems approach is expected to yield implications for improvement in the functioning of the entire system.

To date, there has been no such attempt to perform a systems analysis of the entire communication process for a particular type of innovation (like agriculture, family planning, or education) in a less developed country; a great deal could be gained from such inquiry.

Summary

A *change agent* is a professional who influences innovation decisions in a direction deemed desirable by a change agency. The role of the change agent includes the following: developing a need for change among the clients; establishing a change relationship with them; diagnosing the client's problem; examining the clients' goals and alternatives; then creating the intent to change in the client; encouraging the client to innovate; stabilizing the changed behavior so as to prevent discontinuance; and achieving a terminal relationship with the client. Thus the change agent has a role to play at each stage of the clients' innovation-decision process. However in the case of 2, 4-D weed spray in Columbia, change agent contact was most frequently mentioned at the awareness and trial stages, and least at the persuasion stage.

Essentially, the change agent serves as a communication linkage between his clients and the primary innovation source. As such, the change agent is often subject to role conflict because of his loyalty to two reference groups who have different norms regarding change.

Most change agents have higher contact with clients who are characterized by greater innovativeness, higher social status, and more education. This eliteness bias in change agent contact was found in Colombia and also in the companion investigations in India and Kenya, but the relationships were not very strong.

The change agent-client relationship is characterized by reciprocity in that each expects to exchange with the other. Less elite clients may not perceive potential rewards from interaction with change agents, and this perception may explain their lower contact. *Homophily* is the degree to which pairs of individuals who interact are similar in certain attributes. Communication is more effective when a higher degree of homophily is present. This is further reason for the eliteness bias in change agent contact; they interact with those clients who are most like themselves (that is,

---

[38] Sponsored by Michigan State University, the University of Pittsburgh Consertium for Institution-Building, the Ford Foundation, and the United States Agency for International Development, and conducted jointly by the Department of Communication and the Institute for International Studies in Education at Michigan State University.

[39] Another finding of the Thailand study is that many new educational ideas flow upward from teachers to principals and supervisors, rather than downward, from ministry officials to teachers, as it had expected would be the case.

[40] The analysis of these "relational data" will certainly call for use of relationships (like dyads) as the units of analysis rather than individuals, as has been the case, often inappropriately, in most past social science inquiry (Coleman 1958).

more educated, innovative, and of higher social status). If the source, like a change agent,
has high empathy with his receivers, communication may be effective even when low
homophily is present.

Credibility is the degree to which a communication source or channel is perceived as
trustworthy and competent by the receiver.
Among the peasants in modern Colombian villages, extension change agents were perceived
as highly credible sources for agricultural innovations.

Change agents' programs are more likely to
be successful if they (1) fit the clients' cultural
beliefs and values, (2) involve clients in planning change, (3) increase clients' ability to

evaluate innovations, and (4) use opinion
leaders to spread the program.

Future research is especially needed on explaining change agent success or failure, and
on a systems analysis of vertical communication in change agencies in less developed nations.

A basic assumption that is implied throughout this chapter is that change agents should
use strategies of change so that their efforts
are maximized. Unfortunately, many change
agents simply try to engage in *more* communication activities (such as conducting demonstrations, holding meetings for clients, and so
on). They do not follow strategies of change,
seemingly being too busy to do so.

References

Adams, Don, 1960, "The Monkey and the Fish: Cultural Pitfalls of an
Educational Adviser," *International Development Review*, 2:22–24.
Allahabad Agricultural Institute, 1957, *Extension Evaluation,* Allahabad, India:
Allahabad Agricultural Institute.
Bennis, Warren G., and others, 1962, *The Planning of Change: Readings in the
Applied Behavioral Sciences.* New York: Holt, Rinehart and Winston.
Chou, Teresa Kang Mei, 1966, *Homophily in Interaction Patterns in the
Diffusion of Innovations in Colombian Villages,* M.A. Thesis, Michigan
State University.
Coleman, James, 1958, "Relational Analysis: The Study of Social Organizations
with Survey Methods," *Human Organization,* 16:28–36.
Dahl, Robert A., 1961, *Who Governs? Democracy and Power in an American
City,* New Haven, Conn.: Yale University Press.
Dart, Frances E., 1963, "The Rub of Cultures," *Foreign Affairs,* 41:360–371.
Deutschmann, Paul J., and Orlando Fals Borda, 1962a, *Communication and
Adoption Patterns in an Andean Village,* San Jose, Programs
Interamericano de Información Poplar, Mimeo Report.
Erlich, D., and others, 1957, "Postdecision Exposure to Relevant Information,"
Journal of Abnormal and Social Psychology, 54:98–102.
Fliegel, Frederick C., and others, 1967, *Innovation in India: The Success or
Failure of Agricultural Development Programs in 108 Indian Villages,*
Michigan State University, Department of Communication, Diffusion
of Innovations Research Report 9.
Gans, Herbert J., 1962, *The Urban Villagers: Group and Class in the Life of
Italian-Americans.* New York: Free Press.
Gardner John W., 1964, *Self-Renewal: The Individual and the Innovative
Society,* New York: Harper & Row.
Harzog, William A., Jr., 1967b, "Mass Media Credibility, Exposure, and
Modernization in Rural Brazil," Paper presented at the Association
for Education in Journalism, Boulder, Colo.
Hyman, Herbert H., and others, 1967, *Inducing Social Change in Developing
Communities: An International Survey of Expert Advice.* Geneva:
United Nations Institute for Social Development.
Katz, Robert L., 1963, *Empathy: Its Nature and Uses.* New York: Free Press.
Lippitt, Ronald, and others, 1958, *Dynamics of Planned Change.* New York:
Harcourt, Brace.

McLeod, Jack M., and others, 1967, "Mass Media Exposure and Political Knowledge in Quito, Ecuador," Paper presented at the Association for Education in Journalism, Boulder, Colo.

Mason, Robert G., 1964, "The Use of Information Sources in the Process of Adoption," *Rural Sociology*, 29:40–52.

Merton, Robert K., 1957, *Social Theory and Social Structure*. New York: Free Press.

Miller, Gerald R., 1966, *Speech Communications: A Behavioral Approach*. Indianapolis: Bobbs-Merrill.

Planning Research and Action Institute, 1962, *The Dehati Radio Goshthi Programme: An Evaluation of Its Impact and Organization*. Lucknow, India: Planning Research and Action Institute.

President's Science Advisory Committee, 1967, *The World Food Problem*, Volume 1. Washington, D.C.: U.S. Government Printing Office.

Priess, Jack J., 1954, *Functions of Relevant Power and Authority Groups in the Evaluation of County Agent Performance*, Ph.D. thesis, Michigan State University.

Ramos, Eduardo, 1966, *Client-Change Agent Relationships in Three Colombian Villages*, M.A. thesis, Michigan State University.

Rogers, Everett M., 1962, *Diffusion of Innovations*. New York: Free Press.

———, 1969, *Modernization Among Peasants: The Impact of Communication*. New York: Holt, Rinehart and Winston.

Useem, John, and others, 1963, "Men in the Middle of the Third Culture," *Human Organization*, 22:169–179.

Westley, Bruce H., and Malcolm S. MacLean, Jr., 1957, "A Conceptual Model for Communication Research," *Journalism Quarterly*, 34:31–38.

Whiting, Gordon C., 1967, *Innovation in Brazil: Success and Failure of Agricultural Programs in 76 Minas Gerais Communities*, Michigan State University, Department of Communication, Diffusion of Innovations Research Report 7.

Young, Frank W., and Ruth C. Young, 1962, "The Sequence and Direction of Community Growth: A Cross-Cultural Generalization," *Rural Sociology*, 27:374–386.

16. Training Agents of Social Change in Israel:
Definition of Objectives and a Training Approach[a]

D. Kahneman* • E. O. Schild*

Many sectors of Israeli life are characterized, not only by a rapid rate of change but also by the relative prevalence of *planned* social change. In response to the economic and

social problems ultimately related to the achievement of statehood and the absorption of mass immigration, most public institutions are engaged in inducing and/or controlling

[a] The authors are indebted to Mr. Gershon Tavor of the Israel Agricultural Extension Service and Mr. Naftali Golomb of the Ruppin Adult Agricultural College, who played an important role in the training, and developed the case problems. They also wish to thank Professor E. Katz and Dr. C. W. Greenbaum for their patient criticism and constructive suggestions for this paper as well as Professors S. N. Eisenstadt and M. Horwitz, and Dr. S. N. Herman for their valuable comments.

Reprinted from D. Kahneman and E. O. Schild, "Training Agents of Social Change in Israel: Definition of Objectives and a Training Approach," *Human Organization*, Vol. XXV, No. 1 (Spring 1966), pp. 71–77.

* Department of Psychology, Hebrew University.

change in many spheres of behavior. Recent years have witnessed an increase in the awareness on the part of such institutions that they may profit from a closer acquaintance with modern social science. In addition to the utilization of sociological research and counseling, requests are made for training; many individuals who have been agents of social change for years are now prepared to take some time (usually very little time) to hear what social psychology has to offer.

Thus a demand has arisen for brief, intensive seminars to provide line personnel with principles and skills needed for inducing change in relatively small social units (e.g., a village). The authors have been engaged in developing and conducting a number of seminars of this kind.[1] In this paper we shall describe an approach to training agents of social change, as it has evolved from our experience in these seminars..

Objectives of Training

The introduction of social change involves a broad range of skills and activities. The training approach to be described here focuses on one of the activities of the agent of change,[2] which is perhaps basic to all others: the preliminary analysis of the problem and the planning of the strategy to be followed in achieving the desired change of behavior in the target community. We are here concerned with the issue of deciding *what* to do, rather than with problems of *how* to do it. The acquisition of skills other than planning (e.g., interviewing or the use of audio-visual aids) will not be discussed here.

In attempting to improve the planning approach of practitioners, the social scientist must ask himself: what can present-day knowledge offer the agent of change that is at one time scientifically sound, novel to an audience of experienced practitioners, and relevant to the planning activities of agents of change in real-life situations?

While the planning of most practitioners is neither systematic nor explicit, some implicit theory of factors of change is by necessity implied in the activities of practitioners. Training for adequate planning will therefore have two objectives:

1) Correcting those psychological or sociological assumptions held by practitioners that diverge most seriously from accepted scientific opinion.

2) Providing a systematic approach to analysis and decision-making, designed to highlight the most important features in concrete situations of change. The aim here is not merely to present such an approach to trainees but to achieve positive acceptance and some degree of commitment to application in the field.

In the following sections, we present an accounting sequence for the planning of social change which has been used in several seminars, and discuss some of the factors—cognitive and non-cognitive—which tend to lead the agent of change astray in the planning of his activities. The training situation itself is discussed in the latter part of the paper.

An Accounting Sequence for Planning Social Change

The first stage of any planning involves the collection and evaluation of relevant informa-

---

[1] Most of the seminars referred to in the present paper have been concerned with change in an agricultural framework. Some are organized and financed by the Extension Service of the Israel Ministry of Agriculture; in these seminars the participants are instructors employed by the Ministry to supply advice and promote improvements in immigrant settlements as well as in older, established villages. Other seminars are organized and financed by the kibbutz (collective village) organizations within the framework of the Ruppin Adult Agricultural College; here the participants are kibbutz-members who are to fulfill the task of agricultural manager in their respective villages.

[2] A word on nomenclature: By *agents of charge* we refer to the practitioners in the field, who are the *trainees* in the seminar. The *changees* are those people in the field who are the targets of the agents' efforts. The *trainers* are the social scientists in charge of the seminar.

tion. In the present state of social science, no algorithm for such information collection and evaluation can be constructed for general application to concrete problems of social change. It appears feasible, however, to formulate a sequence of steps to be followed when planning change, and to present a series of questions through which the important factors are brought out and the range of possible plans is gradually narrowed and specified.

Such an accounting sequence will differ from the conceptual tools employed by re-searchers in organizing and structuring scientific investigations.[3] Here we are concerned with an ordered selection of questions to which the practitioner can obtain answers without undue effort. They must provide adequate coverage of the information relevant in a wide range of situations, while emphasizing features most likely to be neglected by practitioners. And finally, they should lead as directly as possible to considerations of possible action. Table 16.1 presents in the left-hand column a summary outline of an accounting

[3] For an example of an accounting scheme for the scientific study of change, see E. Katz, M. L. Levin and H. Hamilton, "Traditions of Research on the Diffusion of Innovation," *American Sociological Review*, XXVIII (1963), 237–262.

TABLE 16.1   Accounting Sequence for Planning Change and Causes of Deficient Planning

Steps of Sequence	*Causes of Deficient Planning*
Planning:	
I Whose behavior is to be changed? What is the precise nature of the change desired?	
II What groups and individuals are likely to play central roles in the process of change or in resistance to change? a) Relevant groups. b) Influentials in these groups. c) Other key individuals particularly affected by the proposed change.	1. Overemphasis of formal as against informal social structure. 2. Analysis of the social structure in terms of social categories rather than in terms of interdependent groups.
III For each key individual—what are the major determinants of the response to the proposed change? a) Motivational determinants—satisfactions or deprivations caused by the change. b) Cognitive determinants—perceived need for change; expectations for agent's behavior and intentions. c) What are, then, the major driving and restraining forces acting on the individual?	3. Stereotyped and undifferentiated view of motives and perceptions as identical for all changees. 4. Exaggeration of the veridicality of perception or of the ease with which distorted perception may be corrected. 5. Insufficient recognition of the role of conformity pressures, of wishes for status and participation, and of personal sympathies and antipathies.
IV What is the structure of personal influence in the community? Who are the individuals to be directly approached by the agent—and who should be left alone or influenced only via other people?	6. Insufficient recognition of the fact that even influentials may be strongly influenced and can be most effectively approached indirectly, via other individuals or groups.
V For each individual to be approached: a) What can the agent do to reduce restraining forces (including how to avoid the needless arousal of antagonism)? to increase driving forces? b) What are the aims in approaching this person: mobilization of active support or neutralization of opposition?	7. Lack of appreciation for the benefits to be had by decreasing restraining forces rather than increasing driving forces. See also (3) and (5) above.
Reevaluation:	
Can the change be obtained within reasonable time and at reasonable cost? What forces may push the agent toward an ineffective course of action?	8. Wish for status among changees. 9. Organizational pressures for quick and conspicuous action.

sequence which we have found useful in the analysis of cases in training seminars. The complete version used in actual work is a detailed workbook in which this outline is elaborated in 200 questions. In terms of the ultimate objectives of training, it is hoped that the practitioners may achieve some skill in following the main outline of this scheme and in covering the main problems with which it is concerned.

It is seen that the sequence here proposed relies heavily on the Lewinian tradition in social psychology, as well as on the sociological studies of the functions of primary groups and interpersonal influence.[4] According to this sequence, the practitioner first clarifies the goals of the change project (Step I) and then undertakes a preliminary survey of the social structure of the changee community, as relevant to the specific change intended (Step II). Information is then collected on the influentials identified in this survey (Step III). Step IV requires the construction of an influence sociomatrix, with key individuals and groups as rows (and columns). This matrix helps to identify certain individuals as targets for direct influence-attempts by the agent of change (e.g., individuals who influence many others, or are the only source of influence for some sub-groups, are unlikely to arouse extreme antagonism, and are themselves relatively less vulnerable to intra-community influences).

Considering both steps III and IV, it should now be possible to list the main individuals to be approached directly, with a fair appreciation of what can be achieved in these encounters and a detailed view of the approach to be taken in such contacts. This information is summarized in Step V. In the common case where informal contacts with influentials in the changee community precede more formal activities, Step V already provides a plan for these informal contacts. When the nature of the formal activities is itself partly dependent

on the response of these influentials, the probable nature and sequence of such formal activities is also likely to emerge at this stage.

In the concluding sections of the accounting sequence, the feasibility of the change project is reevaluated, considering all the information previously analyzed, as well as a new set of factors: the various forces acting on the agent of change, pushing him away from the optimal procedures outlined in previous stages. In actual practice, where planning and execution are not as sharply distinguished as they are here, the same organizational and motivational cross-pressures are likely to lead the agent of change astray already in the stage of choosing a course of action.

One of the major purposes of this sequence is to identify and reduce present or potential sources of resistance to change. Among the many possible sources of resistance, particular emphasis is placed on social determinants and on various irrelevant motives, which are rarely discussed openly by changees (e.g., personal sympathies and antipathies or concern with prestige). In the detailed breakdown of possible forces acting on the changees, wishes for approval, status and freedom of action are prominently mentioned. These are motives that the agent of change is most likely to ignore or frustrate because they appear irrelevant to the problem at hand.

While the accounting scheme is thus not entirely contentless, the use of this or any other set of questions clearly cannot ensure that the agent will achieve valid answers, or draw correct conclusions from the answers obtained. To a considerable extent, the effective use of the sequence depends on the psychological common sense of the agent of change. However, as was stressed above, there are important principles of behavior which are frequently overlooked or misunderstood by practitioners of change. Training in the planning of change must then include the correction of such misconceptions.

[4] For summaries of these traditions, see D. Cartwright, "Achieving Change in People: Some Applications of Group Dynamics Theory," *Human Relations,* IV (1951), 381–392; and E. Katz and P. Lazarsfeld, *Personal Influence,* The Free Press, Glencoe, Ill., 1955.

Causes of Deficient Planning

In the right-hand column of Table 16.1 we have listed some factors that may lead the agent of change astray at each step of the accounting sequence. Most of these factors represent misconceptions in the agents' implicit theory of human behavior, which we have frequently encountered among practitioners in Israel. They seem to express the divergence of common-sense psychology from scientific opinion in three major areas (the numbers refer to the enumeration in Table 16.1):

(1, 2, 5, 6)—Social determinants of behavior: While practitioners clearly realize the existence of social influence, the power of even relatively weak social pressures in controlling behavior[5] comes almost as a shock to many trainees. The pervasiveness of pressures to conformity as well as their range and subtlety[6] are frequently underestimated. The potency of primary groups in determining the flow of information and the response to information[7] is also generally underrated.

(3, 4, 5)—Determinants of cognitions and attitudes: It appears to be a basic assumption of the common sense theory of human behavior that perception is inherently veridical and that cognitions and attitudes are controllable by rational arguments. Behavior and attitudes are thus assumed to be closely attuned to objective reality. Social scientists, on the other hand, stress the functional character of attitudes[8] and the importance of assumptions and expectations in determining perception.[9] Moreover, the prevalence of psycho-logical, rather than logical, consistencies is emphasized in recent psychological works.[10]

(5, 7)—Freedom of choice and the reduction of restraining forces: The advantages of reducing opposition rather than applying pressures[11] are readily accepted by the trainees, but almost never perceived prior to training. While lip-service is commonly paid to the role of personal participation and feelings of free choice, the actual effectiveness of these factors in mediating and maintaining behavioral changes[12] is seldom recognized.

(8, 9)—Deficient planning and the agent's motivation: The potential causes of deficient planning numbered 1 through 7 are based on erroneous assumptions or ignorance of important principles. The causes numbered 8 and 9, on the other hand, represent pressures from below and from above that may distract the otherwise knowledgeable practitioner from the optimal course of action.

---

[5] Cf. e.g., S. E. Asch, *Social Psychology*, Prentice-Hall, New York, 1952; W. S. Verplanck, "The Control of the Content of Conversation: Reinforcement of Statements of Opinion," *Journal of Abnormal and Social Psychology*, II (1955), 668–674.

[6] For a broad summary see T. Shibutani, *Society and Personality*, Prentice-Hall, New York, 1961, Chapters 12, 13.

[7] Cf. E. Katz, "The Two-Step-Flow of Communication: An up-to-date Report on an Hypothesis," *Public Opinion Quarterly*, XXI (1957), 61–78.

[8] Cf. D. Katz, "The Functional Approach to the Study of Attitudes," *Public Opinion Quarterly*, XXIV (1960), 163–204.

[9] Cf. H. Cantril, *The "Why" of Men's Experience*, Macmillan, New York, 1950; J. S. Bruner, "On Perceptual Readiness," *Psychological Review*, LXIV (1957), 123–152.

[10] Cf. R. P. Abelson and M. S. Rosenberg, "Symbolic Psychologic, A Model of Attitudinal Cognition," *Behavioral Science*, III (1958), 1–13.

[11] Cf. K. Levin, "Frontiers in Group Dynamics; Concept, Method and Reality in Social Science; Equilibrium and Social Change," Human Relations, I (1947), 5–41; L. Coch and J. R. P. French, "Overcoming Resistance to Change," *Human Relations*, I (1948), 512–532.

[12] Cf. K. Lewin, "Group Decision and Social Change," in: E. E. Maccoby, T. M. Newcomb and E. L. Hartley (eds.), *Readings in Social Psychology*, (3rd ed.), Holt, New York, 1953, pp. 197–211. On the importance of feelings of choice see e.g., A. R. Cohen "Communication Discrepancy and Attitude Change: A Dissonance Theory Approach," *Journal of Personality*, XXVII (1959), 386–396.

The agent's wish for status among changees is enhanced by the fact that his role is rather ungrateful: changees seldom appreciate the profit to be had from change. The agent may then tend to pursue a strategy that will increase at least his status rewards. As conformity to existing norms and expectations commonly is a safer way to attain status than attempts at change and deviation,[13] the strategy which pays off in status may be detrimental to change-induction.

On the other hand, the organization employing the agent will reward change. But while the successful completion of a project of change may be a protracted affair, the organization will frequently exert pressures for quick and in particular *conspicuous* action. The agent can most easily prove his industry and progress by organizing formal activities in the changee community; informal influence attempts (even when desirable) cannot easily be demonstrated to superiors.[14]

We should perhaps underline that this analysis of the sources of deficient planning is based on experience in Israel only. Even locally, some differences may be observed between different populations of trainees. However, this analysis can be used to derive detailed hypotheses concerning the typical errors of planning to be expected from agents of change who are characterized by this constellation of misconceptions and external pressures. We have found tentative support for these hypotheses in comparing the plans proposed by trainees to deal with case situations to the plans arrived at by following the more formal system outlined in Table 16.1.

We have used the hypotheses presented in Table 16.2 to define objectives for the training of agents of social change: by correcting or modifying the terms listed in the right-hand column, we hope to help the agent of change avoid the characteristic errors listed in the left hand column.

The Approach to Training

In the preceding sections, we have described and analyzed a set of objectives for the training of agents of social change. We now turn to a description of the main phases of a training seminar intended to attain these objectives. The outline refers to a seminar lasting one week. This duration happens in Israel to be a typical compromise between the limitations of organizing institutions in releasing personnel and the trainers' wishes to approximate a cultural island situation.

The Training Program

The program of the seminar is divided into three phases:

(1) Theoretical introduction (15–20 hours). Some central issues in the social psychology of change are discussed with the aim of presenting an alternative to the misconceptions listed earlier in Table 16.1. The topics discussed therefore include: perception as influenced by assumptions and motives; the range of social motives; conflict—driving and restraining forces; dissonance and forced compliance; group cohesiveness and group pressures; personal influence and the flow of communication.

There is a deliberate attempt to prevent arousal of resistance in this stage. While the practical dangers of applying an erroneous psychological theory are emphasised, there is no assault on the trainees' self-image as efficient practitioners. Indeed, the trainees frequently interpret discussions of topics such as the theory of dissonance and the functional character of attitudes as a scientific "debunking" of human nature and engage with cynical enthusiasm in intellectual explorations of

---

[13] Cf. e.g., G. C. Heinans, *The Human Group,* Harcourt & Brace, New York, 1950, pp. 140–141.

[14] The importance of visibility in determining performance has been stressed by Merton (R. K. Merton, *Social Theory and Social Structure,* (2nd ed.), The Free Press, Glencoe, Ill., 1957, pp. 341–357) and Goffman (E. Goffman, *The Presentation of Self in Everyday Life,* Doubleday, New York, 1959, pp. 44–45).

TABLE 16.2 Typical Errors in Practitioners' Plans

Error	*Source of Error**
The practitioner will often:	Lack of systematic prior planning.
At too early a stage commit himself publicly not only to the general objective of the change, but also to details (thus reducing the possibility of arousing feelings of participation and free choice).	Underestimate of changees' want for participation (5).
	Disregard of possibilities for reducing restraining forces (7).
	Wish to enhance own status (8).
	Organizational pressures for quick and positive action (9).
	Overemphasis on formal structure (1).
Proceed too quickly to formal activities without sufficient attention to the need for informal data gathering. Neglect possibilities of utilizing informal processes of influence.	Stereotyped picture of changees' motives and perceptions (3).
	Exaggeration of ease with which distorted perceptions can be corrected (4).
	Insufficient recognition of the role of conformity pressures (5).
	Wish to enhance own status (8).
	Organizational pressure for quick and positive action (9).
Tend to give active roles to early supporters, without testing their status in the changee community and the possibility that they may arouse antagonism among influential changees.	Insufficient recognition of informal social influence structure (1).
	Insufficient recognition of the role of personal sympathies and antipathies (5).
	Wish to enhance own status (8).
	Organizational pressure for immediate results (9).
Use a standard set of rational arguments in all persuasion attempts.	Stereotyped view of changees' motives and perceptions (3).
	Belief in veridicality of perception (4).
	Insufficient recognition of role of irrelevant motives (5).
	Overemphasis of formal structure (1).
Fail to insure that potentially disruptive minority groups are reached.	Emphasis on social categories rather than on interdependent groups (2).
	Insufficient recognition of wishes for participation (5).
Rely on induction of forces, rather than utilizing and affecting own forces, both for individuals and for groups.	Insufficient recognition of group forces acting on influentials (6).
	Lack of appreciation for the importance of reducing restraining forces (7).
	Wish to enhance own status (8)

* Numbers refer to "Causes of Deficient Planning" listed in Table 16.1.

these topics.[15] Moreover, by extensive group participation a high degree of group consensus is attained concerning the main theoretical propositions, so as to ensure that the new facts and concepts are accepted by the trainees as "their" facts and concepts.[16]

(2) Systematic solution of a problem of planned change (18–22 hours). A complex problem is presented in considerable detail, which requires an agent of change (agricultural extension officer, kibbutz manager) to decide on a course of action directed to a given objective. The trainees propose their intuitive solutions after studying the case material on their own. A solution is then sought by filling a workbook based on the accounting sequence outlined in Table 16.1. Trainees perform this task in teams of four, with some guidance and non-directive help from the training staff. After completion of each chapter of the workbook there is a plenary meeting in which the answers of the various teams are compared and analyzed. This work culminates in the preparation of detailed plans by the various teams, including suggested answers to a set of specific questions (such as: "At what stage should the rabbi of the village be approached and with what proposal?"). The plans are compared and an attempt is made to achieve consensus on a final plan in a concluding plenary session.

The main objective of this phase is to illustrate the feasibility and advantages of systematic planning of a change project, including informal preliminary contacts. There is constant confrontation of this approach and the more intuitive suggestions presented earlier, as the possible consequences of various planning errors are exhaustively discussed.

Many trainees discover in this phase some characteristic biases in their approach to the problems of change. They achieve such discoveries on their own or in discussions with a team of peers, and only very rarely do the trainees see themselves under attack by the training staff. Consequently, this main phase of training also arouses little resistance and antagonism.

(3) Discussion of the forces acting on the agent of change (4–6 hours). The question of what a typical agent of change actually would or could do under the conditions of the problem is used to raise the general issues of the pressures which tend to prevent optimal planning and execution of change projects (mainly the points listed as 8 and 9 in Table 16.1). By this time, most trainees have a strong, although perhaps temporary commitment to a planning approach. The consideration at this stage of drawbacks and difficulties of various kinds appears to arouse much cognitive dissonance. It is expected that a moderate degree of dissonance may actually increase the stability and transfer value of whatever learning has taken place in earlier phases.[17] The heated discussions of the personal, organizational, and ethical problems of a planning approach to change, which take place in this phase, appear to provide an indispensable element to the training program.

Some special issues involved in this approach to training are elaborated in the following sections.

The Case Problem

It is our impression that most of the learning which takes place in seminars occurs during the second phase of training, in which a

---

[15] We may recall Goffman's analysis of social interaction as occurring between performer and audience (Goffman, *op. cit.*). The psychological principles offered the trainees make them more proficient as audience, in evaluating the performance and going behind the presentation. In this sense the new cognitions are functional and hence more easily accepted.

[16] Cf. K. Lewin, *Resolving Social Conflicts,* Harper, New York, 1948. Chapters 4, 13.

[17] Cf. J. W. Brehen and A. R. Cohen, *Explorations in Cognitive Dissonance,* Wiley, New York, 1962.

See also D. Papagorgis and W. J. McGuire, "The Generality of Immunity to Persuasion Produced by Pre-exposure to Weakened Counterarguments," *Journal of Abnormal and Social Psychology,* LXII (1961), 475–481.

complex problem of change is solved. The case provides personal experience in the application of a systematic accounting sequence to a problem of change; group interaction and the growing identification with the problem result in a high level of involvement, and provide the basis for the third phase of the seminar. Moreover, the main point of the present approach is underscored in the very task that the trainees perform: they repeatedly discover that some solutions are more correct than others, and that correct solutions can be located early by systematic collection and evaluation of information.

The information concerning a changee community which is potentially available to an agent of change in the practice of his work would probably fill a heavy tome. We undoubtedly appeal to much projective extrapolation on part of the trainees in describing a community in a booklet of 15 to 20 pages. This booklet provides general background information concerning the problem and the proposed change (the agent's objective) as well as sketches of 12 to 15 members of the community, who are either central figures in the problem or representative members of subgroups. The information supplied is generally sufficient to answer, with the aid of some guessing, the many questions of the workbook. This workbook includes only questions, but the answers which the trainees themselves supply allow only a narrow set of satisfactory alternative solutions to the problem.

In most cases—whether fabricated or real —to which we have applied the analysis outlined in Table 16.1, the analysis results in high agreement on the answer to a basic question;

Who should be approached before we actually begin, and how should these initial contacts be conducted?

The answer to this question will usually indicate the probable development of the change project, including its more formal phases. If there is no such correspondence between the direction of initial contacts and subsequent activities, this itself is probably a danger sign: when all steps of a change project are cyrstallized at the outset, the chances of enlisting active cooperation in the changee community are often significantly reduced.

As was mentioned above, the material of the problem is accompanied by a set of questions concerning proposed actions of the agent on both formal and informal levels. The comparison of the trainees' initial answers to the final solution proposed by the group appears to illustrate many of the errors derived in Table 16.2.

Planning and Human Relations

The approach to training described here emphasizes the *planning* of the sequence and content of the interpersonal contacts involved in a project of change. Much is taken for granted in terms of the interpersonal skills required of the agent of change: it is assumed, for instance, that the agent is capable of keeping quiet and listening for extended periods of time, refraining from premature commitments and persuasion attempts. Similarly, we assume that the agent, if motivated to do so, will be able to enter interviews with some estimate of attainable aims and some idea of the approach to be taken. The immediate objective of training is to convince the agent of change that such actions are indeed essential to the achievement of his own objectives.

Many students of training may fear that such an emphasis on planning is liable to foster, or at least justify, a cynical and coldly manipulative approach to interpersonal relations.[18] It is not the purpose of the present paper to discuss the ethics of human manipulation, but some precision is required in the use of this highly loaded term. It may be noted that the rational approach, which appears to treat human beings as objects to be manipulated, often leads to identical results as the most emphatic and subject-oriented approach. Recognizing the motives of others is

---

[18] A sharp distinction between a true human relations approach and manipulation or selling change found e.g., in N. F. Maier *Principles of Human Relations*, Wiley, New York, 1962, pp. 14, 266, 324.

closely similar to seeing the situation from the other's point of view. Attempting to prevent needless frustration of these motives is closely related to considerate behavior. As Skinner has noted in his novel:

> And what a strange discovery for a would-be tyrant, that the only effective technique of control is unselfish.[19]

Obviously, any kind of interpersonal approach becomes objectionable when an agent uses it, in full awareness, against the best interests of the subject. In addition, self-awareness on part of the agent by itself creates an ethical dilemma. A given behavior on the part of the agent of change may be judged sensitive and tactful or appear a cynical play on the weakness of others—depending on how clearly he knows what he is doing.[20] We have found members of kibbutzim relatively most sensitive to this issue: when one deliberately sets out to satisfy a need of the changee, which he is ashamed to admit openly, or of which he is himself unaware, a tacit assumption of equality between the two actors appears to be violated.

Discussion of these problems is encouraged throughout the training period. We have found large differences between populations of trainees in their attitude to this issue. Some groups (e.g., Agricultural Extension Officers) tend to evaluate the agent's actions mainly in terms of their efficacy in producing change. The increased psychological distance from changees which appears implied by this approach is actually welcome. It is our impression that the satisfaction of playing a Machiavellian role may occasionally provide a substitute for the more immediate gratifications which can be obtained by commiting the error of Table 16.2.

Other groups, such as kibbutz managers, attempt to apply the two criteria of ethics and effectiveness in evaluating an agent's performance. Any discrepancy between these criteria almost palpably induced dissonance. We have been impressed by a characteristic mode of handling this dissonance, which appears spontaneously in many trainees. After deciding that a particular wish of a changee is important to his attitude and should be considered, there is a strong tendency to add:

and after all, the man deserves some satisfaction.

Thus, an increased tolerance of the changees' motives may appear as an outcome of a deliberate and dissonance-inducing emphasis on planning.

For all trainees, of course, an important inducement favoring advance planning is that it can be extremely effective in avoiding needless friction. A recurrent issue in the analysis of the problem case is that the forces restraining changees from acceptance of an innovation are very often the agent's own doing—most often an outcome of uncritical application of driving forces. The trainees soon come to realize that many interpersonal crises can be foreseen and avoided by appropriate action —or inaction. Many an encounter which ends in a hopeless tangle of aroused emotions should have been prevented in the first place.

[19] B. F. Skinner, *Walden Two*, Macmillan, New York, 1948, p. 210.
[20] The distinction between calculated and not calculated giving has been analyzed by Homans: (C. C. Homans, *Social Behavior: Its Elementary Forms*, Harcourt, Brace & World, New York, 1961, pp. 298–299.

D. CHANNELS

17. The Components of Communication Networks

Richard R. Fagen*

Let us imagine, for a moment, that we could inject into a political system something like the fluorescent tracers used by doctors in medical diagnosis. Our imaginary fluorescent would be designed to follow the primary channels of political communication. If we were then to put a political system under the fluoroscope and throw the switch, what would we see?

In the first place, the view would depend on which system was on the table. If it were Cuba, we would discover that a host of mass organizations, the military, the mass media, the party, the schools, and special structures such as the Committees for the Defense of the Revolution are used extensively for vertical communication in the system.[1] We would find also a great deal of lateral communication and structural overlap among a rather compact group of party members and top bureaucrats. On the other hand, if the system being examined were the United States, we would get a different picture. Here we would find prominently featured as vertical channels the bureaucracy, various types of interest groups, the mass media, and, intermittently, the political parties. Lateral flows would occur at a great many levels, and the networks within and between important institutions such as the Congress and the State Department would be highly complex.

To continue the image for a moment, the fluoroscopic picture of either system would be altered drastically if we were to catch it in a period of crisis or high excitement. Even in the least complex political systems there are channels which are not normally used but which can be activated under the impact of certain events. In highly complex systems, the differences are well illustrated by imagining the peculiarities revealed if the United States were put under the fluoroscope during a presidential campaign. Certainly anyone mapping communication in and around the party structures and personalities during the campaign would err greatly if he assumed that the observed patterns were characteristic of the modal daily operation of the system. Similarly, in Cuba immediately before and after the Bay of Pigs invasion, channels were activated that had been dormant or quiescent during times when revolutionary politics was functioning as usual.

The more general point is that there is some

[1] Committees for the Defense of the Revolution were first formed by Castro in 1960 to act as a grass-roots defense against counterrevolutionaries. Organized on a geographical basis, they soon became multipurpose citizen groups used by the leadership for recruiting, administering, and proselytizing in the service of the revolution.

Reprinted in part from Richard R. Fagen. "The Components of Communication Networks." *Politics and Communication* (Boston: Little, Brown, 1966), pp. 34–52.

* Professor, Institute of Political Studies, Stanford University.

structural elasticity in the communication patterns observed in any political system at different points of time. The picture revealed by our fluoroscope depends greatly on when we catch the system—with what political problems it is occupied at the time. Always we will observe some core channels in operation, the channels which may be thought of as carrying on the system's continuing political business. In addition we will observe specialized channels, activated in response to special problems and events.

Passing on from the metaphor of the fluoroscope and the patternings of political communication that it might reveal, let us examine types of channels in actual systems. Here we are concerned with what structures and institutions in the society are, or might be, used to carry on communication of consequence to the gross functioning of the political system. A four-fold classification is used: (1) organizations, (2) groups, (3) the mass media, and (4) special channels for interest articulation and aggregation. The classification is not intended to be either exhaustive or conceptually elegant. Rather, its aim is to order in a preliminary manner the diversity of channels and to suggest possible structural points of similarity and difference among systems.

One other word of warning: The typology draws no hard and fast distinction between structures having communication as their primary function and those for which communication is ancillary to other activities. It is tempting at times to isolate the mass media and think of them as somehow the purest and most specialized communication structures; but such a view overlooks the fact that organizations such as the Leninist party are in their own way just as specialized and just as single-mindedly concerned with communication as are the mass media. One way of summarizing the position taken here is to note that the primary function of the mass media is *always* communication, whereas such may not be the case in relevant organizations, groups, and special channels.

Organizations As Channels

As we have already suggested, among the most important political communication channels are institutions such as parties, interest groups, public bureaucracies, unions, and mass organizations capable of linking the elite, the subelite, and broad sectors of the citizenry. We refer to institutions of this sort, national or nearly national in scope and significance, permanent or semipermanent in structure, although not necessarily continuous in operation, as organizational channels.

The comparative study of these channels should take into account at least the following three points.

1. *Organizational Channels of Political Consequence Are Not Necessarily Part of the Political System in the Structural Sense.* This is a restatement of a position taken earlier, but it is well to re-emphasize it here. The basic point is that important organizational channels may not be part of what is normally thought of as the political system. For example, schools and unions in the United States are outside the political system in the structural sense, but at times they function as important channels of political communication. In other systems, the political use of nonpolitical channels is more continuous and complete. Thus Millen, writing about ostensibly independent labor unions in the developing countries, notes:

> The function most expected of the union is that of providing a channel of communication between the political elite—which may be the government in power or a party in opposition —and the masses. In the best situations the channel is two-way. . . . To be effective in this channeling function, a union must have the widest possible mass character, and it must have means for mobilizing its indoctrinated membership or sympathizers for action on command.[2]

The situation referred to by Millen differs from that in the fully developed Leninist system in which governmental penetration and control of unions and other institutions are so complete that those organizations *are* struc-

[2] Bruce H. Millen, *The Political Role of Labor in Developing Countries* (Washington, D. C.: The Brookings Institution, 1963), p. 83.

turally within the political system. In our view, the Leninist system defines one end of a continuum, the end at which few if any organizational channels of political consequence are autonomous. Under the totalitarian "passion for unanimity," all possible organizational channels are incorporated into the political system.[3] But there are other, increasingly noninclusive, structural formates arrayed along the continuum. One task of comparative analysis is to sort out and describe these other formats.

2. *The Political Use of Organizational Channels Is Intermittent or Partial in Many Instances.* Again, this has been touched on previously but bears repeating here. The intermittency may be of two forms. The first is exemplified by the labor union which sometimes serves as a political channel and at other times (or at the same time) performs economic functions such as the training of new workers. This is an example of the multifunctionality of most complex organizations. The second form of intermittency is shown by structures that almost entirely cease to operate when not functioning primarily as channels of political communication. Political parties in some Latin American countries illustrate the type. The key point is that, although the skeleton of the party continues to exist between elections, it is only when the contest is joined that communication, or any activity of major political consequence, takes place. Political parties in the United States operate somewhat in this manner, although their degree of interelection quiescense does not approach the Latin American type.

3. *Organizational Channels Differ Widely in the Political Communication Uses Which They Serve.* This is a version of one of the most widely accepted canons of modern political analysis. The parent proposition reminds us that nominal and structural similarities are a poor guide to political functioning, that the Italian Communist Party and the Chinese Communist Party, despite structural similarities, fit into the operation of the Italian and

Chinese political systems in quite different ways. Likewise, we should not assume that observed structural similarities in organizational channels give us a firm basis for inferring similarities in political functions performed. The basic structures of the Soviet and American public school systems are not dissimilar, but the former is more overtly conceived of and used as a channel for political communication than the latter. In fact, the continuing battle in the United States between those who would teach more "Americanism" in the classroom and those who would mute the issue is, in part, a controversy over the extent to which this organizational channel should be brought explicitly into the service of the political system. The important point is that organizational channels in most systems have substantial flexibility and unused potentiality for political communication. The uses to which channels are put depend not so much on their structural characteristics as on the purposes to which political leaders wish to see them put within the constraints imposed by political, social, and economic environments.

Groups As Channels

The line between an organization and a group, as the words are used here, is not easy to draw. By groups we mean those less permanent, less institutionalized, and frequently less pervasive collectivities which sometimes figure prominently in patterns of political communication. At our terminological extremes, the American Medical Association is clearly an organization and the local "housewives for Johnson" is clearly a group, but discrimination would be more difficult in other examples.

Central to the distinction is the notion that communication in a group is less formal than in an organization, and thus group membership must remain compact enough to allow this looser patterning of communication to endure. Organizations, of course, always contain a number of groups within them, and it is on this basis that the frequently drawn dichot-

[3] Among others, see Carl J. Friedrich and Zbigniew K. Brzezinski, *Totalitarian Dictatorship and Autocracy* (New York: Frederick A. Praeger, Inc., 1961), particularly Part IV.

omy between "formal" and "informal" channels of organizational communication rests. The organization is defined by its formal channels of communication, so some theorists say, and it survives and functions because of the informal channels which spring up both to sustain social groupings and to bypass and supplement hierarchical arrangements. This distinction is not the only one which is central to our argument. We are concerned also with those informal patternings of communication which are *not* embedded in organizations and thus would not show up if we confined our analysis to the group structure of organizational life.

The most familiar example of the primacy of groups in political communication comes from the literature on American voting behavior. Study after study has demonstrated that at election time communication flows not only from the mass media directly to the individual voter, but also from person to person in the face-to-face groups of family and friends to which the citizen belongs.[4] Moreover, it has been argued, the communication of highest political relevance—in the sense that it is the communication which most affects the voting choice—is that which takes place within these groups. It is there that attitudes are formed and changed and choices are made and reinforced.

Nor need we confine our examples to voting for, as other authors have pointed out, groups perform critical communication functions in almost any process of decision that we might wish to examine.[5] From the highest to the lowest levels of the political hierarchy, both intra- and extraorganizational groups act as nodes for the exchange of information and influence. As an example, at the intraorganizational level, there are the coalitions and cliques which give a special flavor to the Congress. At the extraorganizational level are groups such as the top-level *ad hoc* unit assembled by President Kennedy in October 1962, at the time of the Cuban missile crisis. That group was called together because the President perceived that the usual organizational channels were inadequate in the face of the communication demands (information gathering, processing, and evaluation) imposed by the crisis.[6]

In modified form, the three propositions advanced about organizational channels apply also to group channels. That is, the groups of importance are not necessarily structurally part of the political system, their operation as political channels is frequently intermittent or

[4] See particularly Paul F. Lazarsfeld, Bernard Berelson, and Hazel Gaudet, *The People's Choice* (New York: Columbia University Press, 1948), and Bernard R. Berelson, Paul F. Lazarsfeld, and William N. McPhee, *Voting: A Study of Opinion Formation in a Presidential Campaign* (Chicago: University of Chicago Press, 1954). Additional bibliography and insights can be found in Elihu Katz, "The Two-Step Flow of Communication: An Up-To-Date Report on an Hypothesis," *Public Opinion Quarterly*, Vol. XXI, No. 1, Spring 1957, pp. 61–78.

[5] For an excellent overview of the literature on the importance of groups in the political process see Sidney Verba, *Small Groups and Political Behavior* (Princeton, N. J.: Princeton University Press, 1961), particularly Chapter II, "The Primary Group and Politics." Verba's definition differs from ours in that he includes as groups those small decisional units operating with face-to-face communication no matter how institutionalized and formal they might be. Thus, to him the Supreme Court is a group whereas in our terminology it would be a small organization.

[6] In addition to the President, the group included among others Vice-President Lyndon Johnson, Robert Kennedy, Dean Rusk, Robert McNamara, and Douglas Dillon from the Cabinet, and others from the presidential staff, the State Department, the Central Intelligence Agency, and the Defense Department. For more detail on the group and its operation see Henry M. Pachter, *Collision Course: The Cuban Missile Crisis and Coexistence* (New York: Frederick A. Praeger, Inc., 1963), particularly pp. 11ff. See also Theodore C. Sorensen, *Decision-Making in the White House* (New York: Columbia University Press, 1963), *passim.*

partial, and the political uses to which they are put differ widely. Thus, for the purpose of analyzing the pattern of group channels in any system, few real complications are added by the distinction between organizations and groups.

However, in comparing entire systems the distinction becomes important, because, as we move from the more open to the more absolutist political format, we find fewer and fewer key political communication activities performed by groups, except at the very highest levels of decision. The types of political control and predictability sought by absolutist elites are rendered difficult if political communication is carried on in the less formal group channels. The elites prefer organizational or mass media channels in which control and predictability are increased. This is not to claim that groups cease to exist; family, friendship, and intraorganizational groups remain. However, in absolutist systems there is an attempt to relieve such groups of much of their autonomous political communication. Sometimes group communication activities are suppressed, and at other times the activities are formalized to the point at which new organizational channels result. The new organizational channels at first glance may resemble collections of groups by virtue of the small scale of the operating unit or "cell"; but, because of the formalization of communication and the amount of control exercised, the new units are really small organizations. Both techniques of subordination of group life are illustrated by the recent history of Cuba. There reformist, family, and friendship groups have been stilled or coopted by the Castro regime while revolutionary *ad hoc* policy-making and policy-implementing groups have been transformed into bureaucracies with control over newly created organizational channels.

In sum, the mixture of organizational and group channels might well be a structural concomitant of political format. More specifically, it would seem that, where an open and competitive political system is in operation, group channels would proliferate. Where the more absolutist model is successfully in force, the political importance of group channels would diminish.

Mass Media As Channels

A complex political system and its processes are very hard to observe at first hand. What most of us observe are *reports* of certain events and activities which in turn are only the behavioral outcroppings of political processes. For our reports of these events and activities we most frequently depend on the mass media or on others who themselves depend on the mass media.

Structural possibilities for a gigantic and bizarre hoax inhere in this situation. If it were possible to secure the conspiratorial cooperation of two thousand mass media personnel in key places, almost two hundred million Americans and a sizable part of the rest of the world could be led to believe that the President was dead or that atomic weapons were being used on Communist China.[7] Let the President in the flesh shout from the White House lawn that he was very much alive or deny at the top of his lungs that atomic bombs were being used on China, his messages would reach only the most limited audience as

---

[7] It is instructive to speculate on who should be included among the key two thousand personnel. Primarily they would be *gatekeepers* who in turn had the organizational resources needed to perpetrate the hoax on their own organizations, the wire services, radio, TV, and the newspapers.

As to the possibilities of social disorganization which inhere in the hoax, the famous Orson Welles radio broadcast "The War of the Worlds" in 1938 is instructive. Despite repeated warnings that the broadcast, describing an invasion by Martians, was fictional, thousands of listeners became panic stricken. Had the broadcast subject matter been more credible, had all stations carried the same broadcast, and had no warnings regarding its fictional nature been given, the chaos ensuing might well have brought national life to a standstill. See Hadley Cantril. *The Invasion from Mars* (Princeton, N. J.: Princeton University Press, 1940).

long as the conspiracy of the two thousand held. Only with the physical takeover of the national mass media by a centrally controlled agency with internal lines of communication, such as the Army, could the information tide sustaining the hoax be turned.

Though fanciful, the consequences of our imaginary conspiracy are instructive because they remind us how completely most citizens of developed societies depend on the mass media for primary information about the functioning of the national political system. This, of course, does not mean that the content of the media shapes political behavior in any direct and easily predictable manner, even in tightly controlled systems such as the Soviet. On the contrary, most current writing on the mass media and politics goes to some length to point out that the relationship between the two is very complex.[8] However, the existence of national mass media, with all that they imply in increased message capacity, speed, and pervasiveness, changes in a basic way a system's potential for political communication. Structurally, the hoax suggested above would be just as easy to perpetrate in the Soviet Union as in the United States; in fact, because of Soviet centralization of media control, it might well be easier. In either case, under the conditions of the hoax, approximately 0.001 per cent of the citizens are so located in the mass media structures that they could very rapidly reshape some important political images held by the other 99.999 per cent of the population. This is a distinctly modern situation.

Thus, all varieties of political systems that are serviced by well-developed mass media networks also enjoy communication potentialities, for both control and coverage that are not shared by their media-poor relations no matter how extensive the latter's organizational and group channels might be.

To state this point in a slightly different fashion, the growth of mass media in a society alters in the most fundamental manner some aspects of politics. News travels farther and faster in a mass media system, and the "homogenization" and spread of public information is facilitated. Publicity assumes a new role, and a corps of specialists—reporters, columnists, editors, public information officers, and media personalities—is woven into the political process. The citizen participates politically as part of the media audience, tied to, and dependent upon, his newspaper, radio, and television set. But a word of caution is in order. It should not be assumed that the political transformation is complete, for personal contacts, face-to-face communication, and all sorts of nonmedia channels continue to be of vital importance in politics. If there is any single lesson taught by the results of several decades of research on communication processes, it is that the growth of the mass media results in a new mixture of mediated and nonmediated communication. The media do not simply displace or supersede other channels; rather, they link existing networks while giving rise to a host of dependent nets which service, disseminate, and frequently transform their product.

The structural picture of the mass media drawn so far suggests that we are dealing with

[8] See for instance V. O. Key, Jr., *Public Opinion and American Democracy* (New York: Alfred A. Knopf, 1961), particularly Chapters 14 and 15, and Robert E. Lane, *Political Life* (Glencoe, Ill.: The Free Press, 1959), particularly Chapter 19. No attempt has been made here to give the reader a basic understanding of the mass media, their organization, operation, and relation to social life in general. For this purpose, several excellent books are available. For instance, for a basic introduction to the mass media in the United States, see Theodore Peterson, Jay W. Jensen, and William L. Rivers, *The Mass Media and Modern Society* (New York: Holt, Rinehart and Winston, Inc., 1965). For a very useful collection of essays and a good bibliography see Wilbur Schramm, ed., *Mass Communication* (Urbana: University of Illinois Press, 1960). A review of studies of mass media effects can be found in Joseph T. Klapper, *The Effects of Mass Communication* (Glencoe, Ill.: The Free Press, 1960), particularly Part One.

long channels that somehow link informational centers or nodes with individuals and social groupings distant from the centers and from each other. There is some truth in this picture, but at best it is incomplete. For a more general comparative framework we have to consider at least two other types of mass media linkages:

1. *The Media as Lateral Channels.* Speaking of the role of prestige newspapers, such as *The New York Times* and the *Washington Post*, in foreign policy formation, Bernard Cohen notes that,

> By giving policy makers in both branches an insight into the political perceptions of men with important roles in the political process, the press helps to create common understandings or interpretations of political reality. There is thus some significance for the governmental —and hence public—debate on foreign policy in the fact that both Executive officials and Congressmen draw on approximately the same sources for their wider knowledge of "what is going on in the world," and how important it seems to be. Certain kinds of behavior can thus be reasonably predicted, and mutual expectation can become the basis for policy planning. Despite the specialized and confidential character of the State Department's diplomatic channels of information, continuous and meaningful discourse among foreign policy-making officials in all parts of the government, at all times and at all levels, is possible within the bounds set by this independent source of information and intellectual structuring of policy.[9]

Quite literally, important people in Washington and in other capitals around the world talk to each other through the mass media.

Such patterns may be equally prevalent in political systems in which there is otherwise minimal vertical media diffusion. Even in these systems, although there are few opportunities for grass-roots reading, listening, or viewing, the national elite clustered in the capital city have access to the mas media and use them for lateral political communication.

2. *The Media as Links in Other Chains.* In some of the developing countries, two types of persons are most likely to see a movie. The first is the urban dweller, participant in the modern economy at least to the extent that he pays cash to go to the commercial cinema in order to see "the latest." The second is the rural isolate, visited by some administrative arm of government such as community development and treated to an instructional film, frequently on some subject such as postnatal care or the construction of pit latrines. Here we have an example of an organizational channel using the mass media at the final stage as a "multiplier" of messages.

At times the ordering of the organizational and mass media linkages is reversed, as with farm radio forums and "tele-clubs," where the mass media are used for the initial dissemination of information and then structured local organizations continue the discussion and interpretation triggered by the media.[10] In both types of linkage it is noteworthy that mixtures of organizational and media channels are consciously established in order to achieve political goals. Students of communism have long realized how crucial to the operation of political systems such mixed channels can be, and students of political change and development are now acquiring the same awareness.[11]

Before leaving the mass media as channels, one final point should be made. The boundary problem is particularly acute when we attempt to decide *which* media activity has po-

---

[9] Bernard C. Cohen, *The Press and Foreign Policy* (Princeton, N. J.: Princeton University Press, 1963), p. 246.

[10] See J. C. Mathur and Paul Neurath, *An Indian Experiment in Farm Radio Forums* (Paris: UNESCO, 1959); Roger Louis and Joseph Rovan, *Television and Tele-clubs in Rural Communities,* Reports and Papers on Mass Communication, No. 16 (Paris: UNESCO, 1955); and UNESCO, *Rural Television in Japan* (Paris: UNESCO, 1960).

[11] See Ithiel de Sola Pool, "The Mass Media and Politics in the Modernization Process," in Lucian W. Pye, ed., *Communications and Political Development* (Princeton, N. J.: Princeton University Press, 1963).

litical consequences, that is, *when* media channels should be thought of as political communication channels.

The problem becomes more clearly drawn if we examine two types of occurrences. The first is well represented by the "great debates" of 1960 in which Kennedy and Nixon as presidential candidates confronted each other on television before an audience which averaged seventy-one million Americans. Both social scientists and political pundits agree that the debates were the most important single campaign episode serving to overcome Nixon's early lead in voter support.[12] Here the political system consequences of communication in media channels are about as clear-cut and direct as one could hope for in the complexity of dealing with macroeffects in a large national system.

However, consider a second type of example. Eisenstadt quotes an Israeli settler as saying,

> I always like to listen to the news and the radio. It is very important because only in this way can I feel that I know what happens in the State, that I am a real citizen.[13]

We know that the *aggregate* of media experiences like the one above can result in national political transformations of primary importance; but when citizen X listens to program Y it is impossible to link the system consequences to the event in any direct manner. The individual transformations sparked by this type of mediated communication develop for years before they affect the national political system. The consequences are important, but they are often far removed from the subject matter and intent of the original communications.[14]

Specialized Channels for Interest Articulation and Aggregation

Consider two seemingly dissimilar acts: 1. An American housewife walks to her neighbor's basement on election day and casts her ballot for the presidential candidate of her choice. 2. Halfway around the world in Asia a militant leftist student joins a street demonstration and thirty minutes later is swept along in a chanting, rock-throwing attack on the American Embassy. For our purposes can these two behaviors be embedded in some common frame of meaning? Probably yes, for both the voter and the rioter are communicating choice or preference directly up some political hierarchy through special channels that do not fall easily into the typology of organizations, groups, or mass media developed above. This does not mean that organizations, groups, and the mass media do not shape the behavior of the voter and the rioter; of course they do, at least potentially. But the channels used for expression of preference are of an order different from those we have previously discussed.

These channels are used for the articulation and aggregation of interests only under special circumstances. The citizen cannot express himself through these channels whenever he feels the need, as he might on other occasions write a letter to the editor, speak at a union meeting, or complain to the bureaucracy. The social situation has to be "right." It must be election time, or the preconditions for mob action must be present. Thus, the channels are intermittent in operation and in a sense impermanent. In the case of well-institutionalized electoral procedures, the channels can be reconstituted on demand, but, once the com-

---

[12] See Sidney Kraus, ed., *The Great Debates* (Bloomington, Ind.: Indiana University Press, 1962) and Theodore H. White, *The Making of the President, 1960* (New York: Pocket Books, Inc., 1960), particularly Chapter 11. The estimate of audience size is from Frank Stanton, "A CBS View," in Kraus, *op. cit.*, p. 66.

[13] S. N. Eisenstadt, "Communication Systems and Social Structure: An Exploratory Comparative Study," *Public Opinion Quarterly*, Vol. XIX, No. 2, Summer 1955, p. 159.

[14] David Riesman, among others, has discussed the mechanisms through which media-supported character transformations eventually give rise to a new style of politics. See his *The Lonely Crowd* (New Haven: Yale University Press, 1950), particularly Chapters IV and IX.

munication tasks incident to the election are completed, the channels again cease to exist. In the case of the riot, the action forges its own channels, which disappear as the turmoil itself subsides.

The class of events that use or create such channels is not very well defined. The election and the riot seem to fit into the category, and perhaps the boycott and the public opinion poll should be included also. In any event, enough has been said to suggest that we are not dealing simply with a residual category with no common properties of its own. This brief discussion reminds us that in the study of organizations, groups, and the mass media we have not exhausted the possible communication components which the comparative analysis of political systems must note.

Interaction: An Example

As always happens with typologies, much of the richness of real life is lost, particularly when the subject matter is as luxuriant as ours. The communication networks which comprise the "nervous system" of a polity are intricate and complex in the extreme, as every student knows who has tried to trace and lay bare such networks. So, in the interest of ending this discussion on a more empirical note, let us return to the image of the fluoroscope with which the chapter began. Now, however, instead of looking in a general way at macro-differences between national systems, let us confine our attention to one key "node" of a single national system. By so doing, some of the detail can be put back into the picture. In particular, let us focus on the mass media and political communication networks in Washing-ton, D. C.[15] When the fluoroscope is turned on, what do we see?

At first glance, we might be struck by the number and diversity of organizations and individuals specializing in the production, gathering, processing, and dissemination of news and opinion about politics. The public information officers, press secretaries, public relations men, reporters, columnists, editors, and lesser operatives based in Washington must number in the thousands. Many work for the government, many others for the networks, news agencies, newspapers, and magazines, and still others are on commercial, personal, or foreign payrolls. Publicity, in the most general sense, is a very big and, at first glance, a very confusing business in Washington.

If we were to settle back and watch for awhile, certain patterns would emerge and begin to give order and predictability to the picture. We would notice that the specialists interact with each other in regular ways. Daily briefings are held to link official informational centers in the White House and the State Department with the reporters who cover those beats. Furthermore, through press conferences, top public officials on occasion make themselves available for direct interrogation, bypassing the information officers who normally stand between top officialdom and the working press. We would also notice that those who specialize in gathering news and purveying opinion evolve standardized search procedures, tailored to their informational needs. Through personal contacts, including contacts with other members of the working press, the political journalist cultivates the informal sources on which much of his work depends. Although it would not show up on our

[15] Aside from the intrinsic interest and importance of the example (the mass media and political communication in Washington), there are also pragmatic reasons for the choice. At least five books (of quite diverse quality) bear directly on some aspect of the problem. From earliest to most recently published they are Leo C. Rosten, *The Washington Correspondents* (New York: Harcourt, Brace & World, Inc., 1937), Douglass Cater, *The Fourth Branch of Government* (Boston: Houghton Mifflin Company, 1959), Bernard C. Cohen, *The Press and Foreign Policy* (Princeton, N. J.: Princeton University Press, 1963), Dan D. Nimmo, *Newsgathering in Washington* (New York: Atherton Press, 1964), William L. Rivers, *The Opinion-makers* (Boston: The Beacon Press, 1965). The discussion which follows is based on the composite picture which emerges from these five books.

fluoroscope, these all-important formal and informal relationships are eased and maintained by a code of behavior, by certain conventions, confidences, unwritten agreements, niceties, and taboos which make it possible for the mass media specialists to live both with each other and with the various public officials on whom they report and depend.

There are other regularized and important patterns of communication in addition to the face-to-face exchanges just discussed. As suggested earlier, public officials use the mass media for a wide variety of purposes other than simply keeping themselves informed. To understand this second level of patterning we must look not only at the men who make and disseminate news and opinion, but also at the purposes served by the *products* which they turn out. The following list suggests some of the ways in which the mass media are used in political life in Washington.

1. *As an Index of What and Who Is Important, Newsworthy, or Politically Relevant.* It has been pointed out repeatedly that the political world does not order and arrange itself automatically; the media are largely responsible for this. When event X or problem Y appears as the lead article in *The New York Times*, then politicians, officials, and newsmen alike "know" that the event or problem is important. This is "information" of a special type. Prior to presenting information about events, the media tell busy men what events (and opinions) they should be paying attention to or, more precisely, what they *must* pay attention to if they wish to participate fully in political life.

2. *As a Tool for Gauging Public Opinion.* As Cater has pointed out,

In an age of complex and fast-breaking events, the measurement of publicity comes to be taken as a cheap and convenient substitute for public opinion. For the politician and the bureaucrat the headline inch frequently serves as the day-to-day measure of public opinion on a great number of issues. By their responses to this synthetic public opinion they stimulate further publicity and so commences a reflexive cycle that has been known to move news stories

from the inside to the front page and to reshape politics as surely as if public opinion had exerted its sovereign will.[16]

3. *As a Resource for Those with Plans, Problems, or Ambitions.* As the late Senator McCarthy demonstrated so convincingly, those who understand the newsmaking process can move themselves to the center of the political stage very quickly by self-generated publicity, even though as individuals they are not liked or trusted by the working press. Even those who are neither as unscrupulous nor as ambitious as the late senator view the press as a means for securing personal or bureaucratic advantage. The "trial balloon"—in which public reaction to a proposed policy is tested before the policy is officially advocated —is a frequently employed, reputable political tactic. The news leak, the "off-the-record" briefing which removes a potential story from the public domain, and the calculated withholding or distortion of information are a few of the other tactics used by officials and their spokesmen in their continuing efforts both to use and to disarm the press.

In sum, as soon as we look in detail at the web of communication networks active in any important node of a complex system, we realize that no simple typology will capture the richness of the relationships which characterize such a node. Individuals, groups, organizations, and the mass media are all linked together and all interact in the political process; and to equate idealized mass media patterns (a neutral press as watchdog of government) with the operative system is sadly to underestimate the complexity of the real world. In Washington, the mass media are in a real sense the fourth branch of government, not because they keep the other three branches "honest," but because they are the key structures in the public communication network on which functionaries in the other three branches depend. Were we able to gather data in any major capital of the world, most assuredly we would find a similarly complicated interplay and interdependence of com-

[16] Cater, *op. cit.*, pp. 12–13.

munication specialists, public officials, and the mass media. Of course the interdependence would differ from country to country, as would mechanisms of media control, styles of newsgathering, modes of news presentation, and categories of media use. However, the complexity of networks would remain. Thus, although it is possible to reduce any network of political communication to a common set of structural building blocks, it is the total patterning of the network and the uses to which it is put which help us to understand politics. What factors determine the manner in which networks become patterned and used? Why does the process of political communication in Moscow or Cairo or even in London seem so different from political communication in Washington?

E.   CHANGE STRATEGIES

18.   General Strategies for Effecting Changes in Human Systems[a]

Robert Chin* • Kenneth D. Benne**

Discussing general strategies and procedures for effecting change requires that we set limits to the discussion. For, under a liberal interpretation of the title, we would need to deal with much of the literature of contemporary social and behavioral science, basic and applied.

Therefore, we shall limit our discussion to those changes which are planned changes—in which attempts to bring about change are conscious, deliberate, and intended, at least on the part of one or more agents related to the change attempt. We shall also attempt to categorize strategies and procedures which have a few important elements in common but which, in fact, differ widely in other respects. And we shall neglect many of these differences. In addition, we shall look beyond the description of procedures in common sense terms and seek some genotypic characteristics of change strategies. We shall seek the roots of the main strategies discussed, including their

[a] Prepared especially for this volume [1969] and used by permission. This paper is adapted from a paper by Robert Chin prepared for "Designing Education for the Future—An Eight State Project" (Denver, Colo., 1967). Kenneth D. Benne joined in revising and expanding sections of the original paper for inclusion in this volume. In the process of revision, what is in several respects a new paper emerged. The original focus on changing in education has been maintained. Historical roots of ideas and strategies have been explored. The first person style of the original has also been maintained. Citations have been modified to include articles contained in this volume, along with other references.

From Robert Chin and Kenneth D. Benne, "General Strategies for Effecting Changes in Human Systems," *The Planning of Change*, 2d ed., edited by Warren G. Bennis, Kenneth D. Benne, and Robert Chin. (New York: Holt, Rinehart and Winston, 1969), pp. 32–59. Copyright © 1961, 1969 by Holt, Rinehart and Winston, Inc. Reprinted by permission of Holt, Rinehart and Winston, Inc.

* Professor of Psychology, Boston University.
** Professor of Human Relations, Boston Univesity.

variants in ideas and idea systems prominent in contemporary and recent social and psychological thought.

One element in all approaches to planned change is the conscious utilization and application of knowledge as an instrument or tool for modifying patterns and institutions of practice. The knowledge or related technology to be applied may be knowledge of the non-human environment in which practice goes on or of some knowledge-based "thing technology" for controlling one or another feature of the practice environment. In educational practice, for example, technologies of communication and calculation, based upon new knowledge of electronics—audio-visual devices, television, computers, teaching machines—loom large among the knowledges and technologies that promise greater efficiency and economy in handling various practices in formal education. As attempts are made to introduce these new thing technologies into school situations, the change problem shifts to the human problems of dealing with the resistances, anxieties, threats to morale, conflicts, disrupted interpersonal communications, and so on, which prospective changes in patterns of practice evoke in the people affected by the change. So the change agent, even though focally and initially concerned with modifications in the thing technology of education, finds himself in need of more adequate knowledge of human behavior, individual and social, and in need of developed "people technologies," based on behavioral knowledge, for dealing effectively with the human aspects of deliberate change.

The knowledge which suggests improvements in educational practice may, on the other hand, be behavioral knowledge in the first instance—knowledge about participative learning, about attitude change, about family disruption in inner-city communities, about the cognitive and skill requirements of new careers, and so forth. Such knowledge may suggest changes in school grouping, in the relations between teachers and students, in the relations of teachers and principals to parents, and in counseling practices. Here change agents, initially focused on application of behavioral knowledge and the improvement of

people technologies in school settings, must face the problems of using people technologies in planning, installing, and evaluating such changes in educational practice. The new people technologies must be experienced, understood, and accepted by teachers and administrators before they can be used effectively with students.

This line of reasoning suggests that, whether the focus of planned change is in the introduction of more effective thing technologies or people technologies into institutionalized practice, processes of introducing such changes must be based on behavioral knowledge of change and must utilize people technologies based on such knowledge.

A. Types of Strategies for Changing

Our further analysis is based on three types or groups of strategies. The first of these, and probably the most frequently employed by men of knowledge in America and Western Europe, are those we call empirical-rational strategies. One fundamental assumption underlying these strategies is that men are rational. Another assumption is that men will follow their rational self-interest once this is revealed to them. A change is proposed by some person or group which knows of a situation that is desirable, effective, and in line with the self-interest of the person, group, organization, or community which will be affected by the change. Because the person (or group) is assumed to be rational and moved by self-interest, it is assumed that he (or they) will adopt the proposed change if it can be rationally justified and if it can be shown by the proposer(s) that he (or they) will gain by the change.

A second group of strategies we call normative–re-educative. These strategies build upon assumptions about human motivation different from those underlying the first. The rationality and intelligence of men are not denied. Patterns of action and practice are supported by sociocultural norms and by commitments on the part of individuals to these norms. Sociocultural norms are supported by the attitude and value systems of individuals—normative outlooks which undergird their commitments.

Change in a pattern of practice or action, according to this view, will occur only as the persons involved are brought to change their normative orientations to old patterns and develop commitments to new ones. And changes in normative orientations involve changes in attitudes, values, skills, and significant relationships, not just changes in knowledge, information, or intellectual rationales for action and practice.

The third group of strategies is based on the application of power in some form, political or otherwise. The influence process involved is basically that of compliance of those with less power to the plans, directions, and leadership of those with greater power. Often the power to be applied is legitimate power or authority. Thus the strategy may involve getting the authority of law or administrative policy behind the change to be effected. Some power strategies may appeal less to the use of authoritative power to effect change than to the massing of coercive power, legitimate or not, in support of the change sought.[1]

1. Empirical-Rational Strategies

A variety of specific strategies are included in what we are calling the empirical-rational approach to effecting change. As we have already pointed out, the rationale underlying most of these is an assumption that men are guided by reason and that they will utilize some rational calculus of self-interest in determining needed changes in behavior.

It is difficult to point to any one person whose ideas express or articulate the orientation underlying commitment to empirical-rational strategies of changing. In Western Europe and America, this orientation might be better identified with the general social orientation of the Enlightenment and of classical liberalism than with the ideas of any one man. On this view, the chief foes to human rationality and to change or progress based on rationality were ignorance and superstition. Scientific investigation and research represented the chief ways of extending knowledge and reducing the limitations of ignorance. A corollary of this optimistic view of man and his future was an advocacy of education as a way of disseminating scientific knowledge and of freeing men and women from the shackles of superstition. Although elitist notions played a part in the thinking of many classic liberals, the increasing trend during the nineteenth century was toward the universalization of educational opportunity. The common and universal school, open to all men and women, was the principal instrument by which knowledge would replace ignorance and superstition in the minds of people and become a principal agent in the spread of reason, knowledge, and knowledge-based action and practice (progress) in human society. In American experience, Jefferson may be taken as a principal, early advocate of research and of education as agencies of human progress. And Horace Mann may be taken as the prophet of progress through the institutionalization of universal

---

[1] Throughout our discussion of strategies and procedures, we will not differentiate these according to the size of the target of change. We assume that there are similarities in processes of changing, whether the change affects an individual, a small group, an organization, a community, or a culture. In addition, we are not attending to differences among the aspects of a system, let us say an educational system, which is being changed—curriculum, audio-visual methods, team teaching, pupil grouping, and so on. Furthermore, because many changes in communities or organizations start with an individual or some small membership group, our general focus will be upon those strategies which lead to and involve individual changes.

   We will sidestep the issue of defining change in this paper. As further conceptual work progresses in the study of planned change, we shall eventually have to examine how different definitions of change relate to strategies and procedures for effecting change. But we are not dealing with these issues here.

educational opportunity through the common school.[2]

A. Basic Research and Dissemination of Knowledge through General Education

The strategy of encouraging basic knowledge building and of depending on general education to diffuse the results of research into the minds and thinking of men and women is still by far the most appealing strategy of change to most academic men of knowledge and to large segments of the American population as well. Basic researchers are quite likely to appeal for time for further research when confronted by some unmet need. And many people find this appeal convincing. Both of these facts are well illustrated by difficulties with diseases for which no adequate control measures or cures are available—poliomyelitis, for example. Medical researchers asked for more time and funds for research and people responded with funds for research, both through voluntary channels and through legislative appropriations. And the control measures were forthcoming. The educational problem then shifted to inducing people to comply with immunization procedures based on research findings.

This appeal to a combination of research and education of the public has worked in many areas of new knowledge-based thing technologies where almost universal readiness for accepting the new technology was already present in the population. Where such readiness is not available, as in the case of fluoridation technologies in the management of dental caries, general strategy of basic research plus educational (informational) campaigns to spread knowledge of the findings do not work well. The cases of its inadequacy as a single strategy of change have multiplied, especially where "engineering" problems, which involve

a divided and conflicting public or deep resistances due to the threat by the new technology to traditional attitudes and values, have thwarted its effectiveness. But these cases, while they demand attention to other strategies of changing, do not disprove the importance of basic research and of general educational opportunity as elements in a progressive and self-renewing society.

We have noted that the strategy under discussion has worked best in grounding and diffusing generally acceptable thing technologies in society. Some have argued that the main reason the strategy has not worked in the area of people technologies is a relative lack of basic research on people and their behavior, relationships, and institutions and a corresponding lack of emphasis upon social and psychological knowledges in school and college curricula. It would follow in this view that increased basic research on human affairs and relationships and increased efforts to diffuse the results of such research through public education are the ways of making the general strategy work better. Auguste Comte with his emphasis on positivistic sociology in the reorganization of society and Lester F. Ward in America may be taken as late nineteenth-century representatives of this view. And the spirit of Comte and Ward is by no means dead in American academia or in influential segments of the American public.

B. Personnel Selection and Replacement

Difficulties in getting knowledge effectively into practice may be seen as lying primarily in the lack of fitness of persons occupying positions with job responsibilities for improving practice. The argument goes that we need the right person in the right position, if knowledge is to be optimally applied and if rationally based changes are to become the expectation

---

[2] We have indicated the main roots of ideas and idea systems underlying the principal strategies of changing and their subvariants on a chart which appears as figure 18.1 at the end of this essay. It may be useful in seeing both the distinctions and the relationships between various strategies of changing in time perspective. We have emphasized developments of the past twenty-five years more than earlier developments. This makes for historical fore-shortening. We hope this is a pardonable distortion, considering our present limited purpose.

in organizational and societal affairs. This fits with the liberal reformers' frequently voiced and enacted plea to drive the unfit from office and to replace them with those more fit as a condition of social progress.

That reformers' programs have so often failed has sobered but by no means destroyed the zeal of those who regard personnel selection, assessment, and replacement as a major key to program improvement in education or in other enterprises as well. This strategy was given a scientific boost by the development of scientific testing of potentialities and aptitudes. We will use Binet as a prototype of psychological testing and Moreno as a prototype in sociometric testing, while recognizing the extensive differentiation and elaboration which have occurred in psychometrics and sociometrics since their original work. We recognize too the elaborated modes of practice in personnel work which have been built around psychometric and sociometric tools and techniques. We do not discount their limited value as actual and potential tools for change, while making two observations on the way they have often been used. First, they have been used more often in the interest of system maintenance rather than of system change, since the job descriptions personnel workers seek to fill are defined in terms of system requirements as established. Second, by focusing on the role occupant as the principal barrier to improvement, personnel selection and replacement strategies have tended not to reveal the social and cultural system difficulties which may be in need of change if improvement is to take place.

C. SYSTEMS ANALYSTS AS
STAFF AND CONSULTANTS

Personnel workers in government, industry, and education have typically worked in staff relations to line management, reflecting the bureaucratic, line-staff form of organization which has flourished in the large-scale organization of effort and enterprise in the twentieth century. And other expert workers—systems analysts—more attuned to system difficulties

than to the adequacies or inadequacies of persons as role occupants within the system, have found their way into the staff resources of line management in contemporary organizations.

There is no reason why the expert resources of personnel workers and systems analysts might not be used in nonbureaucratic organizations or in processes of moving bureaucratic organizations toward nonbureaucratic forms. But the fact remains that their use has been shaped, for the most part, in the image of the scientific management of bureaucratically organized enterprises. So we have placed the systems analysts in our figure under Frederick Taylor, the father of scientific management in America.

The line management of an enterprise seeks to organize human and technical effort toward the most efficient service of organizational goals. And these goals are defined in terms of the production of some mandated product, whether a tangible product or a less tangible good or service. In persuing this quest for efficiency, line management employs experts in the analysis of sociotechnical systems and in the laying out of more efficient systems. The experts employed may work as external consultants or as an internal staff unit. Behavioral scientists have recently found their way, along with mathematicians and engineers, into systems analysis work.

It is interesting to note that the role of these experts is becoming embroiled in discussions of whether or not behavioral science research should be used to sensitize administrators to new organizational possibilities, to new goals, or primarily to implement efficient operation within perspectives and goals as currently defined. Jean Hills has raised the question of whether behavioral science when applied to organizational problems tends to perpetuate established ideology and system relations because of blinders imposed by their being "problem centered" and by their limited definition of what is "a problem."[3]

We see an emerging strategy, in the use of behavioral scientists as systems analysts and engineers, toward viewing the problem of or-

[3] Jean Hills, "Social Science, Ideology and the Purposes of Educational Administration," *Education Administration Quarterly I* (Autumn 1965), 23–40.

ganizational change and changing as a wide-angled problem, one in which all the input and output features and components of a large-scale system are considered. It is fore-seeable that with the use of high-speed and high-capacity computers, and with the growth of substantial theories and hypotheses about how parts of an educational system operate, we shall find more and more applications for systems analysis and operations research in programs of educational change. In fact, it is precisely the quasi-mathematical character of these modes of research that will make possible the rational analysis of qualitatively different aspects of educational work and will bring them into the range of rational planning—masses of students, massive problems of poverty and educational and cultural deprivation, and so on. We see no necessary incompatibility between an ideology which emphasizes the individuality of the student and the use of systems analysis and computers in strategizing the problems of the total system. The actual incompatibilities may lie in the limited uses to which existing organizers and administrators of educational efforts put these technical resources.

D. Applied Research and Linkage Systems for Diffusion of Research Results

The American development of applied research and of a planned system for linking applied researchers with professional practitioners and both of these with centers for basic research and with organized consumers of applied research has been strongly influenced by two distinctive American inventions—the land-grant university and the agricultural extension system. We, therefore, have put the name of Justin Morrill, author of the land-grant college act and of the act which established the cooperative agricultural exten-

sion system, in Figure 18.1. The land-grant colleges or universities were dedicated to doing applied research in the service of agriculture and the mechanic arts. These colleges and universities developed research programs in basic sciences as well and experimental stations for the development and refinement of knowledge-based technologies for use in engineering and agriculture. As the extension services developed, county agents—practitioners—were attached to the state land-grant college or university that received financial support from both state and federal governments. The county agent and his staff developed local organizations of adult farm men and women and of farm youth to provide both a channel toward informing consumers concerning new and better agricultural practices and toward getting awareness of unmet consumer needs and unsolved problems back to centers of knowledge and research. Garth Jones has made one of the more comprehensive studies of the strategies of changing involved in large-scale demonstration.[4]

All applied research has not occurred within a planned system for knowledge discovery, development, and utilization like the one briefly described above. The system has worked better in developing and diffusing thing technologies than in developing and diffusing people technologies, though the development of rural sociology and of agricultural economics shows that extension workers were by no means unaware of the behavioral dimensions of change problems. But the large-scale demonstration, through the land-grant university cooperative extension service, of the stupendous changes which can result from a planned approach to knowledge discovery, development, diffusion, and utilization is a part of the consciousness of all Americans concerned with planned change.[5]

(1) Applied research and development is

---

[4] Garth Jones, "Planned Organizational Change, a Set of Working Documents," Center for Research in Public Organization, School of Public Administration (Los Angeles: University of Southern California, 1964).

[5] For a review, see Ronald G. Havelock and Kenneth D. Benne, "An Exploratory Study of Knowledge Utilization," in Warren G. Bennis, Kenneth D. Benne, and Robert Chin (eds.), *The Planning of Change*, 2d ed. (New York: Holt, Rinehart and Winston, Inc., 1969), p. 124.

an honored part of the tradition of engineering approaches to problem identification and solution. The pioneering work of E. L. Thorndike in applied research in education should be noted in Figure 18.1. The processes and slow tempo of diffusion and utilization of research findings and inventions in public education is well illustrated in Studies by Paul Mort and his students.[6] More recently, applied research, in its product development aspect, has been utilized in a massive way to contribute curriculum materials and designs for science instruction (as well as in other subjects). When we assess this situation to find reasons why such researches have not been more effective in producing changes in instruction, the answers seem to lie both in the plans of the studies which produced the materials and designs and in the potential users of the findings. Adequate linkage between consumers and researchers was frequently not established. Planned and evaluated demonstrations and experimentations connected with the use of materials were frequently slighted. And training of consumer teachers to use the new materials adaptively and creatively was frequently missing.

Such observations have led to a fresh spurt of interest in evaluation research addressed to educational programs. The fear persists that this too may lead to disappointment if it is not focused for two-way communication between researchers and teachers and if it does not involve collaboratively the ultimate consumers of the results of such research—the students. Evaluation researches conducted in the spirit of justifying a program developed by expert applied researchers will not help to guide teachers and students in their quest for improved practices of teaching and learning, if the concerns of the latter have not been taken centrally into account in the evaluation process.[7]

(2) Recently, attempts have been made to link applied research activities in education with basic researchers on the one hand and with persons in action and practice settings on the other through some system of interlocking roles similar to those suggested in the description of the land grant—extension systems in agriculture or in other fields where applied and development researches have flourished.

The linking of research-development efforts with diffusion-innovation efforts has been gaining headway in the field of education with the emergence of federally supported research and development centers based in universities, regional laboratories connected with state departments of education, colleges and universities in a geographic area, and with various consortia and institutes confronting problems of educational change and changing. The strategy of change here usually includes a well-researched innovation which seems feasible to install in practice settings. Attention is directed to the question of whether or not the innovation will bring about a desired result, and with what it can accomplish, if given a trial in one or more practice settings. The questions of *how* to get a fair trial and *how* to install an innovation in an already going and crowded school system are ordinarily not built centrally into the strategy. The rationalistic assumption usually precludes research attention to these questions. For, if the invention can be rationally shown to have achieved desirable results in some situations, it is assumed that people in other situations will adopt it once they know these results and the rationale behind them. The neglect of the above questions has led to a wastage of much applied research effort in the past.

Attention has been given recently to the roles, communication mechanisms, and processes necessary for innovation and diffusion of

[6] Paul R. Mort and Donald R. Ross, *Principles of School Administration* (New York: McGraw-Hill, Inc., 1957). Paul R. Mort and Francis C. Cornell, *American Schools in Transition: How our Schools Adopt their Practices to Changing Needs* (New York: Bureau of Publications, Teachers College, Columbia University Press, 1941).

[7] Robert Chin, "Research Approaches to the Problem of Civic Training," in F. Patterson (ed.), *The Adolescent Citizen* (New York: The Free Press, 1960).

improved educational practices.[8] Clark and Guba have formulated very specific processes related to and necessary for change in educational practice following upon research. For them, the necessary processes are: *development*, including invention and design; *diffusion*, including dissemination and demonstration; *adoption*, including trial, installation, and institutionalization. Clark's earnest conviction is summed up in this statement: "In a sense, the educational research community will be the educational community, and the route to educational progress will self-evidently be research and development."[9]

The approach of Havelock and Benne is concerned with the intersystem relationships between basic researchers, applied researchers, practitioners, and consumers in an evolved and evolving organization for knowledge utilization. They are concerned especially with the communication difficulties and role conflicts that occur at points of intersystem exchange. These conflicts are important because they illuminate the normative issues at stake between basic researchers and applied researchers, between applied researchers and practitioners (teachers and administrators), between practitioners   and   consumers   (students).

The lines of strategy suggested by their analysis for solving role conflicts and communication difficulties call for transactional and collaborative exchanges across the lines of varied organized interests and orientations within the process of utilization. This brings their analysis into the range of normative–re-educative strategies to be discussed later.

The concepts from the behavioral sciences upon which these strategies of diffusion rest come mainly from two traditions. The first is from studies of the diffusion of traits of culture from one cultural system to another, initiated by the American anthropologist, Franz Boas. This type of study has been carried on by Rogers in his work on innovation and diffusion of innovations in contemporary culture and is reflected in a number of recent writers such as Katz and Carlson.[10] The second scientific tradition is in studies of influence in mass communication associated with Carl Hovland and his students.[11] Both traditions have assumed a *relatively passive recipient of input* in diffusion situations. And actions within the process of diffusion are interpreted from 'the standpoint of an observer of the process. Bauer has pointed out that scientific studies

[8] Matthew B. Miles, *Some Propositions in Research Utilization in Education* (March 1965), in press. Kenneth Wiles, unpublished paper for seminar on Strategies for Curriculum Change (Columbus, Ohio, Ohio State University). Charles Jung and Ronald Lippitt, "Utilization of Scientific Knowledge for Change in Education," in *Concepts for Social Change* (Washington, D. C.: National Educational Association, National Training Laboratories, 1967). Havelock and Benne, *op. cit.*, p. 124. David Clark and Egon Guba, "An Examination of Potential Change Roles in Education," seminar on Innovation in Planning School Curricula (Columbus, Ohio: Ohio State University, 1965).

[9] David Clark, "Educational Research and Development: The Next Decade," in *Implications for Education of Prospective Changes in Society,* a publication of "Designing Education for the Future—an Eight State Project" (Denver, Colo., 1967).

[10] Elihu Katz, "The Social Itinerary of Technical Change: Two Studies on the Diffusion of Innovation," in Bennis and Chin, *op. cit.,* p. 230. Richard Carlson, "Some Needed Research on the Diffusion of Innovations," paper at the Washington Conference on Educational Change (Columbus, Ohio, Ohio State University). Everett Rogers," What are Innovators Like?" in *Change Processes in the Public Schools,* Center for the Advanced Study of Educational Administration (Eugene, Ore.: University of Oregon, 1965). Everett Rogers, *Diffusion of Innovations* (New York: The Free Press, 1962).

[11] Carl Hovland, Irving Janis, and Harold Kelley, *Communication and Persuasion* (New Haven: Yale University Press, 1953).

have exaggerated the effectiveness of mass persuasion since they have compared the total number in the audience to the communications with the much smaller proportion of the audience persuaded by the communication.[12] A clearer view of processes of diffusion must include the actions of the receiver as well as those of the transmitter in the transactional events which are the units of diffusion process. And strategies for making diffusion processes more effective must be transactional and collaborative by design.

E. UTOPIAN THINKING AS A STRATEGY OF CHANGING

It may seem strange to include the projection of utopias as a rational-empirical strategy of changing. Yet inventing and designing the shape of the future by extrapolating what we know of in the present is to envision a direction for planning and action in the present. If the image of a potential future is convincing and rationally persuasive to men in the present, the image may become part of the dynamics and motivation of present action. The liberal tradition is not devoid of its utopias. When we think of utopias quickened by an effort to extrapolate from the sciences of man to a future vision of society, the utopia of B. F. Skinner comes to mind.[13] The title of the Eight State Project, "Designing Education for the Future" for which this paper was prepared, reveals a utopian intent and aspiration and illustrates an attempt to employ utopian thinking for practical purposes.[14]

Yet it may be somewhat disheartening to others as it is to us to note the absence of rousing and beckoning normative statements of what both can and ought to be in man's future in most current liberal-democratic utopias, whether these be based on psychological, sociological, political, or philosophical findings and assumptions. The absence of utopias in current society, in this sense, and in the sense that Mannheim studied them in his now classical study,[15] tends to make the forecasting of future directions a problem of technical prediction, rather than equally a process of projecting value orientations and preferences into the shaping of a better future.

F. PERCEPTUAL AND CONCEPTUAL REORGANIZATION THROUGH THE CLARIFICATION OF LANGUAGE

In classical liberalism, one perceived foe of rational change and progress was superstition. And superstitions are carried from man to man and from generation to generation through the agency of unclear and mythical language. British utilitarianism was one important strand of classical liberalism, and one of utilitarianism's important figures, Jeremy Bentham, sought to purify language of its dangerous mystique through his study of fictions.

More recently, Alfred Korzybski and S. I. Hayakawa, in the general semantics movement, have sought a way of clarifying and rectifying the names of things and processes.[16] While their main applied concern was with personal therapy, both, and especially Hayakawa, were also concerned to bring about changes in social systems as well. People disciplined in general semantics, it was hoped, would see more correctly, communicate more adequately, and reason more effectively and thus lay a realistic common basis for action and changing. The strategies of

[12] Raymond Bauer, "The Obstinate Audience: The Influence Process from the Point of View of Social Communication," in Bennis, Benne, and Chin, *op. cit.*, p. 507.

[13] B. F. Skinner, *Walden Two* (New York: Crowell-Collier and Macmillan, Inc., 1948).

[14] "Designing Education for the Future—an Eight State Project" (Denver, Colo., 1967).

[15] Karl Mannheim, *Ideology and Utopia* (New York: Harcourt, Brace & World, Inc., 1946).

[16] Alfred Korzybski, *Science and Sanity,* 3d ed. (International Non-Aristotelian Library Publishing Company, 1948). S. I. Hayakawa, *Language in Thought and Action* (New York: Harcourt, Brace & World, Inc., 1941).

changing associated with general semantics overlap with our next family of strategies, the normative–re-educative, because of their emphasis upon the importance of interpersonal relationships and social contexts within the communication process.

2. Normative–Re-educative Strategies of Changing

We have already suggested that this family of strategies rests on assumptions and hypotheses about man and his motivation which contrast significantly at points with the assumptions and hypotheses of those committed to what we have called rational-empirical strategies. Men are seen as inherently active, in quest of impulse and need satisfaction. The relation between man and his environmnt is essentially transactional, as Dewey[17] made clear in his famous article on "The Reflex-Arc Concept." Man, the organism, does not passively await given stimuli from his environment in order to respond. He takes stimuli as furthering or thwarting the goals of his ongoing action. Intelligence arises in the process of shaping organism-environmental relations toward more adequate fittings and joining of organismic demands and environmental resources.

Intelligence is social, rather than narrowly individual. Men are guided in their actions by socially funded and communicated meanings, norms, and institutions, in brief by a normative culture. At the personal level, men are guided by internalized meanings, habits, and values. Changes in patterns of action or practice are, therefore, changes, not alone in the rational informational equipment of men, but at the personal level, in habits and values as well and, at the sociocultural level, changes are alterations in normative structures and in institutionalized roles and relationships, as well as in cognitive and perceptual orientations.

For Dewey, the prototype of intelligence in action is the scientific method. And he saw a broadened and humanized scientific method as man's best hope for progress if men could learn to utilize such a method in facing all of the problematic situations of their lives. *Intelligence*, so conceived, rather than *Reason* as defined in classical liberalism, was the key to Dewey's hope for the invention, development, and testing of adequate strategies of changing in human affairs.

Lewin's contribution to normative–re-educative strategies of changing stemmed from his vision of required interrelations between research, training, and action (and, for him, this meant collaborative relationships, often now lacking, between researchers, educators, and activists) in the solution of human problems, in the identification of needs for change, and in the working out of improved knowledge, technology, and patterns of action in meeting these needs. Man must participate in his own re-education if he is to be re-educated at all. And re-education is a normative change as well as a cognitive and perceptual change. These convictions led Lewin[18] to emphasize action research as a strategy of changing, and participation in groups as a medium of re-education.

Freud's main contributions to normative–re-educative strategies of changing are two. First, he sought to demonstrate the unconscious and preconscious bases of man's actions. Only as a man finds ways of becoming aware of these nonconscious wellsprings of his attitudes and actions will he be able to bring them into conscious self-control. And Freud devoted much of his magnificent genius to developing ways of helping men to become conscious of the main springs of their actions and so capable of freedom. Second, in developing therapeutic methods, he discovered and developed ways of utilizing the relationship between change agent (therapist) and client (patient) as a major tool in re-educating the

[17] John Dewey, *Philosophy, Psychology and Social Practice,* Joseph Ratner (ed.) (New York: Capricorn Books, 1967).

[18] Kurt Lewin, *Resolving Social Conflicts* (New York: Harper & Row Publishers, 1948). Kurt Lewin, *Field Theory in Social Science* (New York: Harper & Row Publishers, 1951).

client toward expanded self-awareness, self-understanding, and self-control. Emphasis upon the collaborative relationship in therapeutic change was a major contribution by Freud and his students and colleagues to normative–re-educative strategies of changing in human affairs.[19]

Normative–re-educative approaches to effecting change bring direct interventions by change agents, interventions based on a consciously worked-out theory of change and of changing, into the life of a client system, be that system a person, a small group, an organization, or a community. The theory of changing is still crude but it is probably as explicitly stated as possible, granted our present state of knowledge about planned change.[20]

Some of the common elements among variants within this family of change strategies are the following. First, all emphasize the client system and his (or its) involvement in working out programs of change and improvement for himself (or itself). The way the client sees himself and his problem must be brought into dialogic relationship with the way in which he and his problem are seen by the change agent, whether the latter is functioning as researcher, consultant, trainer, therapist, or friend in relation to the client. Second, the problem confronting the client is not assumed *a priori* to be one which can be met by more adequate technical information, though this possibility is not ruled out. The problem may lie rather in the attitudes, values, norms, and the external and internal relationships of the client system and may require alteration or re-education of these as a condition of its solution. Third, the change agent must learn to intervene mutually and collaboratively along with the client into efforts to define and solve the client's problem(s). The here and now experience of the two provide an important basis for diagnosing the problem and for locating needs for re-education in the interest of solving it. Fourth, nonconscious elements which impede problem solution must be brought into consciousness and publicly examined and reconstructed. Fifth, the methods and concepts of the behavioral sciences are resources which change agent and client learn to use selectively, relevantly, and appropriately in learning to deal with the confronting problem and with problems of a similar kind in the future.

These approaches center in the notion that people technology is just as necessary as thing technology in working out desirable changes in human affairs. Put in this bold fashion, it is obvious that for the normative–re-educative change agent, clarification and reconstruction of values is of pivotal importance in changing. By getting the values of various parts of the client system along with his own, openly into the arena of change and by working through value conflicts responsibly, the change agent seeks to avoid manipulation and indoctrination of the client, in the morally reprehensible meanings of these terms.

We may use the organization of the National Training Laboratories in 1947 as a milestone in the development of normative–re-educative approaches to changing in America. The first summer laboratory program grew out of earlier collaborations among Kurt Lewin, Ronald Lippitt, Leland Bradford, and Kenneth Benne. The idea behind the laboratory was that participants, staff, and students would learn about themselves and their back-home problems by collaboratively building a laboratory in which participants would become both experimenters and subjects in the study of their own developing interpersonal and group behavior within the laboratory setting. It seems evident that the five conditions of a normative–re-educative approach to changing were met in the conception of the training laboratory. Kurt Lewin died before

[19] For Freud, an interesting summary is contained in Otto Fenichel, *Problems of Psychoanalytic Technique* (Albany, N. Y.: NT Psychoanalytic Quarterly Inc., 1941).

[20] W. Bennis, K. Benne, and R. Chin, *The Planning of Change*, 1st ed. (New York: Holt, Rinehart and Winston, Inc., 1961). R. Lippitt, J. Watson and B. Westley, *The Dynamics of Planned Change* (New York: Harcourt, Brace & World, Inc., 1958). W. Bennis, *Changing Organizations* (New York: McGraw-Hill, Inc., 1966).

the 1947 session of the training laboratory opened. Ronald Lippitt was a student of Lewin's and carried many of Lewin's orientations with him into the laboratory staff. Leland Bradford and Kenneth Benne were both students of John Dewey's philosophy of education. Bradford had invented several technologies for participative learning and self-study in his work in WPA adult education programs and as training officer in several agencies of the federal government. Benne came out of a background in educational philosophy and had collaborated with colleagues prior to 1943 in developing a methodology for policy and decision making and for the reconstruction of normative orientations, a methodology which sought to fuse democratic and scientific values and to translate these into principles for resolving conflicting and problematic situations at personal and community levels of human organization.[21] Benne and his colleagues had been much influenced by the work of Mary Follett,[22] her studies of integrative solutions to conflicts in settings of public and business administration, and by the work of Karl Mannheim[23] on the ideology and methodology of planning changes in human affairs, as well as by the work of John Dewey and his colleagues.

The work of the National Training Laboratories has encompassed development and testing of various approaches to changing in institutional settings, in America and abroad, since its beginning. One parallel development in England which grew out of Freud's thinking should be noted. This work developed in efforts at Tavistock Clinic to apply therapeutic approaches to problems of change in industrial organizations and in communities. This work is reported in statements by Elliot Jaques and by Eric Trist.[24] Another parallel development is represented by the efforts of Roethlisberger and Dickson to use personal counseling in industry as a strategy of organizational change.[25] Roethlisberger and Dickson had been strongly influenced by the pioneer work of Elton Mayo in industrial sociology[26] as well as by the counseling theories and methodologies of Carl Rogers.

Various refinements of methodologies for changing have been developed and tested since the establishment of the National Training Laboratories in 1947, both under its auspices and under other auspices as well. For us, the modal developments are worthy of further discussion here. One set of approaches is oriented focally to the improvement of the problem-solving processes utilized by a client system. The other set focuses on helping members of client systems to become aware of their attitude and value orientations and relationship difficulties through a probing of feelings, manifest and latent, involved in the functioning and operation of the client system.[27] Both approaches use the development of "temporary systems" as a medium of re-educa-

[21] Raup, Benne, Smith, and Axtelle, *The Discipline of Practical Judgment in a Democratic Society*, Yearbook No. 28 of the National Society of College Teachers of Education (Chicago: University of Chicago Press, 1943).

[22] Mary Follett, *Creative Experience and Dynamic Administration* (New York: David McKay Company, Inc., 1924).

[23] Karl Mannheim, *Man and Society in an Age of Reconstruction* (New York: Harcourt, Brace & World, Inc., 1940).

[24] Elliot Jaques, *The Changing Culture of a Factory* (New York: Holt, Rinehart and Winston, Inc., 1952). E. L. Trist, "On Socio-Technical Systems," in Bennis, Benne, and Chin, *op. cit.*, 2d. ed., pp. 269–282.

[25] William J. Dickson and F. J. Roethlisberger, *Personal Counseling in an Organization. A Sequel to the Hawthorne Researchers* (Boston: Harvard Business School, 1966).

[26] Elton Mayo, *The Social Problems of an Industrial Civilization* (Cambridge: Harvard University Press, 1945).

[27] Leland Bradford, Jack R. Gibb, and Kenneth D. Benne, *T-Group Theory and Laboratory Method* (New York: John Wiley & Sons, Inc., 1964).

tion of persons and of role occupants in various ongoing social systems.[28]

A. IMPROVING THE PROBLEM-SOLVING CAPABILITIES OF A SYSTEM

This family of approaches to changing rests on several assumptions about change in human systems. Changes in a system, when they are reality oriented, take the form of problem solving. A system to achieve optimum reality orientation in its adaptations to its changing internal and external environments must develop and institutionalize its own problem-solving structures and processes. These structures and processes must be tuned both to human problems of relationship and morale and to technical problems of meeting the system's task requirements, set by its goals of production, distribution, and so on.[29] System problems are typically not social *or* technical but actually sociotechnical.[30] The problem-solving structures and processes of a human system must be developed to deal with a range of sociotechnical difficulties, converting them into problems and organizing the relevant processes of data collection, planning, invention, and tryout of solutions, evaluation and feedback of results, replanning, and so forth, which are required for the solution of the problems.

The human parts of the system must learn to function collaboratively in these processes of problem identification and solution and the system must develop institutionalized support and mechanisms for maintaining and improving these processes. Actually, the model of changing in these approaches is a cooperative, action-research model. This model was suggested by Lewin and developed most elaborately for use in educational settings by Stephen M. Corey.[31]

The range of interventions by outside change agents in implementing this approach to changing is rather wide. It has been most fully elaborated in relation to organizational development programs. Within such programs, intervention methods have been most comprehensively tested in industrial settings. Some of these more or less tested intervention methods are listed below. A design for any organizational development program, of course, normally uses a number of these in succession or combination.

1. Collection of data about organizational functioning and feedback of data into processes of data interpretation and of planning ways of correcting revealed dysfunctions by system managers and data collectors in collaboration.[32]

2. Training of managers and working organizational units in methods of problem solving through self-examination of present ways of dealing with difficulties and through development and tryout of better ways with consultation by outside and/or inside change agents. Usually, the working unit leaves its working place for parts of its training. These laboratory sessions are ordinarily interspersed with on-the-job consultations.

3. Developing acceptance of feedback (research and development) roles and functions within the organization, training persons to fill these roles, and relating such roles strategically to the ongoing management of the organization.

4. Training internal change agents to function within the organization in carrying on needed applied research, consultation, and training.[33]

[28] Matthew B. Miles, "On Temporary Systems," in M. B. Miles (ed.), *Innovation in Education* (New York: Bureau of Publications, Teachers College, Columbia Universtiy Press, 1964), pp. 437–492.

[29] Robert R. Blake and Jane S. Mouton, *The Managerial Grid* (Houston: The Gulf Publishing Company, 1961).

[30] Jay W. Lorsch and Paul Lawrence, "The Diagnosis of Organizational Problems," in Bennis, Benne, and Chin, *op. cit.*, 2d ed., p. 468.

[31] Stephen M. Corey, *Action Research to Improve School Practices* (New York: Bureau of Publications, Teachers College, Columbia University Press, 1953).

[32] See contributions by Miles *et al.*, "Data Feedback and Organizational Change in a School System," in Bennis, Benne, and Chin, *op. cit.*, 2d ed., p. 468. p. 457, and Lorsch and Lawrence.

[33] C. Argyris, "Explorations in Consulting-Client Relationships," Bennis, Benne, and Chin, *op. cit.*, 2d ed., p. 434.

Whatever specific strategies of intervention may be employed in developing the system's capabilities for problem solving, change efforts are designed to help the system in developing ways of scanning its operations to detect problems, of diagnosing these problems to determine relevant changeable factors in them, and of moving toward collaboratively determined solutions to the problems.

B. Releasing and Fostering Growth in the Persons Who Make Up the System to be Changed

Those committed to this family of approaches to changing tend to see the person as the basic unit of social organization. Persons, it is believed, are capable of creative, life-affirming, self- and other-regarding and respecting responses, choices, and actions, if conditions which thwart these kinds of responses are removed and other supporting conditions developed. Rogers has formulated these latter conditions in his analysis of the therapist-client relationship—trustworthiness, empathy, caring, and others.[34] Maslow has worked out a similar idea in his analysis of the hierarchy of needs in persons.[35] If lower needs are met, higher need-meeting actions will take place. McGregor[36] has formulated the ways in which existing organizations operate to fixate persons in lower levels of motivation and has sought to envision an organization designed to release and support the growth of persons in fulfilling their higher motivations as they function within the organization.

Various intervention methods have been designed to help people discover themselves as persons and commit themselves to continuing personal growth in the various relationships of their lives.

1. One early effort to install personal counseling widely and strategically in an organization has been reported by Roethlisberger and Dickson.[37]

2. Training groups designed to facilitate personal confrontation and growth of members in an open, trusting, and accepting atmosphere have been conducted for individuals from various back-home situations and for persons from the same back-home setting. The processes of these groups have sometimes been described as "therapy for normals."[38]

3. Groups and laboratories designed to stimulate and support personal growth have been designed to utilize the resources of nonverbal exchange and communication among members along with verbal dialogue in inducing personal confrontation, discovery, and commitment to continuing growth.

4. Many psychotherapists, building on the work of Freud and Adler, have come to use groups, as well as two-person situations, as media of personal re-education and growth. Such efforts are prominent in mental health approaches to changing and have been conducted in educational, religious, community, industrial, and hospital settings. While these efforts focus primarily upon helping individuals to change themselves toward greater self-clarity and fuller self-actualization, they are frequently designed and conducted in the hope that personal changes will lead to changes in organizations, institutions, and communities as well.

We have presented the two variants of normative–re-educative approaches of chang-

---

[34] Carl Rogers, "The Characteristics of a Helping Relationship," *On Becoming a Person*, (Boston: Houghton Mifflin Company, 1961), pp. 39–58.

[35] Abraham Maslow, *Motivation and Personality* (New York: Harper & Row, Publishers, 1954).

[36] Douglas M. McGregor, "The Human Side of Enterprise," in Bennis, Benne, and Chin, *op. cit.*, 1st ed., pp. 422–431.

[37] Dickson and Roethlisberger, *op. cit.*

[38] James V. Clark "A Healthy Organization," Bennis, Benne, and Chin, *op. cit.*, 2d ed., p. 282. Irving Weschler, Fred Massarik, and Robert Tannenbaum, "The Self in Process: A Sensitivity Training Emphasis," in I. R. Weschler and E. Schein (eds.) *Issues in Training*, Selected Reading Series No. 5 (Washington, D. C., National Training Laboratories).

ing in a way to emphasize their differences. Actually, there are many similarities between them as well, which justify placing both under the same general heading. We have already mentioned one of these similarities. Both frequently use temporary systems—a residential laboratory or workshop, a temporary group with special resources built in, an ongoing system which incorporates a change agent (trainer, consultant, counselor, or therapist) temporarily—as an aid to growth in the system and/or in its members.

More fundamentally, both approaches emphasize experience-based learning as an ingredient of all enduring changes in human systems. Yet both accept the principle that people must learn to learn from their experiences if self-directed change is to be maintained and continued. Frequently, people have learned to defend against the potential lessons of experience when these threaten existing equilibria, whether in the person or in the social system. How can these defenses be lowered to let the data of experience get into processes of perceiving the situation, of constructing new and better ways to define it, of inventing new and more appropriate ways of responding to the situation as redefined, of becoming more fully aware of the consequences of actions, of rearticulating value orientations which sanction more responsible ways of managing the consequences of actions, and so forth? Learning to learn from ongoing experience is a major objective in both approaches to changing. Neither denies the relevance or importance of the noncognitive determinants of behavior—feelings, attitudes, norms, and relationships—along with cognitive-perceptual determinants, in effecting behavioral change. The problem-solving approaches emphasize the cognitive determinants more than personal growth approaches do. But exponents of the former do not accept the rationalistic biases of the rational-empirical family of change strategies, already discussed. Since exponents of both problem-solving and personal growth approaches are com-

mitted to re-education of persons as integral to effective change in human systems, both emphasize norms of openness of communication, trust between persons, lowering of status barriers between parts of the system, and mutuality between parts as necessary conditions of the re-educative process.

Great emphasis has been placed recently upon the releasing of creativity in persons, groups, and organizations as requisite to coping adaptively with accelerated changes in the conditions of modern living. We have already stressed the emphasis which personal growth approaches put upon the release of creative responses in persons being re-educated. Problem-solving approaches also value creativity, though they focus more upon the group and organizational conditions which increase the probability of creative responses by persons functioning within those conditions than upon persons directly. The approaches do differ in their strategies for releasing creative responses within human systems. But both believe that creative adaptations to changing conditions may arise *within* human systems and do not have to be imported from *outside* them as in innovation-diffusion approaches already discussed and the power-compliance models still to be dealt with.

One developing variant of normative–re-educative approaches to changing, not already noted, focuses upon effective conflict management. It is, of course, common knowledge that differences within a society which demand interaccommodation often manifest themselves as conflicts. In the process of managing such conflicts, changes in the norms, policies, and relationships of the society occur. Can conflict management be brought into the ambit of planned change as defined in this volume? Stemming from the work of the Sherifs in creating intergroup conflict and seeking to resolve it in a field-laboratory situation,[39] training in intergroup conflict and conflict resolution found its way into training laboratories through the efforts of Blake and others. Since that time, laboratories for conflict manage-

[39] Muzafer and Carolyn Sherif, *Groups in Harmony and Tension* (New York: Harper & Row, Publishers, 1953).

ment have been developed under NTL and other auspices and methodologies for conflict resolution and management, in keeping with the values of planned change, have been devised. Blake's and Walton's work represent some of the findings from these pioneering efforts.[40]

Thus, without denying their differences in assumption and strategy, we believe that the differing approaches discussed in this section can be seen together within the framework of normative–re-educative approaches to changing. Two efforts to conceptualize planned change in a way to reveal the similarities in assumptions about changing and in value orientations toward change underlying these variant approaches are those by Lippitt, Watson, and Westley and by Bennis, Benne, and Chin.[41]

Another aspect of changing in human organizations is represented by efforts to conceive human organization in forms that go beyond the bureaucratic form which captured the imagination and fixed the contours of thinking and practice of organizational theorists and practitioners from the latter part of the nineteenth through the early part of the twentieth century. The bureaucratic form of organization was conceptualized by Max Weber and carried into American thinking by such students of administration as Urwick.[42] On this view, effective organization of human effort followed the lines of effective division of labor and effective establishment of lines of reporting, control, and supervision from the mass base of the organization up through various levels of control to the top of the pyramidal organization from which legitimate authority and responsibility stemmed.

The work of industrial sociologists like Mayo threw doubt upon the adequacy of such a model of formal organization to deal with the realities of organizational life by revealing the informal organization which grows up within the formal structure to satisfy personal and interpersonal needs not encompassed by or integrated into the goals of the formal organization. Chester Barnard may be seen as a transitional figure who, in discussing the functions of the organizational executive, gave equal emphasis to his responsibilities for task effectiveness and organizational efficiency (optimally meeting the human needs of persons in the organization).[43] Much of the development of subsequent organizational theory and practice has centered on problems of integrating the actualities, criteria, and concepts of organizational effectiveness and of organizational efficiency.

A growing group of thinkers and researchers have sought to move beyond the bureaucratic model toward some new model of organization which might set directions and limits for change efforts in organizational life. Out of many thinkers, we choose four who have theorized out of an orientation consistent with what we have called a normative–re-educative approach to changing.

Rensis Likert has presented an intergroup model of organization. Each working unit strives to develop and function as a group. The group's efforts are linked to other units of the organization by the overlapping membership of supervisors or managers in vertically or horizontally adjacent groups. This view of organization throws problems of delegation, supervision, and internal communication into a new light and emphasizes the importance of linking persons as targets of change and re-education in processes of organizational development.[44]

We have already stressed McGregor's ef-

[40] Robert Blake *et al.*, "The Union Management Inter-Group Laboratory," in Bennis, Benne, and Chin, *op. cit.*, 2d ed., p. 176. Richard Walton, "Two Strategies of Social Change and Their Dilemmas," in Bennis, Benne, and Chin, *op. cit.*, 2d ed., p. 167.

[41] R. Lippitt, J. Watson, and B. Westley, *Dynamics of Planned Change* (New York: Harcourt, Brace & World, Inc., 1958). Bennis, Benne, and Chin, *op. cit.*

[42] Lyndall Urwick, *The Pattern of Management* (Minneapolis: University of Minnesota Press, 1956).

[43] Chester I. Barnard, *The Functions of the Executive* (Cambridge: Harvard University Press, 1938).

[44] Rensis Likert *New Patterns of Management* (New York: McGraw-Hill, Inc., 1961).

forts to conceive a form of organization more in keeping with new and more valid views of human nature and motivation (Theory Y) than the limited and false views of human nature and motivation (Theory X) upon which traditional bureaucratic organization has rested. In his work he sought to move thinking and practice relevant to organization and organizational change beyond the limits of traditional forms. "The essential task of management is to arrange organizational conditions and methods of operation so that people can achieve their own goals best by directing their own efforts toward organizational objectives."[45]

Bennis has consciously sought to move beyond bureaucracy in tracing the contours of the organization of the future.[46] And Shephard has described an organizational form consistent with support for continual changing and self-renewal, rather than with a primary mission of maintenance and control.[47]

3. Power-Coercive Approaches to Effecting Change

It is not the use of power, in the sense of influence by one person upon another or by one group upon another, which distinguishes this family of strategies from those already discussed. Power is an ingredient of all human action. The differences lie rather in the ingredients of power upon which the strategies of changing depend and the ways in which power is generated and applied in processes of effecting change. Thus, what we have called rational-empirical approaches depend on knowledge as a major ingredient of power. In this view, men of knowledge are legitimate sources of power and the desirable flow of influence or power is from men who know to men who don't know through processes of education and of dissemination of valid information.

Normative–re-educative strategies of changing do not deny the importance of knowledge as a source of power, especially in the form of knowledge-based technology. Exponents of this approach to changing are committed to redressing the imbalance between the limited use of behavioral knowledge and people technologies and the widespread use of physical-biological knowledge and related thing technologies in effecting changes in human affairs. In addition, exponents of normative–re-educative approaches recognize the importance of noncognitive determinants of behavior as resistances or supports to changing—values, attitudes, and feelings at the personal level and norms and relationships at the social level. Influence must extend to these noncognitive determinants of behavior if voluntary commitments and reliance upon social intelligence are to be maintained and extended in our changing society. Influence of noncognitive determinants of behavior must be exercised in mutual processes of persuasion within collaborative relationships. These strateiges are oriented against coercive and nonreciprocal influence, both on moral and on pragmatic grounds.

What ingredients of power do power-coercive strategies emphasize? In general, emphasis is upon political and economic sanctions in the exercise of power. But other coercive strategies emphasize the utilization of moral power, playing upon sentiments of guilt and shame. Political power carries with it legitimacy and the sanctions which accrue to those who break the law. Thus getting a law passed against racial imbalance in the schools brings legitimate coercive power behind efforts to desegregate the schools, threatening those who resist with sanctions under the law and reducing the resistance of others who are morally oriented against breaking the law. Economic power exerts coercive influence over the decisions of those to whom it is applied. Thus federal appropriations granting funds to local schools for increased emphasis upon science instruction tends to exercise coercive influence over the decisions of local school officials concerning the emphasis of the school curriculum. In general, power-coercive

[45] McGregor, *op. cit.*, pp. 422–431.
[46] W. G. Bennis, "Changing Organizations," *McGregor Memorial Lectures* (Cambridge, Mass.: M.I.T. Press, February 1966).
[47] H. A. Shephard, "Innovation-Resisting and Innovation-Producing Organizations," *Journal of Business*, vol. 40, no. 4 (October 1967).

strategies of changing seek to mass political and economic power behind the change goals which the strategists of change have decided are desirable. Those who oppose these goals, if they adopt the same strategy, seek to mass political and economic power in opposition. The strategy thus tends to divide the society when there is anything like a division of opinion and of power in that society.

When a person or group is entrenched in power in a social system, in command of political legitimacy and of political and economic sanctions, that person or group can use power-coercive strategies in effecting changes, which they consider desirable, without much awareness on the part of those out of power in the system that such strategies are being employed. A power-coercive way of making decisions is accepted as in the nature of things. The use of such strategies by those in legitimate control of various social systems in our society is much more widespread than most of us might at first be willing or able to admit. This is true in educational systems as well as in other social systems.

When any part of a social system becomes aware that its interests are not being served by those in control of the system, the coercive power of those in control can be challenged. If the minority is committed to power-coercive strategies, or is aware of no alternatives to such strategies, how can they make headway against existing power relations within the system? They may organize discontent against the present controls of the system and achieve power outside the legitimate channels of authority in the system. Thus teachers' unions may develop power against coercive controls by the central administrative group and the school board in a school system. They may threaten concerted resistance to or disregard of administrative rulings and board policies or they may threaten work stoppage or a strike. Those in control may get legislation against teachers' strikes. If the political power of organized teachers grows, they may get legislation requiring collective bargaining between organized teachers and the school board on some range of education issues. The power struggle then shifts to the negotiation table

and compromise between competing interests may become the expected goal of the inter-group exchange. Whether the augmented power of new, relevant knowledge or the generation of common power through joint collaboration and deliberation are lost in the process will depend on the degree of commitment by all parties to the conflict to a continuation and maintenance of power-coercive strategies for effecting change.

What general varieties of power-coercive strategies to be exercised either by those in control as they seek to maintain their power or to be used by those now outside a position of control and seeking to enlarge their power can be identified?

A. Strategies of Nonviolence

Mahatma Gandhi may be seen as the most prominent recent theorist and practitioner of nonviolent strategies for effecting change, although the strategies did not originate with him in the history of mankind, either in idea or in practice. Gandhi spoke of Thoreau's *Essay on Civil Disobedience* as one important influence in his own approach to nonviolent coercive action. Martin Luther King was perhaps America's most distinguished exponent of nonviolent coercion in effecting social change. A minority (or majority) confronted with what they see as an unfair, unjust, or cruel system of coercive social control may dramatize their rejection of the system by publicly and nonviolently witnessing and demonstrating against it. Part of the ingredients of the power of the civilly disobedient is in the guilt which their demonstration of injustice, unfairness, or cruelty of the existing system of control arouses in those exercising control or in others previously committed to the present system of control. The opposition to the disobedient group may be demoralized and may waver in their exercise of control, if they profess the moral values to which the dissidents are appealing.

Weakening or dividing the opposition through moral coercion may be combined with economic sanctions—like Gandhi's refusal to buy salt and other British manufactured commodities in India or like the desegregationists' economic boycott of the products of racially discriminating factories and businesses.

The use of nonviolent strategies for opening up conflicts in values and demonstrating against injustices or inequities in existing patterns of social control has become familiar to educational leaders in the demonstrations and sit-ins of college students in various universities and in the demonstrations of desegregationists against *de facto* segregation of schools. And the widened use of such strategies may be confidently predicted. Whether such strategies will be used to extend collaborative ways of developing policies and normative–re-educative strategies of changing or whether they will be used to augment power struggles as the only practical way of settling conflicts, will depend in some large part upon the strategy commitments of those now in positions of power in educational systems.

B. Use of Political Institutions to Achieve Change

Political power has traditionally played an important part in achieving changes in our institutional life. And political power will continue to play an important part in shaping and reshaping our institutions of education as well as other institutions. Changes enforced by political coercion need not be oppressive if the quality of our democratic processes can be maintained and improved.

Changes in policies with respect to education have come from various departments of government. By far the most of these have come through legislation on the state level. Under legislation, school administrators have various degrees of discretionary powers, and policy and program changes are frequently put into effect by administrative rulings. Judicial decisions have played an important part in shaping educational policies, none more dramatically than the Supreme Court decision declaring laws and policies supporting school segregation illegal. And the federal courts have played a central part in seeking to implement and enforce this decision.

Some of the difficulty with the use of political institutions to effect changes arises from an overestimation by change agents of the capability of political action to effect changes in practice. When the law is passed, the administrative ruling announced, or the judicial decision handed down legitimizing some new policy or program or illegitimizing some traditional practice, change agents who have worked hard for the law, ruling, or decision frequently assume that the desired change has been made.

Actually, all that has been done is to bring the force of legitimacy behind some envisioned change. The processes of re-education of persons who are to conduct themselves in new ways still have to be carried out. And the new conduct often requires new knowledge, new skills, new attitudes, and new value orientations. And, on the social level, new conduct may require changes in the norms, the roles, and the relationship structures of the institutions involved. This is not to discount the importance of political actions in legitimizing changed policies and practices in educational institutions and in other institutions as well. It is rather to emphasize that normative–re-educative strategies must be combined with political coercion, both before and after the political action, if the public is to be adequately informed and desirable and commonly acceptable changes in practice are to be achieved.

C. Changing Through the Recomposition and Manipulation of Power Elites

The idea of practice of a ruling class or of a power elite in social control was by no means original with Karl Marx. What was original with him was his way of relating these concepts to a process and strategy of fundamental social change. The composition of the ruling class was, of course, for Marx those who owned and controlled the means and processes of production of goods and services in a society. Since, for Marx, the ideology of the ruling class set limits to the thinking of most intellectuals and of those in charge of educational processes and of communicating, rationales for the existing state of affairs, including its concentration of political and economic power, is provided and disseminated by intellectuals and educators and communicators within the system.

Since Marx was morally committed to a classless society in which political coercion would disappear because there would be no vested private interests to rationalize and defend, he looked for a counterforce in society to challenge and eventually to overcome the power of the ruling class. And this he found in the economically dispossessed and alienated workers of hand and brain. As this new class gained consciousness of its historic mission and its power increased, the class struggle could be effectively joined. The outcome of this struggle was victory for those best able to organize and maximize the productive power of the instruments of production—for Marx this victory belonged to the now dispossessed workers.

Many of Marx's values would have put him behind what we have called normative–re-educative strategies of changing. And he recognized that such strategies would have to be used after the accession of the workers to state power in order to usher in the classless society. He doubted if the ruling class could be re-educated, since re-education would mean loss of their privileges and coercive power in society. He recognized that the power elite could, within limits, accommodate new interests as these gained articulation and power. But these accommodations must fall short of a radical transfer of power to a class more capable of wielding it. Meanwhile, he remained committed to a power-coercive strategy of changing until the revolutionary transfer of power had been effected.

Marxian concepts have affected the thinking of contemporary men about social change both inside and outside nations in which Marxism has become the official orientation. His concepts have tended to bolster assumptions of the necessity of power-coercive strategies in achieving fundamental redistributions of socioeconomic power or in recomposing or manipulating power elites in a society. Democratic, re-educative methods of changing have a place only after such changes in power allo-

cation have been achieved by power-coercive methods. Non-Marxians as well as Marxians are often committed to this Marxian dictum.

In contemporary America, C. Wright Mills has identified a power elite, essentially composed of industrial, military, and governmental leaders, who direct and limit processes of social change and accommodation in our society. And President Eisenhower warned of the dangerous concentration of power in substantially the same groups in his farewell message to the American people. Educators committed to democratic values should not be blinded to the limitations to advancement of those values, which are set by the less than democratic ideology of our power elites. And normative–re-educative strategists of changing must include power elites among their targets of changing as they seek to diffuse their ways of progress within contemporary society. And they must take seriously Marx's questions about the re-educability of members of the power elites, as they deal with problems and projects of social change.

The operation of a power elite in social units smaller than a nation was revealed in Floyd Hunter's study of decision making in an American city. Hunter's small group of deciders, with their satellite groups of intellectuals, front men, and implementers, is in a real sense a power elite. The most common reaction of educational leaders to Hunter's "discovery" has been to seek ways in which to persuade and manipulate the deciders toward support of educational ends which educational leaders consider desirable—whether bond issues, building programs, or anything else. This is non-Marxian in its acceptance of power relations in a city or community as fixed. It would be Marxian if it sought to build counterpower to offset and reduce the power of the presently deciding group where this power interfered with the achievement of desirable educational goals. This latter strategy, though not usually Marxian inspired in the propaganda sense of that term, has been more characteristic of organized teacher effort in pressing for collective bargaining or of some student demonstrations and sit-ins. In the poverty program, the federal government in its

Figure 18.1. Strategies of Deliberate Changing.

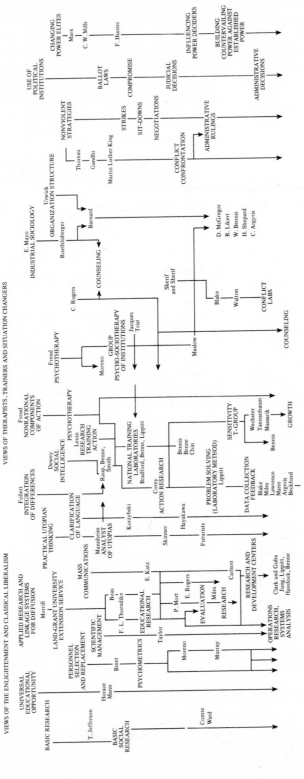

insistence on participation of the poor in making policies for the program has at least played with a strategy of building countervailing power to offset the existing concentration of power in people not identified with the interests of the poor in reducing their poverty.

Those committed to the advancement of normative–re-educative strategies of changing must take account of present actual concentrations of power wherever they work. This does *not* mean that they must develop a commitment to power-coercive strategies to change the distribution of power except when these may be necessary to effect the spread of their own democratically and scientifically oriented methods of changing within society.

19.   Strategies and Tactics of Planned Organizational Change: Case Examples in the Modernization Process of Traditional Societies[a]

Garth N. Jones[*]

Introduction

Traditional societies are caught in a situation that demands wholesale changes in their organizational structures and social dynamics in order to deal with the new complex technological, economic, and political relationships. This being the case, little social science knowledge and technology is available to initiate and manage organizational change in a constructive fashion. Nevertheless, organizational change is an inevitable and universal phenomenon, a characteristic of every human situation. On the other hand, change rarely occurs in a smooth and balanced fashion. Resistance is commonplace with pain and social disorganization generally characterizing the social processes.

Probably, no single group of persons realizes this situation more than the scholars and practitioners who are concerned with community development projects. They have at their disposal the necessary substantive knowledge and means (for example, an improved variety of rice seed) to improve social life. The question is how to incorporate these items into the community (social) organization within a reasonable period of time and in a constructive social way. The task in this regard is essentially to modify and/or structure human behavior in the shortest possible time to meet the needs of organizational change that is required to employ the new knowledge or technology.

From the outset of this article, it should be pointed out that planned and accelerated change is not something peculiar to traditional societies. The assumption of this article is that such change is possible in traditional societies, and may acquire some unique characteristics.

The notion of planned change, i.e., the method of employing social science and technology to assist in the solving of problems of society, is a rather recent development.[1] The purpose of which, in essence, is to make social

Reprinted from Garth N. Jones, "Strategies and Tactics of Planned Organizational Change: Case Examples in the Modernization Process of Traditional Societies," *Human Organization*, Vol. XXIV, No. 3 (Fall 1965), pp. 192–200.

[a] A more detailed treatment is found in Garth N. Jones, *Planned Organizational Change: A Study in Change Dynamics* (New York: Fredrick A. Praeger, 1970).

[*] Professor of Political Science, Colorado State University.

[1] There has occurred a growing literature in the field of planned change. For some of the leading works see: Eli Ginzberg and Ewing W. Reilly, *Effecting Changes in Large Organizations*, Columbia University Press, New York, 1957; Ronald Lippitt, Jean Watson, and Bruce Westley, *The Dynamics of Planned Change*, Harcourt, Brace and Company, New York, 1958; Warren G. Bennis, Kenneth D. Benne, and Robert Chin (eds.), *The Planning of Change*, Holt, Rinehart and Winston, New York, 1961; Paul I. Lawrence, *The Changing of Organizational Behavior Patterns*,

science operational.[2] The role of the social scientist is not only to observe, record, and interpret social phenomena (a passive on-looker), but also to develop and apply theories of social action to influence society (an active social participator or agent of social change).

Both scholars and practitioners in community development and related fields can certainly view the subject of planned change from a practical vantage point. They are directly concerned with how to change the behavior of people in organizational settings so that the organization becomes more effective in utilizing its energies and resources toward obtaining its goals. While the current state of affairs is still to treat the subject at hand largely in a hit or miss manner, substantial progress has occurred in employing more systematic and effective methods. Many case examples may be noted where there has been a conscious, deliberate, and collaborative effort to improve the performance and operation of organizational systems (communities, organizations, and groups) through the application of systematic and appropriate social knowledge and technology. This concept of change is opposed to natural change which refers to change brought about with no apparent deliberateness and no apparent goal-setting upon the part of those involved in it.

The purpose of this article is to examine successful cases on planned organizational change in traditional societies, and to isolate, define, and classify strategies and tactics which performed critical roles in the change processes.[3] The objective is to provide some social tools to facilitate organizational change in the modernization process of traditional communities.

Before analyzing cases on change, some background notes on the nature of planned organizational change would probably be useful.

The Nature of Planned-Organizational Change in Traditional Societies

The whole concept of planned organizational change rests upon the premise that some person, group, or organizational unit (agent of change or social engineer) may work consciously, deliberately, and collaboratively, toward attaining goals of change which have been planned in advance. The purpose is improved performance and operation of organizational systems (client systems) through the application of appropriate knowledge and social technology. The concept is designed to lead a program of action and study, and not to provide a specious description of accomplishment. Involved, among other considerations,

---

Harvard University Graduate School of Business Administration, Boston, 1958; Harriot O. Ronden and Paul R. Lawrence, *Administering Changes,* Harvard University Graduate School of Business Administration, Boston, 1956; Tom Burns and G. M. Stalker, *The Management of Innovation,* Tavistock Publications, Ltd., London, 1961; Charles R. Walker, *Toward the Automatic Factory,* Yale University Press, New Haven, 1957; Robert Tannenbaum, *Introduction of Change in Industrial Organizations: Improving Managerial Performance,* American Management Assoc., Inc., General Mngt., Series No. 186, New York, 1937, and H. G. Barnett, *Innovation: The Basis of Cultural Change,* McGraw-Hill, New York, 1953.

[2] This term is borrowed from the following article by John M. Pfiffner, "Why Not Make Social Science Operational," *Public Administration Review,* XXII (September, 1962), 109–14.

[3] The writer is heavily indebted to Professor John M. Pfiffner, one of the great scholars in public administration, for introducing him to this concept. Several of his unpublished papers, which he designates as "Miscellaneous Papers," were useful for this article, particularly "The Background of Change," 1960: JMP No. 6; Behavioral Research in Administrative Process," 1961: JMP No. 8: "An Operational Focus on Organizational Change," 1961: JMP No. 10 and "Follow-up Papers No. 9 and 10." 1963: JMP No. 12. All were reproduced by the School of Public Administration, University of Southern California.

are mutual goal-setting by one or both parties in the change process, some type of power relationships, and rational planning and action. The final objective sought is that a new situation of social equilibrium will be reached for the proper functioning of the client system, i.e., a condition where all of the significant elements in the social system are in support of each other. In such a state, the individual member of the system is able to find psychological security because of the absence and/or reconciliation of conflicting values, beliefs, and attitudes. In sum, all of the major elements of the social system are in a state of adjustment, both from the place of the individual's position and from that of the organization.[4] Built into the changed state, if it did not exist previously, is a tendency toward movement (change), development, and growth.[5]

Involved in the change processes, in simple analytical terms, are six major elements: (1) agent of change, (2) client system, (3) goals, (4) strategies and tactics, (5) structuring of change, and (6) evaluation. Each of these elements are major topics by themselves, although each in some way or another is inextricably tied to others in some whole.[6] Discussion of one element in the change process usually demands some comment about the nature and actions of the other elements. Only with the utmost care is it possible to discuss in predominate terms one element without making reference to the other(s). As indicated earlier, such an attempt is made in this article. Special

attention is directed toward strategies and tactics of planned organizational change as used in the modernization of traditional societies.

The examination of the subject is restricted to planned organizational change of a constructive nature (in other words, change not based upon violence, revolution, or other destructive measures), as opposed to natural organizational change which refers to changes brought about with no apparent deliberateness and no apparent goal-setting upon the part of those involved in the change process.

The approach in making this examination is to analyze cases dealing with planned organizational change. A case on planned organizational change is regarded as a descriptive and analytic narrative of events which involves the two principal parties to the change process (the agent of change and the client system). The case must include the six elements noted above, and be based upon an actual situation. Its narrative must be reliable and accurate.

The cases selected for this article pertain only to traditional societies. Such a society is so characterized when its ways of behavior continue with little change from generation to generation. Where traditionalism is dominant other characteristics are also present. Professor Everett Hagen sums up these characteristics as follows:

Behavior is governed by custom, not law. The social structure is hierarchical. The individual's position in society is normally inherited rather than achieved. And . . . economic production is low. A traditional so-

[4] Appropriate for the use of equilibrium in the terms of this article is the discussion by Kenneth E. Boulding, *A Reconstruction of Economics,* Wiley & Co., New York, 1950, Chapter 1. In this work equilibrium is viewed as a dynamic system in which the processes of the social system repeat themselves. Many dynamic systems may be either moving toward equilibrium, whereas others may be moving from equilibrium toward system breakdown. In regard to the latter item, some point occurs when the system breaks down and some type of change occurs.

[5] In the change process there is an important difference between development and growth. Development pertains primarily to the improvement of the quality and/or performance of the social system; whereas growth pertains to the increased size and/or magnitude of the social system. The social system could grow but not necessarily develop, i.e., improve its quality and/or performance.

[6] For a treatment of these elements see Garth N. Jones and Aslam Niaz, "Planned Organizational Change: A Classification System for Analysis," revised draft, Los Angeles School of Public Administration, University of Southern California, 1963 dittoed.

ciety, in short, tends to be custombound, hierarchical, ascriptive, and unproductive. . . .[7]

Traditional societies may take many different forms. Some are relatively simple hunting, fishing, or pastoral societies; while others may reach empire size, a large traditional society superimposed on a number of smaller traditional societies.

The typical traditional society rests upon some type of agricultural base with a large peasant population, although this is not necessarily true in all cases.[8]

Strategies and Tactics of Planned Organizational Change

Basic to successful change is the type(s) of strategy and/or tactic employed by the agent of change. Strategy refers to the planning and directing of operations, while tactic relates to the maneuvering of forces into position(s) of advantage. Both aspects involve manipulation of various types and manners, and, therefore, can be treated together to some extent.

Manipulation in the terms of this article is the substitution of judgment in such a way that those influenced are not aware that it is happening. Although this process may be known later, it is not known while the manipulation process is taking place. Manipulation is accomplished by a controlled distortion of the appearance of reality as it is seen by those affected. The actions of those influenced are based on their own judgment of what they perceive, but they are permitted to see only those things that are calculated to call out the kind of judgment desired by the control agent.

To be of maximum value, it is necessary to classify strategies and tactics in some useful manner. The scheme employed here classifies the various strategies and tactics into four groups: coercive, normative, utilitarian, and other change techniques.[9] In the last category are found various types of tactics which are generally employed in connection with some kind of strategy.

In the studies by Jones and Niaz, fourteen various types of strategies and eight tactics have been identified and classified from 112 cases in planned organizational change. These cases covered a large number of human organizational problems found in many different cultural and societal settings.[10] Although the researchers were handicapped with a limited number of cases,[11] the number of traditional societies alone is too many to be digested into this article. Therefore, eleven representative cases, which fit within each of the four major categories, have been selected for discussion purposes.

It is believed that these cases are sufficient to indicate possible pragmatic strategies and tactics that may be useful in the hands of a skilled agent of change in effecting planned organizational change in traditional societies.

---

[7] *On the Theory of Social Change*, The Dorsey Press, Inc., Homewood, Illinois, pp. 55–56.

[8] Hagen, *Ibid.*, in Chapter IV gives an excellent treatment of traditional societies.

[9] The idea of classifying these categories in this way was derived from the system used by Amitai Etzioni to classify goals of organizations. For further details see his *A Comparative Analysis of Complex Organizations*, The Free Press of Glencoe, New York, 1961, particularly 3–70. Dr. Aslam Niaz further applied Etzioni's scheme to the classification of strategies and tactics; in this regard, see his doctoral dissertation. "Strategies of Planned Organizational Change," unpublished doctoral dissertation, University of Southern California, School of Public Administration, Los Angeles, 1963, particularly 46–84. Also see Jones and Niaz, *op. cit.*

[10] For more details see *ibid.*

[11] These cases were examined by the research technique of content analysis. The purpose of the study was to investigate and categorize strategies and tactics of planned organizational changes and to indicate their usefulness in the change process. The research endeavors in this regard have been seriously restricted by a lack of suitable cases. It is hoped that this article will spark off interest on the part of the practitioners in the field and result in more cases from which conclusions based upon empirical research can be reached.

The cases selected illustrate the use of the following strategies and tactics:

Coercive Strategies
   Strategy of Pressure
   Strategy of Stress Induction
Normative Strategies
   Strategy of Participation
   Strategy of Education/Training
Utilitarian Strategies
   Strategy of Placement
   Strategy of Empiricism
Other Change Techniques
   Tactic of Action Research
   Tactic of Technical Modification
   Tactic of Marginality

Coercive Strategies

This category is characterized by non-mutual goal-setting (a goal set by only one party), and imbalanced power relationship. These strategies rest upon the application or the threat of application of physical sanctions, generation of frustration through restriction of movement or controlling through force the satisfaction of needs such as those of food, sex, and comfort.

Two strategies have been selected to illustrate this category: strategy of pressure and strategy of stress induction.

The preliminary findings of Jones and Niaz revealed that this group of strategies was widely employed in traditional societies. This should not imply that the coercive strategies worked to the disadvantage of those types of societies. Under proper circumstance and careful social engineering, they can be effectively used for improving the organizational system of traditional peoples.

STRATEGY OF PRESSURE

This involves the use or show of some kind of force to fulfill predetermined objective(s). Those who are influenced accept displacement of their own judgment and act upon that provided by a superior.

Two case examples will now be discussed to illustrate the use of this type of strategy.

In northern Nigeria, the home of the Hausa tribe, sleeping sickness reached endemic conditions. Field surveys showed that in some areas up to 40 percent of the inhabitants had the disease. Tests revealed that the disease could be controlled by cutting the brush along the streams in which the tsetse fly, the carrier of the disease, bred. The Hausa people disbelieved that sleeping sickness was carried by the fly. Moreover, they regarded certain patches of brush along the streams as sacred and inhabited by spirits who would be angry if their abodes were disturbed. The clearing of the brush was successfully carried out only when pressure was applied by the British colonial officials through the traditional framework of native authority.

While the disease was virtually eliminated, the Hausa people never associated this fact with the cutting of the brush. This was a measure imposed upon them by force from higher authority. Inasmuch as this practice was not incorporated into their cultural system, there were strong indications that this activity would discontinue after the withdrawal of British rule. In sum, the germ theory of disease was beyond their comprehension or willingness to understand. British officials, therefore, felt the strategy of pressure was the only alternative to eradicate the disease.[12]

The Hausa case, although successful as far as short-run goal achievement is concerned, left the administration in a perplexing position in reference to the long-run situation. Another case using the strategy of pressure may be noted where the long-run goal was not left in such a precarious position.

The Gadsden Purchase territory is the home of the Papago Indians, a primitive Indian desert tribe. The severe problem of existence for the Papagos was the dearth of drinking water, and the whole pattern of their lives was built around a simple technology to satisfy this need. Their primary sources of water were from natural ponds in the Arroyos (stream

[12] For some details see Horace Miner, "Culture Change Under Pressure; A Hausa Case," *Human Organization*, XIX (Fall, 1960), 161–167.

channels without streams until a hard rain) fed by the summer rains. The water was muddy, and the source highly unreliable. In 1915, the United States Indian Bureau started to drill wells in the reservation, but this activity was hampered by a lack of funds. When the Civilian Conservation Corp burgeoned in the 1930's, it was possible to drill a large number of wells in areas not yet penetrated by the Indian Bureau.

A spokesman of a village found in one of the driest regions of the reservation was opposed to the sinking of a well within the village area. The village council backed him up. Relations between the Anglo authorities and the Indians were good. The Anglo administrators were caught in a choice of actions. They could respect the local leadership and not drill the well, or they could drill the well and in so doing destroy the existing local leadership. The administrators chose the latter action. They felt that the value of a permanent source of good sanitary water outweighed the value of an individual leader or at the best a few leaders.

In a peculiar quirk of events the anti-forces were caught at night using the well water, and thus discredited in their own community. Since then there has been no opposition to the use of the well.[13]

In summary, it may be useful to compare both cases. The central problem in these cases was to institute technological change in an administered group belonging to a culture other than the agent of change (administrators) against the opposition of the administered group's leadership. This is a typical situation of colonial government or societies which have strong minorities. In both cases, the objectives to some degree were achieved: (1) the breeding places of the tsetse fly were destroyed and thereby the incident of the disease of sleeping sickness reduced and (2) the well was drilled and equipped and the local inhabitants used the water.

At this point, the two cases depart in their common features. Change was completely incorporated into the particular Papago village (i.e., the use of well water); whereas it was doubtful that the Hausa people would continue the practice of cutting the brush along the streams when British colonial authorities withdrew. However, in both cases the strategy of pressure was successfully used to achieve goals. The only question is the length of time that the goals will be maintained.

STRATEGY OF STRESS INDUCTION

This strategy includes any effort (strain or distortion) directed toward disturbing the equilibrium of an organizational system in order to prepare that system for change. The consequence may be a modified system or a complete breakdown in the system that, in turn, develops into a new system.

Traditional societies are particularly susceptible to stress induction in the change process. The case example used here to illustrate this point does not measure up to all of the dimensions of a case on planned organizational change. In spite of its weaknesses, for our purposes, it does make an excellent portrayal of the use of the strategy of stress induction.[14]

The goal for a certain element of an Indian community in Guatemala was to achieve revitalization of its cultural system. The community, Santa Cruz Chinautla, consisted of a total population of 1,672, of which 92.8 percent were classified as Indians of the Pokoman-speaking dialect and the remainder were *Ladinos*, i.e., those with Spanish-Guatemalan orientation. Each of these groups constituted strong cultural systems with the *Ladinos* for many years prior to the revolution of 1944 in the dominant political position. This had led to considerable cultural degeneration of the Indian culture. Central to the Indian culture was a well-established community organization called the *Cofradia* system, the "law of the saints." This organization appeared to be

---

[13] Henry F. Dobyns, "Thirsty Indians: Introduction of Wells among People of an Arid Region," *Human Organization*, XI (Winter, 1952), 33–36.

[14] A more typical case on the use of this strategy within the dimensions of this article is later described under the strategy of education/training, the Vices case.

a fusion of Mayan and Catholic traditions, and was deeply ingrained into the Indian power structure and community affairs.

The newly established constitutional democratic practices of the revolution provided the vehicle by which the Indian cultural group gained complete control of the community government in the second municipal election in 1947.

The rise of the Indians to power brought new and unsuspected crises within the Indian community. The leaders in the *Cofradia* system saw in this political setting a favorable climate by which to regain their power in and reestablish their old ways of life. However, the Indian community was not as fully integrated as formerly and out of this grew two Indian groups: (1) the conservative or supporters of the *Cofradia* system and (2) the radical or the members of the liberal Catholic and the Protestant elements not strongly committed to the *Cofradia* system.

The period from 1944 to 1955 was one full of a series of stress situations for the three principal groups found in Santa Cruz Chinautla: the *Ladinos*, the conservative Indians, and the radical Indians. With each major stress situation, most of them incurred by political forces, there occurred for each individual group a period of reorganization. For the radical Indians and the *Ladinos* the reorganization was of a short duration. For the conservative Indians, however, the stress continued a sequence of reactions analogous to the after-effects of a physical disaster. The group elated by national conditions favorable again for Indian self-government and patterns of life, revitalized its traditional social system. Whether or not this was desirable for the demands of the larger community and the nation constitutes another matter. Significant is that the outcome appears typical for folk, peasant, or underdeveloped communities. The agent of change and the client system will have to wrestle with the question as to whether or not within the revitalized system there is also found a cultural residue in favor of change. In

this particular case, the author felt that he saw such a residue.[15]

Normative Strategies

This category of strategies places emphasis upon normative power as a major source of control. Compliance rests primarily upon the internationalization of directions accepted as proper and legitimate. The techniques of control are usually the manipulation of symbolic rewards, employment of leaders, manipulation of symbols, and administration of rituals.

In this group two types of strategies have been selected for illustration purposes: the strategy of participation and the strategy of education/training.

The preliminary studies of Jones and Niaz revealed that normative strategies were widely employed in all types of organizations. Two case examples will be used to illustrate the use of these strategies.

STRATEGY OF PARTICIPATION

This strategy is no more than involving the individuals concerned into the decision-making process before the actual change is introduced. On the surface this may appear to be a type of strategy not generally suitable for traditional societies. In other words, because of strong cultural commitment to traditional values, other types of strategies appear, off-hand, to be more effective to induce change. The case discussed here conveys the opposite lesson. The endeavor failed because the agents of change did not early involve the client system in the change process.

This case takes place in the same setting and time as a previous one discussed under the strategy of pressure, i.e., the drilling of a well in the reservation of the Papago Indian reservation in the Gadsden Purchase Territory.

The goal was to introduce a new agricultural practice into the social system of the Papago Indians. The Indian Bureau learned of the practice in Sonoran, Mexico, of utilizing flood waters from a single storm in such a

[15] Ruben E. Reina, "Political Crisis and Cultural Revitalization: The Guatemalan Case," *Human Organization*, XVII (Winter, 1958–59), 14–18.

manner as to raise one crop a year on a commercial basis.

This was called the *bolsa* system. The Spanish word *bolsa* means pocket. The water was literally run into a pocket and left there to soak into the ground, after which the land was plowed and harrowed and well-pulverized, and the seed planted.

The Papago Indian extension division saw possibilities for this system, and with the assistance of the Civilian Conservation Corps constructed, with a sizeable investment of energy and capital, a *bolsa*. After several years of frustrations, the project completely failed for technical reasons. Subsequent investigation revealed, among other things, that the *bolsa* was poorly engineered and constructed, climatic conditions in the reservation were not suitable for such an agricultural practice, and an inadequate source of water existed for the acreage prepared for cultivation.

Early, the Indians realized these weaknesses, and, although receptive to Anglo innovations, reverted to their old agricultural practices. In this case they understood better than the Anglo technicians what were the best agricultural practices.

In summary,

> the attempt failed because the administrators did not master the technique they borrowed before introducing it . . .

Furthermore, they

> did not bring the people into the planning . . . with the result that further technical difficulties developed which could have been avoided.

These miscalculations were further compounded because the agents of change were outside of the client system's culture, and unexpected and uncontrollable conditions emerged that they could not cope with in an adequate manner.[16]

STRATEGY OF EDUCATION/TRAINING[17]

Great hopes have been placed upon this strategy as a primary means for planned organizational change. However, education and training are fraught with many problems. They are frequently slow and expensive means, and much time is usually consumed before any effectiveness can be determined. Furthermore, these approaches are often employed without any previous sound conceptualization of the needs of the social system. The development and the effective application of human skill and knowledge constitute a persistent problem in organizational settings. This is particularly a difficult matter in traditional societies. An extensive chain of events is usually necessary before anything of significance results.

First, people must be taught basic skills. This is usually a simple matter; but more in the total educational/training process is involved. The first cannot succeed (this is the second process) unless certain habits, attitudes, and ways of thought and behavior have been created. People must learn to be scientific and progressive in outlook instead of living by ancestral laws and long-tried rules of thumb. Thirdly, the education/training must be grafted upon the old; old values, for example, cannot be discarded overnight.

One of the outstanding success stories of planned organizational change, in which education/training played a crucial role, is the transformation of a semi-feudal Indian hacienda in Peru into a progressive democratic

---

[16] Henry F. Dobyns, "Blunders with Bolsas," *Human Organization,* X (Fall, 1951), 25–32.

[17] In technical terms there is a difference between education and training. However, for this article the two words are used together to relate to the institutional processes (school, family, religious organizations, management training programs etc.) whereby the accumulated ideas, standards, knowledge, technology, and techniques of society are transferred from one person to another. Involved is not only the overall development of the individual for the "good life," but also preparing the individual to meet better certain job requirements of an organization.

community within a five-year period.[18] This experience was the result of an unusual arrangement between the Peruvian government and Cornell University. The endeavor (Peru-Cornell project) operated as a joint enterprise of the Department of Sociology and Anthropology of Cornell University and the Indigenous Institute of Peru. Its primary aims were scientific: the study of the processes and consequences of community development. The project proposed to build into the experiment a more productive and effective social system, and to contribute to the development of a more capable and confident people. All of this was to be accomplished within a short period of time, say five years!

The state of affairs of the *hacienda*, Vicos by name, was not a happy one. The hacienda was over 30,000 acres, in the highlands of northwestern Peru, and inhabited by some 2,000 Quechua-speaking Indians who had a minimum of contact with modern civilization.

Power was so concentrated in the hands of a single person, the patron, that the villagers' fate depended almost entirely upon him. Villagers had almost no say in governmental affairs.

The standard of living was a bare minimum; health and nutritional levels were extremely low; educational facilities (and consequently skills) were almost completely lacking; resistances to the outside world were high, and attitudes toward life were static and pessimistic.

The approach employed was an integrated one. Although a number of strategies were used, two played predominate roles: (1) stress induction and (2) education/training. In fact, it is difficult to separate these two strategies.

The results accomplished by the agents of change within a five-year period were astounding. Let us use the words of the authors to sum up the case:

The Vicosinos, after 400 years of peonage, are about to gain control of their own destiny . . . In October, 1956, democratically, by direct vote of all of its citizens, and for the first time in its history, the people of Vicos elected their own delegates to assume the direction and management of community affairs. At the same time, the Peruvian Government is making it possible for the Vicosinos to purchase the lands on which they have lived as serfs since the Spanish Conquest.[19]

They go on to say that all of this was accomplished with very little expenditure of outside funds, and note four reasons why this situation occurred:

1. The administration took steps to relieve some of the most severe stresses felt by the people . . . This made it possible for the people to have faith in the administration.

2. The administration developed a program of consultation and delegation of responsibility so as to stimulate the development of Indian leadership.

3. The administration and Indian leaders developed a program of education and training, so that the people could gain the knowledge they needed to build a better community.

4. Steps 2 and 3 made it possible for the people themselves to *have faith in themselves*. There resulted a self-propelling social system, in which the benefits people achieved through their own efforts released new hopes and energies, and those hopes and energies in turn produced further rewards.[20]

In final summary, in five years an apathetic and disorganized people were transformed into a dynamic and progressive community. The agents of change had successfully compressed time in a constructive fashion.

Utilitarian Strategies

These strategies are characterized by control over material resources and rewards through the allocation of increased contributions, benefits, and services. These are availa-

---

[18] This case is reported by William F. Whyte and Allan R. Holmberg, "Human Problems of U. S. Enterprise in Latin America," *Human Organization*, XV (Fall, 1956), 15–18. This success story has also been published elsewhere. For a recent account see Leland Stowe, "Miracle at Vicos," *Reader's Digest*, LXXXII (April, 1963), 222–228.

[19] *Ibid.*, p. 18.

[20] *Ibid.*

ble to the client system when it performs in a manner prescribed by the agent of change. Two types of such strategies have been selected for discussion: strategy of placement and strategy of empiricism.

The joint research of Niaz and Jones has not been very fruitful in finding cases using these types of strategies in traditional or transitional societies. On the other hand, a survey of anthropological and related literature indicates that such strategies have frequently been employed to facilitate and bring about change.[21] It appears that scholars and practitioners alike involved with traditional societies have not taken the time to write up case experiences employing these types of strategies. To illustrate the use of these strategies, it will be necessary to include case examples which took place in industrial type societies.

STRATEGY OF PLACEMENT

This strategy could involve two sets of circumstances. One is to assure affected members of a group that they will be taken care of in case of any social changes such as the reduction of employees because of a technological innovation. The other is the placing of the right person(s) in strategic positions when change is desired.

An excellent case example of the former situation occurred in the California State Department of Employment when this agency converted from conventional punch card and electronic accounting machine processing to the newly developed electronic data processing machines. Before this change occurred all permanent employees were assured that none of them would be laid off. Such employees would be transferred to positions elsewhere in the state government or the reduction in force would result as a result of normal personnel turnover. Because of this assurance, the new operation was smoothly installed without incurring any resistance by employees.[22]

During Henry Ford's last years, the Ford Motor Company was near collapse. Henry Ford had a strange relationship with Harry Bennett, a gun-toting character who was all-powerful in the organization. When Henry Ford's grandson, Henry Ford II, became president of the Ford Motor Company he placed able and trustworthy persons in important positions formerly occupied by Harry Bennett and his gang of toughs. The result saved the company, and brought it back to such a position that it became a strong competitor.[23]

STRATEGY OF EMPIRICISM

New practices can frequently be incorporated into a social system on the basis of objective and empirical proof of their value to the system. A good case example of acceptance and rejection of new agricultural practices took place in a small, relatively isolated Costa Rican village, San Juan Norte. In this village attempts were made to introduce three new agricultural practices: the use of chlordane, the cultivation of home vegetable gardens, and the cultivation of POJ sugar cane (*Proefstation Oost Java*, a variety of sugar cane).

In 1951, extension students introduced chlordane, an insecticide, into the village to combat pests. This practice was accepted by the villagers when it was demonstrated to them that it was an effective means to combat insects, particularly ants.

Whereas the introduction of chlordane into the agricultural practices was a success, the same was not the case for the cultivation of home vegetable gardens. This venture failed largely for the reasons that the chlordane endeavor succeeded. No objective proof was furnished as to the feasibility of planting gardens. The agent of change, a school teacher, attempted to cultivate a garden. He made an intensive campaign among villagers and managed to enlist the help of part of them. All

---

[21] A cursory survey of the journal, *Human Organization*, will give sufficient indication as to the extent these strategies have been employed.

[22] Alvin C. Bidwell, John J. Carrell, and Robert R. Blake, "Team Job Training—A New Strategy for Industry," *Training Directors*, XV (October, 1961), 3–23.

[23] Robert Coughlan, "Co-Captains in Ford's Battle for Supremacy," *Life Magazine*, XXXVIII (February 28, 1955), 84–86.

attempts failed for a variety of reasons, and therefore provided no empirical evidence as to the feasibility of this agricultural practice.

The POJ sugar represents a good example of spontaneous change. Fifteen years after the Costa Rican Ministry of Agriculture took steps to disseminte throughout the country the POJ variety of sugar cane, this variety appeared in San Juan Norte. However, its direct introduction was not undertaken by any agent of change, but spontaneously by a villager. Its acceptance was largely conditioned by objective proof of the efficiency of the new variety.

This case concluded that three basic conditions should exist to insure acceptance of an item by a social group: (1) A need for the item must be felt by the members; (2) the item must be compatible with their culture; and (3) the people must have proof of its workability or effectiveness.[24]

Other Change Techniques

In a narrower sense, agents of change employ what is termed here as tactics to facilitate change. This is the maneuvering of forces of various types into positions of advantage. Frequently, this is accomplished in connection with a strategy. In other cases, tactics are used by themselves and may be regarded as strategies.

In this article three types of tactics are noted: (1) action research, (2) technical modification, and (3) marginality. Representative case examples will now be discussed.

Tactic of Action Research

In recent years there has occurred a growing number of accounts where research personnel have become directly involved as manipulator in the change process. This type of action research was used in the previously dis-cussed Vicos case. The researchers in this change situation laid out approximately

130 specific lines of research and development, each matched to a specific developmental goal such as the diversification of agriculture, the development of community leadership etc.[25]

Another interesting case of this nature occurred in Guatemala. Research on nutrition required that school children in several villages receive a different combination of nutrients and submit periodically to examinations to determine their nutritional status. This experiment was threatened by non-cooperation on the part of key persons in several of the villages. An anthropologist was brought into the case to determine the cause of the trouble and to overcome the resistance. Anthropological research disclosed that the growing resistance to the experiment could be attributed to the projects' close identification with one of the two opposing factions in the villages. Effective means were subsequently devised, based upon research, to overcome this resistance.[26]

Tactic of Technical Modification

Cases may be noted where changes in the traditional structure of organizational systems have resulted in an overall increase in performance. An illustration of this type of technical modification occurred in the traditional organizational structure of the Kagor tribe in northern Nigeria. This tribe today may well be the most heavily literate tribal unit in the northern part of Nigeria. The secret of the Kagor's successful development was the planned redefinition of chieftainship carried out under the competent leadership of a village chief (in power at the time the case was written) through councils modeled around traditional tribal institutions and behavior.

---

[24] M. Alers-Montalvo, "Cultural Change in a Costa Rican Village," *Human Organization*, XVI (Winter, 1957), 2–7.

[25] Besides the previous references, see Allan R. Holmberg, "The Research and Development Approach to the Study of Change," *Human Organization*, XVII (Spring, 1958), 12–16 and "Reaching the Heart of South America," *Saturday Review*, XLV (November 3, 1962), 55–62.

[26] Richard N. Adams "A Nutritional Research Program in Guatemala," in Benjamin D. Paul (ed.), *Health, Culture and Community*, Russell Sage Foundation, New York, 1955, 435–458.

The institution of chieftainship was introduced by the British colonial authorities, and was initially incompatible with the Kagor's traditional social structure. It was responsible for considerable social dysfunctionalism, and the admission of undesirable elements. Under the leadership of the chief of the Kagor tribe, the incompatible features were identified and removed and other elements introduced to foster integration and development of the social structure.[27]

TACTIC OF MARGINALITY

Anthropological literature is full of examples where acculturated bilinguals have served a very useful function in the change process because they share the value systems of their own society and that of the innovating society. Such persons have been skillfully employed in the medical program among the Navaho Indians.

In 1956 the Cornell University Medical College established a project of training a small group of Navaho health aids in the middle of the Navaho reservation. The primary purpose was to enable anthropologists to observe the development of the roles of bilinguals in each society in the performance of their work as health aides.

These persons proved to be a positive asset, and provided the vehicle for which significant changes were made and goals accomplished.

This tactic functioned in practice within a broader framework of reference which is conceptualized in this article under two strategies: communication and empiricism.

The acculturated bilinguals were able to bridge effectively the gap of communication, and the transmissions of new technology in the medical field into the social organization of the Navaho. This task was made easier by the highly practical value system of the Navaho. To him "knowledge is power," and, if it can be demonstrated to him that the health aid could facilitate the relief of pain and illness he willingly accepts medical treatment.[28]

General Conclusions

The frame of reference of this article rests upon empirical analysis, i.e., through the research technique of content analysis strategies and tactics of planned organizational change are isolated and defined and some evaluation is made of their roles in the processes of change in traditional societies.

Only an exploratory view of this approach, largely for two reasons, could be taken in this article. First, this research methodology employed is new in this area. Secondly, there is only a limited number of suitable cases on the subject of planned organizational change.

Nevertheless, evidence to date certainly indicates that pragmatic strategies and tactics are available to facilitate organizational change in traditional societies. In other words, by skillfully employing such strategies and tactics it is possible, in a constructive fashion, to telescope and compress the processes of change and development of traditional communities to meet better the needs of modern world society.

The common technique to accelerate change for traditional societies has been through the programs of community development. These programs have been designed to reach village people and to make more effective the use of local initiative and energy for increased production and better living standards. In all of these programs there is a need to adapt improved knowledge and technology to the behavioral patterns of village people, or vice versa. This connotes organizational change, in most cases, of far-reaching consequence.

In final note, it is firmly believed that modern man, equipped with the knowledge of behavioral science, can to a considerable extent control and direct organizational changes rationally, intelligently, and effectively for the goal of a better life. It is hoped that this brief sketch of one possible "bag of tools" may be useful particularly in the hands of community development practitioners toward this end.

[27] M. G. Smith, "Kagoro Political Development," *Human Organization,* XIX (Fall, 1960), 137–149.

[28] John Adair, "The Indian Health Worker in the Cornell-Navaho Project," *Human Organization,* XIX (Summer, 1960), 59–63.

PART TWO

STRATEGIES FOR SOCIAL CHANGE

One of the most salient characteristics of planned social change is the adoption of some general course of action designed to achieve the objectives of change agents or their agencies. Such a course of action is what we shall refer to as strategy. Strategies are the master plans for managing and directing the flow of influence from change agent to change targets (or clients, as the target group will sometimes be called). Those activities which are carried out to implement strategy shall be termed as tactics. There is, of course, an interplay between strategy and tactics. Strategies encompass all perceived relevant circumstances and match actions or tactics with these circumstances.

Four factors appear to exert major influence on strategy development—goals and objectives, the change target resources, and constraints and opportunities. On page 268, we have outlined these four factors. The prime prerequisite for a change agency when attempting social change is a definite set of goals and objectives. These must be clearly articulated and a timetable set for achieving them. Different strategies might be employed depending upon whether the goals are short-run or long-run in nature and whether they must be achieved quickly or are free of such pressure. Another consideration concerns the number of change agents involved and their understanding of the goals. When more than one change agent is employed, it is important that each one has a common understanding of the change agency's goals and objectives. If goals are not understood or similarly perceived by the different agents, then the agents' efforts may be poorly coordinated and possibly in direct conflict. This does not preclude the change agents having different goals. Suboptimization may be desired in which different but compatible goals are pursued by change agents working for the same agency.

In many cases the change agency will find it advantageous to involve its change agents in the process of developing goals and objectives and in the determination of tactics. So doing tends to increase the change agents' involvement in and commitment to their tasks and hence increase their effectiveness. It also enables the agency to utilize the experience of those workers who are closest to the change target in terms of working relationships. Once goals and objectives have been set and strategies and tactics selected and the program placed in operation, there should be a review of the goals, objectives, strategies and tactics in light of the first experiences. Again, the change agents can function as a valuable source of vital information for the leaders of the change agency. A problem does arise here—the desirable time at which a review should take place. Clearly there is an optimal time, but it is not so clear how this is determined. Several factors are involved, such as the nature of the innovation, the change target, change agent, and so on, each receiving a weighted value. However, what might be the optimal time from the standpoint of one factor is not always optimal for another.

A second factor in developing a foundation for determining strategy is the appraisal of the change target. There must be an assessment of the attitudes, beliefs, values, knowledge, and practices prevalent in the client system. Strategies and tactics must be compatible with these. One of the first considerations in appraising the change target is whether the activity or innovation being sponsored involves a modification of some existing behavioral attribute or the introduction of a largely new behavioral attribute. For example, when marketing proper nutrition practices, different strategies are involved depending upon whether the objective is to get housewives to use more of a product that they presently consume in order to increase the intake of protein or whether the objective is to have them start using for the first time an altogether new source of protein.

Another consideration involves the degree to which change targets should be aware of the strategies being directed to them. If the change target system desires change, it would

Outline of Selected Factors Influencing Strategy Development

Goals	Change Target	Resources	Constraints and Opportunities
Mutuality of goals between change agency and change target	Appraisal of change target system by change agent	Change target, change agency and other's resources available for initiating change	Constraints and opportunities associated with change agency
	Is there a felt need?		Constraints and opportunities associated with change target
Magnitude of change intended	What motivates felt need	Resources for sustaining change	
Timetable			Constraints and opportunities inherent in goal's being pursued
Selection of strategy and tactics	Can change target system be segmented	Conversion of resources into social energy	
	Sources and nature of anticipated resistance		Constraints and opportunities inherent in strategies and tactics being pursued

be feasible to make known what approach is being followed. This should bring greater cooperation from the change target. Making strategies known or more obvious can also result in more effective opposition if members of the change target system oppose change.

A third consideration in appraising the change target system is whether there is a felt need to change. The need may have to be defined by the change agent who, through persuasion, or reeducation, or the use of whatever power he has, must convince the change target that a need exists. In other instances the need is evidenced by the active solicitation of assistance from the change agency, which is often the case when management consulting firms are employed. The change target may also demonstrate a felt need by attempts to solve the problem without outside assistance.

While agreeing on the existence of a felt need, the change target and the change agency may not share a common definition of what that felt need is. Such a divergence of opinion is especially prevalent in the civil rights arena involving federal and state governments, on the one hand, and civil rights organizations, on the other hand. The problem is a difficult one to resolve. It can be resolved through attempts by one party to reeducate the other party, through the persuasive expertise of one party, or by one party exerting its power over the other party. The latter approach will produce behavioral change, but it is less certain that it will produce basic and enduring attitudinal change.

Related to the importance of felt needs is the motivation of the change target in seeking or accepting change and in implementing change. Of course, the motivation in most instances is that there is an important need which the desired change can satisfy. This assumes that there is something inherent in the change object uniquely suited to that need. Yet it is not uncommon for change targets to accept change for less direct reasons. Then, generally, the change is made by the change target as a means toward some other end.

It is important, too, that a basis exists for implementing and sustaining the social change. This is true for both the change agency and the change target. While the change agency will generally have sufficient resources to at least initiate a change, it will not necessarily have the resources required to sustain that change over an extended period of time. Thus, the change agency should (and must) choose a strategy with a time factor consistent with the supply of the resources available to sustain a change effort necessary for a given change target. Also, in assessing the change target system, it is necessary to take into account the target's capacity to accept and use assistance.

When assessing the change target system, the change agency also must determine if there are definable segments within the system. To the extent that there are significant subsystems, different strategies and/or tactics may be necessary for each relevant subsystem. For example, in the diffusion of innovations the relevant social system is usually divided into five categories: innovators, early adopters, early majority, late majority, and laggards. Each segment has somewhat different behavioral repertories requiring different strategies. Other bases for defining subsystems, as set forth elsewhere in this volume, are: socioeconomic, for example, family life style, education, race, age; geographic, such as region, city, urban/rural; personality, for example, gregariousness, conservatism, leadership, etc.; and use of the object of change, such as usage rate and level, application of the change, motivation for usage.

There are many other considerations in assessing the change target system. For example: What types and sources of resistance can be expected from the change target with respect to different strategies and tactics? Does the change target system have a preferred strategy? What tactics are inconsistent with knowledge, attitudes, and practices in the system?

Another factor in developing and selecting strategy is a careful appraisal of the resources available to the change agency for implementing a strategy. Different strategies and tactics will involve different mixes of resources. The resources which may be involved are varied: manpower talent, money, time, knowledge of the change target and other relevant parties to the change effort (such as competitors and collaborators), control over channels for directing the flow of influence (such as communication systems), social credit, goodwill, and prestige. These resources may be located within the change agency, in the change target system, or in another relevant social system. It is particularly desirable to have the change target invest his own resources, for this increases his commitment. Even a strategy which involves only token investment by the change target system is preferable to one which requires none, other things being equal.

A final factor in the selection of strategies is to appraise the constraints and opportunities in the general environment within which the change agent must work. Similarly, the change agency must also consider the setting in which the change target will be employing the advocated change. Constraints for either the change agency or change target may come in the form of laws, informal social norms, competing change agents, restrictions in the availability of the resources mentioned above, and the refusal of one of the parties involved to accept a suggested strategy. Opportunities are established for the change agency when the change target acknowledges the need for change and actively seeks assistance. Other favorable conditions include an available and sufficient supply of resources and the ability of the change target system to absorb change with optimal conflict and resistence.

Another set of variables related to constraints and opportunities involves the substance of the strategy. A given strategy will have a number of dimensions, some of which will serve as restraints on its effectiveness while others will function as facilitators. What, then, are the different characteristics or dimensions which can be attached to strategies (and tactics)? Characteristics traditionally associated with innovations seem to be especially relevant descriptions for strategy characteristics. Strategies may vary in terms of the extent of change that they require. Other things being equal, that strategy will be best which involves the least amount of accommodation by the change target for its most effective use. This does not necessarily mean that the advocated change is simple or involves little perturbation· or restructuring of

the change target system. The compatibility or consistency of the strategy with existing values and behavior is important. The complexity of the strategy is also important, particularly if the change target system has an active rather than passive role in implementing the strategy. The more complex a strategy is the greater the difficulty in implementing it and the greater the likelihood of its breaking down. The reversibility of the strategy, another consideration, is partially related to commitment to a given strategy. Once initiated, can a strategy be terminated and, if so, what costs will be involved? How readily can the previous status quo be restored? Divisibility is a related dimension. It concerns the ability to test a strategy on a small scale, or to implement only a part of a strategy on a trial basis.

Other dimensions attached to strategy are: (1) the initial and continuing cost—Is it expensive (in terms of the resources mentioned earlier) to initiate and maintain the strategy? (2) clarity of results—Can the effects of the strategy provide information allowing for continuous modification? (3) risk and uncertainty—What dysfunctional attributes does the strategy have? What is their magnitude and likelihood of occurrence? and, finally, (4) terminality—Is there a unique starting and concluding point or time?

Both for discussion purposes and for broadening our understanding of various strategies it is useful to classify them according to their basic tenor or approach for including social change. However, two things should be stated at the outset. A review of the literature shows particular strategies being classified in different ways. Thus, it is impossible to develop a classification which is mutually exclusive beyond debate. The second point is that any given strategy may legitimately involve more than one philosophy or approach. This part of the book employs a threefold classification system for aligning strategies. Section III presents the first strategy class—power strategist; Section IV, the second strategy class—persuasive strategies; and Section V, the third strategy class—reeducative strategies.

The readings in Section III are primarily concerned with power. Power strategies tend to be coercive in nature. They are those strategies in which force and/or the threat of force is used. The threat of force may be explicit or implicit. It can involve the withholding of a valued commodity, physical or social sanction (punishment), or de facto imposition of the conditions that a change agency wants brought about. The papers in this section focus attention on various power strategies and tactics.

The paper by Samuel Huntington, "Reform and Political Change," distinguishes between revolutionaries and reformers and discusses various strategies open to the reformer. These strategies are termed Fabianism, Blitzkrieg, and Violence. The conditions affecting the use of each strategy is discussed along with normative suggestions. Many of the historical examples presented can be readily projected into today's changing world.

Michael Lipsky in, "Protest as a Political Resource," discusses an important element of power in social change. Lipsky initially addresses situations characterized by relatively little power and discusses the factors accounting for this. Of particular importance is his discussion of what protest leaders may do to increase their power. Equally important and interesting are his six tactics that target groups may employ to blunt the efforts of change agents.

The next two selections are brief statements providing guidelines for organizing and implementing social protest. The paper by Joan Bondurant, "Satyagraha as Applied Socio-Political Action," discusses a nonviolent power strategy associated with Gandhi. It involves a very careful marshalling and exploiting of many resources which constitute the power behind the strategy. As Bondurant indicates at the outset, force is used although the character and result of that force differ from that involved in violent action techniques. The intent of Satyagraha is to precipitate a crisis. Crises help create opportunities for changes in the allocation of power and thus can be strong and effective tools in bringing about change. There may even be an optimum level of crisis as well as an optimal number of crises from the standpoint of inducing change.

Martin Oppenheimer and George Lakey, in

"Direct Action Tactics," examine various forms of demonstrations, noncooperation, intervention as well as the basic mechanics of operating social protest, which is an important consideration. Maximum power can only be exerted if the strategic and tactical mechanisms are functioning properly. This means that the use of resources must be very carefully planned, even to the extent of preselecting stage positions for the various participants.

The Harry Specht paper, "Disruptive Tactics," presents an interesting discussion of the interplay among the perception of change, the response to that perception, the strategy of intervention, and the tactics used. Special attention is given to a range of disruptive tactics that can be used to achieve change. Specht makes a careful distinction between tactics whose objectives are to prevent the change target from operating in its usual way and tactics of violence whose goals are to harm or destroy.

In "The Dynamics of Recent Ghetto Riots" James Hundley, Jr., is concerned with three major aspects of riots. Five general conditions or causal factors preceding riots are treated, four immediate conditions serving as catalyst are discussed, and the internal dynamics of ongoing riots are examined. The discussion lends itself readily to the task of developing prescriptive measures for coping with riots or even for fomenting riots.

Strength in bargaining is a valuable asset and the basis for considerable power as Thomas Schelling in his paper, "An Essay on Bargaining," points out in his discussion of a special circumstance where bargaining power is especially important. This involves "zero-sum" situations where one party's gain is the other party's loss. The characteristics of bargaining are discussed along with a treatment of various ploys useful in a bargaining context. Bargaining is an important topic from the standpoint of social change. In many instances a change in the social system involves a reallocation of resources adversely affecting one party and benefiting another. In such instances a basic conflict occurs which can be removed only through negotiation or bargaining. A third (or more) party may or may not be involved in the process. The bargaining skill possessed by advocates of change will have a direct bearing on the degree of social change which takes place.

It is sometimes desirable to employ more than one type of strategy, particularly when the change target system contains subsystems some of which are more likely to respond better to one strategy while another will be more responsive to a different strategy. Conflict can occur when a mixed strategy approach is used and the different subgroups and their respective strategies cannot be isolated. Different strategies are not necessarily compatible with one another. Richard Walton's paper, "Two Strategies of Social Change and Their Dilemmas," presents a very good picture of the problems in using two sometimes incompatible strategies and tactics. One of the strategies he discusses are what we and the author label power strategies; the other is what he labels an attitude change strategy.

Section IV introduces the subject of persuasive strategies, that is, strategies which attempt to bring about change partly through bias in the manner in which a message is structured and presented. They attempt to create change by reasoning, urging, and inducement. Persuasive strategies can be based in rational appeal as well as emotional appeal and can reflect facts accurately or be totally false. Such strategies include propaganda, advertising, and lobbying among others.

Propaganda is one of the more popular persuasive strategies. It is the attempt to influence people's emotional attitudes and beliefs and, consequently, their actions. Viewed in this way, propaganda encompasses a wide range of communications and behaviors. J. A. C. Brown in "Propaganda and Communication" gives a very good and relatively detailed discussion of the nature and boundaries of propaganda. He contrasts education (a third set of strategies to be discussed later) and propaganda, and describes specific techniques employed in propaganda, such as the use of stereotypes, repetition, and assertion. He aptly identifies suggestion as the fundamental mechanism in all forms of propaganda. Suggestion is the key to inducing in others the acceptance of a specific belief without giving any evidence for it.

Advertising is another persuasive strategy which is coming into increasing use by social change agencies. It may be purely informational but is more generally found to be motivational and persuasive in nature. Milton Rokeach's paper, "Applications to the Field of Advertising," offers a fivefold classification of beliefs and locates the type of belief that advertising is most adept at changing. Among other things he explores problems in trying to change certain kinds of beliefs and how these problems can be approached.

"Social Change Through Issue Advertising," by John Zeigler is an engaging look at one type of social advertising—issue advertising, which he defines as dealing with "certain social issues, and is aimed at changing, clarifying, or repealing laws, or initiating new legislation." It is the use of marketing techniques and know-how as means of achieving social goals. Zeigler presents some insight into how behavioral science knowledge will probably come to be employed in social advertising. He outlines many "rules of thumb" which should serve as guidelines for agencies for whom this form of promotion is available.

Persuasive strategies may invoke a number of different psychosocial appeals. This was made evident by the Brown paper. One appeal, fear, is particularly effective in stimulating change. The reading by Howard Levanthal, "Experimental Studies on Fear," details the results of experimental studies on fear appeals and assesses the conditions affecting their effectiveness. A number of empirical generalizations are made. Fear is seen as a major source of motivation. If used optimally, it can be a very effective tool for change agencies and an essential ingredient of propaganda. With little modification the implications of Levanthal's findings could be extended to several social causes.

Frank Wilder and D. K. Tyagi in "India's New Departures in Mass Motivation for Fertility Control" presents a formula for mass communications strategy in developing societies on the topic of family planning. Their departure from conventional mass communication strategy has not been evaluated scientifically. However, the authors believe it is effective and exportable to other developing societies. Certainly the approach is a promising one and suggests several ways the potential of the mass media as developmental tools might be realized.

One of the necessary conditions for a viable pluralistic society is that its many groups must have and, more importantly, must believe that they have some means of affecting policy decisions. Lobbying is one activity in response to this functional requirement. The Lester Milbrath paper, "Lobbying as a Communication Process" explores lobbying as a communication process involving the communication of facts, arguments, and power. Several strategies and tactics are presented. These came out of a study of one hundred and one Washington, D.C., lobbyists who provided considerable insight into this process and into the difficult and subtle task of persuasion.

Section V concerns a third type of strategy —reeducative strategies. Reeducative strategies rely on the communication of fact and assume man is a rational being capable of discerning fact and adjusting his behavior accordingly. Often this strategy involves the unlearning of something before the new attitude or behavior can be instilled. For this reason we refer to this strategy as reeducative. Such strategy involves three stages.[1] The first is the unfreezing of attitudes and behavior by creating a motivation to learn and change. This might be accomplished by withholding support or approval of the present attitudes and behavior. The second stage is the changing process, which involves developing new cognitions and behavior based upon new information. The final one is the refreezing stage in which the changes are stabilized and integrated into the individual's personality.

One of the most effective tools available for inducing change, at least in the short run, in individuals is the "T" group. The paper by Chris Argyris, "T-Groups for Organizational Effectiveness," suggests that laboratory education, while not a panacea, is a very promising educational process especially in solving or-

ganizational problems. Often very profound changes in individuals can occur under the right circumstances or in the right laboratory environment. Conditions inhibiting and promoting individual or group change are discussed.

Peter Lenrow's paper, "A Framework for Planning Behavior Change in Juvenile Offenders," discusses how the change agency can provide an effective reeducation process for juvenile offenders by coordinating a variety of influence methods in the learning process. Of particular interest is Lenrow's discussion as to why power strategies are ineffective in producing enduring change.

The importance of ancillary matters is often overlooked in discussions of change strategies. It is true regardless of the general type of strategy employed. The paper by Leonard Blumberg, Thomas Shipley, Jr., and Irving Shandler, "Seven Years on Skid Row: Diagnostic and Rehabilitation Center! Philadelphia," discusses such matters in a case study of a reeducative social change program involving the rehabilitation of skid row tenants.

Walter Carmack in a brief paper "Communication and Community Readiness for Social Change" presents a case study of a meticulously planned effort to reeducate a community. The vital role and creative utilization of interpersonal and mass communications in preparing Dallas, Texas, to accept school desegregation is reviewed.

When the basic cognitions and behaviors to be changed are deeply rooted in the individual's concept of self, it is usually necessary to subject him to an intensive and extended reeducative change process. Brainwashing is one such change process and perhaps the most extreme. The paper by Edgar Schein, "The Chinese Indoctrination Program for Chinese Prisoners," is one of the best treatments of this technique available. Among the topics he discusses are direct and indirect attacks on beliefs, attitudes, and values and the manipulation of rewards and punishment.

---

[1] See E. Schein, "The Mechanisms of Change," in W. Bennis, E. Schein, F. Steele and D. Berlew (eds.), *Interpersonal Dynamics* (Homewood, Ill.: Dorsey Press, 1964), pp. 362–378.

SECTION

POWER STRATEGIES

20. Reform and Political Change

Samuel P. Huntington*

Strategy and Tactics of Reform:
Fabianism, Blitzkrieg, and Violence

Revolutions are rare. Reform, perhaps, is even rarer. And neither is necessary. Countries may simply stagnate or they may change in ways which could not be called either revolution or reform. While the line between the two may at times be hazy, they can be distinguished in terms of the speed, scope, and direction of change in the political and social systems. A revolution involves rapid, complete, and violent change in values, social structure, political institutions, governmental policies, and social-political leadership. The more complete these changes, the more total is the revolution. A "great" or "social" revolution means significant changes in all these components of the social and political system.

Changes limited in scope and moderate in speed in leadership, policy, and political institutions may, in turn, be classed as reforms. Not all moderate changes, however, are reforms. The concept of reform implies something about the direction of change as well as something about its scope and rate. A reform, as Hirschman says, is a change in which "the power of hitherto privileged groups is curbed and the economic position and social status of underprivileged groups is correspondingly improved."[1] It means a change in the direction of greater social, economic, or political equality, a broadening of participation in society and polity. Moderate changes in the opposite direction are better termed "consolidations" than reforms.

The way of the reformer is hard. In three

[1] Albert O. Hirschman, *Journeys Toward Progress* (New York, Twentieth Century Fund, 1963, p. 267.

Reprinted from Samuel Huntington, "Reform and Political Change," *Political Order in Changing Societies* (New Haven: Yale University Press, 1968), pp. 344–362. Copyright © 1968 by Yale University.
* Frank G. Thomson Professor of Government, Center for International Affairs, Harvard University.

respects, his problems are more difficult than those of the revolutionary. First, he necessarily fights a two-front war against both conservative and revolutionary. Indeed, to be successful, he may well have to engage in a multifront war with a multiplicity of participants, in which his enemies on one front are his allies on another. The aim of the revolutionary is to polarize politics, and hence he attempts to simplify, to dramatize, and to amalgamate political issues into a single clear-cut dichotomy between the forces of "progress" and those of "reaction." He tries to cumulate cleavages, while the reformer must try to diversify and to disassociate cleavages. The revolutionary promotes rigidity in politics, the reformer fluidity and adaptability. The revolutionary must be able to dichotomize social forces, the reformer to manipulate them. The reformer, consequently, requires a much higher order of *political skill* than does the revolutionary. Reform is rare if only because the political talents necessary to make it a reality are rare. A successful revolutionary need not be a master politician; a successful reformer always is.

The reformer not only must be more adept at the manipulation of social forces than is the revolutionary, but he also must be more sophisticated in the control of social change. He is aiming at some change but not total change, gradual change but not convulsive change. The revolutionary has some interest in all types of change and disorder. Presumably anything which disrupts the status quo is of some value to him. The reformer must be much more selective and discriminating. He has to devote much more attention to the methods, techniques, and timing of changes than does the revolutionary. Like the revolutionary he is concerned with the relation between types of change, but the consequences of these relationships are likely to be even more significant for the reformer than they are for the revolutionary.

Finally, the problem of priorities and choices among different types of reforms is much more acute for the reformer than it is

for the revolutionary. The revolutionary aims first at the expansion of political participation; the politically relevant forces which result are then employed to generate changes in social and economic structure. The conservative opposes both social-economic reform and expanded political participation. The reformer has to balance both goals. Measures promoting social-economic equality usually require the concentration of power, measures promoting political equality the expansion of power. These goals are not inherently contradictory, but, as the experiences of the modernizing monarchs suggest, too great a centralization of power in institutions inherently incapable of expanding power can lead a political system up a blind alley. The reformer thus has to balance changes in social-economic structure against changes in political institutions and to marry the one to the other in such a way that neither is hampered. Leadership and institutions which facilitate one type of reform may be less capable of providing for the other. The military reformer—Mustafa Kemal, Gamal Abdel Nasser, Ayub Khan—is, for instance, notably more successful at promoting social-economic changes than at organizing the participation of new groups in the political system. The Social Democratic or Christian Democratic party leader—Betancourt, Belaunde, Frei—on the other hand, may be better able to identify previously outcast groups with the political system than to bring about social and economic changes.

In theory two broad strategies are open to the reformer who desires to bring about a number of significant changes in social-economic structure and political institutions. One strategy would lead him to make known all his goals at an early time and to press for as many of them as he could in the hope of obtaining as much as possible. The alternative strategy is the foot-in-the-door approach of concealing his aims, separating the reforms from each other, and pushing for only one change at a time. The former is a comprehensive, "root," or blitzkrieg approach; the latter is an incremental, "branch," or Fabian approach.[2] At

[2] See Charles E. Lindblom, "The Science of 'Muddling Through,'" *Public Administration Review*, 19 (Spring 1959), 79–88.

various times in history reformers have essayed both methods. The results of their efforts suggest that for most countries subjected to the strains and dissensions involved in modernization, the most effective method of reform is the combination of a Fabian strategy with blitzkrieg tactics. To achieve his goals the reformer should separate and isolate one issue from another, but, having done this, he should, when the time is ripe, dispose of each issue as rapidly as possible, removing it from the political agenda before his opponents are able to mobilize their forces. The ability to achieve this proper mix of Fabianism and blitzkrieg is a good test of the political skill of the reformer.

In terms of an overall reform program, one can, however, make a logical case for a blitzkrieg strategy. Why should not the reformer make clear his total set of demands immediately, arouse and mobilize the groups which favor change, and through a process of political conflict and political bargaining settle for as much as the balance of forces between change and conservatism permit? If he asks for 100 per cent of what he wants, will he not be sure of getting at least 60 per cent? Or, even better, if he asks for 150 per cent of what he wants, will he not be able to settle for just about everything he can really hope to achieve? Is not this a general strategy of bargaining observable in diplomatic negotiations between states, in labor-management relations, and in the politics of the budgetary process?

The answer to these questions in terms of reform-mongering in a modernizing society is, in general, negative. The comprehensive or blitzkrieg strategy is effective only if the parties to the process are relatively given and unchangeable, if, in short, the structure of the bargaining context is highly stable. The essence of reform-mongering in a modernizing country, however, is to structure the situation so as to influence if not to determine the participants in the political arena. The nature of the demands and the nature of the issues formulated by the reformer in large part shape the allies and the opponents who will play roles in the political process. The problem for the reformer is not to overwhelm a single opponent with an exhaustive set of demands, but to minimize his opposition by an apparently very limited set of demands. The reformer who attempts to do everything all at once ends up accomplishing little or nothing. Joseph II and Kuang Hsu are perfect cases in point. Both attempted simultaneously to push a large number of reforms on a wide variety of fronts, in order to change comprehensively the existing traditional order. They failed because their efforts to attempt so much mobilized so many opponents. Virtually all the social groups and political forces with a stake in the existing society felt themselves threatened; the blitzkrieg or all-out attack simply served to alert and to activate the potential opposition. Here then is the reason why comprehensive reform, in the sense of a dramatic and rapid "revolution from above," never succeeds. It mobilizes into politics the wrong groups at the wrong time on the wrong issues.

The failures of Joseph II and Kuang Hsu contrast markedly with the successful Fabian strategy employed by Mustafa Kemal in the early days of the Turkish Republic. Kemal faced almost all the usual problems of modernization: the definition of the national community, the creation of a modern secular political organization, the inauguration of social and cultural reform, the promotion of economic development. Instead of attempting to solve all these problems simultaneously, however, Kemal carefully separated them one from the other and won acquiescence or even support for one reform from those who would have opposed him on other reforms. The sequence in which the problems were tackled was designed to move from those where Kemal had the greatest support to those which might arouse the greatest controversy. First priority had to be given to the definition of the national community and the delimitation of the ethnic and territorial boundaries of the state. Once a relatively homogeneous ethnic community had been established, the next step—as in the sequels to the Mexican, Russian, and Chinese revolutions—was to create effective modern political institutions for the exercise of authority. It was then possible for those in control to work through the institutions to impose religious, social, cultural, and legal reforms on society. Once traditional forms and customs had been weakened or eliminated, the way was then open for industrialization and economic development. Economic growth, in short, required cultural modernization; cultural modernization required effective political authority; effective political authority had to be rooted in a homogeneous national community. The sequences in which many countries have tackled the problems of modernization have been the products of accident and history. The sequence of change in Turkey, however, was consciously planned by Kemal, and this pattern of unity-authority-equality is the most effective modernization sequence.[3]

Kemal's success in achieving these reforms depended upon his ability to deal with each separately and in effect to suggest at the time that he was handling one that he had no intention of tackling the others. His grand design and ultimate purposes he kept to himself. The first necessity was to create a Turkish national state in Anatolia out of the collapse of the Ottoman Empire. In his struggle to define the national community, Kemal carefully divorced the issue of a limited, integral, homogeneous Turkish nation-state from the type of political authority which would exist in that state. Between 1920 and 1922 the sultan remained in Constantinople while the nationalist movement, under Kemal's leadership, gained strength in the interior. By his successful battles against the Armenians, French, and Greeks, Kemal developed a substantial following. The sultan and the sultanate, however, still retained widespread popular support and sympathy. Kemal consequently separated the

struggle for a national state from opposition to the sultanate. He instead proclaimed one aim of the nationalist movement to be the liberation of the sultan from the control of the British and French forces which had occupied Constantinople. He attacked the sultan's ministers for their collaboration with the foreigners but not the sultan himself. As Kemal subsequently said, "We chose Ferid Pasha's cabinet alone as our target and pretended that we knew nothing about the complicity of the Padishah [Sultan]. Our theory was that the Sovereign had been deceived by the Cabinet and that he himself was in total ignorance of what was really going on."[4] Through this means Kemal was able to align with the nationalist cause those conservatives who still gave primary allegiance to the traditional authority of the sultan.

Once the nationalist victory was assured, Kemal turned his attention to the problem of the political organization of the new state. The nationalists had earlier declared their loyalty to the sovereign, but at the same time they had also proclaimed the sovereignty of the people. Just as earlier he had separated the national issue from the political issue, so now Kemal took pains to separate the political issue from the religious issue. The Ottoman ruler combined the political office of sultan with the religious office of caliph. Kemal knew there would be serious opposition to tampering with the latter position: it gave Turkey special status among Islamic nations. "[If] we lose the Caliphate," one newspaper observed in November 1923, "the State of Turkey, with its five or ten million inhabitants, would lose all importance in the world of Islam, and in the eyes of European politics we would sink to the rank of a petty and insignificant state."[5]

[3] Dankwart A. Rustow, *A World of Nations*, pp. 126–27. On Kemal's strategy and tactics of reform-mongering, see Rustow, "The Army and the Founding of the Turkish Republic," *World Politics*, 11 (July 1959), 545 ff.; Bernard Lewis, *The Emergence of Modern Turkey* (London, Oxford University Press, 1961), p. 254; Richard D. Robinson, *The First Turkish Republic* (Cambridge, Harvard University Press, 1963), pp. 65–66, 69, 80–81; Lord Kinross, *Ataturk* (New York, William Morrow, 1965), p. 430.

[4] Mustapha Kemal, *A Speech Delivered by Ghazi Mustapha Kemal, President of the Turkish Republic, October 1927* (Leipzig, K. F. Koehler, 1929), p. 119.

[5] Quoted in Lewis, p. 257

Conscious of the strength of the religious feelings attached to the caliphate, Kemal in this phase of his reform-mongering limited himself to the elimination of the political elements of traditional authority. In November 1922 the Grand National Assembly abolished the sultanate, but provided for the caliphate to be continued in a member of the Ottoman ruling house chosen by the Assembly. The following summer the Republic People's Party was organized and a new national assembly elected. Shortly thereafter, in October 1923, the capital of the state was transferred from Istanbul— with its multitudinous associations with the Ottoman and, indeed, Byzantine past—to the small town of Ankara in the midst of the Anatolian heartland. A few weeks later the national assembly completed the work of political reconstruction by formally proclaiming Turkey a republic and providing for the election of a president by the assembly. Through this carefully delimited series of steps the imperial political institutions of Ottoman rule were replaced by the modern political structures of a secular republic and a nationalist party.

The political basis of the new society having been laid, Kemal then turned to the problem of religious and cultural reform. Support for these reforms would come primarily from the modernized and Western-oriented bureaucratic and intellectual elite. The principal sources of opposition would be the religious bureaucracy and, potentially, the peasants. To put through the desired social and cultural reforms, it would be necessary to insure the passivity and relative indifference of the latter. Consequently, Kemal carefully divorced this phase of his reforms from any efforts at economic development and change which might tend to stimulate peasant political consciousness and activity. In January 1924 Kemal moved to inaugurate the phase of secularization and two months later he persuaded the national assembly to abolish the caliphate and the religious ministries, to banish all members

of the Ottoman house, to close the separate religious schools and colleges and thus to unify public education, and to abolish the special religious courts which applied Islamic law. To replace the Islamic law, a commission was appointed to draw up a new code, and early in 1926 the assembly approved its recommendation for an adaptation of the Swiss civil code. New codes of commercial, maritime, and criminal law, new civil and criminal procedures, and a new judicial system were also introduced. In 1925 Kemal launched his campaign against the fez as a symbol of religious traditionalism, and its use was prohibited. Also in 1925 the old calendar was abolished and the Gregorian calendar adopted. In 1928 Islam was formally disestablished as the state religion, and in the fall of the same year the shift from Arabic to Roman script was decreed. This latter reform was of fundamental importance: it made it virtually impossible for the new generations educated in the Roman script to acquire access to the vast bulk of traditional literature; it encouraged the learning of European languages; and it greatly eased the problem of increasing literacy.

The accomplishment of these social reforms in the late 1920s prepared the way for an emphasis on economic development in the 1930s. A policy of etatism was proclaimed, and a five year plan adopted in 1934. Throughout the decade great stress was placed on industrial development, particularly in the textile, iron and steel, paper, glass, and ceramics industries. Betwen 1929 and 1938, national income increased 44 per cent, per capita income by 30 per cent, mining production by 132 per cent, and "industry made even more impressive progress."[6]

This sequence of reforms—national, political, social, and economic—reflected a conscious strategy on the part of Kemal. In April 1923 Kemal had issued a manifesto for the Republic People's Party which stressed the political reforms that he was then attempting to put through: the abolition of the sultanate,

[6] Peter F. Sugar, "Economic and Political Modernization: Turkey," in Robert E. Ward and Dankwart A. Rustow, eds., *Political Modernization in Japan and Turkey* (Princeton, Princeton University Press, 1964), p. 174; Z. Y. Hershlag, *Turkey: An Economy in Transition* (The Hague, Van Keulen, 1958), Chaps. 11, 14, 15.

popular sovereignty, representative government, fiscal and administrative reforms. Commenting on this program in 1927 after most of his social-religious reforms had been introduced, Kemal specifically articulated his strategy of attempting only one thing at a time, while maintaining a discreet veil over his long-range goals. The program of 1923, he said,

> contained essentially all that we had carried through up to that day. There were, however, some important and vital questions which had not been included in this programme, such as, for instance, the proclamation of the Republic, the abolition of the Caliphate, the suppression of the Ministry of Education, and that of the Medressas [clerical schools] and Tekkas [religious orders], and the introduction of the hat.
>
> I held the opinion that it was not appropriate to give into the hands of ignorant men and reactionaries the means of poisoning the whole nation by introducing these questions into the programme before the hour had come to do so, because I was absolutely sure that these questions would be settled at the proper time and that the people in the end would be satisfied.[7]

By dealing with each set of issues separately Kemal minimized the opposition to each set of reforms. The opponents of one reform were separated from their potential allies opposed to other reforms. "Those whom the *Gazi* would destroy," Frey accurately observes, "he would first isolate."[8]

A Fabian strategy of isolating one set of issues from another thus tends to minimize the opposition which the reformer confronts at any one time. Similar considerations lead the reformer to employ blitzkrieg tactics in handling each individual issue or set of issues. Then the problem is to enact and to implement legislation embodying a specific reform policy. Celerity and surprise—those two an-

cient principles of war—here become tactical necessities. The existing amount of power in the political system is normally fairly heavily concentrated in the hands of the reforming leader. His need is to put through his reforms before the opposition can mobilize its supporters, expand the number of participants and the amount of power in the system, and thus block the changes. "Both experience and reason," Richelieu observed, "make it evident that what is suddenly presented ordinarily astonishes in such a fashion as to deprive one of the means of opposing it, while if the execution of a plan is undertaken slowly the gradual revelation of it can create the impression that it is only being projected and will not necessarily be executed."[9]

The most successful and rapid racial desegregation in the United States, it has been observed, frequently occurred where those in power introduced abrupt, firm, and irreversible policies without much prior preparation. Such policies brought about effective changes in behavior without attempting to alter attitudes and values. Changes in the latter, however, are likely to follow changes in behavior. A more gradual approach to desegregation did not, on the other hand, increase the likelihood of its acceptance by those in the community opposed to integration. "*Opportunity and time for preparation of public for change is not necessarily related to 'effectiveness' and 'smoothness' of change.* An interval of time for change not only may be used for positive preparation, but may also be used as opportunity to mobilize overt resistance to change."[10]

Again Mustafa Kemal demonstrates the effectiveness of blitzkrieg tactics on individual issues. Typically, in introducing reform, he first held some general discussions of the problem, sounding out in a cautious way the attitudes of different groups. He next had his

[7] Kemal, p. 598.

[8] Frederick W. Frey, "Policital Development, Power and Communications," in Pye, ed., *Communications and Political Development,* pp. 314–15.

[9] Cardinal Richelieu, *Political Testament* (tr. H. B. Hill, Madison, University of Wisconsin Press, 1961), p. 75.

[10] Kenneth Clark, "Desegregation: An Appraisal of the Evidence," *Journal of Social Issues,* 9 (1953), 43; italics in original. See also Ronald Lippitt et al., *The Dynamics of Planned Change* (New York, Harcourt, Brace, 1958), pp. 58–59.

aides secretly prepare a plan for reform. This plan was shown to a few top leaders in politics and society and their support for it secured. At the politically most propitious time, Kemal would then dramatically announce the need for the reform to the party and the national assembly, unveil his plan for change, and demand its immediate approval. The legislation enacting the reform would be promptly passed by the assembly before the opposition could rally its forces and prepare a counterattack. Plans for the proclamation of the Turkish Republic, for instance, were worked out by Kemal and a few of his closest advisers during the summer of 1923. The announcement of this revolutionary idea, "wholly at odds with that of the traditional Moslem state," caused a tremendous "commotion, both in the press of Istanbul and in the lobbies of Parliament, where no serious republican movement had yet existed. Kemal realized that a debate on it might be fatal. The Republic must be forced through by other means before the Opposition had time to unite."[11] At the time, various groups wanted a continuation of traditional rule, the establishment of a constitutional monarch, with or without the Caliph as the monarch, or a multiparty parliamentary democracy. To secure approval of the Republic before these groups could combine their opposition, Kemal arranged a ministerial crisis, plunged the government into seeming anarchy for several days, and then dramatically presented the proposed constitutional change to the party caucus and the assembly, which could do little but to approve it despite the resentment and muttered opposition of many of their members.

Similar tactics were employed by Kemal in putting through his other major reforms. In January 1924, for instance, Kemal determined that the time had come to abolish the Caliphate. He invited the top leaders of the government to go on military maneuvers with him, at which time he secured their agreement to this proposal, to the abolition of the Ministry of Seriat, and to the changes in religious

education. Included in the conference were the editors of leading newspapers, who were locked up with the President for two days, during which time he persuaded them to begin to attack the government for its inaction on the caliphate issue. Hardly a month later, on March 1, Kemal presented his proposals in his opening speech to the Grand National Assembly, arguing that the changes were necessary to safeguard the republic, to unify the national system of education, and to cleanse and elevate the Islamic faith. Again the conservative and religious opposition was given little time to oppose: legislation to accomplish the Gazi's goals was approved on March 3.

Other modernizing reformers have duplicated, sometimes consciously, Kemal's tactics. In Pakistan, for instance, Ayub Khan attempted in many respects to model himself on Mustafa Kemal and, in particular, emulated this blitzkrieg pattern of reform-mongering. "When he is faced with a problem," one observer reported, "he sets up an expert commission to find a solution, and once it has reported he implements the solution rapidly."[12] Such was, for instance, the tactic employed in 1958 to put through land reform. Legislation was drafted by a commission of inquiry, and five days after the commission reported, the legislation was enacted into law.

As this discussion of Fabian strategy and blitzkrieg tactics suggests, the key question for the reformer concerns the rate and the sequence of the mobilization of new groups into politics. The reformer has to attempt to control and to guide this process, to insure that at each time and on each issue his supporters will be stronger than his opponents. Both the revolutionary and the conservative, on the other hand, operate under much less restraint in mobilizing new political participants. Revolution is itself the process of the mobilization of previously excluded groups into politics against the existing political institutions and social-economic structure. Clearly, under some circumstances the limited mobilization which is necessary for reform could lead to the run-

[11] Kinross, p. 431.

[12] Guy Wint, "The 1958 Revolution in Pakistan," *St. Anthony's Papers* (No. 8, 1960), 79.

away mobilization which is the essence of revolution. At the same time, however, mobilization could threaten the reformer from the conservative side. Since reforms involve movements toward greater social, economic, and political equality, they are necessarily opposed by the "vested interests" which benefit from the inequalities of the existing order. Surmounting these interests presents many difficulties to the reformer, but these can usually be overcome so long as the vested interests are unable to mobilize substantial apathetic groups into politics on their side. Such groups usually have little material stake in the existing order, and indeed they would often benefit materially from the proposed reforms. They do have a symbolic stake in the existing society, however, and their values and attitudes are often highly conservative and resistant to change. They may well identify with social and religious institutions whose reform would be to their advantage. It is precisely this which makes the task of the reformer so difficult. There is, as Machiavelli said,

> nothing more difficult to carry out, nor more doubtful of success, nor more dangerous to handle, than to initiate a new order for things. For the reformer has enemies in all those who profit by the old order, and only lukewarm defenders in all those who would profit by the new order, this lukewarmness arising partly from fear of their adversaries, who have the laws in their favour; and partly from the incredulity of mankind, who do not truly believe in anything new until they have had actual experience of it. Thus it arises that on every opportunity for attacking the reformer, his opponents do so with the zeal of partisans, the others only defend him half-heartedly, so that between them he runs great danger.[13]

The dialectic of change is such that the proposals for reform frequently activate previously apathetic groups who now see their important interests threatened. In some measure, the aristocratic resurgence against the rise of the middle class in the late eighteenth century was a movement of this nature. So also was the so-called "backlash" in the twentieth century from lower income white groups against the rise of the Negro in the United States. These developments tend to dichotomize politics and to undermine the position of the reformer. The combination of Fabian strategy and blitzkrieg tactics is designed to reduce this danger and lessen the likelihood that the opponents of reform will have the incentive or the capability to mobilize the masses against change. The mobilization of the masses to political action before the modernization of their values and attitudes constitutes the greatest potential obstacle to the reformer. The competitive mobilization of the masses by both revolutionary and conservative groups also tends, of course, to polarize politics and thus to reduce the support for the reformer. Whoever wins this struggle, the reformer cannot hope to benefit from it. The German communists were notoriously wrong when in 1932 they confidently predicted "Nach Hitler kommen wir"; they were not so wrong, however, in directing their attacks against the middle and thus creating a choice of "Hitler or us."

The effects of broadening political participation vary from one situation to another. In Kemalist Turkey, political activity was largely limited to urban, bureaucratic, elite groups. Within this narrow circle of politics, the modernizing elements in the army and the civil service could exercise a preponderant influence. Consequently, the interests of reform ran counter to the interests of more widespread political participation. The broadening of political participation would have brought more conservative groups into politics and turned the balance against the reformers. Eventually in the 1950s this was precisely what happened, but by then the foundations of the Kemalist state were so strong that only relatively minor movements in the direction of tradition were possible. Foreseeing this danger in the 1920s, however, Kemal did little then to expand political participation. Indeed, as Frey says: "It is the essence of the Ataturk Revolution that it *exploited* the communications bifurcation existing in Turkish society rather than lamenting it or immediately at-

---

[13] Niccolò Machiavelli, *The Prince and the Discourses* (New York, The Modern Library, 1940), pp. 21–22.

tacking it, as a number of other nationalist movements have done. . . . The lack of communications between elite and mass was a vital factor which he used to simplify his task and equate it with his resources."[14] A tension existed in Turkey between the achievement of social and economic equality, on the one hand, and the achievement of political equality, on the other. Progress toward the former depended upon the limitation of the latter, and it was precisely this function which was performed by the one-party political system that existed in Turkey through World War II. The shift to a competitive party system after World War II, in turn, expanded political participation, made politics more democratic, but also slowed down and in some areas even reversed the process of social-economic reform.

The situation confronting reformers in many Latin American countries was just the opposite of that which faced Kemal. In these countries, politics was "right side up," and the political arena was dominated by conservative and oligarchical groups. Consequently, social-economic reform was associated with the broadening of political participation rather than with its limitation. This cumulation of issues and cleavages made politics in Latin America more intense and violent than it was in Turkey and made social revolution seem a much more imminent potentiality. In Turkey the reformer could create political institutions and promote social-economic change without broadening political participation. In Latin America, however, the broadening of political participation was not a brake on social change but a prerequisite to such change. Consequently, in Latin America the conservative seemed more reactionary because he opposed both, while the reformer seemed more revolutionary (and threatening to the conservative) because he had to support both.

In no society do significant social, economic, or political reforms take place without violence or the imminent likelihood of violence. Relatively decentralized and spontaneous violence is a common means through which disadvantaged groups call attention to their grievances and their demands for reform. The active participants in such violence are usually far removed from the centers of power, but the fact of such violence may be effectively used by reformers to push through measures which might otherwise be impossible. Such violence, indeed, may well be encouraged by leaders who are completely committed to working within the existing system and who view the violence as a required stimulus for reforms within that system. The history of reform in the United States—from the Jeffersonians down through abolitionists, populists, the labor movement, and the civil rights movement—is studded with instances of violence and other forms of disorder which helped to trigger changes in governmental policy. In England in the early 1830s riots and other violence played a significant role in consolidating Whig support for the Reform Act of 1832. In India in the 1950s middle-class groups typically employed demonstrations, riots, *satyagraphas*, and other forms of mass protest (usually accompanied by violence) to wrest concessions from the government.[15]

In modernizing countries generally, perhaps the most significant form of illegal and often violent activity for promoting reform is the land invasion. For many reasons discussed below, land reform is of crucial importance to the maintenance of political stability. The achievement of such reform, however, frequently requires the disruption of stability. In Colombia in the late 1920s and early 1930s, for instance, peasants began to occupy private lands. Some haciendas were seized in toto and turned into cooperatives run with the help of communist functionaries. The landowners insisted upon the police and the army acting to restore their property rights. The government,

---

[14] Frey, pp. 313–14 (italics his).

[15] Joseph Hamburger, *James Mill and the Art of Revolution* (New Haven, Yale University Press, 1963), pp 277–78; Myron Weiner, *The Politics of Scarcity*, Chap. 8. On the role of violence in reform in general, see Hirschman, pp. 256–60, and H. L. Nieburg, "The Threat of Violence and Social Change," *American Political Science Review, 56* (Dec. 1962), 865–73.

however, refused to become actively engaged on either side of these local struggles, and instead capitalized on the rural violence to force through parliament—which like most parliaments in modernizing countries was dominated by landlords—a land reform law which legalized the invasions and in effect made property rights dependent upon effective working of the property. Somewhat similarly, in Peru the land invasions which occurred in 1963 at the time of the election of the Belaunde government furnished the trigger necessary to rally support for the reform measures promoted by that government. In both these cases, however, the decentralized violence coincided with the presence in power of a sympathetic and reform-minded administration, just as did the civil rights violence in the mid-1960s in the United States. In most societies, civic peace is impossible without some reform, and reform is impossible without some violence.

The effectiveness of violence in promoting reform stems directly from the extent to which it appears to herald the mobilization into politics of new groups employing new political techniques. In addition, the effectiveness of violence depends upon the existence of feasible policy alternatives, the implementation of which are likely to reduce the disorder. If the violence appears to be a purely anomic response to a general situation and to have diffuse or uncertain targets, it will do little to promote reform. For the latter, both reformers and conservatives must perceive the violence as directly related to action on a particular policy issue. The violence, then, shifts the debate from the merits of the reform to the need for public order. The case for reform, indeed, is never stronger than when it is couched in terms of the need to preserve domestic peace. Its effect then is to swing to the side of reform conservatives interested in the maintenance of order. Since the early days of Vargas in the 1930s, Brazilian elites have often quoted the phrase: "We must make the revolution before the people do." Following the Birmingham riots in 1963, President Kennedy, in somewhat

similar fashion, declared that passage of his civil rights bill was necessary "to get the struggle off the streets and into the courts." Failure to pass the bill, Kennedy warned, would lead to "continued, if not increased, racial strife—causing the leadership on both sides to pass from the hands of reasonable and responsible men to the purveyors of hate and violence." Underscored by the racial violence and disorder which did exist, predictions like this caused even conservative Republicans and Democrats to support civil rights legislation.

The effectiveness of violence and disorder in stimulating reform, however, does not lie in its inherent character. It is not violence per se but rather the shock and the novelty involved in the employment of an unfamiliar or unusual political technique that serves to promote reform. It is the demonstrated willingness of a social group to go beyond the accepted patterns of action which gives impetus to its demands. In effect, such action involves the diversification of political techniques and a threat to existing political organization and procedures. Riots and violence, for instance, were familiar phenomena in England in the early nineteenth century. The scope and intensity of the violence in 1831, however, were new. Commenting on riots at Nottingham and Derby, Melbourne observed that, "such violence and outrage are I believe quite new and unprecedented in this Country; at least I never remember to have heard of Country homes being attacked, plundered, and set on fire in any former times of political ferment."[16] It was the seemingly unprecedented nature of the violence which drove Melbourne to reform. So also in the United States the sit-down strikes of the 1930s and the sit-ins of the 1960s were new tactics whose novelty underwrote the seriousness of the demands of labor and the Negroes. In South Vietnam in 1963 riots and demonstrations were familiar occurrences. The self-immolation of the Buddhist monks, however, represented a dramatic escalation in the level of domestic violence which undoubtedly played a significant role in leading American officials and Vietnamese officers

16 Quoted in Hamburger, p. 278.

to decide on the need for a change in regime.

That it is the novelty of the technique rather than its inherent character which stimulates reform is demonstrated by the fact that repeated use of the technique depreciates its value. In 1963 racial riots in the United States and monkish self-immolations in Vietnam helped to produce significant changes in governmental policy and political leadership. Three years later similar events failed to produce similar consequences. What had once seemed a shocking departure from the political norm now seemed a relatively conventional political tactic. In many praetorian political systems, of course, violence becomes an endemic form of political action and consequently completely loses its capacity to generate significant change. In addition, in non-praetorian systems novel or unusual forms of protest may well be incorporated into the recognized bounds of legitimate political action. As Arthur Waskow has perceptively observed:

To the degree that the politics of disorder is aimed at bringing about change, it is generally invented by people who are "outside" a particular system of political order, and want to bring change about so that they can enter. In doing so, they tend to use new techniques that make sense to themselves out of their own experience, but that look disorderly to people who are thinking and acting inside the system. The Negroes were by no means the first to initiate this process. For example, in the seventeenth and eighteenth centuries, urban lawyers and merchants who could not get the entrenched politicians to pay attention to their grievances (and who were scarcely represented in Parliament) used the illegal and disorderly device of political pamphleteering against the established order. In the same way, nineteenth-century workers who could not get their employers or the elected legislators to pay attention to their demands used unionization and the strike—which at first were illegal—to call attention to their grievances. In both these cases, using the politics of disorder not only

got the users accepted into the political order and got their immediate grievances looked after, but also got the new techniques accepted into the array of authorized and approved political methods. In short, the system of "order" was itself changed. Thus the "criminal libel" of political pamphleteering was enshrined as freedom of the press, and the "criminal conspiracy" of striking was enshrined in the system of free labor unions. One century's disorder became the next century's liberty under ordered law.[17]

One test of the adaptablity of a political system, indeed, may well be its ability to assimilate, to moderate, and to legitimate new techniques of political action employed by groups making new demands upon the system.

The effectiveness of violence or any other novel technique in promoting reform may also decline with its success in stimulating such reforms. If disorder and violence by a group lead the government to make concessions, the propensity of the group to resort to disorder and violence may well increase. The repeated use of the same tactics reduces their impact. At the same time, the willingness of the government to make further concessions presumably decreases. On the one hand, the government undoubtedly argued earlier that its reforms would reduce violence rather than intensify it, and it can understandably be expected to react angrily when this does not turn out to be the case. In addition, the fact that it has made the concessions which it thought desirable and necessary means that the new violence for additional concessions is, in its view, of decreasing legitimacy since it is support of "irresponsible" rather than "reasonable" demands. Consequently, the situation polarizes, with the government feeling that it "must draw the line" against groups "which have gone too far," and the groups feeling that the government has "sold them short" and has "no interest in fundamental change." It is at this point that the impact of reform on the prospects for revolution becomes of decisive significance.

[17] Arthur I. Waskow, *From Race Riot to Sit-In, 1919 and the 1960s* (Garden City, N.Y., Doubleday, 1966), pp. 278–79.

21. Protest as a Political Resource[a]

Michael Lipsky[*]

The frequent resort to protest activity by relatively powerless groups in recent American politics suggests that protest represents an important aspect of minority group and low income group politics.[1] At the same time that Negro civil rights strategists have recognized the problem of using protest as a meaningful political instrument,[2] groups associated with the "war on poverty" have increasingly received publicity for protest activity. Saul Alinsky's Industrial Areas Foundation, for example, continues to receive invitations to help organize low income communities because of its ability to mobilize poor people around the tactic of protest.[3] The riots which dominated urban affairs in the summer of 1967 appear not to have diminished the dependence of some groups on protest as a mode of political activity.

This article provides a theoretical perspec-

[1] "Relatively powerless groups may be defined as those groups which, relatively speaking, are lacking in conventional political resources. For the purposes of community studies, Robert Dahl has compiled a useful comprehensive list. See Dahl, "The Analysis of Influence in Local Communities," *Social Science and Community Action*, Charles R. Adrian, ed. (East Lansing, Michigan, 1960), p. 32. The difficulty in studying such groups is that relative powerlessness only becomes apparent under certain conditions. Extremely powerless groups not only lack political resources, but are also characterized by a minimal sense of political efficacy, upon which in part successful political organization depends. For reviews of the literature linking orientations of political efficacy to socioeconomic status, see Robert Lane, *Political Life* (New York, 1959), ch. 16; and Lester Milbrath, *Political Participation* (Chicago, 1965), ch. 5. Further, to the extent that group cohesion is recognized as a necessary requisite for organized political action, then extremely powerless groups, lacking cohesion, will not even appear for observation. Hence the necessity of selecting for intensive study a protest movement where there can be some confidence that observable processes and results can be analyzed. Thus, if one conceives of a continuum on which political groups are placed according to their relative command of resources, the focus of this essay is on those groups which are near, but not at, the pole of powerlessness.

[2] See, e.g., Bayard Rustin, "From Protest to Politics: The Future of the Civil Rights Movement," *Commentary* (February, 1965), 25–31; and Stokely Carmichael, "Toward Black Liberation," *The Massachusetts Review* (Autumn, 1966.)

[3] On Alinsky's philosophy of community organization, see his *Reveille for Radicals* (Chicago 1945); and Charles Silberman, *Crisis in Black and White* (New York, 1964), ch. 10.

Reprinted from Michael Lipsky, "Protest as a Political Resource," *American Political Science Review*, Vol. LXII, No. 4, (December 1968), pp. 1144–1158.

[a] This article is an attempt to develop and explore the implications of a conceptual scheme for analyzing protest activity. It is based upon my studies of protest organizations in New York City, Washington, D.C., Chicago, San Francisco, and Mississippi, as well as extensive examination of written accounts of protest among low-income and Negro civil rights groups. I am grateful to Kenneth Dolbeare, Murray Edelman, and Rodney Stiefbold for their insightful comments on an earlier draft. This paper was developed while the author was a Staff Associate of the Institute for Research on Poverty at the University of Wisconsin. I appreciate the assistance obtained during various phases of my research from the Rabinowitz Foundation, the New York State Legislative Internship Program, and the Brookings Institution.

[*] Associate Professor of Political Science, Massachusetts Institute of Technology.

tive on protest activity as a political resource. The discussion is concentrated on the limitations inherent in protest which occur because of the need of protest leaders to appeal to four constituencies at the same time. As the concept of protest is developed here, it will be argued that protest leaders must nurture and sustain an organization comprised of people with whom they may or may not share common values. They must articulate goals and choose strategies so as to maximize their public exposure through communications media. They must maximize the impact of third parties in the political conflict. Finally, they must try to maximize chances of success among those capable of granting goals. The tensions inherent in manipulating these four constituencies at the same time form the basis of this discusion of protest as a political process. It is intended to place aspects of the civil rights movement in a framework which suggests links between protest organizations and the general political processes in which such organizations operate.

I. "Protest" Conceptualized

Protest activity as it has been adopted by elements of the civil rights movement and others has not been studied extensively by so-cial scientists. Some of the most suggestive writings have been done as case studies of protest movements in single southern cities.[4] These works generally lack a framework or theoretical focus which would encourage generalization from the cases. More systematic efforts have been attempted in approaching the dynamics of biracial committees in the South,[5] and comprehensively assessing the efficacy of Negro political involvement in Durham, N.C., and Philadelphia, Pa.[6] In their excellent assessment of Negro politics in the South, Matthews and Prothro have presented a thorough profile of Southern Negro students and their participation in civil rights activities.[7] Protest is also discussed in passing in recent explorations of the social-psychological dimensions of Negro ghetto politics[8] and the still highly suggestive, although pre-1960's, work on Negro political leadership by James Q. Wilson.[9] These and other less systematic works on contemporary Negro politics,[10] for all of their intuitive insights and valuable documentation, offer no theoretical formulations which encourage conceptualization about the interaction between recent Negro political activity and the political process.

Heretofore the best attempt to place Negro protest activity in a framework which would generate additional insights has been that of

[4] See, e.g., Jack L. Walker, "Protest and Negotiation: A Case Study of Negro Leadership in Atlanta, Georgia," *Midwest Journal of Political Science*, 7 (May, 1963), 99–124; Jack L. Walker, *Sit-Ins in Atlanta: A Study in the Negro Protest*, Eagleton Institute Case Studies, No. 34 (New York, 1964); John Ehle, *The Free Men* (New York, 1965) [Chapel Hill]; Daniel C. Thompson, *The Negro Leadership Class* (Englewood Cliffs, N.J., 1963) [New Orleans]; M. Elaine Burgess, *Negro Leadership in a Southern City* (Chapel Hill, N.C., 1962) [Durham].

[5] Lewis Killian and Charles Grigg, *Racial Crisis in America: Leadership in Conflict* (Englewood Cliffs, N.J., 1964).

[6] William Keech, "The Negro Vote as a Political Resource: The Case of Durham," (unpublished Ph.D. Dissertation, University of Wisconsin, 1966); John H. Strange, "The Negro in Philadelphia Politics 1963–65," (unpublished Ph.D. Dissertation, Princeton University, 1966).

[7] Donald Matthews and James Prothro, *Negroes and the New Southern Politics* (New York, 1966). Considerable insight on these data is provided in John Orbell, "Protest Participation among Southern Negro College Students," *American Political Science Review*, 61 (June, 1967), 446–456.

[8] Kenneth Clark, *Dark Ghetto* (New York, 1965).

[9] *Negro Politics* (New York, 1960).

[10] A complete list would be voluminous. See, e.g., Nat Hentoff, *The New Equality* (New York, 1964); Arthur Waskow, *From Race Riot to Sit-in* (New York, 1966).

James Q. Wilson.[11] Wilson has suggested that protest activity be conceived as a problem of bargaining in which the basic problem is that Negro groups lack political resources to exchange. Wilson called this "the problem of the powerless."[12]

While many of Wilson's insights remain valid, his approach is limited in applicability because it defines protest in terms of mass action or response and as utilizing exclusively negative inducements in the bargaining process. Negative inducements are defined as inducements which are not absolutely preferred but are preferred over alternative possibilities.[13] Yet it might be argued that protest designed to appeal to groups which oppose suffering and exploitation, for example, might be offering positive inducements in bargaining. A few Negro students sitting at a lunch counter might be engaged in what would be called protest, and by their actions might be trying to appeal to other groups in the system with positive inducements. Additionally, Wilson's concentration on Negro civic action, and his exclusive interest in exploring the protest process to explain Negro civic action, tend to obscure comparison with protest activity which does not necessarily arise within the Negro community.

Assuming a somewhat different focus, protest activity is defined as a mode of political action oriented toward objection to one or more policies or conditions characterized by showmanship or display of an unconventional nature, and undertaken to obtain rewards from political or economic systems while working within the systems. The "problem of the powerless" in protest activity is to activate "third parties" to enter the implicit or explicit bargaining arena in ways favorable to the protesters. This is one of the few ways in which they can "create" bargaining resources. It is intuitively unconvincing to suggest that fifteen people sitting uninvited in the Mayor's office have the power to move City Hall. A better formulation would suggest that the people sitting in may be able to appeal to a wider public to which the city administration is sensitive. Thus in successful protest activity the *reference publics* of protest *targets* may be conceived as explicitly or implicitly reacting to protest in such a way that target groups or individuals respond in ways favorable to the protesters.[14]

It should be emphasized that the focus here is on protest by relatively powerless groups. Illustrations can be summoned, for example, of activity designated as "protest" involving high status pressure groups or hundreds of thousands of people. While such instances may share some of the characteristics of protest activity, they may not represent examples of developing political resources by relatively powerless groups because the protesting groups may already command political resources by virtue of status, numbers or cohesion.

It is appropriate also to distinguish between the relatively restricted use of the concept of protest adopted here and closely related political strategies which are often designated as "protest" in popular usage. Where groups al-

[11] "The Strategy of Protest: Problems of Negro Civic Action," *Journal of Conflict Resolution*, 3 (September, 1961), 291–303. The reader will recognize the author's debt to this highly suggestive article, not least Wilson's recognition of the utility of the bargaining framework for examining protest activity.

[12] *Ibid.*, p. 291.

[13] *Ibid.*, p. 291–292.

[14] See E. E. Schattschneider's discussion of expanding the scope of the conflict, *The Semisovereign People* (New York, 1960). Another way in which bargaining resources may be "created" is to increase the relative cohesion of groups, or to increase the perception of group solidarity as a precondition to greater cohesion. This appears to be the primary goal of political activity which is generally designated "community organization." Negro activists appear to recognize the utility of this strategy in their advocacy of "black power." In some instances protest activity may be designed in part to accomplish this goal in addition to activating reference publics.

ready possess sufficient resources with which to bargain, as in the case of some economic boycotts and labor strikes, they may be said to engage in "direct confrontation."[15] Similarly, protest which represents efforts to "activate reference publics" should be distinguished from "alliance formation," where third parties are induced to join the conflict, but where the value orientations of third parties are sufficiently similar to those of the protesting group that concerted or coordinated action is possible. Alliance formation is particularly desirable for relatively powerless groups if they seek to join the decision-making process as participants.

The distinction between activating reference publics and alliance formation is made on the assumption that where goal orientations among protest groups and the reference publics of target groups are similar, the political dynamics of petitioning target groups are different than when such goal orientations are relatively divergent. Clearly the more similar the goal orientations, the greater the likelihood of protest success, other things being equal. This discussion is intended to highlight, however, those instances where goal orientations of reference publics depart significantly, in direction or intensity, from the goals of protest groups.

Say that to protest some situation, A would like to enter a bargaining situation with B. But A has nothing B wants, and thus cannot bargain. A then attempts to create political resources by activating other groups to enter the conflict. A then organizes to take action against B with respect to certain goals. *Information concerning these goals must be conveyed through communications media (C, D, and E) to F, G, and H, which are B's reference publics.* In response to the reactions of F, G, and H, or in anticipation of their reactions, B responds, *in some way*, to the protesters' demands. This formulation requires the conceptualization of protest activity when un-

dertaken to create bargaining resources as a political process which requires communication and is characterized by a multiplicity of constituencies for protest leadership.

A schematic representation of the process of protest as utilized by relatively powerless groups is presented in Figure 21.1. In contrast to a simplistic pressure group model which would posit a direct relationship between pressure group and pressured, the following discussion is guided by the assumption (derived from observation) that protest is a highly indirect process in which communications media and the reference publics of protest targets play critical roles. It is also a process characterized by reciprocal relations, in which protest leaders frame strategies according to their perception of the needs of (many) other actors.

In this view protest constituents limit the options of protest leaders at the same time that the protest leader influences their perception of the strategies and rhetoric which they will support. Protest activity is filtered through the comunications media in influencing the perceptions of the reference publics of protest targets. To the extent that the influence of reference publics is supportive of protest goals, target groups will dispense symbolic or material rewards. Material rewards are communicated directly to protest constituents. Symbolic rewards are communicated in part to protest constituents, but primarily are communicated to the reference publics of target groups, who provide the major stimuli for public policy pronouncements.

The study of protest as adopted by relatively powerless groups should provide insights into the structure and behavior of groups involved in civil rights politics and associated with the "war on poverty." It should direct attention toward the ways in which administrative agencies respond to "crises." Additionally, the study of protest as a political resource should influence some general con-

---

[15] For an example of "direct confrontation," one might study the three-month Negro boycott of white merchants in Natchez, Miss., which resulted in capitulation to boycott demands by city government leaders. See *The New York Times*, December 4, 1965, p. 1.

Figure 21.1. Schematic Representation of the Process of Protest by Relatively Powerless Groups.

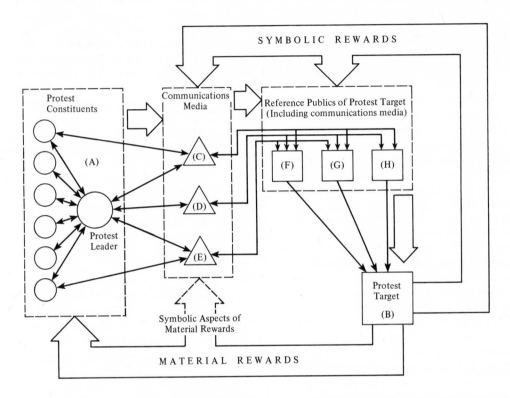

ceptualizations of American political pluralism. Robert Dahl, for example, describes the "normal American political process" as

> one in which there is a high probability that an active and legitimate group in the population can make itself heard effectively at some crucial stage in the process of decision.[16]

Although he agrees that control over decisions is unevenly divided in the population, Dahl writes:

> When I say that a group is heard "effectively," I mean more than the simple fact that it makes a noise; I mean that one or more officials are not only ready to listen to the noise, but expect to suffer in some significant way if they do not placate the group, its leaders, or its

most vociferous members. To satisfy the group may require one or more of a great variety of actions by the responsive leader: pressure for substantive policies, appointments, graft, respect, expression of the appropriate emotions, or the right combination of reciprocal noises.[17]

These statements, which in some ways resemble David Truman's discussion of the power of "potential groups,"[18] can be illuminated by the study of protest activity in three ways. First, what are the probabilities that relatively powerless groups can make themselves heard effectively? In what ways will such groups be heard or "steadily appeased"?[19] Concentration on the process of protest activity may reveal the extent to which, and the conditions under which, relatively powerless

---

[16] *A Preface to Democratic Theory* (Chicago, 1956), pp. 145–146.
[17] *Ibid.*
[18] *The Governmental Process* (New York, 1951), p. 104.
[19] See Dahl, *A Preface to Democratic Theory*, p. 146.

groups are likely to prove effective. Protest undertaken to obstruct policy decisions, for example, may enjoy greater success probabilities than protest undertaken in an effort to evoke constructive policy innovations.[20]

Second, does it make sense to suggest that all groups which make noises will receive responses from public officials? Perhaps the groups which make noises do not have to be satisfied at all, but it is other groups which receive assurances or recognition. Third, what are the probabilities that groups which make noises will receive tangible rewards, rather than symbolic assurances?[21] Dahl lumps these rewards together in the same paragraph, but dispensation of tangible rewards clearly has a different impact upon groups than the dispensation of symbolic rewards. Dahl is undoubtedly correct when he suggests that the relative fluidity of American politics is a critical characteristic of the American political system.[22] But he is less precise and less convincing when it comes to analyzing the extent to which the system is indeed responsive to the relatively powerless groups of the "average citizen."[23]

The following sections are an attempt to demonstrate the utility of the conceptualization of the protest process presented above. This will be done by exploring the problems encountered and the strains generated by protest leaders in interacting with four constituencies. It will be useful to concentrate attention on the maintenance and enhancement needs not only of the large formal organizations which dominate city politics,[24] but also of the ad hoc protest groups which engage them in civic controversy. It will also prove rewarding to examine the role requirements of individuals in leadership positions as they perceive the problems of constituency manipulation. In concluding remarks some implications of the study of protest for the pluralist description of American politics will be suggested.[25]

II. Protest Leadership and Organizational Base

The organizational maintenance needs of relatively powerless, low income, ad hoc protest groups center around the tension generated by the need for leadership to offer symbolic and intangible inducements to protest

[20] Observations that all groups can influence public policy at some stage of the political process are frequently made about the role of "veto groups" in American politics. See *Ibid.*, pp. 104 ff. See also David Reisman, *The Lonely Crowd* (New Haven, 1950), pp. 211 ff., for an earlier discussion of veto-group politics. Yet protest should be evaluated when it is adopted to obtain assertive as well as defensive goals.

[21] See Murray Edelman, *The Symbolic Uses of Politics* (Urbana, Ill., 1964), ch. 2.

[22] See Dahl, *Who Governs?* (New Haven, 1961), pp. 305 ff.

[23] In a recent formulation, Dahl reiterates the theme of wide dispersion of influence. "More than other systems, [democracies] . . . try to disperse influence widely to their citizens by means of the suffrage, elections, freedom of speech, press, and assembly, the right of opponents to criticize the conduct of government, the right to organize political parties, and in other ways." *Pluralist Democracy in the United States* (Chicago, 1967), p. 373. Here, however, he concentrates more on the availability of options to all groups in the system, rather than on the relative probabilities that all groups in fact have access to the political process. See pp. 372 ff.

[24] See Edward Banfield, *Political Influence* (New York, 1961), p. 263. The analysis of organizational incentive structure which heavily influences Banfield's formulation is Chester Barnard, *The Functions of the Executive* (Cambridge, Mass., 1938).

[25] In the following attempt to develop the implications of this conceptualization of protest activity, I have drawn upon extensive field observation and bibliographical research. Undoubtedly, however, individual assertions, while representing my best judgment concerning the available evidence, in the future may require modification as the result of further empirical research.

participation when immediate, material rewards cannot be anticipated, and the need to provide at least the promise of material rewards. Protest leaders must try to evoke responses from other actors in the political process, at the same time that they pay attention to participant organizational needs. Thus relatively deprived groups in the political system not only receive symbolic reassurance while material rewards from the system are withheld,[26] but protest leaders have a stake in perpetuating the notion that relatively powerless groups retain political efficacy despite what in many cases is obvious evidence to the contrary.

The tension embraced by protest leaders over the nature of inducements toward protest participation accounts in part for the style adopted and goals selected by protest leaders. Groups which seek psychological gratification from politics, but cannot or do not anticipate material political rewards, may be attracted to militant protest leaders. To these groups, angry rhetoric may prove a desirable quality in the short run. Where groups depend upon the political system for tangible benefits, or where participation in the system provides intangibe benefits, moderate leadership is likely to prevail. Wilson has observed similar tendencies among Negro leaders of large, formal organizations.[27] It is no less true for leadership of protest groups. Groups whose members derive tangible satisfactions from political participation will not condone leaders who are stubborn in compromise or appear to question the foundations of the system. This coincides with Truman's observation:

> Violation of the "rules of the game" normally will weaken a group's cohesion, reduce its status in the community, and expose it to the claims of other groups.[28]

On the other hand, the cohesion of relatively powerless groups may be strengthened by militant, ideological leadership which questions the rules of the game and challenges their legitimacy.

Cohesion is particularly important when protest leaders bargain directly with target groups. In that situation, leaders' ability to control protest constituents and guarantee their behavior represents a bargaining strength.[29] For this reason Wilson stressed the bargaining difficulties of Negro leaders who cannot guarantee constituent behavior, and pointed out the significance of the strategy of projecting the image of group solidarity when the reality of cohesion is a fiction.[30] Cohesion is less significant at other times. Divided leadership may prove productive by bargaining in tandem,[31] or by minimizing strain among groups in the protest process. Further, community divisions may prove less detrimental to protest aims when strong third parties have entered the dispute originally generated by protest organizations.

The intangible rewards of assuming certain postures toward the political system may not be sufficient to sustain an organizational base. It may be necessary to renew constantly the intangible rewards of participation. And to the extent that people participate in order to achieve tangible benefits, their interest in a protest organization may depend upon the organization's relative material success. Protest leaders may have to tailor their style to present participants with tangible successes, or with the appearance of success. Leaders may have to define the issues with concern for

---

[26] As Edelman suggests, cited previously.

[27] *Negro Politics*, p. 290.

[28] *The Governmental Process*, p. 513.

[29] But cf. Thomas Schelling's discussion of "binding oneself," *The Strategy of Conflict* (Cambridge, Mass., 1960), pp. 22 ff.

[30] "The Strategy of Protest," p. 297.

[31] This is suggested by Wilson, "The Strategy of Protest," p. 298; St. Clair Drake and Horace Cayton, *Black Metropolis* (New York, 1962, rev. ed.), p. 731; Walker, "Protest and Negotiation," p. 122. Authors who argue that divided leadership is dysfunctional have been Clark, p. 156; and Tilman Cothran, "The Negro Protest Against Segregation in the South," *The Annals*, 357 (January, 1965), p. 72.

increasing their ability to sustain organizations. The potential for protest among protest group members may have to be manipulated by leadership if the group is to be sustained.[32]

The participants in protest organizations limit the flexibility of protest leadership. This obtains for two reasons. They restrict public actions by leaders who must continue to solicit active participant support, and they place restraints on the kinds of activities which can be considered appropriate for protest purposes. Poor participants cannot commonly be asked to engage in protest requiring air transportation. Participants may have anxieties related to their environment or historical situation which discourages engagement in some activities. They may be afraid of job losses, beatings by the police, or summary evictions. Negro protest in the Deep South has been inhibited by realistic expectations of retribution.[33] Protests over slum housing conditions are undermined by tenants who expect landlord retaliation for engaging in tenant organizing activity.[34] Political or ethical mores may conflict with a proposed course of action, diminishing participation.[35]

On the other hand, to the extent that fears are real, or that the larger community perceives protest participants as subject to these fears, protest may actually be strengthened. Communications media and potential allies will consider more soberly the complaints of people who are understood to be placing themselves in jeopardy. When young children and their parents made the arduous bus trip from Mississippi to Washington, D.C., to protest the jeopardizing of Head Start funds, the courage and expense represented by their effort created a respect and visibility for their position which might not have been achieved by local protest efforts.[36]

Protest activity may be undertaken by organizations with established relationship patterns, behavior norms, and role expectations. These organizations are likely to have greater access to other groups in the political system, and a demonstrated capacity to maintain themselves. Other protest groups, however, may be ad hoc arrangements without demonstrated internal or external relationship patterns. These groups will have different organizational problems, in response to which it is necessary to engage in different kinds of protest activity.

---

[32] This observation is confirmed by a student of the Southern civil rights movement: "Negroes demand of protest leaders constant progress. The combination of long-standing discontent and a new-found belief in the possibility of change produces a constant state of tension and aggressiveness in the Negro community. But this discontent is vague and diffuse, not specific; the masses do not define the issues around which action shall revolve. This the leader must do." Lewis Killian, "Leadership in the Desegregation Crises: An Institutional Analysis," in Muzafer Sherif (ed.), *Intergroup Relations and Leadership* (New York; 1962), p. 159.

[33] Significantly, Southern-Negro students who actively participated in the early phases of the sit-in movement "tended to be unusually optimistic about race relations and tolerant of whites [when compared with inactive Negro students]. They not only *were* better off, objectively speaking, than other Negroes but *felt* better off." Matthews and Prothro, *op. cit.,* p. 424.

[34] This is particularly the case in cities such as Washington, D.C., where landlord-tenant laws offer little protection against retaliatory eviction. See, e.g., Robert Schoshiuski, "Remedies of the Indigent Tenant: Proposal for Change," *Georgetown Law Journal,* 54 (Winter, 1966), 541 ff.

[35] Wilson regarded this as a chief reason for lack of protest activity in 1961. He wrote: ". . . some of the goals now being sought by Negroes are least applicable to those groups of Negroes most suited to protest action. Protest action involving such tactics as mass meetings, picketing, boycotts, and strikes rarely find enthusiastic participants among upper-income and higher status individuals": "The Strategy of Protest," p. 296.

[36] See *The New York Times,* February 12, 1966, p. 56.

The scarcity of organizational resources also places limits upon the ability of relatively powerless groups to maintain the foundations upon which protest organizations develop. Relatively powerless groups, to engage in political activity of any kind, must command at least some resources. This is not tautological. Referring again to a continuum on which political groups are placed according to their relative command of resources, one may draw a line somewhere along the continuum representing a "threshold of civic group political participation." Clearly some groups along the continuum will possess some political resources (enough, say, to emerge for inspection) but not enough to exercise influence in civic affairs. Relatively powerless groups, to be influential, must cross the "threshold" to engage in politics. Although the availability of group resources is a critical consideration at all stages of the protest process, it is particularly important in explaining why some groups seem to "surface" with sufficient strength to command attention. The following discussion of some critical organizational resources should illuminate this point.

Skilled professionals frequently must be available to protest organizations. Lawyers, for example, play extremely important roles in enabling protest groups to utilize the judicial process and avail themselves of adequate preparation of court cases. Organizational reputation may depend upon a combination of ability to threaten the conventional political system and of exercising statutory rights in court. Availability of lawyers depends upon ability to pay fees and/or the attractiveness to lawyers of participation in protest group activity. Volunteer professional assistance may not prove adequate. One night a week volunteered by an aspiring politician in a housing clinic cannot satisfy the needs of a chaotic political movement.[37] The need for skilled professionals is not restricted to lawyers. For ex-

ample, a group seeking to protest an urban renewal policy might require the services of architects and city planners in order to present a viable alternative to a city proposal.

Financial resources not only purchase legal assistance, but enable relatively powerless groups to conduct minimum programs of political activities. To the extent that constituents are unable or unwilling to pay even small membership dues, then financing the cost of mimeographing flyers, purchasing supplies, maintaining telephone service, paying rent, and meeting a modest payroll become major organizational problems. And to the extent that group finances are supplied by outside individual contributions or government or foundation grants, the long-term options of the group are sharply constrained by the necessity of orienting group goals and tactics to anticipate the potential objections of financial supporters.

Some dependence upon even minimal financial resources can be waived if organizations evoke passionate support from constituents. Secretarial help and block organizers will come forward to work without compensation if they support the cause of neighborhood organizations or gain intangible benefits based upon association with the group. Protest organizations may also depend upon skilled nonprofessionals, such as college students, whose access to people and political and economic institutions often assist protest groups in cutting across income lines to seek support. Experience with ad hoc political groups, however, suggests that this assistance is sporadic and undependable. Transient assistance is particularly typical of skilled, educated, and employable volunteers whose abilities can be applied widely. The die-hards of ad hoc political groups are often those people who have no place else to go, nothing else to do.

Constituent support will be affected by the nature of the protest target and whether pro-

---

[37] On housing clinic services provided by political clubs, see James Q. Wilson, *The Amateur Democrat: Club Politics in Three Cities* (Chicago, 1962), pp. 63–64, 176. On the need for lawyers among low income people, see e.g., *The Extension of Legal Services to the Poor*, Conference Proceedings (Washington, D.C., n.d.), esp. pp. 51–60; and "Neighborhood Law Offices: The New Wave in Legal Services for the Poor," *Harvard Law Review*, 80 (February, 1967), 805–850.

test activity is directed toward defensive or assertive goals. Obstructing specific public policies may be easier than successfully recommending constructive policy changes. Orientations toward defensive goals may require less constituent energy, and less command over resources of money, expertise and status.[38]

III. Protest Leadership and Communications Media

The communications media are extremely powerful in city politics. In granting or withholding publicity, in determining what information most people will have on most issues, and what alternatives they will consider in response to issues, the media truly, as Norton Long has put it, "set . . . the civic agenda."[39] To the extent that successful protest activity depends upon appealing to, and/or threatening, other groups in the community, the communications media set the limits of protest action. If protest tactics are not considered significant by the media, or if newspapers and television reporters or editors decide to overlook protest tactics, protest organizations will not succeed. Like the tree falling unheard in the forest, there is no protest unless protest is perceived and projected.

A number of writers have noticed that the success of protest activity seems directly related to the amount of publicity it receives outside the immediate arena in which protest takes place. This view has not been stated systematically, but hints can be found in many sources. In the literature on civil rights politics, the relevance of publicity represents one of the few hypotheses available concerning the dynamics of successful protest activity.[40]

When protest tactics do receive coverage in the communications media, the way in which they are presented will influence all other actors in the system, including the protesters themselves. Conformity to standards of newsworthiness in political style, and knowledge of the prejudices and desires of the individuals who determine media coverage in political skills, represent crucial determinants of leadership effectiveness.

The organizational behavior of newspapers can partly be understood by examining the maintenance and enhancement needs which direct them toward projects of civic betterment and impressions of accomplishment.[41] But insight may also be gained by analyzing the role requirements of reporters, editors, and others who determine newspaper policy. Reporters, for example, are frequently motivated by the desire to contribute to civic affairs by their "objective" reporting of significant events; by the premium they place on accuracy; and by the credit which they receive for sensationalism and "scoops."

These requirements may be difficult to accommodate at the same time. Reporters demand newsworthiness of their subjects in the short run, but also require reliability and verifiability in the longer run. Factual accuracy may dampen newsworthiness. Sensationalism, attractive to some newspaper editors, may be inconsistent with reliable, verifiable narration of events. Newspapers at first may be attracted to sensationalism, and later demand

---

[38] An illustration of low income group protest organization mobilized for veto purposes is provided by Dahl in "The Case of the Metal Houses." See *Who Governs?*, pp. 192 ff.

[39] Norton Long, "The Local Community as an Ecology of Games," in Long, *The Polity*, Charles Press, ed. (Chicago, 1962), p. 153. See pp. 152–154. See also Roscoe C. Martin, Frank J. Munger, *et al.*, *Decisions in Syracuse: A Metropolitan Action Study* (Garden City, N.Y., 1965) (originally published: 1961), pp. 326–327.

[40] See, e.g., Thompson, *op. cit.*, p. 134, and *passim*; Martin Oppenheimer, "The Southern Student Movement: Year I," *Journal of Negro Education*, 33 (Fall, 1964), p. 397; Cothran, *op. cit.*, p. 72; Pauli Murray, "Protest Against the Legal Status of the Negro," *The Annals*, 357 (January, 1965), p. 63; Allan P. Sindler, "Protest Against the Political Status of the Negroes," *The Annals*, 357 (January, 1965), p. 30.

[41] See Banfield, *op. cit.*, p. 275.

verifiability in the interests of community harmony (and adherence to professional journalistic standards).

Most big city newspapers have reporters whose assignments permit them to cover aspects of city politics with some regularity. These reporters, whose "beats" may consist of "civil rights" or "poverty," sometimes develop close relationships with their news subjects. These relationships may develop symbiotic overtones because of the mutuality of interest between the reporter and the news subject. Reporters require fresh information on protest developments, while protest leaders have a vital interest in obtaining as much press coverage as possible.

Inflated reports of protest success may be understood in part by examining this relationship between reporter and protest leader. Both have role-oriented interests in projecting images of protest strength and threat. In circumstances of great excitement, when competition from other news media representatives is high, a reporter may find that he is less governed by the role requirement of verification and reliability than he is by his editor's demand for "scoops" and news with high audience appeal.[42]

On the other hand, the demands of the media may conflict with the needs of protest group maintenance. Consider the leader whose constituents are attracted solely by pragmatic statements not exceeding what they consider political "good taste." He is constrained from making militant demands which would isolate him from constituents. This constraint may cost him appeal in the press.[43] However, the leader whose organizing appeal requires militant rhetoric may obtain eager press coverage only to find that his inflamatory statements lead to alienation of potential allies and exclusion from the explicit bargaining process.[44]

News media do not report events in the same way. Television may select for broadcast only thirty seconds of a half-hour news conference. This coverage will probably focus on immediate events, without background or explanatory material. Newspapers may give more complete accounts of the same event. The most complete account may appear in the weekly edition of a neighborhood or ethnic newspaper. Differential coverage by news media, the differential news media habits in the general population,[45] are significant factors in permitting protest leaders to juggle con-

[42] For a case study of the interaction between protest leaders and newspaper reporters, see Michael Lipsky, "Rent Strikes in New York City: Protest Politics and the Power of the Poor," (unpublished Ph.D. dissertation, Princeton University, 1967), pp. 139–49. Bernard Cohen has analyzed the impact of the press on foreign policy from the perspective of reporters' role requirements: see his *The Press and Foreign Policy* (Princeton, N.J., 1963), esp. chs. 2–3.

[43] An example of a protest conducted by middle-class women engaged in pragmatic protest over salvaging park space is provided in John B. Keeley, *Moses on the Green*, Inter-University Case Program, No. 45 (University, Ala., 1959).

[44] This was the complaint of Floyd McKissick, National Director of the Congress of Racial Equality, when he charged that ". . . there are only two kinds of statements a black man can make and expect that the white press will report. . . . First . . . is an attack on another black man. . . . The second is a statement that sounds racial, violent, extreme—the verbal equivalent of a riot. . . . [T]he Negro is being rewarded by the public media only if he turns on another Negro and uses his tongue as a switchblade, or only if he sounds outlandish, extremist or psychotic." Statement at the Convention of the American Society of Newspaper Editors, April 20, 1967, Washington, D.C., as reported in *The New York Times*, April 21, 1967, p. 22. See also the remarks of journalist Ted Poston, *ibid.*, April 26, 1965, p. 26.

[45] Matthews and Prothro found, for example, that in their South-wide Negro population sample, 38 percent read Negro-oriented magazines and 17 percent read newspapers written for Negroes. These media treat news of interest to Negroes more completely and sympathetically than do the general media. See pp. 248 ff.

flicting demands of groups in the protest process.

Similar tensions exist in the leader's relationships with protest targets. Ideological postures may gain press coverage and constituency approval, but may alienate target groups with whom it would be desirable to bargain explicitly. Exclusion from the councils of decision-making may have important consequences, since the results of target group deliberations may satisfy activated reference publics without responding to protest goals. If activated reference publics are required to increase the bargaining position of the protest group, protest efforts thereafter will have diminished chances of success.

IV. Protest Leadership and "Third Parties"

I have argued that the essence of political protest consists of activating third parties to participate in controversy in ways favorable to protest goals. In previous sections I have attempted to analyze some of the tensions which result from protest leaders' attempts to activate reference publics of protest targets at the same time that they must retain the interest and support of protest organization participants. This phenomenon is in evidence when Negro leaders, recognized as such by public officials, find their support eroded in the Negro community because they have engaged in explicit bargaining situations with politicians. Negro leaders are thus faced with the dilemma that when they behave like other ethnic group representatives they are faced with loss of support from those whose intense activism has been aroused in the Negro community, yet whose support is vital if they are to remain credible as leaders to public officials.

The tensions resulting from conflicting maintenance needs of protest organizations and activated third parties present difficulties for protest leaders. One way in which these tensions can be minimized is by dividing leadership responsibilities. If more than one group is engaged in protest activity, protest leaders

can, in effect, divide up public roles so as to reduce as much as possible the gap between the implicit demands of different groups for appropriate rhetoric, and what in fact is said. Thus divided leadership may perform the latent function of minimizing tensions among elements in the protest process by permitting different groups to listen selectively to protest spokesmen.[46]

Another way in which strain among different groups can be minimized is through successful public relations. Minimization of strain may depend upon ambiguity of action or statement, deception, or upon effective intergroup communication. Failure to clarify meaning, or falsification, may increase protest effectiveness. Effective intragroup communication may increase the likelihood that protest constituents will "understand" that ambiguous or false public statements have "special meaning" and need not be taken seriously. The Machiavellian circle is complete when we observe that although lying may be prudent, the appearance of integrity and forthrightness is desirable for public relations, since these values are widely shared.

It has been observed that "[t]he militant displays an unwillingness to perform those administrative tasks which are necessary to operate an organization. Probably the skills of the agitator and the skills of the administrator . . . are not incompatible, but few men can do both well."[47] These skills may or may not be incompatible as personality traits, but they indeed represent conflicting role demands on protest leadership. When a protest leader exhausts time and energy conducting frequent press conferences, arranging for politicians and celebrities to appear at rallies, delivering speeches to sympathetic local groups, college symposia and other forums, constantly picketing for publicity and generally making "contacts," he is unable to pursue the direction of office routine, clerical tasks, research and analysis, and other chores.

The difficulties of delegating routine tasks are probably directly related to the skill levels

---

[46] See footnote 31 above.
[47] Wilson, *Negro Politics*, p. 225.

and previous administrative experiences of group members. In addition, to the extent that involvement in protest organizations is a function of rewards received or expected by individuals because of the excitement or entertainment value of participation, then the difficulties of delegating routine, relatively uninteresting chores to group members will be increased. Yet attention to such details affects the perception of protest groups by organizations whose support or assistance may be desired in the future. These considerations add to the protest leader's problem of risking alienation of protest participants because of potentially unpopular cooperation with the "power structure."

In the protest paradigm developed here, "third parties" refers both to the reference publics of target groups and, more narrowly, to the interest groups whose regular interaction with protest targets tends to develop into patterns of influence.[48] We have already discussed some of the problems associated with activating the reference publics of target groups. In discussing the constraints placed upon protest, attention may be focused upon the likelihood that groups seeking to create political resources through protest will be included in the explicit bargaining process with other pressure groups. For protest groups, these constraints are those which occur because of class and political style, status, and organizational resources.

The established civic groups most likely to be concerned with the problems raised by relatively powerless groups are those devoted to service in the public welfare and those "liberally" oriented groups whose potential constituents are either drawn from the same class as the protest groups (such as some trade unions), or whose potential constituents are attracted to policies which appear to serve the interest of the lower class or minority groups (such as some reform political clubs).[49] These civic groups have frequently cultivated

clientele relationships with city agencies over long periods. Their efforts have been reciprocated by agency officials anxious to develop constituencies to support and defend agency administrative and budgetary policies. In addition, clientele groups are expected to endorse and legitimize agency aggrandizement. These relationships have been developed by agency officials and civic groups for mutual benefit, and cannot be destroyed, abridged or avoided without cost.

Protest groups may well be able to raise the saliency of issues on the civic agenda through utilization of communications media and successful appeals or threats to wider publics, but admission to policy-making councils is frequently barred because of the angry, militant rhetorical style adopted by protest leaders. People in power do not like to sit down with rogues. Protest leaders are likely to have phrased demands in ways unacceptable to lawyers and other civic activists whose cautious attitude toward public policy may reflect not only their good intentions but their concern for property rights, due process, pragmatic legislating or judicial precedent.

Relatively powerless groups lack participation of individuals with high status whose endorsement of specific proposals lend them increased legitimacy. Good causes may always attract the support of high status individuals. But such individuals' willingness to devote time to the promotion of specific proposals is less likely than the one-shot endorsement which these people distribute more readily.

Similarly, protest organizations often lack the resources on which entry into the policy-making process depends. These resources include maintenance of a staff with expertise and experience in the policy area. This expertise may be in the areas of the law, planning and architecture, proposal writing, accounting, educational policy, federal grantsmanship or publicity. Combining experience with expertise is one way to create status in issue areas.

---

[48] See Wallace Sayre and Herbert Kaufman, *Governing New York City* (New York, 1960), pp. 257 ff. Also see Banfield, *op. cit.*, p. 267.

[49] See Wilson, *The Amateur Democrats*, previously cited. These groups are most likely to be characterized by broad scope of political interest and frequent intervention in politics. See Sayre and Kaufman, *op. cit.*, p. 79.

The dispensing of information by interest groups has been widely noted as a major source of influence. Over time the experts develop status in their areas of competence somewhat independent of the influence which adheres to them as information-providers. Groups which cannot or do not engage lawyers to assist in proposing legislation, and do not engage in collecting reliable data, cannot participate in policy deliberations or consult in these matters. Protest-oriented groups, whose primary talents are in dramatizing issues, cannot credibly attempt to present data considered "objective" or suggestions considered "responsible" by public officials. Few can be convincing as both advocate and arbiter at the same time.

V. Protest Leadership and Target Groups

The probability of protest success may be approached by examining the maintenance needs of organizations likely to be designated as target groups.[50] For the sake of clarity, and because protest activity increasingly is directed toward government, I shall refer in the following paragraphs exclusively to government agencies at the municipal level. The assumption is retained, however, that the following generalizations are applicable to other potential target groups.

Some of the constraints placed on protest leadership in influencing target groups have already been mentionel in proceeding sections. The lack of status and resources that inhibit protest groups from participating in policy-making conferences, for example, also helps prevent explicit bargaining between protest leaders and city officials. The strain between rhetoric which appeals to protest participants and public statements to which communications media and "third parties" respond favorably also exists with reference to target groups.

Yet there is a distinguishing feature of the maintenance needs and strategies of city agencies which specifically constrains protest organizations. This is the agency director's need to protect "the jurisdiction and income of his organization [by] . . . [m]anipulation of the external environment."[51] In so doing he may satisfy his reference groups without responding to protest group demands. At least six tactics are available to protest targets who are motivated to respond in some way to protest activity but seek primarily to satisfy their reference publics. These tactics may be employed whether or not target groups are "sincere" in responding to protest demands.

1. Target groups may dispense symbolic satisfactions. Appearances of activity and commitment to problems substitute for, or supplement, resource allocation and policy innovations which would constitute tangible responses to protest activity. If symbolic responses supplement tangible pay-offs, they are frequently coincidental, rather than intimately linked, to projection of response by protest targets. Typical in city politics of the symbolic response is the ribbon-cutting, street corner ceremony or the walking-tour press conference. These occasions are utilized not only to build agency constituencies,[52] but to satisfy agency reference publics that attention is being directed to problems of civic concern. In

---

[50] Another approach, persuasively presented by Wilson, concentrates on protest success as a function of the relative unity and vulnerability of targets. See "The Strategy of Protest," pp. 293 ff. This insight helps explain, for example, why protest against housing segregation commonly takes the form of action directed against government (a unified target) rather than against individual homeowners (who present a dispersed target). One problem with this approach is that it tends to obscure the possibility that targets, as collections of individuals, may be divided in evaluation of and sympathy for protest demands. Indeed, city agency administrators under some circumstances act as partisans in protest conflicts. As such, they frequently appear ambivalent toward protest goals: sympathetic to the ends while concerned that the means employed in protest reflect negatively on their agencies.

[51] Sayre and Kaufman, *op. cit.*, p. 253.

[52] See *ibid.*, pp. 253 ff.

this sense publicist tactics may be seen as defensive maneuvers. Symbolic aspects of the actions of public officials can also be recognized in the commissioning of expensive studies and the rhetorical flourishes with which "massive attacks," "comprehensive programs," and "coordinated planning" are frequently promoted.

City agencies establish distinct apparatus and procedures for dealing with crises which may be provoked by protest groups. Housing-related departments in New York City may be cited for illustration. It is usually the case in these agencies that the Commissioner or a chief deputy, a press secretary and one or two other officials devote whatever time is necessary to collect information, determine policy and respond quickly to reports of "crises." This is functional for tenants, who, if they can generate enough concern, may be able to obtain short-cuts through lengthy agency procedures. It is also functional for officials who want to project images of action rather than merely receiving complaints. Concentrating attention on the maintenance needs of city politicians during protest crises suggests that pronouncements of public officials serve purposes independent of their dedication to alleviation of slum conditions.[53]

Independent of dispensation of tangible benefits to protest groups, public officials continue to respond primarily to their own reference publics. Murray Edelman has suggested that:

> Tangible resources and benefits are frequently not distributed to unorganized political group interests as promised in regulatory statutes and the propaganda attending their enactment.[54]

His analysis may be supplemented by suggesting that symbolic dispensations may not only serve to reassure unorganized political group interests, but may also contribute to reducing the anxiety level of organized interests and

wider publics which are only tangentially involved in the issues.

2. Target groups may dispense token material satisfactions. When city agencies respond, with much publicity, to cases brought to their attention representing examples of the needs dramatized by protest organizations, they may appear to respond to protest demands while in fact only responding on a case basis, instead of a general basis. For the protesters served by agencies in this fashion it is of considerable advantage that agencies can be influenced by protest action. Yet it should not be ignored that in handling the "crisis" cases, public officials give the appearance of response to their reference publics, while mitigating demands for an expensive, complex *general* assault on problems represented by the cases to which responses are given. Token responses, whether or not accompanied by more general responses, are particularly attractive to reporters and television news directors, who are able to dramatize individual cases convincingly, but who may be unable to "capture" the essence of general deprivation or of general efforts to alleviate conditions of deprivation.

3. Target groups may organize and innovate internally in order to blunt the impetus of protest efforts. This tactic is closely related to No. 2 (above). If target groups can act constructively in the worst cases, they will then be able to pre-empt protest efforts by responding to the cases which best dramatize protest demands. Alternatively, they may designate all efforts which jeopardize agency reputations as "worst" cases, and devote extensive resources to these cases. In some ways extraordinary city efforts are precisely consistent with protest goals. At the same time extraordinary efforts in the most heavily dramatized cases or the most extreme cases effectively wear down the "cutting-edges" of protest efforts.

Many New York City agencies develop in-

---

[53] See Lipsky, *op. cit.*, chs. 5–6. The appearance of responsiveness may be given by city officials *in anticipation* of protest activity. This seems to have been the Strategy of Mayor Richard Daley in his reaction to the announcement of Martin Luther King's plans to focus civil rights efforts on Chicago. See *The New York Times,* February 1, 1966, p. 11.

[54] See Edelman, *op. cit.*, p. 23.

formal "crisis" arrangements not only to project publicity, as previously indicated, but to mobilize energies toward solving "crisis" cases. They may also develop policy innovations which allow them to respond more quickly to "Crisis" situations. These innovations may be important to some city residents, for whom the problems of dealing with city bureaucracies can prove insurmountable. It might be said, indeed, that the goals of protest are to influence city agencies to handle every case with the same resources that characterize their dispatch of "crisis" cases.[55]

But such policies would demand major revenue inputs. This kind of qualitative policy change is difficult to achieve. Meanwhile, internal reallocation of resources only means that routine services must be neglected so that the "crisis" programs can be enhanced. If all cases are expedited, as in a typical "crisis" response, then none can be. Thus for purposes of general solutions, "crisis" resolving can be self-defeating unless accompanied by significantly greater resource allocation. It is not self-defeating, however, to the extent that the organizational goals of city agencies are to serve a clientele while minimizing negative publicity concerning agency vigilance and responsiveness.

4. Target groups may appear to be constrained in their ability to grant protest goals.[56] This may be directed toward making the protesters appear to be unreasonable in their demands, or to be well-meaning individuals who "just don't understand how complex running a city really is." Target groups may extend sympathy but claim that they lack resources, a mandate from constituents, and/or authority to respond to protest demands. Target groups may also evade protest demands by arguing that "If-I-give-it-to-you-I-have-to-give-it-to-everyone."

The tactic of appearing constrained is particularly effective with established civic groups because there is an undeniable element of truth to it. Everyone knows that cities are financially undernourished. Established civic groups expend great energies lobbying for higher levels of funding for their pet city agencies. Thus they recognize the validity of this constraint when posed by city officials. But it is not inconsistent to point out that funds for specific, relatively inexpensive programs, or for the expansion of existing programs, can often be found if pressure is increased. While constraints on city government flexibility may be extensive, they are not absolute. Protest targets nonetheless attempt to diminish the impact of protest demands by claiming relative impotence.

5. Target groups may use their extensive resources to discredit protest leaders and organizations. Utilizing their excellent access to the press, public officials may state or imply that leaders are unreliable, ineffective as leaders ("they don't really have the people behind them"), guilty of criminal behavior, potentially guilty of such behavior, or are some shade of "left-wing." Any of these allegations may serve to diminish the appeal of protest groups to potentially sympathetic third parties. City officials, in their frequent social and informal business interaction with leaders of established civic groups, may also communicate derogatory information concerning protest groups. Discrediting of protest groups may be undertaken by some city officials while others appear (perhaps authentically) to remain sympathetic to protest demands. These tactics may be engaged in by public officials whether or not there is any validity to the allegations.

6. Target groups may postpone action. The effect of postponement, if accompanied by symbolic assurances, is to remove immediate pressure and delay specific commitments to a future date. That familiar tactic is particularly effective in dealing with protest groups because of their inherent instability. Protest groups are usually comprised of individuals whose intense political activity cannot be sustained except in rare circumstances. Further, to the extent that protest depends upon activating reference publics through strategies

---

[55] See Lipsky, op. cit., pp. 156, 249 ff.
[56] On the strategy of appearing constrained, see Schelling, op. cit., pp. 22 ff.

which have some "shock" value, it becomes increasingly difficult to activate these groups. Additionally, protest activity is inherently unstable because of the strains placed upon protest leaders who must attempt to manage four constituencies (as described herein).

The most frequent method of postponing action is to commit a subject to "study." For the many reasons elaborated in these paragraphs, it is not likely that ad hoc protest groups will be around to review the recommendations which emerge from study. The greater the expertise and the greater the status of the group making the study, the less will protest groups be able to influence whatever policy emerges. Protest groups lack the skills and resource personnel to challenge expert recommendations effectively.

Sometimes surveys and special research are undertaken in part to evade immediate pressures. Sometimes not. Research efforts are particularly necessary to secure the support of established civic groups, which place high priority on orderly procedure and policy emerging from independent analysis. Yet it must be recognized that postponing policy commitments has a distinct impact on the nature of the pressures focused on policymakers.

IV. Conclusion

In this analysis I have agreed with James Q. Wilson that protest is correctly conceived as a strategy utilized by relatively powerless groups in order to increase their bargaining ability. As such, I have argued, it is successful to the extent that the reference publics of protest targets can be activated to enter the conflict in ways favorable to protest goals. I have suggested a model of the protest process which may assist in ordering data and indicating the salience for research of a number of aspects of protest. These include the critical role of communications media, the differential impact of material and symbolic rewards on "feedback" in protest activity, and the reciprocal relationships of actors in the protest process.

An estimation of the limits to protest efficacy, I have argued further, can be gained by recognizing the problems encountered by protest leaders who somehow must balance the conflicting maintenance needs of four groups in the protest process. This approach transcends a focus devoted primarily to characterization of group goals and targets, by suggesting that even in an environment which is relatively favorable to specific protest goals, the tensions which must be embraced by protest leadership may ultimately overwhelm protest activity.

At the outset of this essay, it was held that conceptualizing the American political system as "slack" or "fluid," in the manner of Robert Dahl, appears inadequate because of (1) a vagueness centering on the likelihood that any group can make itself heard; (2) a possible confusion as to which groups tend to receive satisfaction from the rewards dispensed by public officials; and (3) a lumping together as equally relevant rewards which are tangible and those which are symbolic. To the extent that protest is engaged in by relatively powerless groups which must create resources with which to bargain, the analysis here suggests a number of reservations concerning the pluralist conceptualization of the "fluidity" of the American political system.

Relatively powerless groups cannot use protest with a high probability of success. They lack organizational resources, by definition. But even to create bargaining resources through activating third parties, some resources are necessary to sustain organization. More importantly, relatively powerless protest groups are constrained by the unresolvable conflicts which are forced upon protest leaders who must appeal simultaneously to four constituencies which place upon them antithetical demands.

When public officials recognize the legitimacy of protest activity, they may not direct public policy toward protest groups at all. Rather, public officials are likely to aim responses at the reference publics from which they originally take their cues. Edelman has suggested that regulatory policy in practice often consists of reassuring mass publics while at the same time dispensing specific, tangible values to narrow interest groups. It is suggested here that symbolic reassurances are dispensed as much to wide, potentially concerned publics which are not directly affected by regulatory policy, as they are to wide publics comprised of the down-trodden and the deprived, in whose name policy is often written.

Complementing Edelman, it is proposed here that in the process of protest symbolic reassurances are dispensed in large measure because these are the public policy outcomes and actions desired by the constituencies to which public officials are most responsive. Satisfying these wider publics, city officials can avoid pressures toward other policies placed upon them by protest organizations.

Not only should there be some doubt as to which groups receive the symbolic recognitions which Dahl describes, but in failing to distinguish between the kinds of rewards dispensed to groups in the political system, Dahl avoids a fundamental question. It is literally fundamental because the kinds of rewards which can be obtained from politics, one might hypothesize, will have an impact upon the realistic appraisal of the efficacy of political activity. If among the groups least capable of organizing for political activity there is a history of organizing for protest, and if that activity, once engaged in, is rewarded primarily by the dispensation of symbolic gestures without perceptible changes in material conditions, then rational behavior might lead to expressions of apathy and lack of interest in politics or a rejection of conventional political channels as a meaningful arena of activity. In this sense this discussion of protest politics is consistent with Kenneth Clark's observations, that the image of power, unaccompanied by

material and observable rewards, leads to impressions of helplessness and reinforces political apathy in the ghetto.[57]

Recent commentary by political scientists and others regarding riots in American cities seems to focus in part on the extent to which relatively deprived groups may seek redress of legitimate grievances. Future research should continue assessment of the relationship between riots and the conditions under which access to the political system has been limited. In such research assessment of the ways in which access to public officials is obtained by relatively powerless groups through the protest process might be one important research focus.

The instability of protest activity outlined in this article also should inform contemporary political strategies. If the arguments presented here are persuasive, civil rights leaders who insist that protest activity is a shallow foundation on which to seek long-term, concrete gains may be judged essentially correct. But the arguments concerning the fickleness of the white liberal, or the ease of changing discriminatory laws relative to changing discriminatory institutions, only in part explain the instability of protest movements. An explanation which derives its strength from analysis of the political process suggests concentration on the problems of managing protest constituencies. Accordingly, Alinsky is probably on the soundest ground when he prescribes protest for the purpose of building organization. Ultimately, relatively powerless groups in most instances cannot depend upon activating other actors in the political process. Long-run success will depend upon the acquisition of stable political resources which do not rely for their use on third parties.

[57] Clark, *op. cit.*, pp. 154 ff.

22. Satyagraha as Applied Socio-Political Action

Joan V. Bondurant*

Satyagraha is a technique of action. It is characterized by adherence to a stated truth by means of behavior which is not violent but which includes self-suffering. It seeks to effect change and it operates within a conflict situation. As do all techniques of action for effecting change, it employs force. The character and the result of the force of satyagraha are essentially different from those of conventional—violent—techniques of action during conflict.

Satyagraha may use any of several forms of non-violent action. Those which were most commonly employed during the nationalist movement in India are *non-cooperation and civil disobedience. Constructive program* is a positive aspect of satyagraha in action, and is the concomitant of resistance-action.

Non-cooperation may include strike, walkout, *hartal*,[1] and resignation of offices and titles. In principle, non-cooperation is simply the refusal to cooperate with a requirement which is taken to violate fundamental "truths" or refusal to cooperate with those responsible for such violations.

Civil disobedience is the direct contravention of specific laws and may include such activities as non-payment of taxes. Jail-going is a special *non-resistance*[2] activity undertaken in a civil disobedience program. The civil character of satyagraha is maintained by the inviting of and the voluntary submitting to the sanction provided by the law for action contrary to the legal norm.

A special word should be said about fasting and its place in Gandhian satyagraha. Gandhi frequently wrote on the dangers of considering any fast a part of satyagraha. The majority of fasts, he declared, were nothing more than "hunger strikes undertaken without previous preparation and without adequate thought." He repeatedly warned against the indiscriminate use of the fast and was well aware that often "there is violence behind such fasting."[3] Although Gandhi fully believed that fasting could be a most "effective weapon" in the armory of satyagraha,[4] he recognized that its use must be carefully determined.

> Fasting is a fiery weapon. It has its own science. No one, as far as I am aware, has a perfect knowledge of it. Unscientific experimentation with it is bound to be harmful to the one who fasts, and it may even harm the cause espoused. No one who has not earned the right to do so should, therefore, use this weapon. A fast may only be undertaken by him who is associated with the person against whom he fasts. The latter must be directly

---

[1] Voluntary closing of shops and businesses, usually for a twenty-four hour period.

[2] It must be kept firmly in mind that *non-resistance* does not describe satyagraha. Much confusion of thought on Gandhian techniques arises from the failure to distinguish at all times between the active resistance undertaken in satyagraha and the occasional non-resistant effect of such activities as inviting imprisonment. This chapter should make clear the inadequacies of such words as "passive resistance" to express the functioning of satyagraha. It must also be insisted that "non-resistance" in no way characterizes satyagraha and describes only a step in a civil disobedience effort.

[3] *Harijan*, March 11, 1939, as quoted by N. K. Bose, *Studies in Gandhism* (2nd ed., Calcutta: Indian Associated Publishing Co., 1947), p. 159.

[4] *Harijan*, July 26, 1942.

° Affiliation unavailable.

connected with the purpose for which the fast is being undertaken.[5]

In general, fasting may be used as an adjunct to other forms of satyagraha. It should not be considered a form of satyagraha in the sense of mass action. The development of "representative satyagraha" in which individuals are selected to represent the group in offering[6] satyagraha may, however, make use of the fast.

The Essentials of Satyagraha in Action

If one were to lay out a handbook for the conduct of a mass satyagraha campaign based upon the experience with satyagraha in India, the three first chapters might well deal with (1) fundamental rules governing the campaign, (2) the code of discipline, and (3) the steps through which the campaign is to be pursued. Among the points which should enter into such a guide are those outlined below.

Fundamental Rules[7]

(1) *Self-reliance at all times.* Outside aid may, in the proper circumstances, be accepted, but should never be counted upon.

(2) *Initiative in the hands of the satyagrahis.* Through continuous assessment of the conflict situation satyagrahis should, by means of constructive efforts where possible, by positive resistance where indicated, or by tactics of persuasion and adjustment, press the movement ever forward.

(3) *Propagation of the objectives, strategy, and tactics of the campaign.* Propaganda must be made an integral part of the movement. Education of the opponent, the public, and participants must continue apace.

(4) *Reduction of demands to a minimum consistent with truth.* Continuing reassessment of the situation and the objectives with a view to possible adjustment of demands is essential.

(5) *Progressive advancement of the movement* through steps and stages determined to be appropriate within the given situation. Decision as to when to proceed to a further phase of the satyagraha must be carefully weighed in the light of the ever-changing circumstance, but a static condition must be avoided. However, direct action is to be launched only after all other efforts to achieve an honorable settlement have been exhausted.

(6) *Examination of weaknesses* within the satyagraha group. The morale and discipline of the satyagrahis must be maintained through active awareness (by members and leaders alike) of any development of impatience, discouragement, or breakdown of non-violent attitude.

(7) *Persistent search for avenues of cooperation with the adversary on honorable terms.* Every effort should be made to win over the opponent by helping him (where this is consistent with the satyagrahi's true objectives) thereby demonstrating sincerity to achieve an agreement with, rather than a triumph over, the adversary.

(8) *Refusal to surrender essentials in negotiation.* Satyagraha excludes all compromise which affects basic principles or essential portions of valid objectives. Care must be exercised not to engage in bargaining or barter.

(9) *Insistence upon full agreement* on fundamentals before accepting a settlement.

Code of Discipline

The following points were laid down by Gandhi as a code for volunteers in the 1930 movement:[8]

(1) Harbor no anger but suffer the anger of the opponent. Refuse to return the assaults of the opponent.

(2) Do not submit to any order given in anger, even though severe punishment is threatened for disobeying.

(3) Refrain from insults and swearing.

(4) Protect opponents from insult or attack, even at the risk of life.

---

[5] *Harijan,* October 13, 1940, as quoted by N. K. Bose, *op. cit.,* p. 157.

[6] To "offer" satyagraha means to perform an act of satyagraha.

[7] These rules have been adapted and elaborated from N. K. Bose, *op. cit.,* p. 175.

[8] These points are paraphrased from D. G. Tendulkar's account, *Mahatma,* Vol. III (Bombay: Jhaveri and Tendulkar, 1952), p. 17.

(5) Do not resist arrest nor the attachment of property, unless holding property as a trustee.

(6) Refuse to surrender any property held in trust at the risk of life.

(7) If taken prisoner, behave in an exemplary manner.

(8) As a member of a satyagraha unit, obey the orders of satyagraha leaders, and resign from the unit in the event of serious disagreement.

(9) Do not expect guarantees for maintenance of dependents.

Steps in a Satyagraha Campaign[9]

The outline below is applicable to a movement growing out of grievances against an established political order. These steps could be adapted to other conflict situations.

(1) *Negotiation and arbitration.* Every effort to resolve the conflict or redress the grievance through established channels must be exhausted before the further steps are undertaken.

(2) *Preparation of the group for direct action.* Immediately upon recognizing the existence of a conflict situation which might lead to direct action, motives are to be carefully examined, exercises in self-discipline initiated, and the fullest discussion launched within the group regarding issues at stake, appropriate procedures to be undertaken, the circumstance of the opponents, the climate of public opinion, etc. This step often included, for Indian satyagrahis, purificatory fasting.

(3) *Agitation.* This step includes an active propaganda campaign together with such demonstrations as mass-meetings, parades, slogan-shouting.

(4) *Issuing of an ultimatum.* A final strong appeal to the opponent should be made explaining what further steps will be taken if no agreement can be reached. The wording and manner of presentation of the ultimatum should offer the widest scope for agreement, allowing for face-saving on the part of the opponent, and should present a constructive solution to the problem.

(5) *Economic boycott and forms of strike.* Picketing may be widely employed, together with continued demonstrations and education of the public. Sitting *dharna* (a form of sit-down strike) may be employed, as well as non-violent labor strike, and attempts to organize a general strike.

(6) *Non-cooperation.* Depending upon the nature of the issues at stake, such action as non-payment of taxes, boycott of schools and other public institutions, ostracism, or even voluntary exile may be initiated.

(7) *Civil disobedience.* Great care should be exercised in the selection of laws to be contravened. Such laws should be either central to the grievance, or symbolic.

(8) *Usurping of the functions of government.* Shrindharani calls this "assertive satyagraha." Fullest preparations are necessary to make this step effective.

(9) *Parallel government.* The establishment of parallel functions should grow out of step (8), and these should be strengthened in such a way that the greatest possible cooperation from the public can be obtained.

The specific action which is to be undertaken in a given satyagraha movement will, of course, be determined by the nature of the circumstance itself. As in the extensive and intensive preparations for violent combat, much depends upon discipline, leadership, preparation, steadfast purpose, and the adaptation of basic principles and procedures to specific circumstances. An analysis of historic satyagraha campaigns in India indicates directions in which preparation for satyagraha might be developed to strengthen such movements and to avoid potential weaknesses. Gandhi and other Indian leaders accepted all who would join their campaigns. They developed tactics and rules as they moved to meet well-advanced situations of conflict. Had they been able to select their crusaders and to train them for their respective roles in the satyagraha operation, the movements might well have been even more dramatic. Even so, the degree of success with which they met is especially striking when one considers that they worked on an *ad hoc* basis, and that they dealt with a

---

[9] A similar set of progressive steps have been listed in Krishnala Shridarani's classic work *War Without Violence* (New York: Harcourt, Brace, 1939). See pp. 5–42.

mass populace which had no prior understanding of the techniques involved and very
few of whom had any consistent discipline in
the application of these techniques.

The Salt Satyagraha[10]

Note: The Salt Satyagraha was part of the
year-long Civil Disobedience movement of
1930–1931. The following outline touches
upon the entire movement, although many of
the details of that extensive struggle have
been omitted.

DATES, DURATION, AND LOCALE

(1) March 1930–March 1931.
(2) In its extended form, civil disobedience
continued for about one year.
(3) A national movement, with headquarters
in Bombay. Satyagraha activities were launched
in every province.

OBJECTIVES

(1) *Immediate*: Removal of the Salt Acts.
These statutes provided for a government
monopoly of salt. Revenue realized from the
Salt Tax amounted at this time to $25,000,000
out of a total revenue of about $800,000,000.
These laws were held to work a hardship on
the people, especially the poor, and to constitute the taxation of a necessity.
(2) *Long-range*: The Salt Acts were chosen
by Gandhi for contravention in a general civil

disobedience movement because they not only
appeared to be basically unjust in themselves,
but also because they symbolized an unpopular, unrepresentative, and alien government.
British official sources described the object of
the satyagraha as "nothing less than to cause a
complete paralysis of the administrative machinery. . . ." The ultimate objective of civil
disobedience was complete independence.

SATYAGRAHA PARTICIPANTS AND LEADERSHIP

(1) *Gandhi* and other leaders of the Indian
National Congress.
(2) *Secondary leadership*: In the opening
phase, direct participation was limited to disciplined members of Gandhi's ashram at
Ahmedabad, selected by Gandhi to make the
march to the sea. They were described as "soldiers who had been steeled to the disciplines
and hardships which a two hundred mile
march on foot would necessarily entail on
them."
Prominent Congressmen served as organizers in other parts of India. Among these
were Rajagopalachariar in Tamilnad, Vallabhbhai Patel for the whole of Gujarat,
Jawaharlal Nehru in the United Provinces,
Satish Chandra Das Gupta in Bengal, Konda
Venkatappaya in Andhra, and Gopabandhu
Chowdhury in Utkal (Orissa).
(3) *Participants*: After the initial breach of

---

[10] The data for this outline were abstracted from the following sources: Robert
Bernays, *"Naked Faquir"* (New York: H. Holt, 1932); Glorney Bolton, *The
Tragedy of Gandhi* (London: Allen & Unwin, 1934); *Congress Presidential
Addresses*; Sir Reginald Coupland, *The Indian Problem: Report on the Constitu-
tional Problem in India* (New York, etc.: Oxford University Press, 1944); Cumming,
op. cit.; Diwakar, *op. cit.*; Negley Farson, "Indian Hate Lyric" in Eugene Lyons,
ed., *We Cover the World*, by fifteen foreign correspondents (New York: Harcourt,
Brace, 1937); Gregg, *op. cit.*; *India in 1930–31: A Statement Prepared for Presenta-
tion to Parliament in Accordance with the Requirements of the 26th Section of the
Government of India Act* (5 and 6 Geo. V, Chap. 61) (Calcutta: Government of
India Central Publishing Branch, 1932); Alan Campbell Johnson, *Viscount Halifax,
A Biography* (London: Robert Hale, 1941); Webb Miller, *I Found No Peace:
The Journal of a Foreign Correspondent* (New York: The Literary Guild, 1936);
The Indian Annual Register, Nripendra Nath Mitra, ed. (Calcutta: Annual
Register Office, 1930 and 1931), Vols. I and II, 1930, Vols. I and II, 1931; Nehru,
An Autobiography; The New York Times, for this period; Sitaramayya, *op. cit.*;
G. C. Sondhi, ed., *To the Gates of Liberty: Congress Commemoration Volume*
(Calcutta: Swadesh Bharati, 1948); *Young India*, for this period; Correspondence
between the author and R. R. Diwakar, Pyarelal (Nayyar), and R. R. Keithahn.

the salt laws, Indians throughout the country participated.

(4) *Characteristics of participants*: The official government report indicated that the majority of participants were Hindus, but that Muslims did take part, especially on the Frontier. Officials expressed concern that the "Hindu mercantile and industrial community showed active sympathy" and financially supported the movement. Another "unexpected" element among satyagrahis was a large number of Indian women. "Thousands of them—many being of good family and high educational attainments—suddenly emerged from the seclusion of their homes and in some instances actually from *purdah,* in order to join Congress demonstrations and assist in picketing. . . ."

PARTICIPANTS AND LEADERSHIP
OF THE OPPOSITION

(1) *Officials* of the Government of India.

(2) *Police,* both British and Indian.

(3) *Units of the army.*

ORGANIZATION AND CONSTRUCTIVE PROGRAM

(1) *Role of Indian National Congress*: This campaign was conducted as part of an over-all political movement for independence. It was a program adopted by the largest political opposition party in India and so was planned in the light of the organization and constitutional make-up of the Party. The Congress Party delegated to Gandhi full power and responsibility for organizing and leading the campaign (by resolution, 21 March 1930).

(2) *Succession of leadership*: Extensive powers were given to the president of the Congress (then Jawaharlal Nehru) to act on behalf of the executive committee in case it could not meet. The president was empowered to nominate a successor in the event of his removal from action, the successor, in turn, was to have the same power of appointment of a successor. Similar powers were given to provincial and local Congress chiefs.

(3) *Khadi*: The wearing of hand-spun cloth was imperative for all satyagrahis—it became the uniform of the Congress and the movement.

(4) *Other aspects of constructive work*: Welfare and self-sufficiency work was considered one of the ways in which the cause could be promoted. A satyagrahi should "find himself in one of the following states," Gandhi instructed: "1. In prison or in an analogous state, or 2. Engaged in Civil Disobedience, or 3. Under orders at the spinning wheel, or at some constructive work advancing Swaraj."

PREPARATION FOR ACTION

(1) *Public opinion on swaraj*: Prior to the launching of this campaign, the sentiment for full independence was developed through discussion and the deliberations of the Congress Party. On 26 January the Congress, meeting in Lahore, had pledged its members to "carry out the Congress instructions issued from time to time for the purpose of establishing Purna Swaraj" (full independence).

(2) *Training courses*: Volunteers for satyagraha undertook courses of training for direct action, especially in methods of controlling large crowds. Satyagrahis drilled regularly, though they did so without arms.

(3) *Planning for civil disobedience*: The salt laws were selected for contravention. Gandhi planned to lead a march to the sea where satyagrahis would, in violation of the salt monopoly, prepare salt from sea water. Vallabhbhai Patel was chosen to prepare the way for the proposed march. He proceeded along the route to be taken, advising the people of the objectives of the movement, and instructing them in the principles of satyagraha. They were urged to undertake constructive work, to abstain from intoxicants, and to overcome untouchability. (On 7 March Patel was arrested.)

(4) *The Satyagraha Pledge*: The All-India Congress Committee, meeting at Ahmedabad on 21 March 1930, drew up the following pledge to be taken by those volunteering for satyagraha:

1. I desire to join the civil resistance campaign for the Independence of India undertaken by the National Congress.

2. I accept the Creed of the National Congress, that is, the attainment of Purna Swaraj

(complete independence) by the people of India by all peaceful and legitimate means.

3. I am ready and willing to go to jail and undergo all other sufferings and penalties that may be inflicted on me in this campaign.

4. In case I am sent to jail, I shall not seek any monetary help for my family from the Congress funds.

5. I shall implicitly obey the orders of those who are in charge of the campaign.

PRELIMINARY ACTION

(1) *Notice of civil disobedience*: Through the Congress independence resolution adopted at Lahore, subsequently advertised and discussed widely, the intention of the Congress Party to agitate for independence, if necessary through civil disobedience, was made known.

(2) *Gandhi's letter to Lord Irwin, the Viceroy*: On 2 March 1930, Gandhi apprised the Viceroy of the satyagraha plan and reviewed the grievances of the people. Non-violence, he wrote, could be "an intensely active force." It was his purpose, he told the Viceroy, "to set in motion that force, as well against the organised violent force of the British rule as the unorganised violent force of the growing party of violence. . . . The non-violence will be expressed through Civil Disobedience, for the moment confined to the inmates of the Satyagraha Ashram, but ultimately designed to cover all those who choose to join the movement with its obvious limitations."

(3) *The Ultimatum*: In his letter, Gandhi urged a negotiated settlement, barring which, he would lead a satyagraha movement. He further stated the exact day upon which he would proceed, with co-workers, to disregard the provisions of the Salt Acts. "It is, I know, open to you," he told the Viceroy, "to frustrate my design by arresting me. I hope that there will be tens of thousands ready, in a disciplined manner, to take up the work after me, and, in the act of disobeying the Salt Act, to lay themselves open to the penalties of a Law that should never have disfigured the Statute Book." He would, Gandhi said, welcome further discussion, and his letter was in no way a threat but a "simple and sacred duty preemptory on a civil resister." A young Englishman (Reginald Reynolds) who had joined the ashram was selected to deliver the letter.

ACTION

(1) *The march to the sea*: On 12 March, Gandhi and his co-satyagrahis left Ahmedabad for Dandi on the sea coast. He urged villagers along the way to pursue constructive work, to remain non-violent, and to participate in the civil disobedience following the initial breach of the law at Dandi. The march was considered a form of penance and discipline for the beginning of civil disobedience. It also dramatized the issues and attracted nationwide attention.

(2) *The opening of civil disobedience*: The satyagrahis reached Dandi on 5 April. The following morning, after prayers, they proceeded to the beach where they prepared salt from sea water, thus technically breaking the salt laws.

(3) *Gandhi's statement to the press*: Upon breaking the law, Gandhi declared that it was then open to anyone who would take the risk of prosecution to manufacture salt wherever he wished. Villagers were to be instructed concerning the meaning of the salt tax and directed in methods of preparing salt.

(4) *Issuing of leaflets*: Instructions concerning the manufacture of salt were published in the various parts of the country.

(5) *Response from the people*: "It seemed as though a spring had been suddenly released," Nehru wrote. Everywhere people began to make salt. They collected "pots and pans and ultimately succeeded in producing some unwholesome stuff, which we waved about in triumph, and often auctioned for fancy prices." The main thing. Nehru continued, was to commit a breach of the "obnoxious Salt Law. . . . As we saw the abounding enthusiasm of the people and the way salt-making was spreading like a prairie fire, we felt a little abashed and ashamed for having questioned the efficacy of this method when it was first proposed by Gandhiji. And we marvelled at the amazing knack of the man to impress the multitude and make it act in an organised way."

(6) *Hartal*: Throughout the country shops

closed in response to arrests of satyagraha leaders.

(7) *Resignation of offices*: Headmen in villages and subordinate officers resigned in large numbers in sympathy with satyagraha.

(8) *Symbolic acts*: In many parts of India dramatic demonstrations were conducted. In Bombay an "effigy" of the Salt Acts was thrown into the sea as a symbol that British law was dead in the land.

(9) *Succession in leadership*: Jawaharlal Nehru was arrested on 14 April and was succeeded by his father, Motilal Nehru. In other places, leaders of the satyagraha were replaced by appointment following the arrest of the initial leadership. Gandhi, arrested 5 May, was replaced by Abbas Tyabji.

(10) *Non-payment of taxes*: In some areas, as in Bardoli, a program of non-payment of taxes was undertaken.

(11) *Action to control rioting*: Leaders attempted to preserve the non-violent character of satyagraha. In response to the outbreak of riots in Karachi and Calcutta, Gandhi announced: "If non-violence has to fight the people's violence in addition to the violence of the Government it must still perform its arduous task at any cost." (17 April.) Gandhi later (26 April) announced that if satyagrahis who followed him did not fulfill the basic conditions, he himself would practice satyagraha against them.

(12) *Gandhi's second letter to Viceroy*: The Government, in a sort of non-cooperation of its own, refused to arrest Gandhi early in the campaign. The first week of May he explained in a second letter his next move—he would set out for Dharsana where the Government operated a large salt works. There he would demand possession of these works. It would be possible, he said, for the Viceroy to prevent this "raid" in one of the following three ways:

1. by removing the salt tax;
2. by arresting me and my party unless the country can, as I hope it will, replace every one taken away;
3. by sheer goondaism [hooliganism] unless every head broken is replaced as I hope it will be.

(13) *Raids on salt works*: Following Gandhi's arrest on 5 May (just after midnight), volunteers, led by Congress notables, marched to occupy the salt depots. Fresh volunteers stepped in as others were struck down by the police. Organized first-aid units worked to revive victims.

(14) *Non-violent persuasion of police*: Throughout the attack upon the satyagraha raiders, volunteers refrained from striking back or even from deflecting blows. They rushed onto the salt pans, wave upon wave. Where they could, they pleaded with the police to join them. Incidents were reported of policemen refusing to continue the assault. An American journalist, Negley Farson, recorded an incident in which a Sikh, blood-soaked from the assault of a police sergeant, fell under a heavy blow. Congress first-aid volunteers rushed up to rub his face with ice. ". . . he gave us a bloody grin and stood up to receive some more. . . ." The police sergeant was "so sweaty from his exertions that his Sam Browne had stained his white tunic. I watched him with my heart in my mouth. He drew back his arm for a final swing—and then he dropped his hands down by his side. 'It's no use,' he said, turning to me with half an apologetic grin, 'You can't hit a bugger when he stands up to you like that!' He gave the Sikh a mock salute and walked off."

(15) *Economic boycott*: When raids on salt works were halted upon the advent of the monsoon, civil disobedience took other forms including boycott of foreign-made products, especially cloth. Both cloth and liquor shops were persistently picketed.

(16) *Disobedience of ordinances*: As the campaign proceeded, special ordinances designed to suppress publicity and control assembly were promulgated by the Government. These were consistently disobeyed in a general movement to the jails.

(17) *Continuing activities*: The extensive campaign continued throughout the year and involved many manifestations of non-cooperation and civil disobedience.

(18) *Culmination of the movement*: A settlement was reached following talks between Gandhi and the Viceroy, and the Gandhi-

Irwin Agreement was published on 5 March 1931.

(1) *Arrests*: Initially, the Government avoided making mass arrests, partly in response to the "jail-courting" aspects of satyagraha. Finally, however, thousands of satyagrahis were arrested including hundreds of prominent Congress leaders.

(2) *Police action*: From the respective statements made on opposing sides of the movement, it is clear that the police reacted with determination and force. The official report does not acknowledge police excesses. Many non-Indian witnesses, however, testified to the contrary. The biographer of Lord Irwin notes that "the European Sergeants, provoked and overworked, did not always seem inclined to restrain their men." Gandhi, in his letter addressed to the Viceroy, asserted that "the rank and file has been often savagely and in some cases even indecently assaulted." An American journalist, Webb Miller, reported that after one raid on a salt depot he counted, in a hospital, 320 injured, "many still insensible with fractured skulls, others writhing in agony from kicks in the testicles and stomach . . ."

(3) *Determination of the Government*: The Viceroy, addressing both Houses of the legislature on 9 July (1930), asserted that the mass action was "nothing but the application of force under another form, and, when it has as its avowed object the making of Government impossible, a Government is bound either to resist or abdicate." He concluded that the government must "fight it with all our strength."

(4) *Special ordinances*: In an attempt to control the situation, the Government issued numerous ordinances including those providing for press censorship and suppression of objectionable printed matter. In places a ban was placed upon wearing of the white Gandhi cap.

(5) *Viceroy announced Round Table Conference plans*: Lord Irwin announced (12 May) that steps were being taken to arrange a meeting in London of representatives to consider constitutional reforms for India.

(6) *Continuing repression of agitation*: Throughout the early months of 1931 civil disobedience was met by arrests, firings, *lathi* charges, and other police force.

(7) *Gandhi-Irwin Agreement*: Final settlement following talks between Viceroy and Gandhi.

(8) *Fulfillment of the Gandhi-Irwin Agreement*, including repeal of ordinances and release of satyagrahi prisoners.

RESULTS

(1) *Modification of salt regulations*: The immediate objective of the salt satyagraha which opened the over-all civil disobedience movement was, to a large extent, realized. The salt laws were not repealed, but a new official interpretation was effected in the settlement agreed to by Gandhi and Lord Irwin. That interpretation specified that "For the sake . . . of giving relief to certain of the poorer classes," the Government would "extend their administrative provisions, on lines already prevailing in certain places, in order to permit local residents in villages, immediately adjoining areas where salt can be collected or made, to collect or make salt for domestic consumption or sale within such villages, but not for sale to, or trading with, individuals living outside them."

(2) *Other provisions of the Gandhi-Irwin Agreement*: According to the settlement arrived at in discussions between Gandhi and the Viceroy, the Government agreed to the following action:

(a) Amnesty to persons convicted of nonviolent offenses in connection with civil disobedience.

(b) Withdrawal of the restraining ordinances.

(c) Restoration of confiscated, forfeited, or attached properties.

(d) Administrative concession to make salt in certain areas.

In return, civil disobedience was to be ended and, in particular, the following activities discontinued:

(a) Organized defiance of the provisions of any law.

(b) Movement for non-payment of land revenue and other legal dues.

(c) Publication of news-sheets in support of civil disobedience.

(d) Attempts to influence civil and military servants or village officials against government or to persuade them to resign their posts.

(3) *Constitutional reforms*: The settlement included a statement that in further discussions on constitutional reform, representatives of the Congress would be invited to participate, and that in the deliberations of the next Round Table Conference, such questions as federation, reservation of subjects (e.g., defense, external affairs), financial credit, and position of minorities would be included.

Summary Analysis of the Salt Satyagraha

During 1930–1931, satyagraha was employed throughout India to advance the cause of Indian independence. Thousands of localized campaigns in the over-all civil disobedience movement involved hundreds of thousands of persons, many of whom adopted satyagraha as a temporary expedient without fully understanding its basic philosophy. Nevertheless, the movement remained, for the most part, non-violent. The opening campaign led by Gandhi in the march to the sea provided a model of adherence to basic principles and brilliance of strategy. An outstanding characteristic of the other campaigns during these months was the assertion of strong and effective leadership by hundreds of provincial and local Congressmen.

As for the elements of true satyagraha, all are to be found in the salt satyagraha. The immediate objective was the removal of laws which worked a hardship upon the poor. The Salt Acts, establishing a government monopoly over a food necessity, symbolized the further injustice—the subjugation of India by a foreign power. It therefore became the duty of the satyagrahi to disobey the unjust salt laws and to cling to the truth understood to be the right of the Indian people to manufacture salt as they chose. The further truth implications

were understood to lie in a people's right to self-government.

The volunteer satyagrahis who initiated the salt campaign rigorously abided by the principle of non-violence. During the later raids on the salt pans, some satyagrahis destroyed property by cutting wire and otherwise pulling down the fenses surrounding the salt works. Gandhi himself did not lead the raids in which property was destroyed, and he might well have restrained property destruction or considered it a weakness in that phase of the campaign. Some satyagrahis justified the destruction of fences to gain access to the salt pans by arguing that the salt works were public property and should be made available to all citizens. There is no evidence, however, that any physical injury was inflicted by satyagrahis upon their opponents. Violence was, indeed, at work in the successive raids on the salt pans—but it was violence inflicted by police forces upon satyagrahis, many of whom sustained grave and agonizing injury. Wave upon wave of satyagrahis responded to the attack, their action remaining non-violent but nonetheless aggressive. They retaliated, not with violence, but with the several persuasive tactics at their command.

Self-reliance characterized the conduct of the satyagrahis. They signed a pledge to offer civil resistance without expectation of material help for themselves or their families. Again, organized propaganda was published and distributed in the form of bulletins and leaflets, and publicity was further supplied by the press throughout the country in detailed reporting of satyagraha activities. Suppression of satyagraha propaganda and censorship of the press served to extend the opportunities for contravention of the law.

Initiative was retained by the satyagrahis throughout this civil disobedience movement. That action which centered upon contravention of the Salt Acts, progressed from the initial march to the sea and the first production of contraband salt to the subsequent seizure of salt from government depots and the spread of salt-making. Action then extended into the realm of economic boycott accompanied by picketing of cloth and liquor shops. Direct action was not undertaken until every effort had been made for an honorable settlement through negotiation and appeal to the Viceroy. The demand of the satyagrahis that Indians should be free to manufacture salt at will, was at no time relaxed. However, Gandhi remained ever ready to negotiate with the government for a settlement.

This satyagraha proceeded through the early steps of attempted negotiation, of agitation and demonstration, and the issuing of an ultimatum. The opponent was kept informed of intention and procedure. When the settlement was finally effected, following discussions between Gandhi and the Viceroy, the immediate objective—redress of grievances arising from the Salt Acts—was to a substantial degree realized even though the Acts themselves were not abolished. The long-term objective of Swaraj (independence) was, of course, not at once achieved. However, the Gandhi-Irwin Agreement provided that the Congress should participate in the second Round Table Conference to consider constitutional questions involved in the advancement of India along the road towards full independence.

Concluding Note on the Five Campaigns*

Satyagraha, as applied socio-political action, requires a comprehensive program of planning, preparation, and studied execution. To give active expression to the elements which inform the underlying philosophy of satyagraha, attention must be extended to a range of considerations from the choice of the objective through the selection of participants to the terms of final settlement.

Weaknesses in the campaigns examined appear especially where consideration of one or more of the stages of the campaign was slighted. The Vykom campaign showed signs of failure until participation in the satyagraha was narrowed to the religious community directly involved. The Ahmedabad labor satyagraha very nearly collapsed because participants had not been adequately prepared and a thorough-going constructive program had not been planned. The success of the Bardoli campaign was a result of careful attention to every stage of satyagraha. The Rowlatt campaign was discontinued because violence emerged due to inadequate preparation of satyagrahis, failure to delimit the extent of participation, and poor co-ordination of leadership. By 1930 the entire country had been exposed to something of the meaning of non-violent action. The country was more disciplined, as Nehru wrote, and there was a clearer appreciation of the nature of the struggle." Not only was the technique better understood, Nehru continued, "but more important still from Gandhiji's point of view, it was fully realised by every one that he was terribly in earnest about non-violence. There could be no doubt about that now as there probably was in the minds of some people ten years before."[11] The initial action in the salt satyagraha was carefully organized with greater attention to preparation both of the participating satyagrahis and the villagers along the route of the march to the sea. The difficulties experienced later were, in large part, created by a participation more extensive than the leadership could at all times direct. The countrywide response resulted in elements joining the campaign which neither accepted nor fully understood the meaning of non-violent action. The civil disobedience movement extending beyond the initial phase of the salt satyagraha suffered, again, from the failure to develop sufficiently well-defined immediate objectives as intermediary steps to full independence.

The examination of the five campaigns has shown that individual participants in a satyagraha could include members of widely differing economic, social, and religious communities. We have noted participation in satyagraha by laborers, peasants, merchants; by women both from the peasantry and from highly educated and wealthy families; by untouchable Hindus, Brahmans, Muslims—indeed even by the redoubtable Pathan warriors of the Frontier. Leaders, as well as partici-

---

* *Editor's note:* Bondurant examines five satyagraha campaigns. We have chosen to
feature only the "Salt Satyagraha" in this abridgement of her article.
[11] Nehru, *An Autobiography*, p. 209.

pants, included women and members of minority communities. Most of the participants in the campaigns reviewed were employing non-violence for the purpose of achieving specific objectives, and they adopted satyagraha because of its efficacy as a method. For most of those involved, non-violence was a policy, and not a creed. Gandhi's long-time secretary, Pyarelal, expressed this aspect of popular satyagraha movements, in replying to a question I put to him with regard to the necessity of complete belief in non-violence: "It *is* possible to run a satyagraha campaign with people who have no faith in non-violence as a creed provided they sincerely and implicitly follow the rules as a discipline and work under the leadership of unadulterated non-violence. . . ."[12]

The action undertaken in a satyagraha campaign varies distinctly from one circumstance to another. Tactics are evolved to meet the specific situation, both offensively and defensively. Strategy, however, remains broadly the same, based upon the considerations indicated above as steps or stages in a satyagraha campaign. We have noted that satyagraha has been successfully employed in opposition not only to the British Government in India, but against orthodox and entrenched Brahmans, against Indian mill-owners, and against local governments.

The techniques of non-violent action oper-

ating in situations of conflict employ force both defensively and offensively. In the case of Vykom the satygraha was predominatly aggressive in character. In all cases the early emphasis was on persuasion. Non-violent coercion developed in the later phases of the campaigns, especially in the all-India satyagrahas. In the instance of the Ahmedabad satyagraha, Gandhi came to see that his fasting introduced an element of coercion which detracted from the true character of satyagraha. The adherence to persuasion as opposed to coercion was best exemplified in the Vykom satyagraha: after the state had withdrawn its support of the opposition and the roads had been legally opened to untouchables, the satyagrahis did not take advantage of this development to enter the roads against the persisting opposition of the Brahmans. They continued the satyagraha until they had persuaded their opponents that denial of passage to untouchables was morally indefensible.

In examining satyagraha in action, it becomes clear that satyagraha operates as a force to effect change. The effectiveness of its action is governed by criteria centering upon the degree of persuasion effected, the extensiveness of the constructive program, and the degree to which the non-violent character of the action has been preserved.

[12] In a letter to the author, 17 October 1951.

23. Direct Action Tactics

Martin Oppenheimer* • George Lakey**

One catalog of non-violent action lists some sixty-four different methods which have been used throughout history.[1] We are taking from this list those which seem most significant for the current civil rights struggle.

Demonstrations

Demonstrations are primarily expressions of a point of view, and do not of themselves change the power structure as vigorously as

[1] Gene Sharp, *Methods of Nonviolent Action*, Institute for Social Research, Oslo, Norway.

Reprinted by permission of Quadrangle Books from *A Manual for Direct Action* by Martin Oppenheimer and George Lakey, copyright © 1964, 1965 by Martin Oppenheimer, George Lakey and the Friends of Peace Committee.
° Department of Sociology, Lincoln University.
°° Rutgers University.

non-cooperation or direct intervention might. Nevertheless, they do go beyond verbal protest and are considered sufficiently threatening by many authorities to provoke harsh reprisals.

1. Marches and Parades

Technically, the difference between a march and a parade is that a march has a destination of symbolic or immediate importance to the cause, whereas a parade route is chosen for convenience or potential impact on a neighborhood. Both may be short or long. Mass marches and parades can express the solidarity of the campaigners and be an important morale-booster.

A common way of discrediting marches and parades is to describe them as disorderly and violent. You can take two steps to eliminate the validity of this charge:

(a) Have either silence, or singing in unison. Both make a powerful impression of unity and dignity. Slogan-shouting and conversation build an impression of disunity and disorder.

(b) Set up a system of leadership. Experience shows it is helpful to have a marshal and a number of line leaders who, once policy is set, follow the directions of the marshal. The leadership helps in two ways: keeping discipline and building the morale of the marchers. In addition, more efficient decisions can be made in the event of police interference, etc. Leaders should be clearly designated and should set an example for others to follow.

A long march is often called a walk. The best known civil rights walk is the one postman William Moore began through the South, which others continued when he was killed. The Committee for Nonviolent Action has organized two walks for peace and freedom through the South which had to contend with cattle-prods and the like. The effect of a walk can be somewhat like that of the Freedom Rides—to dramatize an issue and give a morale boost to the movement in the towns through which the walkers go.

2. Picketing and Vigiling

The difference between picketing and a vigil is that a vigil is longer and held in a meditative spirit. Often a vigil is held around-the-clock for several days, or it may be daily for weeks or even months. It is also customary for participants in a vigil to stand rather than walk, as in picketing. In a culture like ours where religion is held in high esteem, a vigil is sometimes more effective than picketing; however, it is slightly more wearying and requires more self- and group-discipline. The remarks about orderliness apply here, to both picketing and vigiling.

SAMPLE PICKET OR VIGIL DISCIPLINE[2]

We will try to maintain an attitude of good will at all times, especially in face of provocation.

If violence occurs against us, we will not retaliate but will try to practice forgiveness and forbearance.

We agree that one person is in charge of specific actions and agree to abide by the decisions of the person in charge, even if at the time we do not fully agree with or understand the decision.

If in good conscience we cannot comply with this decision, we will not take contrary action but will withdraw from that phase.

In the event of arrest, we will submit with promptness and composure.

We will try to be prompt in our appointments and to carry out responsibly the tasks we have been assigned.

Here are some suggestions which will help you to organize an effective picket line.[3]

(1) Assemble somewhere other than the place where the picket line will be, then go to the place in a group; this avoids confusion and gives the leader a chance to pass out printed copies of the discipline as well as to conduct registration.

(2) Ask participants to refer questioners, press, or police to the marshal or information officer.

(3) Expect participants to walk erectly and not slouch, call out, laugh loudly, or use pro-

---

[2] Slightly revised from Charles C. Walker, *Organizing for Nonviolent Direct Action,* Cheyrey, Pennsylvania, 1964.

[3] This listing is based on Charles Walker's *Organizing for Nonviolent Direct Action.*

Figure 23.1.   An Organized Picket Line.

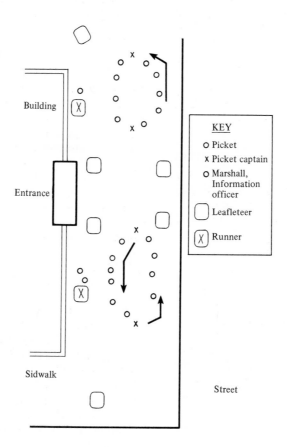

fanity; smoking may be ruled out in some situations.

(4) Assign two leafleteers to each location, so leafleting can go on if one leafleteer gets involved with a questioner.

(5) Instruct leafleteers on how to answer very briefly when asked "What is this all about?" or "Who's doing this?" or "Why don't you people go back to Russia?" or other questions.

(6) Ask leafleteers to pick up all discarded leaflets (to avoid legal entanglements and to show good will).

(7) Keep leaflets in a plastic bag in rainy weather.

(8) Avoid unnecessary scurrying about.

(9) Give instructions in a clear and authoritative voice, but avoid a domineering approach.

(10) Remember that your conduct sets an example for others.

3. Fraternization

This technique has been used in countries occupied by a foreign power, as well as in this country. The idea is to go out of the way to talk with the police or other opponents in a friendly way and to try to persuade them that one's cause is just. Where it has been tried, it has on occasion been amazingly effective, as some instances in Norway under the Nazi occupation testify. But it is not easy.

In the summer of 1964 a group of pacifists conducted a direct action project at a missile site in Quebec Province, Canada, including vigiling and civil disobedience. One of the techniques which they used to communicate was to pass out leaflets addressed "to our brothers in the armed forces," and "to our brothers in the police force." They also made impromptu speeches when soldiers and police were near, explaining their motivation and purpose. As a result, there was some breakdown in military discipline as soldiers went out of their way to join the pacifists in a prayer meeting at the conclusion of the vigil.

4. "Haunting"

This is a means of reminding officials of the immorality of their behavior—volunteers follow them everywhere they go. In India during the Gandhian struggles arrests were made, but the volunteers were replaced by others who "haunted" the authorities until officials were sick of it.

5. Leafleting

Leafleting can do several things for the cause: (a) provide the people with more accurate information than they get in the newspapers; (b) give more people more personal contact with the campaigners (in large communities many people never actually see demonstrators); (c) involve children and others who otherwise might not actively participate in the struggle.

6. Renouncing Honors

There can be some symbolic impact when campaigners renounce honors given them in the past. For example, Negro veterans might send back medals of honor; a Negro "Woman of the Year" might refuse the award from an institution which is part of the power structure; Negro students might send back their American Legion School Awards.

Some of the techniques which come under the heading of demonstrations may become civil disobedience if the city declares them illegal. Injunctions may be issued by courts forbidding marches or picketing. Where the Constitution is in operation, however, these methods do not usually involve breaking the law.

Non-Cooperation

This general category involves methods of direct action in which the campaigners withdraw their usual degree of cooperation with the opponent. The methods may be legal or illegal, depending on local laws.

1. Strike

The strike is one of the best known of all forms of direct action. It has not, however, been used very often in the civil rights struggle. It would be most potent in those areas where Negroes form a very large part of the population or of some economic concern which is important to the area. A form of the strike which might be experimented with is the "token strike." In a token strike all those sympathetic to the cause go off the job for a brief time—perhaps one day or a few hours. This is a way of showing solidarity and seriousness of purpose.

2. Hartal

The Indians under Gandhi developed this device extensively, but it was also used in Budapest at the beginning of the 1956 Hungarian revolution. A Hartal involves staying at home for a full day or more, leaving factories, streets, and places of amusement totally empty. In addition to reducing the chances of "incidents," the stay-at-home may serve to demonstrate to the opponent the degree of unity and self-discipline among the people in a campaign which stresses religious aspects, the day can be seen as a time for meditation and purification.

3. Consumers' Boycott or Selective Buying

From the Montgomery Bus Boycott on, the consumers' boycott has played an important role in the civil rights struggle. This method has its roots in the American Revolution and even further back in history, and has been used throughout the world. Its effectiveness depends on how much the businessman needs the campaigners' patronage for his economic survival.

Here are the advantages of the boycott: (a) it minimizes violence; (b) it promotes solidarity; (c) it does not usually involve civil disobedience. On the other hand, it usually requires a good deal of unity on the part of the protesting community.

4. Renters' Boycott (Rent-Strike)

The refusal to pay rent because of grievances against a landlord may be for a short period (token boycott) or indefinitely. Irish peasants in 1879 were often evicted for refusing rents to rich English landlords. Whether or not eviction takes place depends partly on the number of persons participating and on the nature of the local laws.

In the current civil rights struggle, workers go from house to house, apartment to apartment, talking with people about the injustice of their situation. They invite tenants to an area or house meeting, where the possibilities of united action are stressed. Those who will commit themselves at the meeting begin to strike at once—there is little to be gained by setting a date in the future for the beginning of the action. The action of the few who first volunteer will hopefully begin a wave of others joining the strike.

Guidelines for organization include: being realistic in explaining to the tenants what may happen (no one can guarantee major repairs); staying in close contact with the tenants to offset intimidation; and planning to put the rent money "in escrow," or into a special fund set aside for this purpose. The fund should be carefully accounted for.

Local regulations differ as to eviction possibilities. It is important to get legal counsel, for often constables themselves break the law in the process of eviction. In addition to countering eviction by legal action, picketing the constable and living on the sidewalk in front of the house are direct action tactics which may be tried; numbers of tenants can also obstruct constables' access to the house, thus preventing eviction. This is generally against the law, of course.

5. School Boycott

One of the advantages of the school boycott is that it involves the children in a struggle which will result in their eventual benefit, while still not involving them in a front-line confrontation with its accompanying dangers. The setting up of freedom schools for teaching the young can be a valuable exercise for those in the Negro community who are otherwise difficult to involve.

6. Tax Refusal

This is a drastic tactic, yet it has often been used in struggles in the past in various parts of the world. It can be partial, such as withholding school taxes, or complete. The money which would otherwise go for taxes can be given to the movement for distribution to needy campaigners. Generally opponents feel this tactic more deeply than almost any other, for, if the refusing population is large, it threatens the very survival of the government. Harsh reprisal may therefore be expected. Despite this, the strong moral appeal involved ("Why pay the police who are beating you?") and the strength of the tactic has made tax refusal effective in some campaigns.

Intervention

Direct non-violent intervention consists of physical confrontation rather than withdrawal of cooperation or demonstrating. It carries the conflict into the opponent's camp and often changes the status quo abruptly.

1. Sit-In

The sit-in has been used in the United States mostly in restaurants and at lunch counters. Generally campaigners progressively occupy a large number of all of the available seats and refuse to leave until the Negro members of the group are served, the restaurant closes, the group is arrested, or a certain fixed period of time has gone by. This method can also be used in other situations such as on buses and trains, as in the Freedom Rides. There have been sit-ins in the offices of notables such as mayors and business executives in order to obtain appointments or to symbolize the blocking of freedom in which the official is participating. Legislative halls can be used similarly. Often the sit-in is a perfectly legal activity.

NON-VIOLENT DISCIPLINE OF THE 1960 NASHVILLE STUDENT SIT-IN MOVEMENT

Don't strike back or curse if abused.
Don't laugh out.

Don't hold conversations with the floor workers.

Don't leave your seats until your leader has given you instruction to do so.

Don't block entrances to the stores and the aisles.

Show yourself courteous and friendly at all times.

Sit straight and always face the counter.

Report all serious incidents to your leader.

Refer all information to your leader in a polite manner.

Remember love and nonviolence.

May God bless each of you.

Allied methods are stand-in, where people line up for admission to a theater or similar place; the wade-in, in which campaigners attempt to swim at a segregated beach; and the kneel-in, in which Negroes try to worship at a church which excludes them.

2. The Fast

The fast was used as a method of psychological intervention by, among others, Danilo Dolci[4] when he led 1,000 unemployed fishermen in a twenty-four-hour mass fast on a beach in Sicily. The fast can be of heightened effectiveness when undertaken by persons of high status, such as ministers. Gandhi, the best-known faster, considered this the most difficult of all techniques and emphasized that it should be thought through carefully. This is especially true of the fast unto death. Experience with the fast in Albany, Georgia, by peace walkers, indicates that clarity of purpose and realistic time periods are important. Efforts must be made to overcome the misunderstanding which comes in a society where "good living" is prized and self-denial is looked down upon.

Gandhi believed that fasting is most effective when there is a close relationship between the faster and the opponent.

3. Reverse Strike

This method has been found effective in various situations—e.g., agricultural workers have done more work and worked longer hours than they were paid for, in support of their demand for pay increases. The unemployed in Sicily in 1956 voluntarily repaired a public road that was badly in need of repair in order to call attention to the severe unemployment in the area and the government's failure to deal with it. Although this method looks harmless enough at first glance, it has in practice been regarded as a sufficient threat so that reverse-strikers have been arrested, imprisoned, and even in some cases shot by police attempting to stop them from working! Clearing an unused lot for a playground, despite the fact that the lot belongs to someone else, or to the city, might be a current example. This may involve breaking the law.

4. Non-Violent Interjection and Obstruction

This involves placing one's body between another person and the objective of his work. Civil rights workers in this country have used it at school and other construction sites, to protest the building itself or discrimination in hiring the construction workers. Striking hosiery workers in Reading, Pennsylvania, in 1957, lay down on the sidewalks at the factory gates making it necessary for non-strikers to walk over them to get into the factory, or else stay away from their jobs. In early 1964 at a Cleveland construction site several actionists lay down in front of a bulldozer; a minister, Rev. Bruce Klunder, seeing that the operator might reverse direction, lay down behind the bulldozer and was killed. We should remember that in a confusing situation the operator might not look in both directions before moving his machine.

There is more danger of injury or death when one or a few persons engage in interjection than when a great many participate. An example of the latter case, called obstruction, occurred in Japan in 1956 when 10,000 people physically occupied a site intended for a United States air base. After several days of obstruction the plans for building the air base were abandoned.

Even while this manual is being prepared some individual or group is probably devising still other forms of nonviolent direct action.

---

[4] Dolci, sometimes called "the Italian Gandhi," is a pioneer in applying direct action to community organization.

One of the elements of non-violence is the creativity which it stimulates, and the reader will probably want to experiment with new forms of non-violent struggle. Not all of them will be really effective, and some will collapse as did the World's Fair "stall-in" in April, 1964. In evaluating a new tactic before trying it out, the thoughtful civil rights worker will ask:

(1) Is it clearly related to the issue?
(2) Are the people it will inconvenience really the people heavily involved in the injustice?

(3) Is there chance of direct confrontation between the campaigners and the opponent?
(4) Does the tactic put a major part of the suffering which is inevitable in social change upon our shoulders, rather than upon innocent bystanders?
(5) If direct action, especially interjection and obstruction, involve violation of the law (civil disobedience), are demonstrators prepared to accept the penalties in order to make the point?

If the answer to these questions is "yes," the tactic may be worth trying.

24. Disruptive Tactics[a]

Harry Specht*

There is both confusion and uncertainty about the use of disruptive tactics to bring about planned change in American communities. The confusion, in part, grows out of a major problem the United States faces today —violence, its causes and resolution. Indeed, it is the major problem throughout the world, which we have succeeded so little in dealing with. In addition, in the social sciences as in social work there is neither extensive knowledge about the dynamics of either disruption or violence nor systematic processes the practitioner can use to deal with them.[1]

The idea of government by and through elected officials is being seriously questioned on all sides. Many have lost confidence in the viability of established democratic political structures—students and other young people, minority groups, and the political left. But today, the ubiquity of violence and illegal behavior in American communities is only a reflection of the violence and lawless behavior supported by many of the country's leaders. Thus, the mayor of a large city castigated his police force for not "shooting to kill or to maim" young arsonists and looters; the governor of a large state called rioters "mad dogs"; and the former President lost his credibility when the deception, corruption, and violence of the country's foreign policy became evident.

It seems that Fanon's belief in the cleansing force of violence and the need to use violence as an agent of change is gaining wide support as many white families buy guns to defend themselves against blacks, black action groups arm to protect themselves against the police, and the police increase their arsenals to defend the cities against black insurgents. It is as though the whole country is caught by Fanon's ideas:

For if the last shall be first, . . . this will only come to pass after a murderous and decisive struggle between the two protagonists. That affirmed intention . . . can only triumph if we use all means to turn the scales, including, of course, that of violence.[2]

[1] Raymond C. Mack, "Components of Social Conflict," *Social Problems*, Vol. 12, No. 4 (Spring 1965), pp. 388–397.
[2] Frantz Fanon, *The Wretched of the Earth* (New York: Grove Press, 1963), p. 37.

Reprinted with permission of the National Association of Social Workers from *Social Work*, Vol. 14, No. 2 (April 1969), pp. 5–15.
[a] An earlier version of this paper was presented at the National Conference on Social Welfare, May 29, 1968, in San Francisco, California.
* Associate Professor, School of Social Welfare, University of California, Berkeley.

It is only in a climate of unreason that this mixture of "blood and anger," which can lead to insurrection, becomes thoroughly confused with legitimate dissent and political radicalism. We should not talk of crime in the streets or violence on the campus in shocked dismay when the larger part of the nation's resources are being used to fashion this country into the world's greatest instrument of violence.

A discussion of the moral and ethical, as well as the programmatic, consequences of disruptive tactics used in efforts at planned change presupposes the existence of some organized system of available tactical choices. This paper will first distinguish different kinds of tactics that constitute the spectrum of choices and then discuss disruptive tactics in detail. This order is necessary if the use of disruptive tactics is to be understood as a consciously planned choice made on the basis of moral and ethical considerations as well as strategic objectives. The author uses "strategy" to refer to an over-all plan of action and "tactics" to indicate the more specific actions of moving and directing resources to attain goals. Strategy requires a long-term plan of action based on some theory of cause and effect, while tactics are the somewhat more constant methods of action.

Why Disruption?

What is it about issues that makes them subject to one or another set of tactics? Warren describes the association between different modes of intervention and different responses to issues.[3] (Modes of intervention are categories of tactics.) The range of responses to issues he describes are the following: (1) *issue consensus*, when there is a high possibility of agreement between the action and target system; (2) *issue difference*, when for one reason or another the parties are not in complete agreement but there is a possibility of agreement; and (3) *issue dissensus*, when there is no agreement between the parties. Consensus is associated with collaborative modes of intervention; difference with cam-

paigns of a competitive, persuasive, or bargaining nature; and dissensus with contests in which there is a high degree of conflict between the parties. (Conflict may be considered as an element in all modes of intervention to some degree.) In this paper, disruptive and contest tactics will be associated with dissensus.

The question still remains: Why these responses? The response to an issue, whether rational or not, indicates how the issue is *perceived* by the different parties; perception determines response. By extending Warren's typology, the associations among different perceptions of change, responses to the change, and the kinds of intervention these responses command may be suggested. Table 24.1 combines these elements but adds violence as a fourth mode of intervention based on a perception of change that aims at "reconstruction of the entire system" to which the response is "insurrection."

Perceptions, Responses, Interventions

Collaboration is based on consensual responses to planned changes that are perceived as a rearrangement of resources. For example, the parties to the change are in essential agreement about the co-ordination or reorganization of services. No one thinks they will lose a great deal in the change. Until only recently, there had been a rather narrow concentration on this kind of intervention in social work, based on work with homogeneous and elitist types of community action systems. For the most part, the action system (that undertaking change) and the target system (that being changed) are identical, and the client system (on whose behalf change is sought) is probably not involved at all. The role of the worker is most frequently that of enabler and educator.

Redistribution of resources is a qualitatively different perception of a change. One of the parties expects he will end up with more or less of something (money, facilities, authority) but, because they perceive the need to

[3] Roland I. Warren, *Types of Purposive Social Change at the Community Level*, University Papers in Social Welfare, No. 11 (Waltham, Mass.: Florence Heller Graduate School for Advanced Studies in Social Welfare, Brandeis University, 1965).

TABLE 24.1 Change: Perceptions, Responses, and Modes of Intervention

Perception of Change	Response	Mode of Intervention
Rearrangement of resources	Consensus	Collaboration
Redistribution of resources	Difference	Campaign
Change in status relationships	Dissensus	Contest or disruption
Reconstruction of the entire system	Insurrection[a]	Violence

[a] Insurrection is used here because the word "revolution" can only be applied to a successful insurrection.

remain within the rules of the game—the institutionalized system of competition—the contending parties utilize campaign tactics to persuade, negotiate, bargain, and, eventually, compromise and agree. The action, target, and client systems might be expected to appear as separate entities, with the action system serving as mediator or arbitrator between the other two. The role of the professional change agent is most likely to be that of advocate.

Contest or disruption is generated by a challenge to existing status relationships and this view of change creates an entirely different type of discourse than any of the others mentioned. Contest or disruption is rooted in the competition for power in human relations. Status relationships refer to the social arrangements (the institutionalized system) by which promises, expectations, rights, and responsibilities are awarded, and the social arrangements always give more to some than to others. A threat to the system of relationships in which some people have power over others is the basis for this kind of response whether it involves parents and children, welfare workers and clients, students and teachers, or blacks and whites. None surrenders power voluntarily. The ability to perpetuate these patterns of varied and complex relationships long after the historical conditions that gave rise to them cease to exist is a human quality but also creates conflict.

When community issues are perceived by one group as eliminating or diminishing its power over others, the response will be dissensus; contest and disruption, the result. "To carve out a place for itself in the politico-social

order, a new group may have to fight for a reorientation of many of the values of the old order" is the way Key states this proposition.[4] In these kinds of change efforts, the action and target systems are distinctly separate and the client system is closely aligned or identical with the action system. The role of the community worker is that of partisan or organizer.

A change perceived as intended to overthrow the sovereign power of the state is responded to as insurrection. The mode of intervention associated with it—violence—is not part of the arsenal of tactics available to professional social workers and, therefore, the author will not comment on the relative positions of the action, target, and client systems or the worker's professional role. However, these tactics do pose serious dilemmas for community change agents, which will be discussed in the final section of the paper.

However, it should be said here that the major overriding objective of community organization is to enable communities to create a strategy of reconciliation, to move from insurrection to contest, to campaign, to collaboration. It is necessary for the professional change agent who utilizes the tactics described in this paper to operate with goals that will, as Cloward puts it "eventually heal, not further disrupt."[5]

Examples

The following examples will illustrate the interplay of the three elements that comprise Table 24.1: perceptions, responses, and modes of intervention.

Objectively, fluoridation should present a

[4] V. O. Key, Jr., *Politics, Parties and Pressure Groups* (5th ed.: New York: Thomas Y. Crowell, 1964), p. 48.

[5] Richard A. Cloward, "A Strategy of Disruption." *Center Diary: 16* (January–February 1967), p. 31.

good case for collaborative modes of intervention. It is said to be sensible, scientific, and not only inexpensive, but money-saving. Many health officials and community organizers have approached it with exactly that logical frame of mind because superficially fluoridation would appear to be a rather simple rearrangement of resources that calls for an educational mode of intervention. Yet the issue of fluoridation has been the basis for harsh, vindictive social conflicts in hundreds of communities in the United States.[6]

There appear to be two major sets of reasons for the resistance. First, there are those people who question the effectiveness of the proposed change or who fear that fluoride may be poisonous. This type of resistance does yield to collaborative modes of intervention.[7] But the second basis for resistance does not respond to such methods at all. This is resistance based on the belief that fluoridation infringes on the rights of individuals, that "compulsory medication" usurps the rights of free men. Green supports this contention with concrete findings. His research indicates that indignation over the *presumed* violation of personal freedom is more fundamental than the danger of poisoning. The fear of poisoning symbolizes a disposition to see fluoridation as an insidious attack by a vague constellation of impersonal social forces bent on usurping the powers and prerogatives of the common citizen, and the root cause of this feeling of being victimized experienced by active opponents of fluoridation is the increasing remoteness and impersonality of the sources of power and influence affecting the daily life of the individual.[8] In short, the issue of fluoridation becomes a contest when it is perceived to be a threat to status.

Another example of the delicate balance between perceptions of change as a redistribution of resources and an alteration in status is provided by Marris and Rein in their analysis of community action programs. They pose this question: If community planners had larger grants of money available to them, would it have been easier for them to move the bureaucracies along the lines of the change they desired? This is their answer:

> If the funding agencies had offered more money, they would . . . have given communities a greater incentive to meet the criteria of concerted action. But they would also have raised the stakes in the competition for control of the project's resources. . . . A marginal addition to the city's resources stood at least a chance of insinuating an influence for change, without intruding a challenge to bureaucratic authority too obvious to overlook.[9]

This suggests that an increase in the amount of resources may convert a perception of change from one of a rearrangement or a redistribution to a change in status.

The civil rights movement seems to have shifted in the last five years from a major focus on the rearrangement and redistribution of resources to a greater concern with change in status. Of course, all along, the demands being made by the movement may have *required* change in status for success, but the movement has increasingly recognized that the power of whites over blacks is the issue, as is pointed out in the following statement by Hamilton:

> While there are masses of poor, powerless whites, they do not *perceive* [italics added] their condition as a result of deliberate policy. . . . Many blacks do have such a view.[10]

Memphis, Tennessee, in the events preceding the assassination of Martin Luther King, was not confronting a simple question of the redistribution of resources as in an ordinary

[6] "Trigger for Community Conflict," entire issue of the *Journal of Social Issues*, Vol. 17, No. 4 (October 1961).

[7] Benjamin D. Paul, "Fluoridation and the Social Scientist: A Review," in *ibid.*, p. 5.

[8] *Ibid.*, p. 7.

[9] Peter Marris and Martin Rein, *Dilemmas of Social Reform* (New York: Atherton Press, 1967), p. 158.

[10] Charles Hamilton, "The Meaning of Black Power," reprinted from the *New York Times* in the *San Francisco Chronicle*, "This World," April 21, 1968, p. 25.

TABLE 24.2 The Relationship Between Tactics and Modes of Intervention

Mode of Intervention	Tactics
Collaboration	Joint action
	Cooperation
	Education
Campaign	Compromise
	Arbitration
	Negotiation
	Bargaining
	Mild coercion
Contest or disruption	Clash of position within accepted social norms
	Violation of normative behavior (manners)
	Violation of legal norms
Violence	Deliberate attempts to harm
	Guerilla warfare
	Deliberate attempts to take over government by force

labor dispute. That the striking workers recognized the question of status was quite evident in their signs that read: "I Am a Man!" for indeed it was their manhood they perceived to be at stake. That the mayor of Memphis saw it the same way is clear from his statement that he would be damned if he would be the first southern mayor to bargain collectively with a black union.

Tactics

Modes of intervention comprise sets of tactics. While the purpose of this paper is to discuss disruptive tactics, the idea that there is a dynamic relationship between tactics used for different modes of intervention is helpful in understanding their use. Table 24.2 suggests what this relationship may be.

These behaviors constitute a continuum of interventive modes rather than discrete actions. A strategy for change might utilize tactics from one or more modes of intervention simultaneously, depending on the goals of the action system and the organizational context within which it operates.[11] For example, in *A Manual for Direct Action*, a handbook of action for civil rights and other nonviolent protests, the authors instruct organizers in the use of bargaining and educational tactics along with disruptive tactics, and sometimes all three are directed at the same system.

> Poor negotiation . . . can bring a return to open conflict. . . . [In work with the target system] describe the results of change as *less* threatening than the opponents suppose, and . . . describe the results of not changing . . . as *more* threatening than . . . change. . . . Bring illustrations of successes in other places.[12]

[11] For an interesting discussion of the relationship between these variables *see* Martin Rein and Robert Morris, "Goals, Structures, and Strategies for Community Change," in Mayer N. Zald, ed., *Social Welfare Institutions* (New York: John Wiley & Sons, 1965), pp. 367–382.

[12] Martin Oppenheimer and George Lakey, *A Manual for Direct Action* (Chicago: Quadrangle Books, 1964), p. 24. An interesting related question that cannot be considered in this paper is how the structure of an action system is related to these modes of intervention. All action systems expand and contract throughout their history and one might predict the relationship between organizational structure and tactical choices. For example, movement to insurrection would be accompanied by narrowing the action system and movement from campaign to collaboration by its expansion.

What is meant by disruptive tactics? They are used by one or both parties to a contest. Their purpose has been described as preventing an opponent from continuing to operate, to neutralize, injure, or eliminate him.[13] Warren describes tactics as "processes where deliberate harmful activity is directed toward an opposing party."[14] However, in the strategic viewpoint outlined in this paper, disruptive tactics are considered those that aim in different ways to move the other party toward some acceptable reconciliation. The term "disruptive" seems most appropriate for these tactics because their major objective is to *prevent* the target system from continuing to operate as usual, i.e., to disrupt, but *not* to injure, harm, or destroy. The latter are the goals of the tactics of violence.

Disruptive Tactics

Clash of Position

This tactic is used within accepted social norms and essentially involves such actions as debate, legal disputes, written statements of intent, or public speeches. The objective of this tactic is to bring the issue to the attention of the public, usually in such a way as to mobilize sympathy from the larger community as well as to stir discontent among the "oppressed."

The way in which Gandhi's philosophy of nonviolence has been popularized in the United States often causes Americans to overlook many of the subtle meanings of the elaborate system Gandhi developed, which he called *satyagraha* (search for truth). *Satyagraha* is a complicated and difficult term to define because it embraces both a philosophy of life as well as a methodology of social action and, therefore, is certainly a more developed system than the one described in this paper. It is a refined technique for social and political change that transcends the simple

concepts of civil disobedience, nonviolence, or disruptive behavior.

In the Gandhian view, clash of position comes at quite an advanced stage in dealing with an issue, and a number of other steps are required before a *satyagrahi* makes use of this tactic, such as negotiation, arbitration, reasoning, and other methods designed to win over the opponent. Civil disobedience is, of course, one of the final stages of this action system.[15]

Oglesby and Shaull, in analyzing the process by which the oppressed become revolutionaries, describe a clash of position as the tactic of "mass-based secular prayer." This appeal to a higher power, they say, sometimes results in change. More often, it shows the victim-petitioner that change is more difficult to achieve than he imagined, and this may become "the spiritual low point of the emergent revolutionary's education," for he learns that "the enemy is not a few men, but a whole system."[16]

Violation of Normative Behavior

This tactic refers to actions that might be viewed as a moving away from what may be deemed good manners and involves activities like marches, demonstrations, boycotts, protests, vigils (extended demonstrations), rent strikes, dropping out, haunting (following one's opponent for long periods), renouncing honors, *hartals* (having large masses of people stay at home, a sort of spiritual variation of a general strike), fasts, and interjection (having large masses of people congregate in an area, as, for example, 10,000 Japanese did in 1956 to prevent successfully the use of the site for a U.S. Air Force base). The objectives of these actions are the same as those listed under the heading "clash of position" as well as to generate conscience, discomfort, and guilt in the oppressors and an *esprit de corps* among the oppressed.

[13] Lewis Coser, *The Functions of Social Conflict* (Glencoe, Ill.: Free Press, 1956), p. 8.

[14] Warren, *op. cit.*, p. 29.

[15] Joan V. Bondurant, *Conquest of Violence* (Berkeley: University of California Press, 1965), pp. 40–41.

[16] Carl Oglesby and Richard Shaull, *Containment and Change* (New York: Macmillan Co., 1967), p. 145.

This tactic, more than any others, demonstrates the effects of changing social and legal definitions of behavior. Rent strikes and boycotts, for example, lie in a gray area between violation of normative behavior and violation of law. The increased number of protests by citizens over the last decade has elevated demonstrations and marches to a tactic that is more like a clash of position than anything else. One can hardly announce a grievance today without a public demonstration of some sort. Furthermore, the tactic of choice is, to some degree, specific to the group. For example, only those who have been included in society can drop out; that tactic is available to middle-class college students, not to the hard-core unemployed of the ghetto. Fasting, a technique used with enormous success by Gandhi, is reserved for situations in which there is a rather special relationship of mutual respect between the opposing parties.

Moreover, tactics are *patterned* group behaviors. Whether used consciously or not, the styles of action in different action systems are based on numerous group and organizational variables, such as social class, ideology, resources, and values.

Violation of Legal Norms

This tactic includes techniques like civil disobedience and noncooperation, tax refusal, sit-ins, draft resistance, and other violations of law. Carried to its final stages in *satyagraha,* this tactic includes usurping the functions of government and setting up a parallel government. The objectives of this tactic include all those listed for the other types of disruptive tactics and, in addition, they aim to demonstrate that people feel strongly enough about an issue to expose themselves to the danger of punishment by legal authorities for violating the law.

Civil disobedience presupposes an absence of, or inadequacy in, established law that morally justifies violation of it. The difficult moral question with which action systems must deal is whether they can find it morally correct to disobey an unjust law to protest its injustice or a morally just law to protest another injustice. Based on a philosophical anarchism and the concept of "natural rights," these acts have quite an honorable tradition in American life—a tradition that recognizes that the legal system is and always will be imperfect; the majority, whose wishes the laws (at least theoretically) are supposed to reflect, is itself imperfect; and all moral values have not been and never will be enacted into law.[17]

There are specific requirements of actions classified as nonviolent civil disobedience. They are only utilized after all other remedies have been exhausted and are used openly and selflessly. (That is, the actions have a public character and are carried out with public explanations of the reasons for the action in the name of some higher morality.) Furthermore, they are utilized with an awareness of the consequences for the participants.[18] These tactics are exemplified by the nonviolent resistance to police enforcement of laws. Indeed, the major tenet of those who have committed themselves to these actions expresses a profound faith in the value of the existing legal-political system, and it is the absence of this faith that characterizes changes perceived as insurrection. While rebellion may claim moral justification, unlike civil disobedience its aim is to overthrow the social order, not to change and reconcile. This separation between the legality and the morality of the social order was precisely the distinction Socrates made in recognizing the right of his judges to condemn him to death.

Objectives and Effectiveness

It should be noted that the direction of issues can be from consensus to violence or the reverse, but, as Simmel pointed out in his still relevant seminal work on conflict written in the early 1900's, "the transitions from war to

[17] Vernon Louis Parrington, *Romantic Revolution in America, 1800–1860,* "Main Currents in American Thought" (New York: Harcourt, Brace & Co., 1930), pp. 271–460.

[18] John de J. Pemberton, Jr., "Is There a Moral Right to Violate the Law?" *Social Welfare Forum, 1963* (New York: Columbia University Press, 1965), pp. 194–195.

peace constitute a more serious problem than does the reverse."[19] Certainly, the use of disruptive tactics has the potential for great harm to the group in whose interests they are used. It allows the oppressor to put increasingly fewer limits on himself, freeing him to act disruptively or violently when he might otherwise have been constrained to avoid such behavior. For example, the police in many cities have attacked demonstrators with obvious relish when they used what the police perceived to be tactics of violence, as was the case in the antidraft demonstrations of October 1967 when some student groups attempted to shut down draft centers by violent means. In just this way, Mayor Daley attempted to justify the attacks on demonstrators by the Chicago police during the 1968 Democratic Convention.

Violent tactics can provide the other party with the opportunity to "change the subject," so that the public's concern switches from the issue to the illegal behavior of the demonstrators. Both King and Gandhi always consciously sought to use nonviolent techniques as a rein on the violence of the established ruling class—"to keep the conversation open and the switchblade closed"[20]—and the correctness of their views is borne out by the fact that there were fewer deaths in ten years of nonviolent direct action in the South than in ten days of northern riots.

Stinchcombe asserts that the resort to violent tactics is related to the strengths of social norms governing the use of violence in society. In particular, his comments point up that nonviolent methods are viable only as long as civil authorities continue to accept the responsibility for carefully controlling their own use of violence in dealing with civil disputes. He says:

> The critical question . . . about the violent organizations of a society [i.e., the police and the army] is how far their entry into politics

is governed by an understood set of limiting norms. For if the army and police enter the conflict unconditionally on one or another side of the conflict, supplying a ruling group or a revolutionary group with unlimited power to dispose of its enemies, then competition for place among organizations tends to become unlimited. Because the opposition to currently ruling powers is equally punished, whether it uses speech or riot, opponents are likely to choose the most effective means . . . of combatting government terror [which] are not always peaceful. And a government or revolutionary group supported by the army and police in an unlimited fashion is likely to undertake to root out its opposition, rather than to limit the opposition to approved means of conflict.[21]

To use disruptive tactics, several questions must be considered by the action system: Is the stress that stimulated the use of these tactics recognizable to the opponent? Is there support and reassurance to the opponent whose change is desired that the extent of change is not unlimited? Have encounters opened or closed communication between contending parties? Has there been an adequate process of inquiry and exploration prior to the disruption? In the Gandhian use of disruptive techniques, the major question asked of the *satyagrahi* is whether he has engaged the opponent in a manner designed to transform the complexity of relationships so that new patterns may emerge.[22] When all these attempts fail, violent tactics become a likely alternative.

Tactics of Violence

Insurrection differs from disruption both in the tactics used and the ends sought. It is not a call to resist the immoral acts of legitimate authority, but the withdrawal of legitimacy from the sovereign authority. It ties up the conflict over status relationships with something much larger, whereby the entire system is viewed as impossible to reform.

[19] Georg Simmel. "On Conflict," in Talcott Parsons, ed., *Theories of Society* (New York: Free Press of Glencoe, 1961). p. 1325.

[20] Oglesby and Shaull, *op. cit.* p. 149.

[21] Arthur L. Stinchcombe, "Social Structures and Organizations," in James G. March, ed., *Handbook of Organizations* (Chicago: Rand McNally Co., 1965), p. 97.

[22] Bondurant, *op. cit.*, p. viii.

The leap into revolution leaves "solutions" behind because it has collapsed and wholly redefined the "problems" to which they referred. The rebel is an incorrigible absolutist who makes the one grand claim that the entire system is in error.[23]

The tactics of violence are not available for use by the professional social reformer for several reasons. Quite practically, he cannot practice social work if he is a fugitive from justice, in jail, or dead. But, more important, a professional receives his sanction for practice from the larger society he serves and its legal and political systems. Morally, he may reach the conclusion that the framework is no longer worthy of legitimacy, and it is certainly difficult to argue that the moral basis for that choice does not exist in today's society. But it should be clear that this is the choice that must be made, and the professional should not be confused about what he is undertaking when he commits himself to violence.

This confusion is often encountered among students who think their protest actions should lead to a reversal of policy even if their behavior is violent. But to be a revolutionary requires that one believe that policy *cannot* be changed without replacing the government by force.

The social worker's authority stems from his knowledge, values, skills, and sanction to deal with social welfare institutions and to use social work methods. Although he may give his personal commitment to rebellion, it is improper to use his authority to give legitimacy to the destruction of institutions. This is when the larger strategy that directs a professional's work is especially important because it forces him to test his choice of a specific tactic in relation to its historical perspective. Is the choice of tactics dictated by his view of the long-range struggle and within a professed area of competence? Disruption used without some strategy for change is unlikely to achieve anything but escalation to violence; it certainly will not provide a means for changing the structure of American society.

The task of the intellectual leaders of any community undertaking is to help community action systems maintain freshness and vigor in moving toward goals by elucidating the legal, political, and historical relationships that underlie their efforts.[24] Invariably, revolutionary movements develop with strong, narrow ideologies that monopolize the conduct of the struggle over issues and bind the rebels in a united contempt for all other solutions. Social workers should expect neither support nor quarter from revolutionary groups because, as a rule, they consider others who are struggling on the same side to be more dangerous than the oppressor since they must disallow any who would offer an appealing alternative. They represent the other side of oppression, "killing their way to power."[25] They believe, with Fanon, that "no gentleness can efface the marks of violence; only violence itself can destroy them."[26]

The question for the professional is whether his objective is to enable people to make choices or to assert *his* choice and cast his lot with those who have arrived at *the* solution. Social work operates in a framework of democratic decision-making, and if one decides that the framework is no longer viable, then there is no profession of social work to be practiced.

Dilemma

As long as this country participates in unjust wars of conquest and does not provide the resources needed to deal with domestic crises of racism, poverty, and other social injustices, all professionals will face the dilemma of either working through institutions they believe may be unable to overcome social rot or participating in their destruction. But that awful choice should be made with clarity about the

[23] Oglesby and Shaull, *op. cit.,* p. 146.
[24] Harry Specht, *Urban Community Development,* Publication No. 111 (Walnut Creek, Calif.: Council of Community Services, 1966), p. 44.
[25] Robert Pickus, "Civil Disobedience But Not Violence," *Dissent,* Vol. 15, No. 1 (January–February 1968), p. 21.
[26] Fanon, *op. cit.,* p. 21.

consequences for professional status as well as the objectives to be served.

Guevara was extremely clear about the preconditions for choosing revolutionary tactics:

> It must always be kept in mind that there is a necessary minimum without which the establishment and consolidation of the first center . . . [of guerrilla warfare] is not practicable. People must see clearly the futility of maintaining the fight for social goals within the framework of civil debate. . . . Where a government has come into power through some form of popular vote, fraudulent or not, and maintains at least an appearance of constitutional legality, the guerrilla outbreak cannot be promoted, since the possibilities of peaceful struggle have not yet been exhausted.[27]

These clear guides notwithstanding, many young people attempt to impose the strategies of Fanon, Debray, and Guevara on the American society. Given Guevara's preconditions for revolution, these philosophies of social change in the "Third World" can provide vicarious pleasures for American radicals but not realistic action strategies. Moreover, as Lasch warns:

> While violence as a meaningful strategy is tactically premature in the United States, without other strategic perspectives militancy will carry the day by default and is dangerous because it may support the development of an American fascism.[28]

The New Left and student politics should not be dismissed out of hand. Surely they have created a valuable training ground in which a new generation can test its solutions to social and political problems. However, other persons who are committed to radical social change are often caught between two worlds. They have spent much of their lives working to reform the established order and find their perspective inadequate and their strategy ineffective—or at least they are viewed that way

by young people. It is like the dialogue between mother and son in a poem by Aimé Césaire:

THE MOTHER:

My race—the human race. My religion—brotherhood.

THE REBEL:

My race: that of the fallen. My religion . . . but it's not you that will show it to me with your disarmament. . . . 'tis I myself, with my rebellion and my poor fists clenched and my wooly head. . . .[29]

Conclusion

Perhaps, though, new ways may be found to define the roles of reformer and revolutionary despite their seemingly irreconcilable divergence. For example, Shaull, in coming to grips with this dilemma, suggests that it may be oversimplified. He proposes a "political equivalent" of guerrilla warfare and suggests that greater attention be given to the question of the relationship of those working for radical change and the institutions of the established order. He says: "Service in the framework of a particular institution does not necessarily demand complete subservience to it."[30] In Shaull's view, revolutionaries can contribute to the renewal of institutions by being in but not of these structures, by living as exiles within their own society. Whether this alternative is a viable one or simply Utopian cannot be decided without some exploration but, given the size of this society's institutions and the enormous concentration of power within them, it is certainly an important alternative to consider.

Ultimately, choice of tactics must rest on our beliefs about this society. If we believe it is possible to move the community, we can continue to work for change through its institutions. If it is not possible, then God help us

---

[27] Ernesto Ché Guevara, *Guerrilla Warfare* (New York: Monthly Review Press, 1961), pp. 15–16.

[28] Christopher Lasch, "The Trouble With Black Power," *New York Review of Books,* Vol. 10, No. 4 (February 29, 1968).

[29] Quoted in Fanon, *op. cit.,* p. 86.

[30] Oglesby and Shaull, *op. cit.,* pp. 196–197.

all, for then we must either continue to act in a drama that has lost its purpose or join in the destruction of society. Disruption and violence can contribute to change, but more than that will be required for reconciliation—more than that is required to transform America.

25. The Dynamics of Recent Ghetto Riots[1]

James R. Hundley, Jr.[*]

Introduction

The ghetto riot is a specific case of what sociologists call "crowd" behavior: "The mob, murderous or destructive; the rioting crowd, whether angry or triumphant; crowds engaged in orgies of joy, grief, or religious fervor; audiences which go wild; groups in panic; clusters of gawking spectators—all of these and many other types are manifestations of the crowd."[2] This article will deal with three major aspects of riots as a type of crowd. It will examine the *general conditions* which precede riot outbreaks, the *immediate or proximate conditions* which are critical in providing the catalyst for particular riots, and the *internal dynamics* or main events and behaviors which occur during the course of riots. The analysis is based mainly on research on the five Negro ghetto riots reported below, but also on con- clusions and observations reported in the sociological literature.

During the summers of 1966–1967, three researchers spent three weeks interviewing on the west side of Chicago; the Hough area of Cleveland; the west side of Lansing, Michigan; Newark, New Jersey; and Detroit, Michigan. A total of one hundred and fifty interviews of one-to-three hours each were tape recorded with informants in these communities. Our informants were selected on the basis of two criteria: they witnessed the riot activity for a substantial period of time and/or were familiar with the riot area prior to its outbreak. Many respondents fit both criteria. First, contacts were generally made through the Negro news media, sanctioned Negro leadership, and grass-roots community organizations. Clearly, the most useful informant

[1] *Editor's Note*: In August of 1968 James R. Hundley, Jr. presented this paper at the Annual Meeting of the American Sociological Association in San Francisco. Because Professor Hundley was fully aware of the terminal nature of his condition, his desire in this—his final—paper was to record and synthesize his observations into a general framework for understanding riots. While Professor Hundley also desired to document completely the relationship of his ideas and findings to those in the research literature as well as to document the empirical bases of his conclusions by his own research data, his illness and death prevented the fullest incorporation of these features into the paper. On November 3, 1967, Mr. Hundley died of cancer at age 28. Thus, the paper is necessarily impressionistic and heuristic, rather than being a fully documented, definitive, research report. While the ideas are those Dr. Hundley originally presented, reorganization and shortening of the paper have been necessary to prepare it for publication and several references have been added to the original version. Colleagues and students of Dr. Hundley at Michigan State University helped to prepare the manuscript for publication.

Analysis of Dr. Hundley's research materials continues under the auspices of the sponsors of his research, Michigan State University's School of Police Administration and the National Center on Police and Community Relations.

[2] R. Turner and L. Killian, COLLECTIVE BEHAVIOR 83 (1957).

Reprinted from James Hundley, Jr., "The Dynamics of Recent Ghetto Riots," *Riot in the Cities*, Richard A. Chikota and Michael C. Moran, (eds.) (Rutherford, N.J.: Fairleigh Dickinson Press, 1970), pp. 137–148.

[*] Late Assistant Professor, Department of Sociology, Michigan State University.

when entering a city was the Negro newsman who, in the course of his job, became familiar with the ghetto area, knew its prior conditions, and could move freely through the area while the rioting was occurring.

Before going into the field in the summer of 1966, an interview schedule was prepared based on many of the notions of Smelser, Turner and Killian.[3] Questions were relatively unstructured and open-ended to allow respondents to provide information in their own words. By tape-recording the information from first hand observers immediately after the riot, it was possible to capture as nearly as possible the reality of those outbreaks. The data are, thus, more direct than mass media reports and other printed documents which have supplied the source of information for most of the past research on riots and crowd behavior, but they still lack the definitiveness of systematic, direct observation.

Analysis and interpretation of the data are far from complete at this time. In this article the attempt is to impart a somewhat comprehensive understanding of the dynamics of riots as revealed by this research. The present analysis is thus characterized more by scope than by depth. Specific interview materials (quotations), statistics compiled from the interviews, and statistics on structural conditions in the cities are not presented here, but will appear in subsequent reports. This report summarizes, collapses, and synthesizes general impressions derived from this experience of interviewing. This analysis must, consequently, be regarded as speculative and tentative.

The General Conditions Promoting a Riot Outburst

Five major general causes of crowd outbursts have been identified, each of which must be present in any social situation before a riot can occur. First, potential participants in a crowd must perceive that a crisis exists. The essence of the perceived crisis in the Negro ghetto is that the residents see a gap between the conditions in which they find themselves and what they feel conditions ought to be. The nature of the crisis in ghetto communities revolves around the historic lack of racial equality in the United States, excessive discrimination, a poor educational system, a lack of jobs, poor housing, insufficient welfare systems, and so forth. Ghettoites increasingly use middle-class, white, suburban situations as a point of comparison for evaluating their own situations, and in such comparisons they are clearly relatively deprived.[4]

The second major causal factor in ghetto outbursts is that those involved perceive that the legitimate channels for bringing about change are closed. They see no other way to redress their grievances. White-sanctioned Negro leadership is perceived as those elected officials who respond to the needs of the party or structure and not to the needs of the people they are elected to represent. Urban Negro ghettos seem to place little confidence in the elected officials who could, but do not, represent them. Elected officials are called "Uncle Toms" and, in fact, may be perceived as having taken an office or residential address in the ghetto only in order to be elected. In order to become effective, ghetto residents may have to become a part of a political machine, which inhibits their ability to reflect the community sentiment. Civil rights' groups and other organizations are potential channels for bringing about change in any ghetto. The most striking fact about our recent research was that the various civil rights' organizations were scarcely organized in any of the ghetto areas.

[3] N. Smelser, *Theory of Collective Behavior* especially pp. 47–269 (1963); Turner & Killian, *supra* note 2, especially pp. 83–161. For further comparison of the theoretical approaches of Smelser and Turner & Killian see, J. Hundley, Jr., "A Test of Theories in Collective Behavior: The National Farmers' Organization (NFO)," 1965 (unpublished Ph.D. thesis, Columbus: The Ohio State University), especially pp. 15–86.

[4] For an interesting analysis of the role of relative comparisons in the creation of dissatisfactions see, Davies, "Toward a Theory of Revolution," 27, *American Sociological Rev.*, 1, 5–19 (Feb., 1962).

Most people admitted that these organizations had very little rapport with the ghetto residents. Apparently, civil rights' organizations find it difficult to organize even in the so-called middle-class areas. There are, of course, very good reasons for the lack of formal organizations in the ghetto. The ghettoite is characterized by high in-migration and low levels of education, factors which work against the organization of effective local groups.

The third necessary ingredient to produce a situation conducive of ghetto rioting is the existence of hope in the potential riot participants that rioting will somehow produce a change in present conditions. Many ghettoites express a feeling that they are at their "wits end," "at the end of the line," they "have taken all that they can take," and "Why not riot?" Something beneficial may result from it. Implicit in the statements made by riot participants is the hope that "whitey" will have to respond. He has failed to respond to the needs of the Negro in the past, and to some the only hope left is to force him to respond by rioting.

A fourth condition that must be present before a riot will erupt is that the people must be able to come in close contact. One can expect more crowds in high population density areas. Rioting tends to occur on warm nights, but it is not because the participants are necessarily more irritable. Warm nights and crowded conditions find people out on the stoops or in the streets where they will be more likely to converge on some abnormal event that might occur. Riots tend to occur on week-ends and in the evenings since large numbers of people who are disengaged from normal daytime activities and restraints are more likely to come together and participate in the crowd behavior.

Finally, the fifth major condition that exists is a substantial breakdown in previously accepted relationships between police and community. One of the most glaring conditions in American cities today is a feeling on the ghettoite's part that he has been subjected to discriminating police tactics. The ghettoite is convinced that police are overly brutal, not polite, disrespectful and that Negroes are often arrested indiscriminately and without justification.[5] Many cases of police harassment and intimidation are reported on the part of various people knowledgeable of the ghetto. To what extent these charges are true is quite difficult to determine. Clearly, however, at the heart of most recent ghetto riots is disdain and hatred for the local police department. The Negro ghettoite feels he has no effective channel or adequate legal representation for lodging a complaint against a police officer. Either the sentence imposed on an erring police officer is too light, or no penalty is invoked at all. Normal police grievance procedures are complicated and time consuming. Usually, the ghettoite has not collected sufficient evidence as defined by the police department to prove any misconduct, nor is the typical ghettoite sophisticated enough to see the charge through proper legal channels.[6] The significance of these facts is that respect for law enforcement, as practiced in the ghetto, has eroded and open hostility toward the police is common-place.

How do these general conditions relate to the increasingly rapid rise in the number of riots in America today? Two major factors are suggested: First, the crisis as perceived by Negroes is becoming more acute, and the gap between ghetto living and the white middle class is perceived as increasing.[7] New welfare programs are not closing the gap as hoped. As our respondents related to us, many programs simply have not reached the grass-roots level. Even if money was available, there is a general lack of knowledge and of skilled personnel to develop the various kinds of programs that are needed to eradicate the slum. A major

[5] P. Meyer, *The People Beyond 12th Street: A Survey of Attitudes of Detroit Negroes After the Riot of 1967,* 8–9 (1967) (Sponsored by the Detroit Urban League).

[6] For some further evidence on this point see, *Report of the National Advisory Commission on Civil Disorders,* 310 (Bantam Books ed., 1968).

[7] For evidence that such perceptions are based on fact see, Moynihan, "The Crisis in Welfare," 10, *The Public Interest,* 3–29 (Winter, 1968).

factor in the heightening of the crisis is that more people are declaring that the condition of the Negro is intolerable and must change immediately. Various advocates of the Black Power philosophy, both in SNCC and in other informal local organizations, have been giving the lower-class Negro a rationale for engaging in violence.

The second major factor for the increasing rate of riots from 1966 to 1967, is the growing belief on the part of ghettoites that a riot will bring attention to ghetto problems. As riots occur in one city and the results are communicated, it is perceived that either having a riot or the threat of a riot is a good way to get the immediate attention of various political officials who in the past have been hesitant to act.

The analysis thus far has identified five general conditions promoting riots. Several other reasons have been recently suggested for the increasing high rate of riots. However, these general conditions can be found in most large metropolitan areas. The attempt in the following section is to identify the causes indicating why a riot erupts at a particular time and place.

The Immediate Conditions Producing a Riot

Four main factors seem to be responsible for producing a riot in a ghetto at a particular time. These include:

1. the creation and transmission of rumors offering a riot as one solution or as a possibility,
2. the occurrence of a given event which typifies the kinds of complaints and grievances that a community has,
3. the convergence of large numbers of people around a precipitating event, and
4. the communication of specific grievances throughout the forming crowd so that definite courses of action emerge and are followed among a substantial number of the converging crowd.

Interviews with knowledgeable informants who had their "ears to the ghetto," made it clear that they had picked up a number of cues indicating that a riot was likely to break out at any time. They noticed an increasing number of rumors that something was going to happen.[8] At various times reports were heard that a riot was going to break out at a certain time at a certain place. There was a noticeable increase in discussions about police, white merchants, slum lords, etc. Also noticed was the fact that informal leaders were increasingly sanctioning the notion that something ought to be done now, or "we ought to blow the place up." What these informants are alluding to is the fact that the ghetto community is talking more and more about recent experiences and past events that typify their unfavorable position and the extreme nature of the crisis. This involves a heightening of hostility toward objects in the community that they dislike and the development of a one-sided, extreme definition of certain people who are perceived as responsible for their plight. Among these various definitions is the increasing talk that one of the solutions is to "get out of hand" and riot.

When this communication of hostility and dissatisfaction reaches a certain height, some event usually occurs which typifies the kinds of mal-treatment received by the ghettoites. This may be an arrest in which there is an alleged brutality, e.g., Newark; a heated debate among some officials and a ghettoite, e.g., Chicago; the raiding of an after hours bar, e.g., Detroit. The significance of this event is that it immediately focuses the attention on an overt act of suppression that is met with open hostility not because of the act itself, but because it is representative of a long history of such acts.

Another significant aspect of the precipitating event is that it invokes a substantial convergence of people to the scene of the event. Large numbers of people are in the vicinity, they hear about the event, and come to investigate. They come for many reasons. At this point of convergence, many feel that they have been wronged and that something must be done about the situation. These people may also bring their friends. Other people come who hear about the event and are sim-

---

[8] For a discussion of the role of rumor in crowd behavior see, R. Turner, "Collective Behavior," in *Handbook of Modern Sociology*, 397–409 (R. Faris, ed. 1964).

ply curious. Others come because they are simply passing through the neighborhood and see a large throng of people. Others may be there as instigators or agitators who are attempting to start a riot. Finally, it is clear, particularly in the ghetto, that large numbers of people come to exploit the situation and use the emerging crowd as a cover for normally deviant activities. Other people come because they see it as their role to control potential deviant outbursts. These may be police, city officials; and church, civic, and local leaders. From this conglomerate of people, the riot develops.

The fourth and final specific factor that tends to produce a full-fledged riot is the communication among the mass that something wrong has happened and something must be done immediately to right the wrong. Various rumors are passed through the crowd, suggested courses of action begin to emerge, action is taken, and it is on.

The Internal Dynamics of Recent Crowd Behavior

The Keynoting Process

Now that the preconditions for a riot have been met, and a crowd has gathered, what starts the crowd going? What kinds of interaction-mechanisms solidify the crowd and generate certain purposes?

In the initial phase of a riot, Turner and Killian identify a little understood process called keynoting.[9] This process is defined as the offering of a suggestion for positive action among large numbers of people in an ambiguous situation. A popular contention, supported by Turner and Killian, states that the initial direction of a crowd is determined by the first speakers who can determine the direction of the crowd. This idea comes from an image of the crowd as being highly suggestible and subject to manipulation.[10] We offer some alternative notions to this idea. In the first place, our data indicate that a large number of suggestions are offered from certain informal leaders who come to the fore during the creation of

the crowd. These suggestions are usually not offered from one main speaker area, but from clusterings of people in various locations at the initial crowd scene. The most typical case is a sequence of the most verbal speakers who offer a variety of alternatives. They speak successively and the crowd selects one or two of them. In fact, the crowd tends to split and follow different paths of action that have been suggested to them by these speakers.

Who are these ghettoites who tend to be leaders? They are not generally unknown, anonymous individuals. There is a very definite tendency for the more verbal speakers in the ghetto to take the leadership, especially those with a certain amount of either informal or formal status in local organizations or informal groups. In each city studied there emerged an active, self-appointed leadership made up of the most verbal Negroes who were present both prior to and during the riots.

The Evolving Riot Activities

Recent ghetto riots occur over s substantial number of hours and days. In the first few hours, a course of action may develop which evokes or demands a response by the police or city officials. Official response results in new courses of crowd action. For example, the initial incident in the Chicago riot last year was whether or not a water hydrant would be left running for the youths' enjoyment. Consequently, early leaders demanded that city officials come to the scene and promise better recreational facilities, especially swimming pools and sprinkler attachments. However, once the police had arrested a number of crowd participants rather indiscriminately, the crowd's purpose was to storm the police station, demanding retribution by releasing their blood brothers from jail. In Cleveland, the initial purpose was to correct the transgressions of a white bar owner who reportedly had been calling Negroes vulgar names. In the later stages, the main activity became burning down dilapidated houses that had been con-

[9] Turner & Killian, *supra* note 2 at 117 and 197.
[10] G. Le Bon, *The Crowd* (1965).

demned for urban renewal but had not been removed. These examples indicate how crowd focuses shift, relative to the responses that city officials and police display toward prior action.

A crowd moves on courses of action in the early stages when behavioral deviations go unpunished by the various social control personnel in the area. These may be deviations of informal norms such as extreme statements, vehement conversation, threats, and simply walking into the street, or deviations of various legal norms such as window-breaking, looting, burning, and sniping. A crowd starts on courses of action suggested by certain leaders, but facilitating these actions are crowd participants who are not punished by either the crowd, the existing institutions in the ghetto, or the police. Once these deviations have occurred a sufficient number of times, they tend to become normative and expected as common behaviors of the crowd.

Once the crowd begins to engage in various behaviors through the process of keynoting and because deviations go unpunished, other subsequent factors help determine the specific activities of the rioters. Previous grievances that have been talked about in the community for some period of time represent pre-dispositions to act on the part of the crowd. The verbalized conclusions of the community rumor process, and the heightening of hostility prior to the riot, determine the magnitude and kind of activities. There are heterogenous complaints which result in multiple goals by various segments of the rioting crowd.

Emergent Norms

Once various sections of the crowd deviate and develop a course of action, these behaviors tend to be normative and expected. In this sense, the various acting segments of a crowd hold a creative and emergent set of norms that are guiding their behavior. The crowd sets up its own notion of right and wrong.[11] This notion of right or wrong may be an idea that the Negro needs to be treated with respect by police and that he should not be arrested for "just hanging around and watching the crowd." The emergent norm may be the notion that the Negro section should be allowed to have sprinklers on the fire hydrant just as other city areas have. The crowd may believe that city officials have done nothing about urban renewal and, therefore, want to burn down all the old blighted buildings. The norm might be that white businessmen exploit the Negro, and the only way to solve this is to burn them out completely. At various times, these emergent norms of the crowd tend to be violated either by white passers-by, outside residents in the community, fire departments, or police departments. When these emergent norms are violated, that person or agency may be selected for attack.

The Limits of Deviation

A variety of factors help determine the specific activities of a rioting crowd, but what limits the deviations of a crowd? Crowd behavior is in great part a process of interaction between various participants who are attempting to control the situation and those rioters who continue to adhere to the new norms. Various social control agencies, including police, older ghetto residents, religious and welfare officials, and others, may exert control influences to limit the deviations among a rioting crowd. A second limiting factor is the in-group norms of the rioting recruits. These may be the sparing of Negro-owned businesses, failing to attack women, children, and nuns, or not burning residential homes.

The Crowd Structure

Since crowd behavior is group behavior, an important question is: "What is the group structure of the emerging crowd and how does it change over time?" The early stages of crowd behavior exhibit a rudimentary division of labor. It involves a rather simple relationship between an active core of crowd participants and a relatively passive audience of people who are just standing around watch-

---

[11] For a more general discussion of the emergence of norms in crowd behavior see, Turner & Killian, *supra* note 2 at 394–97.

ing. Noticeable physical space can separate the active core from the passive audience. Quite soon, however, the active core can be divided into the keynoters or activists and their nearby supporters. How is it determined, then, who will be in the active core or in the passive audience? Who will tend to be the activists and who will tend to be the supporters? To answer these questions, we need to examine again the motivations or the reasons people give for coming to the crowd. It is reasonable to expect that the activists are recruited from those who are aggrieved as well as from the instigators and the exploiters. Many of the supporters are friends of the aggrieved, the instigators, and the exploiters. The curious make up the greater portion of the relatively passive audience. Many exploiters and instigators remain in the passive audience or play a supportive role until the opportune time for their deviant purposes becomes apparent.

Once the rioting crowd begins to act along certain lines, the division of activity becomes quite complicated. In recent ghetto riots, the sequence starts with rock and bottle throwing directed toward police and business extablishments. This is then followed by looting. The looting is followed by burning. The window breakers tend to be the more active people, whereas, looters tend to be drawn from a wider range of the population. Early looting of the stores tends to occur in situations where social control agencies have been hesitant to act for some time. Generally, it is after the malicious damage, looting, and burning that the first incidents of sniping are reported.

Our data indicate that most of the brick throwing, early looting, and burning is done by teenage and early twenty-year-old groups of from 5-to-20 individuals. These groups tend to stay together and, in some cases, develop a system of task-sharing. In Chicago, for example, it was noted that large numbers of teenagers would sit under trees near housing developments and rest while other teenage gang members were out engaging in riot activity. Other people reported gangs of teenagers

being demarcated by turbans, white shirts, or no shirts. It was also noticed that gangs would tend to stay in certain areas, indicating that they had divided up the turf. These data support Smelser's notion that the degree of organization of crowd behavior depends upon the amount of prior organization that is recruited to the scene of the crowd.[12] Usually, as time progresses, certain groups engage in violent acts while other groups try to make contact with city officials to obtain promises for a redress of grievances.

In the initial hours of a riot, the crowd is usually characterized by a representative group of ghettoites who verbalize specific concessions and changes desired. The later stages of the life cycle involve larger numbers of instigators and exploiters who use the breakdown of social control and the advantage of the emergent norms to engage in looting, burning, sniping, etc. A final observation is that the curious or the passive audience decreases over the life of a crowd, which facilitates the cessation of the riot. It is no accident that the most extreme form of deviation in ghetto riots—shooting and sniping—usually occurs late on the first night, or the second and third night. A passing curious audience provides little support for these deviations. There is some indication in our data that snipers are associated with instigative and/or exploitive groups.

The Interaction Between the Crowd and Social Control Agencies

In the beginning stages of crowd formation, the presence or absence of police officers can have various effects. In most instances, the very presence of the police creates an event, provides a point of focus, and draws people together among whom rumor can be easily transmitted. In other cases, sending too few officers to a scene results in actions being uncontrolled because not enough policemen are available to break the developing crowd structure. We suggest that if the police activity is seen by the rioters as legitimate, then the presence of small quantities of police will not

---

[12] Smelser, *supra* note 3 at 255.

precipitate a riot. However, even if the original police activity is viewed as legitimate, but the policemen are observed as being rude, impolite, unfair, or brutal, then these activities can precipitate a riot. It appears that the police officers, in their attempt to enforce a higher authority, are perceived by ghetto residents more as a causal factor than a deterrent of riot behavior.

One of the puzzles of recent ghetto riots is why, in some cases, the total withdrawal of police simply enhances riot activity. The success of police withdrawal is contingent upon officers or officials contacting the legitimate leaders of the ghetto community and in allowing them to exert social control. Legitimate leaders will not attempt to exert this control unless police or city officials make immediate concessions or promises. The failure to make immediate concessions reinforces the ghettoites perceptions of the white structure's reluctance to respond, and creates a situation of social suicide for any Negro leader who attempts to approach the crowd with promises of a better tomorrow.

Particularly in the early stages of a riot, police forces are incapable of contolling the situation and resort to observation of riot activities. The very presence of the police, who do not exert control, further promotes the emergence of norms which allow deviant activity. In fact, we have reports of policemen weakly chasing looters, chiding observers, or driving back and forth among looters shouting verbal insults. These non-control activities encourage and promote still more hostile behavior.

Lohman outlines five ways to prevent and control crowds. These recommendations are to isolate the crowd, divide it into small units, create diversions, remove individuals involved in the precipitating event, and remove crowd leaders without force.[13] These basic principles are generally not heeded by police departments. For example, policemen tend to stay around even when a crowd starts to form, and do not quickly remove or isolate individuals involved in the precipitating incident. Police do not take into account the communication process in a crowd and fail to divide it into small units. Instead, they attack along a frontal line much like a military operation.

Other factors determine the length of recent ghetto riots besides the activities of the police. The sooner help comes from outside control agencies, the sooner a riot stops. Prior to Detroit, the national guard had been amazingly successful in controlling crowd behavior immediately upon their arrival. Apart from the sheer force of numbers, calling in the national guard indicates the success of rioters, since they have beaten the "boys in blue." The sooner the larger community seeks out real ghetto leaders and satisfies their grievances, the sooner a riot stops. The more exploiters and instigators in a ghetto, the more likely a riot is to occur and of long duration. Finally, the greater degree of normalcy that is maintained within the ghetto community, the more likely a riot will remain small or cease.

Summary, Implications for Law Enforcement

The following are discussed tentatively as the general conditions which underlie the occurrence of riots: (1) the perception of a crisis in achieving aspirations, (2) the perception that legitimate channels for bringing about changes are blocked, (3) hope on the part of ghettoites that rioting will bring about changes, (4) the possibility that large numbers of people can interact under conditions of reduced social control, and (5) the breakdown of accepted social control mechanisms. The main factors suggested as being responsible for producing a riot at a particular time and place are: (1) the presence of rumors of a riot, (2) an event which typifies grievances and complaints, (3) the physical convergence of large numbers of people around this event, and (4) the arousal of a sense of indignation in the crowd, and the emergence of suggested courses of action for immediate redress. The process by which a crowd develops into a riot involves (1) keynoting or the formation of consensus around suggestions for action, (2) hostile, deviant acts which go unpunished, and (3) the emergence of focused hostility as

13 J. Lohman, *The Police and Minority Groups* 80–86 (1947).

a norm for the crowd, and norms for the types of deviant activities the crowd will sanction. Rioting crowds develop definite group structure, which suggests the possibility of predictable methods for relating to and controlling such crowds by police and others.

Because riot control is such a pressing, immediate need, some additional closing comments on the problem of police-ghetto relations are in order. New and creative approaches to the problems of police and the ghetto are sorely needed. Some kind of credible reviewing mechanism needs to be established to restore faith that police departments will handle grievances of maltreatment, insolence, and brutality. Whether this be a civilian review board, or some variation of this, is not as important as the fact that the community have confidence in what ever mechanism is created. There is a predominant orientation among police departments that the way of solving complicated social problems is by the use of force—more policemen, with more riot helmets, and more sawed-off shotguns. This orientation certainly results in treating symptoms rather than basic causes. There needs to be more policemen recruited from the ghetto, and in many cities more Negro policemen. Some kind of combination of police and social work is particularly needed among older adults as well as among youth. The police find themselves in a position of really not knowing the community, its leaders, or many of its problems. Putting the policeman back on the beat where he comes to know intimately an area might be one partial solution. Also, the policemen assigned to a ghetto need to be rigidly scrutinized. Police departments reflect the society from which they draw recruits—a society which is predominately biased and bigoted toward the Negro. When this predisposition is put together with a policeman's experience of constantly handling the deviant Negro, it results in policemen who personally become very bitter toward all Negroes. Finally, training in riot control techniques based on past research and experience rather than traditional myths is needed. Too many policemen create a scene or incident unknowingly. Sirens blasting and lights flashing, policemen come noisily into a situation and create an event which causes the convergence of people. Other times, they use force indiscriminately and too quickly. Many times, police attack leaders and certain parts of the crowd without breaking up the crowd structure throughout.

The problem of riots must, however, be dealt with in a context which is much broader than that of law enforcement. The basic causes of riots lie deep in our social structure. Negroes increasingly find it impossible to achieve their aspirations by individual and legitimate channels of mobility. Frustrations accumulate and intensify in an environment of threat, distust, and fear. The ghetto riot is an expression of the intensity of these frustrations.

26. An Essay on Bargaining

Thomas C. Schelling*

This chapter presents a tactical approach to the analysis of bargaining. The subject includes both *explicit bargaining* and the *tacit kind* in which adversaries watch and interpret each other's behavior, each aware that his own actions are being interpreted and anticipated, each acting with a view to the expectations that he creates. In economics the subject covers wage negotiations, tariff negotiations, competition where competitors are few, settlements out of court, and the real estate agent and his customer. Outside economics it ranges from the threat of massive retaliation to taking the right of way from a taxi.

Reprinted in part from Thomas C. Schelling, "An Essay on Bargaining," *American Economic Review*, Vol. XLVI, No. 3 (June 1956), pp. 281–306; also included in Thomas C. Schelling, *The Strategy of Conflict* (Cambridge, Mass.: Harvard University Press), 1960.
° Professor, Center for International Affairs, Harvard University.

Our concern will *not* be with the part of bargaining that consists of exploring for mutally profitable adjustments, and that might be called the "efficiency" aspect of bargaining. For example, can an insurance firm save money, and make a client happier, by offering a cash settlement rather than repairing the client's car; can an employer save money by granting a voluntary wage increase to employees who agree to take a substantial part of their wages in merchandise? Instead, we shall be concerned with what might be called the "distributional" aspect of bargaining: the situations in which a better bargain for one means less for the other. When the business is finally sold to the one interested buyer, what price does it go for? When two dynamite trucks meet on a road wide enough for one, who backs up?

These are situations that ultimately involve an element of pure bargaining—bargaining in which each party is guided mainly by his expectations of what the other will accept. But with each guided by expectations and knowing that the other is too, expectations become compounded. A bargain is struck when somebody makes a final, sufficient concession. Why does he concede? Because he thinks the other will not. "I must concede because he won't. He won't because he thinks I will. He thinks I will because he thinks I think he thinks so. . . ." There is some range of alternative outcomes in which any point is better for both sides than no agreement at all. To insist on any such point is pure bargaining, since one always *would* take less rather than reach no agreement at all, and since one always *can* recede if retreat proves necessary to agreement. Yet if both parties are aware of the limits to this range, *any* outcome is a point from which at least one party would have been willing to retreat and the other knows it! There is no resting place.

There is, however, an outcome; and if we cannot find it in the logic of the situation, we may find it in the tactics employed. The purpose of this paper is to call attention to an important class of tactics, of a kind that is peculiarly appropriate to the logic of inde-

terminate situations. The essence of these tactics is some voluntary but irreversible sacrifice of freedom of choice. They rest on the paradox that the power to constrain an adversary may depend on the power to bind oneself; that, in bargaining, weakness is often strength, freedom may be freedom to capitulate, and to burn bridges behind one may suffice to undo an opponent.

Bargaining Power: The Power to Bind Oneself

"Bargaining power," "bargaining strength," "bargaining skill" suggest that the advantage goes to the powerful, the strong, or the skillful. It does, of course, if those qualities are defined to mean only that negotiations are won by those who win. But, if the terms imply that it is an advantage to be more intelligent or more skilled in debate, or to have more financial resources, more physical strength, more military potency, or more ability to withstand losses, then the term does a disservice. These qualities are by no means universal advantages in bargaining situations; they often have a contrary value.

The sophisticated negotiator may find it difficult to seem as obstinate as a truly obstinate man. If a man knocks at a door and says that he will stab himself on the porch unless given $10, he is more likely to get the $10 if his eyes are bloodshot. The threat of mutual destruction cannot be used to deter an adversary who is too unintelligent to comprehend it or too weak to enforce his will on those he represents. The government that cannot control its balance of payments, or collect taxes, or muster the political unity to defend itself, may enjoy assistance that would be denied it if it could control its own resources. And, to cite an example familiar from economic theory, "price leadership" in oligopoly may be an unprofitable distinction evaded by the small firms and assumed perforce by the large one.

Bargaining power has also been described as the power to fool and bluff, "the ability to set the best price for yourself and fool the other man into thinking this was your maximum offer."[1] Fooling and bluffing are cer-

---

[1] J. N. Morgan, "Bilateral Monopoly and the Competitive Output," *Quarterly Journal of Economics,* 63:376n6 (August 1949).

tainly involved; but there are two kinds of fooling. One is deceiving about the facts; a buyer may lie about his income or misrepresent the size of his family. The other is purely tactical. Suppose each knows everything about the other, and each knows what the other knows. What is there to fool about? The buyer may say that, though he'd really pay up to twenty and the seller knows it, he is firmly resolved as a tactical matter not to budge above sixteen. If the seller capitulates, was he fooled? Or was he convinced of the truth? Or did the buyer really not know what he would do next if the tactic failed? If the buyer really "feels" himself firmly resolved, and bases his resolve on the conviction that the seller will capitulate, and the seller does, the buyer may say afterwards that he was "not fooling." Whatever has occurred, it is not adequately conveyed by the notions of bluffing and fooling.

How does one person make another believe something? The answer depends importantly on the factual question, "Is it true?" It is easier to prove the truth of something that is true than of something false. To prove the truth about our health we can call on a reputable doctor; to prove the truth about our costs or income we may let the person look at books that have been audited by a reputable firm or the Bureau of Internal Revenue. But to persuade him of something false we may have no such convincing evidence.

When one wishes to persuade someone that he would not pay more than $16,000 for a house that is really worth $20,000 to him, what can he do to take advantage of the usually superior credibility of the truth over a false assertion? Answer: make it true. How can a buyer make it true? If he likes the house because it is near his business, he might move his business, persuading the seller that the house is really now worth only $16,000 to him. This would be unprofitable; he is no better off than if he had paid the higher price.

But suppose the buyer could make an irrevocable and enforceable bet with some third party, duly recorded and certified, according to which he would pay for the house no more than $16,000, or forfeit $5,000. The seller has lost; the buyer need simply present the truth.

Unless the seller is enraged and withholds the house in sheer spite, the situation has been rigged against him; the "objective" situation— the buyer's true incentive—has been voluntarily, conspicuously, and irreversibly changed. The seller can take it or leave it. This example demonstrates that if the buyer can accept an irrevocable *commitment*, in a way that is unambiguously visible to the seller, he can squeeze the range of indeterminacy down to the point most favorable to him. It also suggests, by its artificiality, that the tactic is one that may or may not be available; whether the buyer can find an effective device for committing himself may depend on who he is, who the seller is, where they live, and a number of legal and institutional arrangements (including, in our artificial example, whether bets are legally enforceable).

If both men live in a culture where "cross my heart" is universally accepted as potent, all the buyer has to do is allege that he will pay no more than $16,000, using this invocation of penalty, and he wins—or at least he wins if the seller does not beat him to it by shouting "$19,000, cross my heart." If the buyer is an agent authorized by a board of directors to buy at $16,000 but not a cent more, and the directors cannot constitutionally meet again for several months and the buyer cannot exceed his authority, and if all this can be made known to the seller, then the buyer "wins"—if, again, the seller has not tied himself up with a commitment to $19,000. Or, if the buyer can assert that he will pay no more than $16,000 so firmly that he would suffer intolerable loss of personal prestige or bargaining reputation by paying more, and if the fact of his paying more would necessarily be known, and if the seller appreciates all this, then a loud declaration by itself may provide the commitment. The device, of course, is a needless surrender of flexibility unless it can be made fully evident and understandable to the seller.

Incidentally, some of the more contractual kinds of commitments are not as effective as they at first seem. In the example of the self-inflicted penalty through the bet, it remains possible for the seller to seek out the third party and offer a modest sum in consideration of the latter's releasing the buyer from the bet, threatening to sell the house for $16,000 if the release is not forthcoming. The effect of the bet—as of most such contractual commitments—is to shift the locus and personnel of the negotiation, in the hope that the third party will be less available for negotiation or less subject to an incentive to concede. To put it differently, a *contractual* commitment is usually the assumption of a contingent "transfer cost," not a "real cost"; and if all interested parties can be brought into the negotiation, the range of indeterminacy remains as it was. But if the third party were available only at substantial transportation cost, to that extent a truly irrevocable commitment would have been assumed. (If bets were made with a number of people, the "real costs" of bringing them into the negotiation might be made prohibitive.)[2]

The most interesting parts of our topic concern whether and how commitments can be taken; but it is worth while to consider briefly a model in which practical problems are absent—a world in which absolute commitments are freely available. Consider a culture in which "cross my heart" is universally recognized as absolutely binding. Any offer accompanied by this invocation is a final offer, and is so recognized. If each party knows the other's true reservation price, the object is to be first with a firm offer. Complete responsibility for the outcome then rests with the other, who

can take it or leave it as he chooses (and who chooses to take it). Bargaining is all over; the commitment (that is, the first offer) wins.

Interpose some communication difficulty. They must bargain by letter; the invocation becomes effective when signed but cannot be known to the other until its arrival. Now when one party writes such a letter, the other may already have signed his own, or may yet do so before the letter of the first arrives. There is then no sale; both are bound to incompatible positions. Each must now recognize this possibility of stalemate and take into account the likelihood that the other already has, or will have, signed his own commitment.

An asymmetry in communication may well favor the one who is (and is known to be) unavailable for the receipt of messages, for he is the one who cannot be deterred from his own commitment by receipt of the other's. (On the other hand, if the one who cannot communicate can feign ignorance of his own inability, the other too may be deterred from his own commitment by fear of the first's unwitting commitment.) If the commitments depend not just on words but on special forms or ceremonies, ignorance of the other party's commitment ceremonies may be an advantage if the ignorance is fully appreciated, since it makes the other aware that only his own restraint can avert stalemate.

Suppose only part of the population belongs

---

[2] Perhaps the "ideal" solution to the bilateral monopoly problem is as follows. One member of the pair shifts his marginal cost curve so that joint profits are now zero at the output at which joint profits originally would have been maximized. He does this through an irrevocable sale-leaseback arrangement; he sells a royalty contract to some third party for a lump sum, the royalties so related to his output that joint costs exceed joint revenue at all other outputs. He cannot now afford to produce at any price or output except that price and output at which the entire original joint profits accrue to him; the other member of the bilateral monopoly sees the contract, appreciates the situation, and accepts his true minimum profits. The "winner" really gains the entire original profit via the lump sum for which he sold royalty rights; this profit does not affect his incentives because it is independent of what he produces. The third party pays the lump sum (minus a small discount for inducement) because he knows that the second party will have to capitulate and that therefore he will in fact get his contingent royalty. The hitch is that the royalty-rights buyer must not be available to the "losing member"; otherwise the latter can force him to renounce his royalty claim by threatening not to reach a bargain, thus restoring the original marginal cost situation. But we may imagine the development of institutions that specialize in royalty purchases, whose ultimate success depends on a reputation for never renegotiating, and whose incentives can thus not be appealed to in any single negotiation.

to the cult in which "cross my heart" is (or is believed to be) absolutely binding. If everyone knows (and is known to know) everyone else's affiliation, those belonging to this particular cult have the advantage. They can commit themselves, the others cannot. If the buyer says "$16,000, cross my heart," his offer is final; if the seller says "$19,000," he is (and is known to be) only "bargaining."

If each does not know the other's true reservation price, there is an initial stage in which each tries to discover the other's and misrepresent his own, as in ordinary bargaining. But the process of discovery and revelation becomes quickly merged with the process of creating and discovering commitments; the commitments permanently change, for all practical purposes, the "true" reservation prices. If one party has, and the other has not, the belief in a binding ceremony, the latter pursues the "ordinary" bargaining technique of *asserting* his reservation price, while the former proceeds to *make* his.

The foregoing discussion has tried to suggest both the plausibility and the logic of self-commitment. Some examples may suggest the relevance of the tactic, although an observer can seldom distinguish with confidence the consciously logical, the intuitive, or the inadvertent use of a visible tactic. First, it has not been uncommon for union officials to stir up excitement and determination on the part of the membership during or prior to a wage negotiation. If the union is going to insist on $2 and expects the management to counter with $1.60, an effort is made to persuade the membership not only that the management could pay $2 but even perhaps that the negotiators themselves are incompetent if they fail to obtain close to $2. The purpose—or, rather, a plausible purpose suggested by our analysis —is to make clear to the management that the negotiators could not accept less than $2 *even if they wished to* because they no longer control the members or because they would lose their own positions if they tried. In other words, the negotiators reduce the scope of their own authority and confront the management with the threat of a strike that the union itself cannot avert, even though it was

the union's own action that eliminated its power to prevent the strike.

Something similar occurs when the United States Government negotiates with other governments on, say, the uses to which foreign assistance will be put, or tariff reduction. If the executive branch is free to negotiate the best arrangement it can, it may be unable to make any position stick and may end by conceding controversial points because its partners know, or believe obstinately, that the United States would rather concede than terminate the negotiations. But, if the executive branch negotiates under legislative authority, with its position constrained by law, and it is evident that Congress will not be reconvened to change the law within the necessary time period, then the executive branch has a firm position that is visible to its negotiating partners.

When national representatives go to international negotiations knowing that there is a wide range of potential agreement within which the outcome will depend on bargaining, they seem often to create a bargaining position by public statements, statements calculated to arouse a public opinion that permits no concessions to be made. If a binding public opinion can be cultivated and made evident to the other side, the initial position can thereby be made visibly "final."

These examples have certain characteristics in common. First, they clearly depend not only on incurring a commitment but on communicating it persuasively to the other party. Second, it is by no means easy to establish the commitment, nor is it entirely clear to either of the parties concerned just how strong the commitment is. Third, similar activity may be available to the parties on both sides. Fourth, the possibility of commitment, though perhaps available to both sides, is by no means equally available; the ability of a democratic government to get itself tied by public opinion may be different from the ability of a totalitarian government to incur such a commitment. Fifth, they all run the risk of establishing an immovable position that goes beyond the ability of the other to concede, and thereby provoke the likelihood of stalemate or breakdown.

Institutional and Structural Characteristics of the Negotiation

Some institutional and structural characteristics of bargaining situations may make the commitment tactic easy or difficult to use, or make it more available to one party than the other, or affect the likelihood of simultaneous commitment or stalemate.

Use of a Bargaining Agent

The use of a bargaining agent affects the power of commitment in at least two ways. First, the agent may be given instructions that are difficult or impossible to change, such instructions (and their inflexibility) being visible to the opposite party. The principle applies in distinguishing the legislative from the executive branch, or the management from the board of directors, as well as to a messenger-carried offer when the bargaining process had a time limit and the principal has interposed sufficient distance between himself and his messenger to make further communication evidently impossible before the time runs out.

Second, an "agent" may be brought in as a principal in his own right, with an incentive structure of his own that differs from his principal's. This device is involved in automobile insurance; the private citizen, in settling out of court, cannot threaten suit as effectively as the insurance company since the latter is more conspicuously obliged to carry out such threats to maintain its own reputation for subsequent accidents.[3]

Secrecy vs. Publicity

A potent means of commitment, and sometimes the only means, is the pledge of one's reputation. If national representatives can arrange to be charged with appeasement for every small concession, they place concession visibly beyond their own reach. If a union with other plants to deal with can arrange to make any retreat dramatically visible, it places its bargaining reputation in jeopardy and thereby becomes visibly incapable of serious compromise. (The same convenient jeopardy is the basis for the universally exploited defense, "If I did it for you, I'd have to do it for everyone else.") But to commit in this fashion publicity is required. Both the initial offer and the final outcome would have to be known; and if secrecy surrounds either point, or if the outcome is inherently not observable, the device is unavailable. If one party has a "public" and the other has not, the latter may try to neutralize his disadvantage by excluding the relevant public; or if both parties fear the potentialities for stalemate in the simultaneous use of this tactic, they may try to enforce an agreement on secrecy.

Intersecting Negotiations

If a union is simultaneously engaged, or will shortly be engaged, in many negotiations while the management has no other plants and deals with no other unions, the management cannot convincingly stake its bargaining reputation while the union can. The advantage goes to the party that can persuasively point to an array of other negotiations in which its own position would be prejudiced if it made a concession in this one. (The "reputation value" of the bargain may be less related to the outcome than to the firmness with which some initial bargaining position is adhered to.) Defense against this tactic may involve, among other things, both misinterpretation of the other party's position and an effort to make the eventual outcome incommensurable with the initial positions. If the subjects under negotiation can be enlarged in the process of negotiation, or the wage figure re-

[3] The formal solution to the right-of-way problem in automobile traffic may be that the winner is the one who first becomes fully and visibly insured against all contingencies; since he then has no incentive to avoid accident, the other must yield and knows it. (The latter cannot counter in kind; no company will insure him now that the first is insured.) More seriously, the pooling of strike funds among unions reduces the visible incentive on each individual union to avoid a strike. As in the bilateral monopoly solution suggested earlier, there is a transfer of interest to a third party with a resulting visible shift in one's own incentive structure.

placed by fringe benefits that cannot be reduced to a wage equivalent, an "out" is provided to the party that has committed itself; and the availability of this "out" weakens the commitment itself, to the disadvantage of the committed party.

Continuous Negotiations

A special case of interrelated negotiations occurs when the same two parties are to negotiate other topics, simultaneously or in the future. The logic of this case is more subtle; to persuade the other that one cannot afford to recede, one says in effect, "If I conceded to you here, you would revise your estimate of me in our other negotiations; to protect my reputation with you I must stand firm." The second party is simultaneously the "third party" to whom one's bargaining reputation can be pledged. This situation occurs in the threat of local resistance to local aggression. The party threatening achieves its commitment, and hence the credibility of its threat, not by referring to what it would gain from carrying out the threat in this particular instance but by pointing to the long-run value of a fulfilled threat in enhancing the credibility of future threats.

The Restrictive Agenda

When there are two objects to negotiate, the decision to negotiate them simultaneously or in separate forums or at separate times is by no means neutral to the outcome, particularly when there is a latent extortionate threat that can be exploited only if it can be attached to some more ordinary, legitimate, bargaining situation. The protection against extortion depends on refusal, unavailability, or inability, to negotiate. But if the object of the extortionate threat can be brought onto the agenda with the other topic, the latent threat becomes effective.

Tariff bargaining is an example. If reciprocal tariffs on cheese and automobiles are to be negotiated, one party may alter the outcome by threatening a purely punitive change in some other tariff. But if the bargaining representatives of the threatened party are confined to the cheese-automobile agenda, and have no instructions that permit them even to take cognizance of other commodities, or if there are ground rules that forbid mention of other tariffs while cheese and automobiles remain unsettled, this extortionate weapon must await another opportunity. If the threat that would be brought to the conference table is one that cannot stand publicity, publicity itself may prevent its effective communication.

The Possibility of Compensation

As Fellner has pointed out, agreement may be dependent on some means of redistributing costs or gains.[4] If duopolists, for example, divide markets in a way that maximizes their combined profits, some initial accrual of profits is thereby determined; any other division of the profits requires that one firm be able to compensate the other. If the fact of compensation would be evidence of illegal collusion, or if the motive for compensation would be misunderstood by the stockholders, or if the two do not sufficiently trust each other, some less optimum level of *joint* profits may be required in order that the initial accrual of profits to the two firms be in closer accordance with an agreed division of gains between them.

When agreement must be reached on something that is inherently a one-man act, any division of the cost depends on compensation. The "agenda" assumes particular importance in these cases, since a principal means of compensation is a concession on some other object. If two simultaneous negotiations can be brought into a contingent relationship with each other, a means of compensation is available. If they are kept separate, each remains an indivisible object.

It may be to the advantage of one party to keep a bargain isolated, and to the other to join it to some second bargain. If there are two projects, each with a cost of three, and each with a value of two to A and a value of

---

[4] W. Fellner, *Competition Among the Few* (New York, 1949), pp. 34–35, 191–97, 231–32, 234.

four to B, and each is inherently a "one-man" project in its execution, and if compensation is institutionally impossbile, B will be forced to pay the entire cost of each as long as the two projects are kept separate. He cannot usefully threaten nonperformance, since A has no incentive to carry out either project by himself. But if B can link the projects together, offering to carry out one while A carries out the other, and can effectively threaten to abandon both unless A carries out one of them, A is left an option with a gain of four and a cost of three, which he takes, and B cuts his cost in half.

An important limitation of economic problems, as prototypes of bargaining situations, is that they tend disproportionately to involve divisible objects and compensable activities. If a drainage ditch in the back of one house will protect both houses; and if it costs $1,000 and is worth $800 to each home-owner; neither would undertake it separately, but we nevertheless usually assume that they will get together and see that this project worth $1,600 to the two of them gets carried out. But if it costs 10 hours a week to be scoutmaster, and each considers it worth 8 hours of his time to have a scout troop but one man must do the whole job, it is far from certain that the neighbors will reach a deal according to which one puts 10 hours on the job and the other pays him cash or does 5 hours' gardening for him. When two cars meet on a narrow road, the ensuing deadlock is aggravated by the absence of a custom of bidding to pay for the right of way. Parliamentary deadlocks occur when logrolling is impracticable. Measures that require unanimous agreement can often be initiated only if several are bundled together.[5]

The Mechanics of Negotiation

A number of other characteristics deserve mention, although we shall not work out their implications. Is there a penalty on the conveyance of false information? Is there a penalty on called bluffs, that is, can one put forth an offer and withdraw it after it has been accepted? Is there a penalty on hiring an agent who pretends to be an interested party and makes insincere offers, simply to test the position of the other party? Can all interested parties be recognized? Is there a time limit on the bargaining? Does the bargaining take the particular structure of an auction, a Dutch auction, a sealed bid system, or some other formal arrangement? Is there a status quo, so that unavailability for negotiation can win the status quo for the party that prefers it? Is renegotiation possible in case of stalemate? What are the costs of stalemate? Can compliance with the agreement be observed? What, in general, are the means of communication, and are any of them susceptible of being put out of order by one party or the other? If there are several items to negotiate, are they negotiated in one comprehensive negotiation, separately in a particular order so that each piece is finished before the next is taken up, or simultaneously through different agents or under different rules?

The importance of many of these structural questions becomes evident when one reflects on parliamentary technique. Rules that permit a president to veto an appropriation bill only in its entirety, or that require each amendment to be voted before the original act is voted on, or a priority system accorded to different kinds of motions, substantially alter the incentives that are brought to bear on each action. One who might be pressured into choosing second best is relieved of his vulnerability if he can vote earlier to eliminate that possibility, thereby leaving only first and third choices about which his preference is known to be so strong that no threat will be made.

Principles and Precedents

To be convincing, commitments usually have to be qualitative rather than quantitative, and to rest on some rationale. It may be difficult to conceive of a really firm commitment to $2.07½; why not $2.02¼? The numerical scale is too continuous to provide good resting places, except at nice round numbers like $2.00. But a commitment to the *principle* of "profit sharing," "cost-of-living increases,"

---

[5] Inclusion of a provision on the Saar in the "Paris Agreements" that ended the occupation of Western Germany may have reflected either this principle or the one in the preceding paragraph.

or any other basis for a numerical calculation that comes out at $2.07½, may provide a foothold for a commitment. Furthermore, one may create something of a commitment by putting the principles and precedents themselves in jeopardy. If in the past one has successfully maintained the principle of, say, non-recognition of governments imposed by force, and elects to nail his demands to that principle in the present negotiation, he not only adduces precedent behind his claim but risks the principle itself. Having pledged it, he may persuade his adversary that he would accept stalemate rather than capitulate and discredit the principle.

Casuistry

If one reaches the point where concession is advisable, he has to recognize two effects: it puts him closer to his opponent's position, and it affects his opponent's estimate of his firmness. Concession not only may be construed as capitulation, it may mark a prior commitment as a fraud, and make the adversary skeptical of any new pretense at commitment. One, therefore, needs an "excuse" for accommodating his opponent, preferably a rationalized reinterpretation of the original commitment, one that is persuasive to the adversary himself.

More interesting is the use of casuistry to release an opponent from a commitment. If one can demonstrate to an opponent that the latter is not committed, or that he has miscalculated his commitment, one may in fact undo or revise the opponent's commitment. Or if one can confuse the opponent's commitment, so that his constituents or principals or audience cannot exactly identify compliance with the commitment—show that "productivity" is ambiguous, or that "proportionate contributions" has several meanings—one may undo it or lower its value. In these cases it is to the opponent's disadvantage that this commitment be successfully refuted by argument. But when the opponent has resolved to make a moderate concession, one may help him by proving that he *can* make a moderate concession consistent with his former position, and that if he does there are no grounds for believing it to reflect on his original principles. One must seek, in other words, a rationalization by which to deny oneself too great a reward from the opponent's concession, otherwise the concession will not be made.[6]

The Threat

When one threatens to fight if attacked or to cut his price if his competitor does, the threat is no more than a communication of one's own incentives, designed to impress on the other the automatic consequences of this act. And, incidentally, if it succeeds in deterring, it benefits both parties.

But more than communication is involved when one threatens an act that he would have no incentive to perform but that is designed to deter through its promise of mutual harm. To threaten massive retaliation against small en-

---

[6] In many textbook problems, such as bilateral monopoly between firms, the ends of the bargaining range are points of zero profits for one or the other party; and to settle for one's minimum position is no better than no settlement at all. But, apart from certain buying and selling situations, there are commonly limits on the range of acceptable outcomes, and the least favorable outcome that one is free to accept may be substantially superior to stalemate. In these cases one's overriding purpose may be to forestall any misguided commitment by the other party. If the truth is more demonstrable than a false position, a conservative initial position is indicated, as it is if any withdrawal from an initial "advanced" position would discredit any subsequent attempt to convey the truth. Actually, though a person does not commonly invite penalties on his own behavior, the existence of an enforceable penalty on falsehood would be of assistance; if one can demonstrate, for example, his cost or income position by showing his income tax return, the penalties on fraud may enhance the value of this evidence.

Even the "pure" bilateral monopoly case becomes somewhat of this nature if the bargaining is conducted by agents or employees whose rewards are more dependent on *whether* agreement is reached than on how favorable the terms of the agreement are.

croachments is of this nature, as is the threat to bump a car that does not yield the right of way or to call a costly strike if the wage is not raised a few cents. The distinctive feature of this threat is that the threatener has no incentive to carry it out either before the event or after. He does have an incentive to bind himself to fulfill the threat, if he thinks the threat may be successful, because the threat and not its fulfillment gains the end; and fulfillment is not required if the threat succeeds. The more certain the contingent fulfillment is, the less likely is actual fulfillment. But the threat's efficacy depends on the credulity of the other party, and the threat is ineffectual unless the threatener can rearrange or display his own incentives so as to demonstrate that he would, *ex post*, have an incentive to carry it out.[7]

We are back again at the commitment. How can one commit himself in advance to an act that he would in fact prefer not to carry out in the event, in order that his commitment may deter the other party? One can of course bluff, to persuade the other falsely that the costs or damages to the threatener would be minor or negative. More interesting, the one making the threat may pretend that he himself erroneously believes his own costs to be small, and therefore would mistakenly go ahead and fulfill the threat. Or perhaps he can pretend a revenge motivation so strong as to overcome the prospect of self-damage; but this option is probably most readily available to the truly revengeful. Otherwise he must find a way to commit himself.

One may try to stake his reputation on fulfillment, in a manner that impresses the threatened person. One may even stake his reputation *with the threatened person himself*, on grounds that it would be worth the costs and pains to give a lesson to the latter if he fails to heed the threat. Or one may try to arrange a legal commitment, perhaps through contracting with a third party.[8] Or if one can turn the whole business over to an agent whose salary (or business reputation) depends on carrying out the threat but who is unalterably relieved of any responsibility for the further costs, one may shift the incentive.

The commitment problem is nicely illustrated by the legal doctrine of the "last clear chance" which recognizes that, in the events that led up to an accident, there was some point at which the accident became inevitable as a result of prior actions, and that the abilities of the two parties to prevent it may not have expired at the same time. In bargaining, the commitment is a device to leave the last clear chance to decide the outcome with the other party, in a manner that he fully appreciates; it is to relinquish further initiative, having rigged the incentives so that the other party must choose in one's favor. If one driver speeds up so that he cannot stop, and the other realizes it, the latter has to yield. A legislative rider at the end of a session leaves the President the last clear change to pass the bill. This doctrine helps to understand some of those cases in which bargaining "strength" inheres in what is weakness by other standards. When a person—or a country—has lost the power to help himself, or the power to avert

---

[7] Incidentally, the deterrent threat has some interesting quantitative characteristics, reflecting the general asymmetry between rewards and punishments. It is not necessary, for example, that the threat promise more damage to the party threatened than to the party carrying it out. The threat to smash an old car with a new one may succeed if believed, or to sue expensively for small damages, or to start a price war. Also, as far as the power to deter is concerned, there is no such thing as "too large" a threat; if it is large enough to succeed, it is not carried out anyway. A threat is only "too large" if its very size interferes with its credibility. Atomic destruction for small misdemeanors, like expensive incarceration for overtime parking, would be superfluous but not exorbitant unless the threatened person considered it too awful to be real and ignored it.

[8] Mutual defense treaties among strong and weak nations might best be viewed in this light, that is, not as undertaken to reassure the small nations nor in exchange for a *quid pro quo*, but rather as a device for surrendering an embarrassing freedom of choice.

mutual damage, the other interested party has no choice but to assume the cost or responsibility. "Coercive deficiency" is the term Arthur Smithies uses to describe the tactic of deliberately exhausting one's annual budgetary allowance so early in the year that the need for more funds is irresistibly urgent.[9]

A related tactic is maneuvering into a status quo from which one can be dislodged only by an overt act, an act that precipitates mutual damage because the maneuvering party has relinquished the power to retreat. If one carries explosives visibly on his person, in a manner that makes destruction obviously inevitable for himself and for any assailant, he may deter assault much more than if he retained any control over the explosives. If one commits a token force of troops that would be unable to escape, the commitment to full resistance is increased. Walter Lippmann has used the analogy of the plate glass window that helps to protect a jewelry store: anyone can break it easily enough, but not without creating an uproar.

Similar techniques may be available to the one threatened. His best defense, of course, is to carry out the act before the threat is made; in that case there is neither incentive nor commitment for retaliation. If he cannot hasten the act itself, he may commit himself to it; if the person to be threatened is already committed, the one who would threaten cannot deter with his threat, he can only make certain the mutually disastrous consequences that he threatens.[10] If the person to be threatened can arrange before the threat is made to share the risk with others (as susggested by the insurance solution to the right-of-way problem mentioned earlier), he may become so visibly unsusceptible to the threat as to dissuade the threatener. Or if by any other means he can either change or misrepresent his own incentives, to make it appear that he would gain in spite of threat fulfillment (or perhaps only that he thinks he would), the threatener may have to give up the threat as costly and fruitless; or if one can misrepresent himself as either unable to comprehend a threat, or too obstinate to heed it, he may deter the threat itself. Best of all may be *genuine* ignorance, obstinancy, or simple disbelief, since it may be more convincing to the prospective threatener; but of course if it fails to persuade him and he commits himself to the threat, both sides lose. Finally, both the threat and the commitment have to be communicated; if the threatened person can be unavailable for messages, or can destroy the communication channels, even through he does so in an obvious effort to avert threat, he may deter the threat itself.[11]

---

[9] A. Smithies, *The Budgetary Process in the United States* (New York, 1955), pp. 40, 56. One solution is the short tether of an apportionment process. See also T. C. Schelling, "American Foreign Assistance," *World Politics*, 7:609–625 (July 1955), regarding the same principle in foreign aid allocations.

[10] The system of supplying the police with traffic tickets that are numbered and incapable of erasures makes it possible for the officer, by writing in the license number of the car before speaking to the driver, to preclude the latter's threat. Some trucks carry signs that say, "Alarm and lock system not subject to the driver's control!" The time lock on bank vaults serves much the same purpose, as does the mandatory secret ballot in elections. So does starting an invasion with a small advance force that, though too small and premature to win the objective, attaches too much "face" to the enterprise to permit withdrawal: the larger force can then be readied without fear of inviting a purely deterrent threat. At many universities the faculty is protected by a rule that denies instructors the power to change a course grade once it has been recorded.

[11] The racketeer cannot sell protection if he cannot find his customer at home; nor can the kidnapper expect any ransom if he cannot communicate with friends or relatives. Thus, as a perhaps impractical suggestion, a law that required the immediate confinement of all interested friends and relatives when a kidnapping occurred might make the prospects for ransom unprofitably dim. The rotation of watchmen and policemen, or their assignment in random pairs, not only limits their exploitation of bribes but protects them from threats.

But the time to show disbelief or obstinacy is before the threat is made, that is, before the commitment is taken, not just before the threat is fulfilled; it does no good to be incredulous, or out of town, when the messenger arrives with the committed threat.

In threat situations, as in ordinary bargaining, commitments are not altogether clear; each party cannot exactly estimate the costs and values to the other side of the two related actions involved in the threat; the process of commitment may be a progressive one, the commitments acquiring their firmness by a sequence of actions. Communication is often neither entirely impossible nor entirely reliable; while certain evidence of one's commitment can be communicated directly, other evidence must travel by newspaper or hearsay, or be demonstrated by actions. In these cases the unhappy possibility of both acts occurring as a result of simultaneous commitment, is increased. Furthermore, the recognition of this possibility of simultaneous commitment becomes itself a deterrent to the taking of commitments.[12]

In case a threat is made and fails to deter, there is a second stage prior to fulfillment in which *both* parties have an interest in undoing the commitment. The purpose of the threat is gone, its deterrence value is zero, and only the commitment exists to motivate fulfillment. This feature has, of course, an analogy with stalemate in ordinary bargaining, stalemate resulting from both parties' getting committed to incompatible positions, or one party's mistakenly committing himself to a position that the other truly would not accept. If there appears a possibility of undoing the commitment, *both* parties have an interest in doing so. How to undo it is a matter on which their interests diverge, since different ways of undoing it lead to different outcomes. Further-

more, "undoing" does not mean neglecting a commitment regardless of reputation; "undoing," if the commitment of reputation was real, means disconnecting the threat from one's reputation, perhaps one's own reputation with the threatened person himself. It is therefore a subtle and tenuous situation in which, though both have an interest in undoing the commitment, they may be quite unable to collaborate in undoing it.

Special care may be needed in defining the threat, both the act that is threatened against and the counter act that is threatened. The difficulty arises from the fact, just noted, that once the former has been done the incentive to perform the later has disappeared. The credibility of the threat before the act depends on how visible to the threatened party is the inability of the threatening party to rationalize his way out of his commitment once it has failed its purpose. Any loopholes the threatening party leaves himself, if they are visible to the threatened party, weaken the visible commitment and hence reduce the credibility of the threat. (An example may be the ambiguous treatment of Quemoy in the Formosa Resolution and Treaty.)

It is essential, therefore, for maximum credibility, to leave as little room as possible for judgment or discretion in carrying out the threat. If one is committed to punish a certain type of behavior when it reaches certain limits, but the limits are not carefully and objectively defined, the party threatened will realize that when the time comes to decide whether the threat must be enforced or not, his interest and that of the threatening party will coincide in an attempt to avoid the mutually unpleasant consequences.

In order to make a threat precise, so that its terms are visible both to the threatened party and to any third parties whose reaction to the

[12] It is a remarkable institutional fact that there is no simple, universal way for persons or nations to assume commitments of the kind we have been discussing. There are numerous ways they can try, but most of them are quite ambiguous, unsure, or only occasionally available. In the "cross-my-heart" society adverted to earlier, bargaining theory would reduce itself to game strategy and the mechanics of communication; but in most of the contemporary world the topic is mainly an empirical and institutional one of who can commit, how, and with what assurance of appreciation by the other side.

whole affair is of value to the adversaries, it may be necessary to introduce some arbitrary elements. The threat must involve overt acts rather than intentions; it must be attached to the visible deeds, not invisible ones; it may have to attach itself to certain ancillary actions that are of no consequence in themselves to the threatening party. It may, for example, have to put a penalty on the carrying of weapons rather than their use; on suspicious behavior rather than observed misdemeanors; on proximity to a crime rather than the crime itself. And, finally, the act of punishment must be one whose effect or influence is clearly discernible.[13]

In order that one be able to pledge his reputation behind a threat, there must be continuity between the present and subsequent issues that will arise. This need for continuity suggests a means of making the original threat more effective; if it can be decomposed into a series of consecutive smaller threats, there is an opportunity to demonstrate on the first few transgressions that the threat will be carried out on the rest. Even the first few become more plausible, since there is a more obvious incentive to fulfill them as a "lesson."

This principle is perhaps most relevant to acts that are inherently a matter of degree. In foreign aid programs the overt act of terminating assistance may be so obviously painful to both sides as not to be taken seriously by the recipient, but if each small misuse of funds is to be accompanied by a small reduction in assistance, never so large as to leave the recipient helpless nor to provoke a diplomatic breach, the willingness to carry it out will receive more credulity; or if it does not at first, a few lessons may be persuasive without too much damage.[14]

The threatening party may not, of course, be able to divide the act into steps. (Both the act to be deterred and the punishment must be divisible.) But the principle at least suggests the unwisdom of defining aggression, or transgression, in terms of some critical degree or amount that will be deemed intolerable. When the act to be deterred is inherently a sequence of steps whose cumulative effect is what matters, a threat geared to the increments may be more credible than one that must be carried out either all at once or not at all when some particular point has been reached. It may even be impossible to define a "critical point" with sufficient clarity to be persuasive.

To make the threatened acts divisible, the acts themselves may have to be modified. Parts of an act that cannot be decomposed may have to be left out; ancillary acts that go with the event, though of no interest in themselves, may be objects to which a threat can effectively be attached. For example, actions that are only preparatory to the main act, and by themselves do no damage, may be susceptible of chronological division and thus be effective objects of the threat. The man who would kick a dog should be threatened with modest punishment for each step toward the dog, even though his proximity is of no interest in itself.

Similar to decomposing a threat into a series is starting a threat with a punitive act that grows in severity with the passage of time. Where a threat of death by violence might not be credited, cutting off the food supply might

[13] During 1950, the Economic Cooperation Administration declared its intention to reward Marshall Plan countries that followed especially sound policies, and to penalize those that did not, through the device of larger or smaller aid allotments. But since the base figures had not been determined, and since their determination would ultimately involve judgment rather than formulas, there would be no way afterwards to see whether in fact the additions and subtractions were made, and the plan suffered from implausibility.

[14] Perhaps the common requirement for amortization of loans at frequent intervals, rather than in a lump sum at the end of the loan period, reflects an analogous principle, as does the custom of giving frequent examinations in a college course to avoid letting a student's failure hinge exclusively on a single grading decision after the course is finished.

bring submission. For moral or public relations purposes, this device may in fact leave the "last clear chance" to the other, whose demise is then blamed on his stubbornness if the threat fails. But in any case the threatener gets his overt act out of the way while it is still preliminary and minor, rather than letting it stand as a final, dreadful, and visible obstacle to his resolution. And if the suffering party is the only one in a position to know, from moment to moment, how near to catastrophe they have progressed, his is the last clear chance in a real sense. Furthermore, the threatener may be embarrassed by his adversary's collapse but not by his discomfort; and the device may therefore transform a dangerous once-for-all threat into a less costly continuous one. Tenants are less easily removed by threat of forcible eviction than by simply shutting off the utilities.[15]

A piecemeal approach may also be used by the threatened person. If he cannot obviate the threat by hastening the entire act, he may hasten some initial stage that clearly commits him to eventual completion. Or, if his act is divisible while the threatener's retaliation comes only in the large economy size, performing it as a series of increments may deny the threatener the dramatic overt act that would trigger his response.

The Promise

Among the legal privileges of corporations, two that are mentioned in textbooks are the right to sue and the "right" to be sued. Who wants to be sued! But the right to be sued is the power to make a promise: to borrow money, to enter a contract, to do business with someone who might be damaged. If suit does arise, the "right" seems a liability in retrospect;

beforehand it was a prerequisite to doing business.

In brief, the right to be sued is the power to accept a commitment. In the commitments discussed up to this point, it was essential that one's adversary (or "partner," however we wish to describe him) not have the power to release one from the commitment; the commitment was, in effect, to some third party, real or fictitious. The promise is a commitment to the second party in the bargain and is required whenever the final action of one or of each is outside the other's control. It is required whenever an agreement leaves any incentive to cheat.[16]

This need for promises is more than incidental; it has an institutional importance of its own. It is not always easy to make a convincing, self-binding, promise. Both the kidnapper who would like to release his prisoner, and the prisoner, may search desperately for a way to commit the latter against informing on his captor, without finding one. If the victim has committed an act whose disclosure could lead to blackmail, he may confess it; if not, he might commit one in the presence of his captor, to create the bond that will ensure his silence. But these extreme possibilities illustrate how difficult, as well as important, it may be to assume a promise. If the law will not enforce price agreements; or if the union is unable to obligate itself to a no-strike pledge; or if a contractor has no assets to pay damages if he loses a suit, and the law will not imprison debtors; or if there is no "audience" to which one can pledge his reputation; it may not be possible to strike a bargain, or at least the same bargain that would otherwise be struck.

Bargaining may have to concern itself with an "incentive" system as well as the division of

---

[15] This seems to be the tactic that avoided an explosion and induced de Gaulle's forces to vacate a province they had occupied in Northern Italy in June 1945, after they had announced that any effort of their allies to dislodge them would be treated as a hostile act. See Harry S Truman, *Year of Decisions* (New York, 1955), pp. 239–42; and Winston S. Churchill, *Triumph and Tragedy*, vol. VI of *The Second World War* (Boston, 1953), pp. 566–68.

[16] The threat may seem to be a promise if the pledge behind it is only one's reputation with his adversary; but it is not a promise from which the second party can unilaterally release the threatener, since he cannot convincingly dissociate his own future estimate of the threatener from the latter's performance.

gains. Oligopolists may lobby for a "fair-trade" law; or exchange shares of stocks. An agreement to stay out of each other's market may require an agreement to redesign the products to be unsuitable in each other's area. Two countries that wish to agree not to make military use of an island may have to destroy the usefulness of the island itself. (In effect, a "third-party commitment" has to be assumed when an effective "second-party commitment" cannot be devised.)[17]

Fulfillment is not always observable. If one sells his vote in a secret election, or a government agrees to recommend an act to its parliament, or an employee agrees not to steal from inventory, or a teacher agrees to keep his political opinions out of class, or a country agrees to stimulate exports "as much as possible," there is no reliable way to observe or measure compliance. The observable outcome is subject to a number of influences, only one of which is covered by the agreement. The bargain may therefore have to be expressed in terms of something observable, even though what is observable is not the intended object of the bargain. One may have to pay the bribed voter if the election is won, not on how he voted; to pay a salesman a commission on sales, rather than on skill and effort; to reward policemen according to statistics on crime rather than on attention to duty; or to punish all employees for the transgressions of one. And, where performance is a matter of degree, the bargain may have to define arbitrary limits distinguishing performance from nonperformance; a specified loss of inventory treated as evidence of theft; a specified increase in exports considered an "adequate" effort; specified samples of performance taken as representative of total performance.[18]

The tactic of decomposition applies to promises as well as to threats. What makes many agreements enforceable is only the recognition of future opportunities for agreement that will be eliminated if mutual trust is not created and maintained, and whose value outweighs the momentary gain from cheating in the present instance. Each party must be confident that the other will not jeopardize future opportunities by destroying trust at the outset. This confidence does not always exist; and one of the purposes of piecemeal bargains is to cultivate the necessary mutual expectations. Neither may be willing to trust the other's prudence (or the other's confidence in the first's prudence, and so forth) on a large issue. But, if a number of preparatory bargains can be struck on a small scale, each may be willing to risk a small investment to create a tradition of trust. The purpose is to let each party demonstrate that he appreciates the need for trust and that he knows the other does too. So, if a major issue has to be negotiated, it may be necessary to seek out and negotiate some minor items for "practice," to establish the necessary confidence in each other's awareness of the long-term value of good faith.

Even if the future will bring no recurrence, it may be possible to create the equivalence of continuity by dividing the bargaining issue into consecutive parts. If each party agrees to send a million dollars to the Red Cross on condition the other does, each may be tempted to cheat if the other contributes first, and each one's anticipation of the other's cheating will inhibit agreement. But if the contribution is divided into consecutive small contributions, each can try the other's good faith for a small price. Furthermore, since each can keep the other on short tether to the finish, no one ever need risk more than one small contribution at a time. Finally, this change in the incentive structure itself takes most of the risk out of the initial contribution; the value of established trust is made obviously visible to both.

Preparatory bargains serve another purpose. Bargaining can only occur when at least one party takes initiative in proposing a bargain. A deterrent to initiative is the information it

---

[17] In an earlier age, hostages were exchanged.

[18] Inability to assume an enforceable promise, like inability to perform the activity demanded, may protect one from an extortionate threat. The mandatory secret ballot is a nuisance to the voter who would like to sell his vote, but protection to the one who would fear coercion.

yields, or may seem to yield, about one's eagerness. But if each has visible reason to expect the other to meet him half way, be- cause of a history of successful bargaining, that very history provides protection against the inference of overeagerness.[19]

[19] Perhaps two adversaries who look forward to some large negotiated settlement would do well to keep avenues open for negotiation of minor issues. If, for example, the number of loose ends in dispute between East and West should narrow down so much that nothing remains to be negotiated but the "ultimate issue" (some final, permanent disposition of all territories and armaments) the possibility of even opening negotiations on the latter might be jeopardized. Or, if the minor issues are not disposed of, but become so attached to the "big" issue that willingness to negotiate on them would be construed as overeagerness on the whole settlement, the possibility of preparatory bargains might disappear.

27. Two Strategies of Social Change and Their Dilemmas

Richard E. Walton*

A group may enter into intergroup contacts with dual change objectives—concessions in substantive areas and improvements in relationships. These two objectives are achieved through quite different strategies, involving power tactics on the one hand and attitude change activities on the other. The present analysis shows that at the tactical level the methods of achieving and employing power are detrimental to the methods of achieving more friendliness and trust, and vice versa. Many dilemmas confront group leaders who would pursue both strategies. The article discusses ways in which leaders attempt to cope with these tactical dilemmas and sometimes integrate the two strategies into a broader strategy of social change. Final comments are devoted to the implications of this discussion for leadership training and the theory and practice of social change.

Change Setting

The type of intergroup setting which is of primary concern here is described by the following assumptions. First, assume a desire on the part of one group to change the allocation of scarce resources between two groups— these could be status, political power, economic advantage or opportunity, geographic occupancy, and so on. Alternately, assume in- compatible preferences regarding social institutions—such as the Berlin Wall, racial segregation, union shop. Second, assume that although the leaders of the groups recognize these areas of conflict they also want to establish a more cooperative set of attitudes between the groups. Third, assume further that there is neither law nor a compulsory arbitration mechanism which can accomplish the desired change or settle the conflict of interest.

Some of our most pressing problems of social change fit these assumptions almost completely and others meet them to a lesser degree. In international relations, for instance, the important substantive conflicts between the United States and the Soviet Union are accompanied by a general desire for more favorable inter-nation attitudes. Moreover, in the present polarized world where the stakes of change can be enormously high, no international legal machinery is available to settle the important issues.

In race relations, the civil rights movement of the last decade has sought social change at times and in places where legal machinery could not be brought to bear to establish and enforce humane treatment for Negroes, to say nothing about equalizing their right to vote, to

Reproduced by special permission from Richard E. Walton, "Two Strategies of Social Change and Their Dilemmas," *The Journal of Applied Behavioral Science*, Vol. II (April–June 1965), pp. 167–179. Published by NTL Institute for Applied Behavioral Science.

* Professor of Business Administration, Graduate School of Business, Harvard University.

use public accommodations, to find housing, to apply for jobs, and so forth. At the same time, the majority of Negro and white leaders have commented upon the necessity for improved intergroup attitudes.

In labor-management relations, also, there are important substantive issues, such as hours, wages, and working conditions, which are neither specified by law nor amenable to resolution by appeal to a higher order of common values. Often these differences are accompanied by a genuine and mutual desire for harmonious intergroup relations.

How does the leadership of a group behave in these situations when they seek a change in the status quo? What actions are instrumental to the change effort?

Two groups of social scientists—viewing the same general situation—offer quite different explanations and advice. One change strategy is advanced by game theorists, diplomatic strategists, and students of revolutions. Their focus is on the building of a power base and the strategic manipulation of power. Another strategy is urged by many social psychologists and by many persons involved in human relations laboratory training. This approach involves overtures of love and trust and gestures of good will, all intended to result in attitude change and concomitant behavior change.

Tactics of the Power Strategy

In recent years there has been an attempt to explicate the rational tactics of power and strategic choice (Schelling, 1960; Rapoport, 1960; Boulding, 1962; Walton & McKersie, 1965). The work in this area suggests that the fixed sum games—those situations in which what one person gains the other loses—require the following tactical operations.

First, in order to establish a basis for negotiation with the other and improve the probable outcome for itself, a group must build its power vis-à-vis the other. Group A can increase its relative power by making group B more dependent upon it and by decreasing its own (A's) dependence upon B. Often the change is sought by groups with a relative power disadvantage. To command attention and establish a basis for a *quid pro quo,* they

must threaten the other with harm, loss, inconvenience, or embarrassment. These threats in international relations range from nuclear war to unilateral cancellation of an official state visit. In civil rights they involve notoriety, demonstrations, consumer boycotts, and sit-ins, lie-ins, and the like. In labor relations they include wildcat strikes, authorized stoppages, unfavorable publicity campaigns. These tactics create a basis for negotiation only if the threats are credible. One important technique for increasing their credibility is to fulfill a given threat once or repeatedly, as required.

A second set of tactical operations is required in order for a group to make maximum use of its potential power. These include biasing the rival group's perceptions of the strength of the underlying preference functions. A leader of group A attempts to overstate his group's needs or preferences for various degrees of achievement of its stated objective. Also, leader A depreciates the importance to B of B's objectives. These operations require the skillful management of ambiguity and uncertainty. They involve manipulating communication opportunities such that B perceives A as being maximally (even if irrationally) committed to a course of action and that the leader of group B does not have a comparable opportunity to commit himself to a different set of actions.

An abundance of illustrative material from international relations is available for each of these tactical operations—for example, the Cuban missile episode, Berlin crises, and the crises over Suez, the Congo, and Viet Nam. Leaders of various civil rights groups have behaved in similar ways. Illustrative encounters are those in Montgomery (school-bus boycotts over public accommodations); Pittsburgh (consumer boycotts over employment); Chicago (lie-ins and demonstrations over de facto segregation in schools); Birmingham (demonstrations over public accommodations); Mississippi ("invading" the state in the interest of voter registration and freedom schools). Analyses of the negotiations in any of the major trade union strikes—such as those in steel in 1959, in rails in 1963, and in autos in 1964—would reveal labor-management behavior which conformed to the tactical operations of the power strategy.

Tactics of the Attitude Change Strategy

Theoretical and empirical work in recent years has identified the conditions and actions which result in change in intergroup relationships (Naess, 1957; Janis & Katz, 1959; Osgood, 1959; Kelman, 1962; Berkowitz, 1962; Sherif, 1962; Deutsch, 1962; Gibb, 1964; Walton & McKersie, 1965). The areas of agreement in these writings may be summarized in terms of the tactics of attitude change.

Increasing the level of attraction and trust between persons or groups involves the following types of operations, considering the leader of group A as the acting party: minimizing the perceived differences between the groups' goals and between characteristics of members of the two groups; communications to B advocating peace; refraining from any actions which might harm members of the rival group (inconvenience, harass, embarrass, or violate them in any way); minimizing or eliminating B's perception of potential threats from A; emphasizing the degree of mutual dependence between the groups; accepting or enhancing the status of the representative of the rival group; ensuring that contacts between groups are on the basis of equal status; attempting to involve many members in intergroup contact; attempting to achieve a high degree of empathy with respect to the motives, expectations, and attitudes of members of group B; adopting a consistent posture of trust toward the other group; being open about A's own plans and intentions; creating a network of social relations involving many mutual associations with third parties.

There is tension between the ideas which underlie the two change strategies outlined above. However, the two groups of social scientists who are associated with these respective change strategies tend to handle this tension either by ignoring it or by depreciating the assumptions, ideas, and tactics of the other. It is true that both systems of ideas treat certain realities of the total social field; and, admittedly, it is possible for one to center one's attention on those particular situations where his ideas by themselves are appropriate and upon those particular aspects of a more complex situation where his ideas apply. The practitioner himself cannot do this. He must deal with the total reality. The leader of a group who is advocating and seeking change directly experiences the tension between these two persuasive systems of ideas.

Social scientists can become more relevant and therefore more helpful to the practitioner if they, too, confront these tensions between ideas, these dilemmas in action programs.

It is important to identify still a third distinct process of change, namely, problem solving. This process can be used whenever the basic nature of the issue is one where there is the potential that arrangements can be invented or created allowing both parties to gain or where one party can gain without the other's sacrificing anything of value to himself. In other words, integrative solutions are logically possible (Blake, 1959). However, this alternative of problem solving is not applicable in the specific intergroup situations assumed here: The substantive conflicts are ones which by the nature of the issues and the parties' basic preferences can be resolved only by dominance-submission or some compromise outcome.

Leadership Dilemmas in Pursuing Both Power and Attitude Change Strategies

If—as we have assumed here—a leader of group A has the objective both of obtaining important concessions from B and of reducing intergroup hostility, he would prefer to pursue simultaneously both change strategies discussed above. But in many respects the strategies place contradictory tactical demands on a leader, forcing him to choose between these strategies or to find some basis on which to integrate the two in some broader strategy of change. Several of the contradictions, dilemmas, and choice points in the tactics of social change are discussed below.

Overstatement of Objectives Versus Deemphasizing Differences

On the one hand, it is often tactical to the power strategy to overstate one's ultimate goals or immediate objectives—in effect, exaggerating the differences between the two groups. The strategy of attitude change, on the other hand, would deemphasize differences. Thus, the United States references to the status of Berlin which overstate our pertinent preferences, needs, and requirements may improve our position in bargaining for new terms there; but these statements run the risk of convincing the Soviet Union that our differences run even deeper than they do and that there is less basis for conciliation and trust than they had believed.

Stereotyping: Internal Cohesion Versus Accurate Differentiation

Stereotyping members of the rival group, focusing on their faults, impugning their motives, questioning their rationality, challenging their competence—these are often employed by leaders and members of the first group to build internal cohesion and willingness to make necessary sacrifices. For example, these tendencies occurred in a moderate form as the Mississippi Summer Project prepared their field staff and student volunteers for their work in "hostile" Mississippi.[1] The tendency to attribute negative attributes to members of the rival group may have aided in the implementation of the almost pure power strategy which characterized this particular project, but this tendency would have been a clear liability in another civil rights project where the objectives included achieving attitude change.

Emphasis on Power to Coerce Versus Trust

If group A increases B's dependence upon A, this may enhance A's power to obtain substantive concessions, but it will not elicit more positive feelings. In fact, it can be argued that the trust-building process requires that A would communicate about A's dependence upon B. A labor union may enhance its power position by making management more aware of the company's vulnerability to a strike. But the same union might elicit more trust if it were to indicate instead how much the union must count upon management.

[1] Personal observation.

Information: Ambiguity Versus Predictability

Whereas ambiguity and uncertainty are often tactical to the power strategy, openness and predictability are essential to the attitude change strategy. Similarly, the first strategy is facilitated when there is limited and disciplined interaction; the second, when there is a more extensive and more open contact pattern. Thus, the power strategy dictates that we restrict the flow of information and people between the Soviet Union and the United States and that the limited contacts be formal and structured and that the agenda of these contacts be quite guarded. Attitude change strategy, on the other hand, calls for freedom of travel, a variety of settings for international contact, and spontaneity and openness in these interchanges.

Threat Versus Conciliation

Review of the tactical operations of the two strategies reveals another important choice point in dual or mixed strategies, namely, What should be the role of threat or harm? When A is primarily pursuing an attitude change strategy, he communicates peaceful plans, he reduces perceived threat to B, and he refrains from actions that harm B. However, to pursue a power strategy in the interest of obtaining substantive gains, A engages in quite different tactics.

Even instances of uncontrolled aggression out of frustration can build bargaining power for the frustrated group and serve as an implicit threat of more aggression if substantive gains are not forthcoming. The Harlem riots in the summer of 1964 illustrate this point. Although it was generally said at the time that these outbursts hurt the civil rights movement (i.e., "had set the movement back several years"), many changes which accommodated the Negroes' demands and needs were soon made in the budgets, plans, and organization of several commissions and departments of New York City. One column headline in the *New York Times*, July 1964, the week following the riots, read "City Accelerates Fight on Poverty: $223,225 Grant Made Amid Reference to Racial Riots." A casual content analysis of items in the news after the riots in Harlem, Rochester, Philadelphia, and elsewhere suggests that there were both substantive gains and attitudinal losses. Notwithstanding the fact that all responsible civil rights leaders deplored the wanton destruction of property and the indiscriminate defiance of legal authorities, their bargaining power was nevertheless strengthened in certain respects.

Hostility Management: Impact Versus Catharsis

This dilemma is related to the preceding one but can present a somewhat more subtle problem for group leadership. Both change strategies involve the purposeful management of hostile feelings. In the power strategy the expression of hostile feelings is managed in a way which creates optimal impact on the other group, communicating strength of interest in the issue or making a threat credible.

The attitude change strategy also involves the expression of hostile feelings, but in a way which creates an optimal impact on the expressing group. Hostility expression is managed in a way which allows catharsis and the reevaluation of one's own group's feelings, but with minimum impact on the other group. Otherwise the hostility level will tend to be maintained or increased.

Coalition Versus Inclusion

One final dilemma relates to the question of whether A tries to involve third parties or publics in a coalition *against* B or in a social group *with* B. Building bargaining power in the interest of substantive change may require A to isolate B and attempt to generate disapproval of B. This has been an important aspect of the strategy of the civil rights movement in the last decade. The movement has tried to identify and isolate those officials and power groups in the South who oppose integration and those national officials in the Republican Party who are unsympathetic with certain legislative and enforcement objectives. This has created a forced choice situation for the moderates and for the uncertain.

However, a strategy of attitude change involves creating a network of social relations among A, B, and others. Applied to the civil rights movement, an emphasis on attitude change would actively encourage dialogue, understanding, and mutual influence among (a) groups in the movement, (b) the middle-of-the-roaders, and (c) the segregationists and other right-wing groups.

Coping with the Dilemmas

How do those who seek both substantive changes opposed by another group and improvements in intergroup attitudes cope with these dilemmas?

If the group's leader sequences the emphasis placed upon these two objectives and their accompanying strategies, this does somewhat ameliorate the tension between the two sets of activities. In international negotiations between the East and the West, both sides have used a freeze-thaw approach. One may first engage in new initiatives intended to make substantive gains or to create a power base for the future, and then make peace overtures. As long as the cycle is not too short in duration and the initiatives and overtures are seen as genuine, a leader can engage in both sets of behaviors and still have them be credible. In race relations, a particular campaign may involve a street demonstration phase (power building) and a negotiation phase (a mixture of power bargaining and relationship building).

Another technique is to have the contradictory strategies implemented by different persons or subgroups. In international relations, power tactics occur in the confrontations between the United States and the Soviet Union in the United Nations General Assembly and Security Council, but their attitude change efforts are implemented by different groups involved in such activities as cultural exchange programs. In race relations, a similar distinction can be made between the programs of CORE and SNCC on the one hand and NAACP and the Urban League on the other. This technique makes it apparent that mixed or dual strategies can be pursued more readily by an organization than by a person, and more readily by a movement than by an organization.

Whether or not the activities are sequenced or assigned to different persons within a group, an important way of coping with these dilemmas is to choose actions which minimize them. Recognition of the tactical requirements of both strategies results in eliminating provocative acts which elicit negative attitudes and add nothing to the power strategy—for example, impeccable dress and demeanor in many civil rights demonstrations or the self-imposed norm of volunteers of the Mississippi Summer Project to avoid mixed racial couples' appearing in public even though eventual acceptance of such a pattern was one of the goals of the movement.

When the relationship between strategies is fully understood by the leader, he can select power tactics which have least negative impact on attitudes and choose attitudinal structuring activities which detract least from the power strategy.

Nonviolence is an attempt to meet the requirements of both strategies, but as a tactic it falls short of achieving an optimal integration. This is true in part because the distinction made between violence and nonviolence is more meaningful to the acting group than to the target group. The distinction usually refers to whether or not there is a physical violation of members of the rival group. In fact, other violations may be experienced by them as equally devastating—such as violation of their traditions and other social norms (integrating schools), assaults on their power base (voting drives). In short, in some situations the only maneuvers which effectively increase bargaining power really do hurt.

Over-all Strategy Consideration

Although in many situations one must engage in the tactics of power only at some disadvantage in terms of achieving attitude change and vice versa, this is not always the case. Especially when one takes a longer-range viewpoint, one may discover that the substantive objectives of the power strategy are more likely to be realized at a later date if an improvement in intergroup attitudes is sought initially. The point is that attitude change may result in some lessening of the substantive conflict. If southern whites as a group were more accepting of Negroes (i.e., developed more favorable attitudes toward them for some independent reason), they would be less adamant on certain substantive issues—for example, segregated schools—and would, as a result, reduce the need for civil rights groups to utilize a power strategy. Moreover, in the case of many of the substantive gains which one may reach through the power strategy—an arms control agreement, a treaty on Berlin, an understanding reached regarding future employment practices affecting Negroes—the fulfillment of these arrangements is dependent upon the level of trust and confidence which exists in the relationship.

Similarly, a longer-range viewpoint may show that the objective of attitude change is more likely to be achieved at a later date if one engages in the power tactics initially. The substantive gains obtained by the power strategy almost always result in temporary setbacks in terms of the level of friendliness and trust between the groups; but in the somewhat longer run, the result may be better affective relations. Consider race relations. One reason why more positive attitudes may develop via the initial power strategy is that the commitment and self-respect which the Negroes usually demonstrate in pursuing the power strategy may engender respect on the part of the larger white community—after the initial heat of conflict has subsided.

Another indirect and eventual way that the power strategy can lead to more favorable attitudinal bonds is through the mechanism of dissonance reduction. If as a result of substantive gains a group must be treated differently (more equal), there is a tendency to regard them differently (more equal) in order to make one's beliefs and attitudes congruent with one's behavior.

There is a third reason why a power strategy designed to obtain substantive concessions may achieve attitude change as well, particularly for a group which is currently less privileged and exercises less power. This refers to an important precondition for achieving a stable and healthy intergroup relationship—equal status and power between groups. This suggests that as long as group A remains at a power disadvantage and there is a potential for achieving power parity, A's mix of power and attitude change tactics will include relatively more power tactics. Thus, the power strategy for the civil rights groups during the last decade has dominated the attitude change strategy. This principle is also illustrated by the warlike actions of the Soviet Union during the period after World War II, when the United States alone possessed the atom bomb.

Whatever the existing balance of power, whenever B makes a move which would build his relative power, A will tend to act primarily in terms of the power strategy. This is illustrated by the United States's bargaining commitment moves when it discovered Soviet missiles in Cuba and when the Soviets attempted to make inroads in the Middle East and the Congo during the Suez and Congo crises respectively.

Implications

Recognition of these dilemmas is the first step toward developing a theory of social action which specifies the conditions under which one should conform to the tactical requirements of one strategy versus the other. But better theory is not enough. The agent of social change needs the behavioral skills required by simultaneously or sequentially mixed strategies. For example, international officials and civil rights leaders should be flexible enough to employ strategies of attitude change when a particular campaign reaches the negotiation phase.

What are the implications for training of leaders of groups advocating major social change? Human relations training generally and laboratory learning in particular are geared to developing insights and skills central to the strategy of attitude change and are less relevant to the power strategy. I suggest that the conception of the problem of change should be broadened to incorporate—as necessary and legitimate—the power strategy.[2] We must understand what demands on leadership behavior are imposed by the power strategy of change both during the phase when power thinking necessarily dominates group leadership and the phase when preserving a power base is merely a consideration in designing an attitude change strategy. If these specialists deplore these power tactics simply because they violate their personal model of preferred social behavior, their advice which *is* appropriate and badly needed by the practitioner will be taken less seriously by him.

---

[2] In the interest of sharpening the issues about our conception of the problem, I offer the following assertions regarding the role of bargaining, power, and violence in social change:

First, bargaining and bargaining tactics (including tactical deception, bluff, commitment, promises, threats, and threat fulfillment) are often necessary in social change situations where there are basic conflicts of interest. Moreover, many of these tactical operations are amoral in such situations.

Second, attempts to create cooperative relations between parties are more effective if there is some parity in their power. Power of a party derives from its capacity to influence some aspect of the fate of the other—either rewards or punishments. Often the only avenue open to a party with less relative power is to increase its capacity to harm (embarrass or inconvenience) the other. Moreover, it may be necessary for the party to engage in a series of maneuvers which are increasingly persuasive in communicating to the other party both a capacity and a willingness to use the power.

Third, where they are used, tactics of nonviolence are effective at least in part because the other group perceives this method as an alternative to violence. The option of violence is indirectly suggested *by advocating nonviolence.*

Fourth, there is experimental evidence that a cooperative bid by A is more effective in eliciting a cooperative response from B when it occurs against a series of noncooperative moves by A. Maybe this paradox also operates in some social situations creating an incentive for initial noncooperation.

References

Berkowitz, L. *Aggression: A social psychological analysis.* New York: McGraw-Hill, 1962.

Blake, R. R. Psychology and the crisis of statesmanship. *Amer. Psychologist,* 1959, 14, 87–94.

Boulding, K. *Conflict and defense: A general theory.* New York: Harper, 1962.

City accelerates fight on poverty. *New York Times,* July 28, 1964, p. 15.

Deutsch, M. A psychological basis for peace. In Q. Wright, W. M. Evan, & M. Deutsch (Eds.), *Preventing World War III: Some proposals.* New York: Simon and Schuster, 1962.

Gibb, J. R. Climate for trust formation. In L. P. Bradford, J. R. Gibb, & K. D. Benne (Eds.), *T-Group theory and laboratory method: Innovation in re-education.* New York: Wiley, 1964.

Janis, I. L., & Katz, D. The reduction of intergroup hostility: Research problems and hypotheses. *J. conflict Resolution,* 1959, 3, 85–100.

Kelman, H. C. Changing attitudes through international activities. *J. soc. Issues,* 1962, 18, 68–87.

Naess, A. A systematization of Gandhian ethics of conflict resolution. *J. conflict Resolution,* 1957, 1, 140–155.

Osgood, C. E. Suggestions for winning the real war with Communism. *J. conflict Resolution,* 1959, 3, 295–325.

Rapoport, A. *Fights, games, and debates.* Ann Arbor: Univer. of Michigan Press, 1960.

Schelling, T. *The strategy of conflict.* Cambridge: Harvard Univer. Press, 1960.

Sherif, M. (Ed.). *Intergroup relations and leadership.* New York: Wiley, 1962.

Walton, R. E., & McKersie, R. B. *A behavioral theory of labor negotiations.* New York: McGraw-Hill, 1965.

IV

PERSUASIVE STRATEGIES

28. Propaganda and Communications

J. A. C. Brown*

Attempts to change the opinions of others are older than recorded history and originated, it must be supposed, with the development of speech. Through speech comes the power to manipulate or persuade people without necessarily resorting to physical force, and before men could speak it is unlikely that they had any opinions to change. Direct violence or the threat of violence may produce submission to the will of another individual or group, but thoughts are created and modified primarily by the spoken or written word so that, although in so-called "brainwashing" words may be supplemented by unpleasant physical treatment, and in commercial advertising by pleasing pictures or music, it is obvious that even in these cases the essential weapons are verbal or at any rate symbolic, and the results aimed at psychological. In general, and with few exceptions, psychological transformations require psychological techniques, and it is with such influences rather than external com-

shall be mainly concerned here. The whole pliance brought about by force alone, that we subject of changing people's minds raises fascinating scientific and moral issues whether it takes the form of religious conversion, political rabble-rousing, health propaganda, the question of the impact of the mass media on popular taste, the impersonal manipulation of the masses allegedly carried out by those in the "opinion business," or the more sinister forms of political indoctrination practised in totalitarian states. In an age of conflicting ideologies when whole nations are being subjected to group persuasion through new means of communication, new techniques, and the pull of mass movements led by demagogues, it is important to find out just how tough or how yielding the human mind really is; how far it is possible to produce genuine change in the individual's or group's way of thinking; and to gain some insight into the means employed to that end. Some authorities take the view that

Reprinted in part from J. A. C. Brown, "Propaganda and Communications," *Techniques of Persuasion* (London: Penguin Books Ltd., 1963), pp. 9–28.
* Affiliation unavailable.

we are all virtually at the mercy of the mass media and baleful methods of group stimulation, whilst others have suggested that brainwashing and similar techniques available to the modern mind-manipulator are not only wellnigh irresistible but lead to real and permanent changes in political or religious outlook. If such beliefs are well-founded, the outlook for civilization as we know it is not pleasant to contemplate; if they are not, then critical examination must be able to show that the mind is a good deal more intractable than those who hold such views seem to suppose. On the other hand, there are sometimes circumstances in which changes of attitude are necessary and desirable, such as the sick attitudes of mental illness or the wrong ones held by many about race, issues in public health, the prevention of accidents, and so on. Most people would agree that the work of the psychiatrist is worth-while and that it is worthy of consideration how public health or safety campaigns may best be run. Whether or not, as ordinarily carried out, such campaigns have any significant effects of the type intended requires careful investigation; and this becomes all the more important if, as there is every reason to believe, well-meant but incompetently conceived propaganda, so far from having merely negative results, can be shown to have positively undesirable ones or even to lead to effects diametrically opposed to those desired.

The Oxford Dictionary defines propaganda as "an association or scheme for propagating a doctrine or practice," and the word takes its origin from the Latin *propagare* which means the gardener's practice of pinning the fresh shoots of a plant into the earth in order to reproduce new plants which will later take on a life of their own. Therefore one implication of the term when it was first used in the sociological sense by the Roman Catholic Church was that the spread of ideas brought about in this way is not one that would take place of itself, but rather a cultivated or artificial generation. In the year 1633, Pope Urban VIII established the Congregatio de Propaganda Fide, otherwise known as "The Congregation of Propaganda" or simply "The Propaganda,"

a committee of cardinals which had, and still has, charge of the foreign missions of the Church. Naturally this was regarded as a beneficent process which by preaching and example attempted to lead the heathen from darkness into light and it was an artificial or cultivated one only in the sense that, without outside intervention, these peoples would never have learned about Christianity. Since the missionaries were well aware of what they were doing, their propaganda was also deliberate and the modern contention that it is possible for propaganda to be unconscious, a favourite theme of Marxists and others, would have conveyed nothing to them.

Within the present century, however, the popular image of propaganda has undergone radical changes and the word has come to acquire overtones implying a process which is frequently sinister, lying, and based on the deliberate attempt on the part of an individual or group to manipulate, often by concealed or underhand means, the minds of others for their own ulterior ends. Superficially, this change can be dated from the official use of propaganda as a weapon in the total warfare of modern times, beginning with the First World War, when lies, political subterfuge, and atrocity stories were unscrupulously employed in an attempt to influence the final result. The exposure of these methods during the interwar years led to a tremendous revulsion of popular feeling amongst the by now predominantly pacific victors, accompanied by avowals of admiration on the part of the defeated some of whom determined to make even better use of the same methods when the occasion arose. But this ambivalent feeling that propaganda is something sly, unpleasant, and frequently silly, yet also a weapon of devastating power for "getting at" people with or without their consent, has far deeper roots than the above explanation might suggest. It arises, in fact, from certain fundamental changes in the nature of communication within technically advanced societies, and the methods employed during the First World War and subsequently were the effect rather than the cause of wholly new developments in the structure and techniques of the modern state. What these developments are must be considered at a later stage; but it is at any rate clear that changing nuances in meaning have made "propaganda" a difficult word to define. It is often employed in a derogatory sense, and in spite of the fact that part of the original meaning was undoubtedly the implication that it was a collective appeal to larger or smaller groups of people made either by an individual or another group, it is now frequently used as indiscriminately as the more recent "brainwashing" to refer to the activities of any unfortunate individual who wishes to convey a piece of unwelcome or unacceptable information to another. Since the greater part of any written or spoken communication is intended to arouse some sort of response in the recipient, it is easy to see why many authorities consider that propaganda is a word which has outlived its usefulness.

If for the moment these complexities are ignored and the dictionary definition extended to apply to any scheme for propagating a doctrine or practice *or for influencing the emotional attitudes of others*, we shall be in a position to glance briefly at the past history of propaganda and the conditions under which it took place. In this way it will be possible to discover some of its other characteristics, and to show how its effectiveness and the form it takes are limited by the structure and the available technical resources of the society which employs it. The obvious reason for amplifying the original definition is that the propagandist is not always doing anything so clear-cut as attempting to spread a specific doctrine or practice; for quite often, as in war propaganda, he is merely trying to arouse strong emotions of hatred or approval for or against another group from motives of expediency, strategy, or plain greed. But emotional pressure, whether it takes the form of arousing positive or negative collective feelings, or simply that of presenting emotionally biased views, is not just something added to propaganda to make it more acceptable. It is fundamental to the whole process. Rational and dispassionate argument employs a totally different technique; and when Socrates by means of questioning rather than by supplying ready-made answers to the problems raised by his pupils brought them to discover the truth for themselves, he was certainly not engaging in propaganda although his pupils' views were changed in the process. The propagandist does not engage in genuine argument because his answers are determined in advance. It follows that, if all propaganda attempts to change minds, not all mind-changing is accomplished by propaganda. In vivid contrast to the Socratic method is that found, for example, in the books of the Old Testament prophets where vehement eloquence is employed to the specific end of turning the Israelites away from the worship of false gods and evil practices towards the worship of Jehovah; for here the means include special pleading, admonition, and the threat of divine retribution. Inasmuch as he is *for* the creation of certain attitudes, the propagandist is necessarily *against* others; and the extirpation of what he regards as false beliefs and doctrines is as much his concern as the propagation of the "right" ones. This suggests the important rule that one can only speak of propaganda when alternative views exist, and it is therefore not propaganda to teach a belief which is universal at a particular time or place. Of course, it sometimes happens that propaganda is carried on for the sole purpose of putting an end to a practice without necessarily replacing it by another, as when public health departments want to stop people from smoking, or the British stopped head-hunting ·in Papua and the self-immolation of Hindu widows on their husbands' funeral pyres' in India. But such campaigns are carried out because the authorities concerned regarded these customs or habits as undesirable and not "good," as those who practice them believe. The alternative view of the campaigners is implicit in their actions.

As people become more literate and, overtly at least, more civilized, the written word comes to play an increasingly important part in the spread of opinions and the creation of emotional attitudes. The existence of books raises two problems fundamental to a study of propaganda: the question of whether it is meaningful to talk of unconscious propaganda, and the issue of censorship. Neither of these problems was created by the written word (although it is easier to control what a man writes than what he says), but obviously we can only know about what went on in the distant past by way of the books which persist long after the spoken words have gone. The works of Herodotus have earned him the title of the father of history, and he has also been less sympathetically described as a hired press agent for the Athenian state. But there is really very little reason to suppose that he was any more aware of his partiality than, until recently, were the writers of our school history books aware of their own imperialist bias because the whole idea of presenting the public with objective information about the world in general is, with some outstanding exceptions, relatively new in human thought. Free expression of opinion has been rare enough and is by no means synonymous with the attempt to be objective which has seldom been regarded as particularly commendable. For centuries of European history "truth" was Catholic truth, and we have seen that in the absence of alternative views it is meaningless to talk about propaganda whether conscious or otherwise. Significantly, the Catholic Congregation of Propaganda only came into existence when the Church began to experience the full impact of new doctrines, and new lands to convert. If by "unconscious propaganda" is meant the sort of bias allegedly shown by Herodotus, it must be remembered that few people in the past, even when they were dimly aware that other standpoints existed, have thought it in any way unnatural to interpret events from that of their own state or religion. This is to exhibit bias, but it is not propaganda unless it is carried out with the purpose of spreading the biased view to those who do not already hold it. It may be supposed that nobody would have been more surprised than Herodotus at any suggestion that Babylonians or Egyptians should not also have held, quite justifiably, their own partial versions of history. Most societies up to the end of the Middle Ages in Europe were controlled by tradition, and such propaganda as took place had to be carried on within the permitted framework and ordinarily by the learned. This view or that might be put forward, but only against the background of a world picture which seemed to represent fixed and unalterable truth; and, for the masses, truth originated in authority rather than in the evidence of their own senses or the conclusions arrived at by independent thought. Periclean Athens stands out as a brief period when men tried deliberately to discount bias and arrive at objective truth, and Thucydides' account of the Peloponnesian War is possibly the first attempt to write impartial history; yet the Athenians executed Socrates for corrupting the youth of the city by getting them to think for themselves. Imperial Rome cared little what religious beliefs its citizens might hold, but cared a great deal for the dignity of the state; and Augustus had Ovid exiled for "a poem and a mistake," while providing state patronage for Virgil, many of whose works are more or less barefaced propaganda against the old republican ideas and for Augustus and the Empire. These are instances of that form of censorship which is an important aspect of propaganda in so far as it selectively suppresses certain views in favour of others.

But it would probably be wrong to regard all suppression of information as being carried out from motives of propaganda. The priesthoods of ancient Egypt and Babylonia, for example, kept their pictographic scripts a closely guarded secret from the common people. But this had nothing to do with propaganda, for whatever meaning we attach to the term can hardly comprise the limitation of religious mysteries to a priestly caste. Eventually reading became democratized with the replacement of the old clumsy scripts by the beginnings of the modern alphabet which enabled traders and scribes to record their transactions or even to write secular literature, but the spread of news was largely limited to the eyes and ears of kings. This was the case in Babylonia and Assyria, and, much later, Julius Caesar had certain items of news posted in the Forum but circulated quite a different version among members of the governing class. During the Middle Ages, much information was carried orally by special messengers, but this too was restricted to the higher clergy and the secular rulers. It must be remembered, however, that in those days news was scarce and precious. No large state of antiquity, as Bertrand Russell has pointed out, was governed from the center to nearly the same extent as is now customary: and the chief reason for this was lack of rapid mobility and therefore of information. Thus, although both Church and state censored forbidden opinions, most limiting of news was based mainly on scarcity together with the not unjustifiable belief that such matters were no concern of the people, who would neither have understood nor wished to hear them. Again, all states from the earliest civilizations right up to the present day have had their state secrets and there have been those matters "which it is not in the public interest to disclose"; but, although this form of censorship may often be abused, it is not ordinarily used as a propaganda weapon.

Propaganda by censorship takes two forms: the selective control of information to favor a particular viewpoint, and the deliberate doctoring of information in order to create an impression different from that originally intended. The most obvious example of the first type is ecclesiastical censorship, which dates from very early in the history of the Church but is best known in the shape of the *Index Librorum Prohibitorum,* traceable from the sixteenth century, whereby all books considered pernicious to Roman Catholics are placed on the Index by the Congregation of the Holy Office. It would be impossible here to give any idea of the great number of important works banned in this way, but an indication of the mental outlook of those responsible is demonstrated by the fact that the Copernican theory was forbidden until as late as 1822. Dante and Galen had also to be removed in the course of time, but Gibbon, Hume, John Stuart Mill, Goldsmith, Sterne, Kant, Voltaire, Croce, Stendhal, and even the works of a number of modern and specifically Catholic writers remain prohibited to the ordinary Catholic, although permission to read forbidden books may be granted to students. This is propaganda because it is selective and deliberately designed to give those toward whom it is di-

rected a partial view of the world in which we live—a world which necessarily includes the opinions of others whether they are true or not. The philosophies of Hume and Kant may be the merest nonsense, but nobody can claim to know anything about philosophy if he has not been permitted to read their works.

A classic example of the second form of propaganda by censorship through doctored information is Bismarck's famous Ems telegram of 1870. The point at issue was whether Leopold of Hohenzollern should succeed to the Spanish throne, a candidature supported by Bismarck and opposed by the French. King William of Prussia and the French ambassador had strolled together in the pleasure garden at Ems discussing the problem, although by this time Leopold, alarmed by the fuss his candidature had aroused, had already resigned it and the threat of war seemed to have been averted. But Bismarck wanted war, and, when William sent a telegram in cipher describing the inoffensive discussion that had taken place at Ems, Bismarck and his colleagues were at first despondent at its unimportant nature. Then the chancellor suddenly saw how he could make use of it to save the situation. By cutting out a few words and sentences and then publishing the abrupt telegram as it was, he could make what had been a fairly polite interview appear as a truculent challenge and a consequent snub. The provocative alterations were made and published, and the press on both sides clamored for war. Thus began the Franco-Prussian War in which 141,000 men were killed.

On a more humble scale is the common practice of theaters when they put up posters giving quotes from important critics which, in many cases, have been cut out of the original context in order to create a favorable impression from what may have been an extremely unfavorable review.

But the spread of control of knowledge and opinions in early times inevitably had a limited impact upon the tradition-bound majority. Only the small educated class was able to read the few available hand-written books well enough to be affected by the censorship of reading-matter, and the loudest voice of any public orator could carry only so far, making it necessary for him to employ messengers or travel about himself if he wanted his communications to get beyond the bounds of the market-place. The wider diffusion of knowledge and the freedom to develop and spread a great diversity of opinions throughout all levels of society, had to wait upon two historical phenomena: the invention of printing by moveable types in 1454, and the Reformation in the following century. The former made it technically possible to spread ideas and factual information far more quickly and widely than ever before, although it could not become fully effective until compulsory education for all had been introduced—an event which did not reach England until as late as 1870, later than in other civilized countries. The Reformation had an effect which was not entirely that foreseen by the Reformers, most of whom were as bigoted and intolerant as their predecessors, since it weakened the Church by splitting it up into so many minor sects that, at least in Protestant countries, its power to stop people thinking and saying what they pleased was greatly reduced. To be fair, it must also be added that by introducing the habit of Bible-reading the Protestants encouraged literacy, and that some of the reformers such as Luther in Germany and Knox in Scotland were largely responsible for setting up education systems along modern lines.

The first publications in England to deal with matters of contemporary public opinion and what we should now describe as news were the early fifteenth-century pamphlets which discussed various social, political, or religious issues generally from a strong partisan point of view; these were followed by the news-letters which, produced by professional London news-writers, gave the reader all the gossip and rumor of the city. The first man to print all the news of the day upon a single sheet in a regular weekly publication with a distinctive title was Nathaniel Butter, who brought out the *Weekly Newes* in 1622. All these publications were strictly censored by the state, with the exception of a brief period of freedom after the Star Chamber (which, unfettered by the law, had been used by

Charles I and his party to persecute their opponents) had finally been abolished in 1641. But this resulted in such a flood of publications that the Long Parliament had to impose an even more rigid censorship on books and reading matter which, in spite of Milton's plea for freedom, was maintained by the Commonwealth. During the Restoration of the monarchy which followed, a Licensing Act in 1662 renewed the royal licensing of printing, and the freedom of the press dates from the failure to renew this act in 1695. The seventeenth and eighteenth centuries were an age of pamphlets which were produced in abundance by such writers as Defoe, Bunyan, Steele, Addison, and many lesser men, and these, like their predecessors, contained propaganda for different shades of opinion. In this respect they were no less partisan than the newspapers; for up to the end of the first quarter of the nineteenth century the English press consisted exclusively of journals of opinion which printed, or distorted, news with the single-minded purpose of converting readers to their own particular point of view. The idea of news as information played a correspondingly small part, and such important events as the Battle of Waterloo might be dismissed in a few lines, swamped by editorial comment and scurrilous gossip. In fact, gossip and scandal often provided the editor with an additional source of income by way of bribery and blackmail, since he could threaten to publish or promise to withhold news of scandals involving prominent public figures according to the price they were willing to pay. Surprisingly, in the light of later developments, it was the growth of commercial advertising that played a major part in making newspapers honest and moderately respectable. For it soon became clear that the gaining of advertisers willing to buy space required a large circulation which could only be achieved by presenting events in a reasonably unbiased way.

From this short historical survey it has been possible to pinpoint some of the more obvious characteristics of propaganda and to show how, as a form of communication, it is influenced by the technical apparatus for spreading communications available at the time. It is now necessary to turn to the views and re-searches of the modern social psychologists who have made a scientific study of the sub-ject. Kimball Young of Queens College, New York, defines propaganda as:

> . . . the more or less deliberately planned and systematic use of symbols, chiefly through sug-gestions and related psychological techniques, with a view to altering and controlling opinions, ideas, and values, and ultimately to changing overt actions along predetermined lines. Prop-aganda may be open and its purpose avowed, or it may conceal its intention. It always has a setting within a social-cultural framework, without which neither its psychological nor its cultural features can be understood.

Leonard W. Doob of Yale, whose *Public Opinion and Propaganda* is one of the most important books on the subject, offers as one of his definitions what is virtually an abbrevi-ated version of the above. Propaganda is, he writes:

> . . . a systematic attempt by an interested in-dividual (or individuals) to control the atti-tudes of groups of individuals through the use of suggestion, and, consequently, to control their actions.

Elsewhere, however, Doob takes into ac-count the content of propaganda and says that it is "the attempt to affect the personalities and to control the behavior of individuals toward ends considered unscientific or of doubtful value in a society at a particular time." As it stands, this seems an inadequate definition, for who is to say what is of "doubt-ful value" at any given time? Apparently the answer is that society itself must judge, since Doob continues:

> . . . the dissemination of a viewpoint con-sidered by a group to be "bad," "unjust," "ugly," or "unnecessary" is propaganda, in terms of that group's standards.

This is undoubtedly how many people de-termine what they are going to describe as "propaganda," but it does not follow that such a subjective definition adequately describes what propaganda really is; for instance, it would exclude what we quite justifiably refer to as health propaganda. However, Doob's point that propaganda always has a setting within a particular social-cultural framework becomes clearer when he contrasts it with education. For the essence of education, he suggests, is its objectivity *in the light of scien-tific truths prevalent at the time*, whilst the essence of propaganda is the attempt to con-trol people's attitudes, often in irrational direc-tions (and always, we might add, by irrational means). Hence it was not propaganda to teach or spread the pre-Copernican picture of the solar system when it was a generally ac-cepted theory prevalent at the time, but it cer-tainly was propaganda when an attempt was made to censor the new theory as it arose or to conceal the fact that an alternative one ex-isted. Somebody has said that freedom of choice presupposes a full appreciation of all the alternatives involved, and one feature common to all propaganda is that it tries to limit our choice deliberately whether by avoiding argument (the bald statement of one point of view to the exclusion of others) or by the emotional and non-objective criticism of the other side and its opinions by the use of caricature, stereotypes, and other means to be discussed later. The uneasy feeling of so many people in the face of propaganda, that an at-tempt is being made to manipulate them by underhand methods, is quite justified. There is nearly always something concealed by the propagandist. What he conceals may be his real aim in engaging in his campaign, the means (suggestion and other psychological tech-niques) employed, the fact that there are alternative views to his own, or the fact that if these are mentioned at all it is only to mis-represent them. Whether the material pre-sented is true or untrue, the operator sincere or insincere, his aims "good" or "bad" is en-tirely irrelevant. What makes behavior propa-ganda is the manner in which the material is presented, just as much as is content.

The problem of unconscious propaganda has already been mentioned, and the issues involved are again best illustrated in the field of education. Superficially it is easy to distin-guish between education and propaganda, since the former aims at independence of judgement, the latter at supplying ready-made judgements for the unthinking. The educator aims at a slow process of development, the propagandist at quick results; the former tells people *how* to think, the latter tells them *what* to think; one strives to produce individual responsibility and an open mind, the other, using mass effects, strives to produce a closed one. Yet the distinction is less easy to make than might be supposed. The Soviet government, for example, like the Catholic Congregation of Propaganda, regard propaganda and education (as conducted by itself) as identical processes; according to the *Soviet Political Dictionary*, propaganda is "the intensive elucidation of the writings of Marx, Engels, Lenin, and Stalin, and of the history of the Bolshevik Party and its tasks." Ozhegov's *Dictionary of the Russian Language* defines "agitation" (which has an unpleasant connotation in the West) as: "Oral and written activity among the broad masses which aims at inculcating certain ideas and slogans for their political education and for attracting them to the solution of the more important social and political tasks." Furthermore, Communists accept the argument of Marx that ideologies reflect the class-struggle which exists in every non-socialist system of production, and that the prevailing ideology of any period will thus be that which favors the economically dominant class; or, as a non-Communist American expressed it more crudely to Mr. Justice Holmes: "Philosophers are men hired by the well-to-do to prove that everything is all right." In this view all non-Communist ideologies (Marx himself unlike his followers excepted the field of science as its conclusions could be verified by empirical methods) are simply unconscious, or sometimes conscious, propaganda. They are not propaganda in the "good" Communist sense which means education, but in the "bad" or reactionary sense which implies the intent to deceive the masses. Of course, there can be no doubt that education, as actually carried out in any country is only rarely unbiased. One social scientist went to the trouble of analyzing a widely used American textbook of arithmetic for schools and found that, in fewer than 200 pages, there were 643 problems which not only dealt with, but stressed the concepts peculiar to capitalism: rent, investments, interest, and so on. One might suppose that it is no sin to take for granted existing economic practices; yet in a socialist country this would be regarded as propaganda and, quite recently, it was reported that Russian educationists were disturbed by the frequency with which the profit motive still reared its ugly head in their own textbooks and were taking steps to change them in a more progressive direction. If arithmetic can be accused of bias, how much more does this apply to the teaching of nationalist values through history, geography, and literature! These are all examples of what Doob means by unconscious propaganda, but the view taken here is that, since it is an inescapable fact that everybody is busy propagating his own point of view most of the time and there is a great deal of truth in Marx's theory about ideologies, the term virtually loses any meaning and is better dropped. None of the practices described above are propaganda unless they are part of a *deliberate* scheme for indoctrination, as happens in totalitarian countries. Doob has further complicated the issue by inferring that sincerity or lack of it on the part of the propagandist should be taken into consideration, and other writers have gone so far as to say that the propagandist is, to some extent, attempting to fool his audience. In this view, sincerity is to be defined as the state of affairs which exists when there is little or no discrepancy between the goals which an individual really seeks and the goals he publicly claims to be seeking. But any such attempt at defining sincerity underestimates the power of the human being for self-deception, and, as Doob himself admits, the propagandist is peculiarly liable to become his own first victim. In any case the issue is irrelevant since the progagandist may be calculatingly deceitful or passionately sincere; it is the method employed which is deceitful whether its operator is fully aware of the fact or not.

The first task of the propagandist is to catch his audience's attention and, in the case of minor and possibly revolutionary political parties or religious bodies attempting to propagate an unfamiliar doctrine, a considerable period of time may have to be spent in building up a receptive frame of mind. This is described by Doob as a "sub-propaganda campaign," and most propagandists prepare the ground in this way, for example by distributing leaflets and posters or by house-to-house visits before embarking on an all-out campaign. Quite commonly, in trying to make his own message stand out against the background of many other competing stimuli, the operator will bring in another and more striking stimulus which, even if it has little or nothing to do with his actual message, is effective in catching the eye or ear in such a way as to cause it to be noted. Examples are the ballyhoo associated with American elections, the rallies of the former Nazi party at Nuremberg which created an impression of invincible power, and, of course, such everyday examples as the pretty girl or handsome male on the posters of cigarette manufacturers or the workman of fabulous strength advertising a certain brand of stout. These are not only attention-catching but by their implications of power, health, enthusiasm, beauty, and masculinity they excite the observer and serve to put him in a more receptive state of mind.

But nobody can create emotions which are not already there, and the propagandist is limited to evoking or stimulating those attitudes suited to his purpose out of the total spectrum existing in his audience, attitudes which may be innate but are more usually socially acquired. Since all the basic motives in man are emotionally conditioned, the expert will make ample use of love, anger, fear, hope, guilt, and any other feelings, emotions, and sentiments useful to the purpose in hand. Ordinarily he will want to arouse a desire for some goal, with a view to suggesting at a later stage that he alone has the means of satisfying that desire; but he may equally trade on the propagandee's feelings of inadequacy or guilt to make him want to "do the right thing." Florists, for instance, in order to increase their sales devise the idea of Mother's Day so that in the long run not only will mother-love manifest itself in the sending of a bunch of flowers, but those who forget to do so will begin to feel thoroughly ashamed of themselves. It is a well-known fact that human emotions become more intense when frustrated, and people are never more prone to suggestion than when there desires for food, shelter, safety, prestige, and the rest have been thwarted—hence the frightening suggestibility of the revolutionary mob. But frustration is a relative term, and it is another common propagandist trick to create in the audience a conviction that they are thwarted no matter how well-provided-for they may actually be: "Why should *your* garden be without its own built-in swimming-pool?"

There are two other important factors which influence suggestibility. Firstly, people are always more suggestible in a crowd, when their individual credulity tends to sink to the lowest common denominator, and secondly, there is good evidence that the arousal of *any* strong emotion may make the individual more suggestible even when that emotion is directed initially *against* the propagandist and his message. As Kimball Young points out, there is more than a passing truth in the old saying that people may go to a revival to scoff but remain to pray. Other lessons the would-be manipulator of people will have to learn are the value of the appeal to authority, since few if any of us ever escape the early conditioning of submission to a powerful parent or parent-substitute, which makes us peculiarly prone to listen to, or even try to emulate, later examples. So, too, the desire to keep up with the "best people" implies the getting and holding of that authority and prestige which we have learned to admire in others. Then there is the old lesson that, although short-run propaganda may be directed towards any age-groups, that designed for complete and thorough indoctrination must be directed to children and youth since they are the most vulnerable to suggestion and persuasion techniques. Revolutionary political parties, religious bodies, and the manufacturers of cigarettes are all equally well aware of this truth. Lastly, propagandists have to learn that with few exceptions campaigns that present first one view and then the opposite—perhaps on the theory that the public should decide rationally between them—are not effective. Of course, in our definition of the term, anyone who did so would, *ipso facto*, cease to be a propagandist.

The fundamental mechanism employed by all forms of propaganda is, as we have seen, suggestion, which may be defined as the attempt to induce in others the acceptance of a specific belief without giving any self-evident or logical ground for its acceptance, whether this exists or not. Research shows that suggestibility increases from the age of four to the age of seven or eight when it reaches a maximum and thereafter declines steadily with increasing age, an observation which leads us to conclude (a) that it originated with the acquiring of language, the ability to communicate and be the object of communication, and (b) that it derives its emotional force from submission to parental authority. The unquestioning acceptance of the parents' words is at its height during these years, and gradual immunization against too easy suggestibility occurs in varying degrees when the child discovers that his parents are not omniscient or omnipotent. With increasing age, ideas and responses become more canalized and fixed, and the person builds up increasingly complex systems of belief, which he makes the basis of his actions and will defend, more or less violently, against attack. Therefore suggestion, although a powerful weapon, is likely to be effective only when the propagandist is able to give the impression that what he is advocating is in line with the propagandee's already-existing beliefs, or when the suggestion he is making is relatively superficial and offers no threat whatever to the convictions of his audience. A good example of suggestion which comes into the second category is demonstrated by an experiment carried out by the two American sociologists Sorokin and Boldyreff, who played the identical gramophone record of a portion of Brahms' First Symphony on two separate occasions to a group of 1,484 high-school and college students. On the first occasion, an introductory talk referred to the piece as superior, musically finer, and more beautiful than the other (actually the same) piece they would later play. At the second playing, the

music was referred to as "an exaggerated imitation of a well-known masterpiece, totally deficient in self-subsistence and beauty." The suggestion that the identical record was different was accepted by no less than 96 per cent of the students; the second suggestion that the first rendering was of a more beautiful piece— i.e. a prestige suggestion coming from a supposed expert—was accepted by 59 per cent, whilst 21 per cent "suspended their judgement" and 16 per cent disagreed. Only 4 per cent of the students, therefore, recognized that both playings were of the same record after they had authoritatively been told otherwise.

The following are some of the more specific techniques employed in propaganda and it will be noted that most of them follow the lines of well-worn channels common to the average human mind (e.g. most people *want* to feel that issues are simple rather than complex, *want* to have their prejudices confirmed, *want* to feel that they "belong" with the implication that others do not, and *need* to pinpoint an enemy to blame for their frustrations). This being the case, the propagandist is likely to find that his suggestions have fallen on fertile soil so long as he delivers his message with an eye to the existing attitudes and intellectual level of his audience.

1. The Use of Stereotypes

It is a natural tendency to "type" people, and in time this picture may become a fixed impression almost impervious to real experience. Hence the stereotypes of the Negro, the Jew, the capitalist, the trade-union leader, or the Communist, and the reactions of members of these groups come to be explained, not in terms of themselves as unique individuals, but in terms of the stereotype. In the early years of this century Sir Charles Goring of the English prison service, who was opposed to the theory of Lombroso, the Italian criminologist, that there is a specific criminal type with certain recognizable physical stigmata, had an artist draw from memory the portraits of many of the inmates of a prison. He made a composite photograph of these and found that it bore a strong resemblance to the conventional stereotype of a criminal. But when a composite picture was made from actual photographs of the same people, it bore no resemblance either to the drawings or to the popular idea of a "criminal type." Clearly the artist had been influenced by his stereotype.

2. The Substitution of Names

The propagandist frequently tries to influence his audience by substituting favorable or unfavorable terms, with an emotional connotation, for neutral ones unsuitable to his purpose. Hence "Red" instead of "Communist" or "Russian," "Union bosses" for presidents of the unions, "Huns" or "Boches" for Germans, "Yids" for Jews. On the other hand, "free enterprise" sounds better than "capitalism" in these times, and the writer of advertising copy is often an adept at substituting long and impressive-sounding words to conceal the true identity of the relatively simple constituents of patent medicines or cosmetics.

3. Selection

The propagandist, out of a mass of complex facts, selects only those that are suitable for his purpose. One would not expect a Conservative politician to go out of his way to mention the Suez incident, nor a Labor one to mention unnecessarily the "groundnut plan." Censorhip is one form of selection and therefore of propaganda.

4. Downright Lying

From the atrocity stories against the Saracens during the Crusades and the ridiculous tales of Belgian priests used as human bell-clappers or the human soap factories of the First World War to the Hitlerian recommendation of the big lie, falsehood has always been part of the propagandist's stock-in-trade.

5. Repetition

The propagandist is confident that, if he repeats a statement often enough, it will in time come to be accepted by his audience. A variation of this technique is the use of slogans and key words, e.g. "Fair Shares for All," "Keep the World Safe for Democracy," "Ein Volk, ein Reich, ein Führe," "Player's Please," "Guinness for Strength," and so on. Such phrases, frequently meaningless, play a large part in politics and advertising, yet what *are* "fair shares"? What *is* "democracy"?

6. Assertion

The propagandist rarely argues but makes bold assertions in favor of his thesis. We have already seen that the essence of propaganda is the presentation of one side of the picture only, the deliberate limitation of free thought and questioning.

7. Pinpointing the Enemy

It is helpful if the propagandist can put forth a message which is not only *for* something, but also *against* some real or imagined enemy who is supposedly frustrating the will of his audience. Hence the Nazi campaigns against the Jews and the "pluto-democracies" which, by careful selection of targets in line with the already existing traditions of the group, had the dual effects (a) of directing aggression away from the propagandist and his party, and (b) of strengthening in-group feelings thus improving party morale.

8. The Appeal to Authority

Suggestion, as mentioned above, is of its nature an appeal to authority. The authority appealed to may be religious, that adhering to a prominent political figure, or, particularly in advertising, the authority of science and the professions. For example; "Doctors in over a thousand skin tests proved X makes your skin younger, softer, lovelier than ever!" Which doctors? And how does one test "loveliness"? Another form taken by the appeal to authority is the appeal to the crowd, or as the Americans describe it, the "bandwagon technique," which implies that "everybody's doing it" and therefore that those who are not are outsiders.

29. Applications to the Field of Advertising

Milton Rokeach*

The advertising man is not the only person who seeks to shape and change other people's beliefs, attitudes, and behavior. There are many kinds of people in our society, professional and nonprofessional, working for pay and for free, who for various combinations of altruistic and selfish reasons are vitally interested in the theory and practice of shaping and changing other people's values, beliefs, attitudes, and behavior. One may point by way of illustration to the psychotherapist, to the teacher, the missionary, the politician, and the lobbyist. All these have in common with the advertising man at least the desire to influence and to persuade others to believe and to act in certain ways they would not otherwise believe and act.

This does not mean that the advertising man wants to change the same sorts of beliefs which, say, the therapist or the politician wants to change. Every human being has many different kinds of beliefs, and every advanced society seems to have encouraged the rise of persuaders who specialize in trying to change some kinds of belief and not other kinds.

What, then, are the different kinds of beliefs that all men hold and what kinds of beliefs does the advertising man wish most to influence? What are the properties of the different kinds of beliefs, and how easily is one kind changed compared with another kind? What special problems arise to plague the advertising man because he specializes in trying to change certain kinds of beliefs and not other kinds; and what can he do about these problems?

Some answers to these questions may be forthcoming by referring briefly to five kinds of beliefs.

Type A beliefs—called primitive beliefs—are all supported by 100 per cent social con-

sensus. Such primitive beliefs are fundamental, taken-for-granted axioms that are not subject to controversy because we believe, and we believe everyone else believes. These beliefs are more resistant to change than other types of beliefs, and also that it is extremely upsetting for Type A beliefs to be seriously brought into question.

And then there is a second kind of primitive belief—Type B—which is also extremely resistant to change. Such beliefs do not depend on social support or consensus but instead arise from deep personal experience. Type B beliefs are incontrovertible and we believe them regardless of whether anyone else believes them. Many of these unshakable beliefs are about ourselves and some of these self-conceptions are positive ones—Type B+ —and some are negative ones—Type B—. The positive ones represent beliefs about what we are capable of, and the negative ones represent beliefs about what we are afraid of. Some illustrations of Type B+ beliefs may be helpful here. Regardless of what others may think of us, we continue to believe ourselves to be intelligent and rational men, able and competent, basically kind and charitable. Type B+ beliefs represent our positive self-images that guide our aspirations and ambitions to become even better, greater, wiser, and nobler than we already are.

Many of us also have Type B— beliefs— negative self-conceptions—which we cling to primitively regardless of whether others may agree with us. We are often beset by phobias, compulsions, obsessions, neurotic self-doubts and anxieties about self-worth, self-identity, and self-competence. These are the kinds of primitive beliefs we only wish we were rid of, and it is these beliefs that the specialized psychotherapist is often asked to change. Other specialized persuaders are generally not

Reprinted from Milton Rokeach, "Applications to the Field of Advertising," *Beliefs, Attitudes and Values* (San Francisco: Jossey-Bass, Inc., 1968), pp. 179–188.
° Professor of Psychology, Michigan State University.

trained or interested in changing Type B— beliefs, but they may be interested in exploiting them without trying to change them.

A third kind of belief—Type C—are authority beliefs, beliefs we all have about which authorities to trust and not to trust. Many facts of physical and social reality have alternative interpretations, are socially controversial, or are not capable of being personally verified or experienced. For these reasons all men need to identify with specific authorities (or reference persons or reference groups) to help them decide what to believe and what not to believe. Is Communism good or bad? Is there a God or isn't there? How do we know the French Revolution actually took place? What about evolution? No man is personally able to ascertain the truth of all such things for himself, so he believes in this or that authority—parents, teachers, religious leaders, scientists—and he is often willing to take authority's word for many things. Thus, we all somehow develop beliefs about which authorities are positive and which are negative, differing from one person to the next, and we look to such authorities for information about what is (and is not) true and beautiful, and good for us.

A fourth kind of belief—Type D—are the beliefs we derive from the authorities we identify with. For example, a devout Catholic has certain beliefs about birth control and divorce because he has taken them over from the authority he believes in. I believe Jupiter has 12 moons not because I have personally seen them but because I trust certain kinds of authorities who have seen them. I am quite prepared to revise my derived belief about Jupiter's moons providing the authorities I trust revise their beliefs. Many people, for example, adhere to a particular religious or political belief system because they identify with a particular authority. Such beliefs can be changed providing the suggestion for change emanates from one's authority, or providing there is a change in one's authority.

Finally, there is a fifth class of beliefs—Type E—inconsequential beliefs. If they are changed, the total system of beliefs is not altered in any significant way. You may believe, for example, that you can get a better shave from one brand of razor blade than another; that a vacation at the beach is more enjoyable than one in the mountains; that Sophia Loren is prettier than Elizabeth Taylor. But, if you can be persuaded to believe the opposite, the change is inconsequential because the rest of your belief system is hardly likely to be affected in any important way.

All these five kinds of beliefs, considered together, are organized into a remarkable piece of architecture which is the total belief system. It has a definable content and a definable structure. And it has a job to do; it serves adaptive functions for the person, in order to maximize his positive self-image and to minimize his negative self-image. Every person has a need to know himself and his world insofar as possible, and a need not to know himself and his world, insofar as necessary. A person's total belief system, with all its five kinds of beliefs, is designed to serve both functions at once.

With these five kinds of beliefs as a frame of reference it is now possible to obtain a somewhat clearer picture of what society's specialized persuaders are trying to do, and which kinds of beliefs they wish most to act upon, to influence, and to change. If we consider first the Type A beliefs that are universally supported by social consensus, it would seem that there are no specialized persuaders whose main business it is to change these kinds of belief. But, as already stated, it would seem to be the business of the professional psychotherapist to change the second kind of primitive belief. The psychotherapists' job is to help us get rid of our negative self-conceptions—Type B— beliefs—and to strengthen our positive self-conceptions—Type B+ beliefs.

Then, there are other specialized persuaders—the political and religious partisans and ideologists of various persuasion. What sorts of beliefs are they mostly concerned with? Their main focus would seem to be the Type C and Type D beliefs—authority beliefs and derived beliefs.

Consider next the kinds of beliefs that another kind of specialized persuader—the advertising man—tries to form and change.

Without in any way denying that the results of advertising may have important economic consequences, it could be suggested from a psychological standpoint that the advertising man has concentrated mainly on forming or changing Type E beliefs—inconsequential beliefs—to the extent that his purpose is to meet the competition, and that he has concentrated mainly on Type D—derived beliefs—to the extent his purpose is to give information. Furthermore, the more competitive the advertising the more it seems to address itself to changing psychologically inconsequential beliefs about the relative merits of one brand over another.

Several implications follow from the preceding analysis. It is tempting to suggest that at least some of the unique characteristics, problems, and embarrassments besetting the advertising industry stem directly or indirectly from its heavy specialization in changing psychologically inconsequential beliefs, and from the additional fact that beliefs that are psychologically inconsequential to the average consumer are highly consequential to all those who need to advertise.

Our findings suggest that inconsequential beliefs are generally easier to change than other kinds of beliefs. This does not mean, however, that the consumer will passively yield to others' efforts to change such beliefs. We generally resist changing *all* our beliefs because we gain comfort in clinging to the familiar and because all our beliefs seem to serve highly important functions for us. So the advertising man, while he has a psychological advantage over other persuaders specializing in changing more central beliefs, still has to find economical ways of changing the less consequential beliefs he specializes in. This he has often tried to do by developing methods for shaking the consumer loose from his belief regarding the virtues of one particular brand over a competitor's in order to make him believe instead that the difference does make a difference. He tries to convince the consumer that there are important benefits to be gained by changing brands, that deeper beliefs and needs will perhaps be better satisfied. The advertising industry has frequently been successful in achieving this aim and, sometimes, miraculously so.

How? The present analysis suggests that the advertiser's goal is often achieved by associating the fifth kind of belief—Type E, the inconsequential beliefs—with other kinds of beliefs tapping psychologically more consequential beliefs and wants. But what other kinds of beliefs are most frequently associated with Type E beliefs?

Theoretically, it is possible to associate, the inconsequential beliefs with Type D, or C, or B+, or B—, or A beliefs, but the advertising industry does not use all these combinations with equal frequency. The associations that seem to occur most frequently in competitive advertising are those between Types E and C (the authority beliefs, as in testimonials) and between Types E and B— (as in the old Lifebuoy ads on B.O. or in the more sophisticated Maiden-Form Bra ads that exploit primitive fears of rejection or primitive self-conceptions concerning insufficient femininity).

Why should these two combinations come up more often than the other possible combinations? One may suspect that this is due to the fact that the advertising industry has been heavily influenced by two theories in psychology—behaviorism and psychoanalysis—both having in common an image of man who is fundamentally an irrational creature, helplessly pushed around on the one hand by irrational guilt, anxiety, self-doubt, and other neurotic self-conceptions (B— beliefs) and, on the other hand, helplessly pushed around by external stimuli which, through reward and punishment, condition him to form arbitrary associations. Advertising has borrowed from psychoanalysis its laws of association and from behaviorism its principles of conditioning; psychoanalysis tells you what to associate with what, and behaviorism tells you how to stamp it in. The inconsequential beliefs have been so often associated with the authority beliefs (Type C) and with the primitive beliefs (Type B—) because the advertising profession has taken over such an irrational image of man from behaviorism and psychoanalysis. In doing so, the advertising industry has come in for a great deal of criticism for a style of advertising that encourages conformity, that is exploitative, debasing, lacking in taste, and insulting to the dignity of man.

Given the facts of our industrial society and, given what Harry C. Groome has in an issue of the *Saturday Review* called the *inevitability* of advertising, the advertising man's general strategy of associating the psychologically inconsequential with the consequential is probably the only one open to him and seems psychologically sound in principle. But given also the five kinds of beliefs previously described, it is now possible to at least explore systematically the other possible combinations to see where they might lead us. What would an ad look like which tries to associate an inconsequential belief (Type E) with a primitive belief which we all share (Type A)?

I recall having seen only one example of such an advertisement, an advertisement that caught my eye like no advertisement has in many years. This ad appeared in the *New Yorker* (September 7, 1963, p. 138). It was entitled "How to keep water off a duck's back." It shows a duck wearing a superbly tailored raincoat. I might add that children seem to be especially delighted in looking at this picture. Here we see an inconsequential belief about a particular brand of raincoat (*London Fog*) associated with a primitive physical belief about the fundamental nature of a certain animal called a duck. By the process of association our primitive belief about the stark-naked duck is momentarily violated; our sanity is threatened, and it is virtually impossible to turn away from the ad until our primitive belief is somehow reestablished or restored to its original state. In the process the viewer is entertained and *London Fog* gains attention. Whether *London Fog* also gains customers remains to be seen.

In this connection, too, the advertiser's attention may be drawn to the television program *Candid Camera* and to the fact that it often entertains mass audiences by having them watch what happens when there is a momentary disruption of a person's primitive belief about physical and social reality—Type A beliefs, those everyone believes. It is perhaps surprising that the advertising industry has not consciously applied the *Candid Camera* ideas for its own uses. (*The London Fog* ad is the only one I remember seeing that seems to use a similar principle.)

Attention may next be drawn to some psychological considerations that would favor an increasing emphasis in advertising on associations between the inconsequential beliefs (Type E) and the primitive beliefs (Type B+), which refer to the positive conceptions we strive to have of ourselves.

Since the end of World War II, an increasing number of distinguished psychologists have revolted against the image of Irrational Man that behaviorism and classical psychoanalysis have both helped build. Contemporary psychoanalysts talk more and more about the conflict-free sphere of ego functioning; the Gestalt psychologists have emphasized for a long time man's search for meaning, understanding, and organization. Carl Rogers has emphasized the drive for growth and maturity within all individuals; Abraham Maslow has familiarized us with man's drive for self-actualization; Gordon Allport and the existentialists talk about being and becoming. Robert White, Harry F. Harlow, D. E. Berlyne, Leon Festinger, and many others have pointed to the fact that man has a need to know, to understand, and to be competent.

Perhaps the major way in which contemporary psychology differs from the psychology of twenty years ago is that Man is now seen to be not only a *rationalizing* creature but also a *rational* creature—curious, exploratory, and receptive to new ideas. This changing image of man has been represented here by the B+ type of beliefs that exist side-by-side with the B— type within the belief system.

One can discern the barest beginnings of this changing image of man on the part of the advertising industry in certain advertisements, and it may surprise you to learn which advertisement I have in mind: the Pepto-Bismol and Anacin ads. There are probably millions of Americans walking around right now with a conception of a stomach that looks like a hollow dumbell standing on end, and with a conception of a mind composed of split-level compartments. In these ads we see that the advertising man concedes that consumers—at least the ones with stomachaches and headaches—have a need to understand why they have stomachaches or headaches.

At the same time, however, the advertising man is also cynically saying that the consumer is too stupid or too irrational to understand anything well. If we were to learn that our children were being taught such conceptions of stomach or head by their teachers, we would demand that such teachers be immediately fired for incompetence. Why, then, should the advertising man be allowed to exploit, for money, the consumer's legitimate need to understand his stomachaches and headaches?

Is there not a better example of the advertising industry's changing conception of man? Yes, I think there is. David Ogilvy has expressed a more dignified and respectful view of the consumer at a conference on creativity early in 1962; he has expressed this view in his book (1963) and in his advertisements on Puerto Rico, and on travel in the United States and abroad. This dignified image of man is not true of all his famous advertisements. For example, his Schweppes ads and his Rolls Royce ads associate an inconsequential belief with unconscious primitive beliefs concerning snobbish strivings of the self—Type E with Type B—. But his travel ads try to associate psychologically inconsequential beliefs with unconscious primitive beliefs—Type B+—concerning a self that strives to become better-realized, better-rounded, and more open to experience. These ads hold out a dignified promise to let the consumer be and become.

Nevertheless, the irrational image of man still predominates in the advertising world. The more inconsequential the benefits of one brand over a competitor's, the more desperately the industry has harangued and nagged and, consequently, irritated its mass audience. It is not easy to convince others that psychologically inconsequential matters are consequential. That the advertising industry attracts such highly talented people, pays them fabulous salaries, and puts them under such terrific pressure can all be attributed to the kinds of beliefs it specializes in changing. It is, consequently, no wonder that the advertising profession is reputed to be among the most guilt-ridden, anxiety-ridden, ulcer-ridden, and death-ridden profession in America.

In closing, therefore, let me emphasize—constructively, I hope—that the advertising man's image of the consumer requires revision in order to bring it more in line not only with the broader and newer image of man outlined here but also with the advertising man's image of himself. To the extent that the advertising man can bring himself to do so, he will gain a new respect from the consumer and in the process gain a renewed respect for himself.

30. Social Change Through Issue Advertising

John A. Zeigler*

Q: John, could you define "issue advertising"?

A: It's advertising that deals with certain social issues, and is aimed at changing, clarifying, or repealing specific laws, or initiating new legislation.

Q: How does it differ from public service advertising?

A: Public service advertising is not aimed at new legislative changes. It's educational, non-controversial, for motherhood and the flag, and "safe" (everyone is against cancer and forest fires).

Q: You've been given the credit for coining the phrase "protest advertising." How does it differ from issue advertising?

A: Protest advertising protests or produces a specific call to action and seldom offers con-

Reprinted from John Zeigler, "Social Change Through Issue Advertising," originally published in *Sociological Inquiry*, Vol. 40. No. 1 (Winter 1970), pp. 159–165.
* President, John Zeigler, Inc.; also Professor, New School for Social Research.

structive solutions or alternatives in the ads. They simply say: "Stop the War" or "Come Demonstrate with Us on Fifth Avenue."

Q: It sounds as if you have a negative feeling toward protest advertising.

A: Not at all. In its way, it's constructive in that it expresses dissent. It's just that I'd rather devote my skills and energy to structuring ads with a solution to social problems. And I believe this is specifically what advertising people are in a position to offer interest groups: *structure* . . . how to put their objectives and rationales down simply and persuasively on paper or on film.

Q: Now, how does issue advertising differ from consumer advertising?

A: Not much; both are salesmanship in print. Someone is trying to persuade someone else to act. Some issue advertising, like our campaign to repeal the draft laws, simply tries to marshall public opinion and create a climate for change. Advertising ill-timed can often be disastrous for an issue, however.

Q: What do you mean?

A: At a certain point a militant tone of voice in an ad *may* be desirable. If it is ill-timed, at a later date when lawmakers are favorably disposed to your argument, your ad might alienate them.

Q: Are there times, due to the political climate, then, that you would recommend a group *not* advertise?

A: Yes. Sometimes even just the threat of advertising your cause may eliminate the necessity for following through with ads. Simply advising a lawmaker you propose to show the public how he intends to vote on your issue may be persuasive enough. An example where advertising was unnecessary was the gun control issue. Fred Papert, who created many ads on this problem after Robert Kennedy was assassinated, said, in effect: "We should never have advertised. We should have taken the money and used it more appropriately in areas other than advertising. The public didn't have to be persuaded that gun control laws were necessary; enough polls substantiated this as the majority voter opinion. Congress was also very aware of voter preference for stronger gun control laws."

Q: What was he advocating, then, as a solution?

A: Let me turn the question around. If your adversary, the National Rifle Association, was swaying lawmakers with dollars or campaign funds, how would *you* use your limited budget to counteract this? Advertising would be a naive waste.

Q: I see what you mean. You're presenting a scary picture.

How did issue advertising get started in the first place?

A: I think the civil rights movement in the South in the early sixties paved the way for the confrontations in print advertising over the Vietnam war. At that point, I think advertising became recognized as a tool for lobbying and nonviolent protest.

Q: What is a successful issue ad?

A: An issue ad is successful if it's changed a law, or achieved any of its stated specific objectives.

Q: Can you name some?

A: Yes. President Johnson acknowledged that the ad Bert Steinhauser of Doyle, Dane, Bernbach created for Citizens Against Rats influenced Congress to pass rat control legislation. The ad showed a large rat next to the headline "Cut this out and put it in bed next to your child." The objective of securing enough names to persuade journalists that clean air is a problem was achieved by Ed McCabe and Carl Ally's campaign for Citizens for Clean Air. At least 300,000 people responded to ads that alerted New Yorkers to the dangerous air they were breathing.

Q: What ads have bombed out?

A: Any ads that have failed to change legislation or achieve their objectives. That would include one of mine: the "Abortion Ad" (Figure 30.1). But we're going back at the lawmakers again next year, and I'm confident we'll win. I don't think, however, you can blame advertising for the failure of an issue; just as you can't blame advertising for the failure of a product. There are too many variables . . . marketing, distribution, sampling; in the case of issue advertising the absence of a strong well-organized group can be a factor.

Figure 30.1.

This Albany politician can force a woman to have a baby whether she wants one or not.

How's that for power?

Unless this man decides to change our current abortion law, he is in effect saying that it's his right to police a woman's reproductive life.

But reliable polls show that a majority (83%) of New Yorkers made their wish quite clear: **"Change our vicious abortion law."**

Even physicians agree. In one poll, 85% of New York State obstetricians said they want the abortion law changed. But the law is still there. So doctors of conscience are forced to break the law to practice modern (and moral) medicine.

Other groups have made the same stand: to cite a few: the New York Civil Liberties Union; the Association of the Bar of the City of New York; the American Public Health Association; Edward P. O'Rourke, Commissioner of Health, City of New York; the American Psychiatric Association; the New York State Council of Churches; the Episcopal Diocese of New York; the Federation of Jewish Philanthropies, and the New York Academy of Medicine.

Prominent political leaders have also favored change: the late U.S. Senator Robert F. Kennedy, Governor Nelson A. Rockefeller, and Mayor John V. Lindsay.

78,000 American women dead every year.
They die after having gone underground to seek out criminal abortionists. In New York alone, 75,000 women risk their lives this way every year. Why? Because we have a law that says professional care from a qualified physician is illegal. As a result, we have a law that encourages crime and causes death.

That's not all. A significant number of all the women who get illegal abortions are married and already mothers. According to Dr. Milton Helpern, Medical Examiner of the City of New York, illegal out-of-hospital abortions are the largest cause of maternal death in New York City. And this statistic doesn't take into consideration the vast number of children left motherless.

Even though most New Yorkers oppose our antiquated law, there is a lot of pressure to keep it on the books. And our lawmakers have failed to act. Now *you* can make your voice heard in Albany: We want the misery and killing stopped. Call your state senator or state assemblyman. If you want to know who he is, call your local Board of Elections or your local League of Women Voters.

Advertisement prepared by the New School for Social Research Workshop: "Social Change Through Issue Advertising".

Q: How does an issue ad campaign get going? How does it start?

A: Well, hopefully, there's a solid organization behind it that's reasonably clear about their objectives. When the Abortion Reform Association came to us, their objective was to change the vicious abortion laws in New York State. They fed every bit of research, facts and data into our group that they had . . . even down to how many politicians were, at that moment, for or against reform. We then had to develop a "rationale" from their objectives.

Q: How do you define "rationale" in the advertising sense?

A: It is the *Unique Selling Proposition:* the reason why I would buy your product (or argument) over a competitive one. It's a sentence or paragraph that presents such a convincing argument I'd feel it wasn't to my best interest if I didn't respond the way you wished. It's also a strategy that perceptively takes into account your own strengths and weaknesses. An important step in developing a rationale or strategy is to position yourself against your competition.

Q: I guess when you consider it, issues do have competitors.

A: Yes, we had a rather wealthy one, as a matter of fact, as we prepared our abortion campaign—the Catholic Church.

Q: John, what media is appropriate for issue advertising?

A: Any and all media. From TV, radio, newspapers and magazines to bumper stickers, placards and buttons. Radio and TV talk shows are very influential in projecting your position before the public.

Q: In short, any form of communication that reaches a sigificant number of people.

A: Exactly. It depends on which audience your strategy is directed toward.

Q: Back to your rationale for the "Abortion" ad.

A: It was that a woman had a right to control her own reproductive system. Her decision to have a baby was simply a matter between her and her physician; the involvement of the Church and politicians would be a misuse of power and a denial of individual rights. It was our responsibility to be sure our client agreed to this rationale.

Q: Apparently they did. What was your next step?

A: Execution: first a strong, engaging powerful headline: "This Albany politician can force a woman to have a baby whether she wants one or not. How's that for power?" Second, a layout that reinforced the headline. Third, body copy that told the complete story and moved the reader to contact lawmakers.

Q: Which was the most important element of this ad?

A: As in all ads—the idea. A great headline, graphics and text will never save a bad idea.

Q: You do use Madison Avenue advertising techniques, do you not?

A: I'm not sure what you mean by "techniques." If you mean the development of a constructive rationale based on reasonable objectives, and an honest execution of this rationale by clear headlines, graphics, and body copy, I'd say "yes," we employ Madison Avenue techniques in issue advertising.

Q: Isn't it critical to be well funded in an issue advertising campaign . . . as well funded as the introduction of a new Detroit car, for instance?

A: No. What's needed is poeple, time and talent. All you need is someone to produce the mechanics of one ad, secure several reprints and use that ad concept to raise money for media placement. An aggressive staff can round up enough funds to push a law through as the result of an ad. Bert Steinhauser only spent $125.00 of his own money for the "Rat" ad. Most issue ads should not only ask for names and people to help, but also for money to extend the campaign. If the ad is persuasive enough, it will raise the money; this has been demonstrated over and over again. I personally erred in not asking for money and enclosing a coupon on two of my abortion ads.

Q: Can we discuss some of these ads on your wall? I see you have them categorized. One group is labeled "good ads." Are these ads that have changed laws?

A: Not necessarily. They may have done a creditable job of informing the public or they may have ingredients within them that are what I would call "effective" advertising elements. The ads may essentially have been a little nudge or a little prod to effecting social change.

Q: What about the "SANE" ad that reads "From the people who brought you Vietnam . . . the anti-ballistic missile system."

A: The cartoon of the kooky generals and Pentagon officials playing with their toy ABM missile does a concise and dramatic job of illustrating the insanity of a proposal that isn't feasible and is incomprehensibly costly.

Q: So, it's a good ad?

A: From that standpoint, yes. I always felt that a second point had to be made in this issue: that Congressmen constantly and on demand appropriate any amount of money to the military out of their fear that their constituents will vote them out of office if they do otherwise. To make Congress aware of the anti-military mood in the country, I feel you first have to alert the public to their own Congressman's fears about the military, military expenditures and misconceptions about how their own constituents feel about military appropriations.

Q: This headline reads "Noise pollution won't kill you. It can only drive you nuts or make you deaf," by Citizens for a Quieter City (Figure 30.2).

A: Yes—this is a good example of honesty and clarity at work. It's a very human headline; it's worded the way people talk and that builds identification with the reader and adds to the believability. They *could* have taken a "scare" or "fear" approach and out of desperation tried to attract people to the cause of noise pollution. Instead, they projected a very "collected" and "together" aura in the way it was worded. The words are calm and deliberate. The *honesty* of the sentence "Noise pollution won't kill you" intrigued me to read further. It's an example of how skilled advertising professionals, in this case Scali McCabe and Sloves, can structure a problem for an issue group in very human terms.

Q: How come you have two political ads in this group? The one reads "Man vs. Machine" with a photo of Eugene McCarthy and the other reads "McCarthy's Machine Needs Money" showing a group of college kids who appear to have just taken time out from their strenuous campaigning to pose for a portrait together.

A: These are examples of brilliant advertising executions. By that I mean copy, layout, photography and typography—as a means of executing the basic idea—all work together in a perfect marriage to "touch" the reader emotionally. That's why good advertising is an art. The advertising man, as an artist, knows how to use his craft to touch people where they live. An artist seldom harangues or screams his message. The creators of these ads also possessed some insight into human psychology; all the elements fuse into one communicative channel: an appeal to the reader's sympathy for the underdog and the little guy who takes on the big guys. Although the "Vs." ad won all the advertising awards, I prefer the "Money" ad. It illustrates the "Machine" with a non-machine: average, appealing kids.

Q: Speaking of kids, since Madison Avenue and advertising are so representative of the "establishment," wouldn't they tend to reject advertising as a means to achieve social change?

A: No. They've already accepted it; picket signs, protest buttons and bumper stickers are all demonstrable workable tools to bring about change.

Q: What about this ad: "Resolution of the Crisis in the Middle East Adopted by the Executive Committee of the National Council of Churches."

A: It suffers from a total lack of clarity and involvement; it's an unfortunate waste of the Council's dollars. It's very similar to many ads that begin "An open letter to . . . ." They could have saved an $8,000 space cost and bought a 10¢ air mail stamp. *If ads are not in some way addressed to me, I won't read them.*

Q: This ad says, "We presidents of student governments and editors of campus newspapers at more than 500 American colleges believe that we should not be forced to fight in the Viet Nam war because the Viet Nam war is unjust and immoral."

A: This is an example of not only a waste of $32,000 but how purposeless, unstructured and diffuse some college students are today. They could have used this space not only to use tons of names to convince Washington

Figure 30.2.

Noise pollution won't kill you.

It can only drive you nuts or make you deaf.

There's so much noise in this city that you'd hardly think there's a need to advertise it.

Noise, after all, is something New Yorkers work with, eat with, try to sleep with, and wake up with—usually when they don't want to.

New York's noise is so pervasive that, except for those few noises loud enough to make themselves heard above the general din, it's usually taken for granted. And it shouldn't be.

Noise is dangerous.

If you stop and think about it, you'll realize that most of the dangerous things in this world are also noisy.

A gunshot is dangerous. It's also noisy.

Breaking glass is noisy. It's also dangerous.

As a result, you instinctively react to noise as a warning of danger. And living with the noise in New York is like having someone fire off a pistol behind your back 24 hours a day.

This is something you can get used to. New Yorkers, after all, can get used to anything.

But while consciously you may be blasé about noise, your body, your nervous system and your subconscious are naive enough to keep right on reacting to it.

It can drive you nuts.

For the past 30 years or so, noise has been known to be a highly effective means of inflicting mental torture.

The Gestapo is said to have rated loud noise on a par with beatings, drugs and electric shock. And in North Korean prison camps, noise was found to be a successful tool for brainwashing.

The reason for this is that loud, unexpected noises are very good at creating emotional stress. When the noise is continual—as it is in New York—so is the stress.

And continual emotional stress, as many psychiatrists believe, is enough to turn a normal adult, with normal problems, into a neurotic — if not an out-and-out psychotic.

In Ohio, for example, a scientist was so maddened by Air Force bombers flying over his house in the middle of the night that he tried to shoot them down with a rifle.

And in Japan, the noise from a pile-driver made a college student find some peace and quiet by sticking his head between the pile and the descending hammer.

If you've been living in the city for a number of years and you haven't gone off the deep end yet, you're still not off the hook. Because if

New York's noise pollution hasn't affected your mind, it's probably affecting your hearing.

It can make you deaf.

Ever since the last century, when blacksmiths and boilermakers started showing up in doctors' offices complaining that they couldn't hear, the medical profession has known that noise can produce deafness.

Yet it wasn't until 1948 that a worker deafened by the noise in his factory was able to collect workmen's compensation for it.

Today, one out of every two factories is noisy enough to make employees eligible for workmen's compensation. And if all these workmen put in claims for the compensation they were entitled to, the outlay would come to several billion dollars.

It's a shame that a subway conductor or a jackhammer operator has to earn his living at the risk of his hearing. But when those who don't work in these occupations are subjected to the same occupational hazards, it's pathetic.

Portable air compressors on New York streets are loud enough to drown out dynamite blasts.

Food blenders in our kitchens are actually louder than Niagara Falls.

Power mowers and poorly-muffled motorcycles are so noisy, they make factories seem like libraries.

As the noise gets louder and louder, the people who have to live with it get deafer and deafer. It used to be that people didn't start to lose their hearing until the age of 70. In big cities today, people start going deaf at 30.

Which seems to indicate that if we don't do something about the noise pollution problem now, in a few years it could automatically solve itself. By making us all too deaf to hear it.

Nobody ever does anything about anything unless people demand it.

In a city the size of New York, a few individuals with legitimate complaints will be dismissed as nuts, lunatics and crackpots.

But if enough "nuts," "lunatics" and "crackpots" get together, there's no telling what they can accomplish.

In Westchester, enough people were sick and tired of having their sleep interrupted by trucks with roaring exhausts to get a noise limit set on the New York State Thruway.

In Florida, enough people had their teeth set on edge by noisy electrical appliances to get a law passed against them.

And in New York, enough people were infuriated by the noise they had to live with in their own apartments to get at least some soundproofing written into a new Building Code.

But while there are enough concerned people to get some of New York's noise shut out of future apartments, there are still far too few to get it shut up for good. And that's why there's such a thing as the Citizens for a Quieter City.

Your financial support is welcome.
Your moral support is essential.

Citizens for a Quieter City is trying to make people aware that the problem of noise pollution exists. And that it doesn't exist as something to be passively accepted as an inevitable burden of the human condition.

To accomplish this, we need your money. For films. For letters. For brochures. For publicity. And for lectures and exhibits. And for more ads like this one.

Your money will also help stimulate research on the problem and its solution.

But what's even more important to us than your money is your name.

We'd like to be able to prove that New Yorkers have already had all the noise pollution they're going to take. With the names of twenty or fifty or a hundred thousand New Yorkers who are every bit as outraged by noise as we are, we should have no trouble doing it.

So please fill out the coupon. And don't feel embarrassed about sending it in without any money. A lot of people's names could be more help to us than a few people's money. Because the one thing we can't afford to do about noise pollution is keep quiet about it.

Quiet!

Citizens for a Quieter City, Inc.
Box 7777, Grand Central Station, New York 10017

☐ I'll be glad to contribute my name.
☐ Here's my contribution of $_____
(All contributions are tax-deductible.)

Name _____
Address _____
City _____ State _____ Zip _____

Advertisement prepared by
Scali, McCabe, Sloves, Inc.
Citizens for a Quieter City   CQC-68-1001
to appear in
Newspapers & magazines

that there were many people opposed to our involvement in the war but also *why* the draft is the *supreme* violation of an individual's rights. It's not enough to protest; those dollars can also be used to *persuade* the public and lawmakers to act. This ad, like so many, suffers from generalization and lack of specificity. Further, it apparently has no rationale and no strategy.

Q: What do you think of the Urban Coalition's campaign "Give a Damn"?

A: I agree with Bob Wilvers of Jack Tinker; it's "establishment advertising" to convince people that someone is "involved" and that the agency who handled it is very "creative." If the objective was to provide jobs and housing, the ads should have told me why it's good business to hire blacks and at least given me a phone number to respond to if I did indeed "Give a Damn"; in short, I'm just fuzzy on what the campaign was all about. But it won a lot of awards.

Q: So what you're saying is that issue advertising tends to be more successful the more clear, direct and specific it gets as well as the more action it generates.

A: Yes, these "establishment do-gooder" ads, in their lack of clarity, succeed only in convincing me that they're manipulating. They're too indirect to convince me they're actually doing something about social problems. Instead of the ads shown here, I'd prefer to see ads saying "These are the laws we helped change" . . . or "Help us change these laws."

This ad, showing a group of blacks, is an example of an establishment ad and reads: "We're proving there's a worthwhile place at Chase Manhattan for men like these. An action report from Chase Manhattan." My reaction is—Oh brother! Business has an obligation to be straight; any black, or any kid for that matter, knows when they're being "conned." I also don't know what they want from me as a reader; I get a *feeling* from them, nevertheless. A *feeling* that "they care." Again, my reaction is: "So what?"

Articulate clearly what you've constructively done about a specific problem, or what you're going to do about it. Otherwise, you leave professionals with the feeling that you've spent thousands of dollars indiscriminately and "hip" citizens with the feeling you're dishonest.

Q: It sounds as if business itself is guilty of producing the "worst" issue ads. Is this your feeling?

A: No. The worst ads are those that have been done about the "black problem." For instance, this one that reads: "Does he make you mad? Scared? Guilty?" and shows a black with a fire bomb. It's a request for funds by the NAACP Legal Defense and Educational Fund. This ad is a threat; I believe the only time people hand over their money when they're *threatened* is at the point of a gun; I react to threats in print by turning the page. In addition, my answer to the headline is, "Yes, he makes me mad"; is that a reason to give money to someone? "Yes, he makes me scared" . . . it's still no reason for me to contribute money to his legal defense. And an emphatic "No", to "does he make you guilty?" I'm sure there are many whites like me who are angry that blacks' individual rights are still being violated; but *I'm* not violating them and therefore I have absolutely no guilt over the "black problem."

The implication of the visual and the headline . . . and that's the essence of the expression of the basic idea of *any ad* . . . is that I should contribute to the Legal Defense Fund because there are kids who throw fire bombs. This is a total absence of logic and reason in this ad, and a complete ignorance of what persuasion and advertising is all about. Irresponsible advertising like this only perpetuates bigotry and racial strife. Educate me, persuade me, use reason and logic, but don't play on my fears unless you can offer a resolution in the ad.

Let me point out that everything I've just said about this ad is my own personal reaction because of my own emotional and philosophical orientations. Nevertheless, this ad obviously appealed to the audience for which it was designed; it was quite successful in raising money. I was told that the key contributors were wired in advance of the ad in a co-ordinated fund-raising campaign and advised when and where the ad would appear. A sophisticated fund-raising effort behind every ad will always help insure its success.

Q: Has issue advertising made the margin for more gutsy advertising in other areas?

A: Well, there is more risk taking and more confrontation in our society today than ever before; and certainly issue ads and posters have helped create this climate. Corporations are less hesitant to be "straight" in their ads. They are increasingly "telling it like it is." They're less and less afraid to name and tackle their competitors head on. Ads comparing one product with another began an upsurge about six years ago; the ad community then panicked and such ads became a "no-no." Now, however, gutsy admakers are "getting competitive."

Q: If you were to put your finger on a *single indispensible ingredient of a successful issue ad*, what would it be?

A: Anger! The ad should first trigger a little fear ("I'm *afraid* if this situation keeps up and how it will affect me and my family") and responsibly mold a person's anger about that issue to motivate him to act. As in direct response or mail order advertising, if he doesn't act before he turns the page, or if he doesn't tear the ad or coupon out, the ad will probably fail.

Q: Are we going to see an upsurge of issue advertising in the future?

A: Yes; there is more and more of it weekly. There's a dichotomy here, however; for every sensible person writing an ad and taking a rational position on paper or film, there is a fascistically oriented person using muscle and threats to bring about change on his terms at the point of a gun. This climate of "confrontation" is both an encouraging sign and a frightening one.

Q: Can you see advertising having a potential dampening effect on violence?

A: There's no question that it could curb the violence in our society; all that's needed is enough dedicated professionals, other manpower and funds.

Q: Are there as many advertising people involved in social change as there should be?

A: I don't believe anyone "should" be involved in issues. It's their own personal choice. I'd like to see more activity on the part of ad people, however, because advertising is a powerful tool for social change. Most interest groups have not yet fully learned how to use advertising skillfully, and ad people can be very helpful to them.

Q: Why *would* advertising people get involved? What's in it for them?

A: Many agency people and agencies are afraid to commit themselves on issues for fear of client retaliation; clients could do much to alleviate this fear and encourage their agencies to get involved. I also think the agency fear is frequently unfounded. I've never heard of a corporation firing an agency because of its efforts on behalf of a political candidate. But if they did risk a commitment to a controversial issue, they would have channeled their own fear and anger about some of the crises of the day into productive vehicles and communications that could change laws. It's a soul-cleansing process; it's been very satisfying to me.

31. Experimental Studies on Fear

Howard Levanthal*

As part of a larger research program on fear arousal and attitude change, my associates and I have conducted a number of experimental studies on smoking (Leventhal, 1965, 1967). The initial theoretical assumptions were compatible with the idea that information can create negative attitudes to smoking, but it was hypothesized that information alone

Reprinted in part from Howard Levanthal, "Experimental Studies on Fear," in Edgar F. Borgatta and Robert R. Evans (eds.) *Smoking, Health, and Behavior* (Chicago: Aldine Publishing Company, 1968), pp. 105–113; copyright © 1968 by Edgar F. Borgatta and Robert R. Evans.
* Professor of Psychology, University of Wisconsin.

was insufficient to create change. Negative attitudes and reductions in smoking were expected to be greatest when anti-smoking propaganda was accompanied by information which aroused fear motivation. More fear would be provoked by more vivid illustrations and statements, and the greater the fear the greater the motivation to accept the anti-smoking recommendation. Fear is seen as the motivation for change. If a response occurs that reduces this fear, the organism learns, i.e., acquires a new attitude or habit pattern.

That this hypothesis is generally true is shown by studies on tetanus inoculations (Dabbs and Leventhal, 1966; Leventhal, Singer, and Jones, 1965; Leventhal, Jones, and Trembly, 1966) and dental hygiene (Leventhal and Niles, 1965; Niles, 1965). In Horn's (1960) study, the effective remote condition actually involved a threat message. While increasing fear by changing the quantity or quality of danger information generally increases acceptance of health recommendations, verbal acceptance is more easily achieved than behavioral change. Verbal acceptance was measured by responses to questions on the importance of preventive measures (attitude) and desires to take the measure (intentions).

Interactions with Fear Level

It was also evident that personality variables played an important role in determining responsiveness to threat communications. For example, in studies of reactions to tetanus (Dabbs and Leventhal, 1966) and automotive accident threats (Leventhal and Trembly, 1968), highly threatening communications increased acceptance for subjects high in self-esteem. Self-esteem was scored by having people describe themselves on an adjective rating scale. Low-esteem subjects, whose self reports appear to indicate maladjustment, may show less acceptance of high than mild messages (Kornzweig, 1967). Along with reduced acceptance, one may find various signs of defense such as fatigue and unwillingness to think about dangers (Leventhal and Trembly, 1968). Self-esteem, therefore, is apparently an important modifier of response to

strong warning of danger, the probability of acceptance being greater among high-esteem or well-adjusted subjects. In their interesting study of smoking clinics, Schwartz and Dubitzky (1968) report data which clearly seem to support this hypothesis.

Esteem is not the only individual difference measure to account for variation in response to threat communications. Patricia Niles (1965) divided subjects on a measure of self-reported vulnerability to cancer. Common sense would suggest that people who feel vulnerable to danger would be more likely to take action to protect themselves. Hochbaum's (1958) retrospective survey supported this hypothesis. He found that individuals taking voluntary chest X-rays were more likely to believe that they were vulnerable to tuberculosis and that they could have the illness and be unaware of it. In a "predictive" survey, Leventhal, Hochbaum, Carriger, and Rosenstock (1960) found that subjects who felt vulnerable to Asian influenza were, subsequently, more likely to take Asian flu shots.

But will vulnerable subjects prove more willing to adopt protective measures when the message is threatening? Niles used three communications, a low-fear, mild-fear and high-fear message, each of which recommended stopping smoking and taking X-rays. At low levels of threat, subjects who regarded themselves as vulnerable behaved the same as those who thought they were invulnerable. But as threat level increased, vulnerable subjects showed no increases in acceptance. Invulnerables, on the other hand, became *increasingly* accepting of the recommendations. Increasing the message's threat value seemed to convince vulnerable subjects that they would fall prey to lung cancer even if they stopped smoking. Their failure to change seemed to reflect "overpersuasion" regarding the inevitability of danger. They were not denying danger, for they were quite fearful and concerned with the impending disaster. But there is no sense in taking protective action against the inevitable.

This interaction between fear and vulnerability is similar in some respects to that between esteem and fear. In fact, Niles' attitude measure of vulnerability was negatively correlated with self-esteem. There are differences, however, in that the esteem effect seems at times to involve denial of the threat rather than resignation to it. Vulnerability is also a narrower conception than self-esteem and in many instances may not be related to any general personality traits. Two such instances are seen in studies of tetanus and response to automotive accidents; subjects without prior inoculation against tetanus (vulnerables) are less accepting of high-threat messages than inoculated subjects (Leventhal and Trembly, 1968), and under high threat, drivers of cars (vulnerables) seem less likely to accept seat belt recommendations than non-drivers (Berkowitz and Cottingham, 1959). It is not easy to see how esteem or some other personality factor would underlie both not having a tetanus shot and driving a car. Yet each separates people into those to whom the threat is more and less relevant.

The vulnerability variable was explored in several studies of smoking and lung cancer. In the first of these investigations, Leventhal and Watts (1967) "varied" vulnerability by dividing the sample into smokers (vulnerable subjects) and nonsmokers (invulnerable subjects). Three levels of fear were used. The "low-fear" condition received statistical information on lung cancer rates and other relatively nonfearful material. In the moderate condition the statistical facts were accompanied by a movie showing a young man's diagnosis of lung cancer and his preparation for surgery. The high-fear communication included all the above information and concluded with a seven-minute color sequence of a lung cancer operation.

In an effort to obtain a more representative sample of participants, a theater was set up in a centrally located building within the New York State Fair grounds. In this way, a wide range of ages, occupations, etc., was sampled. The subjects completed a questionnaire regarding their feelings and their intentions to quit smoking and take X-rays. Because the county health department had located a mobile unit outside the theater, it was also possible to record who took X-rays.

As expected, the communications had a strong impact on reported emotions: subjects who saw the highly fearful communication were the most frightened. (The experimenters noticed that some people looked away and others cried during the high threat film.) The increase in fear occurred for both smokers and nonsmokers. What happened for acceptance of recommendations? For nonsmokers, whose vulnerability to lung cancer is negligible, increasing the fearfulness of the message had no consequences for X-ray behavior; about 45 per cent of the participants took X-rays in each of the three conditions. For smokers, the highly vulnerable subjects, increasing the threat level of the communication inhibited X-ray-taking; there was a steady *decrease* in X-ray-taking going from the low (53 per cent) to moderate (44 per cent) to high (6 per cent) fear communications.

Is the smoker's behavior totally irrational? Does he deny he can get cancer? Does he feel that there is little that can be done to prevent or cure the disease? If smokers deny their vulnerability, or feel they cannot prevent it, they should be less likely to stop smoking after high fear. Five months after the fair a questionnaire was mailed to all participants asking if they had taken X-rays or had tried to reduce smoking and had succeeded in doing so.

One problem with the data was that only half the questionnaires were returned, and it is possible that returns came only from subjects who complied with all the recommendations (including taking X-rays). But this did not seem to be the case, for there was still practically no X-ray-taking in the high-fear group. Smokers wish to avoid detecting cancer by X-rays and to avoid getting it by stopping smoking. The choice then is not fully consistent with either denial or resignation to the danger. There is recognition that quitting smoking is a meaningful way of avoiding cancer and that lung surgery is a doubtful cure. The responses selected are those which are most effective and do not in themselves involve serious danger.

The results of the smoking studies are complex, but they do form a pattern. Raising fear motivation generally increases persuasion; but this finding is importantly qualified, as the most vulnerable subjects seem least accepting as fear level is increased (Niles, 1965) and/or when the action recommended can actually confirm one's vulnerability to cancer (taking X-rays). Both effects suggest that fear-provoking information will increase acceptance only if one *excludes* information which increases the subject's belief that he is definitely vulnerable and will confront the danger. This hypothesis is opposite to common-sense reasoning used in the X-ray (Hochbaum, 1958) and flu studies and in the role-playing studies by Janis and Mann (1965).

To test this hypothesis, Jean Watts (1966) gave recommendations to stop smoking to four groups of subjects. The control group received little information other than the recommendation to stop. One experimental group saw a movie giving statistics on lung cancer in smokers and describing the symptoms and signs of lung cancer. This was intended to create a feeling of personal vulnerability. A second experimental group saw the surgical scenes from the cancer film. No information about symptoms or rates of illness was included in this condition. They had a "good scare" without any emphasis on their personal vulnerability. Finally, a group was used that combined the vulnerability and fear material with the recommendations. The vulnerability message and fear (surgery) message both produced significant decreases in smoking. When they were combined, however, there was no significant decrease in smoking. In fact, the combined messages were significantly poorer than either presented alone.

There are many variables which could make a high-fear message less persuasive than a low. For example, if a communicator appears to be biased, increasing the fearfulness of his communication may strengthen this appearance and increase resistance to persuasion! Authority figures, and perhaps anyone over thirty, could generate resistance in young people on this very basis. But the resistance found by Watts does not appear to involve suspicion of bias in the source or hostility toward him. If anything, the subjects again seem "overper-suaded" of the danger and believe very strongly that smoking will lead to cancer. In fact, in a later study, Watts and Leventhal found that subjects who partially *rejected* a communication (i.e., argued that it was too extreme) were more likely to show reductions in smoking behavior. These results pose an important warning for the mass field program. The combining of techniques, each of which is a successful persuader by itself, may introduce interactions which *reduce* effectiveness.

Overcoming Barriers to Action

It is clear that fear information is not equally effective in establishing attitudinal barriers to smoking for all subjects and for all combinations of information. A strong sense of vulnerability, stimulated by personality dispositions, prior activity (smoking) or information, can generate a sense of inevitability and failure to act. An important point, therefore, is whether anything can be done to bolster the individual's coping ability, and thus insure change in behavior as well as in attitudes.

One procedure which suggested itself was to vary the apparent effectiveness of the recommendation for blocking danger. Extremely effective responses should be more likely to reduce fear and to be learned. If an inadequate or only partially adequate response is recommended, fear will remain and can cause the breakdown in coping.

A second procedure which was suggested was to help the subject understand how *he* can perform the recommended action. The goal was not to convince him of the power of the recommended act, but that he had the ability and know-how to do it. It seemed (Dabbs and Leventhal, 1966) that even if a person believes an act is only minimally effective, he will try it rather than do nothing at all. But "trying it" depends upon "know-how."

To investigate this problem, Leventhal, Watts, and Pagano (1967) designed a study using high- and low-fear communications. At each fear level the groups were split into subgroups, with about one half the subjects at each fear level receiving "specific instructions" on how to quit smoking. The instructions on stopping recommended that the individual list his reasons for smoking and develop arguments counter to them. The message presented sample arguments against various commonly held ideas. For example, the idea that the smoking habit could not be broken was countered by showing that a habit was a chain of reactions which could be disrupted at any number of points. The section counter to the idea that smoking is valuable for relaxation pointed to other pace-breakers which have the same function. To argue against the idea that smoking is pleasurable, the smoker was reminded of various unpleasant aspects of the habit (e.g., shortness of breath, loss of taste, etc.). The bulk of the message, however, consisted of a host of specific points on how to avoid the conditions for smoking. These included suggestions such as not to eat with friends who are smoking, to have excuses to decline cigarettes prepared in advance of situations such as parties where one is likely to smoke, purchasing items in lieu of cigarettes, carrying one's money in a different place, and substituting other activities for smoking. The suggestions were designed specifically for the population under study, in this case college students. To evaluate the persuasive value of these instructions without fear material, a control group was included which was exposed *only* to the specific instruction pamphlet.

It was clear that the high-fear messages led to more frequent reports of fear (subjects felt disgusted, depressed, anxious, fearful, etc.), more negative attitudes toward smoking and stronger intentions to quit. The control condition was lowest on these measures. The subjects were then contacted at three later times to obtain reports on their smoking. One week after the communication, all the experimental groups, high- and low-fear, with or without specific instructions, were smoking less. The control group receiving only specific instructions was unchanged. At one month and again at three months, the fear groups that had received specific instructions continued at a reduced rate of smoking. But the group exposed only to the fear communication began to regress toward its initial level. The control condition was still unchanged. The data look a bit

different depending upon whether we score the average number of cigarettes smoked per group or the proportion of subjects cutting down. The sliding back to old patterns is more pronounced with the proportion scores.

The important point is that instructions alone were insufficient to produce change, and fear alone, either high or low, produced less permanent change. The combination of fear and instructions, while initially no more effective, appeared to have the advantage over a period of time. Two similar investigations on tetanus inoculations yielded rather similar results (Leventhal, Singer, and Jones, 1965; Leventhal, Jones, and Trembly, 1966).

While specific instructions play an important role in turning "good" intentions into performance, the aspects of the instructions (cognitive rules) which are crucial are unknown. There is also little information on the conditions which limit the importance of specific instructions. For example, if they influence the "coping mechanism" they should be of greater value to low- than to high-esteem subjects. There was some evidence to this effect in the Leventhal, Watts, and Pagano study, but definitive evidence is lacking. There are also no clear indications that specific instructions work by changing or reducing the subjects' "fear." Whether they will interact with other aspects of threat information is unknown.

The other hypothesis, that failure to reduce fear with ineffective recommendations would result in less persuasion with high fear communications, has little empirical support. Of the studies varying effectiveness (Dabbs and Leventhal, 1966; Chu, 1966), none suggest that low fear is better than high fear with ineffective recommendations. The findings suggest that, if a recommendation is at least minimally effective, acceptance is greater at high threat levels. Neither of these studies, however, is on smoking behavior.

Findings and Theory

The fear studies show progress in isolating variables which are important modifiers of the relationship of "fear arousal" to attitude and behavior change. The empirical generalizations fall under three headings:

1. Stimulating motivations by means of threat information increases acceptance of recommendations, though the increase is greater for verbal than for overt behavioral compliance.

2. Increasing threat level will not increase acceptance for all people or for all conditions:

(a) Individuals who score high on self-esteem rating scales show more acceptance the more intense the threat. Those with low reported self-esteem are often unchanged or even inhibited by high-threat level.

(b) People for whom the threat is most relevant, i.e., those who are high in vulnerability classified by their prior attitudes or actual behavior, are less likely to respond favorably to threat messages.

(c) Vulnerable subjects are very likely to avoid actions, such as taking X-rays, which may confirm their vulnerability to danger, though they will accept recommendations (stopping smoking) congruent with their desire to avoid vulnerability.

(d) If a communication is designed both to raise fear level and to stimulate feelings of vulnerability to danger, the audience may respond to the anticipated danger as if it is inevitable and fail to take protective action.

3. While threat communications seem to increase motivation to avoid danger they do not appear to be sufficient to insure lasting changes in behavior. Additional information called "specific instructions" is valuable in connecting the person's attitudes to responses suitable for particular situations to insure that his beliefs are translated into action. Thus, what Cartwright (1949) called a behavioral structure is important for lasting change in performance.

The fear studies tell us something about the conditions under which fear communications are likely to dissuade people from smoking. They do not demonstrate, however, that fear communications are the only way or even the best way of doing this. Messages appealing to other negative emotions, such as shame or guilt, or to positive emotions, such as joy, might prove more effective at disrupting the smoking habit. The purpose of these investigations was to study the consequences of fear arousal and to see what conditions limit the impact of fear message. The goal was not to determine which type of emotional appeal was most effective for an anti-smoking message, information which might have relatively little theoretical importance. It would, however, be of both practical and theoretical importance if results similar to those for fear were found in studies of other emotions. For example, our understanding of the process of attitude and behavior change would be advanced considerably if it were known that specific instructions worked the same way for all types of emotional messages, while self-esteem influenced acceptance only for fear and other "negative" emotions.

But a more fundamental question can be raised respecting emotion and motivation. It has been assumed that emotion is motivating; i.e., if it were not for the feelings of fear, the smoker would not bother to alter his beliefs and action. The fear emotion is treated as a biological drive—a source of irritation or discomfort which the person tries to eliminate. According to this drive model, behaviors are learned when they succeed in eliminating the state of discomfort (see Miller, 1951). A number of years ago Harvey Carr (1925) suggested an alternative to the drive formulation which he called a judgmental model of motivation and emotion. According to this formulation, a person can change his attitudes and behavior because he recognizes that they may lead him to a situation of danger. The individual can judge a situation as dangerous and as something to be avoided even if he *does not* become frightened. Thus, he acts to avoid an external danger rather than to reduce or eliminate an internal state of fear.

It is obvious that the judgment of danger is likely to be associated with the emotion of fear. But it is also likely that an experienced person can recognize danger situations even when his emotional responses to the situations have been extinguished. This is an important point, because none of the fear studies show that the strong emotion experienced by the subjects is the "*cause*" of the changes in attitudes and behavior. It may be that some important informational aspect of the communication, and not the subject's fear, is critical in producing the judgment that one is in danger and must act by reducing smoking. If this hypothesis is "true," efforts should be make to identify the informational elements producing the judgment; and information arousing the strong states of fear, if different, should be eliminated from the message. In this way, people might reduce smoking without developing strong antipathies to health communications. Moreover, communications should emphasize those informational ingredients which maximize compliance.

There are a number of observations which lead to the judgmental formulation. The first are the relative magnitudes of the changes for fear and attitudes. The fear differences recorded between high- and low-threat communications are very reliable statistically and are also of large magnitude. The differences in attitudes and behavior between the same treatments, while usually statistically reliable, are typically small. Although one cannot necessarily compare magnitudes on separate dimensions, it does not seem unfair to suggest that it is easier to raise fear than to change beliefs and behavior. If fear is the mediator or "drive" of the acceptance reaction, one might expect the relationship between the two to be a bit more proportional. The lack of proportion would not be surprising if the two responses were related to somewhat different underlying processes.

The second observation was the drive model's failure to predict interactions between fear and other variables. Of course, if fear is only one mediator, and the subject's mode of coping is the other, the lack of proportionality could exist because not all subjects show adaptive coping under high fear. But if the joint determination is of this type, high fear breaking down adaptive coping, factors which facilitate coping might be expected both to reduce the subject's fearfulness and to lead to greater reductions in smoking at high than at low levels of fear motivation. The data indicate, however, factors which have important influences on attitude and behavior change *do not alter fear*! For example, specific instruc-

tions are important in translating attitudes into behavior, yet they do not seem to reduce people's fear. Moreover, the instructions are not typically more effective with high than with moderate threat messages, an interaction that could be expected from the drive model.

It is also doubtful that the interactions of esteem and threat level are mediated by fear. Low-esteem people are not necessarily more frightened when they show resistance to change. The vulnerability results also suggest that cognitive factors and not fear responses (or awareness of fear) mediate compliance.

A third reason for not assigning a mediational role to fear is negative evidence on the fear-reduction hypothesis. The drive model predicts that recommendations which are more effective in reducing fear are accepted more; i.e., the more they eliminate discomfort the more they are believed. In a study on dental hygiene, Leventhal and Singer (1966) found no relationship between attitude change and the degree to which recommendations to avoid dental disease had reduced fear. There is no evidence on this question, however, for the problem of smoking.

We should point out that the judgmental paradigm here proposed does not exclude the possibility that fear reactions serve as mediators for other instrumental behaviors. For example, if a person feels quite frightened and can see no clear reason for his fear, variation in the intensity of his emotional reactions might be the only available guide to action. There are times when this does happen. For example, if fear responses are present after one has successfully eliminated a danger, one might be specifically motivated to reduce unpleasant effects (e.g., take a drink). The neurotic person who typically faces ambiguous danger may also carefully attend to increases and decreases in the intensity of his emotion and choose activities which control fear. Thus, any variable, e.g., age, experience with danger, neurotic history, etc., which can affect the relative strength of the organism's attention to fear versus the environment, could shift the mediators of adaptive activity.

References

Berkowitz, L., and D. R. Cottingham. 1960. The interest and relevance of fear-arousing communications. *Journal of Abnormal Social Psychology*, 60:37–43.

Carr, H. 1925. *Psychology, a study of mental activity*. New York: Longmans, Green.

Cartwright, D. 1949. Some principles of mass persuasion. Selected findings of research in the sale of United States war bonds. *Human Relations*, 2:253–67.

Chu, G. C. 1966. Fear arousal, efficacy, and imminency. *Journal of Personality and Social Psychology*, 4:517–24.

Dabbs, J. M., and H. Leventhal. 1966. Effects of varying the recommendations in a fear-arousing communication. *Journal of Personality and Social Psychology*, 4:525–31.

Hochbaum, G. M. 1958. Public participation in medical screening programs: a socio-psychological study. Washington, D.C.: U.S. Government Printing Office.

Horn, D. 1960. Modifying smoking habits in high school students. *Children*, 7:63–65.

Janis, I. L., and L. Mann. 1965. Effectiveness of emotional role-playing in modifying smoking habits and attitudes. *Journal of Experimental Research in Personality*, 1:84.

Kornzweig, N. D. 1967. Behavior change as a function of fear arousal and personality. Unpublished doctoral dissertation, Yale University.

Leventhal, H. 1965. Fear communications in the acceptance of preventive health practices. *Bulletin of the New York Academy of Medicine*, 41:1144–68.

———. 1967. Fear—for your health. *Psychology Today*, 1:54–58.

———, G. M. Hochbaum, B. K. Carriger, and I. M. Rosenstock. 1960. Epidemic impact on the general population in two cities. In I. Rosenstock *et al.* (Eds.), *The impact of Asian influenza on community life*. Public Health Service Publication No. 706. U.S. Department of Health, Education and Welfare.

———, S. Jones, and G. Trembly. 1966. Sex differences in attitude and behavior change under conditions of fear and specific instructions. *Journal of Experimental Social Psychology*, 2:387–99.

———, and P. Niles. 1965. Persistence of influence for varying durations of exposure to threat stimuli. *Psychological Reports*, 16:223–33.

———, and R. Singer. 1966. Affect arousal and positioning of recommendations in persuasive communications. *Journal of Personality and Social Psychology*, 4:137–46.

———, ———, and S. Jones. 1965. Effects of fear and specificity of recommendation upon attitudes and behavior. *Journal of Personality and Social Psychology*, 2:20–29.

———, and G. Trembly. 1968. Negative emotions and persuasion. *Journal of Personality*, 36:154–68.

———, and J. Watts. 1967. Sources of resistance to fear-arousing communications on smoking and lung cancer. *Journal of Personality*, 34:155–75.

———, ———, and F. Pagano. 1967. Effects of fear and instructions on how to cope with danger. *Journal of Personality and Social Psychology*, 6:313–21.

Miller, N. E. 1951. Learnable drives and rewards. In S. S. Stevens (Ed.), *Handbook of Experimental Psychology*. New York: John Wiley.

Niles, P. 1965. The relationships of susceptibility and anxiety to acceptance of fear-arousing communications. Unpublished doctoral dissertation, Yale University.

Schwartz, J. L., and Dubitzky, M. 1968. Requisites for success in smoking withdrawal. In E. F. Borgatta and R. B. Evans (Eds.), *Smoking, Health and Behavior*. Chicago: Aldine Publishing, pp. 231–47.

Watts, Jean C. 1966. The role of vulnerability in resistance to fear-arousing communications. Unpublished doctoral dissertation, Bryn Mawr College.

32. India's New Departures in Mass Motivation for Fertility Control

Frank Wilder* • D. K. Tyagi**

Imagine that we could construct a "success scale" along which we might rank the several major development fields in which aid-giving agencies (notably of the United States) have sought to assist the developing countries over the past two decades. On such a scale the field of Mass Communications—also known under the aliases of Communications Media, Information, Mass Media Development, Publicity, Propaganda, Mass Education, Audio-Visual Aids and Mass Motivation—would surely land near, and likely at, the bottom.

Perhaps in no other field have we achieved so little, although we seem to have so much to offer; we invested meagerly and sometimes aimlessly, although the potential development return was, and still is, promising.

It is not the purpose of this paper to examine and analyze the unhappy record of the developed countries in assisting the buildup abroad of mass media facilities, techniques, and competence to support national and international development goals. Our purpose is to record the evidence in India of a new and unusual mass communications strategy in that country's family planning program. India's brave radical departures in mass motivation techniques are worth study because they hold promise of unprecedented payoffs at reasonable cost, within the pressing time limits of national fertility control programs in the crucial

developing countries. There may also be lessons, both for foreign aid agencies and host governments, in any development effort where success depends on wide public understanding and participation. However, if only to set the background of the recently implemented Indian formula, let us state some important facts and circumstances in that dark history of efforts to apply mass media techniques in development programs, including family planning:

1. Most development planners recognize at last (albeit 21 years after Gen. George C. Marshall enunciated the European postwar recovery plan that opened an era of global "foreign aid") that the free flow of information and knowledge to and from the people in a developing society is a requisite for (and indeed a spur to) economic and social development.

2. Nonetheless, thus far, no developing country has been assisted to develop resources for mass media development that are commensurate with the enormity and urgency of development needs or responsive to the special non-Western setting in which development must be made to occur—notably in truly traditional rural societies. The gravest deficiency, in both the aid-giving community and the host countries, is a lack of working experts attuned to the special local audience settings

Reprinted from Frank Wilder anl D. K. Tyagi, "India's New Departures in Mass Motivation for Fertility Control," *Demography* (1968), pp. 773–779.

° Ford Foundation Consultant to the Government of India in Mass Communication for Family Planning.

°° Assistant Commissioner (Media), Department of Family Planning.

that must govern selection of media, mode of presentation and message content.

3. The evidence is overwhelming that no developing country (with the apparent new exception of India) has put into motion a wide-scale mass motivation program whose messages are so contrived and presented that they hit the target tellingly and result in widespread new knowledge necessary for timely mass adoption of a new practice. Commercial firms, it is true, have successfully promoted product sales through mass media (largely to literate and urban and semi-urban audiences). It is true also that extension methods, together with radiation from personal experience, have brought spectacular results in agricultural innovation. But mass media utilization, for the spread of awareness, interest, and (possibly) acceptance has been universally marked in the developing countries by one or both of the following disastrous conditions:

a. *The public did not receive message.* Insufficient penetration of the audience results from either (1) a dearth of the standard major media outlets (newspapers, radios and movie facilities) in the target areas; (2) insufficient governmental investment in the personnel and facilities needed and informational materials (posters, pamphlets, exhibits and filmstrips, as well as items for distribution through the press, radio stations and motion picture facilities); (3) a message that lacked luster and prominence, or, most likely, (4) all three.

b. *The public did not understand the message.* This condition is uniquely the result of that great intellectual distance between message-maker and audience. The message-maker is all too frequently an administrator or an artist, and not a trained and seasoned communicator whose concern should be primarily getting the message across. By definition, the message can be got across only within the audience's frames of reference. To make matters worse, most persons designated as mass communications officers themselves shape messages to meet their own sophisticated tastes and those of their colleagues and supervisors. In short, mass communications messages in development

programs have suffered the two extremes of inutility—ineptness or Madison Avenue aptness.

4. Three options in mass media development, or combinations of the three, seem to be available to the developing countries:

a. To continue developing the standard media—that is, the press, radio, motion pictures, posters, pamphlets, exhibits, and (for more developed developing countries) television. (In the light of Indian departures from exclusive use of these media, which will be described later, one may now regard these once-modern media as "traditional.")

b. To introduce new communications technology developed in the West, thereby hurdling years of Western communications evolution. Included here are satellite-based television, electronic typesetting, facsimile transmission, microfiche for libraries, laser beams and the like.

c. To exploit massively as media those widely existing facilities and societal accoutrements with which the public is already intimately familiar and is in frequent day-to-day contact. Some of these facilities and accoutrements are already in use as media—e.g., traveling troupes of entertainers. Some can be transformed into media—e.g., the outsides of railroad rolling stock. Most are characteristically visual, local, and outdoors. None has been effectively used by national development programs.

The Indian Formula

India herself, by virtue of the massive attention she has received from aid-giving countries, exemplified diagrammatically the unhappy record of mass communications at work in a national development program. Then, in the summer of 1966, the Department of Family Planning (within the Ministry of Health and Family Planning) examined its allocations for the use of radio, films, press, exhibitions, and printed materials and decided that no amount of investment in these media would bring the message to India's 560,000 villages in time. Mr. Govind Narain, Secretary of the Department of Family Planning, speaking in August 1968 at the Indian Institue of Mass

Communications, described the Department's motivation in these words:

> Perhaps it is the special nature of family planning that forced upon us the need for reexamining our traditional ways of communicating with the public and of devising new ways to accomplish a communications job that seemed almost impossible. In the first place the success of our total population control programme depends primarily on the individual's acceptance of the idea of preventing pregnancy for his own good. This means that many crores (tens of millions) of individuals must have sufficient information and be highly motivated to adopt one of the several family planning methods. The difficulty here is that we are dealing with the most intimate aspect of human life. The practice of family planning means a radical change in behavior, ranging from the frequent use of a conventional contraceptive device to submission to a surgical procedure such as vasectomy or tubectomy. In dealing with such an intimate and difficult situation, you will appreciate that many of our people, especially in the rural areas, will readily listen to and accept rumors and misinformation about family planning. When you realise that we do not have at our command the benefit of instantaneous dissemination of information, such as through the radio, to the remote villages of our country, you will appreciate our concern to try to find different ways to spread the message of family planning as far and wide as possible.

It should be added that Departmental moves toward more rapid and effective spread of family planning messages were made possible by the unusual phenomenon of a top administrator (the Secretary himself) sensitive to the role of mass communications in development and willing to take risks. In turn, the "education" of such program leaders to the urgency of the mass communications job had been the first priority of the Department's man heading the "Mass Education and Media Section." This office is under the Commissioner, the technical head of the program (and himself a prime target in the crucial early internal "education" drive):

The Indians opted, then, for a combination of the "standard" media (press, radio, motion pictures and printed materials) and any "outdoor" visual medium they could lay their message on. The noteworthy features of the revolutionary Indian strategy, however, are not confined to the add-on of these new media (which, in some cases, amounts to a return to older, truly traditional, media). Two other elements in the Indian strategy differ radically from earlier approaches—the *message* and the use of a special *symbol*.

The Message

First, let us consider the special treatment of the content, or messages, of the information program. To begin with, the Indians chose to ignore those Indian and foreign specialists in advertising, publicity, and mass communications who counselled a changing, phased campaign that would run the gamut in both presentation and message. Slogans would change; designs would change; appeals would change —from "What is Family Planning?" to reproductive biology to "What is the Best Method for Me?" Instead, sizing up the bad void in media coverage in villages and the prospect of bureaucratic delays, they decided to find a message that would be a *direct exhortation to have a specific number of children*; to present this message *in the same form in all media*; to keep it *simple and understandable*; and to *stay with it* until everyone knew, through this message, that family planning is legitimate and what it means. And in sudden realization that no literate Indian in the target group does not know his own language, materials for mass consumption are no longer produced in English; only the 13 major languages are used. The basic design presents visually the stylized front-view faces of a smiling mother and father, a son and a daughter. The message, in words no Indian can fail to understand, says simply: "Have Only Two or Three Children . . . That's Plenty." (The message is warmer and more engaging in the Indian languages than it is in that English translation.) The colors are always the same, bright and attractive. The faces are drawn always in the same style. The same message is verbalized in an appealing song by a popular Indian songwriter and recorded by a singer whose voice is as familiar to Indians as Bing Crosby's once was to Americans.

It should be noted, in passing, that adoption

of the 2-or-3-children slogan was itself a bold and risky step. There is a strong Indian tradition that insists on sons, no matter how many pregnancies it takes. Worse, high officialdom was then concerned with high-parity couples, not the newly married or low-parity couples. Only those few Department officers who forced through the 2-or-3 slogan knew that the fourth child spells death to India's goal of a 2-per-thousand birth rate by 1978.

One obvious major payoff of simplicity and repetition is that they help to hurdle the barrier of illiteracy (which is near-total in many Indian villages). It takes no more than a day or so for an illiterate to know the meaning of that distinctive design he seems to see at every turn. We are convinced that the studies the Indians are planning will show this approach has an overwhelming advantage over the use of several messages in press, radio and films. A high-ranking state family planning official, recently visiting New Delhi, decried the validity of the technique, because "you have put up hundreds of billboards in New Delhi, and we could never do that in the rural areas." He was then told that there are a mere 17 billboards to cover Delhi population of two million. Repetition had created the illusion of saturation.

The largest payoffs, for a fertility control program that lacks time and talent, result from the use of the exhortative message specifying the limits of a "small" family, rather than the loose appeal "Practice Family Planning" or the abstract declaration "A Small Family is a Happy Family." Given normal long delays in message dissemination, why not spell out the meaning of "family planning" in the first awareness message? Can we expect that the words "family planning" in a local language means "birth prevention?" (It certainly does not in any Indian language.) Does the small-family-happy-family message transmit the specific action to be taken? Can fertility programs succeed if people are left to "Have Only Those Children You Can Afford?" And are these not rather elusive concepts for a villager whose personal aspirations do not parallel those of the educated program administrator or the foreign communications advisor?

Finally, the repetition of the simple direct exhortation in the same form, in different "outdoor" media, seen every day by the population at large, provides an illusion of legitimation and, by "airing" the subject of birth control, stimulates public discussion of it.

The Media

It would seem prosaic, even backward, in our television age, to turn to village walls, buses, and billboards to carry a motivational message. However, employing the message techniques already described on such handy media, the Indians appear to be reaping large communications benefits (widespread awareness, considerable primary knowledge, and some inclination toward birth control) with these "new" media.

The first important fact that struck the Indians in their examination of their mass media program was that the press, radio, and films reach only an estimated 20–25 percent of the population, mainly in the urban and semi-urban concentrations—where the need for motivation is least.

Equally revealing was a realistic look at the well-known mobile audiovisual unit as a means of bringing information and knowledge to villagers. In India, the Government's total public information program (both for support of development and for straight information) had at its command a mere 140 such mobile units, known as "cinema vans." That means one unit to cover 4000 villages. The Department of Family Planning, already seized with the need for a massive mass communications effort, had won a fund appropriation for 335 mobile units exclusively for family planning—that is, one for each District (average population 1.6 million). It would be another few years before these 335 additional family planning mobile units would be functioning. Whether all or most of them will be efficiently and effectively functioning at that time is still doubtful. Given full effect operation of these new audiovisual vehicles—meaning a large, trained, and hard-working staff, availability of power, no breakdowns of vehicle or equipment, and sustained logistic support—it would take *eight years for each vehicle to visit each of its 1700 villages once.* (At India's present growth rate, the addition to the population would, by then, be more than 100 million.)

Another old communications media standby, the ordinary printed paper poster, provided another goad that sent the Department searching for other ways to reach their far-flung audience. Posters, they observed, took many months from conception to printing, and sometimes two years or more to the moment of actual public display. Public display itself rarely occurred, since the quantity of posters printed brought only two or three to each clinic, hospital administrator or other appropriate office. The posters were then usually used for display in those very places, where motivation obviously is least needed. When publicly displayed, they found, the average life of posters is about three days: they are either mutilated by children, washed away by rain or used as a smooth foundation for a fresh movie poster. The cost-benefit ratio was clearly so disadvantageous that no one in the busy Department of Family Planning ventured to suggest a specific study to measure it.

In the new strategy, therefore, the Indians began to exploit—in addition to the "standard" media—billboards, buses, matchboxes, rickshas, pocket calendars, newspaper and magazine advertisements, carnival banners, shopping bags, official village civic registers, telephone directories, and—most important— the exterior walls of buildings for huge lasting paintings of the basic design. Also, permanent enamelled metal signs are being distributed to the country's 100,000 post offices, and, after traditional railroad conservatism was painfully overcome, the broad sides of locomotive tenders are being used as traveling billboards.

The Symbol

The third major departure in the Indian mass communications strategy is the *Red Triangle*—a symbol that communicates even as it identifies and represents. It is unadorned, in solid vermillion, and equilateral, with its apex pointed downward.

A development program seeking widespread public participation need not be much concerned with a symbol as a decorative emblem for letterheads and office doors. Where masses of people are as yet untouched by modern contraceptive methods, a symbol should and can act to strengthen the program. The Indians eschewed selection of the conventional sign that attempts to convey meaning through *graphic* representation—that is, a design that seeks to *depict* the idea of family, few children or, somehow, population control. Instead, they sought a design with no prior meaning or connotation, in the belief (now proved correct) that it would soon produce, distinctively and exclusively, an association in the public mind's eye with Family Planning—indeed, would convey awareness of the concept of limiting the number of one's children to two or three.

History's best example of such a nonrepresentational symbol is the Red Cross. This famous symbol, however, has two obvious defects, of which the Red Triangle is free. One is that the Red Cross is suggestive of Christianity, and for this reason it is not used in some Moslem countries. The other is that the Red Cross has come to be recognized widely as representing not only the Red Cross organization (its original purpose), but also medical services, hospital, first aid, drugs, doctors, and facilities or products unrelated to the original purpose. While the Red Triangle is expected to be identified later with products as well as clinics, it will remain, hopefully, within the world of population control programs.

The Indian program must reach out to the minds of some 400 million persons. Illiteracy is widespread, incomes are low, and there is little built-in motivation toward family planning. Effective mass media in the vast rural areas are insufficient. Under those conditions, the special characteristics of the Red Triangle seem to help advance the program significantly. First, it is distinctive. This means it will be identified in people's minds only with family planning and with family planning services and products. (Some intellectuals have read into the Red Triangle the suggestion of images or ideas peculiar to their own conscious and subconscious experience. But the mass of people do not seem to have such established connotations in their minds concerning a vermillion equilateral triangle, its apex pointed downward.) In India, the Red Triangle always appears with the 2-or-3 children message and the "four faces" design.

Second, and more important, the Red Triangle is easy to reproduce anywhere. No artistic talent is needed; it can be quickly painted in the remotest areas by local personnel. It already appears, painted large and prominent, on most of the country's clinics. For use on the clothing of family planning workers, it is easily cut from a piece of red cloth and sewn on. Nor is there any difficulty in making metal or plastic badges.

Because of its bright color, the Red Triangle is clearly visible at some distance. The Red Triangle will soon be displayed wherever contraceptive supplies are sold or distributed, even at drug stores, grocery stores, and tea and cigarette stalls.

But probably of greatest importance is the fact that, unlike elaborate graphic emblems, the Red Triangle can be verbalized in any language in the world. It can be called by name—"The Red Triangle"—even spontaneously by illiterates in their own particular language. This makes it easy for persons to inquire about the location of a clinic and to converse about family planning. They can ask for contraceptives without embarrassment, especially if contraceptive products carry the symbol in their packgaing or carry the brand name, "Red Triangle".

There is no scientifically gathered data to gauge the economic and programmatic soundness of the Indian strategy, although the Department of Family Planning, at this writing, is mapping several needed studies. Nonetheless, informal assessment of results thus far lead us to commend it unqualifiedly for adaptation and application in other developing countries. This apparently visceral conclusion rests only on our conviction that mass communications methods, in their nature and in these settings—unlike clinical methods, for example—lend themselves to sufficiently valid assessment through daily intimate professional (if only visceral) observation. This would be a dangerous premise in a modern marketing situation wherein wide use is made of the press, radio, television, and motion pictures, aimed at an audience that is able to buy, is informed and discriminating, and has several choices. Where all those conditions do *not* exist, and where the primary and urgent goal of mass media utilization is widespread positive public inclination toward contraception, it makes no sense to question the possible payoff of large, bright paintings of a crisp, meaningful, graphic message (at 13 cents a square foot) on outdoor walls in villages.

In the cold light of print, this three-part Indian strategy in mass communications will seem to some of us to be undeserving of the labels, "imaginative," "new," or "revolutionary." Yet, it is all of those. It is imaginative in its insistence on thinking primarily in terms of its audience; it is new in its departure from the "standard" media, although it turned stubbornly to the old and the obvious; it is revolutionary in its upset of existing thinking and trends in mass communications for development. The entire approach is unheard of elsewhere. But it promises to work.

33. Lobbying as a Communication Process[a]

Lester W. Milbrath[*]

Lobbyists and their activities have traditionally been of interest to political scientists because they play a role in the governmental decision process. But just what is that role? Or, to put the question in a more researchable fashion, what kind of model can the analyst

Reprinted from Lester W. Milbrath, "Lobbying as a Communication Process," *Public Opinion Quarterly*, Vol. 24. No. 1 (Spring 1960), pp. 32–53.

[a] I wish to express my appreciation to the Brookings Institution, Duke University, and the Social Science Research Council for support of various stages of this study.

[*] Professor of Political Science, State University of New York at Buffalo.

apply to their activities which will provide the most accurate perspective on their role? The answer to this question must be derived from the larger frame of reference of the over-all governmental decision process.

Social scientists have approached the analysis of governmental decision-making from several different perspectives. For example, some analysts have approached it from the perspective of the role of groups in the process.[1] Others have done research which seemed to indicate that governmental decisions are made by a select power elite,[2] although the elite theory has been challenged by other scholars.[3] One could catalogue additional perspectives on the process, some of which are very provocative,[4] but that is not the purpose of this paper. The purpose, rather, is to present an alternative perspective on the process which may provide some new insights and also lead to a communication model for analyzing the lobbying aspects of the process.

The perspective on the lobbying process reported here is gained from a sample survey of Washington lobbyists. The study focused primarily on lobbyists as individuals who comprise a political skill group rather than on the nature and power of the groups which they represent, as most other studies of lobbying have done. The universe from which the sample was selected included all the individuals with Washington addresses who registered as lobbyists with the Clerk of the House and Secretary of the Senate during the first two quarters of 1956 (the most recent period prior to the field-work phase of the study). One hundred and fourteen names were randomly selected from the total universe of 614; I succeeded in interviewing 101 of these individuals. These interviews were supplemented by interviews with 38 people in Congress, in order to get the perspective of the recipient of lobbying.

The confidential interviews averaged about two hours in length and covered such topics as the occupational history of the respondent; how he happened to get into lobbying; how well he likes the role he plays; what his political background was; what his socioeconomic background was; how he relates to his employer; what role he plays in relation to the government; what tactics and techniques he uses and refers for communicating with governmental decision-makers; and how he evaluates the lobbying process and the role he plays in it. Finally, each respondent was asked to fill out a short personality test.

Under the American system of government, certain individuals, occupying certain governmental offices, are charged by the Constitution

[1] The two outstanding examples probably are: Arthur F. Bentley, *The Process of Government* (Chicago: The University of Chicago Press, 1908), and David B. Truman, *The Government Process* (New York: Alfred A. Knopf, 1951).

[2] Some leading examples here are: Floyd Hunter, *Community Power Structure* (Chapel Hill: University of North Carolina Press, 1953), and his *Top Leadership U.S.A.* (Chapel Hill: University of North Carolina Press, 1959), C. Wright Mills, *The Power Elite* (New York: Oxford University Press, 1956), and Ferdinand Lundberg, *America's Sixty Families* (New York: The Vanguard Press, 1937).

[3] See Robert A. Dahl, "A Critique of the Ruling Elite Model," *The American Political Science Review,* LII (1958), 463–469.

[4] As a result of some recent studies of community politics, Nortoa Long has suggested that community decision-making can be analyzed with a game theory model. His concept is that political decision-making results from the interactive forces of a variety of games being played in any given comunity. The players in one game may be the pawns in another game or may use players in other games as pawns in their own game. The remarkable thing is that community decisions result from the diverging activities and purposes of the games being played. See his "The Local Community as an Ecology of Games," *The American Journal of Sociology,* LXIV (1958), 251–261. Although extensive research would be required for verification, the evidence suggests that national decision-making may also be the result of an ecology of games.

with making decisions which in effect lay down the policies for the country and which have the force of governmental authority and finality behind them. I am thinking mainly here of the President, the members of the Supreme Court, and the members of Congress. The charge has been made that the decisions pronounced by these persons essentially are not their own, but rather they are merely parroting the decisions made by individuals and groups upon whom they are dependent for support. In one sense, close attention to the desires of supporters is considered laudable in a representative democracy. On the other hand, we are distressed if it seems that the decision-maker is following the desires of some special interest and ignoring the general welfare.

Although students of politics have been making educated guesses for some time about the propensity for decision-makers to follow either the general welfare or someone's special welfare, a clear-cut discernment of the influence of such factors as pressure-group activity or political money upon governmental decision-makers can come only from detailed examination of the decision processes of these individuals. Unhappily, it is an extraordinarily difficult research problem to ascertain the bases for judgment made by these decision-makers. Even if the researcher had free access to decision-makers within a context of mutual trust and thirst for truth, it is highly unlikely that these persons could plumb their unconscious and dredge up all the factors that entered into any given decision. Detailed examination of the psychological processes of a decision-maker concerning a given decision would probably, at least at this stage of social science, get bogged down in a mass of unanalyzable detail. Thus, it is not my purpose to present an analytical scheme for assessing the influence of lobbying on the governmental decision process.

My purpose, rather, is to build upon our general knowledge of decision-making to construct a framework showing how lobbying fits into, or plays a role in, the over-all governmental decision process. In decision-making theory, an almost universally accepted concept

is that a decision-maker must have access to ideas, arguments, information, and so forth, before these factors can figure in his decision. Another concept of decision-making suggests, however, that mere accessibility is not enough. Every person has a set of predispositions that derive from a variety of sources, such as conditioned learning experiences, which includes the whole of a person's background as well as the internalized role constraints of his present situation, physiological needs, and inherited physical characteristics and capabilities. These personal predispositions are enduring rather than transitory and condition the behavior of people on a long-term basis, so that we say everyone has a personality. We recognize this when we apply to people such adjectives as *liberal, conservative, manipulative, submissive, sociable, cynical,* and so forth.

The important thing about predispositions, for our analysis, is that they provide a perceptual screen for each individual. Some stimuli are allowed to pass through the screen, while others are stopped. It is a well-known phenomenon that different people viewing the same event may perceive it quite differently. The chairmen of our respective political parties almost invariably arrive at a different interpretation of the factors creating the outcome of an election. Anyone reading congressional hearings extensively must arrive at the conclusion that most members of Congress hear what they want to hear from a witness. The process by which selected stimuli are allowed to pass through the perceptual screen can be referred to as "receptivity."

Anyone wishing to influence the decision of a governmental official, then, must be concerned not only with getting the information to him but also with the problem of presenting it so that the decision-maker will be receptive. The only effective communications are those which get through the perceptual screen. In fact, there is no other way to influence governmental decisions, short of remaking the personalities of decision-makers or replacing them with other persons. The lobbying process, then, is essentially a communication process, and the task of the lobbyist is to figure out how he can handle communications most effectively in order to get through to decision-makers.

Although many lobbyists did not use communication terminology, it was clear that most conceived of their job as one of communication. As the interviews progressed, it seemed that lobbyist communications tended to fall into three categories: facts, arguments, and power. As merchants of information, lobbyists generally have a factual base for their message; especially they provide facts about how a contemplated action will affect the group represented. Because of the constraints of the relationship between lobbyist and decision-maker (to be discussed later), most lobbyists take particular pains never to present anything but accurate facts.

Lobbyists do not depend on facts alone; almost invariably the facts are accompanied by a set of arguments concerning the rightness, wisdom, or justice of the proposed action. Most lobbyists readily admit that these arguments usually present only one side of an issue, but they justify this on the ground that the decision-maker knows the source and is likely to get arguments on the other side from opposing groups. Some lobbyists try to take a posture of objectivity by presenting arguments on both sides of the question, although generally they are also careful that the balance lie in their favor.

Much more difficult and subtle is the task of communicating power. While we recognize that for some officials re-election is not paramount, the majority of elective officials show great respect for power at the polls. In its rawest form, this power can be communicated by defeating an incumbent and substituting a new official who, presumably, will act favorably toward the concerns of the group which put him over. Most lobby groups do not have this much power to throw around; and furthermore it is a rather crude and expensive way to communicate, especially since some competing group or coalition is likely to press vigorously in opposition.

Most lobbyists try to communicate power without going to the trouble and expense of defeating someone at the polls. The accent is on subtley, because an overt threat to defeat an official at the next election unless he "goes along" may serve only to stiffen his resistance. A forthright offer of campaign money to a co-operating decision-maker might be used to smear the donor rather than accomplish its intended purpose. The much publicized contribution to Senator Case, of South Dakota, from a natural-gas lobbyist in early 1956 is an example. Even such a tactic as publicizing the voting records of incumbent members of Congress is looked upon as foolhardy by many lobbyists and resented by many members. Lobbyists prefer to approach officials through constituents, stimulate letter-writing, put on a public relations campaign, and collaborate with other groups as more subtle devices for communicating power.

In addition to its threatening aspects, power can be used in a supportive or positive way. A legislator may be assured of enthusiastic support at the next election by a large membership group as a reward for promotion of a policy that the group wanted. Power has another facet, too: it is not only a relationship about which information can be communicated, but it is also a strong factor influencing decision-makers to keep open channels of communication to groups which hold power. Officials keep open channels of communication for other affective reasons also, such as good will, rapport, rewards for service or favors, and so forth, but political power is a factor they may ignore only at considerable peril.

The lobbyists in this sample were asked to evaluate a series of tactics and techniques for communicating with decision-makers. These tactics can be divided into three broad categories for analytical purposes: (1) techniques for direct personal communication between the lobbyist and decision-maker, (2) techniques for communication through intermediaries, and (3) techniques for keeping channels of communication open. Although these materials have not yet been exhaustively analyzed, the analysis is far enough along to make possible some general comparisons.

Direct Personal Communication

One assumption behind the practice of sending to the capital personal envoys of groups is that direct personal communication is more effective than written communication in gaining access and is more likely to reach the decision-maker when he is in a receptive frame of mind. The presence of a personal envoy at the capital normally tends to give one group a competitive advantage over another without an envoy. As a result, an ever increasing number of groups have sent such envoys. Now, however, there are such a great number and variety of lobbyists competing for the limited time and attention of the decision-makers that the Washington atmosphere has been characterized by some observers as filled with hustle and noise. One result of this competition is that lobbying resources are being diverted from direct communication toward communication through intermediaries who are believed to have better access. Indeed, there are many instances of successful lobbyists who have little or no direct contact with governmental decision-makers. Seventy-five per cent of the lobbyists spent less than 10 per cent of their time calling on members of Congress and no more than another 10 per cent calling on staff assistants to decision-makers.

Personal Presentation of Arguments

Despite this shift toward communication through intermediaries, lobbyists tend to believe that their most effective tactic is the personal presentation of their case to the officeholder, provided they can get in to see him or get him on the phone. Out of the 101 lobbyists interviewed, 65 chose this technique as the one they prefer and generally follow. It is curious that lobbyists spend such a small part of their time calling on members of Congress or their staffs if this tactic is considered so effective. There are several reasons for this. Preparations for these presentations must be careful and thus consume some time in addition to all the other tasks of lobbyists. (About three-fourths of the lobbyists spend more than 40 per cent of their time in the office.) Another factor is that lobbying is only one of the responsibilities of most people who register. In addition to lobbying, they may be executives of their organization; act as a liaison between their organization and the executive depart-

ment of government; carry on a law practice with a variety of clients, many of whom do not have legislative problems; and so forth. But perhaps the most important reason is that lobbyists must be careful not to "carry their pitcher to the well too often," as one Congressman put it. Most lobbyists perceive that they must save up their good will and access for a time when they want to see the decision-maker about something really important. One lobbyist expressed it this way: "I figure I am doing them a favor by not inviting them out to dinner and by not calling on them until I really need something."

All the lobbyists were asked to rate the fourteen communication tactics discussed in this paper on a general scale running from zero for not effective at all to 10 for very effective. These tactics were evaluated primarily as devices for communicating with legislators; however, several are also applicable to communications with decision-makers in the executive branch. The scale wsa presented visually in this form: 0—1—2—3—4—5—6—7—8—9—10, and the techniques to be rated were listed underneath it. Fifty-eight of the lobbyists rated personal presentation of arguments at 10 (or very effective), and the mean score for the entire group was 8.43. This technique rated higher than any other. When mean ratings are broken down by the type of organization the lobbyist represents, and then ranked (see Table 33.1), we discover that personal presentation of arguments is given first rank by all except the representatives of farm groups, church and humanitarian groups, and foreign governments or firms, and even here arguments usually ranked very high.

The personal presentations discussed here are generally oral and incorporate both facts and arguments. Most members of Congress prefer that this statement be very brief and merely summarize the main points. Many lobbyists follow the practice of leaving a short written summary behind for future reference and thus save the decision-maker, or his staff, the trouble of taking notes. Most people in Congress report that they prefer that personal presentations be informative, unbiased, clear, short, sincere, and unaccompanied by pres-

TABLE 33.1   Rank Order of Mean Ratings of Direct Personal Communication by Group Represented

Group	Personal Presentation of Arguments		Presentation of Research Results		Testifying at Hearings	
	Rank	Mean Rating	Rank	Mean Rating	Rank	Mean Rating
Big labor (N = 9)	1	8.3	7	6.1	6	6.4
Small labor (N = 7)	1	9.3	2	9.0	4	7.4
Big farm (N = 2)	7	5.0	3*	7.5	3*	7.5
Small farm (N = 3)	5	7.3	1	8.7	6	6.7
Big trade association (N = 8)	1	8.3	5	6.5	6	6.3
Small trade association (N = 40)	1	8.3	2	7.7	3	6.8
Corporations (N = 14)	1	9.5	2	7.1	3	4.7
Citizen's organizations (N = 5)	1	9.8	2	7.4	3	7.2
Church and humanitarian (N = 3)	3	7.0	5	6.3	4	6.7
Foreign government or firm (N = 2)	3	6.5	4	6.0	1	8.0
More than one type (N = 5)	1	8.6	2	7.4	4	6.4

* Presentation of research results and testifying at hearings were tied.

sure. The threat implied in pressure is painful, and persons who use it will be shunned when they try to gain access in the future. Members of Congress are also skeptical of lobbyists who play the role of advocate without personal conviction about the arguments they present. Members frequently probe for personal conviction and drastically discount the presentations of those who are mere advocates. Lobby groups guard against this by "sidelining" a lobbyist who does not share a particular policy position with the group he represents.

Presenting Research Results

The lobbyists were also asked to rate the presentation of research results. Most of them conceived of this as an integral part of arguments and had difficulty evaluating it separately. On the other hand, some lobbyists made little effort to bolster their arguments with research, either because they felt that their problem was not amenable to research or because they felt the research would not be respected. The representatives of large labor organizations and large trade associations ranked research considerably below arguments. Farm representatives, on the other hand, ranked research above arguments. *Post hoc* reasoning suggests that large labor and trade have sufficient membership to rate tactics related to politics (collaboration with

other groups, constituent contact, letters, etc.) above research. Farm representatives with large memberships also rate these tactics highly, but they still place research above arguments. There is a deep-seated respect for research in the farming industry, and it may be that this colored their response to this tactic.

If one breaks down these mean ratings by the relation of the lobbyist to his employer (Table 33.2), one sees, interestingly, that legislative relations staff persons, who are generally in closer contact with Congress than those in other roles, place less than average emphasis on research. They place greater emphasis on collaboration, constituent contact, hearings, letters, and so forth. There is a generally close relationship between research and arguments, however. Research has an over-all mean rating of 7.4, slightly lower than for arguments, but still higher than the rating for other techniques.

Testifying at Hearings

In contrast with presentation of one's case to a single person, most lobbyists rated testifying at hearings somewhat lower. Only 24 gave it a rating of 10, and the mean for the entire group was 6.55. The rank orders shown in Tables 33.1 and 33.2 disclose that hearings are ranked up close to arguments and research by

TABLE 33.2   Rank Order of Mean Ratings of Direct Personal Communication by Relation of Lobbyist to His Employer

Role of Lobbyist	Personal Presentation of Arguments		Presentation of Research Results		Testifying at Hearings	
	Rank	Mean Rating	Rank	Mean Rating	Rank	Mean Rating
Trade association executive (N = 19)	1	8.2	2*	6.9	5	6.0
Officer of organization (N = 6)	1†	9.0	1†	9.0	6	6.5
Legislative relations staff (N = 12)	2	7.8	7	6.2	4	7.0
Legislative and executive relations staff (N = 17)	1	9.1	4	7.2	2	7.4
Washington representative (N = 16)	1	9.1	2	7.9	3‡	6.3
Lawyer, legal firm (N = 8)	2	7.5	3	7.0	1	7.6
Lawyer, free lance (N = 13)	1	8.1	2	7.5	3	5.7
General counsel in organization (N = 3)	1	9.7	2	8.3	6	6.3
Public relations counsel (N = 2)	4§	5.0	2‖	6.5	2‖	6.5
Lobbyist entrepreneur (N = 3)	1	10.0	2	9.3	3	6.0

* Tied with collaboration with other groups.
† Personal presentation of arguments and presentation of research results were tied.
‡ Tied with contact by constituent.
§ Tied with public relations campaigns.
‖ Presentation of research results and testifying at hearings were tied.

most groups. They are about on a par with collaboration and constituent contact. Interestingly, the mean rating of hearings by corporations was only 4.7, lower than that of any other group; yet the rank order was 3 (above all other techniques except arguments and research), so one might surmise that corporation representatives have a generally more pessimistic view of most of the remaining techniques than do the people representing other kinds of organization.

Since hearings are formal procedures available to nearly anyone wanting to get his point of view before Congress and require only a single presentation, why is it that they are not the clearly preferred technique? Most lobbyists perceive that members of Congress give sporadic attention, at best, to hearing testimony. Furthermore, they are aware that many members of committees have already made up their mind before the hearings begin and there is little the lobbyist can say that will influence them. Another factor is that many hearings are held when only one member of the committee is present, to say nothing of the absence from hearings of all the other members of the House who are not on the committee. Although printed hearing records are

available to members of Congress (also to the public), the average member does not have the time to read them. Despite the limitations of this means of communication, most lobbyists dare not forgo an invitation to go on record favoring or opposing a particular course of action. There is always the possibility that some decision-maker will read their testimony; it is an opportunity for some free publicity; and it is a useful way for the lobbyist to demonstrate to the membership that he is earning his salary. In other words, most lobbyists feel they are expected to testify, or have someone from their group testify, and therefore they nearly always do.

Communication Through Intermediaries

Although lobbying connotes personal representation before government, a far-reaching effort to influence policy-making must include communication with decision-makers through intermediaries. The intermediaries chosen almost invariably have some special relationship to the decision-maker, either a constituent relationship or a close personal relationship. Constituents can be urged to communicate with government in two basic ways. Voting is an indirect but very effective medium of communication. Even if an endorsed candidate does not win, a strong showing of votes indicates the desires and power potential of a large bloc of the incumbent's constituents. The second type of communication is the conventional written or oral message transmitted from the citizen to people in government. Communications through intermediaries are, like the personal presentations of the lobbyist, also designed to communicate facts, arguments, and power. They are especially instrumental in communicating power.

Contact by Constituent and Friend

If the lobbyist believes that he will have difficulty getting an appointment with an elected official or that the official will listen with a closed ear, he may attempt to communicate through a constituent whom he thinks the official respects. The constituent may be asked to phone the officeholder and set up an appointment for the lobbyist, or he may be asked to present the case himself. Sometimes the constituent hastens to Washington and spends a few days calling on his representatives.

The constituent is generally preferred over other intermediaries such as close friends of the decision-maker. This is because many lobbyists feel that the power relationship be-

tween constituent and officeholder more adequately ensures receptiveness to the communication. This is reflected in tactic rankings. The representatives of large membership groups with potential political power (big labor, farm, big trade, church, and humanitarian) give constituent contact a much higher rating then friend contact; where the representatives of other groups give them more equal ratings. Also the highest ratings for constituent contact are given by legislative relations people whose jobs take them into closest contact with Congress. The over-all picture is reported in Table 33.3, where we see that 24 lobbyists gave a rating of 10 to contact by a constituent, whereas only 5 rated contact by a friend that highly. The mean rating for contact by a constituent was 5.9, and for a friend it was only 3.76. The difference in evaluation introduced by the political-power variable is also reflected in the greater variance shown for the constituent-contact rating than for the friend-contact rating.

Letter and Telegram Campaigns

A time-honored lobbying technique is the stimulation of a mass letter-writing and telegram campaign from constituents to their representatives. Most people in Congress are skilled at spotting form letters or telegrams

TABLE 33.3   Ratings of Communication through Intermediaries: Number in Each Category

Rating	Contact by Constituents	Contact by Close Friend	Letter and Telegram Campaigns	Public Relations Campaigns	Publicizing Voting Records
0	14	26	20	21	49
1	3	5	6	2	8
2	6	8	6	2	12
3	8	13	5	3	5
4	2	3	7	2	4
5	11	15	19	15	8
6	7	6	1	2	2
7	4	6	7	11	4
8	8	6	17	17	2
9	12	5	4	5	2
10	24	5	7	17	2
Median	5.79	2.77	4.29	6.14	1.00
Mean	5.90	3.76	4.55	5.55	2.05
No response*	15	16	15	17	16

* Includes 13 in the total sample of 114 who were not interviewed at all.

which are inspired by some organization. They are likely to ignore or discount such a campaign on the ground that it does not accurately represent sentiment in the constituency; on the other hand, if the letters come in a deluge, they must pay attention because of the political weight they represent. Some members may move to counteract the campaign by sending out a mailing to the constituents in an attempt to inform them about the member's position, or they may request an opposing organization to turn out an equal or greater number of letters on the other side, leaving the representative free to vote as he chooses. Lobbyists are aware of these barriers to letters, and the mass campaign is not as widely used as it once was. Those who do use a letter or telegram campaign are generally careful to instruct their people to write each communication individually, speaking their personal thoughts on the subject. The lobbyist's calculation is that the representative will heed such a communication as a true reflection of sentiment.

There was a good deal of variation in the way lobbyists evaluated letter campaigns (Table 33.3): 20 gave it a 0 and 7 gave it a 10. Big labor and big farm lobbyists gave it higher rankings than other lobbyists did. This suggests that organizations with a mass membership enabling them to turn out thousands of letters are more likely to believe that the tactic is effective. Corporation representatives and lobbyists for foreign governments or firms, with no mass membership behind them, ranked letters below the average. Those more intimately associated with a given organization (officers and staff) tended to rank letters higher than those in a more peripheral relationship (lawyers, "PR" men, etc.).

Public Relations Campaigns

A very expensive and indirect method of communication is the public relations campaign. The supposition is that if enough people favor the viewpoint of the organization sponsoring the campaign, this viewpoint and the power behind it will be communicated in various ways to Congress and the administration. It is also hoped that the campaign will

have long-range effects on the voting behavior of the public and thus find policy expression through the selection of governmental decision-makers. Since the effects of a PR campaign are so diffuse and delayed, they are extraordinarily difficult to measure. This is reflected in the wide variance in the lobbyists' ratings: 17 gave it a rating of 10, and 21 gave it a rating of 0 (Table 33.3).

The over-all mean rating for PR campaigns was 5.55, slightly higher than for letter campaigns; yet the pattern of response was very similar to that for letter campaigns. Mass-membership farm and labor lobbyists gave it the highest ratings, while church and humanitarian and foreign government or firm lobbyists gave it the lowest. Lawyers gave it a lower rating than did those closely tied into an organization, while officers of organizations gave it the hghest rating. It is interesting that some lobbyists felt that the tactic had utility, even though they were not sure their message was getting through to the public, not to mention getting from the public back to the decision-makers. They reasoned that the decision-makers are quite likely to conclude that the campaign is very persuasive and convincing many people how they should vote. Therefore, the decision-maker may possibily alter his behavior in the desired way in anticipation of the reaction from his constituents, without receiving direct communication from many of them.

Publicizing Voting Records

Like the public relations campaign, the publicizing of voting records is a device for stimulating communications from the people to their representatives. (Both tactics are also used to generate political power, which has utility for keeping open channels of communication to decision-makers.) Organizations which have considerable power at the polls (labor, farm, and large citizens' organizations) believe that the method is moderately efficacious, while lobbyists from nearly all the other groups rate the method as almost worthless. In fact, many lobbyists actually view the method as dangerous, since a member of Congress whose voting record has been reported unfavorably is likely to resent it and may close the door to them in the future. Many lobbyists and members of Congress felt that voting records are misleading because they do not accurately assess the over-all performance of a member.

Opening Communication Channels

We noted above that it was just as important to the lobbyist to keep his channels of communication to decision-makers open as it was to transmit the communications themselves. Lobbyists give a lot of attention to this problem and guide their behavior so as to create and maintain the open channel. There is a recognized *quid pro quo* relationship between lobbyist and decision-maker. The lobbyist can provide information and perform certain chores that the decision-maker desires. Several of the people in Congress that I interviewed reported that they lined up lobby groups as reinforcements to strengthen their side in policy battles. This practice is so prevalent that it is difficult to discover who is using whom in most instances. The *quid pro quo* for providing services that the decision-maker wants is that he will lend a sympathetic ear when the lobbyist has a problem he wants to present. Mutual confidence is the lubrication which ensures the smooth working of this relationship. The official decision-maker has the upper hand, however, in that he alone has the power to pass out the policy rewards that the lobbyist wants and can turn to many alternative sources for the services he wants. Access and a confidential relationship with officials are so crucial to the task of the lobbyist that most astute lobbyists would not consider jeopardizing them in any way. Many decision-makers use their superior position to guide their relationships with lobbyists and will specify the conditions under which lobbyists are welcome. If the lobbyist does not conform to these expectations, the decision-maker will discard him and turn to someone on whom he can depend. Interestingly, many lobbyists welcome these prescriptions for access because they give structure to a highly unstructured role and give them security in job performance.

One specific result of this relationship is that

very little inaccurate information is presented by lobbyists to public officials. The harried decision-maker frequently utilizes information provided by lobbyists, sometimes without double-checking, in speeches or other public communications. If the information should later prove to be false or biased to the point of serious distortion, the decision-maker is publicly embarrassed and is likely to retaliate by cutting off further access sought by the delinquent lobbyist. Another facet of this relationship is that lobbyists generally are scrupulously careful not to disclose things which are told to them in confidence by a decision-maker; the cost of disclosure would be the cutting off of access.

Entertaining and Parties

One of the popular conceptions of the lobbying process is that most lobbyists depend on entertainment and parties to keep open the channels of communication to decision-makers. The assumption here is that the official will be grateful for the favor and therefore will be receptive to the communications of the lobbyist. Almost the reverse is true. Officials feel they must attend a certain number of "required" social events, and this, coupled with other responsibilities, places them under such time pressure that an evening spent at home with the family seems like a gift. Under such conditions, an invitation by a lobbyist to "do the town" is anything but welcome. Lobbyists are aware that entertainment is an imposition, and it is used very little as a device to keep the channels of communication open.

Nearly all the lobbyists rated both techniques very low (Table 33.4.) Forty-seven gave a rating of 0 to entertainment, and the mean for the group was 1.59. Interestingly, officers of organizations, who generally have more prestige than the average lobbyist and a less restricted expense account, gave entertainment a higher rating than did those in other roles, but even here the mean was only 2.8. Giving a party was felt to have even less utility; 56 rated it 0 and the mean was only 1.24. Only foreign governments or firms and church and humanitarian representatives ranked it much above next-to-the-last place.

TABLE 33.4 Rating of Methods of Opening Communication Channels: Number in Each Category

Rating	Entertaining	Giving a Party	Bribery	Contributing Money	Campaign Work	Collaboration with Other Groups
0	47	56	98	58	54	12
1	15	14	0	5	6	5
2	14	11	0	5	7	0
3	7	3	0	8	6	6
4	4	5	0	7	3	3
5	4	7	0	4	5	13
6	1	0	0	2	1	4
7	5	1	0	1	5	13
8	2	2	0	3	5	12
9	0	0	0	4	1	11
10	0	0	1	2	6	20
Median	1.17	.88	.51	.85	.92	6.50
Mean	1.59	1.24	.10	1.88	2.28	6.16
No response*	15	15	15	15	15	15

* Includes 13 in the total sample of 114 who were not interviewed at all.

Direct Bribery

Contrary to another popular conception, lobbyists have no faith whatsoever in bribery as a device for keeping channels open. Only one lobbyist rated bribery any higher than 0, and he did so with the comment, "If this assumes that the member of Congress is bribable, in that case I'd say 10. There is no surer way to get him to come along with your point of view." But even he was aware that nearly all members of Congress are not open to bribes. A few lobbyists claimed to know of bribes that had been passed, but in every instance their knowledge was second- or third-hand. One Congressman reported that a bribe had been offered him in the guise of a campaign contribution, but, as a result, he reported it to the Justice Department and voted against the lobbyist.

Most lobbyists recognize that the method is not effective and will not have anything to do with it.[5] Most believed that nearly all members of Congress are unbribable. Also, most viewed it as a dangerous gamble, since it could well turn a member of Congress against

the donor instead of producing the desired good will. An official whose ideological rudder is so vacillating that he can be bribed can also be bribed by the other side and does not constitute a very safe investment. Another controlling factor here, according to respondents, is that keeping a bribe secret is an exceedingly difficult task in a "rumor factory" like Washington.

Contributing Political Money and Campaign Work

Since nearly all elected officials have a profound respect for political power, the lobbyist who represents a group with power at the polls finds there is a distinct advantage in keeping channels of communication open to these officials. The tactics of publicizing voting records and conducting public relations campaigns, discussed above, have some utility in producing political power. But what do lobbyists think of direct political actions, such as having members of their groups contribute political money or do volunteer work in the campaign? Both tactics were generally rated quite low, but campaign work, with a mean of

[5] It should be noted that some use is made of small gifts and favors by lobbyists; these are given more to the staffs of decision-makers than to decision-makers themselves, because staff members also have considerable control over access. It is very difficult conceptually to draw firm lines between bribes, campaign contributions, gifts, and favors. Rather than explore such a conceptual tangle in this paper, suffice it to say that the remarks in this section refer primarily to direct bribery.

2.28, usually was ranked higher than political money (mean, 1.88). The higher mean for campaign work can be traced, in part, to the higher rating given to this tactic than to money by the representatives of small labor organizations.

Collaboration with Other Groups

The tactic of collaborating with other groups in planning strategy and making presentations is difficult to categorize, since it has aspects of direct communication, communication through intermediaries, and keeping communication channels open. The tactic is generally highly prized (over-all mean of 6.16), although there was considerable variance in the ratings (see Table 33.4). Those whose lobbyist roles are closest to a given organization (executive, officer, staff) rate it higher than do lawyers and Washington representatives who generally represent more than one group. In fact, full-time legislative relations persons give it the highest ranking, even above presentation of arguments.

Several factors enter into an evaluation of collaboration. From the lobbyist point of view, it distributes the work load so that it is possible to communicate with more people on more issues. This is especially helpful for those groups with a wide range of policy interests. Lobbyists with common interests meet regularly to discuss strategy and exchange information. Not only does collaboration increase the volume and skill of communications, but it also communicates the enhanced power, in terms of numbers of committed persons, that lies behind a policy position. The member of Congress also welcomes joint presentations, because it means a saving of work and tension for him. Congress spends endless hours resolving controversies, and it is a welcome relief to have a controversy settled before it reaches that body.[6] Legislators are so relieved not to have to take a position favoring one group over another that any proposal which carries the backing of most potentially antagonistic groups will almost always be approved.

Summary

The most adequate explanation of the impact of the lobbying process on governmental decision-making would come from a detailed examination of all the influences or pressures producing the behavior of decision-makers. The social scientist is not equipped conceptually or methodologically at this stage to handle such a research problem. On the other hand, he can make some headway in analyzing the lobbying process by viewing it as a communication process. Communication is not necessarily complete when stimuli have been presented by a lobbyist; he must also attempt to guage the receptivity of the decision-maker and, hopefully, get the message through to him. A communication model does not explain all the variables involved in any given decision, but it does include all the variables involved in the lobbying process. The lobbyist has finished his job when he has communicated in the most effective way possible. He cannot control the workings of the decision-maker's mind unless he can remake his personality or, alternatively, get him thrown out of office and replaced by another person. Not only does a communication model encompass the lobby process, but it is also the simplest explanation which accounts for the known evidence.

In general, lobbyists favor face-to-face conversations for the communication of facts and the arguments which support them. However, competition for the limited attention of decision-makers in recent years has forced lobbyists more and more to seek access through intermediaries, especially the constituents of elected officials who have a power relationship to the decision-maker. In order to ensure receptivity, lobbyists also attempt in other ways to communicate subtly the political power behind their groups. Preservation of open communication channels to decision-makers is of such prime importance to lobbyists that the possible cutting off of access can be used as a sanction forcing lobbyists to behave in ways that the decision-makers find desirable.

[6] Corroborating evidence from Vermont is reported in Oliver Garceau and Corinne Silverman, "A Pressure Group and the Pressured," *The American Political Science Review*, XLVIII (1954), 672–691.

SECTION V

REEDUCATIVE STRATEGIES

34. T-Groups for Organizational Effectiveness

Chris Argyris*

What causes dynamic, flexible, and enthusiastically committed executive teams to become sluggish and inflexible as time goes by? Why do they no longer enjoy the intrinsic challenge of their work, but become motivated largely by wages and executive bonus plans?

Why do executives become conformists as a company becomes older and bigger? Why do they resist saying what they truly believe—even when it is in the best interests of the company?

How is it possible to develop a top-management team that is constantly innovating and taking risks?

Is it inevitable that we get things done only when we create crises, check details, arouse fears, and penalize and reward in ways that inadvertently create "heroes" and "bums" among our executive group?

Ask managers why such problems as these exist and their answers typically will be abstract and fatalistic:

"It's inevitable in a big business."
"Because of human nature."
"I'll be damned if I know, but every firm has these problems."
"They are part of the bone and fabric of the company."

Statements like these *are* true. Such problems *are* ingrained into corporate life. But in recent years there has evolved a new way of helping executives develop new inner resources which enable them to mitigate these organizational ills. I am referring to *laboratory education*—or "sensitivity training" as it is sometimes called. Particularly in the form of "T-groups," it has rapidly become one of the most controversial educational experiences now available to management. Yet, as I will advocate in this article, if laboratory education is conducted competently, and if the right people attend, it can be a very powerful educational experience.

How does laboratory education remedy the problems I have mentioned? By striving to expose and modify certain values held by typical executives, values which, unless modified and added to, serve to impair interpersonal effectiveness. As Exhibit 1 explains, these values are ingrained in the pyramidal structure of the business enterprise. The exhibit summarizes several basic causes of management ineffectiveness as isolated by three studies: (1) in a large corporate division—30,000 employees, grossing $500 million per year; (2) a

Reprinted in part from Chris Argyris, "T-Groups for Organizational Effectiveness," *Harvard Business Review*, Vol. 42 (March–April 1964), pp. 60–74. © 1964 by the President and Fellows of Harvard College; all rights reserved.

* Beach Professor of Administrative Science, Yale University.

medium-size company—5,000 employees, grossing in excess of $50 million per year; and (3) a small company—300 employees. The results of these studies are reported in detail elsewhere.[1]

Exhibit I. The Pyramidal Values

There are certain values about effective human relationships that are inherent in the pyramidal structure of the business organization and which successful executives (understandably) seem to hold. Values are learned commands which, once internalized, coerce human behavior in specific directions. This is why an appreciation of these values is basic in understanding behavior.

What are these "pyramidal" values? I would explain them this way.

1. The important human relations—the crucial ones—are those which are related to achieving the organization's objective, i.e., getting the job done, as for example:

> We are here to manufacture shoes, that is our business, those are the important human relationships; if you have anything that can influence those human relationships, fine.

2. Effectiveness in human relationships increases as behavior becomes more rational, logical, and clearly communicated, but effectiveness decreases as behavior becomes more emotional. Let me illustrate by citing a typical conversation:

> "Have you ever been in a meeting where there is a lot of disagreement?"
>
> "All the time."
>
> "Have you ever been in a meeting when the disagreement got quite personal?"
>
> "Well, yes I have, but not very often."
>
> "What would you do if you were the leader of this group?"
>
> "I would say, 'Gentlemen, let's get back to the fact,' or I would say, 'Gentlemen, let's keep personalities out of this.' If it really got bad, I would wish it were five o'clock so I could call it off, and then I would talk to the men individually."

3. Human relationships are most effectively motivated by carefully defined direction, authority, and control, as well as appropriate rewards and penalties that emphasize rational behavior and achievement of the objective.

If these are the values held by most executives, what are the consequences? To the extent that executives believe in these organizational values, the following changes have been found to happen.

(1) There is a *decrease* in receiving and giving information about executives' interpersonal impact on each other. Their interpersonal difficulties tend to be either suppressed or disguised and brought up as rational, technical, intellectual problems. As a result, they may find it difficult to develop competence in dealing with feelings and interpersonal relations. There is a corresponding decrease in their ability to own up to or be responsible for their ideas, feelings, and values. Similarly there is a dropping off of experimentation and risk-taking with new ideas and values.

(2) Along with the decrease in owning, openness, risk-taking, there is an *increase* in the denial of feelings, in closeness to new ideas, and in need for stability (i.e., "don't rock the boat"). As a result, executives tend to find themselves in situations where they are not adequately aware of the human problems, where they do not solve them in such a way that they remain solved without deteriorating the problem-solving process. Thus, if we define interpersonal competence as (a) being aware of human problems, (b) solving them in such a way that they remain solved, without deteriorating the problem-solving process, these values serve to decrease interpersonal competence.

(3) As the executives' interpersonal competence decreases, conformity, mistrust, and dependence, especially on those who are in power, increase. Decision making becomes *less effective*, because people withhold many of these ideas, especially those that are inno-

---

[1] Chris Argyris, *Interpersonal Competence and Organizational Effectiveness* (Homewood, Illinois, Richard D. Irwin, Inc., 1962); *Understanding Organizational Behavior* (Homewood, Illinois, The Dorsey Press, Inc., 1960); and *Explorations in Human Competence* (manuscript, Department of Industrial Administration, Yale University, New Haven, 1964).

vative and risky, and organizational defenses (such as management by crisis, management by detail, and through fear) *increase.* So do such "protective" activities as "JIC" files (just in case the president asks), "information" meetings (to find out what the opposition is planning), and executive politicking.

If this analysis is valid, then we must alter executives' values if we are to make the system more effective. The question arises as to what changes can and *should* be made in these values.

But since executives are far from unknowledgeable, why have they clung to these pyramidal values? First, because they are *not necessarily wrong.* Indeed, they are a necessary part of effective human relationships. The difficulty is that alone they are not enough. By themselves they tend to lead to the above consequence. What is needed is an additional set of values for the executives to hold. Specifically there are three.

1. The important human relationships are not only those related to achieving the organization's objectives but those related to maintaining the organization's internal system and adapting to the environment, as well.

2. Human relationships increase in effectiveness as *all* the relevant behavior (rational and interpersonal) becomes conscious, discussable, and controllable. (The rationality of feelings is as crucial as that of the mind.)

3. In addition to direction, controls, and rewards and penalties, human relationships are most effectively influenced through authentic relationships, internal commitment, psychological success, and the process of confirmation. (These terms are clarified in the body of the article.)

Change Through Education

But how does one change an executive's values? One way is by a process of re-education. First there is an unfreezing of the old values, next the development of the new values, and finally a freezing of the new ones.

In order to begin the unfreezing process, the executives must experience the true ineffectiveness of the old values. This means they must have a "gut" experience of how incomplete the old values are. One way to

achieve this is to give them a task to accomplish in situations where their power, control, and organizational influences are minimized. The ineffectiveness of the old values, if our analysis is correct, should then become apparent.

A second requirement of re-education arises from the fact that the overwhelming number of educational processes available (e.g., lecture, group discussion, and the like) are based on the pyramidal values. Each lecture or seminar at a university has clearly defined objectives and is hopefully staffed by a rational, articulate teacher who is capable of controlling, directing, and appropriately rewarding and penalizing the students. But, as I have just suggested, these represent some of the basic causes of the problems under study. The educator is in a bind. If he teaches by the traditional methods, he is utilizing the very values that he is holding up to be incomplete and ineffective.

To make matters more difficult, if the re-educational process is to be effective, it is necessary to create a *culture* in which the new values can be learned, practiced, and protected until the executives feel confident in using them. Such a culture would be one which is composed of people striving to develop authentic relationships and psychological success. Briefly, *authentic relationships* exist when an individual can behave in such a way as to increase his self-awareness and esteem and, at the same time, provide an opportunity for others to do the same. *Psychological success* is the experience of realistically challenging situations that tax one's capacities. Both are key components of executive competence.

The creation of a re-educational process where the unfreezing of the old values, relearning of the new values, and refreezing of the new values under primary control of the students, embedded in a culture that is rarely found in our society, is an extremely difficult task. Yet an approach to fulfilling these requirements is offered by laboratory education.

Probably because of its novelty, laboratory education has become one of the most talked about, experimented with, lauded, and questioned educational experiences for top executives. The interest of top executives has been so great that the National Training Laboratories (a nonprofit educational organization which administers most of the laboratories) has had to increase the programs many fold in the past ten years.[2]

Any educational experience that is as novel as laboratory education is destined to be controversial. And this is good because reasoned controversy can be the basis for corrections, refinements, and expansions of the process. Research (unfortunately not enough) is being conducted under the auspices of the National Training Laboratories and at various universities such as the University of California, Case Institute of Technology, Columbia, George Washington, Harvard, M.I.T., Michigan, Texas, and Yale, to name a few.

Aims of Program

The first step in a laboratory program is to help the executives teach themselves as much about their behavior as possible. To do so they create their own laboratory in which to experiment. This is why the educational process has been called "laboratory education." The strategy of an experiment begins with a dilemma. A dilemma occurs when, for a given situation, there is no sound basis for selecting among alternatives, or there is no satisfactory alternative to select, or when habitual actions are no longer effective.

What do people do when confronted with a dilemma? Their immediate reaction is to try out older methods of behaving with which they are secure, or else to seek guidance from an "expert." In this way, the anxiety so invariably associated with not knowing what to do can be avoided. In the laboratory, then, the anticipated first reactions by participants to a dilemma are to try traditional ways of responding.

Only when conventional or traditional ways of dealing with a dilemma have been tried—unsuccessfully—are conditions ripe for inventive action. Now people are ready to think, to shed old notions because they have not worked, to experiment, and to explore new ways of reacting to see if they will work. The period when old behavior is being abandoned and when new behavior has yet to be invented to replace it is an "unfrozen" period, at times having some of the aspects of a crisis. It is surrounded by uncertainty and confusion.[3]

Fullest learning from the dilemma-invention situation occurs when two additional types of action are taken:

One is feedback, the process by which members acquaint one another with their own characteristic ways of feeling and reacting in a dilemma-invention situation. Feedback aids in evaluating the consequences of actions that have been taken as a result of the dilemma situation. By "effective" feedback I mean the kind of feedback which minimizes the probability of the receiver or sender becoming defensive and maximizes his opportunity to "own" values, feelings, and attitudes. By "own" I mean being aware of and accepting responsibility for one's behavior.

The final step in the dilemma-invention cycle is generalizing about the total sequence to get a comprehensive picture of the "common case." When this is done, people are searching to see to what extent behavior observed under laboratory conditions fits outside situations. If generalization is not attempted, the richness of dilemma-invention learning is "lost."

T for Training

The core of most laboratories is the T (for training) group.[4] This is most difficult to describe in a few words. Basically it is a group

[2] For information regarding the training laboratories that are available, one may write to Dr. Leland P. Bradford, National Training Laboratories, National Education Association, 1201 10th Street Northwest, Washington, D.C.

[3] See Robert K. Blake and Jane S. Mouton, *The Managerial Grid* (Houston, Texas, Gulf Publishing Co., 1963).

[4] For a detailed summary of research related to laboratory education, see Dorothy Stock, "A Summary of Research on Training Groups," in *T-Group Theory and Laboratory Method; Innovation in Education*, edited by Leland Bradford, Kenneth Benne, and Jack Gibb (New York, John Wiley & Sons, Inc., 1964).

experience designed to provide maximum possible opportunity for the individuals to expose their behavior, give and receive feedback, experiment with new behavior, and develop everlasting awareness and acceptance of self and others. The T-group, when effective, also provides individuals with the opportunity to learn the nature of effective group functioning. They are able to learn how to develop a group that achieves specific goals with minimum possible human cost.

The T-group becomes a learning experience that most closely approximates the values of the laboratory regarding the use of leadership, rewards, penalties, and information in the development of effective groups. It is in the T-group that one learns how to diagnose his own behavior, to develop effective leadership behavior and norms for decision making that truly protect the "wild duck."

Role of Educator

In these groups, some of the learning comes from the educator, but most of it from the members interacting with each other. The "ground rules" the group establishes for feedback are important. With the help of the educator, the group usually comes to see the difference between providing help and attempting to control or punish a member; between analyzing and interpreting a member's adjustment (which is not helpful) and informing him of the impact it has on others. Typically, certain features of everyday group activity are blurred or removed. The educator, for example, does not provide the leadership which a group of "students" would normally expect. This produces a kind of "power vacuum" and a great deal of behavior which, in time, becomes the basis of learning.

There is no agenda, except as the group provides it. There are no norms of group operation (such as *Robert's Rules of Order*) except as the group decides to adopt them. For some time the experience is confusing, tension-laden, frustrating for most participants. But these conditions have been found to be conducive to learning. Naturally, some individuals learn a great deal, while others resist the whole process. It is rare, however, for an individual to end a two-week experience feeling that he has learned nothing.

Usually the T-group begins with the educator making explicit that it is designed to help human beings to—

explore their values and their impact on others,

determine if they wish to modify their old values and desire new ones,

develop awareness of how groups can inhibit as well as facilitate human growth and decision making.

Thus a T-group does not begin without an objective, as far as the educator is concerned. It has a purpose, and this purpose, for the educator, is emotionally and intellectually clear.

However, the educator realizes that the purpose is, at the moment, only intellectually clear to the members. Thus, to begin, the educator will probably state that he has no specific goals in mind for the group. Moreover, he offers no specific agenda, no regulations, no rules, and so on. The group is created so its members can determine their own leadership, goals, and rules.

There is very little that is nondirective about a T-group educator's role. He is highly concerned with growth, and he acts in ways that he hopes will enhance development. He is nondirective, however, in the sense that he does not require others to accept these conditions. As one member of the T-group, he will strive sincerely and openly to help establish a culture that can lead to increased authentic relationships and interpersonal competence.

However, he realizes that he can push those in the group just so far. If he goes too far, he will fall into the trap of masterminding their education. This is a trap in which group members might like to see him fall, since it would decrease their uncomfortableness and place him in a social system similar (in values) to their own. In other words, his silence, the lack of predefined objectives, leadership, agenda, rules, and so on, are not designed to be malicious or hurt people. True, these experiences may hurt somewhat, but the hypothesis is that the pain is "in the service of growth."

At this point, let me assume that you are a member of such a T-group, so that I can tell you what you are likely to experience.

Action and Reaction

At the outset you are likely to expect that the educator will lead you. This expectation is understandable for several reasons:

1. An educator in our culture tends to do precisely this.
2. Because of the newness of the situation, the members may also fear that they are not competent to deal with it effectively. They naturally turn to the educator for assistance. It is common in our culture that when one member of a group has more information than the others as to how to cope with the new, difficult situation, he is expected by the others, *if he cares for them*, to help them cope with the new situation. For example, if I am in a cave with ten other people who are lost and I know how to get out, it would be from their viewpoint the height of noncaring for me to fail to help them get out.
3. Finally, the members may turn to the educator because they have not as yet developed much trust for each other.

The educator may believe it is helpful, during the early stages of a T-group, to tell you that he understands why you feel dependent on him. But he will also add that he believes that learning can take place more effectively if you first develop an increasing sense of trust of one another and a feeling that you can learn from one another.

In my case, when I act as the educator for a T-group, I freely admit that silence is not typical of me and that I need to talk, to be active, to participate. In fact, I may even feel a mild hostility if I am in a situation in which I cannot participate in the way that I desire. Thus, anything you (members) can do to help me "unfreeze" by decreasing your dependence on me would be deeply appreciated. I add that I realize that this is not easy and that I will do my share.

Typically, the members begin to realize that the educator supports those individuals who show early signs of attempting to learn. This is especially true for those who show signs of being open, experimentally minded, and willing to take risks by exposing their behavior. How are these qualities recognized?

There are several cues that are helpful. First, there is the individual who is not highly upset by the initial ambiguity of the situation and who is ready to begin to learn. One sign of such an individual is one who can be open about the confusion that he is experiencing. He is able to own up to his feelings of being confused, without becoming hostile toward the educator or the others. Such an individual is willing to look at his and others' behavior under stress, diagnose it, and attempt to learn from it. Some of these individuals even raise questions about other members' insistance that the educator should get them out of the ambiguous situation.

Some members, on the other hand, react by insisting that the educator has created the ambiguity just to be hostile. You will find that the educator will encourage them to express their concern and hostility as well as help them to see the impact that this behavior (i.e., hostility) is having on him. There are two reasons for the educator's intervention: (1) to reinforce (with feelings) the fact that he is not callous about their feelings and that he is not consciously attempting to be hostile; (2) to unfreeze others to explore their hostility toward him or toward each other. Such explorations can provide rich data for the group to diagnose and from which to learn.

Problem of Mimicking

As the group continues, some members begin to realize that the educator's behavior now may serve for what it is. That is, it may be as valid a model as the educator can manifest of how he would attempt (a) to help create an effective group, and (b) to integrate himself into that group so that he becomes as fully functioning a member as possible. The model is his; he admits owning it, but he is *not* attempting to "sell" it to others or in any way to coerce them to own it.

You may wonder if viewing the educator as a source of "model behavior" would not lead you simply to *mimic* him. (In the technical literature this is discussed as "identification with the leader," or "leader modeling behavior.") Although this may be the case, we should not forget that as you begin to "unfreeze" your previous values and behavior, you will find yourself in the situation of throwing away the old and having nothing new that is concrete and workable. This tends to create states of vacillation, confusion, anxiety, ambivalence, and so on.[5] These states in turn may induce you to "hang on" to the old with even greater tenacity. To begin to substitute the new behavior for the old, you will feel a need to see (1) that you can carry out the new behavior effectively and (2) that the new behavior leads to the desired results.[6]

Under these conditions the members usually try out any bit of behavior that represents the "new." Experimentation not only is sanctioned; it is rewarded. One relatively safe way to experiment is to "try out the educator's behavior." It is at this point that the individual is mimicking. And he should feel free to mimic and *to talk about the mimicking and explore it openly.* Mimicking is helpful if you are aware of and accept the fact that you do not *own* the behavior, for the behavior with which you are experimenting is the educator's. If the educator is not anxious about the mimicking, the member may begin safely to explore the limits of the new behavior. He may also begin to see whether or not the educator's behavior is, for him, realistic.

Individual vs. Group

At the outset the educator tends to provide that assistance which is designated to help the members to—

become aware of their present (usually) low potential for establishing authentic relationships,

become more skillful in providing and receiving nonevaluative descriptive feedback,

minimize their own and others' defensiveness,

become increasingly able to experience and own up to their feelings.

Although interpersonal assistance is crucial, it is also important that the T-group not be limited to such interventions. After the members receive adequate feedback from one another as to their inability to create authentic relationships, they will tend to want to become more effective in their interpersonal relationships. It is at this point that they will need to learn that group structure and dynamics deeply influence the probability of increasing the authenticity of their interpersonal relations. For example:

> As soon as the members realize that they must become more open with those feelings that typically they have learned to hide, they need to establish group norms to sanction the expression of these feelings. Also, if members find it difficult in the group to express their important feelings, this difficulty will tend to be compounded if they feel they must "rush" their contribution and "say something quick," lest someone else take over the communication channels. Ways must be developed by which members are able to use their share of the communication channels. Also, group norms are required that sanction silence and thought, so that members do not feel coerced to say something, before they have thought it through, out of fear that they will not have an opportunity to say anything later.

An example of the interrelationship between interpersonal and group factors may be seen in the problems of developing leadership in a group. One of the recurring problems in the early stages of a T-group is the apparent need on the part of members to appoint a leader or a chairman. Typically, this need is rationalized as a group need because "without an appointed leader a group cannot be effective." For example, one member said, "Look, I think the first thing we need is to elect a leader. Without a leader we are going to get nowhere fast." Another added, "Brother, you are right. Without leadership, there is chaos. People hate to take responsibility and without a leader they will goof off."

There are several ways that your group might consider for coping with this problem,

---

[5] Roger Barker, Beatrice A. Wright, and Mollie R. Gonick, "Adjustment to Physical Handicap and Illness," *Social Science Research Council Bulletin 55,* 1946, pp. 19–54.

[6] Ronald Lippitt, Jeanne Watson, and Bruce Westley, *The Dynamics of Planned Change* (New York, Harcourt, Brace & World, Inc., 1958).

each of which provides important but different kinds of learning:

One approach is to see this as a group problem. How does leadership arise and remain helpful in a group? This level of learning is important and needs to be achieved.

Another possibility is for the group members to explore the underlying assumptions expressed by those individuals who want to appoint leaders. For example, in the case illustrated above, both men began to realize that they were assuming that people "need" appointed leadership because, if left alone, they will not tend to accept responsibility. This implies a lack of confidence in and trust of people. It also implies mistrust of the people around the table. These men were suggesting that without an appointed leader the group will flounder and become chaotic. Someone then took the initiative and suggested that their comments implied a lack of trust of the people around the table. Another individual suggested that another dimension of mistrust might also be operating. He was concerned how he would decide if he could trust the man who might be appointed as the leader. The discussion that followed illustrated to the group the double direction of the problem of trust. Not only do superiors have feelings of mistrust of subordinates, but the latter may also mistrust the former.

One of the defendants of the need for leadership then said, "Look, Mr. B. over there has been trying to say something for half an hour, and hasn't succeeded. If we had a leader, or if he himself were appointed leader temporarily, then he might get his point of view across." Several agreed with the observation. However, two added some further insightful comments. One said, "If we give Mr. B. authority, he will never have to develop his internal strength so that he can get his point across without power behind him." "Moreover," the other added, "if he does get appointed leader, the group will never have to face the problem of how it can help to create the conditions for Mr. B. to express his point of view." Thus we see that attempting to cope with the basic problems of group membership can lead to an exploration of problems of group membership

as well as requirements of effectively functioning groups.

The question of trust, therefore, is a central problem in a T-group, indeed, as it is in any group organization. If this can be solved, then the group has taken an important step in developing authentic relationships. As the degree of trust increases, "functional leadership" will tend to arise spontaneously because individuals in a climate of mutual trust will tend to delegate leadership to those who are most competent for the subject being discussed. In doing so, they also learn an important lesson about effective leadership.

Another kind of learning that usually develops clearly is that the group will not tend to become an effective task-oriented unit without having established effective means to diagnose problems, make decisions, and so on. It is as the group becomes a decision-making unit that the members can "test" the strength and depth of their learning. The pressure and stress of decision making can help to show the degree to which authenticity is apparent rather than real. It can also provide opportunity for further learning, because the members will tend to experience new aspects of themselves as they attempt to solve problems and make decisions.

Further Components

Laboratory education has other components. I have focused in detail on T-groups because of their central role. This by no means describes the total laboratory experience. For example, laboratory education is helpful in diagnosing one's organizational problems.

Diagnosing Problems

When a laboratory program is composed of a group of executives who work in the same firm, the organizational diagnostic experiences are very important. Each executive is asked to come to the laboratory with any agenda or topic that is important to him and to the organization. During the laboratory, he is asked to lead the group in a discussion of the topic. The discussion is taped and observed by the staff (with the knowledge of the members).

WHO LEARNS FROM T-GROUP EXPERIENCES?

People who learn in T-groups seem to possess at least three attributes:

1. A relatively strong ego that is not overwhelmed by internal conflicts.
2. Defenses which are sufficiently low to allow the individual to hear what others say to him (accurately and with minimal threat to his self), without the aid of a professional scanning and filtering system (that is, the therapist, the educator).
3. The ability to communicate thoughts and feelings with minimal distortion. In other words, the operational criterion of minimal threat is that the individual does not tend to distort greatly what he or others say, nor does he tend to condemn others or himself.

This last criterion can be used in helping to select individuals for the T-group experience. *If the individual must distort or condemn himself or others to the point that he is unable to do anything but to continue to distort the feedback that he gives and receives, then he ought not to be admitted to a T-group.*

To put this another way, T-groups, compared to therapy groups, assume a higher degree of health—not illness—that is, a higher degree of self-awareness and acceptance. This is an important point. *Individuals should not be sent to the laboratory if they are highly defensive.* Rather, the relatively healthy individuals capable of learning from others to enhance their degree of effectiveness are the kinds of individuals to be selected to attend.

Once the discussion is completed, the group members listen to themselves on the tape. They analyze the interpersonal and group dynamics that occurred in the making of the decision and study how these factors influenced their decision making. Usually, they hear how they cut each other off, did not listen, manipulated, pressured, created win-lose alternatives, and so on.

Such an analysis typically leads the executives to ask such questions as: Why do we do

this to each other? What do we wish to do about it, if anything?

On the basis of my experience, executives become highly involved in answering these questions. Few hold back from citing interpersonal and organizational reasons why they feel they have to behave as they do. Most deplore the fact that time must be wasted and much energy utilized in this "windmilling" behavior. It is quite frequent for someone to ask, "But if we don't like this, why don't we do something about it?"

Under these conditions, the things learned in the laboratory are intimately interrelated with the everyday "real" problems of the organization. Where this has occurred, the members do not return to the organization with the same degree of bewilderment that executives show who have gone to laboratories full of strangers. In the latter case, it is quite common for the executive to be puzzled as to how he will use what he has learned about human competence when he returns home.[7]

Consultation Groups

Another learning experience frequently used is to break down the participants into groups of four. Sessions are held where each individual has the opportunity both to act as a comsultant giving help and as an individual receiving help. The nature of help is usually related to increasing self-awareness and self-acceptance with the view of enhancing interpersonal competence.

Lectures

As I pointed out above, research information and theories designed to help organizational learning are presented in lectures—typically at a time when it is most clearly related to the learnings that the participants are experiencing in a laboratory.

Role-Playing of "Real" Situations

As a result of the discussions at the laboratory program, many data are collected illustrating situations in which poor communica-

[7] For an example, see Argyris, *Interpersonal Competence and Organizational Effectiveness*, op. cit., Chapter 9.

tions exist, objectives are not being achieved as intended, and so on. It is possible in a laboratory to role-play many of these situations, to diagnose them, to obtain new insights regarding the difficulties, as well as to develop more effective action possibilities. These can be role-played by asking the executives to play their back-home role. For other problems, however, important learnings are gained by asking the superiors to take the subordinates' role.

Developing and Testing Recommendations

In most organizations, executives acknowledge that there are long-range problems that plague an organization, but that they do not have time to analyze them thoroughly in the back-home situation (for example, effectiveness of decentralization). In a laboratory, however, time is available for them to dicuss these problems thoroughly. More important, as a result of their laboratory learnings and with the assistance of the educators, they could develop new-action recommendations. They could diagnose their effectiveness as a group in developing these recommendations—have they really changed; have they really enhanced their effectiveness?

Intergroup Problems

One of the central problems of organizations is the intergroup rivalries that exist among departments. If there is time in a laboratory, this topic should be dealt with. Again, it is best introduced by creating the situation where the executives compete against one another in groups under "win-lose" conditions (i.e., where only one can win and someone must lose).

Correcting Misunderstandings

Any educational activity that is as new and controversial as laboratory education is bound to have misconceptions and misunderstandings built around it. Therefore, I should like to attempt briefly to correct a few of the more commonly heard misunderstandings about laboratory education.

(1) *Laboratory methods in general, and T-groups in particular, are not a set of hidden, manipulative processes by which individuals can be "brainwashed" into thinking, believing, and feeling the way someone might want them to without realizing what is happening to them.*

Central to a laboratory is openness and flexibility in the educational process. It is open in that it is continually described and discussed with the participants as well as constantly open to modification by them.

Along with the de-emphasis of rigidity and emphasis on flexibility, the emphasis is on teaching that kind of knowledge and helping the participants develop those kinds of skills which increase the strength and competence to question, to examine, and to modify. The objectives of a laboratory are to help an individual learn to be able to reject that which he deeply believes is inimical to his self-esteem and to his growth—and this would include, if necessary, the rejection of the laboratory experience.

(2) *A laboratory is not an educational process guided by a staff leader who is covertly in control and by some magic hides this fact from the participants.*

A laboratory means that people come together and create a setting where (as is the case in any laboratory) they generate their own data for learning. This means that they are in control and that any behavior in the laboratory, including the staff member's, is fair game for analysis.

I should like to suggest the hypothesis that if anything is a threat to the participants, it is not the so-called covert control. The experience becomes painful when the participants begin to realize the scope and depth to which the staff is ready "to turn things over to them." Initially this is seen by many participants as the staff abdicating leadership. Those who truly learn come to realize that in doing this the staff is expressing, in a most genuine way, their faith in the potentiality of the participants to develop increasing competence in controlling more of their learning. As this awareness increases, the participants usually begin to see that their cry of "abdication of leadership" is more of a camouflage that hides from them how little they trusted each other and themselves and how over-protected they were in the past from being made to assume some responsibility for their learning.

(3) *The objective of laboratory education is not to suppress conflict and to get everyone to like one another.*

The idea that this is the objective is so patently untrue that I am beginning to wonder if those who use it do not betray their own anxiety more than they describe what goes on in a laboratory. There is no other educational process that I am aware of in which conflict is generated, respected, and cherished. Here conflict, hostility, and frustration become motivations for growth as well as food for learning. It is with these kinds of experiences that participants learn to take risks—the kinds of risks that can lead to an increase in self-esteem. As these experiences are "worked through" and the learnings internalized, participants soon begin to experience a deeper sense of self-awareness and acceptance. These, in turn, lead to an increased awareness and acceptance of others.

And this does *not* necessarily mean liking people. Self-acceptance means that individuals are aware of themselves and care so much about themselves that they open themselves to receiving and giving information (sometimes painful) about their impact on others and others' impact on them, so that they can grow and become more competent.

(4) *Laboratory education does not attempt to teach people to be callous, disrespectful of society, and to dislike those who live a less open life.*

If one truly begins to accept himself, he will be less inclined to condemn nongenuineness in others, but to see it for what it is, a way of coping with a nongenuine world by a person who is (understandably) a nongenuine individual.

(5) *Laboratory education is neither psychoanalysis nor intensive group therapy.*

During the past several years I have been meeting with a group of psychiatrists and clinical psychologists who are trying to differentiate between group therapy and everything else. One problem we discovered is that therapists define therapy as any change. The diffi-

culty with this definition is that it means any change is therapy.

We have concluded that it may be best to conceive of a continuum of "more" or "less" therapy. The more the group deals with unconscious motivations, uses clinical constructs, focuses on "personal past history," and is guided in these activities by the leader, the more it is therapy. Therapy is usually characterized by high proportions of these activities because the individuals who are participating are so conflicted or defensive that they are not able to learn from each other without these activities.

In my view, a T-group is—or should be—a group that contains individuals whose internal conflicts are low enough to learn by:

Dealing with "here and now" behavior (what is going on in the room).

Using relatively nonclinical concepts and nonclinical theory.

Focusing on relatively conscious (or at most preconscious) material.

Being guided increasingly less by the leader and increasingly more by each other.

Accomplishing this in a relatively (to therapy) short time (at the moment, no more than three weeks).

This does not mean that T-groups do not, at times, get into deeper and less conscious problems. They do; and, again, they vary primarily with the staff member's biases. Usually most educators warn the group members against striving to become "two bit" psychologists.

(6) *Laboratory education does not have to be dangerous, but it must focus on feelings.*

Interpersonal problems and personal feelings exist at all levels of the organization, serving to inhibit and decrease the effectiveness of the system. Does it seem to be logical (in fact, moral) for a company to say that it is not going to focus on something that people are already experiencing and feeling? The truth is that people *do* focus on interpersonal problems every hour of the day. They simply do not do it openly.

Now for the argument that the laboratory program can hurt people and is, therefore, dangerous. The facts of life are that people are being hurt every day. I do not know of any laboratory program that did, or could, create for people as much tension as they are experiencing in their everyday work relationships.

It is true that laboratory education does require people to take risks. But does anyone know of any learning that truly leads to growth which does not involve some pain and cost? The value of laboratory education is that it keeps out the people who want to learn "cheaply" and it provides the others with control over how much they wish to learn and what they want to pay for it.

(7) *The objective of laboratory education is to develop effective reality-centerd leaders.*

Some people have expressed concern that if an executive goes through such a learning experience, he might somehow become a weak leader. Much depends on how one defines strong leadership. If strong leadership means unilateral domination and directiveness, then the individual will tend to become "weaker." But why is such leadership strong? Indeed, as I have suggested, it may be weak. Also it tends to develop subordinates who conform, fear to take risks, and are not open, and an organization that becomes increasingly rigid and has less vitality.[8]

Nor can one use the argument that directive leadership has worked and that is why it should remain. There are data to suggest that directive leadership can help an organization under certain conditions (e.g., for routine decisions and under extreme emergencies). But these conditions are limited. If directive leadership is effective beyond these relatively narrow conditions, it may be because of a self-fulfilling prophecy. Directive leadership creates dependence, submissiveness, and conformity. Under these conditions subordinates will tend to be afraid to use their initiative. Consequently, the superior will tend to fill in the vacuum with directive leadership. We now have a closed cycle.

The fact is that directive leaders who learn at a laboratory do not tend to throw away their directive skills. Rather, they seem to use directive leadership where and when it is appropriate. It cannot be emphasized too strongly that there is nothing in laboratory education which requires an individual to throw away a particular leadership pattern. The most laboratory education can do is help the individual see certain unintended consequences and costs of his leadership, and help him to develop other leadership styles *if he wishes.*

(8) *Change is not guaranteed as a result of attendance.*

Sometimes I hear it said that laboratory education is not worthwhile, because some individuals who have attended do not change, or if they do change, it is only for a relatively short period of time.

Let me acknowledge that there is an immense gap in our knowledge about the effectiveness of a laboratory. Much research needs to be done before we know exactly what the payoff is in laboratory education. However, there are a few statements that can be made partially on the basis of research and experience and partially on the basis of theory.

One of the crucial learnings of a laboratory is related to the development of openness and trust in human relationships. These factors are not generated easily in a group. It takes much effort and risk. Those who develop trust in a group learn something very important about it. Trust cannot be issued, inspired, delegated, and transferred. It is an interpersonal factor which has to be *earned* in each relationship. This is what makes trust difficult to develop and precious to have.

Thus, it does not make very much sense to expect that suddenly an individual will act as if he can trust and can be trusted in a setting where this was never true. One executive was needled by the corporate president, who observed that he had not seen any change in the former's behavior. The executive responded: "What makes you think I feel free to change my behavior in front of you?"

This remark points up the possibility that if there is not any observable change, it could mean that the individual has not learned

[8] *Ibid.*

much. But it could also mean that he has learned a great deal, *including* the fact that he ought not to behave differently when he returns. For, it must be emphasized, laboratory education is only a partial attack on the problem of organizational effectiveness. If the changes are to become permanent, one must also change the nature of the organizational structure, managerial controls, incentive systems, reward and penalty systems, and job designs.[9]

Conclusion

While I do not hold up laboratory education as a panacea to remedy all organizational problems, I do feel six conclusions can fairly be drawn:

1. Laboratory education is a very promising educational process. Experience to date suggests that it can help some organizations to *begin* to overcome some of their problems.

2. Laboratory education is *not* a panacea, nor is it a process that can help every organization. Furthermore, it must be followed by changes in the organization, its policies, managerial controls, and even technology. Not all organizations can profit from it; nor do all organizations need similar amounts of it. All these factors should be carefully explored before becoming involved.

3. Not all laboratory programs are alike. Some focus more on interpersonal learning, some on intellectual problem solving, some on small groups, some on intergroups, and some on varying combinations of all of these. Again a careful diagnosis can help one to choose the right combination for the organization, as well as the appropriate educators. Nor are all laboratory programs equally effective. The competence of the educators can vary tremendously, as well as the receptivity of those who attend. The best thing to do is to attempt to attend a laboratory program conducted by competent professionals.

4. Openness, trust, commitment, and risk-taking grow only where the climate is supportive. A one-shot program, even at its best, can only begin the process of unfreezing the executive system. For optimum results, repeat or "booster" programs will be necessary.

5. Although I personally believe that a laboratory program with the "natural" or actual working groups has the greatest probable payoff, it also has the greatest risk. However, one does not have to begin the process this way. There are many different ways to "seed" an organization, hoping to develop increasing trust and risk-taking. The way that will be most effective can best be ascertained by appropriate study of the executive system.

6. Finally, if you ever talk to an individual who has had a successful experience in a laboratory, you may wonder why he seems to have difficulty in describing the experience. I know I still have difficulty describing this type of education to a person who is a stranger to it.

I am beginning to realize that one reason for the difficulty in communication is that the meaningfulness of a laboratory experience varies enormously with each person. Some learn much; some learn little. I find that my learning has varied with the success of the laboratory. Some can hardly wait until it is over; others wish that it would never end. Anyone who understands a laboratory realizes that all these feelings can be real and valid. Consequently, to attempt to describe a laboratory (especially a T-group) to an individual who has never experienced one is difficult because he may be one of those persons who would not have enjoyed the process at all. Therefore, an enthusiastic description may sound hollow.

Another reason why it is difficult to communicate is that the same words can have different meanings to different people. Thus one of the learnings consistently reported by people who have completed a laboratory is that the trust, openness, leveling, risk-taking (and others) take on a new meaning—a meaning that they had not appreciated before the laboratory. This makes it difficult for a person who found laboratory education meaningful to describe it to another. He may want

[9] For a more theoretical discussion of this matter, see Chris Argyris, *Integrating the Individual and the Organization* (New York, John Wiley & Sons, Inc., 1964).

very much to communicate the new meanings of trust, risk-taking, and so on, but he knows, from his own skepticism before the laboratory, that this is a difficult undertaking and that it is not likely to succeed.

The point to all this is that the results of laboratory education are always individualistic; they reflect the individual and the organization. The best way to learn about it is to experience it for one's self.

35. A Framework for Planning Behavior Change in Juvenile Offenders[a]

Peter B. Lenrow[*]

Most people have strongly held views about how to produce change in another person's behavior when it is offensive. Often these beliefs about how to influence people remain implicit and unexamined in the everyday application of influence techniques. For if an influence technique is followed eventually by a desired outcome, the influence agent is likely to conclude that the technique works and that it works for the reasons he used it. He may, of course, be mistaken on both counts: what he did may not have *influenced* the outcome, and if it did, it may have been effective for reasons he has not conceived. Or if application of an influence technique appears to have failed, the influence agent may modify the technique but not his belief about how to change people. To take an example that is comfortably remote from our day-to-day work, consider the belief that casting a spell controls the behavior of another person in a distant village and that it works by summoning evil spirits who frighten him. Such a strongly held belief may persist unexamined even though refinements and innovations are made in the techniques of spell casting. With such comfortably remote examples in mind, those of us who bear responsibility for bringing about constructive changes in other people may properly wonder

what our implicit beliefs are about modifying behavior and how useful they are as a framework for planning programs to bring about change.

In addition, even when we have made our beliefs about modifying behavior explicit and have looked for evidence to check their validity, we find other professional personnel who hold equally explicit views that conflict with our own. Such disagreements, as they occur between juvenile court judges and probation officers, for example, make it difficult for the people who disagree to communicate clearly about a concrete case. Moreover, the disagreements make it difficult to work collaboratively on a plan for bringing about change in that case. We know that it is important in the family setting if parents cannot come to agreement on consistent ways of coping with children's misbehavior. The resulting inconsistency of parental responses often strengthens the child's tendency to misbehave; first, because he finds misbehavior effective in controlling parents by producing a conflict between them, and, second, because there is a fair chance that this time he will not be punished (Bandura & Walters, 1959). There are probably equally important consequences when there is strong disagreement among profes-

Reproduced by special permission from Peter Lenrow, "A Framework for Planning Behavior Change in Juvenile Offenders," *The Journal of Applied Behavioral Science,* Vol. 11, No. 3, (1966), pp. 287–303. Published by NTL Institute for Applied Behavioral Science.

[a] This paper is based on a presentation to juvenile court judges and probation officers in workshops held by The Southwest Center for Law and the Behavioral Sciences, University of Texas School of Law, Wimberley, Texas, Spring, 1965. The workshop was designed to help juvenile court personnel conceptualize their roles as members of a team of change agents with a common frame of reference about the nature of behavioral change.

[*] Assistant Professor of Psychology, University of California, Berkeley.

sionals who share responsibility for preparing and implementing a plan to change a young person's behavior.

I therefore want to examine a number of disagreements about behavior change that are important in work with juvenile offenders, and I will propose a mode of resolving some of them. First, I will make explicit some of the common disagreements about how to change a young person's behavior. The examples will be drawn from the views of court personnel, particularly juvenile court judges and probation officers. I make the assumption that a major goal of the juvenile court is to change the behavior of offenders. I do not assume that the *goal* is to change their basic personality or inner character. It may turn out that this occurs under some conditions, but the *focus* of the present discussion will be on conditions for behavior change.

The major disagreement I will focus on is whether to get the person to act differently and then get the behavior to persist or whether first to change his attitudes and beliefs in ways that will bring about changes in behavior later. This focus of disagreement among court personnel has also been a source of disagreement among social scientists in the past. But over the last eight years, a new way of thinking has developed in the social sciences that reconciles the alternatives that were formerly viewed as incompatible. The major proposal I will make is that this new understanding of behavior change, which has been so successful in reconciling different views among behavioral scientists, may be fruitful in resolving disagreements and reconciling different influence methods used by juvenile judges and other court personnel. I will attempt to illustrate how this new framework for understanding change is useful in evaluating different methods of influencing juvenile offenders. And I will close by suggesting the kinds of questions this new framework provides as a guide in planning programs for behavior change.

Disagreements About Behavior Change

Interviews and questionnaires with juvenile court personnel readily yield contrasting and strongly held views about how to change the behavior of juvenile offenders to bring it more into accord with our society's standards of approved conduct. These views include the general prescription to restrict the offender's behavior to approved conduct by threat of punishment, with privileges conditional on behavior that conforms to authority. This view suggests, "Punish backsliding and make him want to avoid the consequences of his misbehavior." As one judge put it, "Avoid bad company and doing irregular things. . . . If you come back again, whether you like it or not or whether you have supporting witnesses, they'll pin a prison term on you because you have two tags on you now."

Another view that is equally direct in attempting to modify behavior gives less emphasis to punishment and instead prescribes that the offender practice approved behavior —behavior that is characteristic of better socialized people. These prescriptions include, "Join the Boy Scouts, get a job, and stay home in the evening."

A number of other views assume that behavior modification should be more indirect. One emphasis is to try to win the trust of the offender: "I try to reach him, and when he trusts me, he wants to make me proud of him." This view may be coupled with an emphasis on providing opportunities for the offender to develop skills that yield a sense of accomplishment in ways that are socially approved. Such an approach may be endorsed on the grounds that it offers a way to show the offender new paths to self-respect that do not involve antisocial behavior and its attendant punishments. And another view proposes that it is important to find a way to change the norms of the offender, to persuade him to abide by society's norms rather than the ones he has found necessary for obtaining the approval of peers. Some officials try to change the offender's norms by reasoning with him, some by trying to make him feel guilty or ashamed, and some by individualized attention, affection, and a sympathetic approach.

These views may be examined as special cases of a more general contrast in views about behavior change: One view proposes that if you want someone to change a generalized mode of behavior you should punish him when he engages in any of these behaviors and reward him (e.g., with approval and privileges) when he uses acceptable substitutes. The other view proposes that any important mode of behavior to be changed requires first changing the person's way of thinking and feeling about himself and his situations. Changes in the undesirable behaviors will then occur pretty much by themselves as the person tries to make his behavior consistent with the new attitudes.

Each of these contrasting views is of course criticized by proponents of the other view. The proposal to influence antisocial behavior directly by making it more painful and less rewarding than acceptable alternatives does not promise to modify the individual's goals or beliefs and gives no assurance that new behavior will persist. On the other hand, the proposal to induce changes in beliefs and goals by indirect methods involves lengthy treatment, does not promise to stop the antisocial behavior promptly, and may actually be accompanied by an initial increase in disruptive behavior.

Often these two contrasting approaches to behavior change are viewed as mutually exclusive alternatives. For example, separate agencies are evaluated in terms of their general reliance on one of these approaches, and assignment of offenders to one or the other agency is justified by describing them in terms of different types. There is then danger that a decision as to which crude type an offender fits will automatically imply which of several markedly different approaches will be employed. Consequently, the belief that there are mutually exclusive approaches to behavior modification which are appropriate to different types of offenders puts great pressure on the judge and the pretrial investigator to apply the "correct" label to the offender. When they have different evaluations in a given case, the conflict is often intense because radically different approaches to treatment may seem implied by their views of the offender. Each official may be alert to the kind of treatment that the other's typing implies.

It would be useful then to find an approach to planning behavior change for juvenile offenders that reconciles these different views about change. This would not only improve collaboration among court personnel but might eventually have the salutary effect of modifying correctional agencies so that the treatment alternatives they make available to the court are not mutually exclusive (e.g., custodial agencies with limited training only, work camps, and probation).

Integrating Divergent Approaches to Behavior Change

One hope for reconciling the views of court personnel about behavior change would be to learn how the effects of different influence methods are related to one another. Are they mutually exclusive or complementary? Under what conditions? In the behavioral sciences, Herbert Kelman (1958, 1961, 1962, 1963) has developed a general conceptual framework that provides a basis for comparing different methods of producing change. His framework, developed to integrate theories and findings in the behavioral sciences, will serve as a guide for comparing the usefulness of change methods applied to juvenile offenders.

In Kelman's view, it is important to distinguish between two phases of behavior change. The first is a phase in which a person is induced to adopt new behavior; the second is a phase in which the new behavior is transferred to situations outside the one in which it was first acquired. To understand the first phase of behavior change we need to know something about the characteristics of the person to be influenced, the kinds of behavior we want to change, the roles of available influence agents, and the influence techniques available to them.

In principle (and assuming no organic impairment), every person may be motivated to respond to three different kinds of influence. He may be induced to be concerned with the likelihood that his behavior will be rewarded or punished; or concerned to establish a continuing relationship with another person; or concerned to behave in ways that are consistent with and promote his own values. Kelman

(1958, 1961) has shown that a person's behavior may be changed by means of three different processes depending on which of these motivational orientations the influence agent directs himself to and the methods he uses. What are these three processes?

One kind of behavior change, "compliance," occurs under these conditions: the person's primary concern in the influence situation is with obtaining a specific reward or avoiding a specific punishment from an influence agent; the influence agent has power to reward or punish the person; and the influence agent uses techniques that limit the choices available to the person in the influence situation.

Behavior acquired in order to obtain reward or avoid punishment in such situations will persist only under conditions of surveillance by the influence agent, i.e., as long as the person's behavior is observable by the person who controls rewards and punishments.

A second kind of behavior change, "identification," occurs under these conditions: the person is primarily concerned with establishing a satisfying, self-defining relationship with the influence agent; the influence agent has qualities that make a continued relationship with him particularly desirable; and the influence agent defines the role expectations the person must meet in order to maintain an acceptable relationship with the agent. That is, the influence agent makes clear what kind of person the individual must be in order to maintain a valued relationship with him.

New behavior acquired in the process of defining oneself as acceptable in a continuing relationship with the influence agent does not depend on surveillance by the influence agent. Rather it persists so long as the relationship is important to the person who has changed. But the behavior occurs only when the person is engaged in a role that is relevant to his relationship with the influence agent. Thus, while the new behavior occurs in many new situations outside the situation in which the behavior was first acquired, it is still dependent on an external, social support.

A third kind of behavior change, "internalization," occurs under these conditions: the person's primary concern in the influence situation is with the consistency between his behavior and his own concepts of what is worth doing; the influence agent shows himself to be expert and trustworthy; and the influence agent demonstrates new means of promoting the person's independent goals, e.g., his self-respect.

Behavior acquired in this way depends neither on surveillance nor on the relevance of the behavior to a desired relationship with the influence agent; rather, the behavior is shown whenever it is relevant to promoting the person's goals. The behavior thus becomes independent of its original source and integrated with the person's basic values. As such it is manifested in more flexible and discriminating ways.

Problems of Inducing Change

Let us turn now to the relevance of this general framework to the problems of inducing change in the behavior of juvenile offenders. It will be recognized that influence via the process of compliance characterizes the traditional approach of correctional institutions. Correspondingly, influence via the process of identification, and to some extent internalization, generally characterizes the approach of social work. The important point suggested by Kelman's conceptual framework is that each of these approaches to behavior modification may be effective in bringing about change under particular conditions and subject to particular limitations. Second, there is considerable evidence in the behavioral sciences that behavior initially acquired under conditions of compliance may be maintained and generalized via the process of identification. Thus, under special conditions, compliance methods and identification methods may complement one another and have cumulative effects on behavior change.

The special conditions under which this is likely involve the use of rewards and a minimum of punishments by the influence agent. Research findings indicate that reward for conformity to an influence agent's standards produces as much conformity as does punishment. Moreover, reward arouses less resistance. This is important because after punishments terminate, the resistance aroused by previous punishment persists and is accompanied by a drop in conformity compared with that of persons who have been rewarded for conformity (French, Morrison & Levinger, 1960). An influence agent who demonstrates ability to administer rewards fosters imitation of his behavior as he increases his attractiveness (or borrowed reward value) through the repeated association of his characteristics with rewards (Zipf, 1960; Bandura & Walters, 1963). Thus, the relatively greater attractiveness of a rewarding influence agent compared with a punishing one and the fact that he does not arouse resistance (in the form of resentment of his power) lead to a situation in which he can influence behavior via the process of identification. Heavy reliance on punishment or threat of punishment on the other hand, decreases the attractiveness of the influence agent and decreases his effectiveness in altering the behavior of others beyond the immediate social setting. These principles pose a problem we shall return to later: In what kind of setting can rewards appropriately be used as the first step in influencing juvenile offenders?

With these general principles in mind, let us use Kelman's framework to examine the problem of inducing new behavior in juvenile offenders. Working with this framework, we shall want to examine (1) the characteristics of the offenders and the kinds of behavior change necessary for them to show socialized behavior, and (2) the influence agents and techniques appropriate for bringing about these changes.

Individual Differences in Juvenile Offenders

The large literature on individual differences among juvenile offenders has been organized by Jenkins (1955) and recently by Polk (1965) in terms of four main groupings. These groupings may be described in terms of the offender's capacity for self-control over his immediate wants, on the one hand, and his acceptance of the dominant standards of behavior in our society, on the other hand. Occasionally an offense is committed by a boy or a girl who shows high self-control and high commitment to dominant social norms. However, the great bulk of offenses are committed by offenders who can be described in three other groupings: those who show high self-control but are committed to standards of conduct that conflict with the dominant standards in our society; those who show low self-control but are committed to the dominant social norms; and those who show low self-control and are not committed to any stable social norms.

In the past, offenders who show low self-control despite strong adherence to dominant social norms have been called "neurotic" by many researchers, and their offenses have been attributed to a wish for punishment. This complex view has proposed that punishment provides temporary relief from self-condemnation due to excessive moral standards (Freud, 1925; Alexander & Staub, 1931). Many psychotherapists have recommended some form of conventional psychotherapy for these offenders. On the other hand, the offenders who show low self-control and low commitment to any consistent social norms have generally been labeled "psychopaths" and are described as having suffered such early deprivation of consistent mothering that they are incapable of establishing trusting relationships with other people (White, 1956; Jenkins & Hewitt, 1944). They are described as inaccessible to conventional psychotherapy or probationary counseling. Finally, the offenders who show high self-control and commitment to a code of behavior that conflicts with the law have largely been inaccessible to influence via conventional psychotherapy or probationary counseling, which they regard as alien and a threat to their freedom. Some researchers have recommended group work with the entire gang of which the offender is a part (Dumpson, 1949).

Bandura and Walters (1959) have called into question the practice of regarding these four descriptive groups as fundamentally different types of personality problems. Their systematic research presents a persuasive case for the view that antisocial aggression in all four descriptive groups is a learned reaction to the offender's need for dependent relationships with others. Their research indicates that anti-social aggression occurs when the young person's dependency needs are aroused and cannot be expressed because he has learned to regard them as reprehensible or painful. In the case of the offender with high self-control and commitment to a deviant behavior code, his dependency needs are met indirectly by dependence on his gang, while the emphasis on aggression in the gang's code provides a way of denying dependency. In the case of offenders in all four groups, disruptive, antisocial behavior results in apprehension and custody in a dependent relationship for which the youth does not have to take responsibility. Their fear of dependency leads to aggression and externally enforced dependency which they then fear and may react to with further aggression. From this viewpoint, a common objective of attempts to bring about socialized behavior in juvenile offenders would be to use and modify the externally enforced dependency role in a way that permits them to learn more acceptable responses to dependency than antisocial aggression.

The important questions to ask about each offender thus concern the amount and kind of resistance he shows to the dependent role into which he has precipitated himself. Also, how ready is he to enter a dependency relationship that involves less coercion? It may well be that most offenders in the neurotic group accept a dependency relationship authorized by the court and are therefore more accessible to treatment via conventional psychotherapies. But the important information we need in order to plan behavior modification is how readily the individual offender will enter dependency relationships, not whether he is neurotic. Correspondingly, a so-called psychopath may show great anger or mistrust in response to friendly interest and his dependent role in custody. But again the important observation would be how he behaves in a dependent role and how destructive is his behavior when he is not in a controlled environment rather than whether he is psychopathic. The task of influence agents from this viewpoint would be to innovate and devise roles in which offenders who are typically highly resistant to entering a

dependency relationship will accept a dependent position. One of the requirements of this special role would have to be that the offender would not at first be expected to ask for help, confide self-doubts, or manifest emotional responses, since research indicates that boys showing strong antisocial tendencies are more reluctant to express their feelings to others (Jaffee & Polansky, 1962). Let us examine how offenders may be induced via compliance, identification, or internalization to modify their antisocial responses to dependency roles.

Selection of Influence Methods

What kinds of plans do we come up with if we start with the assumption that most offenders have developed their antisocial behavior as a reaction to fear or shame that they connect with dependency needs? If an influence agent uses court sanctions to hold an offender in a dependent role and offers friendly interest, the youth is likely to provoke rejection and punishment in this role by further antisocial behavior (Bandura & Walters, 1959). This repeats his history of parental intolerance or indifference toward his childhood dependency and confirms his sense of being rejected. Hypothetically, it is this view of himself to which he has already reacted with the antisocial behavior that got him apprehended. Thus the treatment would have netted nothing. If the influence agent uses an approach that emphasizes punishments, the offender may comply after testing the agent's power to apply punishments, but the changes via compliance are likely to last only so long as he is under surveillance. How feasible this method will be should depend in part on how costly it is to continue surveillance. The threats of punishment confirm and may increase the offender's sense of being rejected and are likely to lead to further offenses when surveillance ends.

If the influence agent uses a minimum of punishment and employs rewards (such as privileges) that are explicitly contingent on conformity to his standards, compliance may to regard the influence agent as an "easy mark" and regard himself as in control of the situation as long as it lasts. He is likely to regard this role as isolated from the rest of his life. If, however, the influence agent uses a minimum of punishment and provides re-occur and nothing more. The offender is likely wards that are not contingent on conformity to fixed socialized standards, the offender will find himself in a disconcerting, unfamiliar situation. He may be counted on to test whether this situation is really different from previous ones in which he has been rejected and punished. And his testing is likely to involve aggressive, antisocial behavior in an effort to provoke the rejection and punishment he expects. If the influence agent can weather this period of testing, the youth may then develop a strong dependent relationship with the agent (Redl & Wineman, 1952). This puts the agent in a position to induce changes via the process of identification.

How feasible it is for an influence agent to try to hold fast during a period of testing should depend on the ability of the agent to tolerate and understand the provocations, the form that the provocations are likely to take, and the settings available for the testing to go on. If the offender's history indicates that provocation is likely to include destruction of property or bodily injury, it is important for the agent to arrange a setting in which he has a high degree of control over the offender's environment. This requires a minimum of coercive influences, elimination of some opportunities for choice that could be used destructively, and opportunities to employ rewards. Eliminating some choices makes it possible to use a minimum of threats; e.g., if the furniture is unbreakable, aggression toward this property need not be forbidden in this setting. Some residential treatment centers with minimum coercive influences meet these requirements.

The process of testing an influence agent with provocations may be lengthy and may be prolonged by the association of coercive threats with rewards. If the primary influence agent is closely associated with the court, his role will inevitably imply threat of punishment and make it difficult for the agent to be viewed as someone with whom the youth might want to maintain a continuing relationship.

Three ways of modifying the influence agent's role offer promise of decreasing the period of testing and increasing his ability to induce changes via identification as well as compliance. One common practice is to dissociate the primary influence agent from the court insofar as possible (often while the offender is seen concurrently on probationary supervision). Psychologists, psychiatrists, and social workers may thereby work with offenders using rewards almost exclusively. There are, of course, always some limits and they must be firmly applied. Rewards may take the form of a comfortable, private place to meet, few fixed standards to conform to, coffee or food to share, and a group of other offenders to talk to.

This introduces the second way of modifying the role of the influence agent: supplementing his influence with that of a group. If the agent can compose a group that includes a number of influential offenders who have learned to trust him, his ability to give rewards is supplemented by their ability to give approval to new group members. The group is then likely to develop its own norms for behavior that are compatible with the norms of the agent in order to assure the continuation of the group. And the agent's ability to punish can be deemphasized and supplemented by the ability of group members to disapprove of behavior that deviates from the group norms. Thus the agent's ability to influence behavior via compliance is supplemented by the group. In addition, Kelman (1963) points out that membership in the group itself provides rewards in the form of companionship and acceptance. And as these rewards increase the attractiveness of the group, the group provides conditions for change via identification, i.e., change in order to be an acceptable member in terms of the group's norms. Moreover, as members begin to explore the effects of new behavior for achieving self-respect, they can test the effectiveness of their behavior in the group more readily than they might with one adult agent. Such exploration of the effects of new behavior in achieving self-respect may lead via internalization to new patterns of behavior that are relatively independent of group support. Thus the group can potentially enhance the agent's ability to influence behavior via all three processes: compliance, identification, and internalization.

A third way of modifying the role of the influence agent that may be combined with the two other arrangements involves the use of work roles for offenders. If the offender can be provided with an opportunity to work for pay, he may thereby be placed in a situation in which he is willing to enter a dependent relationship, i.e., with an employer. The role is one in which he can obtain rewards for his own efforts and can gain practice in a role that requires socialized behavior. The more the work engages the interests of the youth and offers promise of a continuing vocational role, the more the behavior he initiates in order to get paid will be strengthened by his accepting norms that are part of the vocational role. Thus changes that are initiated via compliance may be made more generalized via identification. There is also a chance that eventually a vocational role that captures an offender's interests will provide opportunities for him to discover new behavior that increases his self-respect. Such changes via internalization would be highly durable.

One bold use of work roles was invented by Charles Slack, a psychologist who hired juvenile offenders in the role of research participants (Slack, 1960). He paid them to come to his research center in order to permit him to learn more about the lives of young people who lived in neighborhoods like theirs. Their job was to talk about whatever interested them and to take a number of interesting tests. This procedure was effective in engaging the interest and continuing participation of offenders who had formerly been inaccessible to all forms of treatment, and his pilot project had promising results. Slack showed initial toleration of deviations from usual middle-class work patterns, was willing to discuss the research procedures and assessment findings with the boys, and employed many rewards that were not contingent on conformity to set

standards. His friendly interest and rewarding behavior in this situation elicited much imitation of his behavior by these offenders. This appears to be a particularly good example of change via the process of identification. And in addition, Slack's observations suggest that as the boys grew interested in the research they developed an interest in understanding their own behavior better. They began to behave like psychotherapy clients who are learning to adopt new views of themselves and to discover that some of their new ways of behaving give them greater self-respect. If such changes via internalization could be demonstrated in a larger project, their persistence would be worth the investment of personnel and wages for the boys.

Before finishing these remarks, a note must be made concerning transfer of new behavior to settings other than the one in which it was acquired. A general rule of thumb would be that the more dissimilar are the influence situation and the situation in which the person is expected to perform newly acquired behavior, the more difficult it is to transfer the new behavior, i.e., get it to persist. On the other hand, the more the influence situation is like the rest of the person's life, the harder it will be to elicit new behavior in the first place. One guideline that these observations suggest is that the closer the offender can remain to his community setting and yet be influenced via identification, the more likely it will be for the behavior to persist after treatment. Second, the more dissimilar the initial influence setting must be made compared with his community setting (in order to induce changes via identification), the more important it will be to provide subsequent influence situations that make gradual his return to the home setting. If a group in which he has acquired new behavior can be maintained intact in his home setting, it will provide a powerful means of sustaining the changes he has begun.

In conclusion, it is worth emphasizing that there is evidence for the effectiveness of both direct efforts to induce behavior change and indirect efforts via modifying the person's attitudes. The important task is to examine the ways in which these approaches can be coordinated to provide optimal influence in a particular case. I have attempted to illustrate how the use of influence agents dissociated from the court, the use of group settings, and the use of work roles provide opportunities for coordinating a variety of influence methods.

References

Alexander, F., & Staub, H. *The criminal, the judge, and the public.* Translated by G. Zilboorg. New York: Macmillan, 1931.

Bandura, A., & Walters, R. H. *Adolescent aggression.* New York: Ronald, 1959.

Bandura, A., & Walters, R. H. *Social learning and personality development.* New York: Holt, 1963.

Dumpson, J. R. An approach to antisocial street gangs. *Fed. Probation,* 1949, 13, 22–29.

French, J. R. P., Jr., Morrison, H. W., & Levinger, G. Coercive power and forces affecting conformity. *J. abnorm. soc. Psychol.,* 1960, 61, 93–101.

Freud, S. Some character types met in psychoanalytic work. In E. Jones (Ed.), *Collected papers.* Vol. IV. London: Hogarth, 1925.

Jaffee, L. D., & Polansky, N. A. Verbal inaccessibility in young adolescents showing delinquent trends. *J. Hlth. Hum. Behav.,* 1962, 3(2), 105–111.

Jenkins, R. L. Adaptive and maladaptive delinquency. *Nerv. Child.,* 1955, 11, 9–11.

Jenkins, R. L., & Hewitt, L. Types of personality structure encountered in child guidance clinics. *Amer. J. Orthopsychiat.,* 1944, 14, 84–94.

Kelman, H. C. Compliance, identification, and internalization: Three processes of attitude change. *J. Conflict Resolution,* 1958, 2, 51–60.

Kelman, H. C. Processes of opinion change. *Publ. Opin. Quart.,* 1961, 25, 57–78.

Kelman, H. C. The induction of action and attitude change. In S. Coopersmith (Ed.), *Proceedings of the XIV International Congress of Applied Psychology, Vol. II. Personality research.* Copenhagen, Denmark: Munksgaard, 1962.

Kelman, H. C. The role of the group in the induction of therapeutic change. *Int. J. Group Psychother.,* 1963, XIII, 399–432.

Polk, F. Moral attitudes, ego strength, and guilt in adolescents reporting deviant behavior. Unpublished doctoral thesis, Univer. of California, Berkeley, 1965.

Redl, F., & Wineman, D. *Controls from within.* Glencoe, Ill.: Free Press, 1952.

Slack, C. W. Experimenter-subject psychotherapy: Introducing a new method of intensive office treatment for unreachable cases. Dittoed manuscript, 1960.

White, R. W. *The abnormal personality.* New York: Ronald, 1956.

Zipf, Sheila G. Resistance and conformity under reward and punishment. *J. abnorm. soc. Psychol.,* 1960. 61, 102–109.

36. Seven Years on Skid Row: Diagnostic and Rehabilitation Center/Philadelphia

Leonard Blumberg* • Thomas E. Shipley, Jr.* • Irving W. Shandler*

The Diagnostic and Rehabilitation Center/ Philadelphia (DRC/P) is an agency originally created to develop ways to relocate homeless men from Skid Row at minimal danger to the health and safety of the larger Philadelphia community. The Center has been open since April 1963, with antecedents going back to 1959. At the time of writing (1970), it had a seven-year history of activity. When it seems appropriate, we will refer to Phase I (1963–1965), and to Phase II (1965–1970). The early phase emphasized the relocation of Skid Row men. The later phase has had a diagnostic-referral-treatment orientation for men with alcohol problems in the context of a Community Mental Health program. The Skid Row men are one of several kinds of people using the Center. In this later period the Skid Row project was oriented to "The Prevention of Skid Row." While the earlier attention on Skid Row men was financed by HHFA-URA-HUD, Phase II of the Skid Row project (as distinct from the Center) has been financed by NIMH. The DRC/P has an extensive program dealing with drug and alcohol abuse outside of Skid Row: however, this program is not the present focus of attention.

Our discussion is organized in terms of (1) the ideology of the Center, (2) the development and changes in the image of the Center by Skid Row men, (3) the role-related relationships at the core of the Center's organization, (4) ways in which social power is manifested and the significance of power phenomena for the Center, and (5) some institutional-organizational trends. From the very beginning the Center's orientation has been interdisciplinary: that is, it was our own explicit intention to create a team approach in which each specialist contributed his skills and knowledge, but no specific area was carved out for his special attention.

Ideology

The Center was established by persons who have a strong conviction that the work of the social scientist should be relevant to the larger society outside the university. We recognize that we walk a tight rope between a meliorative approach, in which the function of "helping" programs may be to adjust people to the society, and a social change approach, in which the social scientist is engaged in changing the local community or the larger society in order to eliminate certain problems that have become manifested in the lives of the citizenry. While initially the project took on a strong meliorative approach, from the very beginning we have been concerned with the prevention of Skid Row and Skid Row conditions, and we recognize that much of this prevention must mean the change of living conditions and certain kinds of land use and real estate practices. Thus in Phase II we have sent community organizers into the community to assess sentiment about local organization for prevention of Skid Row conditions and to organize programs to reach men with gross alcohol problems in the neighborhoods. We confess to some frustration, however, for we found that residents of the near-slum areas where our workers went were more exercized about drug abuse and more interested in drug control programs oriented to youth rather than to working with older men (and women) with alcohol-related problems. We account for this in the following terms: (1) most adults drink, as well as many pre-adults, and heavy drinking is not unusual; (2) the elapsed time for alcohol "addiction" to be apparent is rela-

This paper is a revision of "The Philadelphia Project: An Action Research Program," by the authors which appeared in *Sociology in Action*, edited by Arthur B. Shostak (Homeward, Ill.: The Dorsey Press, 1966), pp. 158–165.

° Diagnostic and Rehabilitation Center, Philadelphia, Pennsylvania.

tively long; (3) there is no apparent relationship between chronic "alcoholism" and felonious crime in comparison with many drugs; and (4) the history of the "great experiment" in Prohibition is combined with an idealistic libertarian demand for the maximum possible individual freedom so that a person is entitled to get drunk if he wants to and for a sentiment that the older people are "too far gone" and "not worth saving" while youth is the future of our society. Further, the DRC/P has no formal responsibility for Skid Row. Consequently, in Phase II, other parts of the Center's program, under fewer grant limitations, have moved to provide diagnostic, referral, and treatment service for younger people with drug problems as well as the organization of community effort with respect to drugs. We recognize of course that this still is on the meliorative side of the continuum, though one would expect that community groups will see larger programs that are important and that must be developed in order to further assist and prevent drug and alcohol abuse problems.

We also believed that social welfare programs and social action programs should include a research component. This would include (1) "pure research" to make a contribution to man's knowledge, (2) administrative research to assess the effectiveness of the program, and (3) the development of summary statistics about agency activity that are necessary for reports to various public agencies and to the United Community Chest. This approach has received a mixed reception among the various publics on which the Center's finances have relied. In Phase I the officials of the Housing and Home Finance Agency showed a lively interest in research design and in implementation that would contribute to the evaluation of the effectiveness of the Section 314 Demonstration grant which they financed, but they showed little interest in research *per se*. Further, they showed virtually no interest in going beyond our submission of a preliminary report to acceptance of the report and in final issuance. Perhaps this was because the report provided only limited evidence that voluntary relocation led to permanent disassociation from the Skid Row way of life and

reaffiliation with the larger community, even when supplemented by diagnostic and referral services. Minimally it seems necessary to have (1) a network of long-term hospitalization and a variety of therapy facilities, (2) short-term detoxification facilities to which police referrals are made, rather than to jail, and (3) a very active style of casework that works with the client "out there" in the community rather than waiting for him to demonstrate motivation for "cure" by coming to the office of the worker. None of these were available on a scale that met the potential need. Further, for those "hard core" Skid Row men (and we do not use the term pejoratively) who identify with Skid Row and who have a settled Skid Row life stye, it is probable that domiciliary facilities calculated to enhance the dignity of these men, despite their pariah status from the point of view of the larger community, is the only "solution." These are hardly encouraging results for socially sensitive governmental personnel who nonetheless must find answers to their problems in terms of their agency's mission as it has been laid out by Congress and upper level policy makers.

In Phase II, NIMH has given considerable support to research and shown considerable interest in design as well as in the action aspects. However, NIMH has been unable to support action under the same grant so that we have had problems finding money to coordinate service with the research design. Further, from time to time we still find it necessary to continue to argue the importance of combined-action research with those action-oriented persons who say "we have enough research—we know what needs to be done—what we need is action." We have heard those comments from various social welfare agency officials, from some university officials, and even from some of our own staff.

On the other hand, there have been important changes in the attitudes of university officials over the seven-year period. In Phase I there were some university officials who argued that it was inappropriate for a university-affiliated agency to engage in any social action —that it should be restricted to research and scholarly publication. During Phase II, however, this view has shifted under the impact of changes in the larger society, especially demands for relevance by students and by black residents of the Temple University locality. Had the program begun after 1965, it might not have been necessary to establish a separate nonprofit corporation. Rather it might have become an affiliate of the School of Social Administration, which took its first class of MSW candidates in the fall of 1969. Now we find the University very much concerned to display its areas of community service, but the tie to the Diagnostic and Rehabilitation Center/Philadelphia is now tenuous, existing only through the released time from teaching of two of the authors and compensated for by the NIMH grant. We have found no ready solution for the desire to exclude research and concentrate on action or to exclude action and concentrate on research, except to continue to collect necessary data insofar as possible and to seek to demonstrate the possibility of implementing the ideology successfully.

The Center began with a casework ideology committed to reaching "out there" beyond the office doors to the client. Initially the program reached Skid Row men through "contact counselors"—interviewers who met the men where they lived. Intake counselors (caseworkers) were more "building bound" but most expressed an active concern for the men. In Phase II the contact counselors were discontinued because the Center was now well known on the Row. However, we have tried to explore the value of "aggressive casework" through an experimental procdeure in which extremely close ties were developed and maintained between client, ex-Skid Row volunteer, and a professionally trained MSW on a twenty-four-hour, on-call, basis. (The results of this program will be published elsewhere.) We are convinced that the intensive program demonstrated that it is possible to develop and maintain a more effective way of working with Skid Row men.

In Phase I there was "resistance" to research from the social work staff. Committed as they were to the full practice of social work skills with their clients, social workers found it next to impossible to live up to experimental plans developed before the project got underway, which they felt was unrealistic. Thus our initial plan called for one sample of Skid Row men to be interviewed and referred to another agency for service, while another sample of Skid Row men would be interviewed and given considerable attention and also be relocated by the staff. Each sample was to be chosen randomly. The research design broke down because the social work staff found it next to impossible to withhold their skills from one population and give it to the other. The arbitrariness of the randomizing procedure alone would have created a considerable problem of rapport with all the men because the staff would have been unable to give the satisfactory explanation for the arbitrariness and treatment of the men. Further, the randomization procedure would fly in the face of efforts to motivate men to come to the Center since many would receive nothing. (Men on the street would quickly know, for there is a very adequate grapevine on Skid Row.)

These problems of adequate data gathering and of research design have persisted into Phase II. Thus, it has been difficult to develop new directions in data collection because the casework staff felt "uncomfortable" with them or because they seem to interfere with the caseworker's perception of their rapport with the client. A similar problem has emerged with respect to standardized medical interview materials. Thus, in Phase I systematic medical data collection was begun, but these materials, while helpful for a medical descriptive statement, were not completely adequate to the style of diagnostic analysis that is usual among physicians. In Phase II we hoped to get enough additional data to allow us to follow the statistical diagnostic model of physicians, but the physicians themselves abandoned the data-gathering procedure in favor of an informal procedure, and it became impossible to do the work that had been planned. Thus, we cannot really say that the service oriented staff learned the basic value of research, although they appreciate the value of administrative performance data to be gathered after a period of years. It is become a perennial task to relate to the social work staff whenever possible, almost on a selling basis, in order to get cooperation for research purposes. This has not been true for all of the casework staff and seems to depend on the earlier training as well as upon idiosyncratic interpersonal elements. On the other hand, there has been reasonable success in maintaining both a research evaluative arm and an action arm within the same agency and maintaining a high level of objectivity. It is entirely possible that the reasonably high level of objectivity is related to the minor alienation between research on the one hand and the service on the other hand.

Our treatment ideology has changed over time. In Phase I the orientation was toward diagnosis and relocation; securing services and treatment for the men was done under the mask of relocation. In later developments the Center was able to secure a grant from the Vocational Rehabilitation Administration for an experimental halfway-house program. This program itself has undergone several stages, and, while we do not wish to completely anticipate reports of its results, our conclusion is that Skid Row men cannot effectively be relocated from Skid Row directly to a halfway house and then to the larger community. If this kind of procedure is to be effective at all, there must be the intervention of a long-term treatment center; even then we are not hopeful that large numbers of Skid Row men can successfully take that route. On the other hand, the Center House, as we now call it, seems to have developed into an effective medium-length therapeutic situation for men who have come from the larger community and will return to the larger community. The Center also actively supported the transformation of a tuberculosis sanitorium into an alcohol and drug treatment hospital, and this facility is a major place of referral for DRC/P clients at the present time. It is worth noting that the two agencies have grown apart despite innumerable conferences between the staffs of the two. Each agency has created its own image in the larger community. Their "misunderstandings" may be due to the fact that the agencies are located in different counties, about 30 miles from each other, that each

agency has become the locus for the career ambitions of its respective personnel as well as the status ambitions of board members because they have adopted different treatment ideologies and because they tend to compete for the same grant dollars.

The treatment orientation of the Center has also been evidenced in the strenuous efforts by staff to secure emergency care for clients. In Phase I there were less than ten beds available, but over the years the number of beds has expanded so that in the near future there will probably be 100 beds available at any one time for detoxification of drunken persons. This does not, of course, begin to meet the massive needs of a metropolitan community the size of the Philadelphia area, but improvements are clearly evident. The problems here relate not only to finance and bed space, but also to the attitudes of admission ward personnel who tend to see the drunken person as suffering from something that he has brought on himself. In the context of scarce general hospital beds, hospital emergency staffs regard the drunken condition as less an urgent illness than some other. We have, however, attempted to meet some of this problem with coordinated work with the National Council on Alcoholism, Delaware Valley Branch, and we have generated videotape and film which we hope will strike at least at the prejudicial elements in the thinking of emergency ward personnel. The project in itself involved not only the staff of the Center, but the volunteer cooperation of a talented senior at Swarthmore College who filled the roles of script writer and actor, along with our physician and the services of the Temple University audiovisual service. How the experimental stage of this subproject will come out remains to be seen.

Our concern for the prevention of Skid Row has changed over time. In Phase I Skid Row was seen primarily as a specially delimited area with a stereotyped population. From a rejection of the subculture hypothesis, we have been persuaded that there is indeed a distinctive style of life into which new residents into the area may become socialized and which is transmitted over time somewhat autonomously from the larger community from which it is partially alienated. However, not all Skid Row residents are part of that subculture. But, at least in eastern and middle-western metropolitan cities, Skid Row as an identifiable "natural area" is apparently disappearing; that is not so much the consequence of urban redevelopment as it is of changes in our social security practices and long-run racial trends.

At the end of Phase I we believed that we had identified an incipient Skid Row area and that there was some evidence that trends in that neighborhood had halted—largely because the neighborhood was being absorbed into the black and Puerto Rican housing market, which was more profitable than the Skid Row housing market, and because a series of inspections by the Department of Licenses and Inspections had tended to have a boomerang effect as local residents and businessmen began to rehabilitate under the impetus of the code inspections. However, during Phase II we found evidence that the basic trends toward Skid Row have continued and that they probably have existed for a long time. These findings forced us to revise our approach to the "prevention of Skid Row." We now believe that such trends are long-time trends and that Skid Row men may indeed move into a neighborhood, having been ejected from an existing or previously existing Skid Row, but that such a neighborhood has developed a lack of "resistance" to these moves as results of trends going over twenty to possibly thirty years. Under these circumstances, in addition, we have found that "incipient Skid Row" areas, as we previously called them, have numbers of men living in a Skid Row style of life who are indigenous to the locality. Some of the Skid Row residents have drifted to the Skid Row area from these neighborhoods and readily move back there given the opportunity. The extent to which this finding is applicable in other cities remains to be explored, however.

Image

The Center's demonstration grant had developed from a census taken in Philadelphia's Skid Row in 1959–1960. In that census white-coated medical school juniors and seniors, addressed as "doctor," had been able to interview approximately 80 percent of the Skid Row men. When the interviewing began on the demonstration grant out of the Center, the interviewing staff largely consisted of middle-class members of the staff. We quickly found that a more effective job of establishing rapport could be done by using some ex-Skid Row men who were involved in an Alcoholics Anonymous program that was the responsibility of one of the staff. In the first six months we found that these ex-Skid Row men on our staff made an important contribution toward the establishment of a favorable image of the Center on the part of the men who still lived on Skid Row. Our ex-Skid Row staff men spoke the slang of the men, they were known to have recently lived on the Row, they knew the problems of alcoholism and "understood" the men, and men on the Row perceived that they were understood; in addition, they knew their way around the area in a way that none of the rest of us possibly could.

An example was the extremely effective job of communication done during the Christmas holidays of 1963 when thirty-one men died of methyl alcohol poisoning from drinking industrial canned heat. The ex-Skid Row men mimeographed a circular and distributed it widely on the Row. When the Center's ex-Skid Row men said "don't drink that squeeze; there's a bad batch on the Row," they were heard and listened to! In recognition of this, the Center's staff has included a number of ex-Skid Row men in such capacities as administrative assistant to the director, interviewer, therapist, messenger, and cook. These men are an integral part of the staff.

This has had its price, however. During Phase I the ex-Skid Row men were still strongly identified with the Row, which facilitated their rapport with the men. It meant, however, that they tended to view the Center as fair game for exploitation; for the sake of the clients, they were inclined to "con" us. A consequence was that we got more volunteers walking into the Center than we had planned for. Looked at in perspective, we see this as something of a trade-off. The image and the rapport contributed by the ex-Skid Row men may have given us better data from those who gave data, but it was at the cost of considerable deviation from the random sample design we had originally planned.

In Phase II, when systematic research design was so important to the NIMH grant, we have found other kinds of problems related to the use of ex-Skid Row men. For instance, we found that ex-Skid Row men are extremely useful in a follow-up of a former client. But follow-up work is extremely frustrating and time consuming. It takes a large number of tries before finding many men and a number of follow-up men have not been able to stay dry.

There is another element to the image of the Center which has emerged. From the very beginning we became aware of the fact that the Center was functionally similar to the missions, that is, we were committed to a parellel activity with parellel consequences, though our procedures in the fulfillment of this function were different. Over the years it has become apparent that for some Skid Row men the halfway house of the Center and the Center itself have been a "waffle"; that is, these men have seen a superlative opportunity for making gains. In effect the Center has become integrated as another one of the Skid Row institutions, though the "nosedive" of the Center is the answering of many questions rather than confessing one's sins to God or some such thing. This gets expressed in another way because there is a population of "hard-core Skid Row men" who are "making it on their own" and with whom we have had relatively little contact. The Center's answer is to remain available and to try to conduct its activities in such a way that at no time are the men debased when they finally do come for some sort of help. Nonetheless, we recognize that for Skid Row men, agencies which stand to assist them are looked at from their perspective as resources to be used rather than anything else.

Role-Related Relationships

The Center's staff is a combination of professionals and nonprofessionals. The professional approach is multidisciplinary—social casework, social group work, medicine, psychiatry, public health, clinical psychology, social psychology, and sociology are all represented. The focus is on a problem population rather than on a single frame of reference or theoretical position. The staff is committed, therefore, to work toward solutions to problems of the Skid Row man, and it recognizes that all the professionals can make a contribution because of their complementary skills. Different disciplines, as such, just get in the way. There are residual interprofessional tensions, but these are largely focused on the "artificiality" introduced into service activities by the researchers, rather than on differences in professional ideologies. These tensions are moderated by the commitment by all persons, whatever their professional role, to the ideology of working for and with Skid Row men so that differences that crop up are regarded as ones to be lived with, to be discussed if possible, to be reconciled if possible, and hopefully to be resolved, rather than as grist for the mill of conflict. They are also limited by the fact that the Center's activities are organized in terms of units derived from separate grants so that people in different grant activities are somewhat insulated from each other.

At the same time, we have noted that professional ideologies have created minor problems for some of the staff outside the Center. To cite just two examples: we wondered whether our osteopathic physician would be permitted to visit some of our Skid Row men in a local hospital, but he was quietly given a staff appointment after some friendly negotiations. Some of our social work staff felt that they would be perceived by their professional peers as professionally offbeat, but in fact they were met with interest and cooperation. (Since the Center serves a population that welfare agencies normally do not reach, and does not compete with, so the Center was possibly not perceived as threatening other agencies.)

Finally, we think that the selection of a social worker with considerable sociological training as the director of the Center has made an important contribution to the moderation of professional role-related tensions. We can develop a post hoc explanation of this—the social worker is the focal point of the relationship that the Skid Row man has with the Center—but the fact is that there was a strong element of chance that matters turned out this way.

Power Structure

Power considerations have been important in the affairs of the Diagnostic and Rehabilitation Center's program. First, and probably most important, is the influence of the Greater Philadelphia Movement in the establishment of the program and in its continuing support. (The Redevelopment Authority of the City of Philadelphia and the State Highway Department already had plans to redevelop the area to the north of Independence Hall.) The Greater Philadelphia Movement, a local civic organization of thirty-five top leaders in commerce, banking, and industry gave impetus to these redevelopment plans. The GPM served as prime contractor for the Skid Row census and for the Phase I Section 314 Demonstration Grant project. When it became necessary to create a nonprofit corporation to receive certain grants, the Skid Row subcommittee of the GPM members were the principal incorporators. The law firm of one of the GPM members is the law firm for the Diagnostic and Rehabilitation Center. The director of the Center has had the ear of the Executive Director of GPM and the GPM Skid Row committee.

While the active support of the power structure, through GPM, has been of immeasurable help, the Center has also had excellent support from the mass media. From the very beginning of the project the mass media saw the Center and its program as good copy. Full cooperation was extended to the representatives of the press, radio, and television. The only request made by the Center was that there be recognition of the special audience on Skid Row. In almost every situation, this request has been honored and each article or TV show (there have been four 30-minute and one 60-minute TV presentations) has been favorably received by the general community, and specifically by the Skid Row men.

Another dimension of power is the Skid Row landlord who can make or break any research sample plan. For example, from the beginning of Phase I it was difficult to get into certain Skid Row hotels in order to interview. In one hotel it was virtually impossible. The hotel owners correctly saw that every man persuaded to leave their hotel and be relocated was money out of their pockets. Legally, the project rested solely upon voluntary cooperation. While we tried to develop ways of using pressure through the City's Department of Licenses and Inspections, we were not very successful. Various types of stratagems were used to get around landlord opposition, the most effective of which was for the interviewer to go to the hotel when the hotel operator was not present. On the other hand, one landlord was able to arrange for advance acquisition of his properties (whether the fact that his brother was a member of the legislature had anything to do with it we cannot say), and he was extremely cooperative.

Many Skid Row landlords received disability checks, old-age insurance checks, and retirement checks of the men living in their places. The man woud endorse the check over to the landlord, who would credit him for rent until the next check arrived, and then take out any money he may have advanced, returning the balance to the man. There was a reasonable probability that the man would then go out and get drunk and be jackrolled while drunk. Not infrequently he did not even have time to get drunk but was mugged shortly after leaving the hotel. He then had to borrow from his landlord until his next check came in. Thus, a system of dependency was established which made it extremely difficult for the man to move from Skid Row even if he wanted to. Where would he get the credit that he needed to survive until the next check? Who would take an interest in him outside of Skid Row? The fact that such interest might be exploitative was irrelevant. We tried to solve this problem through closer relationships with the Department of Public Welfare (a city agency) and the Department of Public Assistance (a state-county agency), and we are convinced it is possible to break the debt dependency relationship although we have not always been able to persuade the men of this.

Power is also evinced through formal governmental authority. The agencies of the city and GPM are concerned that another Skid Row not develop elsewhere in the city. This is a major concern of the Redevelopment Authority, and it is a responsibility of the Department of Licenses and Inspections. Skid Row represents a locale in which homeless men congregate for cheap lodging and food. Under the present housing code it is neither financially feasible nor legally possible to open new Skid Row hotels after the present ones are demolished. Thus, one major source of housing will be eliminated.

The other source of cheap housing is the Gospel missions. While the Center has not maintained good relationships with the missions, it is no secret that the missions are an element of the Skid Row life style that fosters dependency, nor are they an effective force in helping many men to leave the Row. It is our feeling that if the missions, as currently operated, relocate and provide housing on the same basis as they now do, they will draw Skid Row-type men to them and contribute to the formation of a new Skid Row area. From time to time meetings have been held to interpret our program to Skid Row landlords and to clergymen who have an interest in the missions (under the Council of Churches). The plans of some missions are still very much up in the air. It seems probable that one of the least adequate of them will go out of business at the time of site clearance. However, this particular mission also supplies most of the housing for the black men who live in the Skid Row area so that the housing problem for black Skid Row men is likely to be an intensified one. There is a kind of a sadness in this case because this mission was established just after the turn of the century and was regarded as having outstanding facilities for the men of the Tenderloin at that time. The head of the mission has now grown old in service, which included outstanding leadership during the Depression of the 1930s in the effort to serve the large numbers of unemployed and transient males in the city. Another major mission

has undergone a series of changes of directors over the seven-year period and is now beginning to accommodate to its changed circumstances. Its current director is talking about treatment and other facilities rather than a continued high priority upon the "nosedive." But the mission still has a large number of difficulties to overcome during the course of transformation because its board was selected in an earlier period and has a different frame of reference than the present director. Matters are still touch and go. This does not mean that the mission director nor the mission itself has abandoned the religious theme, but that the theme will be moved toward the background. We continue to be sensitive to the importance of the missions in the total picture of Skid Row ("who else gives a damn?") and have been able to interest a Temple University graduate student in religion in a probable doctoral dissertation. It is likely that from this dissertation will come some recommendations, not only to missions, which are seeking to generate a new program, but also to the Center itself with respect to its approach to religion.

Institutional-Organizational Trends

It is to be expected that over the course of the years the agency itself would change, particularly toward increased formalization and institutionalization. The Center, under the impetus of its GPM-dominated board, has successfully achieved United Fund support. Structurally it has become much like other voluntary social welfare agencies with a self-perpetuating board, an executive director, and so forth. There are the usual kinds of questions about a strong board and weak board in these kinds of agencies, and the DRC/P is a strong one which gives the executive director a great deal of autonomy. The executive director is in close touch with the GPM committee and with the board, who are interlocked, and is able to get support in places where "power-structure" influence is helpful.

Internally, a number of changes have become evident; the executive director's primary attention is now centered upon financial problems of the agency as these relate to program.

The agency has evolved a divisional structure with considerable autonomy between the divisions, a tendency that has been facilitated by the grant-contract-project system of funding. However, over time this sort of autonomy will probably disappear, and a unitary system will probably evolve as funding becomes stabilized.

With increasing size and complexity, there is an increasing resort to formal hierarchical communication in order to handle relationships between units of the Center and to make requests for the use of staff among units. These communications across unit-divisional lines are modified by considerable informal communication, however. A large number of efforts have been tried to solve the organizational-communication problems. These have involved staff conferences, educational report meetings, newsletters, and so forth. All have been helpful.

Conclusion

We believe that a multidisciplinary approach can be successful if participants focus attention on the problem at hand rather than on the ideology of their own disciplines. There will be persistent and realistic problems with respect to action-research projects. We cannot maintain that action and research necessarily foster the commonweal. It seems to us, however, that action without research is a treadmill and that research without action neglects important human values.

37. Communication and Community Readiness for Social Change[a]

William R. Carmack*

Man always has sought some means of social control or the ability to motivate his fellows toward desirable social behavior. There is almost universal consensus that social control involves communication, but no precise model relating communication to social action is available.

Moreover, social change is so varied in setting, purpose and scope as to make generalization extremely hazardous. However, we will attempt in this paper to describe one case of social change in a large community and to show the role that communication played in it. We will look for the use and effect of all forms of communication—the print and broadcast media, speeches and person-to-person communication.

A study of the preparation of the community for desegregation of public schools in Dallas, Texas, provides us with an interesting case.[1] Before September, 1961, Dallas was the nation's largest city with a totally segregated school system. The community had expressed itself as favoring this arrangement. However, the Dallas Citizens Council became committed to the need for moving toward desegregation in several phases of community life including the schools.

This organization was formed in 1937 and composed of about 250 heads of the largest corporations in the city. It attempted to work behind the scenes, but has been the subject of a *Fortune* magazine study, two books and comments in numerous articles. Its leadership,

---

[1] The following observations and incidents related to school desegregation in Dallas are based upon the author's investigations there in 1961. A partial report of those investigations is contained in William Carmack and Theodore Freedman, *Dallas, Texas: Factors Affecting School Desegregation* (Field Reports on Desegregation in the South: New York: Anti-Defamation League, 1962).

Reprinted from William R. Carmack, "Communication and Community Readiness for Social Change," *American Journal of Orthopsychiatry*, Vol. 35, No. 3, (April 1965), pp. 539–543. Copyright ©, the American Orthopsychiatric Association, Inc. Reproduced by permission.

[a] Presented at the 1964 annual meeting of the American Orthopsychiatric Association in Chicago, Illinois.

* Chairman, Department of Speech, University of Oklahoma.

a 24-man board, meets monthly to take up "nonpolitical" matters of concern in the city. The decisions of the board have enormous economic and political impact. It was this group that designated from its number the committee to plan the attitude changes necessary to accomplish desegregation peacefully and without incidents such as had taken place in Little Rock, New Orleans and elsewhere.

Let us note the communications aspects of their program of preparation, beginning with the *Who* of communication.

The Dallas leaders were sensitive, perhaps intuitively, to what the ancient Greeks called *ethos* and the modern communications student calls source credibility. They knew that the source of the message suggesting acceptance of change in the racial mores of the community must be a thoroughly acceptable one.

Since the appeal to peaceful acceptance of planned change was to go to all groups within the community, the seven-man committee appointed from among members of the Dallas Citizens Council realized that there must be Negro representation in planning. Accordingly they expanded their group to include seven prominent Negro leaders. The two groups formed a 14-man planning committee which continues to function to this date. The biracial nature of the planning group was widely publicized and undoubtedly was important in securing community-wide acceptance for the group.

Numerous impersonal messages urging acceptance of change were issued, including posters, payroll inserts, bank statement inserts and general advertising. But the real heart of the appeal to the citizens was more personal. Two target groups were identified—the civic leaders and the general public. No short-cut for reaching the community leaders was attempted, but as one of the planning committee members put it, "We simply walked the plan through their offices." This person-to-person communication among peers was highly effective. Obviously it could not be the method used to reach an entire city. The basic instrument of public information and persuasion was a film called "Dallas at the Crossroads," produced for the occasion.

The film was narrated by Walter Cronkite

although he never was identified by name. There was an opening section on civic pride, the inevitability of change and the disastrous effect on other cities of resisting school desegregation. The film moved to a series of short statements by well-known local civic leaders who urged peaceful compliance with the law. A physician warned of the physical harm done by fear. A law school dean urged the necessity of compliance with law. Two lawyers and a judge reviewed the role of legal action in deciding public issues. The mayor of Dallas voiced pride in the city. Next a minister, a labor leader and the editors of both newspapers pledged the support of their groups to peaceful school desegregation. A former mayor pleaded for public cooperation. Finally the chief of police compared violence and mob action to murder and made it clear that those who disobeyed the law would be arrested. The movie closed with schoolchildren pledging allegiance to the flag.

In general, we know that the more personal the message, the more effective it is. It would have been difficult to make a more personal or source-credible public appeal.

Aside from the source, the message or the *What* of communication is a determinant of effectiveness. We already have noted a few of the specific appeals of the film. But whatever the communications medium or the specific message, a single theme appeared in all communication directed toward preparing Dallas for change. The theme selected was civic pride, a theme broad enough to encompass all elements within the population. It continually was stressed that anything less than full compliance with the law was poor citizenship and would reflect discredit on Dallas. This theme might be powerful anywhere, but in Dallas it was doubly appealing. "Big D" is considered by its populace to be the cultural, intellectual and social pacemaker for the nation. In stressing compliance with the law for the good of Dallas the planners had adopted a very appealing theme.

The third important component in mass communications is in the channel. A brief word about the media used in Dallas will suffice.

Every effort was made by the planners of

change to reduce to consistency and harmony all communications offered to the people of Dallas. Personal conferences with publishers of newspapers and owners or managers of radio and TV stations were held. These conferences secured the full cooperation of the mass media in covering the developing plans in such a way as to secure the greatest acceptance and to minimize the possibility of organized or spontaneous resistance. I could raise ethical and philosophical questions about the extent to which the reporting function of the press should be subservient to the community leadership function. But I will content myself here with the observation that the mass media, especially the press, managed the news of school desegregation with a view to the prearranged plan and a full exposure of the basic appeals that had been selected.

As we have seen, considerable personal contact was involved in preparing top community leadership to play its expected role. Where large audiences were involved, however, the planners discouraged personal contact. They preferred to send the film to groups for viewing rather than to supply a speaker. At one point they contemplated the possibility of a speakers' bureau for clubs, churches and other audiences but abandoned the idea because of the difficulty of controlling the speakers who might go out. By sending the film together with written introductions (one set for white and another for Negro audiences) the planners knew precisely what would take place. Moreover, for reasons which I will consider in a moment, they did not release the film for television until late in the campaign.

Aside from personal contact, newspaper coverage, and distribution of the film, the planners used several other techniques for distributing the basic appeals. One hundred thousand copies of a booklet called "Dallas at the Crossroads" were distributed to congregations in churches on a given Sunday. Slips urging peaceful desegregation were inserted into payroll checks and distributed with monthly bank statements. Posters were placed in all bars to reach some who might miss payroll envelopes and bank statements. A 37-page booklet detailing the story and stressing the basic appeals was circulated widely to the out-of-town press in an effort to insure consistency even there. In short, the available channels of communication were fully exploited, and every effort was made to offer a consistent message. Much of the detailed planning that went into this effort was the work of a professional public relations firm employed for the purpose by the Dallas Citizens Council.

A fourth factor to the communications situation, the *To Whom*, focused attention on the audience. Understanding the white community as they did, the planners were able to adapt skillfully to its needs and basic drives. The appeal to civic tranquility, skillfully contrasted with the Little Rock and New Orleans experiences, was highly effective among businessmen. As we have seen earlier, the film was designed to feature the opinion leaders of most other groups—religious, labor, manufacturing, civic, professional and the like. But the problem remained of creating the kind of setting most effective for viewing the film.

The planners reasoned quite correctly that mass exposure on television would insure that more people would see the message, but in a setting which would provide the least impact. More impact could be achieved with smaller, more homogeneous groups in which it would be easier to call to the foreground such personal roles as responsible civic worker, religious man, professional person and the like. So the film was shown on request to organized groups, clubs, Sunday schools, labor meetings and other organizations. It was delivered with a projector and operator free of charge with the request that the group use the prepared introduction and conclude the meeting without discussion or questions. The planners realized that by going through the more effective route of the small group they would miss some individuals, and they did release the film for television viewing by all channels immediately before September 6.

By analyzing the audience in terms of groups as well as individuals and by bringing group opinion leaders into the campaign skillfully the planners were able to make highly effective use of the otherwise rather impersonal mass media.

If they experienced a measure of failure, however, it probably was in the Negro community. Several things militated against their approach. In the first place the Negro community had no organization analogous to the DCC with obvious leadership firmly established. For that reason the seven representatives on the planning committee were not completely representative of the Negro group, and no seven individuals could have been. Further, the means of communication among the Negro group were not as easily manipulated. The plan was not well calculated to involve Negro churches, which were among the more important channels of communication. Consequently, early reaction among Negro residents was scattered with evidence of some disappointment. Considering the token nature of the gains made at the time, this reaction might have been inevitable, no matter how carefully communications had been employed to prepare the group. I should add at this point that integration has proceeded steadily and markedly in almost every aspect of the community's life since 1961. There is considerably less frustration and hostility among Negro leaders at present than there was then.

Perhaps the most remarkable aspect of all was the meticulous planning that went into the communication in preparation for change. Other cities facing similar problems are turning to the leaders of the Dallas experience for help in structuring social change.

The second thing that might help account for the Dallas success was widespread involvement. Everyone who had any legitimate concern in the matter was carefully sought out and involved at all stages. Not only Negro leaders but the power figures of the city among the white community were involved. Moreover, the news media were brought in from the very beginning.

A third interesting aspect of the experience was the highly successful establishment of universally appealing superordinate goals.

Fourth, the Dallas planners made effective use of the concept of reference groups in their appeals to individuals. The testimonials of the prominent professional and political leaders and Walter Cronkite's narration of the film were valuable in this regard. In short, the community was perceived by the planners in terms of groups, not just individuals. The planners rejected mass public speaking as a vehicle and did not rely to any significant degree on television. They approached small groups.

It is not easy to measure effectiveness in communication. First, we do not agree on what constitutes effectiveness. Long ago Aristotle urged that an effective message is one in which all available means of persuasion have been used regardless of the immediate success of the cause with which the communication was identified. Others have insisted on successful accomplishment of objective as the criterion. May I side-step the issue by suggesting that the Dallas case was a general success judged by either criterion. Purposes were accomplished pretty largely, and available means of persuasion were fully exploited.

I see nothing in the Dallas experience to surprise any student of communications theory. Some of what we know theoretically is well illustrated there. I do see in that experience one of the most ingenious and concerted attempts to make full practical use of what we know. And by and large the results are encouraging. Moral and ethical questions are raised that are beyond the scope of this paper. Long-range effectiveness is unclear, but we can at least call the short-run success remarkable.

38.   The Chinese Indoctrination Program for Prisoners of War: A Study of Attempted "Brainwashing"[a]

Edgar H. Schein[o]

In this paper I shall try to present an account of the 'typical' experiences of United Nations prisoners of war in Chinese Communist hands, and to interpret these experiences in a social-psychological framework. Before the return of United Nations prisoners, the "confessions" of such prominent men as Cardinal Mindszenty and William Otis had already aroused considerable interest in so-called brainwashing. This interest was heightened by the widespread rumors of collaboration among United Nations prisoners of war in Korea. Following their repatriation in August 1953, a rash of testimonial articles appeared in the weekly magazines, some attempting to show that the Chinese Communist techniques were so terrifying that no one could withstand them, others roundly condemning the collaborative activities of the so-called "progressives"[1] as having been selfishly motivated under conditions in which resistance was possible. These various accounts fall short because they are too emotionally charged to be objective, and because they fail to have any generality, since they are usually based on the personal experiences of only one man.

The data upon which this paper is based were gathered in an attempt to form a generalized picture of what happened to the average man from the time he was captured until the time he was repatriated. The data were collected during August 1953 at Inchon, Korea, where the repatriates were being processed, and on board the U.S.N.S. *General Black* in transit to the United States from September 1 to September 16.

The method of collecting the data was, in the main, by intensive interviews conducted in Inchon, where the author was a member of one of the processing teams.[2] In the course of the processing, relatively objective tests and projective tests were also given the men;[3] but intensive interviewing was felt to be preferable for gathering the data presented here, because the material to be obtained was highly novel, and because the men had been through a highly traumatic situation which might make the eliciting of *any* information very difficult. It was also recognized that the men might find it difficult to remember, might be reluctant to relate certain of their experiences, and might retrospectively falsify many events.

Of approximately 20 repatriates selected at random at different stages of the repatriation, each was asked to tell in chronological order and in as great detail as possible what had happened to him during his captivity. Emphasis was placed on what the Chinese or North Koreans *did* in their handling of the prisoners and how the men reacted. The men were particularly encouraged to relate the reactions of *others*, in order to avoid arousing anx-

---

[1] Commonly called *pro's* by their fellow prisoners.

[2] As part of the processing, psychiatric interviews were initiated at Inchon during the two or three days that the men were there. The procedure of processing has been described in detail by Henry A. Segal in "Initial Psychiatric Findings of Recently Repatriated Prisoners of War," *Amer. J. Psychiatry* (1954) 111:358–363.

[3] The results of this testing will be reported on in part by H. D. Strassman, Margaret Thaler, and E. H. Schein in "A Prisoner of War Syndrome: Apathy as a Reaction to Severe Stress," *Amer. J. Psychiatry* (1956) 112:998–1003.

Reprinted from Edgar Schein, "The Chinese Indoctrination Program for Prisoners of War," *Psychiatry*, XIX, (May 1956), pp. 149–172.

[a] The views expressed in this paper are those of the author and do not necessarily reflect the official opinion of the Department of the Army.

[o] Professor, School of Industrial Management, Massachusetts Institute of Technology.

iety or guilt over their own behavior and thereby blocking the flow of memories. The interviews varied in length from two to four hours.

From these interviews a picture emerged which was recorded in the form of a composite or typical account of the capture and imprisonment experience. This account was then given to three psychiatrists[4] who together had interviewed 300 men assigned to them at random. It was their job to delete material which, on the basis of their information, was false and to add details which had not been revealed in my 20 interviews.

On board ship I was present at a large number of psychiatric interviews and group therapy sessions, and engaged in many informal discussions with repatriates. Extended late evening "bull sessions" with repatriates were particularly informative.[5]

Many of the traumatic prison-camp experiences could probably not be fully communicated through verbal interviews. However, I believe that the data are sufficiently inclusive and reliable to provide a reasonably accurate account of prisoner-of-war experiences. The picture presented is not to be viewed as the experience of any single person, nor as the experience of all the men. Rather, it represents a composite or typical account which, in all its details, may or may not have been true for any one prisoner.

The Prisoner-of-War Experience

Capture, the March, and Temporary Camps

United Nations soldiers were captured by the Chinese and North Koreans at all stages of the Korean conflict, although particularly large groups were captured during November and December 1950. The conditions under which men were captured varied widely. Some men were captured by having their positions overrun or surrounded; others ran into road blocks and were cut off; still others fought for many days on a shifting front be-

fore they succumbed. The situation in the front lines was highly fluid, and there was a good deal of confusion on both sides. When a position was overrun, the men often scattered and became disorganized.

While the initial treatment of prisoners by the North Koreans was typically harsh and brutal—they often took the prisoner's clothing, gave him little if any food, and met any resistance with immediate severe punishment or death—the Chinese, in line with their overall indoctrination policy, often tried to create an atmosphere of friendliness and leniency. Some men reported that their Chinese captors approached them with outstretched hands, saying, "Congratulations! You've been liberated." It was made clear to the man that he could now join forces with other "fighters for peace." Often the Chinese soldiers pointed out to their captives how lucky they were not to have been captured by the North Koreans. Some men reported incidents of Chinese beating off North Koreans who were "trying to hurt" American prisoners, or of punishing their own guards for being too rough or inconsiderate. The men were usually allowed to keep their clothing, and some consideration was given to the sick and wounded. However, the food and medical attention were only slightly better than that provided by the North Koreans.

For the first six to twenty-four hours after capture, a man was usually in a state of dazed shock, unable to take any kind of integrated action and, later, unable to report any kind of feeling he had had during this period. Following this, he expected death or torture at the hands of his captors, for rumors that this woud happen had been widely circulated in the front lines, often based on stories of men who had fallen into North Korean hands. These fears were, however, quickly dispelled by the friendly attitude of the Chinese soldiers; and this friendly attitude and the emphasis on "peace" was the first and perhaps most signifi-

---

[4] These were Dr. Harvey Strassman, Dr. Patrick Israel, and Dr. Clinton Tempereau; their assistance in reading and commenting on the manuscript was extremely valuable.

[5] The reliability of the material was further checked against the complete Army files on the total group of repatriates.

cant step in making the prisoner receptive to the more formal indoctrination which was to come later.

In the next weeks or months the prisoner was exposed to great physical hardship and to a series of psychological pressures which amounted to a cyclical reactivation of fears and their relief by actual events or by extravagant promises. Implicit in most of what the Chinese said and did was the suggestion that these stresses could be brought to an end by the adoption of a "cooperative" attitude by the prisoner, although at first it was not clear just what this meant.

The men were collected behind the lines and were marched north in groups of varying sizes. The men marched only at night, averaging about 20 miles, and were kept under strict cover in the daytime. Conditions on the march were very hard. Most men reported having great difficulty eating strange and badly prepared foods; however, they were often reminded, whether true or not, that they were getting essentially the same rations as the average Chinese foot soldier. Medical care was almost nonexistent, but this too was depicted as being equally true for Chinese soldiers because of supply shortages. Almost all the men had diarrhea, many had dysentery, and most of them suffered from exposure. Every day would find a few more dead.

Although the columns were not well guarded, few escapes were attempted because the men were too weak, did not know the terrain, were on the whole poorly organized, and were afraid of the North Koreans. The few who did escape were almost always returned to the group within a short time.

During these one- to two-week marches the men became increasingly disorganized and apathetic. They developed a slow plodding gait, called by one man a "prisoner's shuffle." Lines of authority tended to break down, and the prevailing attitude was "every man for himself." Open competition for food, clothing, and shelter made the maintenance of group ties almost impossible. Everything that happened tended to be frustrating and depriving, yet there was no ready outlet for hostility, and no opportunity for constructive resistance. The only *realistic* goal was to get to prison camp where, it was hoped, conditions would be better.[6]

Uppermost in the men's minds were fantasies of food—memories of all the good meals they had had in the past, or plans for elaborate menus in the future. The only competing fantasies concerned loved ones at home, or cars, which seemed symbolically to represent the return to their homes and to freedom.

Arrival at one of the temporary camps was usually a severe disappointment. Many men reported that the only thing that had kept them going on the march was the hope of improved conditions in the camp; but they found the food as bad as ever, living conditions more crowded than before, and a continued lack of consideration for the sick and wounded. Moreover, there was now nothing to do but sit and wait. The news given the men was mostly false, playing up Communist military victories, and was, of course, particularly demoralizing. Many of the men became extremely apathetic and withdrawn, and according to some reports these apathy states sometimes became so severe as to result in death.[7]

The Chinese continually promised improvements in conditions or early repatriation, and failures of these promises to materialize were blamed on obstructions created by United Nations air activity or lack of "cooperation" among the prisoners. It was always made clear

[6] Not all of the men participated in such severe marches. Those captured in 1951 and 1952 were sometimes taken north by truck or under less severe conditions. The sick and wounded were given somewhat more consideration, although never much in the way of medical aid. Numerous incidents were reported of Chinese guards helping men, occasionally even carrying them.

It should also be mentioned that the North Korean civilians seemed ambivalent toward the prisoners. Many of them were sadistic, but many others helped the Americans by hiding them or giving them food and clothing.

[7] For a more complete description of these apathy reactions, see reference footnote 3.

that only certain prisoners could hope to get a break: those who "did well," "cooperated," "learned the truth," and so on. The Chinese distributed propaganda leaflets and required the men to sing Communist songs. Apparently even guards were sensitized to finding potential collaborators among the prisoners by observing their reactions to such activities. Outright indoctrination was not attempted on the marches and in the temporary camps, but those men who finally reached one of the permanent camps were ill-prepared physically and psychologically for the indoctrination pressures they were about to face.

Life in the Permanent Prisoner-of-War Camp

Most of the permanent camps were parts of small Korean villages, often split into several compounds in different parts of the village. The camps were sometimes surrounded by a fence, by barbed wire, or by natural barriers, although sometimes not enclosed at all. While guards were posted at key places, they were not sufficiently plentiful to prevent escapes or excursions to other parts of the village. The camp usually consisted of a series of mud huts in which the men slept on the floor or on straw matting, and a schoolhouse or other permanent building which was used as administrative headquarters, for lectures, and for recreation. The various Chinese officer and enlisted billets were usually scattered through the village. Mess and latrine facilities were very inadequate, and conditions were crowded, but far better than in the temporary camps.

In camp the men were segregated by race, nationality, and rank, and were organized into companies, platoons, and squads. The squads varied in size from 10 to 15 men, who usually shared the same living area. No formal organization was permitted among the prisoners; thus, the Chinese put their own personnel in charge of the platoons and companies, and appointed certain prisoners as squad leaders without consideration of rank.

Although the daily routine in camp varied, the average prisoner arose at dawn, was required to do calisthenics for an hour or more, was assigned to various details—such as gathering wood, carrying water, cooking, repairing

roads, burying other prisoners, and general maintenance of the camp—and then was given a breakfast of potato soup or some form of cereal at around eight o'clock. The rest of the morning and afternoon was usually spent on indoctrination or details. Whether there was a midday meal depended on the attitude of the prisoner, the supply of food, and the general state of the political situation. The main meal was served around five o'clock and usually consisted of vegetables, grains, rice, and occasional bits of pork fat or fish. For men on such a meager diet, details involving many miles of walking or very hard work were especially exhausting.

Recreation varied with the camp and with the political situation. During the first year or so, a heavy emphasis was placed on indoctrination, and recreation was restricted to reading Communist literature, seeing propaganda films, and playing such games as checkers and chess. As the truce talks progressed and repatriation became a possibility, conditions in the camps improved generally. Less emphasis was placed on indoctrination and more leeway was given to the prisoners to engage in recreation of their own choice. The improvement in living conditions made physical recreation more feasible, and the men were permitted to devise athletic fields and equipment. Intercamp "Olympics" conducted by the Chinese—and used by them for their own propaganda purposes—drew wide participation among the more athletically inclined, regardless of their political sentiments.

There are few data available concerning the sexual activities of the prisoners. There were Korean women available in the villages, but men seldom visited them. Reports of homosexuality were very infrequent.

The Indoctrination Program

All of these conditions in the permanent camp were, in actual practice, interlocked with the indoctrination program. This program cannot be viewed as a collection of specific techniques routinely applied, but rather as the creation of a whole set of social conditions within which certain techniques operated. Whether the Chinese manipulation of the social setting to create certain effects was intentional can only be conjectured; intentional or not, it was an important factor in such success as the indoctrination program achieved.

The Removal of Supports to Beliefs, Attitudes, and Values

On matters of opinion, people tend to rely primarily on the opinions of others for determination of whether they themselves are "right" or "wrong"—whether these opinions of others are obtained through mass media of communication or through personal interaction. All of the prisoners' accustomed sources of information concerning daily events on a local, national, or international level were cut off by the Chinese, who substituted their own, usually heavily biased, newspapers, radio broadcasts, and magazines. *The Daily Worker* from various cities was available in the camp libraries, as were numerous magazines and journals from China, Poland, Russia, and Czechoslovakia. The radio news broadcasts heard usually originated in China. And the camp headquarters had no scruples concerning accuracy in the news announcements made over the camp public-address system.

The delivery of mail from home was systematically manipulated; the evidence indicates that all mail which contained information about the war or the truce talks, or which contained favorable personal news, was withheld, while letters containing no general information, or bad personal news were usually delivered.

Personal contact with visitors from outside the camps was very limited, mainly restricted to Communist news correspondents. For most prisoners, there was simply no way to find out accurately what was going on in the world.

The Chinese also attempted to weaken the means of consensual validation by undermining personal contacts among the men. First of all, the men were segregated by race, apparently in order to put special indoctrination pressure on members of certain minorities, especially Negroes. The men were also segregated by rank, in what appeared to be a systematic attempt to undermine the internal structure of the group by removing its leaders. Thus the noncommissioned officers, who were at first in the enlisted camps, were put into a special camp when the Chinese found out that they were quite effective in keeping the other men from various kinds of collaboration. It was reported that this segregation was often followed by a considerable increase in collaboration, particularly among the younger enlisted men.

The Chinese emphasized that rank was no longer of any significance; the entire group was now part of a wider "brotherhood"—the earlier mentioned "fighters for peace"—in which, under communism, everyone was to be equal. The Chinese sometimes put particularly young or inept prisoners in command of the squads to remind the men that former bases of organization no longer counted. While such a procedure aroused only resistance and hostility in most of the prisoners, undoubtedly a few malcontents welcomed the opportunity to gain occupancy of the favored positions that had never been available to them before.

There was also persistent emphasis on undermining all friendships, emotional bonds, and group activities. For instance, the Chinese prohibited all forms of religious expression and ruthlessly persecuted the few chaplains or others who tried to organize or conduct religious services. Bonds to loved ones at home were weakened by the withholding of mail, as the Chinese frequently pointed out to the men that the lack of mail meant that their friends and relatives no longer cared for them.

The systematic use of Chinese spies and also informers from prisoner ranks made it possible for the Chinese to obtain detailed information about almost all activities going on in camp. The men reported that the Chinese were forever sneaking around their quarters and listening to conversations or observing activities from hidden posts, and they also knew that some of their number were acting as informers. These circumstances helped to create a feeling of general distrust, and the only fully safe course was to withdraw from all intimate interaction with other prisoners.

When any semblance of effective organization appeared spontaneously among the men, the Chinese would usually immediately remove and segregate the leaders or key figures; and informal groups which might have supported resistance activities were also usually systematically broken up. The few that were not broken up either were not effective or died because of lack of internal support, thus indicating that this system of social control was highly effective. Usually groups were formed for one of three purposes—to plan for and aid in escapes, to prevent men from collaborating, or for social reasons. According to most reports, the groups organized around escape were highly ineffective. Usually such groups were quickly liquidated by being physically broken up. A few poorly planned escapes were attempted, but the marginal diet, the strangeness of the surrounding terrain, and the carefully built-up fear of the North Koreans all served to minimize escapes. When an escape did occur, the Chinese usually recovered the man easily by offering a bag of rice to anyone turning him in. The groups organized to keep men from collaborating, or to retaliate against them if they did, were usually composed of some of the more outspoken and violent resisters. One such group, labelled the "Ku Klux Klan" by the Chinese because of its militant policy, appeared to be composed mainly of men who had served some time in prison for various infractions of camp rules. They threatened potential collaborators through anonymous notes, but the number of incidents in which they followed through was relatively small. Usually the Chinese discovered their plans and, whenever they became dangerous, disrupted their activities. The third type of group consisted of prisoners who were solely interested in each other's company; one such group, made up primarily of older prisoners, was called "The Old Soldiers' Home."

A few groups remained intact even though the Chinese knew about them, perhaps because the Chinese did not consider them very dangerous, or because their leaders, as spokesmen for the prisoners, provided a valuable sounding board whenever the Chinese wanted to know how the group would react to certain changes in policy. The latter, in fact, gave such groups some power, but if this power was ever misused—that is, if the group supported an escape attempt or a theft of food, for instance—the group was quickly liquidated and its leaders were imprisoned or moved to another camp.

Various other groupings of men existed, some, such as the squad, for administrative reasons, others to support various Chinese enterprises. Soon after capture, the Chinese made a concerted effort to recruit men for a number of "peace committees" whose purpose it was to aid in the indoctrination by conducting personal interviews with resistant prisoners and to deter any resistance activity. They also were charged with such propaganda missions as the preparation of leaflets, peace petitions, and scripts for radio broadcasts—all under the guise of running such innocuous camp activities as recreation. An intercamp peace organization was also formed to draw up peace appeals and petitions to be submitted to the United Nations, carrying, of course, the endorsement of a large number of prisoners.

The members of the camp peace committees and the delegates to intercamp peace rallies were usually selected by a pseudo-democratic method. However, the men who ended up in the key positions were usually those the Chinese wanted, or, in any case, approved of—that is, men who were willing to cooperate with the Chinese, and who had sincerely or falsely convinced their captors that they were sympathetic to the Communist cause. Sometimes the election was held over and over again until the right man was chosen. At other times the men resigned themselves to the fact that all would go more smoothly if they selected at the beginning the man the Chinese wanted, for the group could be dissolved at will anyway.

Each camp also had a number of other committees operating under the peace committee. They were responsible for the daily routine affairs of the camp, such as sanitation, food, recreation, study, and entertainment. The number of noncollaborators who were allowed to be members appeared to depend on the mood of the Chinese and the degree to which they wanted to keep in touch with prisoner opinions. It is likely that with the general improvement in camp conditions in 1952 and 1953, the membership of the various committees became more representative. The peace committees were, by then, largely defunct; they had been exploited as much as possible by the Chinese and no longer served any function in their propaganda campaigns.

Various social groups formed by pro's were left intact—perhaps as a reminder to other prisoners that one way to enter into meaningful relationships with others was through common political activities for the Communists.

One of the most significant facts about the few types of groups that did exist in camp is that they were highly unstable from an internal point of view because of the possible presence of informers and spies. Mutual distrust existed especially in the peace committees and in groups sanctioned by the Chinese, because no member was ever sure whether any other member was really a pro or was just pretending to "go along." If a man was pretending, he had to hide this carefully lest a real pro turn him in to the Chinese. Yet a man who sincerely believed in the Chinese peace effort had to hide this fact from others who might be pretenders, for fear they might harm him directly or blacklist him for the future, at the same time convincing other pro's that he really was sincere.

The members of resistance groups and social groups also had to be wary of each other, because they never knew whether the group had been infiltrated by spies and informers. Furthermore, the fact that the group might be broken up at any time tended to keep any member from becoming too dependent on, or close to, another.[8]

From the point of view of this analysis, the most important effect of the social isolation which existed was the consequent emotional isolation which prevented a man from validating any of his beliefs, attitudes, and values through meaningful interaction with other men at a time when these were under heavy attack from many sources, and when no accurate information was available.

Direct Attacks on Beliefs, Attitudes, and Values

The chief method of direct indoctrination was a series of lectures that all prisoners had to attend at some time during their imprisonment. These lectures were given daily and lasted from two to three hours. Each camp had one or more political instructors who read the lectures from a prepared text. Often one instructor read while another seemed to follow a second copy of the text, as if to make sure that the right material was being presented. The lectures were direct, simple, black-and-white propaganda. They attacked the United Nations and particularly the United States on various political, social, and economic issues, at the same time glorifying the achievements of the Communist countries, and making strong appeals for "peace."

Most men reported that the anti-American material was naïve and seldom based on adequate or correct information about the United States. Even the pro-Communist arguments were sometimes weak and susceptible to attack. Occasionally a well-educated prisoner debated points on communism successfully with instructors who had little knowledge of the classical works of communism. Usually the instructors presented the neo-Communist views of writers such as Mao Tse-tung and were unable to counter the arguments of prisoners who knew Marx and Lenin. The number of prisoners with sufficient education to engage in such arguments was, however, extremely small.

The constant hammering at certain points, combined with all the other techniques used— and in a situation where the prisoners had no access to other information—made it likely that many of the Chinese arguments did filter through enough to make many of the men question some of their former points of view. It is also likely that any appeal for "peace," no matter how false, found a receptive audience among combat-weary troops, especially when

---

[8] Segal (reference footnote 2) has aptly described such prisoner groups as "groups of isolates."

it was pointed out that they were fighting on foreign soil and were intervening in a civil war which was "none of their business." Both lectures and didactic "interrogations" emphasized detailed predictions of what would happen to the prisoners upon repatriation, some of which turned out to be accurate.[9] The Chinese implied that certain problems which would arise would be the result of the "weakness" or "unfairness" of the democratic ideology.

Another direct technique was the distribution of propaganda leaflets and the showing of Communist films glorifying the accomplishments of the Communist regime in Russia and China, and pointing out how much more had been done by communism for the peasant and laborer than by the capatalist system. While such films might have been highly ineffectual under ordinary circumstances, they assumed considerable importance because of the sheer lack of any other audio-visual material.

Perhaps the most effective attack on existing values, beliefs, and attitudes was the use of testimonials from prisoners who were ostensibly supporting Communist enterprises. These included peace petitions, radio appeals, speeches, and confessions. The use of such testimonials had a double effect in that it further weakened group ties while presenting pro-Communist arguments. As long as the men unanimously rejected the propaganda, each of them could firmly hold to the position that his beliefs must be right, even if he could not defend them logically. However, *if even one other man became convinced, it was no longer possible to hold this position.* Each man was then required to begin examining his beliefs and was vulnerable to the highly one-sided arguments that were repeatedly presented.

Of particular importance were the germ-warfare confessions which were extracted from a number of Air Force officers and enlisted men. The Chinese made a movie of one or two of the officers giving their testimony to the "international" commission which they had set up to investigate the problem, and showed

this movie in all the camps. Furthermore, one or two of the officers personally went from camp to camp and explained how United Nations forces had used these bombs; this made a powerful impression on many men who had, until then, dismissed the whole matter as a Chinese propaganda project. The great detail of the accounts, the sincerity of the officers, the fact that they were freely going from camp to camp and did not look as if they were then or had previously been under any duress made it difficult for some men to believe that the accounts could be anything but true.

While it is difficult to determine how many men were convinced that the United Nations forces had used germ bombs, it is evident that serious doubts arose in the minds of many, and some admitted being still in doubt even some weeks after their repatriation. Unquestionably, personal testimonials were on the whole a far more effective propaganda weapon than any amount of direct lecturing, although they both played a part in the overall indoctrination. In general, the older and more experienced prisoners were less susceptible to this kind of propaganda. One sergeant stated that the following kinds of reasons prevented him and others from falling for germ-warfare charges: first, germ bombs are tactically impractical and ineffective; second, the United States would probably not abandon its ethics, and germ bombs would not be consistent with those ethics; and third, even if the United States were to use weapons previously not considered ethical, it would use atom bombs in preference to germ bombs.

The Chinese also used Koreans to give testimonials concerning the barbarity of the United Nations; in one instance women and children told one of the peace committees how United Nations planes had dropped toys which exploded when children tried to pick them up. It is difficult to evaluate the effects of such propaganda, but it is not likely that many prisoners believed stories of such extremity.

[9] The various problems that faced repatriates have been discussed by Segal, reference footnote 2, and by Robert J. Lifton in "Home by ship: Reaction Pattterns of American Prisoners of War Repatriated from North Korea," *Amer. J. Psychiatry* (1954) 110:732–739.

Indirect Attacks on Beliefs, Attitudes, and Values

In the direct attacks which I have been discussing, the source of propaganda was external. In the indirect attacks, a set of conditions was created in which each prisoner of war was encouraged to participate in a way that would make it more possible for him to accept some of the new points of view. One attempt to accomplish this was by means of group discussions following lectures.

Most lectures ended with a series of conclusions—for example, "The South Koreans started the war by invading North Korea," or "The aim of the capitalist nations is world domination." The men were then required to break up into squads, go to their quarters, and discuss the material for periods of two hours or more. At the end of the discussion each squad had to provide written answers to questions handed out during the lecture—the answers, obviously, which had already been provided in the lecture. To "discuss" the lecture thus meant, in effect, to rationalize the predetermined conclusions.[10]

A monitor was assigned to each squad to "aid" the men in the discussion, to make sure that they stayed on the proper topic, and to collect the answers and make sure that they were the "right" ones. Initially, the monitor for most squads was an English-speaking Chinese, but whenever possible the Chinese turned the job over to one of the squad members, usually the one who was most cooperative or sympathetic to the Communist point of view. If one or more members of the squad turned in "wrong" answers—for example, saying that the North Koreans had invaded South Korea —the entire squad had to listen to the lecture again and repeat the group discussion. This procedure might go on for days. The Chinese never tired of repeating the procedure over and over again, apparently believing that group discussion had a better chance of success in converting men to their point of view than individual indoctrination.

The success of such discussions often depended on the degree of supervision. If the monitor was lax, the groups would talk about anything but the required material. But a prisoner-of-war monitor who was actively pro-Communist or a Chinese who had a good understanding of English idiom might obtain considerable discussion. Even when an issue was actively discussed, in many cases it probably reinforced the United Nations position by providing an opportunity for the men to obtain some consensual validation. But in other cases, the deliberation on points of view other than the one they had always held caused them to question certain beliefs and values which in the past had not led to satisfactory conditions for them.

A second means of indirect attack was interrogation. Interrogations were carried on during all stages of internment, but their apparent function and the techniques utilized varied from time to time. Almost all men went through lengthy and repetitive military interrogations, but failure to answer questions seldom led to severe physical punishment. Instead, various psychological pressures were applied. For instance, all information supplied was cross-checked against earlier interrogations and against the information from other men. If an answer did not tally with other information, the respondent had to explain the discrepancy. Continuous pressure to resolve contrary answers often forced a man to tell the truth.

The Chinese tried to create the impression that they could obtain *any* information from *anyone* by the following interrogation technique: If a man continued to refuse to answer a question, despite great fatigue and continued repetition of the question, the interrogator would suddenly pull out a notebook and point out to the man the complete answer

[10] During the last year or so of imprisonment, many of the features of indoctrination which earlier had been compulsory were put on a voluntary basis. Any prisoners who were interested in learning more about communism could attend special lectures and group discussions. The men who participated in such voluntary programs were known as "self-study pro's" and were given many privileges not accorded to other prisoners.

to the question, sometimes in astonishingly accurate detail. The interrogation would then move on to a new topic and the same procedure would be repeated, until the man could not assess whether there was indeed *anything* that the Chinese did *not* know. In most cases the man was told that others had already given information or "confessed," so why should he hold back and suffer?[11]

A further technique was to have the man write out the question and then the answer. If he refused to write it voluntarily, he was asked to copy it from the notebooks, which must have seemed like a harmless enough concession. But the information which he had copied could then be shown to another man as evidence that he had given information of his own volition. Furthermore, it could be used to blackmail him, because he would have a hard time proving that he had merely copied the material.

Another type of interrogation to which almost all men were subjected involved primarily nonmilitary information. The Chinese were very curious about all aspects of life in the Western world and asked many questions about it, often in great detail. They also endeavored, by means of printed forms, to obtain a complete personal history from each prisoner, with particular emphasis on his social-cultural background, his class status, his and his parents' occupational histories, and so on. The purpose was apparently to determine which prisoners' histories might predispose them toward the Communist philosophy and thus make them apt subjects for special indoctrination.

Most men did not give accurate information. Usually the prisoner filled out the form in terms of fictitious characters. But later he would be required to repeat the entire procedure and would usually be unable to remember his earlier answers. He would then be confronted with the discrepancies and would be forced into the fatiguing activity of having to invent justification after justification to resolve them.

If and when the Chinese felt that they had

obtained a relatively true account, it was used in discussion between the interrogator and the prisoner to undermine the prisoner's beliefs and values. Various points in the life history were used to show a man the "errors" of his past life—for example, that he or his parents had been ruthless capitalists exploiting workers, yet had really received only meager benefits from such exploitation. The Chinese were particularly interested in any inconsistencies in the life histories and would focus discussion on them in order to bring to light the motivations involved. Whenever possible, any setbacks that a man had experienced economically or socially were searchingly analyzed, and the blame was laid on the capitalistic system.

The fact that many men were unclear about why they were fighting in Korea was a good lever for such discussions. The interrogator or instructor could point out the basic injustices of foreign intervention in a civil war, and simultaneously could arouse longings for home and the wish that the United Nations had never taken up the fight in the first place. It was not difficult to convince some men that being in Korea was unfair to the Koreans, to themselves, and to their families who wanted them home.

Interrogations might last for hours, days, or even weeks. In some cases the interrogator lived with his subject and tried to create an atmosphere of warmth and friendliness. The main point seemed to be to get the prisoner talking, no matter what he was talking about. The discussions sometimes became effective didactic sessions because of the friendly relationship which the interrogator built up. If there were any weaknesses or inconsistencies in a man's belief systems, once he lowered his guard and began to examine them critically, he was in danger of being overwhelmed by the arguments of the instructor. This did not, of course, occur typically. For many men such critical self-evaluation served as a reinforcement to their own beliefs and actually enabled them to expose weaknesses in the Communist arguments.

---

[11] Many men reported that they felt the Chinese were boasting when they told what they knew—that they were very proud of their ability as interrogators and felt a need to show off to their captors.

Another effective technique for getting the men to question their own beliefs and values was to make them confess publicly to wrong-doings and to "criticize" themselves. Throughout the time that the men were in camp they were required to go through these rituals over and over again, no matter how trivial the offense. These offenses usually were infractions of camp rules. Soon after the men had arrived in permanent camp they were given copies of the camp rules and were required to sign a statement that they would abide by them. Most of the men were far too hungry and cold to read several pages of script covering every aspect of camp life in such minute detail that it was practically impossible not to break one of the rules from time to time. For example, an elaborate set of rules governed where in camp a man was allowed to expectorate.

Sooner or later a minor or major infraction of the rules would occur. The man would be immediately brought up before the camp commander, where his offense would be condemned as a serious crime—one for which he, the commander would point out, could be severely punished, if it were not for the lenient Chinese policy. In line with the great show which the Chinese made of treating the prisoner as a responsible person, the fact that he had agreed in writing to abide by the rules would be emphasized. The prisoner could not now say that he had not read the rules, for this would expose him to further embarrassment. The camp commander would then ask whether the man would admit that he had broken the rule, whether he was sorry that he had done so, and whether he would promise not to behave in such a "criminal" manner in the future. If the offender agreed which seemed at the time to be harmless enough and an easy way to get off, he would be asked to write out a confession.

Sometimes this ended the matter. But frequently the man was required to read his confession to a group of prisoners and to follow it by "self-criticism," which meant that the description of the wrong deed had to be analyzed in terms of the wrong *idea* that lay behind it, that the self had to be "deeply and sincerely" criticized in terms of a number of reasons why the idea and deed were "wrong," and that an elaborate set of promises about future conduct had to be made, along with apologies for the past. Such public self-effacement was a humiliating and degrading experience, and it set a bad precedent for other men who had been attempting to resist getting caught in this net.

Writing out confessions, reading them, and criticizing oneself for minor misconduct in camp did not seem too great a concession at first when viewed against the possibility of physical punishment, torture, or imprisonment. However, these techniques could become a psychological torture once the initial concession had been made. A man who had broken a rule and had gone through the whole ritual of criticism would shortly afterward break another rule, which woud arouse increased hostility on the part of the Chinese and lead to correspondingly greater demands for confession and self-criticism. Men who had confessed at first to trivial offenses soon found themselves having to answer for relatively major ones.[12]

It should be pointed out, however, that the prisoners found numerous ways to obey the letter but not the spirit of the Chinese demands. For example, during public self-criticism sessions they would often emphasize the wrong words in the sentence, thus making the whole ritual ridiculous: "I am sorry I called Comrade Wong *a no-good son-of-a-bitch.*" Another favorite device was to promise never to "get caught" committing a certain crime in the future. Such devices were effective because even those Chinese who knew English

[12] It can be seen that such a technique of "training" a man to confess can ultimately lead to the demand that he confess not only to misdeeds and the "wrong" ideas which lay behind them, but also to "wrong" thoughts and feelings which had not even resulted in action. In conjunction with public self-appraisal, prisoners were also often encouraged to keep diaries of their activities and thoughts. Usually only those prisoners who seriously studied communism kept diaries.

were not sufficiently acquainted with idiom and slang to detect subtle ridicule.

There is also some evidence that the Chinese used enforced idleness or solitary confinement to encourage prisoners to consider the Communist point of view. One of the few activities available, in such circumstances, was to read Communist literature and books by Western authors who directly or indirectly attacked capitalism. The camp libraries were wholly made up of such literature. Those who did not have the strength or inclination to go on physically taxing details found themselves with no alternative but to spend their time reading pro-Communist material. In addition, some read because they felt so emotionally isolated from other prisoners that they could enjoy only solitary activities.

The Eliciting of Collaboration by Rewards and Punishments

For a number of propaganda purposes the Chinese seemed to want certain men to cooperate in specific ways, without caring whether they accepted communism or not. These men did not seem to enjoy as much status as other pro's and were cast off by the Chinese as soon as they had ceased to be useful. Such collaboration was elicited directly by a system of rewards and incentives on the one hand, and threats and punishments on the other.

While it is dangerous to relate complex human behavior to a simple pattern of rewards and punishments, the repatriates' accounts of life in the prisoner-of-war camps make possible a considerable number of inferences concerning the "positive" and "negative" aspects of the social environment, which were important in eliciting the kind of behavior the Chinese wanted. It was made clear to all prisoners, from the time of their capture on, that cooperation with the Chinese would produce a more comfortable state of affairs, while non-cooperation or open resistance would produce a continuing marginal existence. Which rewards were of primary importance to the men

varied with their current condition. On the marches and in the temporary camps physical conditions were so bad that more food, any medication, any clothing or fuel, better and less crowded living conditions, and the like constituted a powerful reward. Promises of early repatriation, or at least of marked improvement of conditions in the permanent camps, were powerful incentives which were chronically exploited.

In the permanent camps there was some improvement in the physical conditions, so that basic necessities became less effective incentives. The promise of early repatriation continued to be a great incentive, however, despite the fact that it had been promised many times before without result. Communicating with the outside world now became a major concern. To let those at home know they were alive, some prisoners began to collaborate by making slanted radio broadcasts or filling their letters with propaganda or peace appeals in order to make sure that they were sent.

As conditions continued to improve, some of the luxury items and smaller accessories to living assumed greater significance. Cigarettes, combs, soap, candy, small items of clothing, a cup of hot tea, a drink of liquor, fresh fruit, and other items of this kind were sought avidly by some men.[13] Obtaining such items from the Chinese was inextricably linked with the degree to which the prisoner was willing to "cooperate." Any tendency toward "cooperation" was quickly followed by an increase in material rewards and promises for the future.

In some cases rewards were cleverly linked with participation in the indoctrination. For example highly valued prizes such as cigarettes or fresh fruit were offered for essays dealing with certain aspects of world politics. The winning entries were published in the camp newspaper or magazine. Usually the winning entry was selected on the basis of its agreement with a Communist point of view, and the winner was usually someone well on

---

[13] A number of men reported that black-market activities flourished among the prisoners. Those items of value which men did not wish to use themselves were bartered or sold to other men. Even valuable medicines could sometimes be obtained only by bartering with pro's who had obtained them from the Chinese.

the road to collaboration anyway, but the whole competition succeeded in getting the men to participate—to consider the various sides of an issue and to examine their previous views critically.

The Chinese also used rewards and punishments to undermine group organization. For example, shortly after capture, a number of men were led to believe that if they made radio broadcasts to the United Nations lines they would be repatriated early. The content of the broadcasts was not specified, but the men agreed to make them in the hope of letting their relatives know that they were alive. These men were then conspicuously assembled in front of other prisoners and were taken to a special location some distance away, where the broadcasts were to be made. In the meantime, other prisoners were encouraged to believe that these men were obtaining special privileges because they were "cooperating" in bringing "peace" to Korea.

The actual content of the radio messages turned out to be a peace appeal which tacitly condemned the United Nations, and a statement that the prisoners were being well treated by the Chinese. When the men saw the messages that they were to read, some of them refused to make the broadcast, despite threats of severe punishment. Other men agreed to make the broadcast but tried to code a message into the prescribed text, and still others hoped that the recipients of the broadcasts would somehow know that they were under duress. At least their families would know that they were alive if they broadcasted something.

When these men rejoined the other prisoners, they found that they had aroused the suspicion and hostility of many, especially since the Chinese showed their "appreciation" by ostentatiously bestowing favors on them. In order to retain these special privileges—and having in any case incurred the hostility or even ostracism of their own group—some of these men continued to collaborate, rationalizing that they were not really harming the United Nations cause. They became self-appointed secret agents and attempted to infiltrate the Chinese hierarchy to gather "intelligence information," in which capacity they felt that they could actually aid the United Nations cause.

Among the most effective rewards used by the Chinese were special privileges and certain symbolic rewards, such as rank and status in the prison hierarchy. Perhaps the most important of the privileges was freedom of movement; the pro's had free access to the Chinese headquarters and could go into town or wherever they wished at any time of the day or night. They were given certain preferred jobs, such as writing for the camp newspaper, and were excused from the more unpleasant chores around the camp. They were often consulted by the Chinese in various policy matters. They received as a status symbol a little peace dove to be worn in the lapel or a Mao Tse-tung button which served as an identification badge. And many rewards were promised them for the future; they were told that they were playing a vital role in the world-wide movement for "peace," and that they could enjoy positions of high rank in this movement if they stayed and continued to work for it.

If one asks why men "fell" for this kind of line—why they were able to believe this kind of promise—one must look to the circumstances described earlier. These men had no sources of contrary information to rely on, and once they had collaborated even a little they were ostracized by their buddies, thus losing the support of the group which might have kept them from collaborating further.

Just as the probability of collaborative behavior could be increased through the use of rewards, the probability of resistance could be decreased through negative or painful stimulation. Usually threats of punishment were used when prisoners refused to "cooperate," and actual punishment was meted out for more aggressive resistance. Threats of death, nonrepatriation, torture, reprisals against families, reduction in food and medication, and imprisonment were all used. While the only one of these threats which was carried out with any degree of consistency was imprisonment, which sometimes involved long periods of solitary confinement, the other threats were nevertheless very effective and the possibility that they might be carried out seemed very real. Especially frightening was the prospect of nonrepatriation, which seemed a likely possibility before the prisoner lists were exchanged at Panmunjom. The threat of death was also effective, for the men knew that they could be killed and listed officially as having died of heart failure or the like.[14] With regard to food and medication, the men could not determine whether they were actually being punished by having these withheld, or whether the meager supply was merely being reserved for "deserving" prisoners.

An effective threat with officers was that of punishing the whole group for which the officer was responsible if he personally did not "cooperate." The incidence of such group punishment was not revealed in the accounts, but it is clear that if an officer did "cooperate" with the Chinese, he was able both to relieve his own fears and to rationalize his cooperation as being the only means of saving the men for whom he was responsible.

Reinforcing all these threats was the vague but powerful fear of the unknown; the men did not know what they were up against in dealing with the Chinese and could not predict the reactions of their captors with any degree of reliability. The only course that led to a consistent reduction in such tension was participation in Chinese enterprises.

Overt punishment varied with the offense, with the political situation, and with the person administering it. Shortly after capture there were numerous incidents of brutality, most of them committed by North Koreans. During early interrogations the Chinese frequently resorted to minor physical punishment such as face-slapping or kicking when answers were not forthcoming, but a prisoner who continued to be silent was usually dismissed without further physical punishment.

Physical punishments in permanent camps had the effect of weakening rather than injuring the men. They varied from severe work details to such ordeals as standing at attention for long periods; being exposed to bright lights or excessive cold; standing on tiptoe with a noose around the neck; being confined in the "cage," a room too small to allow standing, sitting, or lying down; being thrown in the "hole," a particularly uncomfortable form of solitary confinement; or being kept in filthy surroundings and denied certain essentials for keeping clean. Those who were *chronically* uncooperative were permanently segregated from the rest of the group and put into special camps where more severe forms of discipline backed by harsher punishments were in effect. Basically, the "lenient policy" applied only to those men whom the Chinese hoped they could use.

More common forms of punishment for minor infractions were social in character, intended to degrade or embarrass the prisoner in front of his fellows. Public confessions and self-criticisms were the outstanding forms of such punishment, with blackmail being frequently used if a prisoner had once collaborated to any extent. There is *no* evidence that the Chinese used any drugs or hypnotic methods, or offered sexual objects to elicit information, confessions, or collaborative behavior. Some cases of severe physical torture were reported, but their incidence is difficult to estimate.

General Principles in All Techniques

Several general principles underlay the various phases of the Chinese indoctrination, which may be worth summing up at this point. The first of these was *repetition*. One of the chief characteristics of the Chinese was their immense patience in whatever they were doing; whether they were conducting an interrogation, giving a lecture, chiding a prisoner, or trying to obtain a confession, they were always willing to make their demand or assertion over and over again. Many men pointed out that most of the techniques used gained their effectiveness by being used in this repetitive way until the prisoner could no longer sustain his resistance. A second characteristic

---

[14] There is evidence that the Chinese sometimes staged "executions" in order to elicit cooperation. A prisoner might be marched out into a field, an empty gun placed to his head, and the trigger actually pulled. This procedure first created a state of high anxiety and then a state of grateful relief when it was discovered by the prisoner that he would not be executed after all.

was the *pacing of demands.* In the various kinds of responses that were demanded of the prisoners, the Chinese always started with trivial, innocuous ones and, as the habit of responding became established, gradually worked up to more important ones. Thus after a prisoner had once been "trained" to speak or write out trivia, statements on more important issues were demanded of him. This was particularly effective in eliciting confessions, self-criticism, and information during interrogation.

Closely connected with the principle of pacing was the principle of constant *participation* from the prisoner. It was never enough for the prisoner to listen and absorb; some kind of verbal or written response was always demanded. Thus if a man would not give original material in question-and-answer sessions, he was asked to copy something. Likewise, group discussions, autobiographical statements, self-criticisms, and public confessions all demanded an active participation by the prisoner.[15]

In their propaganda campaign the Chinese made a considerable effort to *insert their new ideas into old and meaningful contexts.* In general this was not very successful, but it did work for certain prisoners who were in some way not content with their lot in the United States. The obtaining of autobiographies enabled each interrogator to determine what would be a significant context for the particular person he was dealing with, and any misfortune or setback that the person had suffered served as an ideal starting place for undermining democratic attitudes and instilling communistic ones.

No matter which technique the Chinese were using, they always structured the situation in such a way that the correct response was followed by some form of reward, while an incorrect response was immediately followed by *threats* or *punishment.* The fact that the Chinese had complete control over material resources and had a monopoly of power made it possible for them to manipulate hunger and some other motives at will, thereby giving rewards and punishments their meaning.

Among the various propaganda techniques employed by the Chinese, their use of *prestige suggestion* was outstanding. The average prisoner had no way of disputing the germ-warfare confessions and testimonials of Air Force officers, or the conclusions of an investigation of the germ-warfare charges by ostensibly impartial scientists from many nations.

Among the positive propaganda appeals made, the most effective was probably the *plea for peace.* The Chinese presented an antiwar and laissez-faire ideology which strongly appealed to the war-weary combat soldier.

In addition, the Chinese used a number of *manipulative tricks,* which were usually successful only if the prisoner was not alert because of fatigue or hunger. One such trick was to require signatures, photographs, or personal information for a purpose which sounded legitimate, then using them for another purpose. Some prisoners reported that they were asked to sign "camp rosters" when they first arrived in camp and later found that they had actually signed a peace petition.

In essence, the prisoner-of-war experience in camp can be viewed as a series of problems which each man had to solve in order to remain alive and well integrated. Foremost was the problem of physical privation, which powerfully motivated each man to improve his living conditions. A second problem was to over-

---

[15] The Chinese apparently believed that if they could once get a man to participate he was likely to continue, and that eventually he would accept the attitudes which the participation expressed. However, it may have also been true that the interrogators, for instance, were in danger of losing face with their own group if they could not produce concrete evidence that they had obtained some information; at times they seemed to want any kind of answers, so long as they had something to show in headquarters as proof that they had done their job. Similarly, the material obtained at the end of the group discussions was perhaps used as evidence that the instructors were doing their jobs properly. Thus it is possible that part of the aim was a check by the Chinese on each other.

come the fears of nonrepatriation, death, torture, or reprisals. A third problem was to maintain some kind of cognitive integration, a consistent outlook on life, under a set of conditions where basic values and beliefs were strongly undermined and where systematic confusion about each man's role in life was created. A fourth problem was to maintain a valid position in a group, to maintain friendship ties and concern for others under conditions of mutual distrust, lack of leadership, and systematically created social disorganization. The Chinese had created a set of conditions in which collaboration and the acceptance of communism led to a resolution of conflicts in all these areas.

Reactions to the Indoctrination

It is very difficult to determine after the fact what happened in this highly complex and novel situation—what it was really like for the men who had to spend several years in the Chinese prisoner-of-war camps. Each set of experiences had a highly personal and unique flavor to it, making generalized conclusions difficult.

I may illustrate the problem by discussing *ideological change* and *collaboration*. Both of these were responses to the indoctrination, broadly conceived, *but neither necessarily implies the other*. It was possible for a man to collaborate with the enemy without altering his beliefs, and it was equally possible for a man to be converted to communism to some degree without collaborating.

Obviously, it is necessary to define these responses, even though any precise definition will to some degree distort the actual events. *Collaboration* may be defined as any kind of behavior which helped the enemy: signing peace petitions, soliciting signatures for peace petitions, making radio appeals, writing radio scripts, writing false information home concerning conditions in the camps (or recording statements to this effect), writing essays on communism or working for the Communist-controlled newspaper, allowing oneself to be photographed in "rigged" situations, participating in peace rallies or on peace committees, being friendly with the enemy, asking others to cooperate with the enemy, running errands

for the enemy, accepting special privileges or favors, making false confessions or pro-enemy speeches, informing on fellow prisoners, divulging military information, and so on.

Nothing about ideological conversion is implied in this definition. A man who engaged in any of these collaborative behaviors because he wanted an extra cigarette was just as much a collaborator as one who did so because he wanted to further the Communist cause. Moreover, the definition does not take into account the temporal pattern of such behavior. Many men collaborated at one time during their imprisonment when one set of conditions existed, but did not collaborate at other times under other conditions. The man who moved from collaboration to resistance was obviously different from the man who moved from resistance to collaboration. Perhaps most important of all, this definition says nothing about the particular pattern of motivations or circumstances that drove a man to the first collaborative act and subsequently into a situation in which it was difficult to stop collaborating.

Yet such a concept of collaboration has an advantage in its reference to *overt* behavior. It was such behavior which the other men in camp reacted to and which often formed the basis for later judgments of a man by his government, family, and friends, although different motives were often imputed by different sources for such behavior. The motives that lay behind the behavior are of obvious importance and must be understood, but it should also be recognized that conjectures of motives are more precarious than analyses of behavior.

Ideological change may be defined as a reorganization of political beliefs, which could vary from acquiring mild doubts concerning some aspects of the democratic ideology to the complete abandonment of this ideology and a total embracing of communism. The latter I shall label *conversion*. The problem of measuring the *degree* of ideological change is complicated by the lack of good behavioral criteria for measuring such a process of reorganization of beliefs. One might be tempted to say that anyone could be termed a convert who actively attempted to convince others of the worth of communism, who took all the advanced courses in camp, and who was able to demonstrate in his overt behavior a disregard for democratic values. But such behavior might also characterize a relatively intelligent man who had begun to read Communist literature out of boredom, only to find that both his friends and the Chinese took this as evidence of his genuine interest in communism. He might then be ostracized by his friends and pressed into collaboration by the Chinese, who, it was rumored, severely punished anyone who deceived them.

Of all the prisoners, 21 refused repatriation; one might assume that these represent the total number of converts, but such a criterion is inadequate on at least two grounds. On the one hand, some converts would undoubtedly have been sent back to the United States to spread communism and form a potential fifth column. On the other hand, some collaborators who had not changed ideologically might have been afraid to return, knowing that court-martial proceedings and personal degradation probably awaited them.

One might think that the identification of such men could be made successfully by others who were collaborators and possibly converts. However, anyone who had been and remained a convert would *not* identify other converts. On the other hand, a collaborator who had repudiated communism and his own collaborative activities would be likely to implicate as many others as possible in order to make his own behavior look better. Allegations from known collaborators are therefore very unreliable.

Thus it is more difficult to determine how the prisoners responded to indoctrination techniques ideologically than it is to determine what overt collaboration occurred. What the prisoners *did* is, relatively speaking, a matter

of fact; why they did it is a matter of conjecture. In presenting a classification of types of reactions and the motivation patterns or situations that elicited them, one must rely primarily on the *consensus* of the accounts of the repatriates and must recognize the possible biases that can arise in such an analysis after the fact. I am not implying that each prisoner could be placed into one of the categories to be presented below; it is more likely that each man fell into several categories at any given time, and, moreover, that his motivation-situation complex shifted as different sets of circumstances presented themselves.

The "Get-Alongers"

The predominant reaction of prisoners was to establish a complex compromise between the demands of the Chinese and the demands of their own ideology. This kind of behavior was labeled "playing it cool" by the men, and consisted primarily in a physical and emotional withdrawal from all situations which might arouse basic conflict. Men who reacted in this way were unwilling to do anything that did not have to be done, and learned after some months to "suspend" their feelings about most events, no matter how provoking they might be. This was not an easy adjustment to maintain, since the prisoner had to make some concessions to the Chinese to avoid the more severe physical or psychological pressures, at the same time avoiding cooperating to such an extent as to arouse the suspicion and hostility of his fellow prisoners. The safest course was to withdraw emotionally both from the Chinese and from the rest of the prisoner group; this withdrawal was made easier by the apathy and physical weakness induced by life under marginal conditions.[16]

Most of the men who achieved this kind of compromise successfully without too great a

---

[16] For Puerto Ricans and other foreign nationals whose knowledge of English was very shaky, the problem was easily solved. These men conveniently forgot what little English they knew, and, because the Chinese did not have instructors who could speak their languages, they were permitted to withdraw to a relatively comfortable existence of doing details or routine chores. A few others successfully convinced the Chinese that they were illiterate or in some other way incapacitated for study. Some men resolved the conflict by volunteering for all the heavy or unpleasant details, but obviously such a solution was available only to the physically strong and healthy.

toll on their personality were well integrated and retained secure and stable group identifications from before their prisoner-of-war experience. Their judgment concerning the extent to which they could collaborate safely had to be relatively unimpaired, and they had to be able to evaluate objectively and dispassionately threats made by the Chinese.

At the beginning, while the noncommissioned officers were still in the enlisted camps, many of them were able—partly because of their strong identification with the Army, and partly because of their wider experience—to help the other men carry out such a compromise solution. In many situations they were able to give advice that appears to have been sound from all points of view; thus they would help the other men compose answers to questions that would be sufficiently pro-Communist to satisfy the Chinese but not extreme enough to arouse the suspicion of other prisoners or to be called treasonable. They would also advise the other men on the wisdom of cooperating in the lectures, of trying to escape, and so on.

The Resisters

A number of men developed chronic resistance as their main mode of behavior in camp, refusing to go along with even the most trivial of Chinese requests. This lack of cooperation varied from passive resistance to active, organized obstructionism. Such men were a great trial to the Chinese, who labeled them "reactionaries" and either imprisoned them, if they felt they had some justification, or segregated them in special camps. According to the dynamics involved, these men seem to have fallen into four somewhat separate classes.

THE OBSTRUCTIONIST

These men were characterized by a life-long pattern of indiscriminate resistance to all forms of authority,[17] and had histories of inability to get along in the United Nations Army just as they were unable to get along with the Chinese. They openly defied any attempt to get them to conform, and performed deeds which other prisoners considered heroic, such as withstanding severe torture. Usually these men spent a major part of their internment in the camp prison, in solitary confinement, or in the "hole."

THE IDEALIST OR MARTYR

These men had unusually powerful identifications with groups whose ideology demanded that they actively resist all forms of pressure from the Chinese. The best example would be the man who was deeply religious and whose faith demanded absolute noncooperation with a "Godless enterprise" of the type the Chinese represented.

THE ANXIOUS GUILT-RIDDEN PERSON

This was the man who was afraid of his own inclination to be tempted by the positive rewards that the Chinese offered for collaboration, and who could handle these impulses only by denying them and overreacting in the other direction. He was chronically guilt-ridden over his unpatriotic and antisocial impulses and absolved himself by indulging in exaggerated forms of resistance.

THE WELL-INTEGRATED RESISTANCE LEADER

Probably the majority of resisters fell into this class, although there is no way to estimate their number. Because of extensive experience in difficult situations and a thorough understanding of the military, they were able systematically to organize other men and to set important precedents for resistance. Most of the commissioned and noncommissioned officers fell into this group.[18] The chief characteristic of these men seemed to be their ability to

---

[17] This pattern has been well described by Lifton, reference footnote 9.

[18] I have already mentioned the role of noncommissioned officers in helping the "get-alongers" to maintain a compromise role; my mention of them here is an illustration of the fact that this is not a classification of the men, as such, but a a classification of behavior. Thus, just as the noncommissioned officers displayed leadership in many instances in compromise, so they also functioned as resistance leaders whenever possible.

make valid judgments concerning possible courses of action in a situation in which there was little information on which to base such judgments. They had to be able to guess what Chinese reactions would be, what United Nations reactions would be, and most important, how to handle the other prisoners.

The Cooperators

This group is the most difficult to delineate, since I am attempting to include not only those whom the Chinese considered progressives but all those who collaborated to any significant extent. The accounts of prisoners concerning men who collaborated make possible the discrimination of six somewhat separate patterns of motivation for such behaviors.

THE WEAKLING

This was the man who was chronically unable to resist any form of authority, and who was unable to withstand any degree of physical or psychological discomfort. Such men probably became collaborators very soon after their internment, with a minimum of ideological involvement, because it was the easiest way. They often found that the more they collaborated, the more collaboration was demanded of them. They were highly susceptible to threats of blackmail by the Chinese who could exhibit the evidence of their collaboration to the other prisoners or the United Nations authorities. From the point of view of these men, collaboration was an acceptable adjustment under the physical strains of internment, and they developed elaborate rationalizations to justify their behavior and to convince themselves that they would not suffer for it in the future.

THE OPPORTUNIST

These men exploited the role of pro for all its material benefits, again without any ideological involvement, and with little consideration for the future welfare of themselves or others. They were characterized chiefly by their lack of stable group identification either inside or outside the Army. They met all situations as they arose and tried to make the most out of them for themselves.

THE MISGUIDED LEADER

A minority of commissioned and noncommissioned officers engaged in various types of collaborative activities under the firm impression that they were furthering the United Nations cause and resisting the enemy. Their primary error was one of judgment. They reasoned that the best way to resist indoctrination was to go along with it, to find out what the Chinese were up to, to get into the inner circle so as to better plan resistance. In most cases, they managed merely to set a bad precedent for other prisoners, who felt that if their superiors were getting special privileges they should be getting them as well. These officers, like others, found that once they had begun to collaborate it was difficult to stop. Some of these men were probably weakling types who personally preferred the path of least resistance, but who, because of their responsible positions, had to develop adequate rationalizations. They could not see that their course of action was highly inappropriate; they saw only a justification which met their own needs.

THE BORED OR CURIOUS INTELLECTUAL

Of the very small number of men who had superior education, some turned to Communist literature out of boredom or curiosity, and then found that they had aroused both the hostility of their own group and the expectations of the Chinese that they would collaborate. Only a few managed to interest themselves in the Communist literature without falling into this dilemma. More often, material rewards for the intellectual's interest resulted in his ostracism from his own group, and drove him in the direction of collaboration. Some of these men were fooled by the promise of early repatriation in return for collaboration, and they felt that their collaboration would be sufficiently minor not to damage their own futures. These men, like those previously described, seldom became ideologically confused or converted. Essentially they used bad judgment in an ambiguous situation.

THE "LOW-STATUS" PERSON

The man who was most vulnerable *ideologically* was one who had never enjoyed any kind of secure or rewarding status position either in his home community or in the Army. This type included the younger and less intelligent, the malcontent, and the man whose social reference groups made the attainment of status difficult—that is, the member of various racial, religious, national, or economic minority groups. These men had little realization of the benefits of democracy because they had never experienced them in a meaningful way. They felt that the society was more to blame for their failures than they were. Such men were ready to give serious consideration to an ideology that offered remedies for their misfortunes. As pro's within the Communist hierarchy they could, for the first time, enjoy some measure of status and privilege, and the Chinese wisely promised them important roles in the future of the "peace movement." Some of these men were probably among those who declined repatriation—perhaps out of fear, when they realized how seriously they had jeopardized their position in the Army and at home, perhaps in order to stay with the cause which had for the first time allowed them to be important. It is difficult to determine whether such men underwent a complete ideological conversion, but there is no doubt that they gave serious consideration to the Communist cause, at least to the limit of their intellectual capacity.[19]

The accounts of the repatriates were unclear regarding the reactions of members of the various minority groups, especially the Negroes. The Communist technique of segregating the Negroes and giving them special indoctrination was probably a tactical error. Many Negroes felt that if they were going to be segregated they might as well be segregated in the United States—that there was nothing new or better about communism in this respect. Moreover, the propaganda given them was too extreme; even the very low-status

Negro knew that his circumstances in the United States were not as bad as the Communists painted them.

However, because of the low-status category of most of the Negroes, the positive appeals made to them must have struck responsive chords in some. They had an opportunity to be leaders and to enjoy fully equal status if they became pro's, and they could rationalize that they would be able to improve the position of their race by participating in Communist peace movements which advocated equality. It is not possible to determine to what extent these positive appeals outweighed the deterrents, and thus to estimate the degree to which ideological change occurred among the Negroes. In any case, the Chinese probably could have persuaded more Negroes to collaborate and to embrace communism had they not made the fundamental errors of segregation and poor propaganda.

THE COMMUNIST SYMPATHIZER

This was the man who, even before he had joined the Army, was sympathetic to the Communist cause and who, therefore, felt no conflict about his course of action in the prisoner-of-war camp. However, if there were loyal Communists in the camps, it is unlikely that the Chinese divulged their identity by calling them pro's, since they would be of far more use as undercover agents.

Attitudes Toward Progressives

The reaction of most men toward the pro's was one of perplexity, fear, and hostility. They could not understand how anyone could "swallow the junk" the Chinese were presenting, yet they were afraid that they too might be swayed, for among the pro's were many men like themselves. If the pro was a "weak-minded guy" or a man who did not have the stamina to resist the physical pressures, other

---

[19] The men who were most vulnerable to ideological appeals were not necessarily the ones the Chinese encouraged to become pro's. There is considerable evidence that the Chinese were quite selective in giving important jobs to prisoners and that they favored more mature and stable ones. Thus the younger, less intelligent, and less stable person was exploited by the Chinese in the same manner as he had probably been exploited before. The Chinese made what use they could of such men and then rejected them when they ceased to be useful.

men felt some sympathy for him, but at the same time they resented the extra privileges that his weakness gained for him. If the pro was perceived to be an opportunist, he was hated and threatened with retaliation during internment or following repatriation. If the pro was a person who had status or rank, the men felt perplexed and afraid; they could not decide what they themselves should do, especially if such a pro tried to convince them that it was acceptable to collaborate.

The pro's were very conspicuous in camp by their identification symbols, by their special privileges—which they did not hesitate to flaunt—and by the fact that they usually congregated around camp headquarters. This made them ideal scapegoats and targets for hostility.

They were ostracized by the other prisoners who often refused even to carry on conversations with each other when a pro was present, forcing the pro's into interaction with each other. Thus they tended to form tightly knit groups, which continued even after the end of their internment. The men accused the pro's of informing, imputed to them many motives about which they themselves felt guilty, and attributed any punishment they suffered to some report by a pro. They threatened the pro's with physical violence, but were usually prevented by the Chinese from carrying out such threats. Later, on board ship, the men frequently said that they would now "get even," but the low rate of incidents suggests that no realistic plans underlay the threats. Perhaps most men felt too guilty about their own actual or fantasied collaboration to be comfortable about retaliating against those who had succumbed to the temptations.

The attitudes of the pro's varied with their motivations. Those who had been tricked or "seduced" into collaborating before they could fully realize the consequences remained aloof from other prisoners because they felt guilty and afraid. The opportunists or low-status prisoners felt their collaboration to be entirely justified by the prison-camp situation and viewed noncollaborators as "fools who don't know a good thing when they see it." They tried to persuade others to collaborate—in

some cases because they sincerely believed part of the Chinese propaganda, and in other cases because they knew that the Chinese would reward them still further if they succeeded. Many pro's tried hard to remain liked both by the Chinese and by the other prisoners, but few succeeded. Since the Chinese presented themselves as benevolent captors, the pro's were the only group in camp who could consistently be used as an outlet for all the hostility engendered by the prison-camp situation.

The Effectiveness of the Indoctrination Techniques

By disrupting social organization and by the systematic use of reward and punishment, the Chinese were able to elicit a considerable amount of collaboration. This is not surprising when one considers the tremendous effort the Chinese made to discover the weak points in individual prisoners, and the unscrupulousness with which they manipulated the environment. Only a few men were able to avoid collaboration altogether—those who adopted a completely negativistic position from the moment of capture without considering the consequences for themselves or their fellow prisoners. At the same time the number of men who collaborated to a sufficient extent to be detrimental to the United Nations cause was also very small. The majority collaborated at one time or another by doing things which seemed to them trivial, but which the Chinese were able to turn to their own advantage. Such behavior did not necessarily reflect any defection from democratic values or ideology, nor did it necessarily imply that these men were opportunists or neurotics. Often it merely represented poor judgment in evaluating a situation about which they had little information, and poor foresight regarding the reactions of the Chinese, other prisoners, and people back home.

The extent to which the Chinese succeeded in converting prisoners of war to the Communist ideology is difficult to evaluate because of the previously mentioned hazards in measuring ideological change, and because of the impossibility of determining the *latent* effects of the indoctrination. In terms of *overt* criteria of conversion or ideological change, one can only conclude that, considering the effort devoted to it, the Chinese program was a failure. Only a small number of men decided to refuse repatriation—possibly for reasons other than ideological change[20]—and it was the almost unanimous opinion of the prisoners that most of the pro's were opportunists or weaklings. One can only conjecture, of course, the extent to which prisoners who began to believe in communism managed to conceal their sympathies from their fellows and the degree to which repatriates are now, as a result of their experience, predisposed to find fault with a democratic society if they cannot make a go of it.

It is difficult to determine whether to attribute this relative failure of the Chinese program to the inadequacy of their principles of indoctrination, to their technical inefficiency in running the program, or to both these factors. In actual practice the direct techniques used were usually ineffective because many of the Chinese instructors were deficient in their knowledge of Western culture and the English language. Many of their facts about America were false, making it impossible for them to obtain a sympathetic audience, and many of their attempts to teach by means of group discussion failed because they were not sensitive to the subtle ways in which prisoners managed to ridicule them by sarcasm or other language devices. The various intensive pressures brought to bear on single prisoners and the fostering of close personal relationships between prisoner and instructor were far more effective in producing ideological change, but the Chinese did not have nearly enough trained personnel to indoctrinate more than a handful of men in this intensive manner.

The technique of breaking up both formal and spontaneous organization was effective in creating feelings of social and emotional isolation, but it was never sufficiently extended to make the prisoners completely dependent on

the Chinese. As long as the men lived and "studied" together, there remained opportunities for consensual validation and thus for resisting indoctrination. However, as a means of social control this technique was highly effective, in that it was virtually impossible for the prisoners to develop any program of organized resistance or to engineer successful communication with the outside by means of escapes or clandestine sending out of information.

The most powerful argument against the intellectual appeal of communism was the low standard of living which the men observed in the Korean villages in which they lived. The repatriates reported that they were unable to believe in a system of values which sounded attractive on paper but which was not practiced, and they were not impressed by the excuse that such conditions were only temporary.

Most men returned from prison camp expressing a strong anti-Communist feeling and a conviction that their eyes had, for the first time, been opened to the real dangers of communism. Many men who had taken little interest in politics before returned with the feeling that they now knew what the United States was fighting for in Korea, and expressed a willingness to continue the fight wherever necessary. Hostility toward the Communists was expressed in such violent proposals as blowing up the *Daily Worker* building or deporting all registered Communists to Korea so that they could see the system in operation firsthand. The repatriates' attitude implied that anything labeled "Communist" had to be destroyed, and anything or anyone against communism had to be supported to the greatest possible extent; types of communism or types of approaches in dealing with communism were not evaluated separately.

It was, of course, difficult to determine the strength and stability of sentiments expressed a few days or weeks after repatriation. In some men these feelings undoubtedly repre-

[20] A discussion of some background factors in the lives of these men is presented by Virginia Pasley in *21 Stayed*; New York, Farrar, Strauss & Cudahy, 1955. Unfortunately her study is inconclusive because she did not investigate the background factors in a control group of men who decided to be repatriated.

sented an attempt to overcome the guilt that they felt for having collaborated or wavered in their beliefs. In other men they represented simply the accumulated hostility of two to three years of unrelieved frustration and deprivation. But, curiously, this hostility was seldom verbalized against the Chinese as such; it was always the Communists or the pro's who were the targets. The men were confused about the Chinese because they were so inconsistent; they never felt that they could understand or predict the Chinese reaction to anything.

The summary, it can be said that the Chinese were successful in eliciting and controlling certain kinds of behavior in the prisoner population. They were less successful in changing the beliefs of the prisoners. Yet this lack of success might have been due to the inefficiency of a program of indoctrination which could have been highly effective had it been better supported by adequate information and adequately trained personnel.

Collaboration with the enemy occurs to a greater or lesser extent in any captive population. It occurred in the Japanese and German prisoner-of-war camps during World War II. But never before have captured American soldiers faced a *systematic effort* to make them collaborate and to convert them to an alien political ideology. The only precedent in recent history was the handling of political prisoners by the Nazis, described by Bettelheim.[21] By means of extreme and degrading physical and psychological torture the Nazis attempted to reduce the prison population to an "infantile" state in which the jailer would be viewed with the same awe as the child views his father. Under these conditions, the prisoners tended, in time, to identify with the punitive authority figures and to incorporate many of the values they held, especially with respect to proper behavior in camp. They would curry the favor of the guards, would imitate their style of dress and speech, and would attempt to make other prisoners follow camp rules strictly.

It is possible that such a mechanism also operated in the Chinese prison camps. However, the Nazis attempted, by brutal measures, to reduce their prisoners to docile slave laborers, while the Chinese attempted, by using a "lenient policy" and by treating the prisoners as men in need of "education," to obtain converts who would actively support the Communist point of view. Only those prisoners who showed themselves to be "backward" or "reactionary" by their inability to see the fundamental "truths" of communism were treated punitively.

The essence of this novel approach is to gain complete control over those parts of the physical and social environment which sustain attitudes, beliefs, and values, breaking down interactions and emotional bonds which support the old beliefs and values, and building up new interactions which will increase the probability of the adoption of new beliefs and values. If the only contacts a person is permitted are with persons who *unanimously* have beliefs different from his own, it is very likely that he will find at least some among them with whom, because of growing emotional bonds, he will identify and whose beliefs he will subsequently adopt.

Is the eliciting of collaborative behavior in itself sufficient to initiate the process of ideological change? One might assume that a person who had committed acts consonant with a new ideology might be forced to adopt this ideology in order to rationalize his behavior. This might happen especially if the number of possible rationalizations were limited. The situation in the prison camps, however, allowed the men to develop rationalizations which did not necessarily involve Communist premises. Furthermore, it is likely that whatever rationalizations are adopted, they will not acquire the permanence of beliefs unless supported by social reinforcements. When the prisoners reentered the democratic setting, most of them gave up whatever Communist premises they might have been using to rationalize their collaboration and found new rationalizations that

[21] Bruno Bettelheim, "Individual and Mass Behavior in Extreme Situations," *J. Abnormal and Social Psychol.* (1943) 38:417–452.

attempted to explain, from the standpoint of democratic premises, why they had collaborated. Apart from the technical difficulties the Chinese experienced in running their indoctrination program, they were never able to control social interactions to a sufficient extent to reinforce in meaningful social relationships the Communist rationalizations for collaboration.

Taken singly, there is nothing new or terrifying about the specific techniques used by the Chinese; they invented no mysterious devices for dealing with people. Their method of controlling information by controlling the mass media of communication has been a well-known technique of totalitarian governments throughout history. Their system of propagandizing by means of lectures, movies, reading materials, and testimonials has its counterparts in education and in advertising. Group discussions and other methods requiring participation have their counterparts in education and in psychiatry. The possibility that group discussion may be fundamentally superior to lectures in obtaining stable decisions by participants has been the subject of extensive research in American social psychology. The Chinese methods of interrogation have been widely used in other armies, by the police, by newspaper reporters, and by others interested in aggressively eliciting information. Forced confessions and self-criticism have been widely used techniques in religious movements as a basis for conversion or as a device to perpetuate a given faith. The control of behavior by the manipulation of reward and punishment is obviously the least novel of all the techniques, for men have controlled each other in this way since the beginning of history.

Thus, the only novelty in the Chinese methods was the attempt *to use a combination of all these techniques and to apply them simultaneously* in order to gain complete control over significant portions of the physical and social environment of a group of people. Such an ambitious effort applied on such a large scale is probably unique in the Communist movement, and perhaps in the *Chinese* Communist movement. In order to understand and evaluate this attempt to create ideological uniformity, it is necessary to view the techniques cited in terms of a social-psychological model which does justice to the complexity of this combination. Attempts such as Meerloo's[22] or Winokur's[23] to conceptualize the process of brainwashing in terms of a simple conditioning or learning model seem not only to be premature, but to ignore the most important factor—the simultaneous application of many techniques of social and behavioral control.

Before brainwashing can be properly understood, far more information must be gathered on its operation within China and within the Communist party as a whole; factors which the Chinese have succeeded in manipulating must be built into social-psychological researches on social conformity and attitude change; theoretical models must be constructed which will give a properly weighted emphasis to the variety of factors which probably operate in brainwashing; and personality concepts must be developed which can be used convincingly to categorize the behavior of people subjected to an attack on their most fundamental beliefs and values.

And most important, those who are attempting to understand brainwashing must look at the facts objectively, and not be carried away by hysteria when another country with a different ideology and with different ultimate ends succeeds in eliciting from a small group of Americans behavior that is not consonant with the democratic ideology.

[22] Joost A. M. Meerloo, "Pavlovian Strategy as a Weapon of Menticide," *Amer. J. Psychiatry* (1954) 110:809–813.

[23] George Winokur, " 'Brainwashing'—A Social Phenomenon of Our Time," *Human Organization* (1955) 13:16–18.

PART **THREE**

MANAGEMENT OF SOCIAL CHANGE

Editors' Introduction
to Part III

Every instance of planned social change has a management aspect. The political canvas of the community, the peace demonstration, the school drug abuse program, even violent confrontation—all depend upon the development, management, and direction of human and other resources. The extent of the conscious management input varies, with perhaps a minimum manifested in a gathering of angry people led by a few leaders and a maximum manifested in the operation of large organizations, such as social work agencies, the Peace Corps, and Planned Parenthood Federation, with their formal hierarchies and efficient business procedures.

What do we mean by management? *Management is the process of mobilizing ideas, things, and persons toward the achievement of objectives.* As long as there is a group, a set of objectives, and leadership, there is management.

This does not necessarily mean that people involved in causes are conscious of a management process. Causes are borne out of a womb of discontent. Leaders arise to crystallize issues, project dreams, provide direction, and promise deliverance. Leaders and followers are initially carried along by a plethora of enthusiasm and a scarcity of plans. In fact, many new cause groups resent the appearance of too much "management." They may deny management or even oppose it as potentially corruptive of the group's spirit and mission.

465

But if the cause is to survive and grow, its adherents must eventually recognize and accept the necessity of management. The cause must be turned into a function.[1] This is recognized universally by groups as far apart in their objectives as conservationists, prohibitionists, abortionists, and revolutionaries. They all assent to the "need to organize."

The effectiveness of a group pursuing a cause will depend on many circumstances both outside and under its control. Outside factors—technological, political, economic and cultural—will have an immense effect on the outcome. Within the context set by these forces, the quality of management will make the rest of the difference.

The management process consists of a set of functions that must be carried out in some form. We might say that it consists broadly of the four activities of organizing, planning, implementing, and controlling.[2]

Organizing means developing an administrative structure to initiate and carry out the tasks facing the social enterprise. It consists of defining the authority relationships and job responsibilities within the organization and the relationship of the organization to various supporters, clients, and other organizations.

Planning means determining the proper course of action. It can be subdivided into a number of finer functions, such as fact-finding, forecasting objectives, selecting strategies, and developing a program, budget, procedures and policies. All of these planning functions are formally carried on in large social change agencies such as settlement houses, health organizations, and political parties, and most of them are carried on in less formally organized social enterprises.

Implementing means carrying out the plans and programs of the organization. It consists of such subfunctions as delegating, motivating, coordinating, selling, and innovating. Implementation usually reveals new problems that require recycling to the goal-setting or program planning phase.

Controlling means taking steps to insure the progress of the organization toward its objectives. It involves such functions as establishing a reporting system, developing performance standards, measuring results, taking corrective actions, and administering rewards and sanctions. For a cause to thrive, those involved must experience a sense of progress toward their objectives; otherwise, they get frustrated, lose interest, and drop out. Control is necessary to insure this progress and to signal when new adaptation or social innovation is necessary.

The four management functions are in a logical but not necessarily inalterable sequence. During the lifetime of its activities, a social enterprise may reorganize many times, alter its plans based on the results of previous implementations, and do other things that show adaptation. Furthermore, it will carry on

---

[1] See Porter R. Lee, *Social Work as Cause and Function* (New York: Columbia University Press, 1937), p. 99 "The momentum of the cause will never carry over adequately to the subsequent task of making its fruits permanent. The slow methodical organized effort needed to make enduring the achievement of the cause calls for different motives, different skill, different machinery . . . Zeal is perhaps the most conspicuous trait in adherents to the cause, while intelligence is perhaps most essential in those who administer a function. The emblazoned banner and the shibboleth for the cause, the program and the manual for the function; devoted sacrifice and the flaming spirit for the cause, fidelity, standards, and methods for the function; an embattled host for the cause, an efficient personnel for the function."

[2] There are many ways to state the functions of management, with lists as short as three functions (planning, organizing, and controlling) and as long as eight functions (objective-setting, decision-making, policy formation, planning, organizing, motivating, controlling, and innovating). For a recent attempt at synthesis, see R. Alec MacKensie, "The Management Process in 3-D," *Harvard Business Review* Vol. 47 (November–December 1969), pp. 78–87.

other important functions at various times and at all levels of the organization such as analysis, decision-making, and communication.

It is our contention that those who seek to be effective at social change should approach their problems with a conscious management perspective. The management process will take place regardless of whether it is carried out consciously or not. But to be maximally effective, management has to be conscious: goals and plans must be developed, roles established, persons recruited, directions given, and progress measured. There is a crying need, particularly in the larger social change organizations, for professional managers, men who have both zeal and organizational ability, who know how to mobilize the energies of others for effective actions. This is the major conclusion, for example, in the family planning area:

> A great deal more emphasis needs to be placed on the *administrative* and *organizational* aspects of family planning services. If there is one deficiency in this field that is more serious than any other, I think it's neither lack of an ideal method or inadequacy of our persuasion techniques. *It is a general lack of adequate implemental machinery.* We don't have family planning administrators who know how to furnish services efficiently to great masses of population. We don't have a cadre of people who can organize a governmental program, for example, and apply it to a large population and run it successfully. I believe that the desire for fertility control (motivation) is high enough to give us a good, strong beginning in most of the nations of the world—if we could satisfy it properly. Information is low; practice is lower; we don't have the network of administration and organization to take this program into the field. We need to build it.[3]

To this end, readings have been selected to elucidate the four processes that make up management—organizing, planning, implementing, and controlling. They are presented in Sections VI through IX.

Section VI deals with two major facets of organizing for social change—that of selecting an organizational strategy and that of running an effective organization. Alternative organizational strategies are discussed for community organization work in Jack Rothman's "Three Models of Community Organization Practice." Three quite different patterns of mobilizing community resources for social change are distinguished. The first model, *locality development,* is exemplified by settlement houses, overseas community development programs, and the Peace Corps. These organizations assume that the client population has a will and capacity for self-help which can be energized by the change agency working with them in the role of participants and joint problem solvers. The second model, *social planning,* is exemplified by welfare councils, city planning boards, and the federal bureaucracy. These organizations tend to see the client population as consumers of their effort and spend their time in fact-gathering and program development that can be handed over or sold to the population. The third model, *social action,* is exemplified by civil rights groups, trade unions, militant community organizations, and the New Left. These organizations present themselves as the representatives of client populations who are disadvantaged or exploited and who must organize to fight the existing power structure for their fair share.

The challenge to assess competing models of community organization practice led Robert Pruger and Harry Specht in "Assessing Theoretical Models of Community Organization Practice: Alinsky as a Case in Point" to develop an assessment paradigm which they proceeded to apply to Saul Alinsky's practice model. The paradigm consists of eight elements: problems selected, clients, goals, tactics of change, community involvement, requirements of the change agents, evaluation, and empirical validation. In addition to their interesting findings about the Alinsky model, their assessment approach represents a useful

---

[3] Bernard Berelson, "On Famly Planning Communication," in D. Bogue (ed.), *Mass Communication and Motivation for Birth Control,* (Chicago: University of Chicago, Community and Family Study Center, 1967), p. 49.

paradigm for the comparative evaluation of community organization models.

The extent to which citizen clienteles should be involved in the running of community organizations is next discussed in Sumati Dubey's "Community Action Programs and Citizen Participation: Issues and Confusions." Dubey distinguishes four rationales advanced to support the cause of resident participation: improve program relevancy, more power, better service, and democratic inculcation. Where participation has been established, it has taken the form of either involvement of the clients on the board of directors, or in a staff capacity, or in constituent feedback group capacity. The particular form of client participation depends upon whether the power structure's ultimate interest lies in containment, co-optation, and codetermination. Dubey illustrates these varying approaches in the context of the recent history of community action programs.[4]

The next three articles focus on the problem of running an effective organization. They cover a civil rights organization, a local political organization, and a social service organization, respectively.

In "Setting up an Organization" Martin Oppenheimer and George Lakey provide many practical pointers for the civil rights organizer. Among the issues they discuss are rank-and-file participation, developing staff assignments, managing finances, handling public relations, and conducting meetings. The viewpoint is essentially pragmatic, but based on a good deal of experience and insight into the requisites for organizational effectiveness.

William Singer in "Reflections on Campaign Techniques" deals with similar issues, this time for the local political organization. He draws useful delineations among different personnel (campaign manager, office manager, campaign treasurer, advisers), and different campaign functions (political action, coffee parties, candidate visibility, scheduling, advertising, publicity, volunteers, special events, re-

search, letter writing, telephone campaigns). His discussions of pragmatic organization issues not only applies to political contests, but also is a helpful guide for all groups seeking to take campaigns to the people.

Next the case of effectively running a complex service organization is discussed in Herbert D. Stein's "Administrative Leadership in Complex Service Organizations." Stein notes the tendency of well-intentioned organizations to drift over time into serving the needs of the staff over the needs of the clients. When this is realized, the leadership takes steps to reform the organization toward service, but this too has dysfunctional consequences. Stein then offers several good suggestions based on modern administrative theory for maintaining a responsive organization.

Section VII introduces the important function of planning, which is a task facing all organizations that do not simply wish to "muddle through" their problems. Planning calls, first, for establishing objectives and secondly for developing programs for accomplishing these objectives. In the process of doing this, the change agent must also confront the issue of ethics, which is raised in all forms of planned social intervention.

In "The Hierarchy of Objectives" Charles H. Granger shows the crucial contribution that can be made by clarifying the objectives of an organization or program and placing them in a meaningful hierarchy. Too often the objectives of an organization are not thought through, or are unrealistic, or are imprecise, or are not communicated, or are obsolete. Granger argues and illustrates how these dysfunctional conditions can be avoided.

Amitai Etzioni, in "'Shortcuts' to Social Change?" takes a close look at the social change efficacy of short-run objectives and programs as opposed to presumably more effective longer-run ones. He notes that many social scientists are cynical about expedient measures because these work at the level of symptom rather than cause and create only an

---

[4] An excellent review of some of the recent consequences of citizen participation is found in Jon Van Til and Sally Bould Van Til, "Citizen Participation in Social Policy: The End of the Cycle?" *Social Problems*, Vol. 17, No. 3, (Winter 1970), pp. 313–323.

illusion of progress. Thus, the introduction of better street lighting in a high-crime area may seem to reduce the area's crime rate but in fact may only send the criminal to ply his craft in other areas, since street lights do nothing about the causes of crime. Etzioni takes this and other examples and shows that short-run measures, nevertheless, may be practical in the light of limited resources and might even have some beneficial permanent consequences.

The setting of objectives prepares the way for the work of developing effective programs. The first question that arises is where should the change agency turn for good ideas on which to base its program. Ronald Lippitt in "The Use of Social Research to Improve Social Practice" considers this problem. He distinguishes and illustrates six different ways to identify and utilize change ideas. Change ideas can be gathered from outside of the client system in three ways: through surveying the ideas of professional scientists and workers, through developing feasibility experiments, and through evaluating experiments that have been tried elsewhere. Alternatively, change ideas can be gathered within the client system in three ways: through surveying its members, through training and encouraging them in habits of self-study, and through training them in scientific method. Lippitt concludes by discussing the general problem of the differences between trying to utilize knowledge in the physical sciences and in the social sciences.

The actual shaping of programs to carry out social change objectives can be effectively carried out by using the framework of marketing science, according to Philip Kotler and Gerald Zaltman in their paper "Social Marketing: An Approach to Planned Social Change." The authors, after considering some differences between business and social marketing, show how social planning can be viewed as the problem of developing appropriate products, prices, distribution, and promotion. They present an overall model to guide the planning and feedback relations between the change agency and its markets.

A specific application of the marketing phi-

losophy to the family planning area is made by Julian L. Simon in "Some 'Marketing Correct' Recommendations for Family Planning Campaigns." Simon notes the recommendations of a well-known family planning expert, Donald J. Bogue, agrees with several of them, and takes issue with others that do not seem correct from a marketing point of view. Simon calls for larger and more varied birth control information programs which are based on the hard-nosed criteria that commercial advertisers would use in seeking to get a maximum return on their invested dollars.

The final example of program development is discussed for environmental control in "Teach-In On the Environment." The teach-in is seen as an effective device for informing and dramatizing an important cause to a large number of potential supporters. The article illustrates the extensive thought and planning that must go into the programming of a successful teach-in.

The next two articles raise important ethical questions about the choice of objectives and programs that involve intervention in the affairs of others. Herbert C. Kelman in "Manipulation of Human Behavior: An Ethical Dilemma" poses the essential dilemma: "any manipulation of human behavior inherently violates a fundamental value, but there exists no formula for so structuring an effective change situation that such manipulation is totally absent." He goes on to delineate different types of manipulation associated with the work of the practitioner, the applied researcher, and the basic researcher, and then illustrates specific steps that men in each of these roles can take to mitigate the manipulative aspects of their work.

David Hapgood and Meridan Bennett's paper "Intervening in the Affairs of Others" considers these ethical issues in the context of the Peace Corps program. Peace Corps activities can range from improving crops to trying to implant American values. Very rarely do the American officials of these programs consider which objectives are legitimate and, in fact, whether they have any moral right to disturb the cultural values of another people.

Various new problems and opportunities arise in the attempt to take a social program from the drawing boards to the streets. Section VIII presents various issues related to implementation. In "Introducing Social Innovation" James B. Taylor describes how a change agency that introduces a new program in a community faces a number of potential problems associated with staff relations, working with other community agencies, and client resistances. The project he described was implemented successfully because it utilized, in retrospect, five principles for introducing social innovations: maximum investment, co-optation, equalitarian responsibility, research as creative play, and ideological research leadership. Because of the high spirit and dedication of those involved in the project, it had a substantial impact on the community.

"Educating New York City Residents to Benefits of Medicaid" by Raymond S. Alexander and Simon Podair describes a special campaign which was organized to overcome a disappointing response on the part of New York City residents to a new medical program (Medicaid) which had been offered to them. The original implementation of the program had failed because Medicaid was not explained well, was confused with Medicare, and seemed to be connected with relief. To overcome public misinformation and apathy, the planners reached out to community leaders and prepared mass advertising and specialty advertising (car cards, sound trucks, leaflets). Their well-planned public information campaign resulted in a substantial increase in the enrollment of eligible people in the program.

The great number of specific campaign tactics and techniques are further amplified, this time in the context of stop-smoking efforts, in TB-RD's "Kick the Habit Campaign." This campaign guide is prepared by public relations specialists for the benefit of all local groups throughout the country working to dissuade persons from starting or continuing the smoking habit. It is written not as a theoretical guide, but as a practical campaign document for use by nonscientific workers involved in a cause.

The attempt to implement social programs is bound to encounter various forms of resistance, some anticipated, and others that come as a complete surprise. Goodwin Watson in "Resistance to Change" subdivides resistance forces into those emanating from personality and those emanating from the social system. Personality resistance factors include homeostatis, habit, primacy, selective perception and retention, dependence, superego, self-distrust, and insecurity and regression. Social system resistance factors include conformity to norms, systemic and cultural coherence, vested interests, the "sacrosanct," and rejection of "outsiders." In the light of these sources of resistances Watson presents some recommendations for effective change involving who brings the change, the kinds of change, and the manner of change.

Gerhard Eichholtz and Everett Rogers in "Resistance to Adoption of Audio-Visual Aids by Elementary School Teachers: Constrasts and Similarities to Agricultural Innovation" develop a model to explain the frequent resistance of school systems and teachers to the adoption of new educational media. Called a rejection model (in contrast to an adoption model), it relates various resistances to different psychological states of the target consumer. Along the way the authors compare and contrast generalizations from the two research traditions of rural sociological research and educational diffusion research.

Section IX deals with the fact that control must follow organizing, planning, and implementation if the social enterprise is to stay on course. In "Evaluating Social Action Programs" John W. Evans looks at the evaluation problem from the point of view of the government funder who must determine what programs, techniques, and specific projects to support out of the many vying for funds. He sees the solution as lying in the greater use of cost/benefit analysis and illustrates how this technique would function in the evaluation of antiproverty programs.

Donald T. Campbell in "Reforms as Experiments" looks at the evaluation problem from the point of view of the social scientists. He argues that social reform efforts should be accompanied by well-designed experiments to evaluate their effects. Unfortunately, many past social measurement efforts have faulted in one or more respects to provide conclusive evidence for attempted reforms. Campbell's article, through its many illustrations, helps sensitize the reformer and researcher to the various requirements of well-designed research to improve social knowledge.

In the final article, "Can India Reduce its Birth Rate? A Question of Modernization and Governmental Capacity," Nicholas J. Deme-

rath provides a comparative historical account of the changing efforts of the Indian government to bring into being an effective program of birth rate reduction. This case study of large-scale social change planning cogently demonstrates the role of periodic evaluations of the current program in leading to dramatic redirections of the social effort. Effective social change effort requires a continuous adjustment of means, and even targets, to a constantly evolving environment marked by new problems and new opportunities.

SECTION VI

ORGANIZING FOR SOCIAL CHANGE

A. SELECTING AN ORGANIZATIONAL STRATEGY

39. Three Models of Community Organization Practice[1]

Jack Rothman*

Of the three "primary" areas of practice in social work,[2] community organization was the last to emerge as a definitive method. It remains essentially underdeveloped and ill-de-fined in comparison with casework and group work. It was not until 1939 with the publication of the first Lane report[3] that community organization practice was systematically stud-

Reprinted from Jack Rothman, "Three Models of Community Organization Practice," *Social Work Practice* (New York: Columbia University Press, 1968), pp. 16–47.

* Department of Social Work, University of Michigan.

[1] For their useful suggestions and other contributions to this article I wish to express warm appreciation to my colleagues, Fred Cox, John Erlich, Mitchel Lazarus, and John Tropman.

[2] According to the Council on Social Work Education, there are three "primary" practice areas or "methods of direct service" in social work: casework, group work, and community organization. In addition, there are two "enabling methods: administration and research. (Official Statement of Curriculum Policy for the Master's Degree Program in Graduate Professional Schools of Social Work, adopted by the Board of Directors, 1962.) There is a trend for some schools to treat administration also as a primary method of practice.

[3] Robert P. Lane, "The Field of Community Organization," in *Proceedings of The National Conference of Social Work, 1939* (New York: Columbia University Press, 1939), pp. 495–511, and "Report of Groups Studying the Community Organization Process," in *Proceedings of the National Conference of Social Work, 1940* (New York: Columbia University Press, 1940), pp. 456–73.

ied by social workers, and not until 1947 in papers by Pray[4] and Newstetter[5] that its theoretical and/or philosophical underpinnings were subjected to serious analysis. Definitions of community organization and conceptions regarding its nature vary markedly, even drastically. Consider that in the Curriculum Study of the Council on Social Work Education the largest number of position papers (representing varying approaches) appeared in the volume on community organization.[6] Harper and Dunham[7] in their anthology list thirteen different definitions of community organization and indicate that at least 50 to 100 definitions have been projected in social welfare and sociological literature in the past thirty-five years. Add to this still another endeavor in the more recent Working Definition, a statement prepared by the Community Organization Committee of the National Association of Social Workers.[8] Suffice it to say that a welter of differing, contrasting, and sometimes clashing formulations of community organization practice exists, and that this condition has been a source of immense perplexity and discomfort to the struggling practitioner and to the teacher of community organization.

A similar condition prevails in allied professional fields which have community organization and planning aspects. In a number of these fields, such as education (adult education) and public health (public health education and planning), the community organization dimension is somewhat peripheral and outside the main thrust of the profession—as has been the case in social work. These areas have accordingly likewise suffered from inadequate conceptualization and research efforts. The social planning aspects of city planning have similarly been neglected.

An examination of present practice reveals a considerable degree of variation, transition, and confusion. One observer aptly describes the situation:

> In the past five years, in large measure, under the influence of the federal comprehensive projects, community organization practice has undergone great change. From a method confined largely to Chest and Council social planning and the staffing of national social welfare agencies, it has moved into extensive grass roots organization and participation in political areas. From a method concerned largely with the orderly dispensation of existing welfare services, it has added an emphasis on social change and serving groups in the community by altering institutions and other aspects of their environment. From a method largely utilizing amelioration and consensus, it has consciously moved to include the use of conflict and power. Community organization has added initiating to enabling. It has added working with the impoverished poor to work with the elite; and social agency criticism to social agency support.[9]

With the foregoing as backdrop, we shall endeavor to achieve some greater measure of clarity in conceptualizing community organization practice. One of the difficulties has been that writers on the subject have attempted to set forth a single model or concep-

[4] Kenneth L. M. Pray, "When Is Community Organization Social Work Practise?", in *Proceedings of the National Conference of Social Work, 1947* (New York: Columbia University Press, 1948), pp. 194–204.

[5] Wilber I. Newstetter, "The Social Intergroup Work Process," in *Proceedings of the National Conference of Social Work, 1947* (New York: Columbia University Press, 1948), pp. 205–17.

[6] Harry L. Lurie, *The Community Organization Method in Social Work Education,* Comprehensive Report of the Curriculum Study, 1 of IV (New York: Council on Social Work Education, 1959).

[7] Ernest B. Harper and Arthur Dunham, *Community Organization in Action: Basic Literature and Critical Comments* (New York: Association Press, 1959).

[8] *Defining Community Organization Practice* (New York: National Association of Social Workers, 1962).

[9] Charles Grosser, "The Legacy of the Federal Comprehensive Projects for Community Organization," Twenty-fifth Annual Program Meeting, Council on Social Work Education, 1967, p. 2.

tion of community organization which was presumed to embrace all forms of professional practice. Often these models were actually disparate, touched on different aspects of practice, or made discrepant assumptions about goals, methods, or values. The position advanced here holds that in empirical reality there are different forms of community organization practice and that at this stage in the development of practice theory it would be better to capture and describe these rather than to attempt to establish a grand, all-embracing theory or conception. The implication is that we should speak of community organization *methods* rather than *the* community organization method.

There appear to be at least three important orientations to deliberate or purposive community change in contemporary American communities, both urban and rural, and overseas. We may best refer to them as approaches or models *A*, *B*, and *C*, although they can roughly be given the appellations respectively of *locality development, social planning*, and *social action*. We will use these terms in a particularistic way, as will become clear in the passages which follow. For present purposes, therefore, the reader is cautioned not to interpret these terms in the usual way. These three modes of action are not seen as exhaustive of all actual or potential possibilities. Because of their contemporary significance they have been selected for analysis; for reasons of economy in a single presentation, others have been excluded.

It should also be noted that we are referring to community action which is of a somewhat continuing nature and which includes staff (professionally trained or not) who are responsible for planning or sustaining action processes. Thus the category of events which include sporadic, *ad hoc*, voluntary civic action to obtain a new traffic light or displace an arrogant public official is not included.

Model *A*, locality development, presupposes that community change may be pursued optimally through broad participation of a wide spectrum of people at the local community level in goal determination and action. Its most prototypic form will be found in the literature of a segment of the field commonly termed "community development." As stated by a major U.N. publication: "Community Development can be tentatively defined as a process designed to create conditions of economic and social progress for the whole community with its active participation and the fullest possible reliance on the community's initiative."[10] According to Dunham, some themes emphasized in locality development include democratic procedures, voluntary cooperation, self-help, development of indigenous leadership, and educational objectives.[11]

Some examples of locality development as conceived here include neighborhood work programs conducted by settlement houses; village-level work in some overseas community development programs, including the Peace Corps; community work in the adult education field; and activities of the applied "group dynamics" professionals. Four recent books that express and elaborate community organization method according to Model *A* are those by the Biddles,[12] Goodenough,[13] Franklin,[14] and Clinard.[15] We will draw on the Biddle volume in particular for illustrative purposes.

[10] United Nations, *Social Progress through Community Development* (New York: United Nations, 1955), p. 6.

[11] Arthur Dunham, "Some Principles of Community Development," *International Review of Community Development*, No. 11 (1963), pp. 141–51.

[12] William W. and Loureide J. Biddle, *The Community Development Process: The Rediscovery of Local Initiative* (New York: Holt, Rinehart and Winston, 1965).

[13] Ward H. Goodenough, *Cooperation in Change: an Anthropological Approach to Community Development* (New York: Russell Sage Foundation, 1963).

[14] Richard Franklin, *Patterns of Community Development* (Washington, D.C.: Public Affairs Press, 1966).

[15] Marshall Clinard, *Slums and Community Development* (New York: Free Press, 1966).

Model *B*, the social planning approach, emphasizes a technical process of problem-solving with regard to substantive social problems, such as delinquency, housing, and mental health. Rational, deliberatively planned, and controlled change has a central place in this model. Community participation may vary from much to little, depending on how the problem presents itself and what organizational variables are present. The approach presupposes that change in a complex industrial environment requires expert planners who, through the exercise of technical abilities, including the ability to manipulate large bureaucratic organizations, can skillfully guide complex change processes. By and large, the concern here is with establishing, arranging, and delivering goods and services to people who need them. Building community capacity or fostering radical or fundamental social change does not play a central part.

Within the field of social work the Brandeis University Florence Heller Graduate School for Advanced Studies in Social Welfare has come to typify this approach, and it also finds expression in university departments of public administration, city planning, and so forth. It is practiced in numerous federal bureaus and departments, in social planning divisions of urban renewal authorities, in some community welfare councils (particularly the newer, project-oriented agencies), in various facets of community mental health planning. Some writings which reflect Model *B* include Morris and Binstock,[16] Wilson,[17] and Perloff.[18]

Model *C*, the social action approach, presupposes a disadvantaged segment of the population that needs to be organized, perhaps in alliance with others, in order to make adequate demands on the larger community for increased resources or treatment more in accordance with social justice or democracy. It aims at making basic changes in major institutions or community practices. Social action as employed here seeks redistribution of power, resources, or decision-making in the community and/or changing basic policies of formal organizations. Examples of the social action approach include civil rights and black power groups, such as the Congress on Racial Equality (CORE) and the Student Nonviolent Coordinating Committee (SNCC), Alinsky's Industrial Areas Foundation projects, labor unions, cause organizations and social movements, the welfare rights movement, Mobilization for Youth, political action groups, and student groups associated with the New Left (Students for a Democratic Society [SDS], the Northern Student Movement). Alinsky's *Reveille for Radicals*[19] and scattered writings among the New Left[20] typify the orientation of the social action model. Some more recent writings by social workers also reflect this orientation.[21]

[16] Robert Morris and Robert H. Binstock, *Feasible Planning for Social Change* (New York: Columbia University Press, 1966).

[17] James Q. Wilson, "An Overview of Theories of Planned Change" in Robert Morris, ed., *Centrally Planned Change: Prospects and Concepts* (New York: National Association of Social Workers. 1964), pp. 12–40.

[18] Harvey S. Perloff, ed., *Planning and the Urban Community* (Pittsburgh: Carnegie Institute of Technology, 1961).

[19] Saul Alinsky, *Reveille for Radicals* (Chicago: University of Chicago Press, 1946).

[20] *Thoughts of the Young Radicals* (Washington, D.C.: *The New Republic*, 1966).

[21] Warren Haggstrom, "The Power of the Poor," in Frank Riessman, Jerome Cohen, and Arthur Pearl, eds., *The Mental Health of the Poor* (New York: Free Press, 1964), pp. 205–23; Charles F. Grosser, "Community Development Programs Serving the Urban Poor," *Social Work*, X, No. 3 (1965), 15–21; Richard A. Cloward and Richard M. Elman, "Advocacy in the Ghetto," IV, No. 2 *Trans-Action* (1966). 27–35; George Brager, "Organizing the Unaffiliated in a Low Income Area," *Social Work*, VIII, No. 2. (1963), 34–40; Hyman J. Weiner, "Toward Techniques for Social Change," *Social Work*, VI, No. 2 (1961). 26–35; John Erlich, "Organizing the Poor, a Bibliography," *Poverty and Human Resources Abstract*, I (1966), 167–72.

Several schools of social work have developed specialized programs for training according to these three models. Thus the community development program at the University of Missouri emphasizes Model *A*; the doctoral program in planning at Brandeis University, Model *B*; and the social action program which was based at Syracuse University, Model *C*.

Morris and Binstock suggest a similar threefold division of the field of community planning and action:

> [*A*] . . . to alter human attitudes and behavioral patterns through education, exhortation and a number of other methods for stimulating self-development and fulfillment. [*B*] ". . . to alter social conditions by changing the policies of formal organizations. It is undertaken to modify the amount, the quality, the accessibility, and the range of goods, services, and facilities provided for people." [*C*] ". . . to effect reforms in major legal and functional systems of a society. It relies upon political agitation . . . and a host of other instruments for coping with powerful trends and developments.[22]

Having isolated and set off each of these models or ideal types, it would be well to point out that we are speaking of analytical extremes and that in actual practice these orientations are overlapping rather than discrete.

Practice in any of these orientations may require techniques and approaches that are salient in another orientation. For example, neighborhood social actionists may be required to draw up a social plan in order to obtain funding for desired projects from the Office of Economic Opportunity or from the Urban Renewal Authority (Models *C* and *B*). Or social planners may decide that the most effective way of solving the problem of resistant attitudes toward family planning is through wide discussion and participation in developing a community program (Models *B* and *A*). While such mixtures occur in reality, many organizations in their central tendency may be characterized as reflecting one or another model.

On the other hand, community welfare councils, particularly of the older type that emphasize functional divisions rather than project committees, organizationally represented a blending of Models *A* and *B*. Community development as conducted overseas in developing countries also represents a composite of localized community organization along the lines of Model *A*, together with broad social and economic planning at the national level incorporating Model *B*. This blend may actually constitute a distinct additional model whose characteristics could be explicated independently.

Here, however, we will not attempt to deal with variants or mixed forms which may constitute unique separate models. Instead, for analytical purposes, we will view the three approaches as "pure" forms. The virtue in this is suggested by Morris and Binstock when they refer to their own classification system:

> The categories are somewhat arbitrary, for it is sometimes difficult to say that a particular planning experience fits one category but not another. For these reasons it is particularly important to achieve as narrow a focus as possible in analyzing planning; otherwise a systematic treatment is virtually impossible.

To proceed with the analysis, we will attempt to specify a set of practice variables which will help to describe and compare each of the approaches when they are identified in the ideal-type form. Each of the orientations makes assumptions about the nature of the community situation, the definitions of one's client population or constituency, goal categories of action, conceptions of the general welfare, appropriate strategies of action, and so on. A set of such variables will be treated in the passages that follow. (The reader may find it useful to scan Tables 39.1 and 39.2 at this point.)

1. Goal Categories

Two main goals which have been discussed recurrently in the community organization literature are referred to frequently as "task" and "process." Task goals entail the comple-

---

[22] Morris and Binstock, *op. cit.*, p. 15.

TABLE 39.1   Three Models of Community Organization Practice
According to Selected Practice Variables

	Model A (Locality Development)	Model B (Social Planning)	Model C (Social Action)
1. Goal categories of community action	Self-help; community capacity and integration (process goals)	Problem-solving with regard to substantive community problems (task goals)	Shifting of power relationships and resources; basic institutional change (task or process goals)
2. Assumptions concerning community structure and problem conditions	Community eclipsed, anomie; lack of relationships and democratic problem-solving capacities; static traditional community	Substantive social problems: mental and physical health, housing, recreation	Disadvantaged populations, social injustice, deprivation, inequity
3. Basic change strategy	Broad cross section of people involved in determining and solving their own problems	Fact-gathering about problems and decisions on the most rational course of action	Crystallization of issues and organization of people to take action against enemy targets
4. Characteristic change tactics and techniques	Consensus: communication among community groups and interests; group discussion	Consensus or conflict	Conflict or contest: confrontation, direct action, negotiation
5. Salient practitioner roles	Enabler-catalyst, coordinator; teacher of problem-solving skills and ethical values	Fact-gatherer and analyst, program implementer, facilitator	Activist-advocate: agitator, broker, negotiator, partisan
6. Medium of change	Manipulation of small task-oriented groups	Manipulation of formal organizations and of data	Manipulation of mass organizations and political processes
7. Orientation toward power structure(s)	Members of power structure as collaborators in a common venture	Power structure as employers and sponsors	Power structure as external target of action: oppressors to be coerced or overturned
8. Boundary definition of the community client system or constituency	Total geographic community	Total community or community segment (including "functional" community)	Community segment
9. Assumptions regarding interests of community subparts	Common interests or reconcilable differences	Interests reconcilable or in conflict	Conflicting interests which are not easily reconcilable: scarce resources
10. Conception of the public interest	Rationalist-unitary	Idealist-unitary	Realist-individualist
11. Conception of the client population or constituency	Citizens	Consumers	Victims
12. Conception of client role	Participants in interactional problem-solving process	Consumers or recipients	Employers, constituents, members

tion of a concrete task or the solution of a delimited problem pertaining to the functioning of a community social system—delivery of services, establishment of new services, passing of specific social legislation. Process goals or maintenance goals are more oriented to sys-

tem maintenance and capacity, with aims such as establishing cooperative working relationships among groups in the community, creating self-maintaining community problem-solving structures, improving the power base of the community, stimulating wide interest and

TABLE 39.2   Some Personnel Aspects of Community Organization Models

	Model A (Locality Development)	Model B (Social Planning)	Model C (Social Action)
Agency type	Settlement houses, overseas community development: Peace Corps, Friends Service Committee	Welfare council, city planning board, federal bureaucracy	Alinsky, civil rights, black power, New Left, welfare rights, cause and social movement groups, trade unions
Practice positions	Village worker, neighborhood worker, consultant to community development team, agricultural extension worker	Planning division head, planner	Local organizer
Professional analogues	Adult educator, nonclinical group worker, group dynamics professional, agricultural extension worker	Demographer. social survey specialist, public administrator, hospital planning specialist	Labor organizer, civil rights worker, welfare rights organizer

participation in community affairs, fostering collaborative attitudes and practices, and increasing indigenous leadership. Murray Ross characterizes this set of goals as "community integration" and "community capacity." Process goals are concerned with a generalized or gross capacity of the community system to function over time; task goals, with the solution of delimited functional problems of the system.[23]

In locality development, process goals receive heavy emphasis. The community's capacity to become functionally integrated, to engage in cooperative problem-solving on a self-help basis, and to utilize democratic processes is of central importance. Community practice in adult education makes citizen education the cardinal aim. The applied "group dynamics" professionals likewise assert the priority of "Methodological" goals over "substantive" goals, viewed in terms of personal or community growth.[24] The same orientation if found in the theoretical writings in the field of community development proper where improving the community's "mental health," *qua* community, is sometimes viewed as primary.[25]

In the social planning approach, stress is

[23] For a more extended discussion of this subject see Jack Rothman, "An Analysis of Goals and Roles in Community Organization Practice," *Social Work*, IX, No. 2, (1964), 24–31.

[24] Kenneth D. Benne, "Deliberate Changing as the Facilitation of Growth," in Warren G. Bennis, Kenneth D. Benne, and Robert Chin, eds., *The Planning of Change* (New York: Holt, Rinehart and Winston, 1961).

[25] See, for example, Alan M. Walker. "Some Relations between Community Development and Rogers' Client-centered Therapy," *Community Development Review*, VI, No. 1 (1961), 20–28. ("Community development is essentially a process of community therapy. One of its chief aims as a therapeutic process is the development of more mature individuals through the medium of community betterment. It will, therefore, be helpful to compare theories and methods of community development with those of individual psychiatric therapy, which claims to have much the same end in view.") For a similar position closer to the adult education tradition, see John F. McNaughton, "Seeking Solutions through a Community Workshop in Human Relations," *Adult Leadership*, XI (1963), 227–28, 244. ("This workshop represents the first step in an attempt to improve the psychological health of this community . . . . . resulting from insufficient understanding of each other among the various segments of the community.")

placed on task goals, oriented toward the solution of substantive social problems. Social planning organizations often are mandated specifically to deal with concrete social problems, and their official names signify this— mental health departments, city planning and urban renewal authorities, commissions on physical rehabilitation, or alcoholism, and so on.

The social action approach may lean in the direction of either task goals or process goals. Some social action organizations, such as civil rights groups and cause-oriented organizations (welfare rights, trade unions), emphasize obtaining specific legislative outcomes (higher welfare allotments) or changing specific social practices (hiring more Negroes by corporations). Usually these objectives entail the modification of policies of formal organizations. Other social action groups lean more in the direction of process goals—building a constituency with the ability to acquire and exercise power—as exemplified by Saul Alinsky militant black power movement. This objec- and the Industrial Areas Foundation or the tive of building local-based power and decision-making centers transcends the solution of any given problem situation. Goals are often viewed as results of changing the system rather than tinkering with small-scale or short-range problem situations. These small-scale activities are often pursued, however, because they are feasible and they help to build an organization. Creating power may also be associated with building personal self-esteem. Warren Haggstrom states this proposition as follows: "One way in which the poor can remedy the psychological consequences of their powerlessness and of the image of the poor as worthless is for them to undertake social action that redefines them as potentially worthwhile and individually more powerful."[26]

2. Assumptions Regarding Community Structure and Problem Conditions

In Model *A* (locality development) the local community is frequently seen as overshadowed by the larger society, lacking in fruitful human relationships and problem-solving skills and peopled by isolated individuals suffering from anomie, alienation, disillusionment, and often mental illness. As Ross develops this theme, technological change has pressed society toward greater industrialization and urbanization with little consideration of the effects on social relations:

> The processes of urbanization have almost destroyed "man's feeling of belonging to" a community. . . .
> The problem of developing and maintaining common or shared values (the basic ingredient for cohesion) is made vastly more difficult by industrialization and urbanization. . . .
> The tendency for large subgroups to develop cohesion as separate entities in the community produces social tension, potentially dangerous in any community. . . .
> Democracy will weaken, if not perish, unless supporting institutions are supported and new institutions (to meet new ways of living) are developed. . . .
> The barriers that prevent active participation in the direction of social change inhibit personal development.[27]

Ross sums up his basic assumptions regarding the contemporary community situation:

> This is the problem of man's loss of his essential human dignity. For surely man is being overwhelmed by forces of which he is only dimly aware, which subjugate him to a role of decreasing importance and present him with problems with which he has no means to cope. Aspects of this central problem are the difficulty of full expression of a democratic philosophy and the threats to the mental health of individual members of societies.[28]

---

[26] Warren C. Haggstrom, "The Power of the Poor," in Louis A. Ferman *et al.*, eds., *Poverty in America* (Ann Arbor: University of Michigan Press, 1965), p. 332.

[27] Murray G. Ross, *Community Organization: Theory and Principles* (New York: Harper & Brothers, 1955), pp. 80–83.

[28] *Ibid.*, p. 84.

Alternatively, the community may be seen as tradition-bound, ruled by a small group of conventional leaders, and composed of illiterate populations who lack skills in problem-solving and an understanding of the democratic process. Community development in developing nations frequently proceeds from this supposition.[29]

The planner represented in Model *B* comes to his situation with quite a different viewpoint. He is likely to see the community as comprised of a number of substantive social problem conditions, or a particular substantive problem which is of special interest to him, such as housing, employment, recreation. Warren, while taking account of the outlook set down by Ross, expresses also a perspective that is more congruent with that of the social planners:

> It is apparent that certain types of "problems" are broadly characteristic of contemporary American communities. While most noticeable in the metropolitan areas, most of them are apparent in smaller communities as well. They appear in such forms as the increasing indebtedness of central cities, the spread of urban blight and slums, the lack of adequate housing which people can afford, the economic dependence of large numbers of people in the population, poorly financed and staffed schools, high delinquency and crime rates, inadequate provisions for the mentally ill, the problem of the aged, the need for industrial development, the conflict of local and national agencies for the free donor's dollar, the problem of affording rapid transit for commuters at a reasonable price and at a reasonable profit, and the problem of downtown traffic congestion. This list is almost endless, and each of the problems mentioned could be subdivided into numerous problematical aspects.[30]

The social action practitioner in Model *C* has still a different mind-set. He would more likely view the community as comprised of a hierarchy of privilege and power. There exist islands of deprived, ignored, or powerless populations suffering social injustice or exploitation at the hands of oppressors such as the "power structure," big government, corporations, or the society at large.

Todd Gitlin, former president of the SDS and one of the most articulate spokesmen of the New Left, puts it this way:

> In a supposedly fluid America, it is class that apportions a man's share of justice, health, culture, education, ordinary respect—as any visit to a jail, an emergency room, a theatre, a college or a municipal bureau will illustrate. . . . *Power must be shared among those affected, and resources guaranteed to make this possible.*[31]

Stokely Carmichael, former chairman of SNCC, states the point of view thus:

> President Johnson's concept of the Great Society is preposterous. The definition comes from him, as does the means of entering that society. Excluded people must acquire the opportunity to redefine what the Great Society is, and then it may have meaning.[32]

Again, we caution that the above describes dominant motifs rather than discrete categories. Many social actionists are greatly concerned about apathy and substantive problems, even as some social planners are concerned about the quality of social relations. We are defining dominant central tendencies rather than mutually exclusive properties.

3. Basic Change Strategy

In locality development the change strategy may be characterized as, "Let's all get together and talk this over"—an effort to get a wide range of community people involved in determining their "felt" needs and solving their own problems.

In planning, the basic change strategy is

---

[29] See Goodenough, *op. cit.*

[30] Roland L. Warren, *The Community in America* (Chicago: Rand McNally & Company, 1963), p. 14.

[31] Todd Gitlin, "Power and the Myth of Progress," in *Thoughts of the Young Radicals*, pp. 20, 22.

[32] Stokely Carmichael. "Who Is Qualified?" *ibid.*, p. 34.

one of, "Let's get the facts and take the logical next steps." In other words, let us gather pertinent facts about the problem and then decide on a rational and feasible course of action. The practitioner plays a central part in gathering and analyzing facts and determining appropriate services, programs, and actions. This may or may not be done with the participation of others, depending upon the planner's sense of the utility of participation in the given situation and the organizational context within which he functions.

In social action the change strategy may be articulated as, "Let's organize to destroy our oppressor"—crystallizing issues so that people know who their legitimate enemy is and organizing mass action to bring pressure on selected targets. Such targets may include an organization, such as the urban renewal authority; a person, such as the mayor; or an aggregate of persons, such as slum landlords.

4. Characteristic Change Tactics and Techniques

In locality development, tactics of consensus are stressed—discussion and communication among a wide range of different individuals, groups, and factions.

Warren underlines the importance of cooperative, inclusive techniques for the practice we are designating as locality development:

Because it seeks to organize people to express their own needs and to consider action alternatives with respect to them, the term has been applied to the organization of social action groups of the poor. However, such usage is misleading, since the *organization of one segment of the population in a contest relationship to other segments* which have not been brought into the process violates the major tenet of inclusiveness in community [locality] development principles. This passes no judgment on

its desirability or feasibility, but simply, indicates that in the commonly accepted sense of the term, it is *not* community [locality] development.[33]

In social planning, fact-finding and analytical skills are important. Tactics of conflict or consensus may be employed depending upon the practitioner's analysis of the situation.

In social action conflict, tactics are emphasized including methods such as confrontation and direct action. Ability to mobilize relatively large numbers of people is necessary to carry out rallies, marches, boycotts, and picketing. In his usual direct and colorful way, Alinsky states the issue as follows:

A people's organization is a conflict group. This must be openly and fully recognized. Its sole reason for coming into being is to wage war against all evils which cause suffering and unhappiness. A people's organization is the banding together of multitudes of men and women to fight for those rights which insure a decent way of life. . . . A people's organization is dedicated to an eternal war. . . . A war is not an intellectual debate, and in the war against social evils there are no rules of fair play . . . there can be no compromises.[34]

Elsewhere he adds:

Issues which are non-controversial usually mean that people are not particularly concerned about them; in fact, by not being controversial they cease to be issues. Issues involve differences and controversy. History fails to record a single issue of importance which was not controversial. Controversy has always been the seed of creation.[35]

Warren, in his discussion of types of purposive social change, suggests a variation among conflict tactics: campaign strategies when there are differences among parties but issue consensus can eventually be reached; and contest strategies when the external group

[33] Roland Warren, "Types of Purposive Community Change at the Community Level," Brandeis University, Papers in Social Welfare, No. 11; Florence Heller Graduate School for Studies in Social Welfare, 1965. Italics added.

[34] Alinsky, *op. cit.*, pp. 153–55.

[35] Saul Alinsky, "Citizen Participation and Community Organization in Planning and Urban Renewal" (Chicago: Industrial Areas Foundation, 1962; mimeographed), p. 7.

refuses to recognize the issue or opposes the change agent's proposal so that issue dissensus is quite pervasive and inherent.[36]

5. Practitioner Roles and Medium of Change

In locality development the practitioner's characteristic role is that of an "enabler" or, as more recently suggested by Biddle, "encourager." According to Ross, the enabler role is one of facilitating a process of problem-solving and includes such actions as helping people express their discontents, encouraging organization, nourishing good interpersonal relationships, and emphasizing common objectives.[37] It has a procedural focus and has little to do with selecting specific task objectives or dealing with concrete substantive problems. The Biddles see the encourager as one who

> has been responsible for initiating a growth of initiative in others. He has been party to a process of participant-guided learning of the habits of responsibility, of applied intelligence, and of ethical sensitivity. The indigenous process he has started, or helped to implement, is one of growth in democratic competence.[38]

The practitioner gears himself to the creation of manipulation of small task-oriented groups, and he requires skill in guiding processes of collaborative problem-finding and problem-solving. This role resembles that of Selznick's "institutional leader"—"one who is primarily an expert in the promotion and protection of values" and whose "task is to smooth the path of human interaction, ease communication."[39]

In social planning, more technical or "expert" roles are emphasized, such as fact-finding, implementation of programs, relationships with various bureaucracies and with professionals of various disciplines, and so on. Referring again to Ross, the expert role is suggested as containing these components: community diagnosis, research skill, information about other communities, advice on methods of organization and procedure, technical information, evaluation. In Model *B* the practitioner gears himself to the manipulation of formal organizations (including interorganizational relationships) and to data collection and analysis.

The social action model is likely to incorporate what Grosser calls the "advocate" and "activist" roles. According to Grosser, the advocate is "a partisan in a social conflict, and his expertise is available exclusively to serve client interests."[40] The roles in Model *C* entail the organization of client groups to act on behalf of their interests in a pluralist community arena. The practitioner gears himself to creating and manipulating mass organizations and movements and to influencing political processes. Mass organization is necessary because the constituency has few resources or sources of power outside its sheer numerical strength.

Gamson makes an interesting commentary on the need for mass organization and support in social action projects as he discusses his impressions of a workshop of local social action participants:

> I was reminded of a reaction that I had at the time of the [Cleveland] workshop. We asked the various participants from these groups to describe their successes; I was struck at the time that the descriptions of successes usually did not directly involve influence but other things, things that generated a lot of publicity or involved large numbers of people. My first reaction was, "Aren't they missing something? Shouldn't success be defined in terms of some kind of policy influence rather than this other type of thing?" But I thought about it some more and I decided that they really did have certain kinds of goals, even though they were not articulating them, and that there was something egocentric about my applying my conception of success to them. In fact, I think that they had their finger on something that was

---

[36] Warren, *The Community in America.*

[37] Ross, *op. cit.*

[38] Biddle and Biddle, *op. cit.*, p. 82.

[39] Philip Selznick, *Leadership in Administration: a Sociological Interpretation*, Evanston, Ill.: Row, Petersen & Co., 1957, pp. 27–28.

[40] Charles Grosser, "Community Development Programs Serving the Urban Poor," *Social Work*, X, No. 3 (1965), 18.

quite important. One way of formulating it is to see them as working on a shorter range goal that has to do with mobilization of a constituency or the creation of resources. If you ask what resources these groups have, the major one is the ability to command the energy of a large number of people in the community. This energy will, they hope, eventually get converted into influence.[41]

6. Orientation Toward Power Structure(s)

In locality development the power structure is included within an all-embracing conception of community. All segments of the community are thought of as part of the client system. Hence, members of the power structure are considered to be collaborators in a common venture. One consequence of this might well be that in Model A only goals upon which there can be mutual agreement become legitimate or relevant, the goals which involve incompatible interests are ignored or discarded as inappropriate. Values and constraints narrow the goals to those upon which all factions can agree. Hence, system-change goals are likely to be excluded.

In social planning, the power structure is usually present as sponsor or employer of the practitioner. Sponsors may include a voluntary board of directors or an arm of city government. Morris and Binstock state the case this way: "Realistically, it is difficult to distinguish planners from their employing organizations. In some measure, their interests, motivations, and means are those of their employers."[42] Planners are usually highly trained professional specialists whose services require a considerable financial outlay in salary as well as support in the form of supplies, facilities, and auxiliary technical and clerical personnel. Frequently, planners can only be supported in their work by those in a power position in the society, especially with regard to the posses-

sion of wealth, control of the machinery of government, or a monopoly of prestige. As Rein suggests, much planning is by the "consensus of elites" who are employers and policymakers in planning organizations.[43] Usually this consensus is clothed in strong factual data.

In social action the power structure is seen as an outside target of action; that is to say, the power structure lies outside the client system or constituency itself, as oppositional or oppressive force vis-à-vis the client group. Jack Minnis, an organizer for SNCC, states the position sharply:

> Community organization for action must be approached with the assumption that someone, or group, in the community has the power to make decisions and to implement them. . . . When this identification has been made, it will frequently develop that the groups whose interests will be adversely affected are the same groups who have the power to decide whether or not the objective will be achieved.[44]

The power structure, then, usually represents a force antithetical to the client or constitutent group whose well-being the practitioner is committed to uphold. Those holding power, accordingly, must be coerced or overturned in order that the interests of the client population may find satisfaction.

A practitioner's attitude toward power structures and his capacity to utilize one or another strategy with reference to these are conditional upon the organization within which he operates. The organizational base or structure supporting or sponsoring the practitioner thus is an extremely important variable. In order to attack existing bureaucracies that possess considerable resources and legitimacy the practitioner needs an autonomous power base, perhaps growing out of an indigenous population. (Several excellent treatments of

[41] William Gamson, in John Turner, ed., *Neighborhood Organization for Community Action* (New York: National Association of Social Workers, 1968), p. 131.

[42] Morris and Binstock, *op. cit.*, p. 16.

[43] Martin Rein, "Strategies of Planned Change," American Orthopsychiatric Association, 1965.

[44] Jack Minnis, "The Care and Feeding of Power Structures" (Economic Research and Action Conference, 1964; mimeographed), p. 6.

organizational variables have been made by Zald,[45] Grosser,[46] Brager,[47] and Vinter.[48]

7. Boundary Definition of the Community Client System or Constituency

In locality development the total community, usually a geographic entity, such as a city, neighborhood, or village, is the client system. According to Dunham, "Community Development is concerned with the participation of *all* groups in the community—with both sexes, all age groups, all racial nationality, religious, economic, social and cultural groups."[49] It places "emphasis on the unity of community life."[50]

In social planning the client system might be either a total geographic community or some areal or functional subpart thereof. Community welfare councils and city planners usually conceive of their client groups as comprising the widest cross section of community interests. On the other hand, sometimes the client populations of social planners are more segmented aggregates—a given neighborhood, the mentally ill, the aged, youth, juvenile delinquents, the Jewish community.

In social action the client is usually conceived of as some community subpart or segment which suffers at the hands of the broader community and thus needs the special support of the practitioner. Richard Flacks, former organizer and researcher for SDS, indicates that the objective of action involves "the task of organizing the politically disenfranchised and voiceless so that they can independently and effectively pursue their interests and rights."[51]

In social action practitioners are more likely to think in terms of constituents or fellow partisans[52] rather than in terms of the "client" concept, which may be patronizing or overly detached and clinical.

8. Assumptions Regarding Interests of Community Subparts

In locality development the interests of various groups and factions in the community are seen as basically reconcilable and responsive to the influences of rational persuasion, communication, and mutual good will. The Biddles present a representative set of assumptions concerning differing interests in the community:

> There will always be conflicts between persons and factions. Properly handled, the conflicts can be used creatively.
> Agreement can be reached on specific next steps of improvement without destroying philosophic or religious differences.
> Although the people may express their differences freely, when they become responsible they often choose to refrain in order to further the interest of the whole group and of their idea of community.
> People will respond to an appeal to altruism as well as to an appeal to selfishness.[53]

In social planning there is no pervasive assumption about the degree of intractability of conflicting interests; the approach appears to be pragmatic, oriented toward the particular problem and the actors enmeshed in it. Morris and Binstock set down the social planning orientation as follows:

[45] Mayer N. Zald, "Sociology and Community Organization Practice," in Zald, ed., *Organizing for Community Welfare* (Chicago: Quadrangle Books, 1967), pp. 27–61.

[46] Charles Grosser, "Staff Role in Neighborhood Organization," in Turner, ed., *op. cit.*, pp. 133–45.

[47] George Brager, "Institutional Change: Perimeters of the Possible," *Social Work*, XII, No. 1 (1967), 59–69.

[48] Robert Vinter, "Analysis of Treatment Organization," *Social Work*, XIII, No. 3 (1963), 3–15.

[49] Dunham, *op. cit.*

[50] Arthur Dunham, "Community Development," in *Social Work Yearbook, 1950* (New York: National Association of Social Workers, 1960), p. 184.

[51] Richard Flacks, "Is the Great Society Just a Barbecue?" in *Thoughts of the Young Radicals*, p. 53.

[52] William Gamson, *Power and Discontent* (Homewood, Ill.: Dorsey Press, 1968).

[53] Biddle and Biddle, *op. cit.*, p. 61.

A planner cannot be expected to be attuned to the factional situation within each complex organization from which he is seeking a policy change; nor can he always be aware of the overriding interests of dominant factions. Considerable study and analysis of factions and interests dominate in various types of organizations will be needed before planners will have sufficient guidance for making reliable predictions as to resistance likely in a variety of situations.[54]

The social action model assumes that interests among community subparts are at variance and not reconcilable, and that often coercive influences must be applied (legislation, boycotts, political and social upheavals) before meaningful adjustments can be made. Those who hold power or privilege and profit from the disadvantage of others do not easily give up their advantage; the force of self-interest would make it foolish to expect them to do so. Saul Alinsky states:

> All major controlling interests make a virtue of acceptance—acceptance of the ruling group's policies and decisions. Any movement or organization arising in disagreement, or seeking independent changes and defined by the predominating powers as a threat, is promptly subjugated to castigation, public and private smears, and attacks on its very existence.[55]

9. Conception of the Public Interest

In his brilliant analysis Schubert concludes that the various strands of thinking and writing on the subject can be grouped into three categories in terms of conceptions of the public interest: the rationalist, the idealist, and the realist.[56] The rationalist view postulates a common good that can be arrived at through deliberative processes involving a cross section of interest groups within the population. The common good is determined through expression of various majoritarian interests. The instrumentality of a parliament or congress symbolizes the rationalist outlook. The idealist view holds that the public interest can best be arrived at through the exercise of judgment and conscience on the part of knowledgeable and compassionate advocates of the public interest. This does not necessarily mean communion with the various publics comprising the community. Rather, a small professional or political elite may draw on scientific knowledge, the workings of a higher intellect, and a steadfast moral position to develop decisions or actions on behalf of the public interest.

The realist position views the community as made up of a multitude of conflicting publics or interest groups which endlessly contend with one another in the public arena. Public officials respond to these pressures. Public policy decisions thus register the balance of power at a given point in time. Accordingly, the public interest exists only as a particular transitory compromise resulting from the conflictual resolution of group interaction. Bently was an early advocate of this position, which is reflected by more recent writers who conceive of American society in pluralist terms.

Meyerson and Banfield[57] add to these notions those of unitary and individualist conceptions of the public interest. The unitary conception implies a choosing process in which the outcome is derived from a single set of ends through a central decision. It implies legislators or administrators who are presumed to know the ends of the body politic as a whole and to strive in some central decision-making locus to assert the unitary interests of the whole over the competing lesser interests. The individualist conception acknowledges a valid place for these "lesser" interacting interests and holds that the public interest can only come into being through the "social choice" interplay of these forces upon one another. No single central locus of authority or decision-making can take the place of the free and

---

[54] Morris and Binstock, *op. cit.*, p. 112.

[55] Alinsky, "Citizen Participation and Community Organization in Planning and Urban Renewal," p. 6.

[56] Glendon A. Schubert, *The Public Interest* (Glencoe, Ill.: Free Press, 1960).

[57] Martin Meyerson and Edward C. Banfield, *Politics, Planning and the Public Interest* (Glencoe, Ill.: Free Press, 1955).

open pluralistic interplay in arriving at the common good.

Combining the Schubert and Meyerson-Banfield conceptions, then, and applying them to our models of community organization practice, we conclude as follows:

Locality development has a rationalist-unitary conception of the public interest. It would structure a broad cross section of community groups, focused on the general welfare, utilizing a cooperative decision-making process. The Biddles state it well:

> When the people are free of coercive pressures, and can then examine a wide range of alternatives, they tend to choose the ethically better and intelligently wiser course of action.
>
> There is satisfaction in serving the common welfare, even as in serving self-interest.
>
> A concept of the common good can grow out of group experience that serves the welfare of all in some local area.[58]

The social planning model tends to have an idealist-unitary view of the public interest. Planners, often in collaboration with social scientists, place great stress on the power of knowledge, facts, and theory in arriving at a view of the public interest which is free of the influences of political self-seeking or popular mythology. Thus Morris and Binstock suggest that the planner who seeks to establish goals should base his decisions on an estimate of community need. This is determined through four major avenues: "evidence of demand from the records of service agencies; judgments of experts; population studies; and reanalysis of basic demographic studies."[59] The authors point out that goals cannot be determined by facts alone and that the planner usually arrives at "preference goals" through decisions based on value-tinged judgments as well as on knowledge. And one might add also the sometimes subtle, some-times strong-arm influence of the "consensus of the elites."

The social actionists in Model *C* are usually well acquainted with the grueling interplay of conflicting forces in community change activity. They can be said, in the short run, to take a realist-individualist view of the public interest. As expressed by Tom Hayden, the community organizer, "Realism and sanity would be grounded in nothing more than the ability to face whatever comes" in the confrontation with a multiplicity of community forces and interests.[60] Having no control of, and little access to, a central decision-making apparatus in the community, and usually comprising a small minority of the population, Model *C* practitioners can be effective only as a special interest group confronting others, sometimes attempting to make *ad hoc* coalitions and alliances in the community market place. Rein and Morris refer to this as an "individual rationality" and describe it as follows:

> Individual rationality . . . starts with predetermined, specialized, vested interests . . . places greater stress on pluralistic values and on the inherent legitimacy of each unique and special objective. Proponents of this strategy focus on a rationality of "realism"; it is rooted in tough-mindedness which tries to respond to the world in terms of how it does function rather than how it *ought* to function.[61]

It is the contention of Morris and Rein that change-oriented organizations are most effective when they utilize this individualistic rationality as opposed to a cooperative one, as reflected in the rationalist position.

In long-range terms some social actionists may view the public interest from a idealist-unitary view, with decisions emanating from a revolutionary elite, the working class, clients, and so on.

---

[58] Biddle and Biddle, *op. cit.*, p. 61.

[59] Morris and Binstock, *op. cit.*, p. 42.

[60] Tom Hayden, "The Ability to Face Whatever Comes," in *Thoughts of the Young Radicals*, p. 42.

[61] Martin Rein and Robert Morris, "Goals, Structures, and Strategies for Community Change," in *Social Work Practice, 1962* (New York: Columbia University Press, 1962), p. 135.

10. Conception of the Client Population or Constituency

In locality development, clients are likely to be viewed as normal citizens who possess considerable strengths which are not fully developed and who need the services of a practitioner to help them release and focus these inherent capabilities. The Biddles express this viewpoint as follows:

1. Each person is valuable, unique, and capable of growth toward greater social sensitivity and responsibility.
a. Each person has underdeveloped abilities in initiative, originality, and leadership. These qualities can be cultivated and strengthened.[62]

In social planning, clients are more likely to be thought of as consumers of services, those who will receive and utilize those programs and services which are the fruits of the social planning process—mental health, public housing, recreation, welfare benefits, and so forth. Morris and Binstock specifically refer to "consumers" rather than "clients" in their social planning analytical framework.

In social action, clients or constituents are likely to be considered as victims of "the system," most broadly, or of portions thereof, such as slum landlords, discrimination, employers, city government. Those on behalf of whom action is initiated are often characterized in "underdog" terms.[63]

11. Conception of Client or Constituent Role

In locality development, clients are viewed as active participants in an interactional process with one another and with the practitioner. Considerable stress is placed on groups in the community as the media through which learning and growth take place. Clients engage in an intensive group process of expressing their "felt needs," determining desired goals, and taking appropriate conjoint action.

In planning, clients are recipients of services. They are active in consuming services, not in the determination of policy or goals, a function reserved for the planner or some policy-making instrumentality, such as a board of directors or a commission. According to Morris and Binstock:

Opportunities for members and consumers to determine policy are severely limited because they are not usually organized for this purpose. If they are organized, and if the central issue which brings them together is sufficiently strong, they are likely to withdraw to form a separate organization. If the issue is weak the opportunity to control policy is short-lived because the coalition will fall apart, lacking sufficient incentive to bind together the otherwise diverse constituent elements.[64]

Policy, then, is made by the planner in collaboration with some community group, usually composed of elites, who are presumed to represent either the community-at-large or the best interests of the client group.

In social action the benefiting group is likely to be composed of employers or constituents. In unions the membership ideally runs the organization. Alinsky and the Industrial Areas Foundation will ideally not enter a target area until the people there have gained a controlling and independent voice in the funding of the organization. The concept of the organizer as an employee and servant of the people is stressed. SDS neighborhood functionaries may see themselves as peers and co-partisans working on the basis of complete parity with a constituency of neighborhood residents. This means living in the neighborhood, on a similar income level, and suffering the same deprivations and hardships. The client group, whether employers or constituents, is in the position of determining broad goals and policies. Those not in continual or central participatory roles may participate more sporadically in mass action and pressure group activities, such as marches or boycotts.

[62] Biddle and Biddle, *op. cit.*, p. 60.
[63] These categories are similar, respectively, to those of: (1) clients or patients; (2) customers; and (3) victims as described by Martin Rein, "The Social Service Crisis," *Trans-Action*, I, No. 4 (1964), 3–6.
[64] Morris and Binstock, *op. cit.*, pp. 109–10.

It would be useful here to point out another model of social action (best referred to as social reform) which is close to Model C but varies in one important aspect related to the variable under discussion. A common mode of social action involves activity by a group or coalition of interests which acts vigorously on behalf of some outside client group (community segment) which is at risk or disadvantage. Organizational activity and goal determination take place within the entities who act on the behalf of others, not within the client group itself. Social action to obtain social security legislation, child welfare legislation, better standards of public education, fall into this category. The action system is usually comprised of civic improvement associations (League of Women Voters), liberal politically oriented organizations (Americans for Democratic Action), special interest groups (the Public Education Association), labor organizations, and the like, individually or in coalition. Social action efforts by NASW chapters most frequently take this form.[65] Historically, particularly within social work, many social reform efforts followed this pattern.

Social reform constitutes, in part, a mixture of social action and social planning. Goal categories are of a task nature, a social provision for a disadvantaged group. Assumptions concerning the community situation include both substantive social problems (inadequate housing) and disadvantaged populations (poor people who cannot afford decent housing). The basic change strategy involves the organization of a coalition of concerned interests. Change techniques utilize in large measure campaign tactics, the employment of facts and persuasion to apply pressure on appropriate decision-making bodies. Salient practitioner roles encompass the coalition-builder, fact-gatherer, and legislative technician. The medium of change is through the manipulation of voluntary associations and legislative bodies. The power structure is viewed neutrally in "gatekeeper" terms as decision-making centers that can be influenced through persuasion and/or pressure. The community client system is defined in community segment terms as a population at disadvantage or risk. Interests of community subparts may be reconcilable or in conflict. The conception of the public interest is, as in social action, realist-individualist. Clients are considered victims, and their role is defined as that of potential consumers or recipients.

We have examined the three models horizontally; that is, we have looked at them comparatively in a way that has cut across the practice variables. We may also view the models from a vertical standpoint, by describing each separately in terms of all the listed practice variables. Doing this illustratively in two instances yields a product as follows:

In Model A, locality development, goals of action include self-help and increased community capacity and integration. The community, especially in urban contexts, is seen as eclipsed, fragmented, suffering from anomie, and with a lack of good human relationships and democratic problem-solving skills. The basic change strategy involves getting a broad cross section of people involved in studying and taking action on their problems. Consensus strategies are employed, involving small-group discussion and fostering communication among community subparts (class, ethnic, and so forth). The practitioner functions as an enabler and catalyst as well as a teacher of problem solving skills and ethical values. He is especially skilled in manipulating and guiding small-group interaction. Members of power structures are collaborators in a common effort since the definition of the community client system includes the total geographic community. The practitioner conceives of the community as composed of common interests or reconcilable differences, and he has a rationalist-unitary view of the public interest. Clients are conceived of as citizens engaged in a common community venture, and their role accordingly is one of participating in an interactional problem-solving process.

In the social action model, goals include the

[65] Daniel Thurz, "Social Action as a Professional Responsibility," *Social Work*, XI, No. 3 (1966), 12–21.

shifting of power, resources, and decision-making loci in the society as well as, on a short-range basis, changing the policies of formal organizations. System change is viewed as critical. The community is conceived of as being composed of a hierarchy of privilege and power, with the existence of clusters of deprived populations suffering from disadvantage or social injustice. The basic change strategy involves crystallizing issues and organizing indigenous populations to take action on their own behalf against enemy targets. Change tactics often include conflict techniques, such as confrontation and direct action —rallies, marches, boycotts (as well as "hard-nosed" bargaining). The practitioner functions in the role of activist, agitator, broker, negotiator, and partisan. He is skilled in the manipulation of mass organizations and political processes. Power structures are viewed as an external target of action—oppressors or exploiters who need to be limited or removed. The client group or constituency is a given community segment at disadvantage (blacks, the poor, workers). It is assumed that interests among related parties are at conflict or not easily reconcilable since those who possess power, resources, and prestige are reluctant to relinquish or share them. The conception of the public interest is realist-individualist. Clients are viewed as victims of various forces and interests in the society, and their role is that of employer or constituents with regard to the practitioner, as well as participants in mass action and pressure group activities.

Having come this far, the reader may inquire about the implications of constructing a typology like the foregoing.

In the first place, it is important for a practitioner immersed in the organizational and methodological vortex of one of these models to be aware of his grounding. What are the basic assumptions, orientation toward clients, preferred methods of action, of the situation he is in? In this way, he may perform appropriately, consistent with the expectations of other relevant actors.

Going beyond conformance to what exists, the practitioner may be in a position to create a model of action to deal with specific problems. Some rough rule-of-thumb guidelines can be sketched out in this connection. When populations are homogeneous or when consensus exists among various community subparts and interests, it would be useful to employ locality development. When subgroups are hostile and interests are not reconcilable through usual discussional methods, it may be functional to use social action. When problems are fairly routinized and lend themselves to solution through the application of factual information, social planning would appear to be the preferred mode of action. When the objective is to enhance civic responsibility and competence, Model A would be employed; when to make long-range and unpopular institutional and structural change, Model C; when to solve specific short- and middle-range substantive problems, Model B.

By assessing when one or another mode of action is or is not appropriate, the practitioner takes an analytical, problem-solving stand and does not become the captive of a particular ideological or methodological approach to practice. Practitioners, consequently, should be attuned through training to the differential utility of each approach and should acquire the knowledge and skill which permit them to utilize each of the models as seems appropriate and necessary.

The community practitioner should also become sensitive to the mixed uses of these techniques within a single practice context; for problems require such blending, and organizational structures permit adaptations. Thus the practitioner would be able to make adjustments in a social planning approach that is heedless of functional participation of people, a community development approach that stresses endless group discussion at the expense of addressing compelling community problems, or a social action approach that utilizes conflict when avenues are open for fruitful resolution of issues through discussion or negotiation. Within any given model, aspects of other models may play an important part. Thus in social action the practitioner may employ locality development techniques to a considerable degree within and among his own constituency. A community mental health planner, limited largely to consultation regarding services, might appreciate the contribution to his efforts of external social action programs, viewing them in a positive, supportive way rather than with suspicion or hostility.

The point being made has been stated by Gurin as follows:

> Our field studies have produced voluminous evidence that (various) roles are needed, but not always at the same time and place. The challenging problem, on which we have made a bare beginning, is to define more clearly the specific conditions under which one or another or still other types of practice are appropriate. The skill we shall need in the practitioner of the future is the skill of making a situational diagnosis and analysis that will lead him to a proper choice of the methods most appropriate to the task at hand.[66]

Certain types of mixtures may be more feasible than others. For example, a synthesis of locality development and social planning may be fairly easy to effect. As the Mobilization for Youth experience has demonstrated, social action approaches do not blend readily with either of the other two modes of action. Here, separation in funding, geographical location, or sponsorship may permit dual use of approaches.

In addition to mixing, there is a phasing relationship among the models. A given change project may begin in one mode and then at a later stage move into another. For example, as a social action organization achieves success and attains resources, it may find that it can function most efficiently out of a social planning model. The labor union movement to a degree demonstrates this type of phasing. The practitioner needs to be attuned to appropriate transition points in applying alternative models.

One concluding comment. In the past, social work practices and conceptualizations in community organization were constructed by particularized value orientations to practice. The value system of the profession was seen as restricting practice to a particular formulation. Thus, for many years, the enabler role, and interventions emphasizing cooperative relationships among and across diverse community subparts, was considered the only valid and legitimate avenue of approach in social work. A newer perspective accepts varying value orientations and emphasis within the framework of the profession. The following comment states this proposition well:

> Social work values provide some of the framework for decisions, but they are too broad to provide the specific answers. Social work has general commitments both to the improvement of social institutions and to the enrichment of individual and family life, but no specific formula for determining how these goals can best be achieved at any particular time, not even in an area as central to social work as income maintenance. The profession must therefore be able to encompass a range of ideologies, some of which may be in conflict with one another at certain points.[67]

The three models suggested in this presentation are in the spirit of such a point of view. The locality development practitioner will likely cherish that aspect of the social work value system that emphasizes harmony and communication in human affairs; the social planner will build on social work values that encourage rationality, objectivity, and professional purposiveness; the social actionist will draw on social work value commitments that stress social justice and equality. Each of these value orientations finds support and justification in the traditions of the profession. It would be difficult to claim a priority preeminence for one or the other.

The position taken here accepts the validity of each of these value orientations and encourages the simultaneous development of varying practice models which stem there-

---

[66] Arnold Gurin, "Current Issues in Community Organization Practice and Education," Brandeis University Reprint Series, No. 21, Florence Heller Graduate School for Advanced Studies in Social Welfare, 1966, p. 30.

[67] Wyatt C. Jones and Armand Lauffer, "Implications of the Community Organization Curriculum Project for Practice and Education," Professional Symposium of NASW, National Conference on Social Welfare, 1968, p. 9.

from. In the absence of research or experience which confirms the overarching superiority of only one or the other, the profession can only be enriched and the community benefited by

such multiple and concurrent development of practice technologies. Appropriate mixtures and phasing can be attended to within such a development.

40. Assessing Theoretical Models of Community Organization Practice: Alinsky as a Case in Point

Robert Pruger* • Harry Specht**

Any method of community organization is based on some type of theory about planned change. Frequently the theory which the practitioner uses is implicit and unstated. Regardless of the extent to which their theories are articulated, all practitioners formulate hypotheses about the nature and origin of problems and the institutionalized procedures for bringing about change.[1] They all choose, consciously or not, to take account of certain variables and not others, to consider certain behavior significant and to ignore other behavior.

The elucidation of theory has great value to the practitioner who wants to improve his practice, because it provides a coherent way to organize the factors that have a bearing on his work. To develop sounder systems of practice requires study of the specific conditions under which specific behaviors will change in specific directions. Without such a systematic approach, the practitioner's methods are likely to be inefficient, even haphazard or destructive.

The intention in this paper is to present one means of analyzing theories of community organization in a systematic way. Such an analysis[2] allows for a practical way of inspecting a number of theoretical approaches simultaneously, but does not attempt to defend any

particular theory as more effective than another. Rather, its purpose is to spell out the assumptions and hypotheses underlying methods of practice in order to answer the essential question: What methods produce what changes in what situations?

A brief comment on the present state of theory for community organization practice is necessary lest our title and introductory comments suggest that we believe a genuine theory for community organization practice is imminent. Ideally, a theory of community organization practice would be capable of ordering the vast array of discrete data available about communities, community problems, and methods of intervention. At present, however, there are available only orientations or frameworks which suggest the critical nature of certain variables affecting the behavior of various community systems. In a recent assessment of community organization theory, Kramer and Spect (1) have stated:

There is no community organization theory in the sense of a series of interrelated propositions that explains and predicts community behavior. Indeed, as Warner Bloomberg, Jr., has declared, "there can no more be a 'theory of communities' any more than there can be a 'theory of rocks and stones.'" What are found in innumerable community case studies and

Reprinted from Robert Pruger and Harry Specht, "Assessing Theoretical Models of Community Organization Practice: Alinsky as a Case in Point," *Social Service Review*, Vol. 43, No. 2 (June 1969), pp. 123–135 by permission of the University of Chicago Press.

° Assistant Professor, School of Social Welfare, University of California, Berkeley.
°° Associate Professor, School of Social Welfare, University of California, Berkeley.

[1] The general approach used in this paper is based on the framework described by Ford and Urban (6:3–106).

[2] The approach used here is frequently referred to as an "analytic paradigm"; the varied uses and values of formal paradigms are discussed in detail by Merton (11:13–16).

surveys are various substitutes or facsimilies for a theory such as typologies, ideologies, metaphors, and hypotheses. Most of the descriptive studies have focused on the ecological or demographic character of a community, its institutions and values or its power structure. If the findings do not yield a coherent picture of community life, they at least suggest "sensitizing" concepts or analytic categories that direct attention to the horizontal (local) and vertical (extracommunity) axes of a community, reference groups, monolithic or pluralistic decision-making structures, community influentials, social stratification, status, norms, values, and so forth.

The purpose of this paper is to present an analytic scheme designed to make some order out of the rather fragmented and disparate knowledge used in community organization practice. Four major categories of questions should be included in such an analysis. The first three categories include hypotheses about the causes of the problem, the methods of action planned, and the probable outcomes. The fourth category is an examination of the empirical evidence relating to the first three sections. The remainder of this paper will be a discussion of these categories and their application in an examination of Saul Alinsky's organizing methods.[3]

Propositions About Problems

The first category of questions deals with how the particular community organization method defines the problems to be dealt with. These definitions are based on assumptions

system. We will examine Alinsky's propositions[4] to see how he deals with the following about the structure and function of the social questions: (a) What are the problems to be dealt with? How are they identified and selected? What problems are excluded or treated as marginal? (b) Who is the client, and how is this unit of attention selected?

What Problems are Selected?

Alinsky is concerned about changing those conditions of modern life which alienate men from society, making them—particularly the poor—nonparticipants in the social order. His view is that our societal arrangements not only determine the differential distribution of socially esteemed rewards but also encourage the poor to social adaptations whereby they come to act as if those rewards were not esteemed enough to pursue, and to behave in ways (e.g., with apathy and intraclass hostility) that contribute to the stability of the very social arrangements that victimize them. In their numbers the poor have an option on power, but to become powerful they must organize. Thus Alinsky puts his major focus on the tactics and strategies relevant to the acquisition, elaboration, and use of power. Furthermore, as the poor become oriented to the uses of their own power it is expected that they will effect the structural reform they seek and develop the sense of self-worth that goes with full participation in society.

Alinsky does not often specify his meanings, and the concept of "alienation" as a condition of life among the poor has achieved a central

[3] This is, of course, only one of several systems by which to assess theory. Here we are using a common set of issues and questions which would be applied to any theory. One alternative approach would be to take a single theory (such as that suggested by Ross [18]) and compare others to it. In all cases, the system must provide some stable reference point for the analysis.

Readers unfamiliar with the work of Saul Alinsky may wish to refer to his major work (1).

[4] The term "proposition" includes both assumptions and hypotheses. While the distinction between the two is not of great importance in this paper, it becomes important as this kind of analysis becomes more refined. Essentially, propositions relate variables to one another (26:12). Generally speaking, an assumption is a statement that one accepts as true, while a hypothesis is a conjecture regarding the relationship between variables of a phenomenon which is not asserted to be true. The purpose of scientific research is to determine the credibility of a hypothesis (17:37).

place in his work more by virtue of its frequent repetition than by its controlled usage (21). Most frequently, his uses of the concept seem to be to connote (a) powerlessness (i.e., both the belief among the poor that they cannot influence the outcomes of their lives, and the objective fact of their powerlessness) and (b) the lack of understanding the poor have of the events in which they are caught up.[5] The first definition clearly commits him to the problems of creating and wielding political power; the second probably underlies his concern for popular education.[6]

He does not, however, consider a third possible meaning of alienation, namely, the alienation of the self or the "inability of the individual to find self-rewarding activities that engage him" (21:790). This condition probably has a more even distribution in modern technological society than that suggested by the other two definitions; and a program to attack it would have to go well beyond the mere redistribution of power in society. Alinsky is in the noble tradition of those who have sought a more humane, less brutal materialism; those seeking a more fundamental social reconstruction, however, would have to go well beyond his prescriptions and perspectives (e.g., 14).

Probably the major contribution Alinsky and his associates have made here is in the detailed descriptions of the sequential, strategic phases of organizing instrumental groups in the low-income community—i.e., they have clearly identified the problems to be solved to be the problems of political, rather than social, organization. It is from this insight that the single most important prgrammatic feature, the management of conflict, derives.

A variety of other problems are given a more peripheral place. While popular education is identified as the ultimate objective of what Alinsky calls "People's Organizations," it seems to have a lower claim on organizational resources than does conflict management. Education seems to serve the organizational need to follow conflict strategies rather than the need to develop personal skills which, if possessed, might reduce the readiness to support conflict action. Thus, though the poor are pictured as being oppressed and intimidated by the urban environment, personal skills to manage that environment (from ability to negotiate the subway to making full use of the established social services) are hardly considered. Whatever the defects of the poor (and qualities such as avarice, brutality, malice, and selfishness are mentioned) and whatever the defects of the system, all will be made right by the successful exercise of power.

There is one class of problem Alinsky more than overlooks; he simply denies its existence. This is the problem of the degree and direction of influence exerted on the People's Organization by its own process over time. The following passage provides one entry into the problem:

The substance of a democracy is its people, and if that substance is good—if the people are healthy, interested, informed, participating, filled with a faith in themselves and others— then the structure will inevitably reflect its substance. The very organization of a people so that they become active and aware of their potentialities is a tremendous program in itself. It is the ultimate people's program [1:20].

The minor flaw here is its circuitous reasoning, i.e., if the participants have certain qualities, the organization can only be democratic. However, they must first acquire these qualities from the organization. Far more serious is the fact that it dismissses a subtle, inconvenient reality that all organizations struggle with, but never overcome, and even less resolve as a matter of "inevitable" process—the tendency of structure to powerfully shape substance. Stated in its more familiar form, the larger an institution becomes and the longer it exists, the greater will be the tendency for the pro-

---

[5] "Social objectives, social welfare, the good of the nation, the democratic way of life—all these have become nebulous, meaningless, sterile phrases" (1:67).

[6] "In the last analysis the objective for which any democratic movement must strive is the ultimate objective within democracy—popular education. . . . The very purpose and character of a People's Organization is educational" (1:174).

gram or service of the organization to serve its own needs rather than those of its constituents.

It is not Alinsky's confidence in democracy that is questioned here; as an item of personal faith it is easy to commend it. But to posit the moral justification for waging war, pursuing power, manipulating friend and foe, and doing whatever else is necessary within the law to build a People's Organization, on the belief that the democratic ethic is the inevitable property of People's Organizations is another matter. Michels, in a classic of political sociology, has offered a powerful argument to demonstrate the inevitably undemocratic or oligarchic nature of such organizations (12). Many more recent writers have explicated the role of structural forces in effecting a transfer of sentiment from organizational ends to organizational means.

Alinsky assumes that the People's Organization must, with computerlike precision, make consistently correct moves (at least insofar as the elaboration of its democratic substance is concerned) at each of the many crossroads it comes to. While this is a remarkable faith for someone so critical of ivory towers, it is not sufficient to guarantee the democratic character of People's Organizations. His proud claim, for example, that the "expansion of [native] leadership from a partial role to a more complete one is a natural development that goes hand in hand with the growth of the People's Organization" (1:96), is embarrassed by the finding of political science that identifies specialization of leadership (i.e., leadership limited to one sphere of activity) as a circumstance under which individuals who have the greatest power in a political system do not become a ruling elite.

Who is the Client?

Organizations of the poor are to have the dual role of rehabilitating society as well as the poor themselves. The commitment to conflict as a means of solving problems is implemented by a People's Organization. Alinsky works with a neighborhood or community group, almost exclusively of an urban character. A model statement of bylaws for a People's Organization asserts that the client on whose behalf work is to be done is any organization representative of the people or any portion thereof in that area which participates in the life of the community. An "organization" refers to an officially organized group which has a minimum of ten members (1:222). Writing almost twenty years after Alinsky, Haggstrom says the organization "may be a direct membership neighborhood council or an organization of previously existing organizations" (8:6–7).

Almost all of the material available describes organizational efforts to activate and insure the continuing participation of the poor. While there is little empirical evidence that the organizations include a wide range of religious and class differences, there is, in theory, a vision of all elements of the community united in some shared concern for community improvement. In addition, whereas other theoretical frameworks view social and governmental agencies as potential allies, in Alinsky's scheme they are considered untrustworthy because they cannot be counted on to keep the people's interests paramount. Unaffiliated individuals in poverty neighborhoods and expressive organizations of low-income persons are treated as either nonexistent or irrelevant.

Propositions About Methods of Action

The second major category of questions is directed at an analysis of the specific ways in which systems are to be changed. These propositions aim at answering questions about how the overall goals are interpreted by the agent of intervention, how the change is to be effected, what is expected of the community for change to occur, and what is expected of the change agent.

What are the Goals of Intervention and Who Determines Them?

A distinction must immediately be made between the general organizational ends identified as appropriate by Alinsky and the ends actually pursued by the specific organizations. Only the former can be stated without regard for the resources and strategies available; the latter are inevitably shaped by considerations of strategy and resources, even if they do not always come as a result of deliberate planning.

The three major goals of People's Organizations seem to be:

1. to alter environmental conditions, identified at various places as economic injustice, unequal opportunities, prejudice, unemployment, disease, etc.

2. to alter men's beliefs about themselves, variously identified as feelings of hopelessness, apathy, anonymity, etc.

3. to educate the people, primarily so that they learn more about one another as a basis for greater cooperation and, secondarily, so that they can manage their affairs better.

The hierarchy of these goals is very unclear, especially in regard to the role of education. Within the framework of Alinsky's view of society's shortcomings and his firm moral commitment to brotherhood and equality, he seems to believe that everything is subject to change, and, presumably, that whatever can be changed should be changed. He writes: "A people's program is limited only by the horizon of humanity itself" (1:80). Given the well-known fact that horizons (especially the "horizon of humanity itself") are ever receding before us, it should not be surprising that Alinsky forgives himself the task of ordering its elements.

However, if nowhere else, Alinsky is unmistakably clear about who should be the authors of organizational goals:

In the last analysis of our democratic faith, the answer to all of the issues facing us will be found in the masses of the people themselves, and *nowhere else.*

The substance of a democracy is its people and if that substance is good—if the people are healthy, interested, participating, filled with a faith in themselves and others—then the structure will inevitably reflect its substance. The very organization of a people so that they become active and aware of their potentialities is a tremendous program in itself. It is the ultimate people's program [1:20, 64].

It is, then, the "people" who should define the goals of the People's Organization. Taken as an article of faith or as an alarm to warn against those who would intentionally and with malice aforethought have it otherwise, Alinsky's statements give little reason to doubt his fervid sincerity or praiseworthy values. Fault with his discussion of goals, however, can be found in at least three ways.

First, there is a substantial literature to suggest the complex array of forces that come into play as organizations go about settling on their goals. Wishing, even fervid wishing with all fingers crossed, cannot reduce that complexity; the belief that the people should set the goals, even if poetically expressed, has little bearing on the facts of the case.

Second, a growing number of thinkers and planners concerned with the elaboration of a community development technology, though sympathetic to the notion that the people should be defining organizational goals, doubt the value of treating that ideological point as a fixed limitation on the organizer's (i.e., the outsider's) role. Miller put it as follows:

Many social action programs (e.g., Alinsky, Wilcox, Murrow) emphasize that they do not have a program nor provide a direction of action: the people in a neighborhood should decide what they want to do; the task of the action programs is to help in the program that is developed by the neighborhood and to encourage a frame of mind of doing things for oneself, insisting on being heard by the powers-that-be, etc. Obviously, this approach has much to recommend it. . . . But isn't it also a limited approach emphasizing "spontaneity" and "localness"? Are "grass-roots," knowledgeability, and wisdom enough to handle and solve problems? . . . Consequently, the social actionist needs an ideology . . . if that is a disturbing word, then a goal . . . and the willingness to be involved at many levels, not only as a starter or choke but perhaps even at times as a map-reader [13:1–3].

Third, though not substantial enough a flaw to cast serious doubt on his belief in his own testimony, Alinsky does make one curious remark:

There should not be too much concern with specifics or details of a people's program. The program items are not too significant when one considers the enormous importance of getting people interested and participating in a democratic way [1:79].

The point here is that program goals (with the possible exception of that one elusive, semi-mythical goal that all organizational activity theoretically serves) are themselves also always program means. It seems reasonable, therefore, to consider program goals as being among "the program items [that] are not too significant when one considers the enormous importance of getting people interested and participating in a democratic way." Thus it is possible to conclude that Alinsky leaves goal-setting to the people, not because of some compelling article of the democratic faith, nor even because of the practical argument that only the people are sufficiently wise to perform the task, but simply because it makes no difference what the goals are; they are unimportant. Moreover, in assigning this unimportant task to the people, the organization gains the advantage of high claim to a generally highly esteemed moral point (i.e., being democratic). The crucial activity, however, really is initiating and sustaining a process, and that responsibility is safely in the hands of the Alinsky organizer.

While still avoiding a clear statement of the appropriateness of the organizer as a conscious influence on organizational goals, a recent associate of Alinsky has prescribed a more active role for the organizer than did Alinsky:

An organizer may find it necessary to disagree aggressively with the members, not to convince people of his own point of view on issues, but rather to make it possible to organize, to build effective organization. The people provide the content of action. The organizer has the responsibility to create and maintain the effective democratic structure of action. . . . The organizer, thus, must sometimes assert vigorous, aggressive leadership, even though he is not a member of the organization, and although such leadership should never include projecting his own substantive orientations upon the neighborhood [8:4].

How is Change Effected?

The tactics through which change is achieved can be grouped under two major headings: (a) those tactics that contribute to the creation of a group whose major property is power, but which is also presumed to be efficiently and permanently representative of the larger immediate community; and (b) those tactics that bespeak the most effective use of the organization's power, understood always as the management of conflict situations so that favorable resolution of the conflict is the most likely outcome. The first set of tactics is largely stated as a series of prescriptive, preferred, and proscriptive guides for the organizer's behavior; the second set of tactics has a similar relationship to the organization's behavior.

In reality, of course, the division is not so neat; nor can it even be allowed to appear as such, since a key assumption of Alinsky's scheme is that the proper curve of the organizer's activity is roughly parabolic, i.e., the organizer more or less quickly rises to a point of his maximum influence only more or less quickly to return this power to the organization itself. Thus the organizer always recruits the original group membership, then turns future recruitment over to those already recruited (a prescribed tactic). Sooner or later the organization must maintain its own strength by winning conflicts, securing high levels of participation, and co-opting or outlasting potential competitors to its local power monopoly.

The list of specific tactics is, of course, never complete. The following tactics, drawn from the writings of Alinsky and his associates (1:99–173), are therefore only a sample:

1. Tactics to build the People's Organization (instructions to the organizer):

(a) Become thoroughly familiar with the traditions, conditions, attitudes of the community through informal, low-keyed movement in the community. Identify the specific problems of concern to the people. Do not rely on the organizer's own judgment of the people's problem, nor turn to agency boards or administrators whose leadership is not based on a local constituency.

(b) Bring the people (or more exactly, their leaders) together. Perform a variety of discrete maneuvers so that the coming together is most likely to result in a commitment either to establish a formal organization or effect some easily consummated social action. Among these discrete maneuvers are included the articulation of general issues of concern to the people, avoidance of supplying program specifics, awakening of emotional support for the organization, making arrangements to facilitate attendance (car pools, baby sitting, etc.), asking action-oriented questions, use of the "program ballot," describing what other organizations in similar circumstances have done, and providing alternative courses of action as content for discussion. Once a decision to act has been made, employ other tactics to make sure that the people's intent is carried out.

2. Tactics for the use of power (instructions to the organization):

Over time, continuously deepen the commitment to an ever enlarged scope of group action, with special reference to the requirements of a conflict strategy. Some specific recommended tactics are refusing cooperation with the enemy, "having a fight in the bank," "making positives out of negatives" (e.g., Negroes eating watermelon while staging mass protest marches through white residential areas); carrying out a continuous series of campaigns to keep the opposition off balance; and planning campaigns that tap the skills and interests of the widest possible number of persons in the area, etc.

There is no need in Alinsky's scheme for means or techniques to extinguish the immorality, greediness, or other "bad" behaviors of the people. (The technique known as "creating a new social situation," however, might be considered one.) But this is not oversight on Alinsky's part; rather, it is a reflection of his oft-stated belief that, once the people have

found their head, things can only, and inevitably do, get better. This inevitability guarantees personal transformations (i.e., malevolent, selfish individuals become benevolent cooperators in waging the good war) as well as group transformations (i.e., narrow, reactionary groups or organizations become progressive, militant bastions of democracy).[7]

How is the Community Involved in the Change Process?

In Alinsky's scheme, some element in the community must invite Alinsky in and must offer some assurance of community support for the enterprise and provide finances to cover the work to be done for some specified period of time. A group such as a local church may have, in addition, primary connections with other elements beyond the community, but those community groups who enroll in the People's Organization must be willing to give up that part of their sovereignty which overlaps with the program of the People's Organization. A constitution binding all parties to democratic procedures must be drafted and agreed to; it is the social contract that establishes the organization's legitimacy, and its specific items define the eligibility, obligations, limits, and prerogatives of members. The organization's purpose is therein defined as the instrument through which all the people will be united. While not specifically mentioned in the constitution, it is nevertheless clear that affiliation commits the membership to the view that the major strategy to be pursued is to make latent conflicts between the community and its oppressors manifest; the willingness to accept the People's Organization as setting the discipline for managing conflict is implicit and absolutely essential.

An important feature of this "discipline of conflict" strategy is the refusal to enter into alliances. Alinsky's attack on those most likely to be considered as allies has included special

[7] "The organizer need not be too concerned at the start about the reactionary policies of individual community agencies. He will find that a mixture of the progressive policies of a progressive People's Organization with the individual conservative policies of a conservative neighborhood agency will result in a progressive product. Experience has shown this to be true no matter how wide a gap previously existed between the two agencies" (1:110–11).

classes of persons, such as liberals or intellectuals, and potentially influential programs, such as the war on poverty. Indeed, this is one of the few elements in Alinsky's scheme that he has vociferously kept up to date. His diligence can be likened to that of Madame DeFarge, whose woolly inventory was necessary to insure an absent minded people against a tendency to forget just who their enemies were. An alternate meaning to the purity Alinsky insists upon was provided by Michels in 1915:

> Thus the hatred of the party is directed, not in the first place against the opponents of its own view of the world order, but against the dreaded rivals in the political field, against those who are competing for the same end— power. It is obvious that these are no more than the means vulgarly employed by competitors who wish to steal one another's customers [12:375–76].

Writing as an activist involved in the current scene, Rustin gives still another name to Alinsky's "no-alliance" strategy:

> It is precisely this sense of isolation that gives rise to . . . the tendency within the civil rights movements which, despite its militancy, pursues what I call a "no-win" policy. . . . Spokesmen for this tendency survey the American scene and find no forces prepared to move toward radical solutions. From this they conclude that the only viable strategy is shock; above all, the hypocrisy of white liberals must be exposed. These spokesmen are often described as the radicals of the movement, but they are really its moralists. They seek to change white hearts —by traumatizing them [19:28].

What is Required of the Change Agent?

Alinsky organizers need not have any academic preparation, and in practice they have been drawn from all walks of life. Requirements of the organizer are of two dimensions: (a) what he must be or believe and (b) what he must do. The beliefs that Alinsky delineates for helping the organizer achieve his goals are little more than sentimental absurdities. Thus the organizer "constantly finds his faith in man fortified" (1:114), and he "does what he does

because of his love of his fellow men" (1: 113); moreover, "frequent demonstrations of brutality, selfishness, hate, greed, avarice, and disloyalty among masses of people do not harden the Radical nor lessen his affection for the people" (1:113), and, as icing for this somewhat silly cake, "the Radical cannot suffer personal defeat because in a sense he is selfless" (1:113).

In the practical realm of action, there are major events for which the organizer is responsible and which, presumably, do hasten the group's process as it moves to a self-controlled and sustained readiness to act on its own behalf. Haggstrom defines the realistic but nevertheless immense demands made for skill as the organizer goes about intervening in the life of the group:

> To build organization in low-income areas is something like playing a long game of blindfold chess in which no player is sure of the rules. The chess pieces move themselves; skillful players help get this movement channeled into planned patterns, strategies, and tactics. There are standard beginning lines (e.g., house meetings versus dramatic large public meetings), and some established principles of play ("rub raw the sores of discontent," "the social situation sets the limits for moves"), but much depends on attention to detail, immense energy, and an individual brilliance in capitalizing on whatever happens. Finally, these chess pieces can throw an ineffective player right out of the game. [8:1].

Thus, Alinsky's requirement that the organizer be a saint is modified so that it seems more like the kind of work any immensely skilled, finely tuned artist could perform.

Assessment of Outcomes

There is little in the literature of community organization which can explain how the benefits of intervention are realized in the larger system with which the worker is concerned. With the exception of sociological analyses like those of Warren, Dahl, and Rossi and Dentler (4, 20, 25), there has been a lack of theoretical propositions about how to assess the results of community organization.

How is Outcome Assessed? What is Success? When Does Intervention End?

Success is assessed subjectively by Alinsky, i.e., someone defines the organization as strong and self-directed enough. While Alinsky does not actually state it this way, it seems to be the most likely deduction possible. The primary concern in Alinsky's work is with the condition of the organization rather than the state of the environmental conditions presumed to have required the creation of the organization. And, of course, change that has occurred without benefit of a People's Organization or without the careful cultivation of conflict is ignored and thus is no embarrassment.

One might also judge success, not on the condition of the group or the external world, but on whether the organizer has performed as well as possible under the circumstances. This would be the case if the group dismissed the organizer or took positive steps that violated the moral or other conditions defined in the written and unwritten contract between Alinsky and the organization, or if the organizer himself judged the situation to have reached a point of intractability. On still other grounds, intervention presumably might end simply because the term of the contract had been reached.

Empirical Validation

The last category of the paradigm calls for an examination of the empirical status of the theoretical assumptions included in the other three categories. By this is meant the extent to which the propositions used have been verified by the facts of experience.

In Alinsky's case there is only scanty literature on the changes effected by the People's Organizations. However, if one may define "empirical validation" somewhat loosely, the following observations can be made:

1. Both Alinsky critics and Alinsky sympathizers, though in varying degrees, point to local changes that have been effected:

[Alinsky] organizations have enabled areas to decrease or end exploitation by some absentee landlords and unethical businesses. They have also ended police brutality and secured police protection, street cleaning, and other services which low-income neighborhoods had not previously received at a level equivalent to that of the remainder of the community [9:222].

2. Alinsky does cite one study to support his claim that People's Organizations produce higher degrees of participation in low-income communities than more traditional organizational forms (1:188–89). In addition, by shifting emphasis, one can claim effect on even greater numbers, as does Haggstrom:

Many people are swept into action, not by direct active membership in the organization, but through identification with an acting neighborhood-based mass organization. The organizer has succeeded when he has ensured the creation of such a structure which expands the area of freedom for persons in the action area [8:20].

3. Alinsky's great emphasis on the irreplaceability of indigenous leadership in activating and shaping community effort has found varying degrees of confirmation, or at least support, in the work of organizations committed to community change, such as Mobilization for Youth and the Community Action Program of the War on Poverty. In the case of Mobilization for Youth, which made use of persons representative (in the sense of typical) of the community, problems have developed about maintaining the representative qualities of these persons once they have been made conscious of their leadership positions (7). This outcome suggests a limited viability to the assumption that a single organization or type of organization can plan and engineer a continuing process of community change while maintaning a continuing responsiveness to community residents.

4. Several empirical studies confirm the theory that functional social learning in individuals tends to occur more readily when those individuals have confidence in their capacity to determine the outcome of their lives (e.g., 5). These studies clearly affirm the soundness of Alinsky's major emphasis on participation in the action of a People's Organization as a way of restoring a sense of power to people

socially fixed and disabled by their sense of powerlessness. The relationship of powerlessness and social learning, stated so sharply by Alinsky in 1946, has only grown in importance since then. His critics, however, claim that these benefits are only ephemeral because of the failure to change the outside environment, and thus may lead to a more profound sense of the people's pathetic condition.[8]

In summary, one must note that, in spite of the more than two decades of experience in a large number of American cities, Alinsky-style organizations have not brought any results to bear out his faith that low-income groups easily move from expressive to instrumental concerns. Nor is there evidence that the successful consummation of instrumental activities on one level conditions the readiness of low-income groups to move on to higher levels of instrumental action (3). As yet Alinsky's assumption that these things will occur remains only an article of faith.

It is somewhat ironic that, although we have chosen Saul Alinsky's work to illustrate the use of such an analysis, Alinsky himself would probably deny the value of the effort, inasmuch as it is not based on intimate association with him or any of the activities generated by his Industrial Areas Foundation (16). One who leans so heavily on direct observation and "inside" experience is likely to view the theorist as one who sits down at the typewriter to commit an act of foul play.

Another difficulty lies in the nature of Alinsky's material, particularly his major work, *Reveille for Radicals*. It smacks of distortions which reflect, at best, an ingenuousness of monumental proportions or, at worst, a belief that fraud, if it serve the cause, is less than fraud. In a word, the results claimed for Alinsky organizers are often unbelievable, and there is often the imputation of a high degree of effectiveness to his techniques and strategies which is based largely on the loud squeals arising from the "power structure" he has

threatened to dethrone. Thus, beliefs that Alinsky has a significant contribution to make to the development of an applied theory of community change are often based on the familiar but flimsy notion that where there is smoke there must be fire.

Although the literature by and about Alinsky and his methods is quite meager, the social unrest of the past decade has given him a new relevance. Some of this is reflected in an accelerated writing program among his followers and other writers in the professional literature (e.g., 8, 9, 22, 23, 24), although the largest supply of descriptive material is still randomly distributed among popular magazines and occasional newspaper accounts.[9]

We have selected Alinsky's work for this analysis because, in spite of the negative aspects stated above, few community organization writers have described their methods and techniques in such particularity and color, or revealed them with such frankness. While glorifying irreverence, Alinsky delights in telling us of his hidden motives. While he is often contradictory and inconsistent, his methods and techniques in community organization are described in a detail which can be matched by very few.

The analytic scheme we have used points up many inconsistencies, ambiguities, and contradictions in Alinsky's method of organizing. It also makes clear that Alinsky has developed many ideas and techniques which are of enormous utility to community organization practitioners. Most important, a systematic assessment of the theory used in this particular model of practice reveals these strengths and weaknesses. Parallel assessments of other models of community organization practice would, we believe, yield analytic statements that are more comparable than heretofore. An inventory of such statements would constitute a first significant step in the codification of knowledge for community organization practice.

[8] "Alinsky-organized movements are bound to lead to frustration because they cannot transcend the immediate object of oppression" (2:104; see also 15:35).

[9] Over the years articles about Saul Alinsky have appeared in *Look*, *The New Republic*, *Harper's*, *Fortune*, *Saturday Evening Post*, *National Observer*, *The Reporter*, *Commentary*, and elsewhere.

References

1. Alinsky, Saul. *Reveille for Radicals.* Chicago: University of Chicago Press, 1946.
2. Aronowitz, Stanley. "Poverty, Politics, and Community Organization." *Studies on the Left* 4, no. 3 (1964):103–12.
3. Brager, George, and Specht, Harry. "Mobilizing the Poor for Social Action." In *Social Welfare Forum, 1965.* New York: Columbia University Press, 1965.
4. Dahl, Robert A. *Who Governs?* New Haven, Conn.: Yale University Press, 1961.
5. Evans, John W., and Seeman, Melvin. "Alienation and Learning in a Hospital Setting." *American Sociological Review* 27 (December 1962):772–82.
6. Ford, Donald H., and Urban, Hugh B. *Systems of Psychotherapy: A Comparative Study.* New York: John Wiley & Sons, 1963.
7. Grosser, Charles F. "Local Residents as Mediators between Middle-Class Professional Workers and Lower-Class Clients." *Social Service Review* 40 (March 1966): 56–63.
8. Haggstrom, Warren. "The Organizer." Paper read at the Annual Conference of the Greater Washington Chapter of Americans for Democratic Action, Georgetown University, September 18, 1965.
9. ———. "The Power of the Poor." In *Mental Health of the Poor,* edited by Frank Riessman, Jerome Cohen, and Arthur Pearl. New York: Free Press, 1964.
10. Kramer, Ralph M., and Specht, Harry, eds. *Readings in Community Organization Practice.* Englewood Cliffs, N.J.: Prentice-Hall, 1969.
11. Merton, Robert K. *Social Theory and Social Structure.* Glencoe, Ill.: Free Press, 1957.
12. Michels, Robert. *Political Parties.* New York: Dover Publications, 1959.
13. Miller, S. M. "Social Action Programs: Some Questions." April, 1963. Mimeographed.
14. Polanyi, Karl. "Our Obsolete Market Mentality." *Commentary* 3 (February 1947): 109–17.
15. Riessman, Frank. "Self-Help among the Poor: New Styles of Social Action." *Trans-Action* 2 (September–October 1965):35.
16. Riessman, Frank, and Alinsky, Saul. Exchange of letters in "Feedback from Our Readers." *Trans-Action* 2 (September–October 1965):2.
17. Ripple, Lilian. "Problem Identification and Formulation." In *Social Work Research,* edited by Norman A. Polansky. Chicago: University of Chicago Press, 1960.
18. Ross, Murray G. *Community Organization: Theory and Principles.* New York: Harper & Bros., 1955.
19. Rustin, Bayard. "From Protest to Politics." *Commentary* 39 (February 1965):28.
20. Rossi, Peter H., and Dentler, Robert A. *The Politics of Urban Renewal: The Chicago Findings.* New York: Free Press of Glencoe, 1961.
21. Seeman, Melvin. "On the Meaning of Alienation." *American Sociological Review* 25 (December 1959):783–91.
22. Sherrard, Thomas, and Murray, Richard. "The Church and Neighborhood Community Organization." *Social Work* 10 (July 1965):3–14.
23. Silberman, Charles. *Crisis in Black and White.* New York: Random House, 1964.
24. Von Hoffman, Nicholas. "Finding and Making Leaders." New York: Students for a Democratic Society, n.d. Mimeographed.

25. Warren, Roland L. *The Community in America*. Chicago: Rand McNally
    & Co., 1963.
26. Zetterberg, Hans L. *On Theory and Verification in Sociology*. Totowa,
    N.J.: Bedminster Press, 1963.

41. Community Action Programs and Citizen Participation: Issues and Confusions

Sumati N. Dubey*

The Community Action Program (CAP) of the Economic Opportunity Act of 1964 is defined in the act as fighting poverty by (1) providing service assistance and conducting other activities that give promise of bettering the conditions under which people live, learn, and work, (2) mobilizing and utilizing public and private resources, and (3) developing, conducting, and administering such programs with the maximum feasible participation of the neighborhood residents (i.e., low-income individuals, families, and groups upon whose needs the programs are focused). The central preoccupation of CAPs, consequently, is the planning and development of relevant activities and services as well as effective and efficient allocation of resources. This is to be accomplished through organizational operations whereby the target population participates in setting goals, developing strategies, defining policies, and establishing structures for reaching the legislative objectives.[1]

The mandatory requirement of enlisting the active participation of indigenous people in shaping decisions affecting their own welfare distinguishes the CAP from earlier attempts to involve local groups. In urban renewal projects, for example, citizen participation was sought in order to avoid, or at least to handle, protests that arose among the residents of the areas scheduled for renewal. In other words, whether intentionally or not, programs for resident participation were often used to offset the spontaneous but disruptive activities of local protest groups.[2]

The President's Commission on Juvenile Delinquency and Youth Crime may be the closest forerunner of the CAP from the point of view of resident participation. Administrative guidelines issued by the committee in 1963 called for the involvement of "individuals and organizations in the target community." Local organizations formed to carry out social development programs came to be called "community action agencies." Perhaps the difference between the committee's efforts to involve residents and the CAP's requirement of participation is more a matter of magnitude than of substance.[3]

From the point of view of its ideology and

Reprinted with permission of the National Association of Social Workers, from *Social Work*, Vol. 15, No. 1 (January 1970), pp. 76–84.

° Associate Professor, School of Applied Social Sciences, Case Western Reserve University, Cleveland, Ohio.

[1] Simon Slavin, "Community Action and Institutional Change," in *Social Welfare Forum, 1965* (New York: Columbia University Press, 1965), p. 148.

[2] Frances Fox Piven, "Participation of Residents in Neighborhood Community Action Programs," *Social Work*, Vol. 11, No. 1 (January 1966), pp. 73–74.

[3] Robert F. Kennedy, then attorney general, pointed up the similarities between the juvenile delinquency and CAP programs: "The Juvenile Delinquency Programs . . . created under the [Juvenile Delinquency Control] Act are similar to the Community Action Organization of Title II. So are the techniques, although, of course, the Community Action Program's aims are much broader and will use many more and different techniques." Hearings before the Subcommittee on the War on Poverty Program, March 17–April 14, 1964 (Washington, D.C.: U.S. Government Printing Office, 1964), pp. 304–305.

methods of operation, the CAP can best be conceptualized as a contemporary blend of social action and community development (as defined by the United Nations[4]). The basic similarities between the CAP and the community development concept seem to be that both emphasize involvement of local communities as units of action and decision-making and both require the participation of governments to help these communities in their efforts.

However, there are also some differences. The main one is that in community development (as conducted in developing countries) the greatest emphasis is placed on utilization of surplus human labor as a resource for economic development, while in the CAP the action agenda deals with the inequitable distribution and application of actually and potentially available resources. The CAP objective is to rechannel resources into those local communities suffering most from deprivation, social dislocation, and individual incapacity to meet basic human needs, in order to grant them a substantial share in society's goals and services.[5]

Rationales for Resident Participation

Various rationales for resident participation in CAP antipoverty programs are advanced depending on beliefs about the causes of poverty, commitment to the ideology of social action stemming from the civil rights movement, the degree of commitment to the American value of rugged individualism, and the concern about and belief in the value of coherence and co-ordination among social welfare services.[6] Four basic rationales are given to defend the requirement of resident participation. Each has its own proponents, who do not always agree on a given issue even among themselves.

1. Program Irrelevance and Inadequacy

Programs intended to assimilate the poor into the mainstream of American society, such as public welfare, public housing, social settlements, and social work with hard-core families, are usually initiated and supported from outside the neighborhood and are in effect imposed on the poor.[7] Lacking the basic involvement of the people they try to serve, these programs are generally insufficient, inappropriate, fragmented, and unsuitable to the life-style of the poor, especially of minority groups. Some services even mitigate against the escape of the recipients and their families from the cycle of poverty.[8] In other words, the programs fail to make any lasting positive impact on the conditions of poverty; the majority of service recipients remain poor, live in an atmosphere of apathy and disorganization, and consequently feel hostile toward the very programs supposedly designed to rescue them.[9]

It is therefore considered important to involve the poor in order to obtain a realistic perspective on the appropriateness and effectiveness of social services—a perspective free from biases stemming from considerations of

---

[4] According to the United Nations, the term community development designates the utilization, under a single program, of approaches and techniques that rely on local communities as units of action and attempt to combine outside assistance with organized local self-determination and effort, and that correspondingly seek to stimulate local initiative and leadership as the primary instrument of change. See *Programme of Concerted Action in the Social Field of the United Nations and Specialized Agencies,* Document E/CN/5/291 (New York: United Nations, 1963).

[5] Slavin, *op. cit.,* p. 158.

[6] Daniel P. Moynihan, "What is Community Action?" *The Public Interest,* No. 5 (Fall 1966), pp. 3–8.

[7] Warren C. Haggstrom, "The Power of the Poor," in Frank Riessman and Jerome Cohen, eds., *Mental Health of the Poor* (New York: Free Press, 1964), pp. 214–225.

[8] Frank Riessman, "The New Anti-Poverty Ideology," *Poverty and Human Resources Abstracts,* Vol. 1, No. 4 (July 1966), pp. 5–11.

[9] Haggstrom, *op. cit.,* p. 214.

careerism, political interests, and the public relations needs of agencies and their personnel. It is argued that the poor are in the best position to define their own needs and to suggest appropriate uses of federal funds to meet these needs. Inclusion of the poor in the antipoverty programs, from this point of view, will help overcome a long-standing "colonialism" in both public and private sectors of the social welfare field.[10] The new antipoverty legislation represents a significant breakthrough insofar as it officially recognizes the rights of the poor to participate as policymakers and program developers, operators, and evaluators, in contrast to their more traditional role of passive consumers.[11]

2. Creating a Power Base

Poverty is conceptualized as a situation of enforced dependency and powerlessness wherein the poor have little control over events and decisions affecting them.[12] Banfield observes that concerted action for any purpose necessitates creation of a more or less elaborate system of influence: appropriate people must be persuaded, coerced, inveigled, or otherwise induced to do what is required of them.[13] Where does this influence come from? According to Dahl the possible bases of influence are large, but the most important are money and credit; control over jobs; control over information; social standing; knowledge and expertise; popularity, esteem, or charisma; legality, constitutionality, and officiality; ethnic solidarity; and the right to vote.[14] Rossi points out that the major sources of power with which to induce social change are wealth

and other physical resources, control over prestigious interactions, control over values, threats to property (such as take place in civil disobedience, demonstrations, and so on), and the backing of solidarity interest groups either as voting blocks or as potential votes.[15] The poor, as these authorities imply, do not possess these resources and therefore have relatively little power.

The poor are dependent for their survival on powerful persons and organizations such as slum landlords, public welfare departments, the public housing authority, and local political machines. Welfare payments, exorbitant rent for poor housing, and racial discrimination all contribute toward a condition of impoverishment in which the individual feels worthless and powerless. The poor are not able to deal with the community power structure on equal terms. Their inability to enter into successful negotiation with powerful persons and organizations is due mainly to the lack of necessary resources—expert knowledge, organizational skills, and coercive power —associated with the lowest socioeconomic status. Whenever the poor press their demands by the threat of disruption or other means, the community power structure withholds access to economic resources and brings coercive power to bear through the police, the courts, and administrative regulations in order to defeat such threats.

> This [coercive] power has been and can be mobilized at any time as a direct force to defeat the efforts of self-help organizations [of the poor]. The community can impose direct sanctions—such as the use of police violence,

[10] Richard A. Cloward, "Are the Poor Left Out?" *The Nation* (August 2, 1965), pp. 55–60.

[11] Riessman, *op. cit.*, p. 6.

[12] *See* Kenneth S. Waterman, "Local Issues in the Urban War on Poverty," *Social Work*, Vol. 11, No. 1 (January 1966), pp. 57–63; Kenneth B. Clark, *Dark Ghetto: Dilemmas of Social Power* (New York: Harper & Row, 1965), pp. 11–12; and James Baldwin, *The Fire Next Time* (New York: Dial Press, 1963).

[13] Edward C. Banfield, *Political Influence* (New York: Free Press of Glencoe, 1961).

[14] Robert A. Dahl, "The Analysis of Influence in a Local Community," in Charles Adrian, ed., *Social Science and Community Action* (East Lansing: Michigan State University, 1960), pp. 24–42.

[15] Peter Rossi, "Theory, Research and Practice in Community Organization," in Adrian, ed., *op. cit.*, pp. 9–24.

refusal to rent land to tenant farmers, eviction from a public housing project, and harassment of welfare clients—on members of these organizations as a means of resisting change efforts.[16]

The CAP aims at creating a power base for the poor by delivering to them control over the programs and funds to be funneled into slum and ghetto communities. Cloward points out that under the antipoverty program billions of dollars are likely to be assigned to depressed neighborhoods for use in a wide range of services. To manage these services, huge organizations must be set up. Thousands of jobs are likely to be created and whether these are filled by professionals or by the poor, the new workers will owe allegiance to those who manage the operation. The organizations to be created or expanded, if manned by the poor, are likely to constitute a potentially important source of power for them.[17]

3. Improved Service Delivery

A third rationale lies in the administrative and therapeutic potential of involvement of the poor. One area of increasing concern in the health and welfare field is the problem of service delivery and utilization. In many instances social welfare services seem to be utilized least by those who need them most. Consequently, ways must be found to make these services more available to persons in the lower socioeconomic classes. One such way may be use of area residents as nonprofessional helpers. This has obvious advantages: such indigenous workers tend to bridge the gap between middle-class personnel and the poor—a common obstacle to service delivery—and they supplement the manpower resources that are so scarce in the social welfare field.[18] Riessman observes that the helper therapy principle—the use of people with a specific problem or handicap to help other people with the same problem, with positive results for both—can be especially workable with the poor, since this is culturally congruent with cooperative trends within the lower socioeconomic groups.[19] It is further hoped that nonprofessional staff members, because of their understanding of the culture of poverty, would be able to provide information on the needs and problems of the poor from which realistic programs can be planned.[20]

4. Value of Participatory Democracy

It is usually assumed that every citizen should contribute to the working of the society to the fullest possible extent. In slum communities the primacy of the individual's welfare is generally overshadowed by the interests and manipulations of the "downtown" political apparatus, whose decisions are frequently inconsistent with the values and aspirations of the slum residents. Consequently, new opportunities and channels are needed to enable people to participate in the affairs of *their* community and to express their own opinions.

Predominant Patterns

The term "maximum feasible participation" is subject to various interpretations, and the participation of poverty area residents in CAPs has followed various patterns. Programs

---

[16] Arthur Blum, Magdalena Miranda, and Maurice Meyer, "Goals and Means for Social Change," in John B. Turner, ed., *Neighborhood Organization for Community Action* (New York: National Association of Social Workers, 1963), p. 114.

[17] *Op. cit.*

[18] Alfred H. Katz, "Application of Self-Help Concepts in Current Social Welfare," *Social Work*, Vol. 10, No. 3 (July 1965), pp. 68–74.

[19] Frank Riessman, "The 'Helper' Therapy Principle," *Social Work*, Vol. 10, No. 2 (April 1965), pp. 27–32. *See also* Katz, *op. cit.*; and George Brager, "The Indigenous Worker: A New Approach to the Social Work Technician," *Social Work*, Vol. 10, No. 2 (April 1965), pp. 33–40.

[20] Frank Riessman, "The New Anti-Poverty Ideology"; George Brager and Harry Specht, "Mobilizing the Poor for Social Action," *Social Welfare Forum, 1965* (New York: Columbia University Press, 1965), pp. 197–210.

differ with respect to the number of residents involved, the level of their participation in the organizational structure (e.g., service on an advisory, policy-making, or constituent body), and in the methods used to promote participation (e.g., election, political appointment, or the like). Although information is not available for the entire country, three patterns of participation seem to be emerging:

1. Residents have become involved as policy-makers on boards of directors—either at the city or local level—that define program goals and means. By and large, however, such participation has not taken place to any substantial degree.

2. The poor have performed staff functions in antipoverty programs, generally being referred to as "indigenous" or "non-professional" workers. This is the most prevalent form of participation.

3. They have acted as constituent groups, providing the professional staff with feedback for program evaluation or acting as pressure groups to influence the project's activities.

A number of issues, based on the assumptions discussed previously, are raised with respect to these patterns of participation, among them the following: (1) To what extent and in what ways can and should the poor help determine program goals and the means to achieve them? (2) What is the nature of the partnership among the representatives of the poor, the public interest, the planning expert, and the political bureaucracy?[21] These will be discussed later.

Methods of Promoting Participation

The diversity of methods for involving the poor in the CAPs stems from the lack of specificity in the prescription of maximum feasible participation, from the relative willingness or unwillingness of local politicians to risk a threat to their positions, and from the coalesced strength of the poor in different geographic areas. Shostak identifies three predominant modes of involvement: containment, co-optation, and codetermination.[22]

Containment is designed to keep the aggressive element among the poor under control. This is the predominant mode, for example, in Atlanta and Chicago. The poverty board in Atlanta consists of a majority of whites and a few Negro businessmen—all political appointees—who dictate policy to welfare department personnel. Although two-thirds of Atlanta's poor are Negroes, none of the city's antipoverty programs is run by them. Advisory councils of the poor attached to neighborhood centers are severely limited in their authority over programs. In the case of Chicago's Committee on Urban Opportunity —a citywide board with ninety members— seven persons (the chairmen of the advisory councils of the seven urban progress centers) represent the poverty neighborhoods. The remaining eighty-three members are high-level public officials, corporation executives, welfare officials, labor leaders, clergymen, and so on.

In cities where *co-optation* is the primary mode, the middle-class members of the active ethnic and racial communities (especially the Negro community) are appointed to antipoverty boards to advise politicians on programs. For example, Detroit's antipoverty board consists of indigenous leaders who work with welfare professionals and influential community leaders to provide guidance for the mayor's antipoverty program. The mayor formulates policy with the apparent support of the middle-class Negro community and business and labor leaders.

Codetermination with the poor, the rarest model, is approximated in Philadelphia, where elected spokesmen for the poor join welfare professionals and community leaders in running the city's antipoverty programs. The Philadelphia Anti-Poverty Action Committee consists of elected representatives of the poor, delegates from welfare agencies, religious

---

[21] Piven, *op. cit.*, pp. 73–80.
[22] Arthur B. Shostak, "Containment, Co-optation or Codetermination," *American Child*, Vol. 44, No. 4 (November 1965), pp. 15–19. The examples that follow are taken from this paper.

bodies, organized labor, the business community, NAACP, CORE, and the Urban League. Inclusion of the poor among the decision-makers has had three major effects: (1) Spokesmen for the poor are able to press for an important role for the community action councils. As a result, the councils now recommend candidates for nonprofessional jobs and review the qualifications of professional appointees. (2) The elected representatives have also been able to bring about certain reforms or changes in antipoverty programs. (3) The spokesmen have successfully pressed for swift and concrete results by exerting strong external pressures that help move proposals through the unfamiliar maze of bureaucratic channels and red tape that confront every antipoverty proposal.

Lack of Consensus on Goals

One issue clearly emerging with regard to citizen participation is a lack of consensus on the goal of participation. Is it to promote better utilization of social welfare services by achieving better co-ordination among them? to provide opportunities for participation by the poor in order to enable them to gain power whereby they can personally escape from poverty? to bring about significant social change and eliminate poverty itself?

The issue stems from a theoretical controversy about the causes of poverty and the resultant strategies to deal with it. Where do the causes of poverty rest—in the individual's inabilities, in the social institutions dealing with the poor, or in the social structure that fosters or permits poverty? The Committee on Education and Labor of the House of Representatives identified, in its report on the poverty bill (HR 11377), lack of education, poor health, the absence of marketable skills, and the unstable family life of the poor as causes of their poverty.[23] Accordingly, the bill directed at-

tention to such components of the CAP as expanded and improved services, increased assistance, and necessary facilities in the fields of education, employment, job training and counseling, health services, vocational rehabilitation, housing, home management, and social services.

This conception carries an implicit assumption in the program strategy that the poor are responsible for their poverty, i.e., the defects to be remedied are located within the individual. Consequently, attention is focused on inadequacies of the poor rather than of social institutions and their policies.[24] Participation is thus viewed as a form of social therapy to treat social disintegration and apathy among the poor through self-help.

Those who believe that the causes of poverty lie in the institutional structure of society see participation of the poor as a means of building up a new political force to bring about significant social change. On this basis, militant groups in a number of cities have organized to protest against city administrations.

Degree of Participation

Another issue is related to the degree of resident participation as well as the amount of authority vested in participants. *Community Action Program Guide*, the first policy document issued by the Office of Economic Opportunity, states that a vital feature of every CAP is involvement of the poor (and/or residents of the area) in planning, policy-making, and program operation.[25]

It is widely understood, although not explicitly stated, that OEO expects one-third of the local poverty board members to be drawn from the poor.[26] The direction of the program is to help the poor to help themselves. The guide strongly urges direct involvement of the poor in block elections, petitions and referenda, and neighborhood legal aid associations.

[23] Report of the Committee on Education and Labor, 88th Cong., 2d Sess., June 3, 1964, p. 2.

[24] Slavin, *op. cit.*, pp. 148–150.

[25] *Community Action Program Guide*, I (Washington, D.C.: Office of Economic Opportunity, October 1965), p. 7.

[26] Barbara Carter, "Sargent Shriver and the Role of the Poor," *Reporter*, May 5, 1966, pp. 17–20.

This policy is not always adhered to. Deviations from the policy seem typically to have been forced by local politicans (i.e., mayors and governors) who see a potential threat to their political power. Carter reports that OEO no longer emphasizes representation of the poor on poverty boards, in appeasement of the mayors of Syracuse, Chicago, and Atlanta, who vehemently opposed participation of the poor in the CAPs[27]

There have also been conflicting pronouncements by OEO officials. "Are the poor supposed to make up a third of poverty boards?" Shriver was asked. "No," he replied on November 5, 1965. Yet only two weeks earlier OEO had sent a memorandum to all its regional directors announcing that "we are proposing as a guide that the representatives of the poor be approximately one-third of the membership of a [community action] governing body."[28] On January 12, 1966, Shriver reiterated:

> There is no requirement in this statute that persons have to be poor to serve on a Community Action Committee. The phrase "the poor" is an elliptical way of describing the statutory language. You do not have to be poor to fulfill the statute, and we are not trying to get poor people as such. Is this clear enough.[29]

Pressures from groups that have traditionally presided over public welfare have also been forcing OEO to retreat from its policy of innovation, especially from the technique of arming the poor with power to force a changed institutional structure and/or delivery of services.[30] It is clear that with respect to participation of the poor in CAPs, OEO needs to state its policy firmly and clearly and follow it in a consistent fashion.

Right to Sanction Policy

The right of the poor to sanction a policy must also be clarified. This is important since the poor may be involved for different purposes: they may be involved in policy-making bodies as representatives of the groups a CAP seeks as constituents, they may be target area residents serving on an ad hoc or continuing basis as advisers, or they may be asked to give local sanction to policy created at a higher level. The difference between advice and sanction in dealing with representatives of the poor is critical.[31] In CAPs, involvement of the poor has appeared to represent an attempt to gain legitimation and support of policy, but the poor are rejected when they challenge the central goals and methods of traditional welfare programs. The controversy over the rights of the poor to make decisions is, in fact, the question of distribution of power between the poor and the social welfare network.[32] The dilemma is that a genuine, free, and effective political instrument cannot be created or guaranteed by OEO or any other public program. It will be up to the churches, foundations, and other active organizations to provide "seed money" for the poor to build effective organizations—if they are to be *of* the poor, and not dominated by or dependent on the goodwill and services of agencies and professionals. When a grass-roots organization of the poor comes into being, it might then con-

[27] *Ibid.* Interestingly, in contrast to this above assertion, OEO slashed poverty funds to Los Angeles on the ground that the poor did not have any voice in the poverty board. This policy was again reversed when OEO granted funds to the Atlanta poverty board, which did not have a single poor person on it. When asked about this, Mr. Shriver compared the role of the poor to that of an architect's client who participates in the planning but does not actually design the house.

[28] *Ibid.*

[29] *Ibid.*

[30] Jules Witcover and Erwin Knoll, "Politics and the Poor: Shriver's Second Thought," *Reporter*, December 30, 1965, pp. 23–24.

[31] Melvin B. Mogulof, "Involving Low-Income Neighborhoods in Antidelinquency Programs," *Social Work*, Vol. 10, No. 4 (October 1965), pp. 51–57.

[32] *See* the statement made by Kenneth B. Clark, Hearing of the Subcommittee on Employment, Manpower, and Poverty, 90th Cong., 1967, p. 391.

tract with government programs to operate services for the poor.[33]

The fear of sanctions from the power structure, the lack of expert knowledge, poor formal communication skills, deficiency in organizational skills, preoccupation with survival, and lack of confidence in organizational means as a way of effecting change in their life situation are some of the factors that make participation of the poor in CAPs highly problematic, if not impossible.[34] Verba points out four main conditions for political participation: (1) resources such as information about politics, issues, communication channels, and rules of political participation; skills in written and oral expression; and material and social resources, (2) motivation to participate, (3) structural conduciveness, by which is meant the availability of formal participatory structures, the presence of regularized procedures for participation such as Ombudsmen to process citizen complaints, and the availability of such procedures as periodic elections, and (4) cultural conduciveness such as support of the general norms of democracy. He further points out that these conditions are inequitably distributed in American society—lower-class Americans, especially Negroes, do not possess these resources. Consequently they participate to a significantly lower degree than do the white middle and upper classes.[35]

It has been observed in Cleveland, for example, that those who are struggling to make both ends meet cannot take a fight to the city hall or use coercion or other sanctions. The poor are afraid of going to jail, cannot afford to lose their jobs, and cannot hire lawyers to protect their rights vis-à-vis the police or the public housing authorities. It may be wondered how, with all of these limitations, the poor can participate in social action. Waterman observes that the poor

are politically disconnected and emasculated. Consequently it is almost inevitable that the dominant control and planning of even the Community Action Programs of the War on Poverty, which is to be done at the local level, will not represent those who are poor.[36]

Is Representation a Diversionary Tactic?

Another issue is whether the representation of the poor on antipoverty councils is a diversionary tactic. The effort to involve the poor may be primarily an attempt to divert attention from a far more fundamental problem confronting the poor in this society. In the event the poor take control of the antipoverty programs (and this has not happened), what would they win? They would win control over employment programs—which is not the same as control over the processes that create employment. Participation is therefore irrelevant to the solution of their problems. Many feel that the solution lies in institutional change. The local power structures, although they can affect the lives of individuals, have little freedom to create policies that affect the whole poverty group. Decisions at the local level involve the implementation of national and regional policies rather than the creation of policies that affect major resource allocation.[37]

Who Should Be Involved

The final issue is whom to involve on the antipoverty boards: spokesmen for the poor, residents of the poverty areas who may not themselves be poor, or the poor themselves? There is a tendency in community action agencies to involve self-appointed spokesmen for the poor. Under the guise of involvement some projects have selected Negroes who have only the dimmest notion of what poverty is like. Projects that appoint middle- or upper-class Negroes as representatives of poor Ne-

---

[33] Waterman, *op. cit.*, p. 61.

[34] *See* Blum, Miranda, and Meyer, *op. cit.*, p. 18; and Lee Rainwater, "Neighborhood Action and Lower-Class Life-Style," in Turner, ed., *op. cit.*, pp. 25–39.

[35] Sidney Verba, "Democratic Participation," *Annals*, Vol. 373 (September 1967), pp. 53–78.

[36] *Op. cit.*, p. 60.

[37] Blum, Miranda, and Meyer, *op. cit.*

groes perform a ritual to fulfill the statutory requirements.[38] Kramer's study of CAPs in San Francisco substantiates this assertion:

> The main critical issue among the members of the action system [consisting of welfare professionals, city officials and others] was the identification of appropriate representatives of the poor in the Community Action Program. Although the legislation explicitly prescribed a geographic target area as the basis for representation, this provided few guidelines for the community plan. . . . Usually, some criterion of association with the poor was used, circumventing direct involvement of residents or recipients.[39]

Even when representatives of the poor have been elected,

> in no case were elected poor influential or taken seriously in any major civic decision and in very few cases were they competent or capa-

ble of any genuine rather than condescending involvement.[40]

Summary

The basic rationales advanced for resident participation in CAPs include irrelevance and inadequacy of current programs in regard to the needs of the poor, creation of a power base for the poor, improvement in the service delivery system, and the need of a populace to participate in the democratic process. Residents have been involved in CAPs in the capacity of policy-makers, as staff workers, and as sounding boards for the welfare organizations. The main issues that have arisen in regard to citizen participation in CAPs are the lack of consensus on goals and degrees of participation of residents, their right to sanction policy, and credentials of participants. These issues have considerably affected the workings of the program.

[38] Mogulof, *op. cit.*, pp. 53–54.
[39] Ralph M. Kramer and Clare Denton, "Organization of a Community Action Program: A Comparative Case Study," *Social Work*, Vol. 12, No. 4 (October 1967), p. 78.
[40] Clark, *op. cit.*, p. 392.

B.   RUNNING AN EFFECTIVE ORGANIZATION

42.   Setting Up an Organization

Martin Oppenheimer* • George Lakey**

Once the civil rights worker has analyzed the community and thought about a strategy, he should proceed to set up an organization. Forms of organization, their structures, and their affiliations if any will depend on the job decided on and the personnel available. The worker may want to join an existing group in order to influence it; he may want to set up an

* Department of Sociology, Lincoln University
** Rutgers University

ad hoc or temporary group composed either of individuals or of representatives of other groups; or he may want to create a new group. In recent years most groups tend to be "single-cause" rather than many-purpose, with the exception of some student groups (in some cases, single-cause groups later develop into many-purpose groups). It is generally easier to join an existing group than to set up a new one, and to affiliate rather than to maintain complete independence. There are certain advantages stemming from national affiliation, including financial help, staff help, legal aid, reputation, and aid in moving against concerns and politicians with far-off headquarters in other cities and states.

Organization implies bureaucracy. Every organization has bureaucracy, and this is not necessarily a "dirty" word. It simply means that there is a chain of command or communication through which decisions are carried out. Bureaucracy becomes "dirty" only when decision-making no longer reflects the rank and file membership, and/or when the structure interferes with making decisions. This happens when the structure becomes too large, or when decision-making processes are unclear so that decisiveness is lacking, or when routine alone becomes central in the life of the organization.

Every organization, whether it is the U.S. Army, a business corporation, or a peace or civil rights group, must have a chain of command. Our assumption is that the chain of command should go from the bottom up, that is, should be democratic. This is so because democracy is (a) efficient, more so than dictatorship in the long run; (b) better able to move in the direction of creating a more human society, because it involves people in the determination of their own destinies, hence in the fuller involvement and development of their personalities; and (c) more able to recruit the kind of forces needed really to overcome oppression and injustice, because in the long run movements based on demagogy do not result in justice—the means help to determine the ends.

There are ways in which democratic decision-making and full participation by the rank-

and-file can be undercut. Early in the formation of a group a decision must be made as to structure, and while democratic structure does not guarantee democracy, it does help. A decision must also be made on how decisions are to be taken: by parliamentary or by consensus (the Quaker "sense of the meeting") methods. Both have advantages, and both have disadvantages. Consensus tends to work best when the members of the group have basic agreement on philosophy, while the parliamentary system tends to guarantee representation to organized minorities and recognizes the importance of caucuses. Both systems can be manipulated by persons with the best intentions, not to speak of those with less than the highest moral outlook.

Several kinds of conditions help to undermine democracy aside from outright manipulation, or help make manipulation possible. Wearing the group out with late and boring meetings, or holding the group until most members have gone, leaves the way open for a well-organized minority to railroad ideas through. Having present officers appoint or elect other officers should generally be regarded with suspicion. Nominating committees for officers, rather than nominations from the floor, are another technique for keeping decision-making within a small group. Most important of all is the development of informal person-to-person relationships: shortcuts, doing favors, and the praiseworthy but misdirected desire to want to avoid mistakes— hence letting "experts" do all the jobs. This tends to happen particularly in the midst of crises and emergencies when "we can't afford to make mistakes," and can't take a chance on letting an untrained person do a job and learn at the risk of having him make mistakes. Unless deliberate decisions are made by the group to expand the techniques of the trade, those techniques (such as running a meeting, writing a leaflet, running a mimeo machine, being picket captain, etc.) will remain the property of a few "experts," who tend gradually, and frequently without realizing it, to exclude the rank-and-file members from a real role in the organization.

In civil rights groups conditions of crisis always exist. This makes the situation more serious. In addition, you will run into the argument that decision-making should be limited to those who participate fully in organizational work—something that is not possible for everyone, given the speed of the movement and the constant meetings required. A second-class membership can develop under such circumstances, and a type of clique arises in which the "true revolutionaries," that is, those whose *entire* lives are taken up with the movement, have a different life from the rest of the members, different values, slang, etc. Insofar as such a clique criticizes current values it may have a contribution to make, but when it separates itself from its own rank-and-file, and from the community at large, because of its style of living, it does the movement a disservice. Democracy suffers.

If you need to fight against the growth of non-democratic tendencies in an organization, you must organize your action (that is, form caucuses). This is true whether the non-democratic group is informal, or whether a clearly anti-democratic faction exists. You must organize pro-democratic people to conduct a clear-cut fight on this issue; otherwise, after a time, the organization is doomed to develop in such a way as to undermine its ultimate goals: the democratic and just development of society.

Whether you are conducting a struggle within your own organization or working as a democratic minority in another group, several suggestions may help:

(1) All organizations have three primary functions: policy-making, organization, and education (including both education of the group itself and public relations). Regardless of what body makes policy (conventions, executive committees, etc.) he who is in charge of carrying out policy ultimately determines what happens. The organizer, secretary, coordinator of committees, administrator is the man to watch—or the man to be. This fact can be used either for evil or for good.

(2) You must organize your group into a caucus, meet ahead of meetings, plan strategy, and have a floor leader. Sit in scattered positions throughout the audience. Save your best speaker for last in an exchange from the floor. Know your parliamentary procedure so as not to be outmaneuvered, and to make best use of your numbers.

(3) Remember that you, as a leader, are no good without an organized following, just as an officer is no good without a top-notch first sergeant. The good leader must have a *perspective* (not constantly react to situations only as they arise), *credibility* (not promise what cannot be accomplished, not over- or under-shoot the potential, but keep the group moving at its capacity), and "image" or *personality*. Remember that a leader can be cut down just as surely by apathy as by elections, and that you can sabotage any organization by obeying *all* the rules carefully, just as you can sabotage it by a "slow-down." This, after all, is just another kind of "passive resistance."

(4) The good leader recognizes minority points of view without being bullied by them. Dissenters are a part of the movement unless proven otherwise, and above all they are human beings and must be treated as such. A good leader will insist that arguments be to the point and will not allow "ad hominem" or name-calling arguments which attempt to discredit people's thinking by some form of "guilt by association."

Jobs That Need Doing

The above are general points. What are some of the specific jobs that need doing?[1]

(1) Once the executive committee and the officers have been set up (with clearly established lines of authority, responsibility, and decision-making, and with as little overlap as possible) we are ready to move.

(2) A timetable for action is worthwhile. Persons who have charge of such jobs as publicity, office management, transportation, communication, housing, training, supplies, finances, and literature should be appointed or elected. Special resource persons, when

[1] This section is based partly on Charles Walker, *Organizing for Nonviolent Direct Action*, Cheyney, Pennsylvania, 1961.

needed, should be lined up: workshop leaders, legal counsel, public relations specialists, etc.

(3) Frequently a headquarters in the field must be set up. Select its location carefully for convenience and possible symbolic value. Keep quarters neat and clean. Your headquarters speaks for you; you will want to post notices and posters and possibly open it with a reception and press conference.

(4) Finances are always a tricky matter. Open a special bank account if necessary. Be clear on any tax-exemption problems. Set up a simple bookkeeping system in case your regular bookkeeper is arrested. Your opponents will seek excuses to charge misuse of funds and there may be investigations. Your financial affairs should be kept fanatically clean.

(5) Office supplies, communications equipment (walkie-talkies, etc.), and equipment for meetings must be on hand when they are needed. Make sure your machinery is kept in good repair so that it can function when you need it. The problem of record keeping must be clarified: while you may not wish to have records seized (hence have supporters punished), at the same time it is important to keep track of activities for the sake of accounting for responsibilities, informing new personnel of work in progress when they take over, and helping sociologists and historians in their job for the future.

(6) Secrecy: It is possible to confuse and delay the obtaining of "secret" information by your opponents in various ways. However, if your opponents are determined, this is pointless. It results in *inefficiency* because you have to cover up much that you do from your own members, *authoritarianism* because you cannot tell your members what is going on, and *mistrust*. In any case your opponents, if they are determined, will plant "informers" and/or modern electronic devices in such a way that your activities will be an open book. You may as well open the book and be fully honest about your plans to begin with. You should try to plan tactics (to be discussed later) which do not depend on secrecy for their value.

(7) Register or have records of participants in all projects wherever possible (a) in order to keep them informed prior to the event; (b)

to find out if they have special skills; (c) to keep track of problems as they develop; (d) to follow up later for deeper involvement; (e) to inform attorneys or relatives in case of arrest, accident, or violence. Participants in long-term projects should be insured, if possible.

(8) Participation in a project or membership in an organization should be conditioned upon acceptance of a written discipline, or upon some set of principles or constitution. No exceptions should be made. It is your job to educate people to the acceptance of your principles, but until they do, they should stay out. Such principles do not have to be complicated or numerous. In this way you can cut down on misunderstandings and violations of lines of responsibility and authority, and thus limit the likelihood of violence because of your own people losing control of a demonstration or of themselves. This also helps the morale and public image of the movement, and gives outsiders a sense that the organization is something special to which it is a privilege to belong.

(9) Relations between persons in the group will always be a problem. Boy-girl situations develop. Rules rarely work, so none will be given here. Sloppy public demonstrations of personal affection, needless to say, violate other aspects of most disciplines, and can be handled that way. Sloppy clothing likewise.

(10) Psychological problems also arise. People join movements for all kinds of reasons, and the untrained person will rarely be able to distinguish "real" from stated reasons except in extreme cases. This does not need to become an issue until personal problems interfere with the working of the group. If at all possible, a somewhat older person with experience in family situations should have a kind of leading role in the organization so that he can step in and offer guidance without appearing to interfere in anybody's personal life or making the problem person feel pushed around.

(11) The white participant in civil rights activities, especially (although not exclusively) in the deep South, faces a special problem: how to communicate and live with Negroes in a movement which is primarily of, by,

and for Negroes, and how to survive in action. To varying degrees he may be treated as a second-class participant by Negroes, and frequently, though in very subtle ways, he will be called upon to "prove" his sincerity. This is a difficult role. On the one hand, the white participant should not give in to reverse racism in order to be accepted—he should be accepted because of what he does, and not because of what he is. On the other hand, he must establish contact and communication and maintain them in order to be effective. The white participant should not be afraid to take on an equal role, including a part in the decision-making process, but he should try to establish his credentials as one who has the right to participate because he, too, has put himself on the "firing line." The white participant has many of the problems which face an anthropologist or a sociologist visiting a group with which he is unfamiliar. To be accepted without losing one's own individuality and standards is not easy.

Public Relations

You should not assume that because our cause is just, anyone who is worthwhile will support it—or that anyone who does not support us isn't worth trying to get. Prejudices run deep and must be dealt with. Allies are essential, because (a) civil rights workers are a very small minority in this country and cannot carry enough weight to change society no matter how moral the cause; and (b) certain kinds of allies are important because they lead to the breakdown of significant points of resistance (e.g., ministers, scholars, dignified mothers of white governors). It is therefore important, while not compromising, to try to limit the amount of antagonism from potential allies. This is the key to good "public relations." It involves primarily two things: cutting down on actions which can be misinterpreted to be hostile and negative; and improving the interpretation of all activities. Remember that many people are only looking for an excuse *not* to support the movement. While we cannot avoid creating excuses for those who are really looking for them, we can avoid presenting them on a silver platter.

What we mean when we say "public relations" is really "propaganda." Propaganda, like bureaucracy, is not necessarily a dirty word. It has become dirty because propaganda has come to be associated with lying and distortion of the truth. The distinction is often made between propaganda (which has a distinct message) and education (which leaves conclusions open). But even education is propaganda, because leaving conclusions open is a kind of message, or value, in the direction of democracy.

Before any educational or propaganda campaign is begun, it is important to sit down and analyze your "target population," the people whom you want to move (or in some cases keep in their present state of mind in the face of campaigns by others to move them—propaganda is sometimes defensive). There is, first of all, the hard core of supporters. Then there are friends whom you want to bring in closer. Then there is the vast neutral public. Then there are those in opposition, in various degrees, to the cause. The final objective of all propaganda is to move everyone one step closer to you, or, in cases where there is an offensive against you, to have them not move away from you. Every propaganda item (mass meetings, press releases, leaflets, TV programs, etc.) should be aimed at a particular segment of the population, your "target."

Various publicity methods which you may want to consider include: background information sheets to support press releases for newsmen and community leaders; brief biographical sketches of well-known leaders and participants for "human interest" stories; press releases for dailies, the wire services, special press services (religious, labor, Negro, etc.), neighborhood papers, radio and TV news departments, and commentators and columnists who are sympathetic. You may want to offer advance interviews or tape record special speeches. By all means try to visit key editors, news directors, and special reporters in order to interpret events. Writing letters to the editor should not be neglected, but they should be kept short and to the point.

It is crucial to remember that your job is to inform, not to seek publicity for publicity's sake. Try not to be put into the position of doing things for the press which are not a natural part of the action, no matter how picturesque they may be, but remember to be friendly in your replies to the press, and try to interpret what you do as fully as possible.

When you are speaking "on the record," you should be particularly careful to quote accurately and give only facts of which you are certain. Double-checking is more important than being fast with an answer. If you are the public affairs officer, you should try to do plenty of reading on this complex subject.

Press releases should be clearly marked as to time of release, and should be double-spaced. They should not be too long—two pages at maximum. After a while you will get to know the peculiarities of the local press and you will tailor your releases to meet their requirements of format. All press releases should read like a news story, beginning in the first sentence or two (at most) with Who, What, Where, When, and Why:

> Joe Brotherhood (WHO), chairman of the local chapter of Citizens for Equal Rights, this morning (WHEN) announced a full-scale boycott (WHAT) of all major downtown department stores (WHERE) by Negro citizens. He said the "no-buy" campaign would remain in effect until all the stores hire a satisfactory number of Negro clerks (WHY).
> Brotherhood, 32, who is theology professor at nearby Baptist Seminary, said he had the agreement of four Negro churches and five Negro community groups on the ban. (etc.)

Here are some general cautions for publicity campaigns, leaflets, and other affairs of a public relations nature:

(1) Keep leaflets readable. Don't clutter them up with too much reading material. Start out with something that will hold the reader's attention—"Police Brutality in This Neighborhood," not "Citizens for Equal Rights."

(2) Keep your public relations down to earth. Make your charges believable. Ask people to do something they can really do right now, given their present state of mind. "Come to Freedom School," not "Go Immediately to Register." Don't insult their basic prejudices or beliefs. You want to communicate,

not drive them away (e.g., don't say "your preachers are nothing but Uncle Toms." It's libelous, anyway, to charge a person publicly with being a Communist, or an Uncle Tom!)

(3) Don't promise what you can't deliver. People who disagree with your ideas may gradually come to believe in you as a person if you really show you can deliver. Try small things first. Don't try too much, because failure tends to undermine morale.

(4) Watch your language. Use the English that makes sense to the community in which you are working. Watch your appearance. Appearance is a communicating device. You cannot expect people to raise their own standards of cleanliness, or look up to you as a leader, if you act like a slob. The civil rights worker gives up some of his private rights when he joins the movement.

(5) Keep social affairs social. Don't push too hard on newcomers. Be friendly and make them feel at home. Don't huddle in a corner with the in-group clique. Don't acquire the reputation of having absolutely fixed views, of being dogmatic and inflexible. When in doubt, shake hands.

Conducting a Meeting

It is pointless to try to write a guide to parliamentary procedure in a manual like this. Every organization, over a period of time, develops its own procedures, somewhat based on the parliamentary rules laid down in *Roberts Rules of Order*, but modified to meet specific local conditions. The most important thing to remember about procedure is that its chief purpose is to get business conducted efficiently while protecting the will of the majority and the rights of the minority. Procedures should be amended, changed, thrown out, and invented as long as that chief purpose can get accomplished better.

A typical business *agenda* might read as follows:

(1) *Call* the meeting to *order:* "The meeting will please come to order."

(2) Have the secretary read the *minutes* of the previous meeting, with emphasis on the main points, motions passed, and action ap-

proved. Ask, "Are there any corrections to the minutes?". Then, after all corrections are made, "The minutes stand approved as corrected." Some organizations like to have the rest of the agenda read at this point, with specific topics listed, so that members may know what is ahead.

(3) Have the secretary read short summaries of the more important *corrrespondence*, especially letters from the national office. If action is required, it should be taken either at this point or under old or new business.

(4) *Reports* of special officers (treasurer, particularly, plus membership committee chairman, etc.) and committees (such as the executive committee, special projects committee, housing, education, public accommodations, etc.). After each report, ask for questions or discussion from the floor. There may be motions asking specific action or correcting the actions reported on at this time.

(5) Unfinished, or *old business* should be taken care of next. This is business which has not been covered by committee reports. Ask the floor, "Is there any unfinished business to come before the body?"

(6) *New business* should be next on the agenda. Some new business may have been reported by a committee, such as the executive committee, and this committee may wish to make a more formal report at this point and ask for action. When this is concluded ask, "Is there further new business?"

(7) Some organizations have a place on the agenda for *"Good and Welfare,"* meaning more general gripes. This is a good place to air them and try to cope with such problems out in the open.

(8) "There being no further business, the chair will entertain a motion to *adjourn*."

Before and after many meetings in the civil rights field there may be a short prayer, a moment of silence for meditation, or a short song.

While there is little point in outlining a formal method of procedure, there are some keys to having an orderly meeting:[2]

(1) Before starting a meeting, the chairman should be sure that he has an outline of the business to be considered (the agenda).

(2) Any time an officer or a committee makes a report, there should be a motion to accept or adopt it, or change it, or, sometimes, reject it.

(3) The chairman should always state clearly the motion on which the vote is about to be taken in order that everyone has a clear understanding of the issue. Amendments are usually in order after a motion has been made, and they are voted on before the main motion.

(4) Courtesy to the group is the key to an orderly meeting. Every member has rights equal to every other member.

(5) Only one subject at a time should claim the attention of the group.

(6) The will of the majority must be carried out, and the rights of the minority must be preserved.

[2] These are based on *A Call to Order*, a guide to parliamentary procedure prepared by the United States National Student Association.

43. Reflection on Campaign Techniques

William Singer*

No two political campaigns can be alike. Therefore, any attempt to set down guidelines is, at best, a reflection of past experience which may or may not be applicable in the present circumstances. It does seem, however, that some things, while not entirely transfer-

This political "handbook" was prepared at the request of various political and community leaders of Chicago who were interested in the techniques employed by Singer in his upset election (April 1969). Reprinted by permission.
° Alderman, 44th Ward, City of Chicago.

able from campaign to campaign, have a great deal of merit and ought to be seriously considered, if not adapted to the present campaign. The following is an attempt to indicate a number of campaign aspects which are particularly useful in a relatively small political district, e.g., Alderman, State Representative, Con-Con[1] and, perhaps, even a Congressional district.

1. Key Campaign Personnel

The three most important generalists in the campaign are likely to be the Campaign Manager, the Office Manager and the Campaign Treasurer.

(a) Campaign Manager

There must be one person to whom all staff people can look for direction on a day-to-day basis. The Campaign Manager should be the person who decides whether to order materials, how to organize a blitz, the initial organization of the office, discussions with the press, the candidate's schedule and all other questions which other campaign personnel may ask. The Campaign Manager should be strong enough to make these decisions by himself, and they are not decisions which the candidate should be making.

(b) Office Manager

The Office Manager will organize such things as mailings, telephone campaigns, volunteer workers in the office and all other operations which will be run out of the campaign office. The Office Manager will, of course, take direction from the Campaign Manager; but she should be strong enough to control the operations in the office.

(c) Campaign Treasurer

The Campaign Treasurer should be independent from the operations of the campaign so that he may be more objective in his decisions with respect to money. His job is not to raise money, but to spend money and to control the spending of money. His job is also to negotiate with suppliers and creditors so as to free the Campaign Manager and Office Manager from these financial worries. This person need not be a full-time worker, but should be available to the Office and Campaign Managers at all times.

(d) Other Key Campaign Staff

There is room in every campaign for persons the candidate relies upon and trusts for advice. Titles are unimportant. You can add the title of Campaign Chairman or Campaign Adviser. It doesn't really matter so long as these people are closely advising the candidate *and* so long as they are working together with key regulars on the campaign staff. Thus, it is essential that *small weekly meetings* be held of the key campaign staff members, with the possible exclusion here of the Office Manager. It is at these small meetings where the Campaign Manager, Campaign Treasurer, and a small group of three or four other key advisers should make campaign policy decisions. It may even be necessary to meet twice a week. The existence of these meetings is not necessarily a secret, but what takes place should be restricted to the persons attending. From time to time other persons will attend for various reasons, e.g., the person in charge of advertising and publicity or political action.

2. Component Parts

These are the various functions of the campaign, each of which ought to have a specific chairman.

(a) Political Action

These are fancy words for precinct work, but in these kinds of campaigns it is here that the campaign will be won or lost. A Political Action Chairman who is well-versed in the precincts, who will be able to fire precinct workers when necessary, who will be able to slot and reslot campaign workers into precincts is indispensable. For the most part, political action takes precedence over all of the campaign functions and, therefore, the Political Action Chairman should have first priority on volunteers. It is up to the Chairman to break the district down into workable parts, such as areas, to appoint Area Chairmen, and to work with Area Chairmen in the appointment of Precinct Captains and Precinct Work-

[1] *Editor's Note*: Constitutional Convention.

ers. Of course, in those instances where the candidate is endorsed by a regular party organization, the Political Action Chairman will have to become familiar with the ability of the regular party in their precincts. A staff decision will have to be made as to whether volunteers can or should be brought into areas manned by the regular organization or whether the operations can be merged. These are sticky decisions which must be made at the outset.

(b) Coffee Parties

The coffee parties serve the following functions: (1) to get volunteers for precinct work, election day work, and office work; (2) to increase identification of the candidate; and (3) to raise funds. Each of these results is critical to the campaign and no one of them should be overlooked in setting up the coffees. A Coffee Party Chairman, usually a woman who is able to use the phone during the day, is indispensable. She should, perhaps, have subchairmen working under her in various areas; but should be responsible for coordinating all of the coffees. Her job is to call the prospective hostess, set up the time, call the person handling the candidate's schedule, arrange for a chairman to be there, and arrange for the campaign materials to be at the party. She needs a group of 20 to 30 men or women who will act as chairmen, whom she will also schedule for the parties. (In terms of procedure for the coffees, a detailed sheet is available from my office on how to run the coffee parties.)

(c) Visibility

Visibility means getting the candidate's posters, pictures, bumper stickers, etc., distributed throughout the district. A Visibility Chairman should be someone who has almost full time to devote, who can use the candidate's resources, including lists of coffees, volunteers, persons attending coffees, etc., to ask that signs be put in their windows or that bumper stickers be displayed. He should also be responsible for contacting stores for billboard placement *and* all other imaginative ways of getting the candidate's name physically spread throughout the district. This in-

cludes the kind of election day visibility that is absolutely essential. He should also have a group of volunteers assigned to him, especially during the last few weeks of the campaign.

(d) Scheduling

One person, and only one person, should be in charge of scheduling the candidate. This person should coordinate the schedule of appearances at public places, community groups, coffee parties, and at campaign stops, such as trains and buses. The scheduler should not only be responsible for coordinating dates suggested by persons working in other areas of the campaign, but should seek out places where the candidate should be going, such as community meetings and shopping centers. In addition, the scheduler is also responsible for the candidate's entire day, and the candidate as well as anybody else should clear engagements with the scheduler.

(e) Advertising

This may best be handled by a professional or group of professionals. Their work, however, should be coordinated with the Campaign Manager and other key staff members before anything is committed.

(f) Publicity

If funds are available, a full-time PR person is highly desirable. If funds are not available, a volunteer with experience is the next best. Again, all activities should be checked with the scheduler, the Campaign Manager, and the key staff.

(g) Volunteers

Volunteer operations include going with the candidate to bus and train stops, shopping centers, and, also, blitzes. Volunteers should also be recruited for the office on a regular basis. With respect to the outside volunteer activities, a Volunteer Chairman is quite helpful as it removes this function from the regular office staff. The chairman should coordinate the activities of the volunteers with the activities of the candidate and make sure that volunteers are scheduled to be with the candidate at appropriate times. He can also organize literature blitzes.

(h) Special Events

A few large special events during the campaign are particularly good for workers' morale, publicity, and creating the kind of campaign enthusiasm that is necessary. If one person can handle these special events, again, the office staff is relieved of the burden. These special events can be anything from a large outdoor party for workers or a rally to whatever catchy or gimmicky thing might work in the particular district. The special event might be directed at a particular area or segment of the population or may, again, be just for the workers.

(i) Research and Writing

The candidate will inevitably develop his own basic speech, but it is quite helpful to have a group of people researching the most important issues in the area and, if possible, coming up with a series of position papers. The papers are less important than the advice to the candidate, however; and he should meet regularly with advisers on issues and discuss his positions with them.

(j) Candidate's Personal Staff

The candidate should have a personal secretary to whom he can dictate letters and who can handle personal business for him. He should also have a driver or person who will regularly attend the coffees and other appearances.

(k) Letter Writing

Person-to-person letter writing can be very effective in a local campaign. A chairman for this function can be very useful as he can pinpoint persons who can reach particular groups. If the chairman can get a person to write to 20 to 25 members of a particular group with whom he has stature, this is very effective. Members of the Citizens Committee should be asked to write letters to 20 or 30 of their friends. Actually, the office should have the responsibility of sending out the letters so that there is no expense or effort on the part of the person who is signing his name to the letter. All the chairman has to do is get the person to agree to sign his name to a letter and

work out the language of the letter with the sender. The office staff should take over once the chairman has given the list of names and the draft letter to the Office Manager.

(l) Citizens Committee

One prominent person in the community should act as Chairman of the Citizens Committee, but he should also be someone who will make calls and contact persons who are willing to serve on the committee. From this Citizens Committee various things can be drawn: (1) resources; (2) persons to write letters; (3) coffee parties; and (4) other volunteers.

(m) Telephone Campaign

One way of reaching voters where precincts are not covered on a door-to-door basis is a telephone campaign. This can be done either in the home or at the campaign office, but the latter is highly preferable. If a bank of phones can be set up to be used exclusively for outgoing calls and a general chairman put in charge of calling, the telephone campaign will be much more effective than if left to the individuals in their homes. The chairman, of course, should consult with the campaign strategy team to decide where calling would be most effective. Calling can be done during many hours of the campaign when other things cannot be done. The larger the district or the more inaccessible the voter to individual contact, the more important telephone calling becomes.

3. Finance

The candidate has to be relieved of raising funds himself. He must rely on a finance Chairman and a committee of people who will be responsible for raising the necessary money. Some money will come from the coffees, but the bulk will have to be raised privately. The candidate must be assured that the necessary funds will be forthcoming and that he will not have to spend much of his time raising them. The finance Chairman will work closely with the Campaign Manager and the Campaign Treasurer in determining priorities and allocations.

4. Materials

Depending on the area and the kind of campaign being run, the materials will differ. Standard form, however, would dictate that a basic piece of literature be developed and that this be ready in time for distribution by the precinct workers in their canvass. Where precincts are not covered, a blitz may have to suffice. A second or even a third basic piece is desirable if the funds are available and there has been saturation with the first. Campaign buttons, bumper stickers, and posters, of course, are standard paraphernalia. With respect to bumper stickers, consideration should be given to a small sticker which can be used not only on bumpers, but on car windows, house windows, light poles, stop signs, etc. Reprints of any newspaper stories or editorials are particularly useful. Find the quickest and cheapest printing house in the area and be able to get something run off within 24 to 48 hours.

5. Procedures

These are procedures which may be helpful in seeing that everything is organized and running smoothly.

(a) Staff Meetings

In addition to the weekly key staff meetings, there should also be a weekly or bi-weekly large staff meeting. This should include everyone who has some important role in the campaign. It should be more of a reporting session than a decision-making session, but often in the discussion of activities to date issues will arise which can be discussed at this larger meeting. A final decision may be reserved for the small staff meeting. These larger meetings are also important for morale, and it is a good idea to hold important announcements for these large meetings.

(b) Candidate's Time

At some point in the campaign the areas which must be stressed will become clear, and a staff decision should be made as to how the candidate should spend his time, e.g., door-to-door, shopping centers, coffees, or a combination. Once a decision has been made, everyone on the staff should make sure that the candidate is not deviating from the priorities that have been established.

6. Election Day

There should be an overall Election Day Chairman who will be working closely with the Campaign Manager and the Political Action Chairman. Volunteers who will not be working in the precincts during the campaign, but who can work on election day, must be scheduled according to priorities. On election day they can pass out election day cards, run voters, fill in in precincts, and do telephone calling. Election day procedures will be an important part of the campaign and must be thought out in advance. Materials should be purchased, including the voter cards which on one side should indicate the candidate and his endorsements and on the other side what line on the ballot the candidate is slated.

Finally, mutual confidence between the staff and the candidate is most important. The candidate must have confidence in the staff's ability to run the campaign, as he cannot run it himself. Likewise, the staff must have confidence in the candidate and his ability to see the issues and the problems of the campaign. The candidate is not going to be able to select all of the campaign personnel, and this should be particularly the job of the Campaign Manager who will select the persons responsible for running various aspects of the campaign. Of course, the Campaign Manager should consult the candidate on these selections. But the candidate should and must select a few key persons upon whom he is going to have to place great reliance, and this must be done early in the campaign. From that time on the most important thing for the candidate is exposure and personal contact. This can't be done from his office or on the telephone working out campaign problems.

44. Administrative Leadership in Complex Service Organizations

Herman D. Stein*

There was a story in the newspapers not long ago[1] of the visit to the United States of a British expert in playground design who described school and other public playgrounds in the United States as "an administrator's heaven and a child's hell." The playgrounds, she said, had clearly been built primarily for the ease and economy of their maintenance, and to forestall insurance claims for accidents. They had not been built for the true needs of the children who were supposed to use them. Whether the criticism is fair or not for playgrounds, the vulnerability of complex service organizations to the ailment of turning administrative simplicity into a goal in its own right, whatever the results for consumers, is omnipresent.

Most of us in social work accept the fact that our activities in service agencies *are* to be primarily directed to service, whether in the form of care for hospital patients, treatment of children in child guidance clinics, or help to the economically disadvanaged in the public assistance agency. We are not always as mindful of the fact that as we evolve our administrative structure and patterns, some of this evolution can tend to be in the direction of making it easier for ourselves administratively, to the detriment of our presumed service function.

It has been repeatedly observed[2] that as certain key features of bureaucratization set in, such as an impersonal social climate, proliferation of rules, and status barriers between professionals and clients and between different levels of staff themselves, the total administrative system tends to work more to the advantage of the experts than to its clients. The very features of bureaucracy that can give it the capacity to produce services economically and efficiently, that maintain stability, that provide role security for employees and objective criteria in the treatment of the consumers of its services, can develop a system related primarily to the interests of its staff, particularly its experts, rather than to the interests of its clientele. (A caricature of this phenomenon is the ironic statement sometimes heard in schools, including schools of social work, that "We could run a wonderful school here if it weren't for the students.")

The movement in hospital care for the mentally ill from the custodial institution to the therapeutic milieu provides one of the most vivid illustrations both of the need for loosening up, in the interests of patients, the rigidities of structure and process that emerge with overbureaucratization, and the strains that can develop when the loosening up goes so far that the essential structural requisites of complex formal organization are weakened. Two analyses of processes of debureaucratization in organizations designed for in-patient treatment provide valuable insights. One[3] deals with a specific treatment center for alcoholics; the other,[4] with hospital treatment of the mentally ill generally. In both, the debureaucratization consisted of reducing status differ-

Reprinted from Herman D. Stein, "Administrative Leadership in Complex Service Organizations." *Social Work Practice*, (1965), pp. 42–53. Published by Columbia University Press, New York.

* Affiliation unavailable.

[1] *New York Times*, May 16, 1965, p. 46.

[2] See Earl Rubington, "Organizational Strains and Key Roles," *Administrative Science Quarterly*, IX (1965), 350–69; Herman D. Stein, "Administrative Implications of Bureaucratic Theory," *Social Work*, VI, No. 3 (1961), 14–21.

[3] Rubington, *op. cit.*

[4] William R. Rosengren, "Communication, Organization and Conduct in the 'Therapeutic Milieu,'" *Administrative Science Quarterly*, IX (1964), 70–90.

ences between staff and clients, a flattening of the hierarchical authority system, opening up new channels of communication between staff and patients, providing smaller, decentralized units for care of patients, and promoting an informal, friendly social climate.

These are all moves reflecting the premise that the traditional custodial state hospital type of institution, one prototype of Goffman's[5] profiles of "total institutions," essentially was designed for administrators and staff, not for patients. Both analysts agree that in the situations studied, debureaucratization resulted in a much greater orientation to patient care. The very words changed in the mental hospital from the formal, staff-oriented "going on ward rounds" to the informal, client-directed "chatting with patients."

The strains for patients ease, but in their place come strains for staff. The more personalized relationship of staff to patients, the greater personalization of relationships among staff themselves, the more amorphous systems of communications and control, and reduction in defined roles of authority, apparently create new pressures. As Rosengren put it, the small, nonbureaucratized, total-treatment type of hospital becomes "total" for staff instead of for patients.

While these analyses are directed primarily to consequences in changes of patient care systems, they indirectly reinforce certain other principles. One is that the way to prevent bureaucratic strains in the interests of better service to clients or patients is not to make the organization totally nonbureaucratic and loose in structure and process, but to modify existing conditions and introduce new structure and process focused on patient interests. It is true that nonbureaucratic systems can provide greater latitude for innovation, individualization, professional self-fulfillment, and ready adaptability to change than can more complex formal organizations. They also, however, provide conditions that can make for instability, role confusion, and interpersonal tensions which, if they become severe, can militate

against the interests of clientele. The importance of demonstrating positive affect in interpersonal relationships in the nonbureaucratic structure is such that it may be said that "when it is good, it is very, very good, but when it is bad, it is horrid." There can be a price paid for drastic debureaucratization.

The directions for solutions in complex organizations, one may suggest, are not in substituting role diffusion for role specificity, nor in minimizing hierarchical levels of responsibility, but rather in developing a balance between those elements of structure and process conducive to rational management of the organization, and those elements essential for optimum client service. Decentralization is a case in point. Decentralization may be necessary to attain service objectives in certain kinds of institutions. The smaller size and greater face-to-face relationships permit more individualization and the kinds of treatment relationship that may be necessary. But rational administrative objectives, if the decentralized unit *is* a unit of a larger organization, would require consistency of policy and procedures regarding such elements as staff roles and communication channels. One can avoid overloading the decentralized unit with ritualistic procedures unnecessary to its proper functioning, but one does not remove role requirements, or hierarchial lines of responsibility. It is not easy to have one's bureaucratic cake and eat it too, but the attempt should be constantly made.

The prime principle is to make sure that the service organization exists for service, not for ease of administration. The one is a goal; the other, a means. Minimizing the strains inherent in bureaucratic structure requires approaches consistent with such rational formal organization—that is, consistent with bureaucracy—and central to these approaches is defining responsibility within the structure for determining that all administrative means are related to the ends of service and do not become ends in themselves.

Where research and training are included

[5] Erving Goffman, "On the Characteristics of Total Institutions," in *Asylums* (New York: Doubleday & Co., 1961), pp. 1–125.

with service systems, it is not easy to keep these three objectives in balance, under the best of circumstances. There are, however, certain preconditions for maximizing the reciprocal reinforcement of these systems, and reducing conflict and waste of effort. One is for the organization to have its priorities clear for each system. What is it *primarily* in business for, what secondly, and what comes third? The budgetary and nonbudgetary investments should reflect these priorities. The systems should be differentiated, which is not to say that individuals may not be located in more than one system; but the service, teaching, and research systems as such should be differentiated, not only in such respects as personnel, space, and equipment allocation, but also in terms of administrative responsibilities and, most important, in terms of objectives and expectations.

Organizations geared primarily for service can develop far greater leadership potential with the addition of teaching and research functions, if such preconditions exist, and if there is a pattern of communication and influence among the three systems so that they are individually reinforced in function and effectiveness, and together create an increasingly potent and effective service operation.

The relationship between the needs of the individual and the needs of the organization has come into increasing prominence as a concern in the development of organizational policy as well as in organizational analysis. Thus, Argyris stresses that "the basic impact of formal organization is to make the employees feel dependent, submissive, and passive, and to require them to utilize only a few of their less important abilities,"[6] and calls for a better "mix" of individual needs and organizational demands. Marshall Dimock similarly stresses the incompatibility of bureaucratic structure and personality requirements.[7]

I do not feel that the conflict is inevitable, if thought is given to utilizing the capacities of people in organizations to the fullest, and individualizing them. Fundamental as the problem is for the mental health of our working population, it is equally significant for the welfare of the organization itself. The waste by organizations, in industry, government, and the voluntary sector, incurred by the failure to utilize the human potential, is prodigious.

The essence of the dilemma is that since bureaucratic organizations tend to enhance role specificity, definite and circumscribed job demands, and provide rewards for conformity alone, they may not tap the special abilities, imagination, or views of employees that can well serve the interests of the organizations themselves as well as enhance the sense of individual worth and self-respect of employees.

Several approaches can be taken to reduce this potential conflict. One concerns the planned involvement of personnel in organizational decision-making. Some years ago the term "democratic administration" was popular to connote the proper recognition of all individuals in administration. In its simplistic form, however, this concept is antithetical to hierarchical organization, placing an excessive egalitarian demand on policy involvement without appropriate responsibility and competence.

The concept of "relevant participation"[8] meets this problem by identifying which kinds of policy and operational problems require the participation of which kinds of personnel. In its fullest expression, this concept would invite the participation of every member of an organization, no matter how huge the organization is, in contributing to issues in which their special experience and competence are relevant. A management specialist put it as follows:

The participative principle . . . gives recognition to people as human beings—individually and in their group relations—and it brings

[6] Chris Argyris, *Personality and Organization* (New York: Harper & Brothers, 1957), p. 75, and *Interpersonal Competence and Organizational Effectiveness* (Homewood, Ill.: Dorsey Press, Inc., 1962), pp. 38–54.

[7] Marshall F. Dimock, "Bureaucracy Self-examined," in Robert K. Menton *et al.*, eds., *Reader in Bureaucracy* (Glencoe, Ill.: Free Press, 1952), pp. 397–406.

[8] Stein, *op. cit.*

dignity and meaning to their jobs. It can tap the creative imagination and inventive ingenuity for which we Americans are justly famous. It can banish fear and dependence by giving the members of the organization an opportunity to exert control over their own destinies and to acquire genuine understanding of what are usually felt to be mysterious and arbitrary management actions. It offers, *par excellence*, a way to encourage the development of genuine personal responsibility among all members of the organization, and with it, the freedom which is always lacking when control is centralized.[9]

It should be emphasized that the concept of "relevant participation" includes the participation of clientele, or consumers of service, precisely where and to the extent such participation is relevant. Client participation has been largely neglected, or has been occasionally utilized to give the illusion of involvement without the content of the participation taken seriously.

A second approach involves continuous assessment of special strengths as well as weaknesses of personnel, relevant to the organization's needs, irrespective of the specific occupational roles assigned.

Some years ago, when I was serving as consultant to a middle-sized manufacturing organization, we introduced a policy of having every evaluation made by a superior of a subordinate include consideration of anything the employee was particularly good at or interested in, as well as what he seemed to do poorly. Supervisors were evaluated not only on the same basis, but on the basis of whether they did, indeed, present an appropriate assessment of positives and negatives in their subordinates. There is more to this approach than meets the eye. It took over a year to be understood and to take hold through all levels of the organization from the chief executive down. Permit me to give one illustration of how it worked, at its best:

One twenty-four-year-old employee had been hired as a supply clerk in the central office, where a variety of goods was received that were utilized by designers in fashioning and testing eventual designs for mass production. The clerk's supervisor recommended his dismissal on the basis that his handwriting on shipping orders was often illegible, he was occasionally careless in filling out the form, and he was sometimes away from his desk, just "floating around."

The supervisor was asked by *his* superior whether there was anything the clerk was good at, or interested in, and just why and where he was "floating around." This exploration, which was becoming routine in the organization, led to the information that the clerk spent most of his time, when he was not engaged in receiving and checking supplies, with the designers. When with the designers he asked a variety of technical questions, and inquiry with the designers, in turn, elicited their respect for his quick intelligence and capacity to see the relationship between a handmade design and the sequence and cost of steps in manufacturing.

In this industry, few talents are more precious than the capacity to visualize production processes on the basis of a design. The clerk was reassigned as an assistant in the design section, and served as liaison with the factory. He became more technically qualified, developed his natural conceptual talent, and rapidly moved to important responsibilities. He became a valuable asset to the company, and rose to an executive level within a few years. His handwriting, of course, remained poor.

This was a success story. Others were less dramatic, and some were not successes. Nevertheless, it was possible, in an organization of a thousand people, to individualize. Through a recognition of individual assets and liabilities, made by supervisors throughout the chain of command, the principle was maintained of utilizing and building on the strengths of people, building jobs around these strengths wherever possible, and not insisting that employees only correct their weaknesses, particu-

[9] Douglas McGregor, "Changing Patterns in Human Relations," Society for the Advancement of Management, Cleveland, 1950 (mimeographed); excerpt reprinted in Robert C. Sampson, *The Staff Role in Management: Its Creative Uses* (New York: Harper & Brothers, 1955), p. 85.

larly where these could not be altogether overcome. Both the organization and the individual benefited in ways both expected and unexpected.

The illustration is not from social work, but the concept is hardly less applicable.

A third approach involves flexibility of assignments and testing of capacities, such as the deliberate rotation of tasks within the organization. Such an approach can prevent monotony where the tasks are routine, increase flexibility in the utilization of personnel, and provide a broader perspective on their jobs by individuals seeing another aspect of the organization's effort, from the perspective of changed responsibility. Of course, this should not be overdone to the point where there is discontinuity, group instability, or personal hardship.

Whether it is these or other approaches that are utilized, the essential concept is that there should be a deliberate attempt to maximize individual capacity and ideas. An innovative, forward-looking organization does not develop imaginative ideas at the top only, but in its administrative process, particularly through supervisory channels, helps make it possible for relevant ideas, perceptions, and information to flow freely through all channels of communication, up, down, and sideways. Again, it should be borne in mind that the kinds of approaches referred to, for effective employee utilization in bureaucratic organizations, are themselves bureaucratic in character —they are stated policies, to be pursued throughout the organization, and not vague sentiments to be applied here and there on an individual, use-your-own-judgment basis.

Herbert A. Simon has recently summarized[10] the developments in decision-making theory, research, and practice. He stresses the growth of quantitative decision-making tools in business, the growth of computer methods in decision-making, and the fact that laboratory experimentation in decision-making, following the computation schemes initiated by Bales and Bavelas, has become a thriving enterprise. From this growing body of tested assumptions will come further insights capable of translation into practical terms in our large service agencies. Indeed, some of these directions in the theory of rational choice are finding their way into use now.

Both in the newer decision-making theory and in the older, traditional view of administrative planning, however, the emphasis has typically been on intraorganizational decision-making and planning, as if the organization were a closed system. Of course, it is not, and least so with respect to organizational plans and decisions that are designed to shape its future. There is an external environment to every organization, with which it interacts. These interactions may be conceptualized into major systems for any one organization, affecting: (1) support and maintenance of the organization; (2) administrative policies; (3) structure; (4) operating function.

Leadership within and by an organization requires the capacity of the organization to shape its own destiny to a significant degree, if not entirely. In turn, this necessitates a full understanding of the systems of interaction in which the organization is involved. The components in each of these systems may overlap, but their force will be different. A political special-interest grouping may have considerable influence in the systems of financial support and policies, but have relatively little influence in systems that affect administrative structure or operating function. Agencies that make and receive referrals may have considerable influence in operating function, but little in economic support.

In the case of large, national agencies with decentralized units, the same concepts apply, whether one is referring to the total agency or treating each of its components as an organization in its own right. In the latter case the central headquarters and the other components of the national agency become part of the organization's significant external environment.

No organization operates in limbo, and the

[10] Herbert A. Simon, "Administrative Decision-making," *Public Administration Review*, XXV (1965), 31–37.

more an organization has become large, complex, and bureaucratized, the more does it have interdependent relationships, not only with other organizations but with nonorganizational forces. One of the reasons a large, bureaucratic organization tends to be stable and long-lived is that by the time it gets to be large and complex, it is part of a network of other organizations and major groupings which have investments in the organization's survival. The consequence, however, as in all interdependent relationships, is some degree of loss of autonomy.

One of the most common illusions of personnel in large agencies, even in professional social work agencies, is that the executive, or the board, is really free to make decisions of any kind that affect the interests of the organization. The fact is that there is always a range of constraints on decision-making and agency planning, stemming from the extraorganizational environment as well as from internal organizational considerations.

If the agency does not have a strong planning arm, projecting its aims for the short- and long-range future, it can become simply the passive resultant of external forces shaping the nature of its financial support, its policies, structure, and operative function. Just as there is the illusion of the staff below of the powers of the executive above, so there is often the illusion on the part of those in administrative authority that they are making genuine decisions, guiding the destiny of their organization, when they are merely doing what has become unavoidable in the wake of prior decisions made by other organizations or groups.

For an organization to have optimum control over its own destiny, and particularly where it is concerned with organizational innovation, anticipation of change, and adaptation to change, clear location of responsibility is needed to provide accurate assessments both of the internal organizational system and the extraorganizational systems.[11]

Should an organization such as the Veterans Administration move into different and closer relationships of service for out-patient clients with community agencies, for example, new systems of interactions would develop. Not all such relationships may evolve the way decision-makers in the Veterans Administration or the other agencies concerned may have intended them to be to begin with. Different interests and organizational requirements will have to be negotiated. The direction of such relationships should ideally have been thought through by the initiating agency in advance, along with consequences that could be anticipated and ways of reacting to them. This is the kind of planning responsibility that, however much it should draw on relevant participation of staff at all levels for ideas, reactions, and information, in the last analysis has to be centralized.

William Foote Whyte[12] observes that in the early history of human relations research in industry, with the fascination of the discovery of the "informal organization" and the fact that people were people even when they were working, little attention was given to formal organization and to the impact of the environmental forces that shape systems of behavior within organizations. To this note may be added that the observation that those of us professionally reared in the sciences and professions of human behavior find it congenial to attribute good and bad quality of administration to the personality and intellectual attributes of those in administrative authority.

[11] In this general connection, one should note the increasing attention being paid to interorganizational analysis in the administrative literature. We are still at the level of guiding concepts, however, not of tested research. See Sol Levine and Paul E. White, "Exchange as a Conceptual Framework for the Study of Interorganizational Relationships," *Administrative Science Quarterly*, V (1961), 583–601; Eugene Litwak and Lydia F. Hylton, "Interorganizational Analysis: a Hypothesis on Coordinating Agencies," *Administrative Science Quarterly*, VI (1962), 395–420.

[12] William Foote Whyte, *Man and Organization* (New York: Richard D. Irwin, Inc., 1959).

The news of human factors in organization was not exactly a revelation to us, therefore, although we could not perhaps have systematized our premises. We are, however, less inclined, by training, to concede to structure and process the force which they have, unless we make a special effort to do so.

In complex service organizations, the necessity to be highly cognizant of the repercussions of such structure and process is great indeed. For leadership to be developed within and by such organizations, a perspective is needed which takes into account the personality and group relationship dimensions, on the one hand, and the structural, systemic factors, on the other.

Stress has been placed here on three dimensions of analysis, with deliberate compensatory emphasis on the structural attributes. All of this discussion is related, however, to one basic objective—how our service organizations, in an increasingly complex environment, can do the best job for those they serve and bring out the best in those they employ.

SECTION

PLANNING FOR SOCIAL CHANGE

A.   ESTABLISHING OBJECTIVES

45.   The Hierarchy of Objectives

Charles H. Granger*

Why is a conceptual framework of objectives important in decision making?

What are the most important characteristics of good objectives?

How should objectives be chosen and established?

How can objectives be used profitably by management?

We are all faintly amused by the aptness of the old quotation, "Having lost sight of our objective, we redoubled our efforts." Everyone admits to having been caught in this situation at one time or another. But is it possible that most large organizations are in this predicament a good part of the time?

Evidence indicates that this may indeed be true. The main trouble seems to be a lack of clear understanding of questions such as the above. In discussing these questions I shall use the term *objective* in the relatively broad, nonspecific sense which it commonly has in everyday business language. In this sense an objective is "an aim or end of action"; it is also used as an aim or guide to intermediate decisions and actions. For example, a sales manager might say, "Our objective is to have our salesmen make as many calls as possible"—but he might be very conscious of the fact that a more fundamental objective is to develop high sales volume.

Reprinted from Charles H. Granger, "The Hierarchy of Objectives," *Harvard Business Review,*
    Vol. 42 (May–June 1964), pp. 63–74. © 1964 by the President and Fellows of Harvard College;
    all rights reserved.
° Affiliation unavailable.

Role and Importance

Everyone will admit that objectives are important. But is it really necessary to analyze them? Can they be taken for granted? On a larger scale we have evidence like this:

In a $50-billion-a-year organization, Secretary Robert S. McNamara and professional military people are in serious dispute because of a new way of looking at objectives.

The Roman Catholic Church has called some 2,500 of its highest officials from their pressing daily business to help rethink that organization's objectives.

The American Telephone and Telegraph Company was perhaps saved from government ownership in the 1930's by having thought out its objectives.

Sears, Roebuck and Co. has expanded from being a catalog merchant into a fabulous range of services as a result of a continuing redefinition of its objectives.

Theodore Levitt proposes that some leading industries may be in danger of going the way of the railroads because of inappropriate objectives.[1]

Less dramatic examples, because they are so much more numerous, probably have even greater importance. Think of the waste from the countless decisions made every day which could have been made better if the desired objectives had been more apparent to the decision-maker. In many organizations, if you ask a number of managers to write down their principal objectives, you may get strongly conflicting answers. The results? Research and development money is sometimes spent on projects which are later abandoned because they are inconsistent with broader corporate objectives. Committees spend countless hours thrashing over problems unrelated to the overall purposes of their organizations. Vacillation on acquisition policies is often attributable to inadequately defined objectives. And so on.

Organization planning, marketing planning, R & D planning, financial planning, to say nothing of total corporate planning, properly begin with the question, "What are our overall objectives?" Moreover, proponents of Douglas McGregor's "Theory Y" stress the importance of integrating the objectives of the individual with the objectives of the organization. But how can this be done if the organization's objectives are not really known? It seems that there is a major opportunity for increased effectiveness if our objectives can be made clearer by even a small amount.

Subtle Conflicts

Clarity is not the only question. *Balance* is important, too. Thus:

Many a company is in trouble because customer-service objectives are not properly related to profit objectives.

One utility will tell you (privately) that it ran into a serious earnings problem because its managers overstressed customer-service objectives to the slighting of profit objectives, a condition that took some years to correct.

Some companies recruit too many top-rate college graduates to be consistent with the rather modest objectives of the over-all organization. When after a few years it becomes apparent to these high-potential individuals that the organization does not really intend to pursue very challenging objectives, the result is wasteful high turnover.

Lyndall F. Urwick sums up such problems in a refreshing and often overlooked way:

Unless we have a purpose there is no reason why individuals should try to cooperate together at all or why anyone should try to organize them. This, however, is very easily forgotten. Once an organization is set up, a human group is in being, all the individual and personal motives which have induced persons to join the group, which keep them in the game and playing the game, assume great importance in their minds. Most of us suspect that the main purpose of the undertaking which employs us is to provide us personally with a job. . . . People derive social satisfactions from working together. And they build up, often unconsciously, very elaborate codes of behavior, and loyalties, and affections and antipathies, which may have little or nothing to do with the formal organization of the undertaking, the official relationships which their superiors recognize. . . . Every organization and every part of every organization must be an expression of

[1] "Marketing Myopia," HBR, July–August 1960, p. 45.

the purpose of the undertaking concerned or it is meaningless and therefore redundant.[2]

Is a Theory Necessary?

Management literature is teeming with titles such as "How to Set Objectives," "How We Set Our Objectives," and even with articles on the appropriateness of one objective as opposed to another—profits versus survival, volume versus customer service, and the like. Less attention has been given to the structure of objectives, pseudo-objectives, and constraints. Some sort of conceptual framework embracing the whole range of objectives seems necessary if we are ultimately going to use objectives more effectively. In some orderly way we must relate the "grand design" type of objective with the much more limited objectives lower down in the organization. And we have to examine how one type of objective can be derived from another. Again quoting Urwick:

> We cannot do without theory. It will always defeat practice in the end for a quite simple reason. Practice is static. It does and does well what it knows. It has, however, no principle for dealing with what it doesn't know. . . . Practice is not well adapted for rapid adjustment to a changing environment. Theory is light-footed. It can adapt itself to changed circumstances, think out fresh combinations and possibilities, peer into the future.[3]

Tests of Validity

How can the validity of an objective be tested? What should an objective accomplish? Here are some important criteria to be applied to an objective:

1. *Is it, generally speaking, a guide to action?* Does it facilitate decision making by helping management select the most desirable alternative courses of action?

2. *Is it explicit enough to suggest certain types of action?* In this sense, "to make profits" does not represent a particularly meaningful guide to action, but "to carry on a profitable business in electrical goods" does.

3. *Is it suggestive of tools to measure and control effectiveness?* "To be a leader in the insurance business" and "to be an innovator in child-care services" are suggestive of measuring tools in a helpful way; but statements of desires merely to participate in the insurance field or child-care field are not.

4. *Is it ambitious enough to be challenging?* The action called for should in most cases be something in addition to resting on one's oars. Unless the enterprise sets objectives which involve reaching, there is a hint that the end of the road may be at hand. It might be perfectly appropriate for some enterprises which have accomplished their objectives to quietly disband. However, for an undertaking to have continuity, it needs the vitality of challenging objectives.

5. *Does it suggest cognizance of external and internal constraints?* Most enterprises operate within a framework of external constraints (e.g., legal and competitive restrictions) and internal constraints (e.g., limitations in financial resources). For instance, if objectives are to be a guide to action, it appears that American Motors, because of its particular set of constraints, should have somewhat different objectives than General Motors.

6. *Can it be related to both the broader and the more specific objectives at higher and lower levels in the organization?* For example, are the division's objectives relatable to the corporate objectives, and in turn do they also relate to the objectives of the research department in that division?

If such tests as these are valid indications of the meaningfulness of objectives, then several further propositions become apparent. First, objectives, as aims or ends of action, are intimately involved in a complex of other important considerations or guides to action, such as definitions of the business, internal and external constraints, measurements of success, budgets, and long-range plans. Secondly, there is a ranking or hierarchy of objectives, proceeding in concept from the very broad to

[2] *Notes on the Theory of Organization* (New York, American Management Association, 1952), pp. 18–19.

[3] *Ibid.*, p. 10.

Figure 45.1.   Hierarchy of Objectives in Terms of Level of Need or Activity.

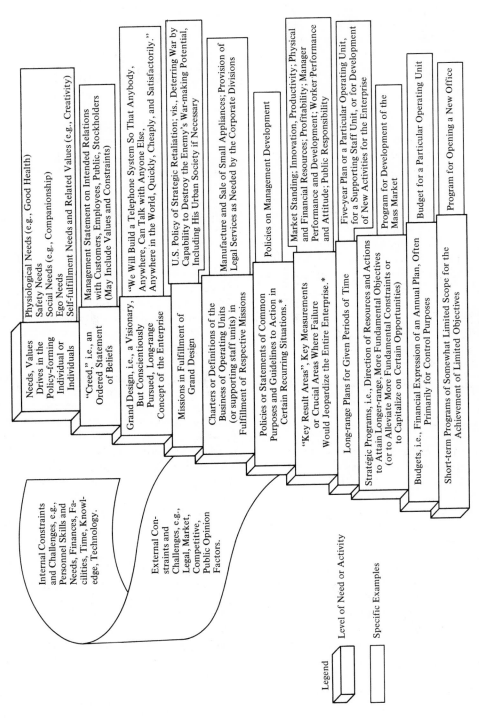

Level of Need or Activity	Specific Examples
Needs, Values Drives in the Policy-forming Individual or Individuals	Physiological Needs (e.g., Good Health) Safety Needs Social Needs (e.g., Companionship) Ego Needs Self-fulfillment Needs and Related Values (e.g., Creativity)
"Creed," i.e., an Ordered Statement of Beliefs	Management Statement on Intended Relations with Customers, Employees, Public, Stockholders (May Include Values and Constraints)
Grand Design, i.e., a Visionary, But Conscientiously Pursued, Long-range Concept of the Enterprise	"We Will Build a Telephone System So That Anybody, Anywhere, Can Talk with Anyone Else, Anywhere in the World, Quickly, Cheaply, and Satisfactorily." U.S. Policy of Strategic Retaliation; vis., Deterring War by Capability to Destroy the Enemy's War-making Potential, Including His Urban Society if Necessary
Missions in Fulfillment of Grand Design	Manufacture and Sale of Small Appliances; Provision of Legal Services as Needed by the Corporate Divisions
Charters or Definitions of the Business of Operating Units (or supporting staff units) in Fulfillment of Respective Missions	Policies on Management Development
Policies or Statements of Common Purposes and Guidelines to Action in Certain Recurring Situations.*	Market Standing; Innovation, Productivity; Physical and Financial Resources; Profitability; Manager Performance and Development; Worker Performance and Attitude; Public Responsibility
"Key Result Areas", Key Measurements or Crucial Areas Where Failure Would Jeopardize the Entire Enterprise.*	Five-year Plan or a Particular Operating Unit, for a Supporting Staff Unit, or for Development of New Activities for the Enterprise
Long-range Plans for Given Periods of Time	Program for Development of the Mass Market
Strategic Programs, i.e., Direction of Resources and Actions to Attain Longer-range, More Fundamental Objectives (or to Alleviate More Fundamental Constraints or to Capitalize on Certain Opportunities)	Budget for a Particular Operating Unit
Budgets, i.e., Financial Expression of an Annual Plan, Often Primarily for Control Purposes	Program for Opening a New Office
Short-term Programs of Somewhat Limited Scope for the Achievement of Limited Objectives	

Internal Constraints and Challenges, e.g., Personnel Skills and Needs, Finances, Facilities, Time, Knowledge, Technology.

External Constraints and Challenges, e.g., Legal, Market, Competitive, Public Opinion Factors.

Legend

Level of Need or Activity

Specific Examples

*May occur at various organization levels.

the specific. Logically, the specific or more limited objectives should not be in conflict with the broad objectives. The second proposition in particular deserves further consideration.

Complete Framework

Much of the confusion which apparently exists about objectives can be alleviated by viewing objectives as a whole framework or complex of "aims or ends of action" and other guiding considerations. In this framework it is not helpful to think there is one overriding consideration, such as "profit," since we must also concede in the next breath that another objective is to "stay within the law." Profit may indeed be the factor to be maximized *in a particular case*, but it cannot be viewed as the sole objective. The concept of a hierarchy is illustrated in Figure 45.1.

Leading Characteristics

Granted the existence of this hierarchy, what is significant about it? What are its important characteristics and implications?

1. *The full range of objectives and guiding considerations is distressingly broad.* No one individual in a large organization could consciously make each decision in light of the total framework of objectives and guiding considerations. Hence, in practice many managers are guided in their decision making by what they themselves view as their own key objectives. This creates quite a problem. Recognition that there is such a problem does not mean that we should shrug our shoulders and ignore the whole subject. It suggests the need for a greater effort to organize and compartmentalize objectives into classes that are useful for each decision-maker in the organization.

2. *The rate of change with time decreases as we go up the scale.* Short-term programs and budgetary objectives may change in less than a year. But long-range plans may exist for several years without major revision, and the "grand design" of an enterprise may last throughout the leadership tenure of its chief executive.

3. *For most enterprises even the broad ob-*

jectives are subject to change in 20 years. The argument is sometimes advanced that the very broad objectives of an enterprise are tied in with human values which are essentially immutable or subject to change only in terms of millennia. A good case could be made for this in terms of some organizations such as the Church. In other fields, however, the "grand design" even of many large organizations has changed within a leadership generation. The airframe industry, Sears, Roebuck and Co., the Tuberculosis Association, and the U.S. Air Force are examples. In smaller organizations it is not unusual to see the needs and values of the leader change—for instance, from financial security to esteem or creative contribution to society—with a discernible change in objectives of the organization. Management consulting firms are keenly aware of the fact that, when a new chief executive comes into power, there is considerable potential for consulting services in helping the organization to rethink and redetail its objectives in line with the new values, creeds, and grand design of the incoming chief executive.

4. *Debates on how specific an objective should be are not especially helpful.* One sometimes encounters the argument that an objective "to earn a fair return for the stockholder" is a pious but meaningless mouthing; 20% pretax return on invested capital (or some such specific target) is advanced as a more appropriate alternative. The scale of objectives in Figure 45.1 suggests that both of these are necessary (along with others). On the one hand, if we intend to use objectives as a tool for measuring progress, we are certainly much better able to do so if we have a certain percentage figure like 20% appropriate to the year. On the other hand, 20% (or any other fixed per cent) may be ridiculous for a recession year when nobody in the industry can even approach the figure; it then becomes meaningless. Thus, to derive a valid measurement we must fall back on our broader objective of fair return to the stockholders.

5. *Debates on the merit of one type of objective as opposed to another are only meaningful in light of the particular circumstances.* For example:

One frequently hears arguments as to whether profitability, public service, or perhaps customer service or survival of the enterprise should be the ascendant objective. Arguments of this kind can quickly degenerate into a chicken-or-egg type of controversy.

Figure 45.1 suggests that the relative merit of a particular type of objective can only be evaluated in light of the particular circumstances being faced—the internal and external constraints, the values of the individuals who control the destiny of the enterprise, and so on. It might be entirely appropriate for a large undertaking, threatened with nationalization or government-directed splitting up which it deems against its best interests, to emphasize public service objectives more than profit objectives. H. Igor Ansoff points out that the near-term profits of many rather large firms are relatively secure anyway.[4]

6. *The obviousness of the need for stated objectives appears to decrease as we approach the upper end of the hierarchy.* Consider the experience of the Defense Department:

> Until the McNamara era, much Congressional debate centered around budgetary allocations in the traditional service categories (Army, Navy, Air Force, and so on), each broken down by personnel, operation and maintenance, procurement, R & D, and military construction. These traditional budget categories represent objectives of a sort and are still being used. But Secretary McNamara and his colleagues revolutionized the concept of objectives in government by taking this line of reasoning: It is not a fundamental objective simply to have so many men in the Marine Corps or to build such and such an Army base. The real objective is maximum national security. Within what might be called a grand design of national security, a number of "missions" were established, including strategic retaliation, continental air and missile defense, and general-purpose warfare capability. Now, for example, the Fleet Ballistic Missile System can be evaluated in terms of its contribution and cost/effectiveness relationships to the mission of the strategic retaliatory forces.

Although the advantages of evaluating the Defense Department program in light of its objectives seem obvious after the fact, and although such a system was long advocated by the Hoover Commission and other bodies, the Defense Department is the only major government department to have done this on a large scale.

This apparent casual approach to objectives is not a phenomenon of government organizations. How many talented leaders from business and other endeavors sit on boards of various churches, educational institutions, charities, and the like, struggling with budgets in cases where the less obvious but more fundamental objectives have not been thought out? It is not an easy job. For example, one large church organization, after much preparatory staff work, required six early-morning-to-late-evening sessions of two days each (including the time of a large group of nationally prominent individuals) to redefine its objectives (the equivalent of grand design, missions, and charters in Figure 45.1) and related matters.

While formalized statements of grand design and missions apparently exist only in a small percentage of business organizations, formalized charters and policy statements are relatively common; long-range plans are becoming much more so, and almost every business has a budget.

7. *The need for broad objectives of the grand design and mission type is not restricted to the very large company.* For example:

> One moderate-size New England company is founded on a variety of specialized technologies in mechanical sealing devices. The head of this company views its *grand design* as "stopping the leaks around the world." Bizarre as this first sounds, it is a perfectly workable concept for a grand design for a highly successful undertaking—which it already is on a moderate scale. From it are spawned *missions* relating to certain markets and applications. There is a network of *charters* relating to various operating divisions both in this country

---

[4] *Business Objectives* (Pittsburgh, Carnegie Institute of Technology, unpublished paper, 1962).

and abroad. This organization seems to have a unified sense of purpose and destiny which it would otherwise lack. The whole management team seems to know where it is going, and the individual managers are excited and enthusiastic about their common purpose.

The unfortunate cases are the organizations which lack such an over-all sense of purpose and are not doing anything to correct it; or perhaps their grand design is substantially accomplished or no longer appropriate to the current environment. These are the business enterprises in declining or static industries, the philanthropies for which the needs are now only marginal, and so on. The objectives of these organizations seem to be "to keep on doing what we have been doing," but the people in them are troubled and perplexed because they see that their results are not particularly satisfactory by a number of standards. A business enterprise in this situation may view its over-all objective as "10% net profit on stockholder investment"—but it does not have a ghost of a chance of achieving it on a consistent basis. People in the organization become engrossed in their personal objectives of holding onto their jobs. If only the board of directors in such cases would insist on having a written statement of the grand design!

8. *Objectives should not only guide action but also stimulate it.* Frederick R. Kappel, chairman of the board at AT&T, observes:

> Unless the business sets demanding and exciting goals, it runs a heavy risk of losing vitality. This is an area where people in top management positions have heavy responsibilities. . . . If these goals fail to stimulate, there is something missing at the top. . . . In the sense that I am using the word, a goal is something presently out of reach; it is something to strive for, to move toward, or to become. It is an aim or purpose so stated that it excites the imagination and gives people something they want to work for, something they don't yet know how to do, something they can be proud of when they achieve it.[5]

Steps in Derivation

When we choose and establish directives, we cannot logically proceed in one step from a grand design to a budget, although companies undoubtedly often attempt this. We are in effect confronted with a situation of goals within goals within goals.

We must start with the given statement of the broader objective (see Figure 45.2). Next comes the process of setting up yardsticks, criteria, "key result areas," or some other form to measure the success of the stated objective. Obviously the more tangible such yardsticks are, the more usable they will be. But if they are going to be specific and realistic (for example, so many dollars in world trade), then it is necessary to consider both the internal resources of the enterprise ("How much physically can we export?") and the environmental conditions ("What share of which world markets can we obtain?"). Hence both an analysis of internal resources and an environmental analysis are called for in setting up realistic and adequately challenging criteria.

The next step requires that management define the range of possible activities which it might use to accomplish the larger objective. For example, the question for a furniture company might be: What balance of emphasis is best between office and home furnishings? The alternatives must be weighed in terms of their effectiveness in accomplishing the objective, on the one hand, and of the consumption of available resources, on the other hand.

As the preferred new subobjectives and subprograms begin to emerge, one can expect numerous conflicts and inconsistencies. In the case of the exporter, for example, protection of domestic sales may not always be consistent with expansion of foreign trade. Hence some sort of reiteration or recycling is called for to minimize the inconsistencies before the final subobjectives can be decided on.

So much for the general process. What are the problems of making it work? What requirements must be observed?

---

[5] *Vitality in a Business Enterprise* (New York, McGraw-Hill Book Company, Inc., 1960.)

Figure 45.2.   Process of Deriving Specific Objectives from Broader Objectives.

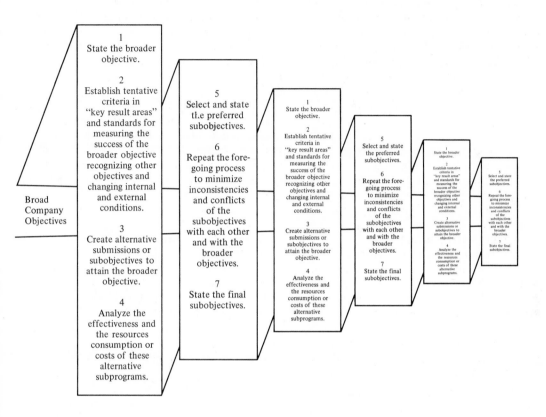

Role of Creativity

Establishing even a subobjective within the framework of a broader objective is a creative act. It involves the conceptual creation of a number of possible subobjectives, testing them against the realities of (1) consistency with internal resources, (2) consistency with environmental conditions, and (3) effectiveness/cost relaitonships in accomplishing the broader objective. Here we see the familiar concepts of creativity: exposure (to the broader objectives, internal and environmental constraints, and challenges), gestation, idea emergence, testing against reality, recycling.

Borrowing from the studies of creativity, we can see that the individual who is creative on the practical level, *provided he has had appropriate exposure to the company situation,* can be very helpful in establishing objectives.

On the other hand, we have to beware of situations in which objectives are set without adequate *exposure* to environmental conditions not all would-be staff planners are conscious of this); likewise we must beware of situations where objectives are set without adequate *analysis* of both internal and environmental conditions (not all line managers are conscious of this).

The creation of a workable grand-design type of objective thus emerges as an especially creative act. There are no broader objectives to be guided by. The creator of the grand design has as tools only his needs, values, and drives, and the company's environmental and internal constraints and challenges.

Motives and Appeals

In setting meaningful objectives, much help can come from creative people—those with high idea-emergence, good at censoring their own ideas against reality, persistent at recycling their ideas for improvement, having adequate exposure to internal and external factors, and possessing adequate drives. Moreover, Douglas McGregor's "Theory Y" approach to management suggests that the higher-order personal drives (such as those based on ego needs and self-fulfillment needs) of these people should be coupled with the objectives of the undertaking for the most effective accomplishment of the mission. This may be especially true in the higher echelons of a large organization. To oversimplify the thought, pay raises and threats of discharge may work with blue-collar workers, but the higher motives may be more effective with the financially more secure managers.

Frederick R. Kappel cites the visionary goal of AT&T—"the big dream stated without equivocation, the dream of good, cheap, fast, worldwide telephone service for everyone." He observes that such a goal is "not a wishful fancy. It is not a speculation. It is a perfectly clear statement that you are going to do something." He then points out three conditions which in his opinion favor setting the right goal at the right time:

1. An instinctive feeling for quality throughout the organization.
2. Freedom to make some mistakes.
3. A recognition of the pressure of external factors.

He further points out that "part of the talent or genius of the goal-setter is the ability to distinguish between the possible and the impossible—but to be willing to get very close to the latter."[6]

Eric Hoffer takes a stronger view, at least in regard to the goals of large undertakings or "mass movements." He suggests that the goals for a vital undertaking should be impossible of achievement (for example, achieving God's Kingdom on earth), and points out that the best climate for setting these visionary goals is among the groups who are down but not quite out.[7] For example, the Black Muslim movement apparently cannot reach the most abject Negroes, who seem to have little interest in anything beyond a day-to-day existence, nor does it apparently appeal much to Negroes who are currently "successful" in American society.

Does this apply to companies in the business world? Are there any indications that the downtrodden business organization, like pre-Hitler Germany, is most susceptible to a brilliant renaissance, and all that it lacks is a deliverer, a leader who electrifies its members with visionary goals? One could say that George Romney did something of this sort with American Motors. But such examples seem rare. Whey aren't there more of them? There is certainly no lack of prospective candidates! Perhaps there is a lack of George Romneys, or perhaps they find themselves called into other fields. But any organization, in however severe straits, can probably boast a few young hotbloods who can establish visionary objectives, but who lack the other qualities of drive and leadership to carry them out.

Need for Renewal

There is probably merit in reestablishing objectives every so often just for the sake of reestablishing them. One might think that if objectives were once set, and if internal and external conditions did not change too much, the objectives would be valid for a good long time. But the same old objectives repeated over and over produce no impact, no challenge.

Perhaps this is a failing of many religious organizations. Canonical types of objectives, produced many years ago by undoubtedly brilliant churchmen, simply do not inspire the organization member of today unless he himself has gone through the process of thinking out the objectives and reached similar conclusions.

Some "Theory Y" practitioners have gone to

---

[6] *Vitality in a Business Enterprise* (New York, McGraw-Hill Book Company, Inc., 1960), pp. 40, 56–58.
[7] *The True Believer* (New York, Harper & Brothers, 1951).

an extreme; they favor changing the objectives at a given level and position every time a new individual comes into the job. In other words, the new appointee, along with his own superior and others with the need to know, sits down and writes a new job description including new objectives for the work. "Theory Y" practitioners claim to have encouraging results with this approach.

Locating Responsibility

Should the superior set the objectives for the individual groups that are subordinate to him? It is apparent that he must at least approve them if he is to discharge his own duties. Beyond this, he probably has broader exposure to internal and environmental conditions than his subordinates. But he may or may not be the creative type who can visualize a whole range of subobjectives, one for each of his various groups, the best of which are chosen after analyzing effectiveness and costs. Some of his subordinates may be better at this creation of alternatives than he is. Certainly they should have had greater exposure in depth (if not in breadth) to internal and environmental constraints, challenges, and opportunities. Accordingly, it would seem that to combine the best of these talents, the objectives for the subgroups should be worked out jointly by the leader of the subgroup and his superior.

How much help can staff give the line in this process? Certainly staff can conduct the internal analyses of resources and the environmental analyses of external conditions, always using the line for appropriate inputs in these analyses. Most line managers are accustomed to using their staffs in a similar capacity. Staff men can also propose and analyze a number of alternative subobjectives, and can sometimes make particularly brilliant contributions in proposing possible alternatives which might otherwise have been overlooked. This can be a major contribution of creative staff workers. Consultants, who are a form of temporary staff, do this frequently.

But the old principle holds true: the people with the ultimate responsibility have to make the ultimate decisions. Furthermore, they have to be brought into the decision-making process at sufficiently fundamental levels so they can have a full understanding of the context in which the final decision choices are being made. No responsible line man could be expected to accept ready-made objectives proposed by a staff person or researcher unless he, the line man, had personally weighed and debated the relation to internal and external conditions and the range of possible alternatives.

Working-Upwards Approach

Now suppose, as is often the case, that a company has not in recent years formally developed a written statement of objectives, and that (as should more often be the case) a member of the board of directors convinces his fellow members that they should have a written statement of objectives. *Where* should the job begin?

One might reason that logic calls for starting at the top of the hierarchy displayed in Figure 45.1, starting with needs, values, and drives of the key individuals, and proceeding on down to creeds, grand designs, missions, and the like. For instance, Secretary Mc-Namara and his associates, in the recent installation of program budgeting in the Defense Department, appear to have gone from a grand design to missions, to program elements (analogous to charters).

However, in our consulting practice with both business and nonbusiness enterprises, my associates and I have found that as a practical measure the top of the scale is *not* the best place to start. We have found that profit objectives in terms of growth in earnings per common share are typically the most readily graspable starting point in business. They lead very understandably to environmental analysis (first in terms of profit results of comparable companies in industry, then to analysis of market requirements, technical trends, and competitive trends in the business environment) and analysis of internal resources.

People seem to have little difficulty in understanding the need and value of analyzing profit goals. Once this understanding has been obtained, it is not too painful to work up and down the hierarchy to fill it out; going *up* to other key result areas, charters, policies, missions, and even grand designs, and *down* long-range plans, strategic programs, budgets, and short-term programs. Suddenly there is a new clarity to the growth directions for the enterprise, the type of management development needed, and the like.

As already indicated, there is a continual process of reiteration. In this reiteration one objective is adjusted in light of another, and in light of new developments in resources and in environmental conditions. Hence it does not really matter that some managers do not readily see the need for defining the higher-level objectives, and that attempts to attack the broader questions of creeds and grand designs make them squirm. When they start with some very tangible aspect such as profits, then work into the other types of objectives as the need to do so becomes demonstrated, they can achieve as good an understanding as anyone can.

Practical Uses

What are the practical uses of objectives? What tangible results come from giving thought and time to the clarification of objectives? An analysis was recently made by the American Management Association of companies that had developed formal company creeds.[8] In all too many cases this analysis indicated that the benefits were along the lines of "having opened up our thinking" or "a beneficial exercise for those who took part," but the practical results were rather hard to measure. This is unfortunate, for there are practical benefits indeed to be obtained.

Better Planning

Probably the most significant use of objectives is in planning. Not many organizations can conscientiously answer the question, "What should we be doing, and how much?" But carefully worked out objectives can narrow the target area, if not altogether pinpoint it. For example:

The new programing system in the Department of Defense is based on the nine types of missions or broad objectives of that organization (e.g., strategic retaliation). For the first time on an overall, formalized basis, the cost of each Defense Department activity has been related to its effectiveness in fulfilling these missions. Alternate systems are presented for top-level considerataion in terms of cost and effectiveness analyses. The practical results include "thumbs down" for the RS-70, the Skybolt missile, and the Nike-Zeus antimissile system.

A major charity had been moving along on its natural momentum, doing an effective job in many ways, but not quite sure of just how large it should grow in the future, what new programs it should be undertaking, and what financial and other plans it should be making to ensure its future effectiveness. It has now developed a number of specific subobjectives in light of a definition of its broader objectives. Practical results are taking place in the way of organizational changes, staff recruitment and development, long-range financing plans, and development of new service programs—all based on a general agreement at the policy-making level of what the organization should look like in 1973.

The management of Sears, Roebuck, in speaking of its objectives, says: "The Company sees itself not so much as a catalog merchant or retailer, but as an organized system for efficient and economical distribution, dedicated to serving the public with a broad range of *goods* and *services* [italics added], and to meeting any change in demand." Probably 90 out of 100 large organizations have some stated objectives of this general type. But the difference is that Sears not only states its objectives; it lives by them. In the last ten years the number of mail-order plants has remained steady at 11, and the number of retail stores has increased slightly from 694 to 748 (although many have been modernized and expanded). But the company is now upgrading itself into a style house, as its recent advertising demonstrates. Here are examples of the variety of Sears Roebuck activities—

It runs a fleet of 5,000 service and installation trucks.

Through Allstate it is the largest stock

[8] Stewart Thompson, *Management Creeds and Philosophies*, Research Study No. 32 (New York, 1958).

company insurer of automobiles in the country, and fourth largest in the fire and casualty field.

It is in the life insurance business.

The Allstate Motor Club and Allstate Tours operate in the travel field.

It has entered the savings and loan business.

Homart Development Company recently opened its first shopping center, with a half-dozen others in various stages of planning.

Sears, Roebuck Acceptance Corp. has about $500 million of installment contracts.

In short, Sears, Roebuck has not occupied itself with perpetuating its existing form. It has arrived at broad objectives and derived a wide and changing range of supporting missions, or subobjectives. All this has led to handsome results, with earnings per share increasing in eight out of the last ten years.

A major drug company has staked out a grand design in the field of human health and well-being. In accordance with this broad objective, the research group has identified some 40 potential and actual program areas—e.g., cardiovascular ailments, fertility control, and cancer. In annual program planning reviews within the research group, scientists and managers go through a series of steps for deriving specific program objectives. They have environmental analysis material on hand—for instance, "If we develop a tranquilizer with such and such characteristics, it will capture X per cent of the market." They also have organized information inputs on the long-range needs in the health field (e.g., dermatology). At the same time they have conducted resources analyses so they know their abilities in certain specialized lines of research.

Choice of Alternatives

The hierarchy of objectives is also valuable in analyzing and choosing alternative courses of action. (This benefit is obviously related to the planning values just discussed, but it deserves separate emphasis.) To use the experience of the drug company again:

To stimulate thinking about alternative courses of action, management encourages scientists to attend association meetings; invites a considerable number of outside technical consultants—usually university people—to meet

with executives; and stresses the study of data from marketing research and the detail sales force.

Three important questions stand out in the criteria for screening the wide range of alternate subprograms—

1. How important is the proposed program? Importance is usually measured in terms of profit potential.

2. Can we do it? This question is usually related to the availability of skills and knowledge to overcome the technical problems involved.

3. What will it cost? Here the company has what amounts to a cost/effectiveness analysis of alternative programs, much along the lines described earlier in the case of the Department of Defense.

Of course, the process of exploring alternatives ends with a good deal of reiteration or recycling to cut out nonessentials here, fill out a program there, and to make the total research effort consistent with a practical budget. In practice, as might be expected, the general program areas do not change radically from year to year. Once a specialized staff and momentum are built up in a given area, a program may last for some time, uncovering new opportunities as time goes along. However, specific detailed projects are changed, and the overall emphasis in the program also changes as a result of management's approach.

Management Development

One of the most interesting uses of a framework of objectives is in management development. Most executives are keenly aware that the difference between their organization and other organizations in its field is its personnel. They recognize that development of its own people is a key issue in the health and success of any enterprise.

Recent theory as well as actual practice in management development has stressed the concept of identifying the objectives of the individual with the objectives of the enterprise. It also stresses making these objectives as specific as possible, and measuring their exact success in meeting them. For example, contrast the effectiveness you might expect in an organization where a supervisor says, "I'm responsible for quality—whatever that means," with effectiveness in an organization where he says:

> I'm responsible for rejects which come off the rotary machines and I've agreed on the standard with the Chief Inspector. Each day I get an analysis of rejects so I can put things right. At present the General Manager and I agree on 2.7 per cent rejects as acceptable, but we have a plan to get this down to 2.2 per cent by next November.[9]

There is ample evidence that this concept of management by objectives and by specific results actually works, and works well. However, the question not always thoroughly explored is, "Are we doing the right thing to begin with?" Possibly the quality control supervisor in the foregoing example is inspecting beautiful products for which there is little demand, for a market where quality is not a key result area, in a situation where the products could better be purchased from the outside, or where the entire company would be better off merged into a larger organization.

If a framework of objectives has been worked out for the whole organization, there is not so much danger of misdirected effort. Top management can be assured that all employees are working toward common purposes which are mutually consistent, appropriately challenging, and realistic in light of both internal and external opportunities and threats. It can be assured that people's potentials are being developed along lines which will increase the effectiveness of the company.

Organizational Efficiency

It should not be inferred from the foregoing discussion that the formal organization structure should be rearranged to conform closely with objectives in various parts of the company. Rearrangement may or may not be appropriate, depending on the circumstances. For example:

In the Department of Defense we find that both the B-52 and the Polaris submarines are program elements in the Strategic Retaliatory Forces. Nevertheless, organizationally they fit into conventional Air Force and Navy formats. Support elements of an organization (for instance, the payroll department) are frequently organized separately as one district entity supporting a number of departments or divisions which may have widely differing objectives. This is done for the sake of efficiency.

Non-Linear Systems, Inc., a specialized California instruments manufacturer with 350 employees, has developed a curious form of organization which ties in closely with the theory of objectives.[10] The company has a president and seven vice presidents, each responsible for an area such as innovation, market standing, profitability, or productivity. It shows evidence of having excellent results with this system.

However, we must not forget that in business true efficiency—unlike the dictionary definition—is not merely producing a certain result at the lowest cost; worthwhile efficiency is producing a *desired* result at the lowest cost. It is a ratio in which cost is the denominator, and the degree of effectiveness in producing some desired result is the numerator. Thus we can hardly consider efficiency without considering a range of objectives. The cost/effectiveness studies in the Department of Defense and "value analysis" studies at General Electric[11] illustrate the application of such thinking to logical cost reduction and efficiency improvement.

Conclusion

It is curious that so many discussions of management begin with exhortations to clarify objectives, and then, as if the nature of objectives were well known, proceed to explore some other aspect of the matter at hand. In reality we know very little about the nature of

[9] John W. Humble, "Programmitis and Crown Princes," *The Manager*, December 1963, p. 47.

[10] See, for example, Arthur H. Kuriloff, "An Experiment in Management, Putting Theory Y to the Test," *Personnel*, November–December 1963, p. 12.

[11] See, for example, Hugh McCullough, "New Concepts in Defense Planning, Programming and Budgeting," *The Federal Accountant*, September 1962, p. 70; also, L. D. Miles, "Purchasing Must Analyze Values," *Purchasing*, January 4, 1960, p. 65.

objectives. And it is abundantly clear that we cannot quickly set up some objectives for an enterprise and then proceed on the assumption that they will be meaningful guides to action.

Taking stock of the little knowledge we do possess, we find that we know a few bare essentials. For instance, there are certain minimum tests which an objective, or a set of objectives, should pass. Thus, objectives—

need not begin with the broad grand design of the enterprise, but all objectives in the hierarchy should be consistent with it;

should make the people in the enterprise reach a bit;

should be realistic in terms of (a) the internal resources of the enterprise, and (b) the external opportunities, threats, and constraints;

should take into account the creative conception of a range of alternatives and the relative effectiveness and cost of each;

should be known to each person so that he understands the goals of his own work and how they relate to the broader objectives of the total enterprise;

should be periodically reconsidered and redefined, not only to take account of changing conditions, but for the salutary effect of rethinking the aims of organizational activities.

Objectives, properly developed and applied, can tell us in what paths, new and old, our total undertakings should be moving. They can guide both the day-to-day activities and the personal development of individuals in an organization. If we in management can clarify the objectives of our undertakings by even a small amount, we can greatly increase the effectiveness and efficiency of our businesses.

46. "Shortcuts" to Social Change?

Amitai Etzioni*

In 1965, when New York City was hit by a "crime wave" (which later turned out to be, in part, a consequence of improved record-keeping), the city increased the number of lights in crime-infested streets. Two of my fellow sociologists described the new anti-crime measure as a "gimmick": it was cheap, could be introduced quickly, was likely to produce momentary results, but would actually achieve nothing. "Treating a symptom just shifts the expression of the malaise elsewhere," one sociologist reminded the other, reciting a favorite dictum of the field. Criminals were unlikely to be rehabilitated by the additional light; they would simply move to other streets. Or, when policemen are put on the subways, there is a rise in hold-ups in the buses. So goes the argument.

The same position is reiterated whenever a shortcut solution, usually technological in nature, is offered to similar problems which are believed to have deep-seated sociological and psychological roots. Because of a shortage of teachers, television education and teaching machines have been introduced into the schools. But most educators call this a "gimmicky" solution, for machines are "superficial" trainers and not "deep" educators. Or, in the instances of individuals who suffer from alcohol or drug addiction, blocking drugs (which kill the craving) and antagonistic drugs (which spoil the satisfaction) are now used. (Among the best known are, respectively, methadone and antabuse.) But, it is said, the source of the addiction lies deep in the personalities of those afflicted and in the social conditions that encourage such addiction. If a person drinks to overcome his guilt or to escape temporarily the misery of his poverty, what good is antabuse to him? It neither reduces his guilt nor his poverty; the only effect it has is to make him physically ill if he con-

Reprinted from Amitai Etzioni, " 'Shortcuts' to Social Change?" *The Public Interest*, No. 12 (Summer 1968), pp. 40–51. © 1968 by National Affairs, Inc.
° Chairman, Department of Sociology, Columbia University.

sumes liquor. Dr. Howard A. Rusk, who writes an influential medical column in *The New York Times*, stated recently:

> One of the most dangerous errors in medicine is to treat symptoms and not get at the underlying pathology of the disease itself. Aspirin and ice packs may lower the fever but at the same time allow the underlying infection to destroy the vital organs of the body. So it is with social sickness.

Until a few years ago, I shared these views. But I was confronted with the following situation: The resources needed to transform the "basic conditions" in contemporary America are unavailable and unlikely to be available in the near future. So far as dollars and cents are concerned, Mayor John V. Lindsay testified before Congress that he needed $100 billion to rebuild New York's slums; at the present rate, it would take forty years before such an amount would be available to eliminate *all* American slums. And that is housing alone! With regard to all needs, a study by the National Planning Association calculated that if the United States sought, by 1985, to realize the modest goals specified by the Eisenhower Commission on National Goals, it would (assuming even a 4 per cent growth rate in GNP) be at least $150 billion a year short.

But even if the economic resources were available, and the political will to use them for social improvement were present, we would still face other severe shortages, principally professional manpower. In the United States in 1966 there were an estimated four to five million alcoholics, 556,000 patients in mental hospitals, and 501,000 out-patients in mental health clinics. To serve them there were about 1,100 psychoanalysts and 7,000 certified psychotherapists. If each therapist could treat fifty patients intensively, a staggering figure by present standards, this would still leave most alcoholic and mental patients without effective treatment. Today most of those in mental hospitals are not treated at all: only 2 per cent of the hospital staffs in 1964 were

psychiatrists, only 10 per cent were professionals of *any* sort; most of the staff are "attendants," more than half of whom have not completed high school and only 8 per cent of whom have had any relevant training.

Thus, we must face the fact that either some shortcuts will have to be found or, in all likelihood, most social problems confronting us will not be treated in the foreseeable future. Forced to reconsider the problem, I decided to re-examine the utility of "shortcuts." For example, do criminals really move to other streets when those they frequent are more brightly illuminated? Or do some of them "shift" to lesser crimes than hold-ups? Or stay home? Do shortcuts deflect our attention from "real issues" and eventually boomerang? In my re-examination,[1] I found some facts which surprised at least me.

Decisions Without Facts

Take, first, the question of crime. It turned out that the sociologist who asserted that, when more guards were put on the subways, criminals shifted to buses, was merely making luncheon conversation; he simply "assumed" this on the a priori proposition that the criminal had to go somewhere. He had neither statistics nor any other kind of information to back up his proposition. I found that the same lack of relevant information held for *all* the situations I examined. One can show this even in such a "heavily researched" area as alcohol addiction.

Alcoholism is very difficult to treat. Most psychoanalysts refuse to treat alcoholics. The rate of remission is notoriously high. Tranquilizers are reported to be effective, but when I asked doctors why they are not used more widely, they suggested that these drugs provided no "basic" treatment and that patients became addicted to tranquilizers instead of alcohol. Searching for the source of this belief, I was directed to a publication of the United States Public Health Service entitled *Alcohol and Alcoholism*, a very competent summary of the knowledge of the field which

---

[1] The study is based on work conducted with the help of the Russell Sage Foundation. For additional discussion, see Amitai Etzioni, *The Active Society* (New York: The Free Press, 1968).

is heavily laced with references to numerous studies. Here I found the following two statements:

[Tranquilizers] are highly effective, but some alcoholics eventually become addicted to the very tranquilizers which helped them break away from their dependency on alcohol.

For most patients . . . [tranquilizers] can produce lasting benefit only as part of a program of psychotherapy.

I wrote to the Public Health Service. Their reply was that

the bases for both of these statements are "social information" rather than substantive research. It is the clinical experience of many physicians (and some therapists) that some alcoholics have a tendency to become dependent on (whatever that means) other substances in addition to alcohol. There is, however, considerable disagreement on the extent to which this is a problem.

Thus, the Public Health Service really does not know if tranquilizers are only a "symptomatic treatment" which results in the shift of the problem from one area to another; it does not know what proportion of alcoholics can be "deeply" helped by these drugs, or even if those who remain addicted to tranquilizers, instead of alcohol, may not be better off than before.

The Case of Drugs

The same confusion exists about drugs. Until 1925, the regulation of drug addiction in the United States was largely in the hands of the medical profession; then it was declared to be a police matter and turned over to the Federal Bureau of Narcotics. The change drove the addicts underground, pushed up the price of narcotics, and prompted the large number of "secondary crimes" (to finance the habit) which are associated with addiction in this country. Drug users were involved in 22.4 per cent of crimes involving property committed in New York City in 1963. While this is less than the more often-cited figures—that addicts are responsible for "half of all crimes"—it is a staggering cost paid for the partial suppression of addiction.

What body of evidence, medical or sociological, led to this rather far-reaching policy change? In fact, the chief reasons had little to do with evidence at all. The central fact was the ambition of the Federal Bureau of Narcotics (formerly the Narcotics Division of the Treasury Department) and of its former head, Harry J. Anslinger. He and his men conducted a systematic and effective campaign—in the courts, Congress, and the press—in favor of the punitive and against the medical approach to addiction because they viewed addicts as criminals.

Or, take the problem of distinctions among drugs. Over the years, many narcotic users, some medical authorities, and several leading social scientists have pointed out that the American drug laws do not distinguish between marijuana and heroin. Marijuana apparently has fewer effects than liquor; several experts argue that, unless one is in the proper company and mood, one does not even gain a "high" feeling from it. Alcoholism causes 11,000 deaths in the United States each year, not counting the thousands of fatalities inflicted by drunken drivers; marijuana per se causes none. Marijuana almost surely is less harmful than cigarettes. Some persons have smoked marijuana for years without visible effects. (Fifty-eight-year-old Mrs. Garnett Brennan, an elementary school principal in Nicasio, California, stated that she had smoked marijuana daily since 1949. Her suspension brought her to the attention of national television and press. She showed none of the symptoms widely expected in persons who have been on narcotics for long periods.) Yet the laws against the *possession* (not just the sale) of marijuana and heroin are equally severe—up to a forty-year jail sentence in some states.

Several authorities in the field have called for legalizing the consumption of marijuana. Those who object argue (1) that marijuana's effects are more severe, especially in accumulation, than has been acknowledged by those who favor its legalization, and (2) that the use of marijuana leads to the use of heroin, in a search for higher "highs," or through the mixing of heroin and marijuana by "pushers."

Lawmakers, police authorities, opinion-makers, campus deans, and citizens continually make decisions on these matters, yet our information is, at best, quite spotty. Despite police attention to drugs for more than forty years, and the extensive attention focused on drug addiction in recent years, Robert Reinhold reported in *The New York Times*, following about two weeks of experts' testimonies in a 1967 Boston trial of two youths accused of possessing marijuana that

> The most striking impression to emerge from the Boston testimony is that there is a paucity of scientific evidence regarding the drug. Witness after witness offered opinion, based on personal observation and anecdotal evidence rather than on scientific experimentation.

On October 17, 1967, James L. Goddard, Commissioner of the United States Food and Drug Administration, stated: "Whether or not marijuana is a more dangerous drug than alcohol is debatable—I don't happen to think it is." He added: "We don't know what its long-term effects are." A few days later, citing no more evidence than Dr. Goddard, Sir Harry Greenfield, chairman of the United Nations Permanent Central Narcotics Board, rejected the "tendentious suggestions" that marijuana was not "very dangerous." Nor has research settled the question whether continuous use of heroin is physiologically debilitating, or whether the symptoms usually associated with the use of heroin are actually the effects of withdrawal. And neither do we know whether a user's inability to function in a social setting is a cause or an effect of his use of heroin.

The main point I wish to make, though, concerns not marijuana but "shortcuts." And the common characteristics of this and other such situations is that the decision-makers *and* experts do not have the information needed to provide the answers. We could, as a shortcut, reduce much of the drug problem by legalizing marijuana. *That* we do know. The rest is conjecture.

Of Taxis and Fire Alarms

Many other questions I have examined are in the same condition. Neither the New York City Police Department nor any other city agency knew what had happened to the criminals who were driven off the lighted streets or off the subways. More recently, there was (or was believed to be) a crime wave in the form of hold-ups of taxi drivers. The police department initiated a new policy which permitted off-duty policemen to "moonlight" as taxi drivers. They were allowed to carry firearms and exercise their regular police prerogatives. This led to a rapid reduction in the number of taxi hold-ups. Good news—unless, as some claim, these muggers were now driven to robbing old ladies. We know that they are not back on the subways (which is relatively easy to establish). Whether they are operating elsewhere in New York City, in other cities, in other illegitimate pursuits, and whether these are less or more costly to society than mugging, or even if they have switched to *legitimate* undertakings, no one knows. The one thing we do know is that the original "symptom" has been reduced.

False fire alarms plague the cities; there were 37,414 such calls in New York City in 1966. In the summer of 1966 the New York City Fire Department installed a whistle device, which is activated when the glass is broken, to call attention to persons who pull the trigger of an alarm box. This, it was believed, would reduce the number of false alarms. "Gimmick," one may say; the exhibitionists who set the alarms now create some other mischief, such as causing real fires in order to see the fire trucks racing at their say-so. But nobody knows if these were actually exhibitionists and what they now do. Have they turned arsonists—or are they taking more tranquilizers? In this case it is not clear if the "symptom" was handled; in 1967 there were more false alarms than in 1966, but the device was not yet universally introduced and not publicized, so it could not deter.

Emotions and Politics

Although almost everybody wants "facts" on which to make decisions, the obvious point is that facts are frequently less powerful in shaping a decision than the long-held prejudices of a person. Many a decision-maker in effect says, "I don't care what the facts are; I am against 'it' because it is evil." In the case of drugs, the methadone programs are a revealing case in point. There is fairly good evidence that methadone kills the craving for heroin (persons on methadone have shot themselves with as much as sixteen units of heroin without attaining a "high"), removes the physiologically debilitating effects of heroin (if it has any) without introducing such effects of its own, and that this treatment enables those who take methadone to function socially more effectively than when they were on heroin.[2] Methadone thus is a "shortcut" *par excellence* because while it solves at least part of the problem, addiction, it does not change the personality which craves for an addicting drug (if there is such a personality), nor does it alter the social setting which encourages the craving.

Although each of the preceding statements in favor of shifting patients from heroin to methadone is not unquestionably substantiated, the critics of the program stress something else: the fact that, in the end, the person is still addicted. A person who regularly takes methadone does seem to become addicted to *it;* at least, it is believed that if a heroin addict stops taking methadone, the craving for heroin will reassert itself. Dr. Robert W. Baird, Director of the Haven Clinic for heroin addicts in New York City, has said that using methadone is "like giving the alcoholic in the Bowery bourbon instead of whiskey in an attempt to get him off his alcoholism." Professor Bernard Barber in his recent book, *Drugs and Society,* reports that in the past the United States Public Health Service "has not accepted any treatment of addicts that left the patient dependent on another drug." Methadone is still legally considered a narcotic and Section 151-392, Regulation No. 5 of the Bureau of Narcotics decrees that treatment by the use of such a drug is by definition not a treatment and hence technically illegal.

Now, if the argument that a person addicted to methadone is still not able to func-

tion in society, or not as well as a fully rehabilitated person (a position taken by some experts), we then have a question of fact: do they or don't they? But the antagonism to such a resolution will not even permit such a question to be seriously raised. The puritanical tradition is still sufficiently strong in American culture so that the use of any substitute drugs, even if less harmful, is regarded as an indulgence. When the American Medical Association in November announced the launching of a year-long scientific study of the effects of marijuana to test the question of its harm, AMA president Dr. Rouse Milford added— before the first day of research—"No good can come from its [marijuana's] use. It's an hallucinogenic drug." Many Americans seem to hold that persons who are attracted to a narcotic should view this as a weakness of the flesh which they should fight and overcome. Similarly, the Food and Drug Administration is not particularly friendly to efforts to find "safe" cigarettes, or blocking or antagonist medication for smokers. It keeps stressing that "Will Power Is the Only Smoking Remedy." Americans, at least when speaking collectively, seem to value a strong person, one able to function without narcotics (however stress-provoking his social environment) and one who seeks a life of achievement and enterprise, not "artistic" existence or nirvana.

Often the underlying prejudice sneaks through when the method of treatment is discussed. When one hears those who prefer the harsh "cold turkey" withdrawal over the painless transition from heroin to methadone, one gains the impression that the heroin users are viewed as sinners, who are to be penalized (or who have to undergo penance) before they are to be considered pure enough to be allowed to return to the flock.

Where there are emotions, politics is not far behind. Politicians have a high sensitivity to voters' sentiments and a low tolerance for risk. If the voters have (or seem to have) puritanical sentiments, a politician prefers "cold turkey" (despite the known fact that 85 to 95 per

---

[2] I benefited from a discussion with Dr. Vincent P. Dole and a visit with his patients on methadone at the Rockefeller University.

cent of all of those thus treated return to the use of heroin once released from supervision) over "soft belly" methadone (despite the fact that the remission rate is *much* lower).

And there is intra-professional politics as well. Were the facts cut and dry, few experts would support an ineffectual program or question one which "works." But as the merits of various approaches are almost always contested, battles rage over funds, prestige, and missions, as for example between the Synanon people (who believe in complete rehabilitation via a version of group therapy), the therapeutic professions (psychiatry, psychotherapy) which have little sympathy for "sheer" chemical-medical treatment, and the methadone doctors and their supporters. Similar battles are fought in other fields, for instance between those who would use teaching machines and television to help alleviate the shortage of teachers and those who consider these "gimmicks" and favor high raises in teachers' salaries and improvement in the teachers' working conditions and status to attract more men and women into the field.

"Fractionating" the Problem

Often a solution to a long-raging controversy over the more effective treatment of a social ill becomes possible once we realize that we have asked the wrong question. Similarly, when we ask whether "shortcuts" really work, we approach the problem in an unproductive way by lumping together too many specific questions.

First, the question must be answered separately from a societal and from a personal vantage point. Some shortcuts "work" for the society, in the limited sense at least that they reduce the societal cost of the problem (not only the dollar and cents cost, but also ancillary social effects), but not the personal costs. For instance, between 1955 and 1965 the number of patients in state mental hospitals declined from 558,922 to 475,761. This decline, however, was not the result of new, therapeutic-oriented, community mental-health centers, but mainly caused by introduction of massive use of tranquilizing drugs, "which do not 'cure' mental illness and often have been

called 'chemical straitjackets.'" Tranquilizers obviously do not change personalities or social conditions. Patients, to put it bluntly, are often so drugged that they doze on their couches at home rather than being locked up in a state mental hospital or wandering in the streets. How effective the shift to "pharmaceutical treatment" (as the prescription of sedatives is called) is depends on the perspective: society's costs are much reduced (the cost of maintaining a patient in a state mental hospital is about seven dollars a day; on drugs—an average of fifteen cents). Personal "costs" are reduced to some degree (most persons, it seems, are less abused at home than in state mental hospitals). But, obviously, heavily drugged people are not effective members of society or happy human beings. Still, a device or procedure which offers a reduction of costs on one dimension (societal *or* personal) without *increasing* the costs on others, despite the fact that it does not "solve" the problem, is truly useful—almost by definition.

It may be argued that by taking society "off the hook" we deflect its attention from the deeper causes of the malaise, in this case of mental illness. But this, in turn, may be countered by stating that because those causes lie so deep, and because their removal requires such basic transformations, basic remedial action is unlikely to be undertaken. *Often our society seems to be "choosing" not between symptomatic (superficial) treatment and "cause" (full) treatment, but between treatment of symptoms and no treatment at all.* Hence, in the examination of the values of many shortcuts, the ultimate question must be: is the society ready or able to provide full-scale treatment of the problem at hand? If no fundamental change is in sight, most people would favor having at least ameliorations and, hence, shortcuts. Moreover, the underlying assumption that amelioration deflects attention may be questioned: studies of radical social change show that it often is preceded by "piecemeal" reforms which, though not originally aimed at the roots of the problem, create a new setting, or spur the mobilization for further action.

Second, shortcuts seem to "work" fully—for

sub-populations and for some problems. It is wrong to ask: "Are teaching machines effective substitutes for teachers?" We should ask: "Are there any teaching needs which machines can effectively serve?" The answer then is quite clear: they seem to function quite well as routine teachers of mechanical skills (typing, driving) and of rudimentary mathematics and language skills. Similarly, machines may be quite effective for those motivated to learn and ineffective for those who need to be motivated. A recent study which compared 400 television lectures with 400 conventional ones at Pennslyvania State University showed the television instruction to be as effective on almost all dimensions studied. It freed teachers for discussion of the television lecture material and for personal tutoring. After all, books are not more personal than television sets.

To put it in more general terms, "gimmicks" may be effective for those in a problem-population whose needs are "shallow", and much less so for those whose problems are deep; and most problem-populations seem to have a significant sub-population whose ills or wants are "shallow." Critics of methadone have argued that it works only for those highly motivated addicts who volunteer to take it. But this is not to be construed as an indictment; while such a treatment may reduce the addiction problem "only" by a third, or a quarter, this constitutes a rather substantial reduction.

The same may be said about procedures for training the hard-core unemployed. These are said to "cream" the population, focusing on those relatively easy to train. Such an approach is damaging only to the extent that the other segments of the unemployed are neglected *because* of such a program and on the assumption that they too can be as readily helped. Otherwise, much can be said in favor of "creaming," if only that it makes most effective use of the resources available.

Debates, indeed fights, among the advocates of various birthcontrol devices—pharmaceutical means (pills), mechanical devices (especially the IUD), sterilization, and the rhythm method—are often couched in terms of one program against all others, especially when the advocates seek to influence the government of a developing nation on the best means of birth control. The Population Council, at least for a while, was "hot" on the IUD. Some drug manufacturers promote the pill. The Catholic church showed more than a passing interest in a rhythm clock (a device to help the woman tell her more from her less fertile periods). In such battles of the experts and "schools," the merits and demerits of each device are often explored without reference to the persons who will use them. Actually, though, merits and demerits change with the attributes of the "target" sub-population. The rhythm methods may be inadequate for most, but when a sub-population for religious reasons will not use other birth control devices, some reduction in birth may well be achieved here by the "gimmicky" rhythm clocks. Pills seems to work fine for "Westernized," routine-minding, middle class women who remember to use them with the necessary regularity. They are much less effective in a population that is less routine in its habits. The IUD may be best where persons who are highly ambivalent about birth control can rely on the loops while forgetting that they are using them.

It is in the nature of shortcuts to be much less expensive in terms of dollars and cents and trained manpower than "deeper" solutions. The HEW cost-benefit analyses reported in *The Public Interest*, No. 8 (Summer 1967) are a case in point. While PPBS is far from a "science of decision-making," it occasionally does provide new insights and raise fresh considerations. If we assume that the following statistics are *roughly* correct, even allowing for a margin of error of 30 to 50 per cent, we still see the technological devices are much less expensive—per life saved—than the "deeper," educational, approaches. The problem was the effectiveness of rival programs in the prevention of "motor vehicle injuries." When various programs were compared in terms of their cost-effectiveness, it was found that the use of technical devices was most economical: $87 per death averted by the use of seat belts and $100 per life saved by the use of restraining devices. The cost of motorcyclist helmets was high in comparison—$3,000 per man; but it was low when compared to the "fundamental" approach of driver education. Here, it is reported, $88,000 is required to avert one death. Of course we may ask for both technological devices *and* education; and the benefit of technological devices by themselves may be slowly exhausted. Still, this data would direct us then to search for more and improved mechanical devices (e.g., seat belts which hold the shoulders and not only the abdomen) rather than spending millions, let us say, on "educational" billboards ("Better Late Than Never"). I am willing to predict—a hazardous business for a sociologist—that the smoking problems will be much reduced by a substitute cigarette (not just a tarless but also a "cool" one, as the hot smoke seems to cause some medical problems) rather than by convincing millions to give up this imbedded symbol of sophistication and—for teenagers—protest.

The Power of Formulas

Not all shortcuts are technological. There is frequently a social problem which can be treated if social definitions are changed; and this can be achieved in part by new legislation. This may seem the most "gimmicky" of all solutions: call it a different name and the problem will go away. Actually, there is much power—both alienating and healing—in societal name calling, and such redefinitions are not at all easy to come by. After years of debate, study, and "politicking," homosexuality was "redefined" in Britain in 1967; it became less of a problem for society and for the homosexuals after Parliament enacted a law which defined intercourse between consenting adults of the same sex in privacy as legal and, in this sense, socially tolerable. The remaining stigma probably more than suffices to prevent "slippage," i.e., even broader tolerance for other kinds of homosexuality, e.g., those affecting minors.

The extent to which such social definitions of what is legitimate, permissible, or deviant can be more easily altered than personality and social structure is an open question; at best, as a rule, only part of a problem can be thus "treated." This approach is superficial or worse when it defines a social or personal

want so as to make it nonexistent (e.g., reducing unemployment by changing the statistical characterization). It is not a "gimmick" in that the problem was created by a social definition —by branding a conduct as undesirable or worse when actually it was one of those "crimes without victims."

Guns, for Instance

There is one area of social conduct where, for reasons which are unclear to me, the blinders fall off, and most social scientists as well as many educated citizens see relationships in their proper dimensions and are willing to accept "shortcuts" for what they are worth. This is the area of violent crime and gun control. Usually, progressive-minded people scoff at gimmicks and favor "basic cures." But it is the conservatives who use the anti-shortcut argument to object to gun control as a means of countering violent crimes. On August 10, 1966, on the tower of the University of Texas, Charles Whitman killed, with his Remington Rifle, thirteen people and wounded thirty-one. This provided some new impetus to the demand to curb the traffic in guns. About sixty bills were introduced in Congress following President Kennedy's assassination, but none has passed; it is still possible to order by mail for about $27 the same kind of weapon, telescopic lenses included, which Lee Harvey Oswald used. The National Rifle Association spokesmen typically argue that criminals would simply turn to other tools —knives, rods, or dynamite—if no guns were available.

But actually this is one of the areas where the value of shortcuts is both logically quite clear and empirically demonstrable. Logically, it is a matter of understanding probabilities. While motives and modes of crime vary, most murders are not carried out in cold blood but by highly agitated persons. Out of 9,250 so-called "willful" killings which took place in the United States in 1964, only 1,350 were committed in the course of committing some other crime such as robbery or a sex offense. The others, 80.1 per cent were committed among friends, neighbors, and in one's family, by "normally" law-abiding citizens, in the course of a quarrel or following one. Obviously, if deadly weapons were harder to come by, the chances of these quarrels being "cooled out," or a third party intervening, would have been much higher and most fatalities would have been averted.

Second, the damage caused is much affected by the tool used. While it is correct to assume that a knife may be used where there is no gun, the probability of *multiple* fatalities is much lower. And a policeman can learn to defend himself from most assaults without having to use a firearm. Most policemen who are killed on duty are killed by guns; all but

one of the fifty-three killed in the United States in 1965, according to official statistics. Hence if the population is disarmed, the fatalities resulting from arming the police can also be saved. Here, as in considering other devices, one must think in terms of multi-factor models and probabilities. No one device, such as a gun-control law, can *solve* the problem. But each additional device may well reduce the probability that a violent act will cause a fatality. This is a "shortcut" in the right direction—even if it doesn't lead you all the way home. Not because I don't want to go all the way at once; but because such trips are often not available.

B.   DEVELOPING PROGRAMS

47.   The Use of Social Research to Improve Social Practice[a]

Ronald Lippitt[*]

My observations in this paper are an attempt to summarize the brief but varied experiences with problems of use of science by the staff of our Center for Research on the Utilization of Scientific Knowledge at the University of Michigan. Our staff teams are involved in projects concerned with the use of scientific resources to help cope with such social problems as delinquency, illegitimate teenage pregnancy, the educational motivation of culturally deprived children, the lack of spread of creative teaching practices, leisure-time programs for central city girls, the

pathology of communication between parents and teenagers and the mental health and productivity problems of work groups in government and industry.

In each project an effort is being made to focus attention and inquiry on the process by which scientific knowledge and scientific personnel can be used to help develop and validate significant improvements in educational and social practice.

First, I would like to identify and illustrate six patterns of use of scientific resources which we see emerging from our work in the area of

Reprinted from Ronald Lippitt, "The Use of Social Research to Improve Social Practice," *American Journal of Orthopsychiatry*, Vol. 35, No. 4 (July 1965), pp. 663–669. Copyright © the American Orthopsychiatric Association, Inc. Reproduced by permission.

[a] Presented at the 1965 Annual Meeting of the American Orthopsychiatric Association, New York, New York.

[*] Program Director, Center for Research on the Utilization of Scientific Knowledge, Institute for Social Research, The University of Michigan, Ann Arbor, Michigan.

social practice. Then I would like to review some of the differences we believe we have discovered between the problem of research utilization in applying social research as contrasted to the use of the biological sciences (e.g. in agricultural practice, medicine or public health) or the use of the physical sciences (e.g. transportation, industrial production or weather prediction). Finally, I would like to focus what seem to emerge as the various roles or functions of the applied behavioral scientist or professional science utilization agent in facilitating the application and diffusion of the practical implications of scientific research and theory.

Summary of Models, Illustrations of Research Utilization Process

Models Which Import Change Resources from Outside the System

I want to distinguish between three patterns of research use which have the characteristic of bringing into the science consumer system (i.e. agency, school system, family) new knowledge and validated practice from outside and three other patterns which have the characteristic of developing the scientific knowledge within the system and then using it as a basis for improvement of practice. In each case I would like to identify briefly the pattern and to illustrate it by a recent or current project of our Research Utilization Center.

The first pattern is one in which the scientist-consultant in communication with a particular practitioner or practice group identifies and defines a problem of practice. This definition is used to guide a process of research knowledge retrieval in which relevant research and theory are brought together and used as a basis for deriving action implications and the design for an improvement of practice or the invention of new practice. Let me briefly describe two recent examples of this research retrieval and derivation procedure:

A recent one-day consultation conference focused on the problems of how the several million citizens of a metropolitan area could be involved in a process of goal setting and feedback in regard to the development of plans for the metropolitan region. A team of professional and political leaders from the metropolitan area spent half the day interviewing invited resource people. Some of these outside resource people were familiar with research and theory in this field, and others were leaders of projects in other metropolitan areas which had attempted to cope with this same problem. With a predeveloped schedule of probes the host team conducted a guided conversation with the visiting resource people. All this retrieved information was tape-recorded. During the second phase of the day the local leadership took active initiative in attempting to formulate implications of this inquiry for the development of a program for their own metropolitan situation and began to project the elements of a design for action that drew from the implications both of previous research and previous practice innovations. The next steps of developmental work also were clarified and agreed on.

A second example started from the definition by elementary school personnel of their problem of "the in-betweeners." These were defined as primarily older, elementary-school, acting-out boys who were too disruptive to be acceptable in the classroom or other educational facilities of the school, but too young and not seriously delinquent enough to be appropriately in the hands of the police and the court. A knowledge retrieval session of school people and scientists from child development, educational psychology, social psychology and sociology identified a variety of relevant research findings. The school people and scientists then focused on producing a series of statements about the possible implications of the findings for "things that should happen to the clients" in order for a significant process of resocialization and education to be achieved. These statements of implications from research findings were used as a springboard for a brain-storming session with the practitioners about possible elements of program design that might most effectively deal with the elements of the problem. An action design emerged which was quite different from anything which either the researchers or the practitioners had visualized originally as an appropriate design for re-education. This design was later tested for feasibility and side effects in two school buildings, evaluated as successful and subsequently diffused to other school buildings.

A second procedure for importing knowledge from outside the system is to conduct outside the system an experimental feasibility test of a design procedure to meet some social practice issue. Such a test is conducted by the applied scientist team under controlled conditions. If the test proves successful, the newly developed model for improved social practice is demonstrated and recommended for adoption. What is taken into the system from outside is a developed and validated model for adoption or adaptation by the client system. This, of course, is comparable to the development of new products in the experimental farm or in the research and development laboratory of the industry.

An example of this procedure in the work of our own staff is the development of the so-called "cross-age socialization design." From previous research several of our staff members had developed the hypothesis that one of the major potentials in most educational and socialization situations was unused. This was the potential influence of older peers on younger peers. It was decided to test out experimentally the feasibility of training 10-, 11-, and 12-year-olds to function as educational aids and socialization agents with 5-, 6-, and 7-year-olds. The experimental farms consisted of a camp and an elementary school where the team of scientists and social engineers had control over all phases of the experimental program. Results indicated that it was feasible to train the older peers to assume creative teaching functions, that there was very significant response on the part of the youngers and that the olders showed great personal growth in their own attitudes and achievement because of their experience of responsibility in collaboration with adults and their learning from the training seminars. It then was possible to present evidence of feasibility and validation from this experimental test to a school system which was concerned about the prob-

lems of achievement and motivation to learn in the young pupils. They adopted the model on a tryout basis and made several creative adaptations in the process of carrying out and evaluating the design.

The third pattern of importation of knowledge is a very exciting one to me. This is the process of identifying creative innovations which have been invented some place else and of developing procedures for getting appropriate documentation about these social inventions so that their relevance to local needs can be considered and the essential features of the practice can be adopted or adapted. It is our observation at the present time that one of the great tragedies in American education and social practice is that a large proportion of the creative inventions which are in line with good research and theory never become visible and never become appropriately transmitted from one setting and practitioner to another. What dissemination does take place is so slight that successful, high quality adoption usually is impossible.

An example of a model for coping with this problem is illustrated in a current project with a state teachers association. A questionnaire nomination procedure has been developed in which all teachers in a school system have an opportunity to fill out a teaching practice nomination sheet identifying whether they feel they have personally invented a teaching practice to cope with the particular type of educational problem (for example, stimulating more motivation to learn) or whether they know of any colleague who has invented a practice. These nomination sheets serve as the basis for work by a screening committee to review the conceptual and research relevance, the practical significance and the potential adoptability of each practice and to select a smaller number of practices for intensive documentation. For example, a nomination survey in four school systems identified about 300 practices which were reduced by the screening committee to 30 for intensive investigation and description. The documentary description emphasizes a concrete description of activity, an identification of necessary skills, a review of the traps and problems of successful use of the practice and ideas for possible improvement of the model from experience of the innovator. The current experiment is attempting to discover what kinds of practices can be communicated in this written form, what kinds require additional steps of observation and what types require more intensive training and consultation. The main point here is that this is a procedure for identifying, describing and importing new models into the system which have been developed by practitioners in other communities, agencies or organizations.

Procedures for Development of the Needed Knowledge Resources Within the System

Let me turn now to the three processes of use of scientific resources which emphasize the local development of the resource knowledge.

The first model is one where the organization or agency contracts with the scientist team to collect diagnostic data relevant to some problem, to analyze the data and then to feed the data about the local situation back to the agency or organization staff for their use. Two brief examples will illustrate this pattern:

Using trained citizen interviewing, the action research team conducted an intensive study in a city of a sample of delinquents and matched nondelinquents, both boys and girls, to assess some of the major factors related to development and maintenance of patterns of delinquent behavior in teenagers of the community. They also conducted an interview study of the key educational and socialization policy leaders of the community concerning their conceptions of delinquency and of delinquency prevention. These data were analyzed by the scientist team and were reported back to the community leaders in a series of community seminars to which the key community leaders were invited. Staff members were available during these seminar sessions to provide consultation on interpretation of the findings and to react to the generalizations and implications being formulated by the community leaders.

The second illustration is a study, in three school systems, of all of the high school girls who dropped out of school because of pre-marital pregnancy. The findings were summarized and fed back to school officials and other key community leaders for their possible use.

The second pattern is one in which the outside applied researchers supervise a self-study process within the organization, community or agency. The researchers train local staff members to collect the information and to participate in the processing of the data, the interpretation of the findings and the working-through process involved in spelling out the implication of the findings for the development of change in educational or social practice.

Our classroom teaching study illustrates this pattern of science utilization. Thirty teachers from seven school systems volunteered to work with us on a diagnostic self-study of their classroom educational climate and the possible implications for changes in their teaching practice. During the spring the action research team provided the teachers with questionnaires to inquire into their own attitudes and orientations. The teachers also were given rating and questionnaire tools to use in eliciting information from their classroom group concerning orientation toward learning, toward the teacher, toward each other and many other aspects of classroom dynamics. During the summer the teachers met regularly with the staff to help tabulate and analyze the data, to develop the concepts needed to work on interpretation and to think through the implications of the findings for possible changes in their own teaching role in the fall. Consultation was provided in this thinking through process and in clarifying the plans for the use of new teaching procedures.

The third model of internal mobilization is quite different from the other two. It focuses on the idea that the practitioner needs direct training in learning to be a consumer of science and of scientific resources in order to be an effective user of scientific knowledge. It is our observation that the desired collaboration between the consumer and the scientist often is impossible because the consumer or practitioner has received no basic training in how to use services of scientists or in how to use inquiry procedures in generating their own basic diagnostic knowledge for the development of their own practice. Let me mention briefly two examples of current work in this very undeveloped area.

One of our activities is focused on training teachers in the techniques of problem solving. We provide them with a tool kit of diagnostic tools and conceptual orientations to assist them in collecting appropriate information and in using it to solve their problems of classroom management. They are trained to be users of two products of science: information-getting methods and conceptual models.

In another project we have developed a laboratory course in behavioral science for elementary schoolchildren. Students have an opportunity to discover who the behavioral scientists are and how their resources can be used as well as to learn to carry through their own inquiry projects on various problems of human relations. It seems clear that part of the current negative orientation toward scientific resources in mental health, education and social welfare results from a serious lack of any concrete education about the nature and the utility of social research and the social scientists.

Some Special Characteristics

From our comparative study of the process of research utilization in agriculture, medicine, public health, industry, mental health and education we have come to the conclusion that there are some very significant differences between the problems and process of research utilization in the area of social research and social practice as compared to these other areas of applied biological and physical science. I would like to summarize briefly several of these differences as we see them:

First, most significant adoptions of new educational or social practice require significant changes in the values, attitudes and skills of the social practitioner. This requires a deeper personal involvement in adopting the new practice than is true in the adoption of new agricultural, industrial or medical practices. There will be more problems of resistance to change and of relearning.

Second, most significant changes in mental health or educational practice really are adaptations rather than adoptions of the innovations of others. What is being passed on is not a thing (e.g., a new seed, new implement, new drug or new machine), but is a new pattern of behavior to be used in a new social context. Therefore, there must be significant features of adaptation in each adoption. One implication of this is that the dissemination of the new practice must therefore include much more orientation of the adopter to the basic principles or conceptions involved in the practice in order to make creative adaptation possible.

A third important difference in our field of social practice is that the concept of "social invention" really has not been developed adequately. There are no adequate procedures for identification, documentary description and validation of new practices. This means that on the one hand there is often a large volume of poorly described nonvalidated practices tempting uncritical adoption efforts by professional colleagues. On the other hand, there is a great volume of creative practice which remains invisible and inaccessible to review and consideration. This means that the diffusion of significant new practice is a very retarded and chaotic situation.

A fourth characteristic of the social practice situation is that the practitioner gets very little feedback about the effectiveness of his adoption effort. The farmer can quickly see that his soil is more fertile or that the new seed produces more corn per acre. The doctor can check whether the new drug reduces infection more rapidly. The engineer can check objectively on the increased output of a new machine. But the teacher or mental health worker typically lacks the criteria and the tools to make this type of check. There is less sense of reward for the effort and very little data for quality control to provide guidance to the practitioner who is making an effort to use a new practice model.

A fifth important difference is that the ways in which mental health and educational practice are organized provide little stimulus for the practitioner to take risks in searching for and using new resources. The practitioner remains relatively invisible to colleagues and supervisors. There are neither competitive challenge nor good communication channels to stimulate sharing and improvement of practice. In addition, there tends to be a high sensitivity to the potentially negative reaction of various publics to changes of practice.

A sixth critical point of difference is that our social practice fields have not developed the networks, procedures and manpower resources necessary to link basic and applied research to operating practice. We lack the in-service training and support needed to stimulate and maintain the upgrading of social practice as social science resources grow and as social technology develops.

I think that all of these facts point to the special challenge we face in our field of making a conscious and concerted effort to focus energy on research utilization.

From the types of studies I have reported we have come to conceive the research utilization function of our staff as requiring that they be *linking agents* at various points in the flow of research use. It has become clear that we have to develop new skills of retrieving and organizing research-based knowledge in such a way that it links to the needs of the social practitioner or client population. Helping the practitioner to clarify his resource needs is, of course, another aspect of this linking responsibility.

But in most cases the appropriate knowledge resources are not enough, as we have seen. There is a necessary linkage function of helping the practitioner work through the implications of new knowledge for specific models of practice and specific operational skills.

As we have noted in several of our examples, another function of the research utilization agent is to serve as inquiry consultant or trainer to assist the client population in carrying through their own diagnostic research and working through the meaning of the findings for changes of practice.

Another necessary linkage function was identified in our look at the diffusion problem. We must find effective and appropriate ways of linking creative innovators to their colleagues to provide for the spread and successful.

Our own experience with graduate seminars and practicums has revealed to me that there is a significant number of students both in the behavioral science departments and in the professional schools who are eager to explore these new roles and acquire the new skills which differ considerably from those of research production being typically taught in the behavioral science departments and from the skills of operating practice being taught in the professional schools. Certainly the training of research utilization agents requires a grounding both in behavioral science discipline and in professional values and technology. This obviously puts a strain on the fairly segregated curriculum designs and training sequences which still exist in most of our graduate programs.

48.   Social Marketing: An Approach to Planned Social Change

Philip Kotler* • Gerald Zaltman**

The authors examine the conditions under which marketing concepts and techniques can be effectively applied to the promotion of social objectives, such as brotherhood, safer driving, and family planning. They believe that social causes could be advanced more successfully through the principles of marketing analysis, planning, and control.

First published in the *Journal of Marketing*, (July 1971), Vol. 35, No. 3, pp. 3–12.
* A. Montgomery Ward Professor of Marketing, Graduate School of Management, Northwestern University.
** Associate Professor of Behavioral Science, Department of Marketing, and Director of Research, Graduate School of Management, and Faculty Associate, Center for the Interdisciplinary Study of Science and Technology, Northwestern University.

In 1952 G. D. Wiebe raised the question "Why can't you sell brotherhood like you sell soap?"[1] This statement implies that sellers of commodities like soap are generally very effective while "sellers" of social causes are generally ineffective. Wiebe examined four social campaigns to determine what conditions or characteristics accounted for their relative success or lack of success. He found that the more the conditions of the social campaign resembled those of a product campaign, the more successful the social campaign. However, because many social campaigns are carried out under quite unmarketlike circumstances, Wiebe also noted clear limitations in the practice of social marketing.

A different view is implied in Joe McGinniss' best-selling book *The Selling of the President 1968*.[2] Its theme seems to be "You can sell a presidential candidate like you sell soap." Once Nixon gave the word: "We're going to build this whole campaign around television . . . you fellows just tell me what you want me to do and I'll do it," the advertising men, public relations men, copywriters, make-up artist, photographers, and others joined together to create the image and the aura that would make this man America's favorite "brand."

These and other cases suggest that the art of selling cigarettes, soap, and steel may have some bearing on the art of selling social causes. People like McGinness—and before him, John K. Galbraith and Vance Packard—believe everything and anything can be sold by Madison Avenue, while people like Wiebe feel this is exaggerated. To the extent that Madison Avenue has this power, some persons would be heartened because of the many good causes in need of an effective social marketing technology and others would despair over the specter of mass manipulation.

Unfortunately, there are few careful discussions of the power and limitations of social marketing. It is the authors' view that social

marketing is a promising framework for planning and implementing social change. At the same time, it is poorly understood and often viewed suspiciously by many behavioral scientists. The application of commercial ideas and methods to promote social goals will be seen by many as another example of business's lack of taste and self-restraint. Yet the application of the logic of marketing to social goals is a natural development and, on the whole, a promising one. It will not disappear by ignoring it or railing against it.

This article discusses the meaning, power, and limitations of social marketing as an approach to planned social change. First, this will require delineating the generic nature of marketing phenomena and some recent conceptual developments in the marketing field. Then there will be a definition of social marketing and an examination of the conditions under which it may be carried out effectively. The instruments of social marketing are defined followed by a systems view of the application of marketing logic to social objectives.

What Is Marketing?

The following statement testifies that there is no universal agreement on what marketing is.

> It has been described by one person or another as a business activity; as a group of related business activities; as a trade phenomenon; as a frame of mind; as a coordinative, integrative function in policy making; as a sense of business purpose; as an economic process; as a structure of institutions; as the process of exchanging or transferring ownership of products; as a process of concentration, equalization, and dispersion; as the creation of time, place and possession utilities; as a process of demand and supply adjustment; and many other things.[3]

In spite of the confusing jumble of definitions, the core idea of marketing lies in *the exchange process. Marketing does not occur unless there are two or more parties, each with something*

[1] G. D. Wiebe, "Merchandising Commodities and Citizenship on Television," *Public Opinion Quarterly*, Vol. 15 (Winter 1951–52), p. 679.

[2] Joe McGinniss, *The Selling of the President 1968* (New York: Trident Press, 1969).

[3] Marketing Staff of the Ohio State University, "A Statement of Marketing Philosophy," *Journal of Marketing*, Vol. 29 (January 1965), p. 43.

to exchange, and both able to carry out communications and distribution. Typically, the
subject of marketing is the exchange of goods
or services for other goods or services or for
money. Belshaw, in an excellent study of marketing exchange and its evolution from traditional to modern markets, shows the exchange
process in marketing to be a fundamental
aspect of both primitive and advanced social
life.[4]

Given that the core idea of marketing lies in
exchange processes, another concept can be
postulated—that of marketing management,
which can be defined as:

> Marketing management is the analysis, plan-
> ning, implementation, and control of programs
> designed to bring about desired exchanges with
> target audiences for the purpose of personal
> and mutual gain. It relies heavily on the
> adaptation and coordination of product, price,
> promotion, and place for achieving effective
> response.[5]

Thus marketing management occurs when
people become conscious of an opportunity to
gain from a more careful planning of their
exchange relations. It should be added here
that although planned social change is not
often viewed from the client's point of view, it
involves very much an exchange relationship
between client and change agent.[6]

The practice of marketing management as
applied to products and services has become
very sophisticated in the last few decades. The
responsibility of launching new products on a
national basis involving the investment and
risk of millions of dollars in the face of the
uncertainties and vicissitudes of consumer and
competitor response has led to an increased
reliance on formal research and planning
throughout the product development and introduction cycle. Marketing management examines the wants, attitudes, and behavior of
potential customers as this might shed light on

designing a desired product and on merchandising, promoting, and distributing it successfully. Management goes through a very formal
process of strategy determination, tactical programming, regional and national implementation, performance measurement, and feedback
control.

Within marketing circles there has been a
shift from a sales to a marketing orientation in
recent decades, although there are still many
believers and practitioners of the former concept. The sales concept holds that the job is
one of finding customers for present products
and convincing them they should buy these
products. The products are considered the
constants, and the sales job is to try to develop
appeals, prices, and services to move attitudes
and behavior toward the product. This sales
concept is implicit in The Selling of the President 1968, since one is not developing a really
new "product" for the job but rather trying to
sell a given one with a little suggestion that it
is somewhat "new and improved." The marketing concept, on the other hand, calls for
most of the effort to be spent on finding out
what a target audience wants and then creating the goods and services to satisfy these
wants. This view seems privately and socially
more acceptable. In private terms, the seller
recognizes that it is easier to create products
and services for existing wants than to try to
alter wants and attitudes toward existing
products. In social terms, it is held that this
philosophy of marketing restores consumer
sovereignty in the determination of the society's product mix and the use of national resources.

In practice, since at any time there are both
products in existence and new products to be
born, most marketing effort is a mixture of
selling and marketing, that is, a change strategy and a response strategy. In both cases
marketing management is becoming a sophis-

[4] Cyril S. Belshaw, Traditional Exchange and Modern Markets (Englewood Cliffs,
N.J.: Prentice-Hall, 1965).

[5] Philip Kotler, Marketing Management: Analysis, Planning and Control, 2d ed.
(Englewood Cliffs, N.J.: Prentice-Hall, 1972).

[6] Arthur H. Niehoff, A Casebook of Social Change (Chicago: Aldine Publishing,
1966); Warren G. Bennis, Kenneth D. Benne, and Robert Chin, The Planning of
Change (New York: Holt, Rinehart and Winston, 1969).

ticated action technology that draws heavily on the behavioral sciences for clues to solving problems of communication and persuasion related to influencing the acceptability of commercial products and services. In the hands of its best practitioners, marketing management is applied behavioral science.

Social Marketing

An increasing number of nonbusiness institutions have begun to examine marketing logic as a means to furthering their institutional goals and products. Marketing men have advised churches on how to increase membership, charities on how to raise money, and art museums and symphonies on how to attract more patrons. In the social sphere, the Advertising Council of America has carried out dozens of campaigns for social objectives, including "Smokey the Bear," "Keep America Beautiful," "Join the Peace Corps," "Buy Bonds," "Go to College," and so on. Social advertising is an established phenomenon on the American scene. Sandage says:

> True, (advertising's) communication function has been confined largely to informing and persuading people in respect to products and services. On the other hand, it can be made equally available to those who wish to inform and persuade people in respect to a city bond issue, cleaning up community crime, the "logic" of atheism, the needs for better educational facilities, the abusive tactics of given law enforcement officers, or any other sentiment held by any individual who wishes to present such sentiment to the public.[7]

Social advertising has become so much of a feature on the American scene that it is no longer a question of whether to use it, but how to use it. It has been very successful in some cases and conspicuously unsuccessful in other cases. At fault to a large extent is the tendency of social campaigners to assign to advertising the primary if not the exclusive

role in accomplishing their social objectives. This ignores the marketing truism that a given marketing objective requires the coordination of the promotional mix with the goods and services mix and with the distribution mix. To this extent, social marketing is a much larger idea than social advertising and even social communication. To emphasize this, the authors define social marketing in the following way:

> Social marketing is the design, implementation, and control of programs calculated to influence the acceptability of social ideas and involving considerations of product planning, pricing, communication, distribution, and marketing research.

It is the explicit use of marketing skills to help translate present social action efforts into more effectively designed and communicated programs that elicit desired audience response. To put it somewhat differently, marketing techniques are the bridging mechanisms between the simple possession of knowledge and the socially useful implementation of what knowledge allows.

Under What Condition Can Social Marketing Be Carried Out Effectively?

Some clues as to the difference between social advertising and social marketing are contained in some early papers by Lazarsfeld and Merton and later by Wiebe trying to explain the failure of social advertising to be very effective.

Lazarsfeld and Merton's Analysis

Paul Lazarsfeld and Robert Merton took exception to the view of many people that mass media can easily be used to control people's minds: "It is our tentative judgment that the social role played by the very existence of the mass media has been commonly overestimated."[8] They saw the effectiveness of mass media for propaganda purposes as depending

---

[7] C. H. Sandage, "Using Advertising to Implement the Concept of Freedom of Speech," in C. H. Sandage and V. Fryburger (eds.), *The Role of Advertising* (Homewood, Ill.: Richard D. Irwin, 1960), pp. 222–223.

[8] Paul F. Lazarsfeld and Robert K. Merton, "Mass Communication, Popular Taste, and Organized Social Action," in William Schramm (ed.), *Mass Communications* (Urbana: University of Illinois Press, 1949), pp. 459–480, at p. 462.

on three conditions, one or more of which is usually lacking in most propaganda situations. The first condition is real or psychological *monopolization* by the media, that is, a condition marked by the absence of counterpropaganda. This characterizes the totalitarian state and accounts for the greater effectiveness of these regimes in molding public opinion through mass media. It is found occasionally in free societies under special circumstances, such as a wartime effort. Part of the effectiveness of the radio performer Kate Smith in selling more than $39 million of bonds in 18 consecutive hours was due to the marathon nature of the event and the fact that everyone's feelings ran with the war, i.e., there was no counterpropaganda. But, in general, most campaigns in a free society in peacetime compete with so many other causes and everyday distractions that the monopoly condition is lacking and reduces the effectiveness of such campaigns.

Lazarsfeld and Merton said the second condition required for effective mass propaganda is *canalization*, the presence of an existing attitudinal base for the feelings that the social communicators are striving to shape. They made the point that typical commercial advertising of products is effective because the task is not one of instilling basic new attitudes or creating significantly new behavior patterns but rather canalizing existing attitudes and behavior in one direction or another. Thus the seller of toothpaste does not have to socialize persons into new dental care habits but rather into which brand to buy of a familiar and desired product. If the pre-existing attitudes are there, then canalization is always an easier task than social reconditioning.

The authors accept this idea but would further add that many business marketing situations also involve the task of reshaping basic attitudes rather than canalizing existing attitudes. For example, consider business firm efforts to influence farmers to change time-honored farming practices, to influence doctors to try out new drugs, and to influence

males to dress with more fashion and flair. Canalization is always easier, but the authors want to emphasize that business marketers, like social marketers, often engage in trying to diffuse fundamentally new products and services requiring major attitudinal reorientations.

Lazarsfeld and Merton call the third condition *supplementation*, by which they mean the effort to follow up mass communication campaigns with programs of face-to-face contacts. In trying to explain the success of the rightist Father Coughlin movement in the thirties, Lazarsfeld and Merton observe:

> This combination of a central supply of propaganda (Coughlin's addresses on a nationwide network), the coordinated distribution of newspapers and pamphlets and locally organized face-to-face discussions among relatively small groups—this complex of reciprocal reinforcement by mass media and personal relations proved spectacularly successful.[9]

This approach, which is standard in many closed societies and organizations, suggests another key difference between social advertising and social marketing. Whereas a social advertising approach contrives only the event of mass media communication and leaves the response to natural social processes, social marketing arranges for a step-down communication process. The message is passed on and discussed in more familiar surroundings to increase its memorability, penetration, and action consequences. Thus supplementation, monopolization, and canalization are critical factors influencing the effectiveness of social marketing effort.

Wiebe's Analysis

An additional contribution was made by Wiebe in his attempt to understand the differential effectiveness of four social campaigns.[10] He explained the relative effectiveness of these campaigns in terms of the audience member's experience with regard to five factors:

1. *The force.* The intensity of the person's motivation toward the goal as a combination of

[9] *Ibid.*
[10] *Ibid.*

his predisposition prior to the message and the stimulation of the message.

2. *The direction.* Knowledge of how or where the person might go to consummate his motivation.

3. *The mechanism.* The existence of an agency that enables the person to translate his motivation into action.

4. *Adequacy and compatibility.* The ability and effectiveness of the agency in performing its task.

5. *Distance.* The audience member's estimate of the energy and cost required to consummate the motivation in relation to the reward.

To show how these factors operate, Wiebe first analyzed the Kate Smith campaign to sell bonds during the Second World War. This campaign was eminently successful, according to Wiebe, because of the presence of force (patriotism), direction (buy bonds), mechanism (banks, post offices, telephone orders), adequacy and compatibility (so many centers to purchase the bonds), and distance (ease of purchase). In fact, extra telephone lines were installed on the night of the campaign at 134 CBS stations to take orders during her appeal. The effort to buy bonds

> . . . was literally reduced to the distance between the listener and his telephone. Psychological distance was also minimized. The listener remained in his own home. There were no new people to meet, no unfamiliar procedures, no forms to fill out, no explanation, no waiting. . . .[11]

In the case of a campaign to recruit Civil Defense volunteers, many of the same factors were present except that the social mechanism was not prepared to handle the large volume of response and this reduced the campaign's success. Teachers, manuals, equipment, and registration and administration procedures were *inadequate*, and many responding citizens were turned away and disappointed after they were led to believe that their services were urgently needed.

The third campaign, a documentary on juvenile delinquency, did not meet with maximum success because of the *absence of a mechanism*. Instead of being directed to an existing agency, people were urged to form neighborhood councils themselves. This certainly takes far more effort than simply picking up the phone to buy a war bond, as Kate Smith suggested, or "stopping in" to register at the nearest Civil Defense unit, as the Civil Defense people suggested.

The fourth campaign revolved around the goal of the Kefauver committee hearings to arouse citizens to "set their house in order." This campaign met with a notable lack of success, however, because citizens were not *directed* to an appropriate mechanism, despite the fact that one existed in principle in the political party organizations. Political party organizations apparently left much to be desired in terms of availability and compatibility. The skepticism prevalent at the time concerning the chances of anything beneficial happening as a result of the hearings was ample evidence that considerable psychological distance existed between the audience and the mechanisms for action.

The Social Marketing Approach

The Lazarsfeld and Merton provisions and the Wiebe factors provide a background against which one can view the conceptual framework used by marketing strategists in striving for a successful product introduction. Marketing people tend to view the problem as one of developing the right *product* backed by the right *promotion* and put in the right *place* at the right *price*. These key variables in the marketing mix have been named the four P's by E. Jerome McCarthy.[12] The authors shall examine each of these variables, designated control variables, in terms of some well-known social issues.

PRODUCT

In business marketing sellers study the needs and wants of target buyers and attempt

---

[11] Wiebe, *op. cit.*, p. 633.

[12] E. Jerome McCarthy, *Basic Marketing: A Managerial Approach*, 3d ed. (Homewood, Ill.: Richard D. Irwin, 1968), pp. 31–33.

to design products and services that meet their desires. If well-designed and affordable, these products will be bought. In social marketing sellers also have to study the target audiences and design appropriate products. They must find a way to "package" the social idea so that it is desirable and "buyable." This corresponds to Wiebe's idea of mechanism.

Product design in the social area is typically more challenging than product design in the business area. Consider the problem of selling "safer driving." The social objective is to create safer driving habits and attitudes in the population. There is no one product that can do this. Various products have to be designed that will make partial contributions to the social objective. A public education media campaign providing tips on safe driving is one such product. The offering of "defensive driving courses" which persons can enroll in is another product. The creation of insurance policies which reduce insurance premiums for safer drivers is still another product. In general, the social marketer keeps his eye on the *core product* (safer driving) and tries to create various tangible products and services which are "buyable" and which advance the social objectives.

The same thinking is required by those who market *altruistic causes* (such as charity giving, blood donation), *personal health causes* (for example, nonsmoking, better nutrition), and *social betterment causes* (such as civil rights, improved housing, better environment). In each case the social marketer must define the change sought, which may be a change in values, beliefs, affects, behavior, or some mixture. He must meaningfully segment the target markets. He must design social products for each market which are "buyable" and which instrumentally serve the social cause. In some social causes the hardest problem will be to innovate appropriate products; in other cases the hardest problem will be to motivate purchase.

PROMOTION

The marketing man's second control variable is promotion, by which he means the communication-persuasion strategy and tactics

that will make the product familiar, acceptable, and even desired by the audience. Wiebe's counterpart to promotion is "force." The social campaign strategist will tend to think of his as mass media communication, but promotion is a much larger idea. To the marketing man, promotion includes the following major activities:

Advertising: Any paid form of nonpersonal presentation and promotion of products, services, or ideas by an identified sponsor.

Personal selling: Any paid form of personal presentation and promotion of products, service, or ideas by an identified sponsor.

Publicity: Any unpaid form of nonpersonal presentation and promotion of products, services, or ideas where the sponsor is unidentified.

Sales Promotion: Miscellaneous paid forms (special programs, incentives, materials, and events) designed to stimulate audience interest and acceptance of a product.

Each of these promotional tools involves complex issues in strategy and tactics. With respect to advertising, the marketer has to determine the size of the total advertising budget, the choice of appeals, the development of attention-getting copy, the selection of effective and efficient media, the time-patterning of the advertising inputs, and the measurement of overall and segment-level results. With respect to personal selling, the marketer has to determine the size of the total sales force, the development of sales territory boundaries and assignments, the development of personal presentation strategies, the degree and type of sales force motivation and supervision, and the evaluation of sales force effectiveness. Publicity calls for arranging for significant news about the product to appear in various media. Sales promotion calls for developing special display, premiums, programs, and events that might be useful in stimulating interest or action.

Each of these activities are specialties in which the specialists have achieved sophisticated levels of knowledge and techniques. This is especially apparent when one examines social campaigns developed by amateurs where the appeals and copy seem very naive.

Even behavioral science consultants to social campaign organizations often fail to make a maximum contribution because of their inability or reluctance to view the issue in broad marketing terms instead of in strictly social or ethical terms.

Nathaniel Martin has criticized the Indian government for failing to handle family planning as a marketing problem.

> Selling birth control is as much a marketing job as selling any other consumer product. And where no manufacturer would contemplate developing and introducing a new product without a thorough understanding of the variables of the market, planners in the highest circles of Indian government have blithely gone ahead without understanding that marketing principles must determine the character of any campaign of voluntary control. The Indians have done only the poorest research. They have mismanaged distribution of contraceptive devices. They have ignored the importance of "customer service." They have proceeded with grossly inadequate undertrained staffs; they have been blind to the importance of promotion and advertising.[13]

This is not to deny that the Indian government has undertaken some innovative promotional approaches. Referral fees are paid to salesmen, barbers, and others who bring in consenting males for sterilization. The consenting male is given a transistor radio or a small payment to cover his costs of being absent from work. Women have been offered gifts for consenting to use intrauterine contraceptive devices. But Martin feels that the total program lacks the qualities of an organized, well-planned, and continuous marketing effort.[14]

An example of careful promotional planning for a social objective is found in the American Cancer Society efforts to raise money for cancer research. In their brochure directed to local units they attempt to educate the volunteer and professional chapters on the handling of newspapers, pictures, company publications, radio and television, movies, special events, and controversial arguments. For example, in terms of special events:

> Dramatic special events attract attention to the American Cancer Society. They bring color, excitement, and glamour to the program. Well planned, they will get excellent coverage in newspapers, on radio and TV, and in newsreels. . . . A Lights-on-Drive, a one-afternoon or one-night House-to-House program have such dramatic appeal that they stir excitement and enthusiasm . . . keep in mind the value of bursts of sound such as fire sirens sounding, loud-speaker trucks, fife and drum corps. . . . A most useful special event is the ringing of church bells to add a solemn, dedicated note to the launching of a drive or education project. This should be organized on a Division or community basis, and the church bell ringing may be the signal to begin a House-to-House canvass. Rehearsals of bell ringing, community leaders tugging at ropes, offer good picture possibilities.[15]

Some readers might be critical of this approach to a worthwhile social objective, but two things should be mentioned. The first is that this should not be identified as the *marketing approach to social objectives.* Many persons mistakenly assume that marketing means hard selling. This is only a particular style of marketing, and it has its critics both inside and outside the profession. There are many firms that market their products with taste and sensitivity: examples include Xerox, Container Corporation, and Hallmark. It is important to recognize that this is not non-marketing but rather a style of marketing that was chosen in the belief of its greater effectiveness in accomplishing the goals of the organization.

[13] Nathaniel A. Martin, "The Outlandish Idea: How a Marketing Man Would Save India," *Marketing/Communications*, Vol. 297 (March 1968), pp. 54–60.

[14] For two analyses of the marketing issues and opportunities in the family planning issue, see Julian L. Simon, "A Huge Marketing Research Task—Birth Control," *Journal of Marketing Research*, Vol. 5 (February 1968), pp. 21–27; and Glen L. Urban, "Ideas on a Decision-Information System for Family Planning," *Industrial Management Review*, Vol. 10 (Spring 1969), pp. 45–61.

[15] *Public Information Guide* (New York: American Cancer Society, 1965), p. 19.

Second, the issue is not whether a particular approach suits one's personal tastes but whether it works. If a "hard" marketing style raises substantially more money for cancer research than a "soft" marketing style, this must be respected by those who think cancer research is more important than personal aesthetics.

PLACE

The third element of the marketing approach to social campaigns calls for providing adequate and compatible distribution and response channels. Motivated persons should know where to go to get the product. Place is equivalent to two of Wiebe's five conditions for an effective mass communication campaign (direction, and adequacy and compatibility). The poor results of many social campaigns can be attributed in part to their failure to suggest clear action outlets for those motivated to acquire the product. The current campaign to get people interested in the pollution problem may suffer from this defect. It is succeeding in making everyone not only aware of environmental pollution but also fearful of it. They want to act. But for the most part they cannot because there is not a clear product to "buy" (such as a petition to sign, an election in which to choose an antipollution candidate, or a pending piece of national legislation). Nor does the average person have a clear picture of the alternative channels of action for expressing his interest in the issue. There are so many ad hoc organizations working without coordination and at times with cross-purpose that the average person is likely to "tune out" from further messages because of personal frustration. Saturation campaigns unaccompanied by the provision of adequate response channels may result in "interest overkill."

The importance of place has been recognized in several campaigns. The most notable example, mentioned earlier, is the Kate Smith bond-selling campaign and its imaginative establishment of telephone order channels during the broadcast. Strategists of anticigarette campaigns have recognized the need for action channels by setting up smoker's clinics in many of the large cities. They could even go further and provide telephone advice and even social calls if the economics would justify these additional channels. Recently, an advertising agency undertook to prepare a campaign called "Pick Your Issue" in which several different social issues would be individually featured. The point would be made that because the busy citizen does not have time to become involved in all issues, this should not be an excuse not to get involved in any issue. The good citizen should "pick an issue." Each issue advertisement will contain information on the organizations that are active in that issue area and inform the citizen on where he might write for further information.

Thus place means arranging for accessible outlets so that motivations can be translated into actions. Planning in this area calls for selecting or developing appropriate outlets, deciding on their number, average size, and locations, and giving them proper motivation to perform their part of the job.

PRICE

The final control variable that must be planned is *price*. Price represents the costs that the buyer must accept in order to get the product. Price includes money costs, opportunity costs, energy costs, and psychic costs. Thus, the cost to persons asked to appear for immunization shots includes any money charge that might be made, any opportunities foregone, the expenditure of energy, and the psychological concerns aroused by inoculation. The cost of giving up smoking is largely psychological. There is actually a financial saving in giving up the habit. The cost of using seat belts is the charge for buying them, the effort to lock and unlock them, and the psychological cost of not being completely sure one is better off in an accident wearing them or not wearing them.

The concept of price is something like Wiebe's concept of distance, along with some of the aspects of adequacy and compatibility. The functioning of his concept can be illustrated in terms of an interesting phenomenon in health care services where many poor patients prefer to patronize unlicensed practitioners and pay a fee instead of going to the regular clinics. In Caracas, Venezuela, for example, although there is a free hospital for the indigent, many of them patronize private clinics which cost them 20 bolivares for consultation. Why? Because while there is no charge at the free hospital, there is a substantial cost to the patient in terms of energy and psychological abuse. When he arrives at the hospital, he queues up to see a social worker. When he is finally interviewed, the social worker asks a lot of questions about his income to determine whether he is really indigent. (Do you have a TV set? How much do you pay? and so on.) Then he sees a number of other hospital staff members for various tests, some of them bringing up the question of his income again. Finally, he sees the doctor who discovers that he really needs to see a specialist who will not be available for a few weeks. Throughout the experience, the person is made to feel inferior and a nuisance. It is no wonder that he wishes to avoid these energy and psychological costs even if it means paying for the services.

But even monetary charges may play a useful role in leading the poor back to free hospital services. In private correspondence, a social psychologist suggested:

> It is a surprising discovery that even free medical care presents a marketing problem. Maybe we should apply dissonance theory and introduce such medical care at a high price to make it look more desirable. Then let us apply a cents-off special introductory offer to make the service attractive.

The marketing man's approach to pricing the social product is based on the assumption that members of a target audience perform a cost-benefit analysis when considering the investment of money, time, or energy to the issue. They somehow process the major benefits and compare them to the major costs and the strength of their motivation to act is directly related to the magnitude of the excess benefit. This type of conceptualization of behavior is found not only in the economist's model of economic man but also in behavioristic theory with its emphasis on rewards and costs, in gestalt theory with its emphasis on

positive and negative valences, and in management theory with its emphasis on incentives and constraints. The marketing man's approach to selling a social product is to think about how the rewards for buying the product can be increased relative to the costs, or the costs reduced relative to the rewards, or trying to find a mix of product, promotion, place, and price that will simultaneously increase the rewards and reduce the costs. The real point is that social marketing calls for giving careful thought to how to present the buyer with manageable, desirable, gratifying, and convenient solutions to a perceived need or problem.

The Social Marketing Planning Process

The "four P's" of marketing management are drawn together in an administrative process framework in Figure 48.1. Information and influences are received from the *environment* by the *change agency*. *Plans and messages* are created which are sent through *channels* to *audiences* and the results are monitored by the *change agency*.

The change agency operates a research unit and a planning unit. The research unit collects several types of information. It monitors the environment—economic, political, technological, cultural, and competitive—for important developments affecting its social policies and objectives. For example, a family planning agency would monitor economic-demographic developments (income and population trends), political developments (liberalization of birth control information), technological developments (new birth control techniques and devices), cultural developments (attitudinal changes toward birth control), and competitive developments (actions of similar and competing groups). The research unit also collects information on the past effectiveness of various programs as well as information on audience attitudes, desires, and behavior.

The change agent's planning unit formulates short-range and long-range social marketing plans on the basis of this information. For example, the family planning organization carefully considers the role of different products, promotions, places, and prices. It would

Figure 48.1.   Social Market Planning System.

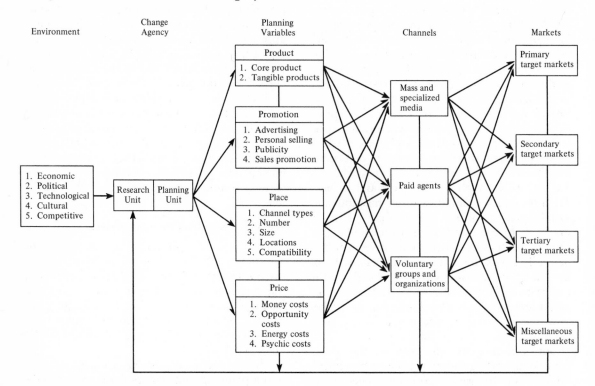

identify the major channels of communication and distribution, such as mass and specialized media, paid agents, and volunteer groups. It would differentiate its programs for its primary target market (large and low-income families), secondary target market (other child-bearing families), tertiary target market (sources of funds and additional volunteer efforts), and miscellaneous target markets (politicians, church groups, etc.). Finally, it would continuously gather effectiveness measures on its different programs for recycling its planning.

This approach represents an application of business marketing principles to the problem of marketing social change. It is already manifest in some of the larger social change agencies. Consider the work, for example, of the National Safety Council. Its staff includes an advertising manager, sales promotion management, Advertising Council of America coordinator, research director, and program director. One of its products is a Defensive Driv-

ing Course. Figure 48.2 shows the various channels through which this course is marketed along with the promotional tools it uses. The National Safety Council reaches potential prospects through business firms, service organizations, schools, and the police and court system. For the decade of the 1970's, the National Safety Council has adopted

. . . a four-point marketing program. . . . One of the first objectives is to increase the sales effectiveness of our existing 150 state and local safety council cooperating agencies. . . . The second part of the program is to create 500 new training agencies in communities not now served by safety councils. . . . A third part of the marketing program will be aimed at selling big industry on adopting DDC as a training course for all employees or selected categories of employees in plant-run training programs. . . . The fourth part of the marketing plan deals with a nationwide promotional effort built around a series of community special-emphasis campaigns running from February 1

Figure 48.2.   Marketing Channels and Tools: Defensive Driving Course.

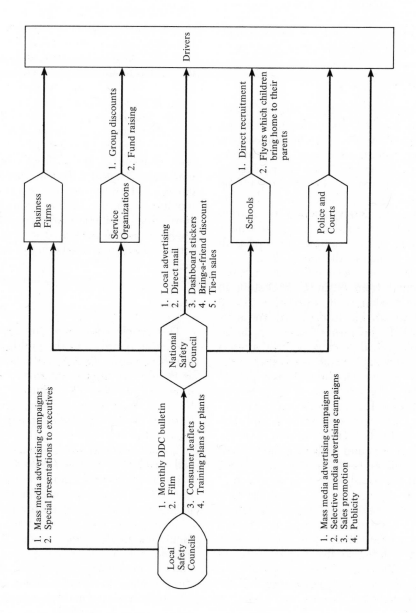

through Memorial Day each year of the decade.[16]

This example illustrates the possibilities of the marketing approach for furthering social causes. These and a few other social agencies have graduated from occasional campaign organizations to full-time marketing organizations which goes through cycles of information gathering, planning, product development, measuring, and reprogramming.

Social Implications of Social Marketing

The authors believe that specific social causes could benefit from marketing thinking and planning. Problems of pollution control, mass transit, private education, drug abuse, and public medicine are in need of innovative solutions and approaches for gaining public attention and support. Marketing men by their training are finely attuned to market needs, product development, issues, and mass communication and promotion techniques, all of which are critical in the social area.

At the same time, social marketing is sufficiently different from business marketing to require fresh thinking and approaches. Social marketing typically has to deal with the market's core beliefs and values whereas business marketing often deals with superficial preferences and opinions. Social marketing must search harder for meaningful *quid pro quos* to gain acceptance or adoption of its products. Social marketing has to work with channel systems that are less well-defined and less pecuniarily motivated. Only through applying marketing concepts and tools to a large number of cases will we begin to learn the powers and limits of the social marketing approach.

In addition, there is the real possibility that the overt marketing of social objectives will be resented and resisted. There will be charges that it is "manipulative" and consequently contributing to bringing the society closer to Orwell's 1984. There will be charges that even if not manipulative, social marketing will increase the amount of "promotional noise" in the society, which they find distasteful both because it emphasizes "trivial differences" and it is noise. Finally, there will be charges that social marketing will increase the costs of promoting social causes beyond the point of net gain either to the specific cause or the society as a whole. In the charities industry professional marketing increases the absolute cost of raising money but usually succeeds in raising more money after costs. But when one considers the macropicture, it is possible that the total amount given to charities may not increase by the same amount as the professional marketing costs.

The authors are concerned with these possible dysfunctional consequences which must obviously be subtracted from the positive good that might be achieved through social marketing. Insofar as social marketing is just emerging, those concerned are encouraged to monitor it closely in the same dispassionate spirit that business marketers have so ably analyzed and documented the many manifestations of business marketing practice over the years.

Summary

This article considered the applicability of marketing concepts to the problem of promoting social causes. Social marketing was defined as the design, implementation, and control of programs calculated to influence the acceptability of social ideas and involving considerations of product planning, pricing, communication, distribution, and marketing research.

Too often social advertising rather than social marketing is practiced by social campaigners. Lazarsfeld and Merton attributed the failure of many social advertising campaigns to the frequent absence of conditions of monopolization, canalization, and supplementation in the social arena. Wiebe, in his examination of four campaigns, concluded that a campaign's effectiveness depended on the presence of adequate force, direction, an adequate and compatible social mechanism,

[16] Chris Imhoff, "DDC's Decisive Decade," *Traffic Safety Magazine*, Vol. 69 (December 1969), pp. 20, 36.

and distance. The marketer sees the success of the campaign as depending on the proper development of product, promotion, place, and price considerations. These concepts were defined and shown to have applicability to social causes. The social marketing process calls for marketing research and the subsequent development of a well-conceived product and appeals moving through mass and specialized communication media and through paid agents and voluntary groups to reach targeted audiences. The marketing style may be hard or soft, depending on what is deemed most effective in accomplishing the social objectives.

A marketing planning approach does not guarantee that the social objectives will be achieved, or that the costs will be acceptable. Yet social marketing appears to represent a bridging mechanism linking the behavioral scientist's knowledge of human behavior with the socially useful implementation of what that knowledge allows. It offers a useful framework for effective social planning at a time when social issues have become more relevant and critical.

49. Some "Marketing Correct" Recommendations for Family Planning Campaigns

Julian L. Simon*

Professor Donald J. Bogue entitled a provocative and interesting article "Some Tentative Recommendations for a 'Sociologically Correct' Family Planning Communication and Motivation Program in India."[1] But family-planning campaigns are an exercise in marketing and advertising (as Bogue himself is the first to admit elsewhere). Therefore, it seems sensible to inquire into *advertising*-correct and *marketing*-correct principles of family planning communication. I shall do so here, mostly in the context of a comparison with the principles that Bogue derived from his examination of relevant sociological principles.

There are eight important areas of *agreement*, points on which advertising and marketing knowledge coincides with Bogue's deductions from sociological theory:

1. At the beginning of a family planning campaign one should emphasize *information and facts* (No. 1).[2] It is common-place that the information content of advertisements for new products is much higher when the products are introduced than later on when the subject is old hat. And family planning campaigns are still at the innovation stage.

2. Logistics are important (No. 6). Advertisers worry about getting store distribution for new products, just as family planning officials ought to be concerned with establishing distribution networks for contraceptive products before beginning their campaigns.

3. The campaign should first aim at the *best prospects* and only later move on successively to the less promising customers (No. 8). This is called "skimming the cream" by sales organization, and it is well known to be efficient, just as it is bound to be efficient in family campaigns.

4. Self-interest (including the welfare of one's children) is a powerful motivating appeal (No. 12). "Show the customer how the product will benefit him"; is perhaps the best-established truth known to advertising men.

5. The audience's distrust of the message and the communicator often reduces the efficiency of

---

[1] In Clyde V. Kiser (ed.), *Research in Family Planning* (Princeton: Princeton University Press, 1962).

[2] The numbers in parentheses refer to the numbered recommendations in Bogue's article for those readers who are interested in making a point-to-point comparison.

Reprinted from Julian L. Simon, "Some 'Marketing Correct' Recommendations for Family Planning Campaigns," *Demography*, Vol. V (1968), pp. 504–507.

* Professor of Economics and Marketing, University of Illinois.

the message (No. 14). This is why advertisers use testimonials by famous or "typical" people to increase believability and to overcome distrust. Family planning campaigns can make good use of the same device.

6. A post-delivery visit to the new mother is a good time to see the family planning idea (No. 22). This fits the marketing man's precept of "Get to the prospect when he is in a buying mood."

7. Impersonal printed messages can be effective. This is what advertising is, of course, and we have long known that it can be more efficient than personal selling in many circumstances. In other circumstances it is most efficient to combine impersonal *and* personal selling.

8. The seller must legitimate the behavior that he wants to stimulate. Family planning campaigns can use traditional authorities to legitimate family planning, just as advertisers use "fifty million Frenchmen" arguments such as "More people drink our beer than any other beer."

Despite this wide area of agreement, there are some major disagreements between Bogue's "sociologically correct" recommendations and the heuristics of advertising. Next come some issues about which the eighty years and billions of dollars of trial-and-error in advertising have given us some well-grounded knowledge.[3]

Bogue says that "most of the communication and almost all the motivation for family planning will be accomplished by private personal communication . . ." (No. 2); and "a major strategy . . . should be to develop a small core of family planners . . . (No. 15). Although marketers have long been aware of the underlying two-step flow-of-influence concept and have propagandized about it for the past ten years, I know of no successful marketing attempt to use this strategy—with the (possibly apocryphal) exception of a silo distributing firm whose product is highly *visible* (which is very much not the case with family-planning practice).

According to Bogue, "The total amount of information to be communicated should be reduced to the smallest amount possible" (No. 21). But mail-order sellers, who can measure the effects of various communication forms better than anyone else, send out *large* amounts of information. A four-page direct-mail letter plus brochure is common-place, as are full-page advertisements full of small type. The governing principle is to give *plenty* of information; if you have something to say people will read or listen to *very long* messages as long as there is something worth reading or listening to. The short-message doctrine is dangerously wrong and is espoused by no respected advertising man for situations that resemble family-planning campaigns.

"The information-disseminating program should be strongly oriented toward husbands and fathers . . ." (No. 3). But advertisers and salesmen try to address themselves to the person who will actually execute the purchase, and contraception is a *female* act, except with condoms. I think that since Bogue made this sociological deduction in 1960, empirical experience in the field has convinced family planners that the correct course is indeed to concentrate on the women—except perhaps if male sterilization is the contraceptive act in question.

This and most of the following points depart not from Bogue's piece but from the family-planning-communication literature in general.

The injunction to concentrate communication efforts in a few places until a "communication threshold" is reached, rather than spreading efforts "too lightly," is frequently found in statements by Freedman and others. The theory is that a single message may fall below the threshold of perception and therefore be waste. But advertising experience suggests the opposite—that two messages are never twice as successful as one—in which case it pays to distribute efforts as *widely* as possible. Recently I summarized all the rele-

---

[3] Despite the claim of marketing knowledge to be heard and used in family planning, there is hardly a reference to the literature of marketing and advertising to be found in discussions of family planning communication. Why?

vant evidence on this point that I could find in the advertising and communications literature.[4]

Some family-planning communicators have shown surprise that messages "wear out," and that it is therefore necessary to offer a variety of message to audiences. But it is well-known among advertising men who have had experience in mail-order operations—which is what a family-planning campaign is—that two different ads that are equally good *ceteris paribus* will produce more total response than will two repetitions of the same ad. There is overwhelming empirical evidence for this, but the conclusion can also be deduced directly from the lack of economies of scale in advertising. The only limits to the number of different messages are (*a*) the cost of producing them, and (*b*) the difficulty of finding a larger number of equally good messages.

The competent advertising man invariably tries out several different messages before deciding which to use as staples. But family planning campaigns have apparently not done any such testing. It is true that during the early stages of introduction of a product or idea, when the messages are heavily informational and factual, there is probably less difference in effectiveness among the messages than later on when there is no longer much to say that is new. Nevertheless, such testing of various messages is bound to result in greater efficiency at *any* stage of the family-planning campaign.

Testing requires that each response can be traced to the message stimulus that caused it. This is difficult to arrange in national package-goods advertising, but in mail-order operations—and family planning can be mail-order type operation in this way—tracing is done simply by keying the coupon or what-have-you as a "box" number, etc. It would be relatively easy to set up a key system to determine whether a clinic visitor was stimulated by a brochure, radio, or home visitor, and whether

the home visitor and salesman A or salesman B. Clinic visitors caused by word-of-mouth cannot be traced in this manner, but it is usually a good assumption that the untraceables are proportional to the traceables. Family-planning officials certainly ought to set up appropriate message-accounting systems.

This last point is perhaps the most important. Conspicuous in its absence from discussions of family-planning campaigns is an explicit consideration of the dollar value of a customer. The final and relevant statistic is the economic value of a prevented birth. This is a difficult problem in cost-benefit analysis and welfare economics, of course, but *without* such a calculation it is logically impossible to appropriate decisions about how much a nation or family-planning group ought to spend to reduce the birth rate. Such calculations of the economic value of a prevented birth are not impossible. Stephen S. Enke,[5] for example, shows how an underdeveloped country such as India can afford to pay a sum larger than the national per capita income for each birth prevented, a figure which tells nations something about how much they can afford to spend (at the margin) to prevent a birth. Another example is in the context of Bogue's program in the West Side Negro ghetto in Chicago. A good number of the children born to women who are contacted by that program are destined to be wards of the community through financial aid to dependent children. One can therefore calculate the cost to the community of an ADC child, and then figure the number of ADC children prevented by a family-planning program. Even the simplest calculation yields startling results. For example, an ADC child undoubtedly costs the community more than $10,000 during its first 16 years. But all out-of-pocket expenses in the West Side experiment *totaled* $4,000, and this means that if that program prevented *only one* ADC birth, it is socially profitable When considered this way, the $12 cost per new

[4] Julian L. Simon, "Are There Economics of Scale in Advertising?" *Journal of Advertising Research* (June, 1965).

[5] Stephen S. Enke, "The Economic Aspects of Slowing Population Growth," *Economics Journal* (March, 1966).

client that is reported by Bogue must be dirt cheap, rather than a "high" cost as his report suggests. (Of course, it is necessary to forge the logical link between number of new clients and number of births prevented, but that estimation job is not too difficult. And by *no* stretch of the imagination would the ratio of births prevented to new clients fall below, say, 1 to 10.)

The dollar value of a customer must also take into account the total births prevented in the *long run*, properly discounted to the present. This is standard practice in mail-order.[6]

In summary, the social psychologists and sociologists who have done yeoman work in the family-planning movement would benefit from an examination of the principles of advertising and marketing, as derived from many years of hard-nosed experience. It might also be well if family planning campaigns took advantage of the experience of professional creators of advertising and of qualified managers of marketing campaigns, rather than depending on their own amateur talents, great as they have shown them to be. This should be all the more valuable as family planning campaigns shift into high gear all over the world in that future which is already upon us.

[6] Julian L. Simon, *How to Start and Operate a Mail-Order Business* (New York: McGraw-Hill, 1965), and "Expenditure Policy for Mail-Order Advertisers," *Journal of Marketing Research* (February, 1967).

50.   Teach-In on the Environment
ENACT*

The first project undertaken by ENACT will be to plan and carry out the necessary organization of a major Teach-In on the Environment.

A teach-in is an extra-curricular effort to reach across the limitations of professional and departmental barriers to inform and to provide opportunities for action. The extraordinary nature of a teach-in can capture and focus the attention of the entire community on specific issues for intensive study, discussion and action. Expert, but diverse, opinions are widely disseminated through formal presentations, panel discussions and workshops. Emphasis is upon individual understanding and involvement.

The result, for many participants, is an informed awareness of the issues, realization of common purpose and a commitment to organized and persistent action.

The teach-in is a newsworthy event; effective publicity can carry the message to a far greater audience in the community and be-

yond than would an equivalent effort invested in seminars and public meetings spread over a longer time interval.

Issues of environmental quality and survival are particularly suitable for the teach-in medium. These are issues in which the general populace must take an interest, and make a new commitment to action, if the problems are to be solved through orderly change. Teach-ins on the environment offer an unusual opportunity to involve a broad spectrum of the community—particularly students—in this enormous challenge.

The Teach-In on the Environment

Coordinated through the ENACT Steering Committee, a number of working committees are preparing the detailed plans for all aspects of the Teach-In. The total effort will involve three phases: (1) the Teach-In Itself, (2) the Momentum Effort, and (3) the Follow-Through.

Reprinted from *Teach-in on the Environment* by ENACT, School of Natural Resources, University of Michigan (Ann Arbor, March 1970), pp. 8–17 (Mimeographed).
* Environmental Action for Survival, 2534 Student Activities Building and/or 146F School of Natural Resources, The University of Michigan, Ann Arbor, Michigan 48104.

The Teach-In Itself

Events during the four-day Teach-In period will be centered on the University campus, in the local schools, and in the general regional community. Some of these events will be occurring simultaneously; others will seek to enlist joint participation from all sectors.

CAMPUS

During the four-day Teach-In period, ENACT will sponsor a structured program of events. Simultaneously, individual departments, schools, and organizations will hold in-house and specialized programs coordinated in the overall events program.

The Teach-In will begin on Wednesday evening (March 11, 1970) with a major kick-off event held in the 14,000 seat Events Building. This program will combine mixed-media presentations, environmentally oriented entertainment by nationally prominent folk singers and a rock band, and two addresses: one by a leader among environmental politicians, the other a leading policy-oriented ecologist. It is hoped that this program can be held with no admission charge.

Thursday (March 12) will be emphasized as a day of events in the local schools (described below). A community rally will be held Thursday evening. Radio and television will be used for special programming in conjunction with the Teach-In, including a "Town Meeting of the Air" on environmental issues. On campus, there will be in-house events in departments, and films and other exhibits will be emphasized. In-house programs in departments will continue during Friday (March 13), but the focus will return to centralized programming, with a series of major speakers during the afternoon. The general topic of these presentations will be kinds of environmental problems and appropriate solutions. During the evening a major panel presentation will deal with problem definition, focusing on a determination of underlying causes. The panel will be followed by a discussion period and by workshops and informal talks with panel participants.

Saturday (March 14) will conclude action

programs in the community ("instant" construction of a vest pocket park, petition canvassing, etc.). Arrangements may be made for a legislative hearing to be held in Ann Arbor that morning dealing with environmental problems. During the afternoon the focus will be upon varieties of roles in change: citizen, government official, specialist, student, etc. Workshops will be held during the later afternoon following up these topics.

The program will conclude on Saturday evening with a major address on the environment and man's future, a synthesizing discussion of the issue and the potential for solving our environmental problems.

Action projects, literature distribution, and publicity events will occur throughout the Teach-In period. An Ecology House will be open on campus at all times for exhibits, music, and informal discussions.

SCHOOLS

A coordinated schedule of events will be conducted in the local elementary and high schools. These events will be largely student planned and administered, although ENACT will provide major speakers, films, and exhibits. Teachers at all levels will be provided with special teaching materials for the period, highlighting many aspects of environmental issues. Teachers' workshops may be held in advance.

A schedule of major assemblies will be arranged to permit multiple appearances by a major speaker particularly attractive to young people. This will serve to keynote the high school events.

COMMUNITY

All media will be used to seek involvement by community groups and individuals. Service clubs and other groups will be encouraged to plan special events during the week to deal with environmental problems. Programs, exhibits, speakers, and workshops on local problems will be scheduled in coordination with existing groups spearheading these efforts. An Environmental Fair will run continuously during the Teach-In period.

Religious groups will be encouraged to give

attention to environmental matters in sermons, Sunday schools, adult meetings, and bulletins.

Legislative and executive declaration of the Teach-In week as "Improve Michigan's Environment Week" will be sought at the state level, with parallel designations in local jurisdictions.

The Momentum Effort

A fundamental part of the organizational and planning work building up to the Teach-In itself will be a staged momentum effort:

University Seminars and Workshops on Man and the Environment. A weekly series of these seminars will be led by both University faculty and guest lecturers, representing fields such as natural science, social sciences, engineering, and design Workshops organized by faculty and students will follow each seminar.

Regional school systems. Speakers will be provided for all elementary and secondary schools for talks both during regular classes and in extra-curricular sessions. A block of night school classes on environmental matters may be scheduled. Educational programs will also be coordinated with nearby universities and junior and community colleges.

Community seminars. Weekly seminars of special interest to the community, focusing especially on local issues, are being scheduled. Community organizations will be informed of the availability of speakers on environmental issues.

Speakers Bureau. ENACT will serve as a registration center for the many graduate students, faculty, and citizens who have indicated a willingness to serve in the momentum effort programs.

Departmental speakers. Many outstanding speakers are brought to campus each semester through funds available to individual departments of schools. Through Teach-In committees established in each school, unconventional speakers, or speakers of interest to large segments of the University will be recommended. ENACT will provide more widespread publicity than is normally given such talks.

Major speakers. During the month prior to the Teach-In itself, one or two major speakers will be scheduled for campus-wide talks under sponsorship of ENACT. Provocative speakers will be sought to assure publicity impact.

Information files. Extensive monitoring of journals, magazines, books, and newspapers for information on specific environmental issues has begun. This information will be indexed and made available to anyone. In addition, a newsletter with information on pertinent issues is being published regularly.

General publicity. Reading lists are already in circulation. Displays will be set up in local bookstores, the public libraries, and elsewhere. Full use of all media is planned.

Action projects. These will be undertaken during all phases: momentum, the Teach-In itself, and follow-through. Appropriate action projects, from many presented, are being considered by several groups within the Steering Committee as well as by Teach-In Committees at the school or department level. The projects may include:

Participatory actions. Organization of groups to undertake a specific project, such as cleaning an area of litter, aid in identifying violators of pollution regulations, design, and implementation of a park area, etc. Emphasis will be placed on interdisciplinary efforts and joint community-university projects.

Demonstrations. Events intended to draw attention to particular problems are planned.

Legislation. Specific legislation at the State level will be selected (or drafted) for promotion and publicity. If possible, legislative hearings will be scheduled in Ann Arbor during the momentum effort.

Litigation. ENACT may bring suit to enjoin some prominent environmental abuse, in order to create public awareness of the law as an effective instrument for environmental action.

The Teach-In itself will culminate a growing momentum of interest and concern. It will focus this concern constructively and it will create a wide demand for continuing action programs. The follow-through from the Teach-In is planned to include the following:

The Follow-Through

Major events of the Teach-In and results of action projects will be publicized at the local, state, and national level as a demonstration of a constructive, broadly based attack on problems of the human environment.

publication of major addresses, panel discussions, and guidelines in pocketbook format for rapid and widespread distribution.

production of videotapes and tape-recordings for use in other schools and on radio and television.

Many on-going action projects and educational programs will be initiated during the momentum effort and the Teach-In itself. Continuation of these projects will be a major function of ENACT.

A major follow-through effort of ENACT will be to maintain interdisciplinary and University-community channels opened by Teach-In events.

As a permanent campus and community organization, ENACT will continue to carry out its stated goals, evolving its procedures, modes of action, and specific projects according to the circumstances. The Teach-In itself will have a major impact on guiding the future work of ENACT to meet identified needs and styles of this campus and community.

Relation to the National Teach-In

On April 22, 1970, teach-ins on the crisis of the environment will be held on many campuses and in many communities throughout the country. The University of Michigan Teach-In must precede this date, which falls after the end of classes (under the University's unusual trimester academic schedule).

ENACT is working in close coordination with the coordinating office of the national movement (Environmental Teach-In, Inc., Washington, D.C.), providing guidelines from our organizational and planning experience to help efforts elsewhere.

The March 11–14 Teach-In will explicitly serve as a keynote or prototype for the national effort to follow National press coverage, participation by as many delegates from other campuses as is possible, and distribution of evaluations of the Michigan events will serve to stimulate and guide the national effort to its maximum effectiveness.

Conclusion

The basic planning philosophy for all activities affiliated with the Teach-In—before, during, after—is to contribute to the building of informed and action-oriented public concern for the human environment. This subject matter, effectively programmed in the Teach-In and follow-through activities, is an ideal vehicle to open communications between campuses and the general citizenry. Resolving in essence to the question of human survival and the quality of human life on a planet of fragile hospitality, this is an issue which must become of far more immediate concern to all sectors of society. Only in this way will effective action be motivated through the numerous channels —economic, political, and social—which contribute to environmental misuse, and which are the necessary means to environmental improvement and protection.

The University of Michigan 1970 Teach-In on the Environment, culminating a staged effort to inform and mobilize concern, can focus public attention on constructive action. Its planned follow-through can broaden and deepen the impact, carrying this urgent issue of environmental quality, with all of its implications for human life, far closer to the concerns and self-interests of all whom it touches.

C. CONFRONTING ETHICS

51. Manipulation of Human Behavior: An Ethical Dilemma for the Social Scientist

Herbert C. Kelman*

The social scientist today—and particularly the practitioner and investigator of behavior change—finds himself in a situation that has many parallels to that of the nuclear physicist. The knowledge about the control and manipulation of human behavior that he is producing or applying is beset with enormous ethical ambiguities, and he must accept responsibility for its social consequences. Even the pure researcher cannot withdraw into the comforting assurance that knowledge is ethically neutral. While this is true as far as it goes, he must concern himself with the question of how this knowledge is *likely* to be used, given the particular historical context of the society in which it is produced. Nor can the practitioner find ultimate comfort in the assurance that he is helping others and doing good. For, not only is the goodness of doing good in itself a matter of ethical ambiguity—a point to which I shall return shortly—but he also confronts the question of the wider social context in which a given action is taken. The production of change may meet the momentary needs of the client—whether it be an individual, an organization, or a community—yet its long-range consequences and its effects on other units of the system of which this client is a part may be less clearly constructive.

There are several reasons why the ethical problems surrounding the study of behavior change are of increasing concern. First, our knowledge about the control of human behavior is increasing steadily and systematically. Relevant information is being developed in various areas within psychology—clinical, social, and experimental—as well as in sociology and anthropology. There is reason to question whether the dangers from that direction are imminent. I have the feeling that the power and sensitivity of scientifically based techniques for controlling and shaping complex human behaviors are often exaggerated. Nevertheless, we are constantly working toward a systematization of this knowledge and we must at least anticipate the day when it will have developed to a point where the conditions necessary for producing a particular change in behavior can be specified with relative precision. Second, there is an increasing readiness and eagerness within our society to use whatever systematic information (or misinformation) about the control of human behavior can be made available. This readiness can be found in different quarters and in response to different motivations. It can be found among therapists and pedagogues, among idealists and agitators, among hucksters and image-makers. Third, social scientists are becoming increasingly respectable, and

Reprinted from Herbert C. Kelman. "Manipulation of Human Behavior: An Ethical Dilemma for the Social Scientist," *Journal of Social Issues*, Vol. 21, No. 2, April 1965, pp. 31–46.

* Richard Cabot Professor of Social Ethics, Department of Social Relations, Harvard University.

many agencies within government, industry, the military, and the fields of public health and social welfare are becoming interested in our potential contributions. Here too there is no imminent danger. We still have a long way to go before becoming truly influential and we may find the road rather bumpy. Nevertheless, we must anticipate the possibility that social scientists will meet with a serious interest in their ideas about behavior control and have an opportunity to put them to the test on a large scale.

For all of these reasons, concern about the implications of our knowledge of behavior control is less and less a matter of hypothetical philosophical speculation. The possibilities are quite real that this knowledge will be used to control human behavior—with varying degrees of legitimacy, effectiveness, and scope. Moreover, this knowledge is being produced in a socio-historical context in which its use on a large scale, for the control of vast populations, is particularly likely. Ours is an age of mass societies, in which the requirements of urbanization and industrialization, together with the availability of powerful media of communication, provide all the necessary conditions for extensive manipulation and control of the behavior of masses. An interest in controlling the behavior of its population is, of course, a characteristic of every society and by no means unique to our age. What *is* unique is that this is done on a mass scale, in a systematic way, and under the aegis of specialized institutions deliberately assigned to this task. Like the nuclear physicist, then, the social scientist is responsible for knowledge that, in the light of the world situation in which it is being produced, has decided explosive possibilities. It behooves us, therefore, to be concerned with the nature of the product that we are creating and the social process to which we are contributing.

The Social Scientist's Dilemma

In their attempts to come to grips with this problem, it seems to me, the practitioner and investigator of behavior change are confronted with a basic dilemma. On the one hand, for those of us who hold the enhancement of man's freedom of choice to be a fundamental value, any manipulation of the behavior of others constitutes a violation of their essential humanity. This would be true regardless of the form the manipulation takes—whether, for example, it be based on threat of punishment or positive reinforcement. Moreover, it would be true regardless of the "goodness" of the cause that this manipulation is designed to serve. Thus, an ethical problem arises not simply from the ends for which behavior control is being used (although this, too, is a major problem in its own right), but from the very fact that we are using it. On the other hand, effective behavior change inevitably involves some degree of manipulation and control, and at least an implicit imposition of the change agent's values on the client or the person he is influencing. There are many situations in which all of us—depending on our particular values—would consider behavior change desirable: for example, childhood socialization, education, psychotherapy, racial integration, and so on. The two horns of the dilemma, then, are represented by the view that any manipulation of human behavior inherently violates a fundamental value, but that there exists no formula for so structuring an effective change situation that such manipulation is totally absent.

In calling attention to the inevitability of behavior control whenever influence is being exerted, I am not suggesting that we should avoid influence under all circumstances. This is not only impossible if there is to be any social life, but it is also undesirable from the point of view of many important social values. Nor am I suggesting that we need not worry about the manipulation inherent in all influence attempts, simply because it is inevitable. The view that we can forget about this problem, because there is nothing we can do about it anyway, ignores the fact that there are important differences in degree and kind of manipulation and that there are ways of mitigating the manipulative effect of various influence attempts even if the effect cannot be eliminated entirely.

This leads me to another very crucial qualification with respect to the first horn of the dilemma that I have presented. In stating that all manipulation of behavior, regardless of its form or of the purpose it is designed to serve, is a violation of the person's essential humanity, I am not suggesting that differences between different types of manipulation are ethically insignificant. The extent to which the influence attempt, despite its manipulative component, allows for or even enhances the person's freedom of choice, the extent to which the relationship between influencer and influencee is reciprocal, the extent to which the situation is oriented toward the welfare of the influencee rather than the welfare of the influencing agent—all of these are matters of great moment from an ethical point of view. In fact, these differences are the major concern of the present analysis. But I consider it essential, as a prophylactic measure, to keep in mind that even under the most favorable conditions manipulation of the behavior of others is an ethically ambiguous act.

It is this first horn of the dilemma that Skinner seems to ignore, as can be seen from his debate with Rogers, several years ago, on issues concerning the control of human behavior (Rogers and Skinner, 1956). Rogers, on the other hand, tends to minimize the second horn of the dilemma.

Skinner is well aware of the inevitability of control in human affairs, and argues for a type of control that is based on intelligent planning and positive reinforcement and is not "exercised for the selfish purposes of the controller" (p. 1057). He makes a number of telling points in responding to his critics. For example, he reminds us that, while we object to external controls, we often ignore psychological constraints that limit freedom of choice to the same or an even greater extent. He asks why a state of affairs that would otherwise seem admirable becomes objectionable simply because someone planned it that way. He points out that control based on the threat and exercise of punishment, which is built into our political and legal institutions, is fully ac-

by government is regarded with suspicion. I find these and other points useful because cepted, but that use of positive reinforcement they help us to focus on forms of control that often remain unrecognized and to consider forms of control that may be ethically superior to current ones but that we tend to reject because of their unorthodox nature. But Skinner fails to see the basis of many of the criticisms directed at him, because he is concerned about the control of human behavior only when that control is aversive, and when it is misused, that is, when it is used for the benefit of the controller and to the detriment of the controllee. He seems unable to see any problem in the mere *use* of control, regardless of technique or purpose. This inability is consistent with his value position, which does not recognize the exercise of choice as a good per se.[1]

My own statement of the first horn of the dilemma is predicated on the assumption that the freedom and opportunity to choose is a fundamental value. To be fully human means to choose. Complete freedom of choice is, of course, a meaningless concept. But the purpose of education and of the arrangement of the social order, as I see it, is to enable men to live in society while at the same time enhancing their freedom to choose and widening their areas of choice. I therefore regard as ethically ambigious any action that limits freedom of choice, whether it be through punishment or reward or even through so perfect an arrangement of society that people do not care to choose. I cannot defend this value because it is not logically derived from anything else. I can, of course, offer supporting arguments for it. First, I can try to show that the desire to choose represents a universal human need, which manifests itself under different historical circumstances (not only under conditions of oppression). Second, I can point out that freedom of choice is an inescapable component of other valued states, such as love, creativity, mastery over the environment, or maximization of one's capacities. Third, I can try

[1] This in turn is related to a point stressed by Rogers, namely Skinner's underestimation of the role of value choices in human affairs in general and in the application of science to social problems in particular.

to argue that valuing free individual choice is a vital protection against tyranny: Quite aside from the notion that power corrupts its user, even the well-motivated, unselfish controlling agent will be tempted to ignore human variability and to do what *he* thinks is good for others rather than what they think is good for themselves—and thus in essence become tyrannical—if he is unhampered by the right to choose as a basic human value. While I can offer these supporting arguments, I recognize that freedom of choice is, in the final analysis, a rock-bottom value for me. Skinner is not concerned with the dilemma presented here because apparently he does not share this fundamental value, even though he is strongly committed to certain other related values, such as the rejection of aversive control and selfish exploitation (albeit without recognizing their status as values).

With Rogers on the other hand, I feel a complete affinity at the value level. He values "man as a self-actualizing process of becoming" and in general proposes that "we select a set of values that focuses on fluid elements of process rather than static attributes" (p. 1063). He favors a society "where individuals carry responsibility for personal decisions" (p. 1064). He regards "responsible personal choice" as "the most essential element in being a person" (p. 1064). But, as I have pointed out, Rogers tends to minimize the second horn of the dilemma presented here: the inevitability of some degree of manipulation in any influence attempt. He makes what appears to me the unrealistic assumption that by choosing the proper goals and the proper techniques in an influence situation one can completely sidestep the problem of manipulation and control. He seems to argue that, when an influencing agent is dedicated to the value of man as a self-actualizing process and selects techniques that are designed to promote this value, he can abrogate his power over the influencee and maintain a relationship untainted by behavior control. This ignores, in my opinion, the dynamics of the influence situation itself. I fully agree that influence attempts designed to enhance the client's freedom of choice and techniques that are consistent with

this goal are ethically superior, and that we should continue to push and explore in this direction. But we must remain aware that the nature of the relationship between influencing agent and influencee is such that inevitably, even in these influence situations, a certain degree of control will be exercised. The assumption that we can set up an influence situation in which the problem of manipulation of behavior is removed, because of the stated purpose and formal structure of the situation, is a dangerous one. It makes us blind to the continuities between all types of influence situations and to the subtle ways in which others can be manipulated. It lulls us into the reassuring certainty that what we are doing is, by definition, good. I would regard it as more in keeping with both the realities of behavior change, and the ethical requirements of minimizing manipulation, to accept the inevitability of a certain amount of control as part of our dilemma and to find a *modus vivendi* in the face of the ethical ambiguities thus created.

Manipulative Uses of Knowledge

Let me proceed to examine briefly the implications of this general dilemma for each of three roles involving social science knowledge about behavior change: the practitioner, as exemplified by the psychotherapist and the group leader or group process trainer; the applied researcher, such as the social scientist in industry or the public opinion pollster; and the basic researcher, such as the investigator of attitude change. These roles are, of course, highly overlapping, but separating them may help us focus on different nuances of the general dilemma.

The Practitioner

The practitioner must remain alert to the possibility that he is imposing his own values on the client; that in the course of helping the client he is actually shaping his behavior in directions that he, the practitioner, has set for him. Thus, psychotherapy, even though it is devoted to what I would consider a highly valuable end—enabling the patient to live more comfortably and achieve his own goals more effectively—is definitely open to the possibility of manipulation. Psychotherapy (at least "good" psychotherapy) is markedly different from brainwashing: the client enters into the relationship voluntarily; the therapist is concerned with helping the patient, rather than with furthering his own ends or the ends of some institution that he represents; influence techniques are designed to free the patient, to enhance his ability to make choices, rather than to narrow his scope. Yet there are some striking similarities between the methods of therapy and those of brainwashing to which the therapist must always remain alert, lest he overstep what is sometimes a rather thin line. The therapist cannot avoid introducing his own values into the therapeutic process. He cannot be helpful to the patient unless he deliberately tries to influence him in the direction of abandoning some behaviors and trying out others. But in doing so he must beware of two types of dangers. One is the failure to recognize that he is engaged in the control of the client's behavior. The other is intoxication with the goodness of what he is doing for and to the client, which in turn leads to a failure to recognize the ambiguity of the control that he exercises. Only if he recognizes these two conditions is he able to take steps to counteract them.

Similar considerations hold for the group leader. Some of the principles of group leadership developed by social psychologists and variously called applied group dynamics, human relations skills, or group process sensitivity are highly congenial to democratic values. They are designed to involve the group in the decision-making process and to foster self-expression on the part of the individual member. Yet the possibilities for manipulation abound. A skillful group leader may be able not only to manipulate the group into making the decision that he desires, but also to create the feeling that this decision reflects the will of the group discovered through the workings of the democratic process. This need not involve a deliberate Machiavellian deception on the part of the group leader; the leader himself may share the illusion that a group product has emerged over which he has exercised no

influence. It is essential, therefore, to be fully aware of the leader's control implicit in these techniques. Some of their proponents argue that, by their very nature, these techniques can be used only for democratic ends. I would question this assumption and, in fact, consider it dangerous because it exempts the group leader from asking those questions that any practitioner of behavior change should keep before his eyes: What am I doing in my relationship to the client? Am I creating a situation in which he can make choices in line with his own values, or am I structuring the situation so that my values dominate?

When the group leader is involved in training others in human relations skills or sensitivity to group process, he is confronted with a further problem. Typically, the trainee is a member of some organization—industrial, governmental, military, educational, religious —in which he will apply the skills he is now learning. The human relations trainer is, thus, in a sense improving the trainee's ability to manipulate others in the service of the organization that he represents. Of course, this is not the goal of the training effort, and trainers always try to communicate the value of the democratic process in group life. But the fact remains that they are training a wide variety of people who will be using these skills for a wide variety of ends. It can certainly be argued that the widespread introduction of human relations skills is likely to have more positive than negative effects from the point of view of a democratic ideology. Perhaps this is true. But it is dangerous to assume that these skills carry their own built-in protection. There is no substitute for a continued attention, on the trainer's part, to questions such as these: Whom am I training? To what uses will they put the skills that I am placing at their disposal? What are the organizational processes in which I am now becoming a partner?

The Applied Researcher

It is essentially these same questions to which the applied social researcher in the broad field of behavior change must address himself. I am here thinking specifically of applied research in the sense that it is done for a client. While the researcher is merely gathering facts, he is nonetheless participating quite directly in the operations of the organization that employs him. If his work is successful, then his findings will be applied to the formulation and execution of the organization's policies. There is thus the real possibility that the investigator is directly helping the organization in its attempts to manipulate the behavior of others—workers in an industry, consumers, or the voting public.

Let us take, for example, the industrial social scientist who studies factors affecting worker morale. On the basis of his recommendations, and often with his direct assistance, management may become more aware of human relations aspects of industrial work and introduce methods designed to improve morale. Ideally, these methods would consist of increased involvement and participation of workers in decisions relating to their jobs. Critics of this type of approach argue that the social scientist is working for management, providing them with information and introducing procedures that are designed to increase productivity at the worker's expense. The assumption in this criticism, to which I think there is some validity, is that the worker is being manipulated so that he experiences a sense of participation and involvement which is not reflected in the reality of his position within the industrial organization. In response to this criticism it can be argued that, considering the over-all lack of satisfaction in industrial work, it is a net good to give the worker some sense of participation and involvement in the work situation, to give him at least a limited opportunity to make choices and thus find some meaning in the job. To be sure, management is interested in these innovations because they expect the changes to increase productivity, but does that necessarily vitiate the advantages from the worker's point of view? This is a rather convincing defense, but in evaluating the pros and cons we must also take into account the social context in which these changes are introduced. What effect does the human relations approach have on unions, which represent the only source of independent power of the industrial worker?

Does it sidestep them, and will it eventually weaken them? What are the general implications of helping the worker adjust to a situation in which he has no real freedom of choice, in any ultimate sense? These questions are not easy to answer, and every social scientist has to decide for himself whether his work in industry is doing more good than harm. In deciding whether or not, and in what way, to do applied social research in industry or elsewhere, the social scientist must ask himself: Whom am I doing this work for? How are my findings likely to be used? Will they increase or decrease the freedom of choice of the people whose behavior will be influenced? What are the social processes, both short-run and long-run, in which I am participating through my research?

Another example of applied social research that raises questions about manipulation of the population is public opinion polling, when used in connection with political campaigns or the political process in general. For instance, in a recent presidential election, computer simulation was used—based on data derived from numerous opinion polls—to predict the responses of various segments of the population to different campaign issues. Information generated by this process was made available to one of the political parties. This type of social research has some troubling implications. It raises the possibility that a candidate might use this information to manipulate the voters by presenting a desirable image, that is, saying what the public presumably wants to hear. In defense against such criticisms, the originators of this technique have pointed out that it represents a systematic way of providing the candidate with relevant information about the interests and concerns of the public, or of particular publics. He can then address himself to those issues with which the public is deeply concerned, thus making his campaign more relevant and meaningful and enhancing the democratic political process. They point out further that this is what candidates try to do anyway—and properly so; all the social scientist does is to help them base their campaigns on more adequate information, rather than on the usually unreliable estimates of politicians. Of course, what assurance do we have that opinion polls and computer simulations based on them will, in fact, be used in this ideal manner to bolster the democratic process, rather than to short-circuit it? The information can be used both to widen and to restrict the citizen's freedom of choice. But, as long as it is information that can help political organizations to manipulate the public more effectively, the researcher must concern himself actively with the question of how it is going to be used and to what kind of process it is going to contribute.

The Basic Researcher

For the man engaged in "basic" research on one or another aspect of behavior change—in contrast to the man who does research for a specific client—it is much easier to take the position that the knowledge he produces is neutral. Yet, since there is a possibility that his product will be used by others for purposes of manipulation, he cannot be completely absolved from responsibility. He must consider the relative probabilities, given the existing socio-historical context, that this knowledge will be used to enhance or to restrict people's freedom of choice. These considerations must enter into his decision whether or not to carry out a given piece of research, and how to proceed with it.

Take, for example, the area of attitude change, with which I myself am strongly identified. Much of the research in this area is clearly dedicated to the discovery of general principles, which can presumably be applied to many situations with differing goals. Yet, because of the nature of the principles and the experimental settings from which they are derived, they can probably be applied most readily, most directly, and most systematically to mass communications. And, because of the nature of our social order, they are particularly likely to be used for purposes of advertising, public relations, and propaganda, forms of mass communication that are least oriented toward enhancing the listener's freedom of choice. There are, of course, many reasons for continuing this line of research, despite the probability that its findings will be used for

manipulative purposes. First, one can argue that extending our general knowledge about processes of attitude change and increasing our understanding of the nature of influence are in themselves liberating forces whose value outweighs the possibility that this knowledge will be used for undesirable ends. Second, such research may not only increase the knowledge of the potential manipulator, but also help in finding ways to counteract manipulative forces, by providing the information needed for effective resistance to manipulation, or by developing knowledge about forms of influence that enhance freedom of choice. Third, one might argue that information about attitude change, despite its potential for manipulative uses, is important for the achievement of certain socially desirable goals, such as racial integration or international understanding.

I obviously find these arguments convincing enough to continue this line of research. But the nagging thought remains that the knowledge I am producing, if it has any scientific merit, may come to be used for ever more effective manipulation of human behavior. Thus, even the basic researcher in the domain of behavior change must always ask himself: Given the realities of our present society, what are the probable uses to which the products of my research are going to be put? What are the social processes to which I am contributing by the knowledge that I feed into them?

Mitigating the Manipulative Aspects of Behavior Change

The very fact that I have presented my position in the form of a dilemma should make it clear that I do not see an ultimate "solution," a way of completely avoiding the ethical ambiguity with which practitioners and researchers in the field of behavior change are confronted. I do feel, however, that there are ways of mitigating the dehumanizing effects of new developments in the field of behavior change. I would like to propose three steps designed to contribute to this end. Stated in their most general form, they would involve: (1) increasing our own and others' active awareness of the manipulative aspects of our work and the ethical ambiguities inherent therein; (2) deliberately building protection against manipulation or resistance to it into the processes we use or study; and (3) setting the enhancement of freedom of choice as a central positive goal for our practice and research. To spell out in somewhat greater detail what these three steps might imply, I would like to examine them from the point of view of each of the three separate (though overlapping) roles that have already been differentiated: the role of the practitioner, of the applied researcher, and of the "basic" researcher in the field of behavior change. The argument that follows is summarized in Table 51.1.

The Practitioner

I have already stressed how essential it is for the practitioner of behavior change to be aware of the fact that he is controlling the client, that he is introducing his own values both in the definition of the situation and in the setting of standards. Thus, in the therapeutic situation, it is not only inevitable but also useful for the therapist to have certain values about what needs to be done in the situation itself and what are desirable directions in which the patient might move, and to communicate these values to the patient. But he must be clear in his own mind that he is bringing these values into the relationship, and he must label them properly for the patient. By recognizing himself that he is engaged in a certain degree of control—and that

this is an ethically ambiguous act, even though his role as therapist requires it—and by making the patient aware of this fact, he provides some safeguards against this control. Among other things, such a recognition would allow the patient, to a limited extent, to "talk back" to the therapist, to argue about the appropriateness of the values that the therapist is introducing. A therapeutic situation is, of course, not a mutual influence situation in the true sense of the word. By definition, it is designed to examine only the patient's values and not those of the therapist. But, from the point of view of reducing the manipulativeness of the situation, it would be important to encourage mutuality at least to the extent of acknowledging that what the therapist introduces into the situation is not entirely based on objective reality, but on an alternative set of values which are open to question. There may be particular therapeutic relationships in which a therapist finds it difficult to acknowledge the values that he brings to them, because his own motivations have become too deeply involved. There may also be institutional settings in which the therapist is required to present the institutional values as the "right" ones, in contrast to the patient's own "wrong" values. These are danger signals, and the therapist may well consider refraining from entering a therapeutic relationship or working in an institutional setting in which he is not free to acknowledge the contribution of his own values.

Second, in addition to increasing awareness

TABLE 51.1 Steps Designed to Mitigate the Manipulative Aspects of Behavior Change in Each of Three Social Science Roles

Desirable Steps	*Practitioner*	*Applied Researcher*	*Basic Researcher*
(1) Increasing awareness of manipulation	Labeling own values to self and clients; allowing client to "talk back"	Evaluating organization that will use findings; considering how, on whom, and in what context they will be used	Predicting probabilities of different uses of research product, given existing socio-historical context
(2) Building protection against or resistance to manipulation into the process	Minimizing own values and maximizing client's values as dominant criteria for change	Helping target group to protect its interests and resist encroachments on its freedom	Studying processes of resistance to control, and communicating findings to the public
(3) Setting enhancement of freedom of choice as a positive goal	Using professional skills and relationship to increase client's range of choices and ability to choose	Promoting opportunities for increased choice on part of target group as integral features of the planned change	Studying conditions for enhancement of freedom of choice and maximization of individual values

of the manipulative aspects of the situation, it is important to build into the change process itself procedures that will provide protection and resistance against manipulation. For the practitioner of behavior change this means structuring the influence situation in such a way that the client will be encouraged to explore his own values and to relate new learnings and new behavioral possibilities to his own value system. At the same time, it is important that the practitioner, be he therapist or group leader, keep to a minimum the direct and indirect constraints that he sets on the influencee. Constraints are, of course, necessary to varying degrees, both for the protection of clients and for keeping the process moving in useful directions. Insofar as possible, however, the situation should be so structured that the influencee determines the direction of the process to a maximal extent. It should be noted that what I am suggesting here is not the same as the use of nondirective techniques. In and of themselves these merely represent a set of formal techniques which may or may not have the desired effect. The crucial point is that the client's own values should be at the center of attention when change is under consideration and should be readily available as criteria against which any induced behavior can be measured. To the extent to which this is true, the patient or the group will be in a better position to resist manipulation in the service of alien values. Often, however, this will require much more than noninterference on the part of the practitioner. It may require active efforts on his part to encourage the client to bring his values to the fore and measure the induced changes against them.

Third, it is important to go beyond providing protection and resistance against manipulation that would encroach on the client's freedom of choice. The actual *enhancement* of freedom of choice should, ideally, be one of the positive goals of any influence attempt. Thus, the terapist should use his professional skills and his relationship to the patient to provide him with new experiences that enhance his ability to choose (and thus to maximize his own values) and with new information that widens his range of choices. Similarly, the group leader should attempt to bring the group to a point where members can make more effective and creative choices, conducive to the achievement of individual and group goals. The enhancement of freedom and creativity as the positive value toward which behavior change should be directed has been discussed most eloquently by Rogers (for example, Rogers and Skinner, 1956).

Needless to say, it would be essential to include in the training of practitioners of behavior change and in their professional standards some consideration of these three desiderata for mitigating the manipulative aspects of their activities. If they learn to acknowledge the role of their own values in the situation, to make active efforts at keeping the client's values in the foreground, and to regard increased freedom of choice as a primary goal, they are less likely to make full use, either unwittingly or by design, of the potential for manipulation that they possess.

The Applied Researcher

In deciding whether to take on a particular piece of research, the applied researcher must keep in mind that the information he is being asked to supply may be used for the manipulation of others, for example, workers in an industry for whom he is doing a morale survey or the voting public if he is working with poll data. The question of *who* is employing him becomes crucial, therefore. He must evaluate the organizations that will be using his findings, and consider how they are likely to use them, whose behavior they will attempt to influence, and in what context this influence will occur. He must consider the probable uses of these findings not only in the short run but also in the long run. Thus, for example, he cannot simply rely on the fact that his contact man in an organization is someone he trusts. If this man is in a peripheral position within the organization, and if the organization is generally undemocratic and exploitative in its orientation, then the long-run prospects are not too reassuring. There is, of course, the possibility that the research itself will have a liberalizing effect on the organization; the probability that this will, in fact, happen must also be estimated. In the final analysis, there can be no foolproof guarantees, but the investigator must at least feel reasonably certain that the net effect of his research will not be a reduction in the freedom of choice of a segment of the population. Each investigator has to draw his own line, with respect to both the probability and the amount of manipulation that he is willing to tolerate. If they are likely to go beyond this line, then he must consider turning down the assignment. Once a researcher has decided to take on an assignment, he must continue to keep the manipulative potential of his findings in mind, and try to counteract it by the way he communicates his findings and the recommendations he bases on them. If his research is, indeed, to have a liberalizing effect on the organization, then he will have to take active steps in this direction.

In order to build some protection against manipulation into the change procedures based on his findings, the researcher should make it a rule to communicate directly with the target group—the group that is to be influenced—and to involve it in the research and in the change process insofar as he has charge of it. Thus, an industrial social scientist employed by management might insist on informing the workers in detail about the purposes and findings of the research and the attempted changes that are likely to result from it. In giving them this information, he would try to help them protect their interests against undue attempts at manipulation and to offer them specific recommendations for resisting encroachments on their freedom of choice. Furthermore, in order to promote freedom of choice as a positive goal, he should make a concerted effort to influence the planned change that will be based on his research so that it will actually leave the target group with greater choice than it had before. In submitting his findings and recommendations to the organization that contracted for the research, he should actively seek and point up opportunities for enhancing freedom of choice on the part of the target group that can be integrated into the planned change.

The two last points both imply a rather active role for the researcher in the planning of change based on his research. I would not want to say that the researcher must always participate directly in the change process itself; there are many times when this would be impossible or inappropriate. But since he is providing information that will, at least in principle, be directly translated into action, it is his responsibility to take some stand with respect to this action. The uses to which the information is put are not only the problem of the contracting organization, but also very much the problem of the man who supplied the information. The researcher should be clear about this, and he should have the support of his profession when he takes an active part in expressing his point of view.

The Basic Researcher

Let me finally, and more briefly, turn to the basic researcher. I have already stated my position that, even though the products of pure research are in a sense neutral, the investigator cannot escape responsibility for their probable consequences. The student of attitude change, for example, must keep in mind that his findings can be used for the systematic manipulation of the population, in ways and for purposes that would produce a net constriction in freedom of choice. In deciding whether or not to proceed with his research, he must try to make some estimate of the probabilities of different uses of his research product, in the light of existing social forces. If he expects restrictive uses to outweigh constructive ones, he would be bound to refrain from engaging in this research. If, on balance, he decides to undertake the research—and there are, of course, many good reasons for doing so—then he must continue to remain alert to its manipulative potential, and must constantly review his decision, particularly as his research emphases shift or as social conditions change.

Researchers in this area also have a special responsibility to be actively concerned with the ways in which the knowledge they produce is used by various agencies in their society. Eternal vigilance to the possibilities of manipulation is, of course, the duty of every citizen. But, as producers of knowledge about manipulation, social scientists are in a position similar to that of the many nuclear physicists who feel a *special* sense of responsibility for the ways in which their knowledge is being used.

Earlier, I suggested that research on attitude change may not only increase the knowledge of the potential manipulator, but also help in finding ways to counteract manipulative forces. So far, research along these lines has been rather limited. If investigators of attitude change and related problems are to mitigate the manipulative potential of their research, they will have to focus more deliberately and more actively on this other line of work. Thus, in order to build some protection against manipulation into the social structure, we will have to extend our research on processes of resistance to control and make a spe-

cial effort to communicate relevant findings to the public. Such an emphasis will contribute to the development of antidotes against manipulation at the same time that research is contributing to the development of knowledge about manipulation itself. From a scientific point of view, such work will be highly germane to the study of attitude change, since it represents an exploration of its limiting conditions.

In order to promote the enhancement of freedom of choice as a positive goal, research will have to focus on the conditions favoring a person's ability to exercise choice and to maximize his individual values. Admittedly, this is a rather value-laden way of stating a problem for basic research. However, if we want our science to contribute to the liberation of man rather than to his dehumanization, this is the kind of problem to which we will have to turn our attention.

References

Rogers, Carl R., and B. F. Skinner. "Some issues concerning the control of human behavior," *Science*, 124 (1956), 1057–1066.

52. Intervening in the Affairs of Others

David Hapgood* • Meridan Bennett*

Visionaries, saints and ascetics, Thoreau led us to hope, cock their ears for the beat of a different drummer. The revolutionary leaders of today certainly follow a different cadence, believing as they do that the huge army of the downtrodden will set the pace for our times.

American civilization, bewitched by its own rhythm, the Big Beat of affluence, is most concerned to protect what it has and will most probably not support the drastic steps needed to create an equal environment of plenty in the third world—this, at any rate, is the gloomy conclusion of economist Robert Heilbroner (in the April 1967 *Commentary*). Whether one concurs with Heilbroner or not, it is a fact that from the midpoint of the twen-

tieth century onward the United States has been intervening in the affairs of other nations with ever-increasing energy. The Peace Corps is part of that movement. It has involved itself in other countries deliberately to effect some kind of change. What kind of change, and where it should be applied, has been one of the most argued-over and elusive aspects of the agency.

In point of fact, the Peace Corps Act makes no mention of directed change. But few, if any, Peace Corps volunteers follow the doctrine that they are working overseas merely to observe new, exotic ways of life, and that their jobs are not intended in some way to work changes in the countries that are their hosts.

Reprinted from David Hapgood and Meridan Bennett, *Agents of Change* (Boston: Little, Brown, 1968), pp. 23–42. Copyright © by David Hapgood and Meridan Bennett. By permission of D.C.: National Training Laboratories, 1966).

° Affiliation not determined.

Certainly no program proposal submitted by field offices around the world to Washington headquarters takes that line. The idea of doing something positive and concrete to effect change and to solve problems in the third world is an implicit assumption of almost everything the Peace Corps has done.

An example: there is a Latin American site containing three volunteers who have labored long and hard to bring a cooperative into existence. The cooperative's members are highland Indians, historically suppressed and exploited by the local mestizos (people of mixed ancestry). The country program under which the three volunteers work originated when the host country and the United States Government signed an instrument, called in diplomatic terms a bilateral agreement, indicating mutual desire to establish a group of American volunteers in the country for the purposes described under the Peace Corps Act. The agreement specified that the volunteers were coming to the host country at its invitation and were to work under programs of the inviting government, with no protections and immunities other than those provided any citizen of that country. On the face of it, the agreement bore no note of compulsion on the part of the United States nor submission on the part of the host country. In this sense the presence of the Peace Corps in that country could not be called "intervention" under international law.

Yet what the volunteers were doing in their remote village must certainly be called interference in the affairs of that forgotten, static community. One of them was articulate on the point: "We're not just here for the good of our souls. We're here to change things. Ninety percent of the people here have no political voice. The few mestizos around are not prevented from gouging them in any way they want. The co-op helps the Indians do something about it."

Despite the punctilious appearance of non-intervention in the official documents, *de facto* intervention is a fair description of the Peace Corps work at almost any volunteer site

around the world. Among the officials in Washington who plan the agency's overseas work, the talk is all about the Peace Corps as a more effective agency of directed change. Arguments rage over whether to favor measurable impact over "intangible" or longer-term benefits to the host countries, but never over whether the Peace Corps should be involved in promoting change in the first place.

The kind of change the Peace Corps might achieve is not easily measured. When AID invests dollars in a project, the economic return on the investment can be calculated. But the Peace Corps creates an intensely personal encounter between volunteers and the people of the third world, and therefore it is working in the much less tangible field of human development. If we are to understand both the peril and the promise of Peace Corps intervention, we must first of all have some understanding of the human environment into which the volunteers are sent.

Despite the endless variety of the third world, ranging from a peaceful African village to the seething slums of Calcutta, poverty imposes some general realities upon the human condition.

The characteristics of the human beings who live in isolation from the means to realize their potential are recognizable anywhere in the world as the heart of the syndrome of poverty: dependency, suspicion, hostility, personal inadequacy. The victim of the syndrome often sees his very survival as beyond his control. The good things in his world appear to him to be strictly limited.[1] This is his economics: the pie is fixed in size; all one can do is to redivide it. He is not motivated to achieve, because by achieving he cuts someone else out of the good, and his society has developed stringent penalties against meddling with the general welfare. As a result, he is suspicious of the people he has grown up with, unwilling to extend them confidence enough to cooperate in mutually beneficial projects, often even too suspicious to place confidence in members of his own family, the last refuge of the isolated man. He meets the

[1] Anthropologist George M. Foster calls this viewpoint the "image of limited good."

outside world with hostility, and frequently the familiar world as well. In dealing with the problems of making a living, of providing shelter and food, of learning to be responsible enough to keep that job, he displays a personal inadequacy which he often articulates in defense of his dependency. Hope is a luxury he cannot afford.

The men who control the institutions under which he lives often exploit him; or, if they actually seek to improve his lot, are incapable of dealing with the complexities of his situation. Malnutrition and disease weaken his ability to perform effectively in a world that increasingly demands effectiveness. These characteristics of poverty prevent the ordinary man of the poor nations from dealing with forces outside himself, which, in the twentieth century, bear in upon him with ever-accelerating speed, worsening his situation and building higher barriers from year to year against his chances for solving his problems.

Whatever security he may have—a certain amount of solidarity in the community immediately surrounding him, the feeling of predictability that a static culture provides, a system of paternalism that denies him choice in his affairs yet shields him from anxiety by removing the need to choose—is being eroded by his inability to deal with forces bearing from the outside. These forces are numerous and often subtle: the ability to read (his father could not), intimations of new and disturbing ideas, the availability of manufactured goods (his father used only what he could make or barter), the existence of roads, the cinema with its fantastic view of pseudo-life, the transistor radio. In most communities where the Peace Corps works, these forces are a fact, and their compound effect is to make the resident of those communities suffer the increasing disintegration of his social fabric.

Change is a threat. The citizen of the underdeveloped world tends to be inflexible, to resist that which is new. If, in fact, the character patterns of people in developing countries had already evolved sufficiently to make change a positive value (as in our culture, where New! Just Out! The Latest Thing! sells everything from religion to razor blades),

there would be little need for a Peace Corps. New technology would be easily absorbed—cows would be vaccinated, fertilizer applied, water boiled, medicare a blooming fact, and zip-top pop waiting in the gloaming.

Change in this century comes unbidden, a disturbing intruder in the midst of traditional, static people whose personalities, formed by tradition, cause them to resist change until poverty becomes a culture of its own. Often the very strangeness, to Westerners, of their personalities causes Americans to characterize them as shiftless, irresponsible, dishonest, ungrateful, and a hundred other adjectives denoting inferiority. Obviously for middle-class Americans to work with sympathy and understanding in such an environment requires the deliberate acquisition of a relative attitude toward culture. The alternative is contempt covered by a mask of charity.

Do Americans have any right to thrust themselves into distant societies so different from their own? In the past the United States, like other great powers, has taken the right largely for granted. The idea that there is an American destiny to intervene in the affairs of others is deeply rooted in the culture, even though the United States has never made an attempt to win a worldwide empire. One has but to review the history of American relations within the Western Hemisphere, or in Asia, or the history of church missions, or, indeed, of America's vigorous and often violent westward expansion to the Pacific, to find this predominant urge in our society. American interventions, from the River Platte to the Mekong Delta, are a matter of record which moments of isolationism and retreat into Fortress America have not obscured. Not all interventions have involved United States troops. Some, like Crossroads Africa and the International Voluntary Service, have been pace-setters for the Peace Corps. Others, originating in the gray areas of government which lie beyond public scrutiny, have suddenly surfaced from the shadows in disaster, like the Bay of Pigs invasion of Cuba. Still others, equally clandestine but less spectacularly disastrous, have toppled regimes from Guatemala to Iran to Saigon. Though the term "Manifest Destiny" was abandoned many years ago, the thrust behind it was never more manifest than during the Presidency of Lyndon B. Johnson, who took office in the Peace Corps' third year.

The motives that have impelled America's interventions in the affairs of others have been varied and, often, unacknowledged. Some, like the Marine forays in the Caribbean of half a century ago, have been crassly economic: the collecting of United States bank loans. The political-military rationale for American cold-war ventures like the Bay of Pigs and Vietnam is familiar. Other forms of intervention have been for professed ethical reasons, as with the saintly, guilt-ridden efforts of Christian missionaries to stop people from eating each other in Borneo. The mixture of morality, self-interest and self-delusion that has characterized so much of this intervention —and which is a clear warning to such a venture as the Peace Corps—is easily discerned in the foreign policy of President Woodrow Wilson. In *We Give to Conquer*, a critique of American aid, Asher Brynes cites this description of that great idealist and great meddler: "In a program of moral imperialism President Wilson placed the weight of the United States behind a continuous, sometimes devious effort to force the Mexican nation to meet his ill-conceived specifications. Though he oozed sympathy, good will and idealism, his basic misunderstanding of the main elements of life in the southern republic brought disaster in its train."

The Peace Corps is a new form of American intervention. Any opinion of the Peace Corps is bound to be colored, therefore, by one's opinion as to the legitimacy of American intervention in general. Is it part of the American power fantasy to assume that we should—or can—direct the modernization of the world, when this inevitably would mean imposing or promoting American qualities of mind and spirit along with American technology? Whenever the United States sends people or money into another society, the act is tinged with imperialism, however mild. Questioning the purpose of American efforts abroad can be painful; the Peace Corps experience has forced many to do just that. Volunteers have

asked, on occasion, if there is really a difference, except in degree, between dropping napalm on Vietnamese to convert them to our form of politics and dropping Peace Corps teachers on Africans to convert them to our form of education. Though the question implies greater conscious intent than the Peace Corps had in its early days, it nonetheless indicates a searching appraisal of national goals.

Two extreme answers will show the range of this issue. One extreme would be to justify the imperialist mission—to update "the white man's burden." The other would be to avoid any form of intervention in other nations.

"The white man's burden" argument says: since our way of life is clearly the best and the *right* way, it is our duty to transmit it to the less fortunate parts of the world. The method involves sending the money and the teachers and the experts to convert them to our way— using, that is, all the tools by which the rich can induce the poor to do or think what the rich want. Often, such peaceful imperialism leads to a more aggressive form. Crusaders are notoriously willing to stick their swords into people who resist the benefits being offered them.

The other extreme, complete American withdrawal from the world abroad, is loaded with its own obvious absurdities. Human questions, in fact, seldom yield to such simple answers as the two extremes we have suggested. American intervention in the third world cannot be halted. Americans are part of the world dialogue. If the Peace Corps is disbanded, other and more massive forms of govenmental intervention will remain and so will the still more important intervention of private interests—missions, trade, exploitation of natural resources by American corporations.

The underdeveloped world is under continuing assaults as well from the other wealthy nations. Almost all the areas where the Peace Corps operates were once under the colonial rule of European powers. Though formerly colonized nations are independent, they frequently continue to maintain an ambiguous relationship with their former rulers. The armies are gone; but the European culture remains. That culture, particularly when its intervention is expressed through education, is generally assumed to be a "good" influence on "backward" peoples. But, on closer examination, that intervention often begins to appear irrelevant to the people's needs, at times absurd, even harmful. Peace Corps volunteers have been forced to view this sort of intervention at first hand in many nations. They have found, time and again, that things are not what they seem: that often, indeed, they are the opposite of what they seem. One example from the Peace Corps experience, admittedly an extreme case, illustrates the strange realities that can exist under a veneer of good intentions when people of one culture intervene in the affairs of another.

In an African country, a former French colony, the Peace Corps sent girl volunteers to work in adult education centers for women. The centers supposedly teach illiterate women to speak, read, and write French, to do simple arithmetic, and to acquire some basic notions of nutrition and hygiene. Most of the students are wives of local officials, themselves literate, and some earn a living trading in the local market. The centers are in small towns, and each is run by an educated African woman and a girl volunteer. To the visitor, the center seems comfortably disorganized and cheerful with the bright colors of African dresses; some women are nursing babies in class. The picture is an attractive one.

Now let us see what goes on in the center. The African teacher is conducting the class; the volunteer is assisting her. The class is reciting an arithmetic lesson, in French. The women's voices drone softly: "two plus two makes four," "five plus four makes nine," "nine plus eight makes seventeen." Then one woman answers: "two plus two makes seventeen." What's that? She says it again. Look at your paper! Before her the woman has a sheet of paper on which she has carefully drawn the arabic numerals: $2+2=4$, $5+4=9$, $9+8=17$. The woman looks down at the paper, and then she says it a third time: "two plus two makes seventeen." The African teacher corrects her sharply and moves on. But the volunteer wonders. That woman is one of the better students, and the class has been on the same

arithmetic lesson for weeks now. Besides, she sells yams in the local market. How can a market woman, of all people, say that "two plus two makes seventeen"? If she did it in the market, she'd go broke in no time.

Exactly, but she does not do it in the market. She knows perfectly well that two and two *yams* are four *yams*. In fact, she can calculate a lot faster in her head than either of her teachers, and she rarely makes a mistake—certainly not the kind she made in class. But in the market she is adding the yams on which her living depends, and she is doing it in her head, and she is working in an African number system that is based on five rather than the Arabic ten. In class, she is doing something entirely different. She is reciting a lesson she has memorized. She has learned to repeat the French phrases for "two plus two . . ." etc., and a couple of the phrases have become confused in her memory. The phrases have no numerical meaning, so she does not realize her error. She has also learned to make certain scratches on paper with her ten-cent ballpoint pen. She makes them very neatly, but she does not see a link between the "4" on the paper and the spoken foreign word for "four", nor between either "four" and four yams. Neither the scratches on the paper, nor the recited foreign phrases, have any connection with the real arithmetic of the marketplace. Similarly, she distinguishes between her written name and her "real" (spoken) name. She recites and writes her lessons because that is what the teacher tells her to do. It is how the Europeans do it. She is not unhappy. She came here out of curiosity, or to be with her friends, or because her husband said to come. Certainly she did not come to learn arithmetic, at which she is already skilled.

The African teacher makes no effort to bridge the gap between market arithmetic and written base-ten numerals. Her job is to make the women recite the lesson properly. Neither she nor her students are stupid, but they are acting out a foreign ritual that has no relevance to their lives. The host government does not appear to care either. If the men running the agency that set up the centers were concerned with teaching arithmetic, they would do it in the local language and they would begin with the difference in number systems. (Amazingly few of the foreigners involved are even aware that this number system, like many of those in Africa, is based on five.) Whether that would serve any purpose is questionable: do the women students have any need in their lives for the ability to write base-ten arithmetic?

The true purpose of the centers is to provide the woman with some of the outward symbols of "modernity." Courses are taught in French in defiance of all apparent sense because the French language is the prime symbol of modernity in nations once ruled by Paris. To the French and to many of the peoples they once ruled, it is well known that God, who is competent in all languages, speaks French by preference. In some centers, a course inaccurately called nutrition was popular. It consisted of learning to prepare and serve a meal in European style: separate plates instead of the common bowl, on the table not on the floor, utensils instead of hands, and a couple of "European" dishes. A capable and charming African teacher listed as her greatest success the European meal served by one of her students; she described it in great detail. Nothing in this feat had the slightest nutritional value, but it was of great importance to the woman, as the teacher realized. Her husband will no longer be ashamed of her: he can show off to his friends a wife who can cook and serve like the Europeans.

In retrospect, the absurdity of what was taking place in the women's centers is evident. With the complicity of both "Westernized" Africans and Europeans, the women were being offered the illusion of progress instead of its substance. Instead of whatever useful changes the West might have to offer, the women were given (and wanted) some of the status-conferring patina of the industrialized West: some writing on a pad, a few words of French, a European meal. To Americans, it is doubtless easier to detect the faults of others' interventions than of their own. (The volunteers in those centers, we should note, tried with some success to make their teaching less irrelevant, but they had no control over the

curriculum.) Time and again volunteers, and the Peace Corps itself, have been forced to search out the underlying meaning of their interventions overseas.

To return to the Latin American site where three volunteers established a co-op, it is clear that American values were imported into the town. The volunteers set out to work a fundamental change. In building a cooperative to supply fertilizer and an improved power source to Indian farmers, they grasped the problems of the day as they saw them and decided to do something concrete. The vague language of diplomatic agreements and legislative enactments did not restrict their decision to intervene. The three volunteers were the kind of people who would have felt uncomfortable in *not* doing something for others born less blessed with opportunity than they. None of the three seemed anxious to bear the "white man's burden." They did not manifest that cool sense of superiority, that aloofness, which too often separates the philanthropist from the philanthropized. Yet in assisting the Indians of the town the volunteers demonstrated a narrowness of cultural vision which prejudiced their efforts. In the first place, they did not make a thorough study of the town. They believed that an agricultural co-op was needed regardless of local circumstances. Had they done their research, they would have discovered that two of the town's mestizos had interests that were being threatened. Had they studied the potential membership of the co-op they would have discovered an almost complete lack of managerial ability. Further, they would have learned that a tractor was far too sophisticated a piece of machinery to be maintained by Indians whose only previous motive power had been their hands. They would therefore have been able to anticipate the amount of training in accountancy, literacy, cooperative management, and mechanical skills that would have been needed to get a rather complex agricultural cooperative off the ground. As it turned out, the volunteers had to carry the whole weight of the co-op on their own shoulders. Thus they inadvertently found themselves carrying—if not the white man's—at least a Peace Corps burden. While the Indians may have obtained some momentary benefit from the co-op, the pattern of their lives was not changed from the centuries-old habit of dependence on and subservience to a dominating outsider. In fact, though the volunteers scarcely realized it, they had stepped in and filled the role of *patron* to this new endeavor, thereby providing yet another demonstration to the Indians of their inability to function without a beneficent and all-powerful master to dictate the conditions of their lives.

In the headlong early days of the Peace Corps, the ambiguities of intervention troubled few if any of those involved. The issues of foreign policy seemed much simpler in those days. There was good and bad in the world, and the American mission was to use the nation's awesome power to combat the bad and help the good people who needed help. Young Americans could do both through the Peace Corps. They were a kind of "good seed" to be sown overseas. In 1961, then-Senator Hubert H. Humphrey said that the Peace Corps "is to be a part of the total foreign policy of the United States . . . to combat the virus of Communist totalitarianism." Secretary of State Dean Rusk added, rather cryptically, that "to make the Peace Corps an instrument of foreign policy would be to rob it of its contribution to foreign policy." The Peace Corps, it seemed, was to win cold-war votes for the United States, but by some undefined methods differing from traditional diplomacy and military action.

The early view of the volunteers' contribution to the people among whom they were to live was best expressed by a Carmack cartoon that first appeared in *The Christian Science Monitor*, then was reproduced in the influential 1961 Colorado State University Research Foundation study of Peace Corps possibilities, *New Frontiers for American Youth*. The cartoon shows a crew-cut youth with a determined but slightly vacuous expression striding out across the globe in the direction indicated by a sign which says: "BATTLE AGAINST HUNGER, INEXPERIENCE, AND APATHY." In his hands the cartoon figure, labeled "U. S. Peace Corps," is carrying standard American hand

tools: shovel, rake, pitchfork, square, saw. One thing was certain: this husky youth in work clothes was going to start out by building things and mucking about in the soil. It was almost as though this American were some kind of god who must return to the earth periodically to replenish his vitality. But how was all this to help the people of the third world? Were Americans to take over all the world's underproductive farms and replace all its hovels with split-levels? The Carmack cartoon seemed to suggest this. To a potential volunteer who did not have the ability to use the tools represented in the cartoon, and most did not, the Peace Corps looked to be an undertaking far beyond his skill. For the official of the Peace Corps who had to make decisions about priorities in assigning volunteers, the agency appeared to wallow in confusion between the problems of building things and the problems of human organization. For the citizen of the third world, this U. S. Peace Corps giant might represent the threat of a new colonialism—an attempt to reconstruct replicas of America abroad. The cartoon was titled, "To Wage a Better Kind of War." It predicted with unconscious accuracy the ironies and ambiguities that would confound the Peace Corps.

Sargent Shriver's policy of rapid expansion, and the easy optimism of the agency's founders, propelled the Peace Corps feet-first into hundreds of exotic situations in those first years. Americans are impressed with size, and the Peace Corps itself seemed to be driven by a need to have as many volunteers as possible in as many places as possible. Each of these places was the site of an experiment in American intervention.

Soon results began flowing into Washington from those experiments. The greatest source of internal criticism in the Peace Corps from the beginning was the volunteers themselves (a source denied AID, for wasted dollars do not complain). Highly motivated and prone to question authority, the volunteers were vocal in their criticisms of what the Peace Corps was doing. More than anyone else, it was the volunteer at the grassroots who questioned the premises of American intervention in the third world. Shriver himself encouraged wide-ranging criticism of everything and everyone, including himself. An important channel of volunteer opinion was the Division of Evaluation, which sent critically minded men into the field to interview volunteers and bring their opinions to the attention of the Washington bureaucracy.

The rapid growth of the Peace Corps was the target of widespread volunteer criticism under Shriver. In the Philippines, Ethiopia, Colombia, and Nigeria, the number of volunteers quickly grew from a few dozen to more than seven hundred. Many volunteers who watched the number of fellow volunteers multiplying around them felt that too many Americans was actually a liability to their mission. That many volunteers, they felt, was too heavy a foreign presence, too much intervention in the nations that were their hosts, too much competition for the largely nonexistent jobs into which they had been sent. This was one criticism to which Shriver turned a deaf ear. Only when Jack Vaughn succeeded him in 1966 did the Peace Corps begin to slow its rate of growth.

The internal debate over numbers of volunteers is helpful in placing the Peace Corps in its perspective as a minor part of the American intervention overseas. Peace Corps people argue whether the agency has too many volunteers in, say, Nigeria; yet the presence of seven hundred Americans, none of them on missions of violence, fades into insignificance compared to the vast network of private and governmental operations abroad. By all the available quantitative measures, the Peace Corps is a very small component of the United States' foreign policy. The total annual budget of the Peace Corps would only run the Defense Department for half a day.

By 1967, Peace Corps volunteers were feeling that, as a voice of America abroad, they were drowned out by the bullhorn roar of other American voices—notably those speaking for military power. Whatever the volunteers had to say in the third world was a whisper; questions raised by war had reached deep into the Peace Corps and had begun to make headlines. For the Peace Corpsman who took seriously the job of creating more life options for the people among whom he was living, the role of America as preserver of world order, by force if necessary, held many horrors. Volunteers around the world had since the beginning been asked to explain their country's failings, not only in the South and the urban ghettoes, but overseas. Volunteers are not required, as a condition of their employment, to give "official" answers. Most volunteers answer critical questions honestly. Sometimes this has meant expressing total disagreement with United States foreign policy. But for many volunteers, disagreement is not enough. Their questioners quickly point out that the Americans with builders' tools have far less strength than the Americans with money and weapons.

The word peace mingles ambiguously with the warlike word corps in the title of the agency, yet rolls off the tongue with surprising ease. Peace, it has frequently been said, requires not only an absence of armed conflict but also the presence of some standard of human dignity. Every culture promotes its own standards of decency. The development of the Peace Corps, as an expression of American standards, parallels almost exactly in time the development of the war in Vietnam. Thus, as an expression of peaceful intent on the part of the United States the small, unspectacular achievements of the Peace Corps have been overshadowed by the doings of the Defense Department.

Volunteers overseas live with an increasingly aggressive image of the United States. Their innocence tends to fall off them in great chunks. Volunteers have worked during periods of violence in such places as India, Pakistan, Nigeria, Cyprus, and many parts of Latin America (not forgetting the Dominican Republic). They are not notably tolerant of the patient, weary lectures of older men like Eric Sevareid, who tell them it's time they learned that peace and war are merely different sides of the same coin. A growing number of volunteers, after their two years' Peace

Corps service, are being drafted. They are thus gaining experience of two diametrically opposed experiments of their nation in intervening in the world.

A dramatic dilemma of American civilization has walked onto the stage of the 1960s. Shall it be the Peace Corpsman, symbolizing independence, self-reliance, and autonomy, or the soldier, with his tools of coercion and destruction? Or shall it (or can it) be a mixture of money, know-how, coercion, and subversion, depending on local circumstances? The dilemma is not only a dilemma of power. It is also a dilemma of purpose.

SECTION

IMPLEMENTING CHANGE PROGRAMS

A. REACHING TARGET AUDIENCES

53. Introducing Social Innovation[a]

James B. Taylor*

This paper reports the processes by which an interdisciplinary research project overcame the usual problems of antagonism among disciplines and succeeded in introducing a number of social innovations into a community. In terms of the experience five "principles" of successful social innovation are suggested: (a) *the principle of maximum investment,* (b) *the principle of co-optation,* (c) *the principle of egalitarian responsibility,* (d) *the principle of research as creative play,* and (e) *the principle of ideological research leadership.* A high degree of staff involvement is made possible by

a relaxation of superego prohibitions against novelty and originality, by allowing maximum feasible participation of all project personnel, and by providing realistically wide but unambiguous boundaries and limits. Under these conditions the research group may take on certain of the emotionally charged, proselyting characteristics of a small social movement and may have an impact on the community out of all proportion to its size.

As the result of having worked for some years in the field of interdisciplinary research,

Reprinted by special permission from James B. Taylor, "Introducing Social Innovation," *The Journal of Applied Behavioral Science,* Vol. VI, No. 1 (1970), pp. 69–77. Published by the NTL Institute for Applied Behavioral Science.

[a] This article is an edited version of a paper read at the American Psychological Association Meeting, San Francisco, California, August 31, 1968.

The research reported herein was supported by Grant RD-1243 P, from the Vocational Rehabilitation Administration (now Social and Rehabilitation Service), U.S. Department of Health, Education, and Welfare, Washington, D.C. 20201.

* Director, Department of Research, The Menninger Foundation.

I am struck by certain troublesome issues which seem to arise time after time. The major one, and the focus of this paper, is the problem of research utilization within the community: How can change be introduced and maintained? The second issue is integrally linked with the first: I refer here to the problems posed by interdisciplinary cooperation.

Ideally, applied social research should lead to improved forms of action, to new ways of doing things, to new social inventions. These inventions should be tested for their utility and then marketed. One could draw an interesting analogy between the marketing of new social inventions and the marketing of any other new product. However, I shall here content myself with observing that major social inventions pose a particularly difficult problem in marketing. If one builds a better mousetrap, it will probably be taken up rather quickly—given enough advertising and adequate retail distribution. A new mousetrap requires no great revolution in anyone's life style or identity; the consumer simply substitutes the new mousetrap for the old one and life goes on unchanged. But a new social form is not introduced so easily. An innovative kind of school, a new way of dealing with poverty, a new procedure for resocializing delinquents, a new technique for rehabilitating the schizophrenic—all are likely to disrupt complex and valued roles, identities, and skills. The disruption may have widespread and ramifying effects, so that whole communities may be challenged and angered. Under such circumstances the new social invention may die of malnutrition, may be forcibly ejected, or may be so changed that it loses its essential character.

The second issue—the problem of interdisciplinary cooperation—is not new. People from different disciplines notoriously have trouble in working together on shared problems. Sometimes people speak of such problems as if the trouble lies only in communication, but I rather think it goes beyond this. I think it is a problem of identity. Most professional education in the social and behavioral sciences requires the student to choose a particular battleground and to stay with it. Much of what passes for training in the "theory" of the discipline is in fact a training for ideological polemic, a training which prepares the student to do effective battle with sibling disciplines. The student learns what is wrong with the outsiders and what is meritorious about his own field. In a word, a professional *identity* is learned, along with ways of defending it. This is a most adaptive kind of training for university life, in which inter- and intradepartmental rivalries sometimes approximate the war of all against all; but it is a somewhat less adaptive training for interdisciplinary research, where a modicum of cooperation and a certain openness are helpful. In the community it is even more disruptive, as professional distance contributes to our Kafka-esque bureaucratic nightmare, and the patient or client is shuttled through a web of agencies and specialist groups, each with its own precious preserve. All of this makes difficult the design and introduction of innovation. One sometimes feels the need for a new adage: "Hell hath no fury like an expert scorned."

I have recently been involved with a rather unusual research and demonstration project which succeeded in avoiding these problems and which produced an unusual degree of social innovation in the Topeka (Kansas) community. Much of its success was fortuitous, by which I mean that things happened out of the internal dynamics of the situation and were not specifically planned in the beginning. Nevertheless, planned or unplanned, the experience points to certain principles which may have more general application. I should like to explore the ways through which this particular project was able to introduce social innovation into the community, with full awareness that I am dealing with a single project and that other ways of successfully introducing innovations also exist.

Inasmuch as preliminary reports have already been published, I do not intend to describe the project itself in great detail. For our purposes I shall concentrate on one aspect of the project: its development as a social unit which produced innovations.

The project, begun in 1963 under a five-year grant from the Vocational Rehabilitation Administration, proposed to develop more effective psychological rehabilitation procedures for low-income people. From the beginning it posed these requirements if it were to succeed:

1. A highly diversified staff must work cooperatively over a five-year period. The heterogeneity of the group is indicated by the fact that its senior personnel included a sociologist, a research psychologist, a psychoanalyst, a child psychiatrist, two clinical psychologists, three social workers, and (for a while) a minister-turned-politician.

2. Research was to be an integral part of the project, with an attempt being made to assess treatment outcome by blind comparison of control and experimental groups. This meant that the work was to be guided by a research design rather than that the research would be appended as an afterthought.

3. From the beginning, it was assumed that the research group would work within the community and would cooperate with all agencies and groups significant in the life of the poor, including public welfare, courts and police, civil rights groups, the schools, public health nurses, and vocational rehabilitation counselors.

4. If the work should suggest a need for new social forms and agencies, these were to be developed as part of the treatment plan insofar as practicable.

I think it apparent that this project was as endangered as any project could be by the difficulties enumerated earlier. As it turned out, however, interdisciplinary wrangles were circumvented; no irreconcilable conflict between action and research emerged; as spin-offs the project contributed to several new institutional forms within the community; and when the research phase terminated, the project continued as a treatment and educational service under local funding. As such, it was in a position to train new generations of psychiatrists and social workers in its techniques and to supply in-service training to a variety of social agencies within the country.

Specifically, this is what happened:

1. The project developed a series of new procedures and perspectives for working with low-income clients. These procedures and perspectives appealed to the clinicians as being both novel and useful. The clinical personnel became so highly invested in their work that when the clinical phase of the project ended they were reluctant to return to traditional forms of practice. This gave them the impetus to develop new patterns of service and new ways of agency functioning within Topeka. All of this took place before there was any scientific evidence that the new techniques and perspectives were in fact unusually effective.

2. During the course of the project the staff remained fairly constant; no major personnel disruptions occurred. True, some staff were lost, but no changes were related to strife within the project.

3. The project staff helped to design and inaugurate an OEO (Office of Economic Opportunity) Community Action Program in Topeka which incorporated perspectives gained in our previous work. Out of this arose further research in the dynamics of community organization.

4. Close working relationships were developed with a variety of community agencies: Our case history evaluations systematically included observations by teachers, notes from public welfare and police records, data from all psychiatric agencies in the city, and consultation with a family's private physician if this were needed. (I would contrast this remarkable cooperation with the oft-reported resistance to innovation supposedly found among old-line social agencies.)

5. Over time a close link was developed and maintained with several neighborhood organizations, with the research group's providing consultations and services.

6. When research funding for the project terminated, the group was able to successfully plead the case for local funding, in part from The Menninger Foundation and in part from the comprehensive mental health program of the county. As a new agency, the project provided training for students in psychiatry at The Menninger Foundation. It gave consultation to a variety of local agencies which ranged from direct intervention

with troubled families to discussion and advice with agency personnel. Thus, the project gave birth to a social institution designed to disseminate findings, techniques, and perspectives to a wide range of allied professions.

Within the space of five years the project has had a rather considerable local impact. Since it has developed its own training program and since the professional *zeitgeist* seems favorable, some national impact may well result. In any case, the project provides a case study for the way in which a particular social institution may grow from a research base, extend itself within a single city, and be instrumental in introducing a range of social innovations.

How did it happen? I suggest that the project exemplifies several principles of social innovation. First, I do not think that innovation would have taken place had the staff been less keenly involved. Let me call this *the principle of maximum investment*. Especially in the early days, the staff seemed almost religious in its commitment, as if nothing else in the clinical world were of any worth. I suspect that the spirit was similar to that of Vienna in the early days of psychoanalysis—a spirit of great in-group solidarity. This high investment gave impetus to the application, as research drew to a close, of newly learned skills in different settings.

Even with such a personal investment, continuation and innovation would not have been possible without an interpenetration of personnel from other groups and agencies. I shall call this *the principle of co-optation*. During the course of the project personnel from the local public welfare office and the Division of Vocational Rehabilitation served as weekly consultants. The legislative representative for the neighborhood, who was also a consultant, eventually joined the staff and then left to head the local OEO program. One leading researcher, the sociologist, was a long-time resident of the city; he had directed the local Urban Renewal Agency and was known and trusted by the most influential members of the community. Less formal relationships developed with public health nurses, parole officers, several school principals, and others. In addition, the part-time clinicians on the research staff were drawn from various psychiatric agencies in Topeka.

Thus, when the research phase concluded, a market for continuing services existed and a variety of agencies were familiar with the work of the project and its potential utility. More than this, some measure of trust and good will had developed, and the agencies were reassured that the project's aim was to help rather than to attack; and it was on this base that further integration and innovation became possible. The highly motivated staff provided a cadre, intent on introducing new social practices. The agency affiliations of the consultants and staff provided a highroad to the introduction of new techniques and perspectives.

Yet there are further questions: How did the staff come to develop its strong sense of solidarity and commitment? How was it that the consultative relations developed so amicably? These phenomena are not always—or often—found in interdisciplinary social science research. In answer, I suggest three other principles: (a) *the principle of egalitarian responsibility*, (b) *the principle of research as creative play*, and (c) *the principle of the research leader as spokesman and ideologist*.

It is the first of these—*the principle of egalitarian responsibility*—which, I believe, was most responsible for the development of group solidarity and commitment. Each member of the research team had an equal hand in formulating, and later in reformulating, the research issues. They were not hired simply to do a routine job; rather they were full professionals engaged in a creative learning task. Even in the initial exploration the team members suggested many of the issues around which the research techniques were organized. This was possible because the research proper was preceded by a six-month period of field exploration in which the clinicians became acquainted with a low-income neighborhood and its inhabitants. The initial research design grew from their observations, feelings, and emergent perceptions. This exploratory period avoided many of the dangers attendant upon premature formalization—the dangers of too quickly freezing the research hypotheses and research design.

Under these conditions no team member was able to set himself up as an authority. The usual issues of status and hierarchy dissolved as the research team struggled with its common task and with its collective feeling of indignation, anger, helplessness, and fear. (Work with low-income families in slum neighborhoods has stresses of its own.) This egalitarianism meant that each member of the group came to feel that he had made a unique contribution and shared a unique responsibility. The social workers, especially, found this experience novel.

As the group began to develop its skills and self-confidence, its solidarity grew. It came to define the psychiatric community as "outsiders" who did not really understand how things were and who adhered to ineffective practices. This was undoubtedly unfair. Such feelings arose in part because the research group was indeed novel and innovative and therefore suspect in the eyes of orthodoxy; in part because the group grew close as it worked together on common tasks, with much communication and mutual support among its members; and in part because deep in their hearts the group members still remained unsure and a little afraid—and fear feeds militance.

The second principle I have here labeled the spirit of *research as creative play*. Like many clinicians, the social workers and psychiatrists were at first overawed by being on a research team. The psychologists had a different problem: they were acquainted with research from their formal training and hence had avoided it thereafter. Research was seen as a kind of behemoth—foreboding, superhuman, faultfinding, arrogant, and carping—but nevertheless a good thing. In a word, research appeared to have all the characteristics of a malignant superego. (I shall not speculate on what in our educational system or research practices gives rise to this unfortunate stereotype.) In any case, as the project progressed a more flexible view began to develop. The clinicians became increasingly free to play with ideas and to question eternal truths without suffering an undue sense of sin.

What was true of the staff was also true of the consultants. They were asked to join because they had a particular area of expertise. Whenever possible, they were paid for their services. We did not approach them in order to teach them but rather as supplicants seeking help. Since they did not have to come as students, they seemed to find it easier to learn and to feel increasingly free to play with ideas and to attempt to think new thoughts. This comparative freedom, with its implications for personal development, also led to a sense of commitment. We did not, of course, achieve utopia. The five years of work included much bickering, acrimony, and temper, sometimes quite intense, but never to the point of disrupting the flow of work.

What I have described is an unusual amount of freedom, which led to a form of organization with high cohesion and much potential for innovation. However, the freedom was within limits. After all, once the patterns for interdisciplinary cooperation have been established and the major parameters of the problem defined, research demands structure and discipline. The person responsible for the technical aspects of research must be able to demand and obtain a willing adherence to the research design. To gain this willing adherence he must act as coordinator, ideologist, and taskmaster. And this, I believe, implies a somewhat different role for research than is commonly found in demonstration projects, where the researcher is often tied onto the project like a tin can on the tail of a dog. If research is indeed creative play, then the *researcher has to be the leader* of the game; he has to give direction, boundaries, and rules to the players. The researcher cannot be only a technician, but rather must take on the additional roles of *administrator and theoretician*.

Obviously this project exemplified one, but only one, model for social innovation. In a way, the model is suspect, for the project is not yet ended; and so far we have no scientific proof that our techniques and insights led to improved functioning for our clients. On the other hand, it is rare for an innovation to become popular solely because its utility is demonstrated. In fact, if one thinks of the last 60 years in psychology, fad and faith seem to have been more important than validity. Any major innovation is likely to take on the character of a social movement in which small cohesive groups with novel perspectives influence the social scene. This was true of psychoanalysis, of Darwinism, and of Newtonian world views; in a smaller way it was true here also. Innovation is a sociological and psychological phenomenon. It is important therefore to analyze the way in which social inventions come to be adopted, apart from and irrespective of their presumed scientific merit.

54. Educating New York City Residents to Benefits of Medicaid

Raymond S. Alexander* • Simon Podair**

A complex health-related law such as Medicaid often creates apathy and incomprehension in the community. The public does not understand the meaning and significance of the law and is confused by conflicting interpretations. Although the need to disseminate information is imperative, often there is no program to inform the public following enactment of health legislation affecting millions of people.

What has distinguished New York City from the rest of New York State, and, in fact, from the rest of the United States, has been the deliberate policy of publicizing and encouraging all eligible persons to enroll in the Medicaid program. The staffs of the city's departments of health and social services were faced with a difficult challenge in interpreting the law to the public and in enrolling eligible persons. Medicaid had been enacted into law on April 1, 1966, with the passage of title 11 of the State Social Welfare Law.

In analyzing the enrollment totals in the spring of 1967, an interdepartmental management group consisting of assistant commissioners from the departments of health and social services discovered that the response to the Medicaid program from people in the general community, who were not actively seeking medical care, was less than enthusiastic. A study was made of reports from the city's health and social service centers to determine why the public was not responding. It revealed a general lack of knowledge as to Medicaid and its benefits, confusion with Medicare, and a belief that one had to be on the welfare rolls to be eligible.

A concerted public information campaign obviously needed to be launched. The results of the study and subsequent recommendations were given to the Commissioner of Health and the Commissioner of Social Services. If the preventive health benefits of Medicaid were to be realized, it was felt that New Yorkers should enroll in advance of serious illness.

Early in May 1967, the Commissioner of Health decided that the full weight of the health department should be put behind a massive enrollment drive to assist the New York City Department of Social Services in carrying out the mandate of the Medicaid legislation.

The campaign was kicked off by the mayor of New York City who designated June as Medicaid Month at a press conference on June 6, 1967. Our entire efforts centered around his proclamation. The program, however, was

Reprinted from Raymond S. Alexander and Simon Podair, "Educating New York City Residents to Benefits of Medicaid," *Public Health Reports,* Vol. 84, No. 9 (September 1969), pp. 767–772.
* Executive Vice-President of Mount Sinai Hospital, Milwaukee, Wisconsin.
** Assistant Director of Public Health Education and Director, Medicaid Health Education, New York City Health Department.

extended 8 weeks beyond June 30 because of its success and the need for followup.

Who were we trying to reach in our mass enrollment drive? More than 3 million persons in New York City were estimated to be eligible under the original New York State Medicaid law, 2 million of whom had not enrolled. Medicaid's eligibility ceiling of a $6,000 annual income for a family of four was higher than the income limit for those receiving public assistance. Within this group were families who had been conditioned to believe that government-supported health care was only for the poor. We felt that these working families above the public assistance level were the ones who most needed Medicaid's preventive and diagnostic services to remain productive wage earners.

Another target group was the aged—one of the country's prime poverty groups in need of expanded community health services. Medicare does not include such high cost services as prescription drugs, dentistry, extensive podiatry, and optical services, but these services are available under Medicaid. The elderly were generally unaware that they could receive medical care through both Medicare and Medicaid.

Once we had selected our target groups, we discovered that there were many obstacles to the success of the enrollment drive. Health educators working with various community groups and neighborhood leaders reported that people who were potentially eligible shied away from registering because of lack of understanding, misconceptions as to the meaning of the program, and reluctance to give data on their financial status. Perhaps the most formidable obstacle was public apathy. Health care connotes problems, pain, and payment of bills. Most people do not become concerned about health care until illness strikes.

Our task was to overcome this apathy and to arouse public interest. But even after the apathy receded, other roadblocks hampered our progress. Enrollment was the responsibility of the department of social services which, in most minds, linked the program with welfare. This link, to many aged persons, was a stigma that interfered with effective communication. "If it's welfare, I don't want it," was the typical reaction of New York's aged.

Content of Campaign

Early in our campaign it became necessary to dispel widespread misinformation. The feeling persisted among aged residents that eligibility for Medicare precluded eligibility for Medicaid. A great deal of confusion also existed regarding income and saving requirements and the extent of services offered. Because this was the first time that such extensive health services were offered, it was difficult to convince an incredulous public of the scope of the program.

To overcome general misunderstanding, apprehension, and apathy, we stressed these basic points:

1. Medicaid was not welfare, but a tax-supported health benefits program available to all residents of New York who met eligibility requirements.

2. An aged person could be eligible for both Medicare and Medicaid and benefit from Medicaid's more extensive services.

3. In order to be eligible for checkups and preventive examinations, New Yorkers had to enroll before onset of illness.

4. It was as much the health department's responsibility as the department of social service's to encourage enrollment.

5. A family of four netting $6,000 after tax deductions was eligible for Medicaid.

6. The health services offered included physician's services, dentistry, optometry, podiatary, drugs, home health and ambulance services, sickroom supplies, eyeglasses, and hearing aids.

By limiting our message to these points, we were able to simplify a program that seemed formidable, even to the informed.

The Health Aspects

Throughout our campaign great stress was placed on the health aspects of Medicaid. It has already been pointed out that although Medicaid was a health services program, enrollment was administered by the department of social services. This arrangement meant that important health concepts could be overshadowed by red tape in enrolling, determining eligibility, and issuing identification cards.

The campaign to publicize Medicaid gave us an opportunity to reach the public with these important health concepts: (a) the preventive medicine features of Medicaid—coverage for regular checkups, immunizations, and dental checkups; (b) the importance of choosing a source of health care, whether a physician in private or group practice or with a clinic; (c) the significance of early detection of disease; (d) the importance of proper treatment of disease; and (e) the contributions of podiatrists, optometrists, and other members of the health team who were formerly overlooked by public health agencies.

These health benefits were brought to the attention of the public as incentives for enrolling in Medicaid. By conducting a health-oriented campaign, we were able to emphasize the practical goals of public health through the means of a publicly funded health care program.

Community Involvement

As in most health programs, dissemination of information was insufficient. To reach the public effectively, we had to focus on community involvement. The organization of the New York City Health Department lent itself to this task.

The department is divided into 30 health districts with a health officer as its administrative head. A key community health worker on the health officer's staff is the health educator. The health educators were mobilized by the bureau of public health education to obtain community support for the enrollment drive. They contacted the major community oriented groups in their neighborhood and discussed the part they could play in our campaign. Special emphasis was placed on reaching the following community leaders.

Professional leaders—ministers, community organizers, social workers, and health workers

Active lay leaders—PTA presidents, church workers, and leaders of older citizens' resident groups

Informal leaders—the owner of the corner grocery where neighbors congregate or an active block worker in the community

Volunteers assisting the local health educator included active community workers from antipoverty agencies and members of the auxiliary police. The auxiliary police are citizen volunteers who assist the police department in emergencies. Their help was obtained through the cooperation of the mayor's New York City Volunteer Council and the Civil Defense Division of the New York City Police Department.

Orientation sessions on Medicaid for the auxiliary police and other volunteers were organized on a borough basis and were led by staff from the departments of health and social services. The purpose of the orientation sessions was to equip volunteers with sufficient knowledge to answer simple questions about Medicaid at the locations.

Essentially the role of the community's leaders in the Medicaid drive, both as individual citizens and as a group, was twofold: (a) to reach their contacts with the overall Medicaid message and (b) to direct persons who might be eligible for Medicaid to the registration centers maintained by the departments of health and social services.

Techniques Used

The techniques used to implement the program were varied. Health workers have questioned the contributions of printed materials and meetings in motivating people for better health. The role of TV and other segments of the mass media has been denigrated, yet the commercial advertisers are quite effective in motivating the public to purchase cigarettes and other products detrimental to health. We did not have the time to engage in community organization in the textbook sense, but we were able to use a variation of this technique—community mobilization.

Neighborhood Medicaid Days

These were held 5 days a week for 12 weeks. Sound trucks with Medicaid banners, manned by the district health educators and volunteers, were stationed at busy street locations to broadcast the points we were trying to make. These locations had been selected by the staffs of the health centers and local community groups to enable the district health educators and volunteers to answer questions of passers-by on Medicaid.

Applicants were not registered at the street locations because of the lack of privacy and the detailed form that had to be completed. Passers-by with complex questions were referred to the special Medicaid registration centers. Persons interested in enrolling were given an application and asked to bring the completed application to a registration center.

Because of people's interest, health educators and volunteers were kept busy answering questions and making referrals to the Medicaid registration centers. At some crowded street locations, persons expressed surprise at the availability of the Medicaid program. Further surprise was evidenced when we described the range of health services. Mingled with this surprise were expressions of approval at the interest of the government in their welfare. Aged residents especially voiced these feelings. One elderly man approached a health educator and said, "Who would think the government would be so good to me."

Most persons were impressed with the availability of complete health care. Dental care, for example, seemed to be of great concern to those who spoke approvingly of the program. The following criticisms were voiced, however.

1. Applicants were unable to obtain a physician who would treat Medicaid patients.
2. There were delays in processing applications.
3. There were delays in receiving a Medicaid card, even after the application had been approved.
4. Persons were unable to reach the Medicaid office because of constantly busy telephones.
5. There were also a few complaints about the type of care given by health practitioners.

Most complaints were administrative and were caused by the lack of leadtime to gear up for the program.

The Neighborhood Medicaid Days removed some of the barriers that had been erected between the residents of New York and the Medicaid program. We were, in a sense, decentralizing the enrollment drive to the streets of the city—the most effective level.

Medicaid Shoppers Days

Some department stores cater to a clientele whose income falls within the Medicaid requirements. We decided to set up Medicaid Shoppers Days at which time we could once again present pertinent information on Medicaid. Our concentration point was the Borough of Brooklyn, and our initial step was to meet with the borough president, a man highly respected by the business community. A meeting was called in the borough president's office which was attended by officials of New York City's Health Services Administration and representatives from the leading department stores in the borough.

After considerable discussion, representatives from three stores agreed to cooperate. At these stores, we were allowed to place an information table, manned by the local health educator, on a selling floor for 1 week. The table was identified with a large sign and contained Medicaid literature. The health educator was kept busy answering questions and directing people to the nearest Medicaid registration center. In essence, we had moved our Neighborhood Medicaid Days indoors.

Distribution of Literature

In addition to distributing literature in the streets and in department stores, we arranged for the distribution of material through banks, post offices, and supermarkets. With the cooperation of the New York City Board of Education, principals distributed a flyer to the children to take home. The flyer stressed that a family of four earning $6,000 after tax deductions was eligible and urged parents to check with registration centers to determine their eligibility. Thus, we reached thousands of parents who were eligible for Medicaid.

We strived for literature distribution within a meaningful context. Picking up a piece of literature in a bank or a supermarket can have more meaning to the person than a flyer thrust into the same person's hands as he is hurrying from a subway station or a bus stop.

Use of Mass Media

For some time, newspapers, radio, and TV had been critical of the Medicaid program of New York City and had publicized its negative aspects. They reported delays in paying practitioners and sluggish processing of Medicaid applications.

Although these criticisms were valid, they were caused by the administrative scope of the program. The department of social services had been diligently trying to solve these difficulties, and they in no way detracted from the fact that persons were receiving health care who had previously suffered from health neglect.

We were able, however, to obtain publicity for our enrollment drive by persuading the press that the city was anxious to meet its responsibilities under the legislation by launching an intensive, well-organized campaign. We asked the press to assist the city in a constructive effort to improve the Medicaid program. We took an aggressive attitude rather than a defensive one. This approach helped negate previous adverse press stories. Major daily and weekly newspapers published stories about our campaign and listed the daily locations for Neighborhood Medicaid Days.

Radio stations in the city broadcast announcements daily, and a leading radio station reached thousands of listeners by broadcasting spot announcements throughout their day's programing. The same station produced a documentary on Medicaid. One TV station broadcast a program in Spanish about Medicaid. Health department officials appeared on TV and radio urging viewers to register for Medicaid if they thought they were eligible. The leading administrators of Medicaid made 25 separate TV and radio broadcasts. Car cards were placed in the city subway system, and posters were distributed to hospital outpatient clinics, health centers, and antipoverty offices.

Evaluation

Our aim was to enroll as many eligible persons as possible, and approximately 450,000 persons applied for Medicaid during and immediately following our campaign. Efforts to enroll eligible persons will continue on an ongoing basis.

Justification for publicizing the services offered by Medicaid is contained in the preamble to the state act which states that "in carrying out this program every effort shall be made to promote maximum public awareness of the availability of and procedure for obtaining such assistance and to facilitate the application for and the provision of such medical assistance."

When cutbacks in Medicaid were being discussed at hearings in Albany some 6 months later, the Commissioner of Health was asked why New York City had such an extensive and expensive publicity campaign. He had to remind the legislators of the intent of the law and of the public health impact of enrollment. He added that the management of newspapers and radio had donated thousands of dollars of free time and space. Compared with the benefits derived by the residents, the cost of reaching more than 450,000 New Yorkers was minimal.

Publicizing the benefits of Medicaid required no special expenditures with the exception of the sound truck which cost $50 a day. Persons assigned to the campaign were regular employees of the department.

New York City was one of the few jurisdictions in the country to organize a massive Medicaid enrollment campaign. The campaign cannot be judged on a purely statistical basis. Its significance lies far beyond the numbers of persons who applied for Medicaid and even beyond increased public understanding. During the drive the departments of health and social services cooperated closely. It was demonstrated that two large public agencies in a metropolis could work together to heighten public interest in health care. The public was introduced to a concept of total health care—not only care by a physician but also to the services provided by dentists, podiatrists, and optometrists. The public could visualize the wide spectrum of health care that should comprise a complete program.

The program also demonstrated that the public will respond to a health program that has a "gut" basis—meeting the people face to face in the streets. Such an approach tends to remove the barriers between professional health workers and residents. We were conducting a public health education campaign that concentrated on a direct approach to people. In such an approach, newspapers, radio, and TV were effective adjuncts.

Summary

On June 6, 1967, officials of New York City's departments of health and social services started a campaign to enroll all persons eligible for Medicaid. Of the more than 3 million persons who were eligible under the original New York State Medicaid law, 2 million had not enrolled.

Keeping eligible persons from enrolling were a general lack of knowledge of Medicaid and its benefits, confusing the program with Medicare, and a belief that one had to be on relief to be eligible.

Target groups for the campaign were families whose income was above the public assistance level and the aged who could obtain additional services not covered by Medicare, such as prescription drugs, dentistry, podiatry, and optical services.

To overcome apathy and arouse public interest, health educators in 30 health districts were mobilized by the bureau of public health education to obtain community support. Many types of volunteers were used—professional leaders, active lay leaders, informal leaders (such as active block workers), volunteers from the police auxiliary, and persons from antipoverty programs.

Techniques used to inform the public about Medicaid were (a) Neighborhood Medicaid Days—sound trucks at busy locations manned by district health educators and volunteers, who answered questions of passers-by, (b) Medicaid Shoppers Days—an information table placed in three department stores in Brooklyn to reach shoppers who might be eligible for Medicaid, and (c) literature distributed in the streets and through department stores, banks, post offices, supermarkets, and schools.

Newspaper, radio, and television publicity, although previously difficult to obtain, were part of the campaign, and health department officials made personal appearances on TV. Car cards were placed in the city subway systems, and posters were distributed to hospital outpatient clinics, health centers, and antipoverty offices to assure widespread publicity.

Approximately 450,000 persons applied for Medicaid during and immediately following the campaign. Among other benefits realized from the effort was the demonstration that two large public agencies in a metropolis could work together to heighten public interest in health care. The public was introduced to the components of wide spectrum health care—preventive medicine, the importance and significance of choosing a source of health care before illness, the significance of early and proper treatment of disease, and the contributions of dentists, podiatrists, optometrists, and other members of the health team.

55. Campaign Guide for the TB-RD Association: Kick the Habit Month

National Tuberculosis and Respiratory Disease Association

Getting Ready for June

June will be busting out all over. With KICK THE HABIT campaigns against cigarette smoking.

This is the message: *KICK THE HABIT. It's a matter of life and breath. Your Christmas Seal association can help.*

This campaign against cigarette smoking is

Permission to reproduce granted by the National Tuberculosis and Respiratory Disease Association.

a natural for every TB-RD association. Possibilities for the campaign are endless. Associations can go big or small with the campaign. But everyone agrees it deserves an all-out effort.

The guide includes ideas both for publicity-getters and solid education efforts. Try to balance both types in your campaign.

What You'll Be Trying to Do

Your objective is simple and straightforward —to encourage people to KICK THE HABIT and to help show them how to do it.

Directly related to this objective is a second one—to encourage and help professional health workers (doctors, nurses, and others) as they do the same job.

What Your Campaign Activities Can Be

You'll have lots more ideas of your own, but here are some starters:

1. Work with volunteers to plan and carry out your campaign.
2. Encourage health workers to help.
3. Plan in advance to evaluate what you've done.
4. Distribute educational materials listed in the illustrated folder.
5. Push education, public information, and publicity as hard as you can.
6. Experiment with group education and withdrawal programs for people who want to quit smoking.

Work with Volunteers— Organize KICK THE HABIT Committees

Committees are the vital key to the success of KICK THE HABIT month and give the local TB-RD association the opportunity to work with important volunteers in every aspect of promotional and program planning.

Organizing a steering committee—composed of health workers, media people, and other appropriate representatives—is an important first step.

Although smaller associations may feel one steering committee can do the job, larger associations may want to add specialized subcommittees such as those suggested below:

MASS MEDIA SUB-COMMITTEE

Top media people from newspapers, TV, radio, and advertising can be brought together for the first time in mid-March to brainstorm approaches to the June promotion. They should meet until all media activities are mapped and can help plan special events such as kick-off luncheons, parades, etc.

WITHDRAWAL PROGRAM SUB-COMMITTEE

A group set up to design the actual "No Smoke" sessions. The Committee may include a psychologist, an adult educator, a physician, and an association staff member. Weekly meetings should assure the development of a good, solid "No Smoke" program. (This is one instance in which a strong leader may do better without a committee. If you have an outstanding teacher who understands the problems of smoking education, from whatever professional field, turn him loose and back him up with the help he needs. Don't burden him with a committee. But be sure he's the right man before you turn him loose—perhaps by setting up an experimental one-session course "to get the feel of things.")

THE STUDENT SUB-COMMITTEE

A group of student leaders from representative schools in the area (an articulate 8th grader or two, several high school youngsters, and representatives from the junior college level). This group is assigned the specific task of developing poster materials, Hi-Y activities, Boys' Club promotions, etc. It should be noted that schools may be closing for vacation in mid-June, but pre-campaign involvement can result in some student participation. A staff representative can meet with this committee.

HEALTH PROFESSIONALS COMMITTEE

This group could consider developing an educational program for MD's, nurses, therapists, technicians, etc., concerning their responsibility to the patients who smoke and how to help them quit.

STAFF COORDINATING SUB-COMMITTEE

In large associations, staff members working on the campaign can meet regularly throughout the planning period and the actual campaign to ensure coordination of activities.

Encourage Health Workers to Help

Doctors, nurses, dentists, adult educators, and many others—they're regularly seeing the people you want to help to stop smoking. And they're in positions to make their recommendations have meaning.

Get to these people. Encourage them to push the anti-smoking cause. Your impact will mushroom as you work through them. (Check back to the guide to distribute the ME QUIT SMOKING? leaflets for promotion ideas with physicians, dentists, and nurses.)

Don't forget hospitals. When a person is sick, his motivation to stop smoking is high.

Be sure to include health workers on your steering committee and your withdrawal program sub-committee, if you have one.

Plan some anti-smoking meetings for health workers and schedule a well-known medical person as speaker. Or you can try to arrange speakers for meetings already scheduled by medical societies and professional groups. (It always helps if you can offer a big name.)

Contact joint interagency committees on nursing and thoracic societies.

Check all other anti-smoking activities in your area so that you won't duplicate programs.

Interagency Councils

Where do interagency councils on smoking fit in the KICK THE HABIT campaign? The campaign is basically a TB-RD association contribution to the total community effort—just as each agency distributes television spot announcements and other educational materials. The NTRDA and its constituent and affiliate associations have been—and will continue to be—among the strongest supporters of interagency programming against smoking. The KICK THE HABIT campaign will not diminish this interest on the part of associations. It may, in fact, lead to stepped-up cooperative effort.

Evaluation

By JUNE 30, you'll have done a lot of work.

You'll want to take some time to try to figure out just how much good you've done, and how things could be done better another time.

Be sure to plan your evaluation IN ADVANCE:

1. In any activity where a count is possible—your withdrawal programs, for example—follow up to see how many people have permanently kicked the habit, not just quit for a couple of weeks. Maybe a postcard followup six months later.

2. Keep a record. How many people came to the meetings? How many people called for information? How many press clips? Radio shows? TV plugs? How many new on-going programs were started? Which new contacts?

3. Bring your committees together one last time, independently or together, to rehash their efforts and say "Next time we'd better do it by . . ."

4. Plan to write up reactions and sum up total efforts to share ideas with other associations. Successful campaigns will make excellent submissions for the 1971 Public Relations Awards.

Materials Available Through Supply Service

Each association has received an illustrated folder with pictures of campaign materials and suggestions for use.

The materials range from bookmarks to radio spot announcements, from billboard posters to booklets packed with information about smoking.

Plan—and order—well ahead on the materials you'll want. Over-order instead of cutting corners; you don't want to be caught in the middle of June with your cupboard bare. You can use up the extras later in the year.

Public Education, Information, and Publicity

An anti-cigarette smoking campaign is a press agent's dream. Your problem is to filter out just the ideas that can work for you, and keep your list of publicity efforts small enough to be practical and effective.

Avoid getting so "gimmicky" that the campaign is taken too lightly. Balance the serious and light approaches.

Here are a few dozen ideas to start with:

1. Decide how you're going to handle pre-campaign publicity.

You can forget about it, arguing that you're not going to get much anyway. This would be a mistake.

You can do news releases (including photos) on formation of committees and similar developments. You know the media in your area; most associations would get some placement.

You can run a teaser campaign using the KICK THE HABIT theme. (KICK *WHAT* HABIT would be the natural reaction.) This has definite potential but would require quite a bit of effort, imagination, and PR know-how.

2. Make sure the key media people in your community are informed about your campaign in advance of kickoff day. Some of these media people will serve on your committees (see page 3), but you'll want to inform the others by letter, visit, phone call, or whatever your previous experience indicates.

3. Arrange for some kickoff day news. The mayor can proclaim KICK THE HABIT month. Include in the festivities other news-makers such as sports figures. Have the newspaper, radio, and TV figures who are supporting your campaign open the gates with news, interviews, commentary, and other mention.

Within a few days after kickoff day, you want everyone in your area to know about the campaign; this means that you have to schedule a number of publicity efforts. News makes news, and special attention to a good start will pay off.

4. But hold back a few ideas so that you'll have some more fuel for the fire each week. Schedule your events so that the media regularly have something new and interesting.

5. At the end of the campaign, a wrap-up story usually is possible. Summarize the good that has been done if you can (how many people said they would quit smoking?)—and recognize the people who volunteered their help.

6. Keep your perspective in your publicity. The campaign should be enjoyable. Cigarette smoking is a most serious problem but you'll only frighten potential converts away if you play too heavily on the death, doom, and des-olation theme. The KICK THE HABIT copy line and art were deliberately selected to bring a light touch; you won't go wrong if you follow its spirit.

And keep things voluntary. Persuasion, yes; force, no. Let's not intimidate and embarrass people who smoke, or make them feel guilty. They already know the facts in outline. Let's try to make it the *in* thing to do to stop smoking.

7. Capitalize on human interest; smoking is loaded with it. People love to talk about their operations; for the same reason they love to talk over their opinions about smoking. Give them a chance. And use their stories—with permission, of course—in your publicity.

8. School will be closed during part of the campaign, but use the drive of youngsters before and during the campaign if you can. A poster contest is an obvious, if sometimes overworked, possibility; prizes could be donated and winners could be displayed in department store windows and other public places. Compositions by 5th graders on why no one should smoke make wonderful reading. More important, get some young people to work with you and dream up their own ideas.

9. Of course, you'll want to go to your clubs and other organizations with speakers, pamphlets, and other activities. Gear up for this in advance of the campaign when there's still room on their programs. And plan the topic for your annual meetings.

10. Try a photography contest of best KICK THE HABIT photos. Get a store to contribute prizes.

11. How about having the celebrity–public-figure–expert of the day make a statement, one each day of the campaign. This probably would best be worked up as an exclusive with an interested newspaper or radio or TV station.

12. Anybody who is anybody should be wearing a KICK THE HABIT sticker during June. It's your job to see that he does when he makes a public appearance, especially on TV. And scatter pretty young girls around to "sticker" everyone who passes. Ask that the stickers be worn regularly by doctors, librarians, pharmacists, etc.

13. Arrange for a second wave of requests for the two leaflets on quitting smoking ("Me Quit Smoking—Why and How"). Check with physicians, nurses, dentists, and others who are distributing it and make sure their supplies are adequate. Ask the press and broadcast media to push the leaflets.

14. Convince a prominent newspaper feature writer who smokes to get in on KICK THE HABIT Campaign and try to give up smoking. Have him/her keep a diary which would be published regularly—a real, honest, personal, hopefully funny, running account of the agonies of giving up smoking.

15. Do same for TV and radio personalities with daily running accounts of the fight. Incidentally, try to convince TV stations not to have their people smoke on camera. One Boston TV station waged a full-scale war on smoking and publicized their "Stop Smoking" campaign, which involved employees and announcers who tried to quit cigarettes.

16. Men are supposed to give up smoking easier than women. Or vice versa: Have big contest between men's group (Rotary, Kiwanis, etc.) and most prominent women's group.

17. Have certain big employers agree to provide free coffee during coffee breaks for first week of June for employees who have given up smoking.

18. Local banks encourage savings accounts of money saved by giving up smoking. Special prizes?

19. Have local psychologist or psychiatrist focus on the human/emotional/personal trauma of quitting.

20. Follow up stories on all kinds of groups, interesting persons who are trying. Report new methods, rewards, etc. (no matter how kooky) developed by people in attempts to quit smoking, "I'll bet you can't quit smoking for a week. If you do, I'll climb to top of courthouse tower and raise banner saying 'John Jones Really Did KICK THE HABIT.'"

21. One of the things sweeping the country is the "call-in" radio programs. People like to hear the sound of their own voice, particularly when they can talk to a "celebrity." Talk the MC into doing a special program of talking with people trying to give up smoking (even those against it); have a doctor present to answer people's medical questions on smoking.

22. Give encouragement to and get publicity coverage on "If at First" clubs—groups of people who have tried to quit lots of times and not yet made it stick. (Mark Twain said, "Giving up smoking is easy. I've done it hundreds of times.") Help people try to quit once more.

23. Encourage newspapers to run small box on front page giving latest capsule news, percentages, etc., in KICK THE HABIT Campaign. Get same info in regularly to certain local radio/TV programs.

24. Tie up with sports celebrities who have given up smoking.

25. Arrange a marathon race or mini-marathon between smokers and non-smokers.

26. Check chart of retail sales of cigarettes and how it's changed over the years.

27. Competitive quitting among a large number of organizations. And emphasize (a) the ones with large constituencies like churches and (b) the ones that have a large number of exhibitionists and PR addicts like some luncheon and service clubs. Try to reach all ethnic and racial groups.

28. Start fund with money that people save by quitting. What could be done with the dough? Give some badly needed bit of hospital equipment (related to respiratory problems) to local hospital? Shouldn't be TB-association sponsored because of fund-raising conflicts—have the money sent to a columnist, newspaper, TV or radio station.

29. How about a survey of the members of your medical society? How many of them have quit smoking? ("More than 100,000 doctors have quit smoking. Do they know something that you don't?" . . . That's the story nationally. What is it in your area?)

30. Set up plastic coffin in city square or town green. (Get a permit first, of course). Have people dump cigarette packs there. Get volunteers to hand cigarette leaflets or stickers to everyone who dumps in a pack. Put KICK THE HABIT and LUNGS ARE FOR LIVING signs on coffin. . . . Or set up a giant plastic football with slot on side so people can

slip in their discarded cigarettes. (Note: this idea and number 31 are similar to recent peace moratorium activities in some communities, and may or may not lend themselves to repetition.)

31. Arrange candlelight parade some night for people who are kicking the habit. (Permit is necessary.) Finish off in some prominent spot with a giant bonfire of people's cigarette packs. Invite a Congressman or public official to ceremonies. Why not have him arrive on fire engine? Alert all media.

32. Dream up some wild way to get your whole town—or part of the town or as many organizations as possible—to quit for the whole month of June. Too much? (Greenfield, Iowa did it.) How about one day or one week, then?

33. Get as many druggists as possible to put a black shroud over their cigarette machines during month of June. Good luck! (It really has been done some places.)

34. What about arranging some KICK THE HABIT skywriting?

35. Take public opinion poll in your area. Find out how many people smoke now. And how many have quit in last five years. Ask how many plan to quit this year. Report results to media.

36. Have man-in-the-street interviews on KICK THE HABIT campaign. Radio and TV. Also features for newspapers.

37. Father's Day is in June. Get groups of fathers to KICK THE HABIT as good example to kids. Do features.

38. Distribute leaflets to employees in industry and businesses, maybe with paycheck. Encourage companies to help pick up the tab.

39. Set up a phone number—dial SMOKERS—so that people can call in and get a recorded message. Have tape machine running so they can leave names and have two cigarette leaflets sent to them.

40. Try to initiate and stimulate programs all around town. In the fire department. The police department. Among other city employees. In unions, businesses, factories. Everywhere.

The Tuberculosis Institute of Chicago and Cook County started smoking and health lectures in the Chicago Police Training Academy. The 7-month police training program now requires each trainee (there are 500 in the current class) to attend a smoking education class. Dramatic demonstrations use calves' lungs to show how breathing works and how smoking damages the lungs. The Chicago *Police Digest* publicized the smoking classes and provided the model for other police training schools.

The Chicago Fire Academy also got in on the act with a similar smoking program which was presented in in-service training and refresher courses for firefighters. A total of 4700 firemen were involved.

41. Contact the program directors of the radio and TV stations in your area, tell them about the KICK THE HABIT campaign and suggest ways in which this campaign can fit into their particular programming needs:

Talk shows are a "natural" for a doctor-dean of a medical school, TB-RD association person to discuss the hazards of smoking and how to go about quitting. Be sure the guests you furnish are—above all—articulate.

Mid-day women's shows also welcome guest speakers, especially when the topic has to do with health. And remember, research has shown that smoking may be hazardous to the unborn child.

Contact the host of a teenage dance show. He might be interested in having a member from your association or a doctor talk to his audience about smoking, during a break in the record playing and dancing. Or he might prefer to include the message as spot announcements in his own special patter.

Contact your local rock station. Since these stations have a young audience, they may be willing to work out an entire day, week or month's worth of programming with you for the KICK THE HABIT Campaign. For instance: before a time check the announcer might say: "It's time to kick the habit at 10:25 AM." Or, it's a great day to KICK THE HABIT, the temperature in _____ is _____ degrees. Aside from these reminders, you might like to supply the disc jockeys with facts about smoking which they could tell their audience about between records.

42. Get teenagers involved. In California, the Tuberculosis and Health Association helped organize a project to get teenagers sending anti-smoking messages to other teenagers. Sixty of them, selected by their peers as leaders, set up their own brand of advertising agency. The project, called "Smoke Out," was run according to techniques used by the local Junior Achievers where youngsters run businesses of their own under the guidance of local businessmen.

Each teenage staff member in the simulated advertising agency chose the position he wanted to fill: account supervisor, copy writer, traffic director, art director, and other jobs. The young advertisers designed billboards, bumper stickers, and wrote radio and television spots, which they also recorded and filmed.

Here are some of their one-liners: "Don't smoke in bed, you might burn a hole in your lungs." "Some of my best friends smoke—I'm going to miss them." "Would you want your sister to marry a smoker?" "My frog smokes, but that's okay because I know he's going to croak anyway."

The campaign, according to teenage public opinion, was a smash.

43. The film *Point of View* is another natural for this campaign. It can be shown to groups or on TV.

44. Triangle Television stations has produced a 20-segment series on how to stop smoking. (This was mentioned in the NTRDA January 1, 1970, *Newsletter*.) Try to encourage a television station in your area to show the entire series during the month of June.

45. June is the month of weddings. Shouldn't young people starting a new life together KICK THE HABIT and make that life longer?

46. Enlist the interest and cooperation of management and union groups.

Sample Press Releases

Here are the beginnings of two sample news releases: NOTE: *Always double-space news releases*

GET YOUR "KICK THE HABIT" STICKER

Got your KICK THE HABIT sticker? During the entire month of June a bevy of young beauties will be distributing these stickers as reminders that it's KICK THE HABIT Month. The promotion is sponsored by the _____ _____ to encourage the area's residents to give up cigarette smoking.

But the stickers are only a part of the promotion. In addition, _____ is two free booklets: "Me Quit Smoking, Why?" and "Me Quit Smoking, How?" These are available free at the Association's offices at _____ _____.

For those who don't want to go it alone, there will be group sessions on how to stop smoking. Several companies in town have agreed to sponsor such programs during working hours, and in addition, other similar courses will be held in the evenings. Additional information on these group programs is also available from the Association's office.

More than 21 million Americans have already given up the cigarette habit, and the _____ feels that it's imperative that every smoker in _____ make a concerted effort to kick the habit this month.

It's a proven fact that smoking contributes to emphysema and causes lung cancer, chronic bronchitis, and other respiratory diseases. It's a matter of life and breath.

"KICK THE HABIT" BEFORE YOU KICK THE BUCKET

If you don't quit cigarette smoking this month, it won't be the fault of _____ _____. They have declared June KICK THE HABIT Month, and 30 full days of activities have been planned, aimed at encouraging people to stop smoking.

The airwaves will be bombarded with messages urging people to stop smoking, and special programs have been produced in cooperation with _____ explaining why you should stop smoking, along with some practical advice on how to KICK THE HABIT.

In addition, there will be several withdrawal programs presented, open to all smokers, on how to break the smoking habit. For those who prefer to go it alone, there are two free booklets available, "Me Quit Smoking, Why?" and "Me Quit Smoking, How?" These book-

lets and information about them may be obtained from the association's offices at _____.
_____.

Withdrawal Programs for Adults Who Want to KICK THE HABIT

It's tough to quit smoking.

That is why some sort of group approach is helpful to lots of people who just can't quite go it alone.

A number of different approaches have been tried. A common one is the five-day withdrawal plan. This usually consists of programs on five consecutive evenings. All kinds of variations can be played on this theme. Although immediate results are good, follow-up shows many people start smoking again within a year.

On the following pages you'll find this information:[1]

1. "Some Thoughts on Smoking Withdrawal Clinics," written by the director of an experimental withdrawal program at Roswell Park Memorial Institute.

2. A rundown on a highly successful withdrawal approach organized by Dr. Donald Fredrickson.

3. An account of a high school smoking withdrawal program conducted by the York County (Pa.) TB and Health Society.

4. Some materials in a no-smoke series organized by the TB-RD Association of King County in Seattle, Washington.

Select any sections for guidance, and then go to it. One possibility not outlined here is setting up a smoking clinic in a hospital—under supervision of physicians. Several associations have helped sponsor this type of clinic.

One item that might be good to kickoff discussions is the "Smoker's Self-Testing Kit," prepared by PHS.

Just one strong suggestion: follow-up with the participants (6 months or a year later) so you can evaluate your efforts. *And another suggestion:* don't get bogged down in a complicated operation that just isn't worth the enormous extra effort for the few people involved. Choose something that you think will work but not bog down.

[1] *Editors' note:* These pages have been omitted here. If the reader desires the material noted, it can be obtained by writing to the National Tuberculosis and Respiratory Disease Association, 1740 Broadway, New York, N. Y. 10019.

B.   MEETING RESISTANCE

56.   Resistance to Change

Goodwin Watson*

All of the forces which contribute to stability in personality or in social systems can be perceived as resisting change. From the standpoint of an ambitious and energetic change agent, these energies are seen as obstructions. From a broader and more inclusive perspective the tendencies to achieve, to preserve, and to return to equilibrium are most salutary.

Reprinted from Goodwin Watson, "Resistance to Change," Goodwin Watson (ed.), *Concepts for Social Change,* Cooperative Project for Educational Development Series, Vol. I (Washington, D.C.: National Training Laboratories, 1966).
* Associate Director, Union for Experimenting Colleges and Universities, Antioch College.

They permit the duration of character, intelligent action, institutions, civilization, and culture.

Lewin's (1951) concept of apparently static systems as in "quasi-stationary equilibrium" has directed attention to the importance of reducing resistance if change is to be accomplished with minimal stress. The more usual strategies of increasing pressures by persuasion and dissuasion raise tensions within the system. If the opposite strategy—that of neutralizing or transforming resistance—be adopted, the forces for change already present in the system-in-situation will suffice to produce movement. For example, administrators may try by exhortation to get teachers to pay more attention to individual differences among pupils. Or, they may analyze the factors which now prevent such attention (e.g. large classes, single textbooks, standard tests) and by removing these pressures release a very natural tendency for teachers to adapt to the different individual pupils.

During the life of a typical innovation or change-enterprise, perceived resistance moves through a cycle. In the early stage, when only a few pioneer thinkers take the reform seriously, resistance appears massive and undifferentiated. "Everyone" knows better; "No one in his right mind" could advocate the change. Proponents are labelled crack-pots and visionaries. In the second stage, when the movement for change has begun to grow, the forces pro and con become identifiable. The position can be defined by its position in the social system and its power appraised. Direct conflict and a show-down mark the third stage, as resistance becomes mobilized to crush the upstart proposal. Enthusiastic supporters of a new idea have frequently underestimated the strength of their opponents. Those who see a favored change as good and needed, find it hard to believe the lengths to which opposition will go to squelch that innovation. This third stage is likely to mean life or death to the proposed reform. Survival is seen as depending on building up power to overcome the enemy. Actually, as Lewin's force-field analysis indicates, an easier and more stable victory can be won by lowering the potency of the opposing forces. The fourth stage, after the decisive battles, finds supporters of the change in power. The persisting resistance is, at this stage, seen as a stubborn, hide-bound, cantankerous nuisance. For a time, the danger of a counterswing of the pendulum remains real. Any conspicuous failure of the reform may mobilize latent opposition which, jointed with the manifest reactionaries, could prove sufficient to shift the balance of power. Strategy in this fourth stage demands wisdom in dealing, not only with the overt opponents, but with the still dissonant elements within the majority which appears, on the whole, to have accepted the innovation. Many teachers of a "new math" today may be less than whole-hearted about its value. In a fifth stage, the old adversaries are as few, and as alienated as were the advocates in the first stage. The strategic situation is now that new change-enterprises are appearing and the one-time fighters for the old innovation (e.g. junior high schools) are being seen as resisters of the emerging change. (Edwards, 1927.)

At each stage of the innovation, from its inception to its defense as status quo, wise strategy requires perceptive analysis of the nature of the resistance. For purposes of this study, we shall focus first on the forces of resistance as they operate within the individual personality. Then we shall inventory the forces most easily identified in the social system. This is, of course, an arbitrary separation, utilized to facilitate the recognition of factors. In reality, the forces of the social system operate within the individuals and those attributed to separate personalities combine to constitute systemic forces. The two work as one.

A. Resistance in Personality

1. Homeostasis

Some of the stabilizing forces within organisms have been described by Cannon (1932) as "homeostasis." The human body has built-in regulatory mechanisms for keeping fairly constant such physiological states as temperature or blood sugar. Exercise increases pulse rate, but "resistance" to this change presently brings the heart-beat back to normal. Appetites rise, are satisfied, and the organism returns to its steady state. Raup (1925) generalized the reversion to *complacency* as the most basic characteristic of the psychological as well as the physiological behavior of man.

The conception of organisms as naturally complacent unless disturbed by intrusive stimuli has had to be modified in recent years because of contradictory evidence showing a hunger for stimulation. Years ago, W. I. Thomas proposed the "desire for new experience" as one of the four most basic wishes underlying human behavior. (Thomas, Znaniecki, 1918–20). Observers of rats, dogs, and chimpanzees have noted an "exploratory motive" strong enough to counterbalance fear of the unknown (Hebb, 1958 p. 171). Experiments with perceptual isolation of human subjects showed that lying quietly awake in a comfortable bed, free from disturbing stimuli, soon became intolerable. People need to interact with a changing environment (Lilly, 1956).

Frequently, educational changes prove temporary. For a time, after sensitivity training, a school principal may be more open and receptive to suggestions from teachers. But with time, the forces which made him behave as he did before training, return him to his own more brusque and arbitrary manner.

2. Habit

Most learning theory has included the assumption that unless the situation changes noticeably, organisms will continue to respond in their accustomed way. At least one psychologist (Stephens, 1965) has argued that the *repetition* of a response—often used as a criterion for having "learned" it—offers no conceptual problem. The model resembles a machine which, unless something significant is altered, will continue to operate in a fixed fashion. There should be no need for repeated exercise or for a satisfying effect to "stamp in" the learned response; once the circuit is connected it should operate until rearranged. Once a habit is established, its operation often becomes satisfying to the organism. Gordon Allport (1937) has introduced the term "functional autonomy" to refer to the fact that ac-

tivities first undertaken as a means to some culminating satisfaction often become intrinsically gratifying. The man accustomed after dinner to his chair, pipe, and newspaper may resist any change in the details of his routine. The term "bus man's holiday" reflects the fact that men sometimes enjoy continuing in free time an activity which has been part of their required work. The concept of functional autonomy is probably too inclusive. Not all activities which are often repeated take on the character of drives. We have no wholly correct basis for predicting which habits will show most intrinsic resistance to change.

Sometimes a new educational practice—e.g. a changed form of teacher's class record book or report card arouses much resistance. After it has been established, perhaps with some persuasion and coercion, it becomes as resistant to change as was its predecessor. The familiar is preferred.

3. Primacy

The way in which the organism first successfully copes with a situation sets a pattern which is unusually persistent. Early habits of speech may be recognized despite much effort in later life to change. A child who has several times heard a story told in certain words is likely to be annoyed if the key phrases are not repeated exactly when the story is re-told. Part of the joy in familiar music is the accord between established expectations and the flow of melody and harmony. Dreams of adults are often located in the settings of childhood. Even in senility, the recent experiences fade first, and the earliest associations persist longest. All later concepts perforce build on some of the earliest generalizations.

It is often observed that teachers, despite in-service courses and supervisory efforts, continue to teach as they themselves were taught. Their image of a teacher was formed in childhood and whenever they hear or read anything about better teaching, this is assimilated to that early and persisting concept.

4. Selective Perception and Retention

Once an attitude has been set up, a person responds to other suggestions within the framework of his established outlook. Situations may be perceived as reenforcing the original attitude when they actually are dissonant. Thus, in one famous experiment, a common stereotype associating Negroes with carrying razors, led observers of a cartoon to think they had seen the razor in the hands of the Negro rather than the white man (Allport, Postman, 1945). Experiments with materials designed to bring about changes in attitude revealed that subjects did not hear clearly, nor remember well, communications with which they disagreed (Watson, Hartmann, 1939; Levine, Murphy, 1943). It is a common observation that people usually prefer news sources, whether in print or broadcast, with which they are already in agreement. (Klapper, 1960). By reading or listening to what accords with their present views; by misunderstanding communications which, if correctly received, would not be consonant with pre-established attitudes; and by conveniently forgetting any learning which would lead to uncongenial conclusions, subjects successfully resist the possible impact of new evidence upon their earlier views. There are relatively few instances in which old prejudices have been changed by better information or persuasive arguments.

The thousands of teachers who are exposed in graduate courses to different philosophies of education from those the teachers are accustomed to employ, may do very well at answering test questions about the new approach, but they carefully segregate in their mind, the new as "theory which, of course, would not work in the practical situation."

5. Dependence

All human beings begin life dependent upon adults who incorporate ways of behaving that were established before the newcomer arrived on the scene. Parents sustain life in the helpless infant and provide major satisfactions. The inevitable outcome is conservative. Children tend to incorporate (imitate, introject) the values, attitudes, and beliefs of those who care for them.

All teachers were once beginners in the lower grades. At that time, their teachers loomed large and influential, whether friendly or hostile. The little pupil had to conform. His later adoption of the kind of teaching he then experienced is as natural as his acceptance of a particular alphabet and number-system.

There may later, in adolescence, be outbursts of rebellion and moves toward independent thought. But the typical adult still agrees far more than he disagrees with his parents on such basic items as language, religion, politics, child-rearing, and what a school should do.

6. Superego

Freud (1922) conceived one of the basic personality functions as engaged in the enforcement of the moral standards acquired in childhood from authoritative adults. From the first "No! No!" said to the baby, on through all the socializing efforts of parents, a code of controls is internalized. When the Oedipus complex is resolved, the child sets standards for himself corresponding to his image of the perfect and omnipotent parent. Any violation of these demanding rules is punished with a severity, the energy of which is derived from the attachment to parents as this operated in the Oedipal period—age three to five.

Here, then, in the Superego, is a powerful agent serving tradition. The repressive constraints which operate—partly unconsciously do not derive from the realities of life in the present or the preceding generation. The Superego of the child corresponds to the Superego of the parent, not to his rational conclusions based on experience. Each mother and father passes on a heritage of taboos which he, in his childhood, acquired from ages past. An individual needs considerable ego-strength to become able to cope realistically with changing life situations in disregard of the unrealistic, perfectionistic demands of his Superego.

There is reason to believe that people who choose occupations in which they try to inculcate higher standards in others (clergymen, teachers, law-enforcement) are persons with extra strong Superego components. They take pride in making severe demands on themselves and on others. They bitterly resist any change which they conceive to be a relaxation of the firmest discipline and the highest expectations of perfection in performance. The influx of less able students into secondary schools and colleges has created almost intolerable conflict in teachers who still require achievement at levels which few can attain.

7. Self-distrust

As a consequence of the dependence of childhood and the stern authority of the tradition-oriented voice of the Superego, children quickly learn to distrust their own impulses. Each says, in effect, "What I would really want is bad! I should not want it!"

John Dewey in *Human Nature and Conduct* (1922) saw the possibility of human betterment in the liberation of the creative impulses of youth. "The young are not as yet subject to the full impact of established customs. Their life of impulsive activity is vivid, flexible, experimenting, curious." What Dewey did not say is that within each young person there are powerful forces condemning and repressing any impulses which do not correspond to the established routines, standards, and institutions of society as it is and has been. The Puritan view that the enjoyable is evil gets a firm hold on children. Every clash between their desires and what adults expect of them, adds an increment to each child's self-rejection: "They must be right; I must be naughty to have such terrible feelings." Thus guilt is mobilized to prevent action for change. Men conclude that they are not worthy of any better life. To be "good" is to accept the *status quo ante*. Agitators and rebels speak with the voice of the evil serpent and should not be heeded.

The author, during the depth of the economic depression, found that most of a sample of unemployed men did not lay the blame for their predicament on faulty social mechanisms. Rather, they internalized the responsibility. They said, "I ought to have stayed on in school"; or "It was my fault that I lost the job; I shouldn't have said what I did!"; or "I should have waited to get married and have a family." Only about one in five wanted to change the economic system; the majority blamed themselves only (Watson, 1941).

Innumerable pupils, parents, teachers, and administrators have felt impulses to alter school procedures. Most of these have been stifled by a feeling which is suggested by the expression: "Who am I to suggest changes in what the wisdom of the past has established?"

8. Insecurity and Regression

A further obstacle to effective participation in social change is the tendency to seek security in the past. The golden age of childhood is a Paradise Lost. When life grows difficult and frustrating, individuals think with nostalgia about the happy days of the past.

The irony is that this frustration-regression sequence enters life at just the time when change would be most constructive. When old ways no longer produce the desired outcome, the sensible recourse would be to experiment with new approaches. But individuals are apt at such a time to cling even more desperately to the old and unproductive behavior patterns. They are dissatisfied with the situation, but the prospect of change arouses even more anxiety, so they seek somehow to find a road back to the old and (as they now see it) more peaceful way of life.

Demands for change in school organization and practice become acute as a result of such social changes as automation, rapid travel to other lands, or racial desegregation. The reaction of insecure teachers, administrators, and parents, is, too often, to try to hold fast to the familiar or even to return to some tried-and-true fundamentals which typify the schools of the past. A candidate for State Superintendent of Schools in California based his successful campaign in the mid-1960's, on return to the old-fashioned. The fact that California had been changing more rapidly in population, occupations, etc., than had any other state, was one factor in the appeal of this program of reaction.

B. Resistance to Change in Social Systems

1. Conformity to Norms

Norms in social systems correspond to habits in individuals. They are customary and expected ways of behaving. Members of the organization demand of themselves and of other members conformity to the institutional norms. This is the behavior described by Whyte in the *Organization Man* (1956). It includes time schedules; modes of dress; forms of address to colleagues, superiors, and subordinates; indications of company loyalty; personal ambition to rise; appropriate consumption; and forms of approved participation in recreation and community life. Teachers, even more than businessmen, have been expected to exemplify certain proper behaviors.

Norms make it possible for members of a system to work together. Each knows what he may expect in the other. The abnormal or anomic is disruptive.

Because norms are shared by many participants, they cannot easily change. Above all, the usual individual cannot change them. He can get himself rejected, for deviate behavior, but the norm will persist. A laboratory experiment (Merei, 1949) showed that even a child with strong leadership qualities was required, nevertheless, to conform to the established play norms of a small group of kindergarten children. An excellent teacher who declined to submit the prescribed advance lesson plans for each week, did not alter the norm; he was fired.

When one person deviates noticeably from the group norm, a sequence of events may be expected. The group will direct an increasing amount of communication toward him, trying to alter his attitude. If this fails, one after another will abandon him as hopeless. Communication to him will decrease. He may be ignored or excluded. He no longer belongs (Festinger, Thibaut, 1951).

The famous experiments, led by Lewin during the war, on altering norms of eating, indicated that changes are better introduced by group-decision than by expecting individuals to pioneer a practice not being used by their associates (Lewin, 1952).

The evidence indicates that if norms are to be altered, this will have to occur throughout the entire operating system. The sad fate of experimental schools and colleges (Miles, 1964) indicates the power of the larger system to impose its norms even on units which have been set apart, for a time, to operate by different standards and expectations.

2. Systemic and Cultural Coherence

The Gestalt principle that parts take on characteristics because of their relationship within the whole, implies that it is difficult to change one part without affecting others. Innovations which are helpful in one area may have side-effects which are destructive in related regions. For example, a technical change which increased the efficiency of piece-workers in a factory enabled them to earn more than supervisors were being paid, so the new technique had to be abandoned. Electronic data processing in another company altered the size and relative responsibilities of related departments, generating considerable resentment (Mann, Neff, 1961). Studying change in a city Y.M.C.A., Sorenson and Dimock (1955) concluded:

> No part of institutional change is an "island unto itself": changes in program call for changes in every other part of the institution. . . . and advance in one sector cannot proceed far ahead of change in other sectors. For example, program groups cannot be changed without officer training. . . . which in turn is contingent upon advisor training. . . . which in turn depends upon staff reeducation. Similarly, changes in staff goals and ways of working are dependent upon administrative procedures, policies and budgets which in turn require changes in Boards and Committees.

A parallel statement for school systems might indicate that a change in teacher-pupil relationships is likely to have repercussions on teacher-principal interaction, on parent-principal contacts, on pressure groups operating on the superintendent, on Board member chances for re-election, and perhaps on the relationship of the local system to state or Federal agencies. Any estimate of resistance which takes account only of the persons primarily and centrally concerned will be inadequate; the repercussions elsewhere may be even more influential in the survival of the innovation.

3. Vested Interests

The most obvious source of resistance is some threat to the economic or prestige interests of individuals. A school consolidation which eliminates some Board members and a principal is unlikely to receive their warm support, although such cases have occurred. The most common resistance to educational improvements which would cost money comes from organized or unorganized taxpayers. Mort (1941) found that desirable school innovations were most likely to be adopted by communities with high financial resources. Poverty has been—at least until the recent anti-poverty program—a block to educational experimenting. The writer (Watson, 1946) found likewise that Y.M.C.A.'s located in communities with high volume of retail sales per capita were more likely to adopt recommended new practices.

A "vested interest" may be in freedom to operate as one pleases, quite as truly as in money-income or title on the door. Centralizing control of school decisions is usually unwelcome to the persons who would otherwise be making decisions in local school neighborhoods or classrooms.

Concern for school taxes and for positions on school boards is likely to center in the upper classes of the community. They are the people who have most power and influence. Newspapers and broadcasting are more accessible to them than to the underprivileged. A few powerful political or financial interests can block programs desired by a large majority of ordinary citizens. The influence of upper-class families on school policies is vividly portrayed in Hollinghead's *"Elmtown's Youth"* (1949).

4. The Sacrosanct

Anthropologists have observed that, within any culture, some activities are easily changed; others are highly resistant to innovation. Generally, the technology is receptive to new ideas and procedures. The greatest resistance concerns matters which are connected with what is held to be sacred. Some women can become managers of business or presidents of colleges in our male-dominated society, but they find it almost impossible to become a priest, rabbi, a bishop or pope in a conservative denomination. Translations of Scriptures into the vernacular have met strong disapproval. The ritual reading of some verses from the Bible or the recitation of a prayer is held onto with far more fervor than is spent on retention of school texts or equipment. Traditional ceremonies are apt to persist despite doubts as to their educational impact. The closer any reform comes to touching some of the taboos or rituals in the community, the more likely it is to be resisted. Introduction of improved technology in underdeveloped countries runs into formidable obstacles if it seems to impinge on religious superstitions, beliefs or practices (Spicer, 1952).

Cultures resist almost as stubbornly, alterations which enter the realm of morals and ethics. Even when few live by the traditional code, it must still be defended as "ideal" (Linton, 1945). A well-recognized illustration is the expectation of sexual continence between puberty and marriage. Kinsey may find very few youths who practice it, but schools, churches, and courts must operate as if the prescription were unquestionable.

There is a clear connection between the operation of the superego in individuals and the taboos persisting in the culture. Both uphold impossibly high standards and react punitively to recognized infractions of the excessive demands.

5. Rejection of "Outsiders"

Most change comes into institutions from "outside." Griffiths studying change in school systems concluded, "The major impetus for change in organizations is from outside" (In Miles, 1964 p. 431).

Few psychological traits of human beings are so universal as that of suspicion and hostility toward strange outsiders. Kohler (1922) observed this kind of behavior among his chimpanzees on the Island of Tenerife many years ago. Wood (1934) has explored, across different cultures, the mixture of curiosity and antagonism toward foreigners. A typical attack on any new proposal is that it doesn't fit our local conditions. Struggles to improve labor and race relations have commonly been discounted as inspired by "outside agitators" or "atheistic Communists." Research, development and engineering units are familiar with the way in which a new project is hampered if it is seen as NIH (not invented here).

The history of experimental demonstration schools is that they were often observed but seldom replicated. "This is fine, but it wouldn't work in our system." Differences in class of children, financial support, equipment, and tradition helped to rationalize the resistance. The genius of agricultural agents a century ago led them away from model farms run by state colleges and toward demonstration projects within the local neighborhood. Farmers accepted what was being done within their country when they could not import new practices from far away.

A major problem in introducing social change is to secure enough local initiative and participation so the enterprise will not be vulnerable as a foreign-importation.

Summary of Recommendations

Our observations on sources of resistance within persons and within institutions can be summarized in some concise principles. These are not absolute laws but are based on generalizations which are usually true and likely to be pertinent. The recommendations are here re-organized to fit three headings: (1) Who brings the change? (2) What kind of change succeeds? and (3) How is it best done?

A. Who Brings the Change?

1. Resistance will be less if administrators, teachers, Board members, and community leaders feel that the project is their own—not one devised and operated by outsiders.

2. Resistance will be less if the project clearly has whole-hearted support from top officials of the system.

B. What Kind of Change?

3. Resistance will be less if participants see the change as reducing rather than increasing their present burdens.

4. Resistance will be less if the project accords with values and ideals which have long been acknowledged by participants.

5. Resistance will be less if the program offers the kind of *new* experience which interests participants.

6. Resistance will be less if participants feel that their autonomy and their security is not threatened.

C. Procedures in Instituting Change

7. Resistance will be less if participants have joined in diagnostic efforts leading them to agree on what the basic problem is and to feel its importance.

8. Resistance will be less if the project is adopted by consensual group decision.

9. Resistance will be reduced if proponents are able to empathize with opponents; to recognize valid objections; and to take steps to relieve unnecessary fears.

10. Resistance will be reduced if it is recognized that innovations are likely to be misunderstood and misinterpreted, and if provision is made for feedback of perceptions of the project and for further clarification as needed.

11. Resistance will be reduced if participants experience acceptance, support, trust, and confidence in their relations with one another.

12. Resistance will be reduced if the project is kept open to revision and reconsideration if experience indicates that changes would be desirable.

References

1. Allport, G. W. *Personality: A Psychological Interpretation.* New York, Holt, Rinehart and Winston, Inc., 1937.
2. Allport, G. W., and L. J. Postman. The basic psychology of rumor. *Transactions of N. Y. Academy of Sciences*, Series II, 1945, 8:61–81.
3. Cannon, W. B. *Wisdom of the Body.* New York, W. W. Norton & Company, Inc., 1932.
4. Dewey, John. *Human Nature and Conduct.* New York, Holt, Rinehart and Winston, Inc., 1922.

5. Dimock, H. S. and Roy Sorenson. *Designing Education in Values: A Case Study in Institutional Change.* New York, Association Press, 1955.
6. Edwards, L. P. *The Natural History of Revolution.* Chicago, University of Chicago Press, 1927.
7. Festinger, Leon and John Thibaut. Interpersonal Communication in Small Groups. *J. Abn. Soc. Psychol.,* 1951, 46:92–99.
8. Freud, Sigmund. *Beyond the Pleasure Principle.* London, Hogarth Press, Ltd., 1922.
9. Hebb, D. O. *A Textbook of Psychology.* Philadelphia, W. B. Saunders Company, 1958.
10. Hollingshead, A. B. *Elmtown's Youth.* New York, John Wiley & Sons, Inc., 1949.
11. Klapper, Joseph T. *Effects of Mass Communication.* New York, The Free Press, 1960.
12. Kohler, Wolfgang. Zur Psychologie des Shimpanzen. *Psychol, Forsehung,* 1922, 1:1–45.
13. Levine, M. M., and G. Murphy. The learning and forgetting of controversial material. *J. Abn. Soc. Psychol.,* 1943, 38:507–517.
14. Lewin, Kurt. *Field Theory in Social Science.* New York, Harper & Row, Publishers, 1951.
15. Lewin, Kurt. Group decision and social change. In G. E. Swanson, T. M. Newcomb and E. L. Hartley, *Readings in Social Psychology.* New York, Holt, Rinehart and Winston, Inc., 1952, pp. 463–473.
16. Linton, Ralph. *The Cultural Background of Personality.* New York, Appleton-Century-Crofts, 1945.
17. Mann, F. C., and F. W. Neff. *Managing Major Change in Organization.* Ann Arbor, Mich. Foundation for Research on Human Behavior, 1961.
18. Merei, F. Group leadership and institutionalization. *Human Rela.* 1949, 2:23–39.
19. Miles, M. B. (Ed.) *Innovation in Education.* New York, Bureau of Publications, Teachers College, Columbia University, 1964.
20. Mort, Paul R., and F. G. Cornell. *American Schools in Transition.* New York, Bureau of Publications, Teachers College, Columbia University, 1941.
21. Raup, R. B. *Complacency: The Foundation of Human Behavior.* Crowell-Collier and Macmillan, Inc., 1925.
22. Spicer, E. H. *Human Problems in Technological Change.* New York, Russell Sage Foundation, 1952.
23. Stephens, J. A. *The Psychology of Classroom Learning.* New York, Holt, Rinehart and Winston, Inc., 1965.
24. Watson, Goodwin. *A Comparison of "Adaptable" versus "Laggard" Y.M.C.A.'s.* New York, Association Press, 1946.
25. Watson, Goodwin. What Makes Radicals? *Common Sense,* 1941, 10:7–9.
26. Watson, W. S., Jr., and G. W. Hartman. The rigidity of a basic attitudinal frame. *J. Abn. Socl. Psychol.,* 1939, 34:314–335.
27. Whyte, William H., Jr. *The Organization Man.* New York, Simon and Schuster, Inc., 1956.
28. Wood, M. M. *The Stranger.* New York, Columbia University Press, 1934.

57. Resistance to the Adoption of Audiovisual Aids by Elementary School Teachers: Contrast and Similarities to Agricultural Innovation

Gerhard Eichholz* • Everett M. Rogers**

In 1955, one of the authors chanced upon an issue of the *Journal of Educational Research* devoted to reviewing research studies on the diffusion of new educational ideas. This was the first convergence between two research traditions, education and rural sociology, that had both been investigating the spread of new ideas for over seventeen years!

The purpose of the present paper is to illustrate the convergence between these two major intellectual traditions focusing on the diffusion of innovations, using data from an investigation of the rejection of audio-visual aids by elementary school teachers.

Traditions of Diffusion Research

Diffusion is the process by which an innovation spreads. The diffusion process is the spread of a new idea from its source of invention or creation to its ultimate users or adopters. Thus diffusion entails the communication or dissemination of an idea, and culminates in its adoption by individuals.

One might expect that various scientists studying the spread of new ideas would be in adequate communication with each other regarding their findings and research methods. Nevertheless, any review of the available literature on the diffusion of innovations must arrive at one conclusion: there has been a very inadequate diffusion of diffusion research findings among those researching the topic.

A *research tradition* is a series of research studies on a similar topic in which successive studies are influenced by preceding investigations. Six major diffusion research traditions

will be briefly described: anthropology, early sociology, rural sociology, education, industrial, medical sociology. Each of these intellectual traditions is shown in Table 57.1. There are important differences among the traditions in terms of the disciplines represented, methods of data-gathering and analysis, units of analysis, and types of findings.

The research tradition that has produced the greatest number of publications and studies on the diffusion of new ideas is rural sociology. Most of these studies deal with the transmission of farm innovations from agricultural scientists to farmers. Rural sociology is probably "the only research tradition within the social sciences that can boast so long and so continuing a concern with the social aspects of diffusion" (Katz, 1961). Most rural sociologists are employed in state universities and conduct their research with funds provided by state agricultural experiment stations. The rural sociology diffusion tradition really got under way with the Ryan and Gross (1943) analysis of the spread of hybrid seed corn in Iowa. Since then, about 300 different publications have appeared to report research findings in this tradition (Rogers, 1962).

The educational research tradition is second largest in number of studies (over 150 are listed in a recent bibliography by Ross, 1958). The educational diffusion studies illustrate strong intercommunication within the tradition, but no close attention to other diffusion traditions. Ross (1958, p. 553), after his review of educational diffusion studies, concluded, "Seldom has dispersed research in some phase of education [educational diffu-

Reprinted with the permission of the publisher from Gerhard Eichholtz and Everett Rogers, "Resistance to Adoption of Audio-Visual Aids by Elementary School Teachers: Contrasts and Similarities to Agricultural Innovation," in Mathew Miles (ed.), *Innovation in Education* (New York: Teachers College Press, Columbia University, © 1964), pp. 299–316.
° Director, Division of Educational Resources, The University of Southern Florida.
°° Professor of Communication, Michigan State University.

TABLE 57.1   A Comparison of the Diffusion Research Traditions*

Tradition	Main Disciplines Represented	Main Method of Data-Gathering and Analysis	Main Unit of Analysis	Major Types of Findings
Anthropology	Anthropology	Participant observation combined with descriptive analysis	Societies or tribes	How idea diffuses from one society to another; consequences of innovation
Early sociology	Sociology	Data from secondary sources and a type of statistical analysis	Mainly communities, but also individuals	S-shaped adopter distribution; correlates of innovativeness
Rural sociology	Sociology	Personal interviews and statistical analysis	Individual farmers	Correlates of innovativeness; characteristics of ideas related to rate of adoption; source of information at adoption process stages; S-shaped adopter distribution
Education	Education	Mailed questionnaire and statistical analysis	School systems	Correlates of innovativeness; S-shaped adopter distribution
Industrial	Ind. economics Ind. history Ind. engineering	Case studies and statistical analysis	Industrial firms	Correlates of innovativeness
Medical sociology	Sociology Public health	Personal interviews and statistical analysis	Individuals	Opinion leadership in diffusion; correlates of innovativeness

* Source: Rogers (1962).

sion] been so well articulated and formed such an integrated pattern as a whole."

The majority of educational diffusion studies have been done at one institution, Columbia University's Teachers College, under the sponsorship of one researcher, Paul Mort. The data were most often gathered by mailed questionnaire from school superintendents or principals. The unit of analysis was the school system in almost all of these investigations.

Diffusion in Education

The Problem of "Lag" in Diffusion

Technology has given education and the educative process a tremendous and some- times bewildering array of innovations. Yet there is criticism of schools for what is commonly called a "lag" in the acceptance of these new ideas. All bowling alleys built within the last few years have an overhead projector installed in every lane for score-keeping, yet it is the exceptional school that has even one overhead projector.[1] Does this constitute a "lag" and is such a "lag" measurable? Mort (1953) defined the lag, and measured it.

A period of about 50 years may elapse between insight into a need and the invention of a solution which will be accepted. Fifteen years typically elapse before it is found in three per cent of the school systems . . . additional twenty

[1] An informal survey (by the authors) of audio-visual equipment available in 25 schools located in a metropolitan school system disclosed that no overhead projectors were used.

years usually suffices for an almost complete diffusion in an area the size of an average state.

Eighty-five years may elapse from insight of a need to complete diffusion. Certainly this may be considered a "lag" when we recall that it was only 58 years after the first successful flight of the Wright brothers that a manned rocket sped into outer space.

Rejection and Adoption

Most of the 500-odd diffusion studies in all traditions mentioned have primarily been concerned with those individuals *adopting* innovations. Resistance or rejection of a given innovation has been mentioned only indirectly. Rejection is treated as a "barrier" to be overcome in most diffusion studies. Rejection of an innovation is considered almost abnormal behavior, to be overcome at any expense by those involved in promoting the new idea. Theoretically, rejection might be considered the opposite of adoption. If adoption is the full-scale use of an innovation, rejection is the non-use of an innovation. If acceptance is worthy of study, rejection should be also. (One example of the importance of rejection is community decisions regarding the fluoridation of water supplies, an idea recommended by the U. S. Public Health Service in the early 1950's. United States communities rejected fluoridation in about 80 per cent of the referenda held in 1961.)

The rejection of an innovation is the antithesis of acceptance. When a given innovation is introduced, the entire population that might use such an innovation are potential adopters or rejecters. The process whereby adopters ultimately use an innovation has five distinct and separate stages (North Central Regional Rural Sociology Subcommittee, 1955). These stages are:

1. *Awareness:* The individual learns of the existence of the innovation.

2. *Interest:* The individual seeks more information and considers the merits of the innovation.

3. *Evaluation:* The individual makes a mental application of the innovation and weighs its merits for his particular situation.

4. *Trial:* The individual applies the innovation on a small scale.

5. *Adoption:* The individual accepts the innovation for continued use on the basis of a previous trial.

Thus the potential accepter moves through five stages to become an actual adopter and full-scale user of an innovation. It can be hypothesized that an individual might follow a similar five-stage process as a potential rejecter, leading to actual rejection based on a trial of a given innovation.

Thus the problem of "lag" in the acceptance of educational innovations is not only one of overcoming barriers, but also that of decreasing the time required in the five-stage process leading to actual acceptance. Furthermore, a study of rejecters might determine if a similar five-stage process leads to rejection, as well as indicate why innovations of proven worth are not immediately acceptable to the very teachers for whom they were designed.

A Study in Rejection

An investigation has been conducted to test a theory of rejection compatible with research findings from adoption studies, and also to explain the "lag" in the adoption of educational innovations. The study attempted to develop a rejection classification for newer educational media (Eichholz, 1961). The newer media were defined as electromechanical innovations such as film projectors, tape recorders, television receivers, etc., and static innovations such as the flannelboard, mock-ups, models, programed instructional materials, etc. The classification system was part of a postulated rejection theory. The theory of rejection attempted to incorporate what is presently known of the adoption process, and to explain some seemingly incongruent behavior on the part of adopters. For example, Johnson and van den Ban (1959) found that some adopters of farm innovations did not continue using them. This phenomenon was labeled a "discontinuance" and seemed to remain an isolated phenomenon, outside of the normal adoption process. Allen (1956) found discontinuances of certain educational practices (including remedial reading) in 12 of 54 schools that he studied.

Figure 57.1 shows a postulated theory of re-

Figure 57.1.   Diagram of a Proposed Rejection Theory.

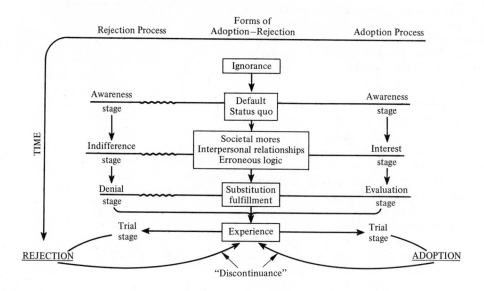

jection combining much of the basic research in adoption. This theory is an attempt to formulate a rejection-adoption theory based primarily on rejection, and incorporates "discontinuances" as a logical result of either the rejection or the adoption process.

Procedure

In an effort to test this theory of rejection and validate the classifications postulated, forty-five teachers in a metropolitan school system were selected for interviews in 1960 on the basis of three criteria:

1. *Grade taught:* 15 teachers were selected from each of the following grade levels: 1–2, 3–4, and 5–6.

2. *Teaching experience:* 15 teachers were selected from each of the following ranges of experience: 1–3 years, 7–10 years, and over 15 years.

3. *Known rejecter:* A short six-question test was given to determine the non-users or rejecters of electromechanical innovations.

The criteria of grade taught and years of teaching experience were used because Kelly (1960) found them to be significant factors in

the adoption of educational innovations. The sample of forty-five teachers made possible a comparison in terms of grade level and teaching experience, with five teachers at each grade level and five at each experience level. A six-item pre-test was given to all teachers; only those teachers found by this test to be rejecters of electromechanical innovations were included in the sample.

Each teacher included in the sample was interviewed with an open-ended questionnaire designed to uncover teachers' feelings toward the newer media. All interviews were over an hour in length, tape recorded, transcribed, and evaluated in terms of attitudes toward specific innovations. These attitude statements were tabulated on the basis of a previously developed rejection classification system. (See *Rejection Responses* below.)

The sample of forty-five teachers came from five elementary schools in a large metropolitan school system. Each school principal was also interviewed concerning his attitudes toward the newer media, and was asked to evaluate each teacher interviewed in his school. An inventory of the newer media available at each school was compiled and checked against the responses of the teachers concerning this equipment. The fact that equipment related to the newer media was available gave added significance to some of the responses.

Some representative responses to illustrate each postulated form of rejection are given below.

Rejection Responses

1. *Rejection through ignorance* was assumed to exist when a given innovation was unknown, or its complexity led to misunderstanding.

We have an opaque projector in the school. I never use it. [The projector available was a micro-projector.]
I don't always know what audio-visual materials are available.
I don't know how to use the movie projector; kind of embarrassed to admit it.

2. *Rejection through default* was expressed by admitting a knowledge of the innovation without any interest in its usage.

I never use a tape recorder . . . just don't use it, that's all. Might be very helpful in speech. I can run it, but we don't have time . . . Let's be honest about it, we don't have time to do everything we want to do with the children.
By the time we get through teaching what we have to teach, there is not too much time left for extras.

3. *Rejection by maintaining the status quo* was expressed when the teacher did not accept an innovation because it had not been used in the past.

I tend to do the teaching process [arithmetic] mechanically, because the book does it that way.
I refuse to tell you that I use these aids all the time. I don't. I am an old-fashioned teacher and feel that we should use the text once in a while.

4. *Rejection through societal mores* was expressed when the teacher thought her society did not find an innovation acceptable, and therefore did not use it herself.

I find that children are watching lots of TV programs they should not be watching, and at hours they should be in bed.
Use the record player once a week. I use it more when the children bring in records. . . . they were rock-and-roll, and I discouraged it because they were not worth listening to.
I don't use the museum. There are only certain classrooms that visit the museum.

5. *Rejection through interpersonal relationships* was expressed by indicating that friends did not use an innovation, or that a particular school environment made using an innovation unacceptable. When some teachers or a principal were enthusiastic over the newer media, these attitudes were similarly reflected by rejecters.

The equipment we have at school is excellent . . . we have enough of everything.
We have three television sets. Don't you think that is very good? But then the principal is very audio-visual minded, and sees that we get things.

On the other hand, indifference toward the newer media in other schools was expressed by rejecters.

The principal doesn't think less of a teacher for not using audio-visual materials. She would probably like to see them used. We never talk about this sort of stuff at teacher's meetings . . . they are all business.

Other personal relationships influence the use of the newer media.

We sort of cooperate . . . we tell each other what we have available and how good we think it is.
I don't use the art program. One of the teachers in the second grade used it and said it was too complicated . . . so she gave it up.

6. *Rejection through erroneous logic* was expressed by giving "rational" but unfounded reasons for the rejection of a worthy innovation.

The upper grades use the A-V materials more than the lower grades do.
I suspect the lower grades use them [newer media] more than we do in the upper grades.

I haven't used quite as many audio-visual materials this year because I have a slower group. Quite often my students think that when they go to see a movie it is fun . . . so I don't use them. I don't use filmstrips either.

7. *Rejection through substitution* was expressed when a teacher spoke of using one practice over another that would have required the use of a particular innovation.

I use two pieces of tag board instead of a screen . . . there is a screen available but this is easier.

If you are going to have a radio program . . . something else will have to be dropped.

I do more work on charts and things like that than on A-V materials.

8. *Rejection through fulfillment* was expressed when a teacher was certain she knew the "best" or "only" way to teach, making any innovation completely unnecessary.

I would not take additional instruction in A-V materials because I think you take those things you are interested in, and I am interested in music and art.

I have a cadet teacher that uses a flannelboard, and the children enjoy it; but I find I can use the blackboard just as well.

I use one film a morning for six weeks. . . . Some have asked why I don't use the radio; but why should I, if I study the material and know what I can present to the children?

9. *Rejection through experience* was expressed by telling of some incident when an innovation was tried and failed.

I signed up one summer to take an audio-visual course, but it was filled.

There are some teachers that order films and ask other teachers to show them.

Now this year I don't use one program that is very good. Sort of ashamed of myself, but I get tired of hearing the same thing year after year.

The children like filmstrips at the beginning because they are a novelty but after a while they get bored.

Results

The findings of this study were not completely conclusive. For example:

1. Attitudes of rejecters were not related to the grade level at which a teacher taught, or to the number of years of teaching experience. This finding is not consistent with the prior findings of Kelly (1960).

2. No teacher, even though classified as a rejecter on the basis of the six-item scale, was a rejecter of *all* the newer media. Every teacher, while rejecting many of the electromechanical innovations, used many of the static innovations.

3. Each form of rejection postulated was expressed by at least 50 per cent of the sample. About 50 per cent of the sample expressed rejection through default, while 93 per cent of the sample expressed rejection through experience.

4. It became obvious that, for the teachers interviewed, the real reasons for rejection and the stated reasons for rejection were not always the same. The postulated forms of rejection could be considered neither complete nor mutually exclusive. Therefore, it became necessary to establish a revised framework for the identification of rejection forms, reducing the nine original postulated forms to five basic forms.

Table 57.2 illustrates the revised framework for the identification of rejection responses. This framework gives typical responses for various forms of rejection, and differentiates between "real" and "stated" reasons for rejection. These forms of rejection appear to be more inclusive and parsimonious. Each form now stands in a direct one-to-one relationship with stages in both adoption and rejection processes. It is further possible to conceptualize a total process that might be known as an adoption-rejection (or "decision") process that incorporates the five forms and five stages of adoption-rejection. Figure 57.2, incorporating the revisions made as a result of this study, shows such a process.

Further Research Needs

This study attempted to define the area of rejection in a limited field. The revised theory and classification of rejection noted here is neither complete nor final. While the classification seems substantiated in the light of the

TABLE 57.2   A Framework for the Identification of Forms of Rejection

Form of Rejection	Cause of Rejection	State of Subject	Anticipated Rejection Responses
1. Ignorance	Lack of dissemination	Uninformed	"The information is not easily available."
2. Suspended judgment	Data not *logically* compelling	Doubtful	"I want to wait and see how good it is, before I try."
3. Situational	Data not *materially* compelling	1. Comparing	"Other things are equally good."
		2. Defensive	"The school regulations will not permit it."
		3. Deprived	"It costs too much to use in time and/or money."
4. Personal	Data not *psychologically* compelling	1. Anxious	"I don't know if I can operate equipment."
		2. Guilty	"I know I should use them, but I don't have time."
		3. Alienated (or estranged)	"These gadgets will never replace a teacher." ("If we use these gadgets, they might replace us.")
5. Experimental	Present or past trials	Convinced	"I tried them once and they aren't any good."

limited sample used, another study is contemplated to further substantiate these findings and to investigate the question of potential adopters-rejecters. There is some reason to believe that a person may be either a potential adopter or a potential rejecter, approaching an innovation with adopter or rejecter "sets." Other questions still unanswered are:

Figure 57.2.   Diagram of Revised Rejection Theory.

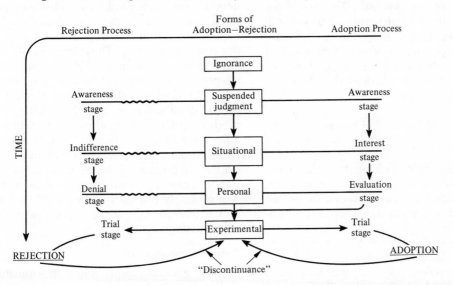

1. What factors differentiate the rejecters and accepters of the newer media?

2. Does a given innovation cause a certain form of rejection, or are all forms of rejection common to all innovation?

3. What happens when a series of many innovations related to teaching methodology is available in a short period of time? Are they adopted as a "cluster"? Is such a cluster or complex of innovations adopted more quickly or slowly than single innovations?

4. Are the means for shortening rejection time common to all forms of rejection, or must each form be treated differently?

5. Can tests be devised to isolate attitudes of rejection on the part of teachers, thereby giving administrators some indication of the potential "lag" they can expect in the acceptance of innovations?

6. Should school administrators be responsible for pressing adoption of the newer media to secure an improved quality of education?

7. Are teachers morally obligated to reject the newer media until such time as they are personally certain of its worth and willing to alter their method of teaching to include the innovation?

Although these and other questions are yet to be answered, technology continues to force upon education a vast and complex number and variety of innovations. Devices from teaching machines to airborne television will meet with resistance. Rejection is the only defense left to a teacher who feels threatened by these innovations. Yet it is on the teachers' acceptance of these innovations that their success ultimately depends.

Similarities to Rural Sociological Research

Common Elements

There are five crucial elements in the analysis of the diffusion of any type of innovation. These elements have been shown to be the same in studies in rural sociology and education.

1. The *innovation*, defined as an idea perceived as new by the individual.

2. The *communication* of the innovation from one individual to another. Diffusion is defined as the process by which an idea spreads.

3. The innovation diffuses through a *social system*, defined as a population of individuals who are functionally differentiated and engaged in collective problem-solving. The social system under analysis in a research study may be all the farmers in a county, all the teachers in a school system, or the members of an aborigine tribe. The farmer, teacher, or aborigine is the unit of analysis in each case. The norms of the system, whether traditional or innovative, affect the diffusion of innovations in that system.

4. Diffusion occurs over *time*. Not all individuals adopt an innovation at the same time. Innovativeness is defined as the degree to which an individual adopts new ideas relatively earlier than other members of his social system. Adopter categories involve the classification of individuals on the basis of their innovativeness: (1) innovators, the first to adopt, (2) early adopters, (3) early majority, (4) late majority, (5) laggards, and (6) nonusers. Adopter categories have been studied both by educational researchers (Ross, 1958) and by rural sociologists (Rogers, 1962).

5. The time differential in adoption or rejection can be explained in part by the forms and *stages* of adoption-rejection. These forms (ignorance, suspended judgment, situational, personal, and experimental) are directly related to the stages found in both the adoption and the rejection process. Thus the time at which any given individual becomes an actual adopter or rejecter will depend on two factors: (1) how quickly he passes through the forms of adoption or rejection, and (2) the predisposition of the individual to either the adoption or the rejection process. It may also be that certain forms of adoption-rejection lead to a greater or lesser time differential. For instance, rejection for situational reasons will probably remain rejection until the situation is altered, in spite of a personal willingness to adopt.

Common Generalizations

Some generalizations found in educational studies seem to be applicable to rural sociological studies (Rogers, 1962). For example, educational researchers have found that schools which are more innovative are characterized by teachers who attend out-of-town educational meetings and who read widely to find new ideas. Similarly, Ryan and Gross (1943) found that farmer-innovators were more likely to travel to metropolitan cities than were laggards. These findings suggest the generalization that *innovativeness varies directly with cosmopoliteness* (defined as the degree to which an individual's orientation is external to a particular social system). This generalization is also supported by evidence from industrial and medical sociology studies (Rogers, 1962).

Another generalization supported by evidence from several research traditions is that *innovativeness varies directly with financial resources*. Rogers (1962) found that innovative farmers operated larger farms, earned higher gross farm incomes, and had a higher net worth than less innovative farmers. Ross (1958) summarizes research evidence to the effect that the more innovative school systems are located in communities with higher average personal incomes and greater school tax support. Similarly, innovativeness has been found to characterize medical doctors with richer patients and industrial firms with larger operations.

Contrasts to Rural Sociological Research

The Unit of Analysis

One of the important differences between the "typical" research study in rural sociology and the "typical" investigation in education of adoption-rejection lies in the unit of analysis. In rural sociology, the unit of analysis is usually the individual farmer.[2] In some 150 educational studies completed to date on the diffusion of innovations, the unit of analysis has been the school or the school system. It should be noted, however, that the study described in this chapter utilizes the individual teacher as the unit of analysis, although school norms relevant to innovativeness were considered. When the school or school system is used

as a unit of analysis, much of the individual variation in innovativeness and other variables is cancelled. The authors, therefore, feel there is a need for further investigation of adoption-rejection using the individual teacher as the unit of analysis, while taking account of school or group norms concerning innovativesness.

Differences in Diffusion-Adoption Rates

Mort (1946, pp. 199–200) found the average school ". . . lags 25 years behind the best practice." Why is the diffusion and adoption of educational ideas so much slower than that of farm innovations or medical drugs? The following reasons are offered.

(1) *The absence of scientific sources of innovation in education*. This is the constant problem of physical versus social research. The drug laboratories and the vast network of agricultural experimental stations make possible accurate and precise measurements under controlled conditions for a given innovation. Education, on the other hand, has only the "campus" or "university" schools and those classes in the nation's schools that are willing to cooperate in experimentation. In either case, the first responsibility is to the student, not to research. Thus, results of innovation trials are often ambiguous, incomplete, and confusing.

(2) *The lack of change agents to promote new educational ideas*. In agriculture, the Extension Service, through a system of county agents, forms a communication link between scientists and farmers. In education, the school principal is probably in a position similar to the county agent; but, as shown in the Eichholz study, only one of the five principals acted in a "change agent" role with his teachers. It should be noted here that the major role of a principal is probably not to promote change but to administer the *status quo*.

(3) *The lack of economic incentive to adopt*. The lack of economic incentive to adopt an innovation is two-fold in nature: (1) The results of adopting an educational innovation are not so easily measured as those fol-

[2] It is interesting to note that a recent rural sociology study (Armstrong, 1959) used Kentucky counties as the unit of analysis in investigating farmer innovativeness.

lowing the adoption of innovations in agriculture. The innovation in agriculture will result in direct economic profit through increased yield. On the other hand, the only measurable result of an educational innovation may be the dollar cost of the innovation itself, since the amount of increased learning through the use of the innovation cannot be easily measured. (2) Teachers are generally paid on the basis of longevity and personal educational attainment. Thus, what is accomplished in the classroom seldom influences the economic level of the teacher. Teachers adopting innovations are paid the same as those rejecting innovations, and the teacher adopting an innovation faces the added risk of possible failure. As Pelley (1948, pp. 170–171) stated, "Unfortunately, there seems to be no possible profit motive in being an educational innovator."

Concluding Comment

The present study illustrates a type of convergence between two of the intellectual traditions dealing with the diffusion of innovations, education and rural sociology. There is need for greater diffusion of diffusion research findings and methods from one tradition to another. The result will be a greater standardization of terminology, a freshness of approach, and a greater sophistication of research methodology.

References

Allen, H. E. The diffusion of educational practices in the school systems of the Metropolitan School Study Council. Unpublished doctoral dissertation, Teachers College, Columbia University, 1956.

Armstrong, J. B. County agent activities and the adoption of soil-building practices. Unpublished master's thesis, University of Kentucky, 1959.

Eichholz, G. Development of a rejection classification for newer educational media. Unpublished doctoral dissertation, The Ohio State University, 1961.

Johnson, D., & van den Ban, A. The dynamics of farm practice change. Paper read at Midwest Sociol. Soc., Lincoln, Nebraska, 1959.

Katz, E. The social itinerary of technical change: two studies on the diffusion of innovation. *Human Organization*, 1961, 20, 70–82.

Kelly, G. B. A study of teachers' attitudes toward audiovisual materials. *Educ. Screen & Audiovisual Guide*, 1960, 39, 119–121.

Mort, P. R. *Principles of school administration*. New York: McGraw-Hill, 1946.

Mort, P. R. *Educational adaptability*. New York: Metropolitan School Study Council, 1953.

North Central Rural Sociology Subcommittee on the Diffusion of Farm Practices. *How farm people accept new ideas*. Iowa Agricultural Extension Service Special Report 15. Ames: The Service, 1955.

Pelley, J. H. Invention in education. Unpublished doctoral dissertation, Teachers College, Columbia University, 1948.

Rogers, E. M. Categorizing the adopters of agricultural practices. *Rural Sociol.*, 1958, 23, 345–354.

Rogers, E. M. *Diffusion of innovations*. New York: Free Press, 1962.

Ross, D. H. *Administration for adaptability: a source book drawing together the results of more than 150 individual studies related to the question of why and how schools improve*. New York: Metropolitan School Study Council, 1958.

Ryan, B., & Gross, N. C. The diffusion of hybrid seed corn in two Iowa communities. *Rural Sociol.*, 1943, 8, 15–24.

SECTION

CONTROLLING CHANGE PROGRAMS

58. Evaluating Social Action Programs

John W. Evans*

Nothing is more important to the *actual* success of social action programs than that we know whether or not they work. If we are sensibly to alter or terminate programs which are not achieving their objectives, or continue and expand those that are, we must have some decent evidence of how effective and efficient these programs are.

All of this should go without saying. Yet odd as it may seem, despite the billions of dollars we have spent in such areas as manpower training, compensatory education, and welfare, and despite the fact that the decision to spend these staggering sums is made in a society known for its hard-nosed practicality,

rationality, and scientific research, we in fact know relatively little about the effectiveness of many of the social action programs which the government has initiated.[1]

There are a number of reasons for this lack of objective, empirical evaluations and it is well to examine them before looking at the present situation and what the future may hold.

The reason most often given as to why we have not produced useful empirical evaluations of large-scale social action programs is that we do not know how. That is, we lack adequate social science methodology, our measuring instruments are too primitive, the

---

[1] In a preliminary draft (June 9, 1969) of a *Study of Federal Program Evaluation Practices*, Joseph S. Wholey at the Urban Institute remarks that, "a large number of major social programs ought to be viewed as quasi-experimental. They were designed on the assumption that certain courses of action would improve education, increase employment, improve housing, or the like. Generally, however, the Federal Government has made no real attempt to evaluate the effectiveness of social programs or local projects within the programs."

Reprinted from John W. Evans, "Evaluating Social Action Programs," *Social Science Quarterly*, Vol. 50, No. 3 (December 1969), pp. 568–581.
° Assistant Commissioner for Planning and Evaluation of U.S. Office of Education.

real world environment is too complex to sort out cause-effect relationships, and so forth. There is no question that the "state of the art" is a very important factor contributing to the underdeveloped state of evaluation, and there is no question that the long catalogue of deficiencies and complexities, recited with hand-wringing despair by both administrators and social scientists, is all true. Our measuring instruments—in the area of cognitive and affective development in children, for example—are far from what we would like to have. The methodological task of sorting out the influence of an education or manpower training program from all the other relevant influences in its participants' lives is indeed so formidable that many say it simply can't be done with any confidence.

In my own view, as true and as formidable as these considerations are, they are not sufficient to account for or justify the dearth of adequate program evaluations. I believe we can greatly improve our basis for assessing social action programs by utilizing the admittedly limited techniques we now have in hand, and I shall have more to say on this below.

One of the most important reasons why objective and empirical evaluations have not become an established, organic part of the decision-making process in the federal government is that empirical evaluation is a mode of thinking that is foreign to the kind of people who have traditionally found themselves in the role of government administrators and program directors. Cabinet members, assistant secretaries, and program directors do not typically come from either a physical or social science background. As a result, when faced with their own and others' concerns about the effectiveness of their programs, their thinking does not naturally turn to the existence and quality of empirical evidence—to matters of criteria, measures, control groups, and the like. This mode of thinking is something which becomes natural only as a result of formal scientific training. Without such thinking, however, the analysis and assessment process must suffer. Sincerity of motivation is confused with effectiveness of results, and inputs (such as dollars and program size) are substi-

tuted for outputs as indicators of program success. Even in the defense area, where hardware problems and the more evaluation-accustomed physical sciences prevail, it took a McNamara to bring this kind of thinking to the top decision levels of the Defense Department.

A second important reason is that the role of program administration and the role of objective evaluation involve conflicting interests. We have not yet arrived at that ideal (and unreal) point in the conduct of affairs in our government where agency heads and program directors see their role as an impartial custodian or overseer of the public interest. It is hard to imagine, for example, the secretary of one of the major departments going to the Congress, reporting that one of his major programs does not appear to be producing any appreciable effect, and recommending that Congress take back the several billion dollars devoted to this program and abolish part of his department. Rather, the program administrator's role seems inevitably to be that of program advocate. To a very considerable extent it is desirable that this should be the case. But the typical process which takes place annually within government agencies preparing for Congressional hearings is not one of developing an even handed presentation of the successes and advantages vs. the failures and difficulties of a program, but rather one of collecting and displaying those things (with limited scrutiny of their validity) which show the program and its accomplishments in a favorable light. This is a situation and a process for which program administrators are not to blame. They know full well from past experience—or at least they believe it to be the case—that if they go before Congress with a report that their program is not working they can expect a cry to go up for their scalp. An admission of program failure will be taken as an admission of personal failure. In this context it does not take the perceptive program administrator long to become wary of hard, clear-cut, empirical evaluations, for they are a two-edged sword. The more attractive course is to go with softer information that is more subject to manipulation.

As a result of all these factors and the pressures they generate (as well as the imperatives of day-to-day operations), it has often been the case that research and evaluation get shunted aside and play second fiddle to program administration and operation. This means, for example, that research and evaluation are organizationally often off to one side in a weaker bureaucratic position relative to the program elements and that funds and staff for the evaluation are allocated sparingly. Within the organization the strong testimonials of the program managers often drown out the weaker and "negative" sounding voices of the research and evaluation staff who are calling for quantitative and objective assessment of program outcomes. In this situation, it is easy to let the political considerations—which are often totally overriding anyway—be the dominant factors in deciding how good a program is and what should be done about it.

Finally, apart from the weaknesses in social science methodology and the foreign and sometimes threatening character of evaluation, there is also the fact that social scientists themselves have shown only limited interest in becoming evaluators. More often than not when they have undertaken evaluation studies, they have not performed well. The problem seems to center around the practical and policy character of the evaluator's role. The socializing experience of graduate school instills in the majority of social scientists a negative definition of practical or applied careers. These are defined as sell-outs of one kind or another and something to be avoided in favor of careers which stress academic, theoretical, and disciplinary goals. When program evaluations are undertaken by academic social scientists, there is a tendency to convert them from a practical or policy task into a theoretical research project or retreat to a focus on models and methodology. The social scientist's scholarly habit of following the analysis where it leads makes him insensitive to and impatient

with deadlines and schedules, with the frequent result that by the time he feels his final report is ready, the problem it addressed has been overtaken by events.

Faced with a theoretically oriented study which he did not want, reaching him too late to be useful and in such voluminous and technically esoteric form that neither he nor his policy people can understand it, the harried administrator throws up his hands. The experience adds to his stereotype of social science as useless to real world decisions, and pushes him a little further if reluctantly toward the conclusion that the only evaluations he can count on are the informal and partisan ones he receives from his program staffs.

Quite apart, then, from the internal organizational considerations, one of the factors contributing to the lack of adequate empirical evaluations of social action programs is the shortage of interested, capable, and practically oriented social scientists to perform them.

Evaluation at OEO

The situation I have outlined above is more of a constructed type than an accurate description of any particular government agency. Indeed, in the last few years considerable progress has been made. Based on the dramatic changes made by McNamara in the Defense Department, President Johnson ordered the Bureau of the Budget to implement a similar Planning, Programming, and Budgeting System (PPBS) throughout the federal government.[2] The essence of this new system is nothing short of a radically different approach to federal decision-making and resource allocation at the highest level. In the defense area, where there has been the greatest effort to apply the PPB System, the intention has been to get away from the traditional interservice power struggle and other ad hoc considerations as the main basis for deciding, for example, whether the Navy should get two new aircraft carriers, the Air Force should get a new bomber, or the Army should be in-

[2] See *The Analysis and Evaluation of Public Expenditures: The PPB System. A Compendium of Papers Submitted to the Sub-committee on Economy in Government of the Joint Economic Committee* (Congress of the United States, 91st Congress, 1969), vols. 1–3.

creased by two divisions. Instead, the PPB System requires that we specify precisely what our military objective is, (say, the defense of a certain area), what the various alternative means for achieving it are (remotely located missiles, mobile naval or troop forces, or whatever) and finally what the relative cost and effectiveness of each of these alternative means is. Thus, in this type of decision-making, resource allocation system, the primary focus is taken off of the means and put where it should be on the objectives, with each means, or program, being assessed in terms of its comparative ability to achieve an objective. Obviously, rigorous evaluation of program effectiveness is central to this kind of decision-making system.

While considerable progress has been made, and the domestic arms of the government are now struggling with the implementation of the PPB System, it is nevertheless still the case that in most government agencies empirical evaluation is not yet the automatic and organic part of the decision-making process that it should be and could be.

Probably one of the better beginnings has been made at the office of Economic Opportunity (OEO). From its early days, OEO had a unit which functioned as an extension of the Director's office called the Office of Research, Plans, Programs, and Evaluation (RPP&E). This office carried out basic research on poverty, prepared short- and long-range plans for the poverty program, and was used by the Director and Deputy Director for advice on major program and policy questions. It eventually acquired the all important budgeting function which allowed its analyses and studies to be more directly influential in important resource allocation decisions (within the limited latitude, of course, which political considerations allowed).

Up until 1968, however, the RPP&E office carried out few formal, empirical evaluations of OEO programs. There were a number of reasons for this, among them the fact that dur-

ing the early years of the War on Poverty most programs were struggling to become operational and overall assessment of their effectiveness did not make much sense at that time. In addition, an early organization decision had created small research and evaluation offices in each of the major program elements (that is, within Job Corps, Head Start, VISTA, and others), and at that time it seemed these offices would collectively provide the needed program evaluations.

By the summer of 1967, however, the then director of RPP&E, Robert A. Levine, an economist, had concluded that depending upon the program offices to produce the needed evaluations of the effectiveness of their programs was not working and that his own office should develop a capability to evaluate the impact of all OEO programs.[3] I was asked to come to OEO in the fall of 1967 and develop the new evaluation function.

After a general review, my small staff and I concluded, as Levine had, that despite the fact that a great deal of money had been spent on evaluation studies by the various program offices, it was not possible to get from these studies a useful answer to the question, "How effective has the program been in achieving its objectives?" We also concluded that it seemed unlikely that the existing organizational arrangement would produce methodologically sophisticated evaluations that focused on the tough questions.

We finally decided that some fairly radical changes would have to be made if the antipoverty programs were to be evaluated in a useful way. We therefore made a number of far reaching recommendations to Bertrand Harding, the then Acting Director of OEO.

We began by proposing a three-fold scheme into which all evaluations be categorized:

Type I. The assessment of overall program impact and effectiveness where the emphasis is on determining the extent to which programs are successful in achieving basic objectives.

[3] See the critical but accurate assessment of early OEO evaluation efforts by Peter Rossi, "Practice, Method, and Theory in Evaluating Social Action Programs," in James L. Sundquist, ed., *On Fighting Poverty* (New York: Basic Books, 1969), pp. 221–223.

Type II. The evaluation of the relative effectiveness of different program strategies and variables where the emphasis is on determining which alternative techniques for carrying out a program are most productive (for example, determining whether one type of curriculum is more effective than another for teaching Head Start children).

Type III. The evaluation of individual projects through site visits and other monitoring activities where the emphasis is on assessing managerial and operational efficiency.

We recommended that primary responsibility for the Type I evaluation of all OEO programs be assigned to the newly created RPP&E Evaluation Division; and that the research and evaluation units in the program offices (Job Corps, Head Start, VISTA, and the others) be responsible for the Type II and Type III evaluations of their respective programs.

There is nothing intellectually elegant about this three-fold distinction. Indeed, it can be argued that separating Type I and Type II evaluations creates an artificial distinction between studies focusing on effectiveness and those focusing on the factors which do or do not contribute to effectiveness. But it seemed clear that if the responsibility for Type I evaluations were left to the programs they would not get done. As noted earlier, there are just too many built-in pressures at the program level that militate against the overall effectiveness question getting properly asked or answered. It seemed important that this type of evaluation be removed from the program level and made an overview function of a staff office which would not be faced with the budgetary choice of reducing program activity in order to fund such evaluations, and which could take an impartial view of all programs. On the other hand, we felt it was important that the Type II evaluations not be removed from the program level because of the need for intimate program knowledge in determining what program variables should be investigated. These considerations led us to make the three-fold distinction and recommend the di-

vision of responsibility between RPP&E and the program offices. Clearly, there were as many practical as conceptual considerations involved.

It should also be pointed out that the three types of evaluation parallel three major organization levels and the different kinds of decisions required at each. At the top level—Congress, the Bureau of the Budget, and the agency director—the question is "What programs?" (Type I); at the level of the program director the question is "What techniques?" (Type I); and at the regional or local level the question is "What projects?" (Type III).

We recommended that the agency set aside as much as 1 per cent of its total appropriation for evaluation of all three types and that one-sixth of this 1 per cent (about $2.8 million) be set aside for the new Evaluation Division to fund priority Type I evaluations.

We further recommended that the new Evaluation Division be given several additional senior level positions to allow the hiring of Ph.D. level professionals and that the program offices be required to submit an annual evaluation plan covering their Type II and Type III evaluations for approval by the new RPP&E Evaluation Division.

These proposals were not greeted with enthusiasm by most of the program heads. Many of them were, understandably, opposed to the idea of outside evaluations of their programs and they protested the levy on their program budgets to fund such evaluations. Numerous meetings were held and memoranda exchanged, but Harding's final decision was to approve all the recommendations. In March of 1968 an official order went out formally establishing the new evaluation division, indicating the division of responsibility between it and the various program offices for the different types of evaluation, and setting aside the necessary funds.[4] In the following months, six professionals were recruited (from the fields of sociology, psychology, mathematics, and systems analysis) and national evaluations were designed and initiated on Head Start, the Community Action Program, five man-

[4] OEO Instruction 72–8, March 6, 1968.

power programs (Job Corps, NYC out-of-school, MDTA institutional, New Careers, and the JOBS program), the Neighborhood Health Centers, the Family Planning Program, Upward Bound, and the Title I-D Special Impact programs.

The Type I evaluation process is intended to provide answers to four fundamental, almost common sense, questions.

1. *Is the program reasonably addressed to the needs of those towards whom it is aimed?* This question merely points up that before launching a training program, for example, we should be sure that the people to be trained are capable of acquiring the skills to be taught, that there is a need for such skills in the labor market, and so forth. As obvious as this point is, it is possible to find examples of programs ill-suited to the needs of the people they were supposed to serve—not necessarily because of misdirection by program managers but because making an accurate assessment of human and social needs requires detailed data on the target population that are often not available.[5] The point here is simply that one of the key steps in evaluating a program is to determine whether or not it really addresses the needs of the population at which it is directed, and this requires not only clear policy but detailed data on the target population as well.

2. *To what extent does the program reach the intended population?* In the absence of information on how well a program achieves its objectives, it is possible to make an evaluative judgment of a program's potential effectiveness on the basis of the extent of its reach.

Other things equal, a program which reaches a large proportion of the intended population is more effective than if it reaches only a small proportion. To make even this level of evaluative judgment, however, requires detailed and extensive data on both the universe of need and the number of people the program is serving.

3. *How successful is the program in achieving its objectives?* Answering this question is getting directly to the problem of determining how well the program is accomplishing what it set out to do. Such an assessment should, of course, be based upon carefully designed and controlled research; but, as I have indicated, in actual practice it is usually based on much less—often little more than impressionistic and subjective judgments. The essence of evaluation is attribution. Therefore the prototypic evaluation should approximate the classic model of experimental design, in which before-after measures are made on a representative sample of program participants and on a comparable control sample of non-participants, preferably randomly assigned. The evaluations we have designed do approximate this model, but many compromises are necessary and approximations are the best we are ever going to get. For example, the requirement of random assignment to program and control groups will, in my opinion, only rarely be feasible for national studies of ongoing programs.

4. *How does the cost of the program compare with the value of its benefits?* Even if we know how well a program fits the needs of its target population, how completely it is reach-

---

[5] The War on Poverty itself provides such examples. One of the basic purposes of the In-School component of the Neighborhood Youth Corps was to supply some kind of employment to poverty kids in order to deter them from dropping out of school. But it appears that economic reasons may not be a major factor in deciding to leave school. There is even some suggestion that by supplying employment and money the program may in fact be counter-productive by encouraging some kids to leave school. There is also the early form of the Small Business Development Program where the qualification requirements resulted in it being nearly impossible to make loans to the group for which the program was intended. Similarly, the basic skills component of several manpower programs, the type of teachers used, the scheduling of classes, and the seeming irrelevance of the material resulted in these programs failing to attract poor, unemployed males—the group at which they were aimed.

ing that population, and how effectively it is accomplishing its objectives, in order to fully evaluate that program we must still determine whether the benefits of the program are greater than its cost or vice versa. This phase of evaluation also requires sophisticated data on both the costs and the benefits of the program—data that are usually not routinely available for most programs.

In sum, if we can answer these four questions about any social action program we will know whether in a general way the program makes sense, how far it is reaching, what effect it is having on those it does reach, and what it is costing to achieve this effect.

Table 58.1 provides a general paradigm for the evaluation of antipoverty programs based on the acquisition of data relating to universe of need, program reach, program effectiveness and program cost for each antipoverty program.

Going down the left-hand Evaluation Data column from A through H will indicate how the completed paradigm would be useful in overall planning and programming. With de-

pendable data for each program on universe of need (A) and program reach (B), we can calculate, and compare programs on, the extent to which they are reaching their target populations (C). A solid figure on program coverage (C) would be useful in planning and budgeting both within a given program and across the total array of programs. Bringing together for all programs the information on their total costs (D) (on which we usually have good data) and information on the number of people they reach (B) (on which we usually don't) would allow us to compute, and compare programs on, the cost per person reached (E). With information on program costs (D), the total universe of need (A), and the present program reach (B), we could determine for each program what the cost of total coverage would be and how much of an increment over present budget outlays this would require (F).

Of course the paradigm oversimplifies some very complex issues. In the first place, some of the cells in the table will turn out to be inappropriate. For example, in evaluating the ex-

TABLE 58.1 Paradigm for the Evaluation of Antipoverty Programs

	Antipoverty Programs[a]								
Evaluation Data	*Job Corps*	*VISTA*	*Community Action Agencies*	*Legal Services*	*Head Start*	*Follow Through*	*Upward Bound*	*Health Services*	*etc.*
A. Universe of need									
B. Program reach									
C. Program coverage ($\frac{A}{B}$)									
D. Program cost									
E. Cost per person reached ($\frac{D}{B}$)									
F. Cost of total coverage (E) (A)[b]									
G. Measures of program effectiveness: 1. Immediate objectives 2. Poverty reduction									
H. Benefit-cost ratio ($\frac{G}{D}$)									

[a] This array of programs is for illustration. It does not reflect the recent organizational changes in OEO or the fact that some programs, e.g., Upward Bound, have been transferred to other agencies.
[b] A correct computation would not be this simple but would take into account the marginal cost required to expand programs at different levels.

tent to which the Community Action Program achieves institutional change, such concepts as universe of need and program reach are not very meaningful. Second, some programs are not aimed so much at individuals as they are at groups, communities, or families, which means that individual measures such as cost per person reached are not relevant. Third, the programs are treated individually, and no provision is made in the table for the cumulative or interactive impact of several programs operating together, though some effort to assess this will have to be made. Finally, meaningful comparisons of the effectiveness of different programs in different functional areas will probably remain essentially intuitive unless a standard measure like the benefit-cost ratio can be developed for all programs. Otherwise, we find ourselves trying to compare the relative values of an educated youth from Job Corps with an improved child from Head Start, with a potential drop-out sent on to college by Upward Bound, with a medically cured mother by Health Services. Assembling program costs is comparatively easy. Ascertaining or even estimating the total individual and social benefits of any program is very difficult, and assigning dollar values to all these benefits may be impossible.

These considerations make it quite clear that we will never achieve a purely mechanical decision-making system. Nevertheless, it is equally clear that developing as much reliable data as we can for each program on its universe of need, its reach, its cost, and its effectiveness will allow us to make much better assessments of our various efforts to move people out of poverty, and to make more rational decisions about the allocation of our limited resources than we are able to do now.

As this is being written, most of the evaluations we have initiated are still in process, so it remains to be seen what impact both the organizational changes and the results of these studies will have. The one major evaluation which has been completed, the one on Head Start, found, to the disappointment of many and the disbelief of some, that Head Start appeared to have few if any lasting cognitive or motivational effects on the children who went through the program. The study has occasioned considerable debate along predictably partisan lines but the well-documented general conclusions of the study are hard to dismiss, and it seems likely the results will have an important influence on the larger decisions yet to be made about Head Start's future.[6]

Some Thoughts About the Future

Out of this entire experience, there are several major conclusions I have come to and I pass them on to others interested in evaluation in the hope that they may comprise a number of lessons which it will not be necessary for us all to learn separately over and over again.

1. My experiences lead me to disagree with the cynic's view that evaluation is generally a waste of time—that partisan political considerations are the overwhelming factor in determining what happens to government social action programs and that empirical evaluation and rational analysis can never hope to be more than an insignificant input in the decision-making process. Irrelevant and often irrational factors still do play a distressingly large role in the assessment of our programs and in the decisions about their future, but my experience in the government leads me to believe —and I think not naively—that the long-run trend is in the other direction. Such a trend is becoming established within the government itself with the Planning, Programming, Bud-

[6] *The Impact of Head Start: An Evaluation of the Effects of Head Start on Children's Cognitive and Affective Development* (The Westinghouse Learning Corporation and Ohio University, June 1969). On the debate over the study see the forthcoming paper by Sheldon White, "The National Impact Study of Head Start," the three-part piece in the Fall 1969 edition of the *Britannica Review of American Education* by Victor Cicirelli, William Madow, and John W. Evans; and Walter Williams and John W. Evans, *Evaluating the War on Poverty*, "The Politics of Evaluation: The Case of Head Start," *The Annals of the American Academy of Political and Social Science* (Sept., 1969).

geting System being pushed strongly by the Bureau of the Budget and increasingly becoming a fixture, if indeed an imperfect one, in most government agencies. But also in the Congress, the press, and the public as well, there is both an increasing demand that judgments and decisions be founded on the best kind of empirical evidence possible and, though it is somewhat more slow in coming, a willingness to accept distasteful judgments about one's favorite (or most hated) program if they appear to be based upon some evidence.

2. An important lesson we must all learn is that our task in evaluating social action programs in the real world is not to produce methodologically perfect studies but rather to *improve decisions* by doing the best that can be done in a timely and relevant way. Evaluation, every bit as much as politics, is the art of the possible. And those of us who practice it and wish to have an impact upon the important events of our time must realize that decisions are going to be made either in the presence or absence of information. This is the nature of the political process and I do not think it is likely to change much in our lifetime if ever. Putting aside important decisions to await the design and completion of an ideal study is not the way Congress and the executive branch work, or indeed the way any program can long operate. Therefore, the task of the evaluator is to bring the best possible information he can to the decision-making point at a time when it can be expected to have some impact. The argument against this position is that some information can be worse than none. Even though this is an obvious and valid point, I believe we should normally assume the reverse. There is no question that in some cases imperfect evaluations and incomplete information will be misleading; but as a general rule, imperfect and incomplete analyses are going to be better than none at all— which is what the alternative is and which, unfortunately, is the basis on which many important decisions have been made.

3. For the reasons cited above, the most important instrumental problem in program evaluation today is not the "poor state of the art"—the inadequacy of measurement techniques, the absence of comprehensive and valid program data systems, or the need for other technical "breakthroughs" in the social sciences. These are very severe problems, which all of us in both the academic and applied areas must continue our efforts to solve. But there is a great deal that can be done with existing admittedly imperfect research and evaluation techniques which can greatly improve our current mode of assessing program effectiveness. There is in my judgment a large gap between the way programs are currently being evaluated and what could be done by a wider application of the research and evaluation techniques we now have in hand. I think we have a long way to go in putting present-day techniques to work before we can legitimately complain that we are stymied in our efforts to improve rational decision-making because of inadequate methodology. Continuing to belabor the point of the "poor state of the art," as so many of us do, is a poor excuse for not getting at the task at hand and it serves only to delay, not to accelerate, the contribution that social science can make to program assessment and policy determination.

4. The single most important step that can be taken to accelerate useful evaluations of government social action programs and insure that such evaluations have impact on decisions is to make evaluation a central part of the management process by giving it a superordinate location within government agencies. As I indicated above, progress along these lines is being made in some agencies, but we still have a long way to go.

It is part of the chronic special pleading of every government bureaucrat that in the next reorganization his element should be "attached to the Director's office." The argument for evaluation, however, is quite different because it rests on the fact that the determination of program effectiveness is a key executive function. Consequently, evaluation is—or should be—a central part of the decision-making and resource allocation process. It is in this respect quite different from the line or operation function of the programs themselves.

The ideal type of organizational arrangement is, in my opinion, one which combines the key executive functions of planning, programming, evaluation (Type I), and *budgeting* in a single staff office which serves as the agency director's key advisor and implementing arm.[7]

There are different ways to categorize types of evaluation and assign organization responsibilities for seeing that they are carried out. My threefold scheme is only one. But regardless of what distinctions and divisions are made, one principle which I believe must be followed is that the responsibility for what I have called Type I evaluations must be removed from the program level.

5. Equal in importance to the organizational location of the evaluation function, is the need for it to be staffed with professionally qualified people. As I noted above, one of the principal reasons for the lack of evaluations and their poor quality has been the shortage of technically competent social scientists within the government to insure that evaluations are methodologically well-designed, relevant to policy and program issues, carried out properly and in a timely fashion by the contracting organization doing the actual work, and reported in a way which allows their results to be understood and used by those at the top levels of the executive and legislative branches who are going to make the actual decisions. Too often well-meaning administrators have attempted to initiate evaluations but their lack of technical expertise has caused the evaluation to run afoul of all of the problems just listed. The result has been worse than just useless studies and wasted money because it has discredited social science and led to the belief that useful empirical evaluations are not practically possible.

If conditions are developing to the point where objective, empirical evaluations are going to play an increasingly important role in government decision-making—as I believe they are—then the problem of the necessary professional manpower must be solved. Increasing numbers of social scientists are going to be needed if methodologically adequate and professionally guided evaluations are actually going to get designed, carried out, and fed into the government decision-making process. I do not believe this can be accomplished by using academically based social scientists on a consulting or short-term contractual basis, though the widespread effort to do this will doubtless continue. Program evaluation and academic research are two different things. They have different goals, they are likely to utilize different methods, they call for different time schedules, and they yield different kinds of results. It is rarely possible to make one the by-product of the other. For this reason, we can continue to expect that social scientists who are primarily interested in theoretical and discipline oriented research are not likely to be interested in the kind of program evaluations that are useful to the government; and as occasionally happens, if they do undertake such studies they are not likely to do a good job from the government's standpoint. What is needed as we look to the future is an increased number of top-notch social scientists who emerge from their graduate studies with a desire to put their skills to work in the applied setting of social action programs. Despite all the talk these days about "relevance," relatively few social scientists with this kind of orientation are emerging from our graduate schools. If we want our disciplines to have the impact on public policy that we continually argue they should, this is a serious problem which must somehow be solved. Otherwise, as things stand now, we as social scientists are in

---

[7] This is ideal when we are talking about individual agencies. The logic for separating the assessment functions from the program can be extended to arguing that the Type I evaluation function should be taken out of individual agencies altogether and placed at the supra-agency level. A number of proposals have been made to create a government-wide evaluation function (for domestic programs) in the executive office of the President, in the Bureau of the Budget, in the Urban Affairs Council, and—to serve the Congress—in the General Accounting Office. This idea has great merit and, in my opinion, will eventually be adopted. But, as of this writing, its time has not yet come.

the untenable position of continually criticizing the government for not basing its judgments and decisions on social science research while at the same time being unwilling to provide the practically oriented professional talent necessary for this to occur.

6. In addition to the requirement for professional staff it is essential that the evaluation function have an invulnerable source of funds. There are different ways this can be accomplished. At OEO we have done it by setting aside a fixed percentage of the total OEO appropriation. This, in my opinion, is better than either designating a fixed amount of money for evaluation or the still more unreliable system of promising that "adequate funds for evaluation will be made available on a project-by-project basis." When budget crises arise, as they always do in all agencies every fiscal year, the research and evaluation budgets are often the first to be raided.

7. Finally, it should be clear that the lot of the evaluator is destined to be a harassed and controversial one and those who contemplate a career in this field should be fully aware of this. The evaluator's problems begin at the beginning of an evaluation but do not end at the end. He can expect opposition from the program staff at the outset because "our programs are not ready to be evaluated yet," "the evaluation does not focus on the right objectives," "there is no way to properly measure success or failure on the objectives of our program," "the evaluation study will not yield definitive conclusions," and so forth.[8] When the evaluation is completed, he can expect to be attacked from both sides regardless of what the findings are. If the findings show the program to be generally successful, the program people will point out that a great deal of money has been spent merely to find out what everyone knew from the beginning anyway. The program detractors will attack the study as unreliable and inconclusive pointing out all its methodological flaws. If the results show the program to be generally unsuccessful, the same charges will be made but from the opposite sides of the fence. Harry Truman's warning, "If you can't stand the heat, stay out of the kitchen," applies to evaluation as well as politics. But for those who can stand the heat, there is an unparalleled professional gratification to be found in the satisfaction that one's work can have an important influence on the key problems of the day.

In sum, there seems little doubt that evaluation is the wave of the future. Powerful forces inside and outside government are no longer content to take argument, exhortation, and anecdotes as the main basis for deciding how billions of dollars should be spent. They have been told by social scientists and others that a more scientific and objective basis for making decisions is possible and they are demanding that it be used. But before objective and empirical evaluations can become a truly influential part of the decision-making process, two things must occur. Within government agencies the evaluation function must be placed in a central location and be given the necessary funds, authority, and professional staff to accomplish its mission. If the necessary number of social science professionals is to be forthcoming to fill these key roles there must be a markedly increased emphasis and interest within the various branches of social science in the practical and policy orientation required for evaluation. While there are considerable pressures and changes inside the federal government that I think are likely to accomplish the first of these changes in the reasonably near future, it is hard to be as optimistic on the second. Most social scientists emerging from their graduate training today eschew this type of professional role.

If social science is to have the impact upon national policy that all of us think it should, this stands a far better chance of achievement, in my opinion, through the application of social science methods to policy problems and program evaluation and through the direct involvement of social scientists in these activities than it does through the continued and largely one-sided emphasis in our respective disciplines on exclusively theoretical and disciplinary concerns.

[8] See the discussion of this problem in Edward A. Suchman's excellent book, *Evaluative Research* (New York: Russell Sage Foundation, 1967), pp. 144–145.

59.   Reforms as Experiments[1]

Donald T. Campbell*

The United States and other modern nations should be ready for an experimental approach to social reform, an approach in which we try out new programs designed to cure specific social problems, in which we learn whether or not these programs are effective, and in which we retain, imitate, modify, or discard them on the basis of apparent effectiveness on the multiple imperfect criteria available. Our readiness for this stage is indicated by the inclusion of specific provisions for program evaluation in the first wave of the "Great Society" legislation, and by the current congressional proposals for establishing "social indicators" and socially relevant "data banks." So long have we had good intentions in this regard that many may feel we are already at this stage, that we already are continuing or discontinuing programs on the basis of assessed effectiveness. It is a theme of this article that this is not at all so, that most ameliorative programs end up with *no* interpretable evaluation (Etzioni, 1968; Hyman & Wright, 1967; Schwartz, 1961). We must look hard at the sources of this condition, and design ways of overcoming the difficulties. This article is a preliminary effort in this regard.

Many of the difficulties lie in the intransigencies of the research setting and in the presence of recurrent seductive pitfalls of interpretation. The bulk of this article will be devoted to these problems. But the few available solutions turn out to depend upon correct administrative decisions in the initiation and execution of the program. These decisions are made in a political arena, and involve political jeopardies that are often sufficient to explain the lack of hard-headed evaluation of effects. Removing reform administrators from the political spotlight seems both highly unlikely, and undesirable even if it were possible. What is instead essential is that the social scientist research advisor understand the political realities of the situation, and that he aid by helping create a public demand for hard-headed evaluation, by contributing to those political inventions that reduce the liability of honest evaluation, and by educating future administrators to the problems and posibilities.

For this reason, there is also an attempt in this article to consider the political setting of program evaluation, and to offer suggestions as to political postures that might further a truly experimental approach to social reform. Although such considerations will be distributed as a minor theme throughout this article, it seems convenient to begin with some general points of this political nature.

[1] The preparation of this paper has been supported by National Science Foundation Grant GS1309X. Versions of this paper have been presented as the Northwestern University Alumni Fund Lecture, January 24, 1968; to the Social Psychology Section of the British Psychological Society at Oxford, September 20, 1968; to the International Conference on Social Psychology at Prague, October 7, 1968 (under a different title); and to several other groups.

The published paper has been modified by the author [as indicated by smaller type face in the body of the article] to improve its usefulness and correct errors [February 1971].

Requests for reprints should be sent to Donald T. Campbell, Department of Psychology, Northwestern University, Evanston, Illinois 60201.

Reprinted from Donald T. Campbell, "Reforms as Experiments," *American Psychologist*, Vol. 24, No. 4 (April 1969), pp. 409–429.
* Professor of Psychology, Northwestern University.

Political Vulnerability from Knowing Outcomes

It is one of the most characteristic aspects of the present situation that *specific reforms are advocated as though they were certain to be successful.* For this reason, knowing outcomes has immediate political implications. Given the inherent difficulty of making significant improvements by the means usually provided and given the discrepancy between promise and possibility, most administrators wisely prefer to limit the evaluations to those the outcomes of which they can control, particularly insofar as published outcomes or press releases are concerned. Ambiguity, lack of truly comparable comparison bases, and lack of concrete evidence all work to increase the administrator's control over what gets said, or at least to reduce the bite of criticism in the case of actual failure. There is safety under the cloak of ignorance. Over and above this tie-in of advocacy and administration, there is another source of vulnerability in that the facts relevant to experimental program evaluation are also available to argue the general efficiency and honesty of administrators. The public availability of such facts reduces the privacy and security of at least some administrators.

Even where there are ideological commitments to a hard-headed evaluation of organizational efficiency, or to a scientific organization of society, these two jeopardies lead to the failure to evaluate organizational experiments realistically. If the political and administrative system has committed itself in advance to the correctness and efficacy of its reforms, it cannot tolerate learning of failure. To be truly scientific we must be able to experiment. We must be able to advocate without that excess of commitment that blinds us to reality testing.

This predicament, abetted by public apathy and by deliberate corruption, may prove in the long run to permanently preclude a truly experimental approach to social amelioration. But our needs and our hopes for a better society demand we make the effort. There are a few signs of hope. In the United States we have been able to achieve cost-of-living and unemployment indices that, however imper-

fect, have embarrassed the administrations that published them. We are able to conduct censuses that reduce the number of representatives a state has in Congress. These are grounds for optimism, although the corrupt tardiness of state governments in following their own constitutions in revising legislative districts illustrates the problem.

One simple shift in political posture which would reduce the problem is the shift from the advocacy of a specific reform to the advocacy of the seriousness of the problem, and hence to the advocacy of persistence in alternative reform efforts should the first one fail. The political stance would become: "This is a serious problem. We propose to initiate Policy A on an experimental basis. If after five years there has been no significant improvement, we will shift to Policy B." By making explicit that a given problem solution was only one of several that the administrator or party could in good conscience advocate, and by having ready a plausible alternative, the administrator could afford honest evaluation of outcomes. Negative results, a failure of the first program, would not jeopardize his job, for his job would be to keep after the problem until something was found that worked.

Coupled with this should be a general moratorium on ad hominum evaluative research, that is, on research designed to evaluate specific administrators rather than alternative policies. If we worry about the invasion-of-privacy problem in the data banks and social indicators of the future (e.g., Sawyer & Schechter, 1968), the touchiest point is the privacy of administrators. If we threaten this, the measurement system will surely be sabotaged in the innumerable ways possible. While this may sound unduly pessimistic, the recurrent anecdotes of administrators attempting to squelch unwanted research findings convince me of its accuracy. But we should be able to evaluate those alternative policies that a given administrator has the option of implementing.

Field Experiments and Quasi-Experimental Designs

In efforts to extend the logic of laboratory experimentation into the "field," and into settings not fully experimental, an inventory of threats to experimental validity has been assembled, in terms of which some 15 to 20 experimental and quasi-experimental designs have been evaluated (Campbell, 1957, 1963; Campbell & Stanley, 1963). In the present article only three or four designs will be examined, and therefore not all of the validity threats will be relevant, but it will provide useful background to look briefly at them all. Following are nine threats to internal validity.[2]

1. *History:* events, other than the experimental treatment, occurring between pretest and posttest and thus providing alternate explanations of effects.

2. *Maturation:* processes within the respondents or observed social units producing changes as a function of the passage of time per se, such as growth, fatigue, secular trends, etc.

3. *Instability:* unreliability of measures, fluctuations in sampling persons or components, autonomous instability of repeated or "equivalent" measures. (This is the only threat to which statistical tests of significance are relevant.)

4. *Testing:* the effect of taking a test upon the scores of a second testing. The effect of publication of a social indicator upon subsequent readings of that indicator.

5. *Instrumentation:* in which changes in the calibration of a measuring instrument or changes in the observers or scores used may produce changes in the obtained measurements.

6. *Regression artifacts:* pseudo-shifts occurring when persons or treatment units have been selected upon the basis of their extreme scores.

7. *Selection:* biases resulting from differential recruitment of comparison groups, producing different mean levels on the measure of effects.

8. *Experimental mortality:* the differential loss of respondents from comparison groups.

9. *Selection-maturation interaction:* interaction selection biases resulting in differential rates of "maturation" or autonomous change.

If a change or difference occurs, these are rival explanations that could be used to explain away an effect and thus to deny that in this specific experiment any genuine effect of the experimental treatment had been demonstrated. These are faults that true experiments avoid, primarily through the use of randomization and control groups. In the approach here advocated, this checklist is used to evaluate specific quasi-experimental designs. This is evaluation, not rejection, for it often turns out that for a specific design in a specific setting the threat is implausible, or that there are supplementary data that can help rule it out even where randomization is impossible. The general ethic, here advocated for public administrators as well as social scientists, is to use the very best method possible, aiming at "true experiments" with random control groups. But where randomized treatments are not possible, a self-critical use of quasi-experimental designs is advocated. We must do the best we can with what is available to us.

Our posture vis-à-vis perfectionist critics from laboratory experimentation is more militant than this: the only threats to validity that we will allow to invalidate an experiment are those that admit of the status of empirical

---

[2] This list has been expanded from the major previous presentations by the addition of *Instability* (but see Campbell, 1968; Campbell & Ross, 1968). This has been done in reaction to the sociological discussion of the use of tests of significance in nonexperimental or quasi-experimental research (e.g., Selvin, 1957; and as reviewed by Galtung, 1967, pp. 358–389). On the one hand, I join with the critics in criticizing the exaggerated status of "statistically significant differences" in establishing convictions of validity. Statistical tests are relevant to at best 1 out of 15 or so threats to validity. On the other hand, I join with those who defend their use in situations where randomization has not been employed. Even in those situations, it is relevant to say or to deny, "This is a trivial difference. It is of the order that would have occurred frequently *had* these measures been assigned to these classes solely by chance." Tests of significance, making use of random reassignments of the actual scores, are particularly useful in communicating this point.

laws more dependable and more plausible than the law involving the treatment. The mere possibility of some alternative explanation is not enough—it is only the *plausible* rival hypotheses that are invalidating. Vis-à-vis correlational studies and common-sense descriptive studies, on the other hand, our stance is one of greater conservatism. For example, because of the specific methodological trap of regression artifacts, the sociological tradition of "ex post facto" designs (Chapin, 1947; Greenwood, 1945) is totally rejected (Campbell & Stanley, 1963, pp. 240–241; 1966, pp. 70–71).

Threats to external validity, which follow, cover the validity problems involved in interpreting experimental results, the threats to valid generalization of the results to other settings, to other versions of the treatment, or to other measures of the effect:[3]

1. *Interaction effects of testing:* the effect of a pretest in increasing or decreasing the respondent's sensitivity or responsiveness to the experimental variable, thus making the results obtained for a pretested population unrepresentative of the effects of the experimental variable for the unpretested universe from which the experimental respondents were selected.

2. *Interaction of selection and experimental treatment:* unrepresentative responsiveness of the treated population.

3. *Reactive effects of experimental arrangements:* "artificiality"; conditions making the experimental setting atypical of conditions of regular application of the treatment. "Hawthorne effects."

4. *Multiple-treatment interference:* where multiple treatments are jointly applied, effects atypical of the separate application of the treatments.

5. *Irrelevant responsiveness of measures:* all measures are complex, and all include irrelevant components that may produce apparent effects.

6. *Irrelevant replicability of treatments:* treatments are complex, and replications of them may fail to include those components actually responsible for the effects.

These threats apply equally to true experiments and quasi-experiments. They are particularly relevant to applied experimentation. In the cumulative history of our methodology, this class of threats was first noted as a critique of true experiments involving pretests (Schanck & Goodman, 1939; Solomon, 1949). Such experiments provided a sound basis for generalizing to other *pretested* populations, but the reactions of unpretested populations to the treatment might well be quite different. As a result, there has been an advocacy of true experimental designs obviating the pretest (Campbell, 1957; Schanck & Goodman, 1939; Solomon, 1949) and a search for nonreactive measures (Webb, Campbell Schwartz, & Sechrest, 1966).

These threats to validity will serve as a background against which we will discuss several research designs particularly appropriate for evaluating specific programs of social amelioration. These are the "interrupted time-series design," the "control series design," "regression discontinuity design," and various "true experiments." The order is from a weak but generally available design to stronger ones that require more administrative foresight and determination.

Interrupted Time-Series Design

By and large, when a political unit initiates a reform it is put into effect across the board, with the total unit being affected. In this setting the only comparison base is the record of previous years. The usual mode of utilization is a casual version of a very weak quasi-experimental design, the one-group pretest-posttest design.

A convenient illustration comes from the 1955 Connecticut crackdown on speeding, which sociologist H. Laurence Ross and I have been analyzing as a methodological illustration (Campbell & Ross, 1968; Glass, 1968;

---

[3] This list has been lengthened from previous presentations to make more salient Threats 5 and 6 which are particularly relevant to social experimentation. Discussion in previous presentations (Campbell, 1957, pp. 309–310; Campbell & Stanley, 1963, pp. 203–204) had covered these points, but they had not been included in the checklist.

Ross & Campbell, 1968). After a record high of traffic fatalities in 1955, Governor Abraham Ribicoff instituted an unprecedentedly severe crackdown on speeding. At the end of a year of such enforcement there had been but 284 traffic deaths as compared with 324 the year before. In announcing this the Governor stated, "With the saving of 40 lives in 1956, a reduction of 12.3% from the 1955 motor vehicle death toll, we can say that the program is definitely worthwhile." These results are graphed in Figure 59.1, with a deliberate effort to make them look impressive.

In what follows, while we in the end decide that the crackdown had some beneficial effects, we criticize Ribicoff's interpretation of his results, from the point of view of the social scientist's proper standards of evidence. Were the now Senator Ribicoff not the man of stature that he is, this would be most unpolitic, because we would be alienating one of the strongest proponents of social experimentation in our nation. Given his character, however, we may feel sure that he shares our interests both in a progressive program of experimental social amelioration, and in making the most hard-headed evaluation possible of these ex-

periments. Indeed, it was his integrity in using every available means at his disposal as Governor to make sure that the unpopular speeding crackdown was indeed enforced that make these data worth examining at all. But the potentials of this one illustration and our political temptation to substitute for it a less touchy one, point to the political problems that must be faced in experimenting with social reform.

Keeping Figure 59.1 and Ribicoff's statement in mind, let us look at the same data presented as a part of an extended time series in Figure 59.2 and go over the relevant threats to internal validity.

History

Both presentations fail to control for the effects of other potential change agents. For instance, 1956 might have been a particularly dry year, with fewer accidents due to rain or snow. Or there might have been a dramatic increase in use of seat belts, or other safety features. The advocated strategy in quasi-experimentation is not to throw up one's hands and refuse to use the evidence because

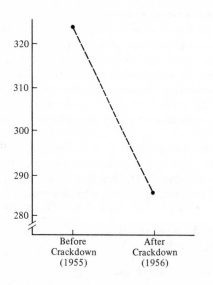

Figure 59.1.   Connecticut   Traffic Fatalities.

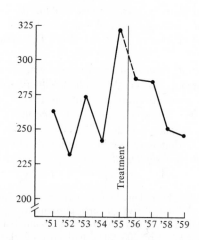

Figure 59.2.   Connecticut   Traffic Fatalities. (Same data as in Figure 59.1 presented as part of an extended time series.)

of this lack of control, but rather to generate by informed criticism appropriate to this specific setting as many *plausible* rival hypotheses as possible, and then to do the supplementary research, as into weather records and safety-belt sales, for example, which would reflect on these rival hypotheses.

Maturation

This is a term coming from criticisms of training studies of children. Applied here to the simple pretest-posttest data of Figure 59.1, it could be the plausible rival hypothesis that death rates were steadily going down year after year (as indeed they are, relative to miles driven or population of automobiles). Here the extended time series has a strong methodological advantage, and rules out this threat to validity. The general trend is inconsistently up prior to the crackdown, and steadily down thereafter.

Instability

Seemingly implicit in the public pronouncement was the assumption that all of the change from 1955 to 1956 was due to the crackdown. There was no recognition of the fact that all time series are unstable even when no treatments are being applied. The degree of this normal instability is the crucial issue, and one of the main advantages of the extended time series is that it samples this instability. The great pretreatment instability now makes the treatment effect look relatively trivial. The 1955–56 shift is less than the gains of both 1954–55 and 1952–53. It is the largest drop in the series, but it exceeds the drops of 1951–52, 1953–54, and 1957–58 by trivial amounts. Thus the unexplained instabilities of the series are such as to make the 1955–56 drop understandable as more of the same. On the other hand, it is noteworthy that after the crackdown there are no year-to-year gains, and in this respect the character of the time series seems definitely to have changed.

The threat of instability is the only threat to which tests of significance are relevant. Box and Tiao (1965) have an elegant Bayesian model for the interrupted time series. Applied by Glass (1968) to our monthly data, with seasonal trends removed, it shows a statistically significant downward shift in the series after the crackdown. But as we shall see, an alternative explanation of at least part of this significant effect exists.

Regression

In true experiments the treatment is applied independently of the prior state of the units. In natural experiments exposure to treatment is often a cosymptom of the treated group's condition. The treatment is apt to be an *effect* rather than, or in addition to being, a cause. Psychotherapy is such a cosymptom treatment, as is any other in which the treated group is self-selected or assigned on the basis of need. These all present special problems of interpretation, of which the present illustration provides one type.

The selection-regression plausible rival hypothesis works this way: Given that the fatality rate has some degree of unreliability, then a subsample selected for its extremity in 1955 would on the average, merely as a reflection of that unreliability, be less extreme in 1956. Has there been selection for extremity in applying this treatment? Probably yes. Of all Connecticut fatality years, the most likely time for a crackdown would be after an exceptionally high year. If the time series showed instability, the subsequent year would on the average be less, *purely as a function of that instability*. Regression artifacts are probably the most recurrent form of self-deception in the experimental social reform literature. It is hard to make them intuitively obvious. Let us try again. Take any time series with variability, including one generated of pure error. Move along it as in a time dimension. Pick a point that is the "highest so far." Look then at the next point. On the average this next point will be lower, or nearer the general trend.

In our present setting the most striking shift in the whole series is the upward shift just prior to the crackdown. It is highly probable that this caused the crackdown, rather than, or in addition to, the crackdown causing the 1956 drop. At least part of the 1956 drop is an artifact of the 1955 extremity. While in principle the degree of expected regression can be computed from the autocorrelation of the series, we lack here an extended-enough body of data to do this with any confidence.

Advice to administrators who want to do genuine reality-testing must include attention to this problem, and it will be a very hard problem to surmount. The most general advice would be to work on chronic problems of a persistent urgency or extremity, rather than reacting to momentary extremes. The administrator should look at the pretreatment time series to judge whether or not instability plus momentary extremity will explain away his program gains. If it will, he should schedule the treatment for a year or two later, so that his decision is more independent of the one year's extremity. (The selection biases remaining under such a procedure need further examination.)

In giving advice to the *experimental* administrator, one is also inevitably giving advice to those *trapped* administrators whose political predicament requires a favorable outcome whether valid or not. To such trapped administrators the advice is pick the very worse year, and the very worst social unit. If there is inherent instability, there is no where to go but up, for the average case at least.

Testing

Two other threats to internal validity need discussion in regard to this design. By *testing* we typically have in mind the condition under which a test of attitude, ability, or personality is itself a change agent, persuading, informing, practicing, or otherwise setting processes of change in action. No artificially introduced testing procedures are involved here. However, for the simple before-and-after design of Figure 59.1, if the pretest were the first data collection of its kind ever publicized, this publicity in itself might produce a reduction in traffic deaths which would have taken place even without a speeding crackdown. Many traffic safety programs assume this. The longer time-series evidence reassures us on this only to the extent that we can assume that the figures had been published each year with equivalent emphasis.[4]

Instrumentation

Instrumentation changes are not a likely flaw in this instance, but would be if recording practices and institutional responsibility had shifted simultaneously with the crackdown. Probably in a case like this it is better to use raw frequencies rather than indices whose correction parameters are subject to periodic revision. Thus per capita rates are subject to periodic jumps as new census figures become available correcting old extrapolations. Analogously, a change in the miles per gallon assumed in estimating traffic mileage for mileage-based mortality rates might explain a shift. Such biases can of course work to disguise a true effect. Almost certainly, Ribicoff's crackdown reduced traffic speed (Campbell & Ross, 1968). Such a decrease in speed increases the miles per gallon actually obtained, producing a concomitant drop in the estimate of miles driven, which would appear as an inflation of the estimate of mileage-based traffic fatalities if the same fixed approximation to actual miles per gallon were used, as it undoubtedly would be.

The "new broom" that introduces abrupt

[4] No doubt the public and press shared the Governor's special alarm over the 1955 death toll. This differential reaction could be seen as a negative feedback servo-system in which the dampening effect was proportional to the degree of upward deviation from the prior trend. Insofar as such alarm reduces traffic fatalities, it adds a negative component to the autocorrelation, increasing the regression effect. This component should probably be regarded as a rival cause or treatment rather than as artifact. (The regression effect is less as the positive autocorrelation is higher, and will be present to some degree insofar as this correlation is less than positive unity. Negative correlation in a time series would represent regression beyond the mean, in a way not quite analogous to negative correlation across persons. For an autocorrelation of Lag 1, high negative correlation would be represented by a series that oscillated maximally from one extreme to the other.)

changes of policy is apt to reform the record keeping too, and thus confound reform treatments with instrumentation change. The ideal experimental administrator will, if possible, avoid doing this. He will prefer to keep comparable a partially imperfect measuring system rather than lose comparability altogether. The politics of the situation do not always make this possible, however. Consider, as an experimental reform, Orlando Wilson's reorganization of the police system in Chicago. Figure 59.3 shows his impact on petty larceny in Chicago—a striking *increase!* Wilson, of course, called this shot in advance, one aspect of his reform being a reform in the bookkeeping. (Note in the pre-Wilson records the suspicious absence of the expected upward secular trend.) In this situation Wilson had no choice. Had he left the record keeping as it was, for the purposes of better experimental design, his resentful patrolmen would have clobbered him with a crime wave by deliberately starting to record the many complaints that had not been getting into the books.[5]

Figure 59.3. Number of Reported Larcenies under $50 in Chicago, Illinois, from 1942 to 1962. (Data from *Uniform Crime Reports of the United States*, 1942–1962.)

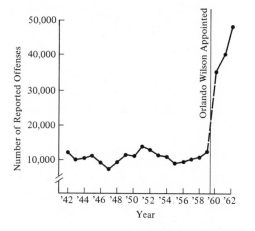

Figure 59.4. Number of Reported Murders and Nonnegligent Manslaughters in Chicago, Illinois, from 1942 to 1962. (Data from *Uniform Crime Reports for the United States*, 1942–1962.)

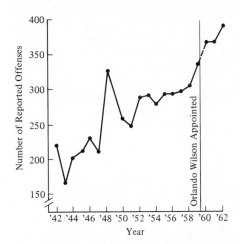

Those who advocate the use of archival measures as social indicators (Bauer, 1966; Gross, 1966, 1967; Kaysen, 1967; Webb et al., 1966) must face up not only to their high degree of chaotic error and systematic bias, but also to the politically motivated changes in record keeping that will follow upon their public use as social indicators (Etzioni & Lehman, 1967). Not all measures are equally susceptible. In Figure 59.4, Orlando Wilson's effect on homicides seems negligible one way or the other.

Irrelevant Responsiveness of Measures

Of the threats to external validity, the one most relevant to social experimentation is *irrelevant responsiveness of measures*. This seems best discussed in terms of the problem of generalizing from indicator to indicator or in terms of the imperfect validity of all measures that is only to be overcome by the use of multiple measures of independent imperfection (Campbell & Fiske, 1959; Webb et al., 1966).

[5] Wilson's inconsistency in utilization of records and the political problem of relevant records are ably documented in Kamisar (1964). Etzioni (1968) reports that in New York City in 1965 a crime wave was proclaimed that turned out to be due to an unpublicized improvement in record keeping.

For treatments on any given problem within any given governmental or business subunit, there will usually be something of a governmental monopoly on reform. Even though different divisions may optimally be trying different reforms, within each division there will usually be only one reform on a given problem going on at a time. But for measures of effect this need not and should not be the case. The administrative machinery should it-

self make multiple measures of potential benefits and of unwanted side effects. In addition, the loyal opposition should be allowed to add still other indicators, with the political process and adversary argument challenging both validity and relative importance, with social science methodologists testifying for both parties, and with the basic records kept public and under bipartisan audit (as are voting rec-

Figure 59.5. Suspension of Licenses for Speeding, as a Percentage of All Suspensions.

Figure 59.7. Arrested while Driving with a Suspended License, as a Percentage of Suspensions.

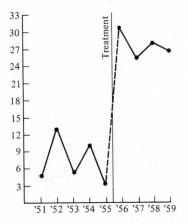

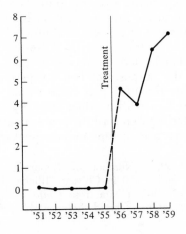

Figure 59.6. Speeding Violations, as a Percentage of All Traffic Violations.

Figure 59.8. Percentage of Speeding Violations Judged Not Guilty.

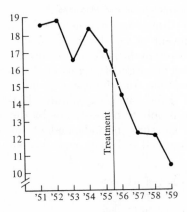

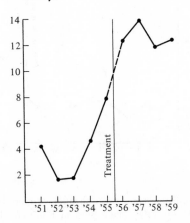

ords under optimal conditions). This competitive scrutiny is indeed the main source of objectivity in sciences (Polanyi, 1966, 1967; Popper, 1963) and epitomizes an ideal of democratic practice in both judicial and legislative procedures.

The next few figures return again to the Connecticut crackdown on speeding and look to some other measures of effect. They are relevant to the confirming that there was indeed a crackdown, and to the issue of side effects. They also provide the methodological comfort of assuring us that in some cases the interrupted time-series design can provide clearcut evidence of effect. Figure 59.5 shows the jump in suspensions of licenses for speeding— evidence that severe punishment was abruptly instituted. Again a note to experimental administrators: with this weak design, *it is only abrupt and decisive changes that we have any chance of evaluating.* A gradually introduced reform will be indistinguishable from the background of secular change, from the net effect of the innumerable change agents continually impinging.

We would want intermediate evidence that traffic speed was modified. A sampling each year of a few hundred five-minute highway movies (random as to location and time) could have provided this at a moderate cost, but they were not collected. Of the public records available, perhaps the data of Figure 59.6, showing a reduction in speeding violations, indicate a reduction in traffic speed. But

the effects on the legal system were complex, and in part undesirable. Driving with a suspended license markedly increased (Figure 59.7), at least in the biased sample of those arrested. Presumably because of the harshness of the punishment if guilty, judges may have become more lenient (Figure 59.8) although this effect is of marginal significance.

The relevance of indicators for the social problems we wish to cure must be kept continually in focus. The social indicators approach will tend to make the indicators themselves the goal of social action, rather than the social problems they but imperfectly indicate. There are apt to be tendencies to legislate changes in the indicators per se rather than changes in the social problems.

To illustrate the problem of the irrelevant responsiveness of measures, Figure 59.9 shows a result of the 1900 change in divorce law in Germany. In a recent reanalysis of the data with the Box and Tiao (1965) statistic, Glass (Glass, Tiao, & Maguire, 1969) has found the change highly significant, in contrast to earlier statistical analyses (Rheinstein, 1959; Wolf, Lüke, & Hax, 1959). But Rheinstein's emphasis would still be relevant: This indicator change indicates no likely improvement in marital harmony, or even in marital stability. Rather than reducing them, the legal change has made the divorce rate a less valid indicator of marital discord and separation than it had been earlier (see also Etzioni & Lehman, 1967).

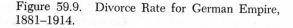

Figure 59.9. Divorce Rate for German Empire, 1881–1914.

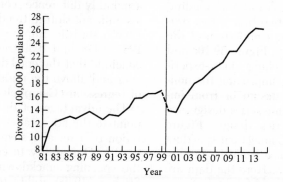

Control Series Design

The interrupted time-series design as discussed so far is available for those settings in which no control group is possible, in which the total governmental unit has received the experimental treatment, the social reform measure. In the general program of quasi-experimental design, we argue the great advantage of untreated comparison groups even where these cannot be assigned at random. The most common of such designs is the nonequivalent control-group pretest-posttest design, in which for each of two natural groups, one of which receives the treatment, a pretest and posttest measure is taken. If the traditional mistaken practice is avoided of matching on pretest scores (with resultant regression artifacts), this design provides a useful control over those aspects of history, maturation, and test-retest effects shared by both groups. But it does not control for the plausible rival hypothesis of *selection-maturation interaction*—that is, the hypothesis that the selection differences in the natural aggregations involve not only differences in mean level, but differences in maturation rate.

This point can be illustrated in terms of the traditional quasi-experimental design problem of the effects of Latin on English vocabulary (Campbell, 1963). In the hypothetical data of Figure 59.10b, two alternative interpretations remain open. Latin may have had effect, for those taking Latin gained more than those not. But, on the other hand, those students taking Latin may have a greater annual rate of vocabulary growth that would manifest itself whether or not they took Latin. Extending this common design into two time series provides relevant evidence, as comparison of the two alternative outcomes of Figure 59.10c and 10d shows. Thus approaching quasi-experimental design from either improving the nonequivalent control-group design or from improving the interrupted time-series design, we arrive at the control series design. Figure 59.11 shows this for the Connecticut speeding crackdown, adding evidence from the fatality rates of neighboring states. Here the data are presented as population-based fatality rates so

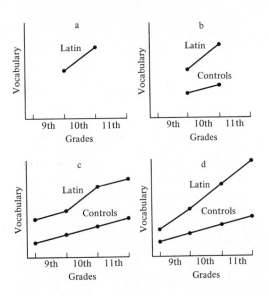

Figure 59.10. Forms of Quasi-experimental Analysis for the Effect of Specific Course Work, Including Control Series Design.

as to make the two series of comparable magnitude.

The control series design of Figure 59.11 shows that downward trends were available in the other states for 1955–56 as due to history and maturation, that is, due to shared secular trends, weather, automotive safety features, etc. But the data also show a general trend for Connecticut to rise relatively closer to the other states prior to 1955, and to steadily drop more rapidly than other states from 1956 on. Glass (1968) has used our monthly data for Connecticut and the control states to generate a monthly difference score, and this too shows a significant shift in trend in the Box and Tiao (1965) statistic. Impressed particularly by the 1957, 1958, and 1959 trend, we are willing to conclude that the crackdown had some effect, over and above the undeniable pseudo-effects of regression (Campbell & Ross, 1968).

The advantages of the control series design point to the advantages for social experimentation of a social system allowing subunit diversity. Our ability to estimate the effects of the speeding crackdown, Rose's (1952) and Stieber's (1949) ability to estimate the effects

Figure 59.11. Control Series Design Comparing Connecticut Fatalities with Those of Four Comparable States.

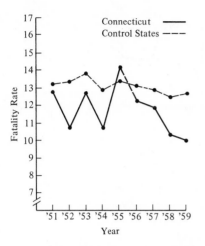

on strikes of compulsory arbitration laws, and Simon's (1966) ability to estimate the price elasticity of liquor were made possible because the changes were not being put into effect in all states simultaneously, because they were matters of state legislation rather than national. I do not want to appear to justify on these grounds the wasteful and unjust diversity of laws and enforcement practices from state to state. But I would strongly advocate that social engineers make use of this diversity while it remains available, and plan cooperatively their changes in administrative policy and in record keeping so as to provide optimal experimental inference. More important is the recommendation that, for those aspects of social reform handled by the central government, a purposeful diversity of implementation be envisaged so that experimental and control groups be available for analysis. Properly planned, these can approach true experiments, better than the casual and ad hoc comparison groups now available. But without such fundamental planning, uniform central control can reduce the present possibilities of reality testing, that is, of true social experimentation. In the same spirit, decentralization of decision making, both within large government and within private monopolies, can provide a useful competition for both efficiency and innovation, reflected in a multiplicity of indicators.

The British Breathalyser Crackdown

One further illustration of the interrupted time series and the control series will be provided. The variety of illustrations so far have each illustrated some methodological point, and have thus ended us as "bad examples." To provide a "good example," an instance which survives methodological critique as a valid illustration of a successful reform, data from The British Road Safety Act of 1967 are provided in Figure 59.12 (Ross, Campbell, & Glass, 1970).

The data on a weekly-hours basis are only available for a composite category of fatalities plus serious injuries, and Figure 59.12 therefore uses this composite for all three bodies of data. The "Week-End-Nights" comprises Friday and Saturday nights from 10:00 P.M. to 4:00 A.M. Here, as expected, the crackdown is most dramatically effective, producing initially more than a 40 per cent drop, leveling off at perhaps 30 per cent, although this involves dubious extrapolations in the absence of some control comparison to indicate what the trend over the years might have been without the crackdown. In this British case, no comparison state with comparable traffic conditions or drinking laws was available. But controls need not always be separate groups of persons, they may also be separate samples of times or stimulus materials (Campbell & Stanley, 1966, pp. 43–47). A cigarette company may use the sales of its main competitor as a control comparison to evaluate a new advertising campaign. One should search around for the most nearly appropriate control comparison. For the Breathalyser crackdown, commuting hours when pubs had been long closed seemed ideal. (The commuting hours figures come from 7:00 A.M. to 10:00 A.M. and 4:00 P.M. to 5:00 P.M. Pubs are open for lunch from 12:00 to 2:00 or 2:30 P.M. and open again at 5:00 P.M.)

These commuting hours data convincingly show no effect, but are too unstable to help much with estimating the long-term effects. They show a different annual cycle than do the week-end nights or the overall figures, and do not go back far enough to provide an adequate base for estimating this annual cycle with precision.

Figure 59.12. British Traffic Fatalities plus Serious Injuries, before and after the Breathalyser Crackdown of October 1967 (seasonally adjusted).

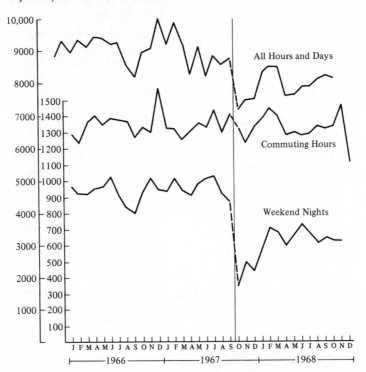

The use of a highly judgmental category such as "serious injuries" provides an opportunity for pseudo-effects due to a shift in the classifiers' standards. The overall figures are available separately for fatalities, and these show a highly significant effect as strong as that found for the serious injury category or the composite shown in Figure 59.12.

More details and the methodological problems are considered in our fuller presentation (Ross, Campbell, Glass, 1970). One further rule for the use of this design needs emphasizing. The *interrupted time series* can only provide clear evidence of effect where the reform is introduced with a vigorous abruptness. A gradually introduced reform has little chance of being distinguished from shifts in secular trends or from the cumulative effect of the many other influences impringing during a prolonged period of introduction. In the Breathalyser crackdown, an intense publicity campaign naming the specific starting date preceded the actual crackdown. Although the impact seems primarily due to publicity and fear rather than an actual increase of arrests, an abrupt initiation date was achieved. Had the enforcement effort changed at the moment the act had passed, with public awareness being built up by subsequent publicity, the resulting data series would have been essentially uninterpretable.

Regression Discontinuity Design

We shift now to social ameliorations that are in short supply, and that therefore cannot be given to all individuals. Such scarcity is inevitable under many circumstances, and can make possible an evaluation of effects that would otherwise be impossible. Consider the heroic Salk poliomyelitis vaccine trials in which some children were given the vaccine while others were given an inert saline placebo injection—and in which many more of these placebo controls would die than would have if they had been given the vaccine. Creation of these placebo controls would have been morally, psychologically, and socially impossible had there been enough vaccine for all. As it was, due to the scarcity, most children that year had to go without the vaccine anyway. The creation of experimental and control groups was the highly moral allocation of that scarcity so as to enable us to learn the true efficacy of the supposed good. The usual medical practice of introducing new cures on a so-called trial basis in general medical practice makes evaluation impossible by confounding prior status with treatment, that is, giving the drug to the most needy or most hopeless. It has the further social bias of giving the supposed benefit to those most assiduous in keeping their medical needs in the attention of the medical profession, that is, the upper and upper-middle classes. The political stance furthering social experimentation here is the recognition of randomization as the most democratic and moral means of allocating scarce resources (and scarce hazardous duties), plus the moral imperative to further utilize the randomization so that society may indeed learn true value of the supposed boon. This is the ideology that makes possible "true experiments" in a large class of social reforms.

But if randomization is not politically feasible or morally justifiable in a given setting, there is a powerful quasi-experimental design available that allows the scarce good to be given to the most needy or the most deserving. This is the regression discontinuity design. All it requires is strict and orderly attention to the priority dimension. The design originated through an advocacy of a tie-breaking experiment to measure the effects of receiving a fellowship (Thistlethwaite & Campbell, 1960), and it seems easiest to explain it in that light. Consider as in Figure 59.13 preaward ability-and-merit dimension, which would have some relation to later success in life (finishing college, earnings 10 years later, etc.). Those higher on the premeasure are most deserving and receive the award. They do better in later

life, but does the award have an effect? It is normally impossible to say because they would have done better in later life anyway. Full randomization of the award was impossible given the stated intention to reward merit and ability. But it might be possible to take a narrow band of ability at the cutting point, to regard all of these persons as tied, and to assign half of them to awards, half to no awards, by means of a tie-breaking randomization.

The tie-breaking rationale is still worth doing, but in considering that design it became obvious that, if the regression of premeasure on later effects were reasonably orderly, one should be able to extrapolate to the results of the tie-breaking experiment by plotting the regression of posttest on pretest separately for those in the award and nonaward regions. If there is no significant difference for these at the decision-point intercept, then the tie-breaking experiment should show no difference. In cases where the tie breakers would show an effect, there should be an abrupt discontinuity in the regression line. Such a discontinuity cannot be explained away by the normal regression of the posttest on pretest, for this normal regression, as extensively sampled within the nonaward area and within the award area, provides no such expectation.

Figure 59.13 presents, in terms of column means, an instance in which higher pretest scores would have led to higher posttest scores

Figure 59.13. Tie-breaking Experiment and Regression Discontinuity Analysis.

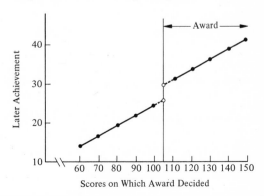

even without the treatment, and in which there is in addition a substantial treatment effect. Figure 59.14 shows a series of paired outcomes, those on the left to be interpreted as no effect; those in the center and on the right as effect. Note some particular cases. In instances of granting opportunity on the basis of merit, like Figure 59.14a and 14b (and Figure 59.13), neglect of the background regression of pretest on posttest leads to optimistic

pseudo-effects: in Figure 59.14a, those receiving the award do do better in later life, though not really because of the award. But in social ameliorative efforts, the setting is more apt to be like Figure 59.14d and 14e, where neglect of the background regression is apt to make the program look deleterious if no effect, or ineffective if there is a real effect.

The design will of course work just as well or better if the award dimension and the deci-

Figure 59.14.   Illustrative Outcomes of Regression Discontinuity Analyses.

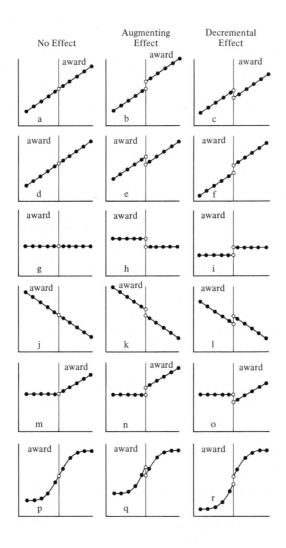

sion base, the pretest measure, are unrelated to the posttest dimension, if it is irrelevant or unfair, as instanced in Figure 59.14g, 14h, and 14i. In such cases the decision base is the functional equivalent of randomization. Negative background relationships are obviously possible, as in Figure 59.14j, 14k, and 14l. In Figure 59.14, m, n, and o are included to emphasize that it is a jump-in intercept at the cutting point that shows effect, and that differences in slope without differences at the cutting point are not acceptable as evidences of effect. This becomes more obvious if we remember that in cases like Figure 59.14m, a tie-breaking randomization experiment would have shown no difference. Curvilinear background relationships, as in Figure 59.14p, 14q, and 14r, will provide added obstacles to clear inference in many instances, where sampling error could make Figure 59.14p look like 14b.

As further illustration, Figure 59.15 provides computer-simulated data, showing individual observations and fitted regression lines, in a fuller version of the no-effect outcome of Figure 59.14a. Figure 59.16 shows an outcome

with effect. These have been generated[6] by assigning to each individual a weighted normal random number as a "true score," to which is added a weighted independent "error" to generate the "pretest." The "true score" plus another independent "error" produces the "posttest" in no-effect cases such as Figure 59.15. In treatment-effect simulations, as in Figure 59.16, there are added into the posttest "effects points" for all "treated" cases, that is, those above the cutting point on the pretest score.

This design could be used in a number of settings. Consider Job Training Corps applicants, in larger number than the program can accommodate, with eligibility determined by need. The setting would be as in Figure 59.14d and 14e. The base-line decision dimension could be per capita family income, with those at below the cutoff getting training. The outcome dimension could be the amount of withholding tax withheld two years later, or the percentage drawing unemployment insurance, these follow-up figures being provided from the National Data Bank in response to

Figure 59.15.   Regression Discontinuity Design: No Effect.

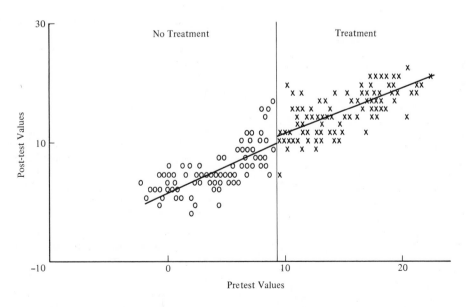

[6] J. Sween & D. T. Campbell, Computer programs for simulating and analyzing sharp and fuzzy regression-discontinuity experiments. In preparation.

Figure 59.16.   Regression Discontinuity Design: Genuine Effect.

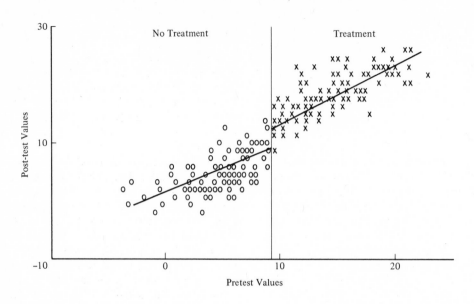

categorized social security numbers fed in, without individual anonymity being breached, without any real invasion of privacy—

by the technique of Mutually Insulated Data Banks. While the plotted points could be named, there is no need that they be named. In a classic field experiment on tax compliance, Richard Schwartz and the Bureau of Internal Revenue have managed to put together sets of personally identified interviews and tax-return data so that statistical analyses such as these could be done, without the separate custodians of either interview or tax returns learning the corresponding data for specific persons (Schwartz and Orleans, 1967; see also Schwartz and Skolnick, 1963).

Applied to the Job Corps illustration, it would work as follows: Separate lists of Job-Corps applicants (with social security numbers) would be prepared for every class interval on per capita family income. To each of these lists an alphabetical designation would be assigned at random. (Thus the $10 per week list might be labeled M; $11, C; $12, Z; $13, Q; $14, N; etc.) These lists would be sent to Internal Revenue, without the Internal Revenue personnel being able to learn anything interpretable about their traineeship status or family income. The Internal Revenue statisti-

cians would locate the withholding tax collected for each person on each list, but would not return the data in that form. Instead, for each list, only the withholding tax amounts would be listed, and these in a newly randomized order. These would be returned to Job Corps research, who could use them to plot a graph like Figures 59.10 or 59.11, and do the appropriate statistical analyses by retranslating the alphabetical symbols into meaningful, base-line values. But within any list, they would be unable to learn which value belonged to which person. (To insure this effective anonymity, it could be specified that no lists shorter than 100 persons be used, the base-line intervals being expanded if necessary to achieve this.) Manniche and Hayes (1957) have spelled out how a broker can be used in a two-staged matching of doubly coded data. Kaysen (1967) and Sawyer and Schechter (1968) have wise discussions of the more general problem.

What is required of the administrator of a scarce ameliorative commodity to use this design? Most essential is a sharp cutoff point on a decision-criterion dimension, on which several other qualitatively similar analytic cutoffs can be made both above and below the award cut. Let me explain this better by explaining why National Merit scholarships were unable to use the design for their actual fellowship decision (although it has been used for their Certificate of Merit). In their operation, diverse committees make small numbers of award decisions by considering a group of candidates and then picking from them the N best to which to award the N fellowships allocated them. This provides one cutting point on an unspecified pooled decision base, but fails to provide analogous potential cutting points above and below. What could be done is for each committee to collectively rank its group of 20 or so candidates. The top N would then receive the award. Pooling cases across committees, cases could be classified according to number of ranks above and below the cutting point, these other ranks being analogous to the award-nonaward cutting point as far as regression onto posttreatment measures was concerned. Such group ranking would be costly of committee time. An equally good procedure, if committees agreed, would be to have each member, after full discussion and freedom to revise, give each candidate a grade, A+, A, A—, B+, B, etc., and to award the fellowships to the N candidates averaging

best on these ratings, with no revisions allowed after the averaging process. These ranking or rating units, even if not comparable from committee to committee in range of talent, in number of persons ranked, or in cutting point, could be pooled without bias as far as a regression discontinuity is concerned, for that range of units above and below the cutting point in which all committees were represented.

It is the dimensionality and sharpness of the decision criterion that is at issue, not its components or validity. The ratings could be based upon nepotism, whimsey, and superstition and still serve. As has been stated, if the decision criterion is utterly invalid we approach the pure randomness of a true experiment. Thus the weakness of subjective committee decisions is not their subjectivity, but the fact that they provide only the one cutting point on their net subjective dimension. Even in the form of average ratings the recommended procedures probably represent some slight increase in committee work load. But this could be justified to the decision committees by the fact that through refusals, etc., it

Figure 59.17. Regression Discontinuity Design: Fuzzy Cutting Point, Pseudo-treatment Effect Only.

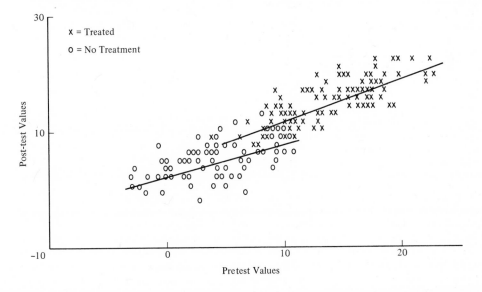

cannot be known at the time of the committee meeting the exact number to whom the fellowship can be offered. Other costs at the planning time are likewise minimal. The primary additional burden is in keeping as good records on the nonawardees as on the awardees. Thus at a low cost, an experimental administrator can lay the groundwork for later scientific follow-ups, the budgets for which need not yet be in sight.

Our present situation is more apt to be one where our pretreatment measures, aptitude measures, reference ratings, etc., can be combined via multiple correlation into an index that correlates highly but not perfectly with the award decision. For this dimension there is a fuzzy cutoff point. Can the design be used in this case? Probably not. Figure 59.17 shows

the pseudo-effect possible if the award decision contributes any valid variance to the quantified pretest evidence, as it usually will. The award regression rides above the nonaward regression just because of that valid variance in this simulated case, there being no true award effect at all. (In simulating this case, the award decision has been based upon a composite of true score plus an independent award error.) Figure 59.18 shows a fuzzy cutting point plus a genuine award effect.[7] The recommendation to the administrator is clear: aim for a sharp cutting point on a quantified decision criterion. If there are complex rules for eligibility, only one of which is quantified, seek out for follow-up that subset of persons for whom the quantitative dimension was determinate. If political patronage necessitates

Figure 59.18.   Regression Discontinuity Design: Fuzzy Cutting Point, with Real Treatment plus Pseudo-treamtent Effect.

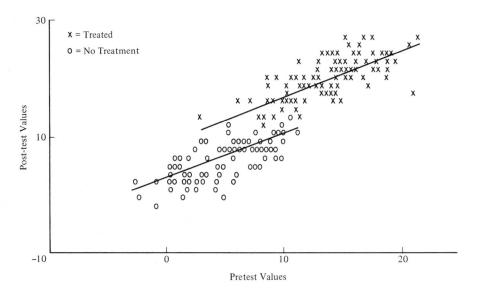

There are some subtle statistical clues that might distinguish these two instances if one had enough cases. There should be increased pooled column variance in the mixed columns for a true effects case. If the data are arbitrarily treated as though there had been a sharp cutting point located in the middle of the overlap area, then there should be no discontinuity in the no-effect case, and some discontinuity in the case of a real effect, albeit an underestimated discontinuity, since there are untreated cases above the cutting point and treated ones below, dampening the apparent effect. The degree of such dampening should be estimable, and correctable, perhaps by iterative procedures. But these are hopes for the future.

some decisions inconsistent with a sharp cut-off, record these cases under the heading "qualitative decision rule" and keep them out of your experimental analysis.

Almost all of our ameliorative programs designed for the disadvantaged could be studied via this design, and so too some major governmental actions affecting the lives of citizens in ways we do not think of as experimental. For example, for a considerable period, quantitative test scores have been used to call up for military service or reject as unfit at the lower ability range. If these cutting points, test scores, names, and social security numbers have been recorded for a number of steps both above and below the cutting point, we could make elegant studies of the effect of military service on later withholding taxes, mortality, number of dependents, etc.

This illustration points to one of the threats to external validity of this design, or of the tie-breaking experiment. The effect of the treatment has only been studied for that narrow range of talent near the cutting point, and generalization of the effects of military service, for example, from this low ability level to the careers of the most able would be hazardous in the extreme. But in the draft laws and the requirements of the military services there may be other sharp cutting points on a quantitative criterion that could also be used. For example, those over 6 feet 6 inches are excluded from service. Imagine a five-year-later follow-up of draftees grouped by inch in the 6 feet 1 inch to 6 feet 5 inches range, and a group of their counterparts who would have been drafted except for their heights, 6 feet 6 inches to 6 feet 10 inches. (The fact that the other grounds of deferment might not have been examined by the draft board would be a problem here, but probably not insurmountable.) That we should not expect height in this range to have any relation to later-life variables is not at all a weakness of this design, and if we have indeed a subpopulation for which there is a sharp numerical cutting point, an internally valid measure of effects would result. Deferment under the present system is an unquantified committee decision. But just as the sense of justice of United States soldiers was quantified through paired comparisons of cases into an acceptable Demobilization Points system at the end of World War II (Guttman, 1946; Stouffer, 1949), so a quantified composite index of deferment priority could be achieved and applied as uniform justice across the nation, providing another numerical cutting point.

In addition to the National Data Bank type of indicators, there will be occasions in which new data collections as by interview or questionnaire are needed. For these there is the special problem of uneven cooperation that would be classified as instrumentation error. In our traditional mode of thinking, completeness of description is valued more highly than comparability. Thus if, in a fellowship study, a follow-up mailed out from the fellowship office would bring a higher return from past winners, this might seem desirable even if the nonawardees' rate of response was much lower. From the point of view of quasi-experimentation, however, it would be better to use an independent survey agency and a disguised purpose, achieving equally low response rates from both awardees and nonawardees, and avoiding a regression discontinuity in cooperation rate that might be misinterpreted as a discontinuity in more important effects.

Randomized Control Group Experiments

Experiments with randomization tend to be limited to the laboratory and agricultural experiment station. But this certainly need not be so. The randomization unit may be persons, families, precincts, or larger administrative units. For statistical purposes the randomization units should be numerous, and hence ideally small. But for reasons of external validity, including reactive arrangements, the randomization units should be selected on the basis of the units of administrative access. Where policies are administered through individual client contacts, randomization at the person level may be often inconspicuously achieved, with the clients unaware that different ones of them are getting different treatments. But for most social reforms, larger administrative units will be involved, such as classrooms, schools, cities, counties, or states. We need to develop the political postures and ideologies that make randomization at these levels possible.

"Pilot project" is a useful term already in our political vocabulary. It designates a trial program that, if it works, will be spread to other areas. By modifying actual practice in this regard, without going outside of the popular understanding of the term, a valuable experimental ideology could be developed. How are areas selected for pilot projects? If the public worries about this, it probably assumes a lobbying process in which the greater needs of some areas are only one consideration, political power and expediency being others. Without violating the public tolerance or intent, one could probably devise a system in which the usual lobbying decided upon the areas eligible for a formal public lottery that would make final choices between matched pairs. Such decision procedures as the drawing of lots have had a justly esteemed position since time immemorial (e.g., Aubert, 1959). At the present time, record keeping for pilot projects tends to be limited to the experimental group only. In the experimental ideology, comparable data would be collected on designated controls. (There are of course exceptions, as in the heroic Public Health Service fluoridation experiments, in which the teeth of Oak Park children were examined year after year as controls for the Evanston experimentals [Blayney & Hill, 1967].)

Another general political stance making possible experimental social amelioration is that of *staged innovation*. Even though by intent a new reform is to be put into effect in all units, the logistics of the situation usually dictate that simultaneous introduction is not possible. What results is a haphazard sequence of convenience. Under the program of staged innovation, the introduction of the program would be deliberately spread out, and those units selected to be first and last would be randomly assigned (perhaps randomization from matched pairs), so that during the transition period the first recipients could be analyzed as experimental units, the last recipients as controls. A third ideology making possible

true experiments has already been discussed: randomization as the democratic means of allocating scarce resources.

This article will not give true experimentation equal space with quasi-experimentation only because excellent discussions of, and statistical consultation on, true experimentation are readily available. True experiments should almost always be preferred to quasi-experiments where both are available. Only occasionally are the threats to external validity so much greater for the true experiment that one would prefer a quasi-experiment. The uneven allocation of space here should not be read as indicating otherwise.

More Advice for Trapped Administrators

But the competition is not really between the fairly interpretable quasi-experiments here reviewed and "true" experiments. Both stand together as rare excellencies in contrast with a morass of obfuscation and self-deception. Both to emphasize this contrast, and again as guidelines for the benefit of those trapped administrators whose political predicament will not allow the risk of failure, some of these alternatives should be mentioned.

Grateful Testimonials

Human courtesy and gratitude being what it is, the most dependable means of assuring a favorable evaluation is to use voluntary testimonials from those who have had the treatment. If the spontaneously produced testimonials are in short supply, these should be solicited from the recipients with whom the program is still in contact. The rosy glow resulting is analogous to the professor's impression of his teaching success when it is based solely upon the comments of those students who come up and talk with him after class. In many programs, as in psychotherapy, the recipient, as well as the agency, has devoted much time and effort to the program and it is dissonance reducing for himself, as well as common courtesy to his therapist, to report improvement. These grateful testimonials can come in the language of letters and conversation, or be framed as answers to multiple-item "tests" in which a recurrent theme of "I am sick," "I am well," "I am happy," "I am sad" recurs. Probably the testimonials will be more favorable as: (a) the more the evaluative meaning of the response measure is clear to the recipient—it is completely clear in most personality, adjustment, morale, and attitude tests; (b) the more directly the recipient is identified by name with his answer; (c) the more the recipient gives the answer directly to the therapist or agent of reform; (d) the more the agent will continue to be influential in the recipient's life in the future; (e) the more the answers deal with feelings and evaluations rather than with verifiable facts; and (f) the more the recipients participating in the evaluation are a small and self-selected or agent-selected subset of all recipients. Properly designed, the grateful testimonial method can involve pretests as well as posttests, and randomized control groups as well as experimentals, for there are usually no placebo treatments, and the recipients know when they have had the boon.

Confounding Selection and Treatment

Another dependable tactic bound to give favorable outcomes is to confound selection and treatment, so that in the published comparison those receiving the treatment are also the more able and well placed. The often-cited evidence of the dollar value of a college education is of this nature—all careful studies show that most of the effect, and of the superior effect of superior colleges, is explainable in terms of superior talents and family connections, rather than in terms of what is learned or even the prestige of the degree. Matching techniques and statistical partialings generally undermatch and do not fully control for the selection differences—they introduce regression artifacts confusable as treatment effects.

There are two types of situations that must be distinguished. First, there are those treatments that are given to the most promising, treatments like a college education which are regularly given to those who need it least. For these, the later concomitants of the grounds of selection operate in the same direction as the treatment: those most likely to achieve any-

way get into the college most likely to produce later achievement. For these settings, the trapped administrator should use the pooled mean of all those treated, comparing it with the mean of all untreated, although in this setting almost any comparison an administrator might hit upon would be biased in his favor.

At the other end of the talent continuum are those remedial treatments given to those who need it most. Here the later concomitants of the grounds of selection are poorer success. In the Job Training Corps example, casual comparisons of the later unemployment rate of those who received the training with those who did not are in general biased against showing an advantage to the training.

> This seems to have been the case in the major Head Start evaluation (Campbell & Erlebacher, 1970).

Here the trapped administrator must be careful to seek out those few special comparisons biasing selection in his favor. For training programs such as Operation Head Start and tutoring programs, a useful solution is to compare the later success of those who completed the training program with those who were invited but never showed plus those who came a few times and dropped out. By regarding only those who complete the program as "trained" and using the others as controls, one is selecting for conscientiousness, stable and supporting family backgrounds, enjoyment of the training activity, ability, determination to get ahead in the world—all factors promising well for future achievement even if the remedial program is valueless. To apply this tactic effectively in the Job Training Corps, one might have to eliminate from the so-called control group all those who quit the training program because they had found a job—but this would seem a reasonable practice and would not blemish the reception of a glowing progress report.

These are but two more samples of well-tried modes of analysis for the trapped administrator who cannot afford an honest evaluation of the social reform he directs. They remind us again that we must help create a political climate that demands more rigorous and less self-deceptive reality testing. We must provide political stances that permit true experiments, or good quasi-experiments. Of the several suggestions toward this end that are contained in this article, the most important is probably the initial theme: Administrators and parties must advocate the importance of the problem rather than the importance of the answer. They must advocate experimental sequences of reforms, rather than one certain cure-all, advocating Reform A with Alternative B available to try next should an honest evaluation of A prove it worthless or harmful.

Multiple Replication in Enactment

Too many social scientists expect single experiments to settle issues once and for all. This may be a mistaken generalization from the history of great crucial experiments in physics and chemistry. In actuality the significant experiments in the physical sciences are replicated thousands of times, not only in deliberate replication efforts, but also as inevitable incidentals in successive experimentation and in utilizations of those many measurement devices (such as the galvanometer) that in their own operation embody the principles of classic experiments. Because we social scientists have less ability to achieve "experimental isolation," because we have good reason to expect our treatment effects to interact significantly with a wide variety of social factors many of which we have not yet mapped, we have much greater needs for replication experiments than do the physical sciences.

The implications are clear. We should not only do hard-headed reality testing in the ini-

tial pilot testing and choosing of which reform to make general law; but once it has been decided that the reform is to be adopted as standard practice in all administrative units, we should experimentally evaluate it in each of its implementations (Campbell, 1967).

Conclusions

Trapped administrators have so committed themselves in advance to the efficacy of the reform that they cannot afford honest evaluation. For them, favorably biased analyses are recommended, including capitalizing on regression, grateful testimonials, and confounding selection and treatment. *Experimental administrators* have justified the reform on the basis of the importance of the problem, not the certainty of their answer, and are committed to going on to other potential solutions if the one first tried fails. They are therefore not threatened by a hard-headed analysis of the reform. For such, proper administrative decisions can lay the base for useful experimental or quasi-experimental analyses. Through the ideology of allocating scarce resources by lottery, through the use of staged innovation, and through the pilot project, true experiments with randomly assigned control groups can be achieved. If the reform must be introduced across the board, the interrupted time-series design is available. If there are similar units under independent administration, a control series design adds strength. If a scarce boon must be given to the most needy or to the most deserving, quantifying this need or merit makes possible the regression discontinuity analysis.

References

Aubert, V. Chance in social affairs. *Inquiry*, 1959, 2, 1–24.

Bauer, R. M. *Social indicators*. Cambridge, Mass.: M.I.T. Press, 1966.

Blayney, J. R., & Hill, I. N. Fluorine and dental caries. *The Journal of the American Dental Association* (Special Issue), 1967, 74, 233–302.

Box, G. E. P., & Tiao, G. C. A change in level of a nonstationary time series. *Biometrika*, 1965, 52, 181–192.

Campbell, D. T. Factors relevant to the validity of experiments in social settings. *Psychological Bulletin*, 1957, 54, 297–312.

Campbell, D. T. From description to experimentation: Interpreting trends as quasi-experiments. In C. W. Harris (Ed.), *Problems in measuring change*. Madison: University of Wisconsin Press, 1963.

Campbell, D. T. Administrative experimentation, institutional records, and nonreactive measures. In J. C. Stanley (Ed.), *Improving experimental design and statistical analysis*. Chicago: Rand McNally, 1967.

Campbell, D. T. Quasi-experimental design. In D. L. Sills (Ed.), *International Encyclopedia of the Social Sciences*. New York: Macmillan and Free Press, 1968, Vol. 5, 259–263.

Campbell, D. T., & Erlebacher, A. How regression artifacts in quasi-experimental evaluations can mistakenly make compensatory education look harmful. In J. Hellmuth (Ed.), *Compensatory education: A national debate*. Vol. III of *The disadvantaged child*. New York: Brunner/Mazel, 1970, 455–463.

Campbell, D. T., & Fiske, D. W. Convergent and discriminant validation by the multitrait-multimethod matrix. *Psychological Bulletin*, 1959, 56, 81–105.

Campbell, D. T., & Ross, H. L. The Connecticut crackdown on speeding: Time-series data in quasi-experimental analysis. *Law and Society Review*, 1968, 3(1), 33–53.

Campbell, D. T., & Stanley, J. C. Experimental and quasi-experimental designs for research on teaching. In N. L. Gage (Ed.), *Handbook of research on teaching*. Chicago: Rand McNally, 1963. (Reprinted as *Experimental and quasi-experimental design for research*. Chicago: Rand McNally, 1966.)

Chapin, F. S. *Experimental design in sociological research*. New York: Harper, 1947.

Etzioni, A. "Shortcuts" to social change? *The Public Interest*, 1968, 12, 40–51.

Etzioni, A., & Lehman, E. W. Some dangers in "valid" social measurement. *Annals of the American Academy of Political and Social Science*, 1967, 373, 1–15.

Galtung, J. *Theory and methods of social research*. Oslo: Universitetsforloget; London: Allen & Unwin; New York: Columbia University Press, 1967.

Glass, G. V. Analysis of data on the Connecticut speeding crackdown as a time-series quasi-experiment. *Law and Society Review*, 1968, 3(1), 55–76.

Glass, G. V., Tiao, G. C., & Maguire, T. O. Analysis of data on the 1900 revision of the German divorce laws as a quasi-experiment. *Law and Society Review*, 1971, 5(4).

Greenwood, E. *Experimental sociology: A study in method*. New York: King's Crown Press, 1945.

Gross, B. M. *The state of the nation: Social system accounting*. London: Tavistock Publications, 1966. (Also in R. M. Bauer, *Social indicators*. Cambridge, Mass.: M.I.T. Press, 1966.)

Gross, B. M. (Ed.), Social goals and indicators. *Annals of the American Academy of Political and Social Science*, 1967, 371, Part 1, May, Pp. i–iii and 1–177; Part 2, September, Pp. i–iii and 1–218.

Guttman, L. An approach for quantifying paired comparisons and rank order. *Annals of Mathematical Statistics*, 1946, 17, 144–163.

Hyman, H. H., & Wright, C. R. Evaluating social action programs. In P. F. Lazarsfeld, W. H. Sewell, & H. L. Wilensky (Eds.), *The uses of sociology*. New York: Basic Books, 1967.

Kamisar, Y. The tactics of police-persecution oriented critics of the courts. *Cornell Law Quarterly*, 1964, 49, 458–471.

Kaysen, C. Data banks and dossiers. *The Public Interest*, 1967, 7, 52–60.

Manniche, E., & Hayes, D. P. Respondent anonymity and data matching. *Public Opinion Quarterly*, 1957, 21(3), 384–388.

Polanyi, M. A society of explorers. In, *The tacit dimension.* (Ch. 3) New York: Doubleday, 1966.

Polanyi, M. The growth of science in society. *Minerva,* 1967, 5, 533–545.

Popper, K. R. *Conjectures and refutations.* London: Routledge and Kegan Paul; New York: Basic Books, 1963.

Rheinstein, M. Divorce and the law in Germany: A review. *American Journal of Sociology,* 1959, 65, 489–498.

Rose, A. M. Needed research on the mediation of labor disputes. *Personnel Psychology,* 1952, 5, 187–200.

Ross, H. L., & Campbell, D. T. The Connecticut speed crackdown: A study of the effects of legal change. In H. L. Ross (Ed.), *Perspectives on the social order: Readings in sociology.* New York: McGraw-Hill, 1968.

Ross, H. L., Campbell, D. T., & Glass, G. V. Determining the social effects of a legal reform: The British "Breathalyser" Crackdown of 1967. *American Behavioral Scientist,* 1970, 13, 493–509.

Sawyer, J., & Schechter, H. Computers, privacy, and the National Data Center: The responsibility of social scientists. *American Psychologist,* 1968, 23, 810–818.

Schanck, R. L., & Goodman, C. Reactions to propaganda on both sides of a controversial issue. *Public Opinion Quarterly,* 1939, 3, 107–112.

Schwartz, R. D. Field experimentation in sociological research. *Journal of Legal Education,* 1961, 13, 401–410.

Schwartz, R. D., & Orleans, S. On legal sanctions. *University of Chicago Law Review,* 1967, 34, 274–300.

Schwartz, R. D., & Skolnick, J. H. Televised communication and income tax compliance. In L. Arons & M. May (Eds.), *Television and human behavior.* New York: Appleton-Century-Crofts, 1963.

Selvin, H. A critique of tests of significance in survey research. *American Sociological Review,* 1957, 22, 519–527.

Simon, J. L. The price elasticity of liquor in the U.S. and a simple method of determination. *Econometrica,* 1966, 34, 193–205.

Solomon, R. W. An extension of control group design. *Psychological Bulletin,* 1949, 46, 137–150.

Stieber, J. W. *Ten years of the Minnesota Labor Relations Act.* Minneapolis: Industrial Relations Center, University of Minnesota, 1949.

Stouffer, S. A. The point system for redeployment and discharge. In S. A. Stouffer et al., *The American soldier. Vol. 2, Combat and its aftermath.* Princeton: Princeton University Press, 1949.

Suchman, E. A. *Evaluative research: Principles and practice in public service and social action programs.* New York: Russell Sage, 1967.

Sween, J., & Campbell, D. T. A study of the effect of proximally auto-correlated error on tests of significance for the interrupted time-series quasi-experimental design. Available from author, 1965. (Multilith)

Thistlethwaite, D. L., & Campbell, D. T. Regression-discontinuity analysis: An alternative to the ex post facto experiment. *Journal of Educational Psychology,* 1960, 51, 309–317.

Walker, H. M., & Lev, J. *Statistical inference.* New York: Holt, 1953.

Webb, E. J., Campbell, D. T., Schwartz, R. D., & Sechrest, L. B. *Unobtrusive measures: Nonreactive research in the social sciences.* Chicago: Rand McNally, 1966.

Wolf, E., Lüke, G., & Hax, H. *Scheidung und Scheidungsrecht: Grundfrägen der Ehescheidung in Deutschland.* Tübigen: J. C. B. Mohr, 1959.

60. Organization and Management Needs of a National Family Planning Program: The Case of India

Nicholas J. Demerath*

Western doctrines and methods of contraception were first promulgated in India by a few welfare leaders in the 1930's when birth control clinics were established in several cities. In 1952 India became the first nation to adopt a policy of birth rate reduction. Today, India and China are the only major nations whose central governments pursue reduction policies; policies for which there are no precedents and no models of success to follow, unlike other national development efforts. In as much as the Indian experience which goes back to 1952 has involved technical assistance by Americans and Europeans and is open to observation, it offers a rare opportunity for social scientific study.

A number of social scientists already have described India's rapid population growth, and analyzed its negative influences on economic development; including, among others, Chandrasekar, Chandrasekaran, Coale and Hoover, Davis, Mahalanobis, Sarkar. Figure 60.1, "Growth of Population in India," comes from a (1966) statistical estimate by the U.S. AID office in New Delhi. With the Malthusian

controls of famine and war presumed inoperative, the prospect of a one billion population by the year 2000 is bleak enough as a matter of human density alone; not to mention the pressures on natural resources, food supplies, public facilities and institutions. As anxieties over food shortage and population surplus become greater, the more numerous will be the studies and reports of demographers, public health physicians, economists and officials. There is also the mounting miscellany by psychologists and sociologists, subsidized by foundations and governments to make a variety of studies, all presumed useful to "family planners"; attitudes and attitude change, communications, human reproduction, marriage customs and family patterns.

Whatever contributions to science may come out of these demographic, economic and behavioral inquiries, their value to Indian population control can be no greater than the capacity of government planners and administrators selectively to use new knowledge in disciplined and effective programs of action. What is this capacity now? Can it be in-

Figure 60.1. Growth of Population in India: How Many People by the Year 2000?

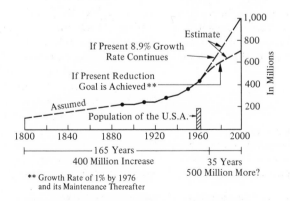

Reprinted from Nicholas J. Demerath, "Organization and Management: Needs of a National Family Planning Program: The Case of India," *Journal of Social Issues*, Vol. XXIII, No. 4 (1967), pp. 179–194.

° Professor of Sociology, Washington University.

creased? These are the questions of this paper and they are the major matters of modernization.

Modernization is a process in which human ends are pursued by means of social activities (a) that are dictated increasingly by theories or doctrines of efficiency or productivity (Stinchcombe, 1966); and (b) that are carried out and disciplined increasingly through managed or instrumental organizations. In the developing societies it is the central government that is the principal agent and organization for most development programs. And it is the government's capacity for disciplined activities, guided by instrumental theory or doctrine, that is the prime element in the society's modernization. India's "National Family Planning Program," that is to say the Center Government's effort through the States to reduce the birth rate, constitutes an instructive case both of the modernization process and the planned control of population; with the effectiveness of the latter being a function of the former.

As Stinchcombe has observed, ". . . imposing the discipline of theories over human activities, is the main political problem of modernization."[1] Furthermore, if activities are to be disciplined by applied theories, some theorists must have authority; and, we would add, their authority must be exerted through managed organizations appropriate to the chosen objectives. Analysis of India's family planning effort, comparing blueprints or plans with actions, shows that these have been the principal problems precisely. Chronologically, the effort has displayed three major phases. These phases serve to organize the analysis which follows.

Stage One (1956–1961)

Blueprint One

It was in 1952 that the Central Ministry of Health received its first appropriation for family planning; $1,300,000 (rupees equivalent) of which only about $600,000 was expended.

But it was not until the second Five-Year Plan period (1956–1960) that the first official planning groups and blue prints for family planning were established on a national scale. Numerous plan and policy boards were created. In 1956 there appeared a Central Family Planning Board, chaired by the Minister of Health, and by 1959 there were state boards in 14 of the 15 states. Top officials were named and by 1959 there were 10 states with Family Planning Officers and, at the Center, a Director of Family Planning responsible to the Director General of Health Services. All of the latter officials and the Health Minister, since 1962, have had medical and public health backgrounds. To plan or to "chalk out" became an ever-greater activity. Two other preliminaries to program action also came to be emphasized, understandably enough: training and research.

There was training in demography, training in family planning methods, and training courses for public health and other community workers. Demographic institutes, medical colleges, schools of nursing, health education agencies were involved in these instructional activities. In addition, special family planning training centers were established at several points, some under the Center and others under the States. Then, traveling teams of trainers were formed, including usually a physician and health educator, or physician and social worker.

Research activities increased. There were demographic studies in government funded centers at Delhi, Calcutta, Trivandrum and Bombay. At medical centers physiological researches were conducted, including investigations of reproduction and of contraceptive techniques and materials. Problems of motivation and communications began to be studied in several small pilot projects.

Action One

Though planning, training and research got most of the attention during the first stage,

---

[1] My definition of modernization is a modification of Stinchcombe's (1966). His elaboration of the concept I accept; particularly the importance he attaches to discipline and authority as the central problems of modernization, and especially in democracies with unsophisticated publics.

there was some program accomplishment in rural clinics and in a few towns and cities. By 1961, 1500 clinics were reported in operation. They provided contraceptives, (condoms, diaphragms, jellies, foam tablets) and advisory services either free or at minimal cost, depending on ability to pay. About five million couples were said to have been "contacted," of whom one-fifth were given appliances, materials or contraceptive advice. In a few states sterilization was promoted and hospitals were being utilized for the operations. Also, several mobile surgical teams were doing the operations, several score a day, at sterilization camps. This method was being promoted by mass advertising and small subsidies were being given the sterilizees as compensation, presumably for time lost from work and for costs of transportation. As of July 1961, about 130,000 sterilizations had been reported, with a preponderence of males over females (Ministry of Health, 1961, 399).

That this action was insufficient, was the central finding of the high level Health Survey and Planning Committee (the Mudaliar Committee) whose report was published in 1961 (Ministry of Health, 1961). The Committee wanted to see the national family planning program become an intensive and broad-scale "mass movement." This was prerequisite to success, though the Committee thought government alone could not launch the movement. They urged efforts to enlist more interest and help from voluntary organizations, like the Indian Family Planning Association, with the Central Government providing financial aid. High priority should be given procurement of larger supplies of contraceptive materials, either by Indian production or import. Expansion of informational efforts was strongly recommended, and family planning education efforts should be coordinated with the education work of other national programs, such as community development and social welfare.

Of particular interest is a supplement to this 1961 report. There, a minority of the Mudaliar Committee went on to urge that quite bold and different steps be taken, if by 1966, Indian population growth rate had not clearly turned downward. In effect, they urged that India take up population planning and control—a more comprehensive stratagem than family planning. The minority proposed (a) graded tax penalties (lesser advantages) beginning with the fourth birth; (b) removal of income tax disadvantages for single persons; (c) no maternity benefits for those who refuse to limit their progeny; (d) limiting government services, like free education, to no more than three children in a family; (e) enlisting the help of all government employees in promoting family planning; and (f) permitting abortion when justified for socio-economic reasons (1961, 406–410). There seems to have been little serious consideration given subsequently to many of these ideas. In 1965 the Minister of Finance did announce certain income tax inducements for smaller families; however, the income tax payers and the highly fertile masses are by no means synonymous.

Stage Two (1962–1964)

Blueprint Two

In April 1963, the Director of Family Planning, as if he were responding to the Mudaliar Committee Report, presented a detailed blueprint for what was termed "the reorganized or extended family planning program." He explained that careful observations by many observers had led him to conclude "the overall progress of the program must be admitted to be remarkable, considering the scope (sic) of the program" (Raina, 84). The progress was documented by tables showing that Center allocations to state governments had risen 200 fold in five years, almost 11 million pieces of "educational materials" had been produced, there were 8,441 service centers. Figures were presented which showed increasing sales of various types of contraceptive supplies between 1956 and 1963.

"To make still further improvements in the programme" the Director reported 25 pages of criticism and then spelled out his reorganization scheme. Heretofore, the key service unit had been mainly a clinic set-up to which women came for rather elaborate medical examination and prescription of contraceptives. Now, a reorganization was needed in the direction of an "extension" approach designed to reach the masses rapidly. Accordingly, the reorganized scheme would emphasize extension education, greater availability of contraceptive supplies, and less dependence on the traditional clinic approach. In addition, there were to be better statistics and evaluation, and a much stronger "ladder" of organization and supervision.

The main program goal was said to be reduction of the nation's birth rate from more than 40 per 1000 to 25 per 1000 population,

possibly by 1973. For this purpose, "operational goals" were defined as achieving for 90 per cent of the married adult population of India three basic pre-conditions of family planning, namely: (a) group acceptance of the smaller family size norm, (b) personal knowledge about family planning methods, and (c) easy availability of supplies and services. The blueprint or "set up" for the states is shown in the chart below. The organization and staffing implications were not spelled out for the nation, but some idea of magnitudes

Figure 60.2.   Family Planning Set Up in States.

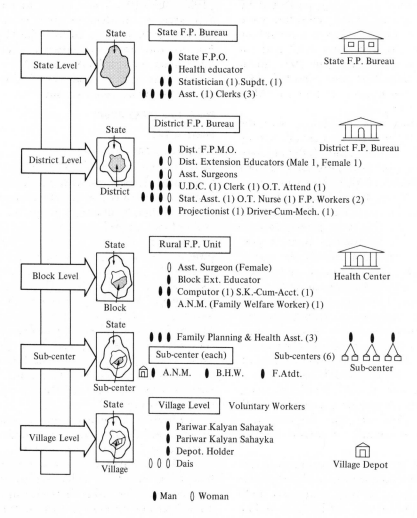

State Level — State — State F.P. Bureau
State F.P. Bureau
● State F.P.O.
● Health educator
●● Statistician (1) Supdt. (1)
●●●● Asst. (1) Clerks (3)

District Level — District — District F.P. Bureau
District F.P. Bureau
● Dist. F.P.M.O.
●○ Dist. Extension Educators (Male 1, Female 1)
●○ Asst. Surgeons
●●● U.D.C. (1) Clerk (1) O.T. Attend (1)
●●●○ Stat. Asst. (1) O.T. Nurse (1) F.P. Workers (2)
●● Projectionist (1) Driver-Cum-Mech. (1)

Block Level — Block — Rural F.P. Unit
Health Center
○ Asst. Surgeon (Female)
● Block Ext. Educator
●● Computor (1) S.K.-Cum-Acct. (1)
● A.N.M. (Family Welfare Worker) (1)

Sub-center — Sub-center
●●● Family Planning & Health Asst. (3)
Sub-center (each)   Sub-centers (6)
Sub-center
● A.N.M.   ● B.H.W.   ● F.Atdt.

Village Level — Village
Village Level   Voluntary Workers
● Pariwar Kalyan Sahayak
● Pariwar Kalyan Sahayka
● Depot. Holder
○○○ Dais   Village Depot

● Man   ○ Woman

can be drawn from Figure 60.2 bearing in mind these facts: India has 15 states and 4 territories. There are 324 districts. There are 5000 rural development blocks, each with about 80,000 people and there are 500,000 villages. Twenty per cent of the estimated 480 million population are in the towns and cities.

At the village and sub-center level, the blueprint provided for female workers (Auxiliary Nurse Midwives), at one per 10,000 population. These ANM's, in addition to performing their routine maternal and child health services, supposedly would educate women for family planning, act as contraceptive "depot holders," refer cases for sterilization and IUCD (Lippes Loop) and then provide follow-up on the cases. One male worker per 20 to 30 thousand population was also blueprinted to do public education, community organization, building and maintaining the contraceptive supply-lines, and organizing camps for sterilization and IUCD's.

The basic unit of operation was to be the Rural Family Planning Unit, coterminous in area with a Community Development Block. This Unit would be attached to the Block Health Unit, where the latter exists; but in absence of a Unit, it could also be set up independently and attached to the Block Development Officer. At block level, a post of Woman Medical Officer was blueprinted. In doing this, the likely acceptance of IUCD as a new family planning method was anticipated. At this level, a full-time Family Planning Extension Educator was planned to join the efforts of leaders and development workers. A Computor was specified to help with vital statistics and program evaluation. Also, a Storekeeper was to be provided to ensure the flow of supplies. At the district level, a consolidated "Family Planning Bureau" was prescribed with enough personnel and supplies to support the total program in all blocks of the district. State and central set ups were left essentially unchanged though their loads, in blueprint, would now be greater under the reorganization. For towns and cities, the reorganized scheme called for "Urban Family Planning Units" (rather than centers or clinics). Presumably, emphasis would go to a mass program to reach all the people in each urban area of 50,000 population. But there was no provision for supporting and coordinating these urban units.

The Government of India (the Center) accepted the blueprint for the reorganized family planning program. In October 1963 there was issued to all state governments a 45 page circular letter with three enclosures. This document specified the basis for financial assistance to the states; dictated line item budgets; spelled out job qualifications and duties at all levels, tables of organization, administrative relations, community relations, training requirements and even specified the bicycle allowances for three positions (Raina, 86–131)!

Action Two

The author of the *1962–1963 Annual Report* and *Blueprint Two* wrote,

> Even such a sympathetic observer as the demographer Kingsley Davis, only 12 years ago, wrote that he doubted whether an official program could be launched in the foreseeable future. Not only is it launched but India's Third Five-Year Plan states that the Family Planning program is at the very center of planned development (Raina, 63).

Just how national was the program's coverage, how effective its implementation, how real its accomplishment, were to become matters of mounting concern over the next two years.

Inaugurating the seventeenth meeting of the Central Family Planning Board in July 1965, Asoka Mehta, Deputy Chairman of the Planning Commission (the Prime Minister is the Chairman), spoke as follows and in a manner accurately described in the reports of the occasion as "impassioned," "spirited," "inspired," "vehement," "raising his voice" (Ministry of Health, 1965, 3). He said,

> We should not waste our time on petty worries of scales and salaries and status. These are undoubtedly important. I do not deny them. But I want to know if there is a famine somewhere and we are fighting it, will we be insisting upon saying what are the patterns of assistance, what are the scales of pay you will give us or what are going to be our service conditions before we can fight the famine? Do we, spe-

cially those of us who are actually engaged in this task, not realise that this is a life and death struggle for us (Ministry of Health 1965, 2–3)?

Mr. Mehta, a development-minded man, clearly thought all was not going well "at the very center of planned development."

That this was the case—despite the larger figures reported on people trained, materials printed, units manned—was revealed clearly in reports of the evaluation of the family planning program by the Planning Commission's Programme Evaluation Organization. The evaluators had visited the states in 1964 and early 1965; with reports and implementation beginning in the summer of 1965.

The evaluation group had not attempted a full-fledged evaluation of the program's impact. Instead, as they pointed out, they studied "the current and emerging problems in the implementation of the 'Reorganized' family planning program" (Planning Commission, 1965, 64). They observed the gap between plans and instrumental capacity. And the critical importance of the gap was now the greater in view of the clinical and administrative advantages of the IUCD or loop which the Indian Council on Medical Research in early 1965 had endorsed for mass utilization.

The findings of the evaluation report (Planning Commission, 1965) provide facts on the 1964 action outcome of "the reorganized and extended" blueprint. At block and district levels, 3195 family planning service units were reported. Over 80 per cent of these were managed by state governments. Local government bodies (towns and cities) were still under-represented, with less than 2.6 of the total. The average population per unit varied from 48,000 in one state (Kerala) to 715,000 in another (Bihar). Staffing of the units was quite deficient; averaging only 1.1 workers full-time equivalent per unit.

In the service units, workers had not learned what they were supposed to do, and with whom they were to do it. Job descriptions and supervisory methods were not known. Local leaders had not been trained in the ways to promote family planning in their areas; indeed, training of all kinds was weak.

At block and district levels also, there were not enough supervisory positions or people. There was a tendency to economize on supervisory posts. Support from district family planning committees was not what it should be, though this could not generally be expected until full-time district staff were available to inform, stimulate and guide district committees. Recruitment of the full district staffs, including district family planning medical officers and family planning extension educators, had not been given a very high priority. Family planning workers were not getting the maximum level of salary, allowances and service benefits which other staff with similar qualifications received. As the evaluation team put it, the "shortages" of staff often were really shortages in appealing conditions of work.

The states lacked assurances of long-term financial support for family planning; and in 10 states for which data were available, only 58 per cent of funds allocated were expended. That Blueprint Two, "the reorganized and extended" program, had been launched in the middle of the Third Plan period, had compounded the financial uncertainties. The state financial authorities had no assurance that subsidies from the Center would be continued or increased in the Fourth Plan, starting in 1966. Therefore, they hesitated to create new positions and to think of expansion. There was widespread caution, delay and inaction.

In the state family planning bureaus, presently sanctioned positions were inadequate to carry out required leadership functions. The state Family Planning Officer was commonly an Assistant Director when, to get the resources and cooperation he needed from other officials, he needed the rank of Deputy Director of Health Services, plus imagination and drive. He would then be aided by helpers at the Assistant Director level to supervise the key aspects of the program. It was noted that state family planning boards were not always very effective, and the state family planning officers needed help in activating these bodies.

Another set of findings on "Action Two" came out of my own travels and observations. During the summer of 1965 I observed family planning work in eight states and five of the largest cities. At the same time I observed and participated in various developments at the Center in New Delhi. My findings pertained mainly to promotion and accomplishment by means of the IUCD or "Lippes loop," and simply paralleled for the most part those reported by the evaluation panel. The loop was the method that began to be emphasized in 1965, and which then was viewed by enthusiasts as "the answer" to the world population problem. There had been real accomplishment in a few states, some of it quite impressive. But as Table 60.1 shows, the all-India picture was very spotty indeed. Five states accounted for about 78 per cent of the 271,386 insertions by the end of November 1965: Gujarat, Maharashtra, Mysore, Punjab, West Bengal. The same five states, at the end of March 1966, had inserted a total of about 73 per cent of the 804,504 IUCD which the Ministry of Health reported for the total national effort. These five states show good accomplishment, but they are the ones that might be expected to top the list: they are highly urbanized and industrialized, compared with the rest of India. Only one of the five leaders, Maharashtra, is among the five most populated states of India (Uttar Pradesh, Bihar, Maha-

rashtra, Andhra Pradesh and Madras, in order). The cumulative total is barely a beginning toward the figure required for any noticeable effect on the birthrate—at least 5,000,000 insertions made in each of several years, and retained; that is, not removed or extruded. Nor do sterilizations (mainly vasectomies performed on men) reported by government—about 1,500,000 over the past 10 years—greatly improve the picture since the great majority of those operated are over 45 years old.

Stage Three (1966–)

Blueprint Three

The Planning Commission's evaluation (1965) concluded with several recommendations that constitute a third blueprint, with a quite different Center set up and changes in Center-State relationships. This evaluation was, in effect, concurred in by two groups of experts sent to India in 1965 by the World Bank and by the United Nations (Technical Assistance): their recommendations in each case resembled closely those of the Planning Commission's panel. A reorganization and enhanced administrative capacity was called for.

TABLE 60.1   IUCD's Inserted May 1, 1965 to March 31, 1966

Name of State or Territory	Cumulative Totals as of		
	July 31	Nov. 30	Mar. 31
1. Andhra Pradesh	—	4,500	9,222
2. Assam	1,731	8,881	27,705
3. Bihar	2	2,331	15,588
4. Gujarat	20,431	51,316	84,949
5. Jammu & Kashmir	—	733	3,051
6. Kerala	575	12,428	35,717
7. Madhya Pradesh	145	2,170	18,987
8. Madras	338	960	3,491
9. Maharashtra	13,257	31,450	129,887
10. Mysore	3,238	21,246	75,900
11. Orissa	187	1,961	6,004
12. Punjab	7,343	39,239	132,263
13. Rajasthan	3,986	6,245	13,663
14. Uttar Pradesh	1,135	8,788	45,347
15. West Bengal	16,233	68,270	164,387
16. Delhi	2,000	10,000	20,113
17. Other (Territories, etc.)	—	868	18,230
TOTAL:	70,601	271,386	804,504

Source: Central Family Planning Directorate

The states should get more technical help from the Center as well as from other, more successful states. Such assistance is needed they said, not only where progress is slow, but also where some extra help might move a state program "over the edge" to success. A "State Consultant Panel" was urged, to include outstanding state workers with experience in special aspects of the program who could be called upon by other states for limited periods to help with specific tasks.

There should be decentralization of certain powers to the states, particularly powers of grant allocation to local voluntary organizations and other bodies. The Center would make the general policies and guidelines for such grants.

In respect to finance, the evaluators recommended (a) each state should have a "masterplan for building up all the component parts of its total family planning program," and the plan should underlay a schematic budget that would assure any unit, once started, of specified budgetary resources for the next ten years, irrespective of the Five-Year Plan period; (b) for better use of funds and greater flexibility of operation, the family planning program should hereafter be handled not as a "centrally sponsored scheme" but as one of the state plan schemes and thus enjoy a specified pattern of central assistance covering the planned and budgeted operations as above; (c) the proportion of Central assistance should be kept at least at 75 per cent of cost, and possibly raised to 100 per cent.

At the Center, the evaluators emphasized the need for much more administrative and financial authority, and a greatly strengthened headquarters staff with sections on planning, contraceptive supplies, administration, training and education and—of key importance— field operations with six regional officers. (The Director of Family Planning had only two or three professional assistants in his office.) The evaluators urged a "Central Family Planning Organization" be established as a Directorate General in the Health Ministry, but to be the "semi-autonomous" arm of a "semi-autonomous Executive Board." The Director General of Family Planning should be called "Com-

missioner of Family Planning" and be ranked an ex-officio Additional Secretary to Government. The panel preferred a five-member Executive Board composed of secretaries in the key ministries because they could be convened more readily than ministers, and could also take action. The Board should be able to exercise full powers of financial sanction and administrative action, including appointment of staff, within the annual budget allocation for the program.

Action Three

Except for reorganization, it is too early to appraise Action Three. The findings and recommendations of the Planning Commission's panel, the World Bank and the U.N. teams, were considered by the Cabinet. Steps toward reorganization began in August 1965. The Family Planning Program did not become a semi-autonomous affair; no Executive Board of Secretaries was created. A Commissioner of Family Planning, a government doctor with managerial experience in the Indian Army, was appointed; but no additional positions were created at the Center for 10 months.

In December of 1965, soon after the new Prime Minister (Mrs. Gandhi) took office, the Health Ministry was redesignated "Ministry of Health and Family Planning" and a full Secretary to government was appointed from the Indian Administrative Service to head a new department of Family Planning. By June 1, 1966, the Secretary, reported to be the personal selection of the Prime Minister and the Minister of Planning, got approval of 30 new supervisory positions in two "wings" of the Department; secretarial and technical. At mid-July, 11 of these jobs had been filled and an Executive Board of the Cabinet Committee was created which, apparently, will work directly with the Secretary.

As with most reorganizations, this one occasioned numerous interpersonal difficulties, factional conflicts and noncooperation at several levels. And there were those who thought the Family Planning Program should be moved to the Ministry of Planning and Social Welfare (formerly the Planning Commission).

Interpretation

I have described a persistent gap between the plans for family planning and the government's capacity to execute. This I have done by comparing blueprints and action over the last 14 years, drawing on government documents and my own observations. One may say of family planning what one observer has said of India's community development program, "the emphasis has been on expansion of schematic pattern at a pace faster than the implementing personnel could organize" (Deshmukh, 1965, 17). The massiveness of India's family planning challenge unquestionably calls for big plans. The population is now estimated at about 490 or 500 million, growing at a rate of about 2.5 per cent or 10 to 12 millions annually, whereas growth of national product is barely ahead.[2] Politically it is no wonder that the Minister of Health and Family Planning announced an unlikely target of 6 million IUCD insertions for 1966–1967, more than six times the 1965–1966 accomplishment. Administratively, though, it is surprising that she did not consult the Secretary or the Commissioner of Family Planning before setting this target. But what is the likelihood that modernization can be induced and government's capacity for disciplined action increased?

There are several favorable factors in the present situation. The creation of a separate Department, appointment of capable men to direct it, the creation of much needed staff positions, the Center's assurance of long-term financial aid to the states, the availability and administrative simplicity of the loop combined with its evident appeal in a ready market requiring only information and service centers to begin with—all these are favorable factors. More important, however, has been the first evidence of consensus in the Cabinet and in the Congress Party that national family planning is not just another health program to be promoted coequally with tuberculosis control, small pox eradication, leprosy control and the like. Instead, it is beginning to get number one priority alongside agriculture, exports and defense; though the politicians probably must have more confidence in the program's capacity before many will commit themselves fully: they need "a winner" in India as elsewhere. Finally, on the favorable side, there are examples now of accomplishment, particularly in the five states, as pointed out earlier.

Of the factors unfavorable to greater government capacity in the foreseeable future, the most basic is the disintegrative or centrifugal tendencies within the nation. India is a new and heterogenous nation with democratic institutions and a federal system whose states possess a degree of constitutional autonomy resembling the United States before the Civil War. The bureaucracy is slowly struggling out of a law-and-order past into a developmental and problem oriented future. And leaders are driven socially and psychologically in a current of change from particularistic to universalistic standards and stratagems.

Observers of Indian administrative behavior have noted other difficulties which may be more emenable to training and personnel development efforts. There is, for example, the penchant for symbols; plans and paper, meetings and assemblies, talk and print. The problem is often thought corrected once the law is passed or the target is announced. The goal is commonly considered won if everyone on a committee assents, if the funds have been appropriated, if the employees have been posted. Numbers games are often substituted for more threatening assessments; numbers of bodies in place, numbers of rupees earmarked, numbers of anything assembled or processed. Also, cooperative action on the job comes hard, for caste-like practices persist regardless of statutory prohibitions.

Every man is an island; each man to his function, his private contract with God. This is the realization of the Gita's selfless action. This is

[2] The Economic Commission for Asia and the Far East reported (1965) that India's gross national product increase, 1952 to 1963, was at an annual rate of 3.3 per cent. Among 12 Asian countries, only Indonesia was lesser (2.8); Japan (10.) and Thailand (6.0) the leaders. India's agricultural product increase is the same as her population growth rate: 2.5 per cent.

caste. In the beginning a no-doubt useful division of labor in a rural society, it has now divorced function from social obligation, position from duties. It has led to the Indian passion for speech-making, for gestures and for symbolic action (Naipaul, 1964, 83).

As observers both Indian and Western frequently note, organizational behavior generally is characterized by deference to age and seniority, to rank and authority and, more subtly, to caste and to color (Harrison, 1960; Misra, 1962; Naipaul, 1964; Srinivas, 1962). Delegation is difficult to practice and responsibility hard to take. It is easier to distrust than to trust. The power to make decisions, even the smallest decisions, is usually held zealously at the top by means of tight review, and by endless noting up and down the parallel hierarchies of administrative generalists and of experts. Organizational goals are set at the top and too seldom translated or broken down for the involvement or understanding of subordinates.

More leaders who inspire and who catalyze group action and cooperation, as well as many more competent managers, are called for. While it is true that India possesses a larger number of intellectuals and professionals than most other societies in transition, their proportion of the population is low and the ratio of managers and organizational leaders is probably even lower. Thus, shortages of personnel qualified to manage and staff a national family planning program is a negative factor alongside the difficulties of communication and cooperation in pursuit of common goals.

Already apparent is an overloading of the family planning elite—overloaded by communications, overloaded by matters for decision (Etzioni, 1965, 487). This elite in the states, the regional offices, and Center needs a very large enhancement of its leadership and management capabilities. This could be done by adding experienced managers from business to those from government, orienting them to family planning problems, and giving them expert social science assistance. Brief, practical management training and development courses for health professionals in supervisory positions could also be helpful; but there is no reason why the Indian family planning effort must be a health function, or that physicians must be its major administrators. Whether the family planning program will get enough strong leadership, and whether a sizeable management input will be made, one cannot say, though it is now the most critical factor in India's family planning accomplishment.

References

Deshmukh, Durgah. Progress of community development. *Kurukshetra*, January 26, 1965.

Economic Commission for Asia and the Far East. 1965 Survey. As reported in the *Economic Times* (Bombay), October 6, 1965.

Etzioni, Amitai. The epigenesis of political unification. In Etzioni, A. (Ed.), *Social change*. New York: Basic Books, 1964.

Harrison, Selig. *India: the most dangerous decades*. New York: Oxford University Press, 1960.

Ministry of Health, Government of India. *Report of the health survey and planning committee*. Madras, Government of India, 1961, Vol. I.

Misra, Vikas. *Hinduism and economic growth*. New York: Oxford University Press, 1962.

Naipaul, V. S. *An area of darkness*. London: Andre Deutsch, 1964.

Planning Commission, Government of India, *Evaluation of the family planning program: reports of assessment teams and the panel of consultants*. New Delhi: Government of India, 1965.

Raina, B. L. *Family planning programme: report for 1962–63*. Ministry of Health, Government of India, New Delhi, (no date).

Srinivas, M. N. *Caste in modern India and other essays*. Bombay: Asia Publishing House, 1962.

Stinchcombe, Arthur. Book review. *American Sociological Review*, April, 1966, XXXI, (2), 266–267.

INDEX
OF AUTHORS